THE
BORZOI
COLLEGE READER

THE
BORZOI
COLLEGE READER

Edited by

CHARLES MUSCATINE

and

MARLENE GRIFFITH

University of California, Berkeley

Alfred · A · Knopf : New York

1966

L. C. catalog card number: 66-10547

THIS IS A BORZOI BOOK,

PUBLISHED BY ALFRED A. KNOPF, INC.

THIRD PRINTING, AUGUST 1966

ACKNOWLEDGMENTS

From "Party of One—Thinking as a Hobby" by William Golding, first published in *Holiday* © 1961 The Curtis Publishing Company. Reprinted by permission of the author.

"On Various Kinds of Thinking" from *The Mind in the Making* by James H. Robinson. Copyright 1921 by Harper & Brothers; renewed 1949 by Bankers Trust Company. Reprinted by permission of Harper & Row, Publishers.

"Propaganda Under a Dictatorship" from *Brave New World Revisited* by Aldous Huxley. Copyright © 1958 by Aldous Huxley, Reprinted by permission of Harper & Row, Publishers, and Chatto and Windus Ltd.

"The Disadvantages of Being Educated" from *Free Speech and Plain Language* by Albert Jay Nock. Copyright 1937 by Albert Jay Nock. By permission of William Morrow and Company, Inc.

"since feeling is first" from *Poems 1923–1954* by e. e. cummings. Copyright 1926 by Horace Liveright; copyright 1954 by e. e. cummings. By permission of Harcourt, Brace & World, Inc.

"The Lord of Creation" by Susanne K. Langer from *Fortune* (January, 1944), 127–128, 130, 132, 134, 136, 139–140, 142, 144, 146, 148, 150, 152, 154. Reprinted by permission.

"Politics and the English Language" from *Shooting an Elephant and Other Essays* by George Orwell. Copyright 1945, 1946, 1949, 1950, by Sonia Brownell Orwell. Reprinted by permission of Harcourt, Brace & World, Inc., and Matin Secker & Warburg Ltd.

"Ultimate Terms in Contemporary Rhetoric" from Chapter 9 of *The Ethics of Rhetoric* by Richard M. Weaver. Copyright 1953 by Henry Regnery Company. Reprinted by permission.

"The Arts of Selling" from *Brave New World Revisited* by Aldous Huxley. Copyright © 1958 by Aldous Huxley. Reprinted by permission of Harper & Row, Publishers, and Chatto and Windus Ltd.

"The Most Cheerful Graveyard in the World" by Paul Jacobs from *The Reporter* (September 18, 1958), 26–30. Copyright 1958 by The Reporter Magazine Company. Reprinted by permission.

"The Article" by Brock Brower from *On Creative Writing* ed. Paul Engle. Copyright © 1963, 1964 by Paul Engle. Reprinted by permission of E. P. Dutton & Co., Inc.

"Philosophical Method of the Americans," "Of the Principal Source of Belief Among Democratic Nations" "Why the Americans Are More Addicted to Practical than to Theoretical Science," and "General Survey of the Subject" from *Democracy in America* by Alexis de Tocqueville. Copyright 1945 by Alfred A. Knopf, Inc. Reprinted by permission of the publisher.

"Love in America" by Raoul de Roussy de Sales from *The Atlantic* (May, 1938), 645–651. Reprinted by permission.

"The Joiners" from Chapter 2 of Part 9 of *America as a Civilization* by Max Lerner. Copyright © 1957 by Max Lerner. Reprinted by permission of Simon and Schuster, Inc.

"What's American About America?" by John A. Kouwenhoven from *Harper's* (July, 1956), 25–33. Reprinted by permission.

[America Is Words, Too] from "Unity and Liberty" in *The American Character* by Denis W. Brogan. © 1956 by Denis W. Brogan. Reprinted by permission of Alfred A. Knopf, Inc.

"Of the Limits to the Authority of Society Over the Individual" by John Stuart Mill from *The Philosophy of John Stuart Mill*. Copyright 1961 by the ed., Marshall Cohen. By permission of Random House, Inc.

[Instinct and Civilization] from Chapter 3 of *Civilization and Its Discontents*, taken from the Standard Edition of *The Complete Psychological Works of Sigmund Freud*, Volume XXI (1927–1931), newly trans. from the German and ed. by James Strachey. Copyright © 1961 by James Strachey. Reprinted by permission of W. W. Norton & Co., Inc., The Hogarth Press Ltd., Sigmund Freud Copyrights Ltd., and Mr. James Strachey.

"The Individual and the Pattern of Culture" from *Patterns of Culture* by Ruth Benedict. Copyright 1934 by Ruth Benedict. Reprinted by permission of Houghton Mifflin Company.

"In Favor of Capital Punishment" by Jacques Barzun from *The American Scholar* (Spring, 1962). Copyright © 1962 by the United Chapters of Phi Beta Kappa. By permission of the publishers.

"The Penalty of Death" from *A Mencken Chrestomathy* by H. L. Mencken. Copyright 1926 by Alfred A. Knopf, Inc.; renewed 1954 by H. L. Mencken. Reprinted by permission of the publisher.

"A Hanging" from *Shooting an Elephant and Other Essays* by George Orwell. Copyright 1945, 1946, 1949, 1950 by Sonia Brownell Orwell. Reprinted by permission of Harcourt, Brace & World, Inc., and Martin Secker & Warburg Ltd.

From "Reflections on the Guillotine" by Albert Camus from *Resistance, Rebellion, and Death* trans. Justin O'Brien. Copyright © 1960 by Alfred A. Knopf, Inc. By permission of the publisher.

"Verdict Guilty—Now What?" from *A Psychiatrist's World* by Dr. Karl Menninger. Copyright © 1959 by Karl Menninger. Reprinted by permission of The Viking Press, Inc.

"Moral Conflict and Psychiatry" by Thomas S. Szasz from *The Yale Review* (Summer, 1960), 555–566. Copyright 1960 by the Yale University Press. Reprinted by permission.

"Law, Morality, and Individual Rights" by David L. Bazelon. Speech delivered before the Federal Bar Association at the National Press Club in Washington, D.C., on April 30, 1963. Reprinted by permission.

"God Sees the Truth, But Waits to Tell" from *The Short Stories of Leo Tolstoy* trans. Arthur Mendel. Copyright © 1960 by Bantam Books, Inc. Reprinted by permission of Bantam Books, Inc.

[The Committee of 100] by Bertrand Russell from *A Matter of Life* ed. Clara Urquhart. Copyright © 1963 by Clara Urquhart. Reprinted by permission of Little, Brown and Co. and Jonathan Cape Ltd.

"Public Statement of Eight Alabama Clergymen" issued April 12, 1963, Pamphlet No. 589A of the American Friends Service Committee. Reprinted by permission of the Protestant Episcopal Church in the Diocese of Alabama, a corporation.

"Letter from Birmingham Jail" from *Why We Can't Wait* by Martin Luther King, Jr. Copyright © 1963 by Martin Luther King, Jr. Reprinted by permission of Harper & Row, Publishers.

"Authority and the Role of Coercion" from *Catholic Viewpoint on Censorship* by Harold C. Gardiner. Copyright © 1958, 1961 by Doubleday & Company, Inc. Reprinted by permission of the publisher.

"The Nature of the Battle Over Censorship" from *Men of Destiny* by Walter Lippmann. Copyright 1927 by The Macmillan Company; renewed 1955 by Walter Lippmann. By permission of the publisher.

"Defense of the Freedom to Read" by Henry Miller from *The Henry Miller Reader* ed. Lawrence Durrell. © 1959 by Henry Miller. Reprinted by permission of the author and the publisher, New Directions, New York.

"U.S.A. v. One Book *Ulysses*" by John M. Woolsey. Reprinted in James Joyce's *Ulysses*. By permission of Random House, Inc.

"Toward a New Definition of Obscenity" by Howard Moody from *Christianity and Crisis* (January 25, 1965), 284–288. © 1965 by Christianity and Crisis, Inc. Reprinted by permission.

"Getting the Story in Vietnam" from *The Making of a Quagmire* by David Halberstam. © Copyright 1965 by David Halberstam. Reprinted by permission of Random House, Inc.

"Technology and the Claims of Community" by Richard H. Rovere from *The American Scholar* (Autumn, 1958), 413–421. Reprinted by permission.

"World Without Walls" by Robert Jungk from *Tomorrow is Already Here* trans. Marguerite Waldman. Copyright 1954 by Robert Jungk. Reprinted by permission of Simon and Schuster, Inc., and Atrium Verlag A.G.

"On Privacy: The American Dream, What Happened to It" by William Faulkner from *Harper's* (July, 1955). Copyright © 1955 by William Faulkner. Reprinted by permission of Harold Ober Associates, Inc.

"The Annihilation of Privacy" by Ashley Montagu from *Saturday Review* (March 31, 1956), 9–11, 32. Reprinted by permission.

"The Reshaping of Privacy" by August Heckscher from *The American Scholar* (Winter, 1958–1959). Copyright © 1958 by the United Chapters of Phi Beta Kappa. By permission of the publishers.

From "Racism: The *ism* of the Modern World" by Ruth Benedict from Chapter 1 of *Race: Science and Politics*, The Viking Press, Inc., and Chapter 1 of *Race and Racism*, Routledge & Kegan Paul Ltd. Copyright 1940 by Ruth Benedict. Reprinted by permission of the publishers.

"The Respective Characteristics of the Three Great Races" by Joseph Arthur, Comte de Gobineau from Chapter 16 of *The Inequality of Human Races* trans. Adrian Collins. Reprinted by permission of G. P. Putnam's Sons.

From "Nation and Race" by Adolf Hitler from Vol. I, Chapter 11 of *Mein Kampf* trans. Ralph Manheim. Copyright 1943 by Houghton Mifflin Company. Reprinted by permission.

"Genetics of Race Equality" by Theodosius Dobzhansky from *Eugenics Quarterly* (December, 1963), 151–160. Reprinted by permission.

"Marrakech" from *Such, Such Were the Joys* by George Orwell. Copyright 1945, 1952, 1953 by Sonia Brownell Orwell. Reprinted by permission of Harcourt, Brace & World, Inc., and Martin Secker & Warburg Ltd.

"The Case for the White Southerner" by Perry Morgan from *Esquire* (January, 1962), 41, 43, 45, 134. © 1961 by Esquire, Inc. Reprinted by permission of Esquire, Inc.

"Letter to the North" by William Faulkner. © Copyright 1956 by William Faulkner. Reprinted by permission of Random House, Inc.

"Faulkner and Desegregation" from *Nobody Knows My Name* by James Baldwin. Copyright © 1956, 1961 by James Baldwin. Reprinted by permission of The Dial Press, Inc.

"My Negro Problem—And Ours" by Norman Podhoretz from *Commentary* (February, 1963), 93–101. Copyright © 1963 by the American Jewish Committee. Reprinted by permission of *Commentary*.

"God's Grandeur" from *Poems of Gerard Manley Hopkins*, Third Edition, ed. W. H. Gardner. Copyright 1948 by Oxford University Press, Inc. Reprinted by permission.

"Why I am an Agnostic" by Clarence Darrow from his *Verdicts Out of Court* ed. Arthur and Lila Weinberg, Chicago, Quadrangle Books, 1963. Reprinted by permission.

"Symbols of Faith" from *Dynamics of Faith* by Paul Tillich. Copyright © 1957 by Paul Tillich. Reprinted by permission of Harper & Row, Publishers.

"Man Against Darkness" by W. T. Stace from *The Atlantic* (September, 1948), 53–58. Reprinted by permission.

"Screwtape Letters 8 and 9" from *The Screwtape Letters and Screwtape Proposes a Toast* by C. S. Lewis. Copyright © 1942 by C. S. Lewis. Reprinted by permission of The Macmillan Company and Geoffrey Bles Ltd.

"The Unbeliever and Christians" by Albert Camus from *Resistance, Rebellion, and Death* trans. Justin O'Brien. Copyright © 1960 by Alfred A. Knopf, Inc. By permission of the publisher.

[The *Bhagavad-Gita* and the Perennial Philosophy], Introduction, by Aldous Huxley from *Song of God: Bhagavad-Gita* trans. Swami Prabhavananda and Christopher Isherwood, Hollywood, Vedanta Press, 1944. Reprinted by permission of the Vedanta Society of Southern California.

[Letter to President Roosevelt] by Albert Einstein from *The Atomic Age* (articles from the *Bulletin of the Atomic Scientists*, 1945–1962) ed. Morton Grodzins and Eugene Rabinowitch, New York, Basic Books, 1963. Reprinted by permission.

"A Petition to the President of the United States" by Leo Szilard from *The Atomic Age* (articles from the *Bulletin of the Atomic Scientists* 1945–1962) ed. Morton Grodzins and Eugene Rabinowitch, New York, Basic Books, 1963. Reprinted by permission.

"A Scientist Rebels" by Norbert Wiener from *The Atlantic* (January, 1947), 46. Reprinted by permission.

"The Scientist Fights for Peace" by Louis N. Ridenour from *The Atlantic* (May, 1947), 80–83. Reprinted by permission.

"The Real Responsibilities of the Scientist" by J. Bronowski. Copyright 1956 by the Educational Foundation for Nuclear Science, Inc., 935 East 60th Street, Chicago, Illinois. Reprinted by permission from the *Bulletin of the Atomic Scientists* (January, 1956).

"Ethics for the Scientist" by John Haybittle. Copyright 1964 by the Educational Foundation for Nuclear Science, Inc., 935 East 60th Street, Chicago, Illinois. Reprinted by permission from the *Bulletin of the Atomic Scientists* (May, 1964).

"The Message of Science" by Paul Weiss from *The Atomic Age* (articles from the *Bulletin of the Atomic Scientists*, 1945–1962) ed. Morton Grodzins and Eugene Rabinowitch, New York, Basic Books, 1963. Reprinted by permission.

[The Grand Academy of Lagado] from Part 3 entitled "A Voyage to Laputa, Balnibarbi, Luggnagg, Glubbdubdrib, and Japan" by Jonathan Swift from *Gulliver's Travels* ed. Herbert Davis, Oxford, Basil Blackwell, 1959. Reprinted by permission.

"The Culture of Machine Living" from *America as a Civilization* by Max Lerner. Copyright © 1957 by Max Lerner. Reprinted by permission of Simon and Schuster, Inc.

"Technical Progress Is Always Ambiguous" by Jacques Ellul from *Technology and Culture* (Fall, 1962), trans. John Wilkinson, The Society for the History of Technology. Reprinted by permission of The University of Chicago Press.

"Sawdust, Seaweed, and Synthetics" by Edgar Ansel Mowrer from *Saturday Review* (December 8, 1956), 11–13, 54–56. Reprinted by permission.

"Nature Fights Back" from *Silent Spring* by Rachel Carson. Copyright © 1962 by Rachel L. Carson. Reprinted by permission of Houghton Mifflin Company.

"The Morning of the Day They Did It" (February 25, 1950) from *The Second Tree from the Corner* by E. B. White. Originally appeared in *The New Yorker*. Copyright 1950 by E. B. White. Reprinted by permission of Harper & Row, Publishers.

"Cyberculture—The Age of Abundance and Leisure" by Alice Mary Hilton from *The Michigan Quarterly Review* (Fall, 1964), 217–229. Reprinted by permission.

"Work" from *The Sane Society* by Erich Fromm. Copyright © 1955 by Erich Fromm. Reprinted by permission of Holt, Rinehart and Winston, Inc.

"Less Work—Less Leisure" by Harvey Swados from *The Nation* (February 22, 1958), 153–158. Reprinted by permission.

"Time on Our Hands" by Russell Lynes from *Harper's* (July, 1958), 34–39. © 1958 by Harper & Row, Publishers, Inc. Reprinted from Harper's Magazine by Special Permission.

"The Disappearing City" by Lewis Mumford from *Architectural Record* (October, 1962), 121, 123, 125, 127–128. Part I of a five-part series entitled "The Future of the City." Reprinted by permission.

"Are Cities Dead?" by Robert Moses from *The Atlantic* (January, 1962), 55–58. Reprinted by permission.

"The Severed Tendon" from *No Further West* by Dan Jacobson. Copyright © 1957, 1958, 1959 by Dan Jacobson. Reprinted by permission of The Macmillan Company and Weidenfeld & Nicolson Ltd.

"The Urban Aesthetic" by John E. Burchard from *Metropolis in Ferment* ed. Martin Meyerson, *The Annals of the American Academy of Political and Social Science* (November, 1957), 112–122. Reprinted by permission.

"Violence in the City Streets" (title of version in *Harper's* [September, 1961], 37–43) by Jane Jacobs. This material appears in another version in *The Death and Life of Great American Cities* by Jane Jacobs. © Copyright 1961 by Jane Jacobs. Reprinted by permission of Random House, Inc.

"How City Planners Hurt Cities" by Jane Jacobs from *Saturday Evening Post* (October 14, 1961), 12, 14. © 1961 by Jane Jacobs. Reprinted by permission.

"The Cultural Importance of Art" from *Philosophical Sketches* by Susanne K. Langer, Baltimore, The Johns Hopkins Press, 1962. Reprinted by permission.

"Notes of a Painter" by Henri-Matisse from *Matisse: His Art and His Public* by Alfred H. Barr, Jr. Copyright 1951 by The Museum of Modern Art, New York. Reprinted with its permission. "Notes d'un pientre" was originally published in *La Grande Revue*, Paris, December 25, 1908. The first complete English translation by Margaret Scolari Barr was published in *Henri-Matisse*, The Museum of Modern Art, 1931, and then again in *Matisse: His Art and His Public*, together with paragraph headings which were added by the author for the convenience of the reader.

"The Function of Art" by Ernst Fischer from *The Necessity of Art* trans. Anna Bostock, London, Penguin Books Ltd., 1963. Reprinted by permission.

"Wanted: An American Novel" editorial from *Life* (September 12, 1955). Reprinted by permission.

[What Can the Artist Do in the World of Today?] from "The Artist and His Time" by Albert Camus from *The Myth of Sisyphus and Other Essays* trans. Justin O'Brien. Copyright © 1955 by Alfred A. Knopf, Inc. By permission of the publisher.

"Why I Write" from *Such, Such Were the Joys* by George Orwell. Copyright 1945, 1952, 1953 by Sonia Brownell Orwell. Reprinted by permission of Harcourt, Brace & World, Inc., and Martin Secker & Warburg Ltd.

"What Use is Poetry?" from *A Clerk of Oxenford* by Gilbert Highet. Copyright 1954 by Gilbert Highet. Reprinted by permission of Oxford Univesity Press, Inc.

"Sailing to Byzantium" from *The Collected Poems of W.B. Yeats*. Copyright 1928 by The Macmillan Company; renewed 1956 by Georgie Yeats. Reprinted with permission of The Macmillan Company and Mr. M.B. Yeats and The Macmillan Company of Canada Ltd.

"For Once, Then, Something" from *Complete Poems of Robert Frost*. Copyright 1923 by Holt, Rinehart and Winston, Inc. Copyright 1951 by Robert Frost. Reprinted by permission of Holt, Rinehart and Winston, Inc.

"Poetry" from *Collected Poems* by Marianne Moore. Copyright 1935 by Marianne Moore; renewed 1963 by Marianne Moore and T.S. Eliot. Reprinted with permission of The Macmillan Company.

"September 1, 1939" from *The Collected Poetry of W. H. Auden*, Random House, Inc., and *Collected Short Poems*, Faber and Faber Ltd. Copyright 1940 by W. H. Auden. Reprinted by permission of the publishers.

"In My Craft or Sullen Art" from *The Collected Poems of Dylan Thomas*, J.M. Dent & Sons, 1946. Copyright 1953 by Dylan Thomas. © 1957 by New Directions and *Death and Entrances. Reprinted by permission of the publishers*, New Directions, New York, and J.M. Dent & Sons, Ltd., London, Literary Executors of the Dylan Thomas Estate.

"Highbrow, Lowbrow, Middlebrow" from *The Tastemakers* by Russell Lynes. Copyright © 1954 by Russell Lynes. Reprinted by permission of Harper & Row, Publishers.

"Fashions in Vulgarity" from *The Cart and the Horse* by Louis Kronenberger. Copyright © 1961 by Louis Kronenberger. Reprinted by permission of Alfred A. Knopf, Inc.

"A Book That Influenced Me" from *Two Cheers for Democracy* by E.M. Forster. Copyright 1951 by E.M. Forster. Reprinted by permission of Harcourt, Brace & World, Inc., and Edward Arnold (Publishers) Ltd.

"How Should One Read a Book?" from *The Second Common Reader* by Virginia Woolf. Copyright 1932 by Harcourt, Brace & World, Inc.; renewed 1960 by Leonard Woolf. Reprinted by permission of Harcourt, Brace & World, Inc., Leonard Woolf, and The Hogarth Press Ltd.

"How Do You Know It's Good?" from *But Will It Sell?* by Marya Mannes. Copyright © 1962 by Marya Mannes. Published by J.B. Lippincott Company.

FOR

Jeffrey and Alison
David and Pamela
Constance, James, and Margaret

WE WISH to thank the many colleagues and friends who have given us their advice during the preparation of this book, especially Mary Arnold, Margaret Barrier, Irving Berg, Robert Bloom, Gaylord Chambers II, Ann Connor, Bernard L. Diamond, David Dushkin, T. J. Kent, Jr., I. Michael Lerner, Allan Metcalf, Henry Morgan, and J. William Ward. We are grateful, too, to Sondra Shair and Martha Platt for bibliographical assistance; to Arlyn Diamond, Susan Scarff, and Estelle Fine for help with the manuscript; and most of all to Joan Glassel, whose support has at every step made the improbable seem possible.

C. M.
M. G.

Berkeley, California
1965

CONTENTS

Contents

Contents /*xix*

INTRODUCTION

To teach the art of critical thinking is the main design of this book. We agree with Aldous Huxley that the survival of our democratic civilization depends on the effort of all concerned to impart rationality, and we can think of no better means to this end than honest reading and honest writing and no better time and place than a beginning college course.

Using "critical" and "honest" as synonyms, we wish also to suggest that there is deep personal value in the kind of reading or writing which tests the idea and leads to discovery or confirmation of what we mean or believe. Critical thinking, reading, and writing are closely interwoven, but all three depend on a sensibility and a mind which are active, not passive. Although each individual will pick up the thread to his own self at a different place, all three can and ultimately do lead him back to a discovery of what he really is and lead him forward to a discovery of what he really wants, both personally and socially. As Emerson suggests, Man Thinking is also Man Being.

Because we believe that critical reading and writing are best taught in an atmosphere of live ideas, we have chosen our reading material from what we consider important areas of intellectual, social, and moral concern, topical, but not soon to become dated. The book is a big one and gives the reader plenty of choice, plenty of variety, and, of course, the option to read in whatever order he may find most stimulating. But our focus is on expository prose, the prose of thought, and our arrangement is by subject matter rather than by rhetorical genre or device.

We have done much of our own teaching in a course whose readings are supposed to help the student "to follow critically the argument of a text, to perceive its structure, and to appreciate its style," and we teach that argument, structure, and style work together. But in both reading and composition we prefer to *begin* with argument, with the main idea, and to consider how structure and style help to express or support it. We believe that the expository essay that makes a point is the heart and soul of the course in composition, and we feel that the other rhetorical categories —description, narration, definition, comparison, and the like—had best be taught as adjuncts to the presentation of a well-buttressed main idea. We include a few stories and poems—partly for refreshment and partly as a reminder that rational argument is not the only way to say things—but we have not attempted to cover genres or topics better dealt with in the study of imaginative writing.

The book is organized in sixteen sections, by topic. From among many respectable topics we have tried to choose only those on which meaningful current debate is possible. We have, thus, been able to collect under each topic pieces representing a variety of arguments, often in direct conflict with each other. The reading presents, then, a wide range of subjects, ideas, and assumptions, and at the same time a continuous dialogue or debate among them. We hope that presenting ideas in the form of issues will help the reader to see that he has something to think about. Suggesting comparison at every point, giving ready occasion to take sides and to criticize, the material is directly suited to generating discussion and writing.

Before each section we have placed an introduction, briefly indicating the main issues raised by the pieces in the section. The sections differ from each other in organization, depending on the nature of the issue and on the availability of writings. In our first two sections, on "The Necessity for Thinking" and "The Right Use of Language," we have not labored to find a compensating number of spokesmen for bad thinking and dishonest use of language, feeling that the reader's own observation will provide material aplenty. Similarly, for the section on "Privacy" we have not been moved to print an adequately villainous statement applauding the invasion of privacy. Under "Technology and Human Values" we have not supplied an essay that praises technology uncritically. The reader cannot help but know that attitude already. All other sections, however, contain overt debate within themselves, and some of the individual essays address themselves specifically to others in the collection.

The reader who makes extensive use of the book may find useful another feature of its organization: the large sections themselves are related to each other in groups and sequences, and there is the continuous possibility of cross-reference between pieces in different sections. Thus, he may wish to read Susanne Langer's "The Lord of Creation" along with Paul Tillich's "Symbols of Faith" for their common interest in symbolism; John Kouwenhoven and Dan Jacobson together on physical aspects of the American scene; or John Stuart Mill and August Heckscher together for their common concern with distinguishing the private and the public spheres of life. Plentiful cross-connections such as these may help the beginning critical reader to appreciate the ultimate interrelatedness of important ideas and issues: to see, for instance, how ideas on language can affect religious thought, how notions of government can be related to topics in anthropology and psychology, how attitudes toward scientific research can influence our opportunities for work, our manner of living, and perhaps even our survival.

While the essays have thus been arranged for the play of their ideas, most of them have also been chosen as rhetorical models, with an eye to their usefulness as guides to the reader's own writing. We have included a few selections from classical sources and some translations of more modern continental authors. But most of the selections are original English essays, both traditional and modern, in a great range of styles and techniques. Of these, all but two or three are either complete works in themselves or are coherent, unabridged sections (usually chapters) of longer works and can be studied as compositional wholes. We have not followed the common practice of making silent changes and omissions, preferring to present the essays as they were written, with the occasional peculiarities and defects of their time and place. In this spirit, we preface each selection with a headnote on its author and with facts on its original publication.

We hope that this small insistence on realism will help the reader to feel the excitement of genuine moral commitment that many of the essays transmit. Good writing, we mean to suggest, comes from a person who not only commands some verbal skill but has something he wants to say. Our ideal essay is a rational statement—propelled by conviction. We agree with Brock Brower: "It is so easy to quote, generalize, qualify, extrapolate *neutrally* around a subject—*Let the reader draw his own conclusions*—instead of facing it directly as something that must be plumbed by a drop-line of pure thought." We are hopeful that in reading writers like Orwell, Camus, Tillich, Langer, Mannes, and many of the others, the reader will also be moved to drop plumblines of his own.

The book is printed without further apparatus, to spare those to whom pedagogical machinery would be an unwelcome distraction. We have prepared instead a separate teacher's guide, available on request from the publisher. The guide contains suggestions for use of the book in college courses, an index showing which essays and passages in the book best illustrate the major rhetorical devices of prose writing, a table of cross-references, and a section of topics for study, including questions on the argument, structure, and style of each essay, and suggested topics for writing.

THE
BORZOI
COLLEGE READER

The Necessity for Thinking

So many of the selections in this book are records of hard thinking, that —in the spirit that nothing should be urged on the reader for which we cannot make a good case—we present here a group of essays about thinking itself. This group and the one that follows, on the right use of language, thus serve as preface and justification to the whole collection.

Perhaps only a few readers nowadays will need to read about thinking in order to be convinced of the necessity for thought. The eminent biochemist Albert Szent-Györgyi, thinking of the possibility of atomic war, has put our dilemma plainly: "If it is our intelligence which led us into trouble it may be our intelligence which can lead us out of it." The essay by Aldous Huxley printed in this section similarly suggests forcible, topical, practical arguments—in this case for thought as necessary protection against political annihilation.

But what we accept rationally we often find hard to put into practice, and for some readers the real controversy over the necessity for thinking is more likely to go on among their own inner impulses than in public debate. It is precisely the recognition of this idea that adds to the persuasiveness of most of these writers and makes of thinking itself a topic of complex interest. Golding's essay is surrounded by his awareness of the problem of distinguishing thought and feeling, and developed within by a witty account of three different kinds of thinking. Robinson's fuller and more philosophical treatment of kinds of thinking is similarly based on his recognition of the unconscious and his wish to distinguish real thinking from emotional prejudice. Emerson's famous essay is the pivotal piece in the group. It relates to the first two with its challenging distinction between "Man Thinking" and man as a "mere thinker" or parroter or bookworm; and its insistence on action and experience—"Only so much do I know, as I have lived"—relates it to the essays of Newman and Nock and to the issues of practical and "liberal" thought, active and contemplative life, and the kinds of education these involve.

In the general spirit of debate, the section ends with a piquantly anti-intellectual poem. Given the absolute necessity of thinking, is thinking all? And if not, does it necessarily come first?

WILLIAM GOLDING

William Gerald Golding, a British author, was born in 1911 and educated at Marlborough grammar school and at Oxford. At first destined for a scientific career, he shifted his attention to literature after two years in the University and published a volume of poems. During World War II he served in the Royal Navy, rising to the command of a rocket-launching ship. Since the war he has devoted himself to teaching and writing, and to his hobbies, which he once described as "thinking, classical Greek, sailing, and archaeology." He is widely known for his strikingly original novels, especially Pincher Martin (1956), describing the feelings of a shipwrecked sailor on an isolated rock in mid-ocean, and Lord of the Flies (1954), a deeply symbolic account of a group of schoolboys who revert to savagery when marooned on an island. The present essay first appeared in the August, 1961, issue of Holiday.

THINKING AS A HOBBY

While I was still a boy, I came to the conclusion that there were three grades of thinking; and since I was later to claim thinking as my hobby, I came to an even stranger conclusion—namely, that I myself could not think at all.

I must have been an unsatisfactory child for grownups to deal with. I remember how incomprehensible they appeared to me at first, but not, of course, how I appeared to them. It was the headmaster of my grammar school who first brought the subject of thinking before me—though neither in the way, nor with the result he intended. He had some statuettes in his study. They stood on a high cupboard behind his desk. One was a lady wearing nothing but a bath towel. She seemed frozen in an eternal panic lest the bath towel slip down any farther; and since she had no arms, she was in an unfortunate position to pull the towel up again. Next to her, crouched the statuette of a leopard, ready to spring down at the top drawer of a filing cabinet labeled A-AH. My innocence interpreted this as the victim's last, despairing cry. Beyond the leopard was a naked, muscular gentleman, who sat, looking down, with his chin on his fist and his elbow on his knee. He seemed utterly miserable.

Some time later, I learned about these statuettes. The headmaster had placed them where they would face delinquent children, because they symbolized to him the whole of life. The naked lady was the Venus of Milo. She was Love. She was not worried about the towel. She was just busy being beautiful. The leopard was Nature, and he was being natural. The naked, muscular gentleman was not miserable. He was Rodin's Thinker, an image of pure thought. It is easy to buy small plaster models of what you think life is like.

I had better explain that I was a frequent visitor to the headmaster's study, because of the latest thing I had done or left undone. As we now say, I was not integrated. I was, if anything, disintegrated; and I was puzzled. Grownups never made sense. Whenever I found myself in a penal position before the headmaster's desk, with the statuettes glimmering whitely above him, I would sink my head, clasp my hands behind my back and writhe one shoe over the other.

The headmaster would look opaquely at me through flashing spectacles.

"What are we going to do with you?"

Well, what *were* they going to do with me? I would writhe my shoe some more and stare down at the worn rug.

"Look up, boy! Can't you look up?"

Then I would look up at the cupboard, where the naked lady was frozen in her panic and the muscular gentleman contemplated the hind-quarters of the leopard in endless gloom. I had nothing to say to the headmaster. His spectacles caught the light so that you could see nothing human behind them. There was no possibility of communication.

"Don't you ever think at all?"

No, I didn't think, wasn't thinking, couldn't think—I was simply waiting in anguish for the interview to stop.

"Then you'd better learn—hadn't you?"

On one occasion the headmaster leaped to his feet, reached up and plonked Rodin's masterpiece on the desk before me.

"That's what a man looks like when he's really thinking."

I surveyed the gentleman without interest or comprehension.

"Go back to your class."

Clearly there was something missing in me. Nature had endowed the rest of the human race with a sixth sense and left me out. This must be so, I mused, on my way back to the class, since whether I had broken a window, or failed to remember Boyle's Law, or been late for school, my teachers produced me one, adult answer: "Why can't you think?"

As I saw the case, I had broken the window because I had tried to hit Jack Arney with a cricket ball and missed him; I could not remember Boyle's Law because I had never bothered to learn it; and I was late for school because I preferred looking over the bridge into the river. In fact, I was wicked. Were my teachers, perhaps, so good that they could not understand the depths of my depravity? Were they clear, untormented people who could direct their every action by this mysterious business of thinking? The whole thing was incomprehensible. In my earlier years, I found even the statuette of the Thinker confusing. I did not believe any of my teachers were naked, ever. Like someone born deaf, but bitterly determined to find out about sound, I watched my teachers to find out about thought.

There was Mr. Houghton. He was always telling me to think. With a modest satisfaction, he would tell me that he had thought a bit himself. Then why did he spend so much time drinking? Or was there more sense in drinking than there appeared to be? But if not, and if drinking were in fact ruinous to health—and Mr. Houghton was ruined, there was no doubt about that—why was he always talking about the clean life and the virtues of fresh air? He would spread his arms wide with the action of a man who habitually spent his time striding along mountain ridges.

"Open air does me good, boys—I know it!"

Sometimes, exalted by his own oratory, he would leap from his desk and hustle us outside into a hideous wind.

"Now, boys! Deep breaths! Feel it right down inside you—huge draughts of God's good air!"

He would stand before us, rejoicing in his perfect health, an open-air man. He would put his hands on his waist and take a tremendous breath. You could hear the wind, trapped in the cavern of his chest and struggling with all the unnatural impediments. His body would reel with shock and his ruined face go white at the unaccustomed visitation. He would stagger back to his desk and collapse there, useless for the rest of the morning.

Mr. Houghton was given to high-minded monologues about the good life, sexless and full of duty. Yet in the middle of one of these monologues, if a girl passed the window, tapping along on her neat little feet, he would interrupt his discourse, his neck would turn of itself and he would watch her out of sight. In this instance, he seemed to me ruled not by thought but by an invisible and irresistible spring in his nape.

His neck was an object of great interest to me. Normally it bulged a bit over his collar. But Mr. Houghton had fought in the First World War alongside both Americans and French, and had come—by who knows what illogic?—to a settled detestation of both countries. If either country happened to be prominent in current affairs, no argument could make Mr.

Houghton think well of it. He would bang the desk, his neck would bulge still further and go red. "You can say what you like," he would cry, "but I've thought about this—and I know what I think!"

Mr. Houghton thought with his neck.

There was Miss Parsons. She assured us that her dearest wish was our welfare, but I knew even then, with the mysterious clairvoyance of childhood, that what she wanted most was the husband she never got. There was Mr. Hands—and so on.

I have dealt at length with my teachers because this was my introduction to the nature of what is commonly called thought. Through them I discovered that thought is often full of unconscious prejudice, ignorance and hypocrisy. It will lecture on disinterested purity while its neck is being remorselessly twisted toward a skirt. Technically, it is about as proficient as most businessmen's golf, as honest as most politicians' intentions, or—to come near my own preoccupation—as coherent as most books that get written. It is what I came to call grade-three thinking, though more properly, it is feeling, rather than thought.

True, often there is a kind of innocence in prejudices, but in those days I viewed grade-three thinking with an intolerant contempt and an incautious mockery. I delighted to confront a pious lady who hated the Germans with the proposition that we should love our enemies. She taught me a great truth in dealing with grade-three thinkers; because of her, I no longer dismiss lightly a mental process which for nine-tenths of the population is the nearest they will ever get to thought. They have immense solidarity. We had better respect them, for we are outnumbered and surrounded. A crowd of grade-three thinkers, all shouting the same thing, all warming their hands at the fire of their own prejudices, will not thank you for pointing out the contradictions in their beliefs. Man is a gregarious animal, and enjoys agreement as cows will graze all the same way on the side of a hill.

Grade-two thinking is the detection of contradictions. I reached grade two when I trapped the poor, pious lady. Grade-two thinkers do not stampede easily, though often they fall into the other fault and lag behind. Grade-two thinking is a withdrawal, with eyes and ears open. It became my hobby and brought satisfaction and loneliness in either hand. For grade-two thinking destroys without having the power to create. It set me watching the crowds cheering His Majesty the King and asking myself what all the fuss was about, without giving me anything positive to put in the place of that heady patriotism. But there were compensations. To hear people justify their habit of hunting foxes and tearing them to pieces by claiming that the foxes liked it. To hear our Prime Minister talk about the great benefit we conferred on India by jailing people like Pandit Nehru and Gandhi. To hear American politicians talk about peace in one sentence and refuse to join the League of Nations in the next. Yes, there were moments of delight.

But I was growing toward adolescence and had to admit that Mr. Houghton was not the only one with an irresistible spring in his neck. I, too, felt the compulsive hand of nature and began to find that pointing out contradiction could be costly as well as fun. There was Ruth, for example, a serious and attractive girl. I was an atheist at the time. Grade-two thinking is a menace to religion and knocks down sects like skittles. I put myself in a position to be converted by her with an hypocrisy worthy of grade three. She was a Methodist—or at least, her parents were, and Ruth had to follow suit. But, alas, instead of relying on the Holy Spirit to convert me, Ruth was foolish enough to open her pretty mouth in argument. She claimed that the Bible (King James Version) was literally inspired. I countered by saying that the Catholics believed in the literal inspiration of Saint Jerome's *Vulgate*, and the two books were different. Argument flagged.

At last she remarked that there were an awful lot of Methodists, and they couldn't be wrong, could they—not all those millions? That was too easy, said I restively (for the nearer you were to Ruth, the nicer she was to be near to) since there were more Roman Catholics than Methodists anyway; and they couldn't be wrong, could they—not all those hundreds of millions? An awful flicker of doubt appeared in her eyes. I slid my arm round her waist and murmured breathlessly that if we were counting heads, the Buddhists were the boys for my money. But Ruth had *really* wanted to do me good, because I was so nice. She fled. The combination of my arm and those countless Buddhists was too much for her.

That night her father visited my father and left, red-cheeked and indignant. I was given the third degree to find out what had happened. It was lucky we were both of us only fourteen. I lost Ruth and gained an undeserved reputation as a potential libertine.

So grade-two thinking could be dangerous. It was in this knowledge, at the age of fifteen, that I remember making a comment from the heights of grade two, on the limitations of grade three. One evening I found myself alone in the school hall, preparing it for a party. The door of the headmaster's study was open. I went in. The headmaster had ceased to thump Rodin's Thinker down on the desk as an example to the young. Perhaps he had not found any more candidates, but the statuettes were still there, glimmering and gathering dust on top of the cupboard. I stood on a chair and rearranged them. I stood Venus in her bath towel on the filing cabinet, so that now the top drawer caught its breath in a gasp of sexy excitement. "A-ah!" The portentous Thinker I placed on the edge of the cupboard so that he looked down at the bath towel and waited for it to slip.

Grade-two thinking, though it filled life with fun and excitement, did not make for content. To find out the deficiencies of our elders bolsters the young ego but does not make for personal security. I found that grade two was not only the power to point out contradictions. It took the

swimmer some distance from the shore and left him there, out of his depth.
I decided that Pontius Pilate was a typical grade-two thinker. "What is
truth?" he said, a very common grade-two thought, but one that is used
always as the end of an argument instead of the beginning. There is a still
higher grade of thought which says, "What is truth?" and sets out to find
it.

But these grade-one thinkers were few and far between. They did not
visit my grammar school in the flesh though they were there in books. I
aspired to them, partly because I was ambitious and partly because I now
saw my hobby as an unsatisfactory thing if it went no further. If you set
out to climb a mountain, however high you climb, you have failed if you
cannot reach the top.

I *did* meet an undeniably grade-one thinker in my first year at Oxford.
I was looking over a small bridge in Magdalen Deer Park, and a tiny
mustached and hatted figure came and stood by my side. He was a
German who had just fled from the Nazis to Oxford as a temporary refuge.
His name was Einstein.

But Professor Einstein knew no English at that time and I knew only
two words of German. I beamed at him, trying wordlessly to convey by
my bearing all the affection and respect that the English felt for him. It
is possible—and I have to make the admission—that I felt here were two
grade-one thinkers standing side by side; yet I doubt if my face conveyed
more than a formless awe. I would have given my Greek and Latin and
French and a good slice of my English for enough German to communicate. But we were divided; he was as inscrutable as my headmaster.
For perhaps five minutes we stood together on the bridge, undeniable
grade-one thinker and breathless aspirant. With true greatness, Professor
Einstein realized that any contact was better than none. He pointed to a
trout wavering in midstream.

He spoke: *"Fisch."*

My brain reeled. Here I was, mingling with the great, and yet helpless
as the veriest grade-three thinker. Desperately I sought for some sign by
which I might convey that I, too, revered pure reason. I nodded
vehemently. In a brilliant flash I used up half of my German vocabulary.

"Fisch. Ja. Ja."

For perhaps another five minutes we stood side by side. Then Professor
Einstein, his whole figure still conveying good will and amiability, drifted
away out of sight.

I, too, would be a grade-one thinker. I was irreverent at the best of
times. Political and religious systems, social customs, loyalties and
traditions, they all came tumbling down like so many rotten apples off a
tree. This was a fine hobby and a sensible substitute for cricket, since you
could play it all the year round. I came up in the end with what must
always remain the justification for grade-one thinking, its sign, seal and
charter. I devised a coherent system for living. It was a moral system,

which was wholly logical. Of course, as I readily admitted, conversion of the world to my way of thinking might be difficult, since my system did away with a number of trifles, such as big business, centralized government, armies, marriage. . . .

It was Ruth all over again. I had some very good friends who stood by me, and still do. But my acquaintances vanished, taking the girls with them. Young women seemed oddly contented with the world as it was. They valued the meaningless ceremony with a ring. Young men, while willing to concede the chaining sordidness of marriage, were hesitant about abandoning the organizations which they hoped would give them a career. A young man on the first rung of the Royal Navy, while perfectly agreeable to doing away with big business and marriage, got as red-necked as Mr. Houghton when I proposed a world without any battleships in it.

Had the game gone too far? Was it a game any longer? In those prewar days, I stood to lose a great deal, for the sake of a hobby.

Now you are expecting me to describe how I saw the folly of my ways and came back to the warm nest, where prejudices are so often called loyalties, where pointless actions are hallowed into custom by repetition, where we are content to say we think when all we do is feel.

But you would be wrong. I dropped my hobby and turned professional.

If I were to go back to the headmaster's study and find the dusty statuettes still there, I would arrange them differently. I would dust Venus and put her aside, for I have come to love her and know her for the fair thing she is. But I would put the Thinker, sunk in his desperate thought, where there were shadows before him—and at his back, I would put the leopard, crouched and ready to spring.

JAMES HARVEY ROBINSON

James Harvey Robinson (1863–1936), American historian and university professor, was educated at Harvard and Freiburg. He taught history at the University of Pennsylvania, and from 1895 to 1919 at Columbia. Resigning in 1919 in protest against the expulsion of a group of professors for their

opposition to World War I, he attacked Columbia president Nicholas Murray Butler for his alleged attempts to suppress freedom of expression at the University. Robinson then helped to found the New School for Social Research in New York City where he taught until 1921, when he retired to devote the rest of his life to writing. Among his dozen volumes of historical and philosophical writing, perhaps the best known to the general public is The Mind in the Making *(1921), subtitled* The Relation of Intelligence to Social Reform. *Chapter II of this book has been excerpted and reprinted so often that it has itself been the subject of an amusing article by Professor David Novarr ("OVKOT," AAUP Bulletin, 1951, Vol. 37). But familiarity has not reduced its value. We reprint the chapter here in full, using the heading of the first section as title for the whole.*

ON VARIOUS KINDS OF THINKING

Good sense is, of all things among men, the most equally distributed; for everyone thinks himself so abundantly provided with it that those even who are the most difficult to satisfy in everything else do not usually desire a larger measure of this quality than they already possess.—DESCARTES.

We see man to-day, instead of the frank and courageous recognition of his status, the docile attention to his biological history, the determination to let nothing stand in the way of the security and permanence of his future, which alone can establish the safety and happiness of the race, substituting blind confidence in his destiny, unclouded faith in the essentially respectful attitude of the universe toward his moral code, and a belief no less firm that his traditions and laws and institutions necessarily contain permanent qualities of reality.

—WILLIAM TROTTER.

1. ON VARIOUS KINDS OF THINKING

The truest and most profound observations on Intelligence have in the past been made by the poets and, in recent times, by story-writers. They have been keen observers and recorders and reckoned freely with the emotions and sentiments. Most philosophers, on the other hand, have exhibited a grotesque ignorance of man's life and have built up systems that are elaborate and imposing, but quite unrelated to actual human affairs. They have almost consistently neglected the actual process of thought and have set the mind off as something apart to be studied by itself. *But no such mind, exempt from bodily processes, animal impulses, savage traditions, infantile impressions, conventional reactions, and traditional knowledge, ever existed,* even in the case of the most abstract of metaphysicians. Kant entitled his great work *A Critique of Pure Reason.* But to the modern student of mind pure reason seems as mythical as the pure gold, transparent as glass, with which the celestial city is paved.

Formerly philosophers thought of mind as having to do exclusively with conscious thought. It was that within man which perceived, remembered, judged, reasoned, understood, believed, willed. But of late it has been shown that we are unaware of a great part of what we perceive, remember, will, and infer; and that a great part of the thinking of which we are aware is determined by that of which we are not conscious. It has indeed been demonstrated that our unconscious psychic life far outruns our conscious. This seems perfectly natural to anyone who considers the following facts:

The sharp distinction between the mind and the body is, as we shall find, a very ancient and spontaneous uncritical savage prepossession. What we think of as "mind" is so intimately associated with what we call "body" that we are coming to realize that the one cannot be understood without the other. Every thought reverberates through the body, and, on the other hand, alterations in our physical condition affect our whole attitude of mind. The insufficient elimination of the foul and decaying products of digestion may plunge us into deep melancholy, whereas a few whiffs of nitrous monoxide may exalt us to the seventh heaven of supernal knowledge and godlike complacency. And *vice versa*, a sudden word or thought may cause our heart to jump, check our breathing, or make our knees as water. There is a whole new literature growing up which studies the effects of our bodily secretions and our muscular tensions and their relation to our emotions and our thinking.

Then there are hidden impulses and desires and secret longings of which we can only with the greatest difficulty take account. They influence our conscious thought in the most bewildering fashion. Many of these unconscious influences appear to originate in our very early years. The older philosophers seem to have forgotten that even they were infants and children at their most impressionable age and never could by any possibility get over it.

The term "unconscious," now so familiar to all readers of modern works on psychology, gives offense to some adherents of the past. There should, however, be no special mystery about it. It is not a new animistic abstraction, but simply a collective word to include all the physiological changes which escape our notice, all the forgotten experiences and impressions of the past which continue to influence our desires and reflections and conduct, even if we cannot remember them. What we can remember at any time is indeed an infinitesimal part of what has happened to us. We could not remember anything unless we forgot almost everything. As

Bergson says, the brain is the organ of forgetfulness as well as of memory. Moreover, we tend, of course, to become oblivious to things to which we are thoroughly accustomed, for habit blinds us to their existence. So the forgotten and the habitual make up a great part of the so-called "unconscious."

If we are ever to understand man, his conduct and reasoning, and if we aspire to learn to guide his life and his relations with his fellows more happily than heretofore, we cannot neglect the great discoveries briefly noted above. We must reconcile ourselves to novel and revolutionary conceptions of the mind, for it is clear that the older philosophers, whose works still determine our current views, had a very superficial notion of the subject with which they dealt. But for our purposes, with due regard to what has just been said and to much that has necessarily been left unsaid (and with the indulgence of those who will at first be inclined to dissent), *we shall consider mind chiefly as conscious knowledge and intelligence, as what we know and our attitude toward it—our disposition to increase our information, classify it, criticize it, and apply it.*

We do not think enough about thinking, and much of our confusion is the result of current illusions in regard to it. Let us forget for the moment any impressions we may have derived from the philosophers, and see what seems to happen in ourselves. The first thing that we notice is that our thought moves with such incredible rapidity that it is almost impossible to arrest any specimen of it long enough to have a look at it. When we are offered a penny for our thoughts we always find that we have recently had so many things in mind that we can easily make a selection which will not compromise us too nakedly. On inspection we shall find that even if we are not downright ashamed of a great part of our spontaneous thinking it is far too intimate, personal, ignoble or trivial to permit us to reveal more than a small part of it. I believe this must be true of everyone. We do not, of course, know what goes on in other people's heads. They tell us very little and we tell them very little. The spigot of speech, rarely fully opened, could never emit more than driblets of the ever renewed hogshead of thought—*noch grösser wie's Heidelberger Fass.* We find it hard to believe that other people's thoughts are as silly as our own, but they probably are.

We all appear to ourselves to be thinking all the time during our waking hours, and most of us are aware that we go on thinking while we are asleep, even more foolishly than when awake. When uninterrupted by some practical issue we are engaged in what is now known as a *reverie.* This is our spontaneous and favorite kind of thinking. We allow our ideas to take their own course and this course is determined by our hopes and fears, our spontaneous desires, their fulfillment or frustration; by our likes and dislikes, our loves and hates and resentments. There is nothing else anything like so interesting to ourselves as ourselves. All thought that is not more or less laboriously controlled and directed will inevitably circle about the beloved Ego. It is amusing and pathetic to observe this tendency in ourselves and in others. We learn politely and generously to overlook this truth, but if we dare to think of it, it blazes forth like the noontide sun.

The reverie or "free association of ideas" has of late become the subject of scientific research. While investigators are not yet agreed on the results, or at least on the proper interpretation to be given to them, there can be no doubt that our reveries form the chief index to our fundamental character. They are a reflection of our nature as modified by often hidden and forgotten experiences. We need not go into the matter further here, for it is only necessary to observe that the reverie is at all times a potent and in many cases an omnipotent rival to every other kind of thinking. It doubtless influences all our speculations in its persistent tendency to self-magnification and self-justification, which are its chief preoccupations, but it is the last thing to make directly or indirectly for honest increase of knowledge.[1] Philosophers usually talk as if such thinking did not exist or were in some way negligible. This is what makes their speculations so unreal and often worthless.

The reverie, as any of us can see for himself, is frequently broken and interrupted by the necessity of a second kind of thinking. We have to make practical decisions. Shall we write a letter or no? Shall we take the subway or a bus? Shall we have dinner at seven or half past? Shall we buy U. S. Rubber or a Liberty Bond? Decisions are easily distinguishable from the free flow of the reverie. Sometimes they demand a good deal of careful pondering and the recollection of pertinent facts; often, however, they are made impulsively. They are a more difficult and laborious thing than the reverie, and we resent having to "make up our mind" when we are tired, or absorbed in a congenial reverie. Weighing a decision, it should be noted, does not necessarily add anything to our knowledge, although we may, of course, seek further information before making it.

2. RATIONALIZING

A third kind of thinking is stimulated when anyone questions our belief and opinions. We sometimes find ourselves changing our minds without any resistance or heavy emotion, but if we are told that we are

---

[1] The poet-clergyman, John Donne, who lived in the time of James I, has given a beautifully honest picture of the doings of a saint's mind: "I throw myself down in my chamber and call in and invite God and His angels thither, and when they are there I neglect God and His angels for the noise of a fly, for the rattling of a coach, for the whining of a door. I talk on in the same posture of praying, eyes lifted up, knees bowed down, as though I prayed to God, and if God or His angels should ask me when I thought last of God in that prayer I cannot tell. Sometimes I find that I had forgot what I was about, but when I began to forget it I cannot tell. A memory of yesterday's pleasures, a fear of to-morrow's dangers, a straw under my knee, a noise in mine ear, a light in mine eye, an anything, a nothing, a fancy, a chimera in my brain troubles me in my prayer."—Quoted by ROBERT LYND, *The Art of Letters,* pp. 46-47.

wrong we resent the imputation and harden our hearts. We are incredibly heedless in the formation of our beliefs, but find ourselves filled with an illicit passion for them when anyone proposes to rob us of their companionship. It is obviously not the ideas themselves that are dear to us, but our self-esteem, which is threatened. We are by nature stubbornly pledged to defend our own from attack, whether it be our person, our family, our property, or our opinion. A United States Senator once remarked to a friend of mine that God Almighty could not make him change his mind on our Latin-America policy. We may surrender, but rarely confess ourselves vanquished. In the intellectual world at least peace is without victory.

Few of us take the pains to study the origin of our cherished convictions; indeed, we have a natural repugnance to so doing. We like to continue to believe what we have been accustomed to accept as true, and the resentment aroused when doubt is cast upon any of our assumptions leads us to seek every manner of excuse for clinging to them. *The result is that most of our so-called reasoning consists in finding arguments for going on believing as we already do.*

I remember years ago attending a public dinner to which the Governor of the state was bidden. The chairman explained that His Excellency could not be present for certain "good" reasons; what the "real" reasons were the presiding officer said he would leave us to conjecture. This distinction between "good" and "real" reasons is one of the most clarifying and essential in the whole realm of thought. We can readily give what seem to us "good" reasons for being a Catholic or a Mason, a Republican or a Democrat, an adherent or opponent of the League of Nations. But the "real" reasons are usually on quite a different plane. Of course the importance of this distinction is popularly, if somewhat obscurely, recognized. The Baptist missionary is ready enough to see that the Buddhist is not such because his doctrines would bear careful inspection, but because he happened to be born in a Buddhist family in Tokio. But it would be treason to his faith to acknowledge that his own partiality for certain doctrines is due to the fact that his mother was a member of the First Baptist church of Oak Ridge. A savage can give all sorts of reasons for his belief that it is dangerous to step on a man's shadow, and a newspaper editor can advance plenty of arguments against the Bolsheviki. But neither of them may realize why he happens to be defending his particular opinion.

The "real" reasons for our beliefs are concealed from ourselves as well as from others. As we grow up we simply adopt the ideas presented to us in regard to such matters as religion, family relations, property, business, our country, and the state. We unconsciously absorb them from our environment. They are persistently whispered in our ear by the group in which we happen to live. Moreover, as Mr. Trotter has pointed out, these judgments, being the product of suggestion and not of reasoning, have the quality of perfect obviousness, so that to question them

. . . is to the believer to carry skepticism to an insane degree, and will be met by contempt, disapproval, or condemnation, according to the nature of the belief in question. When, therefore, we find ourselves entertaining an opinion about the basis of which there is a quality of feeling which tells us that to inquire into it would be absurd, obviously unnecessary, unprofitable, undesirable, bad form, or wicked, we may know that that opinion is a nonrational one, and probably, therefore, founded upon inadequate evidence.[2]

Opinions, on the other hand, which are the result of experience or of honest reasoning do not have this quality of "primary certitude." I remember when as a youth I heard a group of business men discussing the question of the immortality of the soul, I was outraged by the sentiment of doubt expressed by one of the party. As I look back now I see that I had at the time no interest in the matter, and certainly no least argument to urge in favor of the belief in which I had been reared. But neither my personal indifference to the issue, nor the fact that I had previously given it no attention, served to prevent an angry resentment when I heard *my* ideas questioned.

This spontaneous and loyal support of our preconceptions—this process of finding "good" reasons to justify our routine beliefs—is known to modern psychologists as "rationalizing"—clearly only a new name for a very ancient thing. Our "good" reasons ordinarily have no value in promoting honest enlightenment, because, no matter how solemnly they may be marshaled, they are at bottom the result of personal preference or prejudice, and not of an honest desire to seek or accept new knowledge.

In our reveries we are frequently engaged in self-justification, for we cannot bear to think ourselves wrong, and yet have constant illustrations of our weaknesses and mistakes. So we spend much time finding fault with circumstances and the conduct of others, and shifting on to them with great ingenuity the onus of our own failures and disappointments. *Rationalizing is the self-exculpation which occurs when we feel ourselves, or our group, accused of misapprehension or error.*

The little word *my* is the most important one in all human affairs, and properly to reckon with it is the beginning of wisdom. It has the same force whether it is *my* dinner, *my* dog, and *my* house, or *my* faith, *my* country, and *my* God. We not only resent the imputation that our watch is wrong, or our car shabby, but that our conception of the canals of Mars, of the pronunciation of "Epictetus," of the medicinal value of salicine, or the date of Sargon I, are subject to revision.

Philosophers, scholars, and men of science exhibit a common sensitiveness in all decisions in which their *amour propre* is involved. Thousands of argumentative works have been written to vent a grudge. However stately their reasoning, it may be nothing but rationalizing, stimulated by

---

[2] *Instincts of the Herd*, p. 44.

the most commonplace of all motives. A history of philosophy and theology could be written in terms of grouches, wounded pride, and aversions, and it would be far more instructive than the usual treatments of these themes. Sometimes, under Providence, the lowly impulse of resentment leads to great achievements. Milton wrote his treatise on divorce as a result of his troubles with his seventeen-year-old wife, and when he was accused of being the leading spirit in a new sect, the Divorcers, he wrote his noble *Areopagitica* to prove his right to say what he thought fit, and incidentally to establish the advantage of a free press in the promotion of Truth.

All mankind, high and low, thinks in all the ways which have been described. The reverie goes on all the time not only in the mind of the mill hand and the Broadway flapper, but equally in weighty judges and godly bishops. It has gone on in all the philosophers, scientists, poets, and theologians that have ever lived. Aristotle's most abstruse speculations were doubtless tempered by highly irrelevant reflections. He is reported to have had very thin legs and small eyes, for which he doubtless had to find excuses, and he was wont to indulge in very conspicuous dress and rings and was accustomed to arrange his hair carefully.[3] Diogenes the Cynic exhibited the impudence of a touchy soul. His tub was his distinction. Tennyson in beginning his "Maud" could not forget his chagrin over losing his patrimony years before as the result of an unhappy investment in the Patent Decorative Carving Company. These facts are not recalled here as a gratuitous disparagement of the truly great, but to insure a full realization of the tremendous competition which all really exacting thought has to face, even in the minds of the most highly endowed mortals.

And now the astonishing and perturbing suspicion emerges that perhaps almost all that had passed for social science, political economy, politics, and ethics in the past may be brushed aside by future generations as mainly rationalizing. John Dewey has already reached this conclusion in regard to philosophy.[4] Veblen[5] and other writers have revealed the various unperceived presuppositions of the traditional political economy, and now comes an Italian sociologist, Vilfredo Pareto, who, in his huge treatise on general sociology, devotes hundreds of pages to substantiating a similar thesis affecting all the social sciences.[6] This conclusion may be ranked by students of a hundred years hence as one of the several great discoveries of

---

[3] Diogenes Lærtius, book v.
[4] *Reconstruction in Philosophy.*
[5] *The Place of Science in Modern Civilization.*
[6] *Traité de Sociologie Générale, passim.* The author's term *"derivations"* seems to be his precise way of expressing what we have called the "good" reasons, and his *"residus"* correspond to the "real" reasons. He well says, *"L'homme éprouve le besoin de raisonner, et en outre d'étendre un voile sur ses instincts et sur ses sentiments"*— hence, rationalization. (P. 788.) His aim is to reduce sociology to the "real" reasons. (P. 791.)

our age. It is by no means fully worked out, and it is so opposed to nature that it will be very slowly accepted by the great mass of those who consider themselves thoughtful. As a historical student I am personally fully reconciled to this newer view. Indeed, it seems to me inevitable that just as the various sciences of nature were, before the opening of the seventeenth century, largely masses of rationalizations to suit the religious sentiments of the period, so the social sciences have continued even to our own day to be rationalizations of uncritically accepted beliefs and customs.

It will become apparent as we proceed that the fact that an idea is ancient and that it has been widely received is no argument in its favor, but should immediately suggest the necessity of carefully testing it as a probable instance of rationalization.

3. HOW CREATIVE THOUGHT TRANSFORMS THE WORLD

This brings us to another kind of thought which can fairly easily be distinguished from the three kinds described above. It has not the usual qualities of the reverie, for it does not hover about our personal complacencies and humiliations. It is not made up of the homely decisions forced upon us by everyday needs, when we review our little stock of existing information, consult our conventional preferences and obligations, and make a choice of action. It is not the defense of our own cherished beliefs and prejudices just because they are our own—mere plausible excuses for remaining of the same mind. On the contrary, it is that peculiar species of thought which leads us to *change* our mind.

It is this kind of thought that has raised man from his pristine, subsavage ignorance and squalor to the degree of knowledge and comfort which he now possesses. On his capacity to continue and greatly extend this kind of thinking depends his chance of groping his way out of the plight in which the most highly civilized peoples of the world now find themselves. In the past this type of thinking has been called Reason. But so many misapprehensions have grown up around the word that some of us have become very suspicious of it. I suggest, therefore, that we substitute a recent name and speak of "creative thought" rather than of Reason. *For this kind of meditation begets knowledge, and knowledge is really creative inasmuch as it makes things look different from what they seemed before and may indeed work for their reconstruction.*

In certain moods some of us realize that we are observing things or making reflections with a seeming disregard of our personal preoccupations. We are not preening or defending ourselves; we are not faced by the necessity of any practical decision, nor are we apologizing for believing this or that. We are just wondering and looking and mayhap seeing what we never perceived before.

Curiosity is as clear and definite as any of our urges. We wonder what is in a sealed telegram or in a letter in which some one else is absorbed, or what is being said in the telephone booth or in low conversation. This inquisitiveness is vastly stimulated by jealousy, suspicion, or any hint that we ourselves are directly or indirectly involved. But there appears to be a fair amount of personal interest in other people's affairs even when they do not concern us except as a mystery to be unraveled or a tale to be told. The reports of a divorce suit will have "news value" for many weeks. They constitute a story, like a novel or play or moving picture. This is not an example of pure curiosity, however, since we readily identify ourselves with others, and their joys and despair then become our own.

We also take note of, or "observe," as Sherlock Holmes says, things which have nothing to do with our personal interests and make no personal appeal either direct or by way of sympathy. This is what Veblen so well calls "idle curiosity." And it is usually idle enough. Some of us when we face the line of people opposite us in a subway train impulsively consider them in detail and engage in rapid inferences and form theories in regard to them. On entering a room there are those who will perceive at a glance the degree of preciousness of the rugs, the character of the pictures, and the personality revealed by the books. But there are many, it would seem, who are so absorbed in their personal reverie or in some definite purpose that they have no bright-eyed energy for idle curiosity. The tendency to miscellaneous observation we come by honestly enough, for we note it in many of our animal relatives.

Veblen, however, uses the term "idle curiosity" somewhat ironically, as is his wont. It is idle only to those who fail to realize that it may be a very rare and indispensable thing from which almost all distinguished human achievement proceeds. Since it may lead to systematic examination and seeking for things hitherto undiscovered. For research is but diligent search which enjoys the high flavor of primitive hunting. Occasionally and fitfully idle curiosity thus leads to creative thought, which alters and broadens our own views and aspirations and may in turn, under highly favorable circumstances, affect the views and lives of others, even for generations to follow. An example or two will make this unique human process clear.

Galileo was a thoughtful youth and doubtless carried on a rich and varied reverie. He had artistic ability and might have turned out to be a musician or painter. When he had dwelt among the monks at Valambrosa he had been tempted to lead the life of a religious. As a boy he busied himself with toy machines and he inherited a fondness for mathematics. All these facts are of record. We may safely assume also that, along with many other subjects of contemplation, the Pisan maidens found a vivid place in his thoughts.

One day when seventeen years old he wandered into the cathedral of his native town. In the midst of his reverie he looked up at the lamps hanging by long chains from the high ceiling of the church. Then something very difficult to explain occurred. He found himself no longer thinking of the building, worshipers, or the services; of his artistic or religious interests; of his reluctance to become a physician as his father wished. He forgot the question of a career and even the *graziosissime donne*. As he watched the swinging lamps he was suddenly wondering if mayhap their oscillations, whether long or short, did not occupy the same time. Then he tested this hypothesis by counting his pulse, for that was the only timepiece he had with him.

This observation, however remarkable in itself, was not enough to produce a really creative thought. Others may have noticed the same thing and yet nothing came of it. Most of our observations have no assignable results. Galileo may have seen that the warts on a peasant's face formed a perfect isosceles triangle, or he may have noticed with boyish glee that just as the officiating priest was uttering the solemn words, *ecce agnus Dei*, a fly lit on the end of his nose. To be really creative, ideas have to be worked up and then "put over," so that they become a part of man's social heritage. The highly accurate pendulum clock was one of the later results of Galileo's discovery. He himself was led to reconsider and successfully to refute the old notions of falling bodies. It remained for Newton to prove that the moon was falling, and presumably all the heavenly bodies. This quite upset all the consecrated views of the heavens as managed by angelic engineers. The universality of the laws of gravitation stimulated the attempt to seek other and equally important natural laws and cast grave doubts on the miracles in which mankind had hitherto believed. In short, those who dared to include in their thought the discoveries of Galileo and his successors found themselves in a new earth surrounded by new heavens.

On the 28th of October, 1831, two hundred and fifty years after Galileo had noticed the isochronous vibrations of the lamps, creative thought and its currency had so far increased that Faraday was wondering what would happen if he mounted a disk of copper between the poles of a horseshoe magnet. As the disk revolved an electric current was produced. This would doubtless have seemed the idlest kind of an experiment to the stanch business men of the time, who, it happened, were just then denouncing the child-labor bills in their anxiety to avail themselves to the full of the results of earlier idle curiosity. But should the dynamos and motors which have come into being as the outcome of Faraday's experiment be stopped this evening, the business man of to-day, agitated over labor troubles, might, as he trudged home past lines of "dead" cars, through dark streets to an unlighted house, engage in a little creative thought of his own and perceive that he and his laborers would have no modern factories and mines to quarrel about had it not been for the strange practical effects of the idle curiosity of scientists, inventors, and engineers.

The examples of creative intelligence given above belong to the realm of modern scientific achievement, which furnishes the most striking instances of the effects of scrupulous, objective thinking. But there are, of course, other great realms in which the recording and embodiment of acute observation and insight have wrought themselves into the higher life of man. The great poets and dramatists and our modern story-tellers have found themselves engaged in productive reveries, noting and artistically presenting their discoveries for the delight and instruction of those who have the ability to appreciate them.

The process by which a fresh and original poem or drama comes into being is doubtless analogous to that which originates and elaborates so-called scientific discoveries; but there is clearly a temperamental difference. The genesis and advance of painting, sculpture, and music offer still other problems. We really as yet know shockingly little about these matters, and indeed very few people have the least curiosity about them.[7] Nevertheless, creative intelligence in its various forms and activities is what makes man. Were it not for its slow, painful, and constantly discouraged operations through the ages man would be no more than a species of primate living on seeds, fruit, roots, and uncooked flesh, and wandering naked through the woods and over the plains like a chimpanzee.

The origin and progress and future promotion of civilization are ill understood and misconceived. These should be made the chief theme of education, but much hard work is necessary before we can reconstruct our ideas of man and his capacities and free ourselves from innumerable persistent misapprehensions. There have been obstructionists in all times, not merely the lethargic masses, but the moralists, the rationalizing theologians, and most of the philosophers, all busily if unconsciously engaged in ratifying existing ignorance and mistakes and discouraging creative thought. Naturally, those who reassure us seem worthy of honor and respect. Equally naturally those who puzzle us with disturbing criticisms and invite us to change our ways are objects of suspicion and readily discredited. Our personal discontent does not ordinarily extend to any critical questioning of the general situation in which we find ourselves. In every age the prevailing conditions of civilization have appeared quite natural and inevitable to those who grew up in them. The cow asks no questions as to how it happens to have a dry stall and a supply of hay. The kitten laps its warm milk from a china saucer, without knowing anything about porcelain; the dog nestles in the corner of a divan with no sense of obligation to the inventors of upholstery and the manufacturers of down pillows. So we humans accept our breakfasts, our trains and telephones and orchestras and movies, our national Constitution, our moral code and standards of manners, with the simplicity and innocence of a pet rabbit. We have absolutely inexhaustible capacities for appropriating what others do

[7] Recently a re-examination of creative thought has begun as a result of new knowledge which discredits many of the notions formerly held about "reason." See, for example, *Creative Intelligence*, by a group of American philosophic thinkers; John Dewey, *Essays in Experimental Logic* (both pretty hard books); and Veblen, *The Place of Science in Modern Civilization*. Easier than these and very stimulating are Dewey, *Reconstruction in Philosophy*, and Woodworth, *Dynamic Psychology*.

for us with no thought of a "thank you." We do not feel called upon to make any least contribution to the merry game ourselves. Indeed, we are usually quite unaware that a game is being played at all.

We have now examined the various classes of thinking which we can readily observe in ourselves and which we have plenty of reasons to believe go on, and always have been going on, in our fellow-men. We can sometimes get quite pure and sparkling examples of all four kinds, but commonly they are so confused and intermingled in our reverie as not to be readily distinguishable. The reverie is a reflection of our longings, exultations, and complacencies, our fears, suspicions, and disappointments. We are chiefly engaged in struggling to maintain our self-respect and in asserting that supremacy which we all crave and which seems to us our natural prerogative. It is not strange, but rather quite inevitable, that our beliefs about what is true and false, good and bad, right and wrong, should be mixed up with the reverie and be influenced by the same considerations which determine its character and course. We resent criticisms of our views exactly as we do of anything else connected with ourselves. Our notions of life and its ideals seem to us to be *our own* and as such necessarily true and right, to be defended at all costs.

We very rarely consider, however, the process by which we gained our convictions. If we did so, we could hardly fail to see that there was usually little ground for our confidence in them. Here and there, in this department of knowledge or that, some one of us might make a fair claim to have taken some trouble to get correct ideas of, let us say, the situation in Russia, the sources of our food supply, the origin of the Constitution, the revision of the tariff, the policy of the Holy Roman Apostolic Church, modern business organization, trade unions, birth control, socialism, the League of Nations, the excess-profits tax, preparedness, advertising in its social bearings; but only a very exceptional person would be entitled to opinions on all of even these few matters. And yet most of us have opinions on all these, and on many other questions of equal importance, of which we may know even less. We feel compelled, as self-respecting persons, to take sides when they come up for discussion. We even surprise ourselves by our omniscience. Without taking thought we see in a flash that it is most righteous and expedient to discourage birth control by legislative enactment, or that one who decries intervention in Mexico is clearly wrong, or that big advertising is essential to big business and that big business is the pride of the land. As godlike beings why should we not rejoice in our omniscience?

It is clear, in any case, that our convictions on important matters are not the result of knowledge or critical thought, nor, it may be added, are they often dictated by supposed self-interest. Most of them are *pure prejudices* in the proper sense of that word. We do not form them ourselves. They are the whisperings of "the voice of the herd." We have in the last analysis no responsibility for them and need assume none. They are not really our own ideas, but those of others no more well informed or inspired than ourselves, who have got them in the same careless and humiliating manner as we. It should be our pride to revise our ideas and not to adhere to what passes for respectable opinion, for such opinion can frequently be shown to be not respectable at all. We should, in view of the considerations that have been mentioned, resent our supine credulity. As an English writer has remarked:

"If we feared the entertaining of an unverifiable opinion with the warmth with which we fear using the wrong implement at the dinner table, if the thought of holding a prejudice disgusted us as does a foul disease, then the dangers of man's suggestibility would be turned into advantages."[8]

The purpose of this essay is to set forth briefly the way in which the notions of the herd have been accumulated. This seems to me the best, easiest, and least invidious educational device for cultivating a proper distrust for the older notions on which we still continue to rely.

The "real" reasons, which explain how it is we happen to hold a particular belief, are chiefly historical. Our most important opinions—those, for example, having to do with traditional, religious, and moral convictions, property rights, patriotism, national honor, the state, and indeed all the assumed foundations of society—are, as I have already suggested, rarely the result of reasoned consideration, but of unthinking absorption from the social environment in which we live. Consequently, they have about them a quality of "elemental certitude," and we especially resent doubt or criticism cast upon them. So long, however, as we revere the whisperings of the herd, we are obviously unable to examine them dispassionately and to consider to what extent they are suited to the novel conditions and social exigencies in which we find ourselves to-day.

The "real" reasons for our beliefs, by making clear their origins and history, can do much to dissipate this emotional blockade and rid us of our prejudices and preconceptions. Once this is done and we come critically to examine our traditional beliefs, we may well find some of them sustained by experience and honest reasoning, while others must be revised to meet new conditions and our more extended knowledge. But only after we have undertaken such a critical examination in the light of experience and modern knowledge, freed from any feeling of "primary certitude," can we claim that the "good" are also the "real" reasons for our opinions.

I do not flatter myself that this general show-up of man's thought through the ages will cure myself or others of carelessness in adopting ideas, or of unseemly heat in defending them just because we have adopted them. But if the considerations which I propose to recall are really in-

---

[8] Trotter, *op. cit.*, p. 45. The first part of this little volume is excellent.

corporated into our thinking and are permitted to establish our general outlook on human affairs, they will do much to relieve the imaginary obligation we feel in regard to traditional sentiments and ideals. Few of us are capable of engaging in creative thought, but some of us can at least come to distinguish it from other and inferior kinds of thought and accord to it the esteem that it merits as the greatest treasure of the past and the only hope of the future.

ALDOUS HUXLEY

Aldous Leonard Huxley (1894–1963), one of the most well-known of modern English novelists and essayists, came from a family celebrated for intellectual achievement. He was the son of Leonard Huxley, author and editor; grandson of the naturalist Thomas Huxley; and grandnephew of Matthew Arnold. His brother Sir Julian is a distinguished biologist and his half-brother David won the 1963 Nobel Prize in physiology. Huxley studied at Eton and Oxford, despite a serious eye disease which made him almost totally blind for three years. Reading with the aid of a magnifying glass, he graduated from Oxford in 1915 with honors in English literature. In 1919 he joined the staff of Athenaeum, *a London literary magazine, and then followed a steady production of writings in all genres.*

The success of his early novels allowed Huxley to move to Italy in 1923 and thence to France; in 1934 he traveled in the United States, and finally settled in southern California, near Los Angeles. Here he continued to write books, articles, and an occasional movie scenario. He studied Vedanta and other eastern religions, and became interested in the effect of drugs on the mind.

Huxley wrote eleven novels, the best-known being Antic Hay *(1923),* Point Counter Point *(1928),* Brave New World *(1932), and* After Many a Summer Dies the Swan *(1940). Huxley's reputation rests equally on his over twenty volumes of essays and belles lettres, including* On the Margin *(1923),* Jesting Pilate *(1926),* Vulgarity in Literature *(1930),* Ends and

Means *(1937)*, The Perennial Philosophy *(1946)*, Science, Liberty, and Peace *(1946)*, *and* Literature and Science *(1963)*.

Huxley's Brave New World *(1932) has turned out to be devastatingly accurate both as a piece of futuristic science fiction and as a satire on modern technological mass-produced civilization. It has become so widely known that in 1958 Huxley could safely give the title* Brave New World Revisited *to a study of the progress of dehumanization and mental tyranny in the intervening quarter century. Among the three Huxley essays in the present volume, two are taken from* Brave New World Revisited. *The following is Chapter 5.*

PROPAGANDA UNDER A DICTATORSHIP

At his trial after the Second World War, Hitler's Minister for Armaments, Albert Speer, delivered a long speech in which, with remarkable acuteness, he described the Nazi tyranny and analyzed its methods. "Hitler's dictatorship," he said, "differed in one fundamental point from all its predecessors in history. It was the first dictatorship in the present period of modern technical development, a dictatorship which made complete use of all technical means for the domination of its own country. Through technical devices like the radio and the loud-speaker, eighty million people were deprived of independent thought. It was thereby possible to subject them to the will of one man. . . . Earlier dictators needed highly qualified assistants even at the lowest level—men who could think and act independently. The totalitarian system in the period of modern technical development can dispense with such men; thanks to modern methods of communication, it is possible to mechanize the lower leadership. As a result of this there has arisen the new type of the uncritical recipient of orders."

In the Brave New World of my prophetic fable technology had advanced far beyond the point it had reached in Hitler's day; consequently the recipients of orders were far less critical than their Nazi counterparts, far more obedient to the order-giving elite. Moreover, they had been genetically standardized and postnatally conditioned to perform their subordinate functions, and could therefore be depended upon to behave almost as predictably as machines. As we shall see in a later chapter, this conditioning of "the lower leadership" is already going on under the Communist dictatorships. The Chinese and the Russians are not relying merely on the indirect effects of advancing technology; they are working directly on the psychophysical organisms of their lower leaders, subjecting minds and bodies to a system of ruthless and, from all accounts, highly effective conditioning. "Many a man," said Speer, "has been haunted by the nightmare that one day nations might be dominated by technical means. That nightmare was almost realized in Hitler's totalitarian system." Almost, but not quite. The Nazis did not have time—and perhaps did not have the intelligence and the necessary knowledge—to brainwash and condition their lower leadership. This, it may be, is one of the reasons why they failed.

Since Hitler's day the armory of technical devices at the disposal of the would-be dictator has been considerably enlarged. As well as the radio, the loud-speaker, the moving picture camera and the rotary press, the contemporary propagandist can make use of television to broadcast the image as well as the voice of his client, and can record both image and voice on spools of magnetic tape. Thanks to technological progress, Big Brother can now be almost as omnipresent as God. Nor is it only on the technical front that the hand of the would-be dictator has been strengthened. Since Hitler's day a great deal of work has been carried out in those fields of applied psychology and neurology which are the special province of the propagandist, the indoctrinator and the brainwasher. In the past these specialists in the art of changing people's minds were empiricists. By a method of trial and error they had worked out a number of techniques and procedures, which they used very effectively without, however, knowing precisely why they were effective. Today the art of mind-control is in process of becoming a science. The practitioners of this science know what they are doing and why. They are guided in their work by theories and hypotheses solidly established on a massive foundation of experimental evidence. Thanks to the new insights and the new techniques made possible by these insights, the nightmare that was "all but realized in Hitler's totalitarian system" may soon be completely realizable.

But before we discuss these new insights and techniques let us take a look at the nightmare that so nearly came true in Nazi Germany. What were the methods used by Hitler and Goebbels for "depriving eighty million people of independent thought and subjecting them to the will of one man"? And what was the theory of human nature upon which those terrifyingly successful methods were based? These questions can be answered, for the most part, in Hitler's own words. And what remarkably clear and astute words they are! When he writes about such vast abstractions as Race and History and Providence, Hitler is strictly unreadable. But when he writes about the German masses and the methods he used for dominating and directing them, his style changes. Nonsense gives place to sense, bombast to a hard-boiled and cynical lucidity. In his philosophical lucubrations Hitler was either cloudily daydreaming or reproducing other people's half-baked notions. In his comments on crowds and propaganda he was writing of things he knew by firsthand experience. In the words of his ablest biographer, Mr. Alan Bullock, "Hitler was the

greatest demagogue in history." Those who add, "only a demagogue," fail
to appreciate the nature of political power in an age of mass politics. As
he himself said, "To be a leader means to be able to move the masses."
Hitler's aim was first to move the masses and then, having pried them
loose from their traditional loyalties and moralities, to impose upon them
(with the hypnotized consent of the majority) a new authoritarian order
of his own devising. "Hitler," wrote Hermann Rauschning in 1939, "has
a deep respect for the Catholic church and the Jesuit order; not because
of their Christian doctrine, but because of the 'machinery' they have
elaborated and controlled, their hierarchical system, their extremely clever
tactics, their knowledge of human nature and their wise use of human
weaknesses in ruling over believers." Ecclesiasticism without Christianity,
the discipline of a monastic rule, not for God's sake or in order to achieve
personal salvation, but for the sake of the State and for the greater glory
and power of the demagogue turned Leader—this was the goal toward
which the systematic moving of the masses was to lead.

Let us see what Hitler thought of the masses he moved and how he did
the moving. The first principle from which he started was a value
judgment: the masses are utterly contemptible. They are incapable of
abstract thinking and uninterested in any fact outside the circle of
their immediate experience. Their behavior is determined, not by
knowledge and reason, but by feelings and unconscious drives. It is in
these drives and feelings that "the roots of their positive as well as their
negative attitudes are implanted." To be successful a propagandist must
learn how to manipulate these instincts and emotions. "The driving force
which has brought about the most tremendous revolutions on this earth
has never been a body of scientific teaching which has gained power over
the masses, but always a devotion which has inspired them, and often a
kind of hysteria which has urged them into action. Whoever wishes to
win over the masses must know the key that will open the door of their
hearts." . . . In post-Freudian jargon, of their unconscious.

Hitler made his strongest appeal to those members of the lower middle
classes who had been ruined by the inflation of 1923, and then ruined all
over again by the depression of 1929 and the following years. "The
masses" of whom he speaks were these bewildered, frustrated and chronically anxious millions. To make them more masslike, more homogeneously
subhuman, he assembled them, by the thousands and the tens of thousands,
in vast halls and arenas, where individuals could lose their personal identity,
even their elementary humanity, and be merged with the crowd. A man
or woman makes direct contact with society in two ways: as a member
of some familial, professional or religious group, or as a member of a
crowd. Groups are capable of being as moral and intelligent as the individuals who form them; a crowd is chaotic, has no purpose of its own
and is capable of anything except intelligent action and realistic thinking.
Assembled in a crowd, people lose their powers of reasoning and their

capacity for moral choice. Their suggestibility is increased to the point where they cease to have any judgment or will of their own. They become very excitable, they lose all sense of individual or collective responsibility, they are subject to sudden accesses of rage, enthusiasm and panic. In a word, a man in a crowd behaves as though he had swallowed a large dose of some powerful intoxicant. He is a victim of what I have called "herd-poisoning." Like alcohol, herd-poison is an active, extraverted drug. The crowd-intoxicated individual escapes from responsibility, intelligence and morality into a kind of frantic, animal mindlessness.

During his long career as an agitator, Hitler had studied the effects of herd-poison and had learned how to exploit them for his own purposes. He had discovered that the orator can appeal to those "hidden forces" which motivate men's actions, much more effectively than can the writer. Reading is a private, not a collective activity. The writer speaks only to individuals, sitting by themselves in a state of normal sobriety. The orator speaks to masses of individuals, already well primed with herd-poison. They are at his mercy and, if he knows his business, he can do what he likes with them. As an orator, Hitler knew his business supremely well. He was able, in his own words, "to follow the lead of the great mass in such a way that from the living emotion of his hearers the apt word which he needed would be suggested to him and in its turn this would go straight to the heart of his hearers." Otto Strasser called him "a loud-speaker, proclaiming the most secret desires, the least admissible instincts, the sufferings and personal revolts of a whole nation." Twenty years before Madison Avenue embarked upon "Motivational Research," Hitler was systematically exploring and exploiting the secret fears and hopes, the cravings, anxieties and frustrations of the German masses. It is by manipulating "hidden forces" that the advertising experts induce us to buy their wares— a toothpaste, a brand of cigarettes, a political candidate. And it is by appealing to the same hidden forces—and to others too dangerous for Madison Avenue to meddle with—that Hitler induced the German masses to buy themselves a Fuehrer, an insane philosophy and the Second World War.

Unlike the masses, intellectuals have a taste for rationality and an interest in facts. Their critical habit of mind makes them resistant to the kind of propaganda that works so well on the majority. Among the masses "instinct is supreme, and from instinct comes faith. . . . While the healthy common folk instinctively close their ranks to form a community of the people" (under a Leader, it goes without saying) "intellectuals run this way and that, like hens in a poultry yard. With them one cannot make history; they cannot be used as elements composing a community." Intellectuals are the kind of people who demand evidence and are shocked by logical inconsistencies and fallacies. They regard over-simplification as the original sin of the mind and have no use for the slogans, the unqualified assertions and sweeping generalizations which are the propagandist's stock in trade. "All effective propaganda," Hitler wrote, "must be confined to a few bare necessities and then must be expressed in a few stereotyped formulas." These stereotyped formulas must be constantly repeated, for "only constant repetition will finally succeed in imprinting an idea upon the memory of a crowd." Philosophy teaches us to feel uncertain about the things that seem to us self-evident. Propaganda, on the other hand, teaches us to accept as self-evident matters about which it would be reasonable to suspend our judgment or to feel doubt. The aim of the demagogue is to create social coherence under his own leadership. But, as Bertrand Russell has pointed out, "systems of dogma without empirical foundations, such as scholasticism, Marxism and fascism, have the advantage of producing a great deal of social coherence among their disciples." The demagogic propagandist must therefore be consistently dogmatic. All his statements are made without qualification. There are no grays in his picture of the world; everything is either diabolically black or celestially white. In Hitler's words, the propagandist should adopt "a systematically one-sided attitude towards every problem that has to be dealt with." He must never admit that he might be wrong or that people with a different point of view might be even partially right. Opponents should not be argued with; they should be attacked, shouted down, or, if they become too much of a nuisance, liquidated. The morally squeamish intellectual may be shocked by this kind of thing. But the masses are always convinced that "right is on the side of the active aggressor."

Such, then, was Hitler's opinion of humanity in the mass. It was a very low opinion. Was it also an incorrect opinion? The tree is known by its fruits, and a theory of human nature which inspired the kind of techniques that proved so horribly effective must contain at least an element of truth. Virtue and intelligence belong to human beings as individuals freely associating with other individuals in small groups. So do sin and stupidity. But the subhuman mindlessness to which the demagogue makes his appeal, the moral imbecility on which he relies when he goads his victims into action, are characteristic not of men and women as individuals, but of men and women in masses. Mindlessness and moral idiocy are not characteristically human attributes; they are symptoms of herd-poisoning. In all the world's higher religions, salvation and enlightenment are for individuals. The kingdom of heaven is within the mind of a person, not within the collective mindlessness of a crowd. Christ promised to be present where two or three are gathered together. He did not say anything about being present where thousands are intoxicating one another with herd-poison. Under the Nazis enormous numbers of people were compelled to spend an enormous amount of time marching in serried ranks from point A to point B and back again to point A. "This keeping of the whole population on the march seemed to be a senseless waste of time and energy. Only much later," adds Hermann Rauschning, "was there revealed in it a subtle intention based on a well-judged adjustment of ends and means. Marching diverts men's thoughts. Marching kills thought. Marching makes an end of individuality. Marching is the indispensable magic stroke performed in order to accustom the people to a mechanical, quasi-ritualistic activity until it becomes second nature."

From his point of view and at the level where he had chosen to do his dreadful work, Hitler was perfectly correct in his estimate of human nature. To those of us who look at men and women as individuals rather than as members of crowds, or of regimented collectives, he seems hideously wrong. In an age of accelerating over-population, of accelerating over-organization and ever more efficient means of mass communication, how can we preserve the integrity and reassert the value of the human individual? This is a question that can still be asked and perhaps effectively answered. A generation from now it may be too late to find an answer and perhaps impossible, in the stifling collective climate of that future time, even to ask the question.

RALPH WALDO EMERSON

Emerson (1803–1882) is one of the greatest figures in American thought and letters. He spent his childhood in Boston and was trained at Harvard to be a Unitarian minister in the family tradition. Beset by doubts, he resigned from the ministry in 1832 and took up a career of writing and lecturing, during which he continued to work out his transcendentalist philosophy and his ethical doctrine of self-reliance. The present essay was an address delivered to the Phi Beta Kappa chapter at Harvard on August 31, 1837. Its vehement oratorical quality, the memorableness of single phrases, are typical of Emerson, whose style inherits much from the tradition of the New England sermon. Oliver Wendell Holmes called this essay "our intellectual Declaration of Independence." Its appeal to "literary nationalism" (here somewhat muffled by our omission of the final fifth of the essay) is perhaps less important than its recording of a stage in the struggle of a first-class man and thinker to find a way of life that could be pursued with self-reliance and integrity.

THE AMERICAN SCHOLAR

MR. PRESIDENT AND GENTLEMEN:

I greet you on the recommencement of our literary year. Our anniversary is one of hope, and, perhaps, not enough of labor. We do not meet for games of strength or skill, for the recitation of histories, tragedies, and odes, like the ancient Greeks; for parliaments of love and poesy, like the Troubadours; nor for the advancement of science, like our contemporaries in the British and European capitals. Thus far, our holiday has been simply a friendly sign of the survival of the love of letters amongst a people too busy to give to letters any more. As such it is precious as the sign of an indestructible instinct. Perhaps the time is already come when it ought to be, and will be, something else; when the sluggard intellect of this continent will look from under its iron lids and fill the postponed expectation of the world with something better than the exertions of mechanical skill. Our day of dependence, our long apprenticeship to the learning of other lands, draws to a close. The millions that around us are rushing into life, cannot always be fed on the sere remains of foreign harvests. Events, actions arise, that must be sung, that will sing themselves. Who can doubt that poetry will revive and lead in a new age, as the star in the constellation Harp, which now flames in our zenith, astronomers announce, shall one day be the pole-star for a thousand years?

In this hope I accept the topic which not only usage but the nature of our association seem to prescribe to this day,—the AMERICAN SCHOLAR. Year by year we come up hither to read one more chapter of his biography. Let us inquire what light new days and events have thrown on his character and his hopes.

It is one of those fables which out of an unknown antiquity convey an unlooked-for wisdom, that the gods, in the beginning, divided Man into men, that he might be more helpful to himself; just as the hand was divided into fingers, the better to answer its end.

The old fable covers a doctrine ever new and sublime; that there is One Man,—present to all particular men only partially, or through one faculty; and that you must take the whole society to find the whole man. Man is not a farmer, or a professor, or an engineer, but he is all. Man is priest, and scholar, and statesman, and producer, and soldier. In the *divided* or social state these functions are parcelled out to individuals, each of whom aims to do his stint of the joint work, whilst each other performs his. The fable implies that the individual, to possess himself, must sometimes return from his own labor to embrace all the other laborers. But, unfortunately, this original unit, this fountain of power, has been so distributed to multitudes, has been so minutely subdivided and peddled out, that it is spilled into drops, and cannot be gathered. The state of society is one in which the members have suffered amputation from the trunk, and strut about so many walking monsters,—a good finger, a neck, a stomach, an elbow, but never a man.

Man is thus metamorphosed into a thing, into many things. The planter, who is Man sent out into the field to gather food, is seldom cheered by any idea of the true dignity of his ministry. He sees his bushel and his cart, and nothing beyond, and sinks into the farmer, instead of Man on the farm. The tradesman scarcely ever gives an ideal worth to his work, but is ridden by the routine of his craft, and the soul is subject to dollars. The priest becomes a form; the attorney a statute-book; the mechanic a machine; the sailor a rope of the ship.

In this distribution of functions the scholar is the delegated intellect. In the right state he is *Man Thinking*. In the degenerate state, when the victim of society, he tends to become a mere thinker, or still worse, the parrot of other men's thinking.

In this view of him, as Man Thinking, the theory of his office is contained. Him Nature solicits with all her placid, all her monitory pictures; him the past instructs; him the future invites. Is not indeed every man a student, and do not all things exist for the student's behoof? And, finally, is not the true scholar the only true master? But the old oracle said, "All things have two handles: beware of the wrong one." In life, too often, the scholar errs with mankind and forfeits his privilege. Let us see him in his school, and consider him in reference to the main influences he receives.

I. The first in time and the first in importance of the influences upon the mind is that of nature. Every day, the sun; and, after sunset, Night and her stars. Ever the winds blow, ever the grass grows. Every day, men and women, conversing—beholding and beholden. The scholar is he of all men whom this spectacle most engages. He must settle its value in his mind. What is nature to him? There is never a beginning, there is never an end, to the inexplicable continuity of this web of God, but always circular power returning into itself. Therein it resembles his own spirit, whose beginning, whose ending, he never can find,—so entire, so boundless. Far too as her splendors shine, system on system shooting like rays, upward, downward, without centre, without circumference,—in the mass and in the particle, Nature hastens to render account of herself to the mind. Classification begins. To the young mind every thing is individual, stands by itself. By and by, it finds how to join two things and see in them one nature; then three, then three thousand; and so, tyrannized over by its own unifying instinct, it goes on tying things together, diminishing anomalies, discovering roots running under ground whereby contrary and remote things cohere and flower out from one stem. It presently learns that since the dawn of history there has been a constant accumulation and classifying of facts. But what is classification but the perceiving that these objects are not chaotic, and are not foreign, but have a law which is also a law of the human mind? The astronomer discovers that geometry, a pure abstraction of the human mind, is the measure of planetary motion. The chemist finds proportions and intelligible method throughout matter; and science is nothing but the finding of analogy, identity, in the most remote parts. The ambitious soul sits down before each refractory fact; one after another reduces all strange constitutions, all new powers, to their class and their law, and goes on forever to animate the last fibre of organization, the outskirts of nature, by insight.

Thus to him, to this schoolboy under the bending dome of day, is suggested that he and it proceed from one root; one is leaf and one is flower; relation, sympathy, stirring in every vein. And what is that root? Is not that the soul of his soul? A thought too bold; a dream too wild. Yet when this spiritual light shall have revealed the law of more earthly natures,— when he has learned to worship the soul, and to see that the natural philosophy that now is, is only the first gropings of its gigantic hand, he shall look forward to an ever expanding knowledge as to a becoming creator. He shall see that nature is the opposite of the soul, answering to it part for part. One is seal and one is print. Its beauty is the beauty of his own mind. Its laws are the laws of his own mind. Nature then becomes to him the measure of his attainments. So much of nature as he is ignorant of, so much of his own mind does he not yet possess. And, in fine, the ancient precept, "Know thyself," and the modern precept, "Study nature," become at last one maxim.

II. The next great influence into the spirit of the scholar is the mind of the Past,—in whatever form, whether of literature, of art, of institutions, that mind is inscribed. Books are the best type of the influence of the past, and perhaps we shall get at the truth,—learn the amount of this influence more conveniently,—by considering their value alone.

The theory of books is noble. The scholar of the first age received into him the world around; brooded thereon; gave it the new arrangement of his own mind, and uttered it again. It came into him life; it went out from him truth. It came to him short-lived actions; it went out from him immortal thoughts. It came to him business; it went from him poetry. It was dead fact; now, it is quick thought. It can stand, and it can go. It now endures, it now flies, it now inspires. Precisely in proportion to the depth of mind from which it issued, so high does it soar, so long does it sing.

Or, I might say, it depends on how far the process had gone, of transmuting life into truth. In proportion to the completeness of the distillation, so will the purity and imperishableness of the product be. But none is quite perfect. As no air-pump can by any means make a perfect vacuum, so neither can any artist entirely exclude the conventional, the local, the perishable from his book, or write a book of pure thought, that shall be as efficient, in all respects, to a remote posterity, as to contemporaries, or rather to the second age. Each age, it is found, must write its own books;

or rather, each generation for the next succeeding. The books of an older period will not fit this.

Yet hence arises a grave mischief. The sacredness which attaches to the act of creation, the act of thought, is transferred to the record. The poet chanting was felt to be a divine man: henceforth the chant is divine also. The writer was a just and wise spirit: henceforward it is settled the book is perfect; as love of the hero corrupts into worship of his statue. Instantly the book becomes noxious: the guide is a tyrant. The sluggish and perverted mind of the multitude, slow to open to the incursions of Reason, having once so opened, having once received this book, stands upon it, and makes an outcry if it is disparaged. Colleges are built on it. Books are written on it by thinkers, not by Man Thinking; by men of talent, that is, who start wrong, who set out from accepted dogmas, not from their own sight of principles. Meek young men grow up in libraries, believing it their duty to accept the views which Cicero, which Locke, which Bacon, have given; forgetful that Cicero, Locke, and Bacon were only young men in libraries when they wrote these books.

Hence, instead of Man Thinking, we have the bookworm. Hence the book-learned class, who value books, as such; not as related to nature and the human constitution, but as making a sort of Third Estate with the world and the soul. Hence the restorers of readings, the emendators, the bibliomaniacs of all degrees.

Books are the best of things, well used; abused, among the worst. What is the right use? What is the one end which all means go to effect? They are for nothing but to inspire. I had better never see a book than to be warped by its attraction clean out of my own orbit, and made a satellite instead of a system. The one thing in the world, of value, is the active soul. This every man is entitled to; this every man contains within him, although in almost all men obstructed and as yet unborn. The soul active sees absolute truth and utters truth, or creates. In this action it is genius; not the privilege of here and there a favorite, but the sound estate of every man. In its essence it is progressive. The book, the college, the school of art, the institution of any kind, stop with some past utterance of genius. This is good, say they,—let us hold by this. They pin me down. They look backward and not forward. But genius looks forward: the eyes of man are set in his forehead, not in his hindhead: man hopes: genius creates. Whatever talents may be, if the man create not, the pure efflux of the Deity is not his;—cinders and smoke there may be, but not yet flame. There are creative manners, there are creative actions, and creative words; manners, actions, words, that is, indicative of no custom or authority, but springing spontaneous from the mind's own sense of good and fair.

On the other part, instead of being its own seer, let it receive from another mind its truth, though it were in torrents of light, without periods of solitude, inquest, and self-recovery, and a fatal disservice is done. Genius is always sufficiently the enemy of genius by over-influence. The literature of every nation bears me witness. The English dramatic poets have Shakspearized now for two hundred years.

Undoubtedly there is a right way of reading, so it be sternly subordinated. Man Thinking must not be subdued by his instruments. Books are for the scholar's idle times. When he can read God directly, the hour is too precious to be wasted in other men's transcripts of their readings. But when the intervals of darkness come, as come they must,—when the sun is hid and the stars withdraw their shining,—we repair to the lamps which were kindled by their ray, to guide our steps to the East again, where the dawn is. We hear, that we may speak. The Arabian proverb says, "A fig tree, looking on a fig tree, becometh fruitful."

It is remarkable, the character of the pleasure we derive from the best books. They impress us with the conviction that one nature wrote and the same reads. We read the verses of one of the great English poets, of Chaucer, of Marvell, of Dryden, with the most modern joy,—with a pleasure, I mean, which is in great part caused by the abstraction of all *time* from their verses. There is some awe mixed with the joy of our surprise, when this poet, who lived in some past world, two or three hundred years ago, says that which lies close to my own soul, that which I also had well-nigh thought and said. But for the evidence thence afforded to the philosophical doctrine of the identity of all minds, we should suppose some preëstablished harmony, some foresight of souls that were to be, and some preparation of stores for their future wants, like the fact observed in insects, who lay up food before death for the young grub they shall never see.

I would not be hurried by any love of system, by any exaggeration of instincts, to underrate the Book. We all know, that as the human body can be nourished on any food, though it were boiled grass and the broth of shoes, so the human mind can be fed by any knowledge. And great and heroic men have existed who had almost no other information than by the printed page. I only would say that it needs a strong head to bear that diet. One must be an inventor to read well. As the proverb says, "He that would bring home the wealth of the Indies, must carry out the wealth of the Indies." There is then creative reading as well as creative writing. When the mind is braced by labor and invention, the page of whatever book we read becomes luminous with manifold allusion. Every sentence is doubly significant, and the sense of our author is as broad as the world. We then see, what is always true, that as the seer's hour of vision is short and rare among heavy days and months, so is its record, perchance, the least part of his volume. The discerning will read, in his Plato or Shakspeare, only that least part,—only the authentic utterances of the oracle;—all the rest he rejects, were it never so many times Plato's and Shakspeare's.

Of course there is a portion of reading quite indispensable to a wise man. History and exact science he must learn by laborious reading. Colleges, in like manner, have their indispensable office,—to teach elements. But they can only highly serve us when they aim not to drill, but to create; when they gather from far every ray of various genius to their hospitable halls, and by the concentrated fires, set the hearts of their youth on flame. Thought and knowledge are natures in which apparatus and pretension avail nothing. Gowns and pecuniary foundations, though of towns of gold, can never countervail the least sentence or syllable of wit. Forget this, and our American colleges will recede in their public importance, whilst they grow richer every year.

III. There goes in the world a notion that the scholar should be a recluse, a valetudinarian,—as unfit for any handiwork or public labor as a penknife for an axe. The so-called "practical men" sneer at speculative men, as if, because they speculate or *see*, they could do nothing. I have heard it said that the clergy,—who are always, more universally than any other class, the scholars of their day,—are addressed as women; that the rough, spontaneous conversation of men they do not hear, but only a mincing and diluted speech. They are often virtually disfranchised; and indeed there are advocates for their celibacy. As far as this is true of the studious classes, it is not just and wise. Action is with the scholar subordinate, but it is essential. Without it he is not yet man. Without it thought can never ripen into truth. Whilst the world hangs before the eye as a cloud of beauty, we cannot even see its beauty. Inaction is cowardice, but there can be no scholar without the heroic mind. The preamble of thought, the transition through which it passes from the unconscious to the conscious, is action. Only so much do I know, as I have lived. Instantly we know whose words are loaded with life, and whose not.

The world,—this shadow of the soul, or *other me*,—lies wide around. Its attractions are the keys which unlock my thoughts and make me acquainted with myself. I run eagerly into this resounding tumult. I grasp the hands of those next me, and take my place in the ring to suffer and to work, taught by an instinct that so shall the dumb abyss be vocal with speech. I pierce its order; I dissipate its fear; I dispose of it within the circuit of my expanding life. So much only of life as I know by experience, so much of the wilderness have I vanquished and planted, or so far have I extended my being, my dominion. I do not see how any man can afford, for the sake of his nerves and his nap, to spare any action in which he can partake. It is pearls and rubies to his discourse. Drudgery, calamity, exasperation, want, are instructors in eloquence and wisdom. The true scholar grudges every opportunity of action past by, as a loss of power. It is the raw material out of which the intellect moulds her splendid products. A strange process too, this by which experience is converted into thought, as a mulberry leaf is converted into satin. The manufacture goes forward at all hours.

The actions and events of our childhood and youth are now matters of calmest observation. They lie like fair pictures in the air. Not so with our recent actions,—with the business which we now have in hand. On this we are quite unable to speculate. Our affections as yet circulate through it. We no more feel or know it than we feel the feet, or the hand, or the brain of our body. The new deed is yet a part of life,—remains for a time immersed in our unconscious life. In some contemplative hour it detaches itself from the life like a ripe fruit, to become a thought of the mind. Instantly it is raised, transfigured; the corruptible has put on incorruption. Henceforth it is an object of beauty, however base its origin and neighborhood. Observe too the impossibility of antedating this act. In its grub state, it cannot fly, it cannot shine, it is a dull grub. But suddenly, without observation, the selfsame thing unfurls beautiful wings, and is an angel of wisdom. So is there no fact, no event, in our private history, which shall not, sooner or later, lose its adhesive, inert form, and astonish us by soaring from our body into the empyrean. Cradle and infancy, school and playground, the fear of boys, and dogs, and ferules, the love of little maids and berries, and many another fact that once filled the whole sky, are gone already; friend and relative, profession and party, town and country, nation and world, must also soar and sing.

Of course, he who has put forth his total strength in fit actions has the richest return of wisdom. I will not shut myself out of this globe of action, and transplant an oak into a flowerpot, there to hunger and pine; nor trust the revenue of some single faculty, and exhaust one vein of thought, much like those Savoyards, who, getting their livelihood by carving shepherds, shepherdesses, and smoking Dutchmen, for all Europe, went out one day to the mountain to find stock, and discovered that they had whittled up the last of their pine trees. Authors we have, in numbers, who have written out their vein, and who, moved by a commendable prudence, sail for Greece or Palestine, follow the trapper into the prairie, or ramble round Algiers, to replenish their merchantable stock.

If it were only for a vocabulary, the scholar would be covetous of action. Life is our dictionary. Years are well spent in country labors; in town; in the insight into trades and manufactures; in frank intercourse with many men and women; in science; in art; to the one end of mastering in all their facts a language by which to illustrate and embody our perceptions. I learn immediately from any speaker how much he has already lived, through the poverty or the splendor of his speech. Life lies behind us as the quarry from whence we get tiles and copestones for the masonry of to-day. This is the way to learn grammar. Colleges and books only copy the language which the field and the work-yard made.

But the final value of action, like that of books, and better than books, is that it is a resource. That great principle of Undulation in nature, that shows itself in the inspiring and expiring of the breath; in desire and satiety; in the ebb and flow of the sea; in day and night; in heat and cold; and, as yet more deeply ingrained in every atom and every fluid, is known to us under the name of Polarity,—these "fits of easy transmission and reflection," as Newton called them, are the law of nature because they are the law of spirit.

The mind now thinks, now acts, and each fit reproduces the other. When the artist has exhausted his materials, when the fancy no longer paints, when thoughts are no longer apprehended and books are a weariness,—he has always the resource *to live*. Character is higher than intellect. Thinking is the function. Living is the functionary. The stream retreats to its source. A great soul will be strong to live, as well as strong to think. Does he lack organ or medium to impart his truths? He can still fall back on this elemental force of living them. This is a total act. Thinking is a partial act. Let the grandeur of justice shine in his affairs. Let the beauty of affection cheer his lowly roof. Those "far from fame," who dwell and act with him, will feel the force of his constitution in the doings and passages of the day better than it can be measured by any public and designed display. Time shall teach him that the scholar loses no hour which the man lives. Herein he unfolds the sacred germ of his instinct, screened from influence. What is lost in seemliness is gained in strength. Not out of those on whom systems of education have exhausted their culture, comes the helpful giant to destroy the old or to build the new, but out of unhandselled savage nature; out of terrible Druids and Berserkers come at last Alfred and Shakspeare.

I hear therefore with joy whatever is beginning to be said of the dignity and necessity of labor to every citizen. There is virtue yet in the hoe and the spade, for learned as well as for unlearned hands. And labor is everywhere welcome; always we are invited to work; only be this limitation observed, that a man shall not for the sake of wider activity sacrifice any opinion to the popular judgments and modes of action.

I have now spoken of the education of the scholar by nature, by books, and by action. It remains to say somewhat of his duties.

They are such as become Man Thinking. They may all be comprised in self-trust. The office of the scholar is to cheer, to raise, and to guide men by showing them facts amidst appearances. He plies the slow, unhonored, and unpaid task of observation. Flamsteed and Herschel, in their glazed observatories, may catalogue the stars with the praise of all men, and the results being splendid and useful, honor is sure. But he, in his private observatory, cataloguing obscure and nebulous stars of the human mind, which as yet no man has thought of as such,—watching days and months sometimes for a few facts; correcting still his old records;—must relinquish display and immediate fame. In the long period of his preparation he must betray often an ignorance and shiftlessness in popular arts, incurring the disdain of the able who shoulder him aside. Long he must stammer in his speech; often forego the living for the dead. Worse yet, he must accept—how often!—poverty and solitude. For the ease and pleasure of treading the old road, accepting the fashions, the education, the religion of society, he takes the cross of making his own, and, of course, the self-accusation, the faint heart, the frequent uncertainty and loss of time, which are the nettles and tangling vines in the way of the self-relying and self-directed; and the state of virtual hostility in which he seems to stand to society, and especially to educated society. For all this loss and scorn, what offset? He is to find consolation in exercising the highest functions of human nature. He is one who raises himself from private considerations and breathes and lives on public and illustrious thoughts. He is the world's eye. He is the world's heart. He is to resist the vulgar prosperity that retrogrades ever to barbarism, by preserving and communicating heroic sentiments, noble biographies, melodious verse, and the conclusions of history. Whatsoever oracles the human heart, in all emergencies, in all solemn hours, has uttered as its commentary on the world of actions,—these he shall receive and impart. And whatsoever new verdict Reason from her inviolable seat pronounces on the passing men and events of to-day,—this he shall hear and promulgate.

These being his functions, it becomes him to feel all confidence in himself, and to defer never to the popular cry. He and he only knows the world. The world of any moment is the merest appearance. Some great decorum, some fetish of a government, some ephemeral trade, or war, or man, is cried up by half mankind and cried down by the other half, as if all depended on this particular up or down. The odds are that the whole question is not worth the poorest thought which the scholar has lost in listening to the controversy. Let him not quit his belief that a popgun is a popgun, though the ancient and honorable of the earth affirm it to be the crack of doom. In silence, in steadiness, in severe abstraction, let him hold by himself; add observation to observation, patient of neglect, patient of reproach, and bide his own time,—happy enough if he can satisfy himself alone that this day he has seen something truly. Success treads on every right step. For the instinct is sure, that prompts him to tell his brother what he thinks. He then learns that in going down into the secrets of his own mind he has descended into the secrets of all minds. He learns that he who has mastered any law in his private thoughts, is master to that extent of all men whose language he speaks, and of all into whose language his own can be translated. The poet, in utter solitude remembering his spontaneous thoughts and recording them, is found to have recorded that which men in crowded cities find true for them also. The orator distrusts at first the fitness of his frank confessions, his want of knowledge of the persons he addresses, until he finds that he is the complement of his hearers; —that they drink his words because he fulfils for them their own nature; the deeper he dives into his privatest, secretest presentiment, to his wonder he finds this is the most acceptable, most public, and universally true. The people delight in it; the better part of every man feels, This is my music; this is myself.

In self-trust all the virtues are comprehended. Free should the scholar be,—free and brave. Free even to the definition of freedom, "without any hindrance that does not arise out of his own constitution." Brave; for fear is a thing which a scholar by his very function puts behind him. Fear always springs from ignorance. It is a shame to him if his tranquillity, amid dangerous times, arise from the presumption that like children and women his is a protected class; or if he seek a temporary peace by the diversion of his thoughts from politics or vexed questions, hiding his head like an ostrich in the flowering bushes, peeping into microscopes, and turning rhymes, as a boy whistles to keep his courage up. So is the danger a danger still; so is the fear worse. Manlike let him turn and face it. Let him look into its eye and search its nature, inspect its origin,—see the whelping of this lion,—which lies no great way back; he will then find in himself a perfect comprehension of its nature and extent; he will have made his hands meet on the other side, and can henceforth defy it and pass on superior. The world is his who can see through its pretension. What deafness, what stone-blind custom, what overgrown error you behold is there only by sufferance,—by your sufferance. See it to be a lie, and you have already dealt it its mortal blow.

Yes, we are the cowed,—we the trustless. It is a mischievous notion that we are come late into nature; that the world was finished a long time ago. As the world was plastic and fluid in the hands of God, so it is ever to so much of his attributes as we bring to it. To ignorance and sin, it is flint. They adapt themselves to it as they may; but in proportion as a man has any thing in him divine, the firmament flows before him and takes his signet and form. Not he is great who can alter matter, but he who can alter my state of mind. They are the kings of the world who give the color of their present thought to all nature and all art, and persuade men by the cheerful serenity of their carrying the matter, that this thing which they do is the apple which the ages have desired to pluck, now at last ripe, and inviting nations to the harvest. The great man makes the great thing. Wherever Macdonald sits, there is the head of the table. Linnæus makes botany the most alluring of studies, and wins it from the farmer and the herb-woman; Davy, chemistry; and Cuvier, fossils. The day is always his who works in it with serenity and great aims. The unstable estimates of men crowd to him whose mind is filled with a truth, as the heaped waves of the Atlantic follow the moon.

For this self-trust, the reason is deeper than can be fathomed,—darker than can be enlightened. I might not carry with me the feeling of my audience in stating my own belief. But I have already shown the ground of my hope, in adverting to the doctrine that man is one. I believe man has been wronged; he has wronged himself. He has almost lost the light that can lead him back to his prerogatives. Men are become of no account. Men in history, men in the world of to-day, are bugs, are spawn, and are called "the mass" and "the herd." In a century, in a millennium, one or two men; that is to say, one or two approximations to the right state of every man. All the rest behold in the hero or the poet their own green and crude being,—ripened; yes, and are content to be less, so *that* may attain to its full stature. What a testimony, full of grandeur, full of pity, is borne to the demands of his own nature, by the poor clansman, the poor partisan, who rejoices in the glory of his chief. The poor and the low find some amends to their immense moral capacity, for their acquiescence in a political and social inferiority. They are content to be brushed like flies from the path of a great person, so that justice shall be done by him to that common nature which it is the dearest desire of all to see enlarged and glorified. They sun themselves in the great man's light, and feel it to be their own element. They cast the dignity of man from their downtrod selves upon the shoulders of a hero, and will perish to add one drop of blood to make that great heart beat, those giant sinews combat and conquer. He lives for us, and we live in him.

Men, such as they are, very naturally seek money or power; and power because it is as good as money,—the "spoils," so called, "of office." And why not? for they aspire to the highest, and this, in their sleep-walking, they dream is highest. Wake them and they shall quit the false good and leap to the true, and leave governments to clerks and desks. This revolution is to be wrought by the gradual domestication of the idea of Culture. The main enterprise of the world for splendor, for extent, is the up-building of a man. Here are the materials strewn along the ground. The private life of one man shall be a more illustrious monarchy, more formidable to its enemy, more sweet and serene in its influence to its friend, than any kingdom in history. For a man, rightly viewed, comprehendeth the particular natures of all men. Each philosopher, each bard, each actor has only done for me, as by a delegate, what one day I can do for myself. The books which once we valued more than the apple of the eye, we have quite exhausted. What is that but saying that we have come up with the point of view which the universal mind took through the eyes of one scribe; we have been that man, and have passed on. First, one, then another, we drain all cisterns, and waxing greater by all these supplies, we crave a better and more abundant food. The man has never lived that can feed us ever. The human mind cannot be enshrined in a person who shall set a barrier on any one side to this unbounded, unboundable empire. It is one central fire, which, flaming now out of the lips of Etna, lightens the capes of Sicily, and now out of the throat of Vesuvius, illuminates the towers and vineyards of Naples. It is one light which beams out of a thousand stars. It is one soul which animates all men.

· · ·

JOHN HENRY NEWMAN

Newman (1801–1890) was born in London, educated at Oxford, and became an Oxford don. A profoundly religious man, he took Holy Orders in the Anglican Church in 1824. His friendship with such thinkers as Hurrell Froude, John Keble, and Edward Pusey led to the founding of the Oxford Movement, which attempted to combat the rationalistic and "liberal" tendencies in the English church and to establish a firmer basis for its latent tradition of Catholicism. His controversial views led to his withdrawal from Oxford, and in 1845 he became a Roman Catholic. He soon joined the Oratorians, a semi-monastic order, and was Head of the order's house at Egbaston for almost forty years. An attack by Charles Kingsley in 1864 became the occasion for a series of pamphlets, revised and published later as Apologia pro vita sua, *in which Newman gave an account of his religious life and opinions. Its argument, style, and temper did much to restore his standing in British public opinion. The last part of his life was spent amidst universal reverence. He was made Honorary Fellow of Trinity College, Oxford, in 1878 and was created Cardinal in the next year.*

In 1852 Newman was made rector-elect of a projected Catholic University in Dublin. Sensing that the community needed a clear explanation of what a University should be, he delivered a series of nine lectures in Dublin from May 10 to June 7, 1852. They were published that year as Discourses on the Scope and Nature of a University Education *and in his collected works as* The Idea of a University. *His plan for the University fell through, but the lectures have survived as the classical statement of the aims of a liberal education. The present selection (title supplied by us) is the sixth part of the fifth lecture, "Knowledge Its Own End."*

ON LIBERAL KNOWLEDGE

Now bear with me, Gentlemen, if what I am about to say, has at first sight a fanciful appearance. Philosophy, then, or Science, is related to Knowledge in this way:—Knowledge is called by the name of Science or Philosophy, when it is acted upon, informed, or if I may use a strong figure, impregnated by Reason. Reason is the principle of that intrinsic fecundity of Knowledge, which, to those who possess it, is its especial value, and which dispenses with the necessity of their looking abroad for any end to rest upon external to itself. Knowledge, indeed, when thus exalted into a scientific form, is also power; not only is it excellent in itself, but whatever such excellence may be, it is something more, it has a result beyond itself. Doubtless; but that is a further consideration, with which I am not concerned. I only say that, prior to its being a power, it is a good; that it is, not only an instrument, but an end. I know well it may resolve itself into an art, and terminate in a mechanical process, and in tangible fruit; but it also may fall back upon that Reason which informs it, and resolve itself into Philosophy. In one case it is called Useful Knowledge, in the other Liberal. The same person may cultivate it in both ways at once; but this again is a matter foreign to my subject; here I do but say that there are two ways of using Knowledge, and in matter of fact those who use it in one way are not likely to use it in the other, or at least in a very limited measure. You see, then, here are two methods of Education; the end of the one is to be philosophical, of the other to be mechanical; the one rises towards general ideas, the other is exhausted upon what is particular and external. Let me not be thought to deny the necessity, or to decry the benefit, of such attention to what is particular and practical, as belongs to the useful or mechanical arts; life could not go on without them; we owe our daily welfare to them; their exercise is the duty of the many, and we owe to the many a debt of gratitude for fulfilling that duty. I only say that Knowledge, in proportion as it tends more and more to be particular, ceases to be Knowledge. It is a question whether Knowledge can in any proper sense be predicated of the brute creation; without pretending to metaphysical exactness of phraseology, which would be unsuitable to an occasion like this, I say, it seems to me improper to call that passive sensation, or perception of things, which brutes seem to possess, by the name of Knowledge. When I speak of Knowledge, I mean something intellectual, something which grasps what it perceives through the senses; something which takes a view of things; which sees more than the senses convey; which reasons upon what it sees, and while it sees; which invests it with an idea. It expresses itself, not in a mere enunciation, but by an enthymeme: it is of the nature of science from the first, and in this consists its dignity. The principle of real dignity in Knowledge, its worth, its desirableness, considered irrespectively of its results, is this germ within it of a scientific or a philosophical process. This is how it comes to be an end in itself; this is why it admits of being called Liberal. Not to know the relative disposition of things is the state of slaves or children; to have mapped out the Universe is the boast, or at least the ambition, of Philosophy.

Moreover, such knowledge is not a mere extrinsic or accidental advantage, which is ours to-day and another's to-morrow, which may be got up from a book, and easily forgotten again, which we can command or communicate at our pleasure, which we can borrow for the occasion, carry about in our hand, and take into the market; it is an acquired illumination, it is a habit, a personal possession, and an inward endowment. And this is the reason, why it is more correct, as well as more usual, to speak of a University as a place of education, than of instruction, though, when knowledge is concerned, instruction would at first sight have seemed the more appropriate word. We are instructed, for instance, in manual exercises, in the fine and useful arts, in trades, and in ways of business; for these are methods, which have little or no effect upon the mind itself, are contained in rules committed to memory, to tradition, or to use, and bear upon an end external to themselves. But education is a higher word; it implies an action upon our mental nature, and the formation of a character; it is something individual and permanent, and is commonly spoken of in connexion with religion and virtue. When, then, we speak of the communication of Knowledge as being Education, we thereby really imply that that Knowledge is a state or condition of mind; and since cultivation of mind is surely worth seeking for its own sake, we are thus brought once more to the conclusion, which the word "Liberal" and the word "Philosophy" have already suggested, that there is a Knowledge, which is desirable, though nothing come of it, as being of itself a treasure, and a sufficient remuneration of years of labour.

ALBERT JAY NOCK

By the time of his death in 1945 at the age of 72, Albert Jay Nock had achieved a considerable reputation for his "distinguished, humorous, and incisive" style of writing and his intensely iconoclastic views. After a

strictly classical education at St. Stephen's College (now part of Columbia University), he spent some years as a clergyman, then turned to journalism and to critical studies of American involvement in war and diplomacy. He was a great admirer of Henry George, Thomas Jefferson, and François Rabelais, and in his last years a devoted enemy of the New Deal and of Franklin D. Roosevelt. A prolific writer of articles for magazines, he published several collections, including On Doing the Right Thing, and Other Essays *(1928),* The Book of the Journeyman *(1930),* and Free Speech and Plain Language *(1937), from which we take the present essay, first published in* Harper's *in 1932. A more elaborate statement of his views on education will be found in his* The Theory of Education in the United States *(1932).*

THE DISADVANTAGES OF BEING EDUCATED

My interest in education had been comfortably asleep since my late youth, when circumstances waked it up again about six years ago. I then discovered that in the meantime our educational system had changed its aim. It was no longer driving at the same thing as formerly, and no longer contemplated the same kind of product. When I examined it I was as far "out" on what I expected to find as if I had gone back to one of the sawmills familiar to my boyhood in Michigan, and found it turning out boots and shoes.

The difference seemed to be that while education was still spoken of as a "preparation for life," the preparation was of a kind which bore less directly on intellect and character than in former times, and more directly on proficiency. It aimed at what we used to call training rather than education; and it not only did very little with education, but seemed to assume that training *was* education, thus overriding a distinction that formerly was quite clear. Forty years ago a man trained to proficiency in anything was respected accordingly, but was not regarded as an educated man, or "just as good," on the strength of it. A trained mechanic, banker, dentist or man of business got all due credit for his proficiency, but his education, if he had any, lay behind that and was not confused with it. His training, in a word, bore directly upon what he could do or get, while his education bore directly on neither; it bore upon what he could become and be.

Curiosity led me to look into the matter a little more closely, and my observations confirmed the impression that the distinction between training and education was practically wiped out. I noticed, too, that there was a good deal of complaint about this: even professional educators, many of them, were dissatisfied with it. Their complaints, when boiled down, seemed to be that education is too little regarded as an end in itself, and that most of the country's student-population take a too strictly vocational view of what they are doing, while the remainder look at it as a social experience, encouraged largely in order to keep the cubs from being underfoot at home, and reciprocally appreciated mostly because it puts off the evil day when they must go to work; and that our institutions show too much complacency in accommodating themselves to these views.

These complaints, I observed, were not confined to educators; one heard them from laymen as well, and the laymen seemed to be as clear in their minds about the difference between education and training as the professional educators were. For example, one of America's most distinguished artists (whom I am not authorized to quote, and I, therefore, call him Richard Roe) told a friend of mine that when his ship came in he proposed to give magnificent endowments to Columbia, Harvard, Princeton and Yale on the sole condition that they should shut up shop and go out of business forever. Then he proposed to put up a bronze plate over the main entrance to each of these institutions, bearing this legend:

CLOSED

THROUGH THE BENEFACTION

OF

RICHARD ROE

AN HUMBLE PAINTER

IN BEHALF OF EDUCATION

As I saw the situation at the moment, these complaints seemed reasonable. Training is excellent, it can not be too well done, and opportunity for it can not be too cheap and abundant. Probably a glorified crèche for delayed adolescents here and there is a good thing, too; no great harm in it anyway. Yet it struck me as apparently it struck others, that there should also be a little education going on. Something should be done to mature the national resources of intellect and character as well as the resources of proficiency; and, moreover, something should be done to rehabilitate a respect for these resources as a social asset. Full of this idea, I rushed into print with the suggestion that in addition to our present system of schools, colleges and universities which are doing first-class work as training-schools, we ought to have a few educational institutions. My notion was that the educable person ought to have something like an even chance with the ineducable, because he is socially useful. I thought that even a society composed of well-trained ineducables might be improved by having a handful of educated persons sifted around in it every now and then. I, therefore, offered the suggestion, which did not seem exorbitant, that in a population of a hundred and twenty-odd million there should be at least one set of institutions, consisting of a grade-school, a secondary school and an undergraduate college, which should be strictly and rigorously educational, kept in perpetual quarantine against the contagion of training.

II

This was five years ago, and about eighteen months ago I repeated the suggestion. My modest proposal was hardly in print before I received a letter from a friend in the University of Oxford, propounding a point which—believe it or not—had never occurred to me.

But think of the poor devils who shall have gone through your mill! It seems a cold-blooded thing . . . to turn out a lot of people who simply can't live at home. Vivisection is nothing to it. As I understand your scheme, you are planning to breed a batch of cultivated, sensitive beings who would all die six months after they were exposed to your actual civilization. This is not Oxford's superciliousness, I assure you, for things nowadays are precious little better with us. I agree that such people are the salt of the earth, and England used to make some kind of place for them. . . . But now—well, I hardly know. It seems as though some parts of the earth were jolly well salt-proof. The salt melts and disappears, and nothing comes of it.

As I say, I had never thought of that. It had never occurred to me that there might be disadvantages in being educated. I saw at once where my mistake lay. I had been looking at the matter from the point of view of an elderly person to whom such education as he had was just so much clear gain, not from the point of view of a youth who is about to make his start in the world. I saw at once that circumstances, which had been more or less in favour of my educated contemporaries, were all dead against the educated youngster of to-day. Therefore, last year, when I was appointed to deal again with the subject in a public way, I went back on all I had said, and ate my ration of humble-pie with the best grace I could muster.

Every shift in the social order, however slight, puts certain classes irrevocably out of luck, as our vulgarism goes. At the beginning of the sixteenth century the French feudal nobility were out of luck. They could do nothing about it, nobody could do anything about it, they were simply out of luck. Since the middle of the last century, monarchs and a hereditary aristocracy are out of luck. The *Zeitgeist* seems always arbitrarily to be picking out one or another social institution, breathing on it with the devouring breath of a dragon; it decays and dissolves, and those who represent it are out of luck. Up to a few years ago an educated person, even in the United States, was not wholly out of luck; since then, however, an educated young man's chance, or an educated young woman's, is slim. I do not here refer exclusively to the mere matter of picking up a living, although, as I shall show, education is a good bit of hindrance even to that; but also to conditions which make any sort of living enjoyable and worth while.

So in regard to my championship of education it turned out again that everybody is wiser than anybody, at least from the short-time point of view, which is the one that human society invariably takes. Some philosophers think that society is an organism, moving instinctively always towards the immediate good thing, as certain blind worms of a very low order of sensibility move towards food. From the long-time point of view, this may often be a bad thing for the worm; it may get itself stepped on or run over or picked up by a boy looking for fish-bait. Nothing can be done about it, however, for the worm's instinct works that way and, according to these philosophers, so does society's, and the individual member of society has little practical choice but to go along.

Hence our institutions which profess and call themselves educational, have probably done the right thing—the immediate right thing, at any rate—in converting themselves, as our drugstores have done, into something that corresponds only very loosely to their profession. No doubt the lay and professional complaint against this tendency is wrong; no doubt the artist Richard Roe's proposal to close up our four great training-schools is wrong. No doubt, too, our young people are right in instinctively going at education, in the traditional sense of the term, with very long teeth. If I were in their place, I now think I should do as they do; and since I am in the way of recantation, as an old offender who has at last seen the light of grace, I may be allowed to say why I should do so—to show what I now plainly see to be the disadvantages of being educated.

III

Education deprives a young person of one of his most precious possessions, the sense of co-operation with his fellows. He is like a pacifist in 1917, alone in spirit—a depressing situation, and especially, almost unbearably, depressing to youth. "After all," says Dumas's hero, "man is man's brother," and youth especially needs a free play of the fraternal sense; it needs the stimulus and support of association in common endeavour. The survivor of an older generation in America has had these benefits in some degree; he is more or less established and matured and can rub along fairly comfortably on his spiritual accumulations; and besides, as age comes on, emotions weaken and sensitiveness is dulled. In his day, from the spiritual and social point of view, one could afford to be educated—barely and with difficulty afford it perhaps, but education was not a flat liability. It netted enough to be worth its price. At present one can afford only to be trained. The young person's fellows are turning all their energy into a single narrow channel of interest; they have set the whole current of their being in one direction. Education is all against his doing that, while training is all for it; hence training puts him in step with his fellows, while education tends to leave him a solitary figure, spiritually disqualified.

For these reasons: education, in the first place, discloses other channels of interest and makes them look inviting. In the second place, it gives rise to the view that the interest which absorbs his fellows is not worth mortgaging one's whole self, body, mind and spirit, to carry on. In the third place, it shows what sort of people one's fellows inevitably become, through their exclusive absorption in this one interest, and makes it hard to reconcile oneself to the thought of becoming like them. Training, on the other hand, raises no such disturbances; it lets one go on one's chosen way, with no uncertainty, no loss of confidence, as a man of the crowd. Education is divisive, separatist; training induces the exhilarating sense that one is doing with others what others do and thinking the thoughts that others think.

Education, in a word, leads a person on to ask a great deal more from life than life, as at present organized, is willing to give him; and it begets dissatisfaction with the rewards that life holds out. Training tends to satisfy him with very moderate and simple returns. A good income, a home and family, the usual run of comforts and conveniences, diversions addressed only to the competitive or sporting spirit or else to raw sensation—training not only makes directly for getting these, but also for an inert and comfortable contentment with them. Well, these are all that our present society has to offer, so it is undeniably the best thing all round to keep people satisfied with them, which training does, and not to inject a subversive influence, like education, into this easy complacency. Politicians understand this—it is their business to understand it—and hence they hold up "a chicken in every pot and two cars in every garage" as a satisfying social ideal. But the mischief of education is its exorbitance. The educated lad may like stewed chicken and motor-cars as well as anybody, but his education has bred a liking for other things too, things that the society around him does not care for and will not countenance. It has bred tastes which society resents as culpably luxurious, and will not connive at gratifying. Paraphrasing the old saying, education sends him out to shift for himself with a champagne appetite amidst a gin-guzzling society.

Training, on the other hand, breeds no such tastes; it keeps him so well content with synthetic gin that a mention of champagne merely causes him to make a wry face. Not long ago I met a young acquaintance from the Middle West who has done well by himself in a business way and is fairly rich. He looked jaded and seedy, evidently from overwork, and as I was headed for Munich at the moment, I suggested he should take a holiday and go along. He replied, "Why, I couldn't sell anything in

Munich—I'm a business man." For a moment or two I was rather taken aback by his attitude, but I presently recognized it as the characteristic attitude of trained proficiency, and I saw that as things are it was right. Training had kept his demands on life down to a strictly rudimentary order and never tended to muddle up their clear simplicity or shift their direction. Education would have done both; he was lucky to have had none.

It may be plainly seen, I think, that in speaking as he did, my friend enjoyed the sustaining sense of co-operation with his fellows. In his intense concentration, his singleness of purpose, and in the extremely primitive simplicity of his desires and satisfactions, he was completely in the essential movement of the society surrounding him; indeed, if his health and strength hold out, he may yet become one of those representative men like Mr. Ford, the late Mr. Eastman or Mr. Hoover, who take their tone from society in the first instance and in turn give back that tone with interest. Ever since the first westward emigration from the Atlantic seaboard, American civilization may be summed up as a free-for-all scuffle to get rich quickly and by any means. In so far as a person was prepared to accept the terms of this free-for-all and engage in it, so far he was sustained by the exhilaration of what Mr. Dooley called "th' common impulse f'r th' same money." In so far as he was not so prepared, he was deprived of this encouragement.

To mark the tendency of education in these circumstances, we need consider but one piece of testimony. The late Charles Francis Adams was an educated man who overlived the very fag-end of the period when an American youth could afford, more or less hardly, to be educated. He was a man of large affairs, in close relations with those whom the clear consenting voice of American society acclaimed as its representative men, and whose ideals of life were acclaimed as adequate and satisfying; they were the Fords, Eastmans, Owen Youngs, Hoovers, of the period. At the close of his career he wrote this:

> As I approach the end, I am more than a little puzzled to account for the instances I have seen of business success—money-getting. It comes from rather a low instinct. Certainly, as far as my observation goes, it is rarely met in combination with the finer or more interesting traits of character. I have known, and known tolerably well, a good many "successful" men—"big" financially—men famous during the last half-century; and a less interesting crowd I do not care to encounter. Not one that I have ever known would I care to meet again, either in this world or in the next; nor is one of them associated in my mind with the idea of humour, thought or refinement. A set of mere money-getters and traders, they were essentially unattractive and uninteresting. The fact is that money-getting, like everything else, calls for a special aptitude and great concentration; and for it I did not

have the first to any marked degree, and to it I never gave the last. So, in now summing up, I may account myself fortunate in having got out of my ventures as well as I did.

This is by no means the language of a man who, like my acquaintance from the Middle West, is sustained and emboldened by the consciousness of being in co-operation with his fellows—far from it. It will be enough, I think, to intimate pretty clearly the divisive and separatist tendency of education, and to show the serious risk that a young person of the present day incurs in acquiring an education. As matters now stand, I believe that he should not take that risk, and that any one advising or tempting him to take it is doing him a great disservice.

IV

An educated young man likes to think; he likes ideas for their own sake and likes to deal with them disinterestedly and objectively. He will find this taste an expensive one, much beyond his means, because the society around him is thoroughly indisposed towards anything of the kind. It is pre-eminently a society, as John Stuart Mill said, in which the test of a great mind is agreeing in the opinions of small minds. In any department of American life this is indeed the only final test; and this fact is in turn a fair measure of the extent to which our society is inimical to thought. The president of Columbia University is reported in the press as having said the other day that "thinking is one of the most unpopular amusements of the human race. Men hate it largely because they can not do it. They hate it because if they enter upon it as a vocation or avocation it is likely to interfere with what they are doing." This is an interesting admission for the president of Columbia to make—interesting and striking. Circumstances have enabled our society to get along rather prosperously, though by no means creditably, without thought and without regard for thought, proceeding merely by a series of improvisations; hence it has always instinctively resented thought, as likely to interfere with what it was doing. Therefore, the young person who has cultivated the ability to think and the taste for thinking is at a decided disadvantage, for this resentment is now stronger and more heavily concentrated than it ever was. Any doubt on this point may be easily resolved by an examination of our current literature, especially our journalistic and periodical literature.

The educated lad also likes to cultivate a sense of history. He likes to know how the human mind has worked in the past, and upon this knowledge he instinctively bases his expectations of its present and future workings. This tends automatically to withdraw him from many popular movements and associations because he knows their like of old, and knows to a certainty how they will turn out. In the realm of public affairs, for instance, it shapes his judgment of this-or-that humbugging political nostrum that the crowd is running eagerly to swallow; he can match it all the way back to the politics of Rome and Athens, and knows it for precisely what it is. He can not get into a ferment over this-or-that exposure of the almost incredible degradation of our political, social and cultural character; over an investigation of Tammany's misdoings; over the Federal Government's flagitious employment of the income-tax law to establish a sleeping-partnership in the enterprises of gamblers, gangsters, assassins and racketeers; over the wholesale looting of public property through official connivance; over the crushing burden which an ever-increasing bureaucratic rapacity puts upon production. He knows too much about the origin and nature of government not to know that all these matters are representative, and that nothing significant can be done about them except by a self-sprung change of character in the people represented. He is aware, with Edmund Burke, that "there never was for any long time a corrupt representation of a virtuous people, or a mean, sluggish, careless people that ever had a good government of any form." He perceives, with Ibsen, that "men still call for special revolutions, for revolutions in politics, in externals. But all that sort of thing is trumpery. It is the soul of man that must revolt."

Thus in these important directions, and in others more or less like them, the educated youth starts under disadvantages from which the trained youth is free. The trained youth has no incentive to regard these matters except as one or another of them may bear upon his immediate personal interest. Again, while education does not make a gentleman, it tends to inculcate certain partialities and repugnances which training does not tend to inculcate, and which are often embarrassing and retarding. They set up a sense of self-respect and dignity as an arbiter of conduct, with a jurisdiction far outreaching that of law and morals; and this is most disadvantageous. Formerly this disadvantage was not so pressing, but now it is of grave weight. At the close of Mr. Jefferson's first term, some of his political advisers thought it would be a good move for him to make a little tour in the North and let the people see him. He replied, with what now seems an incomprehensible austerity, that he was "not reconciled to the idea of a chief magistrate parading himself through the several States as an object of public gaze, and in quest of an applause which, to be valuable, should be purely voluntary." In his day a chief magistrate could say that and not lose by it; Mr. Jefferson carried every northern State except Connecticut and every southern State except Maryland. At the present time, as we have lately been reminded, the exigencies of politics have converted candidacy for public office into an exact synonym for an obscene and repulsive exhibitionism.

Again, education tends towards a certain reluctance about pushing oneself forward; and in a society so notoriously based on the principle of each man for himself, this is a disadvantage. Charles Francis Adams's younger brother Henry, in his remarkable book called *The Education of Henry Adams*, makes some striking observations on this point. Henry

Adams was no doubt the most accomplished man in America, probably the ablest member of the family which as a whole has been the most notable in American public service since 1776. His youth was spent in acquiring an uncommonly large experience of men and affairs. Yet he says that his native land never offered him but one opportunity in the whole course of his life, and that was an assistant-professorship of history at Harvard, at four dollars a day; and he says further that he "could have wept on President Eliot's shoulder in hysterics, so grateful was he for the rare good-will that inspired the compliment." He recalls that at the age of thirty:

> No young man had a larger acquaintance and relationship than Henry Adams, yet he knew no one who could help him. He was for sale, in the open market. So were many of his friends. All the world knew it, and knew too that they were cheap; to be bought at the price of a mechanic. There was no concealment, no delicacy and no illusion about it. Neither he nor his friends complained; but he felt sometimes a little surprised that, as far as he knew, no one seeking in the labour-market even so much as inquired about their fitness. . . . The young man was required to impose himself, by the usual business methods, as a necessity on his elders, in order to compel them to buy him as an investment. As Adams felt it, he was in a manner expected to black-mail.

Such were the disabilities imposed upon the educated person fifty years ago, when as Adams says, "the American character showed singular limitations which sometimes drove the student of civilized man to despair." Owing to increased tension of the economic system, they are now much heavier. Even more than then, the educated youth emerges, as Adams and his friends did, to find himself "jostled of a sudden by a crowd of men who seem to him ignorant that there is a thing called ignorance; who have forgotten how to amuse themselves; who can not even understand that they are bored."

One might add a few more items to the foregoing, chiefly in the way of spiritual wear and tear—specific discouragements, irritations, disappointments—which in these days fall to the lot of the educated youth, and which the trained youth escapes; but I have mentioned enough for the purpose. Now, it is quite proper to say that the joys and satisfactions of being educated should be brought out as an offset. One can not get something for nothing, nor can one "have it going and coming." If an education is in itself as rewarding a thing as it is supposed to be, it is worth some sacrifice. It is unreasonable to court the joy of making oneself at home in the world's culture, and at the same time expect to get Standard Oil dividends out of it. Granted that your educated lad is out of step, lonesome, short on business acumen and concentration, and all the rest of it—well, he has his education; nobody can get it away from him; his treasure is of the sort that moth and rust do not corrupt, and stock-market operators can not break through and mark down quotations on it. Agreed that if Charles Francis Adams had not been an educated gentleman he might have become another Gould, Fisk, Harriman, Rockefeller, Huntington, Morgan; but given his choice, would he have swapped off his education and its satisfactions for the chance to change places with any of them? Certainly not.

Certainly not; but times have changed. If economic opportunity were now what it was even in Henry Adams's day, a young person just starting out might think twice about balancing the advantages of an education against its disadvantages. In that day, by a little stretching and with a little luck, a young person might come to some sort of compromise with society, but the chance of this is now so remote that no one should take it. Since the closing of the frontier, in or about 1890, economic exploitation has tightened up at such a rate that compromise is hardly possible. It takes every jot of a young person's attention and energy merely to catch on and hang on; and as we have been noticing these last two years, he does not keep going any too well, even at that. The question is not one of being willing to make reasonable sacrifices; it is one of accepting every reasonable prospect of utter destitution. The joys and satisfactions of an education are all that Commencement orators say they are, and more; yet there is force in the Irishman's question, "What's the world to a man when his wife's a widdy?"

v

Things may change for the better, in time; no doubt they will. Economic opportunity may, by some means unforeseen at present, be released from the hold of its present close monopoly. The social value of intellect and character may some day be rediscovered, and the means of their development may be rehabilitated. Were I to be alive when all this happens, I should take up my parable of five years ago, and speak as strongly for education as I did then. But I shall not be alive, and I suspect also that none of the young persons now going out into the world from our training-schools will be alive; so there is no practical point to considering this prospect at present. Hence I can only raise my voice in recantation from the mourner's bench, a convert by force of expediency if not precisely in principle—rice-Christian style, perhaps, and yet, what is one to say? I belong to an earlier time, and for one reason or another the matter of rice does not present itself as an over-importunate problem, but nevertheless I see that the Christians have now "cornered" all the rice, so I can not advise young persons to do as I and my contemporaries did. No, they are right, their training-schools are right; Richard Roe and I are wrong. Let them be honest Christians if they can possibly manage the will-to-believe—one can make astonishing successes with that sometimes by hard trying—but if not, let them be rice-Christians, they can do no better.

Gastein, June, 1932.

---

e. e. cummings (1894-1962)

since feeling is first

since feeling is first
who pays any attention
to the syntax of things
will never wholly kiss you;

wholly to be a fool
while Spring is in the world

my blood approves,
and kisses are a better fate
than wisdom
lady i swear by all flowers. Don't cry
—the best gesture of my brain is less than
your eyelids' flutter which says

we are for each other: then
laugh, leaning back in my arms
for life's not a paragraph

And death i think is no parenthesis

(1926)

The Right Use of Language

"Language" has become a particularly lively subject in recent years. The relatively new science of Linguistics is growing rapidly and noisily, and among the immediate results have been continuing controversies over the proper description of English grammar and over usage versus the rules, in dictionary-making and in speaking generally. Overshadowing the structural and scientific issues, however, still stand the moral ones, at least as venerable as the Greek rhetoricians and sophists—Plato and Aristotle among them— who debated the question of the right use of language and distinguished between eloquence devoted to good persuasion and eloquence devoted to bad. It is the same question, in its modern setting, that is taken up in this group of essays.

We present Mrs. Langer's essay first for a number of reasons. While it touches only peripherally on language itself, it powerfully and clearly describes the mechanism in which language and thought are related— symbolism—and thus provides a link between this and the preceding section. Mrs. Langer's stress on man's unique capacity to manipulate symbols leads directly to a consideration of the political significance of the use of language, a subject taken up in detail by Orwell. Both of these essays, written with World War II vividly in mind, take a special urgency from their setting. Weaver's study, focussing carefully on a few key terms, shows that in postwar America the subject has lost none of its interest. Huxley and Jacobs, respectively, analyze and illustrate, in varying tones, the problem of language in commercial life. We conclude the section with Brock Brower's lively conception of the Article as a new literary form which is giving important expression to the moral function of language.

SUSANNE K. LANGER

Mrs. Langer (born 1895) was educated at Radcliffe College where she received the Ph.D. in 1926. She has taught philosophy at Radcliffe, Wellesley, Smith, and Columbia, and in 1954 became chairman of the Philosophy Department at Connecticut College. She is now Professor Emeritus and research scholar, pursuing investigations in the philosophy of art, expression, and meaning. One of the few notable women in a field traditionally dominated by men, Mrs. Langer has reached a large audience and has had great influence on recent thinking, especially about the arts. Her best-known book is Philosophy in a New Key *(1942), in which, taking her cue from the researches of Ernst Cassirer, she investigates "the symbolism of reason, rite, and art." A collection of her essays and talks was published as* Philosophical Sketches *in 1962. She has also written* An Introduction to Symbolic Logic *(1937),* Feeling and Form *(1953), and* The Problem of Art *(1957). The present essay, clearly deriving from her interest in symbolism, appeared in* Fortune *in January, 1944, at the height of World War II.*

THE LORD OF CREATION

The world is aflame with man-made public disasters, artificial rains of brimstone and fire, planned earthquakes, cleverly staged famines and floods. The Lord of Creation is destroying himself. He is throwing down the cities he has built, the works of his own hand, the wealth of many thousand years in his frenzy of destruction, as a child knocks down its own handiwork, the whole day's achievement, in a tantrum of tears and rage.

What has displeased the royal child? What has incurred his world-shattering tantrum?

The bafflement of the magnificent game he is playing. Its rules and its symbols, his divine toys, have taken possession of the player. For this global war is not the old, hard, personal fight for the means of life, *bellum omnium contra omnes*, which animals perpetually wage; this is a war of monsters. Not mere men but great superpersonal giants, the national states, are met in combat. They do not hate and attack and wrestle as injured physical creatures do; they move heavily, inexorably, by strategy and necessity, to each other's destruction. The game of national states has come to this pass, and the desperate players ride their careening animated toys to a furious suicide.

These moloch gods, these monstrous states, are not natural beings; they are man's own work, products of the power that makes him lord over all other living things—his mind. They are not of the earth, earthy, as families and herds, hives and colonies are, whose members move and fight as one by instinct and habit until a physical disturbance splits them and the severed parts reconstitute themselves as new organized groups. The national states are not physical groups; they are social symbols, profound and terrible.

They are symbols of the new way of life, which the past two centuries have given us. For thousands of years, the pattern of daily life—working, praying, building, fighting, and raising new generations—repeated itself with only slow or unessential changes. The social symbols expressive of this life were ancient and familiar. Tribal gods or local saints, patriarchs, squires, or feudal lords, princes and bishops, raised to the highest power in the persons of emperors and popes—they were all expressions of needs and duties and opinions grounded in an immemorial way of life. The average man's horizon was not much greater than his valley, his town, or whatever geographical ramparts bounded his community. Economic areas were small, and economic problems essentially local. Naturally in his conception the powers governing the world were local, patriarchal, and reverently familiar.

Then suddenly, within some two hundred years, and for many places far less than that, the whole world has been transformed. Communities of different tongues and faiths and physiognomies have mingled; not as of old in wars of conquest, invading lords and conquered population gradually mixing their two stocks, but by a new process of foot-loose travel and trade, dominated by great centers of activity that bring individuals from near and far promiscuously together as a magnet draws filings from many heaps into close but quite accidental contact. Technology has made old horizons meaningless and localities indefinite. For goods and their destinies determine the structure of human societies. This is a new world, a world of persons, not of families and clans, or parishes and manors. The proletarian order is not founded on a hearth and its history. It does not express itself in a dialect, a local costume, a rite, a patron saint. All such traditions by mingling have canceled each other, and disappeared.

Most of us feel that since the old controlling ideas of faith and custom are gone, mankind is left without anchorage of any sort. None of the old social symbols fit this modern reality, this shrunken and undifferentiated world in which we lead a purely economic, secular, essentially homeless life.

But mankind is never without its social symbols; when old ones die, new ones are already in process of birth; and the new gods that have superseded all faiths are the great national states. The conception of them is mystical and moral, personal and devotional; they conjure with names and emblems, and demand our constant profession and practice of the new orthodoxy called "Patriotism."

Of all born creatures, man is the only one that cannot live by bread alone. He lives as much by symbols as by sense report, in a realm compounded of tangible things and virtual images, of actual events and ominous portents, always between fact and fiction. For he sees not only actualities but meanings. He has, indeed, all the impulses and interests of animal nature; he eats, sleeps, mates, seeks comfort and safety, flees pain, falls sick and dies, just as cats and bears and fishes and butterflies do. But he has something more in his repertoire, too—he has laws and religions, theories and dogmas, because he lives not only through sense but through symbols. That is the special asset of his mind, which makes him the master of earth and all its progeny.

By the agency of symbols—marks, words, mental images, and icons of all sorts—he can hold his ideas for contemplation long after their original causes have passed away. Therefore, he can think of things that are not presented or even suggested by his actual environment. By associating symbols in his mind, he combines things and events that were never together in the real world. This gives him the power we call imagination. Further, he can symbolize only part of an idea and let the rest go out of consciousness; this gives him the faculty that has been his pride throughout the ages—the power of abstraction. The combined effect of these two powers is inestimable. They are the roots of his supreme talent, the gift of reason.

In the war of each against all, which is the course of nature, man has an unfair advantage over his animal brethren; for he can see what is not yet there to be seen, know events that happened before his birth, and take possession of more than he actually eats; he can kill at a distance; and by rational design he can enslave other creatures to live and act for him instead of for themselves.

Yet this mastermind has strange aberrations. For in the whole animal kingdom there is no such unreason, no such folly and impracticality as man displays. He alone is hounded by imaginary fears, beset by ghosts and

devils, frightened by mere images of things. No other creature wastes time
in unprofitable ritual or builds nests for dead specimens of its race. Animals
are always realists. They have intelligence in varying degrees—chickens
are stupid, elephants are said to be very clever—but, bright or foolish,
animals react only to reality. They may be fooled by appearance, by
pictures or reflections, but once they know them as such, they promptly
lose interest. Distance and darkness and silence are not fearful to them,
filled with voices or forms, or invisible presences. Sheep in the pasture do
not seem to fear phantom sheep beyond the fence, mice don't look for
mouse goblins in the clock, birds do not worship a divine thunderbird.

But oddly enough, men do. They think of all these things and guard
against them, worshiping animals and monsters even before they conceive of divinities in their own image. Men are essentially unrealistic. With
all their extraordinary intelligence, they alone go in for patently impractical actions—magic and exorcism and holocausts—rites that have no connection with common-sense methods of self-preservation, such as a highly
intelligent animal might use. In fact, the rites and sacrifices by which
primitive man claims to control nature are sometimes fatal to the performers. Indian puberty rites are almost always intensely painful, and
African natives have sometimes died during initiations into honorary
societies.

We usually assume that very primitive tribes of men are closer to
animal estate than highly civilized races; but in respect of practical attitudes, this is not true. The more primitive man's mind, the more fantastic
it seems to be; only with high intellectual discipline do we gradually approach the realistic outlook of intelligent animals.

Yet this human mind, so beclouded by phantoms and superstitions, is
probably the only mind on earth that can reach out to an awareness of
things beyond its practical environment and can also conceive of such
notions as truth, beauty, justice, majesty, space and time and creation.

There is another paradox in man's relationship with other creatures:
namely, that those very qualities he calls animalian—"brutal," "bestial,"
"inhuman"—are peculiarly his own. No other animal is so deliberately
cruel as man. No other creature intentionally imprisons its own kind, or
invents special instruments of torture such as racks and thumbscrews for
the sole purpose of punishment. No other animal keeps its own brethren
in slavery; so far as we know, the lower animals do not commit anything
like the acts of pure sadism that figure rather largely in our newspapers.
There is no torment, spite, or cruelty for its own sake among beasts, as
there is among men. A cat plays with its prey, but does not conquer
and torture smaller cats. But man, who knows good and evil, is cruel for
cruelty's sake; he who has a moral law is more brutal than the brutes, who
have none; he alone inflicts suffering on his fellows with malice afore-
thought.

If man's mind is really a higher form of the animal mind, his morality a specialized form of herd instinct, then where in the course of evolution did he lose the realism of a clever animal and fall prey to subjective fears? And why should he take pleasure in torturing helpless members of his own race?

The answer is, I think, that man's mind is *not* a direct evolution from the beast's mind, but is a unique variant and therefore has had a meteoric and startling career very different from any other animal history. The trait that sets human mentality apart from every other is its preoccupation with symbols, with images and names that *mean* things, rather than with things themselves. This trait may have been a mere sport of nature once upon a time. Certain creatures do develop tricks and interests that seem biologically unimportant. Pack rats, for instance, and some birds of the crow family take a capricious pleasure in bright objects and carry away such things for which they have, presumably, no earthly use. Perhaps man's tendency to see certain forms as *images*, to hear certain sounds not only as signals but as expressive tones, and to be excited by sunset colors or starlight, was originally just a peculiar sensitivity in a rather highly developed brain. But whatever its cause, the ultimate destiny of this trait was momentous; for all human activity is based on the appreciation and use of symbols. Language, religion, mathematics, all learning, all science and superstition, even right and wrong, are products of symbolic expression rather than direct experience. Our commonest words, such as "house" and "red" and "walking," are symbols; the pyramids of Egypt and the mysterious circles of Stonehenge are symbols; so are dominions and empires and astronomical universes. We live in a mind-made world, where the things of prime importance are images or words that embody ideas and feelings and attitudes.

The animal mind is like a telephone exchange; it receives stimuli from outside through the sense organs and sends out appropriate responses through the nerves that govern muscles, glands, and other parts of the body. The organism is constantly interacting with its surroundings, receiving messages and acting on the new state of affairs that the messages signify.

But the human mind is not a simple transmitter like a telephone exchange. It is more like a great projector; for instead of merely mediating between an event in the outer world and a creature's responsive action, it transforms or, if you will, distorts the event into an image to be looked at, retained, and contemplated. For the images of things that we remember are not exact and faithful transcriptions even of our actual sense impressions. They are made as much by what we think as by what we see. It is a well-known fact that if you ask several people the size of the moon's disk as they look at it, their estimates will vary from the area of a dime to that of a barrel top. Like a magic lantern, the mind projects its ideas of things on the screen of what we call "memory"; but like all projections, these ideas are transformations of actual things. They are, in fact, *symbols* of reality, not pieces of it.

A symbol is not the same thing as a sign; that is a fact that psychologists and philosophers often overlook. All intelligent animals use signs; so do we. To them as well as to us sounds and smells and motions are signs of food, danger, the presence of other beings, or of rain or storm. Furthermore, some animals not only attend to signs but produce them for the benefit of others. Dogs bark at the door to be let in; rabbits thump to call each other; the cooing of doves and the growl of a wolf defending his kill are unequivocal signs of feelings and intentions to be reckoned with by other creatures.

We use signs just as animals do, though with considerably more elaboration. We stop at red lights and go on green; we answer calls and bells, watch the sky for coming storms, read trouble or promise or anger in each other's eyes. That is animal intelligence raised to the human level. Those of us who are dog lovers can probably all tell wonderful stories of how high our dogs have sometimes risen in the scale of clever sign interpretation and sign using.

A sign is anything that announces the existence or the imminence of some event, the presence of a thing or a person, or a change in a state of affairs. There are signs of the weather, signs of danger, signs of future good or evil, signs of what the past has been. In every case a sign is closely bound up with something to be noted or expected in experience. It is always a part of the situation to which it refers, though the reference may be remote in space and time. In so far as we are led to note or expect the signified event we are making correct use of a sign. This is the essence of rational behavior, which animals show in varying degrees. It is entirely realistic, being closely bound up with the actual objective course of history—learned by experience, and cashed in or voided by further experience.

If man had kept to the straight and narrow path of sign using, he would be like the other animals, though perhaps a little brighter. He would not talk, but grunt and gesticulate and point. He would make his wishes known, give warnings, perhaps develop a social system like that of bees and ants, with such a wonderful efficiency of communal enterprise that all men would have plenty to eat, warm apartments—all exactly alike and perfectly convenient—to live in, and everybody could and would sit in the sun or by the fire, as the climate demanded, not talking but just basking, with every want satisfied, most of his life. The young would romp and make love, the old would sleep, the middle-aged would do the routine work almost unconsciously and eat a great deal. But that would be the life of a social, superintelligent, purely sign-using animal.

To us who are human, it does not sound very glorious. We want to go places and do things, own all sorts of gadgets that we do not absolutely need, and when we sit down to take it easy we want to talk. Rights and property, social position, special talents and virtues, and above all our ideas, are what we live for. We have gone off on a tangent that takes us far away from the mere biological cycle that animal generations accomplish; and that is because we can use not only signs but symbols.

A symbol differs from a sign in that it does not announce the presence of the object, the being, condition, or whatnot, which is its meaning, but merely *brings this thing to mind*. It is not a mere "substitute sign" to which we react as though it were the object itself. The fact is that our reaction to hearing a person's name is quite different from our reaction to the person himself. There are certain rare cases where a symbol stands directly for its meaning: in religious experience, for instance, the Host is not only a symbol but a Presence. But symbols in the ordinary sense are not mystic. They are the same sort of thing that ordinary signs are; only they do not call our attention to something necessarily present or to be physically dealt with—they call up merely a conception of the thing they "mean."

The difference between a sign and a symbol is, in brief, that a sign causes us to think or act *in face of* the thing signified, whereas a symbol causes us to think *about* the thing symbolized. Therein lies the great importance of symbolism for human life, its power to make this life so different from any other animal biography that generations of men have found it incredible to suppose that they were of purely zoological origin. A sign is always embedded in reality, in a present that emerges from the actual past and stretches to the future; but a symbol may be divorced from reality altogether. It may refer to what is *not* the case, to a mere idea, a figment, a dream. It serves, therefore, to liberate thought from the immediate stimuli of a physically present world; and that liberation marks the essential difference between human and nonhuman mentality. Animals think, but they think *of* and *at* things; men think primarily *about* things. Words, pictures, and memory images are symbols that may be combined and varied in a thousand ways. The result is a symbolic structure whose meaning is a complex of all their respective meanings, and this kaleidoscope of *ideas* is the typical product of the human brain that we call the "stream of thought."

The process of transforming all direct experience into imagery or into that supreme mode of symbolic expression, language, has so completely taken possession of the human mind that it is not only a special talent but a dominant, organic need. All our sense impressions leave their traces in our memory not only as signs disposing our practical reactions in the future but also as symbols, images representing our *ideas* of things; and the tendency to manipulate ideas, to combine and abstract, mix and extend them by playing with symbols, is man's outstanding characteristic. It seems to be what his brain most naturally and spontaneously does. Therefore his primitive mental function is not judging reality, but *dreaming his desires*.

Dreaming is apparently a basic function of human brains, for it is free and unexhausting like our metabolism, heartbeat, and breath. It is easier to dream than not to dream, as it is easier to breathe than to refrain from breathing. The symbolic character of dreams is fairly well established. Symbol mongering, on this ineffectual, uncritical level, seems to be instinctive, the fulfillment of an elementary need rather than the purposeful exercise of a high and difficult talent.

The special power of man's mind rests on the evolution of this special activity, not on any transcendently high development of animal intelligence. We are not immeasurably higher than other animals; we are different. We have a biological need and with it a biological gift that they do not share.

Because man has not only the ability but the constant need of *conceiving* what has happened to him, what surrounds him, what is demanded of him —in short, of symbolizing nature, himself, and his hopes and fears—he has a constant and crying need of *expression*. What he cannot express, he cannot conceive; what he cannot conceive is chaos, and fills him with terror.

If we bear in mind this all-important craving for expression we get a new picture of man's behavior; for from this trait spring his powers and his weaknesses. The process of symbolic transformation that all our experiences undergo is nothing more nor less than the process of *conception*, which underlies the human faculties of abstraction and imagination.

When we are faced with a strange or difficult situation, we cannot react directly, as other creatures do, with flight, aggression, or any such simple instinctive pattern. Our whole reaction depends on how we manage to conceive the situation—whether we cast it in a definite dramatic form, whether we see it as a disaster, a challenge, a fulfillment of doom, or a fiat of the Divine Will. In words or dreamlike images, in artistic or religious or even in cynical form, we must *construe* the events of life. There is great virtue in the figure of speech, "I can *make* nothing of it," to express a failure to understand something. Thought and memory are processes of *making* the thought content and the memory image; the pattern of our ideas is given by the symbols through which we express them. And in the course of manipulating those symbols we inevitably distort the original experience, as we abstract certain features of it, embroider and reinforce those features with other ideas, until the conception we project on the screen of memory is quite different from anything in our real history.

Conception is a necessary and elementary process; what we do with our conceptions is another story. That is the entire history of human culture— of intelligence and morality, folly and superstition, ritual, language, and the arts—all the phenomena that set man apart from, and above, the rest of the animal kingdom. As the religious mind has to make all human history a drama of sin and salvation in order to define its own moral attitudes, so a scientist wrestles with the mere presentation of "the facts" before he can reason about them. The process of *envisaging* facts, values, hopes, and fears underlies our whole behavior pattern; and this process is reflected in the evolution of an extraordinary phenomenon found always, and only, in human societies—the phenomenon of language.

Language is the highest and most amazing achievement of the symbolistic human mind. The power it bestows is almost inestimable, for without it anything properly called "thought" is impossible. The birth of language is the dawn of humanity. The line between man and beast—between the highest ape and the lowest savage—is the language line. Whether the primitive Neanderthal man was anthropoid or human depends less on his cranial capacity, his upright posture, or even his use of tools and fire, than on one issue we shall probably never be able to settle—whether or not he spoke.

In all physical traits and practical responses, such as skills and visual judgments, we can find a certain continuity between animal and human mentality. Sign using is an ever evolving, ever improving function throughout the whole animal kingdom, from the lowly worm that shrinks into his hole at the sound of an approaching foot, to the dog obeying his master's command, and even to the learned scientist who watches the movements of an index needle.

This continuity of the sign-using talent has led psychologists to the belief that language is evolved from the vocal expressions, grunts and coos and cries, whereby animals vent their feelings or signal their fellows; that man has elaborated this sort of communion to the point where it makes a perfect exchange of ideas possible.

I do not believe that this doctrine of the origin of language is correct. The essence of language is symbolic, not signific; we use it first and most vitally to formulate and hold ideas in our own minds. Conception, not social control, is its first and foremost benefit.

Watch a young child that is just learning to speak play with a toy; he says the name of the object, e.g.: "Horsey! horsey! horsey!" over and over again, looks at the object, moves it, always saying the name to himself or to the world at large. It is quite a time before he talks to anyone in particular; he talks first of all to himself. This is his way of forming and fixing the *conception* of the object in his mind, and around this conception all his knowledge of it grows. *Names* are the essence of language; for the *name* is what abstracts the conception of the horse from the horse itself, and lets the mere idea recur at the speaking of the name. This permits the conception gathered from one horse experience to be exemplified again by another instance of a horse, so that the notion embodied in the name is a general notion.

To this end, the baby uses a word long before he *asks for* the object; when he wants his horsey he is likely to cry and fret, because he is reacting to an actual environment, not forming ideas. He uses the animal language of *signs* for his wants; talking is still a purely symbolic process—its practical value has not really impressed him yet.

Language need not be vocal; it may be purely visual, like written lan-

guage, or even tactual, like the deaf-mute system of speech; but it *must
be denotative*. The sounds, intended or unintended, whereby animals communicate do not constitute a language, because they are signs, not names.
They never fall into an organic pattern, a meaningful syntax of even the
most rudimentary sort, as all language seems to do with a sort of driving
necessity. That is because signs refer to actual situations, in which things
have obvious relations to each other that require only to be noted; but
symbols refer to ideas, which are not physically there for inspection, so
their connections and features have to be represented. This gives all true
language a natural tendency toward growth and development, which seems
almost like a life of its own. Languages are not invented; they grow with
our need for expression.

In contrast, animal "speech" never has a structure. It is merely an
emotional response. Apes may greet their ration of yams with a shout of
"Nga!" But they do not say "Nga" between meals. If they could *talk about*
their yams instead of just saluting them, they would be the most primitive
men instead of the most anthropoid of beasts. They would have ideas, and
tell each other things true or false, rational or irrational; they would make
plans and invent laws and sing their own praises, as men do.

The history of speech is the history of our human descent. Yet the
habit of transforming reality into symbols, of contemplating and combining and distorting symbols, goes beyond the confines of language. All
images are symbols, which make us think about the things they mean.

This is the source of man's great interest in "graven images," and in *mere
appearances* like the face of the moon or the human profiles he sees in
rocks and trees. There is no limit to the meanings he can read into natural
phenomena. As long as this power is undisciplined, the sheer enjoyment
of finding meanings in everything, the elaboration of concepts without
any regard to truth and usefulness, seems to run riot; superstition and
ritual in their pristine strength go through what some anthropologists
have called a "vegetative" stage, when dreamlike symbols, gods and ghouls
and rites, multiply like the overgrown masses of life in a jungle. From
this welter of symbolic forms emerge the images that finally govern a
civilization; the great symbols of religion, society, and selfhood.

What does an image "mean?" Anything it is thought to resemble. It is
only because we can abstract quite unobvious forms from the actual
appearance of things that we see line drawings in two dimensions as images
of colored, three-dimensional objects, find the likeness of a dipper in a
constellation of seven stars, or see a face on a pansy. Any circle may
represent the sun or moon; an upright monolith may be a man.

Wherever we can fancy a similarity we tend to see something represented. The first thing we do, upon seeing a new shape, is to assimilate it
to our own idea of something that it resembles, something that is known
and important to us. Our most elementary concepts are of our own actions,
and the limbs or organs that perform them; other things are named by

comparison with them. The opening of a cave is its mouth, the divisions of a river its arms. Language, and with it all articulate thought, grows by this process of unconscious metaphor. Every new idea urgently demands a word; if we lack a name for it, we call it after the first namable thing seen to bear even a remote analogy to it. Thus all the subtle and variegated vocabulary of a living language grows up from a few roots of very general application; words as various in meaning as "gentle" and "ingenious" and "general" spring from the one root "ge" meaning "to give life."

Yet there are conceptions that language is constitutionally unfit to express. The reason for this limitation of our verbal powers is a subject for logicians and need not concern us here. The point of interest to us is that, just as rational, discursive thought is bound up with language, so the life of feeling, of direct personal and social consciousness, the emotional stability of man and his sense of orientation in the world are bound up with images directly given to his senses: fire and water, noise and silence, high mountains and deep caverns, the brief beauty of flowers, the persistent grin of a skull. There seem to be irresistible parallels between the expressive forms we find in nature and the forms of our inner life; thus the use of light to represent all things good, joyful, comforting, and of darkness to express all sorts of sorrow, despair, or horror, is so primitive as to be well-nigh unconscious.

A flame is a soul; a star is a hope; the silence of winter is death. All such images, which serve the purpose of metaphorical thinking, are *natural symbols*. They have not conventionally assigned meanings, like words, but recommend themselves even to a perfectly untutored mind, a child's or a savage's, because they are definitely articulated *forms*, and to see something expressed in such forms is a universal human talent. We do not have to learn to use natural symbols; it is one of our primitive activities.

The fact that sensuous forms of natural processes have a significance beyond themselves makes the range of our symbolism, and with it the horizon of our consciousness, much wider and deeper than language. This is the source of ritual, mythology, and art. Ritual is a symbolic rendering of certain emotional *attitudes*, which have become articulate and fixed by being constantly expressed. Mythology is man's image of his world, and of himself in the world. Art is the exposition of his own subjective history, the life of feeling, the human spirit in all its adventures.

Yet this power of envisagement, which natural symbolism bestows, is a dangerous one; for human beings can envisage things that do not exist, and create horrible worlds, insupportable duties, monstrous gods and ancestors. The mind that can see past and future, the poles and the antipodes, and guess at obscure mechanisms of nature, is ever in danger of seeing what is not there, imagining false and fantastic causes, and courting death instead of life. Because man can play with ideas, he is unrealistic; he is inclined to neglect the all-important interpretation of signs for a rapt contemplation of symbols.

Some twenty years ago, Ernst Cassirer set forth a theory of human mentality that goes far toward explaining the vagaries of savage religions and the ineradicable presence of superstition even in civilized societies: a symbol, he observed, is the embodiment of an idea; it is at once an abstract and a physical fact. Now its great emotive value lies in the concept it conveys; this inspires our reverent attitude, the attention and awe with which we view it. But man's untutored thought always tends to lose its way between the symbol and the fact. A skull represents death; but to a primitive mind the skull *is* death. To have it in the house is not unpleasant but dangerous. Even in civilized societies, symbolic objects—figures of saints, relics, crucifixes—are revered for their supposed efficacy. Their actual power is a power of *expression*, of embodying and thus revealing the greatest concepts humanity has reached; these concepts are the commanding forces that change our estate from a brute existence to the transcendent life of the spirit. But the symbol-loving mind of man reveres the meaning not *through* the articulating form but *in* the form so that the image appears to be the actual object of love and fear, supplication and praise.

Because of this constant identification of concepts with their expressions, our world is crowded with unreal beings. Some societies have actually realized that these beings do not belong to nature, and have postulated a so-called "other world" where they have their normal existence and from which they are said to descend, or arise, into our physical realm. For savages it is chiefly a nether world that sends up spooks; for more advanced cults it is from the heavens that supernatural beings, the embodiments of human ideas—of virtue, triumph, immortality—descend to the mundane realm. But from this source emanates also a terrible world government, with heavy commands and sanctions. Strange worship and terrible sacrifices may be the tithes exacted by the beings that embody our knowledge of nonanimalian human nature.

So the gift of symbolism, which is the gift of reason, is at the same time the seat of man's peculiar weakness—the danger of lunacy. Animals go mad with hydrophobia or head injuries, but purely mental aberrations are rare; beasts are not generally subject to insanity except through a confusion of signs, such as the experimentally produced "nervous breakdown" in rats. It is man who hears voices and sees ghosts in the dark, feels irrational compulsions and holds fixed ideas. All these phantasms are symbolic forms that have acquired a false factual status. It has been truly said that everybody has some streak of insanity; i.e., the threat of madness is the price of reason.

Because we can think of things potential as well as actual, we can be held in nonphysical bondage by laws and prohibitions and commands and by images of a governing power. This makes men tyrants over their own kind. Animals control each other's actions by immediate threats, growls and snarls and passes; but when the bully is roving elsewhere, his former domain is free of him. We control our inferiors by setting up symbols of our power, and the mere idea that words or images convey stands there to hold our fellows in subjection even when we cannot lay our hands on them. There is no flag over the country where a wolf is king; he is king where he happens to prowl, so long as he is there. But men, who can embody ideas and set them up to view, oppress each other by symbols of might.

The envisagements of good and evil, which make man a moral agent, make him also a conscript, a prisoner, and a slave. His constant problem is to escape the tyrannies he has created. Primitive societies are almost entirely tyrannical, symbol-bound, coercive organizations; civilized governments are so many conscious schemes to justify or else to disguise man's inevitable bondage to law and conscience.

Slowly, through ages and centuries, we have evolved a picture of the world we live in; we have made a drama of the earth's history and enhanced it with a backdrop of divinely ordered, star-filled space. And all this structure of infinity and eternity against which we watch the pageant of life and death, and all the moral melodrama itself, we have wrought by a gradual articulation of such vast ideas in symbols—symbols of good and evil, triumph and failure, birth and maturity and death. Long before the beginning of any known history, people saw in the heavenly bodies, in the changes of day and night or of the seasons, and in great beasts, symbolic forms to express those ultimate concepts that are the very frame of human existence. So gods, fates, the cohorts of good and evil were conceived. Their myths were the first formulations of cosmic ideas. Gradually the figures and traditions of religion emerged; ritual, the overt expression of our mental attitudes, became more and more intimately bound to definite and elaborate concepts of the creative and destructive powers that seem to control our lives.

Such beings and stories and rites are sacred because they are the great symbols by which the human mind orients itself in the world. To a creature that lives by reason, nothing is more terrible than what is formless and meaningless; one of our primary fears is fear of chaos. And it is the fight against chaos that has produced our most profound and indispensable images—the myths of light and darkness, of creation and passion, the symbols of the altar flame, the daystar, and the cross.

For thousands of years people lived by the symbols that nature presented to them. Close contact with earth and its seasons, intimate knowledge of stars and tides, made them feel the significance of natural phenomena and gave them a poetic, unquestioning sense of orientation. Generations of erudite and pious men elaborated the picture of the temporal and spiritual realms in which each individual was a pilgrim soul.

Then came the unprecedented change, the almost instantaneous leap of history from the immemorial tradition of the plow and the anvil to the new age of the machine, the factory, and the ticker tape. Often in no more than the length of a life-time the shift from handwork to mass production, and with it from poetry to science and from faith to nihilism, has taken place. The old nature symbols have become remote and have lost their meanings; in the clatter of gears and the confusion of gadgets that fill the new world, there will not be any obvious and rich and sacred meanings for centuries to come. All the accumulated creeds and rites of men are suddenly in the melting pot. There is no fixed community, no dynasty, no family inheritance—only the one huge world of men, vast millions of men, still looking on each other in hostile amazement.

A sane, intelligent animal should have invented, in the course of ten thousand years or more, some sure and obvious way of accommodating indefinite numbers of its own kind on the face of a fairly spacious earth. Modern civilization has achieved the highest triumphs of knowledge, skill, ingenuity, theory; yet all around its citadels, engulfing and demolishing them, rages the maddest war and confusion, inspired by symbols and slogans as riotous and irrational as anything the "vegetative" stage of savage phantasy could provide. How shall we reconcile this primitive nightmare excitement with the achievements of our high, rational, scientific culture?

The answer is, I think, that we are no longer in possession of a definite, established culture; we live in a period between an exhausted age—the European civilization of the white race—and an age still unborn, of which we can say nothing as yet. We do not know what races shall inherit the earth. We do not know what even the next few centuries may bring. But it is quite evident, I think, that we live in an age of transition, and that before many more generations have passed, mankind will make a new beginning and build itself a different world. Whether it will be a "brave, new world," or whether it will start all over with an unchronicled "state of nature" such as Thomas Hobbes described, wherein the individual's life is "nasty, brutish, and short," we simply cannot tell. All we know is that every tradition, every institution, every tribe is gradually becoming uprooted and upset, and we are waiting in a sort of theatrical darkness between the acts.

Because we are at a new beginning, our imaginations tend to a wild, "vegetative" overgrowth. The political upheavals of our time are marked, therefore, by a veritable devil dance of mystical ideologies, vaguely conceived, passionately declared, holding out fanatic hopes of mass redemption and mass beatitudes. Governments vie with each other in proclaiming social plans, social aims, social enterprises, and demanding bloody sacrifices in the name of social achievements.

New conceptions are always clothed in an extravagant metaphorical form, for there is no language to express genuinely new ideas. And in their pristine strength they imbue the symbols that express them with their own mystery and power and holiness. It is impossible to disengage the welter of ideas embodied in a swastika, a secret sign, or a conjuring word from the physical presence of the symbol itself; hence the apparently nonsensical symbol worship and mysticism that go with new movements and visions. This identification of symbolic form and half-articulate meaning is the essence of all mythmaking. Of course the emotive value is incomprehensible to anyone who does not see such figments as expressive forms. So an age of vigorous new conception and incomplete formulation always has a certain air of madness about it. But it is really a fecund and exciting period in the life of reason. Such is our present age. Its apparent unreason is a tremendous unbalance and headiness of the human spirit, a conflict not only of selfish wills but of vast ideas in the metaphorical state of emergence.

The change from fixed community life and ancient local custom to the mass of unpedigreed human specimens that actually constitutes the world in our industrial and commercial age has been too sudden for the mind of man to negotiate. Some transitional form of life had to mediate between those extremes. And so the idol of nationality arose from the wreckage of tribal organization. The concept of the national state is really the old tribe concept applied to millions of persons, unrelated and different creatures gathered under the banner of a government. Neither birth nor language nor even religion holds such masses together, but a mystic bond is postulated even where no actual bond of race, creed, or color may ever have existed.

At first glance it seems odd that the concept of nationality should reach its highest development just as all actual marks of national origins—language, dress, physiognomy, and religion—are becoming mixed and obliterated by our new mobility and cosmopolitan traffic. But it is just the loss of these things that inspires this hungry seeking for something like the old egocentric pattern in the vast and formless brotherhood of the whole earth. While mass production and universal communication clearly portend a culture of world citizenship, we cling desperately to our nationalism, a more and more attenuated version of the old clan civilization. We fight passionate and horrible wars for the symbols of our nations, we make a virtue of self-glorification and exclusiveness and invent strange anthropologies to keep us at least theoretically set apart from other men.

Nationalism is a transition between an old and a new human order. But even now we are not really fighting a war of nations; we are fighting a war of fictions, from which a new vision of the order of nature will someday emerge. The future, just now, lies wide open—open and dark, like interstellar space; but in that emptiness there is room for new gods, new cultures, mysterious now and nameless as an unborn child.

GEORGE ORWELL

Orwell's reputation has shown no sign of decline since his death at 46 in 1950. He is likely to be ranked permanently among the great English essayists. On presenting him an award in 1949, the editors of Partisan Review *commented that his writing "has been marked by a singular directness and honesty, a scrupulous fidelity to his experience that has placed him in that valuable class of the writer who is a witness to his time."*

His real name was Eric Arthur Blair, and he was born in 1903 in Bengal, a province of British India. He attended Eton on a King's Scholarship from 1917 to 1921, then served for five years in the Imperial Police in Burma. Returning to Europe, he spent some poverty-stricken years doing odd jobs, from teaching to dishwashing, while he wrote novels and short stories that did not sell. His Down and Out in Paris and London *(1933) is a vivid record of those years. In 1936 Orwell went to Spain to take part in the Civil War and reported his experiences in* Homage to Catalonia *(1938). Among his other books are the celebrated* Nineteen Eighty-Four *(1949), a terrifying novel picturing the complete victory of totalitarianism,* Animal Farm, a Fairy Story *(1945), and the essay collections* Shooting an Elephant and Other Essays *(1950), and* Such, Such Were the Joys *(1953). The present essay first appeared in the London monthly* Horizon *in 1946 and was reprinted in the 1950 collection.*

POLITICS AND THE ENGLISH
LANGUAGE

Most people who bother with the matter at all would admit that the English language is in a bad way, but it is generally assumed that we cannot by conscious action do anything about it. Our civilization is decadent and our language—so the argument runs—must inevitably share in the general collapse. It follows that any struggle against the abuse of language is a sentimental archaism, like preferring candles to electric light or hansom cabs to aeroplanes. Underneath this lies the half-conscious belief that language is a natural growth and not an instrument which we shape for our own purposes.

Now, it is clear that the decline of a language must ultimately have political and economic causes: it is not due simply to the bad influence of this or that individual writer. But an effect can become a cause, reinforcing the original cause and producing the same effect in an intensified form, and so on indefinitely. A man may take to drink because he feels himself to be a failure, and then fail all the more completely because he drinks. It is rather the same thing that is happening to the English language. It becomes ugly and inaccurate because our thoughts are foolish, but the slovenliness of our language makes it easier for us to have foolish thoughts. The point is that the process is reversible. Modern English, especially written English, is full of bad habits which spread by imitation and which can be avoided if one is willing to take the necessary trouble. If one gets rid of these habits one can think more clearly, and to think clearly is a necessary first step towards political regeneration: so that the fight against bad English is not frivolous and is not the exclusive concern of professional writers. I will come back to this presently, and I hope that by that time the meaning of what I have said here will have become clearer. Meanwhile, here are five specimens of the English language as it is now habitually written.

These five passages have not been picked out because they are especially bad—I could have quoted far worse if I had chosen—but because they illustrate various of the mental vices from which we now suffer. They are a little below the average, but are fairly representative samples. I number them so that I can refer back to them when necessary:

(1) I am not, indeed, sure whether it is not true to say that the Milton who once seemed not unlike a seventeenth-century Shelley had not become, out of an experience ever more bitter in each year, more alien [*sic*] to the founder of that Jesuit sect which nothing could induce him to tolerate.

Professor Harold Laski
(Essay in *Freedom of Expression*).

(2) Above all, we cannot play ducks and drakes with a native battery of idioms which prescribes such egregious collocations of vocables as the Basic *put up with* for *tolerate* or *put at a loss* for *bewilder*.

Professor Lancelot Hogben (*Interglossa*).

(3) On the one side we have the free personality: by definition it is not neurotic, for it has neither conflict nor dream. Its desires,

such as they are, are transparent, for they are just what institutional approval keeps in the forefront of consciousness; another institutional pattern would alter their number and intensity; there is little in them that is natural, irreducible, or culturally dangerous. But *on the other side*, the social bond itself is nothing but the mutual reflection of these self-secure integrities. Recall the definition of love. Is not this the very picture of a small academic? Where is there a place in this hall of mirrors for either personality or fraternity?

Essay on psychology in *Politics* (New York).

(4) All the "best people" from the gentlemen's clubs, and all the frantic fascist captains, united in common hatred of Socialism and bestial horror of the rising tide of the mass revolutionary movement, have turned to acts of provocation, to foul incendiarism, to medieval legends of poisoned wells, to legalize their own destruction of proletarian organizations, and rouse the agitated petty-bourgeoisie to chauvinistic fervor on behalf of the fight against the revolutionary way out of the crisis.

Communist pamphlet.

(5) If a new spirit *is* to be infused into this old country, there is one thorny and contentious reform which must be tackled, and that is the humanization and galvanization of the B.B.C. Timidity here will bespeak canker and atrophy of the soul. The heart of Britain may be sound and of strong beat, for instance, but the British lion's roar at present is like that of Bottom in Shakespeare's *Midsummer Night's Dream*—as gentle as any sucking dove. A virile new Britain cannot continue indefinitely to be traduced in the eyes or rather ears, of the world by the effete languors of Langham Place, brazenly masquerading as "standard English." When the voice of Britain is heard at nine o'clock, better far and infinitely less ludicrous to hear aitches honestly dropped than the present priggish, inflated, inhibited, school-ma'amish arch braying of blameless bashful mewing maidens!

Letter in *Tribune*.

Each of these passages has faults of its own, but, quite apart from avoidable ugliness, two qualities are common to all of them. The first is staleness of imagery; the other is lack of precision. The writer either has a meaning and cannot express it, or he inadvertently says something else, or he is almost indifferent as to whether his words mean anything or not. This mixture of vagueness and sheer incompetence is the most marked characteristic of modern English prose, and especially of any kind of political writing. As soon as certain topics are raised, the concrete melts into the abstract and no one seems able to think of turns of speech that are not hackneyed: prose consists less and less of *words* chosen for the sake of their meaning, and more and more of *phrases* tacked together like the sections of a prefabricated hen-house. I list below, with notes and examples, various of the tricks by means of which the work of prose-construction is habitually dodged:

Dying metaphors. A newly invented metaphor assists thought by evoking a visual image, while on the other hand a metaphor which is technically "dead" (e.g. *iron resolution*) has in effect reverted to being an ordinary word and can generally be used without loss of vividness. But in between these two classes there is a huge dump of worn-out metaphors which have lost all evocative power and are merely used because they save people the trouble of inventing phrases for themselves. Examples are: *Ring the changes on, take up the cudgels for, toe the line, ride roughshod over, stand shoulder to shoulder with, play into the hands of, no axe to grind, grist to the mill, fishing in troubled waters, on the order of the day, Achilles' heel, swan song, hotbed.* Many of these are used without knowledge of their meaning (what is a "rift," for instance?), and incompatible metaphors are frequently mixed, a sure sign that the writer is not interested in what he is saying. Some metaphors now current have been twisted out of their original meaning without those who use them even being aware of the fact. For example, *toe the line* is sometimes written *tow the line.* Another example is *the hammer and the anvil,* now always used with the implication that the anvil gets the worst of it. In real life it is always the anvil that breaks the hammer, never the other way about: a writer who stopped to think what he was saying would be aware of this, and would avoid perverting the original phrase.

Operators or *verbal false limbs.* These save the trouble of picking out appropriate verbs and nouns, and at the same time pad each sentence with extra syllables which give it an appearance of symmetry. Characteristic phrases are *render inoperative, militate against, make contact with, be subjected to, give rise to, give grounds for, have the effect of, play a leading part (role) in, make itself felt, take effect, exhibit a tendency to, serve the purpose of, etc., etc.* The keynote is the elimination of simple verbs. Instead of being a single word, such as *break, stop, spoil, mend, kill,* a verb becomes a *phrase,* made up of a noun or adjective tacked on to some general-purposes verb such as *prove, serve, form, play, render.* In addition, the passive voice is wherever possible used in preference to the active, and noun constructions are used instead of gerunds (*by examination of* instead of *by examining*). The range of verbs is further cut down by means of the *-ize* and *de-* formations, and the banal statements are given an appearance of profundity by means of the *not un-* formation. Simple conjunctions and prepositions are replaced by such phrases as *with respect to, having regard to, the fact that, by dint of, in view of, in the interests of, on the hypothesis that;* and the ends of sentences are saved from anticlimax by such resounding common-places as *greatly to be desired, cannot be left out of account, a development to be expected in the near future, deserving* *of serious consideration, brought to a satisfactory conclusion,* and so on and so forth.

Pretentious diction. Words like *phenomenon, element, individual* (as noun), *objective, categorical, effective, virtual, basic, primary, promote, constitute, exhibit, exploit, utilize, eliminate, liquidate,* are used to dress up simple statement and give an air of scientific impartiality to biased judgments. Adjectives like *epoch-making, epic, historic, unforgettable, triumphant, age-old, inevitable, inexorable, veritable,* are used to dignify the sordid processes of international politics, while writing that aims at glorifying war usually takes on an archaic color, its characteristic words being: *realm, throne, chariot, mailed fist, trident, sword, shield, buckler, banner, jackboot, clarion.* Foreign words and expressions such as *cul de sac, ancien régime, deus ex machina, mutatis mutandis, status quo, gleichschaltung, weltanschauung,* are used to give an air of culture and elegance. Except for the useful abbreviations *i.e., e.g.,* and *etc.,* there is no real need for any of the hundreds of foreign phrases now current in English. Bad writers, and especially scientific, political and sociological writers, are nearly always haunted by the notion that Latin or Greek words are grander than Saxon ones, and unnecessary words like *expedite, ameliorate, predict, extraneous, deracinated, clandestine, subaqueous* and hundreds of others constantly gain ground from their Anglo-Saxon opposite numbers.[1] The jargon peculiar to Marxist writing (*hyena, hangman, cannibal, petty bourgeois, these gentry, lacquey, flunkey, mad dog, White Guard,* etc.) consists largely of words and phrases translated from Russian, German or French; but the normal way of coining a new word is to use a Latin or Greek root with the appropriate affix and, where necessary, the *-ize* formation. It is often easier to make up words of this kind (*deregionalize, impermissible, extramarital, non-fragmentary* and so forth) than to think up the English words that will cover one's meaning. The result, in general, is an increase in slovenliness and vagueness.

Meaningless words. In certain kinds of writing, particularly in art criticism and literary criticism, it is normal to come across long passages which are almost completely lacking in meaning.[2] Words like *romantic, plastic, values, human, dead, sentimental, natural, vitality,* as used in art criticism, are strictly meaningless, in the sense that they not only do not point to

---

[1] An interesting illustration of this is the way in which the English flower names which were in use till very recently are being ousted by Greek ones, *snapdragon* becoming *antirrhinum, forget-me-not* becoming *myosotis,* etc. It is hard to see any practical reason for this change of fashion: it is probably due to an instinctive turning-away from the more homely word and a vague feeling that the Greek word is scientific.

[2] Example: "Comfort's catholicity of perception and image, strangely Whitmanesque in range, almost the exact opposite in aesthetic compulsion, continues to evoke that trembling atmospheric accumulative hinting at a cruel, an inexorably serene timelessness. . . . Wrey Gardiner scores by aiming at simple bull's-eyes with precision. Only they are not so simple, and through this contented sadness runs more than the surface bitter-sweet of resignation." (*Poetry Quarterly.*)

any discoverable object, but are hardly ever expected to do so by the reader. When one critic writes, "The outstanding feature of Mr. X's work is its living quality," while another writes, "The immediately striking thing about Mr. X's work is its peculiar deadness," the reader accepts this as a simple difference of opinion. If words like *black* and *white* were involved, instead of the jargon words *dead* and *living*, he would see at once that language was being used in an improper way. Many political words are similarly abused. The word *Fascism* has now no meaning except in so far as it signifies "something not desirable." The words *democracy, socialism, freedom, patriotic, realistic, justice,* have each of them several different meanings which cannot be reconciled with one another. In the case of a word like *democracy*, not only is there no agreed definition, but the attempt to make one is resisted from all sides. It is almost universally felt that when we call a country democratic we are praising it: consequently the defenders of every kind of régime claim that it is a democracy, and fear that they might have to stop using the word if it were tied down to any one meaning. Words of this kind are often used in a consciously dishonest way. That is, the person who uses them has his own private definition, but allows his hearer to think he means something quite different. Statements like *Marshal Pétain was a true patriot, The Soviet Press is the freest in the world, The Catholic Church is opposed to persecution,* are almost always made with intent to deceive. Other words used in variable meanings, in most cases more or less dishonestly, are: *class, totalitarian, science, progressive, reactionary, bourgeois, equality.*

Now that I have made this catalogue of swindles and perversions, let me give another example of the kind of writing that they lead to. This time it must of its nature be an imaginary one. I am going to translate a passage of good English into modern English of the worst sort. Here is a well-known verse from *Ecclesiastes:*

"I returned and saw under the sun, that the race is not to the swift, nor the battle to the strong, neither yet bread to the wise, nor yet riches to men of understanding, nor yet favour to men of skill; but time and chance happeneth to them all."

Here it is in modern English:

"Objective consideration of contemporary phenomena compels the conclusion that success or failure in competitive activities exhibits no tendency to be commensurate with innate capacity, but that a considerable element of the unpredictable must invariably be taken into account."

This is a parody, but not a very gross one. Exhibit (3), above, for instance, contains several patches of the same kind of English. It will be seen that I have not made a full translation. The beginning and ending of the sentence follow the original meaning fairly closely, but in the middle the concrete illustrations—race, battle, bread—dissolve into the vague phrase "success or failure in competitive activities." This had to be so, because no modern writer of the kind I am discussing—no one capable of using phrases like "objective consideration of contemporary phenomena"—would ever tabulate his thoughts in that precise and detailed way. The whole tendency of modern prose is away from concreteness. Now analyse these two sentences a little more closely. The first contains forty-nine words but only sixty syllables, and all its words are those of everyday life. The second contains thirty-eight words of ninety syllables: eighteen of its words are from Latin roots, and one from Greek. The first sentence contains six vivid images, and only one phrase ("time and chance") that could be called vague. The second contains not a single fresh, arresting phrase, and in spite of its ninety syllables it gives only a shortened version of the meaning contained in the first. Yet without a doubt it is the second kind of sentence that is gaining ground in modern English. I do not want to exaggerate. This kind of writing is not yet universal, and outcrops of simplicity will occur here and there in the worst-written page. Still, if you or I were told to write a few lines on the uncertainty of human fortunes, we should probably come much nearer to my imaginary sentence than to the one from *Ecclesiastes*.

As I have tried to show, modern writing at its worst does not consist in picking out words for the sake of their meaning and inventing images in order to make the meaning clearer. It consists in gumming together long strips of words which have already been set in order by someone else, and making the results presentable by sheer humbug. The attraction of this way of writing is that it is easy. It is easier—even quicker, once you have the habit—to say *In my opinion it is not an unjustifiable assumption that* than to say *I think*. If you use ready-made phrases, you not only don't have to hunt about for words; you also don't have to bother with the rhythms of your sentences, since these phrases are generally so arranged as to be more or less euphonious. When you are composing in a hurry—when you are dictating to a stenographer, for instance, or making a public speech—it is natural to fall into a pretentious, Latinized style. Tags like *a consideration which we should do well to bear in mind* or *a conclusion to which all of us would readily assent* will save many a sentence from coming down with a bump. By using stale metaphors, similes and idioms, you save much mental effort, at the cost of leaving your meaning vague, not only for your reader but for yourself. This is the significance of mixed metaphors. The sole aim of a metaphor is to call up a visual image. When these images clash—as in *The Fascist octopus has sung its swan song, the jackboot is thrown into the melting pot*—it can be taken as certain that the writer is not seeing a mental image of the objects he is naming; in other words he is not really thinking. Look again at the examples I gave at the beginning of this essay. Professor Laski (1) uses five negatives in fifty-three words. One of these is superfluous, making nonsense of the whole passage, and in addition there is the slip *alien* for akin, making further nonsense, and several avoidable pieces of clumsiness which increase the general vagueness. Professor Hogben (2) plays ducks and drakes with a battery which is able to write prescriptions, and, while disapproving of the everyday phrase *put up with*, is unwilling to look *egregious* up in the dictionary and see what it means; (3), if one takes an uncharitable attitude towards it, is simply meaningless: probably one could work out its intended meaning by reading the whole of the article in which it occurs. In (4), the writer knows more or less what he wants to say, but an accumulation of stale phrases chokes him like tea leaves blocking a sink. In (5), words and meaning have almost parted company. People who write in this manner usually have a general emotional meaning—they dislike one thing and want to express solidarity with another—but they are not interested in the detail of what they are saying. A scrupulous writer, in every sentence that he writes, will ask himself at least four questions, thus: What am I trying to say? What words will express it? What image or idiom will make it clearer? Is this image fresh enough to have an effect? And he will probably ask himself two more: Could I put it more shortly? Have I said anything that is avoidably ugly? But you are not obliged to go to all this trouble. You can shirk it by simply throwing your mind open and letting the ready-made phrases come crowding in. They will construct your sentences for you—even think your thoughts for you, to a certain extent—and at need they will perform the important service of partially concealing your meaning even from yourself. It is at this point that the special connection between politics and the debasement of language becomes clear.

In our time it is broadly true that political writing is bad writing. Where it is not true, it will generally be found that the writer is some kind of rebel, expressing his private opinions and not a "party line." Orthodoxy, of whatever color, seems to demand a lifeless, imitative style. The political dialects to be found in pamphlets, leading articles, manifestos, White Papers and the speeches of under-secretaries do, of course, vary from party to party, but they are all alike in that one almost never finds in them a fresh, vivid, home-made turn of speech. When one watches some tired hack on the platform mechanically repeating the familiar phrases—*bestial atrocities, iron heel, bloodstained tyranny, free peoples of the world, stand shoulder to shoulder*—one often has a curious feeling that one is not watching a live human being but some kind of dummy: a feeling which suddenly becomes stronger at moments when the light catches the speaker's spectacles and turns them into blank discs which seem to have no eyes behind them. And this is not altogether fanciful. A speaker who uses that kind of phraseology has gone some distance towards turning himself into a machine. The appropriate noises are coming out of his larynx, but his brain is not involved as it would be if he were choosing his words for himself. If the speech he is making is one that he is accustomed to make over and over again, he may be almost unconscious of what he is saying, as one is when one utters the responses in church. And this reduced state of consciousness, if not indispensable, is at any rate favorable to political conformity.

In our time, political speech and writing are largely the defence of the indefensible. Things like the continuance of British rule in India, the Russian purges and deportations, the dropping of the atom bombs on Japan, can indeed be defended, but only by arguments which are too brutal for most people to face, and which do not square with the professed aims of political parties. Thus political language has to consist largely of euphemism, question-begging and sheer cloudy vagueness. Defenceless villages are bombarded from the air, the inhabitants driven out into the countryside, the cattle machine-gunned, the huts set on fire with incendiary bullets: this is called *pacification*. Millions of peasants are robbed of their farms and sent trudging along the roads with no more than they can carry: this is called *transfer of population* or *rectification of frontiers*. People are imprisoned for years without trial, or shot in the back of the neck or sent to die of scurvy in Arctic lumber camps: this is called *elimination of unreliable elements*. Such phraseology is needed if one wants to name things without calling up mental pictures of them. Consider for instance some comfortable English professor defending Russian totalitarianism. He cannot say outright, "I believe in killing off your opponents when you can get good results by doing so." Probably, therefore, he will say something like this:

"While freely conceding that the Soviet régime exhibits certain features which the humanitarian may be inclined to deplore, we must, I think, agree that a certain curtailment of the right to political opposition is an unavoidable concomitant of transitional periods, and that the rigors which the Russian people have been called upon to undergo have been amply justified in the sphere of concrete achievement."

The inflated style is itself a kind of euphemism. A mass of Latin words falls upon the facts like soft snow, blurring the outlines and covering up all the details. The great enemy of clear language is insincerity. When there is a gap between one's real and one's declared aims, one turns as it were instinctively to long words and exhausted idioms, like a cuttlefish squirting out ink. In our age there is no such thing as "keeping out of politics." All issues are political issues, and politics itself is a mass of lies, evasions, folly, hatred and schizophrenia. When the general atmosphere is bad, language must suffer. I should expect to find—this is a guess which I have not sufficient knowledge to verify—that the German, Russian and Italian languages have all deteriorated in the last ten or fifteen years, as a result of dictatorship.

But if thought corrupts language, language can also corrupt thought. A bad usage can spread by tradition and imitation, even among people who should and do know better. The debased language that I have been discussing is in some ways very convenient. Phrases like *a not unjustifiable as-*

sumption, *leaves much to be desired*, *would serve no good purpose, a consideration which we should do well to bear in mind*, are a continuous temptation, a packet of aspirins always at one's elbow. Look back through this essay, and for certain you will find that I have again and again committed the very faults I am protesting against. By this morning's post I have received a pamphlet dealing with conditions in Germany. The author tells me that he "felt impelled" to write it. I open it at random, and here is almost the first sentence that I see: "[The Allies] have an opportunity not only of achieving a radical transformation of Germany's social and political structure in such a way as to avoid a nationalistic reaction in Germany itself, but at the same time of laying the foundations of a co-operative and unified Europe." You see, he "feels impelled" to write—feels, presumably, that he has something new to say—and yet his words, like cavalry horses answering the bugle, group themselves automatically into the familiar dreary pattern. This invasion of one's mind by ready-made phrases (*lay the foundations, achieve a radical transformation*) can only be prevented if one is constantly on guard against them, and every such phrase anaesthetizes a portion of one's brain.

I said earlier that the decadence of our language is probably curable. Those who deny this would argue, if they produced an argument at all, that language merely reflects existing social conditions, and that we cannot influence its development by any direct tinkering with words and constructions. So far as the general tone or spirit of a language goes, this may be true, but it is not true in detail. Silly words and expressions have often disappeared, not through any evolutionary process but owing to the conscious action of a minority. Two recent examples were *explore every avenue* and *leave no stone unturned*, which were killed by the jeers of a few journalists. There is a long list of flyblown metaphors which could similarly be got rid of if enough people would interest themselves in the job; and it should also be possible to laugh the *not un-* formation out of existence,[3] to reduce the amount of Latin and Greek in the average sentence, to drive out foreign phrases and strayed scientific words, and, in general, to make pretentiousness unfashionable. But all these are minor points. The defence of the English language implies more than this, and perhaps it is best to start by saying what it does *not* imply.

To begin with it has nothing to do with archaism, with the salvaging of obsolete words and turns of speech, or with the setting up of a "standard English" which must never be departed from. On the contrary, it is especially concerned with the scrapping of every word or idiom which has outworn its usefulness. It has nothing to do with correct grammar and syntax, which are of no importance so long as one makes one's meaning clear, or with the avoidance of Americanisms, or with having what is called a "good prose style." On the other hand it is not concerned with fake

---

[3] One can cure oneself of the *not un-* formation by memorizing this sentence: *A not unblack dog was chasing a not unsmall rabbit across a not ungreen field.*

simplicity and the attempt to make written English colloquial. Nor does it even imply in every case preferring the Saxon word to the Latin one, though it does imply using the fewest and shortest words that will cover one's meaning. What is above all needed is to let the meaning choose the word, and not the other way about. In prose, the worst thing one can do with words is to surrender to them. When you think of a concrete object, you think wordlessly, and then, if you want to describe the thing you have been visualizing you probably hunt about till you find the exact words that seem to fit it. When you think of something abstract you are more inclined to use words from the start, and unless you make a conscious effort to prevent it, the existing dialect will come rushing in and do the job for you, at the expense of blurring or even changing your meaning. Probably it is better to put off using words as long as possible and get one's meaning as clear as one can through pictures or sensations. Afterwards one can choose—not simply *accept*—the phrases that will best cover the meaning, and then switch round and decide what impression one's words are likely to make on another person. This last effort of the mind cuts out all stale or mixed images, all prefabricated phrases, needless repetitions, and humbug and vagueness generally. But one can often be in doubt about the effect of a word or a phrase, and one needs rules that one can rely on when instinct fails. I think the following rules will cover most cases:

(i) Never use a metaphor, simile or other figure of speech which you are used to seeing in print.

(ii) Never use a long word where a short one will do.

(iii) If it is possible to cut a word out, always cut it out.

(iv) Never use the passive where you can use the active.

(v) Never use a foreign phrase, a scientific word or a jargon word if you can think of an everyday English equivalent.

(vi) Break any of these rules sooner than say anything outright barbarous.

These rules sound elementary, and so they are, but they demand a deep change of attitude in anyone who has grown used to writing in the style now fashionable. One could keep all of them and still write bad English, but one could not write the kind of stuff that I quoted in those five specimens at the beginning of this article.

I have not here been considering the literary use of language, but merely language as an instrument for expressing and not for concealing or preventing thought. Stuart Chase and others have come near to claiming that all abstract words are meaningless, and have used this as a pretext for advocating a kind of political quietism. Since you don't know what Fascism is, how can you struggle against Fascism? One need not swallow such absurdities as this, but one ought to recognize that the present political chaos is connected with the decay of language, and that one can probably bring about some improvement by starting at the verbal end. If you simplify your English, you are freed from the worst follies of orthodoxy. You cannot speak any of the necessary dialects, and when you make a stupid remark its stupidity will be obvious, even to yourself. Political language—and with variations this is true of all political parties, from Conservatives to Anarchists—is designed to make lies sound truthful and murder respectable, and to give an appearance of solidity to pure wind. One cannot change this all in a moment, but one can at least change one's own habits, and from time to time one can even, if one jeers loudly enough, send some worn-out and useless phrase—some *jackboot, Achilles' heel, hotbed, melting pot, acid test, veritable inferno* or other lump of verbal refuse—into the dustbin where it belongs.

RICHARD M. WEAVER

Professor Weaver was born in Asheville, North Carolina, in 1910 and educated at Kentucky, Vanderbilt, and Louisiana State, where he received the doctorate in 1943. He soon joined the Department of English in the College of the University of Chicago and remained there until his death in 1963. An intense, tough-minded man, he was profoundly displeased with the "pseudoscientific" direction of modern thought. In three of his books he attempts to redirect our attention to the ideas of form, order, and human worth that he feels we have lost in the course of our "progress." These books are Ideas Have Consequences *(1948)*, Visions of Order; the Cultural Crisis of Our Time *(1964), and* The Ethics of Rhetoric *(1957), from which we print here the final chapter. The reader should not allow himself to be put off by the rather technical first two paragraphs; a full understanding of them depends on a knowledge of earlier chapters and is not essential to an appreciation of the rest of the essay.*

ULTIMATE TERMS IN
CONTEMPORARY RHETORIC

We have shown that rhetorical force must be conceived as a power transmitted through the links of a chain that extends upward toward some ultimate source. The higher links of that chain must always be of unique interest to the student of rhetoric, pointing, as they do, to some prime mover of human impulse. Here I propose to turn away from general considerations and to make an empirical study of the terms on these higher levels of force which are seen to be operating in our age.

We shall define term simply here as a name capable of entering into a proposition. In our treatment of rhetorical sources, we have regarded the full predication consisting of a proposition as the true validator. But a single term is an incipient proposition, awaiting only the necessary coupling with another term; and it cannot be denied that single names set up expectancies of propositional embodiment. This causes everyone to realize the critical nature of the process of naming. Given the name "patriot," for example, we might expect to see coupled with it "Brutus," or "Washington," or "Parnell"; given the term "hot," we might expect to see "sun," "stove," and so on. In sum, single terms have their potencies, this being part of the phenomenon of names, and we shall here present a few of the most noteworthy in our time, with some remarks upon their etiology.

Naturally this survey will include the "bad" terms as well as the "good" terms, since we are interested to record historically those expressions to which the populace, in its actual usage and response, appears to attribute the greatest sanction. A prescriptive rhetoric may specify those terms which, in all seasons, ought to carry the greatest potency, but since the affections of one age are frequently a source of wonder to another, the most we can do under the caption "contemporary rhetoric" is to give a descriptive account and withhold the moral until the end. For despite the variations of fashion, an age which is not simply distraught manages to achieve some system of relationship among the attractive and among the repulsive terms, so that we can work out an order of weight and precedence in the prevailing rhetoric once we have discerned the "rhetorical absolutes"—the terms to which the very highest respect is paid.

It is best to begin boldly by asking ourselves, what is the "god term" of the present age? By "god term" we mean that expression about which all other expressions are ranked as subordinate and serving dominations and powers. Its force imparts to the others their lesser degree of force, and fixes the scale by which degrees of comparison are understood. In the absence of a strong and evenly diffused religion, there may be several terms competing for this primacy, so that the question is not always capable of definite answer. Yet if one has to select the one term which in our day carries the greatest blessing, and—to apply a useful test— whose antonym carries the greatest rebuke, one will not go far wrong in naming "progress." This seems to be the ultimate generator of force flowing down through many links of ancillary terms. If one can "make it stick," it will validate almost anything. It would be difficult to think of any type of person or of any institution which could not be recommended to the public through the enhancing power of this word. A politician is urged upon the voters as a "progressive leader"; a community is proud to style itself "progressive"; technologies and methodologies claim to the "progressive"; a peculiar kind of emphasis in modern education calls itself "progressive," and so on without limit. There is no word whose power to move is more implicitly trusted than "progressive." But unlike some other words we shall examine in the course of this chapter, its rise to supreme position is not obscure, and it possesses some intelligible referents.

Before going into the story of its elevation, we must prepare ground by noting that it is the nature of the conscious life of man to revolve around some concept of value. So true is this that when the concept is withdrawn, or when it is forced into competition with another concept, the human being suffers an almost intolerable sense of being lost. He has to know where he is in the ideological cosmos in order to coordinate his activities. Probably the greatest cruelty which can be inflicted upon the psychic man is this deprivation of a sense of tendency. Accordingly every age, including those of rudest cultivation, sets up some kind of sign post. In highly cultivated ages, with individuals of exceptional intellectual strength, this may take the form of a metaphysic. But with the ordinary man, even in such advanced ages, it is likely to be some idea abstracted from religion or historical speculation, and made to inhere in a few sensible and immediate examples.

Since the sixteenth century we have tended to accept as inevitable an historical development that takes the form of a changing relationship between ourselves and nature, in which we pass increasingly into the role of master of nature. When I say that this seems inevitable to us, I mean that it seems something so close to what our more religious forebears considered the working of providence that we regard as impiety any disposition to challenge or even suspect it. By a transposition of terms, "progress" becomes the salvation man is placed on earth to work out; and just as there can be no achievement more important than salvation, so there can be no activity more justified in enlisting our sympathy and support than "progress." As our historical sketch would imply, the term began to be used in the sixteenth century in the sense of continuous development or improvement; it reached an apogee in the nineteenth century, amid noisy demonstrations of man's mastery of nature, and now in the twentieth century it keeps its place as one of the least assailable of the "uncontested terms," despite critical doubts in certain philosophic quarters. It is probably the only term which gives to the average American or West European of today a concept of something bigger than himself, which he is socially impelled to accept and even to sacrifice for. This capacity to demand sacrifice is probably the surest indicator of the "god term," for when a term is so sacrosanct that the material goods of this life must be mysteriously rendered up for it, then we feel justified in saying that it is in some sense ultimate. Today no one is startled to hear of a man's sacrificing health or wealth for the "progress" of the community, whereas such sacrifices for other ends may be regarded as self-indulgent or even treasonable. And this is just because "progress" is the coordinator of all socially respectable effort.

Perhaps these observations will help the speaker who would speak against the stream of "progress," or who, on the other hand, would parry some blow aimed at him through the potency of the word, to realize what a momentum he is opposing.

Another word of great rhetorical force which owes its origin to the same historical transformation is "fact." Today's speaker says "It is a fact" with all the gravity and air of finality with which his less secular-minded ancestor would have said "It is the truth."[1] "These are facts"; "Facts tend to show"; and "He knows the facts" will be recognized as common locutions drawing upon the rhetorical resource of this word. The word "fact" went into the ascendent when our system of verification changed during the Renaissance. Prior to that time, the type of conclusion that men felt obligated to accept came either through divine revelation, or through dialectic, which obeys logical law. But these were displaced by the system of verification through correspondence with physical reality. Since then things have been true only when measurably true, or when susceptible to some kind of quantification. Quite simply, "fact" came to be the touchstone after the truth of speculative inquiry had been replaced by the truth of empirical investigation. Today when the average citizen says "It is a fact" or says that he "knows the facts in the case," he means that he has the kind of knowledge to which all other knowledges must defer. Possibly it should be pointed out that his "facts" are frequently not facts at all in the etymological sense; often they will be deductions several steps removed from simply factual data. Yet the "facts" of his case carry with them this aura of scientific irrefragability, and he will likely regard any questioning of them as sophistry. In his vocabulary a fact is a fact, and all evidence so denominated has the prestige of science.

These last remarks will remind us at once of the strongly rhetorical character of the word "science" itself. If there is good reason for placing "progress" rather than "science" at the top of our series, it is only that the former has more scope, "science" being the methodological tool of "progress." It seems clear, moreover, that "science" owes its present status to

---

[1] It is surely worth observing that nowhere in the King James Version of the Bible does the word "fact" occur.

an hypostatization. The hypostatized term is one which treats as a substance or a concrete reality that which has only conceptual existence; and every reader will be able to supply numberless illustrations of how "science" is used without any specific referent. Any utterance beginning "Science says" provides one: "Science says there is no difference in brain capacity between the races"; "Science now knows the cause of encephalitis"; "Science says that smoking does not harm the throat." Science is not, as here it would seem to be, a single concrete entity speaking with one authoritative voice. Behind these large abstractions (and this is not an argument against abstractions as such) there are many scientists holding many different theories and employing many different methods of investigation. The whole force of the word nevertheless depends upon a bland assumption that all scientists meet periodically in synod and there decide and publish what science believes. Yet anyone with the slightest scientific training knows that this is very far from a possibility. Let us consider therefore the changed quality of the utterance when it is amended to read "A majority of scientists say"; or "Many scientists believe"; or "Some scientific experiments have indicated." The change will not do. There has to be a creature called "science"; and its creation has as a matter of practice been easy, because modern man has been conditioned to believe that the powers and processes which have transformed his material world represent a very sure form of knowledge, and that there must be a way of identifying that knowledge. Obviously the rhetorical aggrandizement of "science" here parallels that of "fact," the one representing generally and the other specifically the whole subject matter of trustworthy perception.

Furthermore, the term "science" like "progress" seems to satisfy a primal need. Man feels lost without a touchstone of knowledge just as he feels lost without the direction-finder provided by progress. It is curious to note that actually the word is only another name for knowledge (L. *scientia*), so that if we should go by strict etymology, we should insist that the expression "science knows" (*i.e.*, "knowledge knows") is pure tautology. But our rhetoric seems to get around this by implying that science is *the* knowledge. Other knowledges may contain elements of quackery, and may reflect the selfish aims of the knower; but "science," once we have given the word its incorporation, is the undiluted essence of knowledge. The word as it comes to us then is a little pathetic in its appeal, inasmuch as it reflects the deeply human feeling that somewhere somehow there must be people who know things "as they are." Once God or his ministry was the depository of such knowledge, but now, with the general decay of religious faith, it is the scientists who must speak *ex cathedra*, whether they wish to or not.

The term "modern" shares in the rhetorical forces of the others thus far discussed, and stands not far below the top. Its place in the general ordering is intelligible through the same history. Where progress is real, there is a natural presumption that the latest will be the best. Hence it is generally thought that to describe anything as "modern" is to credit it with all the improvements which have been made up to now. Then by a transference the term is applied to realms where valuation is, or ought to be, of a different source. In consequence, we have "modern living" urged upon us as an ideal; "the modern mind" is mentioned as something superior to previous minds; sometimes the modifier stands alone as an epithet of approval: "to become modern" or "to sound modern" are expressions that carry valuation. It is of course idle not to expect an age to feel that some of its ways and habits of mind are the best; but the extensive transformations of the past hundred years seem to have given "modern" a much more decisive meaning. It is as if a difference of degree had changed into a difference of kind. But the very fact that a word is not used very analytically may increase its rhetorical potency, as we shall see later in connection with a special group of terms.

Another word definitely high up in the hierarchy we have outlined is "efficient." It seems to have acquired its force through a kind of no-nonsense connotation. If a thing is efficient, it is a good adaptation of means to ends, with small loss through friction. Thus as a word expressing a good understanding and management of cause and effect, it may have a fairly definite referent; but when it is lifted above this and made to serve as a term of general endorsement, we have to be on our guard against the stratagems of evil rhetoric. When we find, to cite a familiar example, the phrase "efficiency apartments" used to give an attractive aspect to inadequate dwellings, we may suspect the motive behind such juxtaposition. In many similar cases, "efficient," which is a term above reproach in engineering and physics, is made to hold our attention where ethical and aesthetic considerations are entitled to priority. Certain notorious forms of government and certain brutal forms of warfare are undeniably efficient; but here the featuring of efficiency unfairly narrows the question.

Another term which might seem to have a different provenance but which participates in the impulse we have been studying is "American." One must first recognize the element of national egotism which makes this a word of approval with us, but there are reasons for saying that the force of "American" is much more broadly based than this. "This is the American way" or "It is the American thing to do" are expressions whose intent will not seem at all curious to the average American. Now the peculiar effect that is intended here comes from the circumstance that "American" and "progressive" have an area of synonymity. The Western World has long stood as a symbol for the future; and accordingly there has been a very wide tendency in this country, and also I believe among many people in Europe, to identify that which is American with that which is destined to be. And this is much the same as identifying it with the achievements of "progress." The typical American is quite fatuous in this regard: to him America is the goal toward which all creation moves; and he judges a country's civilization by its resemblance to the American model. The matter of changing nationalities brings out this point very well. For a citizen of a European country to become a citizen of the United States is considered natural and right, and I have known those so transferring their nationality to be congratulated upon their good sense and their anticipated good fortune. On the contrary, when an American takes out British citizenship (French or German would be worse), this transference is felt to be a little scandalous. It is regarded as somehow perverse, or as going against the stream of things. Even some of our intellectuals grow uneasy over the action of Henry James and T. S. Eliot, and the masses cannot comprehend it at all. Their adoption of British citizenship is not mere defection from a country; it is treason to history. If Americans wish to become Europeans, what has happened to the hope of the world? is, I imagine, the question at the back of their minds. The tremendous spread of American fashions in behavior and entertainment must add something to the impetus, but I believe the original source to be this prior idea that America, typifying "progress," is what the remainder of the world is trying to be like.

It follows naturally that in the popular consciousness of this country, "un-American" is the ultimate in negation. An anecdote will serve to illustrate this. Several years ago a leading cigarette manufacturer in this country had reason to believe that very damaging reports were being circulated about his product. The reports were such that had they not been stopped, the sale of this brand of cigarettes might have been reduced. The company thereupon inaugurated an extensive advertising campaign, the object of which was to halt these rumors in the most effective way possible. The concocters of the advertising copy evidently concluded after due deliberation that the strongest term of condemnation which could be conceived was "un-American," for this was the term employed in the campaign. Soon the newspapers were filled with advertising rebuking this "un-American" type of depreciation which had injured their sales. From examples such as this we may infer that "American" stands not only for what is forward in history, but also for what is ethically superior, or at least for a standard of fairness not matched by other nations.

And as long as the popular mind carries this impression, it will be futile to protest against such titles as "The Committee on un-American activities." While "American" and "un-American" continue to stand for these polar distinctions, the average citizen is not going to find much wrong with a group set up to investigate what is "un-American" and therefore reprehensible. At the same time, however, it would strike him as most droll if the British were to set up a "Committee on un-British Activities" or the French a "Committee on un-French Activities." The American, like other nationals, is not apt to be much better than he has been taught, and he has been taught systematically that his country is a special creation. That is why some of his ultimate terms seem to the general view provincial, and why he may be moved to polarities which represent only local poles.

If we look within the area covered by "American," however, we find significant changes in the position of terms which are reflections of cultural and ideological changes. Among the once powerful but now waning terms are those expressive of the pioneer ideal of ruggedness and self-sufficiency. In the space of fifty years or less we have seen the phrase "two-fisted American" pass from the category of highly effective images to that of comic anachronisms. Generally, whoever talks the older language of strenuosity is regarded as a reactionary, it being assumed by social democrats that a socially organized world is one in which cooperation removes the necessity for struggle. Even the rhetorical trump cards of the 1920's, which Sinclair Lewis treated with such satire, are comparatively impotent today, as the new social consciousness causes terms of centrally planned living to move toward the head of the series.

Other terms not necessarily connected with the American story have passed a zenith of influence and are in decline; of these perhaps the once effective "history" is the most interesting example. It is still to be met in such expressions as "History proves" and "History teaches"; yet one feels that it has lost the force it possessed in the previous century. Then it was easy for Byron—"the orator in poetry"—to write, "History with all her volumes vast has but one page"; or for the commemorative speaker to deduce profound lessons from history. But people today seem not to find history so eloquent. A likely explanation is that history, taken as whole, is conceptual rather than factual, and therefore a skepticism has developed as to what it teaches. Moreover, since the teachings of history are principally moral, ethical, or religious, they must encounter today that threshold resentment of anything which savors of the prescriptive. Since "history" is inseparable from judgment of historical fact, there has to be a considerable community of mind before history can be allowed to have a voice. Did the overthrow of Napoleon represent "progress" in history or the reverse? I should say that the most common rhetorical uses of "history" at the present are by intellectuals, whose personal philosophy can provide it with some kind of definition, and by journalists, who seem to use it unreflectively. For the contemporary masses it is substantially true that "history is bunk."

An instructive example of how a coveted term can be monopolized may be seen in "allies." Three times within the memory of those still young, "allies" (often capitalized) has been used to distinguish those fighting on our side from the enemy. During the First World War it was a supreme term; during the Second World War it was again used with effect; and at the time of the present writing it is being used to designate that nondescript combination fighting in the name of the United Nations in Korea. The curious fact about the use of this term is that in each case the enemy also has been constituted of "allies." In the First World War Germany, Austria-Hungary, and Turkey were "allies"; in the Second, Germany and Italy; and in the present conflict the North Koreans and the Chinese and perhaps the Russians are "allies." But in the rhetorical situation it is not possible to refer to them as "allies," since we reserve that term for the alliance representing our side. The reason for such restriction is that when men or nations are "allied," it is implied that they are united on some sound principle or for some good cause. Lying at the source of this feeling is the principle discussed by Plato, that friendship can exist only among the good, since good is an integrating force and evil a disintegrating one. We do not, for example, refer to a band of thieves as "the allies" because that term would impute laudable motives. By confining the term to our side we make an evaluation in our favor. We thus style ourselves the group joined for purposes of good. If we should allow it to be felt for a moment that the opposed combination is also made up of allies, we should concede that they are united by a principle, which in war is never done. So as the usage goes, we are always allies in war and the enemy is just the enemy, regardless of how many nations he has been able to confederate. Here is clearly another instance of how tendencies may exist in even the most innocent-seeming language.

Now let us turn to the terms of repulsion. Some terms of repulsion are also ultimate in the sense of standing at the end of the series, and no survey of the vocabulary can ignore these prime repellants. The counterpart of the "god term" is the "devil term," and it has already been suggested that with us "un-American" comes nearest to filling that role. Sometimes, however, currents of politics and popular feeling cause something more specific to be placed in that position. There seems indeed to be some obscure psychic law which compels every nation to have in its national imagination an enemy. Perhaps this is but a version of the tribal need for a scapegoat, or for something which will personify "the adversary." If a nation did not have an enemy, an enemy would have to be invented to take care of those expressions of scorn and hatred to which peoples must give vent. When another political state is not available to receive the discharge of such emotions, then a class will be chosen, or a race, or a type, or a political faction, and this will be held up to a practically standardized form of repudiation. Perhaps the truth is that we need the enemy in order to define ourselves, but I will not here venture further into psychological complexities. In this type of study it will be enough to recall that during the first half century of our nation's existence, "Tory" was such a devil term. In the period following our Civil War, "rebel" took its place in the Northern section and "Yankee" in the Southern, although in the previous epoch both of these had been terms of esteem. Most readers will remember that during the First World War "pro-German" was a term of destructive force. During the Second World War "Nazi" and "Fascist" carried about equal power to condemn, and then, following the breach with Russia, "Communist" displaced them both. Now "Communist" is beyond any rival the devil term, and as such it is employed even by the American president when he feels the need of a strong rhetorical point.

A singular truth about these terms is that, unlike several which were examined in our favorable list, they defy any real analysis. That is to say, one cannot explain how they generate their peculiar force of repudiation. One only recognizes them as publicly-agreed-upon devil terms. It is the same with all. "Tory" persists in use, though it has long lost any connection with redcoats and British domination. Analysis of "rebel" and "Yankee" only turns up embarrassing contradictions of position. Similarly we have all seen "Nazi" and "Fascist" used without rational perception; and we see this now, in even greater degree, with "Communist." However one might like to reject such usage as mere ignorance, to do so would only evade a very important problem. Most likely these are instances of the "charismatic term," which will be discussed in detail presently.

No student of contemporary usage can be unmindful of the curious reprobative force which has been acquired by the term "prejudice." Etymologically it signifies nothing more than a prejudgment, or a judgment before all the facts are in; and since all of us have to proceed to a great extent on judgments of that kind, the word should not be any more exciting than "hypothesis." But in its rhetorical applications "prejudice" presumes far beyond that. It is used, as a matter of fact, to characterize unfavorably any value judgment whatever. If "blue" is said to be a better color than "red," that is prejudice. If people of outstanding cultural achievement are praised through contrast with another people, that is prejudice. If one mode of life is presented as superior to another, that is prejudice. And behind all is the implication, if not the declaration, that it is un-American to be prejudiced.

I suspect that what the users of this term are attempting, whether consciously or not, is to sneak "prejudiced" forward as an uncontested term, and in this way to disarm the opposition by making all positional judgments reprehensible. It must be observed in passing that no people are so prejudiced in the sense of being committed to valuations as those who are engaged in castigating others for prejudice. What they expect is that they can nullify the prejudices of those who oppose them, and then get their own installed in the guise of the *sensus communis*. Mark Twain's statement, "I know that I am prejudiced in this matter, but I would be ashamed of myself if I weren't" is a therapeutic insight into the process; but it will take more than a witticism to make headway against the repulsive force gathered behind "prejudice."

If the rhetorical use of the term has any rational content, this probably comes through a chain of deductions from the nature of democracy; and we know that in controversies centered about the meaning of democracy, the air is usually filled with cries of "prejudice." If democracy is taken crudely to mean equality, as it very frequently is, it is then a contradiction of democracy to assign inferiority and superiority on whatever grounds. But since the whole process of evaluation is a process of such assignment, the various inequalities which are left when it has done its work are contradictions of this root notion and hence are "prejudice"— the assumption of course being that when all the facts are in, these inequalities will be found illusory. The man who dislikes a certain class or race or style has merely not taken pains to learn that it is just as good as any other. If all inequality is deception, then superiorities must be accounted the products of immature judgment. This affords plausible ground, as we have suggested, for the coupling of "prejudice" and "ignorance."

Before leaving the subject of the ordered series of good and bad terms, one feels obliged to say something about the way in which hierarchies can be inverted. Under the impulse of strong frustration there is a natural tendency to institute a pretense that the best is the worst and the worst is the best—an inversion sometimes encountered in literature and in social deportment. The best illustration for purpose of study here comes from a department of speech which I shall call "GI rhetoric." The average American youth, put into uniform, translated to a new and usually barren environment, and imbued from many sources with a mission of killing, has undergone a pretty severe dislocation. All of this runs counter to the benevolent platitudes on which he was brought up, and there is little ground for wonder if he adopts the inverted pose. This is made doubly likely by the facts that he is at a passionate age and that he is thrust into an atmosphere of superinduced excitement. It would be unnatural for him not to acquire a rhetoric of strong impulse and of contumacious tendency.

What he does is to make an almost complete inversion. In this special world of his he recoils from those terms used by politicians and other civilians and by the "top brass" when they are enunciating public sentiments. Dropping the conventional terms of attraction, this uprooted and specially focussed young man puts in their place terms of repulsion. To be more specific, where the others use terms reflecting love, hope, and charity, he uses almost exclusively terms connected with excretory and reproductive functions. Such terms comprise what Kenneth Burke has ingeniously called "the imagery of killing." By an apparently universal psychological law, faeces and the act of defecation are linked with the idea of killing, of destruction, of total repudiation—perhaps the word "elimination" would comprise the whole body of notions. The reproductive act is associated especially with the idea of aggressive exploitation. Consequently when the GI feels that he must give his speech a proper show of spirit, he places the symbols for these things in places which would normally be filled by prestige terms from the "regular" list. For specimens of such language presented in literature, the reader is referred to the fiction of Ernest Hemingway and Norman Mailer.

Anyone who has been compelled to listen to such rhetoric will recall the monotony of the vocabulary and the vehemence of the delivery. From these two characteristics we may infer a great need and a narrow means of satisfaction, together with the tension which must result from maintaining so arduous an inversion. Whereas previously the aim had been to love (in the broad sense) it is now to kill; whereas it had been freedom and individuality, it is now restriction and brutalization. In taking revenge for a change which so contradicts his upbringing he is quite capable, as the evidence has already proved, of defiantly placing the lower level above the higher. Sometimes a clever GI will invent combinations and will effect metaphorical departures, but the ordinary ones are limited to a reiteration of the stock terms—to a reiteration, with emphasis of intonation, upon "the imagery of killing."[2] Taken as a whole, this rhetoric is a clear if limited example of how the machine may be put in reverse—of how, consequently, a sort of devil worship may get into language.

A similar inversion of hierarchy is to be seen in the world of competitive sports, although to a lesser extent. The great majority of us in the Western world have been brought up under the influence, direct or indirect, of Christianity, which is a religion of extreme altruism. Its terms of value all derive from a law of self-effacement and of consideration for others, and these terms tend to appear whenever we try to rationalize or vindicate our conduct. But in the world of competitive sports, the direction is opposite: there one is applauded for egotistic display and for success at the expense of others—should one mention in particular American professional baseball? Thus the terms with which an athlete is commended will generally point away from the direction of Christian passivity, although when an athlete's character is described for the benefit of the general public, some way is usually found to place him in the other ethos, as by calling attention to his natural kindness, his interest in children, or his readiness to share his money.

Certainly many of the contradictions of our conduct may be explained through the presence of these small inverted hierarchies. When, to cite one familiar example, the acquisitive, hard-driving local capitalist is made the chief lay official of a Christian church, one knows that in a definite area there has been a transvaluation of values.

---

[2] Compare Sherwood Anderson's analysis of the same phenomenon in *A Story Teller's Story* (New York, 1928), p. 198: "There was in the factories where I worked and where the efficient Ford type of man was just beginning his dull reign this strange and futile outpouring of men's lives in vileness through their lips. Ennui was at work. The talk of the men about me was not Rabelaisian. In old Rabelais there was the salt of infinite wit and I have no doubt that the Rabelaisian flashes that came from our own Lincoln, Washington, and others had point and a flare to them.
But in the factories and in army camps!"

Earlier in the chapter we referred to terms of considerable potency whose referents it is virtually impossible to discover or to construct through imagination. I shall approach this group by calling them "charismatic terms." It is the nature of the charismatic term to have a power which is not derived, but which is in some mysterious way given. By this I mean to say that we cannot explain their compulsiveness through referents of objectively known character and tendency. We normally "understand" a rhetorical term's appeal through its connection with something we apprehend, even when we object morally to the source of the impulse. Now "progress" is an understandable term in this sense, since it rests upon certain observable if not always commendable aspects of our world. Likewise the referential support of "fact" needs no demonstrating. These derive their force from a reading of palpable circumstance. But in charismatic terms we are confronted with a different creation: these terms seem to have broken loose somehow and to operate independently of referential connections (although in some instances an earlier history of referential connection may be made out). Their meaning seems inexplicable unless we accept the hypothesis that their content proceeds out of a popular will that they *shall* mean something. In effect, they are rhetorical by common consent, or by "charisma." As is the case with charismatic authority, where the populace gives the leader a power which can by no means be explained through his personal attributes, and permits him to use it effectively and even arrogantly, the charismatic term is given its load of impulsion without reference, and it functions by convention. The number of such terms is small in any one period, but they are perhaps the most efficacious terms of all.

Such rhetorical sensibility as I have leads me to believe that one of the principal charismatic terms of our age is "freedom." The greatest sacrifices that contemporary man is called upon to make are demanded in the name of "freedom"; yet the referent which the average man attaches to this word is most obscure. Burke's dictum that "freedom inheres in something sensible" has not prevented its breaking loose from all anchorages. And the evident truth that the average man, given a choice between exemption from responsibility and responsibility, will choose the latter, makes no impression against its power. The fact, moreover, that the most extensive use of the term is made by modern politicians and statesmen in an effort to get men to assume more responsibility (in the form of military service, increased taxes, abridgement of rights, etc.) seems to carry no weight either.[3] The fact that what the American pioneer considered freedom has become wholly impossible to the modern apartment-dwelling metropolitan seems not to have damaged its potency. Unless we accept some philosophical interpretation, such as the proposition that freedom consists only in the discharge of responsibility, there

---

[3] One is inevitably reminded of the slogan of Oceania in Orwell's *Nineteen Eighty-four:* "Freedom is Slavery."

seems no possibility of a correlation between the use of the word and circumstantial reality. Yet "freedom" remains an ultimate term, for which people are asked to yield up their first-born.

There is plenty of evidence that "democracy" is becoming the same kind of term. The variety of things it is used to symbolize is too weird and too contradictory for one to find even a core meaning in present-day usages. More important than this for us is the fact, noted by George Orwell, that people resist any attempt to define democracy, as if to connect it with a clear and fixed referent were to vitiate it. It may well be that such resistance to definition of democracy arises from a subconscious fear that a term defined in the usual manner has its charisma taken away. The situation then is that "democracy" means "be democratic," and that means exhibit a certain attitude which you can learn by imitating your fellows.

If rationality is measured by correlations and by analyzable content, then these terms are irrational; and there is one further modern development in the creation of such terms which is strongly suggestive of irrational impulse. This is the increasing tendency to employ in the place of the term itself an abbreviated or telescoped form—which form is nearly always used with even more reckless assumption of authority. I seldom read the abbreviation "U S" in the newspapers without wincing at the complete arrogance of its rhetorical tone. Daily we see "U S Cracks Down on Communists"; "U S Gives OK to Atomic Weapons"; "U S Shocked by Death of Official." Who or what is this "U S"? It is clear that "U S" does not suggest a union of forty-eight states having republican forms of government and held together by a constitution of expressly delimited authority. It suggests rather an abstract force out of a new world of forces, whose will is law and whom the individual citizen has no way to placate. Consider the individual citizen confronted by "U S" or "FBI." As long as terms stand for identifiable organs of government, the citizen feels that he knows the world he moves around in, but when the forces of government are referred to by these bloodless abstractions, he cannot avoid feeling that they are one thing and he another. Let us note while dealing with this subject the enormous proliferation of such forms during the past twenty years or so. If "U S" is the most powerful and prepossessing of the group, it drags behind it in train the previously mentioned "FBI," and "NPA," "ERP," "FDIC," "WPA," "HOLC," and "OSS," to take a few at random. It is a fact of ominous significance that this use of foreshortened forms is preferred by totalitarians, both the professed and the disguised. Americans were hearing the terms "OGPU," "AMTORG" and "NEP" before their own government turned to large-scale state planning Since then we have spawned them ourselves, and, it is to be feared, out of similar impulse. George Orwell, one of the truest humanists of our age, has described the phenomenon thus: "Even in the early decades of the twentieth century, telescoped words and phrases had been one of the characteristic features of political language; and it had been noticed that the tendency to use abbreviations of this kind was most marked in totalitarian countries and totalitarian organizations. Examples were such words as Nazi, Gestapo, Comintern, Inprecor, Agitprop."[4]

I venture to suggest that what this whole trend indicates is an attempt by the government, as distinguished from the people, to confer charismatic authority. In the earlier specimens of charismatic terms we were examining, we beheld something like the creation of a spontaneous general will. But these later ones of truncated form are handed down from above, and their potency is by fiat of whatever group is administering in the name of democracy. Actually the process is no more anomalous than the issuing of pamphlets to soldiers telling them whom they shall hate and whom they shall like (or try to like), but the whole business of switching impulse on and off from a central headquarters has very much the meaning of *Gleichschaltung* as that word has been interpreted for me by a native German. Yet it is a disturbing fact that such process should increase in times of peace, because the persistent use of such abbreviations can only mean a serious divorce between rhetorical impulse and rational thought. When the ultimate terms become a series of bare abstractions, the understanding of power is supplanted by a worship of power, and in our condition this can mean only state worship.

It is easy to see, however, that a group determined upon control will have as one of its first objectives the appropriation of sources of charismatic authority. Probably the surest way to detect the fabricated charismatic term is to identify those terms ordinarily of limited power which are being moved up to the front line. That is to say, we may suspect the act of fabrication when terms of secondary or even tertiary rhetorical rank are pushed forward by unnatural pressure into ultimate positions. This process can nearly always be observed in times of crisis. During the last war, for example, "defense" and "war effort" were certainly regarded as culminative terms. We may say this because almost no one thinks of these terms as the natural sanctions of his mode of life. He may think thus of "progress" or "happiness" or even "freedom"; but "defense" and "war effort" are ultimate sanctions only when measured against an emergency situation. When the United States was preparing for entry into that conflict, every departure from our normal way of life could be justified as a "defense" measure. Plants making bombs to be dropped on other continents were called "defense" plants. Correspondingly, once the conflict had been entered, everything that was done in military or civilian areas was judged by its contribution to the "war effort." This last became for a period of years the supreme term: not God or Heaven or happiness, but successful effort in the war. It was a term to end all other

---

[4] "Principles of Newspeak," *Nineteen Eighty-four* (New York, 1949), p. 310.

terms or a rhetoric to silence all other rhetoric. No one was able to make his claim heard against "the war effort."

It is most important to realize, therefore, that under the stress of feeling or preoccupation, quite secondary terms can be moved up to the position of ultimate terms, where they will remain until reflection is allowed to resume sway. There are many signs to show that the term "aggressor" is now undergoing such manipulation. Despite the fact that almost no term is more difficult to correlate with objective phenomena, it is being rapidly promoted to ultimate "bad" term. The likelihood is that "aggressor" will soon become a depository for all the resentments and fears which naturally arise in a people. As such, it will function as did "infidel" in the mediaeval period and as "reactionary" has functioned in the recent past. Manifestly it is of great advantage to a nation bent upon organizing its power to be able to stigmatize some neighbor as "aggressor," so that the term's capacity for irrational assumption is a great temptation for those who are not moral in their use of rhetoric. This passage from natural or popular to state-engendered charisma produces one of the most dangerous lesions of modern society.

An ethics of rhetoric requires that ultimate terms be ultimate in some rational sense. The only way to achieve that objective is through an ordering of our own minds and our own passions. Every one of psychological sophistication knows that there is a pleasure in willed perversity, and the setting up of perverse shibboleths is a fairly common source of that pleasure. War cries, school slogans, coterie passwords, and all similar expressions are examples of such creation. There may be areas of play in which these are nothing more than a diversion; but there are other areas in which such expressions lure us down the roads of hatred and tragedy. That is the tendency of all words of false or "engineered" charisma. They often sound like the very gospel of one's society, but in fact they betray us; they get us to do what the adversary of the human being wants us to do. It is worth considering whether the real civil disobedience must not begin with our language.

Lastly, the student of rhetoric must realize that in the contemporary world he is confronted not only by evil practitioners, but also, and probably to an unprecedented degree, by men who are conditioned by the evil created by others. The machinery of propagation and inculcation is today so immense that no one avoids entirely the assimilation and use of some terms which have a downward tendency. It is especially easy to pick up a tone without realizing its trend. Perhaps the best that any of us can do is to hold a dialectic with himself to see what the wider circumferences of his terms of persuasion are. This process will not only improve the consistency of one's thinking but it will also, if the foregoing analysis is sound, prevent his becoming a creature of evil public forces and a victim of his own thoughtless rhetoric.

ALDOUS HUXLEY

THE ARTS OF SELLING

This is Chapter 6 of Huxley's Brave New World Revisited *(1958). For information on the author and his writings, see page 25.*

•

The survival of democracy depends on the ability of large numbers of people to make realistic choices in the light of adequate information. A dictatorship, on the other hand, maintains itself by censoring or distorting the facts, and by appealing, not to reason, not to enlightened self-interest, but to passion and prejudice, to the powerful "hidden forces," as Hitler called them, present in the unconscious depths of every human mind.

In the West, democratic principles are proclaimed and many able and conscientious publicists do their best to supply electors with adequate information and to persuade them, by rational argument, to make realistic choices in the light of that information. All this is greatly to the good. But unfortunately propaganda in the Western democracies, above all in America, has two faces and a divided personality. In charge of the editorial department there is often a democratic Dr. Jekyll—a propagandist who would be very happy to prove that John Dewey had been right about the ability of human nature to respond to truth and reason. But this worthy man controls only a part of the machinery of mass communication. In charge of advertising we find an anti-democratic, because anti-rational, Mr. Hyde—or rather a Dr. Hyde, for Hyde is now a Ph.D. in psychology and has a master's degree as well in the social sciences. This Dr. Hyde would be very unhappy indeed if everybody always lived up to John Dewey's faith in human nature. Truth and reason are Jekyll's affair, not his. Hyde is a motivation analyst, and his business is to study human weaknesses and failings, to investigate those unconscious desires and fears by which so much of men's conscious thinking and overt doing is determined. And he does this, not in the spirit of the moralist who would like to make people better, or of the physician who would like to improve their health, but simply in order to find out the best way to take advantage of their ignorance and to exploit their irrationality for the pecuniary benefit of his employers. But after all, it may be argued, "capitalism is dead, consumerism is king"—and consumerism requires the services of expert salesmen versed in all the arts (including the more insidious arts) of persuasion. Under a free enterprise system commercial propaganda by any and every means is absolutely indispensable. But the indispensable is not necessarily the desirable. What is demonstrably good in the sphere of economics may be far from good for men and women as voters or even as human beings. An earlier, more moralistic generation would have been profoundly shocked by the bland cynicism of the motivation analysts. Today we read a book like Mr. Vance Packard's *The Hidden Persuaders*, and are more amused than horrified, more resigned than indignant. Given Freud, given Behaviorism, given the mass producer's chronically desperate need for mass consumption, this is the sort of thing that is only to be expected. But what, we may ask, is the sort of thing that is to be expected in the future? Are Hyde's activities compatible in the long run with Jekyll's? Can a campaign in favor of rationality be successful in the teeth of another and even more vigorous campaign in favor of irrationality? These are questions which, for the moment, I shall not attempt to answer, but shall leave hanging, so to speak, as a backdrop to our discussion of the methods of mass persuasion in a technologically advanced democratic society.

The task of the commercial propagandist in a democracy is in some ways easier and in some ways more difficult than that of a political propagandist employed by an established dictator or a dictator in the making. It is easier inasmuch as almost everyone starts out with a prejudice in favor of beer, cigarettes and iceboxes, whereas almost nobody starts out with a prejudice in favor of tyrants. It is more difficult inasmuch as the commercial propagandist is not permitted, by the rules of his particular game, to appeal to the more savage instincts of his public. The advertiser of dairy products would dearly love to tell his readers and listeners that all their troubles are caused by the machinations of a gang of godless international margarine manufacturers, and that it is their patriotic duty to march out and burn the oppressors' factories. This sort of thing, however, is ruled out, and he must be content with a milder approach. But the mild approach is less exciting than the approach through verbal or physical violence. In the long run, anger and hatred are self-defeating emotions. But in the short run they pay high dividends in the form of psychological and even (since they release large quantities of adrenalin and noradrenalin) physiological satisfaction. People may start out with an initial prejudice against tyrants; but when tyrants or would-be tyrants treat them to adrenalin-releasing propaganda about the wickedness of their enemies—particularly of enemies weak enough to be persecuted—they are ready to follow him with enthusiasm. In his speeches

Hitler kept repeating such words as "hatred," "force," "ruthless," "crush," "smash"; and he would accompany these violent words with even more violent gestures. He would yell, he would scream, his veins would swell, his face would turn purple. Strong emotion (as every actor and dramatist knows) is in the highest degree contagious. Infected by the malignant frenzy of the orator, the audience would groan and sob and scream in an orgy of uninhibited passion. And these orgies were so enjoyable that most of those who had experienced them eagerly came back for more. Almost all of us long for peace and freedom; but very few of us have much enthusiasm for the thoughts, feelings and actions that make for peace and freedom. Conversely almost nobody wants war or tyranny; but a great many people find an intense pleasure in the thoughts, feelings and actions that make for war and tyranny. These thoughts, feelings and actions are too dangerous to be exploited for commercial purposes. Accepting this handicap, the advertising man must do the best he can with the less intoxicating emotions, the quieter forms of irrationality.

Effective rational propaganda becomes possible only when there is a clear understanding, on the part of all concerned, of the nature of symbols and of their relations to the things and events symbolized. Irrational propaganda depends for its effectiveness on a general failure to understand the nature of symbols. Simple-minded people tend to equate the symbol with what it stands for, to attribute to things and events some of the qualities expressed by the words in terms of which the propagandist has chosen, for his own purposes, to talk about them. Consider a simple example. Most cosmetics are made of lanolin, which is a mixture of purified wool fat and water beaten up into an emulsion. This emulsion has many valuable properties: it penetrates the skin, it does not become rancid, it is mildly antiseptic and so forth. But the commercial propagandists do not speak about the genuine virtues of the emulsion. They give it some picturesquely voluptuous name, talk ecstatically and misleadingly about feminine beauty and show pictures of gorgeous blondes nourishing their tissues with skin food. "The cosmetic manufacturers," one of their number has written, "are not selling lanolin, they are selling hope." For this hope, this fraudulent implication of a promise that they will be transfigured, women will pay ten or twenty times the value of the emulsion which the propagandists have so skilfully related, by means of misleading symbols, to a deep-seated and almost universal feminine wish—the wish to be more attractive to members of the opposite sex. The principles underlying this kind of propaganda are extremely simple. Find some common desire, some widespread unconscious fear or anxiety; think out some way to relate this wish or fear to the product you have to sell; then build a bridge of verbal or pictorial symbols over which your customer can pass from fact to compensatory dream, and from the dream to the illusion that your product, when purchased, will make the dream come true. "We no longer buy oranges, we buy vitality. We do not buy just an auto, we buy prestige." And so with all the rest. In toothpaste, for example, we buy, not a mere cleanser and antiseptic, but release from the fear of being sexually repulsive. In vodka and whisky we are not buying a protoplasmic poison which, in small doses, may depress the nervous system in a psychologically valuable way; we are buying friendliness and good fellowship, the warmth of Dingley Dell and the brilliance of the Mermaid Tavern. With our laxatives we buy the health of a Greek god, the radiance of one of Diana's nymphs. With the monthly best seller we acquire culture, the envy of our less literate neighbors and the respect of the sophisticated. In every case the motivation analyst has found some deep-seated wish or fear, whose energy can be used to move the consumer to part with cash and so, indirectly, to turn the wheels of industry. Stored in the minds and bodies of countless individuals, this potential energy is released by, and transmitted along, a line of symbols carefully laid out so as to bypass rationality and obscure the real issue.

Sometimes the symbols take effect by being disproportionately impressive, haunting and fascinating in their own right. Of this kind are the rites and pomps of religion. These "beauties of holiness" strengthen faith where it already exists and, where there is no faith, contribute to conversion. Appealing, as they do, only to the aesthetic sense, they guarantee neither the truth nor the ethical value of the doctrines with which they have been, quite arbitrarily, associated. As a matter of plain historical fact, the beauties of holiness have often been matched and indeed surpassed by the beauties of unholiness. Under Hitler, for example, the yearly Nuremberg rallies were masterpieces of ritual and theatrical art. "I had spent six years in St. Petersburg before the war in the best days of the old Russian ballet," writes Sir Nevile Henderson, the British ambassador to Hitler's Germany, "but for grandiose beauty I have never seen any ballet to compare with the Nuremberg rally." One thinks of Keats—"beauty is truth, truth beauty." Alas, the identity exists only on some ultimate, supramundane level. On the levels of politics and theology, beauty is perfectly compatible with nonsense and tyranny. Which is very fortunate; for if beauty were incompatible with nonsense and tyranny, there would be precious little art in the world. The masterpieces of painting, sculpture and architecture were produced as religious or political propaganda, for the greater glory of a god, a government or a priesthood. But most kings and priests have been despotic and all religions have been riddled with superstition. Genius has been the servant of tyranny and art has advertised the merits of the local cult. Time, as it passes, separates the good art from the bad metaphysics. Can we learn to make this separation, not after the event, but while it is actually taking place? That is the question.

In commercial propaganda the principle of the disproportionately fascinating symbol is clearly understood. Every propagandist has his Art Department, and attempts are constantly being made to beautify the billboards with striking posters, the advertising pages of magazines with lively drawings and photographs. There are no masterpieces; for masterpieces appeal only to a limited audience, and the commercial propagandist is out to captivate the majority. For him, the ideal is a moderate excellence. Those who like this not too good, but sufficiently striking, art may be expected to like the products with which it has been associated and for which it symbolically stands.

Another disproportionately fascinating symbol is the Singing Commercial. Singing Commercials are a recent invention; but the Singing Theological and the Singing Devotional—the hymn and the psalm—are as old as religion itself. Singing Militaries, or marching songs, are coeval with war, and Singing Patriotics, the precursors of our national anthems, were doubtless used to promote group solidarity, to emphasize the distinction between "us" and "them," by the wandering bands of paleolithic hunters and food gatherers. To most people music is intrinsically attractive. Moreover, melodies tend to ingrain themselves in the listener's mind. A tune will haunt the memory during the whole of a lifetime. Here, for example, is a quite uninteresting statement or value judgment. As it stands nobody will pay attention to it. But now set the words to a catchy and easily remembered tune. Immediately they become words of power. Moreover, the words will tend automatically to repeat themselves every time the melody is heard or spontaneously remembered. Orpheus has entered into an alliance with Pavlov—the power of sound with the conditioned reflex. For the commercial propagandist, as for his colleagues in the fields of politics and religion, music possesses yet another advantage. Nonsense which it would be shameful for a reasonable being to write, speak or hear spoken can be sung or listened to by that same rational being with pleasure and even with a kind of intellectual conviction. Can we learn to separate the pleasure of singing or of listening to song from the all too human tendency to believe in the propaganda which the song is putting over? That again is the question.

Thanks to compulsory education and the rotary press, the propagandist has been able, for many years past, to convey his messages to virtually every adult in every civilized country. Today, thanks to radio and television, he is in the happy position of being able to communicate even with unschooled adults and not yet literate children.

Children, as might be expected, are highly susceptible to propaganda. They are ignorant of the world and its ways, and therefore completely unsuspecting. Their critical faculties are undeveloped. The youngest of them have not yet reached the age of reason and the older ones lack the experience on which their new-found rationality can effectively work. In Europe, conscripts used to be playfully referred to as "cannon fodder." Their little brothers and sisters have now become radio fodder and television fodder. In my childhood we were taught to sing nursery rhymes and, in pious households, hymns. Today the little ones warble the Singing

Commercials. Which is better—"Rheingold is my beer, the dry beer," or "Hey diddle-diddle, the cat and the fiddle"? "Abide with me" or "You'll wonder where the yellow went, when you brush your teeth with Pepsodent"? Who knows?

"I don't say that children should be forced to harass their parents into buying products they've seen advertised on television, but at the same time I cannot close my eyes to the fact that it's being done every day." So writes the star of one of the many programs beamed to a juvenile audience. "Children," he adds, "are living, talking records of what we tell them every day." And in due course these living, talking records of television commercials will grow up, earn money and buy the products of industry. "Think," writes Mr. Clyde Miller ecstatically, "think of what it can mean to your firm in profits if you can condition a million or ten million children, who will grow up into adults trained to buy your product, as soldiers are trained in advance when they hear the trigger words, Forward March!" Yes, just think of it! And at the same time remember that the dictators and the would-be dictators have been thinking about this sort of thing for years, and that millions, tens of millions, hundreds of millions of children are in process of growing up to buy the local despot's ideological product and, like well-trained soldiers, to respond with appropriate behavior to the trigger words implanted in those young minds by the despot's propagandists.

Self-government is in inverse ratio to numbers. The larger the constituency, the less the value of any particular vote. When he is merely one of millions, the individual elector feels himself to be impotent, a negligible quantity. The candidates he has voted into office are far away, at the top of the pyramid of power. Theoretically they are the servants of the people; but in fact it is the servants who give orders and the people, far off at the base of the great pyramid, who must obey. Increasing population and advancing technology have resulted in an increase in the number and complexity of organizations, an increase in the amount of power concentrated in the hands of officials and a corresponding decrease in the amount of control exercised by electors, coupled with a decrease in the public's regard for democratic procedures. Already weakened by the vast impersonal forces at work in the modern world, democratic institutions are now being undermined from within by the politicians and their propagandists.

Human beings act in a great variety of irrational ways, but all of them seem to be capable, if given a fair chance, of making a reasonable choice in the light of available evidence. Democratic institutions can be made to work only if all concerned do their best to impart knowledge and to encourage rationality. But today, in the world's most powerful democracy, the politicians and their propagandists prefer to make nonsense of democratic procedures by appealing almost exclusively to the ignorance and irrationality of the electors. "Both parties," we were told in 1956 by the editor of a leading business journal, "will merchandize their candidates and issues by the same methods that business has developed to sell goods. These include scientific selection of appeals and planned repetition. . . . Radio spot announcements and ads will repeat phrases with a planned intensity. Billboards will push slogans of proven power. . . . Candidates need, in addition to rich voices and good diction, to be able to look 'sincerely' at the TV camera."

The political merchandisers appeal only to the weaknesses of voters, never to their potential strength. They make no attempt to educate the masses into becoming fit for self-government; they are content merely to manipulate and exploit them. For this purpose all the resources of psychology and the social sciences are mobilized and set to work. Carefully selected samples of the electorate are given "interviews in depth." These interviews in depth reveal the unconscious fears and wishes most prevalent in a given society at the time of an election. Phrases and images aimed at allaying or, if necessary, enhancing these fears, at satisfying these wishes, at least symbolically, are then chosen by the experts, tried out on readers and audiences, changed or improved in the light of the information thus obtained. After which the political campaign is ready for the mass communicators. All that is now needed is money and a candidate who can be coached to look "sincere." Under the new dispensation, political principles and plans for specific action have come to lose most of their importance. The personality of the candidate and the way he is projected by the advertising experts are the things that really matter.

In one way or another, as vigorous he-man or kindly father, the candidate must be glamorous. He must also be an entertainer who never bores his audience. Inured to television and radio, that audience is accustomed to being distracted and does not like to be asked to concentrate or make a prolonged intellectual effort. All speeches by the entertainer-candidate must therefore be short and snappy. The great issues of the day must be dealt with in five minutes at the most—and preferably (since the audience will be eager to pass on to something a little livelier than inflation or the H-bomb) in sixty seconds flat. The nature of oratory is such that there has always been a tendency among politicians and clergymen to over-simplify complex issues. From a pulpit or a platform even the most conscientious of speakers finds it very difficult to tell the whole truth. The methods now being used to merchandise the political candidate as though he were a deodorant positively guarantee the electorate against ever hearing the truth about anything.

PAUL JACOBS

Paul Jacobs, social scientist and writer, was born in New York City in 1918 and attended C.C.N.Y. and the University of Minnesota. He first became active in the union movement as an organizer and later became a labor consultant and co-publisher of a labor paper. He is a member of the staff of the Fund for the Republic's Center for the Study of Democratic Institutions, and has conducted research projects with various institutes at the University of California. He contributes regularly to the Economist *of London and has written for* The Reporter, Commentary, Commonweal, Atlantic, *and* Harper's. *He is joint editor of* Labor in a Free Society *(1959) and author of* The State of the Unions *(1963), and* Is Curley Jewish? *(1965). The present essay first appeared in* The Reporter, *September 18, 1958.*

THE MOST CHEERFUL
GRAVEYARD IN THE WORLD

Along with amassing a comfortable fortune by convincing Los Angelenos that the only fitting way to begin a "happy Eternal Life" is by being laid to rest, in one way or another, at Forest Lawn Memorial Park, the cemetery he founded in 1917, Dr. Hubert Eaton, or "Digger" as he is known in the trade, has also succeeded in almost completely revising the dying industry.

The Digger, whose official title of "Doctor" is purely honorary, accomplished this revision by the simple but profound device of converting the hitherto prosaic act of dying into a gloriously exciting, well-advertised event, somehow intimately and patriotically connected with the American way of life.

Today, thanks to Eaton, dying in Los Angeles is something to be eagerly anticipated, because it is only after death that one can gain permanent tenure at Forest Lawn. Eaton, in one of his earlier roles—that of "the Builder"—described Forest Lawn as "a place where lovers new and old shall love to stroll and watch the sunset's glow, planning for the future or reminiscing of the past; a place where artists study and sketch; where school teachers bring happy children to see the things they read of in books; where little churches invite, triumphant in the knowledge that from their pulpits only words of Love can be spoken; where memorialization of loved ones in sculptured marble and pictorial glass shall be encouraged but controlled by acknowledged artists; a place where the sorrowing will be soothed and strengthened because it will be God's garden. A place that shall be protected by an immense Endowment Care Fund, the principal of which can never be expended—only the income therefrom used to care for and perpetuate this Garden of Memory.

"This is the Builder's Dream; this is the Builder's Creed."

The Builder's Creed is chiseled into a huge, upright stone slab on Forest Lawn's Cathedral Drive, just outside the Great Mausoleum and hard by the Shrine of Love. Viewed, usually in reverent awe, by more than a million visitors each year, Forest Lawn is, along with Disneyland, a favorite tourist attraction in Southern California, far outdrawing the concrete footprints in front of Grauman's Chinese Theatre.

A smaller inscription underneath the Creed points out that on New Year's Day, 1917, Eaton stood on a hilltop overlooking the small country cemetery which had just been placed in his charge. An unemployed mining engineer, Eaton had gone into the cemetery business after a vein of gold in his mine had suddenly vanished.

"A vision came to the man of what this tiny 'God's Acre' might become; and standing there, he made a promise to The Infinite. When he reached home, he put this promise into words and called it 'The Builder's Creed.' Today, Forest Lawn's almost three hundred acres are eloquent witness that The Builder kept faith with his soul."

Indeed, yes. The "almost three hundred acres" also bear eloquent witness to the fact that Eaton, still digging holes in the ground, worked a vein of gold infinitely more reliable than the one that vanished from his mine—the "Science and Art," as he describes it, "of Persuasion." So strongly does Eaton believe the "profession of salesmanship is the greatest of all professions" that he has established The Foundation for the Science and Art of Persuasion at his alma mater, William Jewell College, Liberty, Missouri.

Forest Lawn reflects Eaton's skill in the "Science." The "country cemetery" with only a "scant dozen acres of developed ground" has grown into Forest Lawn Memorial Park, with a permanent "population" of more than 170,000, increasing at the rate of approximately 6,500 a year.

In fact, business has been so good that there are now two additional Forest Lawn "Memorial Parks" in Los Angeles: Forest Lawn-Hollywood Hills, the focus of a bitter political struggle in the city, and adjacent to it Mount Sinai, designed to attract the growing Jewish population of Los Angeles.

Forest Lawn offers the largest religious painting in the United States, displayed in a building, the Hall of the Crucifixion, specially designed for it. There, for a voluntary contribution of twenty-five cents, the visitor sits comfortably in a large theatre, in one of a "broad sweep of seats, richly upholstered in burgundy, rising tier above tier, matching the splendor of the architecture," and watches the three-thousand-pound curtain open on Jesus at Calvary, forty-five feet high and 195 feet long. A lecture about the painting, supplemented with a moving arrow, is delivered by a tape recording in the special kind of rich, organ-tone voice used throughout Forest Lawn.

There are also hundreds of statues, both originals and reproductions, scattered throughout the three hundred acres. Typical of these is an eighteen-figure group depicting Forest Lawn's solution to the "Mystery of Life." Interpretations of the eighteen figures are supplied: "(17) the atheist, the fool, who grinningly cares not at all; while (18) the stoic sits in silent awe and contemplation of that which he believes he knows but cannot explain with any satisfaction."

At the Court of David there is a huge reproduction of Michelangelo's "David"—with a large fig leaf added by Forest Lawn. An exact copy of the sculptor's "Moses" is displayed at the entrance to the Cathedral Corridor in Memorial Terrace, "the only one," according to Forest Lawn, "cast from clay masks placed directly on the original statue in the Church of Saint Peter in Chains at Rome, Italy."

So that the masks could be made, the Church of Saint Peter had to be closed for a day, something that had not happened before. "I gave a lot of dinners and I bought a lot of wine and I sent a lot of cables and St. Peter's was closed," Eaton modestly explains.

Color photos and post cards of the "Moses" statue can be purchased, along with thousands of other items, at Forest Lawn's souvenir shop. There, browsing visitors can choose from showcases displaying money clips, cocktail napkins, book matches, jigsaw puzzles, and charm bracelets —all decorated with Forest Lawn motifs. Prices range from a modest twenty-nine cents for a key chain to $125 for a glass vase etched with a Forest Lawn scene.

There are brown plastic nutshells containing little photos of Forest Lawn, ladies' compacts, cigarette lighters, cufflinks, salt and pepper shakers, picture frames, demitasse spoons, bookmarks, cups and saucers, pen and pencil sets, glass bells, wooden plaques, ashtrays, place mats and doilies, perfume and powder sets, jackknives, and a great variety of other goodies, all with an appropriate Forest Lawn theme. Books like *The Loved One*, Evelyn Waugh's satire of Forest Lawn, are not on sale in the souvenir shop. (Eaton occasionally expresses resentment over the treatment given the cemetery by novelists—especially by one writer to whom he extended free run of the park only to be parodied later. But Eaton also understands that such novels have brought world-wide publicity to Forest

Lawn and have not adversely affected his sales, which come not from England but from Los Angeles.)

Among the most popular items at the souvenir shop are those showing reproductions of Forest Lawn's three churches, the Church of the Recessional, the Little Church of the Flowers, and the Wee Kirk o' the Heather.

"Providing a dignified setting for final tribute," the three churches "serve also for the joyous and memorable ceremonies of christening and the exchange of marriage vows." Since the churches have opened, more than 43,000 persons have had "memorable" marriages in them. But Forest Lawn makes no money directly from marrying people, and the profits from the souvenir shop are used for the upkeep of the Hall of the Crucifixion. Forest Lawn's real business is burying people.

"The hardest thing in the world to sell," states one of the organization's top officials, "are 'spaces.'" ("Space" is the euphemism used at Forest Lawn for "grave plot.") The reason for the difficulty is that Forest Lawn's sales organization, which comprises about 175 people, concentrates on sales made "Before Need," another phrase in Forest Lawn's own peculiar language of the flowers. Selling cemetery plots "Before Need" rather than "At Time of Need" or "Post Need," although difficult, is very profitable, since under California law a cemetery pays taxes only on its unsold plots. Once a "space" has been sold, it is removed from the tax rolls. Thus it is to the obvious advantage of Forest Lawn to sell off its land as quickly as possible, without waiting for "Need."

There are approximately fifteen hundred individual "spaces" to the acre in Forest Lawn. Prices average $300 per space. There are also rather more elegant neighborhoods at Forest Lawn which are less crowded and therefore more expensive. In the Gardens of Memory, entered only with a special key, there are "memorial sanctuaries designed for families who desire the privacy and protection of crypt interment, but who at the same time long for the open skies and the natural beauty of a verdant garden bathed in sunlight. Under the lawns in the Gardens of Memory have been created a number of monolithically constructed crypts of steel-reinforced concrete."

In the area of ground burial, Forest Lawn has contributed a pleasant innovation. No tombstones are permitted, only markers, set flush with the ground so that there is in fact the pleasant appearance of a park with sweeping green lawns.

But one does not have to be interred to take up permanent residence at Forest Lawn. A number of other arrangements can be made, including being inurned after cremation in the columbarium for as little as $145 or entombed in a mausoleum crypt—which can cost as much as $800,000, as in the case of the Irving Thalberg mausoleum. One can also be placed in a large wall out in the open air. Families may be interred, inurned, or entombed as a unit to maintain "togetherness." Should one feel the need for fresh air while spending the "happy Eternal Life" in a crypt, it is possible, at added cost naturally, to have a ventilating system installed. In the mausoleum, tape-recorded music is played as well.

Inurnment is not restricted to a single form of urn. The law in California, which has a strong undertakers' lobby, provides that after cremation ashes must be buried or placed in a columbarium. A wide variety of urn designs can be seen, ranging from books and loving cups to miniature coffins.

The price for the casket or urn sets the approximate amount paid for the funeral itself, but here the range is far greater than for the "space." The least expensive casket, with the metal screw heads showing, is $115; the most expensive goes for $17,500.

Forest Lawn's rich, creamy advertising presentations combine the hard and the soft sell. On radio and television, the same institutional approach is as manifest as at the cemetery itself. Programs of church services and organ music are announced in deep, sonorous tones, and practically no mention is made of the company's product. The institutional approach is also used on billboards picturing stained-glass windows or the "Moses" statue. However, many of Forest Lawn's billboards are given over to the hard, competitive sell, featuring what is Hubert Eaton's original contribution to the American way of death: the concept of combining in one place mortuary functions, such as embalming, with funeral services and burial, thus obviating the necessity for outside undertakers, florists, funeral chapels, and long processions to the cemetery. Forest Lawn successfully undertook the elimination of the undertaking middleman.

Today, Forest Lawn's hard-sell slogans of "Everything In One Beautiful Place" and "Just One Phone Call" are widely copied, as are the ads which usually feature back or side views, sometimes in color, of two dry-eyed, well-groomed people talking to a distinguished-looking, gray-mustached bank-president or diplomat-type man, identified by a discreet sign on his desk as a "Funeral Counselor." Sometimes only the "Counselor" is shown, answering the "Just One Phone Call" with the dedicated air of a statesman. It is clear from the ads that at Forest Lawn, where the concept of death has been abolished, the standards of accepted behavior demand no vulgar signs of outward grief.

But even though its competitors copy Forest Lawn today, Eaton faced a bitter battle when he first attempted to bring a mortuary into the cemetery. Forest Lawn's permit to operate a mortuary was given only after a determined struggle waged against him by some of the undertakers who foresaw disaster for themselves in the new trend of combined services. It was during this period that Forest Lawn began to build up its own political operations, which today make it the most powerful spokesman for the industry in the state.

There have been a number of occasions when, in its self-interest, Forest Lawn has had to do battle, sometimes in ways that might have been frowned on by the dignified gentlemen in their ads. From the 1930's to the early 1950's, Forest Lawn was in a running argument with the county assessor's office over the tax assessments made on its property, with Forest Lawn always claiming that the assessments were too high and almost always getting them reduced, even as much as fifty per cent, by the county board of supervisors. Some supervisors did consistently oppose Forest Lawn's plea for tax reduction and supported the assessor, but when the votes were taken a majority always supported Forest Lawn.

In 1938, in one of its early appearances before the board of supervisors, Forest Lawn requested a tax reduction, claiming that the vacant property in the land it then owned would remain unsold until 1973. At the time, the county assessor pointed out that Forest Lawn had "acquired additional property when they said it was going to take thirty-five years to sell out what they now have, yet they go to work and buy seventy-five acres adjoining at a big price."

Ten years later, in 1948, the issue of how long it would take to fill Forest Lawn's vacant "spaces" became one of the central points in a bitter political hassle within the Los Angeles City Council, and the cemetery completely reversed its argument of ten years earlier. At issue was Forest Lawn's request for a zoning change to permit the use, as a cemetery, of 480 acres of land adjoining Griffith Park, a public park and playground in the Hollywood area.

Forest Lawn's first request to develop this new cemetery was submitted to and rejected by the city planning commission in 1946. When the request was again rejected in 1948, Forest Lawn appealed, claiming, in contrast to its 1938 plea of unsold land, that "by the year 1965 all of the available grave spaces in existing cemeteries will have been exhausted."

The odds against Forest Lawn's gaining approval for its plan to open a new cemetery seemed formidable. The planning commission opposed it, the park department opposed it, the board of health commissioners opposed it, the water and power commission opposed it, the board of public works opposed it, the Hollywood chamber of commerce opposed it, and a variety of community groups opposed it. But the "Builder's Dream" triumphed, and on March 9, 1948, the city council voted 11-3 to permit the opening of the cemetery.

Never an organization to leave stones unturned, within a few hours Forest Lawn had hastily dug six holes in the ground and buried six bodies in them; a move which, under state law, immediately qualified the area as a commercial graveyard that could not then be disturbed or moved except under very specific circumstances.

"We got the bodies we buried through the county hospital or from their next of kin in advance," states Ugene Blalock, vice-president and general counsel of Forest Lawn, "and we made no charge for our services. If the vote in the council had gone against us, we would have given them a free burial elsewhere."

In fact, however, the council vote has rarely gone against Forest Lawn, even when the city fathers were voting on whether to give Beverly Hills the street where Eaton lives, thus providing the Digger with a more distinguished address. Although he hasn't moved, Eaton now lives in Beverly Hills.

No one is quite sure about the exact basis for Eaton's influence; or if they are, they're not willing to talk about it for the record. Blalock states that Forest Lawn as an institution has not made, as far as he knows, any campaign contribution in eighteen years, although he adds, "Individuals may make political contributions." But politics aside, it is Hubert Eaton, master salesman, who is chiefly responsible for Forest Lawn's success.

It is from Eaton's mind that has come the creation of the Council of Regents of Memorial Court of Honor, twenty-two "outstanding business and professional men" who advise "on all matters concerning the growth of the Memorial Park as a cultural center of religion and fine arts."

Its members, who include the president of Occidental College and the chancellor of the University of Southern California, wear a handsome, flowing red robe, trimmed with velvet, and an elegant round red hat, also trimmed daintily with velvet, while around their necks hangs a kind of Maltese Cross decoration, perhaps the Order of Forest Lawn.

Such touches as these distinguish the imaginative Eaton from his colleagues. Eaton's devotion to salesmanship, as evidenced by his creating special heart-shaped children's sections at Forest Lawn, named Babyland and Lullabyland, began early in life, according to "The Forest Lawn Story," his biography sold at the souvenir shop.

The son of a college professor, Eaton, states the biography, "sat in his little cubbyhole behind his father's bookshelves ostensibly studying but actually eavesdropping on his father's conversations with callers. Invariably they came for advice on one thing or another but more often than not, it was advice on matters affecting money. From these conversations he learned the word salesmanship and what it meant."

It was Eaton, too, who initiated many Forest Lawn public-service activities—the inspirational speaker made available to service clubs, the thirteen half-hour Bible films, and the giving of the Forest Lawn Awards for Persuasive Writing as a "practical service to students and Christian liberal arts colleges."

Long interested in "small, independent, liberal arts colleges" as being "America's last bulwark against the march of Socialism . . ." Eaton believes that "most" college professors are "semi-socialists at heart" who teach young people that salesmanship "smacks of chicanery, demagoguery, of influencing people against their wills . . ."

But Eaton isn't always so serious. Even when he was at college himself, he always had a "good sense of humor." His biography relates that one of his favorite tricks was to persuade a visitor to allow a funnel to be inserted into the top of his trousers and then to make him balance a penny on his chin and try to drop it into the funnel. While the visitor was in this position, young Hubert "or one of his cronies would pour a cup of cold water into the funnel."

Eaton's "good sense of humor changed little in succeeding years," states his biographer, and it certainly hadn't changed much the night when Eaton gave one of his usual huge, lavish parties for a group of friends and guests. It was called "An Enchanted Evening in the South Pacific," of which "Trader" Hubert Eaton was the master of ceremonies. Elaborate Hawaiian acts were presented, and guests received a large, beautifully printed eight-page souvenir program in color, in which Eaton had himself depicted as "Your Happy Planter," jumping from page to page on a golden-shovel pogo stick.

On the cultural level, the printed program carried a large reproduction of the "David" statue, with a fig leaf, a Hawaiian lei, and a girl curled around its neck, all illustrating a poem, "The Secret of Hubie's David," which described just how it was decided to add a fig leaf to Forest Lawn's copy of Michelangelo's "David" in order not to shock "the ladies of L.A."

But surely the greatest of all the improvements that Eaton has made on the past is Forest Lawn itself. Here, what might have been just an ordinary "country cemetery" has been parlayed into a solemn institution, profitable and widely imitated, looking like Edgar Guest's idea of Heaven brought to earth, while representing a social level to which all people can aspire after death. And in the future, says Hubert Eaton, "When the place is all filled up, my idea, from a financial standpoint, has always been to make Forest Lawn into a museum and charge admission."

BROCK BROWER

Born in New Jersey in 1931, Brock Brower was educated at Dartmouth, spent a year at Harvard Law School, and then received a Rhodes Scholarship for study at Oxford. He has been an editor of the University of North Carolina Press, assistant editor of Esquire, *and is now associate editor of* The Transatlantic Review. *Mr. Brower has contributed articles to* Esquire, Mademoiselle, Vogue, The New York Times Magazine, Horizon, *and* The Saturday Evening Post, *and his fiction has appeared in* New

World Writing. *His article on "The Article" is here reprinted from a collection entitled* On Creative Writing, *ed. Paul Engle (New York, 1964).*

THE ARTICLE

Of all extant literary forms, I'm afraid the general article asks the greatest general sufferance of us right at the moment, because it is concurrently in its dotage as journalism and in its nonage as literature. It is, in too many cases, simply senile—a reiterated banality wheezed to formulae for the engineered readerships of certain unreconstructed mass magazines ("What is a good article made of?" singsongs a wordsmith at her forge in *The Writer's Digest*. "STATISTICS, QUOTES, AND ANECDOTES!"). Yet it has proved itself, in some recent instances, to be a precocious instrument —a remarkably free engine for prose that such editors as Norman Podhoretz of *Commentary* and John Fischer of *Harper's* see as the most pertinent and immediate means of expression our culture can offer a writer. As a result, those of us who write it—and try to write it better than the newspapers are written—live in a din of huzzahs and alarums, and none of us knows exactly whether the article is ignominiously sinking, like the old *Collier's*, or emerging triumphant over itself, like a change in the language. The only thing that *is* certain is that it will not "survive"—in the sense that other troubled literary forms, such as the short story and the novel, are predicted to "survive" any current abatement of interest or debility of art—because there are enough of us around who won't *let* it "survive." The article must now either go under along with all magazines that persist in believing some millions of readers can still be united by a single endocrinal response to "a sparkling lead," "a clear, lucid style," "universal reader appeal," et cetera, or become an entirely new and disturbing and quite different thing, put to broad general use much as Norman Mailer and James Baldwin have put it to more intensive personal use in their efforts to sear public awareness with their own convictions.

In other words, the impact of an article is coming to depend more and more upon the writer's individual intelligence and resolve, and less and less upon the corporate noodling of the journal in which it appears; and this shift proves out an interesting juggle that has occurred lately in the handling of our sense of reality. At about the same time that magazines began, I fear, to let reality slip, a number of fine writers—novelists, short story writers, some of the young and uncommitted—began desperately trying to close with reality. "Making a living is nothing; the great difficulty is making a point, making a difference—with words," Elizabeth Hardwick has summed up this impulsive search. These writers found that the point, the difference had to be made with more than fictions—that the "lies like truth" would no longer do for the Truth—and so they turned precipitously to the concreteness of fact. Or perhaps, in the end, Fact actually turned on them, like a cornered assassin, and almost defensively they reached for the first weapon at hand. The article, whatever else it may be, has always been bluntly at hand, if only because it has never been put by any definition out of reach.

It's important to understand how open and available a form it really is —much more so than the short story or novel—despite the false restrictions that popular journalism has imposed upon it. Of course, as long as only journalists wrote the article, it was bound to follow the journalistic crotchets—a "news peg to hang it on," "lots of quotes, high up in the story," "color," "the flavor of the man," and so on *ad nauseam*—but it was never bonded to journalism. In fact, by definition, the article is bonded to no one. The word itself (if a brief look into the N.E.D. can be excused here) comes from the Latin *articulus*, the diminutive of *artus*, or "joint." "*Articulus* in L. was extended from the joint, to the parts jointed on, limbs, members, 'joints' of the finger, etc.; whence *transf.* to the component parts of discourses, writings, actions." An article then is "A literary composition forming materially part of a journal, magazine, encyclopaedia, or other collection, *but treating a specific topic distinctly and independently*." (Italics added.) It serves no genre, no subject matter, no periodical; it should never be written *for*—in that slavish sense—*The Saturday Evening Post, The New Yorker*, or any other master. It should simply be "jointed on" its literary surroundings, as indeed the best articles always are, outlandish among the Contents.

Actually, there is only one specific obligation that touches the form of the article, and it derives from another branch of the above etymology. (Which is my only reason for quoting such wondrous and cumbersome stuff. Usually this is the kind of research a writer of an article does "to have the facts behind him"—and *leave* behind him.) From the same word *articulus* also comes the idea of breaking down a whole into its jointed parts, and treating each part carefully in sequence. For instance, in speaking—as so many of us were painfully taught to do—we *articulate*. "To express distinctly; to give utterance to. . . . To form or fit into a systematically interrelated whole." That is really all an article is obliged to do. It articulates any subject, person, or idea, and it may do so in any style that pleases the writer, so long as he does not fail to exercise at least two of his faculties: his own voice, so that his article will be distinct, and his own reason, so that his article will be independent.

Patently, neither of these faculties has ever been included in the basic equipage of a journalist, which may explain the vapidity of so much that has been published in magazines. Journalism is routinely voiceless, or whenever it gains a voice, it is a street voice, caterwauling for attention, not understanding. But far worse, journalism is routinely mindless. Its vaunted objectivity—its habit of piling the greater fact on top of the lesser fact, like Pelion on top of Ossa on top of a pebble—this is only an escape from the need to reason. When finally faced with a controversial point which demands some interpretation, the journalist is famous for the "Lib-Lab," i.e., "on the one hand, *this,* and on the other hand, *that,*" but neither hand is his. The easy generalization ("the greatest living . . . single most . . . best known . . . fastest rising . . . nonesuch on the immediate horizon") and the endless qualifier ("perhaps") are the two stylistic counterweights with which the journalist maintains his own commitment, and hence his own existence, at constant zero. The total impression is at last one of immobility, as if words indeed made no point, no difference, and the writing strikes us as literally inarticulate—that is, random, disconnected, *disjointed.*

The obvious effect of this practice on our sense of reality is to sap it, and for some time this seemed to be the deliberate case with many magazines. However, nothing can remain unreal for very long and still circulate, so that something of a panic has finally overtaken these magazines, and happily just at the moment when some of the better writers have independently hit upon their own means of articulating reality. In several cases— still far too few—there have been some most fortunate meetings of minds, and the article has begun to appear with both a voice and an independence within it. Put another way, the facts, which would have only been gathered and sieved by a journalist, have been enclosed within a single intelligence, and a mind has set to work, making independent observations that are far more capacitous than those of the tape recorder or the TV camera.

Actually, this is not a new thing, but only a resurrected approach; in fact, one of the best examples of this kind of writing in American letters is an article from *The Southern Literary Messenger,* April, 1836. It appeals to me especially because it shows, long before twentieth-century journalism elaborated itself into a huge staff operation with its own infernal technology, how far superior the work of a single good mind really is.

The subject of this article is what must have been one of the first computers. Or rather, it purported to be such. The machine was an Automaton Chess-Player, displayed by a German named Johann Nepomuk Maelzel, and it played chess against the local human competition (just as IBM7090 has been partially programmed to do) through a dummy seated at a chest, on which were a chessboard and six differently tapered candles. The chest was full of machinery—supposedly—and the dummy, called the Turk, was run by the machinery—supposedly. People had their doubts, of course, though they were allowed in a limited way to examine the mechanism before the Turk started his chess game. But the man who settled those doubts—and proved that a human being *had* to be inside the machine, even if he were a midget—was a writer of occasional articles named Edgar Allan Poe.

Now the remarkable thing about Poe's article, entitled "Maelzel's Chess-Player," is that he disproved the reality of the mechanism—dismantled it and looked inward at its chicane vitals—by simply reasoning it onto the logical scrap heap. He never had to go near the Chess-Player to demolish it. He never got "behind the scenes," or talked intimately with members of the Maelzel household, or met the midget in a bar and got him drunk. He merely observed, reasoned, and concluded. "Ratiocination," Poe was later to call this exercise of intelligence. He even managed by ratiocination to show that the man inside the Chess-Player had to be right-handed—a conclusion that follows irrefutably from the fact that the Turk plays a left-handed game. Poe adduced sixteen other refutations altogether (some of them are given in the selection from "Maelzel's Chess-Player" at the end of this chapter),[1] but two should suffice here to show the style of mind that he brought to bear upon just such a critical question of reality.

3. The Automaton does not invariably win the game. Were the machine a pure machine this would not be the case—it would always win. The *principle* being discovered by which a machine can be made to *play* a game of chess, an extension of the same principle would enable it to *win* a game—a farther extension would enable it to *win all* games—that is, to beat any possible game of an antagonist. A little consideration will convince anyone that the difficulty of making a machine beat all games, is not in the least degree greater, as regards the principle of the operations necessary, than that of making it beat a single game. If then we regard the Chess-Player as a machine, we must suppose, (what is highly improbable,) that its inventor preferred leaving it incomplete to perfecting it—a supposition rendered still more absurd, when we reflect that the leaving it incomplete would afford an argument against the possibility of its being a pure machine —the very argument we now adduce.

4. When the situation of the game is difficult or complex, we never perceive the Turk either shake his head or roll his eyes. It is only when his next move is obvious, or when the game is so circumstanced that to a man in the Automaton's place there would be no necessity for reflection. Now these peculiar movements of the head and eyes are movements customary with persons engaged in meditations, and the ingenious Baron Kempelen would have adapted these movements (were the machine a pure machine) to occasions proper to their display—that is, to occasions of complexity. But the reverse is seen to be the case, and this reverse applies precisely to our supposition of a man in the interior. When engaged in meditation about the game, he has no time to think of setting in motion the mechanism of the Automaton by which are moved the head and the eyes. When the game, however, is obvious, he has time to look about him, and accordingly, we see the head shake and the eyes roll.

In these passages, the *style* of the intelligence is inimitable, but the *role* of the intelligence emphatically is not. In fact, it is precisely the role that

---

[1] Not printed here [Editors' note].

every writer engaging reality must set for his own reason to play—first confrontory, then encompassing, and finally critical. Yet, under the circumstances that usually attend the writing of an article, it is the hardest role to assign independent reason. It is so easily usurped by the "actual assignment—what we want you to do with this one," the pressure of time, the ephemera around the subject, et cetera. The great usurper once was the magazine itself with its Draconic point of view, but this is not now so important as the bad habits this usurpation bred. It is so easy to quote, generalize, qualify, extrapolate *neutrally* around a subject—*Let the reader draw his own conclusions*—instead of facing it directly as something that must be plumbed by a dropline of pure thought.

In writing articles, I've always tried in some way to drop such a line—except when I've been dragooned into assignments that have turned out hopeless and ashen—and I find I'm most comfortable making the effort when I can draw as near as possible to Poe's exercise of pure mind. That is, I prefer to try to imbue an entire matter with an impersonal intelligence which infuses everything like a sudden freshness in the whole air than to set upon a subject with a rush of personality which bestirs everything like too sharp an individual breeze. I suspect this approach (that is, Poe's) is probably best for anybody initially attempting an article—unless he has a Nobel Prize, or expects one soon—but it certainly isn't, by any means, the only style the mind can assume. Much that has been achieved recently with expository prose has been exactly opposite in nature: highly personal, and as far removed from Poe's ratiocination as his terrors are from our own. But this still doesn't change the essential role that reason plays, for there must inevitably be the same force of intelligence in, say, one of James Baldwin's refutations as there is in one of Poe's.

> The American Negro has the great advantage of having never believed the collection of myths to which white Americans cling: that their ancestors were all freedom-loving heroes, that they were born in the greatest country the world has ever seen, or that Americans are invincible in battle and wise in peace, that Americans have always dealt honorably with Mexicans and Indians and all other neighbors or inferiors, that American men are the world's most direct and virile, that American women are pure. Negroes know far more about white Americans than that; it can almost be said, in fact, that they know about white Americans what parents—or, anyway, mothers—know about their children, and that they very often regard white Americans that way. And perhaps this attitude, held in spite of what they know and have endured, helps to explain why Negroes, on the whole, and until lately, have allowed themselves to feel so little hatred. The tendency has really been, insofar as this was possible, to dismiss white people as the slightly mad victims of their own brainwashing. One watched the lives they led. One could not be fooled about that; one

watched the things they did and the excuses that they gave themselves, and if a white man was really in trouble, deep trouble, it was to the Negro's door that he came. And one felt that if one had had that white man's worldly advantages, one would never have become as bewildered and as joyless and as thoughtlessly cruel as he. The Negro came to the white man for a roof or for five dollars or for a letter to the judge; the white man came to the Negro for love. But he was not often able to give what he came seeking. The price was too high; he had too much to lose. And the Negro knew this, too. When one knows this about a man, it is impossible for one to hate him, but unless he becomes a man—becomes equal—it is also impossible for one to love him. Ultimately, one tends to avoid him, for the universal characteristic of children is to assume that they have a monopoly on trouble, and therefore a monopoly on *you*. (Ask any Negro what he knows about the white people with whom he works. And then ask the white people with whom he works what they know about *him*.)

Nothing could conflict more with the immaculately analytic tone of Poe than this homiletic style of Baldwin's, but despite the difference of a century in moral feeling, there is still the same basic probity in both men. Like Poe, Baldwin is also looking closely to see why "the head shakes and the eyes roll." It is the same intrusive act of mind, a stealing inside all reality's dumb shows to find out how false or true the machinery within actually is, whether it is "operating" an automaton or a white man or a Negro or a President or a revolution.

On a practical working level, there are numerous thoughts about writing an article that follow from this insistence upon independent probity, but basically they all come down to the hard fact that if a writer expects to maintain this independence, he must do everything for himself. If a single good mind is to encompass a matter, then other minds become superfluous. The writer himself, for instance, is always his own best researcher, despite what other adjunctive intelligences may contribute, and the rule is that the research is only done when the writer "meets himself coming back the other way," i.e., when among all possible informants, the writer becomes, at least for the moment, the best informed.

Similarly, all the interviewing must be done by the writer himself, *live* —that is, without the excuse of a tape recorder to let him off listening and responding—and all his efforts should be bent upon staging in his own head a kind of symposium attended by his various interviewees. Through him, without ever meeting, they "discuss" the subject. He does not run around collecting opinions, like a pollster. He actively seeks to create a dialogue among people who really only converse through him, and his advantage is that to him each can speak freely, where they might argue with, or shy from, or disdain one another face to face.

And finally, only the writer himself can assume the full burden of knowledge. Behind even the most personal prose, there is always some privacy, or privacies, kept inviolate; there is always information "on the record" and information "off the record." In fact, it is positively the sign of mindless journalistic technology at work when the written instrument exhausts the "available facts." Any writer who is no such technocrat inevitably begins with a much deeper knowledge of his subject than he can possibly put on paper, and the rule is that no writer should set down a word on paper until he knows what he must also leave unsaid.

These are some few of the demands made upon the writer when reason is given its proper role, but they are all made, of course, prior to the actual writing of the article. This is only preparation, and there is still the need to find a voice. That challenge—to discover a voice that will summon reality like a flourish from the horn of Roland—is the hardest to meet in any prose, and it is remarkable how large a success the article has had recently in discovering a variety of such voices. The explanation, of course, is that there has been a heavy borrowing from the house of fiction.

Actually, this is exactly as it should be, though this transposition seems often strangely inhibited. In the past, there existed a much closer tie between expository prose and narrative prose. To return to Poe for a moment, the prose that appears in "Maelzel's Chess-Player" is precisely the prose that he puts in the mouth of his great detective, M. Dupin. "But Truth is often, and in very great degree, the aim of the tale," he wrote in a famous review of Hawthorne's short stories. "Some of the finest tales are tales of ratiocination." As his own indeed proved to be. Even his literary criticism has this same ratiocinative tone as if he only required the one voice to swiftly subsume all forms. The same is true of Melville, whose reportage and fiction (and often their mixture) are given utterance in a single voice that stands reality on its ear. Such descriptions as he offers in *The Encantadas, or Enchanted Isles*, where "No voice, no low, no howl is heard; the chief sound of life here is a hiss," are enough to buckle our senses.

> . . . behold these really wondrous tortoises—none of your schoolboy mud-turtles—but black as widow's weeds, heavy as chests of plate, with vast shells medallioned and orbed like shields, and dented and blistered like shields that have breasted a battle, shaggy, too, here and there, with dark green moss, and slimy with the spray of the sea. These mystic creatures, suddenly translated by night from unutterable solitudes to our peopled deck, affected me in a manner not easy to unfold. They seemed newly crawled forth from beneath the foundations of the world. Yea, they seemed the identical tortoises whereon the Hindoo plants this total sphere. With a lantern I inspected them more closely. Such worshipful venerableness of aspect! Such furry greenness mantling the rude peelings and healing the fissures of their shattered shells. I no more saw three tortoises. They expanded—be-

came transfigured. I seemed to see three Roman Coliseums in magnificent decay.

Yet these tortoises are not what he "imagined" in fiction, but actual beings he "saw" on board ship, and indeed "next evening, strange to say, I sat down with my shipmates, and made a merry repast from the tortoise steaks and tortoise stews." There is no real discrepancy, for Melville's voice is a master instrument, tuned to mundanity as well as dream, and not a vulnerable lute that must be held safely aloof from the vibrations of reality.

Since the nineteenth century, this magisterial range of voice through any number of forms, particularly the article, has been sorely missed, but suddenly—out of a hunger for impressions that only an extreme sense of isolation could have bred—writers have again to attempt it. Nelson Algren writes a travel book that carries him out of his destitute fantasy of Chicago into the real world where he must bring whole nationalities, the Spanish, the French, the English, the Irish, the Turks, around the corner of South Street into his own blind pig. Truman Capote turns profilist, then chronicler of the Moscow *Porgy and Bess* tour, and finally detective, as he offers the police an important clue in a Kansas murder case, the latest grotesque he has chosen from the things of reality to transform directly into an exquisite bibelot of prose. Norman Mailer unleashes a diurnal attack against the culture that has pruned him of his goodly limbs and left him a stark and leafless trunk—a "success"—and out of this shock tactic, out of even the magazine deadline itself, he begins to find his way back from "prophecy" to the novel once more. "The drama of real life will not let down the prose writer," Miss Hardwick comments. "Life inspires. The confession, the revelation, are not reporting, not even journalism. Real life is treated *as if it* were fiction. The concreteness of fact is made suggestive, shadowy, symbolical. The vividly experiencing 'I' begins his search for his art in the newspapers."

And ends by publishing it in the magazines.

So the voice carries over from its beginnings in fiction, and sustains itself at the pitch of real life, perhaps even gains strength, as has certainly been the case with James Baldwin. More than any other writer, Baldwin has achieved his individual voice through the article form. He has even made the article assignment—that purchase order from a magazine for prose on an out-of-stock topic—into an iron link between event and personal vision. In his fiction, this voice has often seemed constricted, even *falsetto,* but set free to find its own natural limits—a liberty which the article form could indulge—it reached a lambency in prose that threw the black sufferings of his people into terrible relief against the white world. At the same time, no writer has set "the vividly experiencing 'I' " to face greater intrinsic peril, simply because every real event for Baldwin seems to catch at some thread in the worn, tacky, durable fabric of his being. He pulls at the thread himself, just a loose end, and then suddenly there is no knowing where the ravel will end or lead us. "On the 19th of December, in 1949, when I had been living in Paris for a little over a year, I was arrested as a receiver of stolen goods and spent eight days in prison," he begins an article for *Commentary*, "Equal in Paris," which I have included in its entirety at the end of this chapter.[2] The stolen goods were only a *drap de lit*, the "theft" only a misunderstanding; the event at bottom was insignificant. But it pulls from Baldwin a thread of existence that supports an awful burden of culture and race and alienation. Yet it never breaks, only delicately shines.

> One had, in short, to come into contact with an alien culture in order to understand that a culture was not a community basket-weaving project, nor yet an act of God; was something neither desirable nor undesirable in itself, being inevitable, being nothing more or less than the recorded and visible effects on a body of people of the vicissitudes with which they had been forced to deal. And their great men are revealed as simply another of these vicissitudes, even if, quite against their will, the brief battle of their great men with them has left them richer.

Am I saying then that only the displaced voice from fiction has sufficient resolve to force a personal articulation of reality upon the article form? Not at all. It is simply that of late the best voices have come over, impassioned or hortatory or simply bully, from fiction, and the writer of an article might better listen to them first if he wishes to find his own voice at all. Obviously no writer need master the short story before trying his hand at an article, but at the same time no writer should ignore the fictional techniques that have so strengthened the embodiment of fact in prose and made it "suggestive, shadowy, symbolical." What the novelists know naturally, the rest of us must learn at our pain.

In my own case, since I invariably keep at an impersonal distance from my subject, my strongest efforts in this area have been bent upon turning fact into imagery in an article. Faced with the usual Augean stable of data, I do not try to sweep it clean—as a journalist would in his Herculean labors—but rather to pick out the most redolent facts and deliberately hoard them for the aura of the stable. That is, I select facts not only as a rationalist, trying to bring an abstract line of reasoning to a conclusion, but also as an imagist, seeking to broach reality for a pattern. It is hard to pick much of an example from what has been a very broadly scattered exercise, but in an article on psychoanalysis, I tried to sum up its early history, while bodying forth the aura of the actual practice, in the following manner:

---

[2] Not printed here [Editors' note].

That first couch was of horsehair. Pyramided high with pillows. *Berggasse 19, Wien IX.* ("After the—well, later when the Professor is no longer with us," the porter said one day to the poet H.D. on her way to her fifty-five-minute "hour," "they will call it Freudgasse." They never did.) For some of his taller patients, it was almost too short, and their feet under the couch rug nearly touched the glowing porcelain stove set narrowly in the corner. From the other corner, behind the couch's hard, slightly elevated headpiece, came the cigar smoke and the fatherly voice. "Today we have tunneled very deep. You have discovered for yourself what I discovered for the race." Around him, the sublimations of a frustrated archaeologist: Greek amphorae, Assyrian and Egyptian statuettes, and other tiny, ancient totems, set all in a row. And over the couch—on the wall usually reserved nowadays for the stark probe of a favored pair of analytical eyes—a large steel engraving of the Temple of Arnak, for this was the only consulting room in the history of psychoanalysis where it was not possible to hang on that wall an honorific portrait of an analyst's chosen St. Analyst.

I wanted to begin with the facts at a particular point in time, but I also wanted these same facts to form an image of reality that would give back a semblance of life, of moment to the prose. My own voice, I'm afraid, is factual, not personal, and I depend much more upon a kind of factual density than upon any vision to help me articulate reality. But this is only one other writer's way of struggling for voice, not the lone arduous path to the one true expository style, and the eventual point is that many voices have lifted themselves above the jibber of mere facts to confound directly the reality behind it.

In fact, one of the best is also one of the most prosaic, that of George Orwell. In a way, Orwell preceded all of us into reality. His prose—which is as spare as experience itself really is—seems to have an absolute correspondence with his moment, his existence; his voice is so quietly suasive that reading him is like joining him. His articles don't end; rather, *he* departs, and leaves behind him both a sense of truth and a sense of embarrassment. In his famous article on "Shooting an Elephant," he ends by telling us:

Afterwards, of course, there were endless discussions about the shooting of the elephant. The owner was furious, but he was only an Indian and could do nothing. Besides, legally I had done the right thing, for a mad elephant has to be killed, like a mad dog, if its owner fails to control it. Among the Europeans opinion was divided. The older men said I was right, the younger men said it was a damn shame to shoot an elephant for killing a coolie, because an elephant was worth more than any damn Coringhee coolie. And afterwards I was very glad that the coolie had been killed; it put me legally in the right and gave me a sufficient pretext for shooting the elephant. I often wondered whether any of the others grasped that I had done it solely to avoid looking a fool.

Orwell has already told us his pathetic reasons for having to shoot the elephant, even as he lies down in the road to do it, but this last is still a shock, the kind of humbling shock that a work of fiction can never bring home. It is, finally, too real.

Orwell, of course, wrote fiction, but in the end he is the strongest argument for the future of the article, for it was in this form that he expressed his best thinking in his most characteristic voice. He could not have told of "A Hanging" or "How the Poor Die" or " 'Such, Such Were the Joys . . .' " without the excuse that journalism offered him (though it was not journalism that he wrote). Fiction helped him find a voice, but it was a voice unnatural to fiction. It had to be heeded elsewhere.

It is quite possible that things have now gone even farther, and fiction itself has become unnatural to the voices *we* heed. In that sense, Baldwin has, much like Orwell, found a more proper form, and it could happen that the next generation of writers in America will not need to "come over" from fiction, but will only look back on it nostalgically as a point of departure. If this is anything like the case, the article obviously will flourish, and might attain the kind of excellence that existed in English prose during the eighteenth century.

But if anything like this *is* to happen, the reasons for writing about reality will have to attain to something like Orwell's humility in truth, for there is no gainsaying the disappointment and denial that will be let loose. "Go, go, go, said the bird:" in T. S. Eliot's poem, "human kind/ Cannot bear very much reality." Few, including most magazine publishers, have any real desire to test the machinery inside, or to discover whether these be automata or men that play the great chess game in the world. Few even wish to be articulate. It is over this guise of indifference—which is really the universal wish to "avoid looking the fool"—that voice and reason will have to triumph. The dead language of journalism has kept the article a corporate instrument in America far too long, but if it can finally achieve the sanctions which so naturally attend fiction, it will emerge as the one form with enough space to contain the risks of actual existence—the only form in which a man has enough room to shoot an elephant and admit his shame and folly.

What Is America?

Ever since its founding, the United States of America has been a subject of intense interest to itself and to the world alike. Although it has one of the oldest of the world's continuous governments, it has nevertheless remained in many ways a "new nation," continuously exciting, continuously the object of both praise and criticism by both natives and foreigners. The modern emergence of the nation as a principal power in world affairs, its taking on of tremendous world-wide responsibilities, gives special intensity to the debate about America. The answers to what America really is, whether there *is* a typically American way of living and thinking, have an increasingly profound importance for us, not only for our self-knowledge, but for their bearing on the future of all nations.

Though many of the essays in this book are more or less relevant to the question, we have collected here a few that take it on quite directly. Four of the authors offer the freshness, objectivity (and perhaps the bias) of the foreigner's point of view. De Tocqueville and Dickens, writing within a few years of each other over a century ago, raise in addition the question of permanence and change in American culture. Professor Lerner, an American, seeks objectivity from the direction of scholarship, describing traits in American culture much as a social scientist would. Professor Kouwenhoven boldly attempts a formal or structural analysis deriving in part from his sensitivity to the fine arts, literature, and architecture. The reader may wish to examine each essay for the author's skill in identifying our most essential traits. The speech of President Kennedy is offered not so much to further the analysis of the American character as to illustrate it.

ALEXIS DE TOCQUEVILLE

Alexis Charles Henri Clérel de Tocqueville was born in Paris in 1805. He studied law, and as the son of an influential aristocratic family, he was given a judicial post in the court at Versailles. After the July Revolution of 1830, De Tocqueville felt increasingly uncertain of his allegiance to the new government, and he succeeded in securing a commission to go to America to study the prison system. Even closer to his heart was the opportunity to study a democratic system of government at first hand and to judge the possibilities of its application in Europe. For nine months in 1831 and 1832 De Tocqueville and his friend and fellow-magistrate Gustave de Beaumont traveled widely in America, visiting prisons, taking notes, writing letters, interviewing prominent people, requesting memoranda on special subjects, and collecting books and documents. On their return, the two young Frenchmen soon completed their prison report; then each turned to his own study of America. De Tocqueville published his book, De la démocratie en Amérique, *in two parts. The first, a description and critical analysis of the American government in the age of Jackson, was published in 1835. The second, a more philosophical study, with greater regard to the general applicability of American traits, came out in 1840.*

De Tocqueville was elected to the French Chamber of Deputies in 1837 and briefly held the post of Minister for Foreign Affairs under Napoleon III, but his major energies were devoted to political thought rather than to politics. He published L'Ancien régime et la revolution *three years before his death in 1859.*

Democracy in America was quickly recognized as an important book and was translated into many languages. The first English translation was made by Henry Reeve, an Englishman, in 1838. This was revised by the American scholar Francis Bowen in 1862. The text of the chapters from Part II that we present below is taken from Phillips Bradley's excellent modern edition (with corrections) of the Bowen translation.

FOUR ESSAYS FROM

DEMOCRACY IN AMERICA

Philosophical Method of the Americans

I THINK that in no country in the civilized world is less attention paid to philosophy than in the United States. The Americans have no philosophical school of their own, and they care but little for all the schools into which Europe is divided, the very names of which are scarcely known to them.

Yet it is easy to perceive that almost all the inhabitants of the United States use their minds in the same manner, and direct them according to the same rules; that is to say, without ever having taken the trouble to define the rules, they have a philosophical method common to the whole people.

To evade the bondage of system and habit, of family maxims, class opinions, and, in some degree, of national prejudices; to accept tradition only as a means of information, and existing facts only as a lesson to be used in doing otherwise and doing better; to seek the reason of things for oneself, and in oneself alone; to tend to results without being bound to means, and to strike through the form to the substance—such are the principal characteristics of what I shall call the philosophical method of the Americans.

But if I go further and seek among these characteristics the principal one, which includes almost all the rest, I discover that in most of the operations of the mind each American appeals only to the individual effort of his own understanding.

America is therefore one of the countries where the precepts of Descartes are least studied and are best applied. Nor is this surprising. The Americans do not read the works of Descartes, because their social condition deters them from speculative studies; but they follow his maxims, because this same social condition naturally disposes their minds to adopt them.

In the midst of the continual movement that agitates a democratic community, the tie that unites one generation to another is relaxed or broken; every man there readily loses all trace of the ideas of his forefathers or takes no care about them.

Men living in this state of society cannot derive their belief from the opinions of the class to which they belong; for, so to speak, there are no longer any classes, or those which still exist are composed of such mobile elements that the body can never exercise any real control over its members.

As to the influence which the intellect of one man may have on that of another, it must necessarily be very limited in a country where the citizens, placed on an equal footing, are all closely seen by one another; and where, as no signs of incontestable greatness or superiority are perceived in any one of them, they are constantly brought back to their own reason as the most obvious and proximate source of truth. It is not only confidence in this or that man which is destroyed, but the disposition to trust the authority of any man whatsoever. Everyone shuts himself up tightly within himself and insists upon judging the world from there.

The practice of Americans leads their minds to other habits, to fixing the standard of their judgment in themselves alone. As they perceive that they succeed in resolving without assistance all the little difficulties which their practical life presents, they readily conclude that everything in the world may be explained, and that nothing in it transcends the limits of the understanding. Thus they fall to denying what they cannot comprehend; which leaves them but little faith for whatever is extraordinary and an almost insurmountable distaste for whatever is supernatural. As it is on their own testimony that they are accustomed to rely, they like to discern the object which engages their attention with extreme clearness; they therefore strip off as much as possible all that covers it; they rid themselves of whatever separates them from it, they remove whatever conceals it from sight, in order to view it more closely and in the broad light of day. This disposition of mind soon leads them to condemn forms, which they regard as useless and inconvenient veils placed between them and the truth.

The Americans, then, have found no need of drawing philosophical method out of books; they have found it in themselves. The same thing may be remarked in what has taken place in Europe. This same method has only been established and made popular in Europe in proportion as the condition of society has become more equal and men have grown more like one another. Let us consider for a moment the connection of the periods in which this change may be traced.

In the sixteenth century reformers subjected some of the dogmas of the ancient faith to the scrutiny of private judgment; but they still withheld it from the discussion of all the rest. In the seventeenth century Bacon in the natural sciences and Descartes in philosophy properly so called abolished received formulas, destroyed the empire of tradition, and overthrew the authority of the schools. The philosophers of the eighteenth century, generalizing at length on the same principle, undertook to submit to the private judgment of each man all the objects of his belief.

Who does not perceive that Luther, Descartes, and Voltaire employed the same method, and that they differed only in the greater or less use which they professed should be made of it? Why did the reformers confine themselves so closely within the circle of religious ideas? Why did Descartes, choosing to apply his method only to certain matters, though he had made it fit to be applied to all, declare that men might judge for themselves in matters philosophical, but not in matters political? How did it happen that in the eighteenth century those general applications were all at once drawn from this same method, which Descartes and his predecessors either had not perceived or had rejected? To what, lastly, is the fact to be attributed that at this period the method we are speaking of suddenly emerged from the schools, to penetrate into society and become the common standard of intelligence; and that after it had become popular among the French, it was ostensibly adopted or secretly followed by all the nations of Europe?

The philosophical method here designated may have been born in the sixteenth century; it may have been more accurately defined and more extensively applied in the seventeenth; but neither in the one nor in the other could it be commonly adopted. Political laws, the condition of society, and the habits of mind that are derived from these causes were as yet opposed to it.

It was discovered at a time when men were beginning to equalize and assimilate their conditions. It could be generally followed only in ages when those conditions had at length become nearly equal and men nearly alike.

The philosophical method of the eighteenth century, then, is not only French, but democratic; and this explains why it was so readily admitted throughout Europe, where it has contributed so powerfully to change the face of society. It is not because the French have changed their former opinions and altered their former manners that they have convulsed the world, but because they were the first to generalize and bring to light a philosophical method by the aid of which it became easy to attack all that was old and to open a path to all that was new.

If it be asked why at the present day this same method is more rigorously followed and more frequently applied by the French than by the Americans, although the principle of equality is no less complete and of more ancient date among the latter people, the fact may be attributed to two circumstances, which it is first essential to have clearly understood.

It must never be forgotten that religion gave birth to Anglo-American society. In the United States, religion is therefore mingled with all the habits of the nation and all the feelings of patriotism, whence it derives a peculiar force. To this reason another of no less power may be added: in America religion has, as it were, laid down its own limits. Religious institutions have remained wholly distinct from political institutions, so that former laws have been easily changed while former belief has remained unshaken. Christianity has therefore retained a strong hold on the public mind in America; and I would more particularly remark that its sway is not only that of a philosophical doctrine which has been adopted upon inquiry, but of a religion which is believed without discussion. In the

United States, Christian sects are infinitely diversified and perpetually modified; but Christianity itself is an established and irresistible fact, which no one undertakes either to attack or to defend. The Americans, having admitted the principal doctrines of the Christian religion without inquiry, are obliged to accept in like manner a great number of moral truths originating in it and connected with it. Hence the activity of individual analysis is restrained within narrow limits, and many of the most important of human opinions are removed from its influence.

The second circumstance to which I have alluded is that the social condition and the Constitution of the Americans are democratic, but they have not had a democratic revolution. They arrived on the soil they occupy in nearly the condition in which we see them at the present day; and this is of considerable importance.

There are no revolutions that do not shake existing belief, enervate authority, and throw doubts over commonly received ideas. Every revolution has more or less the effect of releasing men to their own conduct and of opening before the mind of each one of them an almost limitless perspective. When equality of conditions succeeds a protracted conflict between the different classes of which the elder society was composed, envy, hatred, and uncharitableness, pride and exaggerated self-confidence seize upon the human heart, and plant their sway in it for a time. This, independently of equality itself, tends powerfully to divide men, to lead them to mistrust the judgment of one another, and to seek the light of truth nowhere but in themselves. Everyone then attempts to be his own sufficient guide and makes it his boast to form his own opinions on all subjects. Men are no longer bound together by ideas, but by interests; and it would seem as if human opinions were reduced to a sort of intellectual dust, scattered on every side, unable to collect, unable to cohere.

Thus that independence of mind which equality supposes to exist is never so great, never appears so excessive, as at the time when equality is beginning to establish itself and in the course of that painful labor by which it is established. That sort of intellectual freedom which equality may give ought, therefore, to be very carefully distinguished from the anarchy which revolution brings. Each of these two things must be separately considered in order not to conceive exaggerated hopes or fears of the future.

I believe that the men who will live under the new forms of society will make frequent use of their private judgment, but I am far from thinking that they will often abuse it. This is attributable to a cause which is more generally applicable to democratic countries, and which, in the long run, must restrain, within fixed and sometimes narrow limits, individual freedom of thought.

I shall proceed to point out this cause in the next chapter [which follows].

Of the Principal Source of Belief Among
Democratic Nations

AT different periods dogmatic belief is more or less common. It arises in different ways, and it may change its object and its form; but under no circumstances will dogmatic belief cease to exist, or, in other words, men will never cease to entertain some opinions on trust and without discussion. If everyone undertook to form all his own opinions and to seek for truth by isolated paths struck out by himself alone, it would follow that no considerable number of men would ever unite in any common belief.

But obviously without such common belief no society can prosper; say, rather, no society can exist; for without ideas held in common there is no common action, and without common action there may still be men, but there is no social body. In order that society should exist and, *a fortiori*, that a society should prosper, it is necessary that the minds of all the citizens should be rallied and held together by certain predominant ideas; and this cannot be the case unless each of them sometimes draws his opinions from the common source and consents to accept certain matters of belief already formed.

If I now consider man in his isolated capacity, I find that dogmatic belief is not less indispensable to him in order to live alone than it is to enable him to co-operate with his fellows. If man were forced to demonstrate for himself all the truths of which he makes daily use, his task would never end. He would exhaust his strength in preparatory demonstrations without ever advancing beyond them. As, from the shortness of his life, he has not the time, nor, from the limits of his intelligence, the capacity, to act in this way, he is reduced to take on trust a host of facts and opinions which he has not had either the time or the power to verify for himself, but which men of greater ability have found out, or which the crowd adopts. On this groundwork he raises for himself the structure of his own thoughts; he is not led to proceed in this manner by choice, but is constrained by the inflexible law of his condition. There is no philosopher in the world so great but that he believes a million things on the faith of other people and accepts a great many more truths than he demonstrates.

This is not only necessary but desirable. A man who should undertake to inquire into everything for himself could devote to each thing but little time and attention. His task would keep his mind in perpetual unrest, which would prevent him from penetrating to the depth of any truth or of making his mind adhere firmly to any conviction. His intellect would be at once independent and powerless. He must therefore make his choice from among the various objects of human belief and adopt many opinions without discussion in order to search the better into that smaller number which he sets apart for investigation. It is true that whoever receives an opinion on the word of another does so far enslave his mind, but it is a salutary servitude, which allows him to make a good use of freedom.

A principle of authority must then always occur, under all circumstances, in some part or other of the moral and intellectual world. Its place is variable, but a place it necessarily has. The independence of individual minds may be greater or it may be less; it cannot be unbounded. Thus the question is, not to know whether any intellectual authority exists in an age of democracy, but simply where it resides and by what standard it is to be measured.

I have shown in the preceding chapter how equality of conditions leads men to entertain a sort of instinctive incredulity of the supernatural and a very lofty and often exaggerated opinion of human understanding. The men who live at a period of social equality are not therefore easily led to place that intellectual authority to which they bow either beyond or above humanity. They commonly seek for the sources of truth in themselves or in those who are like themselves. This would be enough to prove that at such periods no new religion could be established, and that all schemes for such a purpose would be not only impious, but absurd and irrational. It may be foreseen that a democratic people will not easily give credence to divine missions; that they will laugh at modern prophets; and that they will seek to discover the chief arbiter of their belief within, and not beyond, the limits of their kind.

When the ranks of society are unequal, and men unlike one another in condition, there are some individuals wielding the power of superior intelligence, learning, and enlightenment, while the multitude are sunk in ignorance and prejudice. Men living at these aristocratic periods are therefore naturally induced to shape their opinions by the standard of a superior person, or a superior class of persons, while they are averse to recognizing the infallibility of the mass of the people.

The contrary takes place in ages of equality. The nearer the people are drawn to the common level of an equal and similar condition, the less prone does each man become to place implicit faith in a certain man or a certain class of men. But his readiness to believe the multitude increases, and opinion is more than ever mistress of the world. Not only is common opinion the only guide which private judgment retains among a democratic people, but among such a people it possesses a power infinitely beyond what it has elsewhere. At periods of equality men have no faith in one another, by reason of their common resemblance; but this very resemblance gives them almost unbounded confidence in the judgment of the public; for it would seem probable that, as they are all endowed with equal means of judging, the greater truth should go with the greater number.

When the inhabitant of a democratic country compares himself in-

dividually with all those about him, he feels with pride that he is the
equal of any one of them; but when he comes to survey the totality of
his fellows and to place himself in contrast with so huge a body, he is
instantly overwhelmed by the sense of his own insignificance and weakness. The same equality that renders him independent of each of his fellow
citizens, taken severally, exposes him alone and unprotected to the influence of the greater number. The public, therefore, among a democratic
people, has a singular power, which aristocratic nations cannot conceive;
for it does not persuade others to its beliefs, but it imposes them and
makes them permeate the thinking of everyone by a sort of enormous
pressure of the mind of all upon the individual intelligence.

In the United States the majority undertakes to supply a multitude of
ready-made opinions for the use of individuals, who are thus relieved from
the necessity of forming opinions of their own. Everybody there adopts
great numbers of theories, on philosophy, morals, and politics, without
inquiry, upon public trust; and if we examine it very closely, it will be
perceived that religion itself holds sway there much less as a doctrine of
revelation than as a commonly received opinion.

The fact that the political laws of the Americans are such that the
majority rules the community with sovereign sway materially increases
the power which that majority naturally exercises over the mind. For
nothing is more customary in man than to recognize superior wisdom in
the person of his oppressor. This political omnipotence of the majority in
the United States doubtless augments the influence that public opinion
would obtain without it over the minds of each member of the community; but the foundations of that influence do not rest upon it. They
must be sought for in the principle of equality itself, not in the more or
less popular institutions which men living under that condition may give
themselves. The intellectual dominion of the greater number would probably be less absolute among a democratic people governed by a king
than in the sphere of a pure democracy, but it will always be extremely
absolute; and by whatever political laws men are governed in the ages of
equality, it may be foreseen that faith in public opinion will become for
them a species of religion, and the majority its ministering prophet.

Thus intellectual authority will be different, but it will not be
diminished; and far from thinking that it will disappear, I augur that it may
readily acquire too much preponderance and confine the action of private
judgment within narrower limits than are suited to either the greatness or
the happiness of the human race. In the principle of equality I very clearly
discern two tendencies; one leading the mind of every man to untried
thoughts, the other prohibiting him from thinking at all. And I perceive
how, under the dominion of certain laws, democracy would extinguish
that liberty of the mind to which a democratic social condition is favorable; so that, after having broken all the bondage once imposed on it by

ranks or by men, the human mind would be closely fettered to the general will of the greatest number.

If the absolute power of a majority were to be substituted by democratic nations for all the different powers that checked or retarded overmuch the energy of individual minds, the evil would only have changed character. Men would not have found the means of independent life; they would simply have discovered (no easy task) a new physiognomy of servitude. There is, and I cannot repeat it too often, there is here matter for profound reflection to those who look on freedom of thought as a holy thing and who hate not only the despot, but despotism. For myself, when I feel the hand of power lie heavy on my brow, I care but little to know who oppresses me; and I am not the more disposed to pass beneath the yoke because it is held out to me by the arms of a million men.

Why the Americans Are More Addicted to Practical Than to Theoretical Science

IF a democratic state of society and democratic institutions do not retard the onward course of the human mind, they incontestably guide it in one direction in preference to another. Their efforts, thus circumscribed, are still exceedingly great, and I may be pardoned if I pause for a moment to contemplate them.

I had occasion, in speaking of the philosophical method of the American people, to make several remarks that it is necessary to make use of here.

Equality begets in man the desire of judging of everything for himself; it gives him in all things a taste for the tangible and the real, a contempt for tradition and for forms. These general tendencies are principally discernible in the peculiar subject of this chapter.

Those who cultivate the sciences among a democratic people are always afraid of losing their way in visionary speculation. They mistrust systems; they adhere closely to facts and study facts with their own senses. As they do not easily defer to the mere name of any fellow man, they are never inclined to rest upon any man's authority; but, on the contrary, they are unremitting in their efforts to find out the weaker points of their neighbor's doctrine. Scientific precedents have little weight with them; they are never long detained by the subtlety of the schools nor ready to accept big words for sterling coin; they penetrate, as far as they can, into the principal parts of the subject that occupies them, and they like to expound them in the popular language. Scientific pursuits then follow a freer and safer course, but a less lofty one.

The mind, it appears to me, may divide science into three parts.

The first comprises the most theoretical principles and those more abstract notions whose application is either unknown or very remote.

The second is composed of those general truths that still belong to pure theory, but lead nevertheless by a straight and short road to practical results.

Methods of application and means of execution make up the third.

Each of these different portions of science may be separately cultivated, although reason and experience prove that no one of them can prosper long if it is absolutely cut off from the two others.

In America the purely practical part of science is admirably understood, and careful attention is paid to the theoretical portion which is immediately requisite to application. On this head the Americans always display a clear, free, original, and inventive power of mind. But hardly anyone in the United States devotes himself to the essentially theoretical and abstract portion of human knowledge. In this respect the Americans carry to excess a tendency that is, I think, discernible, though in a less degree, among all democratic nations.

Nothing is more necessary to the culture of the higher sciences or of the more elevated departments of science than meditation; and nothing is less suited to meditation than the structure of democratic society. We do not find there, as among an aristocratic people, one class that keeps quiet because it is well off; and another that does not venture to stir because it despairs of improving its condition. Everyone is in motion, some in quest of power, others of gain. In the midst of this universal tumult, this incessant conflict of jarring interests, this continual striving of men after fortune, where is that calm to be found which is necessary for the deeper combinations of the intellect? How can the mind dwell upon any single point when everything whirls around it, and man himself is swept and beaten onwards by the heady current that rolls all things in its course?

You must make the distinction between the sort of permanent agitation that is characteristic of a peaceful democracy and the tumultuous and revolutionary movements that almost always attend the birth and growth of democratic society. When a violent revolution occurs among a highly civilized people, it cannot fail to give a sudden impulse to their feelings and ideas. This is more particularly true of democratic revolutions, which stir up at once all the classes of which a people is composed and beget at the same time inordinate ambition in the breast of every member of the community. The French made surprising advances in the exact sciences at the very time at which they were finishing the destruction of the remains of their former feudal society; yet this sudden fecundity is not to be attributed to democracy, but to the unexampled revolution that attended its growth. What happened at that period was a special incident, and it would be unwise to regard it as the test of a general principle.

Great revolutions are not more common among democratic than among other nations; I am even inclined to believe that they are less so. But there prevails among those populations a small, distressing motion, a sort of incessant jostling of men, which annoys and disturbs the mind without exciting or elevating it.

Men who live in democratic communities not only seldom indulge in meditation, but they naturally entertain very little esteem for it. A democratic state of society and democratic institutions keep the greater part of men in constant activity; and the habits of mind that are suited to an active life are not always suited to a contemplative one. The man of action is frequently obliged to content himself with the best he can get because he would never accomplish his purpose if he chose to carry every detail to perfection. He has occasion perpetually to rely on ideas that he has not had leisure to search to the bottom; for he is much more frequently aided by the seasonableness of an idea than by its strict accuracy; and in the long run he risks less in making use of some false principles than in spending his time in establishing all his principles on the basis of truth. The world is not led by long or learned demonstrations; a rapid glance at particular incidents, the daily study of the fleeting passions of the multitude, the accidents of the moment, and the art of turning them to account decide all its affairs.

In the ages in which active life is the condition of almost everyone, men are generally led to attach an excessive value to the rapid bursts and superficial conceptions of the intellect, and on the other hand to undervalue unduly its slower and deeper labors. This opinion of the public influences the judgment of the men who cultivate the sciences; they are persuaded that they may succeed in those pursuits without meditation, or are deterred from such pursuits as demand it.

There are several methods of studying the sciences. Among a multitude of men you will find a selfish, mercantile, and trading taste for the discoveries of the mind, which must not be confounded with that disinterested passion which is kindled in the heart of a few. A desire to utilize knowledge is one thing; the pure desire to know is another. I do not doubt that in a few minds and at long intervals an ardent, inexhaustible love of truth springs up, self-supported and living in ceaseless fruition, without ever attaining full satisfaction. It is this ardent love, this proud, disinterested love of what is true, that raises men to the abstract sources of truth, to draw their mother knowledge thence.

If Pascal had had nothing in view but some large gain, or even if he had been stimulated by the love of fame alone, I cannot conceive that he would ever have been able to rally all the powers of his mind, as he did, for the better discovery of the most hidden things of the Creator. When I see him, as it were, tear his soul from all the cares of life to devote it wholly to these researches and, prematurely snapping the links that bind the body to life, die of old age before forty, I stand amazed and perceive that no ordinary cause is at work to produce efforts so extraordinary.

The future will prove whether these passions, at once so rare and so productive, come into being and into growth as easily in the midst of democratic as in aristocratic communities. For myself, I confess that I am slow to believe it.

In aristocratic societies the class that gives the tone to opinion and has the guidance of affairs, being permanently and hereditarily placed above the multitude, naturally conceives a lofty idea of itself and of man. It loves to invent for him noble pleasures, to carve out splendid objects for his ambition. Aristocracies often commit very tyrannical and inhuman actions, but they rarely entertain groveling thoughts; and they show a kind of haughty contempt of little pleasures, even while they indulge in them. The effect is to raise greatly the general pitch of society. In aristocratic ages vast ideas are commonly entertained of the dignity, the power, and the greatness of man. These opinions exert their influence on those who cultivate the sciences as well as on the rest of the community. They facilitate the natural impulse of the mind to the highest regions of thought, and they naturally prepare it to conceive a sublime, almost a divine love of truth.

Men of science at such periods are consequently carried away towards theory; and it even happens that they frequently conceive an inconsiderate contempt for practice. "Archimedes," says Plutarch, "was of so lofty a spirit that he never condescended to write any treatise on the manner of constructing all these engines of war. And as he held this science of inventing and putting together engines, and all arts generally speaking which tended to any useful end in practice, to be vile, low, and mercenary, he spent his talents and his studious hours in writing only of those things whose beauty and subtlety had in them no admixture of necessity." Such is the aristocratic aim of science; it cannot be the same in democratic nations.

The greater part of the men who constitute these nations are extremely eager in the pursuit of actual and physical gratification. As they are always dissatisfied with the position that they occupy and are always free to leave it, they think of nothing but the means of changing their fortune or increasing it. To minds thus predisposed, every new method that leads by a shorter road to wealth, every machine that spares labor, every instrument that diminishes the cost of production, every discovery that facilitates pleasures or augments them, seems to be the grandest effort of the human intellect. It is chiefly from these motives that a democratic people addicts itself to scientific pursuits, that it understands and respects them. In aristocratic ages science is more particularly called upon to furnish gratification to the mind; in democracies, to the body.

You may be sure that the more democratic, enlightened, and free a nation is, the greater will be the number of these interested promoters of scientific genius and the more will discoveries immediately applicable to productive industry confer on their authors gain, fame, and even power. For in democracies the working class take a part in public affairs;

and public honors as well as pecuniary remuneration may be awarded to those who deserve them.

In a community thus organized, it may easily be conceived that the human mind may be led insensibly to the neglect of theory; and that it is urged, on the contrary, with unparalleled energy, to the applications of science, or at least to that portion of theoretical science which is necessary to those who make such applications. In vain will some instinctive inclination raise the mind towards the loftier spheres of the intellect; interest draws it down to the middle zone. There it may develop all its energy and restless activity and bring forth wonders. These very Americans who have not discovered one of the general laws of mechanics have introduced into navigation an instrument that changes the aspect of the world.

Assuredly I do not contend that the democratic nations of our time are destined to witness the extinction of the great luminaries of man's intelligence, or even that they will never bring new lights into existence. At the age at which the world has now arrived, and among so many cultivated nations perpetually excited by the fever of productive industry, the bonds that connect the different parts of science cannot fail to strike the observer; and the taste for practical science itself, if it is enlightened, ought to lead men not to neglect theory. In the midst of so many attempted applications of so many experiments repeated every day, it is almost impossible that general laws should not frequently be brought to light; so that great discoveries would be frequent, though great inventors may be few.

I believe, moreover, in high scientific vocations. If the democratic principle does not, on the one hand, induce men to cultivate science for its own sake, on the other it enormously increases the number of those who do cultivate it. Nor is it credible that among so great a multitude a speculative genius should not from time to time arise inflamed by the love of truth alone. Such a one, we may be sure, would dive into the deepest mysteries of nature, whatever the spirit of his country and his age. He requires no assistance in his course; it is enough that he is not checked in it. All that I mean to say is this: permanent inequality of conditions leads men to confine themselves to the arrogant and sterile research for abstract truths, while the social condition and the institutions of democracy prepare them to seek the immediate and useful practical results of the sciences. This tendency is natural and inevitable; it is curious to be acquainted with it, and it may be necessary to point it out.

If those who are called upon to guide the nations of our time clearly discerned from afar off these new tendencies, which will soon be irresistible, they would understand that, possessing education and freedom, men living in democratic ages cannot fail to improve the industrial part of science, and that henceforward all the efforts of the constituted authorities ought to be directed to support the highest branches of learning and to foster the nobler passion for science itself. In the present age the human mind must be coerced into theoretical studies; it runs of its own accord to practical applications; and, instead of perpetually referring it to the minute examination of secondary effects, it is well to divert it from them sometimes, in order to raise it up to the contemplation of primary causes.

Because the civilization of ancient Rome perished in consequence of the invasion of the Barbarians, we are perhaps too apt to think that civilization cannot perish in any other manner. If the light by which we are guided is ever extinguished, it will dwindle by degrees and expire of itself. By dint of close adherence to mere applications, principles would be lost sight of; and when the principles were wholly forgotten, the methods derived from them would be ill pursued. New methods could no longer be invented, and men would continue, without intelligence and without art, to apply scientific processes no longer understood.

When Europeans first arrived in China, three hundred years ago, they found that almost all the arts had reached a certain degree of perfection there, and they were surprised that a people which had attained this point should not have gone beyond it. At a later period they discovered traces of some higher branches of science that had been lost. The nation was absorbed in productive industry; the greater part of its scientific processes had been preserved, but science itself no longer existed there. This served to explain the strange immobility in which they found the minds of this people. The Chinese, in following the track of their forefathers, had forgotten the reasons by which the latter had been guided. They still used the formula without asking for its meaning; they retained the instrument, but they no longer possessed the art of altering or renewing it. The Chinese, then, had lost the power of change; for them improvement was impossible. They were compelled at all times and in all points to imitate their predecessors lest they should stray into utter darkness by deviating for an instant from the path already laid down for them. The source of human knowledge was all but dry; and though the stream still ran on, it could neither swell its waters nor alter its course.

Notwithstanding this, China had existed peaceably for centuries. The invaders who had conquered the country assumed the manners of the inhabitants, and order prevailed there. A sort of physical prosperity was everywhere discernible; revolutions were rare, and war was, so to speak, unknown.

It is then a fallacy to flatter ourselves with the reflection that the barbarians are still far from us; for if there are some nations that allow civilization to be torn from their grasp, there are others who themselves trample it underfoot.

General Survey of the Subject

BEFORE finally closing the subject that I have now discussed, I should like to take a parting survey of all the different characteristics of modern society and appreciate at last the general influence to be exercised by the principle of equality upon the fate of mankind; but I am stopped by the difficulty of the task, and, in presence of so great a theme, my sight is troubled and my reason fails.

The society of the modern world, which I have sought to delineate and which I seek to judge, has but just come into existence. Time has not yet shaped it into perfect form; the great revolution by which it has been created is not yet over; and amid the occurrences of our time it is almost impossible to discern what will pass away with the revolution itself and what will survive its close. The world that is rising into existence is still half encumbered by the remains of the world that is waning into decay; and amid the vast perplexity of human affairs none can say how much of ancient institutions and former customs will remain or how much will completely disappear.

Although the revolution that is taking place in the social condition, the laws, the opinions, and the feelings of men is still very far from being terminated, yet its results already admit of no comparison with anything that the world has ever before witnessed. I go back from age to age up to the remotest antiquity, but I find no parallel to what is occurring before my eyes; as the past has ceased to throw its light upon the future, the mind of man wanders in obscurity.

Nevertheless, in the midst of a prospect so wide, so novel, and so confused, some of the more prominent characteristics may already be discerned and pointed out. The good things and the evils of life are more equally distributed in the world: great wealth tends to disappear, the number of small fortunes to increase; desires and gratifications are multiplied, but extraordinary prosperity and irremediable penury are alike unknown. The sentiment of ambition is universal, but the scope of ambition is seldom vast. Each individual stands apart in solitary weakness, but society at large is active, provident, and powerful; the performances of private persons are insignificant, those of the state immense.

There is little energy of character, but customs are mild and laws humane. If there are few instances of exalted heroism or of virtues of the highest, brightest, and purest temper, men's habits are regular, violence is rare, and cruelty almost unknown. Human existence becomes longer and property more secure; life is not adorned with brilliant trophies, but it is extremely easy and tranquil. Few pleasures are either very refined or very coarse, and highly polished manners are as uncommon as great brutality of tastes. Neither men of great learning nor extremely ignorant communities are to be met with; genius becomes more rare, information more diffused. The human mind is impelled by the small efforts of all mankind combined together, not by the strenuous activity of a few men. There is less perfection, but more abundance, in all the productions of the arts. The ties of race, of rank, and of country are relaxed; the great bond of humanity is strengthened.

If I endeavor to find out the most general and most prominent of all these different characteristics, I perceive that what is taking place in men's fortunes manifests itself under a thousand other forms. Almost all extremes are softened or blunted: all that was most prominent is superseded by some middle term, at once less lofty and less low, less brilliant and less obscure, than what before existed in the world.

When I survey this countless multitude of beings, shaped in each other's likeness, amid whom nothing rises and nothing falls, the sight of such universal uniformity saddens and chills me and I am tempted to regret that state of society which has ceased to be. When the world was full of men of great importance and extreme insignificance, of great wealth and extreme poverty, of great learning and extreme ignorance, I turned aside from the latter to fix my observation on the former alone, who gratified my sympathies. But I admit that this gratification arose from my own weakness; it is because I am unable to see at once all that is around me that I am allowed thus to select and separate the objects of my predilection from among so many others. Such is not the case with that Almighty and Eternal Being whose gaze necessarily includes the whole of created things and who surveys distinctly, though all at once, mankind and man.

We may naturally believe that it is not the singular prosperity of the few, but the greater well-being of all that is most pleasing in the sight of the Creator and Preserver of men. What appears to me to be man's decline is, to His eye, advancement; what afflicts me is acceptable to Him. A state of equality is perhaps less elevated, but it is more just: and its justice constitutes its greatness and its beauty. I would strive, then, to raise myself to this point of the divine contemplation and thence to view and to judge the concerns of men.

No man on the earth can as yet affirm, absolutely and generally, that the new state of the world is better than its former one; but it is already easy to perceive that this state is different. Some vices and some virtues were so inherent in the constitution of an aristocratic nation and are so opposite to the character of a modern people that they can never be infused into it; some good tendencies and some bad propensities which were unknown to the former are natural to the latter; some ideas suggest themselves spontaneously to the imagination of the one which are utterly repugnant to the mind of the other. They are like two distinct orders of human beings, each of which has its own merits and defects, its own advantages and its own evils. Care must therefore be taken not to judge the state of society that is now coming into existence by notions derived from a state of society that no longer exists; for as these states of society are exceedingly different in their structure, they cannot be submitted to a just or fair comparison. It would be scarcely more reasonable to require of our contemporaries the peculiar virtues which originated in the social condition of their forefathers, since that social condition is itself fallen and has drawn into one promiscuous ruin the good and evil that belonged to it.

But as yet these things are imperfectly understood. I find that a great number of my contemporaries undertake to make a selection from among the institutions, the opinions, and the ideas that originated in the aristocratic constitution of society as it was; a portion of these elements they would willingly relinquish, but they would keep the remainder and transplant them into their new world. I fear that such men are wasting their time and their strength in virtuous but unprofitable efforts. The object is, not to retain the peculiar advantages which the inequality of conditions bestows upon mankind, but to secure the new benefits which equality may supply. We have not to seek to make ourselves like our progenitors, but to strive to work out that species of greatness and happiness which is our own.

For myself, who now look back from this extreme limit of my task and discover from afar, but at once, the various objects which have attracted my more attentive investigation upon my way, I am full of apprehensions and of hopes. I perceive mighty dangers which it is possible to ward off, mighty evils which may be avoided or alleviated; and I cling with a firmer hold to the belief that for democratic nations to be virtuous and prosperous, they require but to will it.

I am aware that many of my contemporaries maintain that nations are never their own masters here below, and that they necessarily obey some insurmountable and unintelligent power, arising from anterior events, from their race, or from the soil and climate of their country. Such principles are false and cowardly; such principles can never produce aught but feeble men and pusillanimous nations. Providence has not created mankind entirely independent or entirely free. It is true that around every man a fatal circle is traced beyond which he cannot pass; but within the wide verge of that circle he is powerful and free; as it is with man, so with communities. The nations of our time cannot prevent the conditions of men from becoming equal, but it depends upon themselves whether the principle of equality is to lead them to servitude or freedom, to knowledge or barbarism, to prosperity or wretchedness.

CHARLES DICKENS

When Dickens (1812–1870) first arrived in the United States in January, 1842, he was not yet thirty and already a great celebrity. Born into a poor family, he had become a wage-earner at twelve. He had clerked in a lawyer's office, become a stenographer-reporter in the House of Commons, and been launched into continuous fame and fortune by the publication of the Pickwick Papers *in 1837. By the time of the American trip he had published five more novels, including* Oliver Twist, Nicholas Nickleby, *and* The Old Curiosity Shop, *and was received as "a guest of the Nation." He toured most of the country for four months, returned to England in May, and soon thereafter published* American Notes *for General Circulation. This account, and the satirical American scenes in* Martin Chuzzlewit *(1844), did little to endear Dickens to American readers. Dickens, trying to be as complimentary as he could, nevertheless took a dislike to American ways, and his legendary eye for detail betrayed him on every side. Nor was a man of his temperament likely to be pleased with some of the prisons he visited or with the institution of slavery. Dickens belatedly tried to make amends for the tone of the* Notes *in the "Post-script" added after his trip in 1868.*

CONCLUDING REMARKS
FROM AMERICAN NOTES

THERE are many passages in this book, where I have been at some pains to resist the temptation of troubling my readers with my own deductions and conclusions: preferring that they should judge for themselves, from such premises as I have laid before them. My only object in the outset, was, to carry them with me faithfully wheresoever I went: and that task I have discharged.

But I may be pardoned, if on such a theme as the general character of the American people, and the general character of their social system, as presented to a stranger's eyes, I desire to express my own opinions in a few words, before I bring these volumes to a close.

They are, by nature, frank, brave, cordial, hospitable, and affectionate. Cultivation and refinement seem but to enhance their warmth of heart and ardent enthusiasm; and it is the possession of these latter qualities in a most remarkable degree, which renders an educated American one of the most endearing and most generous of friends. I never was so won upon, as by this class; never yielded up my full confidence and esteem so readily and pleasurably, as to them; never can make again, in half a year, so many friends for whom I seem to entertain the regard of half a life.

These qualities are natural, I implicitly believe, to the whole people. That they are, however, sadly sapped and blighted in their growth among the mass; and that there are influences at work which endanger them still more, and give but little present promise of their healthy restoration; is a truth that ought to be told.

It is an essential part of every national character to pique itself mightily upon its faults, and to deduce tokens of its virtue or its wisdom from their very exaggeration. One great blemish in the popular mind of America, and the prolific parent of an innumerable brood of evils, is Universal Distrust. Yet the American citizen plumes himself upon this spirit, even when he is sufficiently dispassionate to perceive the ruin it works; and will often adduce it, in spite of his own reason, as an instance of the great sagacity and acuteness of the people, and their superior shrewdness and independence.

"You carry," says the stranger, "this jealousy and distrust into every transaction of public life. By repelling worthy men from your legislative assemblies, it has bred up a class of candidates for the suffrage, who, in their every act, disgrace your Institutions and your people's choice. It has rendered you so fickle, and so given to change, that your inconstancy has passed into a proverb; for you no sooner set up an idol firmly, than you are sure to pull it down and dash it into fragments: and this, because directly you reward a benefactor, or a public servant, you distrust him, merely because he *is* rewarded; and immediately apply yourselves to find out, either that you have been too bountiful in your acknowledgments, or he remiss in his deserts. Any man who attains a high place among you, from the President downwards, may date his downfall from that moment; for any printed lie that any notorious villain pens, although it militate directly against the character and conduct of a life, appeals at once to your distrust, and is believed. You will strain at a gnat in the way of trustfulness and confidence, however fairly won and well deserved; but you will swallow a whole caravan of camels, if they be laden with unworthy doubts and mean suspicions. Is this well, think you, or likely to elevate the character of the governors or the governed, among you?"

The answer is invariably the same: "There's freedom of opinion here, you know. Every man thinks for himself, and we are not to be easily overreached. That's how our people come to be suspicious."

Another prominent feature is the love of "smart" dealing: which gilds over many a swindle and gross breach of trust; many a defalcation, public and private; and enables many a knave to hold his head up with the best, who well deserves a halter; though it has not been without its retributive operation, for this smartness has done more in a few years to impair the public credit, and to cripple the public resources, than dull honesty, however rash, could have effected in a century. The merits of a broken speculation, or a bankruptcy, or of a successful scoundrel, are not gauged by its or his observance of the golden rule, "Do as you would be done by," but are considered with reference to their smartness. I recollect, on both occasions of our passing that ill-fated Cairo on the Mississippi, remarking on the bad effects such gross deceits must have when they exploded, in generating a want of confidence abroad, and discouraging foreign investment: but I was given to understand that this was a very smart scheme by which a deal of money had been made: and that its smartest feature was, that they forgot these things abroad, in a very short time, and speculated again, as freely as ever. The following dialogue I have held a hundred times: "Is it not a very disgraceful circumstance that such a man as So-and-so should be acquiring a large property by the most infamous and odious means, and notwithstanding all the crimes of which he has been guilty, should be tolerated and abetted by your Citizens? He is a public nuisance, is he not?" "Yes, Sir." "A convicted liar?" "Yes, Sir." "He has been kicked, and cuffed, and caned?" "Yes, Sir." "And he is utterly dishonourable, debased, and profligate?" "Yes, Sir." "In the name of wonder, then, what is his merit?" "Well, Sir, he is a smart man."

In like manner, all kinds of deficient and impolitic usages are referred to the national love of trade; though, oddly enough, it would be a weighty charge against a foreigner that he regarded the Americans as a trading people. The love of trade is assigned as a reason for that comfortless custom, so very prevalent in country towns, of married persons living in hotels, having no fireside of their own, and seldom meeting from early morning until late at night, but at the hasty public meals. The love of trade is a reason why the literature of America is to remain for ever unprotected: "For we are a trading people, and don't care for poetry:" though we *do*, by the way, profess to be very proud of our poets: while healthful amusements, cheerful means of recreation, and wholesome fancies, must fade before the stern utilitarian joys of trade.

These three characteristics are strongly presented at every turn, full in the stranger's view. But, the foul growth of America has a more tangled root than this; and it strikes its fibres, deep in its licentious Press.

Schools may be erected, East, West, North, and South; pupils be taught, and masters reared, by scores upon scores of thousands; colleges may thrive, churches may be crammed, temperance may be diffused, and advancing knowledge in all other forms walk through the land with giant strides: but while the newspaper press of America is in, or near, its present abject state, high moral improvement in that country is hopeless. Year by year, it must and will go back; year by year, the tone of public feeling must sink lower down; year by year, the Congress and the Senate must become of less account before all decent men; and year by year, the memory of the Great Fathers of the Revolution must be outraged more and more, in the bad life of their degenerate child.

Among the herd of journals which are published in the States, there are some, the reader scarcely need be told, of character and credit. From personal intercourse with accomplished gentlemen connected with publications of this class, I have derived both pleasure and profit. But the name of these is Few, and of the others Legion; and the influence of the good, is powerless to counteract the moral poison of the bad.

Among the gentry of America; among the well-informed and moderate: in the learned professions; at the bar and on the bench: there is, as there can be, but one opinion, in reference to the vicious character of these infamous journals. It is sometimes contended—I will not say strangely, for it is natural to seek excuses for such a disgrace—that their influence is not so great as a visitor would suppose. I must be pardoned for saying that there is no warrant for this plea, and that every fact and circumstance tends directly to the opposite conclusion.

When any man, of any grade of desert in intellect or character, can climb to any public distinction, no matter what, in America, without first grovelling down upon the earth, and bending the knee before this monster of depravity; when any private excellence is safe from its attacks; when any social confidence is left unbroken by it, or any tie of social decency and honour is held in the least regard; when any man in that free country has freedom of opinion, and presumes to think for himself, and speak for himself, without humble reference to a censorship which, for its rampant ignorance and base dishonesty, he utterly loathes and despises in his heart; when those who most acutely feel its infamy and the reproach it casts upon the nation, and who most denounce it to each other, dare to set their heels upon, and crush it openly, in the sight of all men: then, I will believe that its influence is lessening, and men are returning to their manly senses. But while that Press has its evil eye in every house, and its black hand in every appointment in the state, from a president to a postman; while, with ribald slander for its only stock-in-trade, it is the standard literature of an enormous class, who must find their reading in a newspaper, or they will not read at all; so long must its odium be upon the country's head, and so long must the evil it works, be plainly visible in the Republic.

To those who are accustomed to the leading English journals, or to the respectable journals of the Continent of Europe; to those who are accustomed to anything else in print and paper; it would be impossible, without an amount of extract for which I have neither space nor inclination, to convey an adequate idea of this frightful engine in America. But if any man desire confirmation of my statement on this head, let him repair to any place in this city of London, where scattered numbers of these publications are to be found; and there, let him form his own opinion.[1]

It would be well, there can be no doubt, for the American people as a whole, if they loved the Real less, and the Ideal somewhat more. It would be well, if there were greater encouragement to lightness of heart and gaiety, and a wider cultivation of what is beautiful, without being eminently and directly useful. But here, I think the general remonstrance, "we are a new country," which is so often advanced as an excuse for defects which are quite unjustifiable, as being, of right, only the slow growth of an old one, may be very reasonably urged: and I yet hope to hear of there being some other national amusement in the United States, besides newspaper politics.

They certainly are not a humorous people, and their temperament always impressed me as being of a dull and gloomy character. In shrewdness of remark, and a certain cast-iron quaintness, the Yankees, or people of New England, unquestionably take the lead; as they do in most other evidences of intelligence. But in travelling about, out of the large cities—as I have remarked in former parts of these volumes—I was quite oppressed by the prevailing seriousness and melancholy air of business: which was so general and unvarying, that at every new town I came to, I seemed to meet the very same people whom I had left behind me, at the last. Such defects as are perceptible in the national manners, seem, to me, to be referable, in a great degree, to this cause: which has generated a dull, sullen persistence in coarse usages, and rejected the graces of life as undeserving of attention. There is no doubt that Washington, who was always most scrupulous and exact on points of ceremony, perceived the tendency towards this mistake, even in his time, and did his utmost to correct it.

I cannot hold with other writers on these subjects that the prevalence of various forms of dissent in America, is in any way attributable to the non-existence there of an established church: indeed, I think the temper of the people, if it admitted of such an Institution being founded amongst them, would lead them to desert it, as a matter of course, merely because

---

[1] NOTE TO THE ORIGINAL EDITION.—Or let him refer to an able, and perfectly truthful article, in *The Foreign Quarterly Review*, published in the present month of October [1842]; to which my attention has been attracted, since these sheets have been passing through the press. He will find some specimens there, by no means remarkable to any man who has been in America, but sufficiently striking to one who has not.

it *was* established. But, supposing it to exist, I doubt its probable efficacy in summoning the wandering sheep to one great fold, simply because of the immense amount of dissent which prevails at home; and because I do not find in America any one form of religion with which we in Europe, or even in England, are unacquainted. Dissenters resort thither in great numbers, as other people do, simply because it is a land of resort; and great settlements of them are founded, because ground can be purchased, and towns and villages reared, where there were none of the human creation before. But even the Shakers emigrated from England; our country is not unknown to Mr. Joseph Smith, the apostle of Mormonism, or to his benighted disciples; I have beheld religious scenes myself in some of our populous towns which can hardly be surpassed by an American camp-meeting; and I am not aware that any instance of superstitious imposture on the one hand, and superstitious credulity on the other, has had its origin in the United States, which we cannot more than parallel by the precedents of Mrs. Southcote, Mary Tofts the rabbit-breeder, or even Mr. Thom of Canterbury: which latter case arose, some time after the dark ages had passed away.

The Republican Institutions of America undoubtedly lead the people to assert their self-respect and their equality; but a traveller is bound to bear those Institutions in his mind, and not hastily to resent the near approach of a class of strangers, who, at home, would keep aloof. This characteristic, when it was tinctured with no foolish pride, and stopped short of no honest service, never offended me; and I very seldom, if ever, experienced its rude or unbecoming display. Once or twice it was comically developed, as in the following case; but this was an amusing incident, and not the rule, or near it.

I wanted a pair of boots at a certain town, for I had none to travel in, but those with the memorable cork soles, which were much too hot for the fiery decks of a steamboat. I therefore sent a message to an artist in boots, importing, with my compliments, that I should be happy to see him, if he would do me the polite favour to call. He very kindly returned for answer, that he would "look round" at six o'clock that evening.

I was lying on the sofa, with a book and a wine-glass, at about that time, when the door opened, and a gentleman in a stiff cravat, within a year or two on either side of thirty, entered, in his hat and gloves; walked up to the looking-glass; arranged his hair; took off his gloves; slowly produced a measure from the uttermost depths of his coat-pocket; and requested me, in a languid tone, to "unfix" my straps. I complied, but looked with some curiosity at his hat, which was still upon his head. It might have been that, or it might have been the heat—but he took it off. Then, he sat himself down on a chair opposite to me; rested an arm on each knee; and, leaning forward very much, took from the ground, by a great effort, the specimen of metropolitan workmanship which I had just pulled off: whistling, pleasantly, as he did so. He turned it over and over; surveyed it with a contempt no language can express; and inquired if I wished him to fix me a boot like *that?* I courteously replied, that provided the boots were large enough, I would leave the rest to him; that if convenient and practicable, I should not object to their bearing some resemblance to the model then before him; but that I would be entirely guided by, and would beg to leave the whole subject to, his judgment and discretion. "You an't partickler, about this scoop in the heel, I suppose then?" says he: "we don't foller that, here." I repeated my last observation. He looked at himself in the glass again; went closer to it to dash a grain or two of dust out of the corner of his eye; and settled his cravat. All this time, my leg and foot were in the air. "Nearly ready, Sir?" I inquired. "Well, pretty nigh," he said; "keep steady." I kept as steady as I could, both in foot and face; and having by this time got the dust out, and found his pencil-case, he measured me, and made the necessary notes. When he had finished, he fell into his old attitude, and taking up the boot again, mused for some time. "And this," he said, at last, "is an English boot, is it? This is a London boot, eh?" "That, Sir," I replied, "is a London boot." He mused over it again, after the manner of Hamlet with Yorick's skull; nodded his head, as who should say, "I pity the Institutions that led to the production of this boot;" rose; put up his pencil, notes, and paper—glancing at himself in the glass, all the time—put on his hat; drew on his gloves very slowly; and finally walked out. When he had been gone about a minute, the door reopened, and his hat and his head reappeared. He looked round the room, and at the boot again, which was still lying on the floor; appeared thoughtful for a minute; and then said "Well, good arternoon." "Good afternoon, Sir," said I: and that was the end of the interview.

There is but one other head on which I wish to offer a remark; and that has reference to the public health. In so vast a country, where there are thousands of millions of acres of land yet unsettled and uncleared, and on every rood of which, vegetable decomposition is annually taking place; where there are so many great rivers, and such opposite varieties of climate; there cannot fail to be a great amount of sickness at certain seasons. But I may venture to say, after conversing with many members of the medical profession in America, that I am not singular in the opinion that much of the disease which does prevail, might be avoided, if a few common precautions were observed. Greater means of personal cleanliness, are indispensable to this end; the custom of hastily swallowing large quantities of animal food, three times a-day, and rushing back to sedentary pursuits after each meal, must be changed; the gentler sex must go more wisely clad, and take more healthful exercise; and in the latter clause, the males must be included also. Above all, in public institutions, and throughout the whole of every town and city, the system of ventilation, and drainage, and removal of impurities requires to be thoroughly revised. There is no local Legislature in America which may not study

Mr. Chadwick's excellent Report upon the Sanitary Condition of our Labouring Classes, with immense advantage.

I have now arrived at the close of this book. I have little reason to believe, from certain warnings I have had since I returned to England, that it will be tenderly or favourably received by the American people; and as I have written the Truth in relation to the mass of those who form their judgments and express their opinions, it will be seen that I have no desire to court, by any adventitious means, the popular applause.

It is enough for me, to know, that what I have set down in these pages, cannot cost me a single friend on the other side of the Atlantic, who is, in anything, deserving of the name. For the rest, I put my trust, implicitly, in the spirit in which they have been conceived and penned; and I can bide my time.

I have made no reference to my reception, nor have I suffered it to influence me in what I have written; for, in either case, I should have offered but a sorry acknowledgment, compared with that I bear within my breast, towards those partial readers of my former books, across the Water, who met me with an open hand, and not with one that closed upon an iron muzzle.

Postscript

AT a Public Dinner given to me on Saturday the 18th of April, 1868, in the City of New York, by two hundred representatives of the Press of the United States of America, I made the following observations among others:

"So much of my voice has lately been heard in the land, that I might have been contented with troubling you no further from my present standing-point, were it not a duty with which I henceforth charge myself, not only here but on every suitable occasion, whatsoever and wheresoever, to express my high and grateful sense of my second reception in America, and to bear my honest testimony to the national generosity and magnanimity. Also, to declare how astounded I have been by the amazing changes I have seen around me on every side,— changes moral, changes physical, changes in the amount of land subdued and peopled, changes in the rise of vast new cities, changes in the growth of older cities almost out of recognition, changes in the graces and amenities of life, changes in the Press, without whose advancement no advancement can take place anywhere. Nor am I, believe me, so arrogant as to suppose that in five-and-twenty years there have been no changes in me, and that I had nothing to learn and no extreme impressions to correct when I was here first. And this brings me to a point on which I have, ever since I landed in the United States last November, observed a strict silence, though sometimes tempted to break it, but in reference to which I will, with your good leave, take you into my confidence now. Even the Press, being human, may be sometimes mistaken or misinformed, and I rather think that I have in one or two rare instances observed its information to be not strictly accurate with reference to myself. Indeed, I have, now and again, been more surprised by printed news that I have read of myself, than by any printed news that I have ever read in my present state of existence. Thus, the vigour and perseverance with which I have for some months past been collecting materials for, and hammering away at, a new book on America has much astonished me; seeing that all that time my declaration has been perfectly well known to my publishers on both sides of the Atlantic, that no consideration on earth would induce me to write one. But what I have intended, what I have resolved upon (and this is the confidence I seek to place in you) is, on my return to England, in my own person, in my own Journal, to bear, for the behoof of my countrymen, such testimony to the gigantic changes in this country as I have hinted at to-night. Also, to record that wherever I have been, in the smallest places equally with the largest, I have been received with unsurpassable politeness, delicacy, sweet temper, hospitality, consideration, and with unsurpassable respect for the privacy daily enforced upon me by the nature of my avocation here and the state of my health. This testimony, so long as I live, and so long as my descendants have any legal right in my books, I shall cause to be republished, as an appendix to every copy of those two books of mine in which I have referred to America. And this I will do and cause to be done, not in mere love and thankfulness, but because I regard it as an act of plain justice and honour."

I said these words with the greatest earnestness that I could lay upon them, and I repeat them in print here with equal earnestness. So long as this book shall last, I hope that they will form a part of it, and will be fairly read as inseparable from my experiences and impressions of America.

May, 1868.

RAOUL DE ROUSSY DE SALES

Raoul de Roussy de Sales (1896–1942), Parisian-born journalist, was sent to this country by the Revue de Paris *in 1932 to cover the New Deal. Two years later he was appointed special American correspondent for the daily* Paris-Midi *and, thereafter, was also correspondent for* Paris-Soir *and* L'Europe nouvelle. *He was twice President of the Association of Foreign Correspondents in the United States, and after the fall of France in 1940 he served as chancellor of the Fighting French delegation. He was co-author of* You Americans *(1939), edited* They Speak for a Nation: Letters from France *(1941), and wrote* The Making of Tomorrow *(1942). His diaries were published posthumously in 1947 under the title* The Making of Yesterday. *The following essay appeared in the May, 1938,* Atlantic Monthly.

LOVE IN AMERICA

I

America appears to be the only country in the world where love is a national problem.

Nowhere else can one find a people devoting so much time and so much study to the question of the relationship between men and women. Nowhere else is there such concern about the fact that this relationship does not always make for perfect happiness. The great majority of the Americans of both sexes seem to be in a state of chronic bewilderment in the face of a problem which they are certainly not the first to confront, but which—unlike other people—they still refuse to accept as one of those gifts of the gods which one might just as well take as it is: a mixed blessing at times, and at other times a curse or merely a nuisance.

The prevailing conception of love, in America, is similar to the idea of democracy. It is fine in theory. It is the grandest system ever evolved by man to differentiate him from his ancestors, the poor brutes who lived in caverns, or from the apes. Love is perfect, in fact, and there is nothing better. But, like democracy, it does not work, and the Americans feel that something should be done about it. President Roosevelt is intent on making democracy work. Everybody is trying to make love work, too.

In either case the result is not very satisfactory. The probable reason is that democracy and love are products of a long and complicated series of compromises between the desires of the heart and the exactions of reason. They have a peculiar way of crumbling into ashes as soon as one tries too hard to organize them too well.

The secret of making a success out of democracy and love in their practical applications is to allow for a fairly wide margin of errors, and not to forget that human beings are absolutely unable to submit to a uniform rule for any length of time. But this does not satisfy a nation that, in spite of its devotion to pragmatism, also believes in perfection.

For a foreigner to speak of the difficulties that the Americans encounter in such an intimate aspect of their mutual relationship may appear as an impertinence. But the truth is that no foreigner would ever think of bringing up such a subject of his own accord. In fact, foreigners who come to these shores are quite unsuspecting of the existence of such a national problem. It is their initial observation that the percentage of good-looking women and handsome men is high on this continent, that they are youthful and healthy in mind and body, and that their outlook on life is rather optimistic.

If the newcomers have seen enough American moving pictures before landing here—and they usually have—they must have gathered the impression that love in America is normally triumphant, and that, in spite of many unfortunate accidents, a love story cannot but end very well indeed. They will have noticed that these love stories which are acted in Hollywood may portray quite regrettable situations at times and that blissful unions get wrecked by all sorts of misfortunes. But they never remain wrecked: even when the happy couple is compelled to divorce, this is not the end of everything. In most cases it is only the beginning. Very soon they will remarry, sometimes with one another, and always— without ever an exception—for love.

The observant foreigner knows, of course, that he cannot trust the movies to give him a really reliable picture of the American attitude towards love, marriage, divorce, and remarriage. But they nevertheless indicate that in such matters the popular mind likes to be entertained by the idea (1) that love is the only reason why a man and a woman should get married; (2) that love is always wholesome, genuine, uplifting, and fresh, like a glass of Grade A milk; (3) that when, for some reason or other, it fails to keep you uplifted, wholesome, and fresh, the only thing to do is to begin all over again with another partner.

Thus forewarned, the foreigner who lands on these shores would be very tactless indeed if he started questioning the validity of these premises. Besides, it is much more likely that he himself will feel thoroughly transformed the moment he takes his first stroll in the streets of New York. His European skepticism will evaporate a little more at each step, and if he considers himself not very young any more he will be immensely gratified to find that maturity and even old age are merely European habits of thought, and that he might just as well adopt the American method, which is to be young and act young for the rest of his life—or at least until the expiration of his visa.

If his hotel room is equipped with a radio, his impression that he has at last reached the land of eternal youth and perfect love will be confirmed at any hour of the day and on any point of the dial. No country in the world consumes such a fabulous amount of love songs. Whether the song is gay or nostalgic, the tune catchy or banal, the verses clever or silly, the theme is always love and nothing but love.

Whenever I go back to France and listen to the radio, I am always surprised to find that so many songs can be written on other subjects. I have no statistics on hand, but I think that a good 75 per cent of the songs one hears on the French radio programmes deal with politics. There are love songs, of course, but most of them are far from romantic, and this is quite in keeping with the French point of view that love is very often an exceedingly comical affair.

In America the idea seems to be that love, like so much else, should be sold to the public, because it is a good thing. The very word, when heard indefinitely, becomes an obsession. It penetrates one's subconsciousness like the name of some unguent to cure heartaches or athlete's foot. It fits in with the other advertisements, and one feels tempted to write to the broadcasting station for a free sample of this thing called Love.

Thus the visitor from Europe is rapidly permeated with a delightful atmosphere of romanticism and sweetness. He wonders why Italy and Spain ever acquired their reputation of being the lands of romance. This, he says to himself, is the home of poetry and passion. The Americans are the real heirs of the troubadours, and station WXZQ is their love court.

To discover that all this ballyhoo about love (which is not confined to the radio or the movies) is nothing but an aspect of the national optimistic outlook on life does not take very long. It usually becomes evident when the foreign visitor receives the confidences of one or more of the charming American women he will chance to meet. This normally happens after the first or second cocktail party to which he has been invited.

II

I wish at this point to enter a plea in defense of the foreign visitor, against whom a great many accusations are often made either in print or in conversation. These accusations fall under two heads. If the foreigner seems to have no definite objective in visiting America, he is strongly suspected of trying to marry an heiress. If for any reason he cannot be suspected of this intention, then his alleged motives are considerably more sinister. Many American men, and quite a few women, believe that the art of wrecking a happy home is not indigenous to this continent, and that in Europe it has been perfected to such a point that to practise it has become a reflex with the visitors from abroad.

It is very true that some foreign visitors come over here to marry for money in exchange for a title or for some sort of glamour. But there are many more foreigners who marry American women for other reasons besides money, and I know quite a few who have become so Americanized that they actually have married for love and for nothing else.

As for the charge that the Europeans are more expert than the Americans in spoiling someone else's marital happiness, it seems to me an unfair accusation. In most cases the initiative of spoiling whatever it is that remains to be spoiled in a shaky marriage is normally taken by one of the married pair, and the wrecker of happiness does not need any special talent to finish the job.

What is quite true, however, is that the American woman entertains the delightful illusion that there *must* be some man on this earth who can understand her. It seems incredible to her that love, within legal bonds or outside of them, should not work out as advertised. From her earliest years she has been told that success is the ultimate aim of life. Her father and mother made an obvious success of their lives by creating her. Her husband is, or wants to be, a successful business man. Every day 130,-000,000 people are panting and sweating to make a success of something or other. Success—the constant effort to make things work perfectly and the conviction that they can be made to—is the great national preoccupation.

And what does one do to make a success?

Well, the answer is very simple: one learns how, or one consults an expert.

That is what her husband does when he wants to invest his money or improve the efficiency of his business. That is what she did herself when she decided to 'decorate' her house. In the American way of life there are no insoluble problems. You may not know the answer yourself, but nobody doubts that the answer exists—that there is some method or perhaps some trick by which all riddles can be solved and success achieved.

And so the European visitor is put to the task on the presumption that the accumulation of experience which he brings with him may qualify him as an expert in questions of sentiment.

The American woman does not want to be understood for the mere fun of it. What she actually wishes is to be helped to solve certain difficulties which, in her judgment, impede the successful development of her inner self. She seldom accepts the idea that maladjustments and misunderstandings are not only normal but bearable once you have made up your mind that, whatever may be the ultimate aim of our earthly existence, perfect happiness through love or any other form of expression is not part of the programme.

III

One of the greatest moral revolutions that ever happened in America was the popularization of Freud's works.

Up to the time that occurred, as far as I am able to judge, America lived in a blissful state of puritanical repression. Love, as a sentiment, was glorified and sanctified by marriage. There was a general impression that some sort of connection existed between the sexual impulses and the vagaries of the heart, but this connection was not emphasized, and the consensus of opinion was that the less said about it the better. The way certain nations, and particularly the French, correlated the physical manifestations of love and its more spiritual aspects was considered particularly objectionable. Love, in other words,—and that was not very long ago,—had not changed since the contrary efforts of the puritanically-minded and the romantic had finally stabilized it midway between the sublime and the parlor game.

The important point is that up to then (and ever since the first Pilgrims set foot on this continent) love had been set aside in the general scheme of American life as the one thing which could not be made to work better than it did. Each one had to cope with his own difficulties in his own way and solve them as privately as he could. It was not a national problem.

Whether or not people were happier under that system is beside the point. It probably does not matter very much whether we live and die with or without a full set of childish complexes and repressions. My own view is that most people are neither complex nor repressed enough as a rule; I wish sometimes for the coming of the Anti-Freud who will complicate and obscure everything again.

But the fact is that the revelations of psychoanalysis were greeted in America as the one missing link in the general programme of universal improvement.

Here was a system, at last, that explained fully why love remained so imperfect. It reduced the whole dilemma of happiness to sexual maladjustments, which in turn were only the result of the mistakes made by one's father, mother, or nurse, at an age when one could certainly not be expected to foresee the consequences. Psychoanalysis integrated human emotions into a set of mechanistic formulas. One learned with great relief that the failure to find happiness was not irreparable. Love, as a sublime communion of souls and bodies, was not a legend, nor the mere fancy of the poets. It was real, and—more important still—practically attainable.

Anybody could have it, merely by removing a few obstructions which had been growing within himself since childhood like mushrooms in a dark cellar. Love could be made to work like anything else.

It is true that not many people are interested in psychoanalysis any more. As a fad or a parlor game, it is dead. Modern débutantes will not know what you are talking about if you mention the Œdipus complex or refer to the symbolic meaning of umbrellas and top hats in dreams. Traditions die young these days. But the profound effect of the Freudian revelation has lasted. From its materialistic interpretation of sexual impulses, coupled with the American longing for moral perfection, a new science has been born: the dialectics of love; and also a new urge for the American people —they want to turn out, eventually, a perfect product. They want to get out of love as much enjoyment, comfort, safety, and general sense of satisfaction, as one gets out of a well-balanced diet or a good plumbing installation.

IV

Curiously enough, this fairly new point of view which implies that human relationships are governed by scientific laws has not destroyed the romantic ideal of love. Quite the contrary. Maladjustments, now that they are supposed to be scientifically determined, have become much more unbearable than in the horse-and-buggy age of love. Husbands and wives and lovers have no patience with their troubles. They want to be cured, and when they think they are incurable they become very intolerant. Reformers always are.

Usually, however, various attempts at readjustment are made with devastating candor. Married couples seem to spend many precious hours of the day and night discussing what is wrong with their relationship. The general idea is that—according to the teachings of most modern psychologists and pedagogues—one should face the truth fearlessly. Husbands and wives should be absolutely frank with one another, on the assumption that if love between them is real it will be made stronger and more real still if submitted, at frequent intervals, to the test of complete sincerity on both sides.

This is a fine theory, but it has seldom been practised without disastrous results. There are several reasons why this should be so. First of all, truth is an explosive, and it should be handled with care, especially in marital life. It is not necessary to lie, but there is little profit in juggling with hand grenades just to show how brave one is. Secondly, the theory of absolute sincerity presupposes that, if love cannot withstand continuous blasting, then it is not worth saving anyway. Some people want their love life to be a permanent battle of Verdun. When the system of defense is destroyed beyond repair, then the clause of hopeless maladjustment is invoked by one side, or by both. The next thing to do is to divorce and find someone else to be recklessly frank with for a season.

Another reason why the method of adjustment through truthtelling is not always wise is that it develops fiendish traits of character which might otherwise remain dormant.

I know a woman whose eyes glitter with virtuous self-satisfaction every time she has had a 'real heart-to-heart talk' with her husband, which means that she has spent several hours torturing him, or at best boring him to distraction, with a ruthless exposure of the deplorable status of their mutual relationship to date. She is usually so pleased with herself after these periodical inquests that she tells most of her friends, and also her coiffeur, about it. 'Dick and I had such a wonderful time last evening. We made a real effort to find out the real truth about each other—or, at least, I certainly did. I honestly believe we have found a new basis of adjustment for ourselves. What a marvelous feeling that is—don't you think so?'

Dick, of course, if he happens to be present, looks rather nervous or glum, but that is not the point. The point is that Dick's wife feels all aglow because she has done her bit in the general campaign for the improvement of marital happiness through truth. She has been a good girl scout.

A man of my acquaintance, who believes in experimenting outside of wedlock, is unable to understand why his wife would rather ignore his experiments. 'If I did not love her and if she did not love me,' he argues, 'I could accept her point of view. But why can't she see that the very fact that I want her to know everything I do is a proof that I love her? If I have to deceive her or conceal things from her, what is the use of being married to her?'

Be it said, in passing, that this unfortunate husband believes that these extramarital 'experiments' are absolutely necessary to prevent him from developing a sense of inferiority, which, if allowed to grow, would destroy not only the love he has for his wife, but also his general ability in his dealings with the outside world.

v

The difference between an American cookbook and a French one is that the former is very accurate and the second exceedingly vague. A French recipe seldom tells you how many ounces of butter to use to make *crêpes Suzette*, or how many spoonfuls of oil should go into a salad dressing. French cookbooks are full of esoteric measurements such as a *pinch* of pepper, a *suspicion* of garlic, or a *generous sprinkling* of brandy. There are constant references to seasoning *to taste*, as if the recipe were merely intended to give a general direction, relying on the experience and innate art of the cook to make the dish turn out right.

American recipes look like doctors' prescriptions. Perfect cooking seems to depend on perfect dosage. Some of these books give you a table of calories and vitamins—as if that had anything to do with the problem of eating well!

In the same way, there is now flourishing in America a great crop of books which offer precise recipes for the things you should do, or avoid doing, in order to achieve happiness and keep the fires of love at a constant temperature. In a recent issue of *Time* magazine, four such books were reviewed together. Their titles are descriptive enough of the purpose of the authors as well as the state of mind of the readers: *Love and Happiness, So You're Going to Get Married, Marriages Are Made at Home, Getting Along Together.*

I have not read all these books, but, according to the reviewer, they all tend to give practical answers to the same mysterious problem of living with someone of the opposite sex. They try to establish sets of little rules and little tricks which will guarantee marital bliss if carefully followed, in the same way that cookbooks guarantee that you will obtain pumpkin pie if you use the proper ingredients properly measured.

As the publisher of one of these books says on the jacket: 'There is nothing in this book about the complicated psychological problems that send men and women to psychoanalysts, but there is a lot in it about the little incidents of daily married life—the things that happen in the parlor, bedroom and bath—that handled one way enable people to live together happily forever after, and handled another way to Reno.'

Time's review of these books is very gloomy in its conclusion: 'Despite their optimistic tone,' it says, 'the four volumes give a troubled picture of United States domestic life—a world in which husbands are amorous when wives are not, and vice versa; where conflicts spring up over reading in bed or rumpling the evening paper . . . the whole grim panorama giving the impression that Americans are irritable, aggravated, dissatisfied people for whom marriage is an ordeal that only heroes and heroines can bear.'

But I believe that the editors of *Time* would be just as dejected if they were reviewing four volumes about American cooking, and for the same reasons. You cannot possibly feel cheerful when you see the art of love or the art of eating thus reduced to such automatic formulas, even if the experts in these matters are themselves cheerful and optimistic. Good food, the pleasures of love, and those of marriage depend on imponderables, individual taste, and no small amount of luck.

VI

Thus the problem of love in America seems to be the resultant of conflicting and rather unrealistic ways of approaching it. Too many songs, too many stories, too many pictures, and too much romance on the one hand, and too much practical advice on the other. It is as if the experience of being in love could only be one of two things: a superhuman ecstasy, the way of reaching heaven on earth and in pairs; or a psychopathic condition to be treated by specialists.

Between these two extremes there is little room for compromise. That the relationship between men and women offers a wide scale of variations seldom occurs to the experts. It is not necessarily true that there is but one form of love worth bothering about, and that if you cannot get the de luxe model, with a life guarantee of perfect functioning, nothing else is worth-while. It is not true either that you can indefinitely pursue the same quest for perfection, or that if a man and a woman have not found ideal happiness together they will certainly find it with somebody else. Life unfortunately does not begin at forty, and when you reach that age, in America or anywhere else, to go on complaining about your sentimental or physiological maladjustments becomes slightly farcical.

It is not easy, nor perhaps of any use, to draw any conclusion from all this, especially for a European who has lost the fresh point of view of the visitor because he lives here, and who is not quite sure of what it means to be a European any more. I sometimes wonder if there is any real difference between the way men and women get along—or do not get along—together on this side of the Atlantic and on the other. There are probably no more real troubles here than anywhere else. Human nature being quite remarkably stable, why should there be? But there is no doubt that the revolt against this type of human inadequacy is very strong indeed here, especially among the women who imagine that the Europeans have found better ways of managing their heart and their senses than the Americans.

If this is at all true, I believe the reason is to be found in a more philosophical attitude on the part of the Europeans towards such matters. There are no theories about marital bliss, no recipes to teach you how to solve difficulties which, in the Old World, are accepted as part of the common inheritance.

Men and women naturally want to be happy over there, and, if possible, with the help of one another; but they learn very young that compromise is not synonymous with defeat. Even in school (I am speaking more particularly of France now) they are taught, through the literature of centuries, that love is a phenomenon susceptible of innumerable variations, but that —even under the best circumstances—it is so intertwined with the other experiences of each individual life that to be overromantic or too dogmatic about it is of little practical use. '*La vérité est dans les nuances,*' wrote Benjamin Constant, who knew a good deal about such matters.

And, speaking of the truly practical and realistic nature of love, it is a very strange thing that American literature contains no work of any note, not even essays, on love as a psychological phenomenon. I know of no good study of the process of falling in and out of love, no analytical description of jealousy, coquettishness, or the development of tediousness. No classification of the various brands of love such as La Rochefoucauld, Pascal, Stendhal, Proust, and many others have elaborated has been attempted from the American angle. The interesting combinations of such passions as ambition, jealousy, religious fervor, and so forth, with love are only dimly perceived by most people and even by the novelists, who, with very few exceptions, seem to ignore or scorn these complicated patterns. These fine studies have been left to the psychiatrists, the charlatans, or the manufacturers of naïve recipes.

The reason for this neglect on the part of real thinkers and essayists may be that for a long time the standards imposed by the puritanical point of view made the whole study more or less taboo with respectable authors. And then the Freudian wave came along and carried the whole problem out of reach of the amateur observer and the artist. In other words, conditions have been such that there has been no occasion to fill this curious gap in American literature.

Of course, nothing is lost. The field remains open, and there is no reason to suppose that love in America will not cease to be a national problem, a hunting ground for the reformer, and that it will not become, as everywhere else, a personal affair very much worth the effort it takes to examine it as such. All that is necessary is for someone to forget for a while love as Hollywood—or the professor—sees it, and sit down and think about it as an eternally fascinating subject for purely human observation.

MAX LERNER

Professor Lerner was born in Minsk, Russia, in 1902 and was brought to the United States in 1907. He received his B.A. from Yale in 1923 and studied law there. In 1927 he received the Ph.D. from the Brookings Graduate School of Economics and Government in Washington, D.C. He has taught at Sarah Lawrence, Harvard, and Williams, and is presently Professor of American Civilization at Brandeis University, where he has also served as Dean of the Graduate School. He has pursued a lively journalistic career between and during stints of teaching. He edited The Nation *from 1936 to 1938, was a radio commentator and editor of* PM *from 1943 to 1948, columnist for the* New York Star *in 1948 and 1949, and since 1949 a world-wide syndicated columnist for the* New York Post. *Among his many books are* It Is Later Than You Think *(1938),* America as a Civilization *(1957), and* The Age of Overkill *(1962). "The Joiners" is Chapter 2 of Part IX of* America as a Civilization.

THE JOINERS

A standard cliché about American society is that the Americans are "joiners" and "belongers." The derisive attack on the symbol of Sinclair Lewis's Babbitt, who belonged to the Elks, Boosters, and a network of other service clubs and lodges, became a stereotype of American social criticism. It is true that the associative impulse is strong in American life: no other civilization can show as many secret fraternal orders, businessmen's "service clubs," trade and occupational associations, social clubs, garden clubs, women's clubs, church clubs, theater groups, political and reform associations, veterans' groups, ethnic societies, and other clusterings of trivial or substantial importance.

When the intellectuals speak scornfully of Americans as "joiners" they usually forget to include themselves: there are more academic organizations in the United States than in the whole of Europe. They have in mind a middle-class American who may be a Shriner or an Elk, a Rotarian, a Legionnaire, a member of a country club or outing club, and at least a dozen other organizations. In the Warner studies of "Yankee City" (Newburyport) which had 17,000 people, there were over 800 associations, about 350 of them more or less permanent. Taking some random figures in the mid-1950s for illustration, the fraternal orders included in the past at least twenty million members; there were about 100,000 women's clubs; there were two million young people who belonged to the rural and small-town "4-H" clubs. At least 100 million Americans were estimated to belong to some kind of national organization.

Max Weber, the German sociologist, visited America in 1905 and spoke of these "voluntary associations" as bridging the transition between the closed hierarchical society of the Old World and the fragmented individualism of the New World, and he saw how crucial a social function these groupings perform in American life. After World War II the students of German society, looking back at the Nazi experience, thought they could trace a connection between the lesser role of such voluntary groups in Germany and the rise of totalitarianism. Their assumption was that when the associative impulse is balked, it may express itself in a more destructive way.

Certainly one of the drives behind "joining" is the integrative impulse of forming ties with like-minded people and thus finding status in the community. Americans joined associations for a number of motives: to "get ahead," to "meet people" and "make contacts," to "get something done," to learn something, to fill their lives. These drives shed some light on the human situation in America. Constantly mobile, Americans need continuities to enable them easily to meet people, make friends, eat and drink with them, call them by their first names. The clubs and lodges help fill the need.

They are at once a way of breaking up "cliques" and "sets" and at the same time forming new ones. They are a means for measuring social distance, narrowing it for those who break in and are included, lengthening it for those who are excluded. For a newcomer in a community it is hard to break the shell of the tight local social groups unless he comes with a recognized stamp from a national organization or makes his way into a local one. Once in it, he joins with the others in a critical surveillance of the next newcomer. This is a way of solving the need in any society both for clannishness and for social flexibility.

In the midst of constant change and turbulence, even in a mass society, the American feels alone. In a society of hierarchy, loneliness is more tolerable because each member knows his position in the hierarchy— lower than some, higher than others, but always known. In a mobile, nonhierarchical society like the American, social position does not have the same meaning as in a vertical scheme of deference and authority. A man's status in the community is a matter of making horizontal connections, which give him his place in what would otherwise be a void. It is this social placing of an American—in church, lodge, service or women's club, eating club, Community Fund drive, veterans' group, country club, political party—that defines his social personality. Through it he gets the sense of effectiveness he does not have as a minor part of the machine process or the corporate organization. Here he can make his way as a person, by his qualities of geniality and friendliness, his ability to talk at a meeting or run it or work in a committee, his organizing capacities, his ardor, his public spirit. Here also he stretches himself, as he rarely does on the job, by working with others for common nonprofit ends.

Thus Americans achieve a sense of collective expression which belies the outward atomism of American life. "Not to belong to a *we* makes you lonesome," says the adolescent girl in Carson McCullers' *The Member of the Wedding*. "When you say *we*, I'm not included, and it's not fair." Since there is little emphasis in America on some mystical community of religion, there is a greater hunger to belong to a "we." This was less true in the earlier history of the nation. The American rarely thought of himself as "lonely" until the twentieth century. Before that time the dominant note in his thinking was that he was a self-sufficient individual. But he is no longer sufficient unto himself. He gets a certain degree of shared experience from his job at the factory or office, and from his trade-union, but he needs a good deal more from personal relations outside his job life. Margaret Mead notes that at their first meeting Americans are distant and ill at ease, but at their second they act like old friends. It is because they have had a shared experience, no matter how slight, which removes their inhibitions and makes them feel expansive because of it. Karen Horney, coming from Germany to America, was compelled to change her whole theory about the neurotic personality when she found how different were the inner sources of conflict in America from those in Germany, and how much of a role loneliness played in American conflicts.

It is a striking fact that friendships in America, especially male friendships, are not as deep as in other cultures. The American male suspects that there is something sissified about a devoted and demonstrative friendship, except between a man and woman, and then it must pass over into love, or perhaps just into sex. In their clubs and associations, however, at first in school clubs and college fraternities and later in secret lodges or women's clubs, Americans find a level of friendship that does not lay them open to the charge of being sentimental. In his clubs a man is not ashamed to call another man "brother," although outside of the lodge, the trade-union, and the church the term "brother" is used sardonically in American speech.

It is the hunger for shared experience that makes the American fear solitude as he does. More than a century ago Emerson spoke of the polar needs of "society and solitude." The days in which Americans pushed into the wilderness to find solitude are largely over. Many of them still leave the crowded cities for "the country," but their search is not so much for solitude as for greater living space and smaller and more compassable groups. Lewis Mumford has made a plea for housing arrangements that will assure each member of the family a room of his own to which he can retreat when the need for solitude comes upon him, to rediscover the shape of his personality. But for many Americans solitude is still too frightening, whether because they dare not face the dilemma of their own personality or because they recognize themselves more easily by reference to their association with others.

There are many ways of dividing American associations into broad types, none wholly satisfactory. The best one can do is to point out some dramatic contrasts between them. There are the occupational and economic groups at one end of the spectrum, geared to self-interest, and the crusading and cultural ones at the other. There are the patriotic societies of the "old Americans" and the newer ethnic societies of minority groups. There are broadly inclusive associations (political parties, trade-unions, *ad hoc* reform groups) at one end, and at the other there are highly personal groups that run all the way from high-school cliques to the adult eating clubs and the "country-club set." There are, as Warner has put it, "secular" organizations and "sacred" ones, matter-of-fact ones and highly ritualistic ones.

Some of these are more saturated with symbolism than others, yet all of them in one way or another deal in symbols and take their appeal from them. The symbolic complexity of American life is largely expressed in these clubs, lodges, and associations, which fulfill to the hilt what Durkheim long ago laid down as the essence of religious groupings—"collective representation." The degree of ritual varies, being very high in the case of Masonic lodges and church groups and less so in the case of *ad hoc* reform groups. Yet the symbolism and the ritual are present, explicitly or implicitly, in all of them.

Behind the urge toward "joining" is the sense of the mysterious and exotic. To belong to a secret order and be initiated into its rites, to be part of a "Temple" with a fancy Oriental name, to parade in the streets of Los Angeles, Chicago, or New York dressed in an Arab fez and burnoose, to have high-sounding titles of potentates of various ranks in a hierarchy: all this has appeal in a nonhierarchical society from which much of the secrecy and mystery of life has been squeezed out. The fraternal groups flourish best in the small towns of the Middle West: the drearier the cultural wasteland of the small town, the greater the appeal of the exotic. Americans have an ambivalent attitude toward secrecy: they want everything out in the open, yet they delight in the secrecy of fraternal groups, as Tom Sawyer's gang of boys in Mark Twain's books did, and as the cellar clubs and the boys' gangs in the big-city slums still do. Much of the appeal of the Ku Klux Klan lies in this mysterious flim-flammery, at once sadistic and grimly prankish. In many ways the American male of adult years is an arrested small boy, playing with dollars and power as he did once with toys or in gangs, and matching the violence of his recreation to the intensity of his loneliness.

This is especially clear in the veterans' groups, like the American Legion or the Veterans of Foreign Wars, which banded together not only for bonuses and other lobbying purposes but through a nostalgia for the ultimate shared experience of killing and facing death. Under the form of vigilant patriotism they are an effort to recapture the adventure of youth and death in a life that seems humdrum by contrast with the memories of war and derring-do. Since they have the self-assurance of being patriots and hunters of subversives, they come to feel that they have earned a license for license. Their political views take on something of the same cast as their prankishness at conventions, and there is a peculiar irony in the spectacle of drunken and boisterous middle-aged men whose leaders deliver solemn speeches about saving the nation. Curiously, some of the men who are pursued by these Hounds of God got themselves into trouble originally by reason of the same proclivity to become joiners, sponsoring a series of liberal and Leftist letterheads through a mixed impulse of gregariousness and reformist action.

For many American women, the women's club fills the emotional void of middle age, helping in the fight against loneliness and boredom. For others it means a chance to act as culture surrogates for their husbands, who are too busy to keep up with the trends in literature, the arts, or the community services. Americans have learned to take the clubwomen with a kindly bantering acceptance, much as in the Helen Hokinson caricatures. The jokes about the ladies' club lecture circuits cannot conceal a measure of pride on the part of a new nation in having wives with leisure enough to spend on veneer, like garden clubs, reading and discussion clubs, parent-teacher associations, and child-study clubs. In every American community the lecture forums, Little Theater groups, concerts and symphonies and poetry readings are in the custody of little groups of devoted people—men as well as women—who combine the sense of community service with a feeling of membership in a cultural elite.

These cultural groups are part of the array of *ad hoc* organizations which Americans form for every conceivable purpose. Some of them are meddlers and priers, seeking to impose their will upon the society by hunting other Americans down and boycotting and censoring their activities; others are formed to combat them with equal militancy. There are vigilante groups and civil liberties groups; there are radical, conservative, liberal, reactionary, and crackpot groups. Each of the three great religious communities—Protestant, Catholic, and Jewish—has its own welfare, charity, social, recreational, social work, and reformist clubs. In fact, the Negroes as well as the newer minority ethnic groups have a more intense participation in associational life than the "old Americans": it is their way of retaining their cohesiveness and morale in the face of the pressures of the majority culture. Cutting across the religious and ethnic divisions are Community Chest drives, hospital societies, private schools, settlement house and welfare groups, and groups built around every conceivable hobby. They go back in their impulse to the idea of self-help, and many of them combine the pressure group with self-interest and "do-goodism." To some degree they embody the fanatical energy drive that has transformed the face of American life.

It is through these associations that Americans avoid the excesses both of state worship and of complete individualism. It is in them, and not in the geographical locality, that the sense of community comes closest to being achieved. Through them also the idea of neighborhood has been re-created in America: for in most American cities the neighbors next door, who may be fellow tenants or fellow houseowners, have little else in common. The real common interests are shared by people working in the same industry or profession, sending their children to the same school, belonging to the same welfare organization or club, fighting for the same causes. Sometimes this involves "sets" and "cliques" which form from the encrustation of shared experience; sometimes it involves common membership in leisure-and-recreation groups whose chief tie is an interchange of taste and experience. But through the sum of these ways the American manages to achieve a functional set of social relations with like-minded people, the core of which is not propinquity of place but community of interests, vocation, preferences, and tastes.

The propensity to join is not new in America. It goes back to the ladies' reading clubs and other cultural groups which spread on the moving frontier and softened some of its rigors, and which were the forerunners of the parent-teacher associations and the civic and forum groups of today. The jungle of voluntary associations was already dense enough for De Tocqueville to note that "in no country in the world has the principle of association been . . . more unsparingly applied to a multitude of different objects than in America." The permissiveness of the state, the openness of an open society, the newness of the surroundings, the need for interweaving people from diverse ethnic groups—or, conversely, of their huddling together inside the ethnic tent until they could be assimilated—all these shaping forces were present from the start. What came later was the breaking up of the rural and small-town life of America and the massing in impersonal cities, bringing a dislocation that strengthened the impulse to join like-minded people.

Yet here again one runs a danger in generalizing about Americans as a nation. There are phases of class and status that must be taken into account. There has been a tendency to believe that because Babbitt was a joiner all joiners and belongers must therefore be Babbitts and must come from the middle classes. But the studies show a different picture. Warner found in Newburyport a direct correlation between the height of the class level and the propensity to join associations. Using his own six class categories (two uppers, two middles, and two lowers), he found that 72 per cent of the people in the upper classes belonged to associations, 64 per cent in the upper middle, 49 per cent in the lower middle, and 39 per cent and 22 per cent in the two lowers respectively.

Moreover, each of the classes tended to join different kinds of groups, for somewhat different purposes, and each of them had a different "style" of behavior within them. The elites used the association chiefly as instruments for the strategic manipulation of the life of the community—through their control of the country clubs, the eating and discussion clubs, the civic associations, the fund-raising drives. Even when they belonged to such middle-class groups as the women's clubs or the businessmen's service clubs, they brought with them a prestige which enabled them to run the show, and sometimes they used their social power as a form of blackmail in extracting larger civic contributions from the parvenu groups. The middle classes used the associations largely as a way of improving their social status and for training themselves in articulateness and leadership. For the lower classes the emphasis was mainly upon church activities. Actually, the figures for their participation in club life would be even lower if it were not for the fact that a large proportion were in the minority ethnic groups and belonged therefore to their ethnic societies. The lower-class "old American" has very few associational ties.

An added word as to why the "low-status" people (as a number of studies have shown) belong to relatively few associations: partly it is because the nature of their work leaves them less time, partly because they lack the needed money for membership, partly because their interests and perspectives are more limited. With more limited life chances there is a corresponding shrinkage of participation in community experience through the associations. In fact, the Lynds found in their *Middletown* studies that the low-income and low-status groups made few visits except in their immediate neighborhood, formed few ties outside it, and had few friendships: their contacts of a more intimate sort were with their "own kin." Thus the low-status groups in America tend to become isolated, and their isolation is all the greater because they are part of a culture in which everybody else "belongs." I have spoken of the differences in class style. One of the striking differences is that the club activities of the lower and middle classes tend to be more symbolic, emotional, and ritualistic: those of the upper classes are more rationalist, with greater emphasis on speeches and discussions.

There are certain common elements, however, in the whole range of associational life. Members are expected to be "active." They belong to committees, take part in campaigns, try to get publicity for their activities in the local press, lay a good deal of stress on fund-raising (especially in the case of the women's groups), and engage in a kind of gift exchange by a reciprocity of contributions which Warner compares to the potlatches of some of the American Indian tribes. A good deal of American humor has concerned itself with club life, including Robert Benchley's classic film on "The Treasurer's Report." But club and committee work has also meant a training in democratic forms and procedures and an instrument for integrating the community.

Some commentators have guessed that Americans are intense joiners because they need some way of alleviating the tensions and anxieties that arise in their competitive living—which would account for the large number of philanthropic, service, and reformist organizations. Certainly the ritual of the fraternal associations may be an answer to the humdrum character of the daily tasks, and the sense of brotherliness and of service may be a way of allaying the accumulated hostilities and guilt feelings. E. D. Chapple, using an anthropological approach to the theory of associations, suggests that a person who has suffered a serious disturbance may get relocated either by some form of ritual (the *rites of passage* mentioned above) or by changes in his "tangent relations," which he achieves by activity in clubs and associations. This is a technical and roundabout way of saying that the American propensity to join meets a need of the personality and mediates disturbances within that personality, and that keeping busy in association work is one way of meeting, avoiding, or channeling tensions within oneself. Yet this seems a negative and partial approach. Like other human beings, Americans don't do things just to avoid trouble or allay guilt. In a deeper and more affirmative sense the joining impulse is part of the expansion of personality, even while it may often help to create some of the insecurities it seeks to allay.

This jibes with what I said above about class differences in community participation. If joining were only an answer to inner tensions, then the low-status groups would be fully as active as the middle classes, or even more so: yet they are much less active. Their lesser activity derives from their lesser income, lesser education, narrower perspectives and life chances. The urge to associate is thus linked with the expansion of perspective and personality, at least in the intermediate stage, since there is plenty of evidence that a highly developed personality tends in the end to seek solitude. But solitude is different from isolation. Another bit of evidence is to be found in the trend toward suburban living. The theory has been that the impersonality of the big city breeds associations. Yet recent experience shows that when people move from the mass city to the more compassable suburb, their participation in club and association life increases deeply. Again this indicates that the American is a joiner because he feels the freedom to expand, to fill out a personality-on-the-make, and he has an inner need to find outer symbols of the fact that he belongs to his culture and has not been left behind by it.

The clubs and associations which he joins do not, however, simplify his life but make it more crowded and complex. The demands on his time and participation multiply. The "new leisure," which is in itself the product of mechanization and the shorter working week, is getting filled in with the beehive activities of common ventures. Keeping up with club work has become one of the new imperatives of middle-class life. What makes it worse for a small group is that the range of leadership is a constricted one, and the most difficult tasks fall upon a few. America has become overorganized and association-saturated. Yet it may be worth the cost since the associations serve as filaments to tie people together in a community of interests less accidental and casual than it may seem.

Such filaments reach across the continent, so that periodically Americans gather in "conventions" of every sort, which serve formally as legislative bodies but actually as ways of tightening the ties of interest by face-to-face encounters. It may be a convention of a political party or of a trade-union or trade association, sales representatives of a big national corporation, scientists or scholars, church groups, or women's clubs, Shriners or Elks or Legionnaires. In the case of a big national organization as many as 100,000 people may descend upon the convention city to stay for a week, although usually it means only a few hundred or few thousand. They outdo one another in antics and pranks; they swarm over the hotels, sustaining the hotel industry, bars, night clubs, and call girls. In the case of conventions called by big corporations or trade associations, the purpose is to build morale and give a personal touch to an otherwise impersonal organization. The dominant note is that of "greeterism," in which the managers and inside groups seek to make the "visiting firemen" feel at home.

But changes have come over American conventions, as over the whole institution of "joining." The "service clubs" such as Kiwanis and Rotarians—a combination of Big Brother, Good Neighbor, and Greeter—are regarded with some amusement even among their own circles. The world of Babbitt exists in perfect form only in the pages of Sinclair Lewis and in the "Americana" items enshrined in the faded issues of Mencken's *American Mercury*. Even the antics of veterans' groups and fraternal orders are coming to be regarded with boredom and annoyance. The emphasis is shifting from adolescent hoopla to the concerns of particular interest and taste groups. Even in the conventions, as Reuel Denney has pointed out, the "greeters" are becoming "meeters"; and the techniques of "participating" sessions, in which work experiences are exchanged, have reached the trade association and corporate meetings.

Yet with all this sobering current of change, Americans as joiners have not wholly lost the *élan* which has made their associational impulse a cross between promotion, interchange of ideas, and the exorcising of loneliness through modern saturnalia.

JOHN A. KOUWENHOVEN

Professor Kouwenhoven, a student of American literature and culture, was born in 1909 and educated at Wesleyan and Columbia. He taught English at a preparatory school from 1932 to 1936 and at Columbia and Bennington from 1936 to 1941. From 1941 to 1954 he was a member of the editorial staff of Harper's *magazine. In 1946 he joined the English faculty of Barnard College, and in 1950 he was made Professor of English and Chairman of the department. Among his principal works are* Adventures of America

1857–1900 *(1938)*, Made in America: The Arts in Modern Civilization *(1948)*, The Columbia Historical Portrait of New York *(1953)*, *and* The Beer Can by the Highway *(1961)*. *The present essay appeared in the July, 1956,* Harper's.

WHAT'S AMERICAN ABOUT AMERICA?

The discovery of America has never been a more popular pastime than it is today. Scarcely a week goes by without someone's publishing a new book of travels in the bright continent. The anthropologists, native and foreign, have discovered that the natives of Middletown and Plainville, U.S.A. are as amazing and as interesting as the natives of such better known communities as the Trobriand Islands and Samoa. Magazines here and abroad provide a steady flow of articles by journalists, historians, sociologists, and philosophers who want to explain America to itself, or to themselves, or to others.

The discoverers of America have, of course, been describing their experiences ever since Captain John Smith wrote his first book about America almost 350 years ago. But as Smith himself noted, not everyone "who hath bin at Virginia, understandeth or knowes what Virginia is." Indeed, just a couple of years ago the Carnegie Corporation, which supports a number of college programs in American Studies, entitled its Quarterly Report "Who Knows America?" and went on to imply that nobody does, not even "our lawmakers, journalists, civic leaders, diplomats, teachers, and others."

There is, of course, the possibility that some of the writers who have explored, vicariously or in person, this country's past and present may have come to understand or know what America really is. But how is the lay inquirer and the student to know which accounts to trust? Especially since most of the explorers seem to have found not one but two or more antipodal and irreconcilable Americas. The Americans, we are convincingly told, are the most materialistic of peoples, and, on the other hand, they are the most idealistic; the most revolutionary, and, conversely, the most conservative; the most rampantly individualistic, and, simultaneously, the most gregarious and herd-like; the most irreverent toward their elders, and, contrariwise, the most abject worshipers of "Mom." They have an unbridled admiration of everything big, from bulldozers to bosoms; and they are in love with everything diminutive, from the "small hotel" in the song to the little woman in the kitchen.

Maybe, as Henry James thought when he wrote *The American Scene*, it is simply that the country is "too large for any human convenience," too diverse in geography and in blood strains to make sense as any sort of unit. Whatever the reason, the conflicting evidence turns up wherever you look, and the observer has to content himself with some sort of pluralistic conception. The philosopher Santayana's way out was to say that the American mind was split in half, one half symbolized by the skyscraper, the other by neat reproductions of Colonial mansions (with surreptitious modern conveniences).

"The American will," he concluded, "inhabits the skyscraper; the American intellect inherits the Colonial mansion." Mark Twain also defined the split in architectural terms, but more succinctly: American houses, he said, had Queen Anne fronts and Mary Ann behinds.

And yet, for all the contrarieties, there remains something which I think we all feel to be distinctively American, some quality or characteristic underlying the polarities which—as Henry James himself went on to say —makes the American way of doing things differ more from any other nation's way than the ways of any two other Western nations differ from each other.

I am aware of the risks in generalizing. And yet it would be silly, I am convinced, to assert that there are not certain things which are more American than others. Take the New York City skyline, for example— that ragged man-made Sierra at the eastern edge of the continent. Clearly, in the minds of immigrants and returning travelers, in the iconography of the ad-men who use it as a backdrop for the bourbon and airplane luggage they are selling, in the eyes of poets and of military strategists, it is one of the prime American symbols.

Let me start, then, with the Manhattan skyline and list a few things which occur to me as distinctively American. Then, when we have the list, let us see what, if anything, these things have in common. Here are a dozen items to consider:

1. The Manhattan skyline
2. The gridiron town plan
3. The skyscraper
4. The Model-T Ford
5. Jazz
6. The Constitution
7. Mark Twain's writing
8. Whitman's *Leaves of Grass*
9. Comic strips
10. Soap operas
11. Assembly-line production
12. Chewing gum

Here we have a round dozen artifacts which are, it seems to me, recognizably American, not likely to have been produced elsewhere. Granted that some of us take more pleasure in some of them than in others—that

many people prefer soap opera to *Leaves of Grass* while others think
Mark Twain's storytelling is less offensive than chewing gum—all twelve
items are, I believe, widely held to be indigenous to our culture. The
fact that many people in other lands like them too, and that some of
them are nearly as acceptable overseas as they are here at home, does
not in any way detract from their obviously American character. It
merely serves to remind us that to be American does not mean to be
inhuman—a fact which, in certain moods of self-criticism, we are inclined
to forget.

What, then, is the "American" quality which these dozen items share?
And what can that quality tell us about the character of our culture,
about the nature of our civilization?

Those engaged in discovering America often begin by discovering the
Manhattan skyline, and here as well as elsewhere they discover apparently
irreconcilable opposites. They notice at once that it doesn't make any
sense, in human or aesthetic terms. It is the product of insane politics,
greed, competitive ostentation, megalomania, the worship of false gods. Its
products, in turn, are traffic jams, bad ventilation, noise, and all the other
ills that metropolitan flesh is heir to. And the net result is, illogically
enough, one of the most exaltedly beautiful things man has ever made.

Perhaps this paradoxical result will be less bewildering if we look for
a moment at the formal and structural principles which are involved in
the skyline. It may be helpful to consider the skyline as we might consider
a lyric poem, or a novel, if we were trying to analyze its aesthetic
quality.

Looked at in this way, it is clear that the total effect which we call
"the Manhattan skyline" is made up of almost innumerable buildings,
each in competition (for height, or glamor, or efficiency, or respect-
ability) with all of the others. Each goes its own way, as it were, in a
carnival of rugged architectural individualism. And yet—as witness the
universal feeling of exaltation and aspiration which the skyline as a whole
evokes—out of this irrational, unplanned, and often infuriating chaos,
an unforeseen unity has evolved. No building ever built in New York
was placed where it was, or shaped as it was, because it would contribute
to the aesthetic effect of the skyline—lifting it here, giving it mass there,
or lending a needed emphasis. Each was built, all those now under
construction are being built, with no thought for their subordination to
any over-all effect.

What, then, makes possible the fluid and ever-changing unity which
does, in fact, exist? Quite simply, there are two things, both simple in
themselves, which do the job. If they were not simple, they would not
work; but they are, and they do.

One is the gridiron pattern of the city's streets—the same basic pattern
which accounts for Denver, Houston, Little Rock, Birmingham, and
almost any American town you can name, and the same pattern which,

in the form of square townships, sections, and quarter sections, was imposed by the Ordinance of 1785 on an almost continental scale. Whatever its shortcomings when compared with the "discontinuous street patterns" of modern planned communities, this artificial geometric grid —imposed upon the land without regard to contours or any preconceived pattern of social zoning—had at least the quality of rational simplicity. And it is this simple gridiron street pattern which, horizontally, controls the spacing and arrangement of the rectangular shafts which go to make up the skyline.

The other thing which holds the skyline's diversity together is the structural principle of the skyscraper. When we think of individual buildings, we tend to think of details of texture, color, and form, of surface ornamentation or the lack of it. But as elements in Manhattan's skyline, these things are of little consequence. What matters there is the vertical thrust, the motion upward; and that is the product of cage or skeleton, construction in steel—a system of construction which is, in effect, merely a three-dimensional variant of the gridiron street plan, extending vertically instead of horizontally.

The aesthetics of cage, or skeleton, construction have never been fully analyzed, nor am I equipped to analyze them. But as a lay observer, I am struck by fundamental differences between the effect created by height in the RCA building at Radio City, for example, and the effect created by height in Chartres cathedral or in Giotto's campanile. In both the latter (as in all the great architecture of the past) proportion and symmetry, the relation of height to width, are constituent to the effect. One can say of a Gothic cathedral, this tower is too high; of a Romanesque dome, this is top-heavy. But there is nothing inherent in cage construction which would invite such judgments. A true skyscraper like the RCA building could be eighteen or twenty stories taller, or ten or a dozen stories shorter without changing its essential aesthetic effect. Once steel cage construction has passed a certain height, the effect of transactive upward motion has been established; from there on, the point at which you cut it off is arbitrary and makes no difference.

Those who are familiar with the history of the skyscraper will remember how slowly this fact was realized. Even Louis Sullivan—greatest of the early skyscraper architects—thought in terms of having to close off and climax the upward motion of the tall building with an "attic" or cornice. His lesser contemporaries worked for years on the blind assumption that the proportion and symmetry of masonry architecture must be preserved in the new technique. If with the steel cage one could go higher than with load-bearing masonry walls, the old aesthetic effects could be counterfeited by dressing the façade as if one or more buildings had been piled on top of another—each retaining the illusion of being complete in itself. You can still see such buildings in New York: the first five stories perhaps a Greco-Roman temple, the next ten a neuter warehouse, and the final five or six an Aztec pyramid. And that Aztec pyramid is simply a cheap and thoughtless equivalent of the more subtle Sullivan cornice. Both structures attempt to close and climax the upward thrust, to provide something similar to the *Katharsis* in Greek tragedy.

But the logic of cage construction requires no such climax. It has less to do with the inner logic of masonry forms than with that of the old Globe-Wernicke sectional bookcases, whose interchangeable units (with glass-flap fronts) anticipated by fifty years the modular unit systems of so-called modern furniture. Those bookcases were advertised in the 'nineties as "always complete but never finished"—a phrase which could with equal propriety have been applied to the Model-T Ford. Many of us remember with affection that admirably simple mechanism, forever susceptible to added gadgets or improved parts, each of which was interchangeable with what you already had.

Here, then, are the two things which serve to tie together the otherwise irrelevant components of the Manhattan skyline: the gridiron ground plan and the three-dimensional vertical grid of steel cage construction. And both of these are closely related to one another. Both are composed of simple and infinitely repeatable units.

It was the French architect, Le Corbusier, who described New York's architecture as "hot jazz in stone and steel." At first glance this may sound as if it were merely a slick updating of Schelling's "Architecture . . . is frozen music," but it is more than that if one thinks in terms of the structural principles we have been discussing and the structural principles of jazz.

Let me begin by making clear that I am using the term jazz in its broadest significant application. There are circumstances in which it is important to define the term with considerable precision, as when you are involved in discussion with a disciple of one of the many cults, orthodox or progressive, which devote themselves to some particular subspecies of jazz. But in our present context we need to focus upon what all the subspecies (Dixieland, Bebop, Swing, or Cool Jazz) have in common; in other words, we must neglect the by no means uninteresting qualities which differentiate one from another, since it is what they have in common which can tell us most about the civilization which produced them.

There is no definition of jazz, academic or otherwise, which does not acknowledge that its essential ingredient is a particular kind of rhythm. Improvisation is also frequently mentioned as an essential; but even if it were true that jazz always involves improvisation, that would not distinguish it from a good deal of Western European music of the past. It is the distinctive rhythm which differentiates all types of jazz from all other music and which gives to all of its types a basic family resemblance.

It is not easy to define that distinctive rhythm. Winthrop Sargeant has described it as the product of two superimposed devices: syncopation and polyrhythm, both of which have the effect of constantly upsetting rhythmical expectations. André Hodeir, in his recent analysis of *Jazz: Its Evolution and Essence*, speaks of "an unending alternation" of syncopations and of notes played *on* the beat, which "gives rise to a kind of expectation that is one of jazz's subtlest effects."

As you can readily hear, if you listen to any jazz performance (whether of the Louis Armstrong, Benny Goodman, or Charlie Parker variety), the rhythmical effect depends upon there being a clearly defined basic rhythmic pattern which enforces the expectations which are to be upset. That basic pattern is the 4/4 or 2/4 beat which underlies all jazz. Hence the importance of the percussive instruments in jazz: the drums, the guitar or banjo, the bull fiddle, the piano. Hence too the insistent thump, thump, thump, thump which is so boring when you only half-hear jazz—either because you are too far away, across the lake or in the next room, or simply because you will not listen attentively. But hence also the delight, the subtle effects, which good jazz provides as the melodic phrases evade, anticipate, and return to, and then again evade the steady basic four-beat pulse which persists, implicitly or explicitly, throughout the performance.

In other words, the structure of a jazz performance is, like that of the New York skyline, a tension of cross-purposes. In jazz at its characteristic best, each player seems to be—and has the sense of being—on his own. Each goes his own way, inventing rhythmic and melodic patterns which, superficially, seem to have as little relevance to one another as the United Nations building does to the Empire State. And yet the outcome is a dazzlingly precise creative unity.

In jazz that unity of effect is, of course, the result of the very thing which each of the players is flouting: namely, the basic 4/4 beat—that simple rhythmic gridiron of identical and infinitely extendible units which holds the performance together. As Louis Armstrong once wrote, you would expect that if every man in a band "had his own way and could play as he wanted, all you would get would be a lot of jumbled up, crazy noise." But, as he goes on to say, that does not happen, because the players know "by ear and sheer musical instinct" just when to leave the underlying pattern and when to get back on it.

What it adds up to, as I have argued elsewhere, is that jazz is the first art form to give full expression to Emerson's ideal of a union which is perfect only "when all the uniters are isolated." That Emerson's ideal is deeply rooted in our national experience need not be argued. Frederick Jackson Turner quotes a letter written by a frontier settler to friends back East, which in simple, unself-conscious words expresses the same reconciling of opposites. "It is a universal rule here," the frontiersman wrote, "to help one another, each one keeping an eye single to his own business."

One need only remember that the Constitution itself, by providing for

a federation of separate units, became the infinitely extendible framework
for the process of reconciling liberty and unity over vast areas and
conflicting interests. Its seven brief articles, providing for checks and
balances between interests, classes, and branches of the government
establish, in effect, the underlying beat which gives momentum and
direction to a political process which Richard Hofstadter has called "a
harmonious system of mutual frustration"—a description which fits a jazz
performance as well as it fits our politics.

The aesthetic effects of jazz, as Winthrop Sargeant long ago suggested,
have as little to do with symmetry and proportion as have those of a
skyscraper. Like the skyscraper, a jazz performance does not build to
an organically required climax; it can simply cease. The "piece" which
the musicians are playing may, and often does, have a rudimentary
Aristotelian pattern of beginning, middle, and end; but the jazz performance need not. In traditional Western European music, themes are
developed. In jazz they are toyed with and dismantled. There is no
inherent reason why the jazz performance should not continue for another
12 or 16 or 24 or 32 measures (for these are the rhythmic cages which
in jazz correspond to the cages of a steel skeleton in architecture). As in
the skyscraper, the aesthetic effect is one of motion, in this case horizontal
rather then vertical.

Jazz rhythms create what can only be called momentum. When the
rhythm of one voice (say the trumpet, off on a rhythmic and melodic
excursion) lags behind the underlying beat, its four-beat measure carries
over beyond the end of the underlying beat's measure into the succeeding one, which has already begun. Conversely, when the trumpet antici-
pates the beat, it starts a new measure before the steady underlying beat
has ended one. And the result is an exhilarating forward motion which
the jazz trumpeter Wingy Manone once described as "feeling an increase
in tempo though you're still playing at the same tempo." Hence the
importance in jazz of timing, and hence the delight and amusement of
the so-called "break," in which the basic 4/4 beat ceases and a soloist
goes off on a flight of rhythmic and melodic fancy which nevertheless
comes back surprisingly and unerringly to encounter the beat precisely
where it would have been if it had kept going.

Once the momentum is established, it can continue until—after an
interval dictated by some such external factor as the conventional length
of phonograph records or the endurance of dancers—it stops. And as
if to guard against any Aristotelian misconceptions about an end, it is
likely to stop on an unresolved chord, so that harmonically as well as
rhythmically everything is left up in the air. Even the various coda-
like devices employed by jazz performers at dances, such as the corny
old "without a shirt" phrase of blessed memory, are harmonically
unresolved. They are merely conventional ways of saying "we quit," not,
like Beethoven's insistent codas, ways of saying, "There now; that ties

off all the loose ends; I'm going to stop now; done; finished; concluded; signed, sealed, delivered."

Thus far, in our discussion of distinctively "American" things, we have focused chiefly upon twentieth-century items. But the references to the rectangular grid pattern of cities and townships and to the Constitution should remind us that the underlying structural principles with which we are concerned are deeply embedded in our civilization. To shift the emphasis, therefore, let us look at item number 7 on our list: Mark Twain's writing.

Mark's writing was, of course, very largely the product of oral influences. He was a born storyteller, and he always insisted that the oral form of the humorous story was high art. Its essential tool (or weapon), he said, is the pause—which is to say, timing. "If the pause is too long the impressive point is passed," he wrote, "and the audience have had time to divine that a surprise is intended—and then you can't surprise them, of course." In other words, he saw the pause as a device for upsetting expectations, like the jazz "break."

Mark, as you know, was by no means a formal perfectionist. In fact he took delight in being irreverent about literary form. Take, for example, his account of the way *Pudd'nhead Wilson* came into being. It started out to be a story called "Those Extraordinary Twins," about a youthful freak consisting, as he said, of "a combination of two heads and four arms joined to a single body and a single pair of legs—and I thought I would write an extravagantly fantastic little story with this freak of nature for hero—or heroes—a silly young miss [named Rowena] for heroine, and two old ladies and two boys for the minor parts."

But as he got writing the tale, it kept spreading along and other people began intruding themselves—among them Pudd'nhead, and a woman named Roxana, and a young fellow named Tom Driscoll, who— before the book was half finished—had taken things almost entirely into their own hands and were "working the whole tale as a private venture of their own."

From this point, I want to quote Mark directly, because in the process of making fun of fiction's formal conventions he employs a technique which is the verbal equivalent of the jazz "break"—a technique of which he was a master.

When the book was finished, and I came to look round to see what had become of the team I had originally started out with— Aunt Patsy Cooper, Aunt Betsy Hale, the two boys, and Rowena the light-weight heroine—they were nowhere to be seen; they had disappeared from the story some time or other. I hunted about and found them—found them stranded, idle, forgotten, and permanently useless. It was very awkward. It was awkward all around; but more particularly in the case of Rowena, because there was a love match on, between her and one of the twins that constituted

the freak, and I had worked it up to a blistering heat and thrown
in a quite dramatic love quarrel [now watch Mark take off like a
jazz trumpeter flying off on his own in a fantastic break] wherein
Rowena scathingly denounced her betrothed for getting drunk, and
scoffed at his explanation of how it had happened, and wouldn't listen
to it, and had driven him from her in the usual "forever" way;
and now here she sat crying and broken-hearted; for she had found
that he had spoken only the truth; that it was not he but the other
half of the freak, that had drunk the liquor that made him drunk;
that her half was a prohibitionist and had never drunk a drop in
his life, and, although tight as a brick three days in the week, was
wholly innocent of blame; and, indeed, when sober was constantly
doing all he could to reform his brother, the other half, who never
got any satisfaction out of drinking anyway, because liquor never
affected him. [Now he's going to get back on the basic beat again.]
Yes, here she was, stranded with that deep injustice of hers torturing
her poor heart.

Now I shall have to summarize again. Mark didn't know what to do
with her. He couldn't just leave her there, of course, after making such
a to-do over her; he'd have to account to the reader for her somehow.
So he finally decided that all he could do was "give her the grand
bounce." It grieved him, because he'd come to like her after a fashion,
"notwithstanding she was such an ass and said such stupid, irritating
things and was so nauseatingly sentimental"; but it had to be done.
So he started Chapter Seventeen with: "Rowena went out in the back
yard after supper to see the fireworks and fell down the well and got
drowned."

It seemed abrupt, [Mark went on] but I thought maybe the
reader wouldn't notice it, because I changed the subject right away
to something else. Anyway, it loosened up Rowena from where she
was stuck and got her out of the way, and that was the main thing.
It seemed a prompt good way of weeding out people that had got
stalled, and a plenty good enough way for those others; so I
hunted up the two boys and said they went out back one night to
stone the cat and fell down the well and got drowned. Next I
searched around and found Aunt Patsy Cooper and Aunt Betsy
Hale where they were aground, and said they went out back one
night to visit the sick and fell down the well and got drowned.
I was going to drown some of the others, but I gave up the idea, partly
because I believed that if I kept that up it would arouse attention,
. . . and partly because it was not a large well and would not hold
any more anyway.

That was a long excursion—but it makes the point: that Mark didn't
have much reverence for conventional story structure. Even his greatest

book, which is perhaps also the greatest book written on this continent —*Huckleberry Finn*—is troublesome. One can scarcely find a criticism of the book which does not object, for instance, to the final episodes, in which Tom rejoins Huck and they go through that burlesque business of "freeing" the old Negro Jim—who is, it turns out, already free. But, as T. S. Eliot was, I think, the first to observe, the real structure of *Huck Finn* has nothing to do with the traditional form of the novel— with exposition, climax, and resolution. Its structure is like that of the great river itself—without beginning and without end. Its structural units, or "cages," are the episodes of which it is composed. Its momentum is that of the tension between the river's steady flow and the eccentric superimposed rhythms of Huck's flights from, and near recapture by, the restricting forces of routine and convention.

It is not a novel of escape; if it were, it would be Jim's novel, not Huck's. Huck is free at the start, and still free at the end. Looked at in this way, it is clear that *Huckleberry Finn* has as little need of a "conclusion" as has a skyscraper or a jazz performance. Questions of proportion and symmetry are as irrelevant to its structure as they are to the total effect of the New York skyline.

There is not room here for more than brief reference to the other "literary" items on our list: Whitman's *Leaves of Grass*, comic strips, and soap opera. Perhaps it is enough to remind you that *Leaves of Grass* has discomfited many a critic by its lack of symmetry and proportion, and that Whitman himself insisted: "I round and finish little, if anything; and could not, consistently with my scheme." As for the words of true poems, Whitman said in the "Song of the Answerer"—

> They bring none to his or her terminus or to be
>   content and full,
> Whom they take they take into space to behold the
>   birth of stars, to learn one of the meanings,
> To launch off with absolute faith, to sweep through
>   the ceaseless rings and never be quiet again.

Although this is not the place for a detailed analysis of Whitman's verse techniques, it is worth noting in passing how the rhythm of these lines reinforces their logical meaning. The basic rhythmical unit, throughout, is a three-beat phrase of which there are two in the first line (accents falling on *none, his,* and *term . . . be, tent,* and *full*), three in the second and in the third. Superimposed upon the basic three-beat measure there is a flexible, nonmetrical rhythm of colloquial phrasing. That rhythm is controlled in part by the visual effect of the arrangement in long lines, to each of which the reader tends to give equal duration, and in part by the punctuation within the lines.

It is the tension between the flexible, superimposed rhythms of the rhetorical patterns and the basic three-beat measure of the underlying framework which unites with the imagery and the logical meaning of the words to give the passage its restless, sweeping movement. It is this tension, and other analogous aspects of the structure of *Leaves of Grass* which give to the book that "vista" which Whitman himself claimed for it. If I may apply to it T. S. Eliot's idea about *Huckleberry Finn*, the structure of the *Leaves* is open at the end. Its key poem may well be, as D. H. Lawrence believed, the "Song of the Open Road."

As for the comics and soap opera, they too—on their own frequently humdrum level—have devised structures which provide for no ultimate climax, which come to no end demanded by symmetry or proportion. In them both there is a shift in interest away from the "How does it come out?" of traditional story telling to "How are things going?" In a typical installment of Harold Gray's *Orphan Annie*, the final panel shows Annie walking purposefully down a path with her dog, Sandy, saying: "But if we're goin', why horse around? It's a fine night for walkin' . . . C'mon, Sandy . . . Let's go . . ." (It doesn't even end with a period, or full stop, but with the conventional three dots or suspension points, to indicate incompletion.) So too, in the soap operas, *Portia Faces Life*, in one form or another, day after day, over and over again. And the operative word is the verb *faces*. It is the process of facing that matters.

Here, I think, we are approaching the central quality which all the diverse items on our list have in common. That quality I would define as a concern with process rather than with product—or, to re-use Mark Twain's words, a concern with the manner of handling experience or materials rather than with the experience or materials themselves. Emerson, a century ago, was fascinated by the way "becoming somewhat else is the perpetual game of nature." And this preoccupation with process is, of course, basic to modern science. "Matter" itself is no longer to be thought of as something fixed, but fluid and ever-changing. Similarly, modern economic theory has abandoned the "static equilibrium" analysis of the neo-classic economists, and in philosophy John Dewey's instrumentalism abandoned the classic philosophical interest in final causes for a scientific interest in "the mechanism of occurrences"—that is, process.

It is obvious, I think, that the American system of industrial mass production reflects this same focus of interest in its concern with production rather than products. And it is the mass-production system, *not* machinery, which has been America's contribution to industry.

In that system there is an emphasis different from that which was characteristic of handicraft production or even of machine manufacture. In both of these there was an almost total disregard of the means of production. The aristocratic ideal inevitably relegated interest in the means exclusively to anonymous peasants and slaves; what mattered to those who controlled and administered production was, quite simply, the finished product. In a mass-production system, on the other hand, it is the process of production itself which becomes the center of interest, rather than the product.

If we are aware of this fact, we usually regard it as a misfortune. We hear a lot, for instance, of the notion that our system "dehumanizes" the worker, turning him into a machine and depriving him of the satisfactions of finishing anything, since he performs only some repetitive operation. It is true that the unit of work in mass production is not a product but an operation. But the development of the system, in contrast with Charlie Chaplin's wonderful but wild fantasy of the assembly line, has shown the intermediacy of the stage in which the worker is doomed to frustrating boredom. Merely repetitive work, in the logic of mass production, can and must be done by machine. It is unskilled work which is doomed by it, not the worker. More and more skilled workers are needed to design products, analyze jobs, cut patterns, attend complicated machines, and co-ordinate the processes which comprise the productive system.

The skills required for these jobs are different, of course, from those required to make hand-made boots or to carve stone ornament, but they are not in themselves less interesting or less human. Operating a crane in a steel mill, or a turret lathe, is an infinitely more varied and stimulating job than shaping boots day after day by hand. A recent study of a group of workers on an automobile assembly line makes it clear that many of the men object, for a variety of reasons, to those monotonous, repetitive jobs which (as we have already noted) should be—but in many cases are not yet—done by machine; but those who *like* such jobs like them because they enjoy the process. As one of them said: "Repeating the same thing you can catch up and keep ahead of yourself . . . you can get in the swing of it." The report of members of a team of British workers who visited twenty American steel foundries in 1949 includes this description of the technique of "snatching" a steel casting with a magnet, maneuvered by a gantry crane running on overhead rails:

> In its operation, the crane approaches a pile of castings at high speed with the magnet hanging fairly near floor level. The crane comes to a stop somewhere short of the castings, while the magnet swings forward over the pile, is dropped on to it, current switched on, and the hoist begun, at the same moment as the crane starts on its return journey. [And then, in words which might equally be applied to a jazz musician, the report adds:] The whole operation requires timing of a high order, and the impression gained is that the crane drivers derive a good deal of satisfaction from the swinging rhythm of the process.

This fascination with process has possessed Americans ever since Oliver Evans in 1785 created the first wholly automatic factory: a flour mill in Delaware in which mechanical conveyors—belt conveyors, bucket conveyors, screw conveyors—are interlinked with machines in a continuous process of production. But even if there were no other visible sign of the national preoccupation with process, it would be enough to point out that it was an American who invented chewing gum (in 1869) and that it is the Americans who have spread it—in all senses of the verb —throughout the world. An absolutely non-consumable confection, its sole appeal is the process of chewing it.

The apprehensions which many people feel about a civilization absorbed with process—about its mobility and wastefulness as well as about the "dehumanizing" effects of its jobs—derive, I suppose, from old habit and the persistence of values and tastes which were indigenous to a very different social and economic system. Whitman pointed out in *Democratic Vistas* more than eighty years ago that America was a stranger in her own house, that many of our social institutions, like our theories of literature and art, had been taken over almost without change from a culture which was not, like ours, the product of political democracy and the machine. Those institutions and theories, and the values implicit in them, are still around, though some (like collegiate gothic, of both the architectural and intellectual variety) are less widely admired than formerly.

Change, or the process of consecutive occurrences, is, we tend to feel, a bewildering and confusing and lonely thing. All of us, in some moods, feel the "preference for the stable over the precarious and uncompleted" which, as John Dewey recognized, tempts philosophers to posit their absolutes. We talk fondly of the need for roots—as if man were a vegetable, not an animal with legs whose distinction it is that he can move and "get on with it." We would do well to make ourselves more familiar with the idea that the process of development is universal, that it is "the form and order of nature." As Lancelot Law Whyte has said, in *The Next Development in Man:*

> Man shares the special form of the universal formative process which is common to all organisms, and herein lies the root of his unity with the rest of organic nature. While life is maintained, the component processes in man never attain the relative isolation and static perfection of inorganic processes. . . . The individual may seek, or believe that he seeks, independence, permanence, or perfection, but that is only through his failure to recognize and accept his actual situation.

As an "organic system" man cannot, of course, expect to achieve stability or permanent harmony, though he can create (and in the great arts of the past, has created) the illusion of them. What he can achieve is a continuing development in response to his environment. The factor which gives vitality to all the component processes in the individual and in society is "not permanence but development."

To say this is not to deny the past. It is simply to recognize that for a variety of reasons people living in America have, on the whole, been better able to relish process than those who have lived under the imposing shadow of the arts and institutions which Western man created in his tragic search for permanence and perfection—for a "closed system." They find it easy to understand what that very American philosopher William James meant when he told his sister that his house in Chocorua, New Hampshire, was "the most delightful house you ever saw; it has fourteen doors, all opening outwards." They are used to living in grid-patterned cities and towns whose streets, as Jean-Paul Sartre observed, are not, like those of European cities, "closed at both ends." As Sartre says in his essay on New York, the long straight streets and avenues of a gridiron city do not permit the buildings to "cluster like sheep" and protect one against the sense of space. "They are not sober little walks closed in between houses, but national highways. The moment you set foot on one of them, you understand that it has to go on to Boston or Chicago."

So, too, the past of those who live in the United States, like their future, is open-ended. It does not, like the past of most other people, extend downward into the soil out of which their immediate community or neighborhood has grown. It extends laterally backward across the plains, the mountains, or the sea to somewhere else, just as their future may at any moment lead them down the open road, the endless-vistaed street.

Our history is the process of motion into and out of cities; of westering and the counter-process of return; of motion up and down the social ladder—a long, complex, and sometimes terrifyingly rapid sequence of consecutive change. And it is this sequence, and the attitudes and habits and forms which it has bred, to which the term "America" really refers.

"America" is not a synonym for the United States. It is not an artifact. It is not a fixed and immutable ideal toward which citizens of this nation strive. It has not order or proportion, but neither is it chaos except as that is chaotic whose components no single mind can comprehend or control. America is process. And in so far as people have been "American"—as distinguished from being (as most of us, in at least some of our activities, have been) mere carriers of transplanted cultural traditions—the concern with process has been reflected in the work of their heads and hearts and hands.

DENIS W. BROGAN

Denis William Brogan, born in Glasgow, Scotland in 1900, was educated at Glasgow University, Oxford, and Harvard. During World War II he headed the American Section of Intelligence of the British Broadcasting Corporation. At present he is Professor of Political Science at Cambridge. He has written several books on England and France, but is best known in the United States for his many books and articles on American culture, character, and politics. Among these are The American Political System *(1933),* The American Character *(1944),* American Themes *(1949),* The Era of Franklin D. Roosevelt *(1952),* Introduction to American Politics *(1955), and* America in the Modern World *(1961). The following essay, to which we have given a title taken from its first sentence, appears in the second part of* The American Character; *it follows a discussion of the problems of American political leaders, ending with an observation on the necessity for oratory in American politics.*

AMERICA IS WORDS, TOO

America is promises but America is words, too. It is built like a church on a rock of dogmatic affirmations. "We hold these truths to be self-evident, that all men are created equal, that they are endowed by their Creator with certain unalienable Rights, that among these are Life, Liberty and the pursuit of Happiness." "We the People of the United States, in order to form a more perfect Union, establish Justice, insure domestic Tranquillity, provide for the common defence, promote the general Welfare, and secure the Blessings of Liberty to ourselves and our Posterity, do ordain and establish this Constitution." These are only two of the most famous assertions of faith in things unseen, of dogmatic articles denied in good faith by many non-Americans but asserted in good faith by millions of Jefferson's countrymen from July 4th, 1776 to this day.

How absurd an ambition for a people to attempt, by a written constitution, to "establish justice"! It is an ambition to make lawyers laugh and philosophers weep. "To promote the general welfare"; what is this entity, so confidently labeled? What would a Marxian or a Machiavellian make of it? What an overleaping ambition of the Supreme Court to apply not known statute or case law but "the rule of reason"! What complacent courage in the founders of the Massachusetts Bay Company to identify the decision of John Winthrop, Richard Saltonstall, and the rest to transplant themselves to New England with "the greatness of the work in regard of the consequence, God's glory and the churches good"! Nevertheless, Massachusetts was founded, and a Saltonstall is governor in this year of grace, 1944, more than three hundred years later. There have been other consequences, too. What (possibly nonspontaneous) wisdom was shown by Lord Baltimore and the other Catholics of Maryland who in 1649 noted the evils arising from "the inforcing of the conscience in matters of Religion" and so came out for the toleration of all Christians—this in an age when the Inquisition was still going strong, a year after the Peace of Westphalia, the year of the massacre at Drogheda by Cromwell, a generation before the revocation of the Edict of Nantes? With what Hebraic confidence in their mission did the people of Massachusetts in 1780 acknowledge "with grateful hearts the goodness of the great Legislator of the universe, in affording us, in the course of His Providence, an opportunity, deliberately and peaceably, without fraud, violence or surprise, of entering into an original, explicit, and solemn compact with each other; and of forming a new constitution of civil government, for ourselves and posterity; and devoutly imploring His direction in so interesting a design, do agree upon, ordain and establish, the following Declaration of Rights and Frame of Government, as the Constitution of the Commonwealth of Massachusetts." Only a lively conviction of divine interest and direction could have justified so extravagant a hope as that by the mere separation of the legislative, executive, and judicial powers the people of Massachusetts or any people could establish a "government of laws and not of men."

But these aspirations, these hopes, extravagant or meaningless as they may seem to the critical, have been fighting words, hopes and beliefs leading to action. So have been the phrases, the slogans, authentic, apocryphal, half-authentic, with which American history and American memory is filled. This is no country where "what Mr. Gladstone said in 1884" is a comic mystery. These echoes from a heroic if overdramatized past resound still. "Give me liberty or give me death!" "In the name of the Great Jehovah and the Continental Congress!" "First in war, first in peace, first in the hearts of his countrymen." "Don't give up the ship." "We have met the enemy and they are ours." "Our federal union, it must be preserved." "Look at Jackson's men, standing like a stone wall!" "With malice toward none." "Public office is a public trust."

"You may fire when ready, Gridley." "Don't cheer, boys! the poor devils are dying." "Make the world safe for democracy." "One third of a nation." The American man-in-the-street may not attribute all these slogans correctly. He may think it was Lawrence of U.S.S. *Chesapeake* who said "Don't give up the ship"; almost uniformly he thinks that it was Washington who warned against "entangling alliances," whereas it was Jefferson. And he *will* mix them up with texts from Scripture. He may have no more knowledge of the historical context than had the badly frightened citizen who, rescued from a lynching bee, protested: "I didn't say I was against the Monroe Doctrine; I love the Monroe Doctrine, I would die for the Monroe Doctrine. I merely said I didn't know what it was." Not all his slogans are reverent. He may, at times, fall back on "Oh, yeah" or the more adequate "however you slice it, it's still baloney." But he knows too much to despise the power of speech, to think that Bryan was adequately described when he was compared to the Platte River of his native Nebraska: "Five inches deep and five miles wide at the mouth." The power of even bad oratory is still great. The power of good oratory is greater.

So the American suspends his irony when a recognized public figure is speaking, or even when he is merely "sounding off." The American audience listens patiently, even happily, to dogmatic and warm statements in favor of the American constitution, home, woman, business, farmer. An American college president (from the deep South) has been known to impose a severe strain on the discipline of the undergraduates of an Oxford college by addressing them as "clean-limbed, clear-eyed boys." A pastor has been known to describe casting a ballot as a "political sacrament." Senator Vest's panegyric on the dog is only recently condemned as too lush, and a tribute to Southern womanhood is engraved on the pedestal of a statue to a forgotten statesman in Nashville, Tennessee.

In Chambers of Commerce, at Rotary Club meetings, at college commencements, in legislatures, in Congress, speech is treated seriously, according to the skill and taste of the user. There is no fear of boss words or of eloquence, no fear of clichés, no fear of bathos. In short, Americans are like all political peoples except the British. It is the countrymen of Burke and Gladstone and Asquith and Churchill who are the exception. But the difference has now the importance of an acquired characteristic. The British listener, above all the English listener, is surprised and embarrassed by being asked to applaud statements whose truth he has no reason to doubt, but whose expression seems to him remarkably abstract and adorned with flowers of old-fashioned rhetoric. It is in Congress, not in the House of Commons, that a speaker can safely conclude a speech on the reorganization of the civil service with a parallel between the Crucifixion and what the then incumbent of the White House had to go through. It is in all kinds of American public meetings that speakers can "slate" and "rap" and "score" and "blast"—to the advantage of headline writers. No words, it seems, can be strong enough to express the passionate feelings involved. It is not quite so bad or good as that; American politicians, American orators, are not so burned-up as they seem. But it must not be forgotten that they are often quite annoyed, quite worried, quite angry; that they are taking really quite a dim view, even when all they can find to express their mood, verbally, is a statement that the American way of life is due to end on the first Tuesday after the first Monday in November every four years. If an American—even a Senator —asks, "Is civilization a failure, or is the Caucasian played out?" it is not necessary to despair. All Americans dislike being beaten at poker and, for the greater gaiety of nations, don't mind saying so.

It is not merely that Americans like slogans, like words. They like absolutes in ethics. They believe that good is good, even if they quarrel over what, in the circumstances, *is* good. It was an American, true, who said: "My country, right or wrong. May she always be right. But, right or wrong, my country!"[1]

But this sentiment is in advance of that of many simple patriots in other lands who cannot conceive that their country could be wrong, who feel no possible risk of moral strain, and who would agree with the British naval officer who thought that even posing the question was improper conduct in an instructor of British naval cadets. To condemn a thing simply as un-American is often foolish, but no more foolish than to condemn a thing merely as un-English. And since the Americans are very articulate about the content of Americanism, while being English is a thing in itself, there is slightly more chance of there being meaning in "un-American" than in "un-English."

This national fondness for oratory, for slogans, has another cause or another result. It was an English Puritan leader on trial for his life who said of the execution of Charles I: "This thing was not done in a corner." It was a very American attitude. What Wilson preached— "open covenants openly arrived at"—is what the American people wants and expects to get. Like Wilson, it exaggerates the degree to which this standard of public negotiation is practicable. It is not always possible to negotiate under the klieg lights of congressional or press publicity. There are sometimes good reasons not only for secret negotiations but for confidential commitments. But they have to be very good reasons, advanced by leaders, native or foreign, in whom the American people have trust—and that trust will not be unlimited. No American leader, certainly not Washington or Lincoln, not Jackson or Jefferson at the height of their power, was thought to be above criticism or even above a certain degree of legitimate suspicion. Whitman, when he wrote of "the never-ending audacity of elected persons," voiced a general Ameri-

---

[1] I have used the popular, not the correct, version of the dictum of Commodore Decatur, U.S.N.

can belief that all leaders bear watching and that they are in duty bound to make frequent reports on the state of the Union, with or without aid of a fireside. The Americans are all, in this connection, from Missouri; they have got to be shown. They have also got to be told, and so has the world. Again, it is a powerful American tradition at work. Every American child used to learn by heart and many still learn by heart a famous plea for telling the world. For the most sacred of all American political scriptures, the Declaration of Independence, opens with a pre-amble justifying publicity. "When, in the course of human events, it be-comes necessary for one people to dissolve the political bands which have connected them with another, and to assume among the Powers of the earth, the separate and equal station to which the Laws of Nature and of Nature's God entitle them, a decent respect to the opinions of mankind requires that they should declare the causes which impel them to the separation."

The Americans expect from their own leaders—and from the leaders of other countries—a regard for the "Laws of Nature and of Nature's God"; they also expect a "decent respect to the opinions of mankind"— publicly manifested in reasons given and discussed with what may seem excessive freedom and candor of comment. It is a view which gives rise to awkwardness and annoyance, but that can't be helped. The ablest modern publicist, native or foreign, is no match for one of the two great-est writers of political prose who have been Presidents of the United States. And, since I have talked so much of the American passion for oratory, for the spoken word, it is worth recalling that Thomas Jeffer-son, one of the finest figures in American history, was also easily the worst public speaker of his time, perhaps of any time.

"A decent respect to the opinions of mankind." It is still a phrase to be remembered. It means that the American man-in-the-street ex-pects to get the low-down on all secret conferences, to have international decisions supplied to him before the participants have had time to put their smiles on and pose for the group photograph. If this demand is not forthcoming from official sources, it is provided from unofficial sources. Commentators of varying degrees of knowledge, candor, truthfulness, in-genuity, intelligence, explain and announce. Wildly conflicting guesses are made with equal confidence, and the reader and listener is given a wide range of confidential misinformation—as is his right. The outsider may wonder at the willing suspension of disbelief on which the commentators can count. He may think that Tom Sawyer was a notably representative American in his insistence on romantic possibilities in face of drab and dreary realities. He may wonder whether an eminent law professor has any particular authority for his views on the connection between British policy and Rumanian oil. He may wonder whether anybody wanting to keep a secret would tell it to Walter Winchell or even dare to enter the Stork Club. But these doubts are irrelevant. For the dispensers of secrets are catering to a public that has a village horror of the successful privacy of its neighbors. This public cannot see why Mr. Roosevelt should want to keep his political intentions quiet, any more than Mr. Tommy Manville keeps his matrimonial intentions quiet. Of course, he may *try*, as a football coach keeps his secret plays quiet if the scouts from other colleges let him. But it is the duty of columnists and Senators to tell all, as soon as they have discovered it or even before. And no agreement that needs to be kept dark for any length of time has any chance of success in the United States. For the American Republic is much more like the Athenian than like the Venetian Republic. And Americans, though they have a great deal to do, have in common with Saint Paul's Athenian audience a continuous eagerness "to tell or to hear some new thing."

But there is more behind it than this passion for information, for an elaborate version of corner-grocery gossip. The American Republic was founded in the days of the "secret du roi," in the days when Wilkes was, with some difficulty, made a martyr of for revealing the secret of Parliament. A world in which great decisions were made by kings or oligarchies in secret, and the results communicated to docile subjects, this was the world against which the founders of the American Republic revolted. True, great things have been done in secret even in America. The Constitution was made in secret—it could not have been made in public even if the art of eavesdropping had in those days been practiced as expertly as it is now. But it was presented, quickly and in its final form, to the American people, presented to be accepted, or rejected or amended. Only so could "We the People of the United States" be committed. Only so can they be committed today.

JOHN FITZGERALD KENNEDY

The thirty-fifth President of the United States was born in Massachusetts in 1917. He studied at the London School of Economics under Harold Laski in 1935 and briefly at Princeton. He then enrolled at Harvard and received a B.S. in 1940. In World War II he served in the Navy as a PT

boat commander and was decorated with the Navy and Marine Corps medal. He ran for Congress in 1946 and served two terms as Representative from the eleventh Massachusetts district. He was senator from 1953 to 1961, and President from 1961 until his assassination in Dallas, Texas, on November 22, 1963. His published writings include Why England Slept *(1940),* Profiles in Courage *(1956), which won a Pulitzer Prize for biography,* The Strategy of Peace *(1960),* To Turn the Tide *(1962), and* A Nation of Immigrants *(1964). His inaugural address was delivered at the Capitol, January 20, 1961.*

INAUGURAL ADDRESS

Vice President Johnson, Mr. Speaker, Mr. Chief Justice, President Eisenhower, Vice President Nixon, President Truman, Reverend Clergy, Fellow Citizens:

We observe today not a victory of party but a celebration of freedom —symbolizing an end as well as a beginning—signifying renewal as well as change. For I have sworn before you and Almighty God the same solemn oath our forebears prescribed nearly a century and three quarters ago.

The world is very different now. For man holds in his mortal hands the power to abolish all forms of human poverty and all forms of human life. And yet the same revolutionary beliefs for which our forebears fought are still at issue around the globe—the belief that the rights of man come not from the generosity of the state but from the hand of God.

We dare not forget today that we are the heirs of that first revolution. Let the word go forth from this time and place, to friend and foe alike, that the torch has been passed to a new generation of Americans— born in this century, tempered by war, disciplined by a hard and bitter peace, proud of our ancient heritage—and unwilling to witness or permit the slow undoing of those human rights to which this Nation has always been committed, and to which we are committed today at home and around the world.

Let every nation know, whether it wishes us well or ill, that we shall pay any price, bear any burden, meet any hardship, support any friend, oppose any foe to assure the survival and the success of liberty.

This much we pledge—and more.

To those old allies whose cultural and spiritual origins we share, we pledge the loyalty of faithful friends. United, there is little we cannot do in a host of cooperative ventures. Divided, there is little we can do —for we dare not meet a powerful challenge at odds and split asunder.

To those new states whom we welcome to the ranks of the free, we pledge our word that one form of colonial control shall not have passed away merely to be replaced by a far more iron tyranny. We shall not always expect to find them supporting our view. But we shall always hope to find them strongly supporting their own freedom—and to remember that, in the past, those who foolishly sought power by riding the back of the tiger ended up inside.

To those peoples in the huts and villages of half the globe struggling to break the bonds of mass misery, we pledge our best efforts to help them help themselves, for whatever period is required—not because the Communists may be doing it, not because we seek their votes, but because it is right. If a free society cannot help the many who are poor, it cannot save the few who are rich.

To our sister republics south of our border, we offer a special pledge—to convert our good words into good deeds—in a new alliance for progress—to assist free men and free governments in casting off the chains of poverty. But this peaceful revolution of hope cannot become the prey of hostile powers. Let all our neighbors know that we shall join with them to oppose aggression or subversion anywhere in the Americas. And let every other power know that this hemisphere intends to remain the master of its own house.

To that world assembly of sovereign states, the United Nations, our last best hope in an age where the instruments of war have far outpaced the instruments of peace, we renew our pledge of support—to prevent it from becoming merely a forum for invective—to strengthen its shield of the new and the weak—and to enlarge the area in which its writ may run.

Finally, to those nations who would make themselves our adversary, we offer not a pledge but a request: that both sides begin anew the quest for peace, before the dark powers of destruction unleashed by science engulf all humanity in planned or accidental self-destruction.

We dare not tempt them with weakness. For only when our arms are sufficient beyond doubt can we be certain beyond doubt that they will never be employed.

But neither can two great and powerful groups of nations take comfort from our present course—both sides overburdened by the cost of modern weapons, both rightly alarmed by the steady spread of the deadly atom, yet both racing to alter that uncertain balance of terror that stays the hand of mankind's final war.

So let us begin anew—remembering on both sides that civility is not a sign of weakness, and sincerity is always subject to proof. Let us never negotiate out of fear. But let us never fear to negotiate.

Let both sides explore what problems unite us instead of belaboring those problems which divide us.

Let both sides, for the first time, formulate serious and precise proposals for the inspection and control of arms—and bring the absolute power to destroy other nations under the absolute control of all nations.

Let both sides seek to invoke the wonders of science instead of its terrors. Together let us explore the stars, conquer the deserts, eradicate disease, tap the ocean depths, and encourage the arts and commerce.

Let both sides unite to heed in all corners of the earth the command of Isaiah—to "undo the heavy burdens . . . [and] let the oppressed go free."

And if a beachhead of cooperation may push back the jungle of suspicion, let both sides join in creating a new endeavor, not a new balance of power, but a new world of law, where the strong are just and the weak secure and the peace preserved.

All this will not be finished in the first one hundred days. Nor will it be finished in the first one thousand days, nor in the life of this Administration, nor even perhaps in our lifetime on this planet. But let us begin.

In your hands, my fellow citizens, more than mine, will rest the final success or failure of our course. Since this country was founded, each generation of Americans has been summoned to give testimony to its national loyalty. The graves of young Americans who answered the call to service surround the globe.

Now the trumpet summons us again—not as a call to bear arms, though arms we need—not as a call to battle, though embattled we are —but a call to bear the burden of a long twilight struggle, year in and year out, "rejoicing in hope, patient in tribulation"—a struggle against the common enemies of man: tyranny, poverty, disease, and war itself.

Can we forge against these enemies a grand and global alliance, North and South, East and West, that can assure a more fruitful life for all mankind? Will you join in that historic effort?

In the long history of the world, only a few generations have been granted the role of defending freedom in its hour of maximum danger. I do not shrink from this responsibility—I welcome it. I do not believe that any of us would exchange places with any other people or any other generation. The energy, the faith, the devotion which we bring to this endeavor will light our country and all who serve it—and the glow from that fire can truly light the world.

And so, my fellow Americans: ask not what your country can do for you—ask what you can do for your country.

My fellow citizens of the world: ask not what America will do for you, but what together we can do for the freedom of man.

Finally, whether you are citizens of America or citizens of the world, ask of us here the same high standards of strength and sacrifice which we ask of you. With a good conscience our only sure reward, with history the final judge of our deeds, let us go forth to lead the land we love, asking His blessing and His help, but knowing that here on earth God's work must truly be our own.

The Individual and Society

"What," asks John Stuart Mill, "is the rightful limit to the sovereignty of the individual over himself? Where does the authority of society begin?" Most of us agree that in a civilized state we cannot always do exactly what we want when we want to. Experience shows that, regardless of principle, as circumstances change the necessary or desirable degrees of freedom change. Sometimes restraint comes from the outside in the form of the law or of public pressure; sometimes from within in the form of conscience; and sometimes, almost invisibly, it comes under the guise of custom or tradition. This section concerns itself in the broadest terms with the relationship between the individual and his culture and society. The following four sections—"Crime and Punishment," "Civil Disobedience," "Censorship," and "Privacy"—take up particular aspects of the relationship.

Mill, in the nineteenth century, clearly recognizes the basic conflict between liberty and authority and predicts that the modern threat to individual liberty will be not the dictatorship of the governing, but of the governed. Freud, a pioneer of twentieth-century thought, offers an explanation of this conflict in psychological terms. He considers it an inevitable condition of civilization and suggests that the search for a satisfactory compromise is a central and continuous task of mankind. Ruth Benedict, a modern anthropologist, sees the relationship very differently, arguing that there "is no proper antagonism between the role of society and that of the individual."

JOHN STUART MILL

Mill (1806–1873), economist, philosopher, and reformer, was one of the most influential nineteenth-century English thinkers. He was the son of James Mill, an economist and historian, who gave him the extraordinary education which Mill later recorded in his Autobiography *(1873). John began Greek at three, Latin at seven, logic at twelve, and at seventeen was writing articles for the* Westminster Review. *Mill early came under the intellectual influence of Jeremy Bentham, and much of his thought reflects the Benthamite, utilitarian principle that social good lies in whatever brings the greatest benefit to the greatest number. Among his most prominent works are* A System of Logic *(1843),* The Principles of Political Economy *(1848),* On Liberty *(1859),* Considerations on Representative Government *(1861), and* Utilitarianism *(1863). Although many of Mill's ideas have passed out of vogue, he continues to be widely read, partly for what is still useful in his philosophy, and partly for his style and his just, exact, and generous character. We present below Chapter 4 of* On Liberty.

OF THE LIMITS TO THE AUTHORITY OF SOCIETY OVER THE INDIVIDUAL

What, then, is the rightful limit to the sovereignty of the individual over himself? Where does the authority of society begin? How much of human life should be assigned to individuality, and how much to society?

Each will receive its proper share, if each has that which more particularly concerns it. To individuality should belong the part of life in which it is chiefly the individual that is interested; to society, the part which chiefly interests society.

Though society is not founded on a contract, and though no good purpose is answered by inventing a contract in order to deduce social obligations from it, every one who receives the protection of society owes a return for the benefit, and the fact of living in society renders it indispensable that each should be bound to observe a certain line of conduct towards the rest. This conduct consists, first, in not injuring the interests of one another; or rather certain interests, which, either by express legal provision or by tacit understanding, ought to be considered as rights; and secondly, in each person's bearing his share (to be fixed on some equitable principle) of the labors and sacrifices incurred for defending the society or its members from injury and molestation. These conditions society is justified in enforcing, at all costs to those who endeavor to withhold fulfilment. Nor is this all that society may do. The acts of an individual may be hurtful to others, or wanting in due consideration for their welfare, without going the length of violating any of their constituted rights. The offender may then be justly punished by opinion, though not by law. As soon as any part of a person's conduct affects prejudicially the interests of others, society has jurisdiction over it, and the question whether the general welfare will or will not be promoted by interfering with it, becomes open to discussion. But there is no room for entertaining any such question when a person's conduct affects the interests of no persons besides himself, or needs not affect them unless they like (all the persons concerned being of full age, and the ordinary amount of understanding). In all such cases there should be perfect freedom, legal and social, to do the action and stand the consequences.

It would be a great misunderstanding of this doctrine, to suppose that it is one of selfish indifference, which pretends that human beings have no business with each other's conduct in life, and that they should not concern themselves about the well-doing or well-being of one another, unless their own interest is involved. Instead of any diminution, there is need of a great increase of disinterested exertion to promote the good of others. But disinterested benevolence can find other instruments to persuade people to their good, than whips and scourges, either of the literal or the metaphorical sort. I am the last person to undervalue the self-regarding virtues; they are only second in importance, if even second, to the social. It is equally the business of education to cultivate both. But even education works by conviction and persuasion as well as by compulsion, and it is by the former only that, when the period of education is past, the self-regarding virtues should be inculcated. Human beings owe to each other help to distinguish the better from the worse, and encouragement to choose the former and avoid the latter. They should be forever stimulating each other to increased exercise of their higher faculties, and increased direction of their feelings and aims towards wise instead of foolish, elevating instead of degrading, objects and contemplations. But neither one person, nor any number of persons, is warranted in saying to another human creature of ripe years, that he shall not do with his life for his own benefit what he chooses to do with it. He is the person most interested in his own well-being: the interest which any other person, except in cases of strong personal attachment, can have in it, is trifling, compared with that which he himself has; the interest which society has in him individually (except as to his conduct to others) is fractional, and altogether indirect: while, with respect to his own feelings and circumstances, the most ordinary man or woman has means of knowledge immeasurably surpassing those that can be possessed by anyone else. The interference of society to overrule his judgment and purposes in what only regards himself, must be grounded on general presumptions; which may be altogether wrong, and even if right, are as likely as not to be misapplied to individual cases, by persons no better acquainted with the circumstances of such cases than those are who look at them merely from without. In this department, therefore, of human affairs, Individuality has its proper field of action. In the conduct of human beings towards one another, it is necessary that general rules should for the most part be observed, in order that people may know what they have to expect; but in each person's own concerns, his individual spontaneity is entitled to free exercise. Considerations to aid his judgment, exhortations to strengthen his will, may be offered to him, even obtruded on him, by others; but he, himself, is the final judge. All errors which he is likely to commit against advice and warning, are far outweighed by the evil of allowing others to constrain him to what they deem his good.

I do not mean that the feelings with which a person is regarded by others, ought not to be in any way affected by his self-regarding qualities or deficiencies. This is neither possible nor desirable. If he is eminent in any of the qualities which conduce to his own good, he is, so far, a proper object of admiration. He is so much the nearer to the ideal perfection of human nature. If he is grossly deficient in those qualities, a sentiment the opposite of admiration will follow. There is a degree of folly, and a degree of what may be called (though the phrase is not unobjectionable) lowness or depravation of taste, which, though it cannot justify doing harm to the person who manifests it, renders him necessarily and properly a subject of distaste, or, in extreme cases, even of contempt: a person could not have the opposite qualities in due strength without entertaining these feelings. Though doing no wrong to anyone, a person may so act as to compel us to judge him, and feel to him, as a fool, or as a being of an inferior order: and since this judgment and feeling are a fact which he would prefer to avoid, it is doing him a service to warn him of it beforehand, as of any other disagreeable consequence to which he exposes himself. It would be well, indeed, if this good office were much more freely rendered than the common notions of politeness at present permit, and if one person could honestly point out to another that he thinks him in fault, without being considered unmannerly or presuming. We have a right, also, in various ways, to act upon our unfavorable opinion of any one, not to the oppression of his individuality, but in the exercise of ours. We are not bound, for example, to seek his society; we have a right to avoid it (though not to parade the avoidance), for we have a right to choose the society most acceptable to us. We have a right, and it may be our duty to caution others against him, if we think his example or conversation likely to have a pernicious effect on those with whom he associates. We may give others a preference over him in optional good offices, except those which tend to his improvement. In these various modes a person may suffer very severe penalties at the hands of others, for faults which directly concern only himself; but he suffers these penalties only in so far as they are the natural, and, as it were, the spontaneous consequences of the faults themselves, not because they are purposely inflicted on him for the sake of punishment. A person who shows rashness, obstinacy, self-conceit—who cannot live within moderate means—who cannot restrain himself from hurtful indulgences—who pursues animal pleasures at the expense of those of feeling and intellect—must expect to be lowered in the opinion of others, and to have a less share of their favorable sentiments, but of this he has no right to complain, unless he has merited their favor by special excellence in his social relations, and has thus established a title to their good offices, which is not affected by his demerits towards himself.

What I contend for is, that the inconveniences which are strictly inseparable from the unfavorable judgment of others, are the only ones to which a person should ever be subjected for that portion of his conduct and character which concerns his own good, but which does not affect the interests of others in their relations with him. Acts injurious to others require a totally different treatment. Encroachment on their rights; infliction on them of any loss or damage not justified by his own rights; falsehood or duplicity in dealing with them; unfair or ungenerous use of advantages over them; even selfish abstinence from defending them against injury—these are fit objects of moral reprobation, and, in grave cases, of moral retribution and punishment. And not only these acts, but the dispositions which lead to them, are properly immoral, and fit subjects of disapprobation which may rise to abhorrence. Cruelty of disposition; malice and ill-nature; that most anti-social and odious of all passions, envy; dissimulation and insincerity; irascibility on insufficient cause, and resentment disproportioned to the provocation; the love of domineering over others; the desire to engross more than one's share of advantages (the πλεονεξία of the Greeks); the pride which derives gratification from the abasement of others; the egotism which thinks self and its concerns more important than everything else, and decides all doubtful questions in his own favor—these are moral vices, and constitute a bad and odious moral character: unlike the self-regarding faults previously mentioned, which are not properly immoralities, and to whatever pitch they may be carried, do not constitute wickedness. They may be proofs of any amount of folly, or want of personal dignity and self-respect; but they are only a subject of moral reprobation when they involve a breach of duty to others, for whose sake the individual is bound to have care for himself. What are called duties to ourselves are not socially obligatory, unless circumstances render them at the same time duties to others. The term duty to oneself, when it means anything more than prudence, means self-respect or self-development; and for none of these is any one accountable to his fellow-creatures, because for none of them is it for the good of mankind that he be held accountable to them.

The distinction between the loss of consideration which a person may rightly incur by defect of prudence or of personal dignity, and the reprobation which is due to him for an offence against the rights of others, is not a merely nominal distinction. It makes a vast difference both in our feelings and in our conduct towards him, whether he displeases us in things in which we think we have a right to control him, or in things in which we know that we have not. If he displeases us, we may express our distaste, and we may stand aloof from a person as well as from a thing that displeases us; but we shall not therefore feel called on to make his life uncomfortable. We shall reflect that he already bears, or will bear, the whole penalty of his error; if he spoils his life by mismanagement, we shall not, for that reason, desire to spoil it still further: instead of wishing to punish him, we shall rather endeavor to alleviate his punishment, by showing him how he may avoid or cure the evils his conduct tends to bring upon him. He may be to us an object of pity, perhaps of dislike, but not of anger or resentment; we shall not treat him like an enemy of society: the worst we shall think ourselves justified in doing is leaving him to himself, if we do not interfere benevolently by showing interest or concern for him. It is far otherwise if he has infringed the rules necessary for the protection of his fellow-creatures, individually or collectively. The evil consequences of his acts do not then fall on himself, but on others; and society, as the protector of all its members, must retaliate on him; must inflict pain on him for the express purpose of punishment, and must take care that it be sufficiently severe. In the one case, he is an offender at our bar, and we are called on not only to sit in judgment on him, but, in one shape or another, to execute our own sentence: in the other case, it is not our part to inflict any suffering on him, except what may incidentally follow from our using the same liberty in the regulation of our own affairs, which we allow to him in his.

The distinction here pointed out between the part of a person's life which concerns only himself, and that which concerns others, many persons will refuse to admit. How (it may be asked) can any part of the conduct of a member of society be a matter of indifference to the other members? No person is an entirely isolated being; it is impossible for a person to do anything seriously or permanently hurtful to himself, without mischief reaching at least to his near connections, and often far beyond them. If he injures his property, he does harm to those who directly or indirectly derived support from it, and usually diminishes, by a greater or less amount, the general resources of the community. If he deteriorates his bodily or mental faculties, he not only brings evil upon all who depended on him for any portion of their happiness, but disqualifies himself for rendering the services which he owes to his fellow-creatures generally; perhaps becomes a burden on their affection or benevolence; and if such conduct were very frequent, hardly any offence that is committed would detract more from the general sum of good. Finally, if by his vices or follies a person does no direct harm to others, he is nevertheless (it may be said) injurious by his example; and ought to be compelled to control himself, for the sake of those whom the sight or knowledge of his conduct might corrupt or mislead.

And even (it will be added) if the consequences of misconduct could be confined to the vicious or thoughtless individual, ought society to abandon to their own guidance those who are manifestly unfit for it? If protection against themselves is confessedly due to children and persons under age, is not society equally bound to afford it to persons of mature years who are equally incapable of self-government? If gambling, or drunkenness, or incontinence, or idleness, or uncleanliness, are as injurious to happiness, and as great a hindrance to improvement, as many or most of the acts prohibited by law, why (it may be asked) should not law, so far as is consistent with practicability and social convenience, endeavor to repress these also? And as a supplement to the unavoidable imperfections of law, ought not opinion at least to organize a powerful police against these vices, and visit rigidly with social penalties those who are known to practise them? There is no question here (it may be said) about restricting individuality, or impeding the trial of new and original experiments in living. The only things it is sought to prevent are things which have been tried and condemned from the beginning of the world until now; things which experience has shown not to be useful or suitable to any person's individuality. There must be some length of time and amount of experience, after which a moral or prudential truth may be regarded as established: and it is merely desired to prevent generation after generation from falling over the same precipice which has been fatal to their predecessors.

I fully admit that the mischief which a person does to himself, may seriously affect, both through their sympathies and their interests, those nearly connected with him, and in a minor degree, society at large. When, by conduct of this sort, a person is led to violate a distinct and assignable obligation to any other person or persons, the case is taken out of the self-regarding class, and becomes amenable to moral disapprobation in the proper sense of the term. If, for example, a man, through intemperance or extravagance, becomes unable to pay his debts, or, having undertaken the moral responsibility of a family, becomes from the same cause incapable of supporting or educating them, he is deservedly reprobated, and might be justly punished; but it is for the breach of duty to his family or creditors, not for the extravagance. If the resources which ought to have been devoted to them, had been diverted from them for the most prudent investment, the moral culpability would have been the same. George Barnwell murdered his uncle to get money for his mistress, but if he had done it to set himself up in business, he would equally have been hanged. Again, in the frequent case of a man who causes grief to his family by addiction to bad habits, he deserves reproach for his unkindness or ingratitude; but so he may for cultivating habits not in themselves vicious, if they are painful to those with whom he passes his life, or who from personal ties are dependent on him for their comfort. Whoever fails in the consideration generally due to the interests and feelings of others, not being compelled by some more imperative duty, or justified by allowable self-preference, is a subject of moral disapprobation for that failure, but not for the cause of it, nor for the errors, merely personal to himself, which may have remotely led to it. In like manner, when a person disables himself, by conduct purely self-regarding, from the performance of some definite duty incumbent on him to the public, he is guilty of a social offence. No person ought to be punished simply for being drunk; but a soldier or a policeman should be punished for being drunk on duty. Whenever, in short, there is a definite damage, or a definite risk of damage, either to an individual or to the public, the case is taken out of the province of liberty, and placed in that of morality or law.

But with regard to the merely contingent, or, as it may be called, constructive injury which a person causes to society, by conduct which neither violates any specific duty to the public, nor occasions perceptible hurt to any assignable individual except himself; the inconvenience is one which society can afford to bear, for the sake of the greater good of human freedom. If grown persons are to be punished for not taking proper care of themselves, I would rather it were for their own sake, than under pretence of preventing them from impairing their capacity of rendering to society benefits which society does not pretend it has a right to exact. But I cannot consent to argue the point as if society had no means of bringing its weaker members up to its ordinary standard of rational conduct, except waiting till they do something irrational, and then punishing them, legally or morally, for it. Society has had absolute power over them during all the early portion of their existence: it has had the whole period of childhood and nonage in which to try whether it could make them capable of rational conduct in life. The existing generation is master both of the training and the entire circumstances of

206/ J O H N S T U A R T M I L L

the generation to come; it cannot indeed make them perfectly wise and good, because it is itself so lamentably deficient in goodness and wisdom; and its best efforts are not always, in individual cases, its most successful ones; but it is perfectly well able to make the rising generation, as a whole, as good as, and a little better than, itself. If society lets any considerable number of its members grow up mere children, incapable of being acted on by rational consideration of distant motives, society has itself to blame for the consequences. Armed not only with all the powers of education, but with the ascendency which the authority of a received opinion always exercises over the minds who are least fitted to judge for themselves; and aided by the *natural* penalties which cannot be prevented from falling on those who incur the distaste or the contempt of those who know them; let not society pretend that it needs, besides all this, the power to issue commands and enforce obedience in the personal concerns of individuals, in which, on all principles of justice and policy, the decision ought to rest with those who are to abide the consequences. Nor is there anything which tends more to discredit and frustrate the better means of influencing conduct, than a resort to the worse. If there be among those whom it is attempted to coerce into prudence or temperance, any of the material of which vigorous and independent characters are made, they will infallibly rebel against the yoke. No such person will ever feel that others have a right to control him in his concerns, such as they have to prevent him from injuring them in theirs; and it easily comes to be considered a mark of spirit and courage to fly in the face of such usurped authority, and do with ostentation the exact opposite of what it enjoins; as in the fashion of grossness which succeeded, in the time of Charles II., to the fanatical moral intolerance of the Puritans. With respect to what is said of the necessity of protecting society from the bad example set to others by the vicious or the self-indulgent; it is true that bad example may have a pernicious effect, especially the example of doing wrong to others with impunity to the wrongdoer. But we are now speaking of conduct which, while it does no wrong to others, is supposed to do great harm to the agent himself: and I do not see how those who believe this, can think otherwise than that the example, on the whole, must be more salutary than hurtful, since, if it displays the misconduct, it displays also the painful or degrading consequences which, if the conduct is justly censured, must be supposed to be in all or most cases attendant on it.

But the strongest of all the arguments against the interference of the public with purely personal conduct, is that when it does interfere, the odds are that it interferes wrongly, and in the wrong place. On questions of social morality, of duty to others, the opinion of the public, that is, of an overruling majority, though often wrong, is likely to be still oftener right; because on such questions they are only required to judge of their own interests; of the manner in which some mode of conduct, if allowed to be practised, would affect themselves. But the opinion of a similar majority, imposed as a law on the minority, on questions of self-regarding conduct, is quite as likely to be wrong as right; for in these cases public opinion means, at the best, some people's opinion of what is good or bad for other people; while very often it does not even mean that; the public, with the most perfect indifference, passing over the pleasure or convenience of those whose conduct they censure, and considering only their own preference. There are many who consider as an injury to themselves any conduct which they have a distaste for, and resent it as an outrage to their feelings; as a religious bigot, when charged with disregarding the religious feelings of others, has been known to retort that they disregard his feelings, by persisting in their abominable worship or creed. But there is no parity between the feeling of a person for his own opinion, and the feeling of another who is offended at his holding it; no more than between the desire of a thief to take a purse, and the desire of the right owner to keep it. And a person's taste is as much his own peculiar concern as his opinion or his purse. It is easy for any one to imagine an ideal public, which leaves the freedom and choice of individuals in all uncertain matters undisturbed, and only requires them to abstain from modes of conduct which universal experience has condemned. But where has there been seen a public which set any such limit to its censorship? or when does the public trouble itself about universal experience? In its interferences with personal conduct it is seldom thinking of anything but the enormity of acting or feeling differently from itself; and this standard of judgment, thinly disguised, is held up to mankind as the dictate of religion and philosophy, by nine tenths of all moralists and speculative writers. These teach that things are right because they are right; because we feel them to be so. They tell us to search in our own minds and hearts for laws of conduct binding on ourselves and on all others. What can the poor public do but apply these instructions, and make their own personal feelings of good and evil, if they are tolerably unanimous in them, obligatory on all the world?

The evil here pointed out is not one which exists only in theory; and it may perhaps be expected that I should specify the instances in which the public of this age and country improperly invests its own preferences with the character of moral laws. I am not writing an essay on the aberrations of existing moral feeling. That is too weighty a subject to be discussed parenthetically, and by way of illustration. Yet examples are necessary, to show that the principle I maintain is of serious and practical moment, and that I am not endeavoring to erect a barrier against imaginary evils. And it is not difficult to show, by abundant instances, that to extend the bounds of what may be called moral police, until it encroaches on the most unquestionably legitimate liberty of the individual, is one of the most universal of all human propensities.

As a first instance, consider the antipathies which men cherish on no better grounds than that persons whose religious opinions are different from theirs, do not practise their religious observances, especially their religious abstinences. To cite a rather trivial example, nothing in the creed or practice of Christians does more to envenom the hatred of Mahomedans against them, than the fact of their eating pork. There are few acts which Christians and Europeans regard with more unaffected disgust, than Mussulmans regard this particular mode of satisfying hunger. It is, in the first place, an offence against their religion; but this circumstance by no means explains either the degree or the kind of their repugnance; for wine also is forbidden by their religion, and to partake of it is by all Mussulmans accounted wrong, but not disgusting. Their aversion to the flesh of the "unclean beast" is, on the contrary, of that particular character, resembling an instinctive antipathy, which the idea of uncleanness, when once it thoroughly sinks into the feelings, seems always to excite even in those whose personal habits are anything but scrupulously cleanly, and of which the sentiment of religious impurity, so intense in the Hindoos, is a remarkable example. Suppose now that in a people, of whom the majority were Mussulmans, that majority should insist upon not permitting pork to be eaten within the limits of the country. This would be nothing new in Mahomedan countries.[1] Would it be a legitimate exercise of the moral authority of public opinion? and if not, why not? The practice is really revolting to such a public. They also sincerely think that it is forbidden and abhorred by the Deity. Neither could the prohibition be censured as religious persecution. It might be religious in its origin, but it would not be persecution for religion, since nobody's religion makes it a duty to eat pork. The only tenable ground of condemnation would be, that with the personal tastes and self-regarding concerns of individuals the public has no business to interfere.

To come somewhat nearer home: the majority of Spaniards consider it a gross impiety, offensive in the highest degree to the Supreme Being, to worship him in any other manner than the Roman Catholic; and no other public worship is lawful on Spanish soil. The people of all Southern Europe look upon a married clergy as not only irreligious, but unchaste, indecent, gross, disgusting. What do Protestants think of these perfectly sincere feelings, and of the attempt to enforce them against

---

[1] The case of the Bombay Parsees is a curious instance in point. When this industrious and enterprising tribe, the descendants of the Persian fire-worshippers, flying from their native country before the Caliphs, arrived in Western India, they were admitted to toleration by the Hindoo sovereigns, on condition of not eating beef. When those regions afterwards fell under the dominion of Mahomedan conquerors, the Parsees obtained from them a continuance of indulgence, on condition of refraining from pork. What was at first obedience to authority became a second nature, and the Parsees to this day abstain both from beef and pork. Though not required by their religion, the double abstinence has had time to grow into a custom of their tribe; and custom, in the East, is a religion.

non-Catholics? Yet, if mankind are justified in interfering with each other's liberty in things which do not concern the interests of others, on what principle is it possible consistently to exclude these cases? or who can blame people for desiring to suppress what they regard as a scandal in the sight of God and man? No stronger case can be shown for prohibiting anything which is regarded as a personal immorality, than is made out for suppressing these practices in the eyes of those who regard them as impieties; and unless we are willing to adopt the logic of persecutors, and to say that we may persecute others because we are right, and that they must not persecute us because they are wrong, we must be aware of admitting a principle of which we should resent as a gross injustice the application to ourselves.

The preceding instances may be objected to, although unreasonably, as drawn from contingencies impossible among us: opinion, in this country, not being likely to enforce abstinence from meats, or to interfere with people for worshipping, and for either marrying or not marrying, according to their creed or inclination. The next example, however, shall be taken from an interference with liberty which we have by no means passed all danger of. Wherever the puritans have been sufficiently powerful, as in New England, and in Great Britain at the time of the Commonwealth, they have endeavored, with considerable success, to put down all public, and nearly all private, amusements: especially music, dancing, public games, or other assemblages for purposes of diversion, and the theatre. There are still in this country large bodies of persons by whose notions of morality and religion these recreations are condemned; and those persons belonging chiefly to the middle class, who are the ascendant power in the present social and political condition of the kingdom, it is by no means impossible that persons of these sentiments may at some time or other command a majority in Parliament. How will the remaining portion of the community like to have the amusements that shall be permitted to them regulated by the religious and moral sentiments of the stricter Calvinists and Methodists? Would they not, with considerable peremptoriness, desire these intrusively pious members of society to mind their own business? This is precisely what should be said to every government and every public, who have the pretension that no person shall enjoy any pleasure which they think wrong. But if the principle of the pretension be admitted, no one can reasonably object to its being acted on in the sense of the majority, or other preponderating power in the country; and all persons must be ready to conform to the idea of a Christian commonwealth, as understood by the early settlers in New England, if a religious profession similar to theirs should ever succeed in regaining its lost ground, as religions supposed to be declining have so often been known to do.

To imagine another contingency, perhaps more likely to be realized than the one last mentioned. There is confessedly a strong tendency

in the modern world towards a democratic constitution of society, accompanied or not by popular political institutions. It is affirmed that in
the country where this tendency is most completely realized—where both
society and the government are most democratic—the United States
—the feeling of the majority, to whom any appearance of a more
showy or costly style of living than they can hope to rival is disagreeable, operates as a tolerably effectual sumptuary law, and that in many
parts of the Union it is really difficult for a person possessing a very
large income, to find any mode of spending it, which will not incur
popular disapprobation. Though such statements as these are doubtless
much exaggerated as a representation of existing facts, the state of things
they describe is not only a conceivable and possible, but a probable
result of democratic feeling, combined with the notion that the public
has a right to a veto on the manner in which individuals shall spend their
incomes. We have only further to suppose a considerable diffusion of
Socialist opinions, and it may become infamous in the eyes of the
majority to possess more property than some very small amount, or any
income not earned by manual labor. Opinions similar in principle to
these, already prevail widely among the artisan class, and weigh op-
pressively on those who are amenable to the opinion chiefly of that class,
namely, its own members. It is known that the bad workmen who form
the majority of the operatives in many branches of industry, are decidedly of opinion that bad workmen ought to receive the same wages
as good, and that no one ought to be allowed, through piecework or
otherwise, to earn by superior skill or industry more than others can
without it. And they employ a moral police, which occasionally becomes
a physical one, to deter skilful workmen from receiving, and employers
from giving, a larger remuneration for a more useful service. If the public
have any jurisdiction over private concerns, I cannot see that these people
are in fault, or that any individual's particular public can be blamed for
asserting the same authority over his individual conduct, which the general public asserts over people in general.

But, without dwelling upon supposititious cases, there are, in our own
day, gross usurpations upon the liberty of private life actually practised,
and still greater ones threatened with some expectation of success, and
opinions proposed which assert an unlimited right in the public not only
to prohibit by law everything which it thinks wrong, but in order to
get at what it thinks wrong, to prohibit any number of things which
it admits to be innocent.

Under the name of preventing intemperance, the people of one English
colony, and of nearly half of the United States, have been interdicted
by law from making any use whatever of fermented drinks, except for
medical purposes: for prohibition of their sale is in fact, as it is intended
to be, prohibition of their use. And though the impracticability of ex-
ecuting the law has caused its repeal in several of the States which had

adopted it, including the one from which it derives its name, an attempt
has notwithstanding been commenced, and is prosecuted with considerable zeal by many of the professed philanthropists, to agitate for a similar
law in this country. The association, or "Alliance" as it terms itself, which
has been formed for this purpose, has acquired some notoriety through
the publicity given to a correspondence between its Secretary and one
of the very few English public men who hold that a politician's opinion
ought to be founded on principles. Lord Stanley's share in this correspondence is calculated to strengthen the hopes already built on him,
by those who know how rare such qualities as are manifested in some
of his public appearances, unhappily are among those who figure in
political life. The organ of the Alliance, who would "deeply deplore the
recognition of any principle which could be wrested to justify bigotry
and persecution," undertakes to point out the "broad and impassable
barrier" which divides such principles from those of the association. "All
matters relating to thought, opinion, conscience, appear to me," he says,
"to be without the sphere of legislation; all pertaining to social act, habit,
relation, subject only to a discretionary power vested in the State itself,
and not in the individual, to be within it." No mention is made of a third
class, different from either of these, viz., acts and habits which are not
social, but individual; although it is to this class, surely, that the act of
drinking fermented liquors belongs. Selling fermented liquors, however,
is trading, and trading is a social act. But the infringement complained
of is not on the liberty of the seller, but on that of the buyer and consumer; since the State might just as well forbid him to drink wine, as
purposely make it impossible for him to obtain it. The Secretary, however, says, "I claim, as a citizen, a right to legislate whenever my social
rights are invaded by the social act of another." And now for the
definition of these "social rights." "If anything invades my social rights,
certainly the traffic in strong drink does. It destroys my primary
right of security, by constantly creating and stimulating social disorder.
It invades my right of equality, by deriving a profit from the creation of a
misery, I am taxed to support. It impedes my right to free moral and
intellectual development, by surrounding my path with dangers, and
by weakening and demoralizing society, from which I have a right to
claim mutual aid and intercourse." A theory of "social rights," the
like of which probably never before found its way into distinct language
—being nothing short of this—that it is the absolute social right of every
individual, that every other individual shall act in every respect exactly
as he ought; that whosoever fails thereof in the smallest particular, violates
my social right, and entitles me to demand from the legislature the
removal of the grievance. So monstrous a principle is far more dangerous
than any single interference with liberty; there is no violation of liberty
which it would not justify; it acknowledges no right to any freedom
whatever, except perhaps to that of holding opinions in secret, without

ever disclosing them: for the moment an opinion which I consider noxious, passes any one's lips, it invades all the "social rights" attributed to me by the Alliance. The doctrine ascribes to all mankind a vested interest in each other's moral, intellectual, and even physical perfection, to be defined by each claimant according to his own standard.

Another important example of illegitimate interference with the rightful liberty of the individual, not simply threatened, but long since carried into triumphant effect, is Sabbatarian legislation. Without doubt, abstinence on one day in the week, so far as the exigencies of life permit, from the usual daily occupation, though in no respect religiously binding on any except Jews, is a highly beneficial custom. And inasmuch as this custom cannot be observed without a general consent to that effect among the industrious classes, therefore, in so far as some persons by working may impose the same necessity on others, it may be allowable and right that the law should guarantee to each, the observance by others of the custom, by suspending the greater operations of industry on a particular day. But this justification, grounded on the direct interest which others have in each individual's observance of the practice, does not apply to the self-chosen occupations in which a person may think fit to employ his leisure; nor does it hold good, in the smallest degree, for legal restrictions on amusements. It is true that the amusement of some is the day's work of others; but the pleasure, not to say the useful recreation, of many, is worth the labor of a few, provided the occupation is freely chosen, and can be freely resigned. The operatives are perfectly right in thinking that if all worked on Sunday seven days' work would have to be given for six days' wages: but so long as the great mass of employments are suspended, the small number who for the enjoyment of others must still work, obtain a proportional increase of earnings; and they are not obliged to follow those occupations, if they prefer leisure to emolument. If a further remedy is sought, it might be found in the establishment by custom of a holiday on some other day of the week for those particular classes of persons. The only ground, therefore, on which restrictions on Sunday amusements can be defended, must be that they are religiously wrong; a motive of legislation which never can be too earnestly protested against. "Deorum injuriæ Diis curæ." It remains to be proved that society or any of its officers holds a commission from on high to avenge any supposed offence to Omnipotence, which is not also a wrong to our fellow-creatures. The notion that it is one man's duty that another should be religious, was the foundation of all the religious persecutions ever perpetrated, and if admitted, would fully justify them. Though the feeling which breaks out in the repeated attempts to stop railway travelling on Sunday, in the resistance to the opening of Museums, and the like, has not the cruelty of the old persecutors, the state of mind indicated by it is fundamentally the same. It is a determination not to tolerate others in doing what is permitted by their religion, because it is not permitted by the persecutor's religion. It is a belief that God not only abominates the act of the misbeliever, but will not hold us guiltless if we leave him unmolested.

I cannot refrain from adding to these examples of the little account commonly made of human liberty, the language of downright persecution which breaks out from the press of this country, whenever it feels called on to notice the remarkable phenomenon of Mormonism. Much might be said on the unexpected and instructive fact, that an alleged new revelation, and a religion founded on it, the product of palpable imposture, not even supported by the *prestige* of extraordinary qualities in its founder, is believed by hundreds of thousands, and has been made the foundation of a society, in the age of newspapers, railways, and the electric telegraph. What here concerns us is, that this religion, like other and better religions, has its martyrs; that its prophet and founder was, for his teaching, put to death by a mob; that others of its adherents lost their lives by the same lawless violence; that they were forcibly expelled, in a body, from the country in which they first grew up; while, now that they have been chased into a solitary recess in the midst of a desert, many in this country openly declare that it would be right (only that it is not convenient) to send an expedition against them, and compel them by force to conform to the opinions of other people. The article of the Mormonite doctrine which is the chief provocative to the antipathy which thus breaks through the ordinary restraints of religious tolerance, is its sanction of polygamy; which, though permitted to Mahomedans, and Hindoos, and Chinese, seems to excite unquenchable animosity when practised by persons who speak English, and profess to be a kind of Christian. No one has a deeper disapprobation than I have of this Mormon institution; both for other reasons, and because, far from being in any way countenanced by the principle of liberty, it is a direct infraction of that principle, being a mere riveting of the chains of one half of the community, and an emancipation of the other from reciprocity of obligation towards them. Still, it must be remembered that this relation is as much voluntary on the part of the women concerned in it, and who may be deemed the sufferers by it, as is the case with any other form of the marriage institution; and however surprising this fact may appear, it has its explanation in the common ideas and customs of the world, which teaching women to think marriage the one thing needful, make it intelligible that many a woman should prefer being one of several wives, to not being a wife at all. Other countries are not asked to recognize such unions, or release any portion of their inhabitants from their own laws on the score of Mormonite opinions. But when the dissentients have conceded to the hostile sentiments of others, far more than could justly be demanded; when they have left the countries to which their doctrines were unacceptable, and established themselves in a remote corner of the earth, which they have been the first to render habitable to human beings; it is difficult to see on what principles but those of tyranny they can be prevented from living there under what laws they please, provided they commit no aggression on other nations, and allow perfect freedom of departure to those who are dissatisfied with their ways. A recent writer, in some respects of considerable merit, proposes (to use his own words) not a crusade, but a *civilizade*, against this polygamous community, to put an end to what seems to him a retrograde step in civilization. It also appears so to me, but I am not aware that any community has a right to force another to be civilized. So long as the sufferers by the bad law do not invoke assistance from other communities, I cannot admit that persons entirely unconnected with them ought to step in and require that a condition of things with which all who are directly interested appear to be satisfied, should be put an end to because it is a scandal to persons some thousands of miles distant, who have no part or concern in it. Let them send missionaries, if they please, to preach against it; and let them, by any fair means (of which silencing the teachers is not one), oppose the progress of similar doctrines among their own people. If civilization has got the better of barbarism when barbarism had the world to itself, it is too much to profess to be afraid lest barbarism, after having been fairly got under, should revive and conquer civilization. A civilization that can thus succumb to its vanquished enemy must first have become so degenerate, that neither its appointed priests and teachers, nor anybody else, has the capacity, or will take the trouble, to stand up for it. If this be so, the sooner such a civilization receives notice to quit, the better. It can only go on from bad to worse, until destroyed and regenerated (like the Western Empire) by energetic barbarians.

SIGMUND FREUD

Sigmund Freud (1856–1939), the founder of psychoanalysis, was born in Moravia but grew up and was educated in Vienna. Here he received his medical degree in 1881 and later became a lecturer in neuropathology and then professor at the University. His early interest in the "psychiatric"

branch of medicine led to a year's study in Paris with the famous neurologist Charcot and later to collaboration with Josef Breuer on the treatment of hysteria by hypnosis. In 1895 they published their findings in Studies in Hysteria. *Breuer soon abandoned this line of inquiry, but Freud continued and soon afterwards replaced hypnosis with free association as a method of treatment. From this step he developed the practice of psychoanalysis as it is known today. Although his theories met with strong resistance and vehement attack, he continued his work in Vienna until the Nazis forced his flight to England in 1938. Freud was a scientist deeply attached to the humanist tradition. A gifted writer, he had the ability to express most complex and often revolutionary concepts with the utmost clarity in almost deceptively simple language. His earlier works deal mainly with psychoanalytic theory; later in his life he also wrote a few non-technical books in which he applied psychoanalytic theory to phenomena of culture. Among these are* The Future of an Illusion *(1927),* Moses and Monotheism *(1939), and* Civilization and Its Discontents *(1929), from which we present—with our title—the third chapter, in the new translation by James Strachey. Footnotes by Strachey appear in brackets; the bibliographical symbols are explained in his edition.*

INSTINCT AND CIVILIZATION

Our enquiry concerning happiness has not so far taught us much that is not already common knowledge. And even if we proceed from it to the problem of why it is so hard for men to be happy, there seems no greater prospect of learning anything new. We have given the answer already [in the previous chapter] by pointing to the three sources from which our suffering comes: the superior power of nature, the feebleness of our own bodies and the inadequacy of the regulations which adjust the mutual relationships of human beings in the family, the state and society. In regard to the first two sources, our judgement cannot hesitate long. It forces us to acknowledge those sources of suffering and to submit to the inevitable. We shall never completely master nature; and our bodily organism, itself a part of that nature, will always remain a transient structure with a limited capacity for adaptation and achievement. This recognition does not have a paralysing effect. On the contrary, it points the direction for our activity. If we cannot remove all suffering, we can remove some, and we can mitigate some: the experience of many thousands of years has convinced us of that. As regards the third source, the social source of suffering, our attitude is a different one. We do not admit it at all; we cannot see why the regulations made by ourselves should not, on the contrary, be a protection and a benefit for every one of us. And yet, when we consider how unsuccessful we have been in precisely this field of prevention of suffering, a suspicion dawns on us that here, too, a piece of unconquerable nature may lie behind—this time a piece of our own psychical constitution.

When we start considering this possibility, we come upon a contention which is so astonishing that we must dwell upon it. This contention holds that what we call our civilization is largely responsible for our misery, and that we should be much happier if we gave it up and returned to primitive conditions. I call this contention astonishing because, in whatever way we may define the concept of civilization, it is a certain fact that all the things with which we seek to protect ourselves against the threats that emanate from the sources of suffering are part of that very civilization.

How has it happened that so many people have come to take up this strange attitude of hostility to civilization?[1] I believe that the basis of it was a deep and long-standing dissatisfaction with the then existing state of civilization and that on that basis a condemnation of it was built up, occasioned by certain specific historical events. I think I know what the last and the last but one of those occasions were. I am not learned enough to trace the chain of them far back enough in the history of the human species; but a factor of this kind hostile to civilization must already have been at work in the victory of Christendom over the heathen religions. For it was very closely related to the low estimation put upon earthly life by the Christian doctrine. The last but one of these occasions was when the progress of voyages of discovery led to contact with primitive peoples and races. In consequence of insufficient observation and a mistaken view of their manners and customs, they appeared to Europeans to be leading a simple, happy life with few wants, a life such as was unattainable by their visitors with their superior civilization. Later experience has corrected some of those judgements. In many cases the observers had wrongly attributed to the absence of complicated cultural demands what was in fact due to the bounty of nature and the ease with which the major human needs were satisfied. The last occasion is especially familiar to us. It arose when people came to know about the mechanism of the neuroses, which threaten to undermine the modicum of happiness enjoyed by civilized men. It was discovered that a person becomes neurotic because he cannot tolerate the amount of frustration which society imposes on him in the service of its cultural ideals, and it was inferred from this that the abolition or reduction of those demands would result in a return to possibilities of happiness.

There is also an added factor of disappointment. During the last few generations mankind has made an extraordinary advance in the natural sciences and in their technical application and has established his control over nature in a way never before imagined. The single steps of this ad-

---

[1] [Freud had discussed this question at considerable length two years earlier, in the opening chapters of *The Future of an Illusion* (1927c).]

vance are common knowledge and it is unnecessary to enumerate them. Men are proud of those achievements, and have a right to be. But they seem to have observed that this newly-won power over space and time, this subjugation of the forces of nature, which is the fulfilment of a longing that goes back thousands of years, has not increased the amount of pleasurable satisfaction which they may expect from life and has not made them feel happier. From the recognition of this fact we ought to be content to conclude that power over nature is not the *only* precondition of human happiness, just as it is not the *only* goal of cultural endeavour; we ought not to infer from it that technical progress is without value for the economics of our happiness. One would like to ask: is there, then, no positive gain in pleasure, no unequivocal increase in my feeling of happiness, if I can, as often as I please, hear the voice of a child of mine who is living hundreds of miles away or if I can learn in the shortest possible time after a friend has reached his destination that he has come through the long and difficult voyage unharmed? Does it mean nothing that medicine has succeeded in enormously reducing infant mortality and the danger of infection for women in childbirth, and, indeed, in considerably lengthening the average life of a civilized man? And there is a long list that might be added to benefits of this kind which we owe to the much-despised era of scientific and technical advances. But here the voice of pessimistic criticism makes itself heard and warns us that most of these satisfactions follow the model of the 'cheap enjoyment' extolled in the anecdote—the enjoyment obtained by putting a bare leg from under the bedclothes on a cold winter night and drawing it in again. If there had been no railway to conquer distances, my child would never have left his native town and I should need no telephone to hear his voice; if travelling across the ocean by ship had not been introduced, my friend would not have embarked on his sea-voyage and I should not need a cable to relieve my anxiety about him. What is the use of reducing infantile mortality when it is precisely that reduction which imposes the greatest restraint on us in the begetting of children, so that, taken all round, we nevertheless rear no more children than in the days before the reign of hygiene, while at the same time we have created difficult conditions for our sexual life in marriage, and have probably worked against the beneficial effects of natural selection? And, finally, what good to us is a long life if it is difficult and barren of joys, and if it is so full of misery that we can only welcome death as a deliverer?

It seems certain that we do not feel comfortable in our present-day civilization, but it is very difficult to form an opinion whether and in what degree men of an earlier age felt happier and what part their cultural conditions played in the matter. We shall always tend to consider people's distress objectively—that is, to place ourselves, with our own wants and sensibilities, in *their* conditions, and then to examine what occasions we should find in them for experiencing happiness or unhappiness. This method of looking at things, which seems objective because it ignores the variations in subjective sensibility, is, of course, the most subjective possible, since it puts one's own mental states in the place of any others, unknown though they may be. Happiness, however, is something essentially subjective. No matter how much we may shrink with horror from certain situations—of a galley-slave in antiquity, of a peasant during the Thirty Years' War, of a victim of the Holy Inquisition, of a Jew awaiting a pogrom—it is nevertheless impossible for us to feel our way into such people—to divine the changes which original obtuseness of mind, a gradual stupefying process, the cessation of expectations, and cruder or more refined methods of narcotization have produced upon their receptivity to sensations of pleasure and unpleasure. Moreover, in the case of the most extreme possibility of suffering, special mental protective devices are brought into operation. It seems to me unprofitable to pursue this aspect of the problem any further.

It is time for us to turn our attention to the nature of this civilization on whose value as a means to happiness doubts have been thrown. We shall not look for a formula in which to express that nature in a few words, until we have learned something by examining it. We shall therefore content ourselves with saying once more that the word 'civilization'[2] describes the whole sum of the achievements and the regulations which distinguish our lives from those of our animal ancestors and which serve two purposes —namely to protect men against nature and to adjust their mutual relations.[3] In order to learn more, we will bring together the various features of civilization individually, as they are exhibited in human communities. In doing so, we shall have no hesitation in letting ourselves be guided by linguistic usage or, as it is also called, linguistic feeling, in the conviction that we shall thus be doing justice to inner discernments which still defy expression in abstract terms.

The first stage is easy. We recognize as cultural all activities and resources which are useful to men for making the earth serviceable to them, for protecting them against the violence of the forces of nature, and so on. As regards this side of civilization, there can be scarcely any doubt. If we go back far enough, we find that the first acts of civilization were the use of tools, the gaining of control over fire and the construction of dwellings. Among these, the control over fire stands out as a quite extraordinary and unexampled achievement,[4] while the others opened up paths

---

[2] ['*Kultur.*' For the translation of this word see the Editor's Note to *The Future of an Illusion.*]

[3] See *The Future of an Illusion.*

[4] Psycho-analytic material, incomplete as it is and not susceptible to clear interpretation, nevertheless admits of a conjecture—a fantastic-sounding one—about the origin of this human feat. It is as though primal man had the habit, when he came in contact with fire, of satisfying an infantile desire connected with it, by putting it out with a stream of his urine. The legends that we possess leave no doubt about the originally phallic view taken of tongues of flame as they shoot upwards. Putting out fire by micturating—a theme to which modern giants, Gulliver in Lilliput and Rabelais' Gargantua, still hark back—was therefore a kind of sexual act with a male,

which man has followed ever since, and the stimulus to which is easily guessed. With every tool man is perfecting his own organs, whether motor or sensory, or is removing the limits to their functioning. Motor power places gigantic forces at his disposal, which, like his muscles, he can employ in any direction; thanks to ships and aircraft neither water nor air can hinder his movements; by means of spectacles he corrects defects in the lens of his own eye; by means of the telescope he sees into the far distance; and by means of the microscope he overcomes the limits of visibility set by the structure of his retina. In the photographic camera he has created an instrument which retains the fleeting visual impressions, just as a gramophone disc retains the equally fleeting auditory ones; both are at bottom materializations of the power he possesses of recollection, his memory. With the help of the telephone he can hear at distances which would be respected as unattainable even in a fairy tale. Writing was in its origin the voice of an absent person; and the dwelling-house was a substitute for the mother's womb, the first lodging, for which in all likelihood man still longs, and in which he was safe and felt at ease.

These things that, by his science and technology, man has brought about on this earth, on which he first appeared as a feeble animal organism and on which each individual of his species must once more make its entry ('oh inch of nature!'[5]) as a helpless suckling—these things do not only sound like a fairy tale, they are an actual fulfilment of every—or of almost every—fairy-tale wish. All these assets he may lay claim to as his cultural acquisition. Long ago he formed an ideal conception of omnipotence and omniscience which he embodied in his gods. To these gods he attributed everything that seemed unattainable to his wishes, or that was forbidden to him. One may say, therefore, that these gods were cultural

---

an enjoyment of sexual potency in a homosexual competition. The first person to renounce this desire and spare the fire was able to carry it off with him and subdue it to his own use. By damping down the fire of his own sexual excitation, he had tamed the natural force of fire. This great cultural conquest was thus the reward for his renunciation of instinct. Further, it is as though woman had been appointed guardian of the fire which was held captive on the domestic hearth, because her anatomy made it impossible for her to yield to the temptation of this desire. It is remarkable, too, how regularly analytic experience testifies to the connection between ambition, fire and urethral erotism. [Freud had pointed to the connection between urination and fire as early as in the 'Dora' case history (1905*e*[1901]). The connection with ambition came rather later. A full list of references will be found in the Editor's Note to the later paper on the subject, 'The Acquisition and Control of Fire' (1932*a*).]

[5] [In English in the original. This very Shakespearean phrase is not in fact to be found in the canon of Shakespeare. The words 'Poore inch of Nature' occur, however, in a novel by George Wilkins, *The Painfull Aduentures of Pericles Prince of Tyre*, where they are addressed by Pericles to his infant daughter. This work was first printed in 1608, just after the publication of Shakespeare's play, in which Wilkins has been thought to have had a hand. Freud's unexpected acquaintance with the phrase is explained by its appearance in a discussion of the origins of *Pericles* in Georg Brandes's well-known book on Shakespeare, a copy of the German translation of which had a place in Freud's library (Brandes, 1896). He is known to have greatly admired the Danish critic (cf. Jones, 1957, 120), and the same book is quoted in his paper on the three caskets (1913*f*).]

ideals. To-day he has come very close to the attainment of this ideal, he
has almost become a god himself. Only, it is true, in the fashion in which
ideals are usually attained according to the general judgement of humanity.
Not completely; in some respects not at all, in others only half way. Man
has, as it were, become a kind of prosthetic[6] God. When he puts on all his
auxiliary organs he is truly magnificent; but those organs have not grown
on to him and they still give him much trouble at times. Nevertheless, he
is entitled to console himself with the thought that this development will
not come to an end precisely with the year 1930 A.D. Future ages will
bring with them new and probably unimaginably great advances in this
field of civilization and will increase man's likeness to God still more. But
in the interests of our investigations, we will not forget that present-day
man does not feel happy in his Godlike character.

We recognize, then, that countries have attained a high level of civilization if we find that in them everything which can assist in the exploitation
of the earth by man and in his protection against the forces of nature—
everything, in short, which is of use to him—is attended to and effectively
carried out. In such countries rivers which threaten to flood the land are
regulated in their flow, and their water is directed through canals to places
where there is a shortage of it. The soil is carefully cultivated and planted
with the vegetation which it is suited to support; and the mineral wealth
below ground is assiduously brought to the surface and fashioned into the
required implements and utensils. The means of communication are ample,
rapid and reliable. Wild and dangerous animals have been exterminated,
and the breeding of domesticated animals flourishes. But we demand other
things from civilization besides these, and it is a noticeable fact that we
hope to find them realized in these same countries. As though we were
seeking to repudiate the first demand we made, we welcome it as a sign
of civilization as well if we see people directing their care too to what
has no practical value whatever, to what is useless—if, for instance, the
green spaces necessary in a town as playgrounds and as reservoirs of fresh
air are also laid out with flower-beds, or if the windows of the houses
are decorated with pots of flowers. We soon observe that this useless
thing which we expect civilization to value is beauty. We require civilized
man to reverence beauty wherever he sees it in nature and to create it in
the objects of his handiwork so far as he is able. But this is far from exhausting our demands on civilization. We expect besides to see the signs
of cleanliness and order. We do not think highly of the cultural level of an
English country town in Shakespeare's time when we read that there was
a big dungheap in front of his father's house in Stratford; we are indignant
and call it 'barbarous' (which is the opposite of civilized) when we find
the paths in the Wiener Wald[7] littered with paper. Dirtiness of any kind

6 [A prosthesis is the medical term for an artificial adjunct to the body, to make
up for some missing or inadequate part: e.g. false teeth or a false leg.]
7 [The wooded hills on the outskirts of Vienna.]

seems to us incompatible with civilization. We extend our demand for cleanliness to the human body too. We are astonished to learn of the objectionable smell which emanated from the *Roi Soleil*;[8] and we shake our heads on the Isola Bella[9] when we are shown the tiny wash-basin in which Napoleon made his morning toilet. Indeed, we are not surprised by the idea of setting up the use of soap as an actual yardstick of civilization. The same is true of order. It, like cleanliness, applies solely to the works of man. But whereas cleanliness is not to be expected in nature, order, on the contrary, has been imitated from her. Man's observation of the great astronomical regularities not only furnished him with a model for introducing order into his life, but gave him the first points of departure for doing so. Order is a kind of compulsion to repeat which, when a regulation has been laid down once and for all, decides when, where and how a thing shall be done, so that in every similar circumstance one is spared hesitation and indecision. The benefits of order are incontestable. It enables men to use space and time to the best advantage, while conserving their psychical forces. We should have a right to expect that order would have taken its place in human activities from the start and without difficulty; and we may well wonder that this has not happened —that, on the contrary, human beings exhibit an inborn tendency to carelessness, irregularity and unreliability in their work, and that a laborious training is needed before they learn to follow the example of their celestial models.

Beauty, cleanliness and order obviously occupy a special position among the requirements of civilization. No one will maintain that they are as important for life as control over the forces of nature or as some other factors with which we shall become acquainted. And yet no one would care to put them in the background as trivialities. That civilization is not exclusively taken up with what is useful is already shown by the example of beauty, which we decline to omit from among the interests of civilization. The usefulness of order is quite evident. With regard to cleanliness, we must bear in mind that it is demanded of us by hygiene as well, and we may suspect that even before the days of scientific prophylaxis the connection between the two was not altogether strange to man. Yet utility does not entirely explain these efforts; something else must be at work besides.

No feature, however, seems better to characterize civilization than its esteem and encouragement of man's higher mental activities—his intellectual, scientific and artistic achievements—and the leading role that it assigns to ideas in human life. Foremost among those ideas are the religious systems, on whose complicated structure I have endeavoured to

---

[8] [Louis XIV of France.]
[9] [The well-known island in Lake Maggiore, visited by Napoleon a few days before the battle of Marengo.]

throw light elsewhere.[10] Next come the speculations of philosophy; and finally what might be called man's 'ideals'—his ideas of a possible perfection of individuals, or of peoples or of the whole of humanity, and the demands he sets up on the basis of such ideas. The fact that these creations of his are not independent of one another, but are on the contrary closely interwoven, increases the difficulty not only of describing them but of tracing their psychological derivation. If we assume quite generally that the motive force of all human activities is a striving towards the two confluent goals of utility and a yield of pleasure, we must suppose that this is also true of the manifestations of civilization which we have been discussing here, although this is easily visible only in scientific and aesthetic activities. But it cannot be doubted that the other activities, too, correspond to strong needs in men—perhaps to needs which are only developed in a minority. Nor must we allow ourselves to be misled by judgements of value concerning any particular religion, or philosophic system, or ideal. Whether we think to find in them the highest achievements of the human spirit, or whether we deplore them as aberrations, we cannot but recognize that where they are present, and, in especial, where they are dominant, a high level of civilization is implied.

The last, but certainly not the least important, of the characteristic features of civilization remains to be assessed: the manner in which the relationships of men to one another, their social relationships, are regulated —relationships which affect a person as a neighbour, as a source of help, as another person's sexual object, as a member of a family and of a State. Here it is especially difficult to keep clear of particular ideal demands and to see what is civilized in general. Perhaps we may begin by explaining that the element of civilization enters on the scene with the first attempt to regulate these social relationships. If the attempt were not made, the relationships would be subject to the arbitrary will of the individual: that is to say, the physically stronger man would decide them in the sense of his own interests and instinctual impulses. Nothing would be changed in this if this stronger man should in his turn meet someone even stronger than he. Human life in common is only made possible when a majority comes together which is stronger than any separate individual and which remains united against all separate individuals. The power of this community is then set up as 'right' in opposition to the power of the individual, which is condemned as 'brute force'. This replacement of the power of the individual by the power of a community constitutes the decisive step of civilization. The essence of it lies in the fact that the members of the community restrict themselves in their possibilities of satisfaction, whereas the individual knew no such restrictions. The first requisite of civilization, therefore, is that of justice—that

---

[10] [Cf. *The Future of an Illusion* (1927c).]

is, the assurance that a law once made will not be broken in favour of an individual. This implies nothing as to the ethical value of such a law. The further course of cultural development seems to tend towards making the law no longer an expression of the will of a small community—a caste or a stratum of the population or a racial group—which, in its turn, behaves like a violent individual towards other, and perhaps more numerous, collections of people. The final outcome should be a rule of law to which all—except those who are not capable of entering a community—have contributed by a sacrifice of their instincts, and which leaves no one—again with the same exception—at the mercy of brute force.

The liberty of the individual is no gift of civilization. It was greatest before there was any civilization, though then, it is true, it had for the most part no value, since the individual was scarcely in a position to defend it. The development of civilization imposes restrictions on it, and justice demands that no one shall escape those restrictions. What makes itself felt in a human community as a desire for freedom may be their revolt against some existing injustice, and so may prove favourable to a further development of civilization; it may remain compatible with civilization. But it may also spring from the remains of their original personality, which is still untamed by civilization and may thus become the basis in them of hostility to civilization. The urge for freedom, therefore, is directed against particular forms and demands for civilization or against civilization altogether. It does not seem as though any influence could induce a man to change his nature into a termite's. No doubt he will always defend his claim to individual liberty against the will of the group. A good part of the struggles of mankind centre round the single task of finding an expedient accommodation—one, that is, that will bring happiness—between this claim of the individual and the cultural claims of the group; and one of the problems that touches the fate of humanity is whether such an accommodation can be reached by means of some particular form of civilization or whether this conflict is irreconcilable.

By allowing common feeling to be our guide in deciding what features of human life are to be regarded as civilized, we have obtained a clear impression of the general picture of civilization; but it is true that so far we have discovered nothing that is not universally known. At the same time we have been careful not to fall in with the prejudice that civilization is synonymous with perfecting, that it is the road to perfection preordained for men. But now a point of view presents itself which may lead in a different direction. The development of civilization appears to us as a peculiar process which mankind undergoes, and in which several things strike us as familiar. We may characterize this process with reference to the changes which it brings about in the familiar instinctual dispositions of human beings, to satisfy which is, after all, the economic task of our lives. A few of these instincts are used up in such a manner that something appears in their place which, in an individual, we describe as a character-trait. The most remarkable example of such a process is found in the anal erotism of young human beings. Their original interest in the excretory function, its organs and products, is changed in the course of their growth into a group of traits which are familiar to us as parsimony, a sense of order and cleanliness—qualities which, though valuable and welcome in themselves, may be intensified till they become markedly dominant and produce what is called the anal character. How this happens we do not know, but there is no doubt about the correctness of the finding.[11] Now we have seen that order and cleanliness are important requirements of civilization, although their vital necessity is not very apparent, any more than their suitability as sources of enjoyment. At this point we cannot fail to be struck by the similarity between the process of civilization and the libidinal development of the individual. Other instincts [besides anal erotism] are induced to displace the conditions for their satisfaction, to lead them into other paths. In most cases this process coincides with that of the *sublimation* (of instinctual aims) with which we are familiar, but in some it can be differentiated from it. Sublimation of instinct is an especially conspicuous feature of cultural development; it is what makes it possible for higher psychical activities, scientific, artistic or ideological, to play such an important part in civilized life. If one were to yield to a first impression, one would say that sublimation is a vicissitude which has been forced upon the instincts entirely by civilization. But it would be wiser to reflect upon this a little longer. In the third place,[12] finally, and this seems the most important of all, it is impossible to overlook the extent to which civilization is built up upon a renunciation of instinct, how much it presupposes precisely the non-satisfaction (by suppression, repression or some other means?) of powerful instincts. This 'cultural frustration' dominates the large field of social relationships between human beings. As we already know, it is the cause of the hostility against which all civilizations have to struggle. It will also make severe demands on our scientific work, and we shall have much to explain here. It is not easy to understand how it can become possible to deprive an instinct of satisfaction. Nor is doing so without danger. If the loss is not compensated for economically, one can be certain that serious disorders will ensue.

But if we want to know what value can be attributed to our view that the development of civilization is a special process, comparable to the normal maturation of the individual, we must clearly attack another problem. We must ask ourselves to what influences the development of

---

[11] Cf. my 'Character and Anal Erotism' (1908*b*), and numerous further contributions, by Ernest Jones [1918] and others.

[12] [Freud had already mentioned two other factors playing a part in the 'process' of civilization: character-formation and sublimation.]

civilization owes its origin, how it arose, and by what its course has been determined.[13]

---

[13] [Strachey notes that "Freud returns to the subject of civilization as a 'process'" in Chapter 6 and again in Chapter 8; and that "He mentions it once more in his open letter to Einstein, *Why War?* (1933*b*)."—Eds.]

RUTH BENEDICT

Ruth Benedict was born in New York City in 1887. After receiving a B.A. degree from Vassar, she taught English in a girls' school and wrote and published some poetry under the name Anne Singleton. In 1914 she married Stanley R. Benedict, a biochemist. Five years later, at the age of thirty-two, Mrs. Benedict enrolled at Columbia, apparently because she wanted "busy work." Thus, almost by accident, she began the study of anthropology under Franz Boas, whom she later described as "the greatest of living anthropologists." She completed her doctorate in 1923 and immediately joined the faculty of Columbia, where she remained until her death in 1948. Mrs. Benedict's research, conducted on periodic field trips, made her a leading authority on the Indians of the American West. She has also been considered a pathfinder in her awareness of the relationship between anthropology and such other social sciences as psychology and sociology. This breadth of attention is evident in her Patterns of Culture *(1934), from which we print the concluding chapter below. Other books by Mrs. Benedict are* The Concept of Guardian Spirit in North America *(1923),* Zuñi Mythology *(1935),* Race: Science and Politics *(1940), and* The Chrysanthemum and the Sword *(1946).*

THE INDIVIDUAL AND THE
PATTERN OF CULTURE

The large corporate behaviour we have discussed is nevertheless the behaviour of individuals. It is the world with which each person is severally presented, the world from which he must make his individual life. Accounts of any civilization condensed into a few dozen pages must necessarily throw into relief the group standards and describe individual behaviour as it exemplifies the motivations of that culture. The exigencies of the situation are misleading only when this necessity is read off as implying that he is submerged in an overpowering ocean.

There is no proper antagonism between the rôle of society and that of the individual. One of the most misleading misconceptions due to this nineteenth-century dualism was the idea that what was subtracted from society was added to the individual and what was subtracted from the individual was added to society. Philosophies of freedom, political creeds of *laissez faire*, revolutions that have unseated dynasties, have been built on this dualism. The quarrel in anthropological theory between the importance of the culture pattern and of the individual is only a small ripple from this fundamental conception of the nature of society.

In reality, society and the individual are not antagonists. His culture provides the raw material of which the individual makes his life. If it is meagre, the individual suffers; if it is rich, the individual has the chance to rise to his opportunity. Every private interest of every man and woman is served by the enrichment of the traditional stores of his civilization. The richest musical sensitivity can operate only within the equipment and standards of its tradition. It will add, perhaps importantly, to that tradition, but its achievement remains in proportion to the instruments and musical theory which the culture has provided. In the same fashion a talent for observation expends itself in some Melanesian tribe upon the negligible borders of the magico-religious field. For a realization of its potentialities it is dependent upon the development of scientific methodology, and it has no fruition unless the culture has elaborated the necessary concepts and tools.

The man in the street still thinks in terms of a necessary antagonism between society and the individual. In large measure this is because in our civilization the regulative activities of society are singled out, and we tend to identify society with the restrictions the law imposes upon us. The law lays down the number of miles per hour that I may drive an automobile. If it takes this restriction away, I am by that much the freer. This basis for a fundamental antagonism between society and the individual is naïve indeed when it is extended as a basic philosophical and political notion. Society is only incidentally and in certain situations regulative, and law is not equivalent to the social order. In the simpler homogeneous cultures collective habit or custom may quite supersede the necessity for any development of formal legal authority. American Indians sometimes say: 'In the old days, there were no fights about hunting grounds or fishing territories. There was no law then, so everybody did what was right.' The phrasing makes it clear that in their old life they did not think of themselves as submitting to a social control imposed upon them from without. Even in our civilization the law is never more than a crude implement of society, and one it is often enough necessary to check in its arrogant career. It is never to be read off as if it were the equivalent of the social order.

Society in its full sense as we have discussed it in this volume is never an entity separable from the individuals who compose it. No individual can arrive even at the threshold of his potentialities without a culture in which he participates. Conversely, no civilization has in it any element which in the last analysis is not the contribution of an individual. Where else could any trait come from except from the behaviour of a man or a woman or a child?

It is largely because of the traditional acceptance of a conflict between society and the individual, that emphasis upon cultural behaviour is so often interpreted as a denial of the autonomy of the individual. The reading of Sumner's *Folkways* usually rouses a protest at the limitations such an interpretation places upon the scope and initiative of the individual. Anthropology is often believed to be a counsel of despair which makes untenable a beneficent human illusion. But no anthropologist with a background of experience of other cultures has ever believed that individuals were automatons, mechanically carrying out the decrees of their civilization. No culture yet observed has been able to eradicate the differences in the temperaments of the persons who compose it. It is always a give-and-take. The problem of the individual is not clarified by stressing the antagonism between culture and the individual, but by stressing their mutual reinforcement. This rapport is so close that it is not possible to discuss patterns of culture without considering specifically their relation to individual psychology.

We have seen that any society selects some segment of the arc of possible human behaviour, and in so far as it achieves integration its institutions tend to further the expression of its selected segment and to inhibit opposite expressions. But these opposite expressions are the congenial responses, nevertheless, of a certain proportion of the carriers of that culture. We have already discussed the reasons for believing that this selection is primarily cultural and not biological. We cannot, therefore, even on theoretical grounds imagine that all the congenial responses of all its people will be equally served by the institutions of any culture. To understand the behaviour of the individual, it is not merely necessary to relate his personal life-history to his endowments, and to measure these against an arbitrarily selected normality. It is necessary also to relate his congenial responses to the behaviour that is singled out in the institutions of his culture.

The vast proportion of all individuals who are born into any society always and whatever the idiosyncrasies of its institutions, assume, as we have seen, the behaviour dictated by that society. This fact is always interpreted by the carriers of that culture as being due to the fact that their particular institutions reflect an ultimate and universal sanity. The actual reason is quite different. Most people are shaped to the form of their culture because of the enormous malleability of their original endowment. They are plastic to the moulding force of the society into which they are born. It does not matter whether, with the Northwest Coast, it requires delusions of self-reference, or with our own civilization the amassing of possessions. In any case the great mass of individuals take quite readily the form that is presented to them.

They do not all, however, find it equally congenial, and those are favoured and fortunate whose potentialities most nearly coincide with the type of behaviour selected by their society. Those who, in a situation in which they are frustrated, naturally seek ways of putting the occasion out of sight as expeditiously as possible are well served in Pueblo culture. Southwest institutions, as we have seen, minimize the situations in which serious frustration can arise, and when it cannot be avoided, as in death, they provide means to put it behind them with all speed.

On the other hand, those who react to frustration as to an insult and whose first thought is to get even are amply provided for on the Northwest Coast. They may extend their native reaction to situations in which their paddle breaks or their canoe overturns or to the loss of relatives by death. They rise from their first reaction of sulking to thrust back in return, to 'fight' with property or with weapons. Those who can assuage despair by the act of bringing shame to others can register freely and without conflict in this society, because their proclivities are deeply channelled in their culture. In Dobu those whose first impulse is to select a victim and project their misery upon him in procedures of punishment are equally fortunate.

It happens that none of the three cultures we have described meets frustration in a realistic manner by stressing the resumption of the original and interrupted experience. It might even seem that in the case of death this is impossible. But the institutions of many cultures nevertheless attempt nothing less. Some of the forms the restitution takes are repugnant to us, but that only makes it clearer that in cultures where frustration is handled by giving rein to this potential behaviour, the institutions of that society carry this course to extraordinary lengths. Among the Eskimo, when one man has killed another, the family of the man who has been murdered may take the murderer to replace the loss within its own group.

The murderer then becomes the husband of the woman who has been widowed by his act. This is an emphasis upon restitution that ignores all other aspects of the situation—those which seem to us the only important ones; but when tradition selects some such objective it is quite in character that it should disregard all else.

Restitution may be carried out in mourning situations in ways that are less uncongenial to the standards of Western civilization. Among certain of the Central Algonkian Indians south of the Great Lakes the usual procedure was adoption. Upon the death of a child a similar child was put into his place. This similarity was determined in all sorts of ways: often a captive brought in from a raid was taken into the family in the full sense and given all the privileges and the tenderness that had originally been given to the dead child. Or quite as often it was the child's closest playmate, or a child from another related settlement who resembled the dead child in height and features. In such cases the family from which the child was chosen was supposed to be pleased, and indeed in most cases it was by no means the great step that it would be under our institutions. The child had always recognized many 'mothers' and many homes where he was on familiar footing. The new allegiance made him thoroughly at home in still another household. From the point of view of the bereaved parents, the situation had been met by a restitution of the *status quo* that existed before the death of their child.

Persons who primarily mourn the situation rather than the lost individual are provided for in these cultures to a degree which is unimaginable under our institutions. We recognize the possibility of such solace, but we are careful to minimize its connection with the original loss. We do not use it as a mourning technique, and individuals who would be well satisfied with such a solution are left unsupported until the difficult crisis is past.

There is another possible attitude toward frustration. It is the precise opposite of the Pueblo attitude, and we have described it among the other Dionysian reactions of the Plains Indians. Instead of trying to get past the experience with the least possible discomfiture, it finds relief in the most extravagant expression of grief. The Indians of the plains capitalized the utmost indulgences and exacted violent demonstrations of emotion as a matter of course.

In any group of individuals we can recognize those to whom these different reactions to frustration and grief are congenial: ignoring it, indulging it by uninhibited expression, getting even, punishing a victim, and seeking restitution of the original situation. In the psychiatric records of our own society, some of these impulses are recognized as bad ways of dealing with the situation, some as good. The bad ones are said to lead to maladjustments and insanities, the good ones to adequate social functioning. It is clear, however, that the correlation does not lie between any one 'bad' tendency and abnormality in any absolute sense. The desire to run away from grief, to leave it behind at all costs, does not foster psychotic behaviour where, as among the Pueblos, it is mapped out by institutions and supported by every attitude of the group. The Pueblos are not a neurotic people. Their culture gives the impression of fostering mental health. Similarly, the paranoid attitudes so violently expressed among the Kwakiutl are known in psychiatric theory derived from our own civilization as thoroughly 'bad'; that is, they lead in various ways to the breakdown of personality. But it is just those individuals among the Kwakiutl who find it congenial to give the freest expression to these attitudes who nevertheless are the leaders of Kwakiutl society and find greatest personal fulfilment in its culture.

Obviously, adequate personal adjustment does not depend upon following certain motivations and eschewing others. The correlation is in a different direction. Just as those are favoured whose congenial responses are closest to that behaviour which characterizes their society, so those are disoriented whose congenial responses fall in that arc of behaviour which is not capitalized by their culture. These abnormals are those who are not supported by the institutions of their civilization. They are the exceptions who have not easily taken the traditional forms of their culture.

For a valid comparative psychiatry, these disoriented persons who have failed to adapt themselves adequately to their cultures are of first importance. The issue in psychiatry has been too often confused by starting from a fixed list of symptoms instead of from the study of those whose characteristic reactions are denied validity in their society.

The tribes we have described have all of them their nonparticipating 'abnormal' individuals. The individual in Dobu who was thoroughly disoriented was the man who was naturally friendly and found activity an end in itself. He was a pleasant fellow who did not seek to overthrow his fellows or to punish them. He worked for anyone who asked him, and he was tireless in carrying out their commands. He was not filled by a terror of the dark like his fellows, and he did not, as they did, utterly inhibit simple public responses of friendliness toward women closely related, like a wife or sister. He often patted them playfully in public. In any other Dobuan this was scandalous behaviour, but in him it was regarded as merely silly. The village treated him in a kindly enough fashion, not taking advantage of him or making a sport of ridiculing him, but he was definitely regarded as one who was outside the game.

The behaviour congenial to the Dobuan simpleton has been made the ideal in certain periods of our own civilization, and there are still vocations in which his responses are accepted in most Western communities. Especially if a woman is in question, she is well provided for even today in our *mores*, and functions honourably in her family and community. The fact that the Dobuan could not function in his culture was not a consequence of the particular responses that were congenial to him, but of the chasm between them and the cultural pattern.

Most ethnologists have had similar experiences in recognizing that the persons who are put outside the pale of society with contempt are not those who would be placed there by another culture. Lowie found among the Crow Indians of the plains a man of exceptional knowledge of his cultural forms. He was interested in considering these objectively and in correlating different facets. He had an interest in genealogical facts and was invaluable on points of history. Altogether he was an ideal interpreter of Crow life. These traits, however, were not those which were the password to honour among the Crow. He had a definite shrinking from physical danger, and bravado was the tribal virtue. To make matters worse he had attempted to gain recognition by claiming a war honour which was fraudulent. He was proved not to have brought in, as he claimed, a picketed horse from the enemy's camp. To lay false claim to war honours was a paramount sin among the Crow, and by the general opinion, constantly reiterated, he was regarded as irresponsible and incompetent.

Such situations can be paralleled with the attitude in our civilization toward a man who does not succeed in regarding personal possessions as supremely important. Our hobo population is constantly fed by those to whom the accumulation of property is not a sufficient motivation. In case these individuals ally themselves with the hoboes, public opinion regards them as potentially vicious, as indeed because of the asocial situation into which they are thrust they readily become. In case, however, these men compensate by emphasizing their artistic temperament and become members of expatriated groups of petty artists, opinion regards them not as vicious but as silly. In any case they are unsupported by the forms of their society, and the effort to express themselves satisfactorily is ordinarily a greater task than they can achieve.

The dilemma of such an individual is often most successfully solved by doing violence to his strongest natural impulses and accepting the rôle the culture honours. In case he is a person to whom social recognition is necessary, it is ordinarily his only possible course. One of the most striking individuals in Zuñi had accepted this necessity. In a society that thoroughly distrusts authority of any sort, he had a native personal magnetism that singled him out in any group. In a society that exalts moderation and the easiest way, he was turbulent and could act violently upon occasion. In a society that praises a pliant personality that 'talks lots'— that is, that chatters in a friendly fashion—he was scornful and aloof. Zuñi's only reaction to such personalities is to brand them as witches. He was said to have been seen peering through a window from outside, and this is a sure mark of a witch. At any rate, he got drunk one day and boasted that they could not kill him. He was taken before the war priests who hung him by his thumbs from the rafters till he should confess to his witchcraft. This is the usual procedure in a charge of witchcraft. However, he dispatched a messenger to the government troops. When they came, his shoulders were already crippled for life, and the officer of the law was left with no recourse but to imprison the war priests who had been responsible for the enormity. One of these war priests was probably the most respected and important person in recent Zuñi history, and when he returned after imprisonment in the state penitentiary he never resumed his priestly offices. He regarded his power as broken. It was a revenge that is probably unique in Zuñi history. It involved, of course, a challenge to the priesthoods, against whom the witch by his act openly aligned himself.

The course of his life in the forty years that followed this defiance was not, however, what we might easily predict. A witch is not barred from his membership in cult groups because he has been condemned, and the way to recognition lay through such activity. He possessed a remarkable verbal memory and a sweet singing voice. He learned unbelievable stores of mythology, of esoteric ritual, of cult songs. Many hundreds of pages of stories and ritual poetry were taken down from his dictation before he died, and he regarded his songs as much more extensive. He became indispensable in ceremonial life and before he died was the governor of Zuñi. The congenial bent of his personality threw him into irreconcilable conflict with his society, and he solved his dilemma by turning an incidental talent to account. As we might well expect, he was not a happy man. As governor of Zuñi, and high in his cult groups, a marked man in his community, he was obsessed by death. He was a cheated man in the midst of a mildly happy populace.

It is easy to imagine the life he might have lived among the Plains Indians, where every institution favoured the traits that were native to him. The personal authority, the turbulence, the scorn, would all have been honoured in the career he could have made his own. The unhappiness that was inseparable from his temperament as a successful priest and governor of Zuñi would have had no place as a war chief of the Cheyenne; it was not a function of the traits of his native endowment but of the standards of the culture in which he found no outlet for his native responses.

The individuals we have so far discussed are not in any sense psychopathic. They illustrate the dilemma of the individual whose congenial drives are not provided for in the institutions of his culture. This dilemma becomes of psychiatric importance when the behaviour in question is regarded as categorically abnormal in a society. Western civilization tends to regard even a mild homosexual as an abnormal. The clinical picture of homosexuality stresses the neuroses and psychoses to which it gives rise, and emphasizes almost equally the inadequate functioning of the invert and his behaviour. We have only to turn to other cultures, however, to realize that homosexuals have by no means been uniformly inadequate to the social situation. They have not always failed to function. In some societies they have even been especially acclaimed. Plato's *Republic* is, of course, the most convincing statement of the honourable estate of homosexuality. It is presented as a major means to the good life, and Plato's high ethical evaluation of this response was upheld in the customary behaviour of Greece at that period.

The American Indians do not make Plato's high moral claims for homosexuality, but homosexuals are often regarded as exceptionally able. In most of North America there exists the institution of the *berdache,* as the French called them. These men-women were men who at puberty or thereafter took the dress and the occupations of women. Sometimes they married other men and lived with them. Sometimes they were men with no inversion, persons of weak sexual endowment who chose this rôle to avoid the jeers of the women. The berdaches were never regarded as of first-rate supernatural power, as similar men-women were in Siberia, but rather as leaders in women's occupations, good healers in certain diseases, or, among certain tribes, as the genial organizers of social affairs. They were usually, in spite of the manner in which they were accepted, regarded with a certain embarrassment. It was thought slightly ridiculous to address as 'she' a person who was known to be a man and who, as in Zuñi, would be buried on the men's side of the cemetery. But they were socially placed. The emphasis in most tribes was upon the fact that men who took over women's occupations excelled by reason of their strength and initiative and were therefore leaders in women's techniques and in the accumulation of those forms of property made by women. One of the best known of all the Zuñis of a generation ago was the man-woman We-wha, who was, in the words of his friend, Mrs. Stevenson, 'certainly the strongest person in Zuñi, both mentally and physically.' His remarkable memory for ritual made him a chief personage on ceremonial occasions, and his strength and intelligence made him a leader in all kinds of crafts.

The men-women of Zuñi are not all strong, self-reliant personages. Some of them take this refuge to protect themselves against their inability to take part in men's activities. One is almost a simpleton, and one, hardly more than a little boy, has delicate features like a girl's. There are obviously several reasons why a person becomes a berdache in Zuñi, but whatever the reason, men who have chosen openly to assume women's dress have the same chance as any other persons to establish themselves as functioning members of the society. Their response is socially recognized. If they have native ability, they can give it scope; if they are weak creatures, they fail in terms of their weakness of character, not in terms of their inversion.

The Indian institution of the berdache was most strongly developed on the plains. The Dakota had a saying, 'fine possessions like a berdache's,' and it was the epitome of praise for any woman's household possessions. A berdache had two strings to his bow, he was supreme in women's techniques, and he could also support his *ménage* by the man's activity of hunting. Therefore no one was richer. When especially fine beadwork or dressed skins were desired for ceremonial occasions, the berdache's work was sought in preference to any other's. It was his social adequacy that was stressed above all else. As in Zuñi, the attitude toward him is ambivalent and touched with malaise in the face of a recognized incongruity. Social scorn, however, was visited not upon the berdache but upon the man who lived with him. The latter was regarded as a weak man who had chosen an easy berth instead of the recognized goals of their culture; he did not contribute to the household, which was already a model for all households through the sole efforts of the berdache. His sexual adjustment was not singled out in the judgment that was passed upon him, but in terms of his economic adjustment he was an outcast.

When the homosexual response is regarded as a perversion, however, the invert is immediately exposed to all the conflicts to which aberrants are always exposed. His guilt, his sense of inadequacy, his failures, are consequences of the disrepute which social tradition visits upon him, and few people can achieve a satisfactory life unsupported by the standards of their society. The adjustments that society demands of them would strain any man's vitality, and the consequences of this conflict we identify with their homosexuality.

Trance is a similar abnormality in our society. Even a very mild mystic is aberrant in Western civilization. In order to study trance or catalepsy within our own social groups, we have to go to the case histories of the abnormal. Therefore the correlation between trance experience and the neurotic and psychotic seems perfect. As in the case of the homosexual, however, it is a local correlation characteristic of our century. Even in our own cultural background other eras give different results. In the Middle Ages when Catholicism made the ecstatic experience the mark of sainthood, the trance experience was greatly valued, and those to whom the response was congenial, instead of being overwhelmed by a catastrophe as in our century, were given confidence in the pursuit of their careers. It was a validation of ambitions, not a stigma of insanity. Individuals who were susceptible to trance, therefore, succeeded or failed in terms of their native capacities, but since trance experience was highly valued, a great leader was very likely to be capable of it.

Among primitive peoples, trance and catalepsy have been honoured in the extreme. Some of the Indian tribes of California accorded prestige principally to those who passed through certain trance experiences. Not all of these tribes believed that it was exclusively women who were so blessed, but among the Shasta this was the convention. Their shamans were women, and they were accorded the greatest prestige in the community. They were chosen because of their constitutional liability to trance and allied manifestations. One day the woman who was so destined, while she was about her usual work, fell suddenly to the ground. She had heard a voice speaking to her in tones of the greatest intensity. Turning, she had seen a man with drawn bow and arrow. He commanded her to sing on pain of being shot through the heart by his arrow, but under the stress of the experience she fell senseless. Her family gathered. She was lying rigid, hardly breathing. They knew that for some time she had had dreams of a special character which indicated a shamanistic calling, dreams of escaping grizzly bears, falling off cliffs or trees, or of being surrounded by swarms of yellow-jackets. The community knew therefore what to expect. After a few hours the woman began to moan gently and to roll about upon the ground, trembling violently. She was supposed to be repeating the song which she had been told to sing and which during the trance had been taught her by the spirit. As she revived, her moaning became more and more clearly the spirit's song until at last she called out the name of the spirit itself, and immediately blood oozed from her mouth.

When the woman had come to herself after the first encounter with her spirit, she danced that night her first initiatory shaman's dance. For three nights she danced, holding herself by a rope that was swung from the ceiling. On the third night she had to receive in her body her power from her spirit. She was dancing, and as she felt the approach of the moment she called out, 'He will shoot me, he will shoot me.' Her friends stood close, for when she reeled in a kind of cataleptic seizure, they had to seize her before she fell or she would die. From this time on she had in her body a visible materialization of her spirit's power, an icicle-like object which in her dances thereafter she would exhibit, producing it from one part of her body and returning it to another part. From this time on she continued to validate her supernatural power by further cataleptic demonstrations, and she was called upon in great emergencies of life and death, for curing and for divination and for counsel. She became, in other words, by this procedure a woman of great power and importance.

It is clear that, far from regarding cataleptic seizures as blots upon the family escutcheon and as evidences of dreaded disease, cultural approval had seized upon them and made of them the pathway to authority over one's fellows. They were the outstanding characteristic of the most respected social type, the type which functioned with most honour and reward in the community. It was precisely the cataleptic individuals who in this culture were singled out for authority and leadership.

The possible usefulness of 'abnormal' types in a social structure, provided they are types that are culturally selected by that group, is illustrated from every part of the world. The shamans of Siberia dominate their communities. According to the ideas of these peoples, they are individuals who by submission to the will of the spirits have been cured of a grievous illness—the onset of the seizures—and have acquired by this means great supernatural power and incomparable vigour and health. Some, during the period of the call, are violently insane for several years; others irresponsible to the point where they have to be constantly watched lest they wander off in the snow and freeze to death; others ill and emaciated to the point of death, sometimes with bloody sweat. It is the shamanistic practice which constitutes their cure, and the extreme exertion of a Siberian séance leaves them, they claim, rested and able to enter immediately upon a similar performance. Cataleptic seizures are regarded as an essential part of any shamanistic performance.

A good description of the neurotic condition of the shaman and the attention given him by his society is an old one by Canon Callaway, recorded in the words of an old Zulu of South Africa:

> The condition of a man who is about to become a diviner is this; at first he is apparently robust, but in the process of time he begins to be delicate, not having any real disease, but being delicate. He habitually avoids certain kinds of food, choosing what he likes, and he does not eat much of that; he is continually complaining of pains in different parts of his body. And he tells them that he has dreamt that he was carried away by a river. He dreams of many things, and his body is muddied [as a river] and he becomes a house of dreams. He dreams constantly of many things, and on awaking tells his friends, 'My body is muddied today; I dreamt many men were killing me, and I escaped I know not how. On waking one part of my body felt different from other parts; it was no longer alike all over.' At last that man is very ill, and they go to the diviners to enquire.
>
> The diviners do not at once see that he is about to have a soft head [that is, the sensitivity associated with shamanism]. It is difficult for them to see the truth; they continually talk nonsense and make false statements, until all the man's cattle are devoured at their command, they saying that the spirit of his people demands cattle, that it may eat food. At length all the man's property is expended, he still being ill; and they no longer know what to do, for he has no more cattle, and his friends help him in such things as he needs.
>
> At length a diviner comes and says that all the others are wrong. He says, 'He is possessed by the spirits. There is nothing else. They move in him, being divided into two parties; some say, "No, we do not wish our child injured. We do not wish it." It is for that reason he does not get well. If you bar the way against the spirits, you will be killing him. For he will not be a diviner; neither will he ever be a man again.'
>
> So the man may be ill two years without getting better; perhaps even longer than that. He is confined to his house. This continues till his hair falls off. And his body is dry and scurfy; he does not like to anoint himself. He shows that he is about to be a diviner by yawning

again and again, and by sneezing continually. It is apparent also from his being very fond of snuff; not allowing any long time to pass without taking some. And people begin to see that he has had what is good given to him.

After that he is ill; he has convulsions, and when water has been poured on him they then cease for a time. He habitually sheds tears, at first slight, then at last he weeps aloud and when the people are asleep he is heard making a noise and wakes the people by his singing; he has composed a song, and the men and women awake and go to sing in concert with him. All the people of the village are troubled by want of sleep; for a man who is becoming a diviner causes great trouble, for he does not sleep, but works constantly with his brain; his sleep is merely by snatches, and he wakes up singing many songs; and people who are near quit their villages by night when they hear him singing aloud and go to sing in concert. Perhaps he sings till morning, no one having slept. And then he leaps about the house like a frog; and the house becomes too small for him, and he goes out leaping and singing, and shaking like a reed in the water, and dripping with perspiration.

In this state of things they daily expect his death; he is now but skin and bones, and they think that tomorrow's sun will not leave him alive. At this time many cattle are eaten, for the people encourage his becoming a diviner. At length [in a dream] an ancient ancestral spirit is pointed out to him. This spirit says to him, 'Go to So-and-so and he will churn for you an emetic [the medicine the drinking of which is a part of shamanistic initiation] that you may be a diviner altogether.' Then he is quiet a few days, having gone to the diviner to have the medicine churned for him; and he comes back quite another man, being now cleansed and a diviner indeed.

Thereafter for life, when he is possessed by his spirits, he foretells events and finds lost articles.

It is clear that culture may value and make socially available even highly unstable human types. If it chooses to treat their peculiarities as the most valued variants of human behaviour, the individuals in question will rise to the occasion and perform their social rôles without reference to our usual ideas of the types who can make social adjustments and those who cannot. Those who function inadequately in any society are not those with certain fixed 'abnormal' traits, but may well be those whose responses have received no support in the institutions of their culture. The weakness of these aberrants is in great measure illusory. It springs, not from the fact that they are lacking in necessary vigour, but that they are individuals whose native responses are not reaffirmed by society. They are, as Sapir phrases it, 'alienated from an impossible world.'

The person unsupported by the standards of his time and place and left naked to the winds of ridicule has been unforgettably drawn in

European literature in the figure of Don Quixote. Cervantes turned upon a tradition still honoured in the abstract the limelight of a changed set of practical standards, and his poor old man, the orthodox upholder of the romantic chivalry of another generation, became a simpleton. The windmills with which he tilted were the serious antagonists of a hardly vanished world, but to tilt with them when the world no longer called them serious was to rave. He loved his Dulcinea in the best traditional manner of chivalry, but another version of love was fashionable for the moment, and his fervour was counted to him for madness.

These contrasting worlds which, in the primitive cultures we have considered, are separated from one another in space, in modern Occidental history more often succeed one another in time. The major issue is the same in either case, but the importance of understanding the phenomenon is far greater in the modern world where we cannot escape if we would from the succession of configurations in time. When each culture is a world in itself, relatively stable like the Eskimo culture, for example, and geographically isolated from all others, the issue is academic. But our civilization must deal with cultural standards that go down under our eyes and new ones that arise from a shadow upon the horizon. We must be willing to take account of changing normalities even when the question is of the morality in which we were bred. Just as we are handicapped in dealing with ethical problems so long as we hold to an absolute definition of morality, so we are handicapped in dealing with human society so long as we identify our local normalities with the inevitable necessities of existence.

No society has yet attempted a self-conscious direction of the process by which its new normalities are created in the next generation. Dewey has pointed out how possible and yet how drastic such social engineering would be. For some traditional arrangements it is obvious that very high prices are paid, reckoned in terms of human suffering and frustration. If these arrangements presented themselves to us merely as arrangements and not as categorical imperatives, our reasonable course would be to adapt them by whatever means to rationally selected goals. What we do instead is to ridicule our Don Quixotes, the ludicrous embodiments of an outmoded tradition, and continue to regard our own as final and prescribed in the nature of things.

In the meantime the therapeutic problem of dealing with our psychopaths of this type is often misunderstood. Their alienation from the actual world can often be more intelligently handled than by insisting that they adopt the modes that are alien to them. Two other courses are always possible. In the first place, the misfit individual may cultivate a greater objective interest in his own preferences and learn how to manage with greater equanimity his deviation from the type. If he learns to recognize the extent to which his suffering has been due to his lack of support in a traditional ethos, he may gradually educate himself to accept his degree of difference with less suffering. Both the exaggerated emotional disturbances of the manic depressive and the seclusion of the schizophrenic add certain values to existence which are not open to those differently constituted. The unsupported individual who valiantly accepts his favourite and native virtues may attain a feasible course of behaviour that makes it unnecessary for him to take refuge in a private world he has fashioned for himself. He may gradually achieve a more independent and less tortured attitude toward his deviations and upon this attitude he may be able to build an adequately functioning existence.

In the second place, an increased tolerance in society toward its less usual types must keep pace with the self-education of the patient. The possibilities in this direction are endless. Tradition is as neurotic as any patient; its overgrown fear of deviation from its fortuitous standards conforms to all the usual definitions of the psychopathic. This fear does not depend upon observation of the limits within which conformity is necessary to the social good. Much more deviation is allowed to the individual in some cultures than in others, and those in which much is allowed cannot be shown to suffer from their peculiarity. It is probable that social orders of the future will carry this tolerance and encouragement of individual difference much further than any cultures of which we have experience.

The American tendency at the present time leans so far to the opposite extreme that it is not easy for us to picture the changes that such an attitude would bring about. Middletown is a typical example of our usual urban fear of seeming in however slight an act different from our neighbours. Eccentricity is more feared than parasitism. Every sacrifice of time and tranquillity is made in order that no one in the family may have any taint of nonconformity attached to him. Children in school make their great tragedies out of not wearing a certain kind of stockings, not joining a certain dancing-class, not driving a certain car. The fear of being different is the dominating motivation recorded in Middletown.

The psychopathic toll that such a motivation exacts is evident in every institution for mental diseases in our country. In a society in which it existed only as a minor motive among many others, the psychiatric picture would be a very different one. At all events, there can be no reasonable doubt that one of the most effective ways in which to deal with the staggering burden of psychopathic tragedies in America at the present time is by means of an educational program which fosters tolerance in society and a kind of self-respect and independence that is foreign to Middletown and our urban traditions.

Not all psychopaths, of course, are individuals whose native responses are at variance with those of their civilization. Another large group are those who are merely inadequate and who are strongly enough motivated so that their failure is more than they can bear. In a society in which the will-to-power is most highly rewarded, those who fail may not be those who are differently constituted, but simply those who are insufficiently endowed. The inferiority complex takes a great toll of suffering in our society. It is not necessary that sufferers of this type have a history of frustration in the sense that strong native bents have been inhibited; their frustration is often enough only the reflection of their inability to reach a certain goal. There is a cultural implication here, too, in that the traditional goal may be accessible to large numbers or to very few, and in proportion as success is obsessive and is limited to the few, a greater and greater number will be liable to the extreme penalties of maladjustment.

To a certain extent, therefore, civilization in setting higher and possibly more worth-while goals may increase the number of its abnormals. But the point may very easily be overemphasized, for very small changes in social attitudes may far outweigh this correlation. On the whole, since the social possibilities of tolerance and recognition of individual difference are so little explored in practice, pessimism seems premature. Certainly other quite different social factors which we have just discussed are more directly responsible for the great proportion of our neurotics and psychotics, and with these other factors civilizations could, if they would, deal without necessary intrinsic loss.

We have been considering individuals from the point of view of their ability to function adequately in their society. This adequate functioning is one of the ways in which normality is clinically defined. It is also defined in terms of fixed symptoms, and the tendency is to identify normality with the statistically average. In practice this average is one arrived at in the laboratory, and deviations from it are defined as abnormal.

From the point of view of a single culture this procedure is very useful. It shows the clinical picture of the civilization and gives considerable information about its socially approved behaviour. To generalize this as an absolute normal, however, is a different matter. As we have seen, the range of normality in different cultures does not coincide. Some, like Zuñi and the Kwakiutl, are so far removed from each other that they overlap only slightly. The statistically determined normal on the Northwest Coast would be far outside the extreme boundaries of abnormality in the Pueblos. The normal Kwakiutl rivalry contest would only be understood as madness in Zuñi, and the traditional Zuñi indifference to dominance and the humiliation of others would be the fatuousness of a simpleton in a man of noble family on the Northwest Coast. Aberrant behaviour in either culture could never be determined in relation to any least common denominator of behaviour. Any society, according to its major preoccupations, may increase and intensify even hysterical, epileptic, or paranoid symptoms, at the same time relying socially in a greater and greater degree upon the very individuals who display them.

This fact is important in psychiatry because it makes clear another group of abnormals which probably exists in every culture: the abnormals who represent the extreme development of the local cultural type. This group is socially in the opposite situation from the group we have discussed, those whose responses are at variance with their cultural standards. Society, instead of exposing the former group at every point, supports them in their furthest aberrations. They have a licence which they may almost endlessly exploit. For this reason these persons almost never fall within the scope of any contemporary psychiatry. They are unlikely to be described even in the most careful manuals of the generation that fosters them. Yet from the point of view of another generation or culture they are ordinarily the most bizarre of the psychopathic types of the period.

The Puritan divines of New England in the eighteenth century were the last persons whom contemporary opinion in the colonies regarded as psychopathic. Few prestige groups in any culture have been allowed such complete intellectual and emotional dictatorship as they were. They were the voice of God. Yet to a modern observer it is they, not the confused and tormented women they put to death as witches, who were the psychoneurotics of Puritan New England. A sense of guilt as extreme as they portrayed and demanded both in their own conversion experiences and in those of their converts is found in a slightly saner civilization only in institutions for mental diseases. They admitted no salvation without a conviction of sin that prostrated the victim, sometimes for years, with remorse and terrible anguish. It was the duty of the minister to put the fear of hell into the heart of even the youngest child, and to exact of every convert emotional acceptance of his damnation if God saw fit to damn him. It does not matter where we turn among the records of New England Puritan churches of this period, whether to those dealing with witches or with unsaved children not yet in their teens or with such themes as damnation and predestination, we are faced with the fact that the group of people who carried out to the greatest extreme and in the fullest honour the cultural doctrine of the moment are by the slightly altered standards of our generation the victims of intolerable aberrations. From the point of view of a comparative psychiatry they fall in the category of the abnormal.

In our own generation extreme forms of ego-gratification are culturally supported in a similar fashion. Arrogant and unbridled egoists as family men, as officers of the law and in business, have been again and again portrayed by novelists and dramatists, and they are familiar in every community. Like the behaviour of Puritan divines, their courses of action are often more asocial than those of the inmates of penitentiaries. In terms of the suffering and frustration that they spread about them there is probably no comparison. There is very possibly at least as great a degree of mental warping. Yet they are entrusted with positions of great influence and importance and are as a rule fathers of families. Their impress both upon their own children and upon the structure of our society is indelible. They are not described in our manuals of psychiatry because they are supported by every tenet of our civilization. They are sure of themselves in real life in a way that is possible only to those who are oriented to the points of the compass laid down in their own culture. Nevertheless a future psychiatry may well ransack our novels and letters and public records for illumination upon a type of abnormality to which it would not otherwise give credence. In every society it is among this very group of the culturally encouraged and fortified that some of the most extreme types of human behaviour are fostered.

Social thinking at the present time has no more important task before it than that of taking adequate account of cultural relativity. In the fields of both sociology and psychology the implications are fundamental, and modern thought about contacts of peoples and about our changing standards is greatly in need of sane and scientific direction. The sophisticated modern temper has made of social relativity, even in the small area which it has recognized, a doctrine of despair. It has pointed out its incongruity with the orthodox dreams of permanence and ideality and with the individual's illusions of autonomy. It has argued that if human experience must give up these, the nutshell of existence is empty. But to interpret our dilemma in these terms is to be guilty of an anachronism. It is only the inevitable cultural lag that makes us insist that the old must be discovered again in the new, that there is no solution but to find the old certainty and stability in the new plasticity. The recognition of cultural relativity carries with it its own values, which need not be those of the absolutist philosophies. It challenges customary opinions and causes those who have been bred to them acute discomfort. It rouses pessimism because it throws old formulas into confusion, not because it contains anything intrinsically difficult. As soon as the new opinion is embraced as customary belief, it will be another trusted bulwark of the good life. We shall arrive then at a more realistic social faith, accepting as grounds of hope and as new bases for tolerance the coexisting and equally valid patterns of life which mankind has created for itself from the raw materials of existence.

Crime and Punishment

Conflicting theories of how to deal with crime are deeply rooted in Western culture. The Mosaic Code is unequivocal: An eye for an eye; a tooth for a tooth. The Sixth Commandment is equally clear: Thou shalt not kill. And the classic statement of forgiveness is, of course, found in the Sermon on the Mount: Whosoever shall smite thee on thy right cheek, turn to him the other also. To the concepts of retribution and forgiveness the modern age has added that of correction and rehabilitation, and all are defended and attacked vigorously in our society.

In the last decades an increasing number of countries and states have passed laws abolishing the death penalty. But at this writing forty-three states in America still allow it. The first four essays in this section present both the practical and the moral issues which continue to be debated. The reader will find Barzun's very direct and Mencken's quite unusual arguments for capital punishment in sharp conflict with those of Orwell and Camus.

A related question which is only now moving into the public orbit is the relationship between mental illness and crime. Is the offender sick or criminal? Do we send him to a hospital or to a prison? Dr. Menninger, who neatly poses the question: "Verdict Guilty—Now What?" tends to regard the offender as sick (although he rightly deplores the non-scientific labeling in which we have just indulged). Dr. Szasz, however, points to some of the dangers inherent in equating crime with illness. Judge Bazelon's speech raises the larger social question of what choices of action are open to the individual who becomes a criminal. The whole question of guilt, punishment, and moral rehabilitation is again raised, this time in pre-Freudian and fictional terms, by Tolstoy's short and simple story with which we conclude the section.

JACQUES BARZUN

Born in France in 1907, Jacques Barzun came to this country when he was twelve years old and later became an American citizen. Admitted to Columbia University shortly before his sixteenth birthday, he became lecturer and researcher in history there and by 1945 rose to full professor. He has been Dean of Faculties and Provost at Columbia since 1958 and Seth Low Professor of History since 1960. A tireless critic of education and society, Professor Barzun is also considered an authority on art and music and an articulate spokesman for the humanist tradition. His many books include Darwin, Marx, Wagner: Critique of a Heritage *(1941),* The Teacher in America *(1945),* Berlioz and the Romantic Century *(1950),* The Modern Researcher *(1957), and* The House of Intellect *(1959). He is also a frequent contributor to periodicals. The essay we present below first appeared in* The American Scholar, *Spring, 1962.*

IN FAVOR OF CAPITAL PUNISHMENT

A passing remark of mine in the *Mid-Century* magazine has brought me a number of letters and a sheaf of pamphlets against capital punishment. The letters, sad and reproachful, offer me the choice of pleading ignorance or being proved insensitive. I am asked whether I know that there exists a worldwide movement for the abolition of capital punishment which has everywhere enlisted able men of every profession, including the law. I am told that the death penalty is not only inhuman but also unscientific, for rapists and murderers are really sick people who should be cured, not killed. I am invited to use my imagination and acknowledge the unbearable horror of every form of execution.

I am indeed aware that the movement for abolition is widespread and articulate, especially in England. It is headed there by my old friend and publisher, Mr. Victor Gollancz, and it numbers such well-known writers as Arthur Koestler, C. H. Rolph, James Avery Joyce and Sir John Barry. Abroad as at home the profession of psychiatry tends to support the cure principle, and many liberal newspapers, such as the *Observer*, are committed to abolition. In the United States there are at least twenty-five state leagues working to the same end, plus a national league and several church councils, notably the Quaker and the Episcopal.

The assemblage of so much talent and enlightened goodwill behind a single proposal must give pause to anyone who supports the other side, and in the attempt to make clear my views, which are now close to unpopular, I start out by granting that my conclusion is arguable; that is, I am still open to conviction, *provided* some fallacies and frivolities in the abolitionist argument are first disposed of and the difficulties not ignored but overcome. I should be glad to see this happen, not only because there is pleasure in the spectacle of an airtight case, but also because I am not more sanguinary than my neighbor and I should welcome the discovery of safeguards—for society *and* the criminal—other than killing. But I say it again, these safeguards must really meet, not evade or postpone, the difficulties I am about to describe. Let me add before I begin that I shall probably not answer any more letters on this arousing subject. If this printed exposition does not do justice to my cause, it is not likely that I can do better in the hurry of private correspondence.

I readily concede at the outset that present ways of dealing out capital punishment are as revolting as Mr. Koestler says in his harrowing volume, *Hanged by the Neck*. Like many of our prisons, our modes of execution should change. But this objection to barbarity does not mean that capital punishment—or rather, judicial homicide—should not go on. The illicit jump we find here, on the threshold of the inquiry, is characteristic of the abolitionist and must be disallowed at every point. Let us bear in mind the possibility of devising a painless, sudden and dignified death, and see whether its administration is justifiable.

The four main arguments advanced against the death penalty are: *1.* punishment for crime is a primitive idea rooted in revenge; *2.* capital punishment does not deter; *3.* judicial error being possible, taking life is an appalling risk; *4.* a civilized state, to deserve its name, must uphold, not violate, the sanctity of human life.

I entirely agree with the first pair of propositions, which is why, a moment ago, I replaced the term capital punishment with "judicial homicide." The uncontrollable brute whom I want put out of the way is not to be punished for his misdeeds, nor used as an example or a warning; he is to be killed for the protection of others, like the wolf that escaped not long ago in a Connecticut suburb. No anger, vindictiveness or moral conceit need preside over the removal of such dangers. But a man's inability to control his violent impulses or to imagine the fatal consequences of his acts should be a presumptive reason for his elimination from society. This generality covers drunken driving and teen-age racing on public highways, as well as incurable obsessive violence; it might be extended (as I shall suggest later) to other acts that destroy, precisely, the moral basis of civilization.

But why kill? I am ready to believe the statistics tending to show that the prospect of his own death does not stop the murderer. For one thing he is often a blind egotist, who cannot conceive the possibility of his own death. For another, detection would have to be infallible to deter the more imaginative who, although afraid, think they can escape discovery. Lastly, as Shaw long ago pointed out, hanging the wrong man will deter as effectively as hanging the right one. So, once again, why kill? If I agree that moral progress means an increasing respect for human life, how can I oppose abolition?

I do so because on this subject of human life, which is to me the heart of the controversy, I find the abolitionist inconsistent, narrow or blind. The propaganda for abolition speaks in hushed tones of the sanctity of human life, as if the mere statement of it as an absolute should silence all opponents who have any moral sense. But most of the abolitionists belong to nations that spend half their annual income on weapons of war and that honor research to perfect means of killing. These good people vote without a qualm for the political parties that quite sensibly arm their country to the teeth. The West today does not seem to be the time or place to invoke the absolute sanctity of human life. As for the clergymen in the movement, we may be sure from the experience of two previous world wars that they will bless our arms and pray for victory when called upon, the sixth commandment notwithstanding.

"Oh, but we mean the sanctity of life *within* the nation!" Very well: is the movement then campaigning also against the principle of self-defense? Absolute sanctity means letting the cutthroat have his sweet will of you, even if you have a poker handy to bash him with, for you might kill. And again, do we hear any protest against the police firing at criminals on the street—mere bank robbers usually—and doing this, often enough, with an excited marksmanship that misses the artist and hits the bystander? The absolute sanctity of human life is, for the abolitionist, a slogan rather than a considered proposition.

Yet it deserves examination, for upon our acceptance or rejection of it depend such other highly civilized possibilities as euthanasia and seemly suicide. The inquiring mind also wants to know, why the sanctity of *human* life alone? My tastes do not run to household pets, but I find

something less than admirable in the uses to which we put animals—
in zoos, laboratories and space machines—without the excuse of the
ancient law, "Eat or be eaten."

It should moreover be borne in mind that this argument about sanctity
applies—or would apply—to about ten persons a year in Great Britain
and to between fifty and seventy-five in the United States. These are the
average numbers of those executed in recent years. The count by itself
should not, of course, affect our judgment of the principle: one life
spared or forfeited is as important, morally, as a hundred thousand. But
it should inspire a comparative judgment: there are hundreds and indeed
thousands whom, in our concern with the horrors of execution, we forget: on the one hand, the victims of violence; on the other, the prisoners
in our jails.

The victims are easy to forget. Social science tends steadily to mark
a preference for the troubled, the abnormal, the problem case. Whether
it is poverty, mental disorder, delinquency or crime, the "patient material" monopolizes the interest of increasing groups of people among the
most generous and learned. Psychiatry and moral liberalism go together;
the application of law as we have known it is thus coming to be regarded
as an historic prelude to social work, which may replace it entirely. Modern literature makes the most of this same outlook, caring only for the
disturbed spirit, scorning as bourgeois those who pay their way and do
not stab their friends. All the while the determinism of natural science
reinforces the assumption that society causes its own evils. A French
jurist, for example, says that in order to understand crime we must first
brush aside all ideas of Responsibility. He means the criminal's and takes
for granted that of society. The murderer kills because reared in a broken
home or, conversely, because at an early age he witnessed his parents
making love. Out of such cases, which make pathetic reading in the
literature of modern criminology, is born the abolitionist's state of
mind: we dare not kill those we are beginning to understand so well.

If, moreover, we turn to the accounts of the crimes committed by
these unfortunates, who are the victims? Only dull ordinary people going
about their business. We are sorry, of course, but they do not interest
science on its march. Balancing, for example, the sixty to seventy criminals
executed annually in the United States, there were the seventy to eighty
housewives whom George Cvek robbed, raped and usually killed during
the months of a career devoted to proving his virility. "It is too bad."
Cvek alone seems instructive, even though one of the law officers who
helped track him down quietly remarks: "As to the extent that his villain-
ies disturbed family relationships, or how many women are still haunted
by the specter of an experience they have never disclosed to another
living soul, these questions can only lend themselves to sterile conjecture."

The remote results are beyond our ken, but it is not idle to speculate about those whose death by violence fills the daily two inches at the back of respectable newspapers—the old man sunning himself on a park bench and beaten to death by four hoodlums, the small children abused and strangled, the middle-aged ladies on a hike assaulted and killed, the family terrorized by a released or escaped lunatic, the half-dozen working people massacred by the sudden maniac, the boatload of persons dispatched by the skipper, the mindless assaults upon schoolteachers and shopkeepers by the increasing horde of dedicated killers in our great cities. Where does the sanctity of life begin?

It is all very well to say that many of these killers are themselves "children," that is, minors. Doubtless a nine-year-old mind is housed in that 150 pounds of unguided muscle. Grant, for argument's sake, that the misdeed is "the fault of society," trot out the broken home and the slum environment. The question then is, What shall we do, not in the Utopian city of tomorrow, but here and now? The "scientific" means of cure are more than uncertain. The apparatus of detention only increases the killer's antisocial animus. Reformatories and mental hospitals are full and have an understandable bias toward discharging their inmates. Some of these are indeed "cured"—so long as they stay under a rule. The stress of the social free-for-all throws them back on their violent modes of self-expression. At that point I agree that society has failed—twice: it has twice failed the victims, whatever may be its guilt toward the killer.

As in all great questions, the moralist must choose, and choosing has a price. I happen to think that if a person of adult body has not been endowed with adequate controls against irrationally taking the life of another, that person must be judicially, painlessly, regretfully killed before that mindless body's horrible automation repeats.

I say "irrationally" taking life, because it is often possible to feel great sympathy with a murderer. Certain *crimes passionnels* can be forgiven without being condoned. Blackmailers invite direct retribution. Long provocation can be an excuse, as in that engaging case of some years ago, in which a respectable carpenter of seventy found he could no longer stand the incessant nagging of his wife. While she excoriated him from her throne in the kitchen—a daily exercise for fifty years—the husband went to his bench and came back with a hammer in each hand to settle the score. The testimony to his character, coupled with the sincerity implied by the two hammers, was enough to have him sent into quiet and brief seclusion.

But what are we to say of the type of motive disclosed in a journal published by the inmates of one of our Federal penitentiaries? The author is a bank robber who confesses that money is not his object:

My mania for power, socially, sexually, and otherwise can feel no degree of satisfaction until I feel sure I have struck the ultimate of submission and terror in the minds and bodies of my victims. . . . It's very

difficult to explain all the queer fascinating sensations pounding and
surging through me while I'm holding a gun on a victim, watching his
body tremble and sweat. . . . This is the moment when all the rationalized hypocrisies of civilization are suddenly swept away and two men
stand there facing each other morally and ethically naked, and right
and wrong are the absolute commands of the man behind the gun.

This confused echo of modern literature and modern science defines
the choice before us. Anything deserving the name of cure for such a
man presupposes not only a laborious individual psychoanalysis, with
the means to conduct and to sustain it, socially and economically, but
also a re-education of the mind, so as to throw into correct perspective
the garbled ideas of Freud and Nietzsche, Gide and Dostoevski, which
this power-seeker and his fellows have derived from the culture and
temper of our times. Ideas are tenacious and give continuity to emotion.
Failing a second birth of heart and mind, we must ask: How soon will
this sufferer sacrifice a bank clerk in the interests of making civilization
less hypocritical? And we must certainly question the wisdom of affording him more than one chance. The abolitionists' advocacy of an unconditional "let live" is in truth part of the same cultural tendency that
animates the killer. The Western peoples' revulsion from power in domestic and foreign policy has made of the state a sort of counterpart of
the bank robber: both having power and neither knowing how to use it.
Both waste lives because hypnotized by irrelevant ideas and crippled by
contradictory emotions. If psychiatry were sure of its ground in diagnos-
ing the individual case, a philosopher might consider whether such dangerous obsessions should not be guarded against by judicial homicide
before the shooting starts.

I raise the question not indeed to recommend the prophylactic execution
of potential murderers, but to introduce the last two perplexities that the
abolitionists dwarf or obscure by their concentration on changing an
isolated penalty. One of these is the scale by which to judge the offenses
society wants to repress. I can for example imagine a truly democratic
state in which it would be deemed a form of treason punishable by death
to create a disturbance in any court or deliberative assembly. The aim
would be to recognize the sanctity of orderly discourse in arriving at
justice, assessing criticism and defining policy. Under such a law, a natural selection would operate to remove permanently from the scene persons who, let us say, neglect argument in favor of banging on the desk
with their shoe. Similarly, a bullying minority in a diet, parliament or
skupshtina would be prosecuted for treason to the most sacred institutions when fists or flying inkwells replace rhetoric. That the mere suggestion of such a law sounds ludicrous shows how remote we are from
civilized institutions, and hence how gradual should be our departure
from the severity of judicial homicide.

I say gradual and I do not mean standing still. For there is one form of barbarity in our law that I want to see mitigated before any other. I mean imprisonment. The enemies of capital punishment—and liberals generally—seem to be satisfied with any legal outcome so long as they themselves avoid the vicarious guilt of shedding blood. They speak of the sanctity of life, but have no concern with its quality. They give no impression of ever having read what it is certain they have read, from Wilde's *De Profundis* to the latest account of prison life by a convicted homosexual. Despite the infamy of concentration camps, despite Mr. Charles Burney's remarkable work, *Solitary Confinement*, despite riots in prisons, despite the round of escape, recapture and return in chains, the abolitionists' imagination tells them nothing about the reality of being caged. They read without a qualm, indeed they read with rejoicing, the hideous irony of "Killer Gets Life"; they sigh with relief instead of horror. They do not see and suffer the cell, the drill, the clothes, the stench, the food; they do not feel the sexual racking of young and old bodies, the hateful promiscuity, the insane monotony, the mass degradation, the impotent hatred. They do not remember from Silvio Pellico that only a strong political faith, with a hope of final victory, can steel a man to endure long detention. They forget that Joan of Arc, when offered "life," preferred burning at the stake. Quite of another mind, the abolitionists point with pride to the "model prisoners" that murderers often turn out to be. As if a model prisoner were not, first, a contradiction in terms, and second, an exemplar of what a free society should not want.

I said a moment ago that the happy advocates of the life sentence appear not to have understood what we know they have read. No more do they appear to read what they themselves write. In the preface to his useful volume of cases, *Hanged in Error*, Mr. Leslie Hale, M.P., refers to the tardy recognition of a minor miscarriage of justice—one year in jail: "The prisoner emerged to find that his wife had died and that his children and his aged parents had been removed to the workhouse. By the time a small payment had been assessed as 'compensation' the victim was incurably insane." So far we are as indignant with the law as Mr. Hale. But what comes next? He cites the famous Evans case, in which it is very probable that the wrong man was hanged, and he exclaims: "While such mistakes are possible, should society impose an irrevocable sentence?" Does Mr. Hale really ask us to believe that the sentence passed on the first man, whose wife died and who went insane, was in any sense *revocable?* Would not any man rather be Evans dead than that other wretch "emerging" with his small compensation and his reasons for living gone?

Nothing is revocable here below, imprisonment least of all. The agony of a trial itself is punishment, and acquittal wipes out nothing. Read the heart-rending diary of William Wallace, accused quite implausibly of having murdered his wife and "saved" by the Court of Criminal Appeals

—but saved for what? Brutish ostracism by everyone and a few years of solitary despair. The cases of Adolf Beck, of Oscar Slater, of the unhappy Brooklyn bank teller who vaguely resembled a forger and spent eight years in Sing Sing only to "emerge" a broken, friendless, useless, "compensated" man—all these, if the dignity of the individual has any meaning, had better have been dead before the prison door ever opened for them. This is what counsel always says to the jury in the course of a murder trial and counsel is right: far better hang this man than "give him life." For my part, I would choose death without hesitation. If that option is abolished, a demand will one day be heard to claim it as a privilege in the name of human dignity. I shall believe in the abolitionist's present views only after he has emerged from twelve months in a convict cell.

The detached observer may want to interrupt here and say that the argument has now passed from reasoning to emotional preference. Whereas the objector to capital punishment *feels* that death is the greatest of evils, I *feel* that imprisonment is worse than death. A moment's thought will show that feeling is the appropriate arbiter. All reasoning about what is right, civilized and moral rests upon sentiment, like mathematics. Only, in trying to persuade others, it is important to single out the fundamental feeling, the prime intuition, and from it to reason justly. In my view, to profess respect for human life and be willing to see it spent in a penitentiary is to entertain liberal feelings frivolously. To oppose the death penalty because, unlike a prison term, it is irrevocable is to argue fallaciously.

In the propaganda for abolishing the death sentence the recital of numerous miscarriages of justice commits the same error and implies the same callousness: what is at fault in our present system is not the sentence but the fallible procedure. Capital cases being one in a thousand or more, who can be cheerful at the thought of all the "revocable" errors? What the miscarriages point to is the need for reforming the jury system, the rules of evidence, the customs of prosecution, the machinery of appeal. The failure to see that this is the great task reflects the sentimentality I spoke of earlier, that which responds chiefly to the excitement of the unusual. A writer on Death and the Supreme Court is at pains to point out that when that tribunal reviews a capital case, the judges are particularly anxious and careful. What a left-handed compliment to the highest judicial conscience of the country! Fortunately, some of the champions of the misjudged see the issue more clearly. Many of those who are thought wrongly convicted now languish in jail because the jury was uncertain or because a doubting governor commuted the death sentence. Thus Dr. Samuel H. Sheppard, Jr., convicted of his wife's murder in the second degree is serving a sentence that is supposed to run for the term of his natural life. The story of his numerous trials, as told by Mr. Paul Holmes, suggests that police incompetence, newspaper demagogy, public envy of affluence and the mischances of legal procedure fashioned the result. But Dr. Sheppard's vindicator is under no illusion as to the conditions that this "lucky" evader of the electric chair will face if he is granted parole after ten years: "It will carry with it no right to resume his life as a physician. His privilege to practice medicine was blotted out with his conviction. He must all his life bear the stigma of a parolee, subject to unceremonious return to confinement for life for the slightest misstep. More than this, he must live out his life as a convicted murderer."

What does the moral conscience of today think it is doing? If such a man is a dangerous repeater of violent acts, what right has the state to let him loose after ten years? What is, in fact, the meaning of a "life sentence" that peters out long before life? Paroling looks suspiciously like an expression of social remorse for the pain of incarceration, coupled with a wish to avoid "unfavorable publicity" by freeing a suspect. The man is let out when the fuss has died down; which would mean that he was not under lock and key for our protection at all. He *was* being punished, just a little—for so prison seems in the abolitionist's distorted view, and in the jury's and the prosecutor's, whose "second-degree" murder suggests killing someone "just a little."[1]

If, on the other hand, execution and life imprisonment are judged too severe and the accused is expected to be harmless hereafter—punishment being ruled out as illiberal—what has society gained by wrecking his life and damaging that of his family?

What we accept, and what the abolitionist will clamp upon us all the more firmly if he succeeds, is an incoherence which is not remedied by the belief that second-degree murder merits a kind of second-degree death; that a doubt as to the identity of a killer is resolved by commuting real death into intolerable life; and that our ignorance whether a maniac will strike again can be hedged against by measuring "good behavior" within the gates and then releasing the subject upon the public in the true spirit of experimentation.

These are some of the thoughts I find I cannot escape when I read and reflect upon this grave subject. If, as I think, they are relevant to any discussion of change and reform, resting as they do on the direct and concrete perception of what happens, then the simple meliorists who expect to breathe a purer air by abolishing the death penalty are deceiving themselves and us. The issue is for the public to judge; but I for one shall not sleep easier for knowing that in England and America and the West generally a hundred more human beings are kept alive in degrading conditions to face a hopeless future; while others—possibly less

---

[1] The British Homicide Act of 1957, Section 2, implies the same reasoning in its definition of "diminished responsibility" for certain forms of mental abnormality. The whole question of irrationality and crime is in utter confusion, on both sides of the Atlantic.

conscious, certainly less controlled—benefit from a premature freedom dangerous alike to themselves and society. In short, I derive no comfort from the illusion that in giving up one manifest protection of the law-abiding, we who might well be in any of these three roles—victim, prisoner, licensed killer—have struck a blow for the sanctity of human life.

H. L. MENCKEN

H. L. Mencken (1880–1956) was perhaps America's most witty, ornery, and controversial newspaperman. Regarded by some as an admirable and fearless critic, he was heartily and openly disliked by others, and received a generous share of criticism which he collected and published as Menckeniana, a Schimpflexicon, *in 1928.*

Born and educated in Baltimore, he worked in his family's tobacco business until his father's death in 1899, when he first became a reporter on the Baltimore Herald Tribune. *He soon rose to editor, and, when the paper stopped publication in 1906, moved to the* Baltimore Sun. *Leaving Baltimore for New York, he became editor of the* Smart Set *(1914–1923), and later, in association with George Jean Nathan, he founded and edited* The American Mercury *(1924–1933). He continued as a prolific writer until suffering a cerebral thrombosis in 1948. He died in Baltimore in 1956.*

The American—as opposed to the English—language was of vital interest to Mencken, and perhaps his best known book is The American Language, *first published in 1919. Four editions and two supplements followed. His many other writings include the three autobiographical volumes* Happy Days *(1940),* Newspaper Days *(1941), and* Heathen Days *(1943); and* Prejudices *(1917–1927), a six-volume collection of his newspaper pieces. The essay printed below, typical of Mencken's outspokenness, is taken from* A Mencken Chrestomathy *(1949).*

THE PENALTY OF DEATH

Of the arguments against capital punishment that issue from uplifters, two are commonly heard most often, to wit:

1. That hanging a man (or frying him or gassing him) is a dreadful business, degrading to those who have to do it and revolting to those who have to witness it.

2. That it is useless, for it does not deter others from the same crime.

The first of these arguments, it seems to me, is plainly too weak to need serious refutation. All it says, in brief, is that the work of the hangman is unpleasant. Granted. But suppose it is? It may be quite necessary to society for all that. There are, indeed, many other jobs that are unpleasant, and yet no one thinks of abolishing them—that of the plumber, that of the soldier, that of the garbage-man, that of the priest hearing confessions, that of the sand-hog, and so on. Moreover, what evidence is there that any actual hangman complains of his work? I have heard none. On the contrary, I have known many who delighted in their ancient art, and practised it proudly.

In the second argument of the abolitionists there is rather more force, but even here, I believe, the ground under them is shaky. Their fundamental error consists in assuming that the whole aim of punishing criminals is to deter other (potential) criminals—that we hang or electrocute A simply in order to so alarm B that he will not kill C. This, I believe, is an assumption which confuses a part with the whole. Deterrence, obviously, is *one* of the aims of punishment, but it is surely not the only one. On the contrary, there are at least half a dozen, and some are probably quite as important. At least one of them, practically considered, is *more* important. Commonly, it is described as revenge, but revenge is really not the word for it. I borrow a better term from the late Aristotle: *katharsis*. *Katharsis*, so used, means a salubrious discharge of emotions, a healthy letting off of steam. A school-boy, disliking his teacher, deposits a tack upon the pedagogical chair; the teacher jumps and the boy laughs. This is *katharsis*. What I contend is that one of the prime objects of all judicial punishments is to afford the same grateful relief (*a*) to the immediate victims of the criminal punished, and (*b*) to the general body of moral and timorous men.

These persons, and particularly the first group, are concerned only indirectly with deterring other criminals. The thing they crave primarily is the satisfaction of seeing the criminal actually before them suffer as he made them suffer. What they want is the peace of mind that goes with the feeling that accounts are squared. Until they get that satisfaction they are in a state of emotional tension, and hence unhappy. The instant they get it they are comfortable. I do not argue that this yearning is noble; I simply argue that it is almost universal among human beings. In the face of injuries that are unimportant and can be borne without damage it may yield to higher impulses; that is to say, it may yield to what is called Christian charity. But when the injury is serious Christianity is adjourned, and even saints reach for their sidearms. It is plainly asking too much of human nature to expect it to conquer so natural an impulse. A keeps a store and has a bookkeeper, B. B steals $700, employs it in playing at dice or bingo, and is cleaned out. What is A to do? Let B go? If he does so he will be unable to sleep at night. The sense of injury, of injustice, of frustration will haunt him like pruritus. So he turns B over to the police, and they hustle B to prison. Thereafter A can sleep. More, he has pleasant dreams. He pictures B chained to the wall of a dungeon a hundred feet underground, devoured by rats and scorpions. It is so agreeable that it makes him forget his $700. He has got his *katharsis*.

The same thing precisely takes place on a larger scale when there is a crime which destroys a whole community's sense of security. Every law-abiding citizen feels menaced and frustrated until the criminals have been struck down—until the communal capacity to get even with them, and more than even, has been dramatically demonstrated. Here, manifestly, the business of deterring others is no more than an afterthought. The main thing is to destroy the concrete scoundrels whose act has alarmed everyone, and thus made everyone unhappy. Until they are brought to book that unhappiness continues; when the law has been executed upon them there is a sigh of relief. In other words, there is *katharsis*.

I know of no public demand for the death penalty for ordinary crimes, even for ordinary homicides. Its infliction would shock all men of normal decency of feeling. But for crimes involving the deliberate and inexcusable taking of human life, by men openly defiant of all civilized order—for such crimes it seems, to nine men out of ten, a just and proper punishment. Any lesser penalty leaves them feeling that the criminal has got the better of society—that he is free to add insult to injury by laughing. That feeling can be dissipated only by a recourse to *katharsis*, the invention of the aforesaid Aristotle. It is more effectively and economically achieved, as human nature now is, by wafting the criminal to realms of bliss.

The real objection to capital punishment doesn't lie against the actual extermination of the condemned, but against our brutal American habit of putting it off so long. After all, every one of us must die soon or late, and a murderer, it must be assumed, is one who makes that sad fact the cornerstone of his metaphysic. But it is one thing to die, and quite another thing to lie for long months and even years under the shadow of death. No sane man would choose such a finish. All of us, despite the Prayer Book, long for a swift and unexpected end. Unhappily, a murderer, under the irrational American system, is tortured for what, to him, must seem a whole series of eternities. For months on end he sits in prison while his lawyers carry on their idiotic buffoonery with writs, injunctions, mandamuses, and appeals. In order to get his money (or that of his friends) they have to feed him with hope. Now and then, by the imbecility of a judge or some trick of juridic science, they actually justify it. But let us say that, his money all gone, they finally throw up their hands. Their client is now ready for the rope or the chair. But he must still wait for months before it fetches him.

That wait, I believe, is horribly cruel. I have seen more than one man sitting in the death-house, and I don't want to see any more. Worse, it is wholly useless. Why should he wait at all? Why not hang him the day after the last court dissipates his last hope? Why torture him as not even cannibals would torture their victims? The common answer is that he must have time to make his peace with God. But how long does that take? It may be accomplished, I believe, in two hours quite as comfortably as in two years. There are, indeed, no temporal limitations upon God. He could forgive a whole herd of murderers in a millionth of a second. More, it has been done.

GEORGE ORWELL

A HANGING

This essay is taken from Orwell's collection Shooting an Elephant and Other Essays *(1950). For information on the author and his writings, see page 74.*

•

It was in Burma, a sodden morning of the rains. A sickly light, like yellow tinfoil, was slanting over the high walls into the jail yard. We were waiting outside the condemned cells, a row of sheds fronted with double bars, like small animal cages. Each cell measured about ten feet by ten and was quite bare within except for a plank bed and a pot for drinking water. In some of them brown silent men were squatting at the inner bars, with their blankets draped round them. These were the condemned men, due to be hanged within the next week or two.

One prisoner had been brought out of his cell. He was a Hindu, a puny
wisp of a man, with a shaven head and vague liquid eyes. He had a thick,
sprouting moustache, absurdly too big for his body, rather like the moustache of a comic man on the films. Six tall Indian warders were guarding
him and getting him ready for the gallows. Two of them stood by with
rifles and fixed bayonets, while the others handcuffed him, passed a chain
through his handcuffs and fixed it to their belts, and lashed his arms tight
to his sides. They crowded very close about him, with their hands always
on him in a careful, caressing grip, as though all the while feeling him to
make sure he was there. It was like men handling a fish which is still alive
and may jump back into the water. But he stood quite unresisting, yielding
his arms limply to the ropes, as though he hardly noticed what was happening.

Eight o'clock struck and a bugle call, desolately thin in the wet air,
floated from the distant barracks. The superintendent of the jail, who was
standing apart from the rest of us, moodily prodding the gravel with his
stick, raised his head at the sound. He was an army doctor, with a grey
toothbrush moustache and a gruff voice. "For God's sake hurry up, Francis," he said irritably. "The man ought to have been dead by this time.
Aren't you ready yet?"

Francis, the head jailer, a fat Dravidian in a white drill suit and gold
spectacles, waved his black hand. "Yes sir, yes sir," he bubbled. "All iss
satisfactorily prepared. The hangman iss waiting. We shall proceed."

"Well, quick march, then. The prisoners can't get their breakfast till this
job's over."

We set out for the gallows. Two warders marched on either side of the
prisoner, with their rifles at the slope; two others marched close against
him, gripping him by arm and shoulder, as though at once pushing and
supporting him. The rest of us, magistrates and the like, followed behind.
Suddenly, when we had gone ten yards, the procession stopped short
without any order or warning. A dreadful thing had happened—a dog,
come goodness knows whence, had appeared in the yard. It came bound-
ing among us with a loud volley of barks, and leapt round us wagging its
whole body, wild with glee at finding so many human beings together. It
was a large woolly dog, half Airedale, half pariah. For a moment it pranced
round us, and then, before anyone could stop it, it had made a dash for
the prisoner and, jumping up, tried to lick his face. Everyone stood
aghast, too taken aback even to grab at the dog.

"Who let that bloody brute in here?" said the superintendent angrily.
"Catch it, someone!"

A warder, detached from the escort, charged clumsily after the dog,
but it danced and gambolled just out of his reach, taking everything as
part of the game. A young Eurasian jailer picked up a handful of gravel
and tried to stone the dog away, but it dodged the stones and came after us
again. Its yaps echoed from the jail walls. The prisoner, in the grasp of

the two warders, looked on incuriously, as though this was another formality of the hanging. It was several minutes before someone managed to catch the dog. Then we put my handkerchief through its collar and moved off once more, with the dog still straining and whimpering.

It was about forty yards to the gallows. I watched the bare brown back of the prisoner marching in front of me. He walked clumsily with his bound arms, but quite steadily, with that bobbing gait of the Indian who never straightens his knees. At each step his muscles slid neatly into place, the lock of hair on his scalp danced up and down, his feet printed themselves on the wet gravel. And once, in spite of the men who gripped him by each shoulder, he stepped slightly aside to avoid a puddle on the path.

It is curious, but till that moment I had never realized what it means to destroy a healthy, conscious man. When I saw the prisoner step aside to avoid the puddle I saw the mystery, the unspeakable wrongness, of cutting a life short when it is in full tide. This man was not dying, he was alive just as we are alive. All the organs of his body were working—bowels digesting food, skin renewing itself, nails growing, tissues forming—all toiling away in solemn foolery. His nails would still be growing when he stood on the drop, when he was falling through the air with a tenth-of-a-second to live. His eyes saw the yellow gravel and the grey walls, and his brain still remembered, foresaw, reasoned—reasoned even about puddles. He and we were a party of men walking together, seeing, hearing, feeling, understanding the same world; and in two minutes, with a sudden snap, one of us would be gone—one mind less, one world less.

The gallows stood in a small yard, separate from the main grounds of the prison, and overgrown with tall prickly weeds. It was a brick erection like three sides of a shed, with planking on top, and above that two beams and a crossbar with the rope dangling. The hangman, a grey-haired convict in the white uniform of the prison, was waiting beside his machine. He greeted us with a servile crouch as we entered. At a word from Francis the two warders, gripping the prisoner more closely than ever, half led half pushed him to the gallows and helped him clumsily up the ladder. Then the hangman climbed up and fixed the rope round the prisoner's neck.

We stood waiting, five yards away. The warders had formed in a rough circle round the gallows. And then, when the noose was fixed, the prisoner began crying out to his god. It was a high, reiterated cry of "Ram! Ram! Ram! Ram!" not urgent and fearful like a prayer or cry for help, but steady, rhythmical, almost like the tolling of a bell. The dog answered the sound with a whine. The hangman, still standing on the gallows, produced a small cotton bag like a flour bag and drew it down over the prisoner's face. But the sound, muffled by the cloth, still persisted, over and over again: "Ram! Ram! Ram! Ram! Ram!"

The hangman climbed down and stood ready, holding the lever.

Minutes seemed to pass. The steady, muffled crying from the prisoner went on and on, "Ram! Ram! Ram!" never faltering for an instant. The superintendent, his head on his chest, was slowly poking the ground with his stick; perhaps he was counting the cries, allowing the prisoner a fixed number—fifty, perhaps, or a hundred. Everyone had changed color. The Indians had gone grey like bad coffee, and one or two of the bayonets were wavering. We looked at the lashed, hooded man on the drop, and listened to his cries—each cry another second of life; the same thought was in all our minds: oh, kill him quickly, get it over, stop that abominable noise!

Suddenly the superintendent made up his mind. Throwing up his head he made a swift motion with his stick. "Chalo!" he shouted almost fiercely.

There was a clanking noise, and then dead silence. The prisoner had vanished, and the rope was twisting on itself. I let go of the dog, and it galloped immediately to the back of the gallows; but when it got there it stopped short, barked, and then retreated into a corner of the yard, where it stood among the weeds, looking timorously out at us. We went round the gallows to inspect the prisoner's body. He was dangling with his toes pointed straight downwards, very slowly revolving, as dead as a stone.

The superintendent reached out with his stick and poked the bare brown body; it oscillated slightly. "*He's* all right," said the superintendent. He backed out from under the gallows, and blew out a deep breath. The moody look had gone out of his face quite suddenly. He glanced at his wrist-watch. "Eight minutes past eight. Well, that's all for this morning, thank God."

The warders unfixed bayonets and marched away. The dog, sobered and conscious of having misbehaved itself, slipped after them. We walked out of the gallows yard, past the condemned cells with their waiting prisoners, into the big central yard of the prison. The convicts, under the command of warders armed with lathis, were already receiving their breakfast. They squatted in long rows, each man holding a tin panikin, while two warders with buckets marched round ladling out rice; it seemed quite a homely, jolly scene, after the hanging. An enormous relief had come upon us now that the job was done. One felt an impulse to sing, to break into a run, to snigger. All at once everyone began chattering gaily.

The Eurasian boy walking beside me nodded towards the way we had come, with a knowing smile: "Do you know, sir, our friend [he meant the dead man] when he heard his appeal had been dismissed, he pissed on the floor of his cell. From fright. Kindly take one of my cigarettes, sir. Do you not admire my new silver case, sir? From the boxwalah, two rupees eight annas. Classy European style."

Several people laughed—at what, nobody seemed certain.

Francis was walking by the superintendent, talking garrulously: "Well, sir, all hass passed off with the utmost satisfactoriness. It was all finished—flick! like that. It iss not always so—oah, no! I have known cases where the doctor wass obliged to go beneath the gallows and pull the prissoner's legs to ensure decease. Most disagreeable!"

"Wriggling about, eh? That's bad," said the superintendent.

"Ach, sir, it iss worse when they become refractory! One man, I recall, clung to the bars of hiss cage when we went to take him out. You will scarcely credit, sir, that it took six warders to dislodge him, three pulling at each leg. We reasoned with him. 'My dear fellow,' we said, 'think of all the pain and trouble you are causing to us!' But no, he would not listen! Ach, he wass very troublesome!"

I found that I was laughing quite loudly. Everyone was laughing. Even the superintendent grinned in a tolerant way. "You'd better all come out and have a drink," he said quite genially. "I've got a bottle of whisky in the car. We could do with it."

We went through the big double gates of the prison into the road. "Pulling at his legs!" exclaimed a Burmese magistrate suddenly, and burst into a loud chuckling. We all began laughing again. At that moment Francis' anecdote seemed extraordinarily funny. We all had a drink together, native and European alike, quite amicably. The dead man was a hundred yards away.

ALBERT CAMUS

Albert Camus, regarded by many as the conscience of his age, was killed in an automobile accident in France at the age of 46. Born in Algeria in 1913, he spent his childhood in extreme poverty. L'envers et l'endroit (*not yet translated into English*) *is a moving record of those years. While he was working his way through the University of Algeria, he became interested in the theater, and for a few years managed and acted with a theatrical company. In 1938 he traveled to Europe for the first time. He returned to Algeria, worked as a journalist for* Alger Républicain *and later for* Paris-Soir *but left in 1942 to join the French Resistance movement; he edited and wrote many articles—then unsigned—for the underground newspaper*

Combat. *After the liberation he continued as editor of* Combat *but resigned in 1945 to devote full time to his writing.*

Camus's reputation blossomed almost overnight. Germaine Brée, a notable student of his work, writes: "Camus's rapid rise to celebrity between 1942 and 1945 is unparalleled in the history of French literature: The Stranger, The Myth of Sisyphus, *the two plays* Caligula *and* The Misunderstanding, *together with Camus's role in the Resistance and the widespread interest in his* Combat *editorials, started his career in meteoric fashion." His fame became international. In 1951 he published* The Rebel, *perhaps the most difficult of his works. In* The Plague *(1947),* The Fall *(1956), and* The Exile and the Kingdom *(1957), a book of short stories, he continued to express his philosophical ideas in fictional terms. In 1957 Camus was awarded the Nobel Prize for literature. The Committee cited his "clearsighted earnestness" which "illuminates the problem of the human conscience of our time."*

Although capital punishment in its broadest sense—the taking away of life—is a recurrent theme in almost all of his work, "Reflections on the Guillotine" (1957) is his one explicit argument on the subject. This long essay was first published in a periodical, and then in Réflexions sur la peine de mort, *a symposium by Arthur Koestler and Camus. Presented here with omissions, it may be read in full in* Resistance, Rebellion, and Death, *ed. and trans. Justin O'Brien (1960).*

FROM REFLECTIONS ON THE GUILLOTINE

Shortly before the war of 1914, an assassin whose crime was particularly repulsive (he had slaughtered a family of farmers, including the children) was condemned to death in Algiers. He was a farm worker who had killed in a sort of bloodthirsty frenzy but had aggravated his case by robbing his victims. The affair created a great stir. It was generally thought that decapitation was too mild a punishment for such a monster. This was the opinion, I have been told, of my father, who was especially aroused by the murder of the children. One of the few things I know about him, in any case, is that he wanted to witness the execution, for the first time in his life. He got up in the dark to go to the place of execution at the other end of town amid a great crowd of people. What he saw that morning he never told anyone. My mother relates merely that he came rushing home, his face distorted, refused to talk, lay down for a moment on the bed, and suddenly began to vomit. He had just discovered the reality hidden under the noble phrases with which it was masked. Instead of thinking of the slaughtered children, he could think of nothing but that quivering body that had just been dropped onto a board to have its head cut off.

Presumably that ritual act is horrible indeed if it manages to overcome the indignation of a simple, straightforward man and if a punishment he considered richly deserved had no other effect in the end than to nauseate him. When the extreme penalty simply causes vomiting on the part of the respectable citizen it is supposed to protect, how can anyone maintain that it is likely, as it ought to be, to bring more peace and order into the community? Rather, it is obviously no less repulsive than the crime, and this new murder, far from making amends for the harm done to the social body, adds a new blot to the first one. Indeed, no one dares speak directly of the ceremony. Officials and journalists who have to talk about it, as if they were aware of both its provocative and its shameful aspects, have made up a sort of ritual language, reduced to stereotyped phrases. Hence we read at breakfast time in a corner of the newspaper that the condemned "has paid his debt to society" or that he has "atoned" or that "at five a.m. justice was done." The officials call the condemned man "the interested party" or "the patient" or refer to him by a number. People write of capital punishment as if they were whispering. In our well-policed society we recognize that an illness is serious from the fact that we don't dare speak of it directly. For a long time, in middle-class families people said no more than that the elder daughter had a "suspicious cough" or that the father had a "growth" because tuberculosis and cancer were looked upon as somewhat shameful maladies. This is probably even truer of capital punishment since everyone strives to refer to it only through euphemisms. It is to the body politic what cancer is to the individual body, with this difference: no one has ever spoken of the necessity of cancer. There is no hesitation, on the other hand, about presenting capital punishment as a regrettable necessity, a necessity that justifies killing because it is necessary, and let's not talk about it because it is regrettable.

But it is my intention to talk about it crudely. Not because I like scandal, nor, I believe, because of an unhealthy streak in my nature. As a writer, I have always loathed avoiding the issue; as a man, I believe that the repulsive aspects of our condition, if they are inevitable, must merely be faced in silence. But when silence or tricks of language contribute to maintaining an abuse that must be reformed or a suffering that can be relieved, then there is no other solution but to speak out and show the obscenity hidden under the verbal cloak. France shares with England and Spain the honor of being one of the last countries this side of the iron curtain to keep capital punishment in its arsenal of repression. The survival of such a primitive rite has been made possible among us only by the thoughtlessness or ignorance of the public, which reacts only with the ceremonial phrases that have been drilled into it. When the imagination sleeps, words are emptied of their meaning: a deaf population absent-mindedly registers the condemnation of a man. But if people are shown the machine, made to touch the wood and steel and to hear the sound of a head falling, then public imagination, suddenly awakened, will repudiate both the vocabulary and the penalty.

When the Nazis in Poland indulged in public executions of hostages, to keep those hostages from shouting words of revolt and liberty they muzzled them with a plaster-coated gag. It would be shocking to compare the fate of those innocent victims with that of condemned criminals. But, aside from the fact that criminals are not the only ones to be guillotined in our country, the method is the same. We smother under padded words a penalty whose legitimacy we could assert only after we had examined the penalty in reality. Instead of saying that the death penalty is first of all necessary and then adding that it is better not to talk about it, it is essential to say what it really is and then say whether, being what it is, it is to be considered as necessary.

So far as I am concerned, I consider it not only useless but definitely harmful, and I must record my opinion here before getting to the subject itself. It would not be fair to imply that I reached this conclusion as a result of the weeks of investigation and research I have just devoted to this question. But it would be just as unfair to attribute my conviction to mere mawkishness. I am far from indulging in the flabby pity characteristic of humanitarians, in which values and responsibilities fuse, crimes are balanced against one another, and innocence finally loses its rights. Unlike many of my well-known contemporaries, I do not think that man is by nature a social animal. To tell the truth, I think just the reverse. But I believe, and this is quite different, that he cannot live henceforth outside of society, whose laws are necessary to his physical survival. Hence the responsibilities must be established by society itself according to a reasonable and workable scale. But the law's final justification is in the good it does or fails to do to the society of a given place and time. For years I have been unable to see anything in capital punishment but a penalty the imagination could not endure and a lazy disorder that my reason condemned. Yet I was ready to think that my imagination was influencing my judgment. But, to tell the truth, I found during my recent research nothing that did not strengthen my conviction, nothing that modified my arguments. On the contrary, to the arguments I already had others were added. Today I share absolutely Koestler's conviction: the death penalty besmirches our society, and its upholders cannot reasonably defend it. Without repeating his decisive defense, without piling up facts and figures that would only duplicate others (and Jean Bloch-Michel's make them useless), I shall merely state reasons to be added to Koestler's; like his, they argue for an immediate abolition of the death penalty.

· · ·

A punishment that penalizes without forestalling is indeed called revenge. It is a quasi-arithmetical reply made by society to whoever breaks its primordial law. That reply is as old as man; it is called the law of retaliation. Whoever has done me harm must suffer harm; whoever has put out my eye must lose an eye; and whoever has killed must die. This is an emotion, and a particularly violent one, not a principle. Retaliation is related to nature and instinct, not to law. Law, by definition, cannot obey the same rules as nature. If murder is in the nature of man, the law is not intended to imitate or reproduce that nature. It is intended to correct it. Now, retaliation does no more than ratify and confer the status of a law on a pure impulse of nature. We have all known that impulse, often to our shame, and we know its power, for it comes down to us from the primitive forests. In this regard, we French, who are properly indignant upon seeing the oil king in Saudi Arabia preach international democracy and call in a butcher to cut off a thief's hand with a cleaver, live also in a sort of Middle Ages without even the consolations of faith. We still define justice according to the rules of a crude arithmetic.[1] Can it be said at least that that arithmetic is exact and that justice, even when elementary, even when limited to legal revenge, is safeguarded by the death penalty? The answer must be no.

Let us leave aside the fact that the law of retaliation is inapplicable and that it would seem just as excessive to punish the incendiary by setting fire to his house as it would be insufficient to punish the thief by deducting from his bank account a sum equal to his theft. Let us admit that it is just and necessary to compensate for the murder of the victim by the death of the murderer. But beheading is not simply death. It is just as different, in essence, from the privation of life as a concentration camp is from prison. It is a murder, to be sure, and one that arithmetically pays for the murder committed. But it adds to death a rule, a public premeditation known to the future victim, an organization, in short, which is in itself a source of moral sufferings more terrible than death. Hence there is no equivalence. Many laws consider a premeditated crime more serious than a crime of pure violence. But what then is capital punishment but the most premeditated of murders, to which no criminal's deed, however calculated it may be, can be compared? For there to be equivalence, the death penalty would have to punish a criminal who had warned his victim of the date at which he would inflict a horrible death

---

[1] A few years ago I asked for the reprieve of six Tunisians who had been condemned to death for the murder, in a riot, of three French policemen. The circumstances in which the murder had taken place made difficult any division of responsibilities. A note from the executive office of the President of the Republic informed me that my appeal was being considered by the appropriate organization. Unfortunately, when that note was addressed to me I had already read two weeks earlier that the sentence had been carried out. Three of the condemned men had been put to death and the three others reprieved. The reasons for reprieving some rather than the others were not convincing. But probably it was essential to carry out three executions where there had been three victims.

on him and who, from that moment onward, had confined him at his mercy for months. Such a monster is not encountered in private life.

There, too, when our official jurists talk of putting to death without causing suffering, they don't know what they are talking about and, above all, they lack imagination. The devastating, degrading fear that is imposed on the condemned for months or years[2] is a punishment more terrible than death, and one that was not imposed on the victim. Even in the fright caused by the mortal violence being done to him, most of the time the victim is hastened to his death without knowing what is happening to him. The period of horror is counted out with his life, and hope of escaping the madness that has swept down upon that life probably never leaves him. On the other hand, the horror is parceled out to the man who is condemned to death. Torture through hope alternates with the pangs of animal despair. The lawyer and chaplain, out of mere humanity, and the jailers, so that the condemned man will keep quiet, are unanimous in assuring him that he will be reprieved. He believes this with all his being and then he ceases to believe it. He hopes by day and despairs of it by night.[3] As the weeks pass, hope and despair increase and become equally unbearable. According to all accounts, the color of the skin changes, fear acting like an acid. "Knowing that you are going to die is nothing," said a condemned man in Fresnes. "But not knowing whether or not you are going to live, that's terror and anguish." Cartouche said of the supreme punishment: "Why, it's just a few minutes that have to be lived through." But it is a matter of months, not of minutes. Long in advance the condemned man knows that he is going to be killed and that the only thing that can save him is a reprieve, rather similar, for him, to the decrees of heaven. In any case, he cannot intervene, make a plea himself, or convince. Everything goes on outside of him. He is no longer a man but a thing waiting to be handled by the executioners. He is kept as if he were inert matter, but he still has a consciousness which is his chief enemy.

When the officials whose job it is to kill that man call him a parcel, they know what they are saying. To be unable to do anything against the hand that moves you from one place to another, holds you or rejects you, is this not indeed being a parcel, or a thing, or, better, a hobbled animal? Even then an animal can refuse to eat. The condemned man cannot. He is given the benefit of a special diet (at Fresnes, Diet No. 4 with extra

---

[2] Roemen, condemned to death at the Liberation of France, remained seven hundred days in chains before being executed, and this is scandalous. Those condemned under common law, as a general rule, wait from three to six months for the morning of their death. And it is difficult, if one wants to maintain their chances of survival, to shorten that period. I can bear witness, moreover, to the fact that the examination of appeals for mercy is conducted in France with a seriousness that does not exclude the visible inclination to pardon, insofar as the law and customs permit.

[3] Sunday not being a day of execution, Saturday night is always better in the cell blocks reserved for those condemned to death.

milk, wine, sugar, jam, butter); they see to it that he nourishes himself. If need be, he is forced to do so. The animal that is going to be killed must be in the best condition. The thing or the animal has a right only to those debased freedoms that are called whims. "They are very touchy," a top-sergeant at Fresnes says without the least irony of those condemned to death. Of course, but how else can they have contact with freedom and the dignity of the will that man cannot do without? Touchy or not, the moment the sentence has been pronounced the condemned man enters an imperturbable machine. For a certain number of weeks he travels along in the intricate machinery that determines his every gesture and eventually hands him over to those who will lay him down on the killing machine. The parcel is no longer subject to the laws of chance that hang over the living creature but to mechanical laws that allow him to foresee accurately the day of his beheading.

That day his being an object comes to an end. During the three quarters of an hour separating him from the end, the certainty of a powerless death stifles everything else; the animal, tied down and amenable, knows a hell that makes the hell he is threatened with seem ridiculous. The Greeks, after all, were more humane with their hemlock. They left their condemned a relative freedom, the possibility of putting off or hastening the hour of his death. They gave him a choice between suicide and execution. On the other hand, in order to be doubly sure, we deal with the culprit ourselves. But there could not really be any justice unless the condemned, after making known his decision months in advance, had approached his victim, bound him firmly, informed him that he would be put to death in an hour, and had finally used that hour to set up the apparatus of death. What criminal ever reduced his victim to such a desperate and powerless condition?

This doubtless explains the odd submissiveness that is customary in the condemned at the moment of their execution. These men who have nothing more to lose could play their last card, choose to die of a chance bullet or be guillotined in the kind of frantic struggle that dulls all the faculties. In a way, this would amount to dying freely. And yet, with but few exceptions, the rule is for the condemned to walk toward death passively in a sort of dreary despondency. That is probably what our journalists mean when they say that the condemned died courageously. We must read between the lines that the condemned made no noise, accepted his status as a parcel, and that everyone is grateful to him for this. In such a degrading business, the interested party shows a praiseworthy sense of propriety by keeping the degradation from lasting too long. But the compliments and the certificates of courage belong to the general mystification surrounding the death penalty. For the condemned will often be seemly in proportion to the fear he feels. He will deserve the praise of the press only if his fear or his feeling of isolation is great enough to sterilize him completely. Let there be no misunderstanding.

Some among the condemned, whether political or not, die heroically, and they must be granted the proper admiration and respect. But the majority of them know only the silence of fear, only the impassivity of fright, and it seems to me that such terrified silence deserves even greater respect. When the priest Bela Just offers to write to the family of a young condemned man a few moments before he is hanged and hears the reply: "I have no courage, even for that," how can a priest, hearing that confession of weakness, fail to honor the most wretched and most sacred thing in man? Those who say nothing but leave a little pool on the spot from which they are taken—who would dare say they died as cowards? And how can we describe the men who reduced them to such cowardice? After all, every murderer when he kills runs the risk of the most dreadful of deaths, whereas those who kill him risk nothing except advancement.

No, what man experiences at such times is beyond all morality. Not virtue, nor courage, nor intelligence, nor even innocence has anything to do with it. Society is suddenly reduced to a state of primitive terrors where nothing can be judged. All equity and all dignity have disappeared. "The conviction of innocence does not immunize against brutal treatment. . . . I have seen authentic bandits die courageously whereas innocent men went to their deaths trembling in every muscle."[4] When the same man adds that, according to his experience, intellectuals show more weakness, he is not implying that such men have less courage than others but merely that they have more imagination. Having to face an inevitable death, any man, whatever his convictions, is torn asunder from head to toe.[5] The feeling of powerlessness and solitude of the condemned man, bound and up against the public coalition that demands his death, is in itself an unimaginable punishment. From this point of view, too, it would be better for the execution to be public. The actor in every man could then come to the aid of the terrified animal and help him cut a figure, even in his own eyes. But darkness and secrecy offer no recourse. In such a disaster, courage, strength of soul, even faith may be disadvantages. As a general rule, a man is undone by waiting for capital punishment well before he dies. Two deaths are inflicted on him, the first being worse than the second, whereas he killed but once. Compared to such torture, the penalty of retaliation seems like a civilized law. It never claimed that the man who gouged out one of his brother's eyes should be totally blinded.

. . .

There are, however, major criminals whom all juries would condemn at any time and in any place whatever. Their crimes are not open to doubt, and the evidence brought by the accusation is confirmed by the

---

[4] Bela Just, *La Potence et la Croix* (Fasquelle).

[5] A great surgeon, a Catholic himself, told me that as a result of his experience he did not even inform believers when they had an incurable cancer. According to him, the shock might destroy even their faith.

confessions of the defense. Most likely, everything that is abnormal and monstrous in them is enough to classify them as pathological. But the psychiatric experts, in the majority of cases, affirm their responsibility. Recently in Paris a young man, somewhat weak in character but kind and affectionate, devoted to his family, was, according to his own admission, annoyed by a remark his father made about his coming home late. The father was sitting reading at the dining-room table. The young man seized an ax and dealt his father several blows from behind. Then in the same way he struck down his mother, who was in the kitchen. He undressed, hid his bloodstained trousers in the closet, went to make a call on the family of his fiancée, without showing any signs, then returned home and notified the police that he had just found his parents murdered. The police immediately discovered the bloodstained trousers and, without difficulty, got a calm confession from the parricide. The psychiatrists decided that this man who murdered through annoyance was responsible. His odd indifference, of which he was to give other indications in prison (showing pleasure because his parents' funeral had attracted so many people—"They were much loved," he told his lawyer), cannot, however, be considered as normal. But his reasoning power was apparently untouched.

Many "monsters" offer equally impenetrable exteriors. They are eliminated on the mere consideration of the facts. Apparently the nature or the magnitude of their crimes allows no room for imagining that they can ever repent or reform. They must merely be kept from doing it again, and there is no other solution but to eliminate them. On this frontier, and on it alone, discussion about the death penalty is legitimate. In all other cases the arguments for capital punishment do not stand up to the criticisms of the abolitionists. But in extreme cases, and in our state of ignorance, we make a wager. No fact, no reasoning can bring together those who think that a chance must always be left to the vilest of men and those who consider that chance illusory. But it is perhaps possible, on that final frontier, to go beyond the long opposition between partisans and adversaries of the death penalty by weighing the advisability of that penalty today, and in Europe. With much less competence, I shall try to reply to the wish expressed by a Swiss jurist, Professor Jean Graven, who wrote in 1952 in his remarkable study on the problem of the death penalty: "Faced with the problem that is once more confronting our conscience and our reason, we think that a solution must be sought, not through the conceptions, problems, and arguments of the past, nor through the hopes and theoretical promises of the future, but through the ideas, recognized facts, and necessities of the present."[6] It is possible, indeed, to debate endlessly as to the benefits or harm attributable to the death penalty through the ages or in an intellectual

---

[6] *Revue de Criminologie et de Police Technique* (Geneva), special issue, 1952.

vacuum. But it plays a role here and now, and we must take our stand here and now in relation to the modern executioner. What does the death penalty mean to the men of the mid-century?

To simplify matters, let us say that our civilization has lost the only values that, in a certain way, can justify that penalty and, on the other hand, suffers from evils that necessitate its suppression. In other words, the abolition of the death penalty ought to be asked for by all thinking members of our society, for reasons both of logic and of realism.

Of logic, to begin with. Deciding that a man must have the definitive punishment imposed on him is tantamount to deciding that that man has no chance of making amends. This is the point, to repeat ourselves, where the arguments clash blindly and crystallize in a sterile opposition. But it so happens that none among us can settle the question, for we are all both judges and interested parties. Whence our uncertainty as to our right to kill and our inability to convince each other. Without absolute innocence, there is no supreme judge. Now, we have all done wrong in our lives even if that wrong, without falling within the jurisdiction of the laws, went as far as the unknown crime. There are no just people—merely hearts more or less lacking in justice. Living at least allows us to discover this and to add to the sum of our actions a little of the good that will make up in part for the evil we have added to the world. Such a right to live, which allows a chance to make amends, is the natural right of every man, even the worst man. The lowest of criminals and the most upright of judges meet side by side, equally wretched in their solidarity. Without that right, moral life is utterly impossible. None among us is authorized to despair of a single man, except after his death, which transforms his life into destiny and then permits a definitive judgment. But pronouncing the definitive judgment before his death, decreeing the closing of accounts when the creditor is still alive, is no man's right. On this limit, at least, whoever judges absolutely condemns himself absolutely.

Bernard Fallot of the Masuy gang, working for the Gestapo, was condemned to death after admitting the many terrible crimes of which he was guilty, and declared himself that he could not be pardoned. "My hands are too red with blood," he told a prison mate.[7] Public opinion and the opinion of his judges certainly classed him among the irremediable, and I should have been tempted to agree if I had not read a surprising testimony. This is what Fallot said to the same companion after declaring that he wanted to die courageously: "Shall I tell you my greatest regret? Well, it is not having known the Bible I now have here. I assure you that I wouldn't be where I now am." There is no question of giving in to some conventional set of sentimental pictures and calling to mind

---

[7] Jean Bocognano: *Quartier des fauves, prison de Fresnes* (Editions du Fuseau).

Victor Hugo's good convicts. The age of enlightenment, as people say, wanted to suppress the death penalty on the pretext that man was naturally good. Of course he is not (he is worse or better). After twenty years of our magnificent history we are well aware of this. But precisely because he is not absolutely good, no one among us can pose as an absolute judge and pronounce the definitive elimination of the worst among the guilty, because no one of us can lay claim to absolute innocence. Capital judgment upsets the only indisputable human solidarity—our solidarity against death—and it can be legitimized only by a truth or a principle that is superior to man.

In fact, the supreme punishment has always been, throughout the ages, a religious penalty. Inflicted in the name of the king, God's representative on earth, or by priests or in the name of society considered as a sacred body, it denies, not human solidarity, but the guilty man's membership in the divine community, the only thing that can give him life. Life on earth is taken from him, to be sure, but his chance of making amends is left him. The real judgment is not pronounced; it will be in the other world. Only religious values, and especially belief in eternal life, can therefore serve as a basis for the supreme punishment because, according to their own logic, they keep it from being definitive and irreparable. Consequently, it is justified only insofar as it is not supreme.

The Catholic Church, for example, has always accepted the necessity of the death penalty. It inflicted that penalty itself, and without stint, in other periods. Even today it justifies it and grants the State the right to apply it. The Church's position, however subtle, contains a very deep feeling that was expressed directly in 1937 by a Swiss National Councillor from Fribourg during a discussion in the National Council. According to M. Grand, the lowest of criminals when faced with execution withdraws into himself. "He repents and his preparation for death is thereby facilitated. The Church has saved one of its members and fulfilled its divine mission. This is why it has always accepted the death penalty, not only as a means of self-defense, but *as a powerful means of salvation.*[8] . . . Without trying to make of it a thing of the Church, the death penalty can point proudly to its almost divine efficacy, like war."

By virtue of the same reasoning, probably, there could be read on the sword of the Fribourg executioner the words: "Lord Jesus, thou art the judge." Hence the executioner is invested with a sacred function. He is the man who destroys the body in order to deliver the soul to the divine sentence, which no one can judge beforehand. Some may think that such words imply rather scandalous confusions. And, to be sure, whoever clings to the teaching of Jesus will look upon that handsome sword as one more outrage to the person of Christ. In the light of this, it is possible to understand the dreadful remark of the Russian condemned man about to be

---

[8] My italics.

hanged by the Tsar's executioners in 1905 who said firmly to the priest who had come to console him with the image of Christ: "Go away and commit no sacrilege." The unbeliever cannot keep from thinking that men who have set at the center of their faith the staggering victim of a judicial error ought at least to hesitate before committing legal murder. Believers might also be reminded that Emperor Julian, before his conversion, did not want to give official offices to Christians because they systematically refused to pronounce death sentences or to have anything to do with them. For five centuries Christians therefore believed that the strict moral teaching of their master forbade killing. But Catholic faith is not nourished solely by the personal teaching of Christ. It also feeds on the Old Testament, on St. Paul, and on the Church Fathers. In particular, the immortality of the soul and the universal resurrection of bodies are articles of dogma. As a result, capital punishment is for the believer a temporary penalty that leaves the final sentence in suspense, an arrangement necessary only for terrestrial order, an administrative measure which, far from signifying the end for the guilty man, may instead favor his redemption. I am not saying that all believers agree with this, and I can readily imagine that some Catholics may stand closer to Christ than to Moses or St. Paul. I am simply saying that faith in the immortality of the soul allowed Catholicism to see the problem of capital punishment in very different terms and to justify it.

But what is the value of such a justification in the society we live in, which in its institutions and its customs has lost all contact with the sacred? When an atheistic or skeptical or agnostic judge inflicts the death penalty on an unbelieving criminal, he is pronouncing a definitive punishment that cannot be reconsidered. He takes his place on the throne of God,[9] without having the same powers and even without believing in God. He kills, in short, because his ancestors believed in eternal life. But the society that he claims to represent is in reality pronouncing a simple measure of elimination, doing violence to the human community united against death, and taking a stand as an absolute value because society is laying claim to absolute power. To be sure, it delegates a priest to the condemned man, through tradition. The priest may legitimately hope that fear of punishment will help the guilty man's conversion. Who can accept, however, that such a calculation should justify a penalty most often inflicted and received in a quite different spirit? It is one thing to believe before being afraid and another to find faith after fear. Conversion through fire or the guillotine will always be suspect, and it may seem surprising that the Church has not given up conquering infidels through terror. In any case, society that has lost all contact with the sacred can find no advantage in a conversion in which it professes to have no interest. Society decrees a sacred punishment and at the same

_____

[9] As everyone knows, the jury's decision is preceded by the words: "Before God and my conscience. . . ."

time divests it both of excuse and of usefulness. Society proceeds sovereignly to eliminate the evil ones from her midst as if she were virtue itself. Like an honorable man killing his wayward son and remarking: "Really, I didn't know what to do with him." She assumes the right to select as if she were nature herself and to add great sufferings to the elimination as if she were a redeeming god.

To assert, in any case, that a man must be absolutely cut off from society because he is absolutely evil amounts to saying that society is absolutely good, and no one in his right mind will believe this today. Instead of believing this, people will more readily think the reverse. Our society has become so bad and so criminal only because she has respected nothing but her own preservation or a good reputation in history. Society has indeed lost all contact with the sacred. But society began in the nineteenth century to find a substitute for religion by proposing herself as an object of adoration. The doctrines of evolution and the notions of selection that accompany them have made of the future of society a final end. The political utopias that were grafted onto those doctrines placed at the end of time a golden age that justified in advance any enterprises whatever. Society became accustomed to legitimizing what might serve her future and, consequently, to making use of the supreme punishment in an absolute way. From then on, society considered as a crime and a sacrilege anything that stood in the way of her plan and her temporal dogmas. In other words, after being a priest, the executioner became a government official. The result is here all around us. The situation is such that this mid-century society which has lost the right, in all logics, to decree capital punishment ought now to suppress it for reasons of realism.

. . .

From the humanitarian idylls of the eighteenth century to the bloodstained gallows the way leads directly, and the executioners of today, as everyone knows, are humanists. Hence we cannot be too wary of the humanitarian ideology in dealing with a problem such as the death penalty. On the point of concluding, I should like therefore to repeat that neither an illusion as to the natural goodness of the human being nor faith in a golden age to come motivates my opposition to the death penalty. On the contrary, its abolition seems to me necessary because of reasoned pessimism, of logic, and of realism. Not that the heart has no share in what I have said. Anyone who has spent weeks with texts, recollections, and men having any contact, whether close or not, with the gallows could not possibly remain untouched by that experience. But, let me repeat, I do not believe, nonetheless, that there is no responsibility in this world and that we must give way to that modern tendency to absolve everything, victim and murderer, in the same confusion. Such purely sentimental confusion is made up of cowardice rather than of generosity and eventually justifies whatever is worst in this world. If you keep on excusing, you eventually give your blessing to the slave camp, to cowardly force, to organized executioners, to the cynicism of great political monsters; you finally hand over your brothers. This can be seen around us. But it so happens, in the present state of the world, that the man of today wants laws and institutions suitable to a convalescent, which will curb him without breaking him and lead him without crushing him. Hurled into the unchecked dynamic movement of history, he needs a natural philosophy and a few laws of equilibrium. He needs, in short, a society based on reason and not the anarchy into which he has been plunged by his own pride and the excessive powers of the State.

I am convinced that abolition of the death penalty would help us progress toward that society. After taking such an initiative, France could offer to extend it to the non-abolitionist countries on both sides of the iron curtain. But, in any case, she should set the example. Capital punishment would then be replaced by hard labor—for life in the case of criminals considered irremediable and for a fixed period in the case of the others. To any who feel that such a penalty is harsher than capital punishment we can only express our amazement that they did not suggest, in this case, reserving it for such as Landru and applying capital punishment to minor criminals. We might remind them, too, that hard labor leaves the condemned man the possibility of choosing death, whereas the guillotine offers no alternative. To any who feel, on the other hand, that hard labor is too mild a penalty, we can answer first that they lack imagination and secondly that privation of freedom seems to them a slight punishment only insofar as contemporary society has taught us to despise freedom.[10]

The fact that Cain is not killed but bears a mark of reprobation in the eyes of men is the lesson we must draw from the Old Testament, to say nothing of the Gospels, instead of looking back to the cruel examples of the Mosaic law. In any case, nothing keeps us from trying out an experiment, limited in duration (ten years, for instance), if our Parliament is still incapable of making up for its votes in favor of alcohol by such a great civilizing step as complete abolition of the penalty. And if, really, public opinion and its representatives cannot give up the law of laziness which simply eliminates what it cannot reform, let us at least —while hoping for a new day of truth—not make of it the "solemn slaughterhouse"[11] that befouls our society. The death penalty as it is now applied, and however rarely it may be, is a revolting butchery, an outrage

---

[10] See the report on the death penalty by Representative Dupont in the National Assembly on 31 May 1791: "A sharp and burning mood consumes the assassin; the thing he fears most is inactivity; it leaves him to himself, and to get away from it he continually braves death and tries to cause death in others; solitude and his own conscience are his real torture. Does this not suggest to you what kind of punishment should be inflicted on him, what is the kind of which he will be most sensitive? *Is it not in the nature of the malady that the remedy is to be found?*" I have italicized the last sentence, for it makes of that little-known Representative a true precursor of our modern psychology.

[11] Tarde.

inflicted on the person and body of man. That truncation, that living and yet uprooted head, those spurts of blood date from a barbarous period that aimed to impress the masses with degrading sights. Today when such vile death is administered on the sly, what is the meaning of this torture? The truth is that in the nuclear age we kill as we did in the age of the spring balance. And there is not a man of normal sensitivity who, at the mere thought of such crude surgery, does not feel nauseated. If the French State is incapable of overcoming habit and giving Europe one of the remedies it needs, let France begin by reforming the manner of administering capital punishment. The science that serves to kill so many could at least serve to kill decently. An anesthetic that would allow the condemned man to slip from sleep to death (which would be left within his reach for at least a day so that he could use it freely and would be administered to him in another form if he were unwilling or weak of will) would assure his elimination, if you insist, but would put a little decency into what is at present but a sordid and obscene exhibition.

I suggest such compromises only insofar as one must occasionally despair of seeing wisdom and true civilization influence those reponsible for our future. For certain men, more numerous than we think, it is physically unbearable to know what the death penalty really is and not to be able to prevent its application. In their way, they suffer that penalty themselves, and without any justice. If only the weight of filthy images weighing upon them were reduced, society would lose nothing. But even that, in the long run, will be inadequate. There will be no lasting peace either in the heart of individuals or in social customs until death is outlawed.

KARL MENNINGER

Dr. Menninger was born in Topeka, Kansas, in 1893, attended Washburn College and the University of Wisconsin, and received his medical degree from Harvard in 1917. He remained in Boston until 1920, working and teaching under Dr. Ernest Southard at Boston Psychopathic Hospital and Harvard Medical School. Dr. Southard's sudden death in 1920 brought Dr.

Menninger back to Topeka where, together with his father and brother, he developed the now famous Menninger Clinic, which has had considerable influence on psychiatric practice in the United States. He has served as Chief of Staff of the Clinic, as Dean of the Menninger School of Psychiatry, and, from 1923 to 1948, as Professor of mental hygiene, criminology, and abnormal psychology at Washburn University. He has also held numerous posts as advisor or consultant. In the light of the article we print below (from Harper's, *August, 1959), it may interest the reader to know that Dr. Menninger has served as vice president of the American League to Abolish Capital Punishment and as Consultant to the Research Staff of the Committee on Rights of the Mentally Ill of the American Bar Association. Among his many books are* The Human Mind *(1930);* Man Against Himself *(1938);* Love Against Hate, *written with Mrs. Menninger (1942);* A Psychiatrist's World *(1959), and* The Vital Balance: the Life Process in Mental Health and Illness *(1963).*

VERDICT GUILTY—NOW WHAT?

Since ancient times criminal law and penology have been based upon what is called in psychology the pain-pleasure principle. There are many reasons for inflicting pain—to urge an animal to greater efforts, to retaliate for pain received, to frighten, or to indulge in idle amusement. Human beings, like all animals, tend to move away from pain and toward pleasure. Hence the way to control behavior is to reward what is "good" and punish what is "bad." This formula pervades our programs of child-rearing, education, and the social control of behavior.

With this concept three out of four readers will no doubt concur.

"Why, of course," they will say. "Only common sense. Take me for example. I know the speed limit and the penalty. Usually I drive moderately because I don't want to get a ticket. One afternoon I was in a hurry; I had an appointment, I didn't heed the signs. I did what I knew was forbidden and I got caught and received the punishment I deserved. Fair enough. It taught me a lesson. Since then I drive more slowly in that area. And surely people are deterred from cheating on their income taxes, robbing banks, and committing rape by the fear of punishment. Why, if we didn't have these crime road blocks we'd have chaos!"

This sounds reasonable enough and describes what most people think —*part of the time.* But upon reflection we all know that punishments and the threat of punishments do *not* deter *some* people from doing forbidden things. Some of them take a chance on not being caught, and this chance is a very good one, too, better than five to one for most crimes. Not even the fear of possible death, self-inflicted, deters some speedsters. Exceeding the speed limit is not really regarded as criminal behavior by most people, no matter how dangerous and self-destructive. It is the kind of a "crime" which respectable members of society commit and condone. This is not the case with rape, bank-robbing, check-forging, vandalism, and the multitude of offenses for which the prison penalty system primarily exists. And from these offenses the average citizen, including the reader, is deterred by quite different restraints. For most of us it is our conscience, our self-respect, and our wish for the good opinion of our neighbors which are the determining factors in controlling our impulses toward misbehavior.

Today it is no secret that our official, prison-threat theory of crime control is an utter failure. Criminologists have known this for years. When pocket-picking was punishable by hanging, in England, the crowds that gathered about the gallows to enjoy the spectacle of an execution were particularly likely to have their pockets picked by skillful operators who, to say the least, were not deterred by the exhibition of "justice." We have long known that the perpetrators of most offenses are never detected; of those detected, only a fraction are found guilty and still fewer serve a "sentence." Furthermore, we are quite certain now that of those who do receive the official punishment of the law, many become firmly committed thereby to a continuing life of crime and a continuing feud with law enforcement officers. Finding themselves ostracized from society and blacklisted by industry they stick with the crowd they have been introduced to in jail and try to play the game of life according to this set of rules. In this way society skillfully converts individuals of borderline self-control into loyal members of the underground fraternity.

The science of human behavior has gone far beyond the common sense rubrics which dictated the early legal statutes. We know now that one cannot describe rape or bank-robbing or income-tax fraud simply as pleasure. Nor, on the other hand, can we describe imprisonment merely as pain. Slapping the hand of a beloved child as he reaches to do a forbidden act is utterly different from the institutionalized process of official punishment. The offenders who are chucked into our county and state and federal prisons are not anyone's beloved children; they are usually unloved children, grown-up physically but still hungry for human concern which they never got or never get in normal ways. So they pursue it in abnormal ways—abnormal, that is, from *our* standpoint.

What might deter the reader from conduct which his neighbors would not like does not necessarily deter the grown-up child of vastly different background. The latter's experiences may have conditioned him to believe that the chances of winning by undetected cheating are vastly greater than the probabilities of fair treatment and opportunity. He knows about the official threats and the social disapproval of such acts. He knows about the hazards and the risks. But despite all this "knowledge," he becomes involved in waves of discouragement or cupidity or excitement or resentment leading to episodes of social offensiveness.

These episodes may prove vastly expensive both to him and to society. But sometimes they will have an aura of success. Our periodicals have only recently described the wealth and prominence for a time of a man described as a murderer. Konrad Lorenz, the great psychiatrist and animal psychologist, has beautifully described in geese what he calls a "triumph reaction." It is a sticking out of the chest and flapping of the wings after an encounter with a challenge. All of us have seen this primitive biological triumph reaction—in some roosters, for example, in some businessmen and athletes and others—*and* in some criminals.

In general, though, the gains and goals of the social offender are not those which most men seek. Most offenders whom we belabor are not very wise, not very smart, not even very "lucky." It is not the successful criminal upon whom we inflict our antiquated penal system. It is the unsuccessful criminal, the criminal who really doesn't know how to commit crimes, and who gets caught. Indeed, until he is caught and convicted a man is technically not even called a criminal. The clumsy, the desperate, the obscure, the friendless, the defective, the diseased—these men who commit crimes that do not come off—are bad actors, indeed. But they are not the professional criminals, many of whom occupy high places. In some instances the crime is the merest accident or incident or impulse, expressed under unbearable stress. More often the offender is a persistently perverse, lonely, and resentful individual who joins the only group to which he is eligible—the outcasts and the anti-social.

And what do we do with such offenders? After a solemn public ceremony we pronounce them enemies of the people, and consign them for arbitrary periods to institutional confinement on the basis of laws written many years ago. Here they languish until time has ground out so many weary months and years. Then with a planlessness and stupidity only surpassed by that of their original incarceration they are dumped back upon society, regardless of whether any change has taken place in them for the better and with every assurance that changes have taken place in them for the worse. Once more they enter the unequal tussle with society. Proscribed for employment by most concerns, they are expected to invent a new way to make a living and to survive without any further help from society.

Intelligent members of society are well aware that the present system is antiquated, expensive, and disappointing, and that we are wasting vast quantities of manpower through primitive methods of dealing with those who transgress the law. In 1917 the famous Wickersham report of the New York State Prison Survey Committee recommended the abolition of jails, the institution of diagnostic clearing houses or classification centers, the development of a diversified institutional system and treatment program, and the use of indeterminate sentences. *Forty-two years have passed.* How little progress we have made! In 1933 the American Psychiatric Association, the American Bar Association, and the American Medical Association officially and jointly recommended psychiatric service for every criminal and juvenile court to assist the court and prison and parole officers with all offenders.

That was twenty-six years ago! Have these recommendations been carried out anywhere in the United States? With few exceptions offenders continue to be dealt with according to old-time instructions, written by men now dead who knew nothing about the present offender, his past life, the misunderstandings accumulated by him, or the provocation given to him.

The sensible, scientific question is: What kind of treatment could be instituted that would deter him or be most likely to deter him? Some of these methods are well known. For some offenders who have the money or the skillful legal counsel or the good luck to face a wise judge go a different route from the prescribed routine. Instead of jail and deterioration, they get the sort of re-education and re-direction associated with psychiatric institutions and the psychiatric profession. Relatively few wealthy offenders get their "treatment" in jail. This does not mean that justice is to be bought, or bought off. But it does mean that some offenders have relatives and friends who *care* and who try to find the best possible solution to the problem of persistent misbehavior, which is NOT the good old jail-and-penitentiary and make-'em-sorry treatment. It is a reflection on the democratic ideals of our country that these better ways are so often—indeed, *usually*—denied to the poor, the friendless, and the ignorant.

If we were to follow scientific methods, the convicted offender would be detained indefinitely pending a decision as to whether and how and when to reintroduce him successfully into society. All the skill and knowledge of modern behavioral science would be used to examine his personality assets, his liabilities and potentialities, the environment from which he came, its effect upon him, and his effects upon it.

Having arrived at some diagnostic grasp of the offender's personality, those in charge can decide whether there is a chance that he can be redirected into a mutually satisfactory adaptation to the world. If so, the most suitable techniques in education, industrial training, group administration, and psychotherapy should be selectively applied. All this may be best done extramurally or intramurally. It may require maximum "security" or only minimum "security." If, in due time, perceptible change occurs, the process should be expedited by finding a suitable spot in society and industry for him, and getting him out of prison control and into civil status (with parole control) as quickly as possible.

The desirability of moving patients out of institutional control swiftly is something which we psychiatrists learned the hard way, and recently. Ten years ago, in the state hospital I know best, the average length of stay was five years; today it is three months. Ten years ago few patients were discharged under two years; today 90 per cent are discharged within the first year. Ten years ago the hospital was overcrowded; today it has eight times the turnover it used to have; there are empty beds and there is no waiting list.

But some patients do not respond to our efforts, and they have to remain in the hospital, or return to it promptly after a trial home visit. And if the *prisoner*, like some of the psychiatric patients, cannot be changed by genuine efforts to rehabilitate him, we must look *our* failure in the face, and provide for his indefinitely continued confinement, regardless of the technical reasons for it. This we owe society for its protection.

There will be some offenders about whom the most experienced are mistaken, both ways. And there will be some concerning whom no one knows what is best. There are many problems for research. But what I have outlined is, I believe, the program of modern penology, the program now being carried out in some degree in California and a few other states, and in some of the federal prisons.

This civilized program, which would save so much now wasted money, so much unused manpower, and so much injustice and suffering, is slow to spread. It is held back by many things—by the continued use of fixed sentences in many places; by unenlightened community attitudes toward the offender whom some want tortured; by the prevalent popular assumption that burying a frustrated individual in a hole for a short time will change his warped mind, and that when he is certainly worse, he should be released because his "time" has been served; by the persistent failure of the law to distinguish between crime as an accidental, incidental, explosive event, crime as a behavior pattern expressive of chronic unutterable rage and frustration, and crime as a business or elected way of life. Progress is further handicapped by the lack of interest in the subject on the part of lawyers, most of whom are proud to say that they are not concerned with criminal law. It is handicapped by the lack of interest on the part of members of my own profession. It is handicapped by the mutual distrust of lawyers and psychiatrists.

The infestation or devil-possession theory of mental disease is an outmoded, pre-medieval concept. Although largely abandoned by psychiatry, it steadfastly persists in the minds of many laymen, including, unfortunately, many lawyers.

On the other hand, most lawyers have no really clear idea of the way in which a psychiatrist functions or of the basic concepts to which he adheres. They cannot understand, for example, why there is no such thing (for psychiatrists) as "insanity." Most lawyers have no conception of the meaning or methods of psychiatric case study and diagnosis. They seem to think that psychiatrists can take a quick look at a suspect, listen to a few anecdotes about him, and thereupon be able to say, definitely, that the awful "it"—the dreadful miasma of madness, the loathsome affliction of "insanity"—is present or absent. Because we all like to please, some timid psychiatrists fall in with this fallacy of the lawyers and go through these preposterous antics.

It is true that almost any offender—like anyone else—when questioned for a short time, even by the most skillful psychiatrist, can make responses and display behavior patterns which will indicate that he is enough like the rest of us to be called "sane." But a barrage of questions is not a psychiatric examination. Modern scientific personality study depends upon various specialists—physical, clinical, and sociological as well as psychological. It takes into consideration not only static and presently observable factors, but dynamic and historical factors, and factors of environmental interaction and change. It also looks into the future for correction, re-education, and prevention.

Hence, the same individuals who appear so normal to superficial observation are frequently discovered in the course of prolonged, intensive scientific study to have tendencies regarded as "deviant," "peculiar," "unhealthy," "sick," "crazy," "senseless," "irrational," "insane."

But now you may ask, "Is it not possible to find such tendencies in any individual if one looks hard enough? And if this is so, if we are all a little crazy or potentially so, what is the essence of your psychiatric distinctions? Who is it that you want excused?"

And here is the crux of it all. We psychiatrists don't want *anyone* excused. In fact, psychiatrists are much more concerned about the protection of the public than are the lawyers. I repeat; psychiatrists don't want anyone excused, certainly not anyone who shows anti-social tendencies. We consider them all responsible, which lawyers do not. And we want the prisoner to take on that responsibility, or else deliver it to someone who will be concerned about the protection of society and about the prisoner, too. We don't want anyone excused, but neither do we want anyone stupidly disposed of, futilely detained, or prematurely released. We don't want them tortured, either sensationally with hot irons or quietly by long-continued and forced idleness. In the psychiatrist's mind nothing should be done in the name of punishment, though he is well aware that the offender may regard either the diagnostic procedure or the treatment or the detention incident to the treatment as punitive. But this is in *his* mind, not in the psychiatrist's mind. And in our opinion it should not be in the public's mind, because it is an illusion.

It is true that we psychiatrists consider that all people have potentialities for antisocial behavior. The law assumes this, too. Most of the time most people control their criminal impulses. But for various reasons and under all kinds of circumstances some individuals become increasingly disorganized or demoralized, and then they begin to be socially offensive. The man who does criminal things is less convincingly disorganized than the patient who "looks" sick, because the former more nearly resembles the rest of us, and seems to be indulging in acts that we have struggled with and controlled. So we get hot under the collar about the one and we call him "criminal" whereas we pityingly forgive the other and call him "lunatic." But a surgeon uses the same principles of surgery whether he is dealing with a "clean" case, say some cosmetic surgery on a face, or a "dirty" case which is foul-smelling and offensive. What we are after is results and the emotions of the operator must be under control. Words like "criminal" and "insane" have no place in the scientific vocabulary any more than pejorative adjectives like "vicious," "psychopathic," "bloodthirsty," etc. The need is to find all the *descriptive* adjectives that apply to the case, and this is a scientific job—not a popular exercise in name-calling. Nobody's insides are very beautiful; and in the cases that require social control there has been a great wound and some of the insides are showing.

Intelligent judges all over the country are increasingly surrendering the onerous responsibility of deciding in advance what a man's conduct will be in a prison and how rapidly his wicked impulses will evaporate there. With more use of the indeterminate sentence and the establishment of scientific diagnostic centers, we shall be in a position to make progress in the science of *treating* anti-social trends. Furthermore, we shall get away from the present legal smog that hangs over the prisons, which lets us detain with heartbreaking futility some prisoners fully rehabilitated while others, whom the prison officials know full well to be dangerous and unemployable, must be released, *against our judgment*, because a judge far away (who has by this time forgotten all about it) said that five years was enough. In my frequent visits to prisons I am always astonished at how rarely the judges who have prescribed the "treatment" come to see whether or not it is effective. What if doctors who sent their seriously ill patients to hospitals never called to see them!

As more states adopt diagnostic centers directed toward getting the prisoners *out* of jail and back to work, under modern, well-structured parole systems, the taboo on jail and prison, like that on state hospitals, will begin to diminish. Once it was a lifelong disgrace to have been in either. Lunatics, as they were cruelly called, were feared and avoided. Today only the ignorant retain this phobia. Cancer was then considered a *shameful* thing to have, and victims of it were afraid to mention it, or have it correctly treated, because they did not want to be disgraced. The time will come when offenders, much as we disapprove of their offenses, will no longer be unemployable untouchables.

To a physician discussing the wiser treatment of our fellow men it seems hardly necessary to add that under no circumstances should we kill them. It was never considered right for doctors to kill their patients, no matter how hopeless their condition. True, some patients in state institutions have undoubtedly been executed without benefit of sentence. They were a nuisance, expensive to keep, and dangerous to release. Various people took it upon themselves to put an end to the matter, and I have even heard them boast of it. The Hitler regime had the same philosophy.

But in most civilized countries today we have a higher opinion of the rights of the individual and of the limits to the state's power. We know, too, that for the most part the death penalty is inflicted upon obscure, impoverished, defective, and friendless individuals. We know that it intimidates juries in their efforts to determine guilt without prejudice. We know that it is being eliminated in one state after another, most recently Delaware. We know that in practice it has almost disappeared—for over seven thousand capital crimes last year there were less than one hundred executions. But vast sums of money are still being spent—let us say wasted—in legal contests to determine whether or not an individual, even one known to have been mentally ill, is now healthy enough for the state to hang him. (I am informed that such a case has recently cost the State of California $400,000!)

Most of all, we know that no state employees—except perhaps some that ought to be patients themselves—want a job on the killing squad, and few wardens can stomach this piece of medievalism in their own prisons. For example, two officials I know recently quarreled because each wished to have the hanging of a prisoner carried out on the other's premises.

Capital punishment is, in my opinion, morally wrong. It has a bad effect on everyone, especially those involved in it. It gives a false sense of security to the public. It is vastly expensive. Worst of all it beclouds the entire issue of motivation in crime, which is so importantly relevant to the question of what to do for and with the criminal that will be most constructive to society as a whole. Punishing—and even killing—criminals may yield a kind of grim gratification; let us all admit that there are times when we are so shocked at the depredations of an offender that we persuade ourselves that this is a man the Creator didn't intend to create, and that we had better help correct the mistake. But playing God in this way has no conceivable moral or scientific justification.

Let us return in conclusion to the initial question: "Verdict guilty— now what?" My answer is that now we, the designated representatives of the society which has failed to integrate this man, which has failed him in some way, hurt him and been hurt by him, should take over. It is *our* move. And our move must be a constructive one, an intelligent one, a purposeful one—not a primitive, retaliatory, offensive move. We, the agents of society, must move to end the game of tit-for-tat and blow-for-blow in which the offender has foolishly and futilely engaged himself and us. We are not driven, as he is, to wild and impulsive actions. With knowledge comes power, and with power there is no need for the frightened vengeance of the old penology. In its place should go a quiet, dignified, therapeutic program for the rehabilitation of the disorganized one, if possible, the protection of society during his treatment period, and his guided return to useful citizenship, as soon as this can be effected.

THOMAS S. SZASZ

Born in Budapest in 1920, Dr. Szasz came to this country in 1938. He received his medical degree from the University of Cincinnati in 1954 and took his psychoanalytic training at the Chicago Institute for Psychoanalysis. He is currently Professor of Psychiatry at the State University of New York. His writings include The Myth of Mental Illness: Foundation of a Theory of Personal Conduct *(1961) and* Law, Liberty, and Psychiatry: An Inquiry into the Social Uses of Mental Health Practices *(1963). The article we present below first appeared in* The Yale Review, *Summer, 1960.*

MORAL CONFLICT AND PSYCHIATRY

With the rapid growth and widespread acceptance of psychiatry in the United States in recent decades, the idea that psychiatry is a medical specialty—concerned with the treatment of so-called mental diseases—has become firmly established. The chief merit of the idea lies, as I see it, in its having helped the medical profession, and people generally, to regard problems in human living in a new light. Until the turn of the century, these problems were categorized as "malingering," and were treated with derision and condemnation. Relabeling them "mental illnesses" led to a more sympathetic and humane attitude. The advantages to be derived from the relabeling, however, went only this far, and no further. Indeed, we might ask at what cost the promotion of some sufferers from the class of malingerers to the class of the mentally ill has been achieved.

There are several penalties attached to regarding problems in human living as manifestations of a so-called mental illness. Perhaps the most important among them is that it has sometimes led to the idea that psychiatry

—like other branches of medicine—is essentially free of moral values. Yet, since psychiatry, or at least some aspects of it, concerns itself with man as a social being, it deals with many of the same problems with which religion and morality (ethics) have dealt in the past. If this is so, it becomes imperative that persons interested in psychiatry and its applications become acquainted with the ethical positions which psychiatrists—both individually and collectively—espouse. It is important, further, that the connections between psychiatry and ethics be kept clearly in mind in all those instances in which psychiatric interventions are undertaken in social situations involving covert moral conflicts. One such situation occurs when psychiatrists participate in the legal disposition of law-breakers, so that a person charged with an offense, instead of being tried for it, may be committed to a state hospital as "mentally ill."

For some time now I have found myself in considerable opposition to certain prevalent psychiatric customs, particularly in regard to psychiatric participation in criminal trials. While my ideas on this subject have been presented previously in several technical papers, I would now like to set them before the general reader. The nature of the subject is such that it rightly concerns the intelligent citizen just as much as it does the psychiatric specialist. In presenting my views, I shall make use of a recently publicized account of a crime, in order to illustrate what may otherwise seem vague or unclear abstractions. My main emphasis, however, is not on this particular case and its special implications, but rather on the general features of the value conflict which I believe it illustrates. If looked for, these may be discerned in many instances in which people who break laws are committed as "insane."

According to an Associated Press news-dispatch dated November 18, 1958, Mrs. Isola Ware Curry, the woman who had stabbed the Reverend Martin Luther King in a Harlem department store some six weeks before, was committed to the Matteawan State Hospital. The dispatch went on to comment: "She never gave a coherent reason for the attack." Mrs. Curry was indicted on a charge of attempted murder in the first degree. Prior to this, however, she had been committed to Bellevue Hospital for pre-trial examination and found "insane" (at the time of the examination). She was not brought to trial for her offense, but was instead committed to an institution which for social purposes functions just like a jail but is called a hospital—a hospital for the "criminally insane."

This sequence of events surprised, I think, no one. An unprovoked attack on an anti-segregationist leader by a Negro woman would—and undoubtedly did—strike the man-on-the-street as "just about as crazy as you can get." Consequently, Mrs. Curry was committable in the public eye. Suppose, however, that the same sort of attack had been made on a segregationist leader; would she still be committable in the public eye, or would her act be interpreted as a political crime based on revenge? Suppose

Mr. King had been attacked by a member of the Ku Klux Klan. Would the attacker have been labeled mentally ill by the general public? Or would his act have been regarded as a political crime?

These questions are by no means irrelevant to Mrs. Curry's act and society's response to it. Involuntary commitment of a person as mentally ill, it must be remembered, is not a purely medical or psychiatric procedure. While the procedure must be based on a medical or psychiatric recommendation, the final decision to commit—or not to commit—is a *judicial* one. I might note here that I am opposed to *all* existing commitment practices. It seems to me, however, that if we are to have such a thing as commitment, it is only proper that the final decision concerning it should be a legal one, for it entails depriving the patient of some of his civil rights. Hence, it would seem obvious that, in our democratic society, no physician should want to—or should be permitted to—exercise this power.

To return to the case of Mrs. Curry: obviously it is not my intention to imply that in having attacked Mr. King she was thinking brightly or acting rightly. Having stabbed her victim in plain view of many witnesses clearly established that she had committed a crime. Hence her trial and conviction could be circumvented in only one way, by pleading "insanity." If this plea is accepted by the authorities charged with the prosecution, it automatically leads to the judgment that the offender was "not responsible for his (or her) criminal actions." On the basis of so-called psychiatric findings, it can be further decided that the offender is "incapable of assisting in his own defense." He can then be committed without being tried. This, apparently, was done in Mrs. Curry's case.

I have no idea what the psychiatric findings were in this case. This is just as well, for I submit that irrespective of what these findings were, they could not *by themselves* justify her commitment to a state hospital. Psychiatric findings of "schizophrenia" or "psychosis" can be demonstrated in millions of people who are not hospitalized. The point here is that since she broke the law, something had to be done, and putting her away *quietly* was, under the circumstances, the socially preferred course to take. This raises the question of what sort of things are involved in this case which make us—and here I refer to that hypothetical entity called "most of us" —uncomfortable, had they been more fully exposed to the light of day.

The main problem which was evaded by the psychiatric short-circuiting of the case is the so-called "Negro problem." This already is so much in the public eye that it would seem to me difficult to justify new attempts to hide it.

There are, of course, some related issues involved in this case. One of these is that this woman acted out a crime which either overtly or nearly so is daily being advocated by the segregationist forces of our society. Thus an act was committed which many people must have greeted with glee. One need not be hypocritical about this. It is well known that when people who stand for one value die, those who stand for an opposing value are happy. When Hitler was in power his death was freely wished for—and undoubtedly prayed for—by many Jews. Other examples could easily be cited. If these are the facts, it is irrational to behave as though everyone shared the same values and goals in life. If the upholding of a democratic law demands the political equality of Negroes—as the Supreme Court has recently re-codified it—it demands equally the open condemnation of taking the law into one's own hands. By not taking Mrs. Curry, or her act, seriously (I am speaking here in a socio-political sense), the need to condemn her act was evaded.

At this point, an objection might be raised against my argument, which might run as follows: "If the attacker had been white and sane, he *would* have been tried, and his act would have been condemned." Let us take each of these points separately. First, the question of color. We are, apparently, especially revolted and perplexed by the fact that a Negro person should have attacked a man who is a leader in the Negro's fight for equality. But in reacting in this way, we merely close our eyes to some further well-known facts about how human beings feel and act.

The tendency for the oppressed to adopt and espouse the ideals of his oppressor is well known. The operation of this tendency may be observed in many situations in which one group oppresses another—for example, in prisoner-of-war camps, concentration camps, and in slave-master relationships of all kinds. Indeed, there is nothing especially mysterious about this. At bottom it is much the same as a free man's admiration of outstanding personalities, whether of an Albert Einstein or a Mickey Mantle. Prominent men possess things or skills which the ordinary man lacks but would like to have. So it is for the prisoner and his captor, slave and master, Negro and white. Psychoanalysts have long ago recognized this phenomenon and called it "identification with the aggressor." More than thirty years ago, in *The Future of an Illusion*, Freud spoke expressly of the "identification of the oppressed with the class that governs and exploits them. . . ." What does this actually mean?

Stripped of technical complexities, it means that a person who has been attacked, violated, and abused—especially if over a long period of time—has, in fact, been abused *twice*. First, by the act itself. Second, by the changes which his captive, submissive position vis-à-vis his exploiters has wrought in his personality, in his inner self. While the first violation is obvious, the second one is not and often escapes attention altogether. Yet of the two, it is probably the more important, for it is the one with the most lasting consequences. The acute harm and indignity of abuse can be stopped and undone by disrupting the relationship responsible for it. Freeing the prisoner, overthrowing the oppressor, liberating the slave—all these put a stop to the specific situation of violation which they are designed to correct.

The second type of harm inflicted upon the oppressed is more insidious and more difficult to correct. Its effect is a modification of the personality: the oppressed adopts the characteristics of being oppressive. He adopts the values and aspirations of the oppressor. Illustrative are such phenomena as the anti-Semitic Jew, or the Negro who wants to be white.

These considerations carry us to the point where we can return to Mrs. Curry's case and ask this question: What would have been considered (by the popular mind, so to speak) as a *reasonable explanation* of her act? Public opinion *defines* reasonableness as concurrence with its own standards, much as Disraeli was said to have characterized an agreeable gentleman as one who agreed with him. Applying this principle to our present case, we must conclude that, in the public mind, all Negroes are lined up on the side of integration. The segregationist Negro is thus made into a theoretical impossibility—a decision which, however, does not make it impossible for him to exist. In regard to the problem of desegregation, then, only two alternatives remain in the public mind: one is that all Negroes are in favor of it, the other that if they are not, they must be "crazy." In this way the very possibility of a Negro espousing the ideals of segregationism is ruled out of existence—and with it a host of historical precedents impressively demonstrating that the oppressed classes *cannot* be relied upon as the steadfast supporters of the value of liberty. The American Founding Fathers belonged to the upper strata of society. So did men like Marx, Lenin, Gandhi, Nehru, and others who, it is true, fought on behalf of the disenfranchised classes of their nations, or of mankind as a whole, but were themselves not really members of these classes.

The possibility that Mrs. Curry's attack on Mr. King was meant to reveal what in fact it manifestly asserted must, therefore, be seriously considered. Why could this attack not be taken on its face value? Why must we assume that it requires some special interpretation which only psychiatrists are able to make? Taking Mrs. Curry's act on its face value would mean that we should regard it as a "show of hands" on her part, informing all and sundry that she stood on the side of those who favored segregationism. Why could her belief that the Negro's "proper place" is to be a slave—and within this belief, her wish to remain a "happy slave" —not be considered a "reasonable explanation" of her act? Many people in our culture hold this belief. Must she be deprived of *the right to share this view* because of her color?

By affixing a so-called psychiatric diagnosis to her—and thus branding her act as "crazy" and ipso facto incomprehensible (except to experts) —the questions raised here were comfortably settled. That she should have a *choice* in regard to the problem of segregation was expressly disallowed. In other words, disposing of Mrs. Curry's case by means of psychiatric—rather than legal—intervention, achieved two major objectives: (1) It deprived her, and by implication others of her race, of the right to commit a crime against a prominent member of her own race. (2) It enabled society—and the public mind—to disguise and evade the moral and socio-psychological dilemmas inherent in her act. These achievements seem clearly to run counter to the values of humanism and democracy. Their malignant implications are even more evident if viewed in the light of the laxity which supposedly characterizes the prosecution of crimes committed by Negroes against Negroes.

What the psychiatrist's job in our society is, is a question which it would require a book, not a brief essay, to answer. I shall limit myself, therefore, to calling attention to two quite independent—and at times conflicting —jobs which psychiatrists take upon themselves. One is to treat people. The other is to harmonize, or tranquilize, interpersonal and social conflicts. I shall make a few comments concerning each.

For our present purposes we shall disregard what psychiatric treatment really consists of and shall focus on the fact that *the therapist's role is to be an agent of the patient*. This role is best illustrated by a private psycho-therapeutic relationship. The psychiatrist's job is to help his patient by clarifying his problems in living. The goal of such a "treatment" generally is to enable the patient, who hires the psychiatrist and pays him for his efforts, to live more effectively in accordance with the values and goals which he himself has set for himself, or may set for himself in the future. This does not mean that the patient's moral conceptions and conduct remain unscrutinized. On the contrary, such scrutiny forms an essential part of the therapy. The point I wished to emphasize was that the therapist is *contractually* (and perhaps otherwise) committed to avoid influencing his patient by any means other than that of talking to him. In a contract so constituted, the psychiatrist may not speak about the patient to others (not even to colleagues), may not testify for or against him in a court of law, and may not hospitalize the patient against his will (i.e., "commit" him as "insane"). The psychoanalytic relationship is the one in which the psychiatrist's role is most clearly defined in this way. Many other psychiatrists' daily work, however, rests on and embodies the same principles.

The psychiatrist's second job I have chosen to call "social tranquilization," and psychiatrists performing this task may then be called "social tranquilizers."

Psychiatrists act in the role of social tranquilizers when they define their task as protecting the harmony of existing (chronic) institutions, such as marriage, social class, profession (as guild), nation, etc. Faced with conflicting values and social aspirations, psychiatrists may now interfere in order to obscure and evade the issues. Relief is offered by focusing the conflicting parties' attention on a substitute problem and its possible solution. For example, a married couple seeking divorce may be advised to have a child or cultivate a common interest. A therapist making such a recommendation is strictly not an agent of either the man or the wife, but rather of marriage, as a social institution.

The psychiatric function of social tranquilization thus consists of two distinct parts. One is to provide relief from tension by means of *distraction;*

the other is to offer *substitute solutions* to problems which are more or less removed from the original sources of tension. In the case of Mrs. Curry, the conflicts over segregation—and the whole so-called Negro problem, in general—appear to be the major primary source of current social tension, especially in the South. Preoccupation with the alleged mental health or illness of those who are for or against segregation may be regarded as a psychiatric contribution to offering a substitute problem; recommendations for easing this problem constitute substitute solutions.

My aim in this essay is limited to making clear what sort of jobs psychiatrists actually perform nowadays. A critical evaluation of the psychological, moral, and political worth of these performances lies beyond the scope of this discussion. Nor is this necessary, for once the essential nature of these tasks has been properly identified, the expert is no longer needed to pass judgment on their worth. This step of evaluating can then be adequately carried out by the intelligently informed public on whose shoulders the ultimate responsibility lies for how it uses its experts. This does not imply that the experts are free of the obligation to examine for themselves how they are being used and to assume individual responsibility for the professional roles which they agree to play. Failure to do this results in blaming "social needs" for medical and psychiatric actions whose effects are destructive of human values. Nazi physicians who "experimented" on their victims offer a recent tragic example.

When psychiatrists act as social tranquilizers, their behavior is based on the tacit premise that the preservation of existing interpersonal and social conditions is a desirable end. The social prestige of psychiatry as a science is used as a means to insure this end. This raises the question of how we decide—either generally, or in any one specific instance—whether to regard change or preservation of the *status quo* as a desirable goal. The notion of so-called mental illness enters into this problem in a crucial way.

How does modern man respond to the endless succession of everyday problems in living with which he must grapple? In trying to answer this question, let us keep in mind such ubiquitous problems as that of the Negro in a Southern community, torn between staying where he is or leaving to settle in the North; or that of a husband or wife, each in some way dissatisfied with the other, trying to decide whether to stay married or get divorced. I want to preface what follows by saying that I do not wish to imply that the mere acts of "staying" and "leaving" are the only solutions possible in the face of such dilemmas; nor that they alone need necessarily "solve" the problem in living with which the individual happens to be struggling. Still, these examples aptly illustrate the kind of problem with which every one of us must struggle more or less constantly as we go through life from adolescence to old age.

There are two distinct patterns of adaptation or "solution" which may be employed in one's efforts to cope with problems in living. One requires active mastery of the difficulty, the other passive acquiescence in the *status quo*. Some ethical systems place a high value on activity, others on passivity. In our own contemporary society, these values can be said to co-exist, albeit not very peacefully. The main source of confusion and difficulty in regard to popular opinion on this subject stems from the fact that we subscribe to a moral double standard about the "rightness" of changing one's circumstances. Thus, we favor an activist position whenever it suits our needs, and espouse the values of maintaining the *status quo* whenever the change promises to be to our disadvantage. This is true equally in interpersonal relationships and in world diplomacy. Here is how it works.

When we find ourselves in a difficult or unpleasant position—faced, for example, with an unsatisfactory job-situation—we consider it a human right and necessity that we have freedom to avail ourselves of all the activity possible in order to change our circumstances. If, however, someone else is in a bad position, and his situation is of advantage to us, we rarely advocate that he have the freedom to alter his situation actively. In other words, we are prone to play the game of social living with rules not equally applicable to all the players. Instead, we like to play with two sets of rules, one for the "free" and another for the "slave." This is, of course, what is meant by a "double standard." No doubt, this makes it a lot easier for those who play with the favorable rules to "win" in the game of life. Moreover, in their understandable eagerness to maintain their advantage, those who play with the rules of the "free" have been very resourceful in their arguments in regard to the differential rules. One of the favorite justifications against adopting uniform rules has been to emphasize that the "slaves" (e.g., the poor, the "insane," the Negro, religious minority groups, etc.) would be *unable* to play with the "free rules"; hence, playing by the "slave rules" is *for them* really to their advantage. This has been an inspired argument and has gained wide acceptance among various classes of discriminated persons.

What I want to emphasize is the existence of an essentially dichotomous attitude toward problems in living. According to one position, man ought to take a passive attitude toward life; according to the other, an active attitude aimed at mastery (in the here and now) is espoused. We find the same dichotomy between the notions of "social action" and "mental illness." Social action is something which a person *does*; for example, revenge for a wrong-doing. Mental illness, on the other hand, is regarded as something that *happens* to a person; it is like falling ill (with, say, pneumonia). It is for this reason that the idea of "punishing" someone who is mentally ill is repugnant to the popular mind. I submit, however, that all this is wrong. For how do we know whether a person is mentally ill? Divesting the question of some of its psychiatric-technical complications (which are partly genuine, but partly manufactured, so to speak), the fact remains that *social deviation* is one of the outstanding occurrences which set in motion a chain of events which may eventually result in the diagnosis of a mental illness. Hence, we have a circular problem. We raise the question of mental illness only in the presence of social deviation; but, when confronted with social deviation, we have no preformed value-free criteria for judging whether to call any given act a (political) crime or a (mental) illness.

How then do we decide what to call it? The answer is simple: *First we decide how we want to deal with the problem or person.* If we want to spirit the culprit away and pull a curtain of secrecy and silence around the issues involved and the social conflicts which may be mobilized by inquiry into them, then we decide that the person responsible is mentally ill. Conversely, if there is no objection to free inquiry into the problem opened up by the socially deviant act—or, even more, if the act can be used to influence particular social issues in certain desired directions—then no recourse to mental illness is taken and the great public drama of a trial follows. Consider in this connection the following examples. Mrs. Curry was committed; but Mr. John Kasper was tried. Ezra Pound was committed; but Alger Hiss was tried. Sacco and Vanzetti, Goering, Hess, and many other political figures have been tried and convicted. Why were not any of the latter considered mentally ill? Psychiatric or psychoanalytic arguments concerning mental mechanisms give us no acceptable answer to this problem. On the contrary, and this is precisely my thesis, shifting the ground to the domain of psychiatry obscures the fundamental fact that in all such cases adjudication of the crime involves us—all of us—in settling a problem of moral and social values. This is usually a painful task but one that must not be shirked. Psychiatric interference thus seems to me to be one of the principal techniques which contemporary society uses to avoid and evade problems of values.

How does this evasion work? The notion of mental illness, commitment to a so-called hospital, and many of the trappings of contemporary psychiatry all point to one thing, namely to the "irresponsibility" of the accused. Thus, at one stroke—and without making it explicit—he is removed from among those who *act* and *do*, and is placed into the class of those to whom (terrible) things *happen*. However, by forgiving someone and asserting that he does not know what he is doing (that is, he is "insane"), we "help" the person at the cost of sacrificing his human dignity and right to self-assertion. But surely, next to killing a man, this act of infantilizing him is one of the worst punishments we can bestow on anyone. For just as killing a man means physical destruction of his body, so demoting him to the class of imbeciles who do not know what they are doing, and hence cannot be taken seriously, is tantamount to killing a man psycho-socially. For we can truly say that man as a person and not merely as a body is alive to the extent—and only to that extent—to which he is free to partake of dignified human relationships. Anything which robs man of either the ability or the opportunity for such relationships contributes to the destruction of his social self.

For those who aspire to a responsible, free, and dignified human life, there can be no shirking of the recognition of the existence and probable inevitability of conflicts of moral value. Such conflicts are just as ubiquitous and unavoidable as personal conflicts. Differences of personal interests or needs cannot be resolved by pretending that they do not exist or by insisting that the other person be molded to one's own needs. While both of these attempts at conflict-solving are time-honored, their limitations are by now well known. Today, many of us are taught to live by making necessary compromises. This can be best accomplished when the specific needs of each of the participants are accurately known and candidly acknowledged. Moreover, compromises lead to the realignment of human needs and values, and so to new conflicts and new compromises. In contrast, efforts at denial or at achieving "total victory" aim at a static solution of the problem; consequently, both are threatened by change. Yet, if anything is characteristic of modern social life it is change. It is for this reason that I suggest that we espouse the very notion of a peaceful, orderly social change as a positive value. There may be much argument, of course, as to what sorts of change are good, and what others bad. This need not concern us here. What does concern us is the role of psychiatry and psychiatrists in contemporary value conflicts. In this regard, it was suggested that the notion of mental illness, as something passive that *happens* to people, rather than as something active, that is, something which people *do* in an effort to adjust, adapt, or communicate, may cause us more trouble than it is worth.

Finally, I have suggested that when psychiatry and psychiatrists, resting their arguments on the notion of mental illness, participate in the social disposition of offenders, they act as social tranquilizers. This means that instead of expediting peaceful social change—which is a covert ethical ideal of science and medicine—psychiatrists acting in this way obstruct change and obscure problems. The conclusion need not strike us as especially strange or novel, for we are already familiar with a similar state of affairs in science in general. The scientific process as a phenomenon of human inventiveness is one thing, institutionalized "science" quite another. The latter may easily be harnessed to obstruct the former, and the history of many scientific societies, organizations, universities, and so forth bears witness to this assertion. In a like manner, psychiatry—either as a science of man or as individual psychotherapy—is one thing; as such, it is intimately tied to the ethical values of human dignity, self-determination, and growth or development through change. Psychiatry as an institutional force is a relatively new thing. It seems to be taking shape and developing in conformity with the characteristics of other institutional forces, which are conservative—in the sense that they oppose *all* change—and hence are inimical to the values of science and democracy.

DAVID L. BAZELON

David L. Bazelon is Chief Judge, U. S. Court of Appeals for the District of Columbia Circuit. Born in 1909, he holds a law degree from Northwestern and has been a judge with the Court since 1949. He has become increasingly well known in legal and psychiatric circles since 1954, when he broke with nineteenth-century precedent—the M'Naghten rule—and adopted a new test of criminal responsibility now known as the Durham rule. The M'Naghten rule permits an insanity plea only if a defendant's mental disorder can be shown to have prevented his knowing right from wrong. The Durham rule does not involve knowing right from wrong but holds instead "that if defendant's unlawful act was the product of mental disease or mental defect, he was not criminally responsible." Deeply concerned over the relationship between mental illness and crime, Judge Bazelon has been lecturer in law and psychiatry at the University of Pennsylvania Law School and Visiting Professor at the Menninger Foundation in Kansas. In 1960 he received the Isaac Ray Award of the American Psychiatric Association. The speech we present below was delivered before the Federal Bar Association in 1963; two later speeches, also concerned with criminal and human responsibility, "The Interface of Law and the Behavioral Sciences," and "The Future of Reform in the Administration of Criminal Justice," have been read into the Congressional Record in 1964 (Vol. 110, No. 68 and Vol. 110, No. 78, respectively).

LAW, MORALITY, AND INDIVIDUAL RIGHTS

For three quarters of a century the first day of May has been an occasion on which people in America have marked their aspirations for a better social order. The May Day demonstrations of the 1880's by American trade unions seeking the eight-hour day are, so far as I am aware, the beginning of this tradition in our country; long, be it noted, before the emergence of Communist regimes which have made May Day an occasion for parading symbols of might rather than of right. Today we find the observance of May first extended from the labor movement to the nation at large and from the limited and long-achieved goal of an eight-hour day to the broader goal upon which depends all social reform and advance in a democratic society: the rule of law.

Remarks in connection with our May first observance of Law Day often cover a broad spectrum: international affairs, communism, democracy, and many aspects of our system of government. Speaking on the eve of Law Day, I want to consider only some aspects of law observance in our own city of Washington. My remarks will be addressed to our observance of the criminal law *and* the rights of individuals. The two must always go together.

The popular concern growing out of our much-publicized crime problem here in the District of Columbia is not with white collar crime or with organized crime, but with crimes of violence, robbery and the like. More precisely, it is with the supposed "excess" of such crimes. Violence has always been with us but now we are really alarmed, and some of us are afraid to be out on the streets. We are alarmed with some cause, but we must retain a proper perspective. As Berl I. Bernhard, staff director of the Civil Rights Commission, pointed out earlier this month, there is a general impression that this District has the highest crime rate among the major cities of the nation, whereas FBI figures show that, in number of crimes per thousand of the population, Washington actually ranks thirteenth among the 25 largest cities. And Mr. Bernhard reports that "compared to a national crime increase of seven per cent for the calendar year 1962 over the year 1961, the crime rate in Washington increased only 4.9 per cent."

Unlawful behavior in the District has been attributed to a variety of causes—the Mallory Rule; the *previously* existing cussedness of the human race; the Durham Rule, of course; and soft sentencing policies—a charge which nicely ignored statistics showing that District of Columbia felons average a longer stay in prison than do felons in the states or in other federal jurisdictions. The average length of time served by felons in the District of Columbia is 40.4 months; in the states it is 28.3 months; and the average of all Federal jurisdictions is 19.5 months. Other alleged causes have included the former inadequate number of juvenile court judges, the absence of corporal punishment and a consequent breakdown of discipline in our school system, and so on. Still other reasons have been reached for and found. Not yet sun-spots, however.

I don't know the whole answer, if there is one, to our crime problem, but I think I know some parts of it. One part was forcefully brought home to me one September when I returned to the city after being away for several weeks. There had been a phenomenal rise in the crime rate during August—something like sixteen or eighteen per cent. I discussed the increase with a friend of mine, a veteran police officer. "For such a marked rise," I said to him, "you must have some sort of explanation." "Oh yes, it's quite simple," he replied, "You see, August was a very wet month." When I pressed him further, he pointed out: "These people wait on the street corner each morning around 6:00 or 6:30 for a truck to pick them up and take them to a construction site. If it's raining, that truck doesn't come, and the men are going to be idle that day. If the bad weather keeps up for three days," he continued, "we know we are going to have trouble on our hands—and sure enough, there invariably follows a rash of purse-snatchings, house-breakings and the like." Then he added: "These people have to eat like the rest of us, you know."

Thus one gets a painfully sharp illustration of the direct relationship between unemployment, poverty and crime—a theme to which James B. Conant has drawn attention in his significant study, "Slums and Suburbs." The mass of school drop-outs who are without employment and without hope of employment constitute the combustible material which Conant fears will burst into a crime explosion on a scale we have never known.

Both crime *and* morality have their generative conditions. So we need a probing awareness of the conditions of physical and mental life which are essential to the standards of law and morality we have adopted. We must face up to the absence of the essential conditions and not merely cluck our tongues about it. Only then will there be any real chance of altering personal circumstances and behavior in the right direction.

This was recognized by the District Commissioners' Crime Council of which former U. S. Attorney Oliver Gasch was co-chairman. It pointed out that:

> all of the police forces, public recreational facilities, and wholesome activity programs that money can buy will not miraculously turn a youth from anti-social behavior, if his share of city life reveals only deprivation and discrimination. Substandard housing . . . unequal job opportunities and many other discriminatory practices . . . lend themselves most powerfully to the creation of a psychological climate hardly conducive to good citizenship.

We must ask ourselves these questions: Does the citizen of a free, affluent society have a right to health and development, and to the adequate upbringing on which these depend? Do we want this included in our concept of modern democratic citizenship? If we do, then the illnesses and other failures of our citizens who have been denied such an upbringing must be recognized as failures of society as well. An alternative view is that society need accept only limited responsibility for the sick and miseducated individuals it creates; need give only limited recognition, for example, to mental illness and mental retardation in criminal proceedings; need not recognize that such disabilities are a large part of the problem of crime and that social illness accounts for much of the remainder. By that alternative, "we," the more successful part of society, get off easy.

When rules are enforced against individuals who lack the training and capacity to follow them, the rules become instruments of oppression. It is not always the moral prescriptions that are wrong. What is always wrong is our failure to recognize the conditions that are essential for their observance. For I take it that morality is a real thing, but also that its functioning is based on real conditions; the educative conditions which give an inner structure to the individual, and the interwoven social conditions in the context of which the individual acts out his fate.

Many people feel that any discussion of criminal law and morality which does not concentrate on the issue of free will evades the real question. I am neither a philosopher nor a theologian and have no desire to discuss free will in the usual abstract terms. I am satisfied that the concept of morality relates to choices—real choices, the grounds of which are never exclusively spiritual, because they also concern the multiform conditions of social life. If belief in free will necessarily assumes that there is always a choice and that all choices are equally available to differently situated actors, then I heartily disagree. Intellectual, physical and emotional capacity, wealth, social status, all extend or limit the area of choice. To impose moral responsibility where there is no real choice is exactly what leads to Sunday morality, since it equates the illusion of choice with actual choice. We would all do well to return again and again to the irony of Anatole France when he said: "The law, in its majestic equality, forbids the rich as well as the poor to sleep under the bridges, to beg in the streets, and to steal bread."

One evades all sorts of disturbing problems if one talks in terms of complete free will instead of examining the range of actually available choices; attributes anti-social conduct to inborn evil instead of questioning how the evil got there; adheres to the strict responsibility of criminals and ignores the other side of the coin, responsibility *for* criminals.

What *are* "society's responsibilities"? They can be discussed from scores of viewpoints, including the educational and job opportunities we offer our young and our reaction when badly socialized human beings annoy us by getting into trouble. But I suggest that most problems concerning the responsibility of society finally come down to a question of the *allocation of resources*—material and emotional; what we give and what we fail to give; finally, understanding and money. One might even say, love and money.

This assertion of society's responsibilities may smack of "welfare-ism." But is there really any other way of looking at the matter? The most violent opponent of the welfare state concept probably acts much like a welfare state toward his own family. Even if he rules his roost with an unforgiving iron hand, he would never admit that he had been parsimonious toward his children with his affections and his funds. Even when Social Darwinism was in vogue, its most convinced exponent was paternalistic at home. He may have been a stern Victorian father but he took seriously his responsibilities toward his dependents.

Social Darwinism, like isolationism, persists in America only as a nostalgic dream. It persists sub rosa, as a mood, but it has ceased to be intellectually respectable. The Balanced Budget promises to take its place as the Number One rationalization of social irresponsibility. Though Social Darwinism is not the pleasing source of self-righteousness it once was, the motif of economy in the allocation of resources still accomplishes what Social Darwinism intended. It is not easy for the strong and fortunate to give up the idea that the weak and miserable should be left to their own scant resources. There is probably no area in the entire administration of the criminal law which is not affected by preoccupation with economy of money and economy of human feeling. That our wealthy society approaches its responsibilities in forma pauperis, as it were, is a national scandal. It daily contradicts the democratic humanism under which we profess to live.

While we debate how and whether to attack the roots of the problem, what measures do we and should we take against those who endanger us by violent crimes? No one would deny that we need vigorous law enforcement. But should this entail, for example, the use of terror evoked by the threat of setting beasts against human beings? I refer, of course, to the use of police dogs. Although I am not aware that this use has reduced the crime rate, the police assert that it is effective. Assume for the moment that it is. A full-scale reign of terror might be effective, too. But could we respect ourselves if we instituted one? Can we pretend that resort to such tactics will foster respect for the law and not merely respect for brute force? By measures such as these, perhaps you can force even the most unsocialized and anti-social people into a kind of submission—and not have to bother to look for the reasons for their plight. But at what a price! I have been told by the head of a municipal police force that, as a practical matter, only respect for the law can insure public safety upon the thousands of city blocks of a large metropolis. It isn't feasible to maintain a policeman on each block twenty-four hours a day, even if that were thought desirable.

Many people persist in thinking that withdrawal of legal rights and safeguards from those accused of crime would have a beneficial effect. We are told that crimes cannot adequately be solved if the police are not permitted to make arrests for investigation. And we hear that the rules established in the Mallory and Durham decisions increase our crime rate by enticing lawbreakers from outlying areas into the District of Columbia. I doubt that the perpetrators of crime calculate nicely the length of time during which they may be interrogated by the police before deciding where to snatch a purse, or consider that, if caught, their chance of landing in a mental hospital instead of a prison may be greater here than it would be elsewhere.

I suspect that the causes of aberrant behavior run a good bit deeper than this, and that the factors which trigger it are less subject to rationalization. But suppose I am wrong. Suppose, for instance, it could be shown that the Durham Rule increases the crime rate. Then we should have to weigh the morality of punishing mentally disordered people by putting them in prison or by putting them to death. Perhaps we could even go so far as to abolish the insanity defense. But, as Justice Cardozo remarked: "if insanity is not to be a defense, let us say so frankly and even brutally, but let us not mock ourselves with a definition that palters with reality. Such a method is neither good morals nor good science nor good law."

Some of the measures which are advocated to deal with the problem of crime raise serious issues under our Bill of Rights. We have generally assumed that we are not subject to arrest unless the police have probable cause to think we have committed a crime. But the police tell us they need to make arrests without probable cause and solely for investigation in order to solve crimes. Such experience as we have had since the District Commissioners' courageous action to halt arrests for investigation does not bear out this contention. But even if the position of the police should later prove to be factually correct, we should have to decide whether such arrests violate the Fourth Amendment, as the local bar is convinced that they do; and if so, then whether the Fourth Amendment must be abandoned in an attempt to stem the crime wave. But we should heed the warning of Justice Douglas in *Jones v. United States* that "Though the police are honest and their aims are worthy, history shows they are not appropriate guardians of the privacy which the Fourth Amendment guarantees."

I urge that we face the constitutional issues which lurk in some of the proposed "solutions" to the crime problem. I do not mean that we should see if the words of the Constitution can be juggled so as to reach a desired end, but whether what is planned would in fact offend the letter and the spirit of the Constitution. I suspect that sub rosa infringements of constitutional guarantees are more dangerous than frontal attacks. With the latter we can see just how far our basic principles are being surrendered: with the former, the erosion may go a long way before we understand what is happening.

We should be aware that if the protections of the Bill of Rights are restricted we shall, in practice, be affecting directly the rights of only one section of our population. When we talk about arrests for investigation, lengthy police interrogation prior to arraignment, and the like, the subject under discussion is not you or me. *We* don't get arrested without probable cause because, to put it plainly, we don't "look" as if we would commit acts of violence and we do look as if it might not pay to trifle with our rights. Nor would you or I be subjected to long interrogation by the police without the benefit of counsel. Nor do you and I live in neighborhoods where the police dragnet is used, and where suspects are subjected to wholesale arrest.

So the issue really comes down to whether we should further whittle away the protections of the very people who most need them—the people who are too ignorant, too poor, too ill-educated to defend themselves. On Law Day it is appropriate to inquire whether we can expect to induce a spirit of respect for law in the people who constitute our crime problem by treating them as beyond the pale of the Constitution.

Though the direct effect of restricting constitutional guarantees would at first be limited in this way, indirectly and eventually we should all be affected. Initially the tentacles of incipient totalitarianism seize only the scapegoats of society, but over time they may weaken the moral fibre of society to the point where none of us will remain secure.

A debate earlier this month at a meeting of the District of Columbia Bar Association showed the healthy concern of the legal profession with the perennial and inevitable conflict between police demands and constitutional mandates. The overwhelming vote which followed that debate demonstrated that lawyers are still in their rightful place at the forefront of the movement to protect civil rights. There could have been no better prelude to Law Day than that.

Our attitude toward crime reflects our view of the value of the individual in society. In our deepest democratic and national commitments, we are a society of individuals. It is for the protection of individuals and of society that one who is accused of crime is deemed innocent until proved guilty and is afforded all the other legal safeguards. In protecting him, we protect ourselves. In a sense the entire system of criminal jurisprudence is "symbolic," since every part of it stands for something more than itself, namely, the preservation of the worth of each individual in the society of individuals. We must deter not only crime, but also the debasement of the individual.

LEO N. TOLSTOY

Count Tolstoy (1828–1910), author of War and Peace *(1865–69) and* Anna Karenina *(1875–77), is considered one of the greatest novelists of all time; he was also an important social and moral philosopher. His daughter Alexandra writes that while he attended the University of Kazan, "philosophical thoughts and the urge for self-improvement were interwoven with ambitious dreams of becoming rich, famous, distinguished, and educated." He began to study oriental languages, then switched to law, but was a poor student and left the University after two years. He retired to the country where he worked out for himself a comprehensive program of study which included law, practical medicine, agriculture, and mathematics in addition to languages and philosophy. He became increasingly committed to the simple life, and his diary at the time foreshadows his later intense concern with social, religious, and educational reform. The story we print below, translated by Arthur Mendel, was written in 1871 for a children's primer, designed to teach children to read by providing them with "interesting artistic stories rich in meaning, yet without any dull moralizing." It became popular with adults as well, and Tolstoy himself considered it one of his finest works.*

GOD SEES THE TRUTH, BUT WAITS TO TELL

In the town of Vladimir there lived a young merchant named Aksenov. He owned two shops and his own house. A handsome fellow with fair curly hair, he was the life of the party and the first to strike up a song. When he was younger, Aksenov used to drink a lot, and when he had drunk too much would get into brawls; but since his marriage, he had given up drinking except for occasional lapses.

One summer day, Aksenov had to travel to a fair at Nizhni. When he began to say good-by to his family, his wife said to him:

"Ivan Dmitrievich, don't go today. I had a bad dream about you."

Aksenov chuckled and said:

"Are you afraid that I'll go off on a binge at the fair?"

"I don't know myself what I fear, but it was such a strange thing that I dreamed—you had come back from another town and had taken off your hat, and I saw that your hair had gone completely gray."

Aksenov laughed.

"That means there'll be profits! You'll see, I'll have good fortune and bring you rich gifts."

Then he said good-by and left.

When he had gone half the way, he met a merchant friend of his and they stopped for the night. They drank tea together and went to sleep in adjoining rooms. Aksenov did not like to sleep long. He awoke in the middle of the night and, since it was easier to travel while it was still cool, he woke the coachman and told him to harness the horses. Then he went to the soot-covered cabin of the innkeeper, paid his bill, and left.

After he had gone forty versts, he stopped again, fed the horses, and rested on the front porch of the inn. At dinner time, he went out onto the back porch, asked for a samovar, took a guitar and began to play. Suddenly a troika with ringing bells drove up to the inn. An official and two soldiers got out of the carriage. The official went up to Aksenov and asked him who he was and where he was from. Aksenov told him what he wanted to know and asked if he would like to join him for tea. But the official continued to question him: "Where did you sleep last night? Were you alone or with a merchant? Did you see the merchant in the morning? Why did you leave the inn so early?" Aksenov wondered why he was being asked these things. He told him all that had occurred, then added, "But why are you questioning me like this? I'm not some kind of thief or bandit. I am traveling on my own business, and there's nothing for you to question me about."

Then the official called a soldier and said:

"I am the district police officer, and I am asking you these questions because the merchant you stayed with last night has been found with his throat cut. Show me your things. Search him!"

They went into the cabin, took out his suitcase and bag, untied them and began to search. Suddenly, the officer pulled out a knife from the bag and shouted:

"Whose knife is this?"

Aksenov looked. He saw that they had found a knife covered with blood in his bag, and he was frightened.

"And why is there blood on the knife?"

Aksenov wanted to answer, but could not speak.

"I . . . I don't know . . . I . . . knife . . . I, not mine . . ."

Then the officer said:

"In the morning they found a merchant with his throat cut. There is no one besides you who could have done it. The cabin was locked from the inside, and no one except you had been inside. You have in your bag a knife covered with blood, and, in fact, guilt is written all over your face. Now tell us, how did you kill him and how much money did you steal?"

Aksenov swore that he did not do it, that he had not seen the merchant since they had drunk tea together, that the only money he had was his own eight thousand rubles, that the knife was not his. But his voice broke, his face was pale, and he shook with fear as though he were guilty.

The officer called a soldier and told him to bind Aksenov and take him out to a cart. When they bound his feet and lifted him onto the cart, Aksenov crossed himself and began to cry. They took away his bags and money and sent him to jail in a nearby town. Inquiries were made in Vladimir to find out what sort of man Aksenov was. All the merchants and inhabitants of Vladimir noted that when he was younger Aksenov drank and caroused, but that he was a good man.

Then he was brought to trial and charged with the murder of a merchant from Riazan and the theft of twenty thousand rubles.

His wife was grief-stricken and did not know what to think. Her children were young: one was still at the breast. She took them all and went to the town where her husband was imprisoned. At first they refused to let her in, but she implored the prison authorities, and they took her to her husband. When she saw him in prison clothes, chained, and with thieves, she collapsed and for a long time remained unconscious. Then she placed her children about her, sat beside him, and began to tell him about things at home and to ask about all that had happened to him. He told her everything.

"And what now?" she asked.

"We must petition the Tsar. They cannot let an innocent man perish!"

His wife said that she had already sent a petition to the Tsar but that it had not been allowed to reach him.

Aksenov was silent and only grew more despondent.

"It wasn't for nothing that, you remember, I dreamed of your turning gray," his wife said. "Look, you are already beginning to gray from grief. You should not have gone."

She began to run her fingers through his hair and said:

"Vanya, my dearest one, tell your wife the truth; didn't you do it?"

"And you too suspect me?" He covered his face with his hands and wept. A guard came in then and said that his wife and children had to leave. Aksenov said good-by to his family for the last time.

When his wife had left, Aksenov began to think about all that had been said. When he recalled that his wife too had suspected him and that she had asked if he killed the merchant, he said to himself:

"Clearly, only God can know the truth, and one must turn to God alone and from God alone await mercy." From that time on Aksenov ceased sending petitions, ceased hoping, and only prayed to God. He was sentenced to flogging and hard labor. The sentence was carried out. They flogged him with a knout, and when the knout wounds had closed, they herded him along with other convicts to Siberia.

For twenty-six years Aksenov lived in Siberian servitude. The hair of his head turned as white as snow and his beard grew long, thin and gray. All his joyfulness vanished. He grew hunched, moved along quietly, spoke little, never laughed and often prayed to God.

While in prison Aksenov learned to make boots. With the money he earned he bought the *Lives of the Saints* and read it when there was light enough in the prison. On holidays he went to the prison church where he read the Gospels and, since his voice was still good, sang in the choir. The prison officials liked Aksenov for his humility, and his fellow prisoners respected him and called him "Grandpa" and "Godly one." When there were any petitions concerning prison conditions, the other prisoners always sent Aksenov to present them to the officials; and when quarrels arose among them, the prisoners always went to him to judge the case.

No one from Aksenov's home wrote him, and he did not even know if his wife and children were still alive.

One day they brought some new convicts to the prison. In the evening all the old convicts gathered around the new ones and began to ask them what town or village they were from and why they had been exiled. Aksenov also sat down on one of the long, elevated shelf-bunks near the new inmates and dejectedly listened to what they said.

One of the new convicts was a tall, robust old man of about sixty with a clipped, gray beard. He was telling of his arrest.

"So, fellows, I was sent here for no reason at all. I unharnessed a horse from a coachman's sleigh. They grabbed me. 'Thief,' they said. I told them that I had only wanted to get where I was going faster and that I had let the horse go. In fact, the coachman was a friend of mine. 'All right?' I asked. 'No, you stole the horse,' they said. Now, I have stolen things, but they didn't know what or where. I've done things that should have landed me here long ago, although they never caught me. But there's no justice at all in their driving me here this time. Lies! I've been in Siberia before, although I didn't stay long."

"Where are you from?" one of the convicts asked.

"Our family comes from Vladimir, local tradespeople. My name is Makar, Makar Semenovich, in full."

Aksenov raised his head and asked:

"Semenych, have you ever heard anything about the Aksenov merchants in Vladimir? Are they alive?"

"Who hasn't heard of them! Rich merchants, although their father is in Siberia, a sinner like ourselves, no doubt. And you, Grandpa, what are you in for?"

Aksenov did not like to talk about his own misfortune. He sighed and said:

"For my sins I have spent these twenty-six years in hard labor."

"And what sort of sins?" Makar Semenov asked.

"Those worth this punishment," Aksenov said, and he wanted to say no more about it. But the other prisoners told the newcomer why Aksenov had been sent to Siberia. They told him how someone had killed a merchant and had planted a knife on Aksenov and that for this Aksenov had been falsely convicted.

When Makar Semenov heard this and looked at Aksenov, he slapped his knees with his hands and said:

"Well that's something! That's really something! How you've aged Grandpa!"

They asked him why he was so surprised and where he had seen Aksenov, but Makar Semenov did not answer and only said:

"It's a miracle, lads, the way people meet."

At these words Aksenov began to wonder if this man knew something about the murder of the merchant, and he asked:

"Have you heard of this affair before, Semenych, or have you seen me before?"

"Of course I've heard about it! News travels quickly. But it happened long ago, and you forget what you've heard."

"Did you ever hear, perhaps, who killed the merchant?" Aksenov then asked.

Makar Semenov laughed and said:

"The one whose knife they found in your bag probably did it. And if someone did plant a knife on you, well, a man's not a thief until he's caught, you know. But how could anyone have put a knife in your bag? Wasn't it right by your head? You would have heard something."

As soon as Aksenov heard these words he realized that it was this very man who had killed the merchant. He got up and walked off. All that night he could not fall asleep, but lay deeply depressed. He recalled the past. He saw his wife as she had been on that last day when he left for the fair. It was as though she stood there alive before him. He saw her face and her eyes. He heard her voice speak to him and laugh. He saw his children as they were then, little ones, one in a little coat, the other at the breast. And he remembered how he himself had been then—young and gay. He recalled how he had sat on the porch at the inn where they arrested him, how he had played the guitar and how happy he had been. And he remembered the place where they had whipped him, the executioner, the crowd gathered around, the chains, the convicts, the whole twenty-six years of prison life: and he remembered his age. So great a gloom came upon him that he wanted to kill himself.

"And all because of that scoundrel!" Aksenov thought.

He felt such fury toward Makar Semenov that he wanted to revenge himself even though it cost him his own life. He prayed all night, but could not calm down. The next day, he did not go near Makar Semenov and did not look at him.

This went on for two weeks. Aksenov could not sleep nights, and he was so forlorn he did not know where to turn.

One night while he was walking about the prison barracks he noticed handfuls of dirt being thrown from beneath one of the long shelf-bunks shared by the prisoners. He stopped to look. Suddenly, Makar Semenov jumped out from under the bunk and with a frightened expression looked at Aksenov. Aksenov wanted to move on in order not to face him, but Makar grabbed his arm and told him how he had been digging a passage beneath the wall and carrying dirt out in his boot tops and how he had been scattering the dirt in the street when the prisoners were sent off to work.

"Just be quiet about this, old fellow, and I'll take you along. If you talk, they'll whip me. But I won't let you get away—I'll kill you."

Looking at the scoundrel, Aksenov shook with rage. He jerked his arm away and said:

"There's no reason for me to leave here, and there's no need to kill me— you killed me long ago. And whether or not I tell about you depends on how God directs my soul."

The next day as they were leading the convicts off to work, a guard noticed Makar Semenov scattering dirt. They searched the barracks and found the hole. The warden came to the barracks and asked all of them: "Who dug this hole?" They all denied doing it. Those who knew the truth did not betray Makar Semenov because they knew that he would be whipped half to death. Then the warden turned to Aksenov. He knew that Aksenov was an honorable man and said:

"Old man, you are truthful—tell me before God who did this?"

Makar Semenov stood as though nothing had happened, looking at the warden, but not turning to look at Aksenov. Aksenov's lips and hands trembled and for a long time he could not speak. He thought to himself: "Why should I protect him, why should I forgive him when he has ruined my life? Let him pay for my torments. But if I tell, they'll flog him. And what if I have been wrong about him? In any case will things be any easier for me?"

The warden asked him again:

"Well, old man, tell the truth, who dug the hole?"

Aksenov glanced at Makar Semenov and said:

"I cannot tell, your excellency. God has not directed me to do so. I will not tell. It is in your power to do what you want with me."

No matter how hard the warden tried to persuade him, Aksenov said nothing more. So, they did not discover who had dug the hole.

The next night, as Aksenov lay on his bed and had just about fallen asleep, he heard someone come up to him and sit on the bunk at his feet. He looked in the dark and recognized Makar.

"What more do you want of me? What are you doing here?" he asked.

Makar Semenov was silent. Aksenov raised himself and said:

"What do you want? Get out of here or I'll call the guard."

Makar Semenov bent close to Aksenov and in a whisper said:

"Ivan Dmitrich, forgive me!"

"For what shall I forgive you?"

"I killed the merchant and planted the knife on you. I wanted to kill you too, but I heard noises outside. I slipped the knife into your bag and climbed out the window."

Aksenov was silent and did not know what to say. Makar Semenov dropped from the bunk, bowed to the ground and said:

"Ivan Dmitrich, forgive me. For God's sake, forgive me. I'll confess that I killed the merchant. They'll pardon you, and you can go home."

"It's easy for you to talk," Aksenov said, "but how I have suffered! Where can I go now? . . . My wife is dead, my children have forgotten me. There's no place for me."

Makar Semenov did not rise, but beat his head on the ground and said:

"Ivan Dmitrich, forgive! When they whipped me with a knout it was easier for me than it is now to look at you. . . . But you pitied me before when you didn't betray me. Forgive me for Christ's sake! Forgive me, forgive this accursed wretch." And he began to sob.

When Aksenov heard Makar Semenov weeping, he began to cry himself and said:

"God will forgive you. Perhaps I am a hundred times worse than you."

Suddenly, his soul grew calm. He ceased to yearn for his home and he no longer wanted to leave prison, but only thought of his final hour.

In spite of what Aksenov had said, Makar Semenov confessed his guilt. When they issued the order permitting Aksenov to return home, he was already dead.

Civil Disobedience

When the conscience of the individual is in conflict with the law, which should yield? The issue was expressed fatefully for the United States by Thomas Jefferson in the Declaration of Independence. Today again specific laws and mores are being challenged by men who do not challenge the general principle of law and order. Once again the issue has become a focal point of national debate.

Many people say that civil disobedience within a civilized state is by definition immoral. This argument is felt to be especially cogent in a democracy, where law is man-made and adjustable. We voluntarily relinquish some of our freedom and accept the necessity and authority of the law in order to protect the community and guard it against anarchy. Defiance, then, strikes not only at specific laws but also at the concept of law and order and thus at the system itself. This is the position which Plato presents so forcefully in *The Crito*, part of which is printed below. The counter-argument is presented by Thoreau, one of the most dedicated individualists in our history, who argues for the supreme sovereignty of the individual conscience. Bertrand Russell and Martin Luther King, using both rational argument and passionate appeal, present the case for non-violent civil disobedience today. In weighing their arguments, the reader may also wish to consider two related ideas. One is that such acts as the illegal sit-in may be likened to the strike and picketing of a few generations ago; they are forms of social protest which are attempting to qualify for public acceptance and legality. The other, a paradox pointed out by George Orwell in his essay on Gandhi, is that modern civil disobedience can only be effective in a democratic community. "It is difficult to see," says Orwell, "how Gandhi's methods [passive resistance] could be applied in a country where opponents of the regime disappear in the middle of the night and are never heard of again. Without a free press and the right of assembly, it is impossible not merely to appeal to outside opinion, but to bring a mass movement into being, or even to make your intentions known to your adversary."

PLATO

Plato, one of the greatest philosophers of the western world, was born in Athens. Originally named Aristocles, he was surnamed Plato because of his broad shoulders or—as some would have it—his broad forehead. Early in his life he became a student of Socrates, and his subsequent writings are evidence of the profound influence his teacher had on him. After Socrates' trial, conviction, and death in 399 B.C., Plato spent thirteen years away from Athens, in Italy, Egypt, and parts of Greece. He returned in 386 B.C. and founded the Academy in which he taught until his death in 347 B.C. Aristotle was his student. Plato's extant works are in the form of conversations, or dialogues, in which the leading speaker is usually Socrates. Perhaps the best known of the dialogues is The Republic, *in which Socrates explores the nature of the ideal state. Plato records the last days of Socrates in three early dialogues,* The Apology, The Crito, *and* The Phaedo. The Apology *presents Socrates' speech at his trial on charges of corrupting youth and believing in Gods other than the State's divinities.* The Phaedo *records Socrates' last conversation before death. In* The Crito, *Crito visits Socrates in prison and tries to persuade him to escape. We print below, from the Jowett translation, third edition, Socrates' argument for submitting to the death penalty that the law had imposed on him.*

FROM THE CRITO

Socrates . . . Ought a man to do what he admits to be right, or ought he to betray the right?

Crito. He ought to do what he thinks right.

Soc. But if this is true, what is the application? In leaving the prison against the will of the Athenians, do I wrong any? or rather do I not wrong those whom I ought least to wrong? Do I not desert the principles which were acknowledged by us to be just—what do you say?

Cr. I cannot tell, Socrates; for I do not know.

Soc. Then consider the matter in this way:—Imagine that I am about to play truant (you may call the proceeding by any name which you like), and the laws and the government come and interrogate me: 'Tell us, Socrates,' they say; 'what are you about? are you not going by an act of yours to overturn us—the laws, and the whole state, as far as in you lies? Do you imagine that a state can subsist and not be overthrown, in which the decisions of law have no power, but are set aside and trampled upon by individuals?' What will be our answer, Crito, to these and the like words? Any one, and especially a rhetorician, will have a good deal to say on behalf of the law which requires a sentence to be carried out. He will argue that this law should not be set aside; and shall we reply, 'Yes; but the state has injured us and given an unjust sentence.' Suppose I say that?

Cr. Very good, Socrates.

Soc. 'And was that our agreement with you?' the law would answer; 'or were you to abide by the sentence of the state?' And if I were to express my astonishment at their words, the law would probably add: 'Answer, Socrates, instead of opening your eyes—you are in the habit of asking and answering questions. Tell us,—What complaint have you to make against us which justifies you in attempting to destroy us and the state? In the first place did we not bring you into existence? Your father married your mother by our aid and begat you. Say whether you have any objection to urge against those of us who regulate marriage?' None, I should reply. 'Or against those of us who after birth regulate the nurture and education of children, in which you also were trained? Were not the laws, which have the charge of education, right in commanding your father to train you in music and gymnastic?' Right, I should reply. 'Well then, since you were brought into the world and nurtured and educated by us, can you deny in the first place that you are our child and slave, as your fathers were before you? And if this is true you are not on equal terms with us; nor can you think that you have a right to do to us what we are doing to you. Would you have any right to strike or revile or do any other evil to your father or your master, if you had one, because you have been struck or reviled by him, or received some other evil at his hands?—you would not say this? And because we think right to destroy you, do you think that you have any right to destroy us in return, and your country as far as in you lies? Will you, O professor of true virtue, pretend that you are justified in this? Has a philosopher like you failed to discover that our country is more to be valued and higher and holier far than mother or father or any ancestor, and more to be regarded in the eyes of the gods and of men of understanding? also to be soothed, and gently and reverently entreated when angry, even more than a father, and either to be persuaded, or if not persuaded, to be obeyed? And when we are punished by her, whether with imprisonment or stripes, the punishment is to be endured in silence; and if she leads us to wounds or death in battle, thither we follow as is right; neither may any one yield or retreat or leave his rank, but whether in battle or in a court of law, or in any other place, he must do what his city and his country order him; or he must change their view of what is just: and if he may do no violence to his father or mother, much less may he do violence to his country.' What answer shall we make to this, Crito? Do the laws speak truly, or do they not?

Cr. I think that they do.

Soc. Then the laws will say, 'Consider, Socrates, if we are speaking truly that in your present attempt you are going to do us an injury. For, having brought you into the world, and nurtured and educated you, and given you and every other citizen a share in every good which we had to give, we further proclaim to any Athenian by the liberty which we allow him, that if he does not like us when he has become of age and has seen the ways of the city, and made our acquaintance, he may go where he pleases and take his goods with him. None of us laws will forbid him or interfere with him. Any one who does not like us and the city, and who wants to emigrate to a colony or to any other city, may go where he likes, retaining his property. But he who has experience of the manner in which we order justice and administer the state, and still remains, has entered into an implied contract that he will do as we command him. And he who disobeys us is, as we maintain, thrice wrong; first, because in disobeying us he is disobeying his parents; secondly, because we are the authors of his education; thirdly, because he has made an agreement with us that he will duly obey our commands; and he neither obeys them nor convinces us that our commands are unjust; and we do not rudely impose them, but give him the alternative of obeying or convincing us;—that is what we offer, and he does neither.

'These are the sort of accusations to which, as we were saying, you, Socrates, will be exposed if you accomplish your intentions; you, above all other Athenians.' Suppose now I ask, why I rather than anybody else? they will justly retort upon me that I above all other men have acknowledged the agreement. 'There is clear proof,' they will say, 'Socrates, that we and the city were not displeasing to you. Of all Athenians you have been the most constant resident in the city, which, as you never leave, you may be supposed to love. For you never went out of the city either to see the games, except once when you went to the Isthmus, or to any other place unless when you were on military service; nor did you travel as other men do. Nor had you any curiosity to know other states or their laws: your affections did not go beyond us and our state; we were your special favourites, and you acquiesced in our government of you; and here in this city you begat your children, which is a proof of your satisfaction. Moreover, you might in the course of the trial, if you had liked, have fixed the penalty at banishment; the state which refuses to let you go now would have let you go then. But you pretended that you preferred death to exile, and that you were not unwilling to die. And now you have forgotten these fine sentiments, and pay no respect to us the laws, of whom you are the destroyer; and are doing what only a miserable slave would do, running away and turning your back upon the compacts and agreements which you made as a citizen. And first of all answer this very question: Are we right in saying that you agreed to be governed according to us in deed, and not in word only? Is that true or not?' How shall we answer, Crito? Must we not assent?

Cr. We cannot help it, Socrates.

Soc. Then will they not say: 'You, Socrates, are breaking the covenants and agreements which you made with us at your leisure, not in any haste or under any compulsion or deception, but after you have had seventy years to think of them, during which time you were at liberty to leave the city, if we were not to your mind, or if our covenants appeared to you to be unfair. You had your choice, and might have gone either to Lacedaemon or Crete, both which states are often praised by you for their good government, or to some other Hellenic or foreign state. Whereas you, above all other Athenians, seemed to be so fond of the state, or, in other words, of us her laws (and who would care about a state which has no laws?), that you never stirred out of her; the halt, the blind, the maimed were not more stationary in her than you were. And now you run away and forsake your agreements. Not so, Socrates, if you will take our advice; do not make yourself ridiculous by escaping out of the city.

'For just consider, if you transgress and err in this sort of way, what good will you do either to yourself or to your friends? That your friends will be driven into exile and deprived of citizenship, or will lose their property, is tolerably certain; and you yourself, if you fly to one of the neighbouring cities, as, for example, Thebes or Megara, both of which are well governed, will come to them as an enemy, Socrates, and their government will be against you, and all patriotic citizens will cast an evil eye upon you as a subverter of the laws, and you will confirm in the minds of the judges the justice of their own condemnation of you. For he who is a corrupter of the laws is more than likely to be a corrupter of the young and foolish portion of mankind. Will you then flee from well-ordered cities and virtuous men? and is existence worth having on these terms? Or will you go to them without shame, and

talk to them, Socrates? And what will you say to them? What you say
here about virtue and justice and institutions and laws being the best
things among men? Would that be decent of you? Surely not. But if
you go away from well-governed states to Crito's friends in Thessaly,
where there is great disorder and licence, they will be charmed to hear
the tale of your escape from prison, set off with ludicrous particulars
of the manner in which you were wrapped in a goatskin or some other
disguise, and metamorphosed as the manner is of runaways; but will there
be no one to remind you that in your old age you were not ashamed
to violate the most sacred laws from a miserable desire of a little more
life? Perhaps not, if you keep them in a good temper; but if they are
out of temper you will hear many degrading things; you will live, but
how?—as the flatterer of all men, and the servant of all men; and doing
what?—eating and drinking in Thessaly, having gone abroad in order
that you may get a dinner. And where will be your fine sentiments
about justice and virtue? Say that you wish to live for the sake of your
children—you want to bring them up and educate them—will you take
them into Thessaly and deprive them of Athenian citizenship? Is this
the benefit which you will confer upon them? Or are you under the
impression that they will be better cared for and educated here if you
are still alive, although absent from them; for your friends will take care
of them? Do you fancy that if you are an inhabitant of Thessaly they
will take care of them, and if you are an inhabitant of the other world
that they will not take care of them? Nay; but if they who call themselves friends are good for anything, they will—to be sure they will.

'Listen, then, Socrates, to us who have brought you up. Think not
of life and children first, and of justice afterwards, but of justice first,
that you may be justified before the princes of the world below. For
neither will you nor any that belong to you be happier or holier or
juster in this life, or happier in another, if you do as Crito bids. Now
you depart in innocence, a sufferer and not a doer of evil; a victim, not
of the laws but of men. But if you go forth, returning evil for evil, and
injury for injury, breaking the covenants and agreements which you
have made with us, and wronging those whom you ought least of all to
wrong, that is to say, yourself, your friends, your country, and us, we
shall be angry with you while you live, and our brethren, the laws in
the world below, will receive you as an enemy; for they will know that
you have done your best to destroy us. Listen, then, to us and not to
Crito.'

This, dear Crito, is the voice which I seem to hear murmuring in my
ears, like the sound of the flute in the ears of the mystic; that voice, I say,
is humming in my ears, and prevents me from hearing any other. And
I know that anything more which you may say will be vain. Yet speak,
if you have anything to say.

Cr. I have nothing to say, Socrates.

Soc. Leave me then, Crito, to fulfil the will of God, and to follow whither he leads.

THOMAS JEFFERSON

On June 11, 1776, the Continental Congress appointed a committee of five—Thomas Jefferson, Benjamin Franklin, John Adams, Robert Livingston, and Roger Sherman—to prepare a declaration of independence. It was decided that Jefferson should first write a draft. He did so, drawing heavily on the natural rights political philosophy of the time, but, as he says, he turned to "neither book nor pamphlet" in its preparation. A few changes were made by Adams and Franklin, and it was then presented to Congress on June 28. On July 2 and 3 Congress debated the form and content of the Declaration, made a few further changes, and on July 4 approved it without dissent. We here credit Jefferson with authorship, although we print the amended and official version taken from the United States Senate Manual.

DECLARATION OF
INDEPENDENCE

(In Congress July 4, 1776)

The Unanimous Declaration of the Thirteen
United States of America

When in the Course of human events, it becomes necessary for one people to dissolve the political bands which have connected them with another, and to assume among the powers of the earth, the separate and equal station to which the Laws of Nature and of Nature's God entitle them, a decent respect to the opinions of mankind requires that they should declare the causes which impel them to the separation.

We hold these truths to be self-evident, that all men are created equal, that they are endowed by their Creator with certain unalienable Rights, that among these are Life, Liberty and the pursuit of Happiness. That to secure these rights, Governments are instituted among Men, deriving their just powers from the consent of the governed, That whenever any Form of Government becomes destructive of these ends, it is the Right of the People to alter or to abolish it, and to institute new Government, laying its foundation on such principles and organizing its powers in such form, as to them shall seem most likely to effect their Safety and Happiness. Prudence, indeed, will dictate that Governments long established should not be changed for light and transient causes; and accordingly all experience hath shewn that mankind are more disposed to suffer, while evils are sufferable, than to right themselves by abolishing the forms to which they are accustomed. But when a long train of abuses and usurpations, pursuing invariably the same Object evinces a design to reduce them under absolute Despotism, it is their right, it is their duty, to throw off such Government, and to provide new Guards for their future security. Such has been the patient sufferance of these Colonies; and such is now the necessity which constrains them to alter their former Systems of Government. The history of the present King of Great Britain is a history of repeated injuries and usurpations, all having in direct object the establishment of an absolute Tyranny over these States. To prove this, let Facts be submitted to a candid world.

He has refused his Assent to Laws, the most wholesome and necessary for the public good.

He has forbidden his Governors to pass Laws of immediate and pressing importance, unless suspended in their operation till his Assent should be obtained; and when so suspended, he has utterly neglected to attend to them.

He has refused to pass other Laws for the accommodation of large districts of people, unless those people would relinquish the right of Representation in the Legislature, a right inestimable to them and formidable to tyrants only.

He has called together legislative bodies at places unusual, uncomfortable, and distant from the depository of their public Records, for the sole purpose of fatiguing them into compliance with his measures.

He has dissolved Representative Houses repeatedly, for opposing with manly firmness his invasions on the rights of the people.

He has refused for a long time, after such dissolutions, to cause others to be elected; whereby the Legislative powers, incapable of Annihilation, have returned to the People at large for their exercise; the State remaining in the mean time exposed to all the dangers of invasion from without, and convulsions within.

He has endeavoured to prevent the population of these States; for that purpose obstructing the Laws for Naturalization of Foreigners; refusing to pass others to encourage their migrations hither, and raising the conditions of new Appropriations of Lands.

He has obstructed the Administration of Justice, by refusing his Assent to Laws for establishing Judiciary powers.

He has made Judges dependent on his Will alone, for the tenure of their offices, and the amount and payment of their salaries.

He has erected a multitude of New Offices, and sent hither swarms of Officers to harass our people, and eat out their substance.

He has kept among us, in times of peace, Standing Armies without the Consent of our legislatures.

He has affected to render the Military independent of and superior to the Civil power.

He has combined with others to subject us to a jurisdiction foreign to our constitution, and unacknowledged by our laws; giving his Assent to their Acts of pretended Legislation:

For quartering large bodies of armed troops among us:

For protecting them, by a mock Trial, from punishment for any Murders which they should commit on the Inhabitants of these States:

For cutting off our Trade with all parts of the world:

For imposing Taxes on us without our Consent:

For depriving us in many cases, of the benefits of Trial by Jury:

For transporting us beyond Seas to be tried for pretended offences:

For abolishing the free System of English Laws in a neighbouring Province, establishing therein an Arbitrary government, and enlarging its Boundaries so as to render it at once an example and fit instrument for introducing the same absolute rule into these Colonies:

For taking away our Charters, abolishing our most valuable Laws, and altering fundamentally the Forms of our Governments:

For suspending our own Legislatures, and declaring themselves invested with power to legislate for us in all cases whatsoever.

He has abdicated Government here, by declaring us out of his Protection and waging War against us.

He has plundered our seas, ravaged our Coasts, burnt our towns, and destroyed the lives of our people.

He is at this time transporting large Armies of foreign Mercenaries to compleat the works of death, desolation and tyranny, already begun with circumstances of Cruelty & perfidy scarcely paralleled in the most barbarous ages, and totally unworthy the Head of a civilized nation.

He has constrained our fellow Citizens taken Captive on the high Seas to bear Arms against their Country, to become the executioners of their friends and Brethren, or to fall themselves by their Hands.

He has excited domestic insurrections amongst us, and has endeavoured to bring on the inhabitants of our frontiers, the merciless Indian Savages, whose known rule of warfare is an undistinguished destruction of all ages, sexes and conditions.

In every stage of these Oppressions We have Petitioned for Redress in the most humble terms: Our repeated Petitions have been answered only by repeated injury. A Prince, whose character is thus marked by every act which may define a Tyrant, is unfit to be the ruler of a free people.

Nor have We been wanting in attentions to our British brethren. We have warned them from time to time of attempts by their legislature to extend an unwarrantable jurisdiction over us. We have reminded them of the circumstances of our emigration and settlement here. We have appealed to their native justice and magnanimity, and we have conjured them by the ties of our common kindred to disavow these usurpations, which would inevitably interrupt our connections and correspondence. They too have been deaf to the voice of justice and of consanguinity. We must, therefore, acquiesce in the necessity, which denounces our Separation, and hold them, as we hold the rest of mankind. Enemies in War, in Peace Friends.

WE, THEREFORE, the REPRESENTATIVES OF THE UNITED STATES OF AMERICA, IN GENERAL CONGRESS, Assembled, appealing to the Supreme Judge of the world for the rectitude of our intentions, do, in the Name, and by authority of the good People of these Colonies, solemnly PUBLISH and DECLARE, That these United Colonies are, and of Right ought to be FREE AND INDEPENDENT STATES; that they are Absolved from all Allegiance to the British Crown, and that all political connection between them and the State of Great Britain, is and ought to be totally dissolved; and that as FREE AND INDEPENDENT STATES, they have full Power to levy War, conclude Peace, contract Alliances, establish Commerce, and to do all other Acts and Things which INDEPENDENT STATES may of right do. And for the support of this Declaration, with a firm reliance on the protection of divine Providence, we mutually pledge to each other our Lives, our Fortunes and our sacred Honor.

HENRY DAVID THOREAU

A social rebel with high principles, a man who loved nature and solitude, Thoreau is considered by some a memorable individualist, by others a perennial adolescent, and by still others as both. E. B. White has called him a "regular hairshirt of a man." Born in Concord, Mass., in 1817, he was educated at Harvard and after graduation returned to Concord where he first taught school and on later occasions supported himself by making pencils. He became a friend of Emerson, who was at the time leader of Concord's intellectual and spiritual life; he joined the Transcendental Club and contributed frequently to its journal, The Dial. *Some have said that Thoreau was the answer to Emerson's plea for an American Scholar (see page 31). From July 4, 1845, to September 6, 1847, Thoreau lived in a hut at nearby Walden Pond, an experience which he recorded in his most famous work,* Walden. *His stay there was interrupted for one day in the summer of 1845 when he was arrested for not paying the Massachusetts poll tax. He explained his refusal as an act of protest against a government which sanctioned the Mexican War, a war he considered in the interests of Southern slave holders; he later wrote an eloquent defense of civil disobedience which was first published in 1849. This essay, which has become an American classic, is reprinted in full below; the text is that of the Riverside edition of Thoreau's works.*

CIVIL DISOBEDIENCE

I heartily accept the motto,—"That government is best which governs least;" and I should like to see it acted up to more rapidly and systematically. Carried out, it finally amounts to this, which also I believe,—"That government is best which governs not at all;" and when men are prepared for it, that will be the kind of government which they will have. Government is at best but an expedient; but most governments are usually, and all governments are sometimes, inexpedient. The objections which have been brought against a standing army, and they are many and weighty, and deserve to prevail, may also at last be brought against a standing government. The standing army is only an arm of the standing government. The government itself, which is only the mode which the people have chosen to execute their will, is equally liable to be abused and perverted before the people can act through it. Witness the present Mexican war, the work of comparatively a few individuals using the standing government as their tool; for, in the outset, the people would not have consented to this measure.

This American government,—what is it but a tradition, though a recent one, endeavoring to transmit itself unimpaired to posterity, but each instant losing some of its integrity? It has not the vitality and force of a single living man; for a single man can bend it to his will. It is a sort of wooden gun to the people themselves. But it is not the less necessary for this; for the people must have some complicated machinery or other, and hear its din, to satisfy that idea of government which they have. Governments show thus how successfully men can be imposed on, even impose on themselves, for their own advantage. It is excellent, we must all allow. Yet this government never of itself furthered any enterprise, but by the alacrity with which it got out of its way. *It* does not keep the country free. *It* does not settle the West. *It* does not educate. The character inherent in the American people has done all that has been accomplished; and it would have done somewhat more, if the government had not sometimes got in its way. For government is an expedient by which men would fain succeed in letting one another alone; and, as has been said, when it is most expedient, the governed are most let alone by it. Trade and commerce, if they were not made of India-rubber, would never manage to bounce over the obstacles which legislators are continually putting in their way; and, if one were to judge these men wholly by the effects of their actions and not partly by their intentions, they would deserve to be classed and punished with those mischievous persons who put obstructions on the railroads.

But, to speak practically and as a citizen, unlike those who call themselves no-government men, I ask for, not at once no government, but *at once* a better government. Let every man make known what kind of government would command his respect, and that will be one step toward obtaining it.

After all, the practical reason why, when the power is once in the hands of the people, a majority are permitted, and for a long period continue, to rule is not because they are most likely to be in the right, nor because this seems fairest to the minority, but because they are physically the strongest. But a government in which the majority rule in all cases cannot be based on justice, even as far as men understand it. Can there not be a government in which majorities do not virtually decide right and wrong, but conscience?—in which majorities decide only those questions to which the rule of expediency is applicable? Must the citizen ever for a moment, or in the least degree, resign his conscience to the legislator? Why has every man a conscience, then? I think that we should be men first, and subjects afterward. It is not desirable to cultivate a respect for the law, so much as for the right. The only obligation which I have a right to assume is to do at any time what I think right. It is truly enough said, that a corporation has no conscience; but a corporation of conscientious men is a corporation *with* a conscience. Law never made men a whit more just; and, by means of their respect for it, even the well-disposed are daily made the agents of injustice. A common and natural result of an undue respect for law is, that you may see a file of soldiers, colonel, captain, corporal, privates, powder-monkeys, and all, marching in admirable order over hill and dale to the wars, against their wills, ay, against their common sense and consciences, which makes it very steep marching indeed, and produces a palpitation of the heart. They have no doubt that it is a damnable business in which they are concerned; they are all peaceably inclined. Now, what are they? Men at all? or small movable forts and magazines, at the service of some unscrupulous man in power? Visit the Navy-Yard, and behold a marine, such a man as an American government can make, or such as it can make a man with its black arts,—a mere shadow and reminiscence of humanity, a man laid out alive and standing, and already, as one may say, buried under arms with funeral accompaniments, though it may be,—

> "Not a drum was heard, not a funeral note,
>   As his corse to the rampart we hurried;
> Not a soldier discharged his farewell shot
>   O'er the grave where our hero we buried."

The mass of men serve the state thus, not as men mainly, but as machines, with their bodies. They are the standing army, and the militia, jailers, constables, posse comitatus, etc. In most cases there is no free exercise whatever of the judgment or of the moral sense; but they put themselves on a level with wood and earth and stones; and wooden men can perhaps be manufactured that will serve the purpose as well. Such command no more respect than men of straw or a lump of dirt. They have the same sort of worth only as horses and dogs. Yet such as these even are commonly esteemed good citizens. Others—as most legislators, politicians, lawyers, ministers, and office-holders—serve the state chiefly with their heads; and, as they rarely make any moral distinctions, they are as likely to serve the Devil, without *intending* it, as God. A very few, as heroes, patriots, martyrs, reformers in the great sense, and *men*, serve the state with their consciences also, and so necessarily resist it for the most part; and they are commonly treated as enemies by it. A wise man will only be useful as a man, and will not submit to be "clay," and "stop a hole to keep the wind away," but leave that office to his dust at least:—

> "I am too high-born to be propertied,
>   To be a secondary at control,
>   Or useful serving-man and instrument
>   To any sovereign state throughout the world."

He who gives himself entirely to his fellow-men appears to them useless and selfish; but he who gives himself partially to them is pronounced a benefactor and philanthropist.

How does it become a man to behave toward this American government to-day? I answer, that he cannot without disgrace be associated with it. I cannot for an instant recognize that political organization as *my* government which is the *slave's* government also.

All men recognize the right of revolution; that is, the right to refuse allegiance to, and to resist, the government, when its tyranny or its inefficiency are great and unendurable. But almost all say that such is not the case now. But such was the case, they think, in the Revolution of '75. If one were to tell me that this was a bad government because it taxed certain foreign commodities brought to its ports, it is most probable that I should not make an ado about it, for I can do without them. All machines have their friction; and possibly this does enough good to counterbalance the evil. At any rate, it is a great evil to make a stir about it. But when the friction comes to have its machine, and oppression and robbery are organized, I say, let us not have such a machine any longer. In other words, when a sixth of the population of a nation which has undertaken to be the refuge of liberty are slaves, and a whole country is unjustly overrun and conquered by a foreign army, and subjected to military law, I think that it is not too soon for honest men to rebel and revolutionize. What makes this duty the more urgent is the fact that the country so overrun is not our own, but ours is the invading army.

Paley, a common authority with many on moral questions, in his chapter on the "Duty of Submission to Civil Government," resolves all civil obligation into expediency; and he proceeds to say, "that so long as the interest of the whole society requires it, that is, so long as the established government cannot be resisted or changed without public inconveniency, it is the will of God that the established government be obeyed, and no longer. . . . This principle being admitted, the justice of every particular case of resistance is reduced to a computation of the quantity of the danger and grievance on the one side, and of the probability and expense of redressing it on the other." Of this, he says, every man shall judge for himself. But Paley appears never to have contemplated those cases to which the rule of expediency does not apply, in which a people, as well as an individual, must do justice, cost what it may. If I have unjustly wrested a plank from a drowning man, I must restore it to him though I drown myself. This, according to Paley, would be inconvenient. But he that would save his life, in such a case, shall lose it. This people must cease to hold slaves, and to make war on Mexico, though it cost them their existence as a people.

In their practice, nations agree with Paley; but does any one think that Massachusetts does exactly what is right at the present crisis?

"A drab of state, a cloth-o'-silver slut,
  To have her train borne up, and her soul trail in the dirt."

Practically speaking, the opponents to a reform in Massachusetts are not a hundred thousand politicians at the South, but a hundred thousand merchants and farmers here, who are more interested in commerce and agriculture than they are in humanity, and are not prepared to do justice to the slave and to Mexico, *cost what it may*. I quarrel not with far-off foes, but with those who, near at home, coöperate with, and do the bidding of, those far away, and without whom the latter would be harmless. We are accustomed to say, that the mass of men are unprepared; but improvement is slow, because the few are not materially wiser or better than the many. It is not so important that many should be as good as you, as that there be some absolute goodness somewhere; for that will leaven the whole lump. There are thousands who are *in opinion* opposed to slavery and to the war, who yet in effect do nothing to put an end to them; who, esteeming themselves children of Washington and Franklin, sit down with their hands in their pockets, and say that they know not what to do, and do nothing; who even postpone the question of freedom to the question of free-trade, and quietly read the prices-current along with the latest advices from Mexico, after dinner, and, it may be, fall asleep over them both. What is the price-current of an honest man and patriot to-day? They hesitate, and they regret, and sometimes they petition; but they do nothing in earnest and with effect. They will wait, well disposed, for others to remedy the evil, that they may no longer have it to regret. At most, they give only a cheap vote, and a feeble countenance and Godspeed, to the right, as it goes by them. There are nine hundred and ninety-nine patrons of virtue to one virtuous man. But it is easier to deal with the real possessor of a thing than with the temporary guardian of it.

All voting is a sort of gaming, like checkers or backgammon, with a slight moral tinge to it, a playing with right and wrong, with moral questions; and betting naturally accompanies it. The character of the voters is not staked. I cast my vote, perchance, as I think right; but I am not vitally concerned that that right should prevail. I am willing to leave it to the majority. Its obligation, therefore, never exceeds that of expediency. Even voting *for the right* is *doing* nothing for it. It is only expressing to men feebly your desire that it should prevail. A wise man will not leave the right to the mercy of chance, nor wish it to prevail through the power of the majority. There is but little virtue in the action of masses of men. When the majority shall at length vote for the abolition of slavery, it will be because they are indifferent to slavery, or because there is but little slavery left to be abolished by their vote. *They* will then be the only slaves. Only *his* vote can hasten the abolition of slavery who asserts his own freedom by his vote.

I hear of a convention to be held at Baltimore, or elsewhere, for the selection of a candidate for the Presidency, made up chiefly of editors, and men who are politicians by profession; but I think, what is it to any independent, intelligent, and respectable man what decision they may come to? Shall we not have the advantage of his wisdom and honesty, nevertheless? Can we not count upon some independent votes? Are there not many individuals in the country who do not attend conventions? But no: I find that the respectable man, so called, has immediately drifted from his position, and despairs of his country, when his country has more reason to despair of him. He forthwith adopts one of the candidates thus selected as the only *available* one, thus proving that he is himself *available* for any purposes of the demagogue. His vote is of no more worth than that of any unprincipled foreigner or hireling native, who may have been bought. O for a man who is a *man*, and, as my neighbor says, has a bone in his back which you cannot pass your hand through! Our statistics are at fault: the population has been returned too large. How many *men* are there to a square thousand miles in this country? Hardly one. Does not America offer any inducement for men to settle here? The American has dwindled into an Odd Fellow,—one who may be known by the development of his organ of gregariousness, and a manifest lack of intellect and cheerful self-reliance; whose first and chief concern, on coming into the world, is to see that the Almshouses are in good repair; and, before yet he has lawfully donned the virile garb, to collect a fund for the support of the widows and orphans that may be; who, in short, ventures to live only by the aid of the Mutual Insurance company, which has promised to bury him decently.

It is not a man's duty, as a matter of course, to devote himself to the eradication of any, even the most enormous wrong; he may still properly have other concerns to engage him; but it his duty, at least, to wash his hands of it, and, if he gives it no thought longer, not to give it practically his support. If I devote myself to other pursuits and contemplations, I must first see, at least, that I do not pursue them sitting upon another man's shoulders. I must get off him first, that he may pursue his contemplations too. See what gross inconsistency is tolerated. I have heard some of my townsmen say, "I should like to have them order me out to help put down an insurrection of the slaves, or to march to Mexico;— see if I would go;" and yet these very men have each, directly by their allegiance, and so indirectly, at least, by their money, furnished a substitute. The soldier is applauded who refuses to serve in an unjust war by those who do not refuse to sustain the unjust government which makes the war; is applauded by those whose own act and authority he disregards and sets at naught; as if the state were penitent to that degree that it hired one to scourge it while it sinned, but not to that degree that it left off sinning for a moment. Thus, under the name of Order and Civil Government, we are all made at last to pay homage to and support our own meanness. After the first blush of sin comes its indifference; and from immoral it becomes, as it were, *un*moral, and not quite unnecessary to that life which we have made.

The broadest and most prevalent error requires the most disinterested virtue to sustain it. The slight reproach to which the virtue of patriotism is commonly liable, the noble are most likely to incur. Those who, while they disapprove of the character and measures of a government, yield to it their allegiance and support are undoubtedly its most conscientious supporters, and so frequently the most serious obstacles to reform. Some are petitioning the state to dissolve the Union, to disregard the requisitions of the President. Why do they not dissolve it themselves,—the union between themselves and the state,—and refuse to pay their quota into its treasury? Do not they stand in the same relation to the state that the state does to the Union? And have not the same reasons prevented the state from resisting the Union which have prevented them from resisting the state?

How can a man be satisfied to entertain an opinion merely, and enjoy *it?* Is there any enjoyment in it, if his opinion is that he is aggrieved? If you are cheated out of a single dollar by your neighbor, you do not rest satisfied with knowing that you are cheated, or with saying that you are cheated, or even with petitioning him to pay you your due; but you take effectual steps at once to obtain the full amount, and see that you are never cheated again. Action from principle, the perception and the performance of right, changes things and relations; it is essentially revolutionary, and does not consist wholly with anything which was. It not only divides states and churches, it divides families; ay, it divides the *individual,* separating the diabolical in him from the divine.

Unjust laws exist: shall we be content to obey them, or shall we endeavor to amend them, and obey them until we have succeeded, or shall we transgress them at once? Men generally, under such a government as this, think that they ought to wait until they have persuaded the majority to alter them. They think that, if they should resist, the remedy would be worse than the evil. But it is the fault of the government itself that the remedy *is* worse than the evil. *It* makes it worse. Why is it not more apt to anticipate and provide for reform? Why does it not cherish its wise minority? Why does it cry and resist before it is hurt? Why does it not encourage its citizens to be on the alert to point out its faults, and *do* better than it would have them? Why does it always crucify Christ, and excommunicate Copernicus and Luther, and pronounce Washington and Franklin rebels?

One would think, that a deliberate and practical denial of its authority was the only offense never contemplated by government; else, why has it not assigned its definite, its suitable and proportionate penalty? If a man who has no property refuses but once to earn nine shillings for the state, he is put in prison for a period unlimited by any law that I know, and determined only by the discretion of those who placed him there; but if he should steal ninety times nine shillings from the state, he is soon permitted to go at large again.

If the injustice is part of the necessary friction of the machine of government, let it go, let it go: perchance it will wear smooth,—certainly the machine will wear out. If the injustice has a spring, or a pulley, or a rope, or a crank, exclusively for itself, then perhaps you may consider whether the remedy will not be worse than the evil; but if it is of such a nature that it requires you to be the agent of injustice to another, then, I say, break the law. Let your life be a counter friction to stop the machine. What I have to do is to see, at any rate, that I do not lend myself to the wrong which I condemn.

As for adopting the ways which the state has provided for remedying the evil, I know not of such ways. They take too much time, and a man's life will be gone. I have other affairs to attend to. I came into this world, not chiefly to make this a good place to live in, but to live in it, be it good or bad. A man has not everything to do, but something; and because he cannot do *everything*, it is not necessary that he should do *something* wrong. It is not my business to be petitioning the Governor or the Legislature any more than it is theirs to petition me; and if they should not hear my petition, what should I do then? But in this case the state has provided no way: its very Constitution is the evil. This may seem to be harsh and stubborn and unconciliatory; but it is to treat with the utmost kindness and consideration the only spirit that can appreciate or deserves it. So is all change for the better, like birth and death, which convulse the body.

I do not hesitate to say, that those who call themselves Abolitionists should at once effectually withdraw their support, both in person and property, from the government of Massachusetts, and not wait till they constitute a majority of one, before they suffer the right to prevail through them. I think that it is enough if they have God on their side, without waiting for that other one. Moreover, any man more right than his neighbors constitutes a majority of one already.

I meet this American government, or its representative, the state government, directly, and face to face, once a year—no more—in the person of its tax-gatherer; this is the only mode in which a man situated as I am necessarily meets it; and it then says distinctly, Recognize me; and the simplest, the most effectual, and, in the present posture of affairs, the indispensablest mode of treating with it on this head, of expressing your little satisfaction with and love for it, is to deny it then. My civil neighbor, the tax-gatherer, is the very man I have to deal with,—for it is, after all, with men and not with parchment that I quarrel,—and he has voluntarily chosen to be an agent of the government. How shall he ever know well what he is and does as an officer of the government, or as a man, until he is obliged to consider whether he shall treat me, his neighbor, for whom he has respect, as a neighbor and well-disposed man, or as a maniac and disturber of the peace, and see if he can get over this obstruction to his neighborliness without a ruder and more impetuous thought or speech corresponding with his action. I know this well, that if one thousand, if one hundred, if ten men whom I could name,—if ten *honest* men only,—ay, if *one* HONEST man, in this State of Massachusetts, *ceasing to hold slaves*, were actually to withdraw from this copartnership, and be locked up in the county jail therefor, it would be the abolition of slavery in America. For it matters not how small the beginning may seem to be: what is once well done is done forever. But we love better to talk about it: that we say is our mission. Reform keeps many scores of newspapers in its service, but not one man. If my esteemed neighbor, the State's ambassador, who will devote his days to the settlement of the question of human rights in the Council Chamber, instead of being threatened with the prisons of Carolina, were to sit down the prisoner of Massachusetts, that State which is so anxious to foist the sin of slavery upon her sister,—though at present she can discover only an act of inhospitality to be the ground of a quarrel with her,—the Legislature would not wholly waive the subject the following winter.

Under a government which imprisons any unjustly, the true place for a just man is also a prison. The proper place to-day, the only place which Massachusetts has provided for her freer and less desponding spirits, is in her prisons, to be put out and locked out of the State by her own act, as they have already put themselves out by their principles. It is there that the fugitive slave, and the Mexican prisoner on parole, and the Indian come to plead the wrongs of his race should find them; on that separate, but more free and honorable ground, where the State places those who are not *with* her, but *against* her,—the only house in a slave State in which a free man can abide with honor. If any think that their influence would be lost there, and their voices no longer afflict the ear of the State, that they would not be as an enemy within its walls, they do not know by how much truth is stronger than error, nor how much more eloquently and effectively he can combat injustice who has experienced a little in his own person. Cast your whole vote, not a strip of paper merely, but your whole influence. A minority is powerless while it conforms to the majority; it is not even a minority then; but it is irresistible when it clogs by its whole weight. If the alternative is to keep all just men in prison, or give up war and slavery, the State will not hesitate which to choose. If a thousand men were not to pay their tax-bills this year, that would not be a violent and bloody measure, as it would be to pay them, and enable the State to commit violence and shed innocent blood. This is, in fact, the definition of a peaceable revolution, if any such is possible. If the tax-gatherer, or any other public officer, asks me, as one has done, "But what shall I do?" my answer is, "If you really wish to do anything, resign your office." When the subject has refused allegiance, and the officer has resigned his office, then the revolution is accomplished. But even suppose blood should flow. Is there not a sort of blood shed when the conscience is wounded? Through this wound a man's real manhood and immortality flow out, and he bleeds to an everlasting death. I see this blood flowing now.

I have contemplated the imprisonment of the offender, rather than the seizure of his goods,—though both will serve the same purpose,—because they who assert the purest right, and consequently are most dangerous to a corrupt State, commonly have not spent much time in accumulating property. To such the State renders comparatively small service, and a slight tax is wont to appear exorbitant, particularly if they are obliged to earn it by special labor with their hands. If there were one who lived wholly without the use of money, the State itself would hesitate to demand it of him. But the rich man—not to make any invidious comparison—is always sold to the institution which makes him rich. Absolutely speaking, the more money, the less virtue; for money comes between a man and his objects, and obtains them for him; and it was certainly no great virtue to obtain it. It puts to rest many questions which he would otherwise be taxed to answer; while the only new question which it puts is the hard but superfluous one, how to spend it. Thus his moral ground is taken from under his feet. The opportunities of living are diminished in proportion as what are called the "means" are increased. The best thing a man can do for his culture when he is rich is to endeavor to carry out those schemes which he entertained when he was poor. Christ answered the Herodians according to their condition. "Show me the tribute-money," said he;—and one took a penny out of his pocket;—if you use money which has the image of Cæsar on it, and which he has made current and valuable, that is, *if you are men of the State*, and gladly enjoy the advantages of Cæsar's government, then pay him back some of his own when he demands it. "Render therefore to Cæsar that which is Cæsar's, and to God those things which are God's,"—leaving them no wiser than before as to which was which; for they did not wish to know.

When I converse with the freest of my neighbors, I perceive that, whatever they may say about the magnitude and seriousness of the question, and their regard for the public tranquillity, the long and the short of the matter is, that they cannot spare the protection of the existing government, and they dread the consequences to their property and families of disobedience to it. For my own part, I should not like to think that I ever rely on the protection of the State. But, if I deny the authority of the State when it presents its tax-bill, it will soon take and waste all my property, and so harass me and my children without end. This is hard. This makes it impossible for a man to live honestly, and at the same time comfortably, in outward respects. It will not be worth the while to accumulate property; that would be sure to go again. You must hire or squat somewhere, and raise but a small crop, and eat that soon. You must live within yourself, and depend upon yourself always tucked up and ready for a start, and not have many affairs. A man may grow rich in Turkey even, if he will be in all respects a good subject of the Turkish government. Confucius said: "If a state is governed by the principles of reason, poverty and misery are subjects of shame; if a state is not governed by the principles of reason, riches and honors are the subjects of shame." No: until I want the protection of Massachusetts to be extended to me in some distant Southern port, where my liberty is endangered, or until I am bent solely on building up an estate at home by peaceful enterprise, I can afford to refuse allegiance to Massachusetts, and her right to my property and life. It costs me less in every sense to incur the penalty of disobedience to the State than it would to obey. I should feel as if I were worth less in that case.

Some years ago, the State met me in behalf of the Church, and commanded me to pay a certain sum toward the support of a clergyman whose preaching my father attended, but never I myself. "Pay," it said, "or be locked up in the jail." I declined to pay. But, unfortunately, another man saw fit to pay it. I did not see why the schoolmaster should be taxed to support the priest, and not the priest the schoolmaster; for I was not the State's schoolmaster, but I supported myself by voluntary subscription. I did not see why the lyceum should not present its tax-bill, and have the State to back its demand, as well as the Church. However, at the request of the selectmen, I condescended to make some such statement as this in writing:—"Know all men by these presents, that I, Henry Thoreau, do not wish to be regarded as a member of any incorporated society which I have not joined." This I gave to the town clerk; and he has it. The State, having thus learned that I did not wish to be regarded as a member of that church, has never made a like demand on me since; though it said that it must adhere to its original presumption that time. If I had known how to name them, I should then have signed off in detail from all the societies which I never signed on to; but I did not know where to find a complete list.

I have paid no poll-tax for six years. I was put into a jail once on this account, for one night; and, as I stood considering the walls of solid stone, two or three feet thick, the door of wood and iron, a foot thick, and the iron grating which strained the light, I could not help being struck with the foolishness of that institution which treated me as if I were mere flesh and blood and bones, to be locked up. I wondered that it should have concluded at length that this was the best use it could put me to, and had never thought to avail itself of my services in some way. I saw that, if there was a wall of stone between me and my townsmen, there was a still more difficult one to climb or break through before they could get to be as free as I was. I did not for a moment feel confined, and the walls seemed a great waste of stone and mortar. I felt as if I alone of all my townsmen had paid my tax. They plainly did not know how to treat me, but behaved like persons who are underbred. In every threat and in every compliment there was a blunder; for they thought that my chief desire was to stand the other side of that stone wall. I could not but smile to see how industriously they locked the door on my meditations, which followed them out again without let or hindrance, and *they* were really all that was dangerous. As they could not reach me, they had resolved to punish my body; just as boys, if they cannot come at some person against whom they have a spite, will abuse his dog. I saw that the State was half-witted, that it was timid as a lone woman with her silver spoons, and that it did not know its friends from its foes, and I lost all my remaining respect for it, and pitied it.

Thus the State never intentionally confronts a man's sense, intellectual or moral, but only his body, his senses. It is not armed with superior wit or honesty, but with superior physical strength. I was not born to be forced. I will breathe after my own fashion. Let us see who is the strongest. What force has a multitude? They only can force me who obey a higher law than I. They force me to become like themselves. I do not hear of *men* being *forced* to live this way or that by masses of men. What sort of life were that to live? When I meet a government which says to me, "Your money or your life," why should I be in haste to give it my money? It may be in a great strait, and not know what to do: I cannot help that. It must help itself; do as I do. It is not worth the while to snivel about it. I am not responsible for the successful working of the machinery of society. I am not the son of the engineer. I perceive that, when an acorn and a chestnut fall side by side, the one does not remain inert to make way for the other, but both obey their own laws, and spring and grow and flourish as best they can, till one, perchance, over-shadows and destroys the other. If a plant cannot live according to its nature, it dies; and so a man.

The night in prison was novel and interesting enough. The prisoners in their shirt-sleeves were enjoying a chat and the evening air in the doorway, when I entered. But the jailer said, "Come, boys, it is time to lock up;" and so they dispersed, and I heard the sound of their steps returning into the hollow apartments. My room-mate was introduced to me by the jailer as "a first-rate fellow and a clever man." When the door was locked, he showed me where to hang my hat, and how he managed matters there. The rooms were whitewashed once a month; and this one, at least, was the whitest, most simply furnished, and probably the neatest apartment in the town. He naturally wanted to know where I came from, and what brought me there; and, when I had told him, I asked him in my turn how he came there, presuming him to be an honest man, of course; and, as the world goes, I believe he was. "Why," said he, "they accuse me of burning a barn; but I never did it." As near as I could discover, he had probably gone to bed in a barn when drunk, and smoked his pipe there; and so a barn was burnt. He had the reputation of being a clever man, had been there some three months waiting for his trial to come on, and would have to wait as much longer; but he was quite domesticated and contented, since he got his board for nothing, and thought that he was well treated.

He occupied one window, and I the other; and I saw that if one stayed there long, his principal business would be to look out the window. I had soon read all the tracts that were left there, and examined where former prisoners had broken out, and where a grate had been sawed off, and heard the history of the various occupants of that room; for I found that even here there was a history and a gossip which never circulated beyond the walls of the jail. Probably this is the only house in the town where verses are composed, which are afterward printed in a circular form, but not published. I was shown quite a long list of verses which were composed by some young men who had been detected in an attempt to escape, who avenged themselves by singing them.

I pumped my fellow-prisoner as dry as I could, for fear I should never see him again; but at length he showed me which was my bed, and left me to blow out the lamp.

It was like traveling into a far country, such as I had never expected to behold, to lie there for one night. It seemed to me that I never had heard the town-clock strike before, nor the evening sounds of the village; for we slept with the windows open, which were inside the grating. It was to see my native village in the light of the Middle Ages, and our Concord was turned into a Rhine stream, and visions of knights and castles passed before me. They were the voices of old burghers that I heard in the streets. I was an involuntary spectator and auditor of whatever was done and said in the kitchen of the adjacent village-inn,—a wholly new and rare experience to me. It was a closer view of my native town. I was fairly inside of it. I never had seen its institutions before. This is one of its peculiar institutions; for it is a shire town. I began to comprehend what its inhabitants were about.

In the morning, our breakfasts were put through the hole in the door, in small oblong-square tin pans, made to fit, and holding a pint of chocolate, with brown bread, and an iron spoon. When they called for the vessels again, I was green enough to return what bread I had left; but my comrade seized it, and said that I should lay that up for lunch or dinner.

Soon after he was let out to work at haying in a neighboring field, whither he went every day, and would not be back till noon; so he bade me good-day, saying that he doubted if he should see me again.

When I came out of prison,—for some one interfered, and paid that tax,—I did not perceive that great changes had taken place on the common, such as he observed who went in a youth and emerged a tottering and gray-headed man; and yet a change had to my eyes come over the scene,—the town, and State, and country,—greater than any that mere time could effect. I saw yet more distinctly the State in which I lived. I saw to what extent the people among whom I lived could be trusted as good neighbors and friends; that their friendship was for summer weather only; that they did not greatly propose to do right; that they were a distinct race from me by their prejudices and superstitions, as the Chinamen and Malays are; that in their sacrifices to humanity they ran no risks, not even to their property; that after all they were not so noble but they treated the thief as he had treated them, and hoped, by a certain outward observance and a few prayers, and by walking in a particular straight though useless path from time to time, to save their souls. This may be to judge my neighbors harshly; for I believe that many of them are not aware that they have such an institution as the jail in their village.

It was formerly the custom in our village, when a poor debtor came out of jail, for his acquaintances to salute him, looking through their fingers, which were crossed to represent the grating of a jail window, "How do ye do?" My neighbors did not thus salute me, but first looked at me, and then at one another, as if I had returned from a long journey. I was put into jail as I was going to the shoemaker's to get a shoe which was mended. When I was let out the next morning, I proceeded to finish my errand, and, having put on my mended shoe, joined a huckleberry party, who were impatient to put themselves under my conduct; and in half an hour,—for the horse was soon tackled,—was in the midst of a huckleberry field, on one of our highest hills, two miles off, and then the State was nowhere to be seen.

This is the whole history of "My Prisons."

I have never declined paying the highway tax, because I am as desirous of being a good neighbor as I am of being a bad subject; and as for supporting schools, I am doing my part to educate my fellow-countrymen now. It is for no particular item in the tax-bill that I refuse to pay it. I simply wish to refuse allegiance to the State, to withdraw and stand aloof from it effectually. I do not care to trace the course of my dollar, if I could, till it buys a man or a musket to shoot one with,—the dollar is innocent,—but I am concerned to trace the effects of my allegiance. In fact, I quietly declare war with the State, after my fashion, though I will still make what use and get what advantage of her I can, as is usual in such cases.

If others pay the tax which is demanded of me, from a sympathy with the State, they do but what they have already done in their own case, or rather they abet injustice to a greater extent than the State requires. If they pay the tax from a mistaken interest in the individual taxed, to save his property, or prevent his going to jail, it is because they have not considered wisely how far they let their private feelings interfere with the public good.

This, then, is my position at present. But one cannot be too much on his guard in such a case, lest his action be biased by obstinacy or an undue regard for the opinions of men. Let him see that he does only what belongs to himself and to the hour.

I think sometimes, Why, this people mean well, they are only ignorant; they would do better if they knew how: why give your neighbors this pain to treat you as they are not inclined to? But I think again, This is no reason why I should do as they do, or permit others to suffer much greater pain of a different kind. Again, I sometimes say to myself, When many millions of men, without heat, without ill will, without personal feeling of any kind, demand of you a few shillings only, without the possibility, such is their constitution, of retracting or altering their present demand, and without the possibility, on your side, of appeal to any other millions, why expose yourself to this overwhelming brute force? You do not resist cold and hunger, the winds and the waves, thus obstinately; you quietly submit to a thousand similar necessities. You do not put your head into the fire. But just in proportion as I regard this as not wholly a brute force, but partly a human force, and consider that I have relations to those millions as to so many millions of men, and not of mere brute or inanimate things, I see that appeal is possible, first and instantaneously, from them to the Maker of them, and, secondly, from them to themselves. But if I put my head deliberately into the fire, there is no appeal to fire or to the Maker of fire, and I have only myself to blame. If I could convince myself that I have any right to be satisfied with men as they are, and to treat them accordingly, and not according, in some respects, to my requisitions and expectations of what they and I ought to be, then, like a good Mussulman and fatalist, I should endeavor to be satisfied with things as they are, and say it is the will of God. And, above all, there is this difference between resisting this and a purely brute or natural force, that I can resist this with some effect; but I cannot expect, like Orpheus, to change the nature of the rocks and trees and beasts.

I do not wish to quarrel with any man or nation. I do not wish to split hairs, to make fine distinctions, or set myself up as better than my neighbors. I seek rather, I may say, even an excuse for conforming to the laws of the land. I am but too ready to conform to them. Indeed, I have reason to suspect myself on this head; and each year, as the tax-gatherer comes round, I find myself disposed to review the acts and position of the general and State governments, and the spirit of the people, to discover a pretext for conformity.

> "We must affect our country as our parents,
>   And if at any time we alienate
>   Our love or industry from doing it honor,
>   We must respect effects and teach the soul
>   Matter of conscience and religion,
>   And not desire of rule or benefit."

I believe that the State will soon be able to take all my work of this sort out of my hands, and then I shall be no better a patriot than my fellow-countrymen. Seen from a lower point of view, the Constitution, with all its faults, is very good; the law and the courts are very respectable; even this State and this American government are, in many respects, very admirable, and rare things, to be thankful for, such as a great many have described them; but seen from a point of view a little higher, they are what I have described them; seen from a higher still, and the highest, who shall say what they are, or that they are worth looking at or thinking of at all?

However, the government does not concern me much, and I shall bestow the fewest possible thoughts on it. It is not many moments that I live under a government, even in this world. If a man is thought-free, fancy-free, imagination-free, that which *is not* never for a long time appearing *to be* to him, unwise rulers or reformers cannot fatally interrupt him.

I know that most men think differently from myself; but those whose lives are by profession devoted to the study of these or kindred subjects content me as little as any. Statesmen and legislators, standing so completely within the institution, never distinctly and nakedly behold it. They speak of moving society, but have no resting-place without it. They may be men of a certain experience and discrimination, and have no doubt invented ingenious and even useful systems, for which we sincerely thank them; but all their wit and usefulness lie within certain not very wide limits. They are wont to forget that the world is not governed by policy and expediency. Webster never goes behind government, and so cannot speak with authority about it. His words are wisdom to those legislators who contemplate no essential reform in the existing government; but for thinkers, and those who legislate for all time, he never once glances at the subject. I know of those whose serene and wise speculations on this theme would soon reveal the limits of his mind's range and hospitality. Yet, compared with the cheap professions of most reformers, and the still cheaper wisdom and eloquence of politicians in general, his are almost the only sensible and valuable words, and we thank Heaven for him. Comparatively, he is always strong, original, and, above all, practical. Still, his quality is not wisdom, but prudence. The lawyer's truth is not Truth, but consistency or a consistent expediency. Truth is always in harmony with herself, and is not concerned chiefly to reveal the justice that may consist with wrong-doing. He well deserves to be called, as he has been called, the Defender of the Constitution. There are really no blows to be given by him but defensive ones. He is not a leader, but a follower. His leaders are the men of '87. "I have never made an effort," he says, "and never propose to make an effort; I have never countenanced an effort, and never mean to countenance an effort, to disturb the arrangement as originally made, by which the various States came into the Union." Still thinking of the sanction which the Constitution gives to slavery, he says, "Because it was a part of the original compact,—let it stand." Notwithstanding his special acuteness and ability, he is unable to take a fact out of its merely political relations, and behold it as it lies absolutely to be disposed of by the intellect,—what, for instance, it behooves a man to do here in America to-day with regard to slavery,—but ventures, or is driven, to make some such desperate answer as the following, while professing to speak absolutely, and as a private man,—from which what new and singular code of social duties might be inferred? "The manner," says he, "in which the governments of those States where slavery exists are to regulate it is for their own consideration, under their responsibility to their constituents, to the general laws of propriety, humanity, and justice, and to God. Associations formed elsewhere, springing from a feeling of humanity, or any other cause, have nothing whatever to do with it. They have never received any encouragement from me, and they never will."

They who know of no purer sources of truth, who have traced up its stream no higher, stand, and wisely stand, by the Bible and the Constitution, and drink at it there with reverence and humility; but they who behold where it comes trickling into this lake or that pool, gird up their loins once more, and continue their pilgrimage toward its fountain-head.

No man with a genius for legislation has appeared in America. They are rare in the history of the world. There are orators, politicians, and eloquent men, by the thousand; but the speaker has not yet opened his mouth to speak who is capable of settling the much-vexed questions of the day. We love eloquence for its own sake, and not for any truth which it may utter, or any heroism it may inspire. Our legislators have not yet learned the comparative value of free-trade and of freedom, of union, and of rectitude, to a nation. They have no genius or talent for comparatively humble questions of taxation and finance, commerce and manufactures and agriculture. If we were left solely to the wordy wit of legislators in Congress for our guidance, uncorrected by the seasonable experience and the effectual complaints of the people, America would not long retain her rank among the nations. For eighteen hundred years, though perchance I have no right to say it, the New Testament has been written; yet where is the legislator who has wisdom and practical talent enough to avail himself of the light which it sheds on the science of legislation?

The authority of government, even such as I am willing to submit to, —for I will cheerfully obey those who know and can do better than I, and in many things even those who neither know nor can do so well,—is still an impure one: to be strictly just, it must have the sanction and consent of the governed. It can have no pure right over my person and property but what I concede to it. The progress from an absolute to a limited monarchy, from a limited monarchy to a democracy, is a progress toward a true respect for the individual. Even the Chinese philosopher was wise enough to regard the individual as the basis of the empire. Is a democracy, such as we know it, the last improvement possible in government? Is it not possible to take a step further towards recognizing and organizing the rights of man? There will never be a really free and enlightened State until the State comes to recognize the individual as a higher and independent power, from which all its own power and authority are derived, and treats him accordingly. I please myself with imagining a State at last which can afford to be just to all men, and to treat the individual with respect as a neighbor; which even would not think it inconsistent with its own repose if a few were to live aloof from it, not meddling with it, nor embraced by it, who fulfilled all the duties of neighbors and fellow-men. A State which bore this kind of fruit, and suffered it to drop off as fast as it ripened, would prepare the way for a still more perfect and glorious State, which also I have imagined, but not yet anywhere seen.

BERTRAND RUSSELL

Bertrand Russell, philosopher, mathematician, educator, prolific essayist, controversial social critic, and pacifist leader, was born in England in 1872, the son of a family prominent in English history since the early sixteenth century. Educated (and since 1944 a Fellow) at Trinity College, Cambridge, he has also taught or lectured at Harvard, Chicago, UCLA, and many other schools in this country. His career has been both dis-

tinguished and lively and has often brought him into the center of public attention. He won early renown for his Principia Mathematica *(1910–1913), written with Alfred North Whitehead, and early notoriety when he served a jail sentence as a conscientious objector in World War I. His academic visit to America in 1940 caused a furor when a New York State Supreme Court order forbade his appointment as Professor of Philosophy at CCNY, presumably because of his controversial views on sex and marriage, and when unsuccessful attempts were made to oust him from a lectureship at Harvard that same year. In 1950 he won the Nobel Prize for literature "in recognition of his manysided and significant authorship in which he has constantly figured as a defender of humanity and freedom of thought." In the last decade, Russell has devoted a large part of his efforts to pacifist activities. In 1961 he was once again jailed, this time for inciting pacifist demonstrators to a "breach of peace." More recently he has founded the Bertrand Russell Peace Foundation and the Atlantic Peace Foundation. This essay below, which we have entitled "The Committee of 100," is taken from* A Matter of Life *(1963), a collection of essays (edited by Clara Urquhart) concerned with "the moral sickness of which nuclear danger is but the most frightening symptom."*

Russell's bibliography is so extensive that we can do no more than suggest a few of his best known volumes. These include Introduction to Mathematical Philosophy *(1919),* Sceptical Essays *(1928),* Marriage and Morals *(1929),* Education and the Social Order *(1932),* In Praise of Idleness *(1935),* A History of Western Philosophy *(1945),* Authority and the Individual *(1949),* Why I Am Not a Christian *(1957), and* Has Man a Future? *(1963).*

THE COMMITTEE OF 100

The Committee of 100, as your readers are aware, calls for non-violent civil disobedience on a large scale as a means of inducing the British Government (and others, we hope, in due course) to abandon nuclear weapons and the protection that they are supposed to afford. Many critics have objected that civil disobedience is immoral, at any rate where the government is democratic. It is my purpose to combat this view, not in general, but in the case of non-violent civil disobedience on behalf of certain aims advocated by the Committee of 100.

It is necessary to begin with some abstract principles of ethics. There are, broadly speaking, two types of ethical theory. One of these, which is exemplified in the Decalogue, lays down rules of conduct which are supposed to hold in all cases, regardless of the effects of obeying them. The other theory, while admitting that some rules of conduct are valid in a very great majority of cases, is prepared to consider the consequences of actions and to permit breaches of the rules where the consequences of obeying the rules are obviously undesirable. In practice, most people adopt the second point of view, and only appeal to the first in controversies with opponents.

Let us take a few examples. Suppose a physically powerful man, suffering from hydrophobia, was about to bite your children, and the only way of preventing him was to kill him. I think very few people would think you unjustified in adopting this method of saving your children's lives. Those who thought you justified would not deny that the prohibition of murder is *almost* always right. Probably they would go on to say that this particular sort of killing should not be called 'murder'. They would define 'murder' as 'unjustifiable homicide'. In that case, the precept that murder is wrong becomes a tautology, but the ethical question remains: 'What sort of killing is to be labelled as murder?' Or take, again, the commandment not to steal. Almost everybody would agree that in an immense majority of cases it is right to obey this commandment. But suppose you were a refugee, fleeing with your family from persecution, and you could not obtain food except by stealing. Most people would agree that you would be justified in stealing. The only exceptions would be those who approved of the tyranny from which you were trying to escape.

There have been many cases in history where the issue was not so clear. In the time of Pope Gregory VI, simony was rife in the Church. Pope Gregory VI, by means of simony, became Pope and did so in order to abolish simony. In this he was largely successful, and final success was achieved by his disciple and admirer, Pope Gregory VII, who was one of the most illustrious of Popes. I will not express an opinion on the conduct of Gregory VI, which has remained a controversial issue down to the present day.

The only rule, in all such doubtful cases, is to consider the consequences of the action in question. We must include among these consequences the bad effect of weakening respect for a rule which is usually right. But, even when this is taken into account, there will be cases where even the most generally acceptable rule of conduct should be broken.

So much for general theory. I will come now one step nearer to the moral problem with which we are concerned.

What is to be said about a rule enjoining respect for law? Let us first consider the arguments in favour of such a rule. Without law, a civilized community is impossible. Where there is general disrespect for the law, all kinds of evil consequences are sure to follow. A notable example was the failure of prohibition in America. In this case it became obvious that the only cure was a change in the law, since it was impossible to obtain general respect for the law as it stood. This view prevailed, in spite of the fact that those who broke the law were not actuated by what are called conscientious motives. This case made it obvious that respect for the law has two sides. If there is to be respect for the law, the law must be generally considered to be worthy of respect.

The main argument in favour of respect for law is that, in disputes between two parties, it substitutes a neutral authority for private bias which would be likely in the absence of law. The force which the law can exert is, in most such cases, irresistible, and therefore only has to be invoked in the case of a minority of reckless criminals. The net result is a community in which most people are peaceful. These reasons for the reign of law are admitted in the great majority of cases, except by anarchists. I have no wish to dispute their validity save in exceptional circumstances.

There is one very large class of cases in which the law does not have the merit of being impartial as between the disputants. This is when one of the disputants is the state. The state makes the laws and, unless there is a very vigilant public opinion in defence of justifiable liberties, the state will make the law such as suits its own convenience, which may not be what is for the public good. In the Nuremberg trials war criminals were condemned for obeying the orders of the state, though their condemnation was only possible after the state in question had suffered military defeat. But it is noteworthy that the powers which defeated Germany all agreed that failure to practise civil disobedience may deserve punishment.

Those who find fault with the particular form of civil disobedience which I am concerned to justify maintain that breaches of the law, though they may be justified under a despotic régime, can never be justified in a democracy. I cannot see any validity whatever in this contention. There are many ways in which nominally democratic governments can fail to carry out principles which friends of democracy should respect. Take, for example, the case of Ireland before it achieved independence. Formally, the Irish had the same democratic rights as the British. They could send representatives to Westminster and plead their case by all the received democratic processes. But, in spite of this, they were in a minority which, if they had confined themselves to legal methods, would have been permanent. They won their independence by breaking the law. If they had not broken it, they could not have won.

There are many other ways in which governments, which are nominally democratic, fail to be so. A great many questions are so complex that only a few experts can understand them. When the bank rate is raised or lowered, what proportion of the electorate can judge whether it was right to do so? And, if anyone who has no official position criticizes the action of the Bank of England, the only witnesses who can give authoritative evidence will be men responsible for what has been done, or closely connected with those who are responsible. Not only in questions of finance, but still more in military and diplomatic questions, there is in every civilized state a well-developed technique of concealment. If the government wishes some fact to remain unknown, almost all major organs of publicity will assist in concealment. In such cases it often happens that the truth can only be made known, if at all, by persistent and self-sacrificing efforts involving obloquy and perhaps disgrace. Sometimes, if the matter rouses sufficient passion, the truth comes to be known in the end. This happened, for example, in the Dreyfus Case. But where the matter is less sensational the ordinary voter is likely to be left permanently in ignorance.

For such reasons democracy, though much less liable to abuses than dictatorship, is by no means immune to abuses of power by those in authority or by corrupt interests. If valuable liberties are to be preserved there have to be people willing to criticize authority and even, on occasion, to disobey it.

Those who most loudly proclaim their respect for law are in many cases quite unwilling that the domain of law should extend to international relations. In relations between states the only law is still the law of the jungle. What decides a dispute is the question of which side can cause the greatest number of deaths to the other side. Those who do not accept this criterion are apt to be accused of lack of patriotism. This makes it impossible not to suspect that law is only valued where it already exists, and not as an alternative to war.

This brings me at last to the particular form of non-violent civil disobedience which is advocated and practised by the Committee of 100. Those who study nuclear weapons and the probable course of nuclear war are divided into two classes. There are, on the one hand, people employed by governments, and, on the other hand, unofficial people who are actuated by a realization of the dangers and catastrophes which are probable if governmental policies remain unchanged. There are a number of questions in dispute. I will mention a few of them. What is the likelihood of a nuclear war by accident? What is to be feared from fall-out? What proportion of the population is likely to survive an all-out nuclear war? On every one of these questions independent students find that official apologists and policy-makers give answers which, to an unbiased inquirer, appear grossly and murderously misleading. To make known to the general population what independent inquirers believe to be the true answers to these questions is a very difficult matter. Where the truth is difficult to ascertain there is a natural inclination to believe what official authorities assert. This is especially the case when what they assert enables people to dismiss uneasiness as needlessly alarmist. The major organs of publicity feel themselves part of the Establishment and are very reluctant to take a course which the Establishment will frown on. Long and frustrating experience has proved, to those among us who have endeavoured to make unpleasant facts known, that orthodox methods, alone, are insufficient. By means of civil disobedience a certain kind of publicity becomes possible. What we do is reported, though as far as possible our reasons for what we do are not mentioned. The policy of suppressing our reasons, however, has only very partial success. Many people are roused to inquire into questions which they had been willing to ignore. Many people, especially among the young, come to share the opinion that governments, by means of lies and evasions, are luring whole populations to destruction. It seems not unlikely that, in the end, an irresistible popular movement of protest will compel governments to allow their subjects to continue to exist. On the basis of long experience, we are convinced that this object cannot be achieved by law-abiding methods alone. Speaking for myself, I regard this as the most important reason for adopting civil disobedience.

Another reason for endeavouring to spread knowledge about nuclear warfare is the extreme imminence of the peril. Legally legitimate methods of spreading this knowledge have been proved to be very slow, and we believe, on the basis of experience, that only such methods as we have adopted can spread the necessary knowledge before it is too late. As things stand, a nuclear war, probably by accident, may occur at any moment. Each day that passes without such a war is a matter of luck, and it cannot be expected that luck will hold indefinitely. Any day, at any hour, the whole population of Britain may perish. Strategists and negotiators play a leisurely game in which procrastination is one of the received methods. It is urgent that the populations of East and West compel both sides to realize that the time at their disposal is limited and that, while present methods continue, disaster is possible at any moment, and almost certain sooner or later.

There is, however, still another reason for employing non-violent civil disobedience which is very powerful and deserves respect. The programmes of mass extermination, upon which vast sums of public money are being spent, must fill every humane person with feelings of utter horror. The West is told that communism is wicked; the East is told that capitalism is wicked. Both sides deduce that the nations which favour either are to be 'obliterated', to use Khrushchev's word. I do not doubt that each side is right in thinking that a nuclear war would destroy the other side's 'ism', but each side is hopelessly mistaken if it thinks that a nuclear war could establish its own 'ism'. Nothing that either East or West desires can result from a nuclear war. If both sides could be made to understand this, it would become possible for both sides to realize that there can be no victory for either, but only total defeat for both. If this entirely obvious fact were publicly admitted in a joint statement by Khrushchev and Kennedy, a compromise method of coexistence could be negotiated giving each side quite obviously a thousand times more of what it wants than could be achieved by war. The utter uselessness of war, in the present age, is completely obvious except to those who have been so schooled in past traditions that they are incapable of thinking in terms of the world that we now have to live in. Those of us who protest against nuclear weapons and nuclear war cannot acquiesce in a world in which each man owes such freedom as remains to him to the capacity of his government to cause many hundreds of millions of deaths by pressing a button. This is to us an abomination, and rather than seem to acquiesce in it we are willing, if necessary, to become outcasts and to suffer whatever obloquy and whatever hardship may be involved in standing aloof from the governmental framework. This thing is a horror. It is something in the shadow of which nothing good can flourish. I am convinced that, on purely political grounds, our reasoned case is unanswerable. But, beyond all political considerations, there is the determination not to be an accomplice in the worst crime that human beings have ever contemplated. We are shocked, and rightly shocked, by Hitler's extermination of six million Jews, but the governments of East and West calmly contemplate the possibility of a massacre at least a hundred times greater than that perpetrated by Hitler. Those who realize the magnitude of this horror cannot even *seem* to acquiesce in the policies from which it springs. It is this feeling, much more than any political calculation, that gives fervour and strength to our movement, a kind of fervour and a kind of strength which, if a nuclear war does not soon end us all, will make our movement grow until it reaches the point where governments can no longer refuse to let mankind survive.

MARTIN LUTHER KING, Jr.

Martin Luther King was born in Georgia in 1929 and educated at Morehouse College, Crozer Theological Seminary, and Boston University. He became a Baptist minister in Montgomery, Alabama, in 1954. The next year he launched the now famous Montgomery bus boycott. Since then Dr. King has become a forceful advocate of non-violent disobedience in the civil rights struggle. Founder and President of the Southern Christian Leadership Conference, he was a leader of the 1963 "March on Washington" and a participant in many of the demonstrations against segregation which followed in its wake. In 1964 he received the Nobel Peace Prize.

A leading spokesman for civil rights, his writings include Stride

Toward Freedom (1958), Strength to Love (1963), and Why We Can't Wait (1964), which includes a revised version of the letter printed below, and an author's note in which he says that "This response to a published statement by eight fellow clergymen from Alabama . . . was composed under somewhat constricting circumstances. Begun on the margins of the newspaper in which the statement appeared while I was in jail, the letter was continued on scraps of writing paper supplied by a friendly Negro trusty, and concluded on a pad my attorneys were eventually permitted to leave me. Although the text remains in substance unaltered, I have indulged in the author's prerogative of polishing it for publication." For its greater immediacy, we present here the unrevised version of the letter, together with the public statement which occasioned it.

PUBLIC STATEMENT BY EIGHT
ALABAMA CLERGYMEN

April 12, 1963

We the undersigned clergymen are among those who, in January, issued "An Appeal for Law and Order and Common Sense," in dealing with racial problems in Alabama. We expressed understanding that honest convictions in racial matters could properly be pursued in the courts, but urged that decisions of those courts should in the meantime be peacefully obeyed.

Since that time there had been some evidence of increased forbearance and a willingness to face facts. Responsible citizens have undertaken to work on various problems which cause racial friction and unrest. In Birmingham, recent public events have given indication that we all have opportunity for a new constructive and realistic approach to racial problems.

However, we are now confronted by a series of demonstrations by some of our Negro citizens, directed and led in part by outsiders. We recognize the natural impatience of people who feel that their hopes are slow in being realized. But we are convinced that these demonstrations are unwise and untimely.

We agree rather with certain local Negro leadership which has called for honest and open negotiation of racial issues in our area. And we believe this kind of facing of issues can best be accomplished by citizens of our own metropolitan area, white and Negro, meeting with their knowledge and experience of the local situation. All of us need to face that responsibility and find proper channels for its accomplishment.

Just as we formerly pointed out that "hatred and violence have no sanction in our religious and political traditions," we also point out that such actions as incite to hatred and violence, however technically peaceful those actions may be, have not contributed to the resolution of our local problems. We do not believe that these days of new hope are days when extreme measures are justified in Birmingham.

We commend the community as a whole, and the local news media and law enforcement officials in particular, on the calm manner in which these demonstrations have been handled. We urge the public to continue to show restraint should the demonstrations continue, and the law enforcement officials to remain calm and continue to protect our city from violence.

We further strongly urge our own Negro community to withdraw support from these demonstrations, and to unite locally in working peacefully for a better Birmingham. When rights are consistently denied, a cause should be pressed in the courts and in negotiations among local leaders, and not in the streets. We appeal to both our white and Negro citizenry to observe the principles of law and order and common sense.

Signed by:
C. C. J. CARPENTER, DD., LL.D., Bishop of Alabama
JOSEPH A. DURICK, D.D., Auxiliary Bishop, Diocese of Mobile-Birmingham
Rabbi MILTON L. GRAFMAN, Temple Emanu-El, Birmingham, Alabama
Bishop PAUL HARDIN, Bishop of the Alabama-West Florida Conference of the Methodist Church
Bishop NOLAN B. HARMON, Bishop of the North Alabama Conference of the Methodist Church
GEORGE M. MURRAY, D.D., LL.D., Bishop Coadjutor, Episcopal Diocese of Alabama
EDWARD V. RAMAGE, Moderator, Synod of the Alabama Presbyterian Church in the United States
EARL STALLINGS, Pastor, First Baptist Church, Birmingham, Alabama

LETTER FROM BIRMINGHAM JAIL

Martin Luther King, Jr.
Birmingham City Jail
April 16, 1963

Bishop C. C. J. Carpenter
Bishop Joseph A. Durick
Rabbi Milton L. Grafman
Bishop Paul Hardin
Bishop Nolan B. Harmon
The Rev. George M. Murray
The Rev. Edward V. Ramage
The Rev. Earl Stallings

My dear Fellow Clergymen,

While confined here in the Birmingham City Jail, I came across your recent statement calling our present activities "unwise and untimely." Seldom, if ever, do I pause to answer criticism of my work and ideas. If I sought to answer all of the criticisms that cross my desk, my secretaries would be engaged in little else in the course of the day and I would have no time for constructive work. But since I feel that you are men of genuine good will and your criticisms are sincerely set forth, I would like to answer your statement in what I hope will be patient and reasonable terms.

I think I should give the reason for my being in Birmingham, since you have been influenced by the argument of "outsiders coming in." I have the honor of serving as president of the Southern Christian Leadership Conference, an organization operating in every Southern state with headquarters in Atlanta, Georgia. We have some eighty-five affiliate organizations all across the South—one being the Alabama Christian Movement for Human Rights. Whenever necessary and possible we share staff, educational, and financial resources with our affiliates. Several months ago our local affiliate here in Birmingham invited us to be on call to engage in a nonviolent direct action program if such were deemed necessary. We readily consented and when the hour came we lived up to our promises. So I am here, along with several members of my staff, because we were invited here. I am here because I have basic organizational ties here. Beyond this, I am in Birmingham because injustice is here. Just as the eighth century prophets left their little villages and carried their "thus saith the Lord" far beyond the boundaries of their home town, and just as the Apostle Paul left his little village of Tarsus and carried the gospel of

Jesus Christ to practically every hamlet and city of the Graeco-Roman world, I too am compelled to carry the gospel of freedom beyond my particular home town. Like Paul, I must constantly respond to the Macedonian call for aid.

Moreover, I am cognizant of the interrelatedness of all communities and states. I cannot sit idly by in Atlanta and not be concerned about what happens in Birmingham. Injustice anywhere is a threat to justice everywhere. We are caught in an inescapable network of mutuality tied in a single garment of destiny. Whatever affects one directly affects all indirectly. Never again can we afford to live with the narrow, provincial "outside agitator" idea. Anyone who lives inside the United States can never be considered an outsider anywhere in this country.

You deplore the demonstrations that are presently taking place in Birmingham. But I am sorry that your statement did not express a similar concern for the conditions that brought the demonstrations into being. I am sure that each of you would want to go beyond the superficial social analyst who looks merely at effects, and does not grapple with underlying causes. I would not hesitate to say that it is unfortunate that so-called demonstrations are taking place in Birmingham at this time, but I would say in more emphatic terms that it is even more unfortunate that the white power structure of this city left the Negro community with no other alternative.

In any nonviolent campaign there are four basic steps: (1) collection of the facts to determine whether injustices are alive; (2) negotiation; (3) self-purification; and (4) direct action. We have gone through all of these steps in Birmingham. There can be no gainsaying of the fact that racial injustice engulfs this community. Birmingham is probably the most thoroughly segregated city in the United States. Its ugly record of police brutality is known in every section of this country. Its unjust treatment of Negroes in the courts is a notorious reality. There have been more unsolved bombings of Negro homes and churches in Birmingham than any city in this nation. These are the hard, brutal, and unbelievable facts. On the basis of these conditions Negro leaders sought to negotiate with the city fathers. But the political leaders consistently refused to engage in good faith negotiation.

Then came the opportunity last September to talk with some of the leaders of the economic community. In these negotiating sessions certain promises were made by the merchants—such as the promise to remove the humiliating racial signs from the stores. On the basis of these promises Rev. Shuttlesworth and the leaders of the Alabama Christian Movement for Human Rights agreed to call a moratorium on any type of demonstrations. As the weeks and months unfolded we realized that we were the victims of a broken promise. The signs remained. As in so many experiences of the past we were confronted with blasted hopes, and the dark shadow of a deep disappointment settled upon us. So we had no alternative except that of preparing for direct action, whereby we would present our very bodies as a means of laying our case before the conscience of the local and national community. We were not unmindful of the difficulties involved. So we decided to go through a process of self-purification. We started having workshops on nonviolence and repeatedly asked ourselves the questions, "Are you able to accept blows without retaliating?" "Are you able to endure the ordeals of jail?"

We decided to set our direct action program around the Easter season, realizing that with the exception of Christmas, this was the largest shopping period of the year. Knowing that a strong economic withdrawal program would be the by-product of direct action, we felt that this was the best time to bring pressure on the merchants for the needed changes. Then it occurred to us that the March election was ahead, and so we speedily decided to postpone action until after election day. When we discovered that Mr. Connor was in the run-off, we decided again to postpone action so that the demonstrations could not be used to cloud the issues. At this time we agreed to begin our nonviolent witness the day after the run-off.

This reveals that we did not move irresponsibly into direct action. We too wanted to see Mr. Connor defeated; so we went through postponement after postponement to aid in this community need. After this we felt that direct action could be delayed no longer.

You may well ask, "Why direct action? Why sit-ins, marches, etc.? Isn't negotiation a better path?" You are exactly right in your call for negotiation. Indeed, this is the purpose of direct action. Nonviolent direct action seeks to create such a crisis and establish such creative tension that a community that has constantly refused to negotiate is forced to confront the issue. It seeks so to dramatize the issue that it can no longer be ignored. I just referred to the creation of tension as a part of the work of the nonviolent resister. This may sound rather shocking. But I must confess that I am not afraid of the word tension. I have earnestly worked and preached against violent tension, but there is a type of constructive nonviolent tension that is necessary for growth. Just as Socrates felt that it was necessary to create a tension in the mind so that individuals could rise from the bondage of myths and half-truths to the unfettered realm of creative analysis and objective appraisal, we must see the need of having nonviolent gadflies to create the kind of tension in society that will help men rise from the dark depths of prejudice and racism to the majestic heights of understanding and brotherhood. So the purpose of the direct action is to create a situation so crisis-packed that it will inevitably open the door to negotiation. We, therefore, concur with you in your call for negotiation. Too long has our beloved Southland been bogged down in the tragic attempt to live in monologue rather than dialogue.

One of the basic points in your statement is that our acts are untimely. Some have asked, "Why didn't you give the new administration time to act?" The only answer that I can give to this inquiry is that the new administration must be prodded about as much as the outgoing one before it acts. We will be sadly mistaken if we feel that the election of Mr. Boutwell will bring the millennium to Birmingham. While Mr. Boutwell is much more articulate and gentle than Mr. Connor, they are both segregationists dedicated to the task of maintaining the status quo. The hope I see in Mr. Boutwell is that he will be reasonable enough to see the futility of massive resistance to desegregation. But he will not see this without pressure from the devotees of civil rights. My friends, I must say to you that we have not made a single gain in civil rights without determined legal and nonviolent pressure. History is the long and tragic story of the fact that privileged groups seldom give up their privileges voluntarily. Individuals may see the moral light and voluntarily give up their unjust posture; but as Reinhold Niebuhr has reminded us, groups are more immoral than individuals.

We know through painful experience that freedom is never voluntarily given by the oppressor; it must be demanded by the oppressed. Frankly I have never yet engaged in a direct action movement that was "well timed," according to the timetable of those who have not suffered unduly from the disease of segregation. For years now I have heard the word "Wait!" It rings in the ear of every Negro with a piercing familiarity. This "wait" has almost always meant "never." It has been a tranquilizing thalidomide, relieving the emotional stress for a moment, only to give birth to an ill-formed infant of frustration. We must come to see with the distinguished jurist of yesterday that "justice too long delayed is justice denied." We have waited for more than three hundred and forty years for our constitutional and God-given rights. The nations of Asia and Africa are moving with jet-like speed toward the goal of political independence, and we still creep at horse and buggy pace toward the gaining of a cup of coffee at a lunch counter.

I guess it is easy for those who have never felt the stinging darts of segregation to say wait. But when you have seen vicious mobs lynch your mothers and fathers at will and drown your sisters and brothers at whim; when you have seen hate filled policemen curse, kick, brutalize, and even kill your black brothers and sisters with impunity; when you see the vast majority of your twenty million Negro brothers smothering in an airtight cage of poverty in the midst of an affluent society; when you suddenly find your tongue twisted and your speech stammering as you seek to explain to your six-year-old daughter why she can't go to the public amusement park that has just been advertised on television, and see tears welling up in her little eyes when she is told that Funtown is closed to colored children, and see the depressing clouds of inferiority begin to form in her little mental sky, and see her begin to distort her little personality by unconsciously developing a bitterness toward white people; when you have to concoct an answer for a five-year-old son asking in agonizing pathos: "Daddy, why do white people treat colored people so mean?"; when you take a cross country drive and find it necessary to sleep night after night in the uncomfortable corners of your automobile because no motel will accept you; when you are humiliated day in and day out by nagging signs reading "white" men and "colored"; when your first name becomes "nigger" and your middle name becomes "boy" (however old you are) and your last name becomes "John," and when your wife and mother are never given the respected title "Mrs."; when you are harried by day and haunted by night by the fact that you are a Negro, living constantly at tip-toe stance never quite knowing what to expect next, and plagued with inner fears and outer resentments; when you are forever fighting a degenerating sense of "nobodiness";—then you will understand why we find it difficult to wait. There comes a time when the cup of endurance runs over, and men are no longer willing to be plunged into an abyss of injustice where they experience the bleakness of corroding despair. I hope, sirs, you can understand our legitimate and unavoidable impatience.

You express a great deal of anxiety over our willingness to break laws. This is certainly a legitimate concern. Since we so diligently urge people to obey the Supreme Court's decision of 1954 outlawing segregation in the public schools, it is rather strange and paradoxical to find us consciously breaking laws. One may well ask, "How can you advocate breaking some laws and obeying others?" The answer is found in the fact that there are two types of laws. There are *just* laws and there are *unjust* laws. I would be the first to advocate obeying just laws. One has not only a legal but moral responsibility to obey just laws. Conversely, one has a moral responsibility to disobey unjust laws. I would agree with Saint Augustine that "An unjust law is no law at all."

Now what is the difference between the two? How does one determine when a law is just or unjust? A just law is a man-made code that squares with the moral law or the law of God. An unjust law is a code that is out of harmony with the moral law. To put it in the terms of Saint Thomas Aquinas, an unjust law is a human law that is not rooted in eternal and natural law. Any law that uplifts human personality is just. Any law that degrades human personality is unjust. All segregation statutes are unjust because segregation distorts the soul and damages the personality. It gives the segregator a false sense of superiority and the segregated a false sense of inferiority. To use the words of Martin Buber, the great Jewish philosopher, segregation substitutes an "I-it" relationship for the "I-thou" relationship, and ends up relegating persons to the status of things. So segregation is not only politically, economically, and sociologically unsound, but it is morally wrong and sinful. Paul Tillich has said that sin is separation. Isn't segregation an existential expression of man's tragic separation, an expression of his awful estrangement, his terrible sinfulness? So I can urge men to obey the 1954 decision of the Supreme Court because it is morally right, and I can urge them to disobey segregation ordinances because they are morally wrong.

Let us turn to a more concrete example of just and unjust laws. An unjust law is a code that a majority inflicts on a minority that is not binding on itself. This is *difference* made legal. On the other hand a just law is a code that a majority compels a minority to follow that it is willing to follow itself. This is *sameness* made legal.

Let me give another explanation. An unjust law is a code inflicted upon a minority which that minority had no part in enacting or creating because they did not have the unhampered right to vote. Who can say the legislature of Alabama which set up the segregation laws was democratically elected? Throughout the state of Alabama all types of conniving methods are used to prevent Negroes from becoming registered voters and there are some counties without a single Negro registered to vote despite the fact that the Negro constitutes a majority of the population. Can any law set up in such a state be considered democratically structured?

These are just a few examples of unjust and just laws. There are some instances when a law is just on its face but unjust in its application. For instance, I was arrested Friday on a charge of parading without a permit. Now there is nothing wrong with an ordinance which requires a permit for a parade, but when the ordinance is used to preserve segregation and to deny citizens the First Amendment privilege of peaceful assembly and peaceful protest, then it becomes unjust.

I hope you can see the distinction I am trying to point out. In no sense do I advocate evading or defying the law as the rabid segregationist would do. This would lead to anarchy. One who breaks an unjust law must do it *openly, lovingly* (not hatefully as the white mothers did in New Orleans when they were seen on television screaming "nigger, nigger, nigger") and with a willingness to accept the penalty. I submit that an individual who breaks a law that conscience tells him is unjust, and willingly accepts the penalty by staying in jail to arouse the conscience of the community over its injustice, is in reality expressing the very highest respect for law.

Of course there is nothing new about this kind of civil disobedience. It was seen sublimely in the refusal of Shadrach, Meshach, and Abednego to obey the laws of Nebuchadnezzar because a higher moral law was involved. It was practiced superbly by the early Christians who were willing to face hungry lions and the excruciating pain of chopping blocks, before submitting to certain unjust laws of the Roman Empire. To a degree academic freedom is a reality today because Socrates practiced civil disobedience.

We can never forget that everything Hitler did in Germany was "legal" and everything the Hungarian freedom fighters did in Hungary was "illegal." It was "illegal" to aid and comfort a Jew in Hitler's Germany.

But I am sure that, if I had lived in Germany during that time, I would have aided and comforted my Jewish brothers even though it was illegal. If I lived in a communist country today where certain principles dear to the Christian faith are suppressed, I believe I would openly advocate disobeying these antireligious laws.

I must make two honest confessions to you, my Christian and Jewish brothers. First I must confess that over the last few years I have been gravely disappointed with the white moderate. I have almost reached the regrettable conclusion that the Negroes' great stumbling block in the stride toward freedom is not the White Citizens' "Counciler" or the Ku Klux Klanner, but the white moderate who is more devoted to "order" than to justice; who prefers a negative peace which is the absence of tension to a positive peace which is the presence of justice; who constantly says "I agree with you in the goal you seek, but I can't agree with your methods of direct action"; who paternalistically feels that he can set the time-table for another man's freedom; who lives by the myth of time and who constantly advises the Negro to wait until a "more convenient season." Shallow understanding from people of good will is more frustrating than absolute misunderstanding from people of ill will. Lukewarm acceptance is much more bewildering than outright rejection.

I had hoped that the white moderate would understand that law and order exist for the purpose of establishing justice, and that when they fail to do this they become the dangerously structured dams that block the flow of social progress. I had hoped that the white moderate would understand that the present tension in the South is merely a necessary phase of the transition from an obnoxious negative peace, where the Negro passively accepted his unjust plight, to a substance-filled positive peace, where all men will respect the dignity and worth of human personality. Actually, we who engage in nonviolent direct action are not the creators of tension. We merely bring to the surface the hidden tension that is already alive. We bring it out in the open where it can be seen and dealt with. Like a boil that can never be cured as long as it is covered up but must be opened with all its pus-flowing ugliness to the natural medicines of air and light, injustice must likewise be exposed, with all of the tension its exposing creates, to the light of human conscience and the air of national opinion before it can be cured.

In your statement you asserted that our actions, even though peaceful, must be condemned because they precipitate violence. But can this assertion be logically made? Isn't this like condemning the robbed man because his possession of money precipitated the evil act of robbery? Isn't this like condemning Socrates because his unswerving commitment to truth and his philosophical delvings precipitated the misguided popular mind to make him drink the hemlock? Isn't this like condemning Jesus because His unique God consciousness and never-ceasing devotion to His will precipitated the evil act of crucifixion? We must come to see, as federal courts have consistently affirmed, that it is immoral to urge an individual to withdraw his efforts to gain his basic constitutional rights because the quest precipitates violence. Society must protect the robbed and punish the robber.

I had also hoped that the white moderate would reject the myth of time. I received a letter this morning from a white brother in Texas which said: "All Christians know that the colored people will receive equal rights eventually, but is it possible that you are in too great of a religious hurry? It has taken Christianity almost 2000 years to accomplish what it has. The teachings of Christ take time to come to earth." All that is said here grows out of a tragic misconception of time. It is the strangely irrational notion that there is something in the very flow of time that will inevitably cure all ills. Actually time is neutral. It can be used either destructively or constructively. I am coming to feel that the people of ill will have used time much more effectively than the people of good will. We will have to repent in this generation not merely for the vitriolic words and actions of the bad people, but for the appalling silence of the good people. We must come to see that human progress never rolls in on wheels of inevitability. It comes through the tireless efforts and persistent work of men willing to be co-workers with God, and without this hard work time itself becomes an ally of the forces of social stagnation.

We must use time creatively, and forever realize that the time is always ripe to do right. Now is the time to make real the promise of democracy, and transform our pending national elegy into a creative psalm of brotherhood. Now is the time to lift our national policy from the quicksand of racial injustice to the solid rock of human dignity.

You spoke of our activity in Birmingham as extreme. At first I was rather disappointed that fellow clergymen would see my nonviolent efforts as those of the extremist. I started thinking about the fact that I stand in the middle of two opposing forces in the Negro community. One is a force of complacency made up of Negroes who, as a result of long years of oppression, have been so completely drained of self-respect and a sense of "somebodiness" that they have adjusted to segregation, and of a few Negroes in the middle class who, because of a degree of academic and economic security, and because at points they profit by segregation, have unconsciously become insensitive to the problems of the masses. The other force is one of bitterness and hatred and comes perilously close to advocating violence. It is expressed in the various black nationalist groups that are springing up over the nation, the largest and best known being Elijah Muhammad's Muslim movement. This movement is nourished by the contemporary frustration over the continued existence of racial discrimination. It is made up of people who have lost faith in America, who have absolutely repudiated Christianity, and who have concluded that the white man is an incurable "devil." I have tried to stand between these two forces saying that we need not follow the "do-nothingism" of the complacent or the hatred and despair of the black nationalist. There is the more excellent way of love and nonviolent protest. I'm grateful to God that, through the Negro church, the dimension of nonviolence entered our struggle. If this philosophy had not emerged I am convinced that by now many streets of the South would be flowing with floods of blood. And I am further convinced that if our white brothers dismiss us as "rabble rousers" and "outside agitators"—those of us who are working through the channels of nonviolent direct action—and refuse to support our nonviolent efforts, millions of Negroes, out of frustration and despair, will seek solace and security in black nationalist ideologies, a development that will lead inevitably to a frightening racial nightmare.

Oppressed people cannot remain oppressed forever. The urge for freedom will eventually come. This is what has happened to the American Negro. Something within has reminded him of his birthright of freedom; something without has reminded him that he can gain it. Consciously and unconsciously, he has been swept in by what the Germans call the *Zeitgeist*, and with his black brothers of Africa, and his brown and yellow brothers of Asia, South America, and the Caribbean, he is moving with a sense of cosmic urgency toward the promised land of racial justice. Recognizing this vital urge that has engulfed the Negro community, one should readily understand public demonstrations. The Negro has many pent-up resentments and latent frustrations. He has to get them out. So let him march sometime; let him have his prayer pilgrimages to the city hall; understand why he must have sit-ins and freedom rides. If his repressed emotions do not come out in these nonviolent ways, they will come out in ominous expressions of violence. This is not a threat; it is a fact of history. So I have not said to my people, "Get rid of your discontent." But I have tried to say that this normal and healthy discontent can be channeled through the creative outlet of nonviolent direct action. Now this approach is being dismissed as extremist. I must admit that I was initially disappointed in being so categorized.

But as I continued to think about the matter I gradually gained a bit of satisfaction from being considered an extremist. Was not Jesus an extremist in love? "Love your enemies, bless them that curse you, pray for them that despitefully use you." Was not Amos an extremist for justice— "Let justice roll down like waters and righteousness like a mighty stream." Was not Paul an extremist for the gospel of Jesus Christ—"I bear in my body the marks of the Lord Jesus." Was not Martin Luther an extremist— "Here I stand; I can do none other so help me God." Was not John Bunyan an extremist—"I will stay in jail to the end of my days before I make a butchery of my conscience." Was not Abraham Lincoln an extremist—"This nation cannot survive half slave and half free." Was not Thomas Jefferson an extremist—"We hold these truths to be self evident that all men are created equal." So the question is not whether we will be extremist but what kind of extremist will we be. Will we be extremists for hate or will we be extremists for love? Will we be extremists for the preservation of injustice—or will we be extremists for the cause of justice? In that dramatic scene on Calvary's hill three men were crucified. We must never forget that all three were crucified for the same crime—the crime of extremism. Two were extremists for immorality, and thus fell below their environment. The other, Jesus Christ, was an extremist for love, truth, and goodness, and thereby rose above His environment. So, after all, maybe the South, the nation, and the world are in dire need of creative extremists.

I had hoped that the white moderate would see this. Maybe I was too optimistic. Maybe I expected too much. I guess I should have realized that few members of a race that has oppressed another race can understand or appreciate the deep groans and passionate yearnings of those that have been oppressed, and still fewer have the vision to see that injustice must be rooted out by strong, persistent, and determined action. I am thankful, however, that some of our white brothers have grasped the meaning of this social revolution and committed themselves to it. They are still all too small in quantity, but they are big in quality. Some like Ralph McGill, Lillian Smith, Harry Golden, and James Dabbs have written about our struggle in eloquent, prophetic, and understanding terms. Others have marched with us down nameless streets of the South. They have languished in filthy, roach-infested jails, suffering the abuse and brutality of angry policemen who see them as "dirty nigger lovers." They, unlike so many of their moderate brothers and sisters, have recognized the urgency of the moment and sensed the need for powerful "action" antidotes to combat the disease of segregation.

Let me rush on to mention my other disappointment. I have been so greatly disappointed with the white Church and its leadership. Of course there are some notable exceptions. I am not unmindful of the fact that each of you has taken some significant stands on this issue. I commend you, Rev. Stallings, for your Christian stand on this past Sunday, in welcoming Negroes to your worship service on a non-segregated basis. I commend the Catholic leaders of this state for integrating Springhill College several years ago.

But despite these notable exceptions I must honestly reiterate that I have been disappointed with the Church. I do not say that as one of those negative critics who can always find something wrong with the Church. I say it as a minister of the gospel, who loves the Church; who was nurtured in its bosom; who has been sustained by its spiritual blessings and who will remain true to it as long as the cord of life shall lengthen.

I had the strange feeling when I was suddenly catapulted into the leadership of the bus protest in Montgomery several years ago that we would have the support of the white Church. I felt that the white ministers, priests, and rabbis of the South would be some of our strongest allies. Instead, some have been outright opponents, refusing to understand the freedom movement and misrepresenting its leaders; all too many others have been more cautious than courageous and have remained silent behind the anesthetizing security of stained glass windows.

In spite of my shattered dreams of the past, I came to Birmingham with the hope that the white religious leadership of this community would see the justice of our cause and, with deep moral concern, serve as the channel through which our just grievances could get to the power structure. I had hoped that each of you would understand. But again I have been disappointed.

I have heard numerous religious leaders of the South call upon their worshippers to comply with a desegregation decision because it is the law, but I have longed to hear white ministers say follow this decree because integration is morally right and the Negro is your brother. In the midst of blatant injustices inflicted upon the Negro, I have watched white churches stand on the sideline and merely mouth pious irrelevancies and sanctimonious trivialities. In the midst of a mighty struggle to rid our nation of racial and economic injustice, I have heard so many ministers say, "Those are social issues with which the Gospel has no real concern," and I have watched so many churches commit themselves to a completely other-worldly religion which made a strange distinction between body and soul, the sacred and the secular.

So here we are moving toward the exit of the twentieth century with a religious community largely adjusted to the status quo, standing as a tail light behind other community agencies rather than a headlight leading men to higher levels of justice.

I have travelled the length and breadth of Alabama, Mississippi, and all the other Southern states. On sweltering summer days and crisp autumn mornings I have looked at her beautiful churches with their spires pointing heavenward. I have beheld the impressive outlay of her massive religious education buildings. Over and over again I have found myself asking: "Who worships here? Who is their God? Where were their voices when the lips of Governor Barnett dripped with words of interposition and nullification? Where were they when Governor Wallace gave the clarion call for defiance and hatred? Where were their voices of support when tired, bruised, and weary Negro men and women decided to rise from the dark dungeons of complacency to the bright hills of creative protest?"

Yes, these questions are still in my mind. In deep disappointment, I have wept over the laxity of the Church. But be assured that my tears have been tears of love. There can be no deep disappointment where there is not deep love. Yes, I love the Church; I love her sacred walls. How could I do otherwise? I am in the rather unique position of being the son, the grandson, and the great grandson of preachers. Yes, I see the Church as the body of Christ. But, oh! How we have blemished and scarred that body through social neglect and fear of being nonconformist.

There was a time when the Church was very powerful. It was during that period when the early Christians rejoiced when they were deemed worthy to suffer for what they believed. In those days the Church was not merely a thermometer that recorded the ideas and principles of popular opinion; it was a thermostat that transformed the mores of society. Wherever the early Christians entered a town the power structure got disturbed and immediately sought to convict them for being "disturbers of the peace" and "outside agitators." But they went on with the conviction that they were a "colony of heaven" and had to obey God rather than man. They were small in number but big in commitment. They were too God-intoxicated to be "astronomically intimidated." They brought an end to such ancient evils as infanticide and gladiatorial contest.

Things are different now. The contemporary Church is so often a weak, ineffectual voice with an uncertain sound. It is so often the arch-supporter of the status quo. Far from being disturbed by the presence of the Church, the power structure of the average community is consoled by the Church's silent and often vocal sanction of things as they are.

But the judgment of God is upon the Church as never before. If the Church of today does not recapture the sacrificial spirit of the early Church, it will lose its authentic ring, forfeit the loyalty of millions, and be dismissed as an irrelevant social club with no meaning for the twentieth century. I am meeting young people every day whose disappointment with the Church has risen to outright disgust.

Maybe again I have been too optimistic. Is organized religion too inextricably bound to the status quo to save our nation and the world? Maybe I must turn my faith to the inner spiritual Church, the church within the Church, as the true *ecclesia* and the hope of the world. But again I am thankful to God that some noble souls from the ranks of organized religion have broken loose from the paralyzing chains of conformity and joined us as active partners in the struggle for freedom. They have left their secure congregations and walked the streets of Albany, Georgia, with us. They have gone through the highways of the South on torturous rides for freedom. Yes, they have gone to jail with us. Some have been kicked out of their churches and lost the support of their bishops and fellow ministers. But they have gone with the faith that right defeated is stronger than evil triumphant. These men have been the leaven in the lump of the race. Their witness has been the spiritual salt that has preserved the true meaning of the Gospel in these troubled times. They have carved a tunnel of hope through the dark mountain of disappointment.

I hope the Church as a whole will meet the challenge of this decisive hour. But even if the Church does not come to the aid of justice, I have no despair about the future. I have no fear about the outcome of our struggle in Birmingham, even if our motives are presently misunderstood. We will reach the goal of freedom in Birmingham and all over the nation, because the goal of America is freedom. Abused and scorned though we may be, our destiny is tied up with the destiny of America. Before the pilgrims landed at Plymouth, we were here. Before the pen of Jefferson etched across the pages of history the majestic words of the Declaration of Independence, we were here. For more than two centuries our fore-parents labored in this country without wages; they made cotton "king"; and they built the homes of their masters in the midst of brutal injustice and shameful humiliation—and yet out of a bottomless vitality they continued to thrive and develop. If the inexpressible cruelties of slavery could not stop us, the opposition we now face will surely fail. We will win our freedom because the sacred heritage of our nation and the eternal will of God are embodied in our echoing demands.

I must close now. But before closing I am impelled to mention one other point in your statement that troubled me profoundly. You warmly commended the Birmingham police force for keeping "order" and "preventing violence." I don't believe you would have so warmly commended the police force if you had seen its angry violent dogs literally biting six unarmed, nonviolent Negroes. I don't believe you would so quickly commend the policemen if you would observe their ugly and inhuman treatment of Negroes here in the city jail; if you would watch them push and curse old Negro women and young Negro girls; if you would see them slap and kick old Negro men and young Negro boys; if you will observe them, as they did on two occasions, refuse to give us food because we wanted to sing our grace together. I'm sorry that I can't join you in your praise for the police department.

It is true that they have been rather disciplined in their public handling of the demonstrators. In this sense they have been rather publicly "nonviolent." But for what purpose? To preserve the evil system of segregation. Over the last few years I have consistently preached that nonviolence demands that the means we use must be as pure as the ends we seek. So I have tried to make it clear that it is wrong to use immoral means to attain moral ends. But now I must affirm that it is just as wrong, or even more so, to use moral means to preserve immoral ends. Maybe Mr. Connor and his policemen have been rather publicly nonviolent, as Chief Prichett was in Albany, Georgia, but they have used the moral means of nonviolence to maintain the immoral end of flagrant racial injustice. T. S. Eliot has said that there is no greater treason than to do the right deed for the wrong reason.

I wish you had commended the Negro sit-inners and demonstrators of Birmingham for their sublime courage, their willingness to suffer, and their amazing discipline in the midst of the most inhuman provocation. One day the South will recognize its real heroes. They will be the James Merediths, courageously and with a majestic sense of purpose, facing jeering and hostile mobs and the agonizing loneliness that characterizes the life of the pioneer. They will be old, oppressed, battered Negro women, symbolized in a seventy-two year old woman of Montgomery, Alabama, who rose up with a sense of dignity and with her people decided not to ride the segregated buses, and responded to one who inquired about her tiredness with ungrammatical profundity: "My feets is tired, but my soul is rested." They will be young high school and college students, young ministers of the gospel and a host of the elders, courageously and nonviolently sitting in at lunch counters and willingly going to jail for conscience sake. One day the South will know that when these disinherited children of God sat down at lunch counters they were in reality standing up for the best in the American dream and the most sacred values in our Judeo-Christian heritage, and thus carrying our whole nation back to great wells of democracy which were dug deep by the founding fathers in the formulation of the Constitution and the Declaration of Independence.

Never before have I written a letter this long (or should I say a book?). I'm afraid that it is much too long to take your precious time. I can assure you that it would have been much shorter if I had been writing from a comfortable desk, but what else is there to do when you are alone for days in the dull monotony of a narrow jail cell other than write long letters, think strange thoughts, and pray long prayers?

If I have said anything in this letter that is an overstatement of the truth and is indicative of an unreasonable impatience, I beg you to forgive me. If I have said anything in this letter that is an understatement of the truth and is indicative of my having a patience that makes me patient with anything less than brotherhood, I beg God to forgive me.

I hope this letter finds you strong in the faith. I also hope that circumstances will soon make it possible for me to meet each of you, not as an integrationist or a civil rights leader, but as a fellow clergyman and a Christian brother. Let us all hope that the dark clouds of racial prejudice will soon pass away and the deep fog of misunderstanding will be lifted from our fear-drenched communities and in some not too distant tomorrow the radiant stars of love and brotherhood will shine over our great nation with all of their scintillating beauty.

Yours for the cause of
Peace and Brotherhood

MARTIN LUTHER KING, JR.

Censorship

Censorship is at least as old as the ancient world. Protagoras' treatise, *Concerning Gods*, was burned in fifth-century B.C. Athens; the attacks on Cleon in Aristophanes' *The Acharnians* led to an Athenian "censorship" law; and the Romans had, of course, their Censors. But it was the invention of printing which brought forth the more systematic censorship of the modern world.

Until the nineteenth century, political and religious censorship caused the greatest debate. Milton's classic *Areopagitica*—not reprinted here because of its great length—attacked the licensing act of 1643 "in order to deliver the press from the restraints with which it was encumbered." "God," writes Milton, " trusts [man] with the gift of reason to be his own chooser"; he thus presents an argument against censorship of any kind.

To show that political censorship is still an issue today, we do not need to turn to the obvious example of the totalitarian governments. Although we in America tend to take "freedom of the press" for granted, we accept direct censorship for "security" reasons, and, as the essay by David Halberstam shows, our press can be subjected to powerful indirect censorship, both from the government and from itself. The ancient concern with moral censorship—often debated today in terms of pornography and obscenity—is taken up in six of our essays. Plato and Father Gardiner speak for the necessity of censorship in moral education. Walter Lippmann explains it as basically a conservative implement, used to defend the existing order against rebel attack. Henry Miller and Judge Woolsey present different stances against literary censorship; and the Reverend Howard Moody proposes to change the whole moral ground of the controversy, offering a new definition of obscenity itself.

Censorship

PLATO

FROM THE REPUBLIC

We present below two excerpts from The Republic—*one from Book II and one from Book X—the Jowett translation, third edition. For information on Plato and his works, see page 311.*

•

[Socrates is speaking to Adeimantus]

. . .

You know also that the beginning is the most important part of any work, especially in the case of a young and tender thing; for that is the time at which the character is being formed and the desired impression is more readily taken.

Quite true.

And shall we just carelessly allow children to hear any casual tales which may be devised by casual persons, and to receive into their minds ideas for the most part the very opposite of those which we should wish them to have when they are grown up?

We cannot.

Then the first thing will be to establish a censorship of the writers of fiction, and let the censors receive any tale of fiction which is good, and reject the bad; and we will desire mothers and nurses to tell their children the authorised ones only. Let them fashion the mind with such tales, even more fondly than they mould the body with their hands; but most of those which are now in use must be discarded.

Of what tales are you speaking? he said.

You may find a model of the lesser in the greater, I said; for they are necessarily of the same type, and there is the same spirit in both of them.

Very likely, he replied; but I do not as yet know what you would term the greater.

Those, I said, which are narrated by Homer and Hesiod, and the rest of the poets, who have ever been the great story-tellers of mankind.

But which stories do you mean, he said; and what fault do you find with them?

A fault which is most serious, I said; the fault of telling a lie, and, what is more, a bad lie.

But when is this fault committed?

Whenever an erroneous representation is made of the nature of gods and heroes,—as when a painter paints a portrait not having the shadow of a likeness to the original.

Yes, he said, that sort of thing is certainly very blameable; but what are the stories which you mean?

First of all, I said, there was that greatest of all lies, in high places, which the poet told about Uranus, and which was a bad lie too,—I mean what Hesiod says that Uranus did, and how Cronus retaliated on him. The doings of Cronus, and the sufferings which in turn his son inflicted upon him, even if they were true, ought certainly not to be lightly told to young and thoughtless persons; if possible, they had better be buried in silence. But if there is an absolute necessity for their mention, a chosen few might hear them in a mystery, and they should sacrifice not a common [Eleusinian] pig, but some huge and unprocurable victim; and then the number of the hearers will be very few indeed.

Why, yes, said he, those stories are extremely objectionable.

Yes, Adeimantus, they are stories not to be repeated in our State; the young man should not be told that in committing the worst of crimes he is far from doing anything outrageous; and that even if he chastises his father when he does wrong, in whatever manner, he will only be following the example of the first and greatest among the gods.

I entirely agree with you, he said; in my opinion those stories are quite unfit to be repeated.

Neither, if we mean our future guardians to regard the habit of quarrelling among themselves as of all things the basest, should any word be said to them of the wars in heaven, and of the plots and fightings of the gods against one another, for they are not true. No, we shall never mention the battles of the giants, or let them be embroidered on garments; and we shall be silent about the innumerable other quarrels of gods and heroes with their friends and relatives. If they would only believe us we would tell them that quarrelling is unholy, and that never up to this time has there been any quarrel between citizens; this is what old men and old women should begin by telling children; and when they grow up, the poets also should be told to compose for them in a similar spirit. But the narrative of Hephaestus binding Here his mother, or how on another occasion Zeus sent him flying for taking her part when she was being beaten, and all the battles of the gods in Homer—these tales must not be admitted into our State, whether they are supposed to have an allegorical meaning or not. For a young person cannot judge what is allegorical and what is literal; anything that he receives into his mind at that age is likely to become indelible and unalterable; and therefore it is most important that the tales which the young first hear should be models of virtuous thoughts.

There you are right, he replied; but if any one asks where are such models to be found and of what tales are you speaking—how shall we answer him?

I said to him, You and I, Adeimantus, at this moment are not poets, but founders of a State: now the founders of a State ought to know the general forms in which poets should cast their tales, and the limits which must be observed by them, but to make the tales is not their business.

Very true, he said; but what are these forms of theology which you mean?

Something of this kind, I replied:—God is always to be represented as he truly is, whatever be the sort of poetry, epic, lyric or tragic, in which the representation is given.

Right.

And is he not truly good? and must he not be represented as such?

Certainly.

And no good thing is hurtful?

No, indeed.

And that which is not hurtful hurts not?

Certainly not.

And that which hurts not does no evil?

No.

And can that which does no evil be a cause of evil?

Impossible.

And the good is advantageous?

Yes.

And therefore the cause of well-being?

Yes.

It follows therefore that the good is not the cause of all things, but of the good only?

Assuredly.

Then God, if he be good, is not the author of all things, as the many assert, but he is the cause of a few things only, and not of most things that occur to men. For few are the goods of human life, and many are the evils, and the good is to be attributed to God alone; of the evils the causes are to be sought elsewhere, and not in him.

That appears to me to be most true, he said.

Then we must not listen to Homer or to any other poet who is guilty of the folly of saying that two casks

'Lie at the threshold of Zeus, full of lots, one of good, the other of evil lots,'

and that he to whom Zeus gives a mixture of the two

'Sometimes meets with evil fortune, at other times with good;'

but that he to whom is given the cup of unmingled ill,

'Him wild hunger drives o'er the beauteous earth.'

And again—

'Zeus, who is the dispenser of good and evil to us.'

And if any one asserts that the violation of oaths and treaties, which was really the work of Pandarus, was brought about by Athene and Zeus, or that the strife and contention of the gods was instigated by Themis and Zeus, he shall not have our approval; neither will we allow our young men to hear the words of Aeschylus, that

'God plants guilt among men when he desires utterly to destroy a house.'

And if a poet writes of the sufferings of Niobe—the subject of the tragedy in which these iambic verses occur—or of the house of Pelops, or of the Trojan war or on any similar theme, either we must not permit him to say that these are the works of God, or if they are of God, he must devise some explanation of them such as we are seeking; he must say that God did what was just and right, and they were the better for being punished; but that those who are punished are miserable, and that God is the author of their misery—the poet is not to be permitted to say; though he may say that the wicked are miserable because they require to be punished, and are benefited by receiving punishment from God; but that God being good is the author of evil to any one is to be strenuously denied, and not to be said or sung or heard in verse or prose by any one whether old or young in any well-ordered commonwealth. Such a fiction is suicidal, ruinous, impious.

I agree with you, he replied, and am ready to give my assent to the law.

Let this then be one of our rules and principles concerning the gods, to which our poets and reciters will be expected to conform—that God is not the author of all things, but of good only. . . .

[*Socrates is speaking to Glaucon*]

. . .

Hear and judge: The best of us, as I conceive, when we listen to a passage of Homer, or one of the tragedians, in which he represents some pitiful hero who is drawling out his sorrows in a long oration, or weeping, and smiting his breast—the best of us, you know, delight in giving way to sympathy, and are in raptures at the excellence of the poet who stirs our feelings most.

Yes, of course I know.

But when any sorrow of our own happens to us, then you may observe that we pride ourselves on the opposite quality—we would fain be quiet and patient; this is the manly part, and the other which delighted us in the recitation is now deemed to be the part of a woman.

Very true, he said.

Now can we be right in praising and admiring another who is doing that which any one of us would abominate and be ashamed of in his own person?

No, he said, that is certainly not reasonable.

Nay, I said, quite reasonable from one point of view.

What point of view?

If you consider, I said, that when in misfortune we feel a natural hunger and desire to relieve our sorrow by weeping and lamentation, and that this feeling which is kept under control in our own calamities is satisfied and delighted by the poets;—the better nature in each of us, not having been sufficiently trained by reason or habit, allows the sympathetic element to break loose because the sorrow is another's; and the spectator fancies that there can be no disgrace to himself in praising and pitying any one who comes telling him what a good man he is, and making a fuss about his troubles; he thinks that the pleasure is a gain, and why should he be supercilious and lose this and the poem too? Few persons ever reflect, as I should imagine, that from the evil of other men something of evil is communicated to themselves. And so the feeling of sorrow which has gathered strength at the sight of the misfortunes of others is with difficulty repressed in our own.

How very true!

And does not the same hold also of the ridiculous? There are jests which you would be ashamed to make yourself, and yet on the comic stage, or indeed in private, when you hear them, you are greatly amused by them, and are not at all disgusted at their unseemliness;—the case of pity is repeated;—there is a principle in human nature which is disposed to raise a laugh, and this which you once restrained by reason, because you were afraid of being thought a buffoon, is now let out again; and having stimulated the risible faculty at the theatre, you are betrayed unconsciously to yourself into playing the comic poet at home.

Quite true, he said.

And the same may be said of lust and anger and all the other affections, of desire and pain and pleasure, which are held to be inseparable from every action—in all of them poetry feeds and waters the passions instead of drying them up; she lets them rule, although they ought to be con-trolled, if mankind are ever to increase in happiness and virtue.

I cannot deny it.

Therefore, Glaucon, I said, whenever you meet with any of the eulo-gists of Homer declaring that he has been the educator of Hellas, and that he is profitable for education and for the ordering of human things, and that you should take him up again and again and get to know him and regulate your whole life according to him, we may love and honour those who say these things—they are excellent people, as far as their lights extend; and we are ready to acknowledge that Homer is the greatest of poets and first of tragedy writers; but we must remain firm in our conviction that hymns to the gods and praises of famous men are the only poetry which ought to be admitted into our State. For if you go beyond this and allow the honeyed muse to enter, either in epic or lyric verse, not law and the reason of mankind, which by common consent have ever been deemed best, but pleasure and pain will be the rulers in our State. . . .

HAROLD C. GARDINER

Harold C. Gardiner was born in Washington, D.C., in 1904 and educated at St. Andrew on Hudson, Woodstock College, and Cambridge University, where he received the Ph.D. In 1935 he was ordained as a priest in the Catholic Church. He has been Board Chairman of the Catholic Book of the Month Club, a member of the Catholic Press Association, and since 1940, literary editor of America, *a national Catholic weekly. His many books include* The Great Books: A Christian Appraisal, *4 vols. (1949–1952);* Fifty Years of the American Novel *(1951);* Catholic Viewpoint on Censorship *(1957), from which we reprint Chapter 1 below;* In All Conscience, *with F. Getlein (1960); and* Movies, Words and Art *(1961).*

AUTHORITY AND THE ROLE OF COERCION

It may seem like taking a very long running start indeed in order to essay a modest broad jump, but any discussion of the problems of modern, and especially American, censorship cannot be sensibly undertaken without laying first a basis for argumentation by sketching the Catholic philosophy on the state and on human freedom. It is to be hoped that the term "Catholic philosophy" will not annoy those not of the Catholic faith who may chance to read these words. The phrase is not used in the sense of describing a "sectarian" system of thought. The philosophy referred to is indeed more aptly termed the *philosophia perennis,* for its roots lie far back in the Judaic and Greco-Roman world, were developed by the medieval Christian philosophers, and have borne fruit in the thinking of the framers of our Declaration of Independence. Many philosophers, political scientists, thinkers on the problems of government and the relations of Church and state hold, at least in general outline, the philosophy of the state and of human freedom that will be sketched in this and the following chapter.

To begin at the beginning, this philosophy holds that the state is a "natural" institution. This means that man, by his very nature, spontaneously but inevitably forms a community with his fellow men; that man is, of his very nature, a "social" being. Since man's nature comes from God, and since man's impulses toward communal living are a natural consequence of his being man, this gravitation is also God-given. This is seen most obviously in the institution of marriage. The first society to which man is naturally drawn, both by the exigencies of his nature and by his historical development, is the familial society. This seminal society, however, proves itself to be inadequate for the fulfillment of man's deepest desires and needs, and so man is induced again by the very bent of his nature to associate with other families—for mutual sociability, protection, comfort, development, and so on.

But, together with his impulses toward societal living, man, even in society, still possesses his individual will, his particular desires and ambitions. Given this fact, itself another God-given attribute, society is faced immediately with the problem of a number of individuals and families trying to get along together for some common purpose, toward some mutually agreed goal—protection against outside inimical forces, let us say, or the development of agricultural ways and means. Obviously there arises the necessity of some compromise; individual differences must be resolved; somebody, or some group selected to deliberate and speak for the whole community, has to make the decisions. And so arises, just as naturally and just as clearly God-given in origin as man's societal nature itself, the institution of authority.

It is not to be thought that authority in a community takes its origin from deficiency. The necessity of authority does not spring from sin—as though only in a group of fallible and fumbling human beings is authority a necessity. Far from being a necessary evil, authority results from the very perfection of the human beings it is destined to weld into community life. Authority arises from the fact of each individual's free will:

it is because each one has free will that individuality must be harnessed, so to speak, if the individuals are to pull as a team for the cohesion and advancement of the community.

Authority in a community, then, has more than what is called a "substitutional" function—that is, a function that makes up for some inherent deficiency in the body to be governed. To be sure, some of the obvious instances of authority that spring to mind show us authority being exercised because there is some sort of "deficiency" in those governed. So parents, for example, exercise their authority over minor children because the children cannot yet know what is best for them. But even if children became overnight as wise and kind and prudent as their parents, parental authority would still exist (though its open exercise might be minimized) because of the very fact that common action in the family demands a source from which decisions must come.

Now the reason for this rather long disquisition on a fundamental concept, which most men of good will find no difficulty in accepting, is that a consequence that is largely overlooked may be brought to light. The consequence is simply and perhaps, to some, startlingly this: authority is not only to be respected but *loved*. If the common purpose of a family—mutual love, peace, prosperity, and so on—is a purpose worthy of love, then the authority that directs the family to that purpose is worthy of love, and not only because authority is the human instrument through which the common purpose may be achieved, but because, just as the family and its essential purposes are natural (i.e., God-instituted), so the authority is natural (i.e., God-instituted).

This is true not merely from a consideration of the origin of society and of the authority which is necessary for the very existence of society, but from a consideration of the purpose or end for which society exists. That end or purpose, in general, is the common good, the good of society as a whole as distinguished from the good of the individuals who make up the whole. Individuals dwell in familial society in such fashion that desires, ambitions, modes of action that might be most delectable for the individual are forgone, sacrificed (or sublimated, as the current phrase goes) for the sake of the good of the whole family. Mother's craving for the mink coat or father's passion for golf yields—or should—to the needs of the family for decent prosperity. Individuals and families dwelling in civil society also conspire, or should conspire, to a common end, which we call the common good and which can be summed up in the phrase "peace and prosperity." An individual or a family yields to some extent its dominion over its wealth and property through the machinery of taxes, for example, not because they like to, but because it is for the common good.

Authority, therefore, is to be respected and loved, not only because it comes, reductively, as the philosophers would say, from God, but because, in its legitimate exercise, it also leads (reductively) to God, because such exercise of authority leads to the common good which is also willed by God.

This philosophy of authority is not only down-to-earth, it reaches to heaven in its sublimity. It may sound like the veriest idealism, but it is not for that reason utopian. Common sense alone will tell us that, if authority is not loved, the vagaries to which any exercise of human authority is subject will sooner or later bring that authority to be feared or hated. It is perhaps almost inevitable, because of the earthiness of our human emotions, that a neutral and sort of bloodless respect for authority cannot long hold the field. This is especially true since authority is not infrequently vested in a person or a party one feels he cannot validly respect. In such a case, if the *principle* of authority is not loved, its imposition by one who is not respected comes easily to bring law and order under fear, suspicion, and hatred. Then one will obey because he must, not because he loves the common good which is, of itself, as the goal of societal action, lovable.

As has been hinted above, it does not follow from this line of thought that any and every *enactment* of authority must be loved. Some enactments may be onerous (such as the paying of taxes) but just; in this case the enactment must be respected, not only in thought, but in actual fulfillment. Other enactments may be ill-considered (such as our late Prohibition law) or unjust; in this case there is recourse, in a properly constituted state, to redress. So we have the system of constitutional checks and balances by which the enactments of the legislative arm are subject to review by the judiciary; thus the goal of the common good, though lost sight of for a time, may be restored as the only proper purpose of the state.

But the principle remains unshaken. Authority, as the necessary instrument by which the parts of the societal whole may conspire to a common end, is an object of love.

The particular relevance of this principle to the problem of censorship will become clear, it is to be hoped, throughout the whole course of this book. Its particular relevance here depends on another aspect of law and authority which must now fit into this preliminary chapter.

One of the essential postulates of law is authority's coercive power. If a society is to strive with any hope of success toward a common goal —peace and prosperity in a commonwealth—the authority governing that society must not only be able to pass laws and to reassess those laws constantly as circumstances change (the role of the interpretations of our Supreme Court); it must also be enabled to enforce those laws and to exact penalties for their violation. This is obviously the point at which respect for authority, let alone love for it, as we have been considering above, comes in for its severest test. It is one thing to be all in favor of sane traffic laws and even to love them in a theoretical sort of way while you are snug in your armchair or gleefully watching some road hog getting his comeuppance at the hands of a traffic cop. It is quite another thing to love the authority that slaps a ticket on you because you temporarily forgot your respect for (and love of) the law. Coercion is never pleasant for those being coerced and, quite obviously, coercion can overstep proper bounds and turn into injustice and tyranny. But coercion that is exercised as a means to prevent the frustration of the common good is as worthy of respect and love as is the authority it is designed to uphold.

One consideration that may serve to put the coercive aspect of law and authority into proper perspective is a consideration of the educative or pedagogical quality of coercion. Restrictions merely for the sake of restriction are never proper or valid, either morally or politically. Such restrictions would be purely the result of the whim of the authority— or, worse, of malice. Restrictions are valid only if they are for the sake of a greater good, a greater liberty. To be restrained to drive your car at not more than fifty miles an hour is an improper infringement of your liberty, *unless* that very restriction allows drivers in general (and pedestrians) a reasonably assured freedom from danger to life and limb.

This principle is so valid that not even the restrictions which God's law puts on our human actions are good *merely* because they are restrictions. The negative precepts of the Ten Commandments look always to a positive freedom. "Thou shalt not commit adultery" means that if you avoid this threat to the stability, happiness, and holiness of married union you will be freed from a burden so that you may go on from there to the fullness of married life as God intends it. The negative precepts, accordingly, may be looked upon as simply clearing away the roadblocks thrown up by our pride and sensuality so that the greater freedom may operate, and that freedom is positive and glorious: "You shall *love* God with your whole heart and with your whole soul and with all your mind, and your neighbor as yourself," or, more gloriously still, "as Christ has loved you."

If the coercive aspect of law and authority is looked on in this way, as a means toward a greater freedom, the pedagogical aspect of coercion becomes clear. Coercion by way of consequence instructs the members of a society (family or state), although the instruction may be painful, that there *is* a common good which the offending member may have been habitually ignoring or temporarily forgetting. St. Thomas Aquinas has much to say on this matter of the pedagogical value of coercion, especially in his *Summa Theologica* (1a–2ae, 95, 1). Here, for instance, is one commentary on the teaching of the Saint:

"Every man needs education and virtuous training. Paternal training, whose proper instrument is persuasion, provides sufficiently for the training of youths who are prone to virtue; on the contrary, those who are prone to vice must be prevented by coercion from doing wrong. . . . By compelling bad boys from doing wrong, a twofold result is secured: first, the tranquillity of honest people is assured; secondly, the bad boys themselves get used to acting honestly, so that they may finally become virtuous, having become able to do voluntarily what they previously did by fear of punishment.

"This elevated conception of the pedagogical function of coercion rests upon the psychological fact that a good habit generated by fear, although non-virtuous in its origin, makes virtue easier, the substitution of good will for fear taking place easily when the exterior acts of virtue have become habitual. Coercion, in the long run, paves the way for persuasion, because habitual automatism turns to voluntariness."[1]

The skeptic or the cynic will probably retort that this concept of the pedagogical value of coercion is a pipe dream and that it is extremely doubtful that the wrongdoer is ever so persuaded by force and restraint that he comes to will and love the good. This happy result is certainly to be discerned frequently enough in the sanctuary of conscience: the sinner, restrained by the fear of hell, for instance, can and does come to love the good. But the point of this discussion is quite other. It may be that in the sphere of external activity—in civic, social, and political life—the mere fact of restraint or coercion rarely convinces the wrongdoer of the good to be desired. It may be that the extortionist or the blackmailer or the arsonist, clapped into jail to restrain his felonious acts, is simply biding his time and meditating ways and means to resume his ill-advised manner of life.

But those who are not so coerced, those who are concerned with the problems of respect for law and authority—they are the ones who ought to be able to consider with dispassion this whole matter of the coercive aspect of authority. The sorry fact of the matter is, however, that all too frequently the very ones who ought to be concerned with the very highest and most exalted concepts of the law are often the ones who, perhaps all unwittingly, are whittling away at one of the very foundations of respect for law—the foundation of its coercive power. So, in this matter of censorship, protests by such organizations as the American Civil Liberties Union against any and all exercises of "censorship" all too often sound as though they are based on the assumption that all coercion exercised by authority is a bad and evil thing, both in itself and in its consequences. Thus, for instance, the following statement issued by the Authors League of America (as reported in the New York *Times* for May 9, 1957):

"[The League has noted] with increasing concern, in the decade since the Second World War, a drift in our national life toward censorship. . . . The impetus in this authoritarian drift is coming mainly from groups who above all should hold totalitarianism in abhorrence: a few religious organizations and a few patriotic organizations, where zeal has overcome wisdom . . .

---

[1] Yves Simon, *Nature and Functions of Authority* (Milwaukee: Marquette University Press, 1940), p. 54.

"The Authors League denies the right of any individual or group in the United States to set limits on the freedom to write, which includes the freedom of publication, distribution and performance of writings."

The obvious drift of this statement, of course, is directed toward groups which endeavor to "censor" outside the operation of the law; but two overtones, it is to be suspected, are also evident. The first is that "censorship" is *ipso facto* "totalitarian." This is a point to be proved, not merely asserted. Beyond that seems to lie the confusion against which this whole chapter is directed: namely, that all coercion or restraint imposed by society on the individual is wrong.

This consideration, however, needs further development in the following chapter, in which we shall discuss more fully the problem of human freedom in the face of legitimate authority. Underlying the false estimate of coercion as being merely a negating and restrictive aspect of authority is the equally false assumption that whatever, especially in a democracy, curtails freedom (but what *type* of freedom is rarely defined, though here lies the specific problem) impedes "progress." The Catholic concept, on the other hand, holds that the very idea of human progress implies necessarily the correlative idea of measure and restraint, internally in a man's own conscience and motives, and externally through the operation of law and of social forces which are not formally legal.

The suspicion that the coercive aspects of authority and law are not to be tolerated by free men is a holdover from the philosophic liberalism of the nineteenth century. The most familiar expression of this bent of mind is found in the cant expression that "ideas have to make their way in the market place." Perhaps the most cogent phrasing of this philosophy is found in the following passage:

"If we refrain from coercing a man for his own good, it is not because his good is indifferent to us, but because it cannot be furthered by coercion. The difficulty is founded on the nature of the good, itself, which on its personal side depends on the spontaneous flow of feeling checked and guided not by external restraint, but by rational self-control. To try to form character by coercion is to destroy it in the making. Personality is not built up from without but grows from within, and the function of the outer order is not to create it, but to provide for it the most suitable conditions for growth. Thus, to the common question whether it is possible to make men good by Act of Parliament, the reply is that it is not possible to compel morality because morality is the act or character of a free agent, but that it is possible to create the conditions under which morality can develop, and among these not the least important is freedom from compulsion by others."[2]

Commenting on this statement, Yves Simon pithily remarks: "The point

---

[2] L. T. Hobhouse, *Liberalism* (New York: Holt, 1911), p. 143.

is, precisely, that good habits possibly determined by coercion are to be numbered among these 'conditions under which morality can develop.' "[3]

Again, these liberals and their modern progeny claim that "an absolute freedom of thought and expression [is] justified, their idea being that in any circumstances whatever, truth can but profit by unrestricted freedom."[4] Let truth go out and jostle with error in the market place, they proclaim, do not restrain or limit error and the expression of it, and the truth will always win out. Now, certainly the Catholic position entertains the utmost respect for the power of truth (*magna est veritas et praevalebit*) and for its ultimate triumph, but that respect is not so naïve as to believe that here and now, in these circumstances, when the truth should already have won and its delayed victory imperils the common good, error must be left uncontrolled. Professor Simon puts his finger on this liberal philosophical error when he says:

"The contribution of error to the development of truth is but a happy occurrence, whose regularity is not guaranteed by any steady principle. Liberals ascribe to accidental occurrences a regularity that accident does not admit of. At the *heart of Liberalism* lies an almost religious belief in a kind of Demiurge immanent in the stream of contingent events, or better, identical with the very stream of contingencies. . . . Owing to this benevolent Spirit of Nature, contingency and chance are supposed to result indefectibly in happy achievements. Wrong use of the human freedom, in the long run at least, does not matter. Regarding both truth-values and economic values, the Liberal confidently relies upon the *laissez faire laissez passer* system. Liberalism is an *optimistic naturalism*."[5]

Another aspect of the "optimistic naturalism" of philosophic liberalism is the rather naïve idolatry of the power of mere education, and by that is meant any educative process that insists exclusively on the freedom to examine and learn. With reference to the problem of censorship, the argument would run that if only "good" books, movies, and what not were made increasingly widespread for the consuming public they would inevitably drive out the "bad." This stand is based, as will be evident, on the prior assumption that the truth will always vanquish error if allowed to compete on an equal footing. But any "equal footing" rests on the further assumption that all men are equal in taste, inclination to virtue, powers of self-control, and a host of other qualities. Surely it is a fact of experience, which even the foes of all and every censorship are themselves constrained to admit, that some people who have indeed been exposed to "good" literature throughout many years of education still seem to prefer the "art" and "girlie" magazines to the reasonably priced classics that can be found on the very same newsstands.

This is not to underestimate the power of education but simply to restate that the educative process, no less than the process of law, neces-

---

[3] *Op. cit.*, p. 56.   [4] *Ibid.*, p. 59.   [5] *Ibid.*, pp. 61–62.

sarily entails a restrictive or coercive element. If the goal of education is a glorious and positive "do"—*do* grow into the full stature of integral manhood—it can be reached only by some inculcation of many a "don't"—*don't* dissipate your energies, debauch your potentialities by running after goals that are unworthy of a man. C. S. Lewis, in his thoughtful and challenging little book, *The Abolition of Man,* has much to say on this entire subject. Here is a small passage which underlines the thought that education alone is not enough to make a man virtuous:

"It still remains true that no justification of virtue will enable a man to be virtuous. Without the aid of *trained* [emphasis supplied] emotions, the intellect is powerless against the animal organism. I had sooner play cards with a man who was quite sceptical about ethics, but bred to believe that 'a gentleman does not cheat,' than against an irreproachable moral philosopher who had been brought up among sharpers. In battle it is not syllogisms that will keep the reluctant nerves and muscles to their post in the third hour of the bombardment."[6]

But the training of the emotions, of the will, of just and noble sentiments, what Plato calls the "spirited element," is something that implicates all sorts of restraining elements in education. The young trainee cannot be thrown out, naked and unarmed, into the market place of clashing ideas and expected to see at once—or perhaps ever—the beauty and force of the truth. Mere exposure to "facts" will never add up to human education. As Mr. Lewis remarks of one he calls the "Innovator" (he is the holder of the thesis that man will always obey the truth if exposed to it): "[He] is trying to get a conclusion in the imperative mood out of premises in the indicative mood; and though he continues trying to all eternity he cannot succeed, for the thing is impossible."[7] To put the potential reader, for instance, in the presence of "good" and "bad" literature, before an openly pornographic book and a wholesome one, and say, "See, the one is good and the other bad," will never, of itself, induce in the reader the conclusion, "I ought to read the one and avoid the other." The premises for that conclusion have to come from a deeper source than the mere struggle between truth and error in the market place. Part of the source is the restrictive or coercive aspect of both law and education.

This stage of our discussion leads immediately into the thorny problem of the proper balance between law (and education) and human freedom. Before we go on to that, however, let us try to gather together some conclusions.

The Catholic viewpoint is that law is to be loved because it is rational and because of its origin and purpose. Its origin is from God; its ultimate purpose is rationally to assure greater freedom.

---

[6] C. S. Lewis, *The Abolition of Man* (New York: Macmillan, 1947), p. 15.
[7] *Ibid.*, p. 20.

One of the necessary postulates of law (or of the exercise of law through authority) is the community's coercive power, the restriction and punishment of evil-doing, of infringements of the law. This onerous element is not less to be loved than the expansive aspects, for it is destined for the same purpose, to facilitate the exercise of freedom.

It follows, therefore, that society, which has the right and duty to establish laws for the common good, has, by the same title, the right *and the duty* to exercise coercion. It would seem superfluous to emphasize this truth were it not for the fact that most of the controversy about censorship seems to rest fundamentally at exactly this crux. A great number of those who oppose censorship in any shape or form deny implicitly (though they may never advert to the fact) that society has the *right* to censor—especially the state in a pluralistic society like the one in which we live. We aver in these pages that the state not only has the *right* but is solemnly bound by the *duty* to censor, under certain circumstances.

It seems odd that this can apparently be the stand of opponents of censorship, since they are quite ready to admit other coercive powers of the state. No one of them would question the right of the state to arrest traffic-law violators, for instance, or to throw dope peddlers into jail, but when it comes to any restrictions or controls in the matter of freedom of expression, they will not only deny the state's duty to protect the common good, but will even call into question its right.

It is hard, no doubt, to reconcile the divergent statements of such organizations as the American Civil Liberties Union. In the "Statement on Censorship Activity by Private Organizations and the National Office of Decent Literature," issued to the press in May 1957, for instance, we read, on the one hand: "Since *any kind* [emphasis supplied] of censorship infringes that constitutionally guaranteed freedom of the press which protects the free exchange of ideas in our country, it is imperative that the American people be warned of the danger in which their freedom stands." Again: "The First and Fourteenth Amendments to the United States Constitution, and the constitutions of the several States, prohibit governmental abridgment of freedom of the press. If one may read, one must be able to buy; if one may buy, others must be able to print and sell." But on the other hand, the American Civil Liberties Union is constrained to recognize that the phrase, "any kind of censorship," is far too wide, for it goes on to state: "If curbs are to be placed on freedom of the press, and these curbs must be based on a clear and present danger of a substantive harm from the publication, they can be imposed only by our courts, through full legal process."

If the Constitution prohibits governmental abridgment of freedom of the press, how can the courts be exercising "full legal process" when they impose curbs, even under "clear and present danger"?

I do not see how the Union can have it both ways, and I believe their fundamental drive is to abolish all kinds of control on all possible kinds of expression and that their stand is that the "full legal process" under which the courts now act is itself unconstitutional. And this, if I am not reading too sinister a purpose into the convictions of men of good will, springs, it seems incontrovertible to me, from a false concept of the nature of coercion in the authority of government.

A further example. In *The Freedom to Read*, published for the National Book Committee, the authors state: "We have argued on philosophic grounds [we shall advert to these arguments in our next chapter] that censorship is unsound, impractical and undesirable." Yet in the very next sentence they go on to say: "On political grounds, recognizing that censorship in the broad sense has been and is being practiced, we shall consider how its operation can be kept strictly in conformity with law and the preservation of rights, in order that it shall not impede directly or indirectly the freedom of expression by which, among other consequences, the dangers of censorship may become more generally recognized."[8] But, again, here is an inconsistency. If censorship is indeed "unsound, impractical and undesirable," then any "law" dealing with it ought to be concerned wholly and solely with eliminating it, lock, stock, and barrel.

The thought will not die that we are back at a basic misapprehension —that any restriction of "freedom" is a block to "progress," and hence that any coercive aspects of the law are always, by their nature, bad aspects and should therefore not only be held to a minimum, which all admit, but eliminated altogether.

Inevitably we come at this point to a consideration of "freedom." Is it an absolute? What is it? Is it the only and essentially indispensable atmosphere under which "progress" can flourish? Before we essay some thoughts on this and, obviously, on its connection with the problems of censorship, let us close this chapter with a pertinent thought from St. Thomas:

"Laws are passed to ensure the smooth running of the commonwealth. Unrestricted rights are not allowed in any civil constitution. Even in a democratic state, where the whole people exercise power, rights are not absolute but relative, though from the equal liberty of all subjects under the law the state may be described as predominantly equalitarian. The statutes passed by a democracy may be just, not because they reach pure and perfect justice, but because they fit the purpose of the regime."[9]

Perhaps, after all is said and done, the opponents of all and any censorship, who are, it would seem, the proponents of freedom as an absolute,

---

8 By Richard McKeon, Robert K. Merton, and Walter Gellhorn (New York: R. R. Bowker Co., 1957), p. 11.
9 Commentary in *V Ethics*, lect. 2. This quotation from St. Thomas is taken from the rich store to be found in *St. Thomas Aquinas: Philosophical Texts*, by Thomas Gilby (New York: Oxford Press, 1951), especially from the sections on "Law" and "Community and Society," pp. 352–93.

are devoted to a false ideal of law which does not take sufficiently into account the fact that law, as we know it, is for poor, fallible, striving human beings who *need* the pedagogy of coercion and restraint no less than the expansive skies of liberty and freedom.

WALTER LIPPMANN

Walter Lippmann has been called the Dean of American newspapermen. Born in 1889, he was educated at Harvard and then taught philosophy there as an assistant to George Santayana. He joined the staff of The New Republic *at its founding in 1914, interrupted his journalistic career to serve as assistant to the Secretary of War—doing special work on peace negotiating—and then moved to an editorial position on the* New York World. *In 1931 he joined the staff of the* New York Herald Tribune. *His writings have been syndicated in newspapers throughout the country, and his column "Today and Tomorrow" won him Pulitzer Prizes in 1958 and 1962. The 1958 award cited the "wisdom, perception, and high sense of responsibility with which he has commented for many years on national and international affairs." He has also received numerous honorary degrees and such foreign decorations as the Legion of Honor from France and the Order of Leopold from Norway. His many books include* Liberty and the News *(1920),* Public Opinion *(1922),* The Good Society *(1937),* The Public Philosophy *(1955),* The Coming Tests with Russia *(1961), and* Western Unity and the Common Market *(1962). The essay we present below is Chapter 8 of* Men of Destiny, *first published in 1928.*

THE NATURE OF THE BATTLE
OVER CENSORSHIP

Not long ago I was at work in my study writing, when, as was her custom, the lady across the way burst into song. There was something about that lady's voice which prevented the use of a human intelligence, and I called upon the janitor to give her my compliments and then silence her. She replied with a good deal of conviction that this was a free country and she would sing when the spirit moved her; if I did not like it, I could retire to the great open spaces.

The lady and I both love liberty, I think. But she loves her liberty whereas I love mine. There does not seem to be a theory of liberty which can be used to decide between us. Lord Acton, for example, was a great historian of the problem of liberty, but as between the lady and myself, I see no help from him when he says that "by liberty I mean the assurance that every man shall be protected in doing what he believes his duty against the influence of authority and majorities, custom and opinion." It was the lady's custom to feel it her duty to practice her singing at the precise moment when I felt it my duty to write an article. The janitor never seemed so completely convinced as I was that mine was much the higher form of duty until he had had a chance on the day after Christmas to compare the lady's gift with mine. Then apparently he read John Stuart Mill, learned that "the sole end for which mankind are warranted, individuals or collectively, in interfering with the liberty of action of any of their number, is self-protection." I got protection and it cost me a box of Corona Coronas, twenty-five dollars, and an old overcoat.

I am somewhat persuaded that no one has ever succeeded in defining the area of liberty more precisely than I did in this case. The classic attempts by Milton and Mill end, if you examine them, in vagueness and compromise. Milton, for example, would have granted freedom of opinion to every one but the Papists and the Atheists; Mill was prepared to suppress any one who did "evil" to "others," leaving it to the others, it would seem, to decide what was evil. Had Milton been asked why Papists and Atheists should be denied the freedom he asked for Dissenters, he would probably have said that they would abuse their freedom. Mill argued that if you gave too much liberty to some men there would be none left for other men. He may have been right, but when you admit this to be true you have disposed of the claim that there is a clear and universal doctrine of liberty.

A theory of liberty is usually stated in general terms, but in fact its real meaning in concrete cases is derived from the nature of these cases themselves. Milton worked out his doctrine of liberty as a weapon which the Puritans could use against the Stuarts; Mill wrote for Victorian England during the ascendancy of the middle class, in that short interval between the downfall of the squirearchy and before the rise of the great corporations. He addressed himself to a section of the English people which did not then contemplate the possibility of really serious divisions of opinion.

The history of Luther's ideas shows how closely related is a theory of liberty to the specific needs of the man who preaches it. When Luther first came into conflict with the Holy See he stood very much alone. There was at that time no Protestant Church, the German princes had not taken him up, he had not worked out a Protestant theology. At this juncture he made his famous utterance on behalf of liberty, saying that "Princes are not to be obeyed when they command submission to superstitious errors, but their aid is not to be invoked in support of the word of God." Facing a bull of excommunication, living in fear of assassination, he preached that heretics must be converted by Scripture and not by fire, otherwise the hangman would be the greatest doctor. But later when the religious revolution had won in Germany, it developed, like all revolutions, beyond anything that Luther had desired. In the name of that right of private judgment and dissent which he had proclaimed against Leo X, there arose heresies within the heresy, the sects of Zwingli and the Anabaptists, and the red jacobinism of the Peasants' War. Luther was horrified at these threats against the security of the Church he had founded. "Out of the gospel and divine truth come devilish lies," he cried, "from the blood in our body comes corruption." The devil, he said, having failed to put him down by the help of the Pope, was seeking his destruction through the preachers of treason and blood. He exhorted the nobles to crush the rebels without mercy. "If there are innocent persons among them, God will surely save and preserve them as He did with Lot and Jeremiah."

Lord Acton, from whom I have taken this account, says that in appealing to the sword Luther had in reality reverted to his original teaching, and that the notion of liberty, whether civil or religious, was hateful to his despotic nature and contrary to his interpretation of Scripture. It remains a fact that Luther had at one time preached the revolutionary doctrine of the right of private judgment, and that this doctrine was worked out to justify his own rebellion against Rome.

II

Heywood Broun and Margaret Leech say in their book on Anthony Comstock that "anything remotely bearing upon sex was to his mind obscene." This helps to explain Comstock, but it is quite misleading if it is meant as an account of Comstockery. This crusading is not a one-man affair, and the psychopathology of the vice crusader does not, I think, give a convincing explanation of his success in enlisting the support of the community. Obviously American society from the Civil War to the World War was not composed entirely or even largely of Anthony Comstocks. Yet for forty years the vice crusade was carried on with the consent of the community punctuated only here and there by the jeers of a minority. Comstock got his support not because of what he

believed about the uncleanness of sex but because of what he did toward
suppressing those particular manifestations of sex which respectable people wished to have suppressed.

The patrons of his society, the public officials, the clergy, and the
fathers and mothers who backed him were not much interested in, and
many were no doubt embarrassed by, his idiotic assaults on September
Morn and the nude classics. They were thinking of the tons of plainly
indecent books and pictures he destroyed rather than the occasional
masterpiece which he insulted.

A realistic study of censorship will show, I believe, that it is almost
wholly directed against the unadjusted outsiders. It is not the idea as
such which the censor attacks, whether it be heresy or radicalism or
obscenity. He attacks the circulation of the idea among the classes which
in his judgment are not to be trusted with the idea.

The censor himself may be cited as proof of this assertion that the
danger is believed to be not in the idea itself but in the peculiar corrupti-
bility of a certain part of the community. The censor exposes himself
daily to every corrupting influence. I do not know, of course, what goes
on in the dreams of those who compile the Index Expurgatorius, spend
their days reading bolshevik pamphlets in the Department of Justice,
see all the prohibited films and read all the dirty books. They may in their
unconscious minds come to doubt God, insult the flag, and despise
chastity. But whatever the private consequences may be, outwardly the
censors remain doubly convinced of the sanctity of the institution they
are protecting. No one has ever been known to decline to serve on a
committee to investigate radicals on the ground that so much exposure
to their doctrines would weaken his patriotism, nor on a vice commission on the ground that it would impair his morals. Anything may
happen inside the censor, but what counts is that in his outward appearances after his ordeal by temptation he is more than ever a paragon of
the conforming virtues. Perhaps his appetites are satisfied by an inverted
indulgence, but to a clear-sighted conservative that does not really
matter. The conservative is not interested in innocent thoughts. He is
interested in loyal behavior.

Apart from certain residual tabus which have the power to cause irrational fear, the essence of censorship has always been, not to suppress
subversive ideas as such, but to withhold them from those who are young
or unprivileged or otherwise undependable. The purpose of censorship
is to prevent overt rebellion against the state, the church, the family, and
the economic system. Where there is no danger of overt action there is
rarely any interference with freedom.

That is why there has so often been amazing freedom of opinion within
an aristocratic class which at the same time sanctioned the ruthless suppression of heterodox opinion among the common people. When the
Inquisition was operating most effectively against the bourgeois who

had lapsed into heresy, the princes of the Church and the nobles enjoyed the freedom of the Renaissance. There are indeed historians who point out that the Inquisition was not concerned with Jews, Mohammedans and infidels but almost entirely with Christians who had lapsed. For the evil which the Inquisition attacked was not disbelief as such but disloyalty to the Church.

An old Roman maxim said: *de internis non iudicat praetor*, the judge is not concerned with subjective things. Neither is the censor. He does not bother about the internal freedom of an aristocracy, the free speculation which has long been practiced within the Jesuit order, the private candor of politicians and journalists, the unimpressed realism of bankers about business men. Opinions in such a medium are free because they are safe. There is no organic disposition to run wild because the mind is free.

For purposes of argument the advocates of censorship will often pretend that they are worried about the intrinsic viciousness of an idea. Advocates of censorship are often muddle-headed and therefore not clear as to why they are doing what they are doing. But actions speak louder than words, and when you look at censorship as a whole it is plain that it is actually applied in proportion to the vividness, the directness, and the intelligibility of the medium which circulates the subversive idea. The moving picture is perhaps the most popular medium of expression there is; it speaks clearly to the lowest and the most immature intelligence. It is therefore forbidden to present many scenes which the theater is free to present. There are less theaters and the seats cost more. In America, at least, the theater is now largely confined to the metropolitan centers, and it is patronized by a well-to-do, comparatively mature, and sophisticated audience. It is only when a play goes into a long run and begins to be seen by the very general public, as was "The Captive," for example, that the authorities are compelled to pay much attention to protests from the guardians of morality. The scandal about "The Captive" was at bottom its success. Had it been played for a limited run in a theater attended by the sophisticated, it would not have been clubbed to death. But when "The Captive" had run four months on Broadway it had exhausted its mature audience; it was then being patronized by much simpler people, and it was from them and from those who heard from them that the demand for suppression arose and gradually became irresistible.

The newspapers and magazines of general circulation are much freer than the stage. They discuss regularly matters which if presented on the stage would bring out the police reserves. Men are much less moved by what they read than by what they see, and literacy is a recent and uncertain accomplishment of the human race. The proprietors of the tabloids found this out a few years ago and it has been a very profitable discovery. They have produced a new type of paper which is consciously adapted to a low and hurried intelligence. But the essence of tabloid journalism is that it caters with extreme skill to the unadjusted and unprivileged part of the community. It offers them not rebellion but vicarious satisfaction, and therefore it is a kind of narcotic bolshevism as distinguished from the stimulant bolshevism that Lenin preached. There is some protest against the tabloids, but it is not as yet very severe, because the tabloids are in effect a substitute for rebellion rather than a cause of it. Nevertheless they are suspect because, like the moving picture, they reach the suspect classes, and one may confidently predict that if censorship is ever applied to American newspapers it will be due to some breach of the peace which is ascribed to the tabloids. Unless they turn respectable, as some of them show signs of doing, the logic of their formula will compel them to explore newer and newer excitements. They will experiment until at last they bring down upon themselves the wrath of the established community.

The novel is even freer than the press to-day because it is an even denser medium of expression. And in the jargon of a learned treatise a man may if he likes discuss with equanimity the advantages and disadvantages of incest among the Egyptian Pharaohs, or assassination as a method of social reform. For the practical limitations on the freedom of thought and speech are fixed by the estimate of those who have the power to suppress as to how effectively a dangerous idea is being presented to those who might be disposed to rebel.

III

Any one who with a moderately objective mind examines our own great controversies about freedom and suppression cannot fail, I think, to realize how little their avowed theory has to do with the attitude men take. The arguments which men used to justify the nullification of the Fifteenth Amendment in Georgia are now heard in Massachusetts to justify the nullification of the Eighteenth Amendment. The same corporate interests which object to regulation at home as an intolerable form of paternalism insist when they go abroad that the government shall protect them as if they were helpless children. The word "liberty" as used to-day may mean the open shop if an employer is speaking, a closed shop if a labor leader is speaking. There is no commonly accepted definition of liberty. The government of human affairs consists in finding a compromise among conflicting interests: liberty is the watchword used by an interest to justify it in doing what it would like to do, and authority is the watchword of an interest that does not wish to be interfered with by some other interest while it is doing what it wishes to do.

In concrete questions the verbal encounter throws little light on the issue. Suppression through some form of censorship is a means of defense, and, speaking broadly, suppression is practiced by the guardians of the state, the church, the family, and property. The support of censorship is to be found among those who feel themselves to be in harmony with the purposes of the institution that is attacked—that is to say, among officials and party workers and the classes who depend most upon the protection of the state, among churchmen and the devout, among parents, teachers, the guardians of the young, among the elderly and the sexually settled, and also among the impotent and inhibited—all those in short whose manner of life would become confused if the particular institution were radically altered. They are the reserves of conservatism from which are mobilized the legions of defense against the irregular forces of the outsiders—the immature, the unprivileged, the unsettled, and the unadjusted, by whom rebellions are made.

The defenders of authority assume that a considerable part of the people, including all children, are not attached by fixed and reliable habits to the existing order. Being unattached they are impressionable, and might therefore be seduced by agitators. They do not have within themselves, inherent in their characters, that interested loyalty to things as they are which makes men immune to subversive influences. In matters of this sort we must remember that the words "right" and "wrong" mean simply friendly or hostile to the purposes of the institution in question; that is why it is said that the outsiders do not have the interest of the institution sufficiently at heart to feel instinctively the difference between right and wrong. They cannot be allowed to judge for themselves because they are without the premises of sound judgment. They are not unconsciously loyal, and their impressions have to be controlled by the insiders who are intuitively right-minded.

The rationalist argument for liberty, as stated for example by Mill, does not meet this powerful dogma squarely. That, it seems to me, is why the stock theories of liberty are persuasive only to the party which is in rebellion and to a few neutrals who are not vitally concerned with the quarrel. The doctrinaires of liberty base their theory on the assumption that almost all men have the ability to weigh evidence and choose reasonably. Whether almost all men have the ability or not, they certainly do not use it. They are governed by their interests as they conceive them by consulting their feelings about them. The men who ever reach a conclusion which is contrary to their bias and their convenience are too few to make any important difference in the course of events. I have taken into account the fact that some men will sacrifice their lives, their fortunes, and their reputations in the pursuit of an ideal or under the compulsion of some deep necessity of which they may not be wholly aware. The hero and the saint would not be so distinguished if their conduct were normal. For the run of men and women, who make up human society, the thing which decides their attitude in a concrete and critical issue is not evidence, argument and repartee, but whether they are attached to or repelled by the institution which is under fire.

The neutrally-minded person with a somewhat liberal disposition often

misunderstands this conflict because it does not really touch him. He
merely apprehends it as he apprehends the news that forty miners have
been trapped in a mine. But your rebel knows his side of the conflict
as the doomed miners know their anguish, in a way that a disinterested
mind can never know it. The rebel feels his rebellion not as a plea for this
or that reform but as an unbearable tension in his viscera. He must break
down the cause of his frustration or jump out of his own skin. The true
conservative has the same sort of organic need: his institution is to him
a mainstay of his being; it exists not as an idea but in the very structure
of his character, and the threat to destroy it fills him with anxiety and
with fury.

The battles of liberty are organic conflicts between the adjusted
and the unadjusted.

March, 1927.

HENRY MILLER

*Henry Miller is an American novelist who was born in New York City
in 1891. At 18 he spent two months at City College, then traveled in
the Southwest and Alaska with the money his father had given him to go
to Cornell University. When he returned home the next year he went to
work in his father's tailor shop; later he became an employment manager
for Western Union Telegraph Company; and still later he operated a
Greenwich Village speakeasy. In 1930 he took up residence in France for
nine years. He returned to New York in 1940, traveled widely, wrote
voluminously, and for a long time settled in Big Sur, California.*

*Because of its history in United States courts, the best known of Mr.
Miller's many novels is probably* Tropic of Cancer *(1934). Among his
other books are* Tropic of Capricorn *(1938),* Sexus *(1949),* Plexus *(1953),*
The Colossus of Maroussi *(1941), and more recently* Nexus *(1960),* To
Paint Is to Love Again *(1960), and* Stand Still Like the Hummingbird
*(1962). He has also written several pieces on literary censorship, among
them the letter we print below, addressed to a Norwegian lawyer.*

DEFENSE OF THE FREEDOM
TO READ

Big Sur, California
February 27, 1959

Mr. Trygve Hirsch
Oslo, Norway

Dear Mr. Hirsch:

To answer your letter of January 19th requesting a statement of me which might be used in the Supreme Court trial to be conducted in March or April of this year. . . . It is difficult to be more explicit than I was in my letter of September 19th, 1957, when the case against my book *Sexus* was being tried in the lower courts of Oslo. However, here are some further reflections which I trust will be found *à propos*.

When I read the decision of the Oslo Town Court, which you sent me some months ago, I did so with mingled feelings. If occasionally I was obliged to roll with laughter—partly because of the inept translation, partly because of the nature and the number of infractions listed—I trust no one will take offense. Taking the world for what it is, and the men who make and execute the laws for what they are, I thought the decision as fair and honest as any theorem of Euclid's. Nor was I unaware of, or indifferent to, the efforts made by the Court to render an interpretation beyond the strict letter of the law. (An impossible task, I would say, for if laws are made for men and not men for laws, it is also true that certain individuals are made for the law and can only see things through the eyes of the law.)

I failed to be impressed, I must confess, by the weighty, often pompous or hypocritical, opinions adduced by scholars, literary pundits, psychologists, medicos and such like. How could I be when it is precisely such single-minded individuals, so often wholly devoid of humor, at whom I so frequently aim my shafts?

Rereading this lengthy document today, I am more than ever aware of the absurdity of the whole procedure. (How lucky I am not to be indicted as a "pervert" or "degenerate," but simply as one who makes sex pleasurable and innocent!) Why, it is often asked, when he has so much else to give, did he have to introduce these disturbing, controversial scenes dealing with sex? To answer that properly, one would have to go back to the womb—with or without the analyst's guiding hand. Each one—priest, analyst, barrister, judge—has his own answer, usually a ready-made one. But none go far enough, none are deep enough, inclusive enough. The divine answer, of course, is—first remove the mote from your own eye!

If I were there, in the dock, my answer would probably be—"Guilty! Guilty on all ninety-seven counts! To the gallows!" For when I take the short, myopic view, I realize that I was guilty even before I wrote the book. Guilty, in other words, because I am the way I am. The marvel is that I am walking about as a free man. I should have been condemned the moment I stepped out of my mother's womb.

In that heart-rending account of my return to the bosom of the family which is given in *Reunion in Brooklyn*, I concluded with these words, and I meant them, each and every one of them: "I regard the entire world as my home. I inhabit the earth, not a particular portion of it labeled America, France, Germany, Russia. . . . I owe allegiance to mankind, not to a particular country, race or people. I answer to God, not to the Chief Executive, whoever he may happen to be. I am here on earth to work out my own private destiny. My destiny is linked with that of every other living creature inhabiting this planet—perhaps with those on other planets too, who knows? I refuse to jeopardize my destiny by regarding life within the narrow rules which are laid down to circumscribe it. I dissent from the current view of things, as regards murder, as regards religion, as regards society, as regards our well-being. I will try to live my life in accordance with the vision I have of things eternal. I say 'Peace to you all!' and if you don't find it, it's because you haven't looked for it."

It is curious, and not irrelevant, I hope, to mention at this point the reaction I had upon reading Homer recently. At the request of the publisher, Gallimard, who is bringing out a new edition of *The Odyssey*, I wrote a short Introduction to this work. I had never read *The Odyssey* before, only *The Iliad*, and that but a few months ago. What I wish to say is that, after waiting sixty-seven years to read these universally esteemed classics, I found much to disparage in them. In *The Iliad*, or "the butcher's manual," as I call it, more than in *The Odyssey*. But it would never occur to me to request that they be banned or burned. Nor did I fear, on finishing them, that I would leap outdoors, axe in hand, and run amok. My boy, who was only nine when he read *The Iliad* (in a child's version), my boy who confesses to "liking murder once in a while," told me he was fed up with Homer, with all the killing and all the nonsense about the gods. But I have never feared that this son of mine, now going on eleven, still an avid reader of our detestable "Comics," a devotee of Walt Disney (who is not to my taste at all), an ardent movie fan, particularly of the "Westerns," I have never feared, I say, that he will grow up to be a killer. (Not even if the Army claims him!) I would rather see his mind absorbed by other interests, and I do my best to provide them, but, like all of us, he is a product of the age. No need, I trust, for me to elaborate on the dangers which confront us all, youth especially, in *this* age. The point is that with each age the menace varies. Whether it be witchcraft, idolatry, leprosy, cancer, schizophrenia, communism, fascism, or what, we have ever to do battle. Seldom do we really vanquish the enemy, in whatever guise he presents himself. At best we become immunized. But we never know, nor are we able to prevent in advance, the dangers which lurk around the corner. No matter how knowledgeable, no matter how wise, no matter how prudent and cautious, we all have an Achilles' heel. Security is not the lot of man. Readiness, alertness, responsiveness—these are the sole defenses against the blows of fate.

I smile to myself in putting the following to the honorable members of the Court, prompted as I am to take the bull by the horns. Would it please the Court to know that by common opinion I pass for a sane, healthy, normal individual? That I am not regarded as a "sex addict," a pervert, or even a neurotic? Nor as a writer who is ready to sell his soul for money? That, as a husband, a father, a neighbor, I am looked upon as "an asset" to the community? Sounds a trifle ludicrous, does it not? Is this the same *enfant terrible*, it might be asked, who wrote the unmentionable *Tropics, The Rosy Crucifixion, The World of Sex, Quiet Days in Clichy?* Has he reformed? Or is he simply in his dotage now?

To be precise, the question is—are the author of these questionable works and the man who goes by the name of Henry Miller one and the same person? My answer is yes. And I am also one with the protagonist of these "autobiographical romances." That is perhaps harder to swallow. But why? Because I have been "utterly shameless" in revealing every aspect of my life? I am not the first author to have adopted the confessional approach, to have revealed life nakedly, or to have used language supposedly unfit for the ears of school girls. Were I a saint recounting his life of sin, perhaps these bald statements relating to my sex habits would be found enlightening, particularly by priests and medicos. They might even be found instructive.

But I am not a saint, and probably never will be one. Though it occurs to me, as I make this assertion, that I have been called that more than once, and by individuals whom the Court would never suspect capable of holding such an opinion. No, I am not a saint, thank heavens! nor even a propagandist of a new order. I am simply a man, a man born to write, who has taken as his theme the story of his life. A man who has made it clear, in the telling, that it was a good life, a rich life, a merry life, despite the ups and downs, despite the barriers and obstacles (many of his own making), despite the handicaps imposed by stupid codes and conventions. Indeed, I hope that I have made more than that clear, because whatever I may say about my own life which is only *a* life, is merely a means of talking about life itself, and what I have tried, desperately sometimes, to make clear is this, that I look upon life itself as good, good no matter on what terms, that I believe it is *we* who make it unlivable, *we*, not the gods, not fate, not circumstance.

Speaking thus, I am reminded of certain passages in the Court's decision which reflect on my sincerity as well as on my ability to think straight. These passages contain the implication that I am often deliberately obscure as well as pretentious in my "metaphysical and surrealistic" flights. I am only too well aware of the diversity of opinion which these "excursi" elicit in the minds of my readers. But how am I to answer such accusations, touching as they do the very marrow of my literary being? Am I to say, "You don't know what you are talking about"? Ought I to muster impressive names—"authorities"—to counterbalance these judgments? Or would it not be simpler to say, as I have before— "Guilty! Guilty on all counts, your Honor!"

Believe me, it is not impish, roguish perversity which leads me to pronounce, even quasi-humorously, this word "guilty." As one who thoroughly and sincerely believes in what he says and does, even when wrong, is it not more becoming on my part to admit "guilt" than attempt to defend myself against those who use this word so glibly? Let us be honest. Do those who judge and condemn me—not in Oslo necessarily, but the world over—do these individuals truly believe me to be a culprit, to be "the enemy of society," as they often blandly assert? What is it that disturbs them so? Is it the existence, the prevalence, of immoral, amoral, or unsocial behavior, such as is described in my works, or is it the exposure of such behavior in print? Do people of our day and age really behave in this "vile" manner or are these actions merely the product of a "diseased" mind? (Does one refer to such authors as Petronius, Rabelais, Rousseau, Sade, to mention but a few, as "diseased minds"?) Surely some of you must have friends or neighbors, in good standing too, who have indulged in this questionable behavior, or worse. As a man of the world, I know only too well that the appanage of a priest's frock, a judicial robe, a teacher's uniform provides no guarantee of immunity to the temptations of the flesh. We are all in the same pot, we are all guilty, or innocent, depending on whether we take the frog's view or the Olympian view. For the once I shall refrain from pretending to measure or apportion guilt, to say, for example, that a criminal is more guilty, or less, than a hypocrite. We do not have crime, we do not have war, revolution, crusades, inquisitions, persecution and intolerance because some among us are wicked, mean-spirited, or murderers at heart; we have this malignant condition of human affairs because all of us, the righteous as well as the ignorant and the malicious, lack true forbearance, true compassion, true knowledge and understanding of human nature.

To put it as succinctly and simply as possible, here is my basic attitude toward life, my prayer, in other words: "Let us stop thwarting one another, stop judging and condemning, stop slaughtering one another." I do not implore you to suspend or withhold judgment of me or my work. Neither I nor my work is that important. (One cometh, another goeth.) What concerns me is the harm you are doing to yourselves. I mean by perpetuating this talk of guilt and punishment, of banning and proscribing, of whitewashing and blackballing, of closing your eyes when convenient, of making scapegoats when there is no other way out. I ask you pointblank—does the pursuance of your limited role enable you to get the most out of life? When you write me off the books, so to speak, will you find your food and wine more palatable, will you sleep better, will you be a better man, a better husband, a better father than before? These are the things that matter—what happens to *you*, not what you do to *me*.

I know that the man in the dock is not supposed to ask questions, he is there to answer. But I am unable to regard myself as a culprit. I am simply "out of line." Yet I am in the tradition, so to say. A list of my precursors would make an impressive roster. This trial has been going on since the days of Prometheus. Since before that. Since the days of the Archangel Michael. In the not too distant past there was one who was given the cup of hemlock for being "the corrupter of youth." Today he is regarded as one of the sanest, most lucid minds that ever was. We who are always being arraigned before the bar can do no better than to resort to the celebrated Socratic method. Our only answer is to return the question.

There are so many questions one could put to the Court, to any Court. But would one get a response? Can the Court of the Land ever be put in question? I am afraid not. The judicial body is a sacrosanct body. This is unfortunate, as I see it, for when issues of grave import arise the last court of reference, in my opinion, should be the public. When justice is at stake responsibility cannot be shifted to an elect few without injustice resulting. No Court could function if it did not follow the steel rails of precedent, taboo and prejudice.

I come back to the lengthy document representing the decision of the Oslo Town Court, to the tabulation of all the infractions of the moral code therein listed. There is something frightening as well as disheartening about such an indictment. It has a medieval aspect. And it has nothing to do with justice. Law itself is made to look ridiculous. Once again let me say that it is not the courts of Oslo or the laws and codes of Norway which I inveigh against; everywhere in the civilized world there is this mummery and flummery manifesting as the Voice of Inertia. The offender who stands before the Court is not being tried by his peers but by his dead ancestors. The moral codes, operative only if they are in conformance with natural or divine laws, are not safeguarded by these flimsy dikes; on the contrary, they are exposed as weak and ineffectual barriers.

Finally, here is the crux of the matter. Will an adverse decision by this court or any other court effectively hinder the further circulation of this book? The history of similar cases does not substantiate such an eventuality. If anything, an unfavorable verdict will only add more fuel to the flames. Proscription only leads to resistance; the fight goes on underground, becomes more insidious therefore, more difficult to cope with. If only one man in Norway reads the book and believes with the author that one has the right to express himself freely, the battle is won. You cannot eliminate an idea by suppressing it, and the idea which is linked with this issue is one of freedom to read what one chooses. Freedom, in other words, to read what is bad for one as well as what is good for one —or, what is simply innocuous. How can one guard against evil, in short, if one does not know what evil is?

But it is not something evil, not something poisonous, which this book *Sexus* offers the Norwegian reader. It is a dose of life which I administered to myself first, and which I not only survived but thrived on. Certainly I would not recommend it to infants, but then neither would I offer a child a bottle of *aqua vite*. I can say one thing for it unblushingly —compared to the atom bomb, it is full of life-giving qualities.

Henry Miller.

JOHN M. WOOLSEY

John Munro Woolsey (1877–1945) was educated at Yale University and the Columbia Law School, where he founded the Columbia Law Review. *He was admitted to the New York Bar in 1901 and worked in private law offices—specializing in admiralty law—until he was appointed U. S. District Judge by President Hoover in 1929. It was in this capacity that he handed down the celebrated decision on James Joyce's novel* Ulysses. *The decision was upheld by the Federal Circuit Court of Appeals, and the Random House 1934 edition of* Ulysses *thus became the first legally*

printed edition of the book in any English-speaking country. The decision is here reprinted from the Modern Library edition of Ulysses.

U. S. A. v. ONE BOOK *ULYSSES*

UNITED STATES DISTRICT COURT

SOUTHERN DISTRICT OF NEW YORK

United States of America, *Libelant* v. One Book called "Ulysses" Random House, Inc., *Claimant*	OPINION A. 110-59

On cross motions for a decree in a libel of confiscation, supplemented by a stipulation—hereinafter described—brought by the United States against the book "Ulysses" by James Joyce, under Section 305 of the Tariff Act of 1930, Title 19 United States Code, Section 1305, on the ground that the book is obscene within the meaning of that Section, and, hence, is not importable into the United States, but is subject to seizure, forfeiture and confiscation and destruction.

United States Attorney—by Samuel C. Coleman, Esq., and Nicholas Atlas, Esq., of counsel—for the United States, in support of motion for a decree of forfeiture, and in opposition to motion for a decree dismissing the libel.

Messrs. Greenbaum, Wolff & Ernst,—by Morris L. Ernst, Esq., and Alexander Lindey, Esq., of counsel—attorneys for claimant Random House, Inc., in support of motion for a decree dismissing the libel, and in opposition to motion for a decree of forfeiture.

WOOLSEY, J:

The motion for a decree dismissing the libel herein is granted, and, consequently, of course, the Government's motion for a decree of forfeiture and destruction is denied.

Accordingly a decree dismissing the libel without costs may be entered herein.

I. The practice followed in this case is in accordance with the suggestion made by me in the case of *United States v. One Book Entitled "Contraception"*, 51 F. (2d) 525, and is as follows:

After issue was joined by the filing of the claimant's answer to the libel for forfeiture against "Ulysses", a stipulation was made between the United States Attorney's office and the attorneys for the claimant providing:

1. That the book "Ulysses" should be deemed to have been annexed to and to have become part of the libel just as if it had been incorporated in its entirety therein.

2. That the parties waived their right to a trial by jury.

3. That each party agreed to move for decree in its favor.

4. That on such cross motions the Court might decide all the questions of law and fact involved and render a general finding thereon.

5. That on the decision of such motions the decree of the Court might be entered as if it were a decree after trial.

It seems to me that a procedure of this kind is highly appropriate in libels for the confiscation of books such as this. It is an especially advantageous procedure in the instant case because on account of the length of "Ulysses" and the difficulty of reading it, a jury trial would have been an extremely unsatisfactory, if not an almost impossible, method of dealing with it.

II. I have read "Ulysses" once in its entirety and I have read those passages of which the Government particularly complains several times. In fact, for many weeks, my spare time has been devoted to the consideration of the decision which my duty would require me to make in this matter.

"Ulysses" is not an easy book to read or to understand. But there has been much written about it, and in order properly to approach the consideration of it it is advisable to read a number of other books which have now become its satellites. The study of "Ulysses" is, therefore, a heavy task.

III. The reputation of "Ulysses" in the literary world, however, warranted my taking such time as was necessary to enable me to satisfy myself as to the intent with which the book was written, for, of course, in any case where a book is claimed to be obscene it must first be determined, whether the intent with which it was written was what is called, according to the usual phrase, pornographic,—that is, written for the purpose of exploiting obscenity.

If the conclusion is that the book is pornographic that is the end of the inquiry and forfeiture must follow.

But in "Ulysses", in spite of its unusual frankness, I do not detect anywhere the leer of the sensualist. I hold, therefore, that it is not pornographic.

IV. In writing "Ulysses", Joyce sought to make a serious experiment in a new, if not wholly novel, literary genre. He takes persons of the lower middle class living in Dublin in 1904 and seeks not only to describe what they did on a certain day early in June of that year as they went about the City bent on their usual occupations, but also to tell what many of them thought about the while.

Joyce has attempted—it seems to me, with astonishing success—to show how the screen of consciousness with its ever-shifting kaleidoscopic impressions carries, as it were on a plastic palimpsest, not only what is in the focus of each man's observation of the actual things about him, but also in a penumbral zone residua of past impressions, some recent and some drawn up by association from the domain of the subconscious. He shows how each of these impressions affects the life and behavior of the character which he is describing.

What he seeks to get is not unlike the result of a double or, if that is possible, a multiple exposure on a cinema film which would give a clear foreground with a background visible but somewhat blurred and out of focus in varying degrees.

To convey by words an effect which obviously lends itself more appropriately to a graphic technique, accounts, it seems to me, for much of the obscurity which meets a reader of "Ulysses". And it also explains another aspect of the book, which I have further to consider, namely, Joyce's sincerity and his honest effort to show exactly how the minds of his characters operate.

If Joyce did not attempt to be honest in developing the technique which he has adopted in "Ulysses" the result would be psychologically misleading and thus unfaithful to his chosen technique. Such an attitude would be artistically inexcusable.

It is because Joyce has been loyal to his technique and has not funked its necessary implications, but has honestly attempted to tell fully what his characters think about, that he has been the subject of so many attacks and that his purpose has been so often misunderstood and misrepresented. For his attempt sincerely and honestly to realize his objective has required him incidentally to use certain words which are generally considered dirty words and has led at times to what many think is a too poignant preoccupation with sex in the thoughts of his characters.

The words which are criticized as dirty are old Saxon words known to almost all men and, I venture, to many women, and are such words as would be naturally and habitually used, I believe, by the types of folk whose life, physical and mental, Joyce is seeking to describe. In respect of the recurrent emergence of the theme of sex in the minds of his characters, it must always be remembered that his locale was Celtic and his season Spring.

Whether or not one enjoys such a technique as Joyce uses is a matter of taste on which disagreement or argument is futile, but to subject that technique to the standards of some other technique seems to me to be little short of absurd.

Accordingly, I hold that "Ulysses" is a sincere and honest book and I think that the criticisms of it are entirely disposed of by its rationale.

V. Furthermore, "Ulysses" is an amazing *tour de force* when one considers the success which has been in the main achieved with such a difficult objective as Joyce set for himself. As I have stated, "Ulysses" is not an easy book to read. It is brilliant and dull, intelligible and obscure by turns. In many places it seems to me to be disgusting, but although it contains, as I have mentioned above, many words usually considered dirty, I have not found anything that I consider to be dirt for dirt's sake. Each word of the book contributes like a bit of mosaic to the detail of the picture which Joyce is seeking to construct for his readers.

If one does not wish to associate with such folk as Joyce describes, that is one's own choice. In order to avoid indirect contact with them one may not wish to read "Ulysses"; that is quite understandable. But when such a real artist in words, as Joyce undoubtedly is, seeks to draw a true picture of the lower middle class in a European city, ought it to be impossible for the American public legally to see that picture?

To answer this question it is not sufficient merely to find, as I have found above, that Joyce did not write "Ulysses" with what is commonly called pornographic intent, I must endeavor to apply a more objective standard to his book in order to determine its effect in the result, irrespective of the intent with which it was written.

VI. The statute under which the libel is filed only denounces, in so far as we are here concerned, the importation into the United States from any foreign country of "any obscene book". Section 305 of the Tariff Act of 1930, Title 19 United States Code, Section 1305. It does not marshal against books the spectrum of condemnatory adjectives found, commonly, in laws dealing with matters of this kind. I am, therefore, only required to determine whether "Ulysses" is obscene within the legal definition of that word.

The meaning of the word "obscene" as legally defined by the Courts is: tending to stir the sex impulses or to lead to sexually impure and lustful thoughts. *Dunlop* v. *United States*, 165 U. S. 486, 501; *United States* v. *One Book Entitled "Married Love"*, 48 F. (2d) 821, 824; *United States* v. *One Book Entitled "Contraception"*, 51 F. (2d) 525, 528; and compare *Dysart* v. *United States*, 272 U. S. 655, 657; *Swearingen* v. *United States*, 161 U. S. 446, 450; *United States* v. *Dennett*, 39 F. (2d) 564, 568 (C. C. A. 2); *People* v. *Wendling*, 258 N. Y. 451, 453.

Whether a particular book would tend to excite such impulses and thoughts must be tested by the Court's opinion as to its effect on a person with average sex instincts—what the French would call *l'homme moyen sensuel*—who plays, in this branch of legal inquiry, the same role of hypothetical reagent as does the "reasonable man" in the law of torts and "the man learned in the art" on questions of invention in patent law.

The risk involved in the use of such a reagent arises from the inherent tendency of the trier of facts, however fair he may intend to be, to make his reagent too much subservient to his own idiosyncrasies. Here, I have attempted to avoid this, if possible, and to make my reagent herein more objective than he might otherwise be, by adopting the following course:

After I had made my decision in regard to the aspect of "Ulysses", now under consideration, I checked my impressions with two friends of mine who in my opinion answered to the above stated requirement for my reagent.

These literary assessors—as I might properly describe them—were called on separately, and neither knew that I was consulting the other. They are men whose opinion on literature and on life I value most highly. They had both read "Ulysses", and, of course, were wholly unconnected with this cause.

Without letting either of my assessors know what my decision was, I gave to each of them the legal definition of obscene and asked each whether in his opinion "Ulysses" was obscene within that definition.

I was interested to find that they both agreed with my opinion: that reading "Ulysses" in its entirety, as a book must be read on such a test as this, did not tend to excite sexual impulses or lustful thoughts but that its net effect on them was only that of a somewhat tragic and very powerful commentary on the inner lives of men and women.

It is only with the normal person that the law is concerned. Such a test as I have described, therefore, is the only proper test of obscenity in the case of a book like "Ulysses" which is a sincere and serious attempt to devise a new literary method for the observation and description of mankind.

I am quite aware that owing to some of its scenes "Ulysses" is a rather strong draught to ask some sensitive, though normal, persons to take. But my considered opinion, after long reflection, is that whilst in many places the effect of "Ulysses" on the reader undoubtedly is somewhat emetic, nowhere does it tend to be an aphrodisiac.

"Ulysses" may, therefore, be admitted into the United States.

JOHN M. WOOLSEY
UNITED STATES DISTRICT JUDGE

December 6, 1933

HOWARD MOODY

Howard Moody graduated from Yale Divinity School in 1951 and served for five years as Minister to Students at Ohio State University before he became Minister of the Judson Memorial Church in Greenwich Village, New York City. Judson Church is a very unusual one. Strongly involved with its community, it has a Center for delinquent children, works with narcotics addicts, and provides an international and interracial house for students in the metropolitan area. The Judson Poets' Theater received five awards for off-Broadway plays in the 1963–64 season, and the Judson Dance Theater is one of the outstanding avant-garde dance groups in the City. Active in civic and community affairs, Mr. Moody served as a delegate to the 1962 White House Conference on Narcotics Addiction and has lectured at the New School for Social Research. He is also the author of The Fourth Man *(1964), a collection of essays on modern American culture. The essay we present below first appeared in the journal* Christianity and Crisis, *January 25, 1965.*

TOWARD A NEW DEFINITION OF OBSCENITY

It was no accident that one of the issues in the Presidential campaign was the "breakdown" of morality and the "deterioration of decency." We are obviously in the midst of what is simultaneously a moral and an artistic revolution, and it is usually difficult to tell where one leaves off and the other begins. All the way from the police department "put-down" of "dirty poetry" in coffeehouses in the early Fifties to the recent persecution of that most tragic of all shamans, Lenny Bruce, we have felt the reverberations of a battle that is as old as the country itself.

In the last few years slick-paper sex magazines like Ralph Ginzburg's

Eros, as well as classics like *Fanny Hill,* have been banned and unbanned with disarming regularity. More recently the new wave of off-beat film makers experimenting with weird and strange themes have been arrested and their films banned from public places. Everything from topless bathing suits for women to bottomless bathing suits for men (in a Greenwich Village sportswear shop) are subjects for legal action.

To some people the foregoing is merely evidence of the decadence and coming destruction of American civilization, while to others it is the dawn of a new day of freedom of expression and the demise of shackling censorship. Whatever one's point of view as to the significance of the present revolution, it will be impossible to understand the present situation without knowing something of the history of the problem. How continuously, and sometimes obsessively, we as a people have been bent upon what Morris Ernst and Alan Schwartz have called "the search for the obscene." (*Censorship: The Search for the Obscene* [Macmillan] is their valuable study of this question from which I have drawn much of the legal-historical material in this article.)

Though the Puritans have often been blamed for "blue laws" and censorship, they actually were a great deal freer than they are often given credit for. In his revealing volume *The Not-Quite Puritans* Henry Lawrence refers to no fewer than 66 *confessions* to fornication in one small town between 1761-65 (that was only those who confessed).

As a matter of fact, our first anti-obscenity law did not come into existence until the nineteenth century. Our forefathers, the Revolutionists and fashioners of the Constitution, did not seem so concerned with obscenity or pornography (and don't think there wasn't plenty around, cf. *The Fyfteen Plagues of a Maidenhead* and Ben Franklin's *Advice to a Young Man on Choosing a Mistress,* a ribald essay not published but freely circulated). Their concern is contained in the words of the First Amendment about Congress making no law abridging freedom of speech, religion and the press.

The real beginning of censorship—the establishment of prudery by legal sanctions—was the work not of Puritans and Pilgrims but of nine-teenth-century Protestants. This will come as a surprise to those who label Roman Catholics as the book banning "bad boys" of censorship and the first antagonists of pornography. After all it was Anthony Comstock, a fanatical 24-year-old grocery clerk, who with the decisive help of the YMCA badgered the country and the Congress into passing a law that still governs obscenity in the mails. State after state followed the Congress and enacted "Comstock Laws." The major support for Comstock came, ironically enough, from the Babylon of sin and iniquity, New York City. The crusaders were not Irish Catholics; their top leadership was from the Protestant social hierarchy of New York, and J. P. Morgan's name led all the rest.

The leaders of censorship crusades used several means to gain their end, beginning with the law. From the late 1880's on, the crusaders have been confounded in attempts to get a definitive ruling on the meaning of obscenity in the courts of the land. The definition in the Comstock Law was terribly unclear, and since that time the courts have played the "synonyms game" (obscene is "dirty," "lewd," "lascivious," "scurrilous").

The protesters seemed to be disturbed by several matters as they pressed by law for the banning of books, and later films. They were deeply offended by "dirty words." One of the most important court cases was the Woolsey case, named after Judge John M. Woolsey, which dealt with the question of whether James Joyce's *Ulysses* might be distributed in this country. The basic objection to this book was the use of "four-letter words." The counsel, Morris Ernst, gave a historic exposition. The following is his dialogue with the judge.

> *Counsel:* Judge, as to the word "fuck," one etymological dictionary gives its derivation as from *facere*—to make—the farmer fucked the seed into the soil. This, Your Honor, has more integrity than a euphemism used every day in every modern novel to describe precisely the same event.
> *Judge Woolsey:* For example . . .
> *Counsel:* "They slept together." It means the same thing.
> *Judge Woolsey:* (smiling) But, Counselor, that isn't even usually the truth!

The final opinion of Judge Woolsey was that *Ulysses*, in spite of its vulgar language, did not excite sexual impulses or lustful thoughts and that its net effect was only that of a somewhat tragic and very powerful commentary on the inner lives of men and women.

This was the beginning of a whole series of significant legal cases on "obscenity" and attempts to control pornography.

One of the most important cases on obscenity was the *Roth* case, which involved an outright challenge to an obscenity law and its constitutionality under the First Amendment. Justice Harlan's decision in this case ought to be read by every fair-minded person interested in the problem of freedom and censorship.

Roth had been convicted by a lower court for selling books that "tend to stir sexual impulses and lead to sexually impure thoughts." This would, of course, condemn much of the world's great literature, and, moreover, Justice Harlan asserts: ". . . in no event do I think that limited federal interest in this area can extend to mere 'thoughts.' The federal power has no business, whether under the postal or commerce laws, to bar the sale of books because they might lead to any kind of 'thoughts.'"

And in sections of the decision Justice Brennan's understanding of human nature is comparable to his judicial wisdom. He says:

However, sex and obscenity are not synonymous; obscene material is material dealing with sex in a manner appealing to prurient interest. The portrayal of sex, e.g. literature, art and scientific works, is not itself sufficient reason to deny material the constitutional protection of freedom of speech and press. Sex, as a great and mysterious moving force in human life, has indisputably been a subject of absorbing interest to mankind through the ages; it is one of the vital problems of human interest and public concern.

The culmination of the long court battle was the Supreme Court's decision last June declaring *Tropic of Cancer* and the film *The Lovers* not to be obscene.

The peddlers of prudery also used another technique for the enforcement of their morality on the community as a whole: social and religious sanction. This was an effective weapon as long as a people dominated by a common Protestant ethos or Christian moral understanding controlled both legally and socially the normally accepted standards of behavior for the society. However, with the "passing of Christendom," and the accompanying breakdown of religious authority, control has become much more difficult.

The censors in more recent years have used more desperate techniques such as that of quasi-legal and police action. Since the higher courts keep refusing to make irrevocably clear what is obscene, censors are driven to vigilante tactics that are extra-legal, highly undemocratic and probably unconstitutional. Self-appointed citizens' clean-books councils are springing up all over the country. Their tactics are intimidation, and their appeals are sloganeering. Operating under the very appealing objective of "keeping filth and smut from our children," they move on to cleaning from libraries such books as *Brave New World, Black Boy, Catcher in the Rye* and others.

One of the more renowned private citizens' groups in this country is an interfaith organization in New York City called *Operation Yorkville*, which has garnered financial support and the backing of religious and political leaders for its task of guarding the morals of the city's youth. Most recently its chief targets of "malignancy" are the American Civil Liberties Union, the Supreme Court of the United States and every Court of Appeals judge who refuses to accept their "book-burning" standards. In order to punish the "pushers of pornography," methods are used, including accusations, that violate the rights of others.

One would not for a moment deny the right of these individuals acting in concert to make their point of view felt by means of persuasion. But when they use intimidating threats and slanderous name-calling as in the recent attack on the Supreme Court Justices for their June 22 ruling as "nurturing degeneracy," then these groups have gone beyond the boundary of what constitutes responsible citizens' action.

The question that comes to the Church and to individual Christians at this point is what should be our posture in the midst of these revolutions going on about us? I think Christians should look carefully at the confusion regarding the meaning of obscenity and then make a major contribution by raising our own standard for judging obscenity. The Supreme Court, in its most recent case prior to last June's decision, defined it as follows:

> Obscene material is material which deals with sex in a manner appealing to prurient interest, and the test of obscenity is whether to the *average* person, applying contemporary community standards, the dominant theme of the material appeals to *prurient* interest (Justice Brennan: *Roth* v. *U.S.*, 1957).

The dictionary defines *prurient* as "having an uneasy or morbid desire or curiosity: given to the indulgence of lewd ideas; impure minded." It is almost too obvious to say that even the wisest gods, let alone mortal men, would have an exceedingly difficult time deciding under this definition what is obscene, who is an average person, whose community standard, and what constitutes dominant theme. More basic than such highly ambiguous matters is the larger question of the legitimacy of using sex (even in a prurient way) as the sole basis for determining what is obscene. Here we are up against the most important aspect of the definition of obscenity: at least two of the important grounds for censorship are "dirty words" and "sexual subjects."

Relative to the matter of vulgar language, what righteous indignation can we Christians muster about our Anglo-Saxon forebears? Can we really pretend that the use of "coarse" and "vulgar" words is somehow tantamount to an affront to God Almighty? (Do we have to be so ashamed of the "bawdy" talk of Martin Luther?) Vulgar speech and four-letter words are not blasphemous or immoral, and our shame and prudery over them are basically class matters. (Even the derivation of the word "lewd" is interestingly traced to a *lewdefrere*, a lay brother; unlearned, unlettered, rude, artless, belonging to lower orders.) Vulgar and bawdy language may well be objected to on the basis of aesthetics and social manners, but it is hardly justifiable to make a moral or theological case against raw language as the Church has tended to do.

I remember my father telling me as a youth that uttering the profanity "Goddamn" was the unforgivable sin of blasphemy as well as the breaking of the Third Commandment. It is the Christian's devious manner of avoiding the hard truth that "taking God's name in vain" is a far more profound sin than profanity. It is not the vulgar utterance from our lips but our deeds that truly profane human life. Christ always warned that you can't judge a man by his speech. Not everyone who says words like "Lord, Lord," even spoken with great reverence and piety, "does the truth" of those words; conversely many people who speak roughly in the raw language of vulgarity live in awe of and respect for the mystery of humanity.

The true profanity against God is to refuse to take him seriously; the truly "dirty" word is the one used to deny and to denigrate the humanness of another person. Language is symbolic, not literal; when a person speaks in raw language he may be trying to say something that nice and prosaic words will not communicate.

My point here is that, from a theological or ethical perspective, "dirty words" are a terribly inadequate base from which to write a definition of obscenity.

In the same way, we do not do justice to the Christian perspective upon human evil and immorality if we see *sex* as the dominant determinative factor in the judgment of what is obscene. Sex, by our understanding of creation, is vital and a potent force in human behavior, though shot through with human sin and distortion. To make sex the sole determinative factor in defining "obscenity" or "pornography" or "filth" is to relegate it to the shadowy regions of immorality (depending on who says it in what community and how much). This completely fails to explain what all Christian faith and tradition teaches us is really *obscene* in this world.

For Christians the truly obscene ought not to be slick-paper nudity, nor the vulgarities of dirty old or young literati, nor even "weirdo" films showing transvestite orgies or male genitalia. What is obscene is that material, whether sexual or not, that has as its basic motivation and purpose the degradation, debasement and dehumanizing of persons. The dirtiest word in the English language is not "fuck" or "shit" in the mouth of a tragic shaman, but the word "NIGGER" from the sneering lips of a Bull Connor. Obscenity ought to be much closer to the biblical definition of blasphemy against God and man.

The censor tells us that the "filth" must be stopped because it is leading our children into acts of violence, rape, narcotic addiction and prostitution. They say that young minds are being poisoned and perverted by "pornographic books."

Are we really worried about the pornographic pictures peddled by shady characters on street corners? I remember all those "dirty" comic books in high school, i.e., *Popeye, Maggie and Jiggs*—they made me feel I was "illicit" and they made me laugh, but I wasn't moved to ravish my teacher as a result.

I do not conceive that a picture is "dirty" because sex is its dominant theme. (The tragic disservice of slick-paper sex magazines is not that they display nudes in suggestive poses but that they become anti-sexual by pushing sex to the point of satiety, thus making it a deadly bore.) A picture is not dirty that shows a man and woman in one of the 57 recommended positions for intercourse (unaesthetic perhaps, possibly bad taste, but hardly obscene!). The dirty or obscene is the one that shows the police dogs being unleashed on the Negro demonstrators in Birmingham. The "lewdest" pictures of all—more obscene than all the tawdry products of the "smut industry"—are the pictures of Dachau, the ovens, and the grotesque pile of human corpses.

Let us as Christians write a new definition of obscenity based on the dehumanizing aspects of our contemporary culture. Can we not see the hypocrisy of our prudery when we spend time, words and money trying to prevent the magazine *Eros* from going through the mails and never raise an eyebrow about the tons of material that vilify human beings and consign whole ethnic groups to the lowest kind of animality? Do we not have to admit the duplicity that allows our police to *guard* George Lincoln Rockwell as he mouths blasphemous obscenities of the most inhuman order on public streets, while the same police are used to *harass* Lenny Bruce in the confines of a night club while he vulgarly satirizes our human hypocrisies?

Should we not as Christians raise a new standard of "obscenity" not obsessed with sex and vulgar language, but defined rather as that material which has as its dominant theme and purpose the debasement and depreciation of human beings—their worth and their dignity. Such a definition might include some material dealing with sex but this would be a minor aspect of pornography. The "words" that would offend us and from which we want our young protected would not be "Anglo-Saxon" but English, French, German, which carried within their etymology and meaning outrages against human individuals and groups.

The pornographic pictures would be those that showed humans being violated, destroyed, physically beaten. (The prize obscene film might be a three-minute documentary of a fully clothed man, twitching and writhing as the shock of electricity applied by our officials burns through his body.)

All the resources of our Christian teaching and tradition, all the theological armament in the Church could be called up in the warfare against "the new obscenity." The significant concomitant of this is that it would lessen the distortion and perversion of sex in our society that the present definition of obscenity has created. A further advantage to this new understanding would be that the Church and many literary critics would be saved the embarrassment of having to defend every mediocre form of literature and art against the wild attacks of the book-banners.

We would be saved the somewhat ludicrous spectacle of "far-out ministers" and "hip theologians" eloquently testifying in court for what may be lousy literature or atrocious art. (There was a laughable scene in the recent court case against Lenny Bruce when a minister was forced into justifying why he didn't use four-letter words in his homiletical exercises on Sunday. I can already see some enterprising seminary developing a new course in "The Use of Pornography in Preaching.")

Norman Podhoretz has stated the matter succinctly: ". . . it is the extent to which law has forced criticism into hypocrisy that, in order to defend freedom of expression, one must always be exaggerating the literary merits of any piece of erotica that happens to get published."

If it is asserted that this position skirts dangerously close to "license" and the accompanying breakdown of moral order, I can only reply that it is one of the hard truths of Christian tradition that we have been released to a freedom whose burden is a terrible risk. This freedom of the Christian man has already sent Christians in our time against the law, to prison and even to death. With this new definition of obscenity we will run a risk by allowing our children and ourselves to see "obscene pictures" of the instant destruction of 200,000 persons at Hiroshima with one bomb—the risk that we may come to accept this as a natural and realistic way of solving conflicts between men and nations. This is a real danger, but the alternative is mental slavery, a restricted thought process, a closed society. Consequently in the battles of censorship in a pluralistic society Christians may find themselves coming down regularly against the inroads of censorship at the risk of being called licentious and immoral.

It may be, as some politicians claimed in the past campaign, that this nation is in a state of moral decadence. If so, I am convinced that the evidence of this is not to be found in salacious literature, erotic art or obscene films but in the "soul-rot" that comes from the moral hypocrisy of straining at the gnat of sexuality and swallowing the camel of human deterioration and destruction.

Protestant Christian liberals in this country have been very adept at accommodating Christian faith and ethics to the social and economic revolutions of the past 30–40 years. However, we display every evidence of being ill at ease and unprophetic in relating our Christian insights and teachings to the moral and sexual revolutions in American life. There are a few clues that the wind is changing, but much more study and reflection in honesty is needed.

DAVID HALBERSTAM

David Halberstam was born in New York City in 1934 and educated at Harvard, where he was Managing Editor of the Crimson. *After four years with the* Nashville Tennessean, *he joined the Washington Bureau of the* New York Times *in 1960. First a correspondent in the Congo, he was later transferred to South Vietnam and is currently on the metropolitan staff of the* Times. *In 1964 he won a Pulitzer Prize for his coverage of Vietnam and also the Louis M. Lyons award for conscience and integrity in journalism—awarded by the Nieman Fellows of Harvard—for reporting "the truth as [he] saw it [in the Vietnam conflict] . . . without yielding to unrelenting pressures." Author of a novel,* The Noblest Roman *(1961), Mr. Halberstam has more recently written* The Making of a Quagmire *(1965), a book about Vietnam. The article we reprint below first appeared in* Commentary, *January, 1965.*

GETTING THE STORY IN VIETNAM

In most underdeveloped countries the relationship between the American embassy and the American reporter is fairly simple and generally straightforward. A reporter arriving in, say, a country in Africa will go to see officials of the American mission almost immediately. From them he can count on hearing the local American position, but he can also count on getting a relatively detached, if limited, view of the local government, its relations with the U.S., with the Eastern bloc, and with its neighbors. For example, when I was in the Congo for the New York *Times* in 1961 and 1962, the line went something like this: Prime Minister Adoula is better than most people think and considering the kind of country this is, really better than you might expect. As for Tshombe, don't be fooled by his anti-Communist stand. He is an anti-Communist, but he is also following a policy which he hopes will turn the rest of the Congo over to the Communists, so that his Katanga secession will look even better to the West.

This was a sensible viewpoint; it was supported, among other things, by the fact that Tshombe's deputies were always voting with the radical left in the assembly in an attempt to topple the moderate government. But it was far from the whole story. The rest of the story was that the Americans wanted to minimize Tshombe's considerable charm and ability and to make him seem just another tribal leader in Katanga, when he actually had far broader support. Thus, when I wrote a long article on him for the Sunday *Times* magazine, the State Department sent a cable to the USIS man in Leopoldville complaining that I had been too sympathetic, and suggesting that I be talked into doing an equally sympathetic piece on Adoula.

But if the State Department often makes the mistake of thinking that New York *Times* reporters are *its* reporters, the relation between American ambassadors and American reporters in most underdeveloped countries is generally one of mutual respect; if anything, reporters—and New York *Times* reporters in particular—may be treated too well. The reporter constantly has to remind himself that an ambassador in a small country where there is no immediate crisis may regard him as the best way to break through State Department channels and get his problems to the White House for breakfast.

In Vietnam, however, relationships such as these simply did not exist. Some were later to claim that the difficulties which arose between the press and the American mission were the result of poor handling or inept news management. But in fact the conflict went much deeper. The job of the reporters in Vietnam was to report the news, whether or not the news was good for America. To the ambassadors and generals, on the other hand, it was crucial that the news be good, and they regarded any other interpretation as defeatist and irresponsible. For beginning in late 1961, when President Kennedy sent General Maxwell D. Taylor to Vietnam on a special mission to see what could be done to keep the country from falling to the Communists, the American commitment there underwent a radical change. From the position of a relatively cool backstage adviser—a position not too different from the one it holds in many other underdeveloped countries—the U.S. became actively involved. Over 16,000 American troops were sent in where there had only been about 600 advisers before, and American aid was boosted to one-and-a-half million dollars a day. Thus the Kennedy administration committed itself fully to Vietnam, placing the nation's prestige in Southeast Asia squarely into the hands of the Ngo family, and putting its own political future in jeopardy.

In effect, the Taylor mission argued that the war could be won, and could be won under the existing government—provided the Vietnamese military were retrained in new methods of counter-guerrilla warfare. Taylor's report recommended that helicopters and amphibious personnel carriers be given to the Vietnamese army to increase its mobility. The report also outlined programs designed to break through Diem's overly centralized and personalized government so that American aid might filter down to the peasants. Finally, Taylor suggested a series of political reforms: broadening the base of the government by taking in non-Ngo anti-Communist elements; making the national assembly more than a rubber stamp; easing some of the tight restrictions on the local press. Above all, Taylor said, the government had to interest itself in the welfare of the peasant, and to this end, Diem, who was not himself corrupt or unjust, must be persuaded to stop tolerating the corruption and injustice of local officials.

The U.S. administration and some of its representatives in the field believed that the Diem government's domestic policies could be changed by all-out American support and that the government could thereby also be led into instituting reforms it had been unwilling to make on its own. Ambassador Frederick Nolting, Jr. emphasized, however, that because of Diem's peculiar psychological makeup, only support which was full and enthusiastic could influence him. It was in line with this position that Vice-President Lyndon Johnson, when visiting Vietnam in the summer of 1961 as Kennedy's personal representative, praised Diem as an Asian Winston Churchill. When, on the plane out of Saigon, a reporter tried to talk to the Vice-President about Diem's faults, Johnson snapped, "Don't tell me about Diem. He's all we've got out there."

It is not surprising, then, that by 1962 the Americans were giving in to the Ngo family on virtually everything. Having failed to get reforms, American officials said that these reforms were being instituted; having failed to improve the demoralized state of the Vietnamese army, the Americans spoke of a new enthusiasm in the army; having failed to change the tactics of the military, they talked about bold new tactics which were allegedly driving the Communists back. For the essence of American policy was: *There is no place else to go.* Backing out of South Vietnam entirely would virtually turn Southeast Asia over to the Communists and could have disastrous repercussions in the next Presidential election. To extend the U.S. commitment would involve the country in another Korean war, and it was by no means certain that the American people were prepared to support such a war. Finding a new leader might be possible, but Diem and Nhu had allowed no national hero to emerge. Consequently, there seemed no alternative to the Taylor-Kennedy policy of helping the country to help itself—sending in advisers, helicopters, pilots, fighter bombers, and pilot-trainers—while stopping short of committing American combat troops to a war against Asians on Asian soil without atomic weapons.

Because a sensitive administration back home wanted to hear that this policy was succeeding, and because of the belief that if the Americans expressed enough enthusiasm Diem would come to trust them and be more receptive to their suggestions for reform, optimism about the situation in Vietnam became an essential element of American policy itself. Not only were members of the mission regularly optimistic in their reports and in their comments to the press, but visiting VIPs were deliberately used to make things look even better. Thus, a general or some other high official from Washington would arrive in Vietnam, spend one day in Saigon being briefed and meeting the Ngo family, and another day or two in the field touring selected strategic hamlets and units. Then at the airport on his way home he would hold a press conference in which he would declare that the war was being won, that the people were rallying to the government, and that he had been impressed by the determination of that great leader, President Diem.

But with the increase in American equipment and American participation, more American reporters also arrived, and they saw little reason to be optimistic. They were told of a new popular enthusiasm for the government; they heard the American officials talk of reforms; they would pick up their American papers and read stories from Washington about new experts on guerrilla war, about special Washington staffs on counterinsurgency, about books on the subject being rushed into print to inform the American public. Then they would go into the field and see the same tired old government tactics, the same hack political commanders in charge, the same waste of human resources.

I myself arrived in Saigon in September of 1962—a time of singularly bad feeling. François Sully, the *Newsweek* correspondent and for seventeen years a resident of Indo-China, had just been ordered out by the government—or rather by Madame Nhu. Though at first the American authorities had referred to the expulsion as a misunderstanding which would soon be cleared up, it was obvious that there was no misunderstanding at all. As far as anyone could tell, Sully was being expelled because he had offended Madame Nhu in a *Newsweek* article: a quotation from her about the guerrillas—"The enemy has more drive"—had been used under a photo of her paramilitary girl's organization, a cadre which she called "my little darlings," and which drew better pay than the government soldiers in the field. Cables from *Newsweek*'s highest executives pointing out that Sully had nothing to do with writing captions, were of no avail.

The expulsion of a colleague is a serious business for reporters, and in this case the arbitrariness and malice of the decision made it worse. Since Sully's departure was followed shortly by that of Jim Robinson of NBC, and since we all soon began to receive personal warnings of various kinds from agents of the government, we knew that the threat of expulsion hung over all of us. This meant that each man had to censor himself to a certain extent and to decide whether a particular story was important enough to be worth the risk of expulsion. I, for example, tried to avoid stories that would upset the Ngo family without shedding light on the serious issues of the country. On the other hand, in the early spring of 1963, when the military situation was deteriorating in the Delta, and then in June when it became clear that the government lacked the capacity to handle the Buddhist crisis, I decided that it was necessary to take the risk of expulsion and to write very frankly about the events involved.

What was perhaps even more disturbing than Sully's expulsion itself was the reaction of the highest American officials to it; obviously they were not in the least unhappy to see him go. He was, as one of the highest political officers at the time told me, "just a *pied noir*"—a low life. He had caused trouble for the American mission by writing solely about negative aspects of the country, and adopting a doomsday attitude toward the war. From the very beginning, then, I could see that the relation between the American mission and the American press in Vietnam was quite different from that which existed anywhere else in the world. Although the embassy occasionally chided the Ngo government for its attacks on the press, such high officials as Ambassador Nolting, General Paul Donald Harkins, and the CIA chief John H. Richardson were basically more sympathetic to the government viewpoint. They felt we were inaccurate and biased; they thought the war was being won, and they longed for control over us. "The American commitment," said an official mission white paper prepared in January 1963 for General Earle Wheeler, Chief of Staff of the Army, and rewritten once by Nolting because it was not strong enough, "has been badly hampered by irresponsible, astigmatic and sensationalized reporting."

The sources of this conflict between the press and the American mission can be seen very clearly in a comparison of the personalities of Ambassador Nolting and my predecessor as *Times* correspondent in Vietnam, Homer Bigart. Nolting is a gracious and considerate Virginian, a former philosophy professor who went into diplomacy in World War II and has been a career diplomat ever since. He had never been in the Far East before being assigned to Saigon, and because of the pressure from Washington, he badly wanted to take what the Vietnamese government was telling him at face value. If he was shown a piece of paper saying that local officials were going to do something, he was satisfied that it would be done. Though he had held an important job in NATO, he had never been much involved with reporters before, and he had almost no understanding of the press. "You're always looking for the hole in the doughnut, Mr. Halberstam," he once said to me. An extremely hard worker, he was caught in an almost impossible situation: a wartime alliance in which he was bending over backward to alleviate his ally's suspicions, at a time when his every gesture simply convinced the very same ally to take America's continued support for granted. The net effect was of a mythical partnership, for the last thing in the world the Ngo family wanted was a partnership with anyone, particularly the U.S. Still, his position would have been more sympathetic if he had not fed the fire himself. He was reporting that the war was being won, and he was pressuring his subordinates to tell him only good news; to reassure Washington, he had to believe that American policy was more successful than it actually was.

Nolting's job was difficult, but it was made even more difficult by the almost psychotic preoccupation of Diem and his family with the Western press—the one element operating in Saigon other than the Vietcong they could not control. Diem resented any criticism of his family; and since his family was in fact his government, he became angry at a wide assortment of stories. Diem and the Nhus believed that the American press was Communist-infiltrated; paradoxically the Nhus also believed that some of the reporters were CIA agents, and part of a vast underground American conspiracy against them. Hence, for example, when the first Buddhist monk burned himself to death, Diem was convinced that the act had been staged and paid for by an American television team—despite the fact that there had not been a single television man on the scene.

Every time we wrote something Diem disliked he would accuse American officials of having deliberately leaked it to us. (Actually, the source was often one of his own supposedly loyal palace intimates.) Nolting did his best to keep us from finding out anything which reflected badly on the government, but the city was filled with dissident Americans and especially Vietnamese who talked freely; it is a national characteristic of the Vietnamese that they cannot keep a secret. But unlike Diem, who could control the Vietnamese press, Nolting could not get the American reporters "on the team."

The prototype of a non-team player is Homer Bigart. A highly experienced correspondent, winner of two Pulitzer prizes for foreign reporting, Bigart has great prestige among his colleagues. He is no scholar; if he reads books it is a well kept secret, and his facility in foreign languages can be gauged by the legend about him which has it that if a Frenchman were to offer him a cigarette, he would answer: "*Je ne* smoke *pas.*" He is not one of the new breed of reporters—Yale or Harvard and a Nieman fellowship—but wherever he goes in the world he sheds light, writing simply, incisively, and informatively.

In Saigon, Bigart was fifty-five years old, and his stomach frequently bothered him. But in what was essentially a young man's assignment—a relentless, ruthless grind under tropical conditions—basic professional pride drove him on and he outworked every young reporter in town. The embassy officials who accused Sully of being a *pied noir*, and the rest of us of being too young, were obviously dazzled by Bigart's reputation and intimidated by his capacity to find out things they were trying to hide. Eventually they even tried to discredit his reporting by sly allusions to his age and health. When he left Vietnam there was a great sigh of relief from American officials on the scene.

As the situation in Vietnam continued to deteriorate militarily and politically, the antagonism of the chiefs of the American mission toward American reporters grew. In the spring of 1963, the Buddhist protest began, and for four months the reporters—and Washington—watched with a sense of hopelessness Diem's inability to deal with the swelling religious-political protest. The mission's proud boasts that Diem could handle his population and that the embassy could influence the Ngo family were stripped naked during the four-month crisis. On August 21, the entire policy seemed to collapse: after months of promising U. S. officials that he would be conciliatory toward the Buddhists, Nhu—without informing the Americans—raided Vietnam's pagodas in a veritable blood bath. The embassy not only was caught cold and ignorant when it happened, but then was unable to tell who had led the raid and inaccurately blamed it on the military. Reporters, who had predicted that something of this nature was likely to happen, described the raid and identified the raider correctly. In a sense, this meant the end of the old policy, but it ironically unleashed a new wave of criticism against the reporters.

My own first experience of this new wave came in early September, when a friend sent me a column from the New York *Journal-American* in which I was accused of being soft on Communism and of preparing the way through my dispatches in the *Times* for a Vietnamese Fidel Castro. I showed the clipping to a friend in the embassy. "Well, I think you have to expect this sort of thing," he said. "There may be more." He was right; there was more. A few days later, Joseph Alsop, after a brief visit to Vietnam, attacked a group of "young crusaders" in the Saigon press corps who, he said, were generally accurate in their reporting but were responsible for the near-psychotic state of mind among the inhabitants of GiaLong Palace. Being criticized by Alsop is no small honor in this profession; those of us whom he called the "young crusaders" knew that our stock was rising. At the same time, having covered the complex evolution of the Buddhist crisis for four long months, and having spotted the Buddhists as an emerging political force long before the American embassy, we were amazed to see ourselves charged by another visiting reporter with not having understood the political implications of the crisis. And having covered the disintegration of the Delta for more than a year-and-a-half and gone on more than thirty missions in this area, some of us were equally amazed to see ourselves charged by Mr. Alsop with not having visited what he quaintly referred to as "the front."

Alsop was not our only critic. The Kennedy administration—embarrassed by what was beginning to look like a major foreign policy failure, and angered by its ineptitude in allowing the pagoda crackdown to take place, in not having diagnosed it correctly when it did take place, and in not having any answer when it finally did analyze the situation correctly—took to attacking our reporting as inaccurate, the work of a handful of emotional and inexperienced young men. In addition, the President's press secretary, Pierre Salinger, and other White House staff members more interested in their chief's political standing at home than in the status of the war in Vietnam, would knowingly inform White House reporters that we in Vietnam never went on operations.

At the Pentagon, in the higher reaches where the realities of the war rarely penetrated, the criticism was particularly vehement. Defense Department reporters were told by Major General Victor Krulak, the Pentagon's specialist on counter-insurgency, that he simply could not understand what was happening in Vietnam. Experienced correspondents such as the free-lancer Richard Tregaskis and Marguerite Higgins (then of the *Herald Tribune*, now of *Newsday*) were finding that the war was being won, while a bunch of inexperienced young reporters kept writing defeatist stories about the political side. When Maggie Higgins was in Saigon, General Krulak told a representative of *Time* magazine, young Halberstam met her at a bar and showed her a photo of some dead bodies; he asked her if she had ever seen dead bodies, and when she said yes, he burst into tears. Krulak took great delight in passing this story around—whether it was his or Miss Higgins's invention I will never know. In any case, the long knives were really out. "It's a damn good thing you never belonged to any left-wing groups or anything like that," a friend of mine high up in the State Department told me after I left Saigon, "because they were really looking for stuff like that."

On October 22, Arthur Ochs Sulzberger, the new publisher of the *Times*, went by the White House to pay a courtesy call on the President of the United States. It was a time when, except for Vietnam, the administration was riding high and feeling very cocky: Kennedy was sure his 1964 opponent would be Goldwater and was confidently expecting a big victory. Almost the first question the President asked Mr. Sulzberger was what he thought of his young man in Saigon. Mr. Sulzberger answered that he thought I was doing fine. The President suggested that perhaps I was too close to the story, too involved (this is the most insidiously damaging thing that can be said about a reporter). No, Mr. Sulzberger answered, he did not think I was too involved. The President asked if perhaps Mr. Sulzberger had been thinking of transferring me to another assignment. No, said Mr. Sulzberger, the *Times* was quite satisfied with the present distribution of assignments. (At that particular point I was supposed to take a two-week breather, but the *Times* immediately cancelled my vacation.)

But the most curious attack of all on the Saigon press corps came from *Time* magazine. A dispute had long been simmering between *Time*'s editors in New York and its reporters in the field in Vietnam, a far sharper division than the usual one between field and office. The *Time* reporters in the field felt strongly that the magazine was giving too optimistic a view of the war. Periodically, Charles Mohr, *Time*'s chief correspondent in Southeast Asia (who had once been described by Henry Luce himself as "A reporter—and how!") would return to New York for conferences where he would argue for tougher coverage on Vietnam. But his editors, who had lunched with Secretary McNamara and other Pentagon officials and had seen the most secret of charts and the most secret of arrows, would explain patiently to him that he understood only a portion of "the big picture."

In April 1963, Richard M. Clurman, one of the foremost defenders of working reporters among *Time*'s executives, visited Saigon, met with some of the working reporters, talked with their sources, and interviewed Diem, Nhu, and Nolting. After that, matters improved somewhat, and during most of the Buddhist crisis Mohr was relatively pleased with what he was getting into the magazine. But then things took a turn for the worse again. In August 1963, a brilliant cover story he sent in on Madame Nhu was edited to underemphasize her destructive effect on the society, and several weeks later, a long and detailed piece he did on the Saigon press corps analyzing the root of the controversy and praising the work of the reporters was killed.

Finally, in early September, with Washington still searching for answers, Mohr was asked to do a roundup on the entire state of the war in Vietnam. He and his colleague, Mert Perry, put vast amounts of energy into the legwork, and the story he filed was the toughest written to that date by a resident correspondent. It began with this lead: "The war in Vietnam is being lost." Not everyone in Vietnam, Mohr noted, "would be willing to go so far at this point. But those men who know Vietnam best and have given the best of their energies and a portion of their souls to this program are suddenly becoming passionate on this subject." Washington, he continued, had asked all Saigon officials for detailed reports on what was happening, and it had given these officials a chance "to bare their souls. Much of what they write may be diluted by the time it reaches Washington. However, these men realize that they are in the middle of a first class major foreign policy crisis and that history will be a harsh judge. 'I am laying it on the line,' said one. 'Now is the time for the truth. There are no qualifications in what I write.' Another said: 'I am going on the record in black and white. The war will be lost in a year, but I gave myself some leeway and said three years.' Another said that his program in the countryside is 'dead.' One source said American military reporting in the country 'has been wrong and false—lies really. We are now paying the price.'"

This was strong stuff, and it left no doubt that American policy had **failed**. But it was not what the editors of *Time* magazine wanted to hear.

Mohr's story was killed in New York, and an optimistic piece was printed instead bearing no relation to the copy he had filed, and assuring the world that "government troops are fighting better than ever." Since this was not what most sources—the New York *Times*, the AP, the UPI, *Newsweek*, CBS, NBC—were reporting at the time, an explanation was needed. Accordingly, Otto Fuerbringer, the managing editor of *Time*, summoned a writer into his office and (as Stanley Karnow, Mohr's predecessor as *Time* bureau chief in Southeast Asia put it in *Nieman Reports*) with "nothing but his own preconceptions to guide him, dictated the gist of an article for his magazine's Press Section." Karnow called the piece that finally appeared "a devastating compendium of bitter innuendoes and clever generalities, all blatantly impeaching American correspondents in Vietnam for distorting the news." The war, it hinted, was going better than one would gather from the small incestuous clique of reporters who sat around the Caravelle Bar in Saigon interviewing each other and never venturing forth to the countryside. It was a staggering piece, for it not only indicted all of us, but two of *Time*'s own men as well. The upshot was that they both resigned, Mohr eventually going to the *Times*, where he soon became the White House correspondent, and Perry to the Chicago *Daily News*.

No one becomes a reporter to make friends, but neither is it pleasant in a situation like the war in Vietnam to find yourself completely at odds with the views of the highest officials of your country. The pessimism of the Saigon press corps was of the most reluctant kind: many of us came to love Vietnam, we saw our friends dying all around us, and we would have liked nothing better than to believe that the war was going well and that it would eventually be won. But it was impossible for us to believe those things without denying the evidence of our own senses. The enemy was growing stronger day by day, and if nothing else we would have been prevented from sending tranquilizing stories to our papers by a vision of the day when the Vietcong walked into Saigon and *Time* righteously demanded to know where those naïve reporters were now who had been telling the world that all was going well with the war in Vietnam. And so we had no alternative but to report the truth in the hope that we might finally break through the optimism that prevailed so obstinately in high places in America.

Privacy

Does an individual have a *right* to be left alone? The Fourth Amendment protects private property against improper search and seizure, but does it protect personality? The "right to privacy" in its modern sense owes its legal acceptance to an article published by two young lawyers, Samuel D. Warren and Louis D. Brandeis, in the *Harvard Law Review* in 1890. They argue that "the right to life has come to mean the right to enjoy life—the right to be let alone"; in defense of this right they invoke what they call "the principle . . . of an inviolate personality."

The following writers are all concerned with the fact that in modern America this principle is not universally respected. Richard Rovere's essay serves as a general introduction to the subject of privacy in a technological age. In a more journalistic vein, Robert Jungk explores the uses of specific technological and psychological devices in industry. Ashley Montagu attempts to enlarge the subject of loss of privacy by reminding us of the increasing attack on our senses by noise, music, and advertising. Faulkner sees the problem from yet another point of view. Speaking as a writer, he deplores the apparent confusion in the public mind between a man's work and a man's life. The concluding selection, by August Heckscher, takes issue with some of the points raised by Mr. Rovere but also continues the theme raised by Faulkner. "What is disturbing today," he writes, "is not merely the decline of privacy; it is equally the decline of a public sphere."

RICHARD H. ROVERE

Mr. Rovere was born in 1915 and educated at Bard College and Columbia University. He has held editorial positions with Harper's, *the* London Spectator, The American Scholar, *and* The New Yorker. *A prolific commentator on American politics, his books include* The Eisenhower Years *(1956),* Senator Joe McCarthy *(1959),* The Orwell Reader, *which he edited in 1956, and* The American Establishment and Other Reports, Opinions, and Speculations *(1962). He is a regular contributor to* The New Yorker *(Letter from Washington) and a frequent contributor to other magazines. The following essay appeared in* The American Scholar, *Autumn, 1958, as the first of a series on the invasion of privacy.*

TECHNOLOGY AND THE CLAIMS OF COMMUNITY

It is repeatedly asserted by solicitous groups and individuals that the right of privacy—described once by Mr. Justice Brandeis as the "right to be let alone . . . the most comprehensive of rights and the right most valued by civilized men"—is in sorry shape in this Republic today. The evidence is impressive. Wire tapping is epidemic; even where it is illegal, it flourishes, and some authorities believe that the number of telephones being monitored on any given day runs into the hundreds of thousands. "Bugging," the use of concealed electronic devices by absentee eavesdroppers, is an almost universal practice among policemen, private detectives, and both public and private investigators. People describing themselves as "investigators" are as numerous and as pestiferous, it often seems, as flies in late September. Each day, more and more of us are required to tell agencies of government more and more about ourselves;

and each melancholy day, government agencies are telling more and more about us. Someone in the F.B.I.—not Mr. Hoover, certainly, but someone —slips a "raw" file to a favored congressman; the President instructs the Bureau of Internal Revenue to turn over income tax returns to an investigating committee; the Defense Department gives medical records to an insurance adjuster. The existence of the files, apart from their disclosure, may itself be regarded as a violation of privacy; we are compelled to leave bits and pieces of ourselves in many places where we would just as soon not be.

Broadly speaking, invasions of privacy are of two sorts, both on the increase. There are those, like wire tapping and bugging and disclosure of supposedly confidential documents, that could conceivably be dealt with by changes in law or public policy. Then there are those that appear to be exercises of other rights—for example, freedom of speech, of the press, of inquiry. A newspaper reporter asks an impertinent personal question; the prospective employer of a friend wishes to know whether the friend has a happy sex life; a motivational researcher wishes to know what we have against Brand X deodorant; a magazine wishing to lure more advertisers asks us to fill out a questionnaire on our social, financial and intellectual status. Brandeis' "right to be let alone" is unique in that it can be denied us by the powerless as well as by the powerful—by a teen-ager with a portable radio as well as by a servant of the law armed with a subpoena.

Most of those who publicly lament the decline of privacy talk as if they believe that the causes are essentially political; they seem to feel that enemies of individual rights are conspiring to destroy privacy just as certain of them have sought, in recent years, to destroy the right to avoid self-incrimination. Some also see privacy eroding as a consequence of a diminishing respect for it. I think there may be something in both points, although a good deal less in the first than in the second; but it seems to me that the really important causes lie elsewhere—in our advancing technology and in the growing size and complexity of our society. Until the early part of this century, the right of privacy was seldom invoked. Though its broadest and most binding guarantee is in the Fourth Amendment to the Constitution, which affirms "the right of the people to be secure in their persons, houses, papers, and effects" and prohibits unreasonable searches and seizures, it was not until 1905 that a court squarely upheld the right of privacy. The jurisdiction was Georgia, and the court laid it down as a common-law proposition that "the right of privacy has its foundations in the instincts of nature." In a thinly populated land, with government touching only lightly on the everyday lives of citizens and with a technology so primitive that people had to depend on their own eyes and ears to know what others were up to, men armed with the Fourth Amendment and with the squirrel gun permitted them under the Second Amendment could pretty well attend to their own privacy.

Mostly, one supposes, it was not thought of as a "right" to be protected but as a condition of life cherished by some and merely accepted by others.

But then came the camera, the telephone, the graduated income tax, and later the tape recorder, the behavioral scientist, television (now being used to follow us as we move about supermarkets and department stores as a kind of radar for the light-fingered), the professional social worker, "togetherness" and a host of other developments that are destructive of privacy as a right and as a condition. Soundproofing is the only technological contribution I can think of that has been an aid to the right to be let alone. The rest have lent themselves to invasions of privacy, and the end is not yet in sight. Wire tapping, for example, is now in the process of being fully automated; where formerly the number of wires that could be tapped was limited by the number of personnel that could be assigned to sitting around all day waiting for a conversation to intercept, today innumerable phones can be monitored entirely by machines. Someday, no doubt, we shall be spied upon from space platforms equipped with television cameras. And all this time the welfare state has been developing—in the main, of course, as a response to technology. It may be that a disrespect for privacy has been on the increase, too, but what is certain is that those of a trespassing inclination are infinitely better equipped today and have infinitely more excuses for their incursions. I rather think this is the essential thing, for I believe that if the Georgia court was correct in saying that the "instincts of nature" provided foundations for the right of privacy, the same thing may also be cited as a source of motive power for those who assume the right to violate privacy. Was it not Senator McCarthy who screamed bloody murder when the Post Office Department ran a "mail cover" on his correspondence? (In a mail cover, postal officials do not open mail but examine envelopes and wrappings with a view to learning the identity of a victim's correspondents.) No doubt his outrage was as genuine as it was noisy. There is a hermit spirit in each of us, and also a snooper, a census taker, a gossipmonger and a brother's keeper.

Technology has forced the surrender of a measure of privacy in many different ways. It may be a man's business whether he drinks or not, but if he wishes to drive a car or fly an airplane or perform brain operations, society's need to inquire into his drinking habits must surely override his right to privacy in this serious matter. Government is society's instrument in such affairs, and the more responsibilities we saddle it with, the more we require it to take a hand in our lives. If we wish it to protect us against quacks, frauds, swindlers, maniacs and criminals, we must give it powers of prosecution, punishment and licensing. We can be reasonably certain that its tendency will be to go too far (the American Civil Liberties Union reports with distress that in some places tile layers must now be licensed by public authority), but we may—indeed, it seems to me that most of us do—judge its excesses to be less dangerous than complete laissez faire or laissez passer. Technology has made us all a great deal more dependent upon one another than we ever were in the past and necessarily, therefore, less able to protect our own privacy. Once we could labor alone—now there is a division of labor which relates my work to yours. Once we traveled alone—now our mobility is collectivized, and while we have a legitimate concern over the habits of the man at the controls, whose private life we find it necessary to investigate, we also constitute ourselves a captive audience and a group of hostages to those in whom the instincts of nature that lead to compulsive trespassing are more powerful than those that make sometime recluses of us all.

In my view, which may be eccentric, it gains us nothing to denounce J. Edgar Hoover or those who descend to what Mr. Justice Holmes called the "dirty business" of wire tapping—or even to expend rhetoric on the death of solitude in our kind of civilization, as William Faulkner now and then does when he feels himself affronted by the attentions of the press. If there is any way at all out of the fish bowl, it will be found only by facing some hard facts of life today. For one thing, there is no stopping the technology that extends our senses by wires and waves and electrical impulses. For another, it is difficult—if, indeed, it is possible—to distinguish, morally and practically, between the use of these devices and the use of the senses unaided. I think that wire tapping is a dirty business, but I am not sure that I can find much logic to support my belief so long as I am willing to countenance the older, unmechanized ways by which society apprehends criminals. What is the moral difference between tapping a telephone wire and straining one's ears to overhear a conversation believed by the participants to be private? What is the moral difference between putting an ear to a keyhole and bugging a room? Or between using any and all bugging devices and planting spies and informers in the underworld? Or between carrying a concealed tape recorder to an interview and carrying a concealed plan to commit to memory as much of the talk as the memory can retain? Society needs detectives, or so at least I believe, and the means they employ have never been lovely and have almost always involved the violation of privacy.

So far as morality is concerned, I doubt if a valid distinction can be made between primitive and advanced techniques. But a practical distinction can be made, and in fact has been made (wire tapping *is* either outlawed or restricted by law in every American jurisdiction), and the rationale is not very different from that which proscribes mechanical devices in most sports. Whether or not wire tapping is dirty business in the Holmesian sense, it is dirty pool, and this applies, or soon will, one suspects, to most other gadgets. It may be no more immoral than other means used for the same end—any more than killing with thermonuclear weapons is more immoral than killing with a club—but somehow the advantage it gives to the police side is offensive to sportsmanship, and the numbers that can be bagged by automated spying, like the numbers that can be killed by a hydrogen bomb, make it seem more offensive to our humanity. Against this, it can be argued that crime and subversion have also benefited by science and that their adversaries should not have to fight a horse cavalry war against them. But the fact of the matter is that it is not narcotics peddlers whose privacy has been more efficiently violated by the use of the new techniques; the net has not been drawn tighter against society's enemies—it has simply been spread for a larger catch. And here another practical distinction can be made, even though a moral one comes hard. It is one thing to deceive and trap a dope pusher by almost any means available, and quite another to tap the phone of, let us say, a philanthropic foundation on the chance of turning up a relationship between it and some citizen of a heretical turn of mind. To be sure, the underworld members of the Apalachin rally have every bit as much right to privacy as Robert M. Hutchins. But the law in its wisdom has found a way to draw a line between the two without denying their equality; this is the doctrine of "probable cause," embodied as the condition for seizure and arrest in the same Fourth Amendment that keeps most of us out of the broad net of policemen merely fishing for evidence in our homes and among our papers and effects.

It seems to me that it is by no means too late for law and public policy to deal with violations of privacy that are undertaken by zealous guardians of the peace and the public order. In all probability, wire tapping and the many forms of bugging can never be wholly eliminated, even where they are outlawed and the penalties for their use are severe; they suit the police mentality too well, and they may be easily employed without fear of detection. Moreover, there are circumstances in which even the most ardent civil libertarians would be forced to approve their use. But the third degree and the rubber truncheon also suit the police mentality, and free societies have managed to reduce their use to a point where they are not regarded as essential characteristics of the machinery of law enforcement. Probable cause, with high standards for the determination of probability, would seem a basic safeguard against present excesses. Another would be an extension of the rule of the inadmissibility of wire-tap evidence; this, of course, is the rule in the federal courts today, and it has not stopped the F.B.I. and God knows how many other government agencies from tapping wires in the hope of learning where admissible evidence may be turned up. But there is no reason why the rule of inadmissibility might not be strengthened in such a way as to give ordinary criminal defendants a chance at acquittals and reversals whenever the prosecution's case has been made by playing dirty pool. The police, like merchants, do not care for profitless ventures, and somewhere, no doubt, there is a point at which most of the profit can be taken out of the indiscriminate wire tapping and bugging that is being employed today. Mr. Justice Murphy used to say that there was no means of preserving the liberties of citizens so efficacious as making the denial of those liberties disadvantageous to the police power.

Nothing will be done, however, along this line unless a certain amount of public pressure builds up against a catch-as-catch-can view of law enforcement and in defense of the right of privacy. And even if abuses of the police power were checked, we would be left with all those invasions that are the work not of the police power, but of other public authorities and of a multitude of private ones. Here, as I see it, we encounter problems far knottier than those posed by technology in the service of law and order. We were willed a social order dedicated to the sovereignty of the individual but, again thanks mainly to technology, dependent for its functioning largely on the interdependence of lives. My behavior affects my neighbor in a hundred ways undreamed of a century ago. My home is joined to his by pipes and cables, by tax and insurance rates. If my labor is not immediately dependent on his, it is on that of other men down the street and across the continent. When I move about, my life is at my neighbor's mercy—and his, of course, at mine. I may build a high fence, bolt the doors, draw the blinds and insist that my time to myself is mine alone, but his devices for intrusion are limitless. My privacy can be invaded by a ringing telephone as well as by a tapped one. It can be invaded by an insistent community that seeks to shame me into getting up off my haunches to do something for the P.T.A. or town improvement or the American Civil Liberties Union—possibly, for this worthy organization, making a survey of invasions of privacy. My "right to be let alone" is a right I may cherish and from time to time invoke, but it is not a right favored by the conditions of the life I lead and am, by and large, pleased to be leading. If I were to think of it as any sort of absolute right, I would be as blind to the world about me as those who used to believe that the United States could assert and by itself defend its right to be let alone. No kind of sovereignty has ever been absolute, but in the last century or so the decline has been staggering.

The meaningful invasions that are a consequence of the condition of our lives are, to be sure, those undertaken more or less in the name of the whole community: by organs of government other than the police, by the press, by education, by business. Against them, the law can offer few defenses without denying other freedoms and committing new invasions of privacy. The press has a right to describe Nathan Leopold's release from prison; whether it will exercise that right in the face of eloquent pleas not to do so is a matter of conscience and taste. In general, our rule is that those who lead part of their lives in public—politicians, entertainers, writers and others, including celebrated criminal defendants, who court the public favor in one way or another—have forfeited the right to invoke the common-law doctrine that "a person who unreasonably and seriously interferes with another's interest in not having his affairs known to others . . . is liable to the other." In England, Randolph

Churchill may raise the roof because the press is, in his view, too nosey about the private life of Princess Margaret, but here there would be no one to defend the proposition that the press and public should be kept in the dark about the President's health, as the British public was once kept in the dark about the health of Randolph Churchill's father. And the same tests of public interest and relevance that apply in the community of the nation apply in every subcommunity. To a degree, we can control our privacy by controlling our mode of existence, and if we can never retain anything like complete mastery, we can at least attempt an approach to it. But the costs are heavy and to many, probably most, Americans excessive.

It is common for Europeans to say that privacy will die in America because we care nothing about it. "An American has no sense of privacy," Bernard Shaw wrote. "He does not know what it means. There is no such thing in the country." Foreigners frequently profess to be scandalized by American institutions that seem to them destructive of the very idea of privacy—the standard sleeping car, for instance, and the now ubiquitous portable radio. Alistair Cooke has said that while in England good manners consist in not intruding oneself upon others, here they consist in being tolerant of those who lead their private life in public and remain a good sport about all noisy intrusions. I think the differences are real but insignificant. The British may piously talk of the royal family's right to privacy, but their gutter press makes more lives miserable than ours does. The French set great store by privacy, but they allow their police a license that Americans would never tolerate. (The French police operate on the theory that their work would be quite impossible if they were not allowed to run mail covers, ransack telegraph files and tap wires.) We are perhaps the most gregarious and community-minded of people and have developed social and technological interdependence further than any other, but it is still, I think, universally acknowledged that the man who tells another to "mind your own business" has justice on his side and speaks the common law. We are all in the same fix, and we all have to strike the same balance between our need for others and our need for ourselves alone.

ROBERT JUNGK

Robert Jungk was born in Berlin of Austrian Jewish parents in 1913. During the Third Reich he started an underground press service, was forced to flee, but founded another anti-Nazi information bulletin in Czechoslovakia. When Prague fell, he continued his work in Paris; when Paris fell, he worked in Switzerland. There he became a correspondent for the London Observer *and also attained a Ph.D. in modern history at Zurich University. Since 1950 Mr. Jungk has been an American citizen, living in Los Angeles when not on one of his reporting trips. His books include* Brighter Than a Thousand Suns *(1958) and* Children of the Ashes: The Story of a Rebirth *(1961). The present essay is a chapter from his* Tomorrow Is Already Here *(1954).*

WORLD WITHOUT WALLS

An editor of *Ammunition,* a magazine published by the International Union of Automobile Workers, made the sharpest criticism I have yet heard of certain aspects of industrial psychology. He said to me: "During the war a 'soul engineer' in a factory whose men we organize asked them whom they hated most. At that time our adversaries naturally came first. If that man were to put the question today he would probably find that the leader in such an unpopularity contest was himself; the 'deep psychology' with which the human-relations programs are honoring us has become simply a new name for spying, a new way of driving and oppressing."

This prejudice is by no means universal. Many trade-unionists are entirely in sympathy with the efforts of the industrial psychologists. They take exception only when the new techniques of soul cure are misused. But that, they say, unfortunately occurs too often.

Perhaps a more eloquent complaint was one I heard from a man at the employing end, Mr. L., the personnel chief of a motor-parts factory. "Some of the things you'll see in my department will astonish and perhaps alarm you. They do me too." These were his surprising words when I handed him my letter of introduction from a close friend of his.

"I am not altogether blameless myself," he admitted. "It was I who first brought these Messrs. 'Soul Bunglers' and their assistants into the works. I had a great respect for science and hoped to accomplish something genuinely helpful to our people. But what came of it? A sniffing around and an agitation, a silly fooling with questionnaires, statistics and dozens of tests. And in return there's not a trace of healthy human understanding left. On paper the production in our factory seems to have risen through these methods. Despite the figures, I doubt it. But even if it were so, the price we pay is too high. Our factory has become a world without walls, without respect for individuality, without regard for private life. Why don't I draw the conclusion and leave? You ought to be able to figure that out without much psychology. I'm over fifty."

With these words, Mr. L. sent me to Mr. H., who, although he nominally works under the chief who views the new methods with horror, has in actual fact the final say in the personnel department. H., a man of about forty, has the smooth porcelain face and courteous manners of the intelligent middle-grade general staff officer, a type one comes across on subcommittees of the Joint Chiefs of Staff in Washington.

H., as he told me, discovered his calling to personnel management when he was in the Army. Driven more or less by chance into a department that used psychological tests to discover the particular aptitudes of recruits and placed them accordingly, he became, when the war was over, a specialist in choice and guidance of personnel.

Even at first glance his office resembles a laboratory. The walls are papered with colored charts, complicated statistical exhibits and graphic curves which look like illustrations of the quantum theory. In these psychographs, productometers, motive profiles, sociograms and communication charts, each worker appears as a fractional number—a decimal part of a total sum.

"The great new development in our field," affirms Mr. H., "is the inclusion of the complete personality of the employee in our evaluations. The theory and practice of scientific management have made considerable strides in the past fifteen years. Former tests contented themselves with noting the surface aspects of the candidate, such as mental reaction and signs of physical skill. Today with the help of personality tests we try to look deeper into the motives of our people. How is their emotional stability? Are they honest? Are they loyal? Do they get on with their fellow workers? What is the state of their private life? Are they married? Have they sex problems? Do they spend their money easily? What is their relationship with their parents? What with their children? Have they got inhibitions? Are they aggressive?

"Each of our employees is appraised according to forty personality traits, beginning with his upbringing, continuing through his capacity for remembering names, on to his political orientation. We don't, of course, wish to exert any direct influence on his political opinions, but as an expression of his personality, these, too, seem implicitly important and informative."

"These tests must be very long and expensive," I interposed.

Mr. H. was not of that opinion. Actually, he said, they saved the firm substantial sums. To put the wrong man in the wrong place, to give responsibility to a person incapable of taking it—these were the things that really cost money. According to his own calculations—he had splendidly illustrated memoranda on the subject to show me—the firm had saved 14.3 per cent in the past year on repairs alone because more carefully chosen people operated the machines. "A single workman can cost us thousands of dollars in damages through a mistake in the handling of a valuable machine. We invest two thousand dollars' worth of instruction in each new worker and see no point in losing it simply because we haven't adequately tested the man's character before engaging him. One single foreman who lets his childish aggressions react on the workers under him can release all sorts of protest responses, which then appear in the form of five-figure losses in the production statistics."

H. proudly showed me the interview rooms in which people seeking jobs were interrogated, given forms to fill in or watched by a tester for their reactions to certain psychological tables. With naïve pride he showed me the files kept in connection with everyone holding or aspiring to a post. There was the information of a local credit office regarding his financial circumstances, reports of his teachers and former chiefs, reports of a detective agency about his private life.

"We leave nothing to chance," said Mr. H., "and we've been proved right."

At all events, this system of "personal weighing" introduced into the firm under his guidance still held, he regretfully admitted, a large gap. "What's the use of all the tests for our lower and middle-grade employees if we, the managers, don't submit ourselves to equally severe ones?" he asked. "Something must and will be altered here. Capability must be the decisive factor in leadership. Not influence or seniority. There are any number of firms which do put their leading people through such tests and have thereby lopped off a great deal of deadwood. Well, one can't have everything right away. . . ." He looked me in the face with an air of aggressive self-consciousness and I guessed at once what he had in mind. Over the head of his superior, Mr. L., the guillotine of personality tests was already suspended.

Advocates of industrial psychology can produce a number of strong arguments for increased psychological penetration of the working world.

They believe that the advantages to be gained by probing deeply into personality and private life far outweigh the disadvantages. The people who are tested, they say, are themselves generally grateful for having been prevented from taking up posts they would have been unable to fill. At the same time the continual observation of all employees makes possible the speedier advancement of many a gifted person who would formerly have remained unnoticed.

But in practice, many cases contradict this friendly picture. Since it is a matter of mass choice, the tests are apt to be applied hurriedly, superficially and mechanically. Only too often distorted results are produced and the fate of a capable person endangered by the faulty inferences of a soul engineer with too much work piled on his desk. Despite such errors, which no one denies, American industry keeps to its new system of psychological choice and guidance because, as the personnel chief of a California airplane factory told me, there is no other feasible standard for allotting posts.

"What could we go by otherwise?" he asked. "Hundreds of people about whom we know nothing come into my department in the course of a month asking for employment. When the factories were small and the job seekers came chiefly from the neighborhood, it was easy to dispense with tests. One knew his neighbors, friends, teachers, former employers. But nowadays people travel thousands of miles to find work in a region that suits them. Look at today's application list alone: a man from Vermont, another from Arkansas, a third from Chicago, a fourth from Portland. We can't, really, rely altogether on their word."

An assiduous young psychologist in General Motors who looks after about two hundred thousand people defended the system as follows: "Our concerns have grown to such dimensions that the relationship between the upper and middle ranks and the mass of workers has naturally become less familiar than formerly. In a little business of about a hundred men the chief used to know his people and the people knew each other fairly well. It was easy then to find out which people deserved advancement or a rise in wages. The psychological test is unhappily a necessary substitute for years of close acquaintance. Now we are obliged to conduct mass interrogations regularly, if only to be able to ascertain the general mood in the works."

One of the main difficulties in the way of a fair application of psychological tests is the scarcity of trained psychologists. In 1950, when thousands of firms were demanding the help of soul engineers, there were only three hundred qualified industrial psychologists in existence. Therefore, only the largest firms can, for the present, maintain house psychologists. The others must have recourse to special concerns, such as the Psychological Corporation of New York, thoroughly serious firms, in the midst of the many spurious ones that have followed the trend and plunged into the tempting business of soul guidance.

The fees demanded by the psychological advisory firms are high. They are generally consulted, for the first time, when strong signs of social unrest appear in some part of a factory organism. A sudden fall in the production figures not to be accounted for by technical deficiencies, an unusual accumulation of defective products, quarrels in one or more departments and threats of strike are usually the occasion.

The Psychological Corporation, when the alarm is given, moves in at once with its specialists and the whole bag of tricks for the investigation of psychological unrest. The inevitable questionnaires are distributed, personal interviews held with the staff of the business from top to bottom, and on occasion, if simple methods prove inadequate, microphones concealed here and there for the reception of "candid reactions"—that is, expressions of the employees not intended for the ears of the observers.

The diagnosis reached through the investigation, if the business is very large, is obtained by the collation of the facts according to a definite system, stamping on perforated cards and calculations of the average value. The ostensible mood can then be exactly stated in percentages. Such a "report on mood," regarded as a model in professional circles, was made, for example, on behalf of General Motors, on the strength of over a hundred thousand depositions. In order to disguise the true purpose the interrogation was camouflaged as a prize essay; valuable awards in the form of automobiles were offered for the best answers to the question "Why I like my job."

When a firm of psychological advisers has made its report and pointed out ways to a psychological cure, it does not fail to recommend regular psychological guidance as a prescription for prevention of further difficulties and to offer its own services in this respect at a reduced subscription price.

Such a service comprises a test program to eliminate from the start all possible troublemakers and failures among the prospective employees; secondly, comes a "merit rating" program which again scrutinizes the employees and establishes their capacities at regular intervals, considering whether a man is under- or overpaid, whether he ought to be dismissed or promoted; finally, a "morale-building" program, which is responsible for the maintenance of a good mood and working spirit in the business.

If the first psychological "emergency treatment" has been successful, there is every chance that the direction of a business with a modern outlook will secure the permanent collaboration of a firm of soul engineers, especially one which can prove, by application of practical psychology on its own behalf, that its services will cost the client practically nothing since they can be deducted from income tax. In this way the firm of Rohrer, Hibler and Replogle, founded in Chicago in 1945 by the legal psychologist Perry L. Rohrer, acquired one hundred and seventy-five permanent clients in the course of five years. Its specialty is the "development of suitable manager material." First, one of the firm's eighteen qualified psychologists is commissioned to make a series of quick analyses. He maps out, in a few sittings, an exact personal-development history of every man in a responsible position, puts the patient through a series of deep psychological tests and then tries to rebuild him by a lightning treatment on the basis of his acquired experiences. Professional psychologists would probably not think much of the seriousness of these soul treatments if they were told that the conferences between manager and industrial psychologist often take place "during a game of golf or over a glass of beer."

Individual treatment of this sort is too expensive for middle-size businesses. In firms of this class the technique of the group interview is practiced with considerable success. Eight or ten candidates for employment or promotion are brought together in the same room. They are given a general discussion theme closely connected with their work—in an airplane concern, for example, "The advantages and disadvantages of air-freight traffic"—and left to themselves for a prearranged period of generally about an hour. But only in appearance, for at least three observers belonging to the advisory firm are listening to the debates and marking each candidate according to various criteria: Is he too aggressive? Is he too passive? Is he convincing? Amiable? Does he have personal magnetism? Capacities of leadership? Is he patient or does he easily become irritable?

"The ideal arrangement for such a group interview," writes Harold Fields, one of the testers in the employ of the city of New York, "is a room in which the candidates sit around a table. The walls are of glass, transparent from the outside and like a mirror on the inside. Behind them sits the invisible testing committee. Openings in the wall make it possible to hear what is being said in the room."

The so-called self-valuation techniques have also begun to find favor. Employees who work in the same group are provided with questionnaires in which they are requested to state in confidence to the soul engineer their opinion of their nearest fellow worker. In this way the psychological examiner is said to obtain an exact picture of the "social build-up of the group." He can then, for example, remove a particular harmful element from this body and introduce instead an active optimistic element.

While the participants in such interviews at least know that they are being watched and appraised, this is not true in the case of many of the newer psychological screenings. Sales personnel in department stores and shops are regularly examined for their abilities by testers of the Willmark Corporation who pose as customers. These investigators, to make the deception complete, go to the length of purchasing wares which are later returned to the firm. A report on each sales person is prepared on a form, stating among other things whether he has been friendly or sullen, whether he tried, by suggestive sales technique, to encourage the customer to buy more, whether he kept the disciplinary rules of the business, how he took leave of the customer. It is a matter of pride with the Willmark Service System and its thirty-three branches all over America that virtually none of its sales analysts is ever unmasked by one of his victims.

Some firms use the system of keeping an applicant waiting at length in an anteroom while they have him watched through television cameras or simply by a schooled secretary. Before the man has even had a chance to speak with the chief of personnel he has been unwittingly judged and condemned. For they believe it possible to determine by the degree of friendliness with which he greets the secretary, the assurance with which he expresses his wish, the calm or nervousness with which he waits, whether he uses his time to read the magazines at his disposal or to look ahead of him in boredom, trepidation or annoyance, whether he is suitable for the vacant post.

The American partiality for mechanical patents has created a large series of machines for judging and assessing human beings. Tape-recording instruments, television equipment, cameras and complicated calculating machines are introduced. The chronograph, invented by the anthropologist, Eliot Chaple, is said to be able to measure the initiative, skill, friendliness and other qualities of the good salesman with ninety-per-cent exactitude.

But the most uncanny of the machines is the polygraph, now employed by at least three hundred American firms and popularly called the lie detector. When it became known that this apparatus had been installed by important government offices of national defense, for use in the selection of their personnel, a storm was raised in the press against such a violation of the rights of personal freedom. This practice is said to have then been abandoned. But the business world was untouched by the wave of protest, and there the polygraph is used more and more.

At first the lie detector was employed only by the police for the purpose of obtaining confessions. Then the private-detective agencies added polygraph departments in order to be able to offer their clients this new service. Banks, insurance companies and similar types of enterprise in which there was danger of embezzlement began to make use of the new apparatus with great success. Department stores and chain stores followed suit. They started the practice of sending their employees every three months for a polygraph test, on the correct assumption that fear of such an examination would eliminate or substantially reduce the small thefts from the stockrooms customary in such businesses. When the armaments industry was obliged to conceal more and more of its work, the trial by lie detector was made a prerequisite to the engagement of any person whose function it would be to deal with confidential orders of the armed forces.

How precisely the lie detector, which has been constantly bettered since its beginnings, can work I learned for myself when the polygraph specialists of the Los Angeles police consented to put me through a test. It was agreed that I should answer a number of personal questions, sometimes truly, sometimes with a lie. The questions of the examiner were to be so formulated as to be answered with a *yes* or *no*. I lied about my age, my birthday, my actions at a certain hour the previous day and the sum of money I had in my wallet. Although it was only a game, with no emotions of fear or guilt to assist the discovery, the tester recognized three lies out of four with certainty and one with near certainty. The most astonishing feature was its ability to detect not only a lie but a doubt. I had hesitated in my mind as to whether I had sixteen or eighteen dollars on me. This hesitation was plainly noted by the instrument even though I naturally did not alter the expression of my face.

I had occasion later to accompany a private polygraph specialist to his work in the personnel division of an aircraft factory near Los Angeles. He allowed me, after I had been presented as his assistant—a white lie of which the tester was not ashamed—to participate in a real truth trial.

It took place in a room without windows which even in the daytime was artificially illuminated with soft indirect lighting, a semi-twilight intended to remove any irritation and have a relaxing effect. There was no sound from without, the temperature was mild and even and the walls were painted a friendly cream color.

The girl to be tested sat down in a comfortable leather armchair with a high back which was turned to the desk. To her were now deftly attached a number of hooks and buckles. The tester chatted with her informally meanwhile about general topics.

"Do you still live in the same Motor Court as when you applied for the interview?" he asked sympathetically. "That wouldn't do in the long run. Myself, I shouldn't be able to bear it. Those car noises early in the morning when the overnight guests move on . . ."

"Oh, no," she prattled, very rapidly. "We had such a stroke of luck and found a little place right away with a built-in kitchen corner. Altogether everything has gone so smoothly up to now. When I saw your advertisement in our local paper in Allentown I said to Bill—that's my husband—there's our chance to go west at last. He agreed right away and here we are."

"That's fine," said the tester. "When you come out here quite new you often have trouble finding a place to live."

"Yes," she said, "we were specially lucky."

"Now make yourself quite comfortable," said the examiner; "what's the excitement? there's no need for it."

"The whole thing's a bit unusual. I feel as if I were on the electric chair with that stuff around my arm and on my chest."

"I won't hurt you," the man assured her as he turned the second contact button. "The sling round your right upper arm measures your blood pressure, the rubber coil over the chest your breathing and the two metal disks on the joints of your hands the moisture of the skin. If you find the test disagreeable, you are, of course, free to refuse it."

"If all this is really necessary for getting the job . . ."

"I fear it is necessary. It's for a position of confidence, you know. Just answer my questions truthfully. That's all I ask of you."

Before him on the table lay the questionnaire which the applicant had filled in.

"Your name is Erna Krazinsky?"

"Yes."

"You were born in Troy, New Jersey?"

"Yes."

"Your last post was with Johnson and Johnson?"

"Yes."

"You left the post voluntarily?"

"Yes."

"Or were you dismissed?"

"No . . . I said voluntarily."

"Please answer only *yes* or *no*," he repeated in his kind, imperturbable voice.

"Did you eat meat yesterday evening?"

"Yes."

"Is your father still alive?"

"No."

"Did you come to California ten days ago?"

"Yes."

"You were never before in California?"

"No."

"You went to high school for four years?"

"Yes."

"Are you married?"

"Yes."

"You have children?"

"No."

"You are twenty-six years old?"

"Yes."

"Were you ever divorced?"

"No."

"Good, Mrs. Krazinsky," said the tester, "the torture is over. Was it really so bad?" He loosened the various bindings with which she had been attached to the chair and patted her laughingly on the shoulder. "You've done your bit well," he said kindly.

"May I possibly know the result?" asked the candidate, raising a coquettish eye to him as she smoothed her skirt.

"Sorry," said the interviewer, "the result is naturally confidential. But we'll soon write to you."

When she had passed through the door, he wrote on the upper left-hand side of the questionnaire a large 45.

"That means," he explained to me, "that Mrs. Krazinsky is only 45 per cent truthful. So she hasn't the faintest chance of getting the job. For the posts advertised only candidates 100 per cent honest are considered. Besides, she knew she practically hadn't a chance, else she wouldn't have made that attempt at flirting just before she left. But the polygraph doesn't react to flirting."

The rectangular box standing on the tester's desk had, then, weighed and found wanting. With its buttons, its tension gauge and the paper drum covered with curving signs written on it by automatic pencils, it resembled in many ways the control instruments I had seen on the boards of power houses, steel smelters and atomic factories. There they disclosed the pressure of a boiler, the strength of a current. Here they measured heartbeats, breathing, cold sweat, blood pressure, and it was possible to infer thereby what had taken place in the innermost thoughts of a man.

"Mrs. Krazinsky has lied certainly twice, probably three times," stated the tester. "She did not come to California ten days ago for the first time. That's certain. Every time the conversation touched on the topic the polygraph needles deflected. Here at the very beginning, when we were still chatting about indifferent things, the curves run even. But when I —quite innocently, by the way, and without intending to put a test question—spoke of the housing shortage for newcomers, the apparatus reacted so clearly that I decided to put the question again later on. And this time the deflection was even greater. In between came neutral questions which I knew would be answered truthfully. Hardly anyone lies when you ask what he's eaten. By such questions I establish the normal level of excitement. Anything that goes beyond it is suspicious."

"Why do you think she lied on that particular point?" I asked.

"Oh, there are a number of possible reasons. Perhaps she only wanted to arouse the interviewer's sympathy by making it seem she had come here all the way from Pennsylvania just for the sake of this job. It may be, too, that she's worked in one or more firms round about Los Angeles and been dismissed from all of them. That seems to be the most likely. Because, look, the question about the last post brings another strong hook on all four measuring curves. And do you see the jump here at the question about whether she's married? The blood-pressure gauge and the skin contact gauge show that something is not in order there. The breathing gauge and the heart curve are unclear. There's something odd about that, too. Probably she lives with someone she isn't married to."

Certainly the use of the lie detector for personnel selection represents the limit of the psychotechnical invasion of personality, and it would be unfair to judge all the accomplishments of industrial psychology by the exaggerations for which it is responsible.

But even the far more innocent and ethically unobjectionable techniques of counseling, the public-opinion polls and the promotion of happy industrial relations, have indirect effects all too reminiscent of similar phenomena in the totalitarian states. Knowing that before and during their employment they are being watched by people in whose hands lie their economic fate, many who wish to keep their jobs speak in a way that does not reflect their true feelings.

Millions of Americans, as soon as they cross the threshold of their place of work, step, partly consciously, partly almost unconsciously, into roles which correspond to what the soul engineers expect of them. They are happy, and "keep smiling" even when they do not feel so inclined. They act as though they were "well balanced" and "perfectly normal" even when they have a tremendous urge to kick over the traces. They strain every fiber to suppress their natural aggressiveness and to be "good companions" with whom everyone easily gets along, even when they would like to break into loud curses at the man at the next desk. And above all, they behave as though they were loyal to the firm through thick and thin, even if they find more to criticize in it than to praise.

This standard mask of the "jolly good fellow," of the "easy going guy," of the "sweet girl," grows onto some of them as a second face. It is no longer a question of the inner conscience, of a true impulse of the soul, but of codes of behavior coming from the outside. To judge how the wind from the heights of the directors' office will blow, how the potential giver of an order would like the salesman to behave, to guess how a superior pictures the man whom he will promote, this is the most important asset in the battle for a living. In place of rules and regulations imposed by the authorities appears a far stricter self-censorship. Be sure to do nothing striking or unusual, which could be regarded as neurotic, as egotistical, as maladjusted or perhaps even revolutionary.

Thus in the "world without walls" which has increasingly come to be, the type of man on which America's greatness was based is becoming rarer and rarer; the strong, free man guided by his own conscience, constantly searching for something new. Since four out of five Americans today are employees (as against one in five a hundred years ago), a profound alteration in the national character is taking place, a contradiction of the democratic tradition and a cause of concern to every friend of America.

WILLIAM FAULKNER

William Faulkner (1897–1962) lived most of his life in Oxford, Mississippi. He left high school to work in his grandfather's bank, served as a pilot in the Royal Canadian Air Force during World War I, and enrolled at the University of Mississippi in the fall of 1919 but withdrew without taking a degree. Discouraged at trying to earn a living by writing, he took a job as night superintendent of a power plant in the summer of 1929. The publication of the novel Sanctuary *the next year won him a popular following, financial security, and marked the turning point of his career, which culminated in his receiving the Nobel Prize for literature in 1949. From 1957 until his death in 1962 he was a writer in residence at the University of Virginia.*

In Sartoris *(1929), Faulkner first created Yoknapatawpha, a fictional Mississippi county which became the locale for a number of his best novels. His fiction is vividly memorable for its unique style and its dense, uncompromising portrayal of Southern life. Some of his best known books are* The Sound and the Fury *(1929);* As I Lay Dying *(1930);* Absalom, Absalom! *(1936);* Light in August *(1950);* The Snopes Trilogy: *The* Hamlet *(1940),* The Town *(1957), and* The Mansion *(1959); and* A Fable *(1954), for which he received the Pulitzer Prize. Although long recognized as a major American writer, Faulkner never felt himself to be a public figure and considered his life to be out of the public domain. This attitude is clearly reflected in the article we present below from* Harper's, *July, 1955.*

ON PRIVACY: THE AMERICAN DREAM, WHAT HAPPENED TO IT

This was the American Dream: a sanctuary on the earth for individual man: a condition in which he could be free not only of the old established closed-corporation hierarchies of arbitrary power which had oppressed him as a mass, but free of that mass into which the hierarchies of church and state had compressed and held him individually thralled and individually impotent.

A dream simultaneous among the separate individuals of men so asunder and scattered as to have no contact to match dreams and hopes among the old nations of the Old World which existed as nations not on citizenship but subjectship, which endured only on the premise of size and docility of the subject mass; the individual men and women who said as with one simultaneous voice: "We will establish a new land where man can assume that every individual man—not the mass of men but individual men—has inalienable right to individual dignity and freedom within a fabric of individual courage and honorable work and mutual responsibility."

Not just an idea, but a condition: a living human condition designed to be co-eval with the birth of America itself, engendered, created, and simultaneous with the very air and word America, which at that one stroke, one instant, should cover the whole earth with one simultaneous suspiration like air or light. And it was, it did: radiating outward to cover even the old weary repudiated still-thralled nations, until individual men everywhere, who had no more than heard the name, let alone knew where America was, could respond to it, lifting up not only their hearts but the hopes too which until now they did not know—or anyway dared not remember—that they possessed.

A condition in which every man would not only not be a king, he wouldn't even want to be one. He wouldn't even need to bother to need to be the equal of kings because now he was free of kings and all their similar congeries; free not only of the symbols but of the old arbitrary hierarchies themselves which the puppet-symbols represented—courts and cabinets and churches and schools—to which he had been valuable not as an individual but only as that integer, his value compounded in that immutable ratio to his sheer mindless numbers, that animal increase of his will-less and docile mass.

The dream, the hope, the condition which our forefathers did not bequeath to us, their heirs and assigns, but rather bequeathed us, their successors, to the dream and the hope. We were not even given the chance then to accept or decline the dream, for the reason that the dream already owned and possessed us at birth. It was not our heritage because we were its, we ourselves heired in our successive generations to the dream by the idea of the dream. And not only we, their sons born and bred in America, but men born and bred in the old alien repudiated lands, also felt that breath, that air, heard that promise, that proffer that there was such a thing as hope for individual man. And the old nations themselves, so old and so long-fixed in the old concepts of man as to have thought themselves beyond all hope of change, making oblation to that new dream of that new concept of man by gifts of monuments and devices to mark the portals of that inalienable right and hope:

"There is room for you here from about the earth, for all ye individually homeless, individually oppressed, individually unindividualized."

A free gift left to us by those who had mutually travailed and individually endured to create it; we, their successors, did not even have to earn, deserve it, let alone win it. We did not even need to nourish and feed it. We needed only to remember that, living, it was therefore perishable and must be defended in its crises. Some of us, most of us perhaps, could not have proved by definition that we knew exactly what it was. But then, we didn't need to: who no more needed to define it than we needed to define that air we breathed or that word, which, the two of them, simply by existing simultaneously—the breathing of the American air which made America—together had engendered and created the dream on that first day of America as air and motion created temperature and climate on the first day of time.

Because that dream was man's aspiration in the true meaning of the word aspiration. It was not merely the blind and voiceless hope of his heart: it was the actual inbreathe of his lungs, his lights, his living and unsleeping metabolism, so that we actually lived the Dream. We did not live *in* the dream: we lived the Dream itself, just as we do not merely live *in* air and climate, but we live Air and Climate; we ourselves individually representative of the Dream, the Dream itself actually audible in the strong uninhibited voices which were not afraid to speak cliché at the very top of them, giving to the cliché-avatars of "Give me liberty or give me death" or "This to be self-evident that all individual men were created equal in one mutual right to freedom" which had never lacked for truth anyway, assuming that hope and dignity and truth, a validity and immediacy absolving them even of cliché.

That was the Dream: not man created equal in the sense that he was created black or white or brown or yellow and hence doomed irrevocably to that for the remainder of his days—or rather, not doomed with equality but blessed with equality, himself lifting no hand but instead lying curled and drowsing in the warm and airless bath of it like the yet-wombed embryo; but liberty in which to have an equal start at equality with all other men, and freedom in which to defend and preserve that equality by means of the individual courage and the honorable work and the mutual responsibility. Then we lost it. It abandoned us, which had supported and pro-

tected and defended us while our new nation of new concepts of
human existence got a firm enough foothold to stand erect among the
nations of the earth, demanding nothing of us in return save to remember
always that, being alive, it was therefore perishable and so must be held
always in the unceasing responsibility and vigilance of courage and
honor and pride and humility. It is gone now. We dozed, slept, and it
abandoned us. And in that vacuum now there sound no longer the strong
loud voices not merely unafraid but not even aware that fear existed,
speaking in mutual unification of one mutual hope and will. Because
now what we hear is a cacophony of terror and conciliation and compromise babbling only the mouth-sounds, the loud and empty words
which we have emasculated of all meaning whatever—freedom, democracy, patriotism—with which, awakened at last, we try in desperation
to hide from ourselves that loss.

Something happened to the Dream. Many things did. This, I think,
is a symptom of one of them.

About ten years ago a well known literary critic and essayist, a good
friend of long standing, told me that a wealthy widely circulated weekly
pictorial magazine had offered him a good price to write a piece about
me—not about my work or works, but about me as a private citizen, an
individual. I said No, and explained why: my belief that only a writer's
works were in the public domain, to be discussed and investigated and
written about, the writer himself having put them there by submitting
them for publication and accepting money for them; and therefore he not
only would but must accept whatever the public wished to say or do
about them from praise to burning. But that, until the writer committed
a crime or ran for public office, his private life was his own; and not only
had he the right to defend his privacy, but the public had the duty to do
so since one man's liberty must stop at exactly the point where the next
one's begins; and that I believed that anyone of taste and responsibility
would agree with me.

But the friend said No. He said:

"You are wrong. If I do the piece, I will do it with taste and responsibility. But if you refuse me, sooner or later someone will do it who will
not bother about taste or responsibility either, who will care nothing about
you or your status as a writer, an artist, but only as a commodity:
merchandise: to be sold, to increase circulation, to make a little money."

"I don't believe it," I said. "Until I commit a crime or announce for
office, they can't invade my privacy after I ask them not to."

"They not only can," he said, "but once your European reputation gets
back here and makes you financially worth it, they will. Wait and see."

I did. I did both. Two years ago, by mere chance during a talk with an
editor in the house which publishes my books, I learned that the same
magazine had already set on foot the same project which I had declined
eight years before; I don't know whether the publishers were formally

notified or if they just heard about it by chance too, as I did. I said No
again, recapitulating the same reasons which I still believed were not even
arguable by anyone possessing the power of the public press, since the
qualities of taste and responsibility would have to be inherent in that power
for it to be valid and allowed to endure. The editor interrupted.

"I agree with you," he said. "Besides, you don't need to give me reasons.
The simple fact that you don't want it done is enough. Shall I attend to it
for you?" So he did, or tried to. Because my critic friend was still right.
Then I said:

"Try them again. Say 'I ask you: please don't.'" Then I submitted the
same *I ask you: please don't* to the writer who was to do the piece. I don't
know whether he was a staff writer designated to the job, or whether he
volunteered for it, or perhaps himself sold his employers on the idea.
Though my recollection is that his answer implied, "I've got to, if I refuse
they will fire me," which is probably correct, since I got the same answer
from a staff-member of another magazine on the same subject.

And if that was so, if the writer, a member of the craft he served, was
victim too of that same force of which I was victim—that irresponsible
use which is therefore misuse and which in its turn is betrayal, of that
power called Freedom of the Press which is one of the most potent and
priceless of the defenders and preservers of human dignity and rights—
then the only defense left me was to refuse to co-operate, have anything
to do with the project at all. Though by now I knew that that would not
save me, that nothing I could do would stop them.

Perhaps they—the writer and his employer—didn't believe me, could
not believe me. Perhaps they dared not believe me. Perhaps it is impossible
now for any American to believe that anyone not hiding from the police
could actually not want, as a free gift, his name and photograph in any
printed organ, no matter how base or modest or circumscribed in circulation. Though perhaps the matter never reached this point: that both of
them—the publisher and the writer—knew from the first, whether I did
or not, that the three of us, the two of them and their victim, were all
three victims of that fault (in the sense that the geologist uses the term)
in our American culture which is saying to us daily: "Beware!," the three
of us faced as one not with an idea, a principle of choice between good
and bad taste or responsibility or lack of it, but with a fact, a condition
in our American life before which all three of us were (at that moment)
helpless, at that moment doomed.

So the writer came with his group, force, crew, and got his material
where and how he could and departed and published his article. But
that's not the point. The writer is not to be blamed since, empty-handed,
he would (if my recollection is right) have been fired from the job
which deprived him of the right to choose between good and bad taste.
Nor the employer either, since to hold his (the employer's) precarious own
in a craft can compel even him, head and chief of one of its integral com-

ponents, to serve the mores of the hour in order to survive among his rival ones.

It's not what the writer said, but that he said it. That he—they—published it, in a recognized organ which, to be and remain recognized, functions on the assumption of certain inflexible standards; published it not only over the subject's protests but with complete immunity to them; an immunity not merely assumed to itself by the organ but an immunity already granted in advance by the public to which it sold its wares for a profit. The terrifying (not shocking; we cannot be shocked by it since we permitted its birth and watched it grow and condoned and validated it and even use it individually for our own private ends at need) thing is that it could have happened at all under those conditions. That it could have happened at all with its subject not even notified in advance. And even when he, the victim, was warned by accident in advance, he was still completely helpless to prevent it. And even after it was done, the victim had no recourse whatever since, unlike sacrilege and obscenity, we have no laws against bad taste, perhaps because in a democracy the majority of the people who make the laws don't recognize bad taste when they see it, or perhaps because in our democracy bad taste has been converted into a marketable and therefore taxable and therefore lobbyable commodity by the merchandising federations which at the same simultaneous time create the market (not the appetite: that did not need creating: only pandering to) and the product to serve it, and bad taste by simple solvency was purified of bad taste and absolved. And even if there had been grounds for recourse, the matter would still have remained on the black side of the ledger since the publisher could charge the judgment and costs to operating loss and the increased sales from the publicity to capital investment.

The point is that in America today any organization or group, simply by functioning under a phrase like Freedom of the Press or National Security or League Against Subversion, can postulate to itself complete immunity to violate the individualness—the individual privacy lacking which he cannot be an individual and lacking which individuality he is not anything at all worth the having or keeping—of anyone who is not himself a member of some organization or group numerous enough or rich enough to frighten them off. That organization will not be of writers, artists, of course; being individuals, not even two artists could ever confederate, let alone enough of them. Besides, artists in America don't have to have privacy because they don't need to be artists as far as America is concerned. America doesn't need artists because they don't count in America; artists have no more place in American life than the employers of the weekly pictorial magazine staff-writers have in the private life of a Mississippi novelist.

But there are the other two occupations which are valuable to American life, which require, demand privacy in order to endure, live. These are science and the humanities, the scientists and the humanitarians: the pioneers in the science of endurance and mechanical craftsmanship and self-discipline and skill like Colonel Lindbergh who was compelled at last to repudiate it by the nation and culture one of whose mores was an inalienable right to violate his privacy instead of an inviolable duty to defend it, the nation which assumed an inalienable right to abrogate to itself the glory of his renown yet which had neither the power to protect his children nor the responsibility to shield his grief; the pioneers in the simple science of saving the nation like Dr. Oppenheimer who was harassed and impugned through those same mores until all privacy was stripped from him and there remained only the qualities of individualism whose possession we boast since they alone differ us from animals—gratitude for kindness, fidelity to friendship, chivalry toward women, and the capacity to love—before which even his officially vetted harassers were impotent, turning away themselves (one hopes) in shame, as though the whole business had had nothing whatever to do with loyalty or disloyalty or security or insecurity, but was simply to batter and strip him completely naked of the privacy lacking which he could never have become one of that handful of individuals capable of serving the nation at a moment when apparently nobody else was, and so reduce him at last to one more identity-less integer in that identityless anonymous unprivacied mass which seems to be our goal.

And even that is only a point of departure. Because the sickness itself goes much further back. It goes back to that moment in our history when we decided that the old simple moral verities over which taste and responsibility were the arbiters and controls, were obsolete and to be discarded. It goes back to that moment when we repudiated the meaning which our fathers had stipulated for the words "liberty" and "freedom," on and by and to which they founded us as a nation and dedicated us as a people, ourselves in our time keeping only the mouth-sounds of them. It goes back to the moment when we substituted license in the place of liberty—license for any action which kept within the proscription of laws promulgated by confederations of the practitioners of the license and the harvesters of the material benefits. It goes back to that moment when in place of freedom we substituted immunity for any action to any recourse, provided merely that the act be performed beneath the aegis of the empty mouth-sound of freedom.

At which instant truth vanished too. We didn't abolish truth; even we couldn't do that. It simply quit us, turned its back on us, not in scorn nor even contempt nor even (let us hope) despair. It just simply quit us, to return perhaps when whatever it will be—suffering, national disaster, maybe even (if nothing else will serve) military defeat—will have taught us to prize truth and pay any price, accept any sacrifice (oh yes, we are brave and tough too; we just intend to put off having to be as long as possible) to regain and hold it again as we should never have let it go: on its own compromiseless terms of taste and responsibility. Truth—that long clean clear simple undeviable unchallengeable straight and shining line, on one side of which black is black and on the other white is white, has now become an angle, a point of view having nothing to do with truth nor even with fact, but depending solely on where you are standing when you look at it. Or rather—better—where you can contrive to have him standing whom you are trying to fool or obfuscate when he looks at it.

Across the board in fact, a parlay, a daily triple: truth and freedom and liberty. The American sky which was once the topless empyrean of freedom, the American air which was once the living breath of liberty, are now become one vast down-crowding pressure to abolish them both, by destroying man's individuality as a man by (in that turn) destroying the last vestige of privacy without which man cannot be an individual. Our very architecture itself has warned us. Time was when you could see neither from inside nor from outside through the walls of our houses. Time is when you can see from inside out though still not from outside in through the walls. Time will be when you can do both. Then privacy will indeed be gone; he who is individual enough to want it even to change his shirt or bathe in, will be cursed by one universal American voice as subversive to the American way of life and the American flag.

If (by that time) walls themselves, opaque or not, can still stand before that furious blast, that force, that power rearing like a thunder-clap into the American zenith, multiple-faced yet mutually conjunctived, bellowing the words and phrases which we have long since emasculated of any significance or meaning other than as tools, implements, for the further harassment of the private individual human spirit, by their furious and immunized high priests: "Security." "Subversion." "Anti-Communism." "Christianity." "Prosperity." "The American Way." "The Flag."

With odds at balance (plus a little fast footwork now and then of course) one individual can defend himself from another individual's liberty. But when powerful federations and organizations and amalgamations like publishing corporations and religious sects and political parties and legislative committees can absolve even one of their working units of the restrictions of moral responsibility by means of such catch-phrases as "Freedom" and "Salvation" and "Security" and "Democracy," beneath which blanket absolution the individual salaried practitioners are themselves freed of individual responsibility and restraint, then let us beware. Then even people like Dr. Oppenheimer and Colonel Lindbergh and me (the weekly magazine staff-writer too if he really was compelled to choose between good taste and starvation) will have to confederate in our turn to preserve that privacy in which alone the artist and scientist and humanitarian can function.

Or to preserve life itself, breathing; not just artists and scientists and humanitarians, but the parents by law or biology of doctors of osteopathy too. I am thinking of course of the Cleveland doctor convicted recently of the brutal slaying of his wife, three of whose parents—his wife's father and his own father and mother—with one exception did not even outlive that trial regarding which the Press itself, which kept the sorry business on most of the nation's front pages up to the very end, is now on record as declaring that it was overcovered far beyond its value and importance.

I am thinking of the three victims. Not the convicted man: he will doubtless live a long time yet; but of the three parents, two of whom died —one of them anyway—because, to quote the Press itself, "he was wearied of life," and the third one, the mother, by her own hand, as though she had said, *I can bear no more of this.*

Perhaps they died solely because of the crime, though one wonders why the coincidence of their deaths was not with the commission of the murder but with the publicity of the trial. And if it was not solely because of the tragedy itself that one of the victims was "wearied of life" and another obviously said, *I can bear no more*—if they had more than that one reason to relinquish and even repudiate life, and the man was guilty as the jury said he was, just what medieval witch-hunt did that power called Freedom of the Press, which in any civilized culture must be accepted as that dedicated paladin through whose inflexible rectitude truth shall prevail and justice and mercy be done, condone and abet that the criminal's very progenitors be eliminated from the earth in expiation of his crime? And if he was innocent as he said he was, what crime did that champion of the weak and the oppressed itself participate in? Or (to repeat) not the artist. America has not yet found any place for him who deals only in things of the human spirit except to use his notoriety to sell soap or cigarettes or fountain pens or to advertise automobiles and cruises and resort hotels, or (if he can be taught to contort fast enough to meet the standards) in radio or moving pictures where he can produce enough income tax to be worth attention. But the scientist and the humanitarian, yes: the humanitarian in science and the scientist in the humanity of man, who might yet save that civilization which the professionals at saving it—the publishers who condone their own battening on man's lust and folly, the politicians who condone their own trafficking in his stupidity and greed, and the churchmen who condone their own trading on his fear and superstition—seem to be proving that they can't.

ASHLEY MONTAGU

Born in London in 1905, Ashley Montagu has had a lively scholarly career. He attended the University of London, where he thinks he was the first student to study physical anthropology, while also studying psychology, cultural anthropology, and sociology. In 1927 he came to the United States to study paleontology with W. K. Gregory, decided to settle here, and received his doctorate in cultural anthropology. Professor and Chairman of the Anthropology Department at Rutgers University from 1949 to 1955, he has also taught at the New School for Social Research, the University of Delaware, and the University of California at Santa Barbara. In 1950 he was one of the social scientists who helped draft the UNESCO statement on Race. Among his many books are Man's Most Dangerous Myth: The Fallacy of Race *(1942),* The Natural Superiority of Women *(1953),* The Biosocial Nature of Man *(1956),* Man: His First Million Years *(1957), and* Race, Science, and Humanity *(1963). The article we reprint below first appeared in the* Saturday Review, *March 31, 1956.*

THE ANNIHILATION OF PRIVACY

In recent years the increasing isolation of the individual and the fragmentation of social relationships in an age of anxiety have become matters of frequent comment. In a now famous book published in 1941, "Escape from Freedom," Dr. Erich Fromm pointed out that modern society affects man simultaneously in two distinct, yet related, ways. Man becomes more independent and he becomes more isolated, alone, and afraid. Man flees from freedom because freedom has thrown him upon his own resources, to sink or swim by his own efforts, and I am going to suggest that man's flight from this kind of anxious freedom serves to foster the conditions which minister to the shrinkage of his personality and the ever-growing invasion of his privacy.

In T. S. Eliot's "The Cocktail Party" one of the characters remarks:

> . . . Do you know—
> It no longer seems worth while to *speak* to anyone! . . .
> No . . . it isn't that I *want* to be alone,
> But that everyone's alone—or so it seems to me.
> They make noises, and think they are talking to each other;
> They make faces, and think they understand each other.
> And I'm sure they don't. . . .

The fear of being "desocialized," of being alone, is a healthy fear, for the biosocial nature of man is directed toward *relatedness* as the process of living. To be or feel alone is both unnatural and unhealthy. Man is socially the most highly developed of all creatures. Interaction with other human beings is an environmental necessity to him. No man can survive as an island entire of himself. No man wants to be an island. But every human being wants and needs to replenish his resources for being social by having a room of his own, as it were, a sanctuary to which he can retire and in which he can be alone with himself, undisturbed by the rumors and alarums of the outside world. I am going to suggest that the increasing loss of privacy from which Western man is suffering, particularly in the United States of America, serves, among other things, to reduce rather than to increase the chances of the individual being able to discover what those things are that are right and healthy for him, as a human being, to do. And that from this fact spring certain serious psychological consequences.

A genuinely healthy society holds together by the respect which men give to men, by the recognition of the biosocial needs of man for relatedness, and the making available of the means by which that relatedness can be achieved. Such a society, instead of providing men with instruments that make them less than themselves, affords them the means of becoming instruments of something greater than themselves. In spite of the superficial appearances our society lamentably fails to afford such opportunities to the majority of individuals. We teach the three "R's," but we teach them as techniques for the achievement of limited objectives. Our educational attitudes are not directed toward "drawing out" but toward "pumping in." Our value system is a conflicting one, in which the worship of God is taught on the one hand and of Mammon on the other. The pursuit of life in reality reduces itself to the pursuit of a living, "liberty" assumes the form of economic liberty, and "happiness" resolves itself into getting whatever one can out of life by whatever means one can. In the United States we have achieved the highest standard of living in the world—but it is seldom, if ever, added, it is at the highest cost of ulcers, mental breakdowns, homicide, violent crime, juvenile delinquency, alcoholic, and drug addiction rates, in the entire world. Can it be that something is somewhere wrong? That there are causes for all this breakdown, death, and destruction of human beings—that these causes are traceable ones?

Today anyone who chooses can cause your phone to ring and invade your privacy whether you like it or not. Whether you like it or not anyone who chooses to do so can know everything—both true and false— that it is possible to know about you, in fact, more than you know about yourself. In this our Government sets the example, for the Federal Bureau of Investigation has millions of such records on file in Washington. The files of the Congressional Committee on Un-American Activities are open to anyone who cares to use them. Then there are the manpower lists, the biographical reference works, specialty lists, credit ratings, telephone books, Black Books, Red Books, Who Knows What Books, the scandal-mongering yellow press, private eyes, public eyes, FBI's, wiretapping, TV and radio brainwashing, and so on. Privacy has gone with the waves. "Big Brother" of George Orwell's powerful and prophetic novel, "Nineteen Eighty-Four," is already watching you. A life of one's own is already well-nigh impossible, and the paradox is observed that in a world in which the private life of the individual daily shrinks, and his social life with his fellow human beings is reduced to the narrowest dimensions, that his life should become increasingly more public.

Small-town gossip was at one time the only medium through which such publicity could be achieved—or rather thrust upon one. But that was a very primitive medium compared with the devices at our disposal in the modern age. Today we have gossip sheets with huge circulations which specialize in the exposure of the most intimate details of the individual's life—whether such details are true or false matters not one bit. Duly elected members of the Congress use their positions for political and private purposes to institute public Congressional Inquisitions during which the reputations of those whom they wish to destroy are nakedly exposed to the public gaze. If the Government sets the example for such antinomian indecencies, it is not surprising that innumerable individuals have set themselves up in everything ranging from one-man vigilante committees to group organizations dedicated to the investigation of the private life of any and every individual whom they choose to pillory. These individuals and organizations are more than willing, they are anxious, to supply anyone who asks for it with such information. And if it isn't asked for they will supply it whenever they can. As a consequence of such publicity many persons have been deprived of the right to earn a living.

It has even been suggested that this kind of desecration of men's privacy be put on a "scientific" basis. Dr. W. H. Sheldon, for example, in a book entitled "Varieties of Delinquent Youth" (Harper's, 1949), has suggested that since "we have begun to forget *who are* the biologically best" people . . . this difficulty could be overcome "if standardized photographic records of even a few hundred thousands of a well-sampled population were to be kept for so short a time as half a dozen generations, together with biographical summaries embracing the physiological, psychiatric, and social adventures of this sample population. . . ." And he goes on to suggest that at a very small cost "we could keep central files of standardized photographs of the entire population."

And, of course, these photographs will be in the nude. Thus will the last of our privacies be stripped from us. Our warts and our wrinkles, not to mention more private parts of our anatomy, would become the vicarious property of the public custodian. The possibilities are very interesting.

Since we are now in the Cinderella-land of photography it should be mentioned that telephoto lenses are now able to pick up scenes over great distances, and that it is now possible to do this with television and sound and other recording devices. Such devices have already been used by crime investigators and the military. Their application to civilian life is already creeping in.

In addition to the one-way glass screens through which one can be observed without being aware of it, there are schools in the United States today in which the principal can listen in on the classroom, and hospitals in which the nurse can listen in on the patient. Television for similar purposes is just around the corner. Here, too, the possibilities are very interesting.

In the realm of sound or rather *noise* it must be said that the offenses committed this way in the United States are unparalleled for sheer barbarism anywhere else in the world. Many years ago Schopenhauer wrote an essay "On Noise." It is many years since I read it, but I vividly recall how scorching Schopenhauer was on the sudden sharp brain-stopping, thought-killing explosive cracking of the whips of coachmen and others. What Schopenhauer would have had to say on the din and discord created by the automobile horns of today, the noises of starting and gear-shifting, the backfiring of trucks and buses, and the screeching and groaning of brakes and tires—all to the accompaniment of a perfusion of essence of gasoline exhaust fumes—can only be guessed at.

Public noises, sanctioned and created by public agencies, are among the most barbarous and stupid of destroyers of the individual's inalienable right to quietude. At all times of the day and night their licensed discords are encouraged to break in on one. Consider the piercing shrieks that suddenly fracture the smog-laden air when the police in their cars are bent on getting somewhere in a hurry. The principal function of the sirens when the police are hurrying to the scene of a crime is, I presume, to announce their impending arrival to the criminals so that the latter may make a leisurely getaway. To these iniquities of the police-car sirens add those of ambulances, rescue squads, and the clanging of fire-engine bells (the least offensive of the noises).

How thick-skinned must one grow in order not to understand that the sudden noise of sirens constitutes a nerve-wracking violation of one's privacy, and a damaging assault upon one's nervous system? For nothing is more effective than such noises in producing an unpleasant jumpiness of the nervous system. It is not without significance that in no other civilized land in the world does one encounter such noisome sirens as those of the police cars in the United States. How far gone must one be not to know that the last thing on earth a sick or injured person wants to hear while he is being driven to a hospital is the clanging signal or siren of the ambulance. This only serves to disturb him and contribute to his anxiety—as well as to that of everyone else. Surely, some other means could be devised which would enable such vehicles to gain a speedy right of way—if only by the adoption of more pleasant sounds or signals?

Urbanites who think to escape these impertinences of noise by moving to the country may find that factory whistles or sirens or both can be uncomfortably annoying, and what is perhaps even more hard to bear, every so often one will be awakened from sleep by the community fire-siren, which whines and moans and groans until all the fireman have appeared—and all sleep has vanished. Effective signals under rural conditions are highly necessary, but, again, surely some less barbarous means to summon firemen could be devised? It is done in other parts of the world.

Ah, public-address systems. These are instruments of torture which are at the disposal of anyone who has anything from moth-eaten ratskins to political self-aggrandizement to peddle. Wherever you may be your eardrums may suddenly be assaulted by the inescapable abomination issuing from a mobile public-address unit. Seated in your own home your privacy may be similarly blasted by the outbreak of obstreperousness issuing from such a mobile unit.

Thus, in whatever environment one may be, the opportunity of being quietly with oneself is inexorably diminishing, for there is no longer any time of the day during which one cannot be broken in on by the uninvited gate-crashers of the sound barrier without so much as a by-your-leave.

In addition to the varieties of noise another widespread technique, developed within the last 100 years, for the invasion of privacy is advertising. Advertising in its proper place is undoubtedly a desirable means of making people acquainted with what they might otherwise fail to know. But when I want to contemplate the beauties of the land I would prefer that contemplation to be uninterrupted by the impertinence of the huckster's misshapen and misplaced art which, like some pathological sequestrum, too often suggests that it would be better for not being at all. Certainly, there are some landscapes which are so dreary that they are lent greater interest by almost any kind of hoarding, there can be no criticism here, but where the natural beauty of the land is picturesque enough we can dispense with the dubious embellishments of the advertisers. Increasingly, however, as one travels about the country one has occasion to observe that no longer is it true that "every prospect pleases," but that it is more than ever true that this is so because "only man is vile." No other creature defaces its natural habitat with such unnatural excrescences as does man. Perhaps we shall someday live to see the whole of nature taken over by the advertising fraternity. The sea alone, I believe, has thus far resisted their efforts—but it is only a matter of time before they will conquer even that element. Skywriting, public addresses from the sky, advertising blimps and planes, are no longer novelties. Just think of the artificial satellites!

But for the time being let us keep to the earth and the advertisers. One of the most insidious forms which the depletion of privacy takes is mail advertising. I am not for a moment suggesting that large numbers of individuals do not like receiving advertising in their mail. On the contrary, it is clear that innumerable persons do enjoy receiving this kind of mail, especially where the other kind is likely to be somewhat thin. For the advertising people such persons become like so many puppets who can, in certain numbers, be moved in the desired direction. I will not discuss, but only refer to, the untold thousands of acres of beautiful trees that are sacrificed in order to manufacture the paper upon which the advertisers impress their blandishments.

Those of us who are affronted by the time-wasting litter represented by so much of the advertising mail we receive are probably in the minority, and I shall not dwell upon this kind of invasion of their privacy, which is after all one of the minor invasions. But I do think that one of the little considered consequences of mail advertising is well worth some attention, and that is the reducing effects it has upon the reading habits of the population. There are large numbers of people whose reading is virtually restricted to the advertising they receive through the mail. Such readers are to be found not only among the isolated rural dwellers, but also among many who live in the larger urban centers of this world. What with the telephone, radio, movies, television, and the other distractions that modern life has to offer, the reading of the advertising mail fits comfortably into the necessity to be entertained, and will do service for a good deal of the reading of other kinds which might otherwise have been done.

With the toleration which is increasingly exhibited toward these encroachments upon our privacy goes an increasing callousness to them. We grow accustomed to the transgressions upon our being, the violations of our privacy, and the infringement of our right to be alone with ourselves whenever we choose. This is life as we know it, and the harder it grows the more hardened do we become to it. In becoming so hardened we become cut off from the best that is within ourselves and the best that we could make of ourselves and of the world in which we live. We become increasingly insensitive to all those things to which we should be most sensitive—above all, to human need. In the crowded cities in which we live in loneliness we live more and more for ourselves, in environments in which the modes and opportunities for spontaneous and unreserved social participation are reduced to a minimum. The struggle for existence and the gigantism of our cities have largely served to bring this isolation about, and at the same time to produce the state of mind which invites every kind of intrusion that will serve to reduce one's isolation. It is in this way that isolation comes to be confused with privacy, and the privacy of isolation is unwanted. Since in isolation (which is lack of desired social contact) privacy is excessive the individual is only too glad to sacrifice his privacy for less isolation.

The unsatisfied desire, the longing, for social participation leads to the fear of being alone, and the desire for occasional solitude tends to be overcome by the fear of being alone. In this manner the need for privacy may eventually be completely submerged in the overpowering need to be *with*—overpowering because it has been so inadequately satisfied by normal means. When such an annihilation of privacy is achieved man is indeed in danger—he is in danger of self-annihilation, of becoming a living automaton at the mercy of anyone who knows how to make him tick. In such a society one becomes grateful to "Big Brother" for assuming the task of directing the life one is no longer capable of directing oneself. In this way does the annihilation of privacy lead to the annihilation of the person, and of society, for the healthy society depends upon the ability of man to reflect upon what a true society is—and without the privacy to reflect man and society are lost.

Many men in contemporary society are very much in the state of Browning's "Paracelsus":

> I give the fight up: let there be an end,
> A privacy, an obscure nook for me.
> I want to be forgotten even by God.

Shall we ever recover our hearts? It is a question—and it is a question that can be successfully and happily answered only if each of us will do what is required—namely, to return to the fellowship of man. This is the answer to the individual's plaint

> And how am I to face the odds
> Of man's bedevilment and God's?
> I, a stranger and afraid,
> In a world I never made.

AUGUST HECKSCHER

August Heckscher, journalist and author, was born in 1913 and educated at Yale and Harvard. After World War II he served first as editor of the Auburn Citizen Advertiser, *later became chief editorial writer of the* New York Herald Tribune, *and is now serving as director of the Twentieth Century Fund. President Kennedy appointed him as special consultant on the arts for 1962–1963. His books include* These Are the Days *(1936),* A Pattern of Politics *(1947),* The Politics of Woodrow Wilson *(1956),* Diversity of Words *(written with Raymond Aron, 1957), and* The Public Happiness *(1962). He has also been a frequent contributor to magazines. The article we print below first appeared in* The American Scholar, *Winter, 1958–1959, as the second in an* American Scholar *series on the invasion of privacy.*

THE RESHAPING OF PRIVACY

The decline of privacy, one of the more depressing features of the time, takes many forms; some of them are more obvious than others. One hardly needs to emphasize the inquisitorial spirit that has characterized the past decade. A man's beliefs and convictions, even the degree of his enthusiasm or doubt, have been matters for public inquiry. More than that, the opinions of his parents—or of his own distant and perhaps indiscreet youth—have seemed fit subjects for the authorities to investigate. The fact that these excesses have abated for the time being should not blind us to the serious incursions of which Congress and other public bodies have been guilty.

More subtle than these official acts, but no less hostile to the realm of privacy, has been a general disposition to emphasize the external and the superficial. The widely deplored trend to conformity, seen from this point of view, is the result of a common disregard for the secluded and inward qualities that at other times have been judged the heart of life. Conceivably, men and women could manage to go along in their behavior with the drift of things, keeping their thoughts and feelings to themselves. But this could only be true of a people for whom a rich inner life was habitual. Americans, on the contrary, live in the open, and when they all say the same things, they are very likely to be thinking the same things, too. When they are behaving as one, they are likely to be feeling as one. And so the prevailing readiness to follow catchwords and fads, to blend as inconspicuously as possible with the group, can only be taken as proof that the domain of the private has been disconcertingly reduced.

A de-emphasis of privacy has affected in a very general way the conduct of our democracy. It is not only, as I have already suggested, that Congress deems itself privileged to pry into the lives of the people, but that the people feel entitled to pry into processes of government and into aspects of their elected officials that have traditionally been screened from immediate surveillance. Where no secrecy is permitted, diplomacy becomes virtually extinct. As for negotiations between states, they can scarcely be carried on when each move and countermove of the bargaining process forms the substance of headlines within the hour. In such circumstances things must be said upon each side to captivate the crowd. The result is a lowering of the whole level of discourse between public men. I am tempted to mention, besides, the frantic kind of curiosity that allows the public to suppose that it is entitled to know the innermost biological details concerning the health of its representatives. That it should feel a responsibility for judging the fitness of a President to carry on his tasks is one thing; that it should, beyond that, consider it its privilege to subject his most intimate bodily functions to direct scrutiny could only happen where the foundations of privacy have been eroded.

That privacy has been diminished in these and in many other ways may be taken as beyond much argument. Why this has come about is more disputable. Mr. Rovere, opening this series of discussions in this journal, has suggested that the complexity of a modern technological society inevitably subjects the citizens to a degree of surveillance that would not have been thought tolerable in earlier times. I would be more inclined to feel that a decay of the inner life precedes the invasion from the outside—as usually happens when the overthrow of states is involved. Moreover, the idea of "technological imperatives" does not seem convincing to me. The machine is used by man to further his own ends, and it can protect privacy (if that is what we desire) as well as circumscribe it. Yet the matter is not so one-sided as it is commonly made to appear; for if privacy has diminished, it has also, in many cases, been extended during epochs when the machine was exerting its sway. Meanwhile, the public sphere tends to shrink, and much that was formerly carried on in the broad daylight of competition, rivalry and discussion is done today mutedly, almost furtively.

The most obvious paradox in this regard is the growth of secrecy concomitant with the decline of privacy. It might have been assumed that a people which is inclined to make public professions of faith about almost everything, to perform in the broad light of day many actions that formerly were reserved for the sphere of intimacy, would have comparatively little fear of the dark. But the opposite is true. While men and women have been leaving less and less to be guessed at about themselves, they have been suspecting others of having the most sinister designs, conceived in a mysterious inner world. The habit of peering into everything has been accompanied by the conviction that secret plots are being successfully hatched. The two attitudes are related, of course: spying and conspiracy have often proved to be opposite sides of the same coin. Yet it might have been hoped that a people bred to the tradition of democracy could have matched its own openness of manner with a general faith in sunlight and fresh air.

The extension of privacy, or at any rate the diminution of the public sphere, can be observed in the newer tendencies of the educational world. Education in this country has had a tradition of being deeply public; it not only drew into its stream the widest possible representation of the citizenry, but its aim was to fit men for the broadest tasks. However much the development of the individual personality might be involved, the primary concern of education was the transmission of the culture of society as a whole. In the modern, coeducational college, however, the drift is toward communal values that minimize what is essentially public and play up the importance of the student's subjective and emotional problems. Where social life dominates intellectual life, the private affairs of men and women become inevitably more preoccupying than public learning. Extracurricular activities, instead of reflecting the political forum or the arena of combat, take their pattern from the suburban community. The curriculum becomes infected with strong doses of home economy or social hygiene, while the higher learning is threatened by specialization and the private jargons of increasingly narrow and isolated disciplines.

The city has always been a public place; the "man in the street" is a man alert to the conflicting current of opinions, aware of fads and fashions, although he is never wholly taken in by any of them. But in suburbia there are no streets; for that matter, there are no men, at least during the hours between eight and six. It is a place of women and of homes. The women never quite withdraw into these homes, and yet never entirely emerge from them. If it is argued that suburbia provides no privacy, it can be argued with equal justification that it provides no public arena—no square, no market place, no political responsibility. Here, to a disconcerting degree, men and women lead an existence without the disruption, the challenge and the risk of public duty. At the same time, they do not find any corresponding satisfaction in inner lives complexly woven and deeply lived.

In short, what is disturbing today is not merely the decline of privacy;

it is equally the decline of a public sphere. We are so used, indeed, to praising the privacy we seem in danger of losing that we have almost forgotten what virtue there can be in its opposite. It has not always been so. For the Athenians of the classic age, private life was always conceived as something unworthy of man at his best. It was in the public realm that he found the means to excellence and virtue; here, and here alone, he could perform the deeds that made his fame live and achieve results more durable than his own brief existence. The slave was not permitted to enter this realm; the barbarian never had the wit to organize and establish it. Both were something less than men. In comparison to the rivalry and excitement of the forum, the household was for the Greeks only a place where the necessities of life were fulfilled. Its darkness originated in the secrecy, and even the degradation, surrounding the rites of birth and death. The Greeks had never heard of such a word as "publicity," with its suggestion that something essentially private has been trumpeted forth. They never had to worry about "public relations," which is too often a way of debasing essentially intimate qualities, such as kindness and friendship, by misapplying them in the context of the group.

The derangement of the private and the public spheres in American life is nowhere so vividly or so sadly illustrated as by the teen-ager. A denial of responsibility marks a retreat into a special teen-age world, the substance of which is all mist and fog. The citizen of this world has no public role; rather he defiantly displays many types of conduct that might more decently have remained hidden. The public sphere is the home of speech and action; it is here that a man can hope to be "the doer of great deeds and the speaker of great words." Yet speech and action are, in this sense, denied the teen-ager. Living in a private world, he communicates in what is very largely a private tongue, with the English language either blurred or else deliberately (and often amusingly) transformed by slang. More often he cannot communicate at all, being unable to give objectivity to his feelings or to materialize his intent. As for action, the teen-ager can, of course, make movements and even on occasion appear quite agitated. But what he does has not the individuality, the clearness of outline, the definite beginning and end that distinguish the performance of deeds from animal behavior or instinctive conduct.

Doubtless, teen-agers have always been much as they are now; what is striking is the degree to which they are catered to in the United States and accepted as representative. In their elevation to something close to a model in our civilization, we see writ large certain tendencies that are apparent at all levels. Almost everywhere, as with the teen-agers, we find behavior taking the place of action, private jargons taking the place of public speech, and a retreat from the forum into the clique. The picture window, serving in the typical housing development more as a means for having others look in than for letting the owner look out, stands as a perfect symbol of the confusion of realms, a confusion that spreads from the teen-ager to society as a whole. Vacancy or conformity at the core, combined with the display before others of what should be an inner privacy, is a situation more menacing, and certainly more difficult to cure, than a deliberate attack upon one's personal citadel.

The idea that the private and public realms are coexistent, and that the real problem is a right relationship between them rather than the disproportionate elevation of one or the other, we owe to a remarkable study that has been published within the year. *The Human Condition*, by Hannah Arendt, is one of those rare books that can be read many times, from many points of view, always revealing some new facet, some unexpected richness of perspective or understanding. I should like to draw on it here for the illumination it casts upon our concern with privacy. There are two levels of existence, Miss Arendt maintains: that of necessity and that of freedom; that of mere survival and that of adventure, choice, courage, fame. In the classic age the former was kept from view. The slaves and the women had no share in the citizenship of the time; but to free men there always was open the chance of rising to a kind of second life, a leap into freedom and full manhood. Similarly, the Middle Ages gave through the church the possibility of crossing over every day from the mundane and secular into the glory of the sacred. In each case, a form of immortality was the reward. The danger of both approaches was that portions of life were robbed of the vitality and meaning that might have been achieved. The Greeks robbed the private sphere; the Middle Ages, the secular. However, each gave to a man's existence the clearness that comes from understanding one thing supremely well, and neither invited the soul to wander amid the murk—between public and private, between heaven and earth. Men at their best were human beings; they were even divine beings. They were never a statistic or a uniformity, moving listlessly amid the unindividualized mass.

The trouble with men who live their lives in public is that they tend, when they are in private, not to be very interesting. Socrates with his eternal questions may well have seemed rather a bore to his family. Of Gladstone there is the well-known complaint that he treated a personal encounter as if it were a mass meeting. In the ideal society the vitality of the private sphere counterbalances that of the public sphere, and enrichment and deepening of individuality accompany the doing of great deeds and the speaking of great words. Christianity played a major role in bringing about this enhancement of personality. Much later, as Miss Arendt points out, Rousseau gave a whole new dimension to the realm of intimacy. It might seem a paradox—although I hope that by now it will not seem so —that one man should have both deepened the content of privacy and, in his political philosophy, vastly extended the involvement of the citizen in the public sphere.

Miss Arendt's theme is that the activities of life fall properly into either the public or the private realm, and that a society is disordered when there is confusion between them. The transplanting of an action not only distorts it; its very nature may be altered in the process. Take something as simple as gossip, for example. Inherently private, gossip can perform a highly useful function, as anyone who has lived in a smaller community will testify. It ventilates the closed circles of existence and provides a channel for the kind of human discourse without which a society remains unwarmed and impersonal. When it is not deliberately malicious, it permits the standards of the community to evolve and make themselves felt without undue harshness for any individual. But gossip corrupted by publicity, deprived of the free, amorphous quality of talk, and congealed in print, loses its humanity; it becomes essentially political, but without the broader issues and the tests of responsibility that are appropriate to the political sphere.

A more dramatic and basic example of the transformation of an act through its transposition from one realm to another is provided by Miss Arendt in a penetrating discussion of the ethic of goodness. The essence of virtue, she says, is that it be personal, hidden from the world—indeed, hidden almost from the well-doer himself, so that his right hand knows not what the left hand has accomplished. Goodness must be of the spirit, fleeting, serving no end but its own, leaving behind (at least in the good man) no visible trace. As soon as this quality is made public, subject to organization and accountability, it ceases to be goodness. Righteousness passes over into self-righteousness and the sin of pride is born. Public charity can of course accomplish many admirable results in the world; but the point is precisely that these results *are* in the world. They are no longer of the spirit; and however socially useful they may be, they do not meet the radical test of Christian virtue.

Consumption, like all the essential tasks of the household, has traditionally been part of the private realm; it has been one with that side of a man's life in which his elementary physical and biological needs are satisfied. Miss Arendt argues convincingly that one of the most significant sources of the contemporary world's confusion of values lies in the transfer of consumption from a private to a public function. Consider man in a simpler state: he is compelled by his condition to labor for the sustenance of daily life; he makes and consumes what is required by nature, with nothing left over to provide the occasion for freedom or for choice. Because of its origins in necessity, labor has in the past been essentially private, undertaken within the household and performed by men lacking the essential rights of citizenship. It is only in the modern world that we have seen it brought forth and made a dominant factor of the public scene. The result, as Miss Arendt points out, has been to improve vastly the conditions of labor; but it has also been to blur the difference between labor and the higher forms of work and action that are essentially of the public sphere.

Just as labor has been brought out from its former seclusion in this way, so has consumption, until in the Western countries today the phrase used to describe the basic conditions under which we live is "a consumer society." That has long seemed to me a curious, disturbing phrase, yet not until I read Miss Arendt's book did I perceive its full import. What we are doing by its use is to belittle the status of free individuals, putting the purchaser of an automobile or television set in the position of one who actually annihilates and digests these things—as a savage, who was incapable of understanding their purpose, might do. At the same time, we are belittling the goods themselves—often wonders of technological precision—by implying that they are not durable but are absorbed as soon as they are produced. (We go further, of course, and by deliberate obsolescence insure that the semipermanent shall be made scarcely more lasting than a thing of paper.) By talking of "consumers" and "consumer goods" we describe our society in terms that emphasize what is most circumscribed and is least touched by a public spirit.

In every great society the decisive element has been very different from the rather pitiful individuals who produced and consumed the necessities of life. What has been decisive has been the men who lived by action: the users, the possessors, those who have availed themselves of what is at hand, creating out of durable things new combinations and possibilities of the spirit. Even today we find here and there a few individuals who in their attitude toward physical things endeavor deliberately to set themselves above the role of mere consumers. These are the people who pride themselves on a car that is old enough to be a real possession or wear a tweed jacket frazzled at the elbow. Such people may not necessarily rise to the test of great words and great deeds, but they do try to affirm, sometimes a little quaintly or ostentatiously, that they are something more than drones condemned to spend their lives in a dreary round of consumption.

It is in the home that the plethora of today's goods is consumed; and the cult of the home, as a result, has developed in alarming proportions. The authors of utopias have usually been careful to insist that the home shall be comfortable, and yet never so preoccupying as to draw men and women completely away from the public sphere in which their characters as citizens are developed. Anyone judging the present-day American scene must be struck by the disproportion between the lavishness of the country's interior gadgetry and the impoverishment of so many of its public facilities. The kitchen seems to take a higher rank than the school; the car than the highway upon which its usefulness depends. While this withdrawal has been taking place, while an orgy of consumption has been going on within, the home has lost many of the higher functions formerly associated with it. It has ceased to be a center of education and discipline; it has lost its character as a focus of authority. Recreation has become largely a matter of the household, with the withering of ceremonial and festive aspects of great popular gatherings; but this has happened at a time when the entertainment that does go on within the home has been largely reduced to watching television.

Our concern is with the restoration of privacy, free from invasions by the public. Yet we have seen how differently the problem can present itself. Actually there seems today to be a retreat into privacy, and at the same time a disposition to flaunt areas of life hitherto hidden in the public light. The privacy lacks substance and depth, while the publicly performed portions of our life lack the edge of excellence, risk and high responsibility. What seems actually to have happened is that we move largely in a sphere that is neither that of personality nor of politics, but one that must be called the social sphere. Here the emphasis is on behavior rather than action. Individuality gives way to the uniformity that can be measured and controlled, leaving room neither for great actions on the one hand, nor for inwardness and conscience on the other. The social sphere is, needless to say, important. Its rules of conduct, its overt and superficial conformities, keep men from hopeless divisions. Through it are provided the audience and the stage for political action; through it, also, the individual is kept from too complete a submersion in self. The social is the sphere of necessary unity and practical compromise; but when it becomes dominant, devouring the realms of the private and the public alike, life lacks both inward depth and external adventure.

What has happened to privacy, therefore, may be said to be less an invasion than a corruption. Its meaning can be restored only when we see it once more in relation to a clearly conceived and vital public realm. The home can generate emotionally enriching experiences when it is part of a community more maturely developed than contemporary suburbia. The student can move with a sense of inner rewards when the modern university in its social organization takes on again something of the atmosphere of a free city. Life in general can be rewarding to the individual in proportion as there is a chance for lucid communication and meaningful action on a broad stage. In the inherited tradition we have had the themes of personal intimacy and of public responsibility both amply developed; if we seem to have fulfilled neither, but to have fallen into a misty mid-region of social conformity, it may not be because of pestiferous officials or because of the dictates of the machine. It may be because, lacking clarity of concepts and rigor of philosophical views, we have failed to distinguish between the things that belong to ourselves and those that belong to the polis.

Social Implications of Race

The opening pages of Ruth Benedict's book *Race: Science and Politics* (1940) serve as a better introduction to this section than any we could devise. Arthur de Gobineau's chapter demonstrates a theoretical position of the nineteenth century, one which Hitler later used to sanction his devastating policy and which thus illustrates crudely how "social science" can be used to further political ends. Professor Dobzhansky, writing in 1963, brings a modern scientific mind to bear on the concepts of "race" and "equality." Orwell's description of a North African city as seen through the eyes of a white European sounds a note of warning, and serves to introduce the last four selections. They present, from varying points of view and in varying styles and tone, the American dilemma of Negro and White.

RUTH BENEDICT

FROM RACISM: THE ISM OF THE MODERN WORLD

As an introduction to this section, we reprint here the opening pages of the first chapter of Ruth Benedict's Race: Science and Politics *(1940). For information on the author and her writing, see page 225.*

•

As early as the late 1880's a French pro-Aryan, Vacher de Lapouge, wrote: "I am convinced that in the next century millions will cut each other's throats because of 1 or 2 degrees more or less of cephalic index." On the surface it appears a fantastic reason for world wars, and it was certainly a reason new under the sun. Was he right? What could it mean? The cephalic index is the quotient of the greatest breadth of the head divided by its length, and some tribes and peoples over the world run to high indices and some to low. Narrow heads are found among uncivilized primitives and among powerful and cultivated Western Europeans; broad heads are too. Neither the narrow heads of the whole world nor the broad heads stack up to show any obvious monopoly of glorious destiny or any corner on ability or virtue. Even in any one European nation or in America men of achievement have been some of them narrow-headed and some broad-headed. What could it mean that "millions will cut each other's throats" because of the shape of the top of their skulls?

In the long history of the world men have given many reasons for killing each other in war: envy of another people's good bottom land or of their herds, ambition of chiefs and kings, different religious beliefs, high spirits, revenge. But in all these wars the skulls of the victims on both sides were generally too similar to be distinguished. Nor had the war leaders incited their followers against their enemies by referring to the shapes of their heads. They might call them the heathen, the barbarians, the heretics, the slayers of women and children, but never our enemy Cephalic Index 82.

It was left for high European civilization to advance such a reason for war and persecution and to invoke it in practice. In other words, racism is a creation of our own time. It is a new way of separating the sheep from the goats. The old parable in the New Testament separated mankind as individuals: on the one hand those who had done good, and on the other those who had done evil. The new way divides them by hereditary bodily characteristics—shape of the head, skin colour, nose form, hair texture, colour of the eyes—and those who have certain hallmarks are known by these signs to be weaklings and incapable of civilization, and those with the opposite are the hope of the world. Racism is the new Calvinism which asserts that one group has the stigmata of superiority and the other has those of inferiority. According to racism we know our enemies, not by their aggressions against us, not by their creed or language, not even by their possessing wealth we want to take, but by noting their hereditary anatomy. For the leopard cannot change his spots and by these you know he is a leopard.

For the individual, therefore, racism means that damnation or salvation in this world is determined at conception; an individual's good life cannot tip the balance in his favour and he cannot live a bad life if his physical type is the right sort. By virtue of birth alone each member of the "race" is high caste and rightly claims his place in the sun at the expense of men of other "races." He need not base his pride upon personal achievement nor upon virtue; he was born high caste.

From this postulate racism makes also an assertion about race: that the "good" anatomical hallmarks are the monopoly of a pure race which has always throughout history manifested its glorious destiny. The racialists have rewritten history to provide the scion of such a race with a long and glamorous group ancestry as gratifying as an individual coat of arms, and they assure him that the strength and vigour of his race are immutable and guaranteed by the laws of Nature. He must, however, guard this pure blood from contamination by that of lesser breeds, lest degeneration follow and his race lose its supremacy. All over the world for the last generation this doctrine has been invoked in every possible kind of conflict: sometimes national, between peoples as racially similar as the French and Germans; sometimes across the colour line, as in Western fears of the Yellow Peril; sometimes in class conflicts, as in France; sometimes in conflicts between immigrants who arrived a little earlier and those who came a little later, as in America. It has become a bedlam.

Where all people claim to be tallest, not all can be right. In this matter of races, can the sciences to which they all appeal judge among the babel of contradictory claims and award the decision? Or is it a matter of false premises and bastard science? It is essential, if we are to live in this modern world, that we should understand Racism and be able to judge its arguments. We must know the facts first of Race, and then of this doctrine that has made use of them. For Racism is an *ism* to which everyone in the world today is exposed; for or against, we must take sides. And the history of the future will differ according to the decision which we make.

JOSEPH ARTHUR, COMTE DE GOBINEAU

Joseph Arthur de Gobineau (1816–1882), French diplomat, Orientalist, and man of letters, was educated first by private tutors and later at a college in Switzerland. In 1849 he was appointed "chef de cabinet" by Alexis de Tocqueville, then Foreign Minister, and subsequently served in many other diplomatic posts. His writings include books on Asiatic religion and philosophy and on the Renaissance, but of most interest to us here is his four-volume Essai sur l'inégalité des races humaines *(1853–1855), translated in 1915 by Adrian Collins as* The Inequality of Human Races. *In these volumes M. Gobineau proposes that Aryan racial purity can be maintained only by preserving and strengthening the Nordic strains, a theory which later became fashionable in German intellectual circles and must have influenced Nazi ideology. We present below the concluding chapter of this work, originally entitled "Recapitulation: The Respective Characteristics of the Three Great Races; the Superiority of the White Type, and, Within this Type, of the Aryan Family."*

THE RESPECTIVE CHARACTERISTICS OF THE THREE GREAT RACES

I have shown the unique place in the organic world occupied by the human species, the profound physical, as well as moral, differences separat-

ing it from all other kinds of living creatures. Considering it by itself, I
have been able to distinguish, on physiological grounds alone, three great
and clearly marked types, the black, the yellow, and the white. However
uncertain the aims of physiology may be, however meagre its resources,
however defective its methods, it can proceed thus far with absolute
certainty.

The negroid variety is the lowest, and stands at the foot of the ladder.
The animal character, that appears in the shape of the pelvis, is stamped on
the negro from birth, and foreshadows his destiny. His intellect will always
move within a very narrow circle. He is not however a mere brute, for
behind his low receding brow, in the middle of his skull, we can see signs of
a powerful energy, however crude its objects. If his mental faculties are
dull or even non-existent, he often has an intensity of desire, and so of
will, which may be called terrible. Many of his senses, especially taste and
smell, are developed to an extent unknown to the other two races.[1]

The very strength of his sensations is the most striking proof of his
inferiority. All food is good in his eyes, nothing disgusts or repels him.
What he desires is to eat, to eat furiously, and to excess; no carrion is too
revolting to be swallowed by him. It is the same with odours; his inordinate
desires are satisfied with all, however coarse or even horrible. To these
qualities may be added an instability and capriciousness of feeling, that
cannot be tied down to any single object, and which, so far as he is concerned, do away with all distinctions of good and evil. We might even say
that the violence with which he pursues the object that has aroused his
senses and inflamed his desires is a guarantee of the desires being soon
satisfied and the object forgotten. Finally, he is equally careless of his own
life and that of others: he kills willingly, for the sake of killing; and this
human machine, in whom it is so easy to arouse emotion, shows, in face
of suffering, either a monstrous indifference or a cowardice that seeks a
voluntary refuge in death.

The yellow race is the exact opposite of this type. The skull points
forward, not backward. The forehead is wide and bony, often high and
projecting. The shape of the face is triangular, the nose and chin showing none of the coarse protuberances that mark the negro. There is
further a general proneness to obesity, which, though not confined to
the yellow type, is found there more frequently than in the others.
The yellow man has little physical energy, and is inclined to apathy; he
commits none of the strange excesses so common among negroes. His
desires are feeble, his will-power rather obstinate than violent; his longing for material pleasures, though constant, is kept within bounds. A rare
glutton by nature, he shows far more discrimination in his choice of food.
He tends to mediocrity in everything; he understands easily enough
anything not too deep or sublime. He has a love of utility and a respect

[1] "Taste and smell in the negro are as powerful as they are undiscriminating. He
eats everything, and odours which are revolting to us are pleasant to him" (Pruner).

for order, and knows the value of a certain amount of freedom. He is practical, in the narrowest sense of the word. He does not dream or theorize; he invents little, but can appreciate and take over what is useful to him. His whole desire is to live in the easiest and most comfortable way possible. The yellow races are thus clearly superior to the black. Every founder of a civilization would wish the backbone of his society, his middle class, to consist of such men. But no civilized society could be created by them; they could not supply its nerve-force, or set in motion the springs of beauty and action.

We come now to the white peoples. These are gifted with reflective energy, or rather with an energetic intelligence. They have a feeling for utility, but in a sense far wider and higher, more courageous and ideal, than the yellow races; a perseverance that takes account of obstacles and ultimately finds a means of overcoming them; a greater physical power, an extraordinary instinct for order, not merely as a guarantee of peace and tranquillity, but as an indispensable means of self-preservation. At the same time, they have a remarkable, and even extreme, love of liberty, and are openly hostile to the formalism under which the Chinese are glad to vegetate, as well as to the strict despotism which is the only way of governing the negro.

The white races are, further, distinguished by an extraordinary attachment to life. They know better how to use it, and so, as it would seem, set a greater price on it; both in their own persons and those of others, they are more sparing of life. When they are cruel, they are conscious of their cruelty; it is very doubtful whether such a consciousness exists in the negro. At the same time, they have discovered reasons why they should surrender this busy life of theirs, that is so precious to them. The principal motive is honour, which under various names has played an enormous part in the ideas of the race from the beginning. I need hardly add that the word honour, together with all the civilizing influences connoted by it, is unknown to both the yellow and the black man.

On the other hand, the immense superiority of the white peoples in the whole field of the intellect is balanced by an inferiority in the intensity of their sensations. In the world of the senses, the white man is far less gifted than the others, and so is less tempted and less absorbed by considerations of the body, although in physical structure he is far the most vigorous.[2]

Such are the three constituent elements of the human race. I call them secondary types, as I think myself obliged to omit all discussion of the Adamite man. From the combination, by intermarriage, of the varieties of these types come the tertiary groups. The quaternary formations are produced by the union of one of these tertiary types, or of a pure-blooded

---

[2] Martius observes that the European is superior to the coloured man in the pressure of the nervous fluid (*Reise in Brasilien*, vol. i, p. 259).

tribe, with another group taken from one of the two foreign species.

Below these categories others have appeared—and still appear. Some of these are very strongly characterized, and form new and distinct points of departure, coming as they do from races that have been completely fused. Others are incomplete, and ill-ordered, and, one might even say, anti-social, since their elements, being too numerous, too disparate, or too barbarous, have had neither the time nor the opportunity for combining to any fruitful purpose. No limits, except the horror excited by the possibility of infinite intermixture, can be assigned to the number of these hybrid and chequered races that make up the whole of mankind.

It would be unjust to assert that every mixture is bad and harmful. If the three great types had remained strictly separate, the supremacy would no doubt have always been in the hands of the finest of the white races, and the yellow and black varieties would have crawled for ever at the feet of the lowest of the whites. Such a state is so far ideal, since it has never been beheld in history; and we can imagine it only by recognizing the undisputed superiority of those groups of the white races which have remained the purest.

It would not have been all gain. The superiority of the white race would have been clearly shown, but it would have been bought at the price of certain advantages which have followed the mixture of blood. Although these are far from counterbalancing the defects they have brought in their train, yet they are sometimes to be commended. Artistic genius, which is equally foreign to each of the three great types, arose only after the intermarriage of white and black. Again, in the Malayan variety, a human family was produced from the yellow and black races that had more intelligence than either of its ancestors. Finally, from the union of white and yellow, certain intermediary peoples have sprung, who are superior to the purely Finnish tribes as well as to the negroes.

I do not deny that these are good results. The world of art and great literature that comes from the mixture of blood, the improvement and ennoblement of inferior races—all these are wonders for which we must needs be thankful. The small have been raised. Unfortunately, the great have been lowered by the same process; and this is an evil that nothing can balance or repair. Since I am putting together the advantages of racial mixtures, I will also add that to them is due the refinement of manners and beliefs, and especially the tempering of passion and desire. But these are merely transitory benefits, and if I recognize that the mulatto, who may become a lawyer, a doctor, or a business man, is worth more than his negro grandfather, who was absolutely savage, and fit for nothing, I must also confess that the Brahmans of primitive India, the heroes of the Iliad and the Shahnameh, the warriors of Scandinavia—the glorious shades of noble races that have disappeared—give us a higher and more brilliant idea of humanity, and were more active, intelligent, and trusty instruments of civilization and grandeur than the peoples, hybrid a hundred times over, of the present day. And the blood even of these was no longer pure.

However it has come about, the human races, as we find them in history, are complex; and one of the chief consequences has been to throw into disorder most of the primitive characteristics of each type. The good as well as the bad qualities are seen to diminish in intensity with repeated intermixture of blood; but they also scatter and separate off from each other, and are often mutually opposed. The white race originally possessed the monopoly of beauty, intelligence, and strength. By its union with other varieties, hybrids were created, which were beautiful without strength, strong without intelligence, or, if intelligent, both weak and ugly. Further, when the quantity of white blood was increased to an indefinite amount by successive infusions, and not by a single admixture, it no longer carried with it its natural advantages, and often merely increased the confusion already existing in the racial elements. Its strength, in fact, seemed to be its only remaining quality, and even its strength served only to promote disorder. The apparent anomaly is easily explained. Each stage of a perfect mixture produces a new type from diverse elements, and develops special faculties. As soon as further elements are added, the vast difficulty of harmonizing the whole creates a state of anarchy. The more this increases, the more do even the best and richest of the new contributions diminish in value, and by their mere presence add fuel to an evil which they cannot abate. If mixtures of blood are, to a certain extent, beneficial to the mass of mankind, if they raise and ennoble it, this is merely at the expense of mankind itself, which is stunted, abased, enervated, and humiliated in the persons of its noblest sons. Even if we admit that it is better to turn a myriad of degraded beings into mediocre men than to preserve the race of princes whose blood is adulterated and impoverished by being made to suffer this dishonourable change, yet there is still the unfortunate fact that the change does not stop here; for when the mediocre men are once created at the expense of the greater, they combine with other mediocrities, and from such unions, which grow ever more and more degraded, is born a confusion which, like that of Babel, ends in utter impotence, and leads societies down to the abyss of nothingness whence no power on earth can rescue them.

Such is the lesson of history. It shows us that all civilizations derive from the white race, that none can exist without its help, and that a society is great and brilliant only so far as it preserves the blood of the noble group that created it, provided that this group itself belongs to the most illustrious branch of our species.

Of the multitude of peoples which live or have lived on the earth,

ten alone have risen to the position of complete societies. The remainder
have gravitated round these more or less independently, like planets
round their suns. If there is any element of life in these ten civilizations
that is not due to the impulse of the white races, any seed of death that
does not come from the inferior stocks that mingled with them, then
the whole theory on which this book rests is false. On the other hand,
if the facts are as I say, then we have an irrefragable proof of the nobility
of our own species. Only the actual details can set the final seal of truth
on my system, and they alone can show with sufficient exactness the
full implications of my main thesis, that peoples degenerate only in consequence of the various admixtures of blood which they undergo; that
their degeneration corresponds exactly to the quantity and quality of
the new blood, and that the rudest possible shock to the vitality of a
civilization is given when the ruling elements in a society and those developed by racial change have become so numerous that they are clearly
moving away from the homogeneity necessary to their life, and it therefore becomes impossible for them to be brought into harmony and so
acquire the common instincts and interests, the common logic of existence,
which is the sole justification for any social bond whatever. There is
no greater curse than such disorder, for however bad it may have made
the present state of things, it promises still worse for the future.

NOTE.—The "ten civilizations" mentioned in the last paragraph are as
follows. They are fully discussed in the subsequent books of the "Inequality of Races," of which the present volume forms the first.
I. The Indian civilization, which reached its highest point round the
Indian Ocean, and in the north and east of the Indian Continent, southeast of the Brahmaputra. It arose from a branch of a white people, the
Aryans.
II. The Egyptians, round whom collected the Ethiopians, the Nubians,
and a few smaller peoples to the west of the oasis of Ammon. This society was created by an Aryan colony from India, that settled in the
upper valley of the Nile.
III. The Assyrians, with whom may be classed the Jews, the Phœni-
cians, the Lydians, the Carthaginians, and the Hymiarites. They owed their
civilizing qualities to the great white invasions which may be grouped
under the name of the descendants of Shem and Ham. The Zoroastrian
Iranians who ruled part of Central Asia under the names of Medes,
Persians, and Bactrians, were a branch of the Aryan family.
IV. The Greeks, who came from the same Aryan stock, as modified
by Semitic elements.
V. The Chinese civilization, arising from a cause similar to that operating in Egypt. An Aryan colony from India brought the light of civilization to China also. Instead however of becoming mixed with black

peoples, as on the Nile, the colony became absorbed in Malay and yellow races, and was reinforced, from the north-west, by a fair number of white elements, equally Aryan but no longer Hindu.

VI. The ancient civilization of the Italian peninsula, the cradle of Roman culture. This was produced by a mixture of Celts, Iberians, Aryans, and Semites.

VII. The Germanic races, which in the fifth century transformed the Western mind. These were Aryans.

VIII.–X. The three civilizations of America, the Alleghanian, the Mexican, and the Peruvian.

Of the first seven civilizations, which are those of the Old World, six belong, at least in part, to the Aryan race, and the seventh, that of Assyria, owes to this race the Iranian Renaissance, which is, historically, its best title to fame. Almost the whole of the Continent of Europe is inhabited at the present time by groups of which the basis is white, but in which the non-Aryan elements are the most numerous. There is no true civilization, among the European peoples, where the Aryan branch is not predominant.

In the above list no negro race is seen as the initiator of a civilization. Only when it is mixed with some other can it even be initiated into one.

Similarly, no spontaneous civilization is to be found among the yellow races; and when the Aryan blood is exhausted stagnation supervenes.

ADOLF HITLER

Adolf Hitler (1889–1945), Austrian born, became the Nazi Dictator of Germany. After a brief and unsuccessful venture in art (he was refused admission to the Viennese Academy) and after a number of years of odd jobs and poverty, he left Vienna in 1913 and settled in Munich. During World War I he volunteered in the Bavarian army and rose to the rank of Corporal. He returned to Munich in 1918 and began dabbling in politics. In 1920, with a handful of followers, he founded his own party which grew into the National Socialist German Workers' (Nazi) party. The Munich

Putsch of 1923, an abortive attempt to overthrow the state government of Bavaria, gained him national attention and a thirteen-month jail sentence. It was during these months in jail that Hitler wrote the first volume of Mein Kampf (My Struggle), *published in 1925, which he intended to call "A Four and One-Half Year Struggle against Lies, Stupidity, and Cowardice: Settling Accounts with the Destroyers of the Nationalist Socialist Movement." The second volume was published in the following year, 1926. The book enjoyed only a small circulation at first, but a few years before Hitler came to power sales began to rise and soon* Mein Kampf *was a best seller second only to the Bible. Hitler was made chancellor in 1933 and after Hindenburg's death in 1934 was elected Führer for life. He is thought to have committed suicide in Berlin, on April 29, 1945.*

Today Hitler's name has become a byword for psychotic inhumanity; Mein Kampf *has been called a satanic Bible. Partly autobiographical, it not only outlines his program for world conquest but also broadcasts his hatred of Jews and his aim to restore to the Aryan "race" its sense of superiority. The selection we reprint below is the beginning of the eleventh chapter of Volume 1 of* Mein Kampf, *translated by Ralph Manheim.*

NATION AND RACE

There are some truths which are so obvious that for this very reason they are not seen or at least not recognized by ordinary people. They sometimes pass by such truisms as though blind and are most astonished when someone suddenly discovers what everyone really ought to know. Columbus's eggs lie around by the hundreds of thousands, but Columbuses are met with less frequently.

Thus men without exception wander about in the garden of Nature; they imagine that they know practically everything and yet with few exceptions pass blindly by one of the most patent principles of Nature's rule: the inner segregation of the species of all living beings on this earth.

Even the most superficial observation shows that Nature's restricted form of propagation and increase is an almost rigid basic law of all the innumerable forms of expression of her vital urge. Every animal mates only with a member of the same species. The titmouse seeks the titmouse, the finch the finch, the stork the stork, the field mouse the field mouse, the dormouse the dormouse, the wolf the she-wolf, etc.

Only unusual circumstances can change this, primarily the compulsion of captivity or any other cause that makes it impossible to mate within the same species. But then Nature begins to resist this with all possible means, and her most visible protest consists either in refusing further capacity for propagation to bastards or in limiting the fertility of later offspring; in most cases, however, she takes away the power of resistance to disease or hostile attacks.

This is only too natural.

Any crossing of two beings not at exactly the same level produces a medium between the level of the two parents. This means: the offspring will probably stand higher than the racially lower parent, but not as high as the higher one. Consequently, it will later succumb in the struggle against the higher level. Such mating is contrary to the will of Nature for a higher breeding of all life. The precondition for this does not lie in associating superior and inferior, but in the total victory of the former. The stronger must dominate and not blend with the weaker, thus sacrificing his own greatness. Only the born weakling can view this as cruel, but he after all is only a weak and limited man; for if this law did not prevail, any conceivable higher development of organic living beings would be unthinkable.

The consequence of this racial purity, universally valid in Nature, is not only the sharp outward delimitation of the various races, but their uniform character in themselves. The fox is always a fox, the goose a goose, the tiger a tiger, etc., and the difference can lie at most in the varying measure of force, strength, intelligence, dexterity, endurance, etc., of the individual specimens. But you will never find a fox who in his inner attitude might, for example, show humanitarian tendencies toward geese, as similarly there is no cat with a friendly inclination toward mice.

Therefore, here, too, the struggle among themselves arises less from inner aversion than from hunger and love. In both cases, Nature looks on calmly, with satisfaction, in fact. In the struggle for daily bread all those who are weak and sickly or less determined succumb, while the struggle of the males for the female grants the right or opportunity to propagate only to the healthiest. And struggle is always a means for improving a species' health and power of resistance and, therefore, a cause of its higher development.

If the process were different, all further and higher development would cease and the opposite would occur. For, since the inferior always predominates numerically over the best, if both had the same possibility of preserving life and propagating, the inferior would multiply so much more rapidly that in the end the best would inevitably be driven into the background, unless a correction of this state of affairs were undertaken. Nature does just this by subjecting the weaker part to such severe living conditions that by them alone the number is limited, and by not permitting the remainder to increase promiscuously, but making a new and ruthless choice according to strength and health.

No more than Nature desires the mating of weaker with stronger individuals, even less does she desire the blending of a higher with a lower race, since, if she did, her whole work of higher breeding, over perhaps hundreds of thousands of years, might be ruined with one blow.

Historical experience offers countless proofs of this. It shows with terrifying clarity that in every mingling of Aryan blood with that of lower peoples the result was the end of the cultured people. North America, whose population consists in by far the largest part of Germanic elements who mixed but little with the lower colored peoples, shows a different humanity and culture from Central and South America, where the predominantly Latin immigrants often mixed with the aborigines on a large scale. By this one example, we can clearly and distinctly recognize the effect of racial mixture. The Germanic inhabitant of the American continent, who has remained racially pure and unmixed, rose to be master of the continent; he will remain the master as long as he does not fall a victim to defilement of the blood.

The result of all racial crossing is therefore in brief always the following:

(a) Lowering of the level of the higher race;

(b) Physical and intellectual regression and hence the beginning of a slowly but surely progressing sickness.

To bring about such a development is, then, nothing else but to sin against the will of the eternal creator.

And as a sin this act is rewarded.

When man attempts to rebel against the iron logic of Nature, he comes into struggle with the principles to which he himself owes his existence as a man. And this attack must lead to his own doom.

Here, of course, we encounter the objection of the modern pacifist, as truly Jewish in its effrontery as it is stupid! 'Man's rôle is to overcome Nature!'

Millions thoughtlessly parrot this Jewish nonsense and end up by really imagining that they themselves represent a kind of conqueror of Nature; though in this they dispose of no other weapon than an idea, and at that such a miserable one, that if it were true no world at all would be conceivable.

But quite aside from the fact that man has never yet conquered Nature in anything, but at most has caught hold of and tried to lift one or another corner of her immense gigantic veil of eternal riddles and secrets, that in reality he invents nothing but only discovers everything, that he does not dominate Nature, but has only risen on the basis of his knowledge of various laws and secrets of Nature to be lord over those other living creatures who lack this knowledge—quite aside from all this, an idea cannot overcome the preconditions for the development and being of humanity, since the idea itself depends only on man. Without human beings there is no human idea in this world, therefore, the idea as such is always conditioned by the presence of human beings and hence of all the laws which created the precondition for their existence.

And not only that! Certain ideas are even tied up with certain men. This applies most of all to those ideas whose content originates, not in an exact scientific truth, but in the world of emotion, or, as it is so beautifully and clearly expressed today, reflects an 'inner experience.' All these ideas, which have nothing to do with cold logic as such, but represent only pure expressions of feeling, ethical conceptions, etc., are chained to the existence of men, to whose intellectual imagination and creative power they owe their existence. Precisely in this case the preservation of these definite races and men is the precondition for the existence of these ideas. Anyone, for example, who really desired the victory of the pacifistic idea in this world with all his heart would have to fight with all the means at his disposal for the conquest of the world by the Germans; for, if the opposite should occur, the last pacifist would die out with the last German, since the rest of the world has never fallen so deeply as our own people, unfortunately, has for this nonsense so contrary to Nature and reason. Then, if we were serious, whether we liked it or not, we would have to wage wars in order to arrive at pacifism. This and nothing else was what Wilson, the American world savior, intended, or so at least our German visionaries believed—and thereby his purpose was fulfilled.

In actual fact the pacifistic-humane idea is perfectly all right perhaps when the highest type of man has previously conquered and subjected the world to an extent that makes him the sole ruler of this earth. Then this idea lacks the power of producing evil effects in exact proportion as its practical application becomes rare and finally impossible. Therefore, first struggle and then we shall see what can be done. Otherwise mankind has passed the high point of its development and the end is not the domination of any ethical idea but barbarism and consequently chaos. At this point someone or other may laugh, but this planet once moved through the ether for millions of years without human beings and it can do so again some day if men forget that they owe their higher existence, not to the ideas of a few crazy ideologists, but to the knowledge and ruthless application of Nature's stern and rigid laws.

Everything we admire on this earth today—science and art, technology and inventions—is only the creative product of a few peoples and originally perhaps of *one* race. On them depends the existence of this whole culture. If they perish, the beauty of this earth will sink into the grave with them.

However much the soil, for example, can influence men, the result of the influence will always be different depending on the races in question. The low fertility of a living space may spur the one race to the highest achievements; in others it will only be the cause of bitterest poverty and final undernourishment with all its consequences. The inner nature of peoples is always determining for the manner in which outward influences will be effective. What leads the one to starvation trains the other to hard work.

All great cultures of the past perished only because the originally creative race died out from blood poisoning.

The ultimate cause of such a decline was their forgetting that all culture depends on men and not conversely; hence that to preserve a certain culture the man who creates it must be preserved. This preservation is bound up with the rigid law of necessity and the right to victory of the best and stronger in this world.

Those who want to live, let them fight, and those who do not want to fight in this world of eternal struggle do not deserve to live.

Even if this were hard—that is how it is! Assuredly, however, by far the harder fate is that which strikes the man who thinks he can overcome Nature, but in the last analysis only mocks her. Distress, misfortune, and diseases are her answer.

The man who misjudges and disregards the racial laws actually forfeits the happiness that seems destined to be his. He thwarts the triumphal march of the best race and hence also the precondition for all human progress, and remains, in consequence, burdened with all the sensibility of man, in the animal realm of helpless misery.

*   *   *

It is idle to argue which race or races were the original representative of human culture and hence the real founders of all that we sum up under the word 'humanity.' It is simpler to raise this question with regard to the present, and here an easy, clear answer results. All the human culture, all the results of art, science, and technology that we see before us today, are almost exclusively the creative product of the Aryan. This very fact admits of the not unfounded inference that he alone was the founder of all higher humanity, therefore representing the prototype of all that we understand by the word 'man.' He is the Prometheus of mankind from whose bright forehead the divine spark of genius has sprung at all times, forever kindling anew that fire of knowledge which illumined the night of silent mysteries and thus caused man to climb the path to mastery over the other beings of this earth. Exclude him—and perhaps after a few thousand years darkness will again descend on the earth, human culture will pass, and the world turn to a desert.

·   ·   ·

THEODOSIUS DOBZHANSKY

Professor Dobzhansky, born in Russia in 1900, is an internationally known authority on genetics and evolution. As a Fellow of the International Education Board of the Rockefeller Foundation, he worked at Columbia University and at the California Institute of Technology from 1927 to 1929. He was invited to stay on at the California Institute of Technology, joined its faculty, and by 1936 was named full professor. In 1940 he returned to Columbia as Professor of Zoology. As specialist, Professor Dobzhansky has devoted over thirty years of study to the mechanics of heredity in the fruit fly; as humanist, he has been concerned with the philosophical and social implications of modern biology. His writings include Genetics and the Origin of Species *(1937), which earned him the Daniel Giraud Elliot medal and prize from the National Academy of Sciences in 1941;* Heredity, Race and Society, *in collaboration with L. C. Dunn (1946);* Evolution, Genetics, and Man *(1955);* The Biological Basis of Human Freedom *(1956); and* Mankind Evolving: The Evolution of the Human Species *(1962). The article we present below first appeared in* Eugenics Quarterly, *December, 1963.*

GENETICS OF RACE EQUALITY

The crucial fact of our age is that people almost everywhere now take the idea of human equality quite seriously. It is no longer accepted as nature's law that people with darker skins are destined to be servants and those with lighter ones, masters. Children of those at the bottom of the social ladder no longer acquiesce in being placed automatically in a similar position. Everybody is entitled to equality. But what is equality? On the authority of the Declaration of Independence, it is a self-evident truth "that all men were created equal." Yet we hear that biology and genetics have demonstrated conclusively that men are unequal. Do biology and genetics really contradict what the Declaration of Independence holds to be self-evident? Or are the words "equal" and "unequal" being used in different senses? Just what have biology and genetics discovered that is relevant to the probem of equality or inequality?

Two geometric figures are said to be equal if they are identical in size and shape and coincide when superimposed on each other. Human equality, whether of persons or of groups, obviously means nothing of this sort. We generally have no difficulty distinguishing between persons whom we meet; the similarity of so-called identical twins strikes us as something unusual and remarkable. In fact, no two persons, not even identical twins, are ever truly identical. Every human being is in some respects unlike any other. This is not something that modern biology has recently found, but a matter of simple observation, so amply documented by the experience of everyone that its validity can hardly be questioned. Every person is, indeed, an individual, unique and unrepeatable. However, diversity and unlikeness, whether of individuals or of groups such as races, should not be confused with inequality. Nor should the affirmation of equality be taken to imply identity or uniformity.

Biology and genetics have some relevance to the problem of human equality. They have ushered in a new understanding of the nature and causes of human diversity. This nature resides in the remarkable chemical substances, the deoxyribonucleic acids, which are the principal constituents of the genes carried in the chromosomes of cell nuclei. Human genes are products of the evolutionary history of the human species, or the changes which were taking place in response to the environments in which our ancestors were living.

At this point one is tempted to discuss technicalities, which, although interesting and even fascinating in their own right, are not absolutely indispensable to our main theme. I shall resist the temptation. The essentials, developed from the seminal discoveries made by Gregor Mendel almost a century ago, can be stated quite simply. How many kinds of genes we inherit from our ancestors is not known with precision; there are at least thousands, and there may be tens of thousands, of genes carried in each human sex cell. An individual carries, then, thousands or tens of thousands of *pairs* of genes—one member of each pair being of maternal and the other of paternal origin.

What happens when the individual comes, in its turn, to form sex cells—egg cells or spermatozoa? It follows from Mendel's findings that each sex cell receives one or the other, the maternal or the paternal, member of every gene pair, but not a mixture of the two. A sex cell which receives a maternal copy of a gene A may, however, receive either the maternal or the paternal copy of the gene B, of the gene C, etc. Taking 1000 as a minimum estimate of the number of genes, it turns out that an individual is potentially capable of forming 2^{1000} kinds of sex cells containing different assortments of the maternal and paternal (or grand-maternal and grandpaternal) genes. I say *potentially*, because 2^{1000} is a number far greater than that of the atoms in the universe. Even if only one tenth—i.e. 100—of the maternal and paternal genes are different, the potentially possible number of kinds of sex cells is 2^{100}, which is a 31-place figure, vastly greater than the number of the sex cells produced.

All this adds up to something pretty simple after all: not even brothers and sisters, children of the same parents, are at all likely to have the same genes. No matter how many people may be born, despite any possible "population explosion," a tremendous majority of the potentially possible human nature will never be realized. A carping critic may remark that we hardly needed to learn genetics to discover what we know from everyday observation, that no two persons are ever alike. Genetics does, however, demonstrate something less commonplace when applied to analysis of the racial diversity among men.

Since our neighbors and even our closest relatives are all distinguishably different persons, it is not in the least surprising that people living in remote lands, or people whose ancestors came from such lands, are more noticeably different. We are inclined, however, to treat the diversity of groups in a manner rather different from diversity of individuals. If asked to describe your brother, or a cousin, or a fellow next door, you will probably say that he is somewhat taller (or shorter), darker (or lighter), heavier (or slimmer) than you, and you may add that he is inclined to be kind or easily angered, lazy or impatient, etc. A person whose ancestors lived in America before Columbus is, however, likely to be referred to as an Indian, and one whose ancestors came from trop-ical Africa, as a Negro.

Up to a point, this is, of course, legitimate. People of African ancestry usually have such conspicuous traits as a dark skin, kinky hair, broad nose, full lips, etc. One should not, however, forget that individual Indians, or Negroes, differ among themselves as much as do persons of the white race or any other race or group. When a group of people is given a name, a stereotype is likely to be invented; and oddly enough, the fewer persons of a given group one knows, the more rigid are the stereotypes of what all Indians, or Negroes, or Irishmen, or Jews are supposed to be. Most unreasonable of all, persons are then likely to be treated not according to what they are as individuals but according to the stereotype of the group to which they belong. This is as unwar-rantable biologically as it is ethically iniquitous.

Biologists have found between a million and two million species of animals and plants. An individual animal belongs to a certain species. It is, for example, either a horse *(Equus caballus)*, or an ass *(Equus asinus)*, or a sterile species hybrid (mule); but it cannot belong to two species at the same time. When anthropologists and biologists started to describe and classify races of men and animals, they treated races the same way as they treated species. Each was catalogued and given a name. But then difficulties arose. Biologists are sometimes in doubt as to whether certain forms should be regarded as belonging to the same or to two different species; however, with enough material, and given careful study, the doubts can usually be resolved. There is, however, no agreement among anthropologists concerning how many races there are in the human species. Opinions vary from three to more than two hundred. This is not a matter of insufficient data; the more studies are made on human populations, the less clear-cut the races become.

The difficulty is fundamental. Biological species are genetically closed systems; races are genetically open ones. Species do not interbreed and do not exchange genes, or do so rarely; they are reproductively isolated. The gene pools of the species man, chimpanzee, gorilla, and orang are quite separate; gene interchanges do not occur between these species. The biological meaning of this separation is evolutionary independence. Two species may have arisen from a common ancestor who lived long ago, but they embarked on separate evolutionary courses when they became species. No matter how favorable a new gene arising by mutation in the human species may be, it will not benefit the species chimpanzee nor vice versa.

Not so with races. Mankind, the human species, was a single evolutionary unit, at least, since mid-Pleistocene (the Ice Age). It continues to be a single unit, all segregations and apartheids notwithstanding. Wherever different human populations are sympatric—i.e. geographically intermingled in a common territory as castes or as religions or linguistic groups—some miscegenation and gene exchange crops up. More important still is the interbreeding and gene flow among populations of neighboring territories. It is a relative innovation in mankind that some racially distinct populations live sympatrically, like Negroes and Whites over a considerable part of the United States. Before, say, 2000 B.C., the human races, like races of most animal species, were largely allopatric, living in different territories. However, the peripheral gene flow, the gene exchange between allopatric but neighboring populations, whether human or animal, is and always was a regular occurrence.

This continuous, sometimes slow, but unfailing gene flow between neighboring clans, tribes, nations, and races upholds the biological and evolutionary unity of mankind. There may be no recorded case of a marriage of an Eskimo with, say, a Melanesian or a Bushman, but there are genetic links between all these populations via the geographically intervening groups. In contrast with distinct species, a beneficial change arising in any population anywhere in the world may become a part of the common biological endowment of all races of mankind. This genetic oneness of mankind has been growing steadily since the development of material cultures has made travel and communication between the inhabitants of different countries progressively more and more rapid and easy. What should be stressed however, is that mankind has not become a meaningful biological entity just recently, since men began to travel often and far. The human species was such an entity even before it became recognizably human.

Races, on the contrary, are not, and never were, groups clearly defined biologically. The gene flow between human populations makes race boundaries always more or less blurred. Consider three groups of people, for example: Scandinavians, Japanese, and Congolese. Every individual will probably be easily placeable in one of the three races—White, Mongoloid, and Negroid. It will however, be far from easy to delimit these races if one observes also the inhabitants of the countries geographically intermediate between Scandinavia, Japan, and Congo, respectively. Intermediate countries have intermediate populations, or populations which differ in some characteristics from all previously outlined races. One may try to get out of the difficulty by recognizing several intermediate races; or else, one may speculate that the races were nicely distinct at some time in the past, and got mixed up lately owing to miscegenation. This helps not at all. The more races one sets up, the fuzzier their boundaries become. And the difficulty is by no means confined to man; it occurs as well in many biological species where it cannot be blamed on recent miscegenation.

Populations which inhabit different countries differ more often in relative frequencies of genetically simple traits than in any single trait being present in all individuals of one population and always absent in another population. Not only are the differences thus relative rather than absolute; but, to make things more complex still, the variations of different characters are often independent or at least not strongly correlated. Some populations may be clearly different in a gene A but rather similar in a gene B, while other populations may be different in B but less so in A. This makes the drawing of any lines separating different races a rather arbitrary procedure, and results in the notorious inability of anthropologists to agree on any race classification yet proposed. Race classifiers might have indeed preferred to find simple and tidy races, in which every person would show just the characteristics that his race is supposed to possess. Nature has not been obliging enough to make the races conform to this prescription. Exactly the same difficulties which a student of races encounters in the human species are met with also by zoologists who are working with species of nonhuman animals, and arguments have actually been put forward that animals have no races, or at least that the races should not be described and named. Where, then, are races found? If they are nowhere to be found, then what are these visibly different populations of the human species which are usually referred to as races?

Much needed light on the nature of population or race difference came from studies on the genetics of chemical constituents of the human blood.

As far back as 1900, Landsteiner discovered four blood types, or blood groups, distinguishable by simple laboratory tests. These blood groups—called O, A, B, and AB—are inherited very simply, according to Mendel's laws. Brothers and sisters and parents and children may, and quite often do, differ in blood types. An enormous number of investigations have been made, especially in recent years, on the distribution of the blood types among peoples in various parts of the world. Any race or population can be described in terms of the percentages of the four blood types. Almost everywhere persons of all four types are found, but in different proportions. Thus B and AB bloods are commonest among peoples of central Asia and India, A bloods in western Europe and in some American Indians, while many American Indian tribes belong predominantly or even exclusively to the group O.

Several other blood group systems have been discovered, including the Rhesus system, usually referred to as the Rh factor. The genes for these blood groups behave in general like those for the "classical" O-A-B-AB blood types. For example, one of the variants (alleles) of the Rhesus gene occurs much more often in the populations of Africa than elsewhere. But mark this well—this gene does occur, albeit infrequently, in human populations almost everywhere in the world, and it is quite certain that it has not spread so widely owing to a Negro admixture in recent centuries.

These facts are profoundly significant. Consider the following situation, which is by no means unusual. A person of European origin, say an Englishman or a Frenchman, has O-type blood, while his brother has B blood. In this particular respect, these brothers differ from each other, while one of them resembles many American Indians with O bloods, and the other matches numerous persons in Asia and elsewhere who have B bloods. Or else, one of the brothers may have the kind of Rhesus blood type most characteristic of the Africans, and the other brother may have blood more like a majority of his European neighbors. Such characteristics, of which the persons concerned are usually quite unaware, may become vitally important in some circumstances. If an individual with O-type blood needs a blood transfusion, then O-type blood from a donor of no matter what race will be safe, while the blood of the recipient's brother may be dangerous if that brother has A, B, or AB blood.

Though not different in principle from the blood types, the genetics of skin color and similar traits is considerably more complex. The color difference between Negro and White skin is due to joint action of several genes, each of which by itself makes the skin only a little darker or lighter. Geneticists have studied the inheritance of skin pigmentation for half a century, yet exactly how many genes are involved is still unknown. The skin color is obviously variable among the so-called "white" as well as among the "black" peoples, some individuals being darker and others, lighter. If we were able to map the geographic distribution of each separate skin color gene as thoroughly as it has been done for some blood group genes, the race differences would probably be resolved into gene frequency differences. It is fair to say that the studies on blood types and similar traits have, so far at least, helped more to understand races than to classify them.

Thus every race includes persons with diverse genetic endowments. Genetic studies show that race differences are compounded of the same kinds of genetic elements in which individuals within a race also differ. An individual must always be judged according to what he is, not according to the place of origin of his ancestors. Races may be defined as populations which differ in frequencies, or in prevalence, of some genes. Race differences are relative, not absolute.

This modern race concept, based on findings of genetics, appears to differ from the traditional view so much that it has provoked some misunderstanding and opposition. The use of traits like the blood groups to elucidate the nature of the races of which mankind is composed may seem a questionable procedure. To distinguish races, should one use, rather, traits like the skin pigmentation in place of the blood types? Some blood types can be found almost anywhere in the world; on the other hand, pale skins (other than albino) do not occur among the natives of equatorial Africa or of New Guinea, and black skins are not found among the natives of Europe. This objection is beside the point. The blood types are useful because their genetic nature is relatively simple and well understood. The classification of the human races need not be based on any one trait; the behavior of the blood types helps, however, to understand the behavior of other traits, including the skin color.

To sum up, the races of man are not integrated biological entities of the sort biological species are. Race boundaries are blurred by the more or less slow but long-sustained gene exchange. The number of races that should be recognized is arbitrary in the sense that it is a matter of convention and convenience whether one should give names to only a few "major" or also to a larger number of "minor" races. An anthropologist who maintains that there are exactly five or any other fixed number of races, or who resolves to cut the Gordian Knot—mankind has no races— is nurturing illusions. On the other hand, there need be nothing arbitrary about race differences; human populations are racially distinct if they differ in the frequencies of some genes, and not distinct if they do not so differ. The presence of race differences can be ascertained, and if they are present, their magnitude can be measured.

The problem that inevitably arises in any discussion of individual and race equality is how consequential the differences among humans really are. Man's bodily structures do not differentiate him very strikingly from other living creatures; it is the psychic, intellectual, or spiritual side of human nature that is truly distinctive of Man. Physical race differences supply only the externally visible marks by which the geographic origin of people, or rather of their ancestors, can be identified. The blood types, nose shapes, and skin colors of people whom we meet are so much less important to us than their dispositions, intelligence, and rectitude. It is a person's personality that matters.

The diversity of personalities would seem to be as great, and surely more telling, than the diversity of skin colors or other physical traits. And, though the biological basis of both kinds of diversity is the same in principle, it is different enough in its outward manifestations that the difference constitutes a genuine problem. This is the perennial nature-nurture problem. The confusion and polemics with which it was beset for a long time were due in part to the problem having been wrongly stated—which human traits are due to heredity and which to environment. No trait can arise unless the heredity of the organism makes it possible, and no heredity operates outside of environments. A meaningful way is to ask what part of the diversity observed in a given population is conditioned by the genetic differences between persons composing this population, and what part is due to the upbringing, education, and other environmental variables. Furthermore, the issue must be investigated and solved separately for each function, trait or characteristic that comes under consideration. Suppose one collects good data on the genetic and environmental components of the observed diversity in the intelligence quotients, or on the resistance to tuberculosis. This would not tell us anything about the diversity of temperaments or about resistance to cancer.

Even correctly stated, the nature-nurture problem remains a formidable one. Dogmatic statements abound on both the hereditarian and the environmentalist side of the controversy, and they usually say much about their authors but not much about the subject at issue. The plain truth is that it is not known just how influential are the genetic variables in psychic or personality traits or how plastic these traits might be in different environments that can be contrived by modern technology, medicine, and educational methods. There is no way in practice to arrange for a large group of people to be brought up under controlled and uniform conditions in order to see how similar or different they would develop. The converse experiment—observing identical twins, individuals with similar heredities brought up in different environments—is possible, but opportunities for such observations are scarcer than one would wish they were.

Some partisans of human equality got themselves in the untenable position of arguing that mankind is genetically uniform with respect to intelligence, ability, and other psychic traits. Actually it is, I think, fair to say that whenever any variable trait in man was at all adequately studied genetically, evidence was found of at least some, though perhaps slight, contribution of genetic differences. Being equal has to be compatible with being different, and different in characters that are relevant to the specifically human estate, not alone in "skin-deep" traits like skin color.

The current civil rights movement in the United States has elicited a rash of racist pamphlets which pretend to prove, very "scientifically" of course, that races cannot be equal because they differ in the average brain size, the average I.Q., etc. Now, there is no reason to believe that small differences in the brain volumes are any indication of different mental capacities; the I.Q. tests are not reliable when administered to people of different sociocultural backgrounds, and in any case they cannot be taken as anything approaching a measurement of human worth. Be all that as it may, the striking fact—which not even the racists can conceal—is that the race differences in the averages are much smaller than the variations within any race. In other words, large brains and high I.Q.'s of persons of every race are much larger and higher than the averages for their own or any other race. And conversely, the low variants in every race are much below the average for any race. This is a situation quite analogous to what is known about race differences in such traits as blood groups and is in perfect accord with theoretical expectations in populations which exchange genes.

It is impossible in an article such as the present one to summarize and to evaluate critically the abundant but often unreliable and contradictory data on the nature-nurture situation in man. It is more useful to consider here some fundamentals that must be kept in mind in dealing with such data. An all too often forgotten and yet most basic fact is that the genes determine, not traits or characters, but the ways in which the organism responds to the environments. One inherits, not the skin color and intelligence, but only genes which make the development of certain colors and intelligence possible. To state the same thing with a slightly different emphasis, the gene complement determines the path which the development of a person will take, given the sequence of the environments which this person encounters in the process of living. Any developmental process, whether physiological or psychological, can be influenced or modified by genetic as well as by environmental variables. The realization of heredity is manageable, within limits, by physiological and social engineering. What the limits are depends upon our understanding of the developmental processes involved. Modern medicine is able to control the manifestations of some hereditary diseases which not so long ago were incurable. This does not make hereditary defects and diseases harmless or unimportant; even if they can be cured, it is better for the individual and for his society to have no necessity of being cured. This does give substance to the hope that hereditary need be, not destiny, but conditioning.

Although the mode of inheritance of physical and psychic traits in man is fundamentally the same, their developmental plasticity—the ability to respond to modifying influences of the environment—is different. There is no known way to alter the blood group with which a person is born; it is possible to modify one's skin color, making it somewhat darker or lighter by sun tanning or by lack of sun exposure; the development of personality traits is very much dependent on the family and social environments in which an individual is brought up and lives. The great lability of psychic traits is at least one of the reasons why it is so hard, not only to measure precisely the role played by heredity in their variations, but even to prove unambiguously that some of these traits are influenced by heredity at all. The more environmentally labile is a trait, the more critical it is for its investigation to have the environment under control; this is difficult or impossible to achieve with man.

The great environmental plasticity of psychic traits in man is no biological accident. It is an important, even crucial, evolutionary adaptation which distinguishes man from other creatures, including those nearest to him in the zoological system. It is by brain, not by brawn, that man controls his environment. Mankind's singular and singularly powerful adaptive instrument is culture. Culture is not inherited through genes, it is acquired by learning from other human beings. The ability to learn, and thus to acquire a culture and to become a member of a society is, however, given by the genetic endowment that is mankind's distinctive biological attribute. In a sense, human genes have surrendered their primacy in human evolution to an entirely new, nonbiological or superorganic agent, culture. However, it should not be forgotten that this agent is entirely dependent on the human genotype.

A pseudobiological fallacy—dangerous because it is superficially so plausible—alleges that the differences in psychic traits among human individuals and races are genetically fixed to about the same extent as they are among races or breeds of domestic animals. This overlooks the fact that the behavior of a breed of horses or of dogs is always a part of a complex of characters that are deliberately selected by the breeders to fit the animals for its intended use. A hunting dog with a temperament of a Pekingese, a great Dane behaving like a fox terrier, a draft horse as high-strung as a race horse or vice versa—all these monstrosities would be worthless or even dangerous to their human masters. Man has seen to it that the genes that stabilize the desirable behavior traits in his domestic animals be fixed and the genes that predispose for variable or undesirable behavior be eliminated.

What is biologically as well as sociologically requisite in man is the exact opposite—not to fix rigidly his qualities, but to be able to learn whatever mode of behavior fits a job to be done, the mores of the group of which one happens to be a member, a conduct befitting the circumstances and opportunities. Man's paramount adaptive trait is his educability. The biological evolution of mankind has accordingly so shaped the human genotype that an educability is a universal property of all non-pathological individuals. It is a diagnostic character of mankind as a species, not of only some of its races. This universality is no accident either. In all cultures, primitive or advanced, the vital ability is to be able to learn whatever is necessary to become a competent member of some group or society. In advanced civilizations the variety of function has grown so enormously that learning has come to occupy a considerable fraction of the life span. Even where, as in India, the society was splintered for centuries into castes specialized for different occupations, the ability to learn new professions or trades has been preserved.

Champions of human equality have traditionally been environmentalists, conspicuously distrustful of genetic determinisms. Historically their attitude has been useful in counterbalancing the influence of those racist hereditarians who tried to justify the denial of equality of opportunity to most people on the pretext that the latter are genetically inferior. The environmentalists, however, went too far in their protest. They simply failed to understand that to be equal is not the same thing as to be alike. Equality is a sociological, not a biological, ideal. A society may grant equality to its citizens, but it cannot make them alike. What is more, in a society composed of genetically identical individuals, equality would be meaningless; individuals would have to be assigned for different occupations by drawing lots or in some other arbitrary manner. The ideal of equality of opportunity is precious, because it holds out a hope that persons and groups diverse in their endowments may enjoy a feeling of belonging and of partnership and may work for the common good in whatever capacity without loss of their human dignity. Men must be dealt with primarily on the basis of their humanity and also on the basis of their potentialities and accomplishments as individuals; the practice of treating them according to their race or color is a nefarious one.

Genetic diversity is a blessing, not a curse. Any society—particularly any civilized society—has a multitude of diverse vocations and callings to be filled, and new ones are constantly emerging. The human genetically secured educability enables most individuals of all races to be trained for most occupations. This is certainly the basic and fundamental adaptive quality of all mankind; yet this is in no way incompatible with a genetically conditioned diversity of preferences and special abilities. Music is an obnoxious noise to some, ecstatic pleasure to others. Some have a bodily frame that can be trained for championship in wrestling, or running, or sprinting, or weight lifting. Some can develop phenomenal abilities for chess playing, or painting, or composing poetry. Can anybody develop a skill in any of these occupations if he makes sufficient effort? Possibly many people could, to some extent. The point is, however, that what comes easily to some requires great exertion from others, and even then the accomplishment is mediocre at best. The willingness to strive derives, however, at least in part, from a feeling that the labor is rewarded by the thrill of accomplishment or in some other way. There is little stimulus to exert oneself if the results of the exertions are likely to be pitifully small. And it is also possible that there is such a thing as predisposition to striving and effort.

It is a perversion of the ethic of equality to endeavor to reduce everybody to a uniform level of achievement. "From each according to his ability" is the famous motto of Marxian socialism, and it behooves democracy to grant no less recognition to the diversity of human individualities. This is not an apology for "rugged individualism"; the "ruggedness" amounts often to indifference or even contempt for individualities of others. Equality is, however, not an end in itself, but a means to an end, which can only be the self-actualization of human individuals and the fullest possible realization of their socially valuable capacities and potentialities. Individuals and groups will arrange their lives differently, in accordance with their diverse notions of what form of happiness they wish to pursue. Their contributions to mankind's store of achievements will be different in kind and in magnitude. The point is, however, that everybody should be able to contribute to the limit of his ability. To deny the equality of opportunity to persons or groups is evil, because it results in wastage of talent, ability, and aptitude, besides being contrary to the basic ethic of humanity.

GEORGE ORWELL

MARRAKECH

This essay, written in 1939, is included in George Orwell's collection entitled Such, Such Were the Joys *(1953). For information on the author and his writings, see page 74.*

•

As the corpse went past the flies left the restaurant table in a cloud and rushed after it, but they came back a few minutes later.

The little crowd of mourners—all men and boys, no women—threaded their way across the market-place between the piles of pomegranates and the taxis and the camels, wailing a short chant over and over again. What really appeals to the flies is that the corpses here are never put into coffins, they are merely wrapped in a piece of rag and carried on a rough wooden bier on the shoulders of four friends. When the friends get to the burying-ground they hack an oblong hole a foot or two deep, dump the body in it and fling over it a little of the dried-up, lumpy earth, which is like broken brick. No gravestone, no name, no identifying mark of any kind. The burying-ground is merely a huge waste of hummocky earth, like a derelict building-lot. After a month or two no one can even be certain where his own relatives are buried.

When you walk through a town like this—two hundred thousand inhabitants, of whom at least twenty thousand own literally nothing except the rags they stand up in—when you see how the people live, and still more how easily they die, it is always difficult to believe that you are walking among human beings. All colonial empires are in reality founded upon that fact. The people have brown faces—besides, there are so many of them! Are they really the same flesh as yourself? Do they even have names? Or are they merely a kind of undifferentiated brown stuff, about as individual as bees or coral insects? They rise out of the earth, they sweat and starve for a few years, and then they sink back into the nameless mounds of the graveyard and nobody notices that they are gone. And even the graves themselves soon fade back into the soil. Sometimes, out for a walk, as you break your way through the prickly pear, you notice that it is rather bumpy underfoot, and only a certain regularity in the bumps tells you that you are walking over skeletons.

I was feeding one of the gazelles in the public gardens.

Gazelles are almost the only animals that look good to eat when they are still alive, in fact, one can hardly look at their hindquarters without thinking of mint sauce. The gazelle I was feeding seemed to know that this thought was in my mind, for though it took the piece of bread I was holding out it obviously did not like me. It nibbled rapidly at the bread, then lowered its head and tried to butt me, then took another nibble and then butted again. Probably its idea was that if it could drive me away the bread would somehow remain hanging in mid-air.

An Arab navvy working on the path nearby lowered his heavy hoe and sidled slowly towards us. He looked from the gazelle to the bread and from the bread to the gazelle, with a sort of quiet amazement, as though he had never seen anything quite like this before. Finally he said shyly in French:

"*I could eat some of that bread.*"

I tore off a piece and he stowed it gratefully in some secret place under his rags. This man is an employee of the Municipality.

When you go through the Jewish quarters you gather some idea of what the medieval ghettoes were probably like. Under their Moorish rulers the Jews were only allowed to own land in certain restricted areas, and after centuries of this kind of treatment they have ceased to bother about overcrowding. Many of the streets are a good deal less than six feet wide, the houses are completely windowless, and sore-eyed children cluster everywhere in unbelievable numbers, like clouds of flies. Down the centre of the street there is generally running a little river of urine.

In the bazaar huge families of Jews, all dressed in the long black robe and little black skull-cap, are working in dark fly-infested booths that look like caves. A carpenter sits cross-legged at a prehistoric lathe, turning chair-legs at lightning speed. He works the lathe with a bow in his right hand and guides the chisel with his left foot, and thanks to a lifetime of sitting in this position his left leg is warped out of shape. At his side his grandson, aged six, is already starting on the simpler parts of the job.

I was just passing the coppersmiths' booths when somebody noticed that I was lighting a cigarette. Instantly, from the dark holes all round, there was a frenzied rush of Jews, many of them old grandfathers with flowing grey beards, all clamouring for a cigarette. Even a blind man somewhere at the back of one of the booths heard a rumour of cigarettes and came crawling out, groping in the air with his hand. In about a minute I had used up the whole packet. None of these people, I suppose, works less than twelve hours a day, and every one of them looks on a cigarette as a more or less impossible luxury.

As the Jews live in self-contained communities they follow the same trades as the Arabs, except for agriculture. Fruit-sellers, potters, silversmiths, blacksmiths, butchers, leatherworkers, tailors, water-carriers, beggars, porters—whichever way you look you see nothing but Jews. As a matter of fact there are thirteen thousand of them, all living in the space of a few acres. A good job Hitler wasn't here. Perhaps he was on his way, however. You hear the usual dark rumours about the Jews, not only from the Arabs but from the poorer Europeans.

"Yes, mon vieux, they took my job away from me and gave it to a Jew. The Jews! They're the real rulers of this country, you know. They've got all the money. They control the banks, finance—everything."

"But," I said, "isn't it a fact that the average Jew is a labourer working for about a penny an hour?"

"Ah, that's only for show! They're all moneylenders really. They're cunning, the Jews."

In just the same way, a couple of hundred years ago, poor old women used to be burned for witchcraft when they could not even work enough magic to get themselves a square meal.

All people who work with their hands are partly invisible, and the more important the work they do, the less visible they are. Still, a white skin is always fairly conspicuous. In northern Europe, when you see a labourer ploughing a field, you probably give him a second glance. In a hot country, anywhere south of Gibraltar or east of Suez, the chances are that you don't even see him. I have noticed this again and again. In a tropical landscape one's eye takes in everything except the human beings. It takes in the dried-up soil, the prickly pear, the palm tree and the distant mountain, but it always misses the peasant hoeing at his patch. He is the same colour as the earth, and a great deal less interesting to look at.

It is only because of this that the starved countries of Asia and Africa are accepted as tourist resorts. No one would think of running cheap trips to the Distressed Areas. But where the human beings have brown skins their poverty is simply not noticed. What does Morocco mean to a Frenchman? An orange-grove or a job in Government service. Or to an Englishman? Camels, castles, palm trees, Foreign Legionnaires, brass trays, and bandits. One could probably live there for years without noticing that for nine-tenths of the people the reality of life is an endless, back-breaking struggle to wring a little food out of an eroded soil.

Most of Morocco is so desolate that no wild animal bigger than a hare can live on it. Huge areas which were once covered with forest have turned into a treeless waste where the soil is exactly like broken-up brick. Nevertheless a good deal of it is cultivated, with frightful labour. Every-thing is done by hand. Long lines of women, bent double like inverted capital L's, work their way slowly across the fields, tearing up the prickly weeds with their hands, and the peasant gathering lucerne for fodder pulls it up stalk by stalk instead of reaping it, thus saving an inch or two on each stalk. The plough is a wretched wooden thing, so frail that one can easily carry it on one's shoulder, and fitted underneath with a rough iron spike which stirs the soil to a depth of about four inches. This is as much as the strength of the animals is equal to. It is usual to plough with a cow and a donkey yoked together. Two donkeys would not be quite strong enough, but on the other hand two cows would cost a little more to feed. The peasants possess no harrows, they merely plough the soil several times over in different directions, finally leaving it in rough fur-rows, after which the whole field has to be shaped with hoes into small oblong patches to conserve water. Except for a day or two after the rare rainstorms there is never enough water. Along the edges of the fields chan-nels are hacked out to a depth of thirty or forty feet to get at the tiny trickles which run through the subsoil.

Every afternoon a file of very old women passes down the road outside my house, each carrying a load of firewood. All of them are mummified with age and the sun, and all of them are tiny. It seems to be generally the case in primitive communities that the women, when they get beyond a certain age, shrink to the size of children. One day a poor old creature who could not have been more than four feet tall crept past me under a vast load of wood. I stopped her and put a five-sou piece (a little more than a farthing) into her hand. She answered with a shrill wail, almost a scream, which was partly gratitude but mainly surprise. I suppose that from her point of view, by taking any notice of her, I seemed almost to be violating a law of nature. She accepted her status as an old woman, that is to say as a beast of burden. When a family is travelling it is quite usual to see a father and a grown-up son riding ahead on donkeys, and an old woman following on foot, carrying the baggage.

But what is strange about these people is their invisibility. For several weeks, always at about the same time of day, the file of old women had hobbled past the house with their firewood, and though they had registered themselves on my eyeballs I cannot truly say that I had seen them. Firewood was passing—that was how I saw it. It was only that one day I happened to be walking behind them, and the curious up-and-down motion of a load of wood drew my attention to the human being beneath it. Then for the first time I noticed the poor old earth-coloured bodies, bodies reduced to bones and leathery skin, bent double under the crushing weight. Yet I suppose I had not been five minutes on Moroccan soil before I noticed the overloading of the donkeys and was infuriated by it. There is no question that the donkeys are damnably treated. The Moroccan donkey is hardly bigger than a St. Bernard dog, it carries a load which in the British Army would be considered too much for a fifteen-hands mule, and very often its pack-saddle is not taken off its back for weeks together. But what is peculiarly pitiful is that it is the most willing creature on earth, it follows its master like a dog and does not need either bridle or halter. After a dozen years of devoted work it suddenly drops dead, whereupon its master tips it into the ditch and the village dogs have torn its guts out before it is cold.

This kind of thing makes one's blood boil, whereas—on the whole—the plight of the human beings does not. I am not commenting, merely pointing to a fact. People with brown skins are next door to invisible. Anyone can be sorry for the donkey with its galled back, but it is generally owing to some kind of accident if one even notices the old woman under her load of sticks.

As the storks flew northward the Negroes were marching southward —a long, dusty column, infantry, screw-gun batteries, and then more infantry, four or five thousand men in all, winding up the road with a clumping of boots and a clatter of iron wheels.

They were Senegalese, the blackest Negroes in Africa, so black that sometimes it is difficult to see whereabouts on their necks the hair begins. Their splendid bodies were hidden in reach-me-down khaki uniforms, their feet squashed into boots that looked like blocks of wood, and every tin hat seemed to be a couple of sizes too small. It was very hot and the men had marched a long way. They slumped under the weight of their packs and the curiously sensitive black faces were glistening with sweat.

As they went past a tall, very young Negro turned and caught my eye. But the look he gave me was not in the least the kind of look you might expect. Not hostile, not contemptuous, not sullen, not even inquisitive. It was the shy, wide-eyed Negro look, which actually is a look of profound respect. I saw how it was. This wretched boy, who is a French citizen and has therefore been dragged from the forest to scrub floors and catch syphilis in garrison towns, actually has feelings of reverence before a white skin. He has been taught that the white race are his masters, and he still believes it.

But there is one thought which every white man (and in this connection it doesn't matter twopence if he calls himself a socialist) thinks when he sees a black army matching past. "How much longer can we go on kidding these people? How long before they turn their guns in the other direction?"

It was curious, really. Every white man there had this thought stowed somewhere or other in his mind. I had it, so had the other onlookers, so had the officers on their sweating chargers and the white N.C.O.'s marching in the ranks. It was a kind of secret which we all knew and were too clever to tell; only the Negroes didn't know it. And really it was like watching a flock of cattle to see the long column, a mile or two miles of armed men, flowing peacefully up the road, while the great white birds drifted over them in the opposite direction, glittering like scraps of paper.

[1939]

PERRY MORGAN

Perry Morgan is Managing Editor of the Charlotte (N.C.) News. *Educated at the University of Georgia, he has also studied as a Nieman Fellow at Harvard. He has worked on newspapers in Georgia, Michigan, Virginia, and North Carolina and has won several prizes for editorial and news writing. The article we reprint below first appeared in the January, 1962, issue of* Esquire.

THE CASE FOR THE WHITE SOUTHERNER

When the good citizens of New Rochelle, New York, were accused last year of admitting Jim Crow to their schools, they denied it. When they were taken to court, they resisted. When the judge looked and saw old Jim sitting there plain as day and ordered his removal, a solid citizen of New Rochelle cried: "Nobody understands our situation."

New Rochelle is located in the Piety Belt that denounces racial discrimination and has it, too. The law is against it, but the majority of people are for it. Beginning in 1930, Judge Irving R. Kaufman found, the New Rochelle school board had confined Negro pupils exclusively to one school. This was the Lincoln School (presumably after Abraham Lincoln who signed the Emancipation Proclamation) from which transfers were denied even though all-white schools had twice as many vacant seats as children registered at Lincoln. Even after Judge Kaufman ordered Jim Crow expelled, a school board majority concocted a desegregation plan designed to sneak old Jim back into school by the side door. The judge, however, was adamant.

The Piety Belt is a varied land populated by people of good conscience. Their forefathers, according to much-loved myth, fought a war to free the slaves. And for the century since, by preachment and earnest exhortation, they have urged the white Southerner to conquer the evil in his heart and treat the Negro as a free and equal American. They have looked away to Dixie Land with fury and scorn and earnestly have hoped the down-trodden Negro would never doubt the constancy of their faith.

Abundance of precept, however, has been accompanied by a stringent shortage of example in the Piety Belt. Negroes migrating into the North early noted that, although the law was on their side, the people lacked some of the warmth and fellowship to which they were accustomed. "Up North," the saying sprang up, "they don't care how high you get just so you don't get too close; down South, they don't care how close you get, just so you don't get too high." The point has not lost its sharpness.

The South has been given far too much credit for ingenuity in shaping the law to its own purposes. The Southern lawyer seeking to circumvent the Supreme Court decision really had to look no farther than Philadelphia to find the model for what in the South the Northern press sniffily defines as "token integration." According to a Public Affairs Committee study by Will Maslow and Richard Cohen, "more Negro children attend what are in fact segregated schools in the major cities of the North than attend officially segregated schools in urban areas of the South." Note the authors: "When Lieutenant Nellie Forbush, the Navy nurse in *South Pacific*, tells the world she hails from Little Rock, she is greeted from Maine to Madagascar with hoots, catcalls and other indigenous expressions of disapproval . . . yet Little Rock . . . has fewer Negroes than the South Side of Chicago. More significant, school segregation is as prevalent in that corner of Chicago as it is in the Arkansas capital." So much for the soul of John Brown—in bivouac.

The non-Southerner naturally has ready excuses for this paradox. It is difficult to admit guilt. Having hidden his complicity in the crime of slavery for a century he cannot bring himself to face the fact now that the victim has caught up with him. His schools stagger from crisis to crisis under the weight of a vast influx of Negro children who lack the capacity to keep up with their white classmates. Achievement levels are dropping. The more affluent whites are fleeing. One school superintendent told *Look* Magazine's George B. Leonard, Jr. that a third of the children in his elementary schools may end up not only unemployed, but unemployable. But, as Leonard wrote, this is a shrouded crisis. Though Dr. James B. Conant has deplored the lack of statistics, school officials cannot publicly face the "delicate and complex matter of racial prejudice." Instead, "they cling to the vain old hope that racial prejudice will disappear if you pretend race does not exist."

So earnest is the innocent resident of the Piety Belt in his explanations that he forgets the white Southerner has heard them all before. In fact, he holds the patents on them. The Negro came to *him* on Yankee slave ships from the jungle. Yet in trying to shake the Northerner from his silly pretensions, *Look* indulged its own in a headline saying *"America's large cities are paying the grim price of a century of rural and Southern educational neglect."*

Southern neglect? God in heaven! By his standards of the time the Northerner perhaps had excuse for visiting unmerciful vengeance upon the whites of the defeated Confederacy. But what of the freed man in whose name, and out of strategic necessity, the Civil War was given a sacred cause through Lincoln's Emancipation Proclamation? Leaving the freed man and the white man together in a pit of poverty, pain and ignorance, the victorious Northerner turned to a feast of prosperity whose cynicism sickened and dismayed Henry Adams and other sensitive souls.

On reflection, though, it is not quite accurate to say the North merely wrought ruin and departed. More precisely, with a host of exploiting devices, it leeched out of a destroyed region many of the pitiful resources left for its meager sustenance. Long before Franklin D. Roosevelt rediscovered America's own viciously exploited colony to the South, the Piety Belt was grieving for the downtrodden in faraway corners of the world.

The white Southerner and the Negro climbed out of the pit together, and unassisted. It was a long, grim and demeaning journey, and if it scarred the Negro it also scarred the white. For its part in the crime of slavery, as Gerald Johnson has written, the South has paid and paid and paid. It owes neither the North nor the world apologies for its stewardship of the human dilemma deposited on American shores three centuries ago. What qualifications the Negro now brings in support of his demand for full participation in the world's most difficult citizenship, he has from the white Southerner. If he goes North with an inferior education, he was given that by a white man who has never been able to afford adequate schools for his own children.

The Southerner has believed a lot of comforting bushwa about his own region—moonlight, magnolias and all the rest. But having some little experience with the Negro problem, he is altogether disinclined to believe the North's nonsense too. He has observed that wherever the two races exist together in significant numbers—in London, Capetown or New Rochelle—walls are thrown up, and that when laws oppose, the walls somehow curve around the laws.

The case for the white Southerner is that he is a human being with a normal complement of virtues and vices. If he himself has been too much concerned with defending and vaunting his virtues, the North has been overly fascinated with condemning his vices. A Union officer made that point a century ago, as W. D. Workman has recalled, and so did Harriet Beecher Stowe when she got around to looking for herself.

Let the misunderstood citizen of affluent New Rochelle mark well this unique fact: twice in a hundred years the South has been forced to recast the laws, the mood and the mind of its people. In both cases, though it had no model for judgment, the nation decided to substitute revolutionary for evolutionary processes. The latter, to be sure, were still working injustices when the Supreme Court interrupted in 1954, but they had wrought profound changes too. The South at that point had begun rapidly to repair the spiritual and material ravages of a grim host of decades of poverty, ignorance, pain, disease and economic exploitation. A growing middle class was bringing a new stability to political processes flawed and half-paralyzed by the racial factor. The region had begun to surmount the bleak, crippling pessimism that was the natural inheritance of the past and to take new and promising initiatives even in the field of race relations. Great strides had been taken in education, medicine and agriculture. The fabled Southern female was slaving in field and factory, and sometimes both, to send sons and daughters to college and break once and for all the harsh grip of hoe and row. The winds of hope and progress, in sum, were quickening.

Then came May 17, 1954, and an historic decision concerned as much with conjectural foreign-policy needs for a purer national image as with the needs of the American Negro. Never before, not even in the Dred Scott case which wrecked the court's power and prestige on the reefs of Northern outrage, had there issued a writ touching so profoundly and personally the lives of so many millions of individuals. Yet out of his profound innocence, the Northerner fully expected the South—by taking thought—to swiftly swallow its sociological medicine, cleanse the national conscience and miraculously reorder its ancient social rhythms.

Be it noted that the court itself had no such expectations. Far less momentous writs of the court had failed before to run beyond the narrow bounds of the District of Columbia. Less than two decades had passed since the court had prevented its dismemberment by reversing —lock, stock, and barrel—its whole philosophy toward the New Deal.

The court, nonetheless, had set out to make a social laboratory out of a vast region whose history had led, in Robert Penn Warren's phrase, to a massive "fear of abstraction—the instinctive fear that the massiveness of experience, the concreteness of life, will be violated." Now, suddenly, so far as the rank-and-file Southerner knew, the most fearful of all abstractions had been struck into the law of the land. Once again, the vast engine of the Federal Government that had ground his fathers down was to undertake a transformation of his and his children's lives. Once again, the national press would smoke with moral rebuke and condemnation. Already, the NAACP was promising to wrap up the whole revolution in a year or two and, as at least one NAACP official gave as his personal opinion, intermarriage certainly *was* one goal of the revolution.

If this travail would make the world love America more, the Southerner asked himself, what would it do to his children? The very essence of the Supreme Court decision was admission that in the mass the Negro was culturally inferior. And the white schools themselves, despite tax support proportionally greater than the national average, sorely needed strengthening. Thus it was that the most liberal Southerner—and the South has a strain of liberalism unsurpassed for courage and toughness —was forced to ponder earnestly when the learned and gentle William Polk asked: "If the Negro is entitled to lift himself by enforced association with the white man, why should not the white man be entitled to prevent himself from being pulled down by enforced association with the Negro?"

And there were other questions for the heart: What would happen to the virtues of that paternalism which had bound black and white together in a relationship that, however unprogressive, was often warmly human in its sharing? If the Southerner *knew* he did not understand the lesser figure in this bond, was it not frightening to be forced to comprehend that this friendly, agreeable and sympathetic soul that jollied him and nursed his children was in reality a total stranger who changed vocabularies at quitting time?

Walter Lippmann once remarked that "all deliberate speed" in, say, Alabama might mean admission of Negro students to graduate schools of white universities by the tenth anniversary of the court's ruling. Lippmann offered a piercing insight into the fantastic complexity of rejiggering human attitudes plus calm acceptance that wherever such engineering is attempted social turbulence, fear and instability clog and distort the normal channels of social and political leadership. This, really, was not so strange a point—having been written down indelibly in blood and anguish throughout human history. But unhappily, American understanding that is capable of leaping an ocean often sinks midstream in the Potomac River.

As applied to Algeria, for example, the faithful reader of The New York *Times* and auditor of national television understands the difficulty very well. He sees clearly, for it has been movingly and expertly explained, why proud French generals, exquisitely mannered and magnificently educated, yielded to righteousness, insolence and finally to armed rebellion against the great de Gaulle himself at a moment when the very existence of France seemed at stake. Nor can the literate Northerner have failed to understand why in the teeth of the furies and the face of inevitable defeat the French *colon* incessantly riots to retain a way of life that must—and will—go with the wind. The parallels, of course, cannot be drawn too closely, but it says something meaningful about the universal frailties of the human condition.

But, in fairness, the Southerner who would be understood must not overly complain about the myopia of the Northern eye as it skims swiftly over the iron segregation of its Negro ghettos to focus intently upon the South. For if the Supreme Court decisions created opportunities and even felt necessities for false prophecy and senseless doctrine in the South, the market also turned bullish in the North.

Hearken to that admirable and sincerely self-righteous Senator from Illinois, Paul Douglas, regularly informing the South that it simply must throw off the palpable sins of segregation, get right with God and be born again in the image of the Americans for Democratic Action. Yes, verily, and let us not fret so much with the deliberateness of our speed. Keating of New York pats his foot. Ditto Javits and so also Clark of Pennsylvania and other evangelists of instant racial equality.

Let us not impute a lack of charity to these gentlemen. Indeed, they have the faith of their fathers. To befriend a recalcitrant South, they are ready at the drop of a hat to enact a force bill or to employ with Federal monies sociological shepherds to lead the region to redemption. And though all this piety falls sweetly upon the ears of Harlem and South Chicago, with their balances of power and their largely separate and patently unequal schools, it would be idle to charge these gentlemen with insincerity. Moreover, it would be immaterial. The Ku Klux Klan has been full of thugs who wielded the whip with absolute—and terrible— sincerity. John Brown, sainted by the sages of Concord for exploits including the insane murder and mutilation of five non-slaveholders in one night, was the acme of sincerity.

In the light of this heritage, then, which later unconstitutionally forced the fateful Fourteenth Amendment upon the South, does not Paul Douglas' impatience begin to seem entirely reasonable? And, in fact, isn't it understandable if just a bit insane that the last Democratic National Convention would declare an intention to abolish *all* literacy tests for voting in order finally and fully to extend the franchise to the Negro in the South . . . even in those many places where, as stubborn fact has it, he outnumbers the white? The answer is yes, of course, if one is prepared to admit that in the light of the Southerner's entirely different heritage the nation in 1954 would have foreseen that Faubus' rabble would for a time drown out the never-stilled voices of hope, faith and charity in the South. The answer is yes, if one is prepared, as the editors of The New York *Times* are not, to comprehend the resentment of Southerners when with merciless stupidity and frightening innocence "freedom riders" depart the ghettos and, with headlines and television cameras going on before, venture forth to tempt the violent boob from his lair.

Let us not turn so quickly away from this violent man, however. He, too, has a history. Perhaps he is kin to the tenant, Gudger, from whose barren, wasted life James Agee fashioned, in the 1930's, poignant prose for his *Let Us Now Praise Famous Men:*

"Gudger has no home, no land, no mule: none of the more important farming implements. He must get all of these of his landlord (who), for his share of the corn and cotton, also advances him rations money during four months of the year, March through June, and his fertilizer. Gudger pays him back with his labor and with the labor of his family. At the end of the season he pays him back further; with half his corn, with half his cottonseed. Out of his own half of these crops he also pays him back the rations money, plus interest, and his share of the fertilizer, plus interest, and such other debts, plus interest, as he may have incurred. What is left, once doctor bills and other debts have been deducted, is his year's earnings. . . ." Or perhaps this man screaming in the street was related to Ricketts who, with hope of good times, "went $400 into debt on a fine young pair of mules. One of the mules died before it had made its first crop; and the other died the year after; against his fear, amounting to full horror, of sinking to the half-crop level where nothing is owned, Ricketts went into debt for other, inferior mules; his cows went one by one into debts and desperate exchanges and by sickness; he got congestive chills; his wife got pellagra; a number of his children died; he got appendicitis and lay for days on end under the icecap; his wife's pellagra got into her brain; for ten consecutive years now, though they have lived on so little rations money and have turned nearly all their cottonseed money toward their debts, they have not cleared or had any hope of clearing a cent at the end of the year."

In all his variety from a Klansman plotting an atrocity to a school-board member secretly urging Negroes to apply for admission to the upper-class schools to the wan little interracial groups meeting in the church parlor, the white Southerner is a creature of a heritage that he can no more reject than a mother can reject her children. Splotched with evil, to be sure, that heritage also is compounded of triumphs of endurance, of courage, of selflessness that moved a world. Simply because it is gone does not mean it is forgotten or, indeed, could be forgotten. For if the "good Southerner" could break the bonds with the "bad Southerner" to whom he is bound irrevocably by ties, of blood, religion, race, memory, myth and love of land, where would he seek a new code of conduct? Not in the North, surely, for the Southerner knows in his bones what the historians know in fact: that the North has no moral credentials to preach in this matter, that whatever virtues that region may accidentally have earned by "freeing the slaves" was corrupted by a conscienceless "Reconstruction" of a freed man without freedom and a white man without hope or even youth. For the Negro there was no jubilee-jubilo. For neither white nor black was there a Marshall Plan.

The Southerner's senses told him rightly he had no corner on the corrupting of the American dream. He knew that the zeal of the abolitionist was not the reflection of a higher Northern morality—that to the North there was also greed, cynicism and calculation. He knew there was a reason that when the Supreme Court first came to the Fourteenth Amendment that charter of human freedom was converted to one of corporate privilege.

All this is remembered by the defeated as naturally as it is forgotten by the victorious. All this is the stubborn stuff of the barrier reef in the Potomac that keeps the white Northerner and Southerner forever strangers and prolongs the sterile ritual of finger-pointing that has woven both Paul Douglas and Orval Faubus into the sardonic and not-so-secret mirth of Negro intellectuals. Connoisseurs of that humor must await with relish the answer to the riddle: "What's the difference between a group of distressed Negroes being driven into a church by a white mob in Montgomery and another group being driven out of a church by a white mob in Chicago?" Only a dense literalist would torture that riddle with legalisms.

The legalisms remain, of course, and the white Southerner will make his peace with them. And though some of his number take secret pride in having been able with courage and statecraft to hew a path to compliance through a dense thicket of difficulties, he does not forget that the New Order requires most of the "poor white" Southerner who has been given least. He wonders, watching the flight to the suburbs and the proliferation of private pools, clubs and schools, if the grand design of 1954 does not trend North and South toward integration of the impoverished. Knowing something of the Negro's own intense concern for shadings of color that can reject as "too dark" a baby offered for adoption, he ponders earnestly whether the sociologists in their toneless tracts have not assumed too much in their vaunted knowledge of human nature. He understands the Negro professional man's remark to Harry Ashmore that he can always get a contribution for the cause but never an apartment in a New York Jewish neighborhood. He admires the frankness of another successful Negro who, having come up from squalor by dint of great determination, found himself "too busy to practice sociology." He can simultaneously admire the courage of a young Negro sit-in demonstrator, detest the white louts profaning the Confederate flag and wonder all the while whether the sit-ins will sabotage better job opportunities for Negroes. He is bound to wonder, too, if the Negro ever will turn from the faults of the white man's society to grapple with those grievous failings of his own that crowd the dockets of crime, disease and illegitimacy. For as the North ceaselessly has reminded the white Southerner, there is a limit to the number of excuses to be found in deprivation.

Writing that, I see in my mind's eye a white woman with a fifth-grade education, who, driven finally from the tyranny of the field, took a town job that paid $26 a month for sixteen hours a day in labor and transit, and who from this meager sum bought schoolbooks for three children; who, after washing their single sets of clothes at midnight, rose for work at 4 a.m. to leave biscuit dough in the oven and a stern note not to be late for school; who in all her life never bought unless she could pay and carries within her still a fierce independence that denies her pleasure from any gift, but who finds pleasure in giving. She is a Baptist who voted for Kennedy, but, may Myrdal forgive her, she is "prejudiced" against the Negro.

Not for the white Southerner is the sweet and innocent assurance of the slogan. No man better than he knows from mourning a dozen "New Souths" that died a-borning how swiftly the high rhetoric of progress can collapse into a wail and turn him back to the bleak rewards of the beloved and immemorial land.

He moves hesitantly, uncertainly into the New Order. Some of him dares to hope that this time a truly expanding economy will bathe both races in prosperity's magical sprays of tolerance. But he would also hope that some of the virtues of the old might be retained and perhaps even recognized beyond his borders: that in the new patterns the old civility and generosity and, yes, even the romanticism might find a cranny.

For if his fathers' dreams of a noble breed of learned men carried within itself a fatal flaw, was it otherwise so wild a dream? Was it one that a man—glimpsing it, as it were, in a smashed antique mirror—could quite relinquish in an age when men moved as ants beneath the edifice of the Great Machine?

The white Southerner will not fail his nation, nor himself. Out of the aged anguish and conflict of the human heart, the strongest of him will accommodate the pressures of the New Order into something comprehensible to the kin of Gudger and Ricketts and to the Negro who in the company of the white Southerner has at least learned to read the Declaration of Independence.

It may be true that the white Southerner could have done better in the past and that today he could move more swiftly to accommodate the New Order in the tangled skein of the old. Many of his own courageous prophets tell him so, and millions of his number are not averse to taking new paths laid out with care and reason.

It may be, as this loyal son believes, that the grinding mills of the New Order will in time refine the South's great virtues into a new statecraft that will not suffer by comparison with the wisdom and vision of the old.

Certain it is that few beyond are equipped to judge the Southerner's stewardship of the human dilemma the North so long ignored, but soon must face.

The white Southerner fears not history's judgment so much as the misjudgments of the non-Southerner who, armored in innocence and shielded by mass anonymity, sometimes forgets that allegiance to high principle purchases neither wisdom nor political responsibility.

WILLIAM FAULKNER

LETTER TO THE NORTH

Only on very rare occasions did Faulkner feel it necessary to speak out on public problems. He did so in the following article, published in Life, *March 5, 1956. For information on the author and his writings, see page 437.*

•

My family has lived for generations in one same small section of north Mississippi. My great-grandfather held slaves and went to Virginia in command of a Mississippi infantry regiment in 1861. I state this simply as credentials for the sincerity and factualness of what I will try to say.

From the beginning of this present phase of the race problem in the South, I have been on record as opposing the forces in my native country which would keep the condition out of which this present evil and trouble has grown. Now I must go on record as opposing the forces outside the South which would use legal or police compulsion to eradicate that evil overnight. I was against compulsory segregation. I am just as strongly against compulsory integration. Firstly of course from principle. Secondly because I don't believe compulsion will work.

There are more Southerners than I who believe as I do and have taken the same stand I have taken, at the same price of contumely and insult and threat from other Southerners which we foresaw and were willing to accept because we believed we were helping our native land which we love, to accept a new condition which it must accept whether it wants to or not. That is, by still being Southerners, yet not being a part of the general majority Southern point of view; by being present yet detached, committed and attainted neither by Citizens' Council nor NAACP; by being in the middle, being in a position to say to any incipient irrevocability: "Wait, wait now, stop and consider first."

But where will we go, if that middle becomes untenable? If we have to vacate it in order to keep from being trampled? Apart from the legal aspect, apart even from the simple incontrovertible immorality of discrimination by race, there was another simply human quantity which drew us to the Negro's side: the simple human instinct to champion the underdog.

But if we, the (comparative) handful of Southerners I have tried to postulate, are compelled by the simple threat of being trampled if we don't get out of the way, to vacate that middle where we could have worked to help the Negro improve his condition—compelled to move for the reason that no middle any longer exists—we will have to make a new choice. And this time the underdog will not be the Negro, since he, the Negro, will now be a segment of the topdog, and so the underdog will be that white embattled minority who are our blood and kin. These non-Southern forces will now say, "Go then. We don't want you because we won't need you again." My reply to that is, "Are you sure you won't?"

So I would say to the NAACP and all the organizations who would compel immediate and unconditional integration: "Go slow now. Stop now for a time, a moment. You have the power now; you can afford to withhold for a moment the use of it as a force. You have done a good job, you have jolted your opponent off-balance and he is now vulnerable. But stop there for a moment; don't give him the advantage of a chance to cloud the issue by that purely automatic sentimental appeal to that same universal human instinct for automatic sympathy for the underdog simply because he is under."

And I would say this too. The rest of the United States knows next to nothing about the South. The present idea and picture which they hold of a people decadent and even obsolete through inbreeding and illiteracy—the inbreeding a result of the illiteracy and the isolation—as to be a kind of species of juvenile delinquents with a folklore of blood and violence, yet who, like juvenile delinquents, can be controlled by firmness once they are brought to believe that the police mean business, is as baseless and illusory as that one a generation ago of (oh yes, we subscribed to it too) columned porticoes and magnolias. The rest of the United States assumes that this condition in the South is so simple and so uncomplex that it can be changed tomorrow by the simple will of the national majority backed by legal edict. In fact, the North does not even recognize what it has seen in its own newspapers.

I have at hand an editorial from the New York *Times* of February 10th on the rioting at the University of Alabama because of the admission of Miss Lucy, a Negro. The editorial said: "This is the first time that force and violence have become part of the question." That is not correct. To all Southerners, no matter which side of the question of racial equality they supported, the first implication, and—to the Southerner—even promise, of force and violence was the Supreme Court decision itself. After that, by any standards at all and following as inevitably as night and day, was the case of the three white teen-agers, members of a field trip group from a Mississippi high school (and, as teen-agers do, probably wearing the bright particolored blazers or jackets blazoned across the back with the name of the school) who were stabbed in passing on a Washington street by Negroes they had never seen before and who apparently had never seen them before either; and that of the Till boy and the two Mississippi juries which freed the defendants from both charges; and of the Mississippi garage attendant killed by a white man because, according to the white man, the Negro filled the tank of the white man's car full of gasoline when all the white man wanted was two dollars' worth.

This problem is far beyond a mere legal one. It is even far beyond the moral one it is and still was a hundred years ago in 1860, when many Southerners, including Robert Lee, recognized it as a moral one at the very instant when they in turn elected to champion the underdog because that underdog was blood and kin and home. The Northerner is not even aware yet of what that war really proved. He assumes that it merely proved to the Southerner that he was wrong. It didn't do that because the Southerner already knew he was wrong and accepted that gambit even when he knew it was the fatal one. What that war should have done, but failed to do, was to prove to the North that the South will go to any length, even that fatal and already doomed one, before it will accept alteration of its racial condition by mere force of law or economic threat.

Since I went on record as being opposed to compulsory racial inequality, I have received many letters. A few of them approved. But most of them were in opposition. And a few of these were from Southern Negroes, the only difference being that they were polite and courteous instead of being threats and insults, saying in effect: "Please, Mr. Faulkner, stop talking and be quiet. You are a good man and you think you are helping us. But you are not helping us. You are doing us harm. You are playing into the hands of the NAACP so that they are using you to make trouble for our race that we don't want. Please hush, you look after your white folks' trouble and let us take care of ours." This one in particular was a long one, from a woman who was writing for and in the name of the pastor and the entire congregation of her church. It went on to say that the Till boy got exactly what he asked for, coming down there with his Chicago ideas, and that all his mother wanted was to make money out of the role of her bereavement. Which sounds exactly like the white people in the South who justified and even defended the crime by declining to find that it was one.

We have had many violent inexcusable personal crimes of race against race in the South, but since 1919 the major examples of communal race tension have been more prevalent in the North, like the Negro family who were refused acceptance in the white residential district in Chicago, and the Korean-American who suffered for the same reason in Anaheim,

Calif. Maybe it is because our solidarity is not racial, but instead is the majority white segregationist plus the Negro minority like my correspondent above, who prefer peace to equality. But suppose the line of demarcation should become one of the race; the white minority like myself compelled to join the white segregation majority no matter how much we oppose the principle of inequality; the Negro minority who want peace compelled to join the Negro majority who advocate force, no matter how much that minority wanted only peace?

So the Northerner, the liberal, does not know the South. He can't know it from his distance. He assumes that he is dealing with a simple legal theory and a simple moral idea. He is not. He is dealing with a fact: the fact of an emotional condition of such fierce unanimity as to scorn the fact that it is a minority and which will go to any length and against any odds at this moment to justify and, if necessary, defend that condition and its right to it.

So I would say to all the organizations and groups which would force integration on the South by legal process: "Stop now for a moment. You have shown the Southerner what you can do and what you will do if necessary; give him a space in which to get his breath and assimilate that knowledge; to look about and see that (1) Nobody is going to force integration on him from the outside; (2) That he himself faces an obsolescence in his own land which only he can cure; a moral condition which not only must be cured but a physical condition which has got to be cured if he, the white Southerner, is to have any peace, is not to be faced with another legal process or maneuver every year, year after year, for the rest of his life."

JAMES BALDWIN

James Baldwin was born in Harlem in 1924, the oldest of nine children, and graduated from DeWitt Clinton High School where he was editor of the literary magazine. After the death of his father in 1943 he lived in Greenwich Village, working by day as handyman, office boy, or factory worker and writing at night. A Rosenwald Fellowship received in 1948

enabled him to go to Paris, where he wrote his first two novels, Go Tell
It on the Mountain *(1952) and* Giovanni's Room *(1956), and the essays
published as* Notes of a Native Son *(1955). In 1957 he returned to America and since then has become one of the most articulate literary spokesmen of the civil rights movement.* The Fire Next Time *(1963), two
searing articles, or letters, on the relationship between the American
Negro and the American white man, secured his reputation as an essayist.
Baldwin's writing has won him many awards, among them a Guggenheim
Fellowship (1954), a* Partisan Review *Fellowship (1956), and the National Institute of Arts and Letters Award (1956).* Nobody Knows My
Name, *a collection of essays, was selected as one of the outstanding books
of 1961 by the Notable Book Council of the American Library Association. The essay we present below is Chapter 7 of this collection.*

FAULKNER AND DESEGREGATION

Any real change implies the breakup of the world as one has always known
it, the loss of all that gave one an identity, the end of safety. And at such
a moment, unable to see and not daring to imagine what the future will
now bring forth, one clings to what one knew, or thought one knew;
to what one possessed or dreamed that one possessed. Yet, it is only when
a man is able, without bitterness or self-pity, to surrender a dream he has
long cherished or a privilege he has long possessed that he is set free—
he has set himself free—for higher dreams, for greater privileges. All
men have gone through this, go through it, each according to his degree,
throughout their lives. It is one of the irreducible facts of life. And remembering this, especially since I am a Negro, affords me almost my
only means of understanding what is happening in the minds and hearts
of white Southerners today.

For the arguments with which the bulk of relatively articulate white
Southerners of good will have met the necessity of desegregation have no
value whatever as arguments, being almost entirely and helplessly dishonest, when not, indeed, insane. After more than two hundred years
in slavery and ninety years of quasi-freedom, it is hard to think very highly
of William Faulkner's advice to "go slow." "They don't mean go slow,"
Thurgood Marshall is reported to have said, "they mean don't go." Nor
is the squire of Oxford very persuasive when he suggests that white
Southerners, left to their own devices, will realize that their own social
structure looks silly to the rest of the world and correct it of their own
accord. It has looked silly, to use Faulkner's rather strange adjective, for
a long time; so far from trying to correct it, Southerners, who seem to be
characterized by a species of defiance most perverse when it is most de-

spairing, have clung to it, at incalculable cost to themselves, as the only conceivable and as an absolutely sacrosanct way of life. They have never seriously conceded that their social structure was mad. They have insisted, on the contrary, that everyone who criticized it was mad.

Faulkner goes further. He concedes the madness and moral wrongness of the South but at the same time he raises it to the level of a mystique which makes it somehow unjust to discuss Southern society in the same terms in which one would discuss any other society. "Our position is wrong and untenable," says Faulkner, "but it is not wise to keep an emotional people off balance." This, if it means anything, can only mean that this "emotional people" have been swept "off balance" by the pressure of recent events, that is, the Supreme Court decision outlawing segregation. When the pressure is taken off—and not an instant before—this "emotional people" will presumably find themselves once again on balance and will then be able to free themselves of an "obsolescence in [their] own land" in their own way and, of course, in their own time. The question left begging is what, in their history to date, affords any evidence that they have any desire or capacity to do this. And it is, I suppose, impertinent to ask just what Negroes are supposed to do while the South works out what, in Faulkner's rhetoric, becomes something very closely resembling a high and noble tragedy.

The sad truth is that whatever modifications have been effected in the social structure of the South since the Reconstruction, and any alleviations of the Negro's lot within it, are due to great and incessant pressure, very little of it indeed from within the South. That the North has been guilty of Pharisaism in its dealing with the South does not negate the fact that much of this pressure has come from the North. That some—not nearly as many as Faulkner would like to believe—Southern Negroes prefer, or are afraid of changing, the status quo does not negate the fact that it is the Southern Negro himself who, year upon year, and generation upon generation, has kept the Southern waters troubled. As far as the Negro's life in the South is concerned, the NAACP is the only organization which has struggled, with admirable single-mindedness and skill, to raise him to the level of a citizen. For this reason alone, and quite apart from the individual heroism of many of its Southern members, it cannot be equated, as Faulkner equates it, with the pathological Citizen's Council. One organization is working within the law and the other is working against and outside it. Faulkner's threat to leave the "middle of the road" where he has, presumably, all these years, been working for the benefit of Negroes, reduces itself to a more or less up-to-date version of the Southern threat to secede from the Union.

Faulkner—among so many others!—is so plaintive concerning this "middle of the road" from which "extremist" elements of both races are driving him that it does not seem unfair to ask just what he has been doing there until now. Where is the evidence of the struggle he has been carrying on there on behalf of the Negro? Why, if he and his enlightened confreres in the South have been boring from within to destroy segregation, do they react with such panic when the walls show any signs of falling? Why—and how—does one move from the middle of the road where one was aiding Negroes into the streets—to shoot them?

Now it is easy enough to state flatly that Faulkner's middle of the road does not—cannot—exist and that he is guilty of great emotional and intellectual dishonesty in pretending that it does. I think this is why he clings to his fantasy. It is easy enough to accuse him of hypocrisy when he speaks of man being "indestructible because of his simple will to freedom." But he is not being hypocritical; he means it. It is only that Man is one thing—a rather unlucky abstraction in this case—and the Negroes he has always known, so fatally tied up in his mind with his grandfather's slaves, are quite another. He is at his best, and is perfectly sincere, when he declares, in *Harpers*, "To live anywhere in the world today and be against equality because of race or color is like living in Alaska and being against snow. We have already got snow. And as with the Alaskan, merely to live in armistice with it is not enough. Like the Alaskan, we had better use it." And though this seems to be flatly opposed to his statement (in an interview printed in *The Reporter*) that, if it came to a contest between the federal government and Mississippi, he would fight for Mississippi, "even if it meant going out into the streets and shooting Negroes," he means that, too. Faulkner means everything he says, means them all at once, and with very nearly the same intensity. This is why his statements demand our attention. He has perhaps never before more concretely expressed what it means to be a Southerner.

What seems to define the Southerner, in his own mind at any rate, is his relationship to the North, that is to the rest of the Republic, a relationship which can at the very best be described as uneasy. It is apparently very difficult to be at once a Southerner and an American; so difficult that many of the South's most independent minds are forced into the American exile; which is not, of course, without its aggravating, circular effect on the interior and public life of the South. A Bostonian, say, who leaves Boston is not regarded by the citizenry he has abandoned with the same venomous distrust as is the Southerner who leaves the South. The citizenry of Boston do not consider that they have been abandoned, much less betrayed. It is only the American Southerner who seems to be fighting, in his own entrails, a peculiar, ghastly, and perpetual war with all the rest of the country. ("Didn't you say," demanded a Southern woman of Robert Penn Warren, "that you was born down here, used to live right near here?" And when he agreed that this was so: "Yes . . . but you never said where you living now!")

The difficulty, perhaps, is that the Southerner clings to two entirely antithetical doctrines, two legends, two histories. Like all other Americans, he must subscribe, and is to some extent controlled by the beliefs and the principles expressed in the Constitution; at the same time, these beliefs and principles seem determined to destroy the South. He is, on the one hand, the proud citizen of a free society and, on the other, is committed to a society which has not yet dared to free itself of the necessity of naked and brutal oppression. He is part of a country which boasts that it has never lost a war; but he is also the representative of a conquered nation. I have not seen a single statement of Faulkner's concerning desegregation which does not inform us that his family has lived in the same part of Mississippi for generations, that his great-grandfather owned slaves, and that his ancestors fought and died in the Civil War. And so compelling is the image of ruin, gallantry and death thus evoked that it demands a positive effort of the imagination to remember that slaveholding Southerners were not the only people who perished in that war. Negroes and Northerners were also blown to bits. American history, as opposed to Southern history, proves that Southerners were not the only slaveholders, Negroes were not even the only slaves. And the segregation which Faulkner sanctifies by references to Shiloh, Chickamauga, and Gettysburg does not extend back that far, is in fact scarcely as old as the century. The "racial condition" which Faulkner will not have changed by "mere force of law or economic threat" was imposed by precisely these means. The Southern tradition, which is, after all, all that Faulkner is talking about, is not a tradition at all: when Faulkner evokes it, he is simply evoking a legend which contains an accusation. And that accusation, stated far more simply than it should be, is that the North, in winning the war, left the South only one means of asserting its identity and that means was the Negro.

"My people owned slaves," says Faulkner, "and the very obligation we have to take care of these people is morally bad." "This problem is . . . far beyond the moral one it is and still was a hundred years ago, in 1860, when many Southerners, including Robert Lee, recognized it as a moral one at the very instant they in turn elected to champion the underdog because that underdog was blood and kin and home." But the North escaped scot-free. For one thing, in freeing the slave, it established a moral superiority over the South which the South has not learned to live with until today; and this despite—or possibly because of—the fact that this moral superiority was bought, after all, rather cheaply. The North was no better prepared than the South, as it turned out, to make citizens of former slaves, but it was able, as the South was not, to wash its hands of the matter. Men who knew that slavery was wrong were forced, nevertheless, to fight to perpetuate it because they were unable to turn against "blood and kin and home." And when blood and kin and home were defeated, they found themselves, more than ever, committed: committed, in effect, to a way of life which was as unjust and crippling as it was inescapable. In sum, the North, by freeing the slaves of their masters, robbed the masters of any possibility of freeing themselves of the slaves.

When Faulkner speaks, then, of the "middle of the road," he is simply speaking of the hope—which was always unrealistic and is now all but smashed—that the white Southerner, with no coercion from the rest of the nation, will lift himself above his ancient, crippling bitterness and refuse to add to his already intolerable burden of blood-guiltiness. But this hope would seem to be absolutely dependent on a social and psychological stasis which simply does not exist. "Things have been getting better," Faulkner tells us, "for a long time. Only six Negroes were killed by whites in Mississippi last year, according to police figures." Faulkner surely knows how little consolation this offers a Negro and he also knows something about "police figures" in the Deep South. And he knows, too, that murder is not the worst thing that can happen to a man, black or white. But murder may be the worst thing a man can do. Faulkner is not trying to save Negroes, who are, in his view, already saved; who, having refused to be destroyed by terror, are far stronger than the terri- fied white populace; and who have, moreover, fatally, from his point of view, the weight of the federal government behind them. He is trying to save "whatever good remains in those white people." The time he pleads for is the time in which the Southerner will come to terms with himself, will cease fleeing from his conscience, and achieve, in the words of Robert Penn Warren, "moral identity." And he surely believes, with Warren, that "Then in a country where moral identity is hard to come by, the South, because it has had to deal concretely with a moral problem, may offer some leadership. And we need any we can get. If we are to break out of the national rhythm, the rhythm between complacency and panic."

But the time Faulkner asks for does not exist—and he is not the only Southerner who knows it. There is never time in the future in which we will work out our salvation. The challenge is in the moment, the time is always now.

NORMAN PODHORETZ

Norman Podhoretz was born in New York City and educated at Columbia College and Cambridge University, England, where he was a Fulbright Scholar and a Kellet Fellow. A precociously talented writer and critic, he was appointed editor of Commentary *in 1960, at the age of thirty. He has been a frequent contributor to magazines, and recently published a ten-year collection of his articles, entitled* Doings and Undoings: The Fifties and After in American Writing *(1964). The article we print below first appeared in* Commentary, *February, 1963.*

MY NEGRO PROBLEM—AND OURS

> If we—and . . . I mean the relatively conscious whites and the relatively conscious blacks, who must, like lovers, insist on, or create, the consciousness of the others—do not falter in our duty now, we may be able, handful that we are, to end the racial nightmare, and achieve our country, and change the history of the world.
>
> —JAMES BALDWIN

Two ideas puzzled me deeply as a child growing up in Brooklyn during the 1930's in what today would be called an integrated neighborhood. One of them was that all Jews were rich; the other was that all Negroes were persecuted. These ideas had appeared in print; therefore they must be true. My own experience and the evidence of my senses told me they were not true, but that only confirmed what a day-dreaming boy in the provinces—for the lower-class neighborhoods of New York belong as surely to the provinces as any rural town in North Dakota—discovers very early: *his* experience is unreal and the evidence of his senses is not to be trusted. Yet even a boy with a head full of fantasies incongruously synthesized out of Hollywood movies and English novels cannot altogether deny the reality of his own experience—especially when there is so much deprivation in that experience. Nor can he altogether gainsay the evidence of his own senses—especially such evidence of the senses as comes from being repeatedly beaten up, robbed, and in general hated, terrorized, and humiliated.

And so for a long time I was puzzled to think that Jews were supposed to be rich when the only Jews I knew were poor, and that Negroes were supposed to be persecuted when it was the Negroes who were doing the only persecuting I knew about—and doing it, moreover, to *me*. During the early years of the war, when my older sister joined a left-wing youth organization, I remember my astonishment at hearing her passionately denounce my father for thinking that Jews were worse off than Negroes. To me, at the age of twelve, it seemed very clear that Negroes were better off than Jews—indeed, than *all* whites. A city boy's world is contained within three or four square blocks, and in my world it was the whites, the Italians and Jews, who feared the Negroes, not the other way around. The Negroes were tougher than we were, more ruthless, and on the whole they were better athletes. What could it mean, then, to say that they were badly off and that we were more fortunate? Yet my sister's opinions, like print, were sacred, and when she told me about exploitation and economic forces I believed her. I believed her, but I was still afraid of Negroes. And I still hated them with all my heart.

It had not always been so—that much I can recall from early childhood. When did it start, this fear and this hatred? There was a kindergarten in the local public school, and given the character of the neighborhood, at least half of the children in my class must have been Negroes. Yet I have no memory of being aware of color differences at that age, and I know from observing my own children that they attribute no significance to such differences even when they begin noticing them. I think there was a day—first grade? second grade?—when my best friend Carl hit me on the way home from school and announced that he wouldn't play with me any more because I had killed Jesus. When I ran home to my mother crying for an explanation, she told me not to pay any attention to such foolishness, and then in Yiddish she cursed the *goyim* and the *schwartzes*, the *schwartzes* and the *goyim*. Carl, it turned out, was a *schwartze*, and so was added a third to the categories into which people were mysteriously divided.

Sometimes I wonder whether this is a true memory at all. It is blazingly vivid, but perhaps it never happened: can anyone really remember back to the age of six? There is no uncertainty in my mind, however, about the years that followed. Carl and I hardly ever spoke, though we met in school every day up through the eighth or ninth grade. There would be embarrassed moments of catching his eye or of his catching mine—for whatever it was that had attracted us to one another as very small children remained alive in spite of the fantastic barrier of hostility that had grown up between us, suddenly and out of nowhere. Nevertheless, friendship would have been impossible, and even if it had been possible, it would have been unthinkable. About that, there was nothing anyone could do by the time we were eight years old.

Item: The orphanage across the street is torn down, a city housing project begins to rise in its place, and on the marvelous vacant lot next to the old orphanage they are building a playground. Much excitement and anticipation as Opening Day draws near. Mayor LaGuardia himself comes to dedicate this great gesture of public benevolence. He speaks of neighborliness and borrowing cups of sugar, and of the playground he says that children of all races, colors, and creeds will learn to live together in harmony. A week later, some of us are swatting flies on the playground's inadequate little ball field. A gang of Negro kids, pretty much our own age, enter from the other side and order us out of the park. We refuse, proudly and indignantly, with superb masculine fervor. There is a fight, they win, and we retreat, half whimpering, half with bravado. My first nauseating experience of cowardice. And my first appalled realization that there are people in the world who do not seem to be afraid of anything, who act as though they have nothing to lose. Thereafter the playground becomes a battleground, sometimes quiet, sometimes the scene of athletic competition between Them and Us. But rocks are thrown as often as baseballs. Gradually we abandon the place and use the streets instead. The streets are safer, though we do not admit this to ourselves. We are not, after all, sissies—that most dreaded epithet of an American boyhood.

Item: I am standing alone in front of the building in which I live. It is late afternoon and getting dark. That day in school the teacher had asked a surly Negro boy named Quentin a question he was unable to answer. As usual I had waved my arm eagerly ("Be a good boy, get good marks, be smart, go to college, become a doctor") and, the right answer bursting from my lips, I was held up lovingly by the teacher as an example to the class. I had seen Quentin's face—a very dark, very cruel, very Oriental-looking face—harden, and there had been enough threat in his eyes to make me run all the way home for fear that he might catch me outside.

Now, standing idly in front of my own house, I see him approaching from the project accompanied by his little brother who is carrying a baseball bat and wearing a grin of malicious anticipation. As in a nightmare, I am trapped. The surroundings are secure and familiar, but terror is suddenly present and there is no one around to help. I am locked to the spot. I will not cry out or run away like a sissy, and I stand there, my heart wild, my throat clogged. He walks up, hurls the familiar epithet ("Hey, mo'f——r"), and to my surprise only pushes me. It is a violent push, but not a punch. A push is not as serious as a punch. Maybe I can still back out without entirely losing my dignity. Maybe I can still say, "Hey, c'mon Quentin, whaddya wanna do *that* for. I dint do nothin' to *you*," and walk away, not too rapidly. Instead, before I can stop myself, I push him back—a token gesture—and I say, "Cut that out, I don't wanna fight, I ain't got nothin' to fight about." As I turn to walk back into the building, the corner of my eye catches the motion of the bat his little brother has handed him. I try to duck, but the bat crashes colored lights into my head.

The next thing I know, my mother and sister are standing over me, both of them hysterical. My sister—she who was later to join the "progressive" youth organization—is shouting for the police and screaming imprecations at those dirty little black bastards. They take me upstairs, the doctor comes, the police come. I tell them that the boy who did it was a stranger, that he had been trying to get money from me. They do not believe me, but I am too scared to give them Quentin's name. When I return to school a few days later, Quentin avoids my eyes. He knows that I have not squealed, and he is ashamed. I try to feel proud, but in my heart I know that it was fear of what his friends might do to me that had kept me silent, and not the code of the street.

Item: There is an athletic meet in which the whole of our junior high school is participating. I am in one of the seventh-grade rapid-advance classes, and "segregation" has now set in with a vengeance. In the last three or four years of the elementary school from which we have just graduated, each grade had been divided into three classes, according to "intelligence." (In the earlier grades the divisions had either been arbitrary or else unrecognized by us as having anything to do with brains.) These divisions by IQ, or however it was arranged, had resulted in a preponderance of Jews in the "1" classes and a corresponding preponderance of Negroes in the "3's," with the Italians split unevenly along the spectrum. At least a few Negroes had always made the "1's," just as there had always been a few Jewish kids among the "3's" and more among the "2's" (where Italians dominated). But the junior high's rapid-advance class of which I am now a member is overwhelmingly Jewish and entirely white—except for a shy lonely Negro girl with light skin and reddish hair.

The athletic meet takes place in a city-owned stadium far from the school. It is an important event to which a whole day is given over. The winners are to get those precious little medallions stamped with the New York City emblem that can be screwed into a belt and that prove the wearer to be a distinguished personage. I am a fast runner, and so I am assigned the position of anchor man on my class's team in the relay race. There are three other seventh-grade teams in the race, two of them all Negro, as ours is all white. One of the all-Negro teams is very tall—their anchor man waiting silently next to me on the line looks years older than I am, and I do not recognize him. He is the first to get the baton and crosses the finishing line in a walk. Our team comes in second, but a few minutes later we are declared the winners, for it has been discovered that the anchor man on the first-place team is not a member of the class. We are awarded the medallions, and the following day our home-room teacher makes a speech about how proud she is of us for being superior athletes as well as superior students. We want to believe that we deserve the praise, but we know that we could not have won even if the other class had not cheated.

That afternoon, walking home, I am waylaid and surrounded by five Negroes, among whom is the anchor man of the disqualified team. "Gimme my medal, mo'f——r," he grunts. I do not have it with me and I tell him so. "Anyway, it ain't yours," I say foolishly. He calls me a liar on both counts and pushes me up against the wall on which we sometimes play handball. "Gimme my mo'f——n' medal," he says again. I repeat that I have left it home. "Le's search the li'l mo'f——r," one of them suggests, "he prolly got it *hid* in his mo'f——n' *pants*." My panic is now unmanageable. (How many times had I been surrounded like this and asked in soft tones, "Len' me a nickle, boy." How many times had I been called a liar for pleading poverty and pushed around, or searched, or beaten up, unless there happened to be someone in the marauding gang like Carl who liked me across that enormous divide of hatred and who would therefore say, "Aaah, c'mon, le's git someone else, *this* boy ain't got no money on 'im.") I scream at them through tears of rage and self-contempt, "Keep your f——n' filthy lousy black hands offa me! I swear I'll get the cops." This is all they need to hear, and the five of them set upon me. They bang me around, mostly in the stomach and on the arms and shoulders, and when several adults loitering near the candy store down the block notice what is going on and begin to shout, they run off and away.

I do not tell my parents about the incident. My team-mates, who have also been waylaid, each by a gang led by his opposite number from the disqualified team, have had their medallions taken from them, and they never squeal either. For days, I walk home in terror, expecting to be caught again, but nothing happens. The medallion is put away into a drawer, never to be worn by anyone.

Obviously experiences like these have always been a common feature of childhood life in working-class and immigrant neighborhoods, and Negroes do not necessarily figure in them. Wherever, and in whatever combination, they have lived together in the cities, kids of different groups have been at war, beating up and being beaten up: micks against kikes against wops against spicks against polacks. And even relatively homogeneous areas have not been spared the warring of the young: one block against another, one gang (called in my day, in a pathetic effort at gentility, an "S.A.C.," or social-athletic club) against another. But the Negro-white conflict had—and no doubt still has—a special intensity and was conducted with a ferocity unmatched by intramural white battling.

In my own neighborhood, a good deal of animosity existed between the Italian kids (most of whose parents were immigrants from Sicily) and the Jewish kids (who came largely from East European immigrant families). Yet everyone had friends, sometimes close friends, in the other "camp," and we often visited one another's strange-smelling houses, if not for meals, then for glasses of milk, and occasionally for some special event like a wedding or a wake. If it happened that we divided into warring factions and did battle, it would invariably be half-hearted and soon patched up. Our parents, to be sure, had nothing to do with one another and were mutually suspicious and hostile. But we, the kids, who all spoke Yiddish or Italian at home, were Americans, or New Yorkers, or Brooklyn boys: we shared a culture, the culture of the street, and at least for a while this culture proved to be more powerful than the opposing cultures of the home.

Why, *why* should it have been so different as between the Negroes and us? How was it borne in upon us so early, white and black alike, that we were enemies beyond any possibility of reconciliation? Why did we hate one another so?

I suppose if I tried, I could answer those questions more or less adequately from the perspective of what I have since learned. I could draw upon James Baldwin—what better witness is there?—to describe the sense of entrapment that poisons the soul of the Negro with hatred for the white man whom he knows to be his jailer. On the other side, if I wanted to understand how the white man comes to hate the Negro, I could call upon the psychologists who have spoken of the guilt that white Americans feel toward Negroes and that turns into hatred for lack of acknowledging itself as guilt. These are plausible answers and certainly there is truth in them. Yet when I think back upon my own experience of the Negro and his of me, I find myself troubled and puzzled, much as I was as a child when I heard that all Jews were rich and all Negroes persecuted. How could the Negroes in my neighborhood have regarded the whites across the street and around the corner as jailers? On the whole, the whites were not so poor as the Negroes, but they were quite poor enough, and the years were years of Depression. As for white hatred of the Negro, how could guilt have had anything to do with it? What share had these Italian and Jewish immigrants in the enslavement of the Negro? What share had they—downtrodden people themselves breaking their own necks to eke out a living—in the exploitation of the Negro?

No, I cannot believe that we hated each other back there in Brooklyn because they thought of us as jailers and we felt guilty toward them. But does it matter, given the fact that we all went through an unrepresentative confrontation? I think it matters profoundly, for if we managed the job of hating each other so well without benefit of the aids to hatred that are supposedly at the root of this madness everywhere else, it must mean that the madness is not yet properly understood. I am far from pretending that I understand it, but I would insist that no view of the problem will begin to approach the truth unless it can account for a case like the one I have been trying to describe. Are the elements of any such view available to us?

At least two, I would say, are. One of them is a point we frequently come upon in the work of James Baldwin, and the other is a related point always stressed by psychologists who have studied the mechanisms of prejudice. Baldwin tells us that one of the reasons Negroes hate the white man is that the white man refuses to *look* at him: the Negro knows that in white eyes all Negroes are alike; they are faceless and therefore not altogether human. The psychologists, in their turn, tell us that the white man hates the Negro because he tends to project those wild impulses that he fears in himself onto an alien group which he then punishes with his contempt. What Baldwin does *not* tell us, however, is that the principle of facelessness is a two-way street and can operate in both directions with no difficulty at all. Thus, in my neighborhood in Brooklyn, *I* was as faceless to the Negroes as they were to me, and if they hated me because I never looked at them, I must also have hated them for never looking at *me*. To the Negroes, my white skin was enough to define me as the enemy, and in a war it is only the uniform that counts and not the person.

So with the mechanism of projection that the psychologists talk about: it too works in both directions at once. There is no question that the psychologists are right about what the Negro represents symbolically to the white man. For me as a child the life lived on the other side of the play-ground and down the block on Ralph Avenue seemed the very embodi-ment of the values of the street—free, independent, reckless, brave, masculine, erotic. I put the word "erotic" last, though it is usually stressed above all others, because in fact it came last, in consciousness as in im-portance. What mainly counted for me about Negro kids of my own age was that they were "bad boys." There were plenty of bad boys among the whites—this was, after all, a neighborhood with a long tradition of crime as a career open to aspiring talents—but the Negroes were *really* bad, bad in a way that beckoned to one, and made one feel inadequate. *We* all went home every day for a lunch of spinach-and-potatoes; *they* roamed around during lunch hour, munching on candy bars. In winter *we* had to wear itchy woolen hats and mittens and cumbersome galoshes; *they* were bare-headed and loose as they pleased. *We* rarely played hookey, or got into serious trouble in school, for all our street-corner bravado; *they* were defiant, forever staying out (to do what delicious things?), forever mak-ing disturbances in class and in the halls, forever being sent to the principal and returning uncowed. But most important of all, they were *tough;* beautifully, enviably tough, not giving a damn for anyone or anything. To hell with the teacher, the truant officer, the cop; to hell with the whole of the adult world that held *us* in its grip and that we never had the cour-age to rebel against except sporadically and in petty ways.

This is what I saw and envied and feared in the Negro: this is what finally made him faceless to me, though some of it, of course, was actually there. (The psychologists also tell us that the alien group which becomes the object of a projection will tend to respond by trying to live up to what is expected of them.) But what, on his side, did the Negro see in me that made me faceless to *him?* Did he envy me my lunches of spinach-and-potatoes and my itchy woolen caps and my prudent behavior in the face of authority, as I envied him his noon-time candy bars and his bare head in winter and his magnificent rebelliousness? Did those lunches and caps spell for him the prospect of power and riches in the future? Did they mean that there were possibilities open to me that were denied to him? Very likely they did. But if so, one also supposes that he feared the impulses within himself toward submission to authority no less powerfully than I feared the impulses in myself toward defiance. If I represented the jailer to him, it was not because I was oppressing him or keeping him down: it was because I symbolized for him the dangerous and probably pointless temptation toward greater repression, just as he symbolized for me the equally perilous tug toward greater freedom. I personally was to be rewarded for this repression with a new and better life in the future, but how many of my friends paid an even higher price and were given only gall in return.

We have it on the authority of James Baldwin that all Negroes hate whites. I am trying to suggest that on their side all whites—all American whites, that is—are sick in their feelings about Negroes. There are Negroes, no doubt, who would say that Baldwin is wrong, but I suspect them of being less honest than he is, just as I suspect whites of self-deception who tell me they have no special feeling toward Negroes. Special feelings about color are a contagion to which white Americans seem susceptible even when there is nothing in their background to account for the susceptibility. Thus everywhere we look today in the North, we find the curious phenomenon of white middle-class liberals with no previous personal experience of Negroes—people to whom Negroes have always been faceless in virtue rather than faceless in vice—discovering that their abstract commitment to the cause of Negro rights will not stand the test of a direct confrontation. We find such people fleeing in droves to the suburbs as the Negro population in the inner city grows; and when they stay in the city we find them sending their children to private school rather than to the "integrated" public school in the neighborhood. We find them resisting the demand that gerrymandered school districts be re-zoned for the purpose of overcoming de facto segregation; we find them judiciously considering whether the Negroes (for their own good, of course) are not perhaps pushing too hard; we find them clucking their tongues over Negro militancy; we find them speculating on the question of whether there may not, after all, be something in the theory that the races are biologically different; we find them saying that it will take a very long time for Negroes to achieve full equality, no matter what anyone does; we find them deploring the rise of black nationalism and expressing the solemn hope that the leaders of the Negro community will discover ways of containing the impatience and incipient violence within the Negro ghettos.[1]

But that is by no means the whole story; there is also the phenomenon of what Kenneth Rexroth once called "crow-jimism." There are the broken-down white boys like Vivaldo Moore in Baldwin's *Another Country* who go to Harlem in search of sex or simply to brush up against something that looks like primitive vitality, and who are so often punished by the Negroes they meet for crimes that they would have been the last ever to commit and of which they themselves have been as sorry victims as any of the Negroes who take it out on them. There are the writers and intellectuals and artists who romanticize Negroes and pander to them, assuming a guilt that is not properly theirs. And there are all the white liberals who permit Negroes to blackmail them into adopting a double standard of moral judgment, and who lend themselves—again assuming the responsibility for crimes they never committed—to cunning and contemptuous exploitation by Negroes they employ or try to befriend.

And what about me? What kind of feelings do I have about Negroes today? What happened to me, from Brooklyn, who grew up fearing and envying and hating Negroes? Now that Brooklyn is behind me, do I fear them and envy them and hate them still? The answer is yes, but not in the same proportions and certainly not in the same way. I now live on the upper west side of Manhattan, where there are many Negroes and many Puerto Ricans, and there are nights when I experience the old apprehensiveness again, and there are streets that I avoid when I am walking in the dark, as there were streets that I avoided when I was a child. I find that I am not afraid of Puerto Ricans, but I cannot restrain my nervousness whenever I pass a group of Negroes standing in front of a bar or sauntering down the street. I know now, as I did not know when I was a child, that power is on my side, that the police are working for me and not for them. And knowing this I feel ashamed and guilty, like the good liberal I have grown up to be. Yet the twinges of fear and the resentment they bring and the self-contempt they arouse are not to be gainsaid.

But envy? Why envy? And hatred? Why hatred? Here again the intensities have lessened and everything has been complicated and qualified by the guilts and the resulting over-compensations that are the heritage of the enlightened middle-class world of which I am now a member. Yet just as in childhood I envied Negroes for what seemed to me their superior masculinity, so I envy them today for what seems to me their

[1] For an account of developments like these, see "The White Liberal's Retreat" by Murray Friedman in the January 1963 *Atlantic Monthly*.

superior physical grace and beauty. I have come to value physical grace
very highly, and I am now capable of aching with all my being when I
watch a Negro couple on the dance floor, or a Negro playing baseball
or basketball. They are on the kind of terms with their own bodies that
I should like to be on with mine, and for that precious quality they seem
blessed to me.

The hatred I still feel for Negroes is the hardest of all the old feelings
to face or admit, and it is the most hidden and the most overlarded by
the conscious attitudes into which I have succeeded in willing myself.
It no longer has, as for me it once did, any cause or justification (except,
perhaps, that I am constantly being denied my right to an honest expression of the things I earned the right as a child to feel). How, then,
do I know that this hatred has never entirely disappeared? I know it from
the insane rage that can stir in me at the thought of Negro anti-Semitism;
I know it from the disgusting prurience that can stir in me at the sight
of a mixed couple; and I know it from the violence that can stir in me
whenever I encounter that special brand of paranoid touchiness to which
many Negroes are prone.

This, then, is where I am; it is not exactly where I think all other white
liberals are, but it cannot be so very far away either. And it is because
I am convinced that we white Americans are—for whatever reason, it
no longer matters—so twisted and sick in our feelings about Negroes that
I despair of the present push toward integration. If the pace of progress
were not a factor here, there would perhaps be no cause for despair:
time and the law and even the international political situation are on the
side of the Negroes, and ultimately, therefore, victory—of a sort, anyway
—must come. But from everything we have learned from observers who
ought to know, pace has become as important to the Negroes as substance.
They want equality and they want it *now,* and the white world is yielding to their demand only as much and as fast as it is absolutely being compelled to do. The Negroes know this in the most concrete terms
imaginable, and it is thus becoming increasingly difficult to buy them
off with rhetoric and promises and pious assurances of support. And so
within the Negro community we find more and more people declaring
—as Harold R. Isaacs recently put it in these pages[2]—that they want *out:*
people who say that integration will never come, or that it will take a
hundred or a thousand years to come, or that it will come at too high a
price in suffering and struggle for the pallid and sodden life of the American middle class that at the very best it may bring.

The most numerous, influential, and dangerous movement that has
grown out of Negro despair with the goal of integration is, of course,
the Black Muslims. This movement, whatever else we may say about it,
must be credited with one enduring achievement: it inspired James Bald-

---

[2] "Integration and the Negro Mood," December 1962.

win to write an essay[3] which deserves to be placed among the classics of our language. Everything Baldwin has ever been trying to tell us is distilled here into a statement of overwhelming persuasiveness and prophetic magnificence. Baldwin's message is and always has been simple. It is this: "Color is not a human or personal reality; it is a political reality." And Baldwin's demand is correspondingly simple: color must be forgotten, lest we all be smited with a vengeance "that does not really depend on, and cannot really be executed by, any person or organization, and that cannot be prevented by any police force or army: historical vengeance, a cosmic vengeance based on the law that we recognize when we say, 'Whatever goes up must come down.'" The Black Muslims Baldwin portrays as a sign and a warning to the intransigent white world. They come to proclaim how deep is the Negro's disaffection with the white world and all its works, and Baldwin implies that no American Negro can fail to respond somewhere in his being to their message: that the white man is the devil, that Allah has doomed him to destruction, and that the black man is about to inherit the earth. Baldwin of course knows that this nightmare inversion of the racism from which the black man has suffered can neither win nor even point to the neighborhood in which victory might be located. For in his view the neighborhood of victory lies in exactly the opposite direction: the transcendence of color through love.

Yet the tragic fact is that love is not the answer to hate—not in the world of politics, at any rate. Color is indeed a political rather than a human or a personal reality and if politics (which is to say power) has made it into a human and a personal reality, then only politics (which is to say power) can unmake it once again. But the way of politics is slow and bitter, and as impatience on the one side is matched by a setting of the jaw on the other, we move closer and closer to an explosion and blood may yet run in the streets.

Will this madness in which we are all caught never find a resting-place? Is there never to be an end to it? In thinking about the Jews I have often wondered whether their survival as a distinct group was worth one hair on the head of a single infant. Did the Jews have to survive so that six million innocent people should one day be burned in the ovens of Auschwitz? It is a terrible question and no one, not God himself, could ever answer it to my satisfaction. And when I think about the Negroes in America and about the image of integration as a state in which the Negroes would take their rightful place as another of the protected minorities in a pluralistic society, I wonder whether they really believe in their hearts that such a state can actually be attained, and if so *why* they should wish to survive as a distinct group. I think I know why the Jews

---

[3] Originally published last November in the *New Yorker* under the title "Letter From a Region in My Mind," it has just been reprinted (along with a new introduction) by Dial Press under the title *The Fire Next Time.*

once wished to survive (though I am less certain as to why we still do):
they not only believed that God had given them no choice, but they
were tied to a memory of past glory and a dream of imminent redemption.
What does the American Negro have that might correspond to this? His
past is a stigma, his color is a stigma, and his vision of the future is the hope
of erasing the stigma by making color irrelevant, by making it disappear as
a fact of consciousness.

I share this hope, but I cannot see how it will ever be realized unless
color does *in fact* disappear: and that means not integration, it means
assimilation, it means—let the brutal word come out—miscegenation.
The Black Muslims, like their racist counterparts in the white world,
accuse the "so-called Negro leaders" of secretly pursuing miscegenation
as a goal. The racists are wrong, but I wish they were right, for I believe
that the wholesale merging of the two races is the most desirable
alternative for everyone concerned. I am not claiming that this alternative
can be pursued programmatically or that it is immediately feasible as
a solution; obviously there are even greater barriers to its achievement
than to the achievement of integration. What I am saying, however, is that
in my opinion the Negro problem can be solved in this country in no other
way.

I have told the story of my own twisted feelings about Negroes here,
and of how they conflict with the moral convictions I have since developed, in order to assert that such feelings must be acknowledged as
honestly as possible so that they can be controlled and ultimately disregarded in favor of the convictions. It is *wrong* for a man to suffer because
of the color of his skin. Beside that clichéd proposition of liberal thought,
what argument can stand and be respected? If the arguments are the arguments of feeling, they must be made to yield; and one's own soul is not the
worst place to begin working a huge social transformation. Not so long
ago, it used to be asked of white liberals, "Would you like your sister to
marry one?" When I was a boy and my sister was still unmarried, I would
certainly have said no to that question. But now I am a man, my sister is
already married, and I have daughters. If I were to be asked today whether
I would like a daughter of mine "to marry one," I would have to answer:
"No, I wouldn't *like* it at all. I would rail and rave and rant and tear my
hair. And then I hope I would have the courage to curse myself for raving
and ranting, and to give her my blessing. How dare I withhold it at the
behest of the child I once was and against the man I now have a duty
to be?"

The Future of Religion

There is nothing new about religious controversy. Amenhotep IV was in conflict with the Egyptian priesthood; Socrates was accused of subverting the gods; the early Christians were thought to be undermining the Roman state; and in more modern times numerous wars have been waged in the name of God. The issue of freedom of religion was basic to the founding of this country. But not until the late nineteenth century was the *future* of religion seriously questioned. "God is dead!" proclaimed Nietzsche and ushered in a modern period of doubt, disillusion, and re-affirmation. Paul Tillich has suggested that the predicament of modern man is that he "has lost an answer to the question: What is the meaning of life? Where do we come from, where do we go to? What shall we do, what should we become in the short stretch between birth and death?" Possibly only as these questions continue to be asked can we attempt to discover answers, either new or old.

In one way or another, all the writers we present below are concerned with these questions. The reader may wish to weigh the statements of Father Hopkins, Tillich, and Lewis—three men of faith—against those of Darrow, Camus, and Stace, who speak as agnostic, unbeliever, and atheist, respectively. In the final selection, Huxley strikes a conciliatory, philosophical note: he attempts to describe a "perennial philosophy" by abstracting the "Highest Common Factor" present in all religions.

GERARD MANLEY HOPKINS
(1844–1889)

GOD'S GRANDEUR

The world is charged with the grandeur of God.
   It will flame out, like shining from shook foil;
   It gathers to a greatness, like the ooze of oil
Crushed. Why do men then now not reck his rod?
Generations have trod, have trod, have trod;
   And all is seared with trade; bleared, smeared with toil;
   And wears man's smudge and shares man's smell: the soil
Is bare now, nor can foot feel, being shod.

And for all this, nature is never spent;
   There lives the dearest freshness deep down things;
And though the last lights off the black West went
   Oh, morning, at the brown brink eastward, springs—
Because the Holy Ghost over the bent
   World broods with warm breast and with ah! bright wings.

(1877)

CLARENCE DARROW

Clarence Darrow is probably best known for his distinguished career in criminal law. Born in Ohio (1857–1938), he attended one year of law school at the University of Michigan, spent his second year in an attorney's office, and was admitted to the Ohio bar the third year, at the age of 21. He soon left Ohio for Chicago and became the most sought-after and controversial criminal lawyer of his time. His most famous cases include the defense of the child-murderers, Leopold and Loeb, for whom he won a life sentence instead of the death penalty, and the Scopes Trial in 1925—known as the Monkey Trial—which created a national and international furor. Darrow, an outspoken agnostic, defended John Scopes, a Dayton, Tennessee, science teacher who had taught evolution and thus broken a state law prohibiting "the teaching in public schools of any theories that deny the divine creation of man as taught in the Bible." The prosecuting attorney was William Jennings Bryan, a Fundamentalist. Darrow put Bryan on the stand, cross-examined him regarding his Fundamentalist beliefs, and won what was considered a triumphant victory, although Scopes was formally convicted and sentenced to a nominal fine of $100. Bryan died five days later. The reader may wish to keep this case in mind when reading the essay we present below, reprinted here from Verdicts Out of Court, *ed. Arthur and Lila Weinberg (1963). It was originally written in 1929 for a symposium in which Darrow was joined by a rabbi, a Protestant bishop, and a Catholic judge. Among Darrow's other writings are two autobiographical books,* Farmington *(1904) and* The Story of My Life *(1932), and a number of socio-legal works, including* Resist Not Evil *(1904),* Eye for an Eye *(1904), and* Crime: Its Cause and Its Treatment *(1922).*

WHY I AM AN AGNOSTIC

An agnostic is a doubter. The word is generally applied to those who doubt the verity of accepted religious creeds or faiths. Everyone is an agnostic as to the beliefs or creeds they do not accept. Catholics are agnostic to the Protestant creeds, and the Protestants are agnostic to the Catholic creed. Anyone who thinks is an agnostic about something, otherwise he must believe that he is possessed of all knowledge. And the proper place for such a person is in the madhouse or the home for the feebleminded. In a popular way, in the western world, an agnostic is one who doubts or disbelieves the main tenets of the Christian faith.

I would say that belief in at least three tenets is necessary to the faith of a Christian: a belief in God, a belief in immortality, and a belief in a supernatural book. Various Christian sects require much more, but it is difficult to imagine that one could be a Christian, under any intelligent meaning of the word, with less. Yet there are some people who claim to be Christians who do not accept the literal interpretation of all the Bible, and who give more credence to some portions of the book than to others.

I am an agnostic as to the question of God. I think that it is impossible for the human mind to believe in an object or thing unless it can form a mental picture of such object or thing. Since man ceased to worship openly an anthropomorphic God and talked vaguely and not intelligently about some force in the universe, higher than man, that is responsible for the existence of man and the universe, he cannot be said to believe in God. One cannot believe in a force excepting as a force that pervades matter and is not an individual entity. To believe in a thing, an image of the thing must be stamped on the mind. If one is asked if he believes in such an animal as a camel, there immediately arises in his mind an image of the camel. This image has come from experience or knowledge of the animal gathered in some way or other. No such image comes, or can come, with the idea of a God who is described as a force.

Man has always speculated upon the origin of the universe, including himself. I feel, with Herbert Spencer, that whether the universe had an origin—and if it had—what the origin is will never be known by man. The Christian says that the universe could not make itself; that there must have been some higher power to call it into being. Christians have been obsessed for many years by Paley's argument that if a person passing through a desert should find a watch and examine its spring, its hands, its case and its crystal, he would at once be satisfied that some intelligent being capable of design had made the watch. No doubt this is true. No civilized man would question that someone made the watch. The reason he would not doubt it is because he is familiar with watches and other appliances made by man. The savage was once unfamiliar with a watch and would have had no idea upon the subject. There are plenty of crystals and rocks of natural formation that are as intricate as a watch, but even to intelligent man they carry no implication that some intelligent power must have made them. They carry no such implication because no one has any knowledge or experience of someone having made these natural objects which everywhere abound.

To say that God made the universe gives us no explanation of the beginning of things. If we are told that God made the universe, the question immediately arises: Who made God? Did he always exist, or was there same power back of that? Did he create matter out of nothing, or is his existence co-extensive with matter? The problem is still there. What is the origin of it all? If, on the other hand, one says that the universe was not made by God, that it always existed, he has the same difficulty to confront. To say that the universe was here last year, or millions of years ago, does not explain its origin. This is still a mystery. As to the question of the origin of things, man can only wonder and doubt and guess.

As to the existence of the soul, all people may either believe or disbelieve. Everyone knows the origin of the human being. They know that it came from a single cell in the body of the mother, and that the cell was one out of ten thousand in the mother's body. Before gestation the cell must have been fertilized by a spermatozoön from the body of the father. This was one out of perhaps a billion spermatozoa that was the capacity of the father. When the cell is fertilized a chemical process begins. The cell divides and multiplies and increases into millions of cells, and finally a child is born. Cells die and are born during the life of the individual until they finally drop apart, and this is death.

If there is a soul, what is it, and where did it come from, and where does it go? Can anyone who is guided by his reason possibly imagine a soul independent of a body, or the place of its residence, or the character of it, or anything concerning it? If man is justified in any belief or disbelief on any subject, he is warranted in the disbelief in a soul. Not one scrap of evidence exists to prove any such impossible thing.

Many Christians base the belief of a soul and God upon the Bible. Strictly speaking, there is no such book. To make the Bible, sixty-six books are bound into one volume. These books were written by many people at different times, and no one knows the time or the identity of any author. Some of the books were written by several authors at various times. These books contain all sorts of contradictory concepts of life and morals and the origin of things. Between the first and the last nearly a thousand years intervened, a longer time than has passed since the discovery of America by Columbus.

When I was a boy the theologians used to assert that the proof of the divine inspiration of the Bible rested on miracles and prophecies. But a miracle means a violation of a natural law, and there can be no proof imagined that could be sufficient to show the violation of a natural law;

even though proof seemed to show violation, it would only show that we were not acquainted with all natural laws. One believes in the truthfulness of a man because of his long experience with the man, and because the man has always told a consistent story. But no man has told so consistent a story as nature.

If one should say that the sun did not rise, to use the ordinary expression, on the day before, his hearer would not believe it, even though he had slept all day and knew that his informant was a man of the strictest veracity. He would not believe it because the story is inconsistent with the conduct of the sun in all the ages past.

Primitive and even civilized people have grown so accustomed to believing in miracles that they often attribute the simplest manifestations of nature to agencies of which they know nothing. They do this when the belief is utterly inconsistent with knowledge and logic. They believe in old miracles and new ones. Preachers pray for rain, knowing full well that no such prayer was ever answered. When a politician is sick, they pray for God to cure him, and the politician almost invariably dies. The modern clergyman who prays for rain and for the health of the politician is no more intelligent in this matter than the primitive man who saw a separate miracle in the rising and setting of the sun, in the birth of an individual, in the growth of a plant, in the stroke of lightning, in the flood, in every manifestation of nature and life.

As to prophecies, intelligent writers gave them up long ago. In all prophecies facts are made to suit the prophecy, or the prophecy was made after the facts, or the events have no relation to the prophecy. Weird and strange and unreasonable interpretations are used to explain simple statements, that a prophecy may be claimed.

Can any rational person believe that the Bible is anything but a human document? We now know pretty well where the various books came from, and about when they were written. We know that they were written by human beings who had no knowledge of science, little knowledge of life, and were influenced by the barbarous morality of primitive times, and were grossly ignorant of most things that men know today. For instance, Genesis says that God made the earth, and he made the sun to light the day and the moon to light the night, and in one clause disposes of the stars by saying that "he made the stars also." This was plainly written by someone who had no conception of the stars. Man, by the aid of his telescope, has looked out into the heavens and found stars whose diameter is as great as the distance between the earth and the sun. We now know that the universe is filled with stars and suns and planets and systems. Every new telescope looking further into the heavens only discovers more and more worlds and suns and systems in the endless reaches of space. The men who wrote Genesis believed, of course, that this tiny speck of mud that we call the earth was the center of the universe, the only world in space, and made for man, who was the only being worth considering.

These men believed that the stars were only a little way above the earth, and were set in the firmament for man to look at, and for nothing else. Everyone today knows that this conception is not true.

The origin of the human race is not as blind a subject as it once was. Let alone God creating Adam out of hand, from the dust of the earth, does anyone believe that Eve was made from Adam's rib—that the snake walked and spoke in the Garden of Eden—that he tempted Eve to persuade Adam to eat an apple, and that it is on that account that the whole human race was doomed to hell—that for four thousand years there was no chance for any human to be saved, though none of them had anything whatever to do with the temptation; and that finally men were saved only through God's son dying for them, and that unless human beings believed this silly, impossible and wicked story they were doomed to hell? Can anyone with intelligence really believe that a child born today should be doomed because the snake tempted Eve and Eve tempted Adam? To believe that is not God-worship; it is devil-worship.

Can anyone call this scheme of creation and damnation moral? It defies every principle of morality, as man conceives morality. Can anyone believe today that the whole world was destroyed by flood, save only Noah and his family and a male and female of each species of animal that entered the Ark? There are almost a million species of insects alone. How did Noah match these up and make sure of getting male and female to reproduce life in the world after the flood had spent its force? And why should all the lower animals have been destroyed? Were they included in the sinning of man? This is a story which could not beguile a fairly bright child of five years of age today.

Do intelligent people believe that the various languages spoken by man on earth came from the confusion of tongues at the Tower of Babel, some four thousand years ago? Human languages were dispersed all over the face of the earth long before that time. Evidences of civilizations are in existence now that were old long before the date that romancers fix for the building of the Tower, and even before the date claimed for the flood.

Do Christians believe that Joshua made the sun stand still, so that the day could be lengthened, that a battle might be finished? What kind of person wrote that story, and what did he know about astronomy? It is perfectly plain that the author thought that the earth was the center of the universe and stood still in the heavens, and that the sun either went around it or was pulled across its path each day, and that the stopping of the sun would lengthen the day. We know now that had the sun stopped when Joshua commanded it, and had it stood still until now, it would not have lengthened the day. We know that the day is determined by the rotation of the earth upon its axis, and not by the movement of the sun. Everyone knows that this story simply is not true, and not many even pretend to believe the childish fable.

What of the tale of Balaam's ass speaking to him, probably in Hebrew? Is it true, or is it a fable? Many asses have spoken, and doubtless some in Hebrew, but they have not been that breed of asses. Is salvation to depend on a belief in a monstrosity like this?

Above all the rest, would any human being today believe that a child was born without a father? Yet this story was not at all unreasonable in the ancient world; at least three or four miraculous births are recorded in the Bible, including John the Baptist and Samson. Immaculate conceptions were common in the Roman world at the time and at the place where Christianity really had its nativity. Women were taken to the temples to be inoculated of God so that their sons might be heroes, which meant, generally, wholesale butchers. Julius Caesar was a miraculous conception —indeed, they were common all over the world. How many miraculous-birth stories is a Christian now expected to believe?

In the days of the formation of the Christian religion, disease meant the possession of human beings by devils. Christ cured a sick man by casting out the devils, who ran into the swine, and the swine ran into the sea. Is there any question but what that was simply the attitude and belief of a primitive people? Does anyone believe that sickness means the possession of the body by devils, and that the devils must be cast out of the human being that he may be cured? Does anyone believe that a dead person can come to life? The miracles recorded in the Bible are not the only instances of dead men coming to life. All over the world one finds testimony of such miracles; miracles which no person is expected to believe, unless it is his kind of a miracle. Still at Lourdes today, and all over the present world, from New York to Los Angeles and up and down the lands, people believe in miraculous occurrences, and even in the return of the dead. Superstition is everywhere prevalent in the world. It has been so from the beginning, and most likely will be so unto the end.

The reasons for agnosticism and skepticism are abundant and compelling. Fantastic and foolish and impossible consequences are freely claimed for the belief in religion. All the civilization of any period is put down as a result of religion. All the cruelty and error and ignorance of the period has no relation to religion. The truth is that the origin of what we call civilization is not due to religion but to skepticism. So long as men accepted miracles without question, so long as they believed in original sin and the road to salvation, so long as they believed in a hell where man would be kept for eternity on account of Eve, there was no reason whatever for civilization: life was short, and eternity was long, and the business of life was preparation for eternity.

When every event was a miracle, when there was no order or system or law, there was no occasion for studying any subject, or being interested in anything excepting a religion which took care of the soul. As man doubted the primitive conceptions about religion, and no longer accepted the literal, miraculous teachings of ancient books, he set himself to understand nature. We no longer cure disease by casting out devils. Since that time, men have studied the human body, have built hospitals and treated illness in a scientific way. Science is responsible for the building of railroads and bridges, of steamships, of telegraph lines, of cities, towns, large buildings and small, plumbing and sanitation, of the food supply, and the countless thousands of useful things that we now deem necessary to life. Without skepticism and doubt, none of these things could have been given to the world.

The fear of God is not the beginning of wisdom. The fear of God is the death of wisdom. Skepticism and doubt lead to study and investigation, and investigation is the beginning of wisdom.

The modern world is the child of doubt and inquiry, as the ancient world was the child of fear and faith.

PAUL TILLICH

A profound and compassionate thinker, Tillich (1886–1965) was one of the great modern theologians. He was born and educated in Germany and was well on his way to a distinguished academic career when he was dismissed from his post as Professor of Philosophy at the University of Frankfurt because of his outspoken criticism of the Nazi movement. In 1933, at the age of 47, he emigrated to the United States at the invitation of Union Theological Seminary in New York, where he taught until 1954. That year he was appointed to the Divinity School Faculty at Harvard, and in 1962 he was named as the first Duveen Professor of Theology at the University of Chicago. His books include The Shaking of the Foundations *(1948) and* The New Being *(1955), two volumes of sermons;* The Protestant Era *(1948);* The Courage to Be *(1952);* Love, Power, and Justice *(1954); and* Dynamics of Faith *(1957), from which we present Chapter 3.*

SYMBOLS OF FAITH

1. THE MEANING OF SYMBOL

Man's ultimate concern must be expressed symbolically, because symbolic language alone is able to express the ultimate. This statement demands explanation in several respects. In spite of the manifold research about the meaning and function of symbols which is going on in contemporary philosophy, every writer who uses the term "symbol" must explain his understanding of it.

Symbols have one characteristic in common with signs; they point beyond themselves to something else. The red sign at the street corner points to the order to stop the movements of cars at certain intervals. A red light and the stopping of cars have essentially no relation to each other, but conventionally they are united as long as the convention lasts. The same is true of letters and numbers and partly even words. They point beyond themselves to sounds and meanings. They are given this special function by convention within a nation or by international conventions, as the mathematical signs. Sometimes such signs are called symbols; but this is unfortunate because it makes the distinction between signs and symbols more difficult. Decisive is the fact that signs do not participate in the reality of that to which they point, while symbols do. Therefore, signs can be replaced for reasons of expediency or convention, while symbols cannot.

This leads to the second characteristic of the symbol: It participates in that to which it points: the flag participates in the power and dignity of the nation for which it stands. Therefore, it cannot be replaced except after an historic catastrophe that changes the reality of the nation which it symbolizes. An attack on the flag is felt as an attack on the majesty of the group in which it is acknowledged. Such an attack is considered blasphemy.

The third characteristic of a symbol is that it opens up levels of reality which otherwise are closed for us. All arts create symbols for a level of reality which cannot be reached in any other way. A picture and a poem reveal elements of reality which cannot be approached scientifically. In the creative work of art we encounter reality in a dimension which is closed for us without such works. The symbol's fourth characteristic not only opens up dimensions and elements of reality which otherwise would remain unapproachable but also unlocks dimensions and elements of our soul which correspond to the dimensions and elements of reality. A great play gives us not only a new vision of the human scene, but it opens up hidden depths of our own being. Thus we are able to receive what the play reveals to us in reality. There are within us dimensions of which we cannot become aware except through symbols, as melodies and rhythms in music.

Symbols cannot be produced intentionally—this is the fifth characteristic. They grow out of the individual or collective unconscious and cannot function without being accepted by the unconscious dimension of our being. Symbols which have an especially social function, as political and religious symbols, are created or at least accepted by the collective unconscious of the group in which they appear.

The sixth and last characteristic of the symbol is a consequence of the fact that symbols cannot be invented. Like living beings, they grow and they die. They grow when the situation is ripe for them, and they die when the situation changes. The symbol of the "king" grew in a special period of history, and it died in most parts of the world in our period. Symbols do not grow because people are longing for them, and they do not die because of scientific or practical criticism. They die because they can no longer produce response in the group where they originally found expression.

These are the main characteristics of every symbol. Genuine symbols are created in several spheres of man's cultural creativity. We have mentioned already the political and the artistic realm. We could add history and, above all, religion, whose symbols will be our particular concern.

2. RELIGIOUS SYMBOLS

We have discussed the meaning of symbols generally because, as we said, man's ultimate concern must be expressed symbolically! One may ask: Why can it not be expressed directly and properly? If money, success or the nation is someone's ultimate concern, can this not be said in a direct way without symbolic language? Is it not only in those cases in which the content of the ultimate concern is called "God" that we are in the realm of symbols? The answer is that everything which is a matter of unconditional concern is made into a god. If the nation is someone's ultimate concern, the name of the nation becomes a sacred name and the nation receives divine qualities which far surpass the reality of the being and functioning of the nation. The nation then stands for and symbolizes the true ultimate, but in an idolatrous way. Success as ultimate concern is not the national desire of actualizing potentialities, but is readiness to sacrifice all other values of life for the sake of a position of power and social predominance. The anxiety about not being a success is an idolatrous form of the anxiety about divine condemnation. Success is grace; lack of success, ultimate judgment. In this way concepts designating ordinary realities become idolatrous symbols of ultimate concern.

The reason for this transformation of concepts into symbols is the character of ultimacy and the nature of faith. That which is the true ultimate transcends the realm of finite reality infinitely. Therefore, no finite reality can express it directly and properly. Religiously speaking,

God transcends his own name. This is why the use of his name easily becomes an abuse or a blasphemy. Whatever we say about that which concerns us ultimately, whether or not we call it God, has a symbolic meaning. It points beyond itself while participating in that to which it points. In no other way can faith express itself adequately. The language of faith is the language of symbols. If faith were what we have shown that it is not, such an assertion could not be made. But faith, understood as the state of being ultimately concerned, has no language other than symbols. When saying this I always expect the question: Only a symbol? He who asks this question shows that he has not understood the difference between signs and symbols nor the power of symbolic language, which surpasses in quality and strength the power of any nonsymbolic language. One should never say "only a symbol," but one should say "not less than a symbol." With this in mind we can now describe the different kinds of symbols of faith.

The fundamental symbol of our ultimate concern is God. It is always present in any act of faith, even if the act of faith includes the denial of God. Where there is ultimate concern, God can be denied only in the name of God. One God can deny the other one. Ultimate concern cannot deny its own character as ultimate. Therefore, it affirms what is meant by the word "God." Atheism, consequently, can only mean the attempt to remove any ultimate concern—to remain unconcerned about the meaning of one's existence. Indifference toward the ultimate question is the only imaginable form of atheism. Whether it is possible is a problem which must remain unsolved at this point. In any case, he who denies God as a matter of ultimate concern affirms God, because he affirms ultimacy in his concern. God is the fundamental symbol for what concerns us ultimately. Again it would be completely wrong to ask: So God is nothing but a symbol? Because the next question has to be: A symbol for what? And then the answer would be: For God! God is symbol for God. This means that in the notion of God we must distinguish two elements: the element of ultimacy, which is a matter of immediate experience and not symbolic in itself, and the element of concreteness, which is taken from our ordinary experience and symbolically applied to God. The man whose ultimate concern is a sacred tree has both the ultimacy of concern and the concreteness of the tree which symbolizes his relation to the ultimate. The man who adores Apollo is ultimately concerned, but not in an abstract way. His ultimate concern is symbolized in the divine figure of Apollo. The man who glorifies Jahweh, the God of the Old Testament, has both an ultimate concern and a concrete image of what concerns him ultimately. This is the meaning of the seemingly cryptic statement that God is the symbol of God. In this qualified sense God is the fundamental and universal content of faith.

It is obvious that such an understanding of the meaning of God makes the discussions about the existence or nonexistence of God meaningless. It is meaningless to question the ultimacy of an ultimate concern. This element in the idea of God is in itself certain. The symbolic expression of this element varies endlessly through the whole history of mankind. Here again it would be meaningless to ask whether one or another of the figures in which an ultimate concern is symbolized does "exist." If "existence" refers to something which can be found within the whole of reality, no divine being exists. The question is not this, but: which of the innumerable symbols of faith is most adequate to the meaning of faith? In other words, which symbol of ultimacy expresses the ultimate without idolatrous elements? This is the problem, and not the so-called "existence of God"—which is in itself an impossible combination of words. God as the ultimate in man's ultimate concern is more certain than any other certainty, even that of oneself. God as symbolized in a divine figure is a matter of daring faith, of courage and risk.

God is the basic symbol of faith, but not the only one. All the qualities we attribute to him, power, love, justice, are taken from finite experiences and applied symbolically to that which is beyond finitude and infinity. If faith calls God "almighty," it uses the human experience of power in order to symbolize the content of its infinite concern, but it does not describe a highest being who can do as he pleases. So it is with all the other qualities and with all the actions, past, present and future, which men attribute to God. They are symbols taken from our daily experience, and not information about what God did once upon a time or will do sometime in the future. Faith is not the belief in such stories, but it is the acceptance of symbols that express our ultimate concern in terms of divine actions.

Another group of symbols of faith are manifestations of the divine in things and events, in persons and communities, in words and documents. This whole realm of sacred objects is a treasure of symbols. Holy things are not holy in themselves, but they point beyond themselves to the source of all holiness, that which is of ultimate concern.

3. SYMBOLS AND MYTHS

The symbols of faith do not appear in isolation. They are united in "stories of the gods," which is the meaning of the Greek word "mythos" —myth. The gods are individualized figures, analogous to human personalities, sexually differentiated, descending from each other, related to each other in love and struggle, producing world and man, acting in time and space. They participate in human greatness and misery, in creative and destructive works. They give to man cultural and religious traditions, and defend these sacred rites. They help and threaten the human race, especially some families, tribes or nations. They appear in epiphanies and incarnations, establish sacred places, rites and persons, and thus create a cult. But they themselves are under the command and threat of a fate which is beyond everything that is. This is mythology as developed most impressively in ancient Greece. But many of these characteristics can be found in every mythology. Usually the mythological gods are not equals. There is a hierarchy, at the top of which is a ruling god, as in Greece; or a trinity of them, as in India; or a duality of them, as in Persia. There are savior-gods who mediate between the highest gods and man, sometimes sharing the suffering and death of man in spite of their essential immortality. This is the world of the myth, great and strange, always changing but fundamentally the same: man's ultimate concern symbolized in divine figures and actions. Myths are symbols of faith combined in stories about divine-human encounters.

Myths are always present in every act of faith, because the language of faith is the symbol. They are also attacked, criticized and transcended in each of the great religions of mankind. The reason for this criticism is the very nature of the myth. It uses material from our ordinary experience. It puts the stories of the gods into the framework of time and space although it belongs to the nature of the ultimate to be beyond time and space. Above all, it divides the divine into several figures, removing ultimacy from each of them without removing their claim to ultimacy. This inescapably leads to conflicts of ultimate claims, able to destroy life, society, and consciousness.

The criticism of the myth first rejects the division of the divine and goes beyond it to one God, although in different ways according to the different types of religion. Even one God is an object of mythological language, and if spoken about is drawn into the framework of time and space. Even he loses his ultimacy if made to be the content of concrete concern. Consequently, the criticism of the myth does not end with the rejection of the polytheistic mythology.

Monotheism also falls under the criticism of the myth. It needs, as one says today, "demythologization." This word has been used in connection with the elaboration of the mythical elements in stories and symbols of the Bible, both of the Old and the New Testaments—stories like those of the Paradise, of the fall of Adam, of the great Flood, of the Exodus from Egypt, of the virgin birth of the Messiah, of many of his miracles, of his resurrection and ascension, of his expected return as the judge of the universe. In short, all the stories in which divine-human interactions are told are considered as mythological in character, and objects of demythologization. What does this negative and artificial term mean? It must be accepted and supported if it points to the necessity of recognizing a symbol as a symbol and a myth as a myth. It must be attacked and rejected if it means the removal of symbols and myths altogether. Such an attempt is the third step in the criticism of the myth. It is an attempt which never can be successful, because symbol and myth are forms of the human consciousness which are always present. One can replace one myth by another, but one cannot remove the myth from man's spiritual life. For the myth is the combination of symbols of our ultimate concern.

A myth which is understood as a myth, but not removed or replaced, can be called a "broken myth." Christianity denies by its very nature any unbroken myth, because its presupposition is the first commandment: the affirmation of the ultimate as ultimate and the rejection of any kind of idolatry. All mythological elements in the Bible, and doctrine and liturgy should be recognized as mythological, but they should be maintained in their symbolic form and not be replaced by scientific substitutes. For there is no substitute for the use of symbols and myths: they are the language of faith.

The radical criticism of the myth is due to the fact that the primitive mythological consciousness resists the attempt to interpret the myth of myth. It is afraid of every act of demythologization. It believes that the broken myth is deprived of its truth and of its convincing power. Those who live in an unbroken mythological world feel safe and certain. They resist, often fanatically, any attempt to introduce an element of uncertainty by "breaking the myth," namely, by making conscious its symbolic character. Such resistance is supported by authoritarian systems, religious or political, in order to give security to the people under their control and unchallenged power to those who exercise the control. The resistance against demythologization expresses itself in "literalism." The symbols and myths are understood in their immediate meaning. The material, taken from nature and history, is used in its proper sense. The character of the symbol to point beyond itself to something else is disregarded. Creation is taken as a magic act which happened once upon a time. The fall of Adam is localized on a special geographical point and attributed to a human individual. The virgin birth of the Messiah is understood in biological terms, resurrection and ascension as physical events, the second coming of the Christ as a telluric, or cosmic, catastrophe. The presupposition of such literalism is that God is a being, acting in time and space, dwelling in a special place, affecting the course of events and being affected by them like any other being in the universe. Literalism deprives God of his ultimacy and, religiously speaking, of his majesty. It draws him down to the level of that which is not ultimate, the finite and conditional. In the last analysis it is not rational criticism of the myth which is decisive but the inner religious criticism. Faith, if it takes its symbols literally, becomes idolatrous! It calls something ultimate which is less than ultimate. Faith, conscious of the symbolic character of its symbols, gives God the honor which is due him.

One should distinguish two stages of literalism, the natural and the reactive. The natural stage of literalism is that in which the mythical and the literal are indistinguishable. The primitive period of individuals and groups consists in the inability to separate the creations of symbolic imagination from the facts which can be verified through observation and experiment. This stage has a full right of its own and should not be disturbed, either in individuals or in groups, up to the moment when man's questioning mind breaks the natural acceptance of the mythological visions as literal. If, however, this moment has come, two ways are possible. The one is to replace the unbroken by the broken myth. It is the objectively demanded way, although it is impossible for many people who prefer the repression of their questions to the uncertainty which appears with the breaking of the myth. They are forced into the second stage of literalism, the conscious one, which is aware of the questions but represses them, half consciously, half unconsciously. The tool of repression is usually an acknowledged authority with sacred qualities like the Church or the Bible, to which one owes unconditional surrender. This stage is still justifiable, if the questioning power is very weak and can easily be answered. It is unjustifiable if a mature mind is broken in its personal center by political or psychological methods, split in its unity, and hurt in its integrity. The enemy of a critical theology is not natural literalism but conscious literalism with repression of and aggression toward autonomous thought.

Symbols of faith cannot be replaced by other symbols, such as artistic ones, and they cannot be removed by scientific criticism. They have a genuine standing in the human mind, just as science and art have. Their symbolic character is their truth and their power. Nothing less than symbols and myths can express our ultimate concern.

One more question arises, namely, whether myths are able to express every kind of ultimate concern. For example, Christian theologians argue that the word "myth" should be reserved for natural myths in which repetitive natural processes, such as the seasons, are understood in their ultimate meaning. They believe that if the world is seen as a historical process with beginning, end and center, as in Christianity and Judaism, the term "myth" should not be used. This would radically reduce the realm in which the term would be applicable. Myth could not be understood as the language of our ultimate concern, but only as a discarded idiom of this language. Yet history proves that there are not only natural myths but also historical myths. If the earth is seen as the battleground of two divine powers, as in ancient Persia, this is an historical myth. If the God of creation selects and guides a nation through history toward an end which transcends all history, this is an historical myth. If the Christ—a transcendent, divine being—appears in the fullness of time, lives, dies and is resurrected, this is an historical myth. Christianity is superior to those religions which are bound to a natural myth. But Christianity speaks the mythological language like every other religion. It is a broken myth, but it is a myth; otherwise Christianity would not be an expression of ultimate concern.

W. T. STACE

Walter Terence Stace was born in England in 1886 and educated at Trinity College, Dublin University. He joined the British Civil Service in 1910 and served in Ceylon for twenty-two years. In 1932 he accepted a position teaching philosophy at Princeton University, where he taught until his retirement in 1955; he is today Professor Emeritus. His writings include The Philosophy of Hegel *(1924),* The Destiny of Western Man *(1942),* Religion and the Modern Mind *(1952),* The Teachings of the Mystics *(1961), and* Mysticism and Philosophy *(1961). The article we reprint below originally appeared in* The Atlantic Monthly, *September, 1948.*

MAN AGAINST DARKNESS

I

The Catholic bishops of America recently issued a statement in which they said that the chaotic and bewildered state of the modern world is due to man's loss of faith, his abandonment of God and religion. For my part I believe in no religion at all. Yet I entirely agree with the bishops. It is no doubt an oversimplification to speak of *the* cause of so complex a state of affairs as the tortured condition of the world today. Its causes are doubtless multitudinous. Yet allowing for some element of oversimplification, I say that the bishops' assertion is substantially true.

M. Jean-Paul Sartre, the French existentialist philosopher, labels himself an atheist. Yet his views seem to me plainly to support the statement of the bishops. So long as there was believed to be a God in the sky, he says, men could regard him as the source of their moral ideals. The universe, created and governed by a fatherly God, was a friendly habitation for man. We could be sure that, however great the evil in the world, good in the end would triumph and the forces of evil would be routed.

With the disappearance of God from the sky all this has changed. Since the world is not ruled by a spiritual being, but rather by blind forces, there cannot be any ideals, moral or otherwise, in the universe outside us. Our ideals, therefore, must proceed only from our own minds; they are our own inventions. Thus the world which surrounds us is nothing but an immense spiritual emptiness. It is a dead universe. We do not live in a universe which is on the side of our values. It is completely indifferent to them.

Years ago Mr. Bertrand Russell, in his essay *A Free Man's Worship*, said much the same thing.

> Such in outline, but even more purposeless, more void of meaning, is the world which Science presents for our belief. Amid such a world, if anywhere, our ideals henceforward must find a home. . . . Blind to good and evil, reckless of destruction, omnipotent matter rolls on its relentless way; for man, condemned today to lose his dearest, tomorrow himself to pass through the gate of darkness, it remains only to cherish, ere yet the blow falls, the lofty thoughts that ennoble his little day; . . . to worship at the shrine his own hands have built; . . . to sustain alone, a weary but unyielding Atlas, the world that his own ideals have fashioned despite the trampling march of unconscious power.

It is true that Mr. Russell's personal attitude to the disappearance of religion is quite different from either that of M. Sartre or the bishops or myself. The bishops think it a calamity. So do I. M. Sartre finds it "very distressing." And he berates as shallow the attitude of those who think that without God the world can go on just the same as before, as if nothing had happened. This creates for mankind, he thinks, a terrible crisis. And in this I agree with him. Mr. Russell, on the other hand, seems to believe that religion has done more harm than good in the world, and that its disappearance will be a blessing. But his picture of the world, and of the modern mind, is the same as that of M. Sartre. He stresses the *purposelessness* of the universe, the facts that man's ideals are his own creations, that the universe outside him in no way supports them, that man is alone and friendless in the world.

Mr. Russell notes that it is science which has produced this situation. There is no doubt that this is correct. But the way in which it has come about is not generally understood. There is a popular belief that some particular scientific discoveries or theories, such as the Darwinian theory of evolution, or the views of geologists about the age of the earth, or a series of such discoveries, have done the damage. It would be foolish to deny that these discoveries have had a great effect in undermining religious dogmas. But this account does not at all go to the root of the matter. Religion can probably outlive any scientific discoveries which could be made. It can accommodate itself to them. The root cause of the decay of faith has not been any particular discovery of science, but rather the general spirit of science and certain basic assumptions upon which modern science, from the seventeenth century onwards, has proceeded.

II

It was Galileo and Newton—notwithstanding that Newton himself was a deeply religious man—who destroyed the old comfortable picture of a friendly universe governed by spiritual values. And this was effected, not by Newton's discovery of the law of gravitation nor by any of Galileo's brilliant investigations, but by the general picture of the world which these men and others of their time made the basis of the science, not only of their own day, but of all succeeding generations down to the present. That is why the century immediately following Newton, the eighteenth century, was notoriously an age of religious skepticism. Skepticism did not have to wait for the discoveries of Darwin and the geologists in the nineteenth century. It flooded the world immediately after the age of the rise of science.

Neither the Copernican hypothesis nor any of Newton's or Galileo's particular discoveries were the real causes. Religious faith might well have accommodated itself to the new astronomy. The real turning point between the medieval age of faith and the modern age of unfaith came when the scientists of the seventeenth century turned their backs upon what used to be called "final causes." The final cause of a thing or event meant the purpose which it was supposed to serve in the universe, its cosmic purpose. What lay back of this was the presupposition that there is a cosmic order or plan and that everything which exists could in the last analysis be explained in terms of its place in this cosmic plan, that is, in terms of its purpose.

Plato and Aristotle believed this, and so did the whole medieval Christian world. For instance, if it were true that the sun and the moon were created and exist for the purpose of giving light to man, then this fact would explain why the sun and the moon exist. We might not be able to discover the purpose of everything, but everything must have a purpose. Belief in final causes thus amounted to a belief that the world is governed by purposes, presumably the purposes of some overruling mind. This belief was not the invention of Christianity. It was basic to the whole of Western civilization, whether in the ancient pagan world or in Christendom, from the time of Socrates to the rise of science in the seventeenth century.

The founders of modern science—for instance, Galileo, Kepler, and Newton—were mostly pious men who did not doubt God's purposes. Nevertheless they took the revolutionary step of consciously and deliberately expelling the idea of purpose as controlling nature from their new science of nature. They did this on the ground that inquiry into purposes is useless for what science aims at: namely, the prediction and control of events. To predict an eclipse, what you have to know is not its purpose but its causes. Hence science from the seventeenth century onwards became exclusively an inquiry into causes. The conception of purpose in the world was ignored and frowned on. This, though silent and almost unnoticed, was the greatest revolution in human history, far outweighing in importance any of the political revolutions whose thunder has reverberated through the world.

For it came about in this way that for the past three hundred years there has been growing up in men's minds, dominated as they are by science, a new imaginative picture of the world. The world, according to this new picture, is purposeless, senseless, meaningless. Nature is nothing but matter in motion. The motions of matter are governed, not by any purpose, but by blind forces and laws. Nature on this view, says White-head—to whose writings I am indebted in this part of my paper—is "merely the hurrying of material, endlessly, meaninglessly." You can draw a sharp line across the history of Europe dividing it into two epochs of very unequal length. The line passes through the lifetime of Galileo. European man before Galileo—whether ancient pagan or more recent Christian—thought of the world as controlled by plan and purpose. After Galileo European man thinks of it as utterly purposeless. This is the great revolution of which I spoke.

It is this which has killed religion. Religion could survive the discoveries that the sun, not the earth, is the center; that men are descended from simian ancestors; that the earth is hundreds of millions of years old. These discoveries may render out of date some of the details of older theological dogmas, may force their restatement in new intellectual frameworks. But they do not touch the essence of the religious vision itself, which is the faith that there is plan and purpose in the world, that the world is a moral order, that in the end all things are for the best. This faith may express itself through many different intellectual dogmas, those of Christianity, of Hinduism, of Islam. All and any of these intellectual dogmas may be destroyed without destroying the essential religious spirit. But that spirit cannot survive destruction of belief in a plan and purpose of the world, for that is the very heart of it. Religion can get on with any sort of astronomy, geology, biology, physics. But it cannot get on with a purposeless and meaningless universe.

If the scheme of things is purposeless and meaningless, then the life of man is purposeless and meaningless too. Everything is futile, all effort is in the end worthless. A man may, of course, still pursue disconnected ends, money, fame, art, science, and may gain pleasure from them. But his life is hollow at the center. Hence the dissatisfied, disillusioned, restless, spirit of modern man.

The picture of a meaningless world, and a meaningless human life, is, I think, the basic theme of much modern art and literature. Certainly

it is the basic theme of modern philosophy. According to the most characteristic philosophies of the modern period from Hume in the eighteenth
century to the so-called positivists of today, the world is just what it is,
and that is the end of all inquiry. There is no reason for its being what
it is. Everything might just as well have been quite different, and there
would have been no reason for that either. When you have stated what
things are, what things the world contains, there is nothing more which
could be said, even by an omniscient being. To ask any question about
why things are thus, or what purpose their being so serves, is to ask a
senseless question, because they serve no purpose at all. For instance, there
is for modern philosophy no such thing as the ancient problem of evil.
For this once famous question presupposes that pain and misery, though
they seem so inexplicable and irrational to us, must ultimately subserve
some rational purpose, must have their places in the cosmic plan. But this
is nonsense. There is no such overruling rationality in the universe. Belief
in the ultimate irrationality of everything is the quintessence of what is
called the modern mind.

It is true that, parallel with these philosophies which are typical of
the modern mind, preaching the meaninglessness of the world, there has
run a line of idealistic philosophies whose contention is that the world is
after all spiritual in nature and that moral ideals and values are inherent
in its structure. But most of these idealisms were simply philosophical
expressions of romanticism, which was itself no more than an unsuccessful
counterattack of the religious against the scientific view of things. They
perished, along with romanticism in literature and art, about the beginning
of the present century, though of course they still have a few adherents.

At the bottom these idealistic systems of thought were rationalizations
of man's wishful thinking. They were born of the refusal of men to
admit the cosmic darkness. They were comforting illusions within the
warm glow of which the more tender-minded intellectuals sought to
shelter themselves from the icy winds of the universe. They lasted a little
while. But they are shattered now, and we return once more to the vision
of a purposeless world.

III

Along with the ruin of the religious vision there went the ruin of
moral principles and indeed of all values. If there is a cosmic purpose, if
there is in the nature of things a drive towards goodness, then our moral
systems will derive their validity from this. But if our moral rules do
not proceed from something outside us in the nature of the universe—
whether we say it is God or simply the universe itself—then they must
be our own inventions. Thus it came to be believed that moral rules must
be merely an expression of our own likes and dislikes. But likes and dislikes are notoriously variable. What pleases one man, people, or culture
displeases another. Therefore morals are wholly relative.

This obvious conclusion from the idea of a purposeless world made its appearance in Europe immediately after the rise of science, for instance in the philosophy of Hobbes. Hobbes saw at once that if there is no purpose in the world there are no values either. "Good and evil," he writes, "are names that signify our appetites and aversions; which in different tempers, customs, and doctrines of men are different. . . . Every man calleth that which pleaseth him, good; and that which displeaseth him, evil."

This doctrine of the relativity of morals, though it has recently received an impetus from the studies of anthropologists, was thus really implicit in the whole scientific mentality. It is disastrous for morals because it destroys their entire traditional foundation. That is why philosophers who see the danger signals, from the time at least of Kant, have been trying to give to morals a new foundation, that is, a secular or nonreligious foundation. This attempt may very well be intellectually successful. Such a foundation, independent of the religious view of the world, might well be found. But the question is whether it can ever be a *practical* success, that is, whether apart from its logical validity and its influence with intellectuals, it can ever replace among the masses of men the lost religious foundation. On that question hangs perhaps the future of civilization. But meanwhile disaster is overtaking us.

The widespread belief in "ethical relativity" among philosophers, psychologists, ethnologists, and sociologists is the theoretical counterpart of the repudiation of principle which we see all around us, especially in international affairs, the field in which morals have always had the weakest foothold. No one any longer effectively believes in moral principles except as the private prejudices either of individual men or of nations or cultures. This is the inevitable consequence of the doctrine of ethical relativity, which in turn is the inevitable consequence of believing in a purposeless world.

Another characteristic of our spiritual state is loss of belief in the freedom of the will. This also is a fruit of the scientific spirit, though not of any particular scientific discovery. Science has been built up on the basis of determinism, which is the belief that every event is completely determined by a chain of causes and is therefore theoretically predictable beforehand. It is true that recent physics seems to challenge this. But so far as its practical consequences are concerned, the damage has long ago been done. A man's actions, it was argued, are as much events in the natural world as is an eclipse of the sun. It follows that men's actions are as theoretically predictable as an eclipse. But if it is certain now that John Smith will murder Joseph Jones at 2.15 P.M. on January 1, 1963, what possible meaning can it have to say that when that time comes John Smith will be *free* to choose whether he will commit the murder or not? And if he is not free, how can he be held responsible?

It is true that the whole of this argument can be shown by a competent philosopher to be a tissue of fallacies—or at least I claim that it can. But the point is that the analysis required to show this is much too subtle to be understood by the average entirely unphilosophical man. Because of this, the argument against free will is generally swallowed whole by the unphilosophical. Hence the thought that man is not free, that he is the helpless plaything of forces over which he has no control, has deeply penetrated the modern mind. We hear of economic determinism, cultural determinism, historical determinism. We are not responsible for what we do because our glands control us, or because we are the products of environment or heredity. Not moral self-control, but the doctor, the psychiatrist, the educationist, must save us from doing evil. Pills and injections in the future are to do what Christ and the prophets have failed to do. Of course I do not mean to deny that doctors and educationists can and must help. And I do not mean in any way to belittle their efforts. But I do wish to draw attention to the weakening of moral controls, the greater or less repudiation of personal responsibility which, in the popular thinking of the day, result from these tendencies of thought.

IV

What, then, is to be done? Where are we to look for salvation from the evils of our time? All the remedies I have seen suggested so far are, in my opinion, useless. Let us look at some of them.

Philosophers and intellectuals generally can, I believe, genuinely do something to help. But it is extremely little. What philosophers can do is to show that neither the relativity of morals nor the denial of free will really follows from the grounds which have been supposed to support them. They can also try to discover a genuine secular basis for morals to replace the religious basis which has disappeared. Some of us are trying to do these things. But in the first place philosophers unfortunately are not agreed about these matters, and their disputes are utterly confusing to the non-philosophers. And in the second place their influence is practically negligible because their analyses necessarily take place on a level on which the masses are totally unable to follow them.

The bishops, of course, propose as remedy a return to belief in God and in the doctrines of the Christian religion. Others think that a new religion is what is needed. Those who make these proposals fail to realize that the crisis in man's spiritual condition is something unique in history for which there is no sort of analogy in the past. They are thinking perhaps of the collapse of the ancient Greek and Roman religions. The vacuum then created was easily filled by Christianity, and it might have been filled by Mithraism if Christianity had not appeared. By analogy they think that Christianity might now be replaced by a new religion, or even that Christianity itself, if revivified, might bring back health to men's lives.

But I believe that there is no analogy at all between our present state and that of the European peoples at the time of the fall of paganism. Men had at that time lost their belief only in particular dogmas, particular embodiments of the religious view of the world. It had no doubt become incredible that Zeus and the other gods were living on the top of Mount Olympus. You could go to the top and find no trace of them. But the imaginative picture of a world governed by purpose, a world driving towards the good—which is the inner spirit of religion—had at that time received no serious shock. It had merely to re-embody itself in new dogmas, those of Christianity or some other religion. Religion itself was not dead in the world, only a particular form of it.

But now the situation is quite different. It is not merely that particular dogmas, like that of the virgin birth, are unacceptable to the modern mind. That is true, but it constitutes a very superficial diagnosis of the present situation of religion. Modern skepticism is of a wholly different order from that of the intellectuals of the ancient world. It has attacked and destroyed not merely the outward forms of the religious spirit, its particularized dogmas, but the very essence of that spirit itself, belief in a meaningful and purposeful world. For the founding of a new religion a new Jesus Christ or Buddha would have to appear, in itself a most unlikely event and one for which in any case we cannot afford to sit and wait. But even if a new prophet and a new religion did appear, we may predict that they would fail in the modern world. No one for long would believe in them, for modern men have lost the vision, basic to all religion, of an ordered plan and purpose of the world. They have before their minds the picture of a purposeless universe, and such a world-picture must be fatal to any religion at all, not merely to Christianity.

We must not be misled by occasional appearances of a revival of the religious spirit. Men, we are told, in their disgust and disillusionment at the emptiness of their lives, are turning once more to religion, or are searching for a new message. It may be so. We must expect such wistful yearnings of the spirit. We must expect men to wish back again the light that is gone, and to try to bring it back. But however they may wish and try, the light will not shine again,—not at least in the civilization to which we belong.

Another remedy commonly proposed is that we should turn to science itself, or the scientific spirit, for our salvation. Mr. Russell and Professor Dewey both make this proposal, though in somewhat different ways. Professor Dewey seems to believe that discoveries in sociology, the application of scientific method to social and political problems, will rescue us. This seems to me to be utterly naïve. It is not likely that science, which is basically the cause of our spiritual troubles, is likely also to produce the cure for them. Also it lies in the nature of science that, though it can teach us the best means for achieving our ends, it can never tell us what ends to pursue. It cannot give us any ideals. And our trouble is about ideals and ends, not about the means for reaching them.

V

No civilization can live without ideals, or to put it in another way, without a firm faith in moral ideas. Our ideals and moral ideas have in the past been rooted in religion. But the religious basis of our ideals has been undermined, and the superstructure of ideals is plainly tottering. None of the commonly suggested remedies on examination seems likely to succeed. It would therefore look as if the early death of our civilization were inevitable.

Of course we know that it is perfectly possible for individual men, very highly educated men, philosophers, scientists, intellectuals in general, to live moral lives without any religious convictions. But the question is whether a whole civilization, a whole family of peoples, composed almost entirely of relatively uneducated men and women, can do this.

It follows, of course, that if we could make the vast majority of men as highly educated as the very few are now, we might save the situation. And we are already moving slowly in that direction through the techniques of mass education. But the critical question seems to concern the time-lag. Perhaps in a few hundred years most of the population will, at the present rate, be sufficiently highly educated and civilized to combine high ideals with an absence of religion. But long before we reach any such stage, the collapse of our civilization may have come about. How are we to live through the intervening period?

I am sure that the first thing we have to do is to face the truth, however bleak it may be, and then next we have to learn to live with it. Let me say a word about each of these two points. What I am urging as regards the first is complete honesty. Those who wish to resurrect Christian dogmas are not, of course, consciously dishonest. But they have that kind of unconscious dishonesty which consists in lulling oneself with opiates and dreams. Those who talk of a new religion are merely hoping for a new opiate. Both alike refuse to face the truth that there is, in the universe outside man, no spirituality, no regard for values, no friend in the sky, no help or comfort for man of any sort. To be perfectly honest in the admission of this fact, not to seek shelter in new or old illusions, not to indulge in wishful dreams about this matter, this is the first thing we shall have to do.

I do not urge this course out of any special regard for the sanctity of truth in the abstract. It is not self-evident to me that truth is the supreme value to which all else must be sacrificed. Might not the discoverer of a truth which would be fatal to mankind be justified in suppressing it, even in teaching men a falsehood? Is truth more valuable than goodness and beauty and happiness? To think so is to invent yet another absolute, another religious delusion in which Truth with a capital T is substituted for God. The reason why we must now boldly and honestly face the truth that the universe is nonspiritual and indifferent to goodness, beauty, happiness, or truth is not that it would be wicked to suppress it, but simply that it is too late to do so, so that in the end we cannot do anything else but face it. Yet we stand on the brink, dreading the icy plunge. We need courage. We need honesty.

Now about the other point, the necessity of learning to live with the truth. This means learning to live virtuously and happily, or at least contentedly, without illusions. And this is going to be extremely difficult because what we have now begun dimly to perceive is that human life in the past, or at least human happiness, has almost wholly depended upon illusions. It has been said that man lives by truth, and that the truth will make us free. Nearly the opposite seems to me to be the case. Mankind has managed to live only by means of lies, and the truth may very well destroy us. If one were a Bergsonian one might believe that nature deliberately puts illusions into our souls in order to induce us to go on living.

The illusions by which men have lived seem to be of two kinds. First, there is what one may perhaps call the Great Illusion—I mean the religious illusion that the universe is moral and good, that it follows a wise and noble plan, that it is gradually generating some supreme value, that goodness is bound to triumph in it. Secondly, there is a whole host of minor illusions on which human happiness nourishes itself. How much of human happiness notoriously comes from the illusions of the lover about his beloved? Then again we work and strive because of the illusions connected with fame, glory, power, or money. Banners of all kinds, flags, emblems, insignia, ceremonials, and rituals are invariably symbols of some illusion or other. The British Empire, the connection between mother country and dominions, is partly kept going by illusions surrounding the notion of kingship. Or think of the vast amount of human happiness which is derived from the illusion of supposing that if some nonsense syllable, such as "sir" or "count" or "lord" is pronounced in conjunction with our names, we belong to a superior order of people.

There is plenty of evidence that human happiness is almost wholly based upon illusions of one kind or another. But the scientific spirit, or the spirit of truth, is the enemy of illusions and therefore the enemy of human happiness. That is why it is going to be so difficult to live with the truth.

There is no reason why we should have to give up the host of minor illusions which render life supportable. There is no reason why the lover should be scientific about the loved one. Even the illusions of fame and glory may persist. But without the Great Illusion, the illusion of a good, kindly, and purposeful universe, we shall *have* to learn to live. And to ask this is really no more than to ask that we become genuinely civilized beings and not merely sham civilized beings.

I can best explain the difference by a reminiscence. I remember a fellow student in my college days, an ardent Christian, who told me that if he did not believe in a future life, in heaven and hell, he would rape, murder, steal, and be a drunkard. That is what I call being a sham civilized being. On the other hand, not only could a Huxley, a John Stuart Mill, a David Hume, live great and fine lives without any religion, but a great many others of us, quite obscure persons, can at least live decent lives without it.

To be genuinely civilized means to be able to walk straightly and to live honorably without the props and crutches of one or another of the childish dreams which have so far supported men. That such a life is likely to be ecstatically happy I will not claim. But that it can be lived in quiet content, accepting resignedly what cannot be helped, not expecting the impossible, and thankful for small mercies, this I would maintain. That it will be difficult for men in general to learn this lesson I do not deny. But that it will be impossible I would not admit since so many have learned it already.

Man has not yet grown up. He is not adult. Like a child he cries for the moon and lives in a world of fantasies. And the race as a whole has perhaps reached the great crisis of its life. Can it grow up as a race in the same sense as individual men grow up? Can man put away childish things and adolescent dreams? Can he grasp the real world as it actually is, stark and bleak, without its romantic or religious halo, and still retain his ideals, striving for great ends and noble achievements? If he can, all may yet be well. If he cannot, he will probably sink back into the savagery and brutality from which he came, taking a humble place once more among the lower animals.

C. S. LEWIS

Clive Staples Lewis (1898–1963) was for most of his life a Fellow and Tutor at Magdalen College, Oxford, and was universally admired in academic circles for his work on medieval and renaissance English literature. But his interests carried his name far beyond the University. He was also an accomplished lecturer, writer of children's books, novelist, moralist, and, of primary concern to us here, apologist for religion. He gave up Christianity at about fourteen but later embraced the Anglican faith. "I didn't want to," he once said. "I'm not in the least the religious type. I

want to be let alone, to feel I'm my own master; but since the facts seemed to be just the opposite, I had to give in." He records the spiritual history of his early years in Surprised by Joy *(1955). The Screwtape Letters originally appeared in serial form in* The Guardian *and was published as a book in 1942. It consists of thirty-one letters in a one-way correspondence from a devil to his willing but ignorant nephew-in-training. In it Lewis presents his religious thinking, though with the evident special talents of the novelist and student of satire and allegory. The eighth and ninth letters are reprinted here from the text published by Geoffrey Bles in 1961. Among Lewis's many other books are* The Pilgrim's Regress *(1933),* The Allegory of Love *(1936),* Christian Behavior *(1943),* The Abolition of Man *(1943),* Perelandra *(1944),* English Literature in the Sixteenth Century *(1954),* An Experiment in Criticism *(1961), and* The Discarded Image *(1964).*

SCREWTAPE LETTERS 8 AND 9

8

My dear Wormwood,

So you "have great hopes that the patient's religious phase is dying away", have you? I always thought the Training College had gone to pieces since they put old Slubgob at the head of it, and now I am sure. Has no one ever told you about the law of Undulation?

Humans are amphibians—half spirit and half animal. (The Enemy's determination to produce such a revolting hybrid was one of the things that determined Our Father to withdraw his support from Him.) As spirits they belong to the eternal world, but as animals they inhabit time. This means that while their spirit can be directed to an eternal object, their bodies, passions, and imaginations are in continual change, for to be in time means to change. Their nearest approach to constancy, therefore, is undulation—the repeated return to a level from which they repeatedly fall back, a series of troughs and peaks. If you had watched your patient carefully you would have seen this undulation in every department of his life—his interest in his work, his affection for his friends, his physical appetites, all go up and down. As long as he lives on earth periods of emotional and bodily richness and liveliness will alternate with periods of numbness and poverty. The dryness and dullness through which your patient is now going are not, as you fondly suppose, your workmanship; they are merely a natural phenomenon which will do us no good unless you make a good use of it.

To decide what the best use of it is, you must ask what use the Enemy wants to make of it, and then do the opposite. Now it may surprise you to learn that in His efforts to get permanent possession of a soul, He relies on the troughs even more than on the peaks; some of His special favourites have gone through longer and deeper troughs than anyone else. The reason is this. To us a human is primarily food; our aim is the absorption of its will into ours, the increase of our own area of selfhood at its expense. But the obedience which the Enemy demands of men is quite a different thing. One must face the fact that all the talk about His love for men, and His service being perfect freedom, is not (as one would gladly believe) mere propaganda, but an appalling truth. He really *does* want to fill the universe with a lot of loathsome little replicas of Himself—creatures whose life, on its miniature scale, will be qualitatively like His own, not because He has absorbed them but because their wills freely conform to His. We want cattle who can finally become food; He wants servants who can finally become sons. We want to suck in, He wants to give out. We are empty and would be filled; He is full and flows over. Our war aim is a world in which Our Father Below has drawn all other beings into himself: the Enemy wants a world full of beings united to Him but still distinct.

And that is where the troughs come in. You must have often wondered why the Enemy does not make more use of His power to be sensibly present to human souls in any degree He chooses and at any moment. But you now see that the Irresistible and the Indisputable are the two weapons which the very nature of His scheme forbids Him to use. Merely to over-ride a human will (as His felt presence in any but the faintest and most mitigated degree would certainly do) would be for Him useless. He cannot ravish. He can only woo. For His ignoble idea is to eat the cake and have it; the creatures are to be one with Him, but yet themselves; merely to cancel them, or assimilate them, will not serve. He is prepared to do a little over-riding at the beginning. He will set them off with communications of His presence which, though faint, seem great to them, with emotional sweetness, and easy conquest over temptation. But He never allows this state of affairs to last long. Sooner or later He withdraws, if not in fact, at least from their conscious experience, all those supports and incentives. He leaves the creature to stand up on its own legs—to carry out from the will alone duties which have lost all relish. It is during such trough periods, much more than during the peak periods, that it is growing into the sort of creature He wants it to be. Hence the prayers offered in the state of dryness are those which please Him best. We can drag our patients along by continual tempting, because we design them only for the table, and the more their will is interfered with the better. He cannot "tempt" to virtue as we do to vice. He wants them to learn to walk and must therefore take away His hand; and if only the will to walk is really here He is pleased even with their stumbles. Do not be deceived, Wormwood. Our cause is never more in danger than when a human, no longer desiring, but still intending, to do our Enemy's will, looks round upon a universe from which every trace of Him seems to have vanished, and asks why he has been forsaken, and still obeys.

But of course the troughs afford opportunities to our side also. Next week I will give you some hints on how to exploit them,

Your affectionate uncle
Screwtape

9

My dear Wormwood,

I hope my last letter has convinced you that the trough of dullness or "dryness" through which your patient is going at present will not, of itself, give you his soul, but needs to be properly exploited. What forms the exploitation should take I will now consider.

In the first place I have always found that the Trough periods of the human undulation provide excellent opportunity for all sensual temptations, particularly those of sex. This may surprise you, because, of course, there is more physical energy, and therefore more potential appetite, at the Peak periods; but you must remember that the powers of resistance are then also at their highest. The health and spirits which you want to use in producing lust can also, alas, be very easily used for work or play or thought or innocuous merriment. The attack has a much better chance of success when the man's whole inner world is drab and cold and empty. And it is also to be noted that the Trough sexuality is subtly different in quality from that of the Peak—much less likely to lead to the milk and water phenomenon which the humans call "being in love", much more easily drawn into perversions, much less contaminated by those generous and imaginative and even spiritual concomitants which often render human sexuality so disappointing. It is the same with other desires of the flesh. You are much more likely to make your man a sound drunkard by pressing drink on him as an anodyne when he is dull and weary than by encouraging him to use it as a means of merriment among his friends when he is happy and expansive. Never forget that when we are dealing with any pleasure in its healthy and normal and satisfying form, we are, in a sense, on the Enemy's ground. I know we have won many a soul through pleasure. All the same, it is His invention, not ours. He made the pleasures: all our research so far has not enabled us to produce one. All we can do is to encourage the humans to take the pleasures which our Enemy has produced, at times, or in ways, or in degrees, which He has forbidden. Hence we always try to work away from the natural condition of any pleasure to that in which it is least natural, least redolent of its Maker, and least pleasurable. An ever increasing craving for an ever diminishing pleasure is the formula. It is more certain; and it's better *style*. To get the man's soul and give him *nothing* in return—that is what really gladdens our Father's heart. And the troughs are the time for beginning the process.

But there is an even better way of exploiting the Trough; I mean through the patient's own thoughts about it. As always, the first step is to keep knowledge out of his mind. Do not let him suspect the law of undulation. Let him assume that the first ardours of his conversion might have been expected to last, and ought to have lasted, forever, and that his present dryness is an equally permanent condition. Having once got this misconception well fixed in his head, you may then proceed in various ways. It all depends on whether your man is of the desponding type who can be tempted to despair, or of the wishful-thinking type who can be assured that all is well. The former type is getting rare among the humans. If your patient should happen to belong to it, everything is easy. You have only got to keep him out of the way of experienced Christians (an easy task now-a-days), to direct his attention to the appropriate passages in scripture, and then to set him to work on the desperate design of recovering his old feelings by sheer will-power, and the game is ours. If he is of the more hopeful type your job is to make him acquiesce in the present low temperature of his spirit and gradually become content with it, persuading himself that it is not so low after all. In a week or two you will be making him doubt whether the first days of his Christianity were not, perhaps, a little excessive. Talk to him about "moderation in all things". If you can once get him to the point of thinking that "religion is all very well up to a point", you can feel quite happy about his soul. A moderated religion is as good for us as no religion at all—and more amusing.

Another possibility is that of direct attack on his faith. When you have caused him to assume that the trough is permanent, can you not persuade him that "his religious phase" is just going to die away like all his previous phases? Of course there is no conceivable way of getting by reason from the proposition "I am losing interest in this" to the proposition "This is false". But, as I said before, it is jargon, not reason, you must rely on. The mere word *phase* will very likely do the trick. I assume that the creature has been through several of them before—they all have—and that he always feels superior and patronising to the ones he has emerged from, not because he has really criticized them but simply because they are in the past. (You keep him well fed on hazy ideas of Progress and Development and the Historical Point of View, I trust, and give him lots of modern Biographies to read? The people in them are always emerging from Phases, aren't they?)

You see the idea? Keep his mind off the plain antithesis between True and False. Nice shadowy expressions—"It was a phase"—"I've been through all that"—and don't forget the blessed word "Adolescent",

Your affectionate uncle
Screwtape

ALBERT CAMUS

THE UNBELIEVER AND CHRISTIANS

Camus made the following statement at the Dominican Monastery of Latour-Maubourg in 1948. The English translation by Justin O'Brien appears in Resistance, Rebellion, and Death *(New York, 1960). For information about the author and his writings, see page 261.*

•

Inasmuch as you have been so kind as to invite a man who does not share your convictions to come and answer the very general question that you are raising in these conversations, before telling you what I think unbelievers expect of Christians, I should like first to acknowledge your intellectual generosity by stating a few principles.

First, there is a lay pharisaism in which I shall strive not to indulge. To me a lay pharisee is the person who pretends to believe that Christianity is an easy thing and asks of the Christian, on the basis of an external view of Christianity, more than he asks of himself. I believe indeed that the Christian has many obligations but that it is not up to the man who rejects them himself to recall their existence to anyone who has already accepted them. If there is anyone who can ask anything of the Christian, it is the Christian himself. The conclusion is that if I allowed myself at the end of this statement to demand of you certain duties, these could only be duties that it is essential to ask of any man today, whether he is or is not a Christian.

Secondly, I wish to declare also that, not feeling that I possess any absolute truth or any message, I shall never start from the supposition that Christian truth is illusory, but merely from the fact that I could not accept it. As an illustration of this position, I am willing to confess this: Three years ago a controversy made me argue against one among you, and not the least formidable. The fever of those years, the painful memory of two or three friends assassinated had given me the courage to do so. Yet I can assure you that, despite some excessive expressions on the part of François Mauriac, I have not ceased meditating on what he said. At the end of this reflection—and in this way I give you my opinion as to the usefulness of the dialogue between believer and unbeliever—I have come to admit to myself, and now to admit publicly here, that for the fundamentals and on the precise point of our controversy François Mauriac got the better of me.

Having said that, it will be easier for me to state my third and last principle. It is simple and obvious. I shall not try to change anything that I think or anything that you think (insofar as I can judge of it) in order to reach a reconciliation that would be agreeable to all. On the contrary, what I feel like telling you today is that the world needs real dialogue, that falsehood is just as much the opposite of dialogue as is silence, and that the only possible dialogue is the kind between people who remain what they are and speak their minds. This is tantamount to saying that the world of today needs Christians who remain Christians. The other day at the Sorbonne, speaking to a Marxist lecturer, a Catholic priest said in public that he too was anticlerical. Well, I don't like priests who are anticlerical any more than philosophers that are ashamed of themselves. Hence I shall not, as far as I am concerned, try to pass myself off as a Christian in your presence. I share with you the same revulsion from evil. But I do not share your hope, and I continue to struggle against this universe in which children suffer and die.

. . .

And why shouldn't I say here what I have written elsewhere? For a long time during those frightful years I have waited for a great voice to speak up in Rome. I, an unbeliever? Precisely. For I knew that the spirit would be lost if it did not utter a cry of condemnation when faced with force. It seems that that voice did speak up. But I assure you that millions of men like me did not hear it and that at that time believers and unbelievers alike shared a solitude that continued to spread as the days went by and the executioners multiplied.

It has been explained to me since that the condemnation was indeed voiced. But that it was in the style of the encyclicals, which is not at all clear. The condemnation was voiced and it was not understood! Who could fail to feel where the true condemnation lies in this case and to see that this example by itself gives part of the reply, perhaps the whole reply, that you ask of me. What the world expects of Christians is that Christians should speak out loud and clear, and that they should voice their condemnation in such a way that never a doubt, never the slightest doubt, could rise in the heart of the simplest man. That they should get away from abstraction and confront the blood-stained face history has taken on today. The grouping we need is a grouping of men resolved to speak out clearly and to pay up personally. When a Spanish bishop blesses political executions, he ceases to be a bishop or a Christian or even a man; he is a dog just like the one who, backed by an ideology, orders that execution without doing the dirty work himself. We are still waiting, and I am waiting, for a grouping of all those who refuse to be dogs and are resolved to pay the price that must be paid so that man can be something more than a dog.

. . .

And now, what can Christians do for us?

To begin with, give up the empty quarrels, the first of which is the quarrel about pessimism. I believe, for instance, that M. Gabriel Marcel would be well advised to leave alone certain forms of thought that fascinate him and lead him astray. M. Marcel cannot call himself a democrat and at the same time ask for a prohibition of Sartre's play. This is a position that is tiresome for everyone. What M. Marcel wants is to defend absolute values, such as modesty and man's divine truth, when the things that should be defended are the few provisional values that will allow M. Marcel to continue fighting someday, and comfortably, for those absolute values. . . .

By what right, moreover, could a Christian or a Marxist accuse me, for example, of pessimism? I was not the one to invent the misery of the human being or the terrifying formulas of divine malediction. I was not the one to shout *Nemo bonus* or the damnation of unbaptized children. I was not the one who said that man was incapable of saving himself by his own means and that in the depths of his degradation his only hope was in the grace of God. And as for the famous Marxist optimism! No one has carried distrust of man further, and ultimately the economic fatalities of this universe seem more terrible than divine whims.

Christians and Communists will tell me that their optimism is based on a longer range, that it is superior to all the rest, and that God or history, according to the individual is the satisfying end-product of their dialectic. I can indulge in the same reasoning. If Christianity is pessimistic as to man, it is optimistic as to human destiny. Well, I can say that, pessimistic as to human destiny, I am optimistic as to man. And not in the name of a humanism that always seemed to me to fall short, but in the name of an ignorance that tries to negate nothing.

This means that the words "pessimism" and "optimism" need to be clearly defined and that, until we can do so, we must pay attention to what unites us rather than to what separates us.

. . .

That, I believe, is all I had to say. We are faced with evil. And, as for me, I feel rather as Augustine did before becoming a Christian when he said: "I tried to find the source of evil and I got nowhere." But it is also true that I, and a few others, know what must be done, if not to reduce evil, at least not to add to it. Perhaps we cannot prevent this world from being a world in which children are tortured. But we can reduce the number of tortured children. And if you don't help us, who else in the world can help us do this?

Between the forces of terror and the forces of dialogue, a great unequal battle has begun. I have nothing but reasonable illusions as to the outcome of that battle. But I believe it must be fought, and I know that certain men at least have resolved to do so. I merely fear that they will occasionally feel somewhat alone, that they are in fact alone, and that after an interval of two thousand years we may see the sacrifice of Socrates repeated several times. The program for the future is either a permanent dialogue or the solemn and significant putting to death of any who have experienced dialogue. After having contributed my reply, the question that I ask Christians is this: "Will Socrates still be alone and is there nothing in him and in your doctrine that urges you to join us?"

It may be, I am well aware, that Christianity will answer negatively. Oh, not by your mouths, I am convinced. But it may be, and this is even more probable, that Christianity will insist on maintaining a compromise or else on giving its condemnations the obscure form of the encyclical. Possibly it will insist on losing once and for all the virtue of revolt and indignation that belonged to it long ago. In that case Christians will live and Christianity will die. In that case the others will in fact pay for the sacrifice. In any case such a future is not within my province to decide, despite all the hope and anguish it awakens in me. I can speak only of what I know. And what I know—which sometimes creates a deep longing in me—is that if Christians made up their minds to it, millions of voices—millions, I say—throughout the world would be added to the appeal of a handful of isolated individuals who, without any sort of affiliation, today intercede almost everywhere and ceaselessly for children and for men.

ALDOUS HUXLEY

THE *BHAGAVAD GITA* AND THE PERENNIAL PHILOSOPHY

The following essay first appeared as the Introduction to Swami Prabhavananda and Christopher Isherwood's translation of the Bhagavad Gita *(1944). For information about Huxley and his writing, see page 25.*

•

More than twenty-five centuries have passed since that which has been called the Perennial Philosophy was first committed to writing; and in the course of those centuries it has found expression, now partial, now complete, now in this form, now in that, again and again. In Vedanta and Hebrew prophecy, in the Tao Teh King and the Platonic dialogues, in the Gospel according to St. John and Mahayana theology, in Plotinus and the Areopagite, among the Persian Sufis and the Christian mystics of the Middle Ages and the Renaissance—the Perennial Philosophy has spoken almost all the languages of Asia and Europe and has made use of the terminology and traditions of every one of the higher religions. But under all this confusion of tongues and myths, of local histories and particularist doctrines, there remains a Highest Common Factor, which is the Perennial Philosophy in what may be called its chemically pure state. This final purity can never, of course, be expressed by any verbal statement of the philosophy, however undogmatic that statement may be, however deliberately syncretistic. The very fact that it is set down at a certain time by a certain writer, using this or that language, automatically imposes a certain sociological and personal bias on the doctrines so formulated. It is only in the act of contemplation, when words and even personality are transcended, that the pure state of the Perennial Philosophy can actually be known. The records left by those who have known it in this way make it abundantly clear that all of them, whether Hindu, Buddhist, Hebrew, Taoist, Christian or Mohammedan, were attempting to describe the same essentially indescribable Fact.

The original scriptures of most religions are poetical and unsystematic. Theology, which generally takes the form of a reasoned commentary on the parables and aphorisms of the scriptures, tends to make its appearance at a later stage of religious history. The Bhagavad Gita occupies an intermediate position between scripture and theology; for it combines the poetical qualities of the first with the clear-cut methodicalness of the second. The book may be described, writes Ananda K. Coomaraswamy in his admirable 'Hinduism and Buddhism,' "as a compendium of the whole Vedic doctrine to be found in the earlier Vedas, Brahmanas and Upanishads, and being therefore the basis of all the later developments, it can be regarded as the focus of all Indian religion." But this 'focus of Indian religion' is also one of the clearest and most comprehensive summaries of the Perennial Philosophy ever to have been made. Hence its enduring value, not only for Indians, but for all mankind.

At the core of the Perennial Philosophy we find four fundamental doctrines.

First: the phenomenal world of matter and of individualized consciousness—the world of things and animals and men and even gods—is the manifestation of a Divine Ground within which all partial realities have their being, and apart from which they would be nonexistent.

Second: human beings are capable not merely of knowing *about* the Divine Ground by inference; they can also realize its existence by a direct intuition, superior to discursive reasoning. This immediate knowledge unites the knower with that which is known.

Third: man possesses a double nature, a phenomenal ego and an eternal Self, which is the inner man, the spirit, the spark of divinity within the soul. It is possible for a man, if he so desires, to identify himself with the spirit and therefore with the Divine Ground, which is of the same or like nature with the spirit.

Fourth: man's life on earth has only one end and purpose: to identify himself with his eternal Self and so to come to unitive knowledge of the Divine Ground.

In Hinduism the first of these four doctrines is stated in the most categorical terms. The Divine Ground is Brahman, whose creative, sustaining and transforming aspects are manifested in the Hindu trinity. A hierarchy of manifestations connects inanimate matter with man, gods, High Gods and the undifferentiated Godhead beyond.

In Mahayana Buddhism the Divine Ground is called Mind or the Pure Light of the Void, the place of the High Gods is taken by the Dhyani-Buddhas.

Similar conceptions are perfectly compatible with Christianity and have in fact been entertained, explicitly or implicitly, by many Catholic and Protestant mystics, when formulating a philosophy to fit facts observed by super-rational intuition. Thus, for Eckhart and Ruysbroeck, there is an Abyss of Godhead underlying the Trinity, just as Brahman underlies

Brahma, Vishnu and Shiva. Suso has even left a diagrammatic picture of the relations subsisting between Godhead, triune God and creatures. In this very curious and interesting drawing a chain of manifestation connects the mysterious symbol of the Divine Ground with the three Persons of the Trinity, and the Trinity in turn is connected in a descending scale with angels and human beings. These last, as the drawing vividly shows, may make one of two choices. They can either lead the life of the outer man, the life of separative selfhood; in which case they are lost (for, in the words of the Theologia Germanica, 'nothing burns in hell but the self'). Or else they can identify themselves with the inner man, in which case it becomes possible for them, as Suso shows, to ascend again, through unitive knowledge, to the Trinity and even, beyond the Trinity, to the ultimate Unity of the Divine Ground.

Within the Mohammedan tradition such a rationalization of the immediate mystical experience would have been dangerously unorthodox. Nevertheless, one has the impression, while reading certain Sufi texts, that their authors did in fact conceive of *al haqq*, the Real, as being the Divine Ground or Unity of Allah, underlying the active and personal aspects of the Godhead.

The second doctrine of the Perennial Philosophy—that it is possible to know the Divine Ground by a direct intuition higher than discursive reasoning—is to be found in all the great religions of the world. A philosopher who is content merely to know about the ultimate Reality— theoretically and by hearsay—is compared by Buddha to a herdsman of other men's cows. Mohammed uses an even homelier barnyard metaphor. For him the philosopher who has not realized his metaphysics is just an ass bearing a load of books. Christian, Hindu and Taoist teachers write no less emphatically about the absurd pretensions of mere learning and analytical reasoning. In the words of the Anglican Prayer Book, our eternal life, now and hereafter, 'stands in the knowledge of God'; and this knowledge is not discursive but 'of the heart,' a super-rational intuition, direct, synthetic and timeless.

The third doctrine of the Perennial Philosophy, that which affirms the double nature of man, is fundamental in all the higher religions. The unitive knowledge of the Divine Ground has, as its necessary condition, self-abnegation and charity. Only by means of self-abnegation and charity can we clear away the evil, folly and ignorance which constitute the thing we call our personality and prevent us from becoming aware of the spark of divinity illuminating the inner man. But the spark within is akin to the Divine Ground. By identifying ourselves with the first we can come to unitive knowledge of the second. These empirical facts of the spiritual life have been variously rationalized in terms of the theologies of the various religions. The Hindus categorically affirm that thou art That—that the indwelling Atman is the same as Brahman. For orthodox Christianity there is not an identity between the spark and God. Union of the human spirit with God takes place—union so complete that the word 'deification' is applied to it; but it is not the union of identical substances. According to Christian theology, the saint is 'deified,' not because Atman *is* Brahman, but because God has assimilated the purified human spirit into the divine substance by an act of grace. Islamic theology seems to make a similar distinction. The Sufi, Mansur, was executed for giving to the words 'union' and 'deification' the literal meaning which they bear in the Hindu tradition. For our present purposes, however, the significant fact is that these words are actually used by Christians and Mohammedans to describe the empirical facts of metaphysical realization by means of direct, super-rational intuition.

In regard to man's final end, all the higher religions are in complete agreement. The purpose of human life is the discovery of Truth, the unitive knowledge of the Godhead. The degree to which this unitive knowledge is achieved here on earth determines the degree to which it will be enjoyed in the posthumous state. Contemplation of truth is the end, action the means. In India, in China, in ancient Greece, in Christian Europe, this was regarded as the most obvious and axiomatic piece of orthodoxy. The invention of the steam engine produced a revolution, not merely in industrial techniques, but also and much more significantly in philosophy. Because machines could be made progressively more and more efficient, Western man came to believe that men and societies would automatically register a corresponding moral and spiritual improvement. Attention and allegiance came to be paid, not to Eternity, but to the Utopian future. External circumstances came to be regarded as more important than states of mind about external circumstances, and the end of human life was held to be action, with contemplation as a means to that end. These false and, historically, aberrant and heretical doctrines are now systematically taught in our schools and repeated, day in, day out, by those anonymous writers of advertising copy who, more than any other teachers, provide European and American adults with their current philosophy of life. And so effective has been the propaganda that even professing Christians accept the heresy unquestioningly and are quite unconscious of its complete incompatibility with their own or anybody else's religion.

These four doctrines constitute the Perennial Philosophy in its minimal and basic form. A man who can practice what the Indians call Jnana yoga (the metaphysical discipline of discrimination between the real and the apparent) asks for nothing more. This simple working hypothesis is enough for his purposes. But such discrimination is exceedingly difficult and can hardly be practiced, at any rate in the preliminary stages of the spiritual life, except by persons endowed with a particular kind of mental constitution. That is why most statements of the Perennial Philosophy have included another doctrine, affirming the existence of one or more human Incarnations of the Divine Ground, by whose mediation and grace the worshipper is helped to achieve his goal—that unitive knowledge of the Godhead, which is man's eternal life and beatitude. The Bhagavad Gita is one such statement. Here, Krishna is an Incarnation of the Divine Ground in human form. Similarly, in Christian and Buddhist theology, Jesus and Gotama are Incarnations of divinity. But whereas in Hinduism and Buddhism more than one Incarnation of the Godhead is possible (and is regarded as having in fact taken place) for Christians there has been and can be only one.

An Incarnation of the Godhead and, to a lesser degree, any theocentric saint, sage or prophet is a human being who knows Who he is and can therefore effectively remind other human beings of what they have allowed themselves to forget: namely, that if they choose to become what potentially they already are, they too can be eternally united with the Divine Ground.

Worship of the Incarnation and contemplation of his attributes are for most men and women the best preparation for unitive knowledge of the Godhead. But whether the actual knowledge itself can be achieved by this means is another question. Many Catholic mystics have affirmed that, at a certain stage of that contemplative prayer in which, according to the most authoritative theologians, the life of Christian perfection ultimately consists, it is necessary to put aside all thoughts of the Incarnation as distracting from the higher knowledge of that which has been incarnated. From this fact have arisen misunderstandings in plenty and a number of intellectual difficulties. Here, for example, is what Abbot John Chapman writes in one of his admirable Spiritual Letters. "The problem of *reconciling* (not merely uniting) mysticism with Christianity is more difficult. The Abbot (Abbot Marmion) says that St. John of the Cross is like a sponge full of Christianity. You can squeeze it all out, and the full mystical theory remains. Consequently fifteen years or so I hated St. John of the Cross and called him a Buddhist. I loved St. Teresa, and read her over and over again. She is first a Christian, only secondarily a mystic. Then I found that I had wasted fifteen years, so far as prayer was concerned." And yet, he concludes, in spite of its 'Buddhistic' character, the practice of mysticism (or, to put it in other terms, the realization of the Perennial Philosophy) makes good Christians. He might have added that it also makes good Hindus, good Buddhists, good Taoists, good Moslems and good Jews.

The solution to Abbot Chapman's problem must be sought in the domain, not of philosophy, but of psychology. Human beings are not born identical. There are many different temperaments and constitutions; and within each psycho-physical class one can find people at very different stages of spiritual development. Forms of worship and spiritual discipline which may be valuable for one individual may be useless or even positively harmful for another belonging to a different class and standing, within that class, at a lower or higher level of development. All this is clearly set forth in the Gita, where the psychological facts are linked up with general cosmology by means of the postulate of the *gunas*. Krishna, who is here the mouthpiece of Hinduism in all its manifestations, finds it perfectly natural that different men should have different methods and even apparently different objects of worship. All roads lead to Rome—provided, of course, that it is Rome and not some other city which the traveller really wishes to reach. A similar attitude of charitable inclusiveness, somewhat surprising in a Moslem, is beautifully expressed in the parable of Moses and the Shepherd, told by Jalaluddin Rumi in the second book of the Masnavi. And within the more exclusive Christian tradition these problems of temperament and degree of development have been searchingly discussed in their relation to the way of Mary and the way of Martha in general, and in particular to the vocation and private devotions of individuals.

We now have to consider the ethical corollaries of the Perennial Philosophy. "Truth," says St. Thomas Aquinas, "is the last end for the entire universe, and the contemplation of truth is the chief occupation of wisdom." The moral virtues, he says in another place, belong to contemplation, not indeed essentially, but as a necessary predisposition. Virtue, in other words, is not the end, but the indispensable means to the knowledge of divine reality. Shankara, the greatest of the Indian commentators on the Gita, holds the same doctrine. Right action is the way to knowledge; for it purifies the mind, and it is only to a mind purified from egotism that the intuition of the Divine Ground can come.

Self-abnegation, according to the Gita, can be achieved by the practice of two all-inclusive virtues—love and non-attachment. The latter is the same thing as that 'holy indifference,' of which St. François de Sales is never tired of insisting. "He who refers every action to God," writes Camus, summarizing his master's teaching, "and has no aims save His Glory, will find rest everywhere, even amidst the most violent commotions." So long as we practice this holy indifference to the fruits of action, "no lawful occupation will separate us from God; on the contrary, it can be made a means of closer union." Here the word 'lawful' supplies a necessary qualification to a teaching which, without it, is incomplete and even potentially dangerous. Some actions are intrinsically evil or inexpedient; and no good intentions, no conscious offering of them to God, no renunciation of the fruits can alter their essential character. Holy indifference requires to be taught in conjunction not merely with a set of commandments prohibiting crimes, but also with a clear conception of what in Buddha's Eightfold Path is called 'right livelihood.' Thus, for the Buddhist, right livelihood was incompatible with the making of deadly weapons and of intoxicants; for the mediaeval Christian, with the taking of interest and with various monopolistic practices which have since come to be regarded as legitimate good business. John Woolman, the American Quaker, provides a most enlightening example of the way in which a man may live in the world, while practicing perfect non-attachment and remaining acutely sensitive to the claims of right livelihood. Thus, while it would have been profitable and perfectly lawful for him to sell West Indian sugar and rum to the customers who came to his shop, Woolman refrained from doing so, because these things were the products of slave labour. Similarly, when he was in England, it would have been both lawful and convenient for him to travel by stage coach. Nevertheless, he preferred to make his journeys on foot. Why? Because the comforts of rapid travel could only be bought at the expense of great cruelty to the horses and the most atrocious working conditions for the post-boys. In Woolman's eyes, such a system of transportation was intrinsically undesirable, and no amount of personal non-attachment could make it anything but undesirable. So he shouldered his knapsack and walked.

In the preceding pages I have tried to show that the Perennial Philosophy and its ethical corollaries constitute a Highest Common Factor, present in all the major religions of the world. To affirm this truth has never been more imperatively necessary than at the present time. There will never be enduring peace unless and until human beings come to accept a philosophy of life more adequate to the cosmic and psychological facts than the insane idolatries of nationalism and the advertising man's apocalyptic faith in Progress towards a mechanized New Jerusalem. All the elements of this philosophy are present, as we have seen, in the traditional religions. But in existing circumstances there is not the slightest chance that any of the traditional religions will obtain universal acceptance. Europeans and Americans will see no reason for being converted to Hinduism, say, or Buddhism. And the people of Asia can hardly be expected to renounce their own traditions for the Christianity professed, often sincerely, by the imperialists who, for four hundred years and more, have been systematically attacking, exploiting and oppressing, and are now trying to finish off the work of destruction by 'educating' them. But happily there is the Highest Common Factor of all religions, the Perennial Philosophy which has always and everywhere been the metaphysical system of the prophets, saints and sages. It is perfectly possible for people to remain good Christians, Hindus, Buddhists or Moslems and yet to be united in full agreement on the basic doctrines of the Perennial Philosophy.

The Bhagavad Gita is perhaps the most systematic scriptural statement of the Perennial Philosophy. To a world at war, a world that, because it lacks the intellectual and spiritual prerequisites to peace, can only hope to patch up some kind of precarious armed truce, it stands pointing, clearly and unmistakably, to the only road of escape from the self-imposed necessity of self-destruction. For this reason we should be grateful to Swami Prabhavananda and Mr. Isherwood for having given us this new version of the book—a version which can be read, not merely without that dull aesthetic pain inflicted by all too many English translations from the Sanskrit, but positively with enjoyment.

The Responsibility
of the Scientist

The atomic bombing of Hiroshima and Nagasaki by the United States in 1945 began a new era of passionate thought concerning the ethical problems of science. Atomic warfare rudely upset the security of such ideas as "disinterested research." It became suddenly more difficult for many scientists to pursue "pure" research, secure from responsibility for its ultimate practical applications. The paradoxical capacity of science for good and for evil had, of course, long before become apparent to civilized man. The only difference was well described by the British scientist Jacob Bronowski in his *Science and Human Values:* "Nothing happened in 1945 except that we changed the scale of our indifference to man; and conscience, in revenge, for an instant became immediate to us."

The first three documents we present in this section—by Einstein, Szilard, and Wiener—dramatize sharply the crisis of civic duty and conscience experienced by many scientists in the war years and after. Ridenour, specifically answering Wiener, vigorously argues for the validity of both disinterested research and military preparedness, and against the notion that scientists have any special long-term moral responsibility. Bronowski offers further analysis of these issues, attempting to define the proper roles of scientists, citizens, and governments. Haybittle renews the case for the scientist's special responsibility and opens another question: To what extent can science itself offer guidance in moral problems? Weiss's essay makes the affirmative case for the humaneness of the "scientific spirit." Most of the concrete discussions of science in these essays are by physicists and deal particularly with atomic science because the "philosophical" literature in this field is unusually rich. We trust that the reader will have no difficulty in transposing the arguments into terms of the slower but no less spectacular explosions in biology and in the behavioral sciences that are taking place even now.

ALBERT EINSTEIN

Einstein (1879–1955), the twentieth century's greatest scientist, was an ardent pacifist. Nevertheless, he felt it his duty to send a letter to President Franklin D. Roosevelt in 1939, informing him of the possibilities of nuclear warfare. The letter was drafted by Leo Szilard and delivered by Alexander Sachs, an economist with ready access to the President. It ultimately led to the government's atomic bomb project. We have taken the text of the letter from The Atomic Age, *ed. Morton Grodzins and Eugene Rabino-witch (New York, 1963).*

LETTER TO
PRESIDENT ROOSEVELT

August 2, 1939

F. D. Roosevelt
President of the United States
White House
Washington, D.C.

Sir:

Some recent work by E. Fermi and L. Szilard, which has been communicated to me in manuscript, leads me to expect that the element uranium may be turned into a new and important source of energy in the immediate future. Certain aspects of the situation which has arisen seem to call for watchfulness and, if necessary, quick action on the part of the Administration. I believe therefore that it is my duty to bring to your attention the following facts and recommendations:

In the course of the last four months it has been made probable—

through the work of Joliot in France as well as Fermi and Szilard in America—that it may become possible to set up a nuclear chain reaction in a large mass of uranium, by which vast amounts of power and large quantities of new radium-like elements would be generated. Now it appears almost certain that this could be achieved in the immediate future.

This new phenomenon would also lead to the construction of bombs, and it is conceivable—though much less certain—that extremely powerful bombs of a new type may thus be constructed. A single bomb of this type, carried by boat and exploded in a port, might very well destroy the whole port together with some of the surrounding territory. However, such bombs might very well prove to be too heavy for transportation by air.

The United States has only very poor ores of uranium in moderate quantities. There is some good ore in Canada and the former Czechoslovakia, while the most important source of uranium is Belgian Congo.

In view of this situation you may think it desirable to have some permanent contact maintained between the Administration and the group of physicists working on chain reactions in America. One possible way of achieving this might be for you to entrust with this task a person who has your confidence and who could perhaps serve in an inofficial capacity. His task might comprise the following:

a) to approach Government Departments, keep them informed of the further development, and put forward recommendations for Government action, giving particular attention to the problem of securing a supply of uranium ore for the United States;

b) to speed up the experimental work, which is at present being carried on within the limits of the budgets of University laboratories, by providing funds, if such funds be required, through his contacts with private persons who are willing to make contributions for this cause, and perhaps also by obtaining the co-operation of industrial laboratories which have the necessary equipment.

I understand that Germany has actually stopped the sale of uranium from the Czechoslovakian mines which she has taken over. That she should have taken such early action might perhaps be understood on the ground that the son of the German Under-Secretary of State, von Weizsäcker, is attached to the Kaiser-Wilhelm-Institut in Berlin where some of the American work on uranium is now being repeated.

Yours very truly,

(signed) ALBERT EINSTEIN

LEO SZILARD

Szilard (1898–1964) was one of the great physicists of the century. Born in Hungary, he received the Ph.D. from the University of Berlin in 1922. When Hitler came to power in 1933, he went to Vienna, then to London, and in 1938 came to the United States. With Enrico Fermi he created the first nuclear chain reaction in 1942, and was among the first scientists to urge the government to produce an atomic bomb. After the bomb was made, however, he sought to prevent its military use. A number of fruitless attempts resulted finally in his circulating this petition, which was signed by sixty-nine scientists. It arrived in the office of the Secretary of War after the final decision had been made to drop the first two bombs. Szilard's petition and Secretary Stimson's article in explanation, "The Decision to Use the Atomic Bomb," may be found in the volume The Atomic Age, *ed. M. Grodzins and E. Rabinowitch (New York, 1963).*

A PETITION TO THE PRESIDENT OF THE UNITED STATES

July 17, 1945

Discoveries of which the people of the United States are not aware may affect the welfare of this nation in the near future. The liberation of atomic power which has been achieved places atomic bombs in the hands of the Army. It places in your hands, as Commander-in-Chief, the fateful decision whether or not to sanction the use of such bombs in the present phase of the war against Japan.

We, the undersigned scientists, have been working in the field of atomic power. Until recently we have had to fear that the United States might be attacked by atomic bombs during this war and that her only defense might lie in a counterattack by the same means. Today, with the defeat of Germany, this danger is averted and we feel impelled to say what follows:

The war has to be brought speedily to a successful conclusion and attacks by atomic bombs may very well be an effective method of warfare. We feel, however, that such attacks on Japan could not be justified, at least not unless the terms which will be imposed after the war on Japan were made public in detail and Japan were given an opportunity to surrender.

If such public announcement gave assurance to the Japanese that they could look forward to a life devoted to peaceful pursuits in their homeland and if Japan still refused to surrender, our nation might then, in certain circumstances, find itself forced to resort to the use of atomic bombs. Such a step, however, ought not to be made at any time without seriously considering the moral responsibilities which are involved.

The development of atomic power will provide the nations with new means of destruction. The atomic bombs at our disposal represent only the first step in this direction and there is almost no limit to the destructive power which will become available in the course of their future development. Thus a nation which sets the precedent of using these newly liberated forces of nature for purposes of destruction may have to bear the responsibility of opening the door to an era of devastation on an unimaginable scale.

If after this war a situation is allowed to develop in the world which permits rival powers to be in uncontrolled possession of these new means of destruction, the cities of the United States as well as the cities of other nations will be in continuous danger of sudden annihilation. All the resources of the United States, moral and material, may have to be mobilized to prevent the advent of such a world situation. Its prevention is at present the solemn responsibility of the United States—singled out by virtue of her lead in the field of atomic power.

The added material strength which this lead gives to the United States brings with it the obligation of restraint, and if we were to violate this obligation our moral position would be weakened in the eyes of the world and in our own eyes. It would then be more difficult for us to live up to our responsibility of bringing the unloosened forces of destruction under control.

In view of the foregoing, we, the undersigned, respectfully petition: first, that you exercise your power as Commander-in-Chief to rule that the United States shall not resort to the use of atomic bombs in this war unless the terms which will be imposed upon Japan have been made public in detail and Japan, knowing these terms, has refused to surrender; second, that in such an event the question whether or not to use atomic bombs be decided by you in the light of the considerations presented in this petition as well as all the other moral responsibilities which are involved.

NORBERT WIENER

Wiener (1894–1964), son of a Harvard professor, was a child prodigy and received his Ph.D. in mathematics from Harvard at the age of nineteen. He spent over forty years on the faculty of the Massachusetts Institute of Technology, receiving many honors for his contributions in mathematics, engineering, and logical science. His work on cybernetics—the science of communications and control—has led to his reputation as the "father of automation." He was also an exceptional linguist, philosopher, and student of literature. This open letter, published in the Atlantic Monthly, January, 1947, was addressed to a research scientist of an aircraft corporation.

A SCIENTIST REBELS

SIR:—

I have received from you a note in which you state that you are engaged in a project concerning controlled missiles, and in which you request a copy of a paper which I wrote for the National Defense Research Committee during the war.

As the paper is the property of a government organization, you are of course at complete liberty to turn to that government organization for such information as I could give you. If it is out of print as you say, and they desire to make it available for you, there are doubtless proper avenues of approach to them.

When, however, you turn to me for information concerning controlled missiles, there are several considerations which determine my reply. In the past, the comity of scholars has made it a custom to furnish scientific information to any person seriously seeking it. However, we must face these facts: The policy of the government itself during and after the war, say in the bombing of Hiroshima and Nagasaki, has made it clear that to provide scientific information is not a necessarily innocent act, and may entail the gravest consequences. One therefore cannot escape reconsidering the established custom of the scientist to give information to every person who may inquire of him. The interchange of ideas which is one of the great traditions of science must of course receive certain limitations when the scientist becomes an arbiter of life and death.

For the sake, however, of the scientist and the public, these limitations should be as intelligent as possible. The measures taken during the war by our military agencies, in restricting the free intercourse among scientists on related projects or even on the same project, have gone so far that it is clear that if continued in time of peace this policy will lead to the total irresponsibility of the scientist, and ultimately to the death of science. Both of these are disastrous for our civilization, and entail grave and immediate peril for the public.

I realize, of course, that I am acting as the censor of my own ideas, and it may sound arbitrary, but I will not accept a censorship in which I do not participate. The experience of the scientists who have worked on the atomic bomb has indicated that in any investigation of this kind the scientist ends by putting unlimited powers in the hands of the people whom he is least inclined to trust with their use. It is perfectly clear also that to disseminate information about a weapon in the present state of our civilization is to make it practically certain that that weapon will be used. In that respect the controlled missile represents the still imperfect supplement to the atom bomb and to bacterial warfare.

The practical use of guided missiles can only be to kill foreign civilians indiscriminately, and it furnishes no protection whatsoever to civilians in this country. I cannot conceive a situation in which such weapons can produce any effect other than extending the kamikaze way of fighting to whole nations. Their possession can do nothing but endanger us by encouraging the tragic insolence of the military mind.

If therefore I do not desire to participate in the bombing or poisoning of defenseless peoples—and I most certainly do not—I must take a serious responsibility as to those to whom I disclose my scientific ideas. Since it is obvious that with sufficient effort you can obtain my material, even though it is out of print, I can only protest *pro forma* in refusing to give you any information concerning my past work. However, I rejoice at the fact that my material is not readily available, inasmuch as it gives me the opportunity to raise this serious moral issue. I do not expect to publish any future work of mine which may do damage in the hands of irresponsible militarists.

I am taking the liberty of calling this letter to the attention of other people in scientific work. I believe it is only proper that they should know of it in order to make their own independent decisions, if similar situations should confront them.

NORBERT WIENER

LOUIS N. RIDENOUR

Dr. Ridenour (1911–1959) received his B.S. from the University of Chicago and his Ph.D. in physics from the California Institute of Technology. He taught at the University of Pennsylvania from 1938 to 1947 and was Professor of Physics there when he published the present article (May, 1947, Atlantic Monthly*) in answer to Norbert Wiener. At the time of his death he was vice president of Lockheed Aircraft Corporation. His primary interest was in radar. He was Adviser on Radar to Air Force General Spaatz in World War II and won the President's Medal for Merit for his work on radar development. Author of* Bibliography in an Age of Science *(in collaboration) (1951), he also edited* Radar System Engineering *(1947) and* Modern Physics for the Engineer *(1954).*

THE SCIENTIST FIGHTS
FOR PEACE

Now that the war is officially over, everyone seems to be trying to guarantee the peace in his own individual way. The wrangles and name-calling among the various peace-lovers parallel some of the worst features of a war, though they stop short of bloodletting.

I am sure that there are few people who love peace more devoutly, or who wish more profoundly to guarantee and preserve it, than Norbert Wiener. Yet I find myself in violent disagreement with his views as stated in his letter, "A Scientist Rebels." The issues involved are so important that the point of view of a scientist opposed to Wiener should be clearly stated.

Fundamentally, our disagreement turns on two points.

The first concerns the social responsibility of the scientist. Wiener clearly believes that the scientist is the armorer of modern war, and as such holds a responsibility of unique importance. I feel that the social responsibility of the scientist is unique in no important way. It is identical with the social responsibility of every other thinking man, except for one special and temporary thing. It is necessary today to educate the non-scientific public to the Promethean nature of atomic energy and the true character of science (for example, that it contains no secrets). This education must be done, so that all the people can participate in the decisions they will have to make concerning the organization of society in such a form that wars become less likely.

This educational job was splendidly begun by our government with the publication of the Smyth Report—a step that has recently been criticized by men who do not understand the meaning and the scope of the stupendous educational enterprise we have only just begun. Such an attitude toward the publication of the Smyth Report is the best possible evidence that, if the instruction of all people in these matters is not done promptly and well, we shall continue to wriggle out of the thinking that is demanded of us, using the well-worn old loopholes: "Not such a terrible weapon"; "Every offensive weapon brings a countermeasure"; "We'll keep the secret"; "We'll keep ahead in armaments"; "Let's have a cheap preventive war"; and so on.

Secondly, Wiener wishes to dissociate himself utterly from any activity connected with preparation for war, even to the extent of doing everything he can to make those preparations ineffective. I regard it as deplorable that our nation is preparing for war, and I prefer to leave to others the actual work involved; but so long as it is the policy of our nation to prepare for war, I shall certainly not attempt to impede such preparations. In fact, I have tried to help them by pointing out a way in which our anxiety to increase our military strength is harming our potential military performance: the hysterical insistence on secrecy in nuclear physics is slowing our progress in that field. I conceive the duty of the peace-lover to be that of working for a world in which national arms are no longer desired by a majority of the people of this country or of the world. Meanwhile, I do not believe in the wisdom, propriety, or effectiveness of attempts to sabotage the preparation of arms when these arms are as widely believed to be necessary as they are today.

Wiener's views in these matters are best stated in his own words. The occasion for the letter that was printed in the January *Atlantic* was that Wiener had been asked, by an employee of an aircraft company engaged in work on guided missiles, for a copy of a National Defense Research Committee report he had written during the war. This report was out of print, and Wiener's correspondent had assumed that the simplest way to get a copy was to appeal to the author. In denying the request, Wiener said:—

The policy of the government itself during and after the war . . . has made it clear that to provide scientific information is not a necessarily innocent act. . . . The interchange of ideas which is one of the great traditions of science must of course receive certain limitations when the scientist becomes an arbiter of life and death. . . .

The measures taken during the war by our military agencies, in restricting the free intercourse among scientists . . . [will] if continued in time of peace . . . lead to the total irresponsibility of the scientist, and ultimately to the death of science. Both of these are disastrous for our civilization, and entail grave and immediate peril for the public. . . .

I will not accept a censorship in which I do not participate. . . . To disseminate information about a weapon in the present state of our civilization is to make it practically certain that that weapon will be used. . . .

The practical use of guided missiles can only be to kill foreign civilians indiscriminately. . . . Their possession can do nothing but endanger us by encouraging the tragic insolence of the military mind. . . .

I do not expect to publish any future work of mine which may do damage in the hands of irresponsible militarists.

No doubt Wiener's letter sounded eminently sensible, and even lofty, to many who read it. The motives that lie back of it are certainly lofty, and with them I have no quarrel. But the assumptions on which it rests are open to the gravest question. Wiener encourages his readers to believe that, since technology is the daughter of science, and war is increasingly shaped by technology, the scientist has a unique moral and social responsibility. He must guide his work along peaceful channels; he must suppress such of his findings as apply to war.

This simply does not fit with the basic character of science. By definition, science consists of a completely open-minded probing into the unknown. No man can say what will be found as the result of a given investigation; and certainly no man can predict the nature of the practical engineering outcome of a given scientific investigation. Lee De Forest, the inventor of the three-electrode vacuum tube that is the basis of all present-day electronics, is said to be appalled at the babel and cacophony his invention has loosed upon the world. But De Forest was an inventor, not a scientist. The inventor or the engineer knows the goal of his work; the scientist has no goal but truth. He may have a preconception, based on existing theory, of what he will find in a given experiment, but he is ready to discard this in a moment if his results fail to bear it out.

To continue with our example, then: if De Forest is amazed at the results his invention has brought, imagine how Clerk Maxwell and Heinrich Hertz would feel if they could spend a day with the networks. Before Maxwell, the notion of electromagnetic radiation—radio waves—had never been conceived; before Hertz, radio waves had never knowingly been generated by man. With sufficient imagination, De Forest might have foreseen mass entertainment as the result of his improvement in the existing wireless communication art. It is altogether unthinkable that either Maxwell or Hertz could have had the slightest notion that he was providing a medium for the advertising of soap.

This essential unknowability of the practical ends of scientific investigation makes it senseless to speak, as some do, of "the planning of science for human betterment." This bit of Marxist doctrine is widely met nowadays, even in the best circles, and Professor Wiener does himself and his colleagues a disservice by embracing it. Since we cannot guess how technology will use the still unknown results of a proposed scientific investigation, we must therefore conclude that either science as a whole is good for mankind or it is not. We can "plan" science only to the extent of turning it off or on. Since science, through technology, really means material civilization, the question becomes: Is material civilization good for mankind or is it not? There are arguments on both sides of that question, but clearly its resolution is by no means the concern of the scientist alone.

Other meaningless phrases are finding their way into conversation and the public prints. According to this country's announced policy for the international control of atomic energy, we desire "the interchange of scientific information for peaceful purposes." What can this possibly mean? Either scientific information is exchanged or it is not. No man can say what the practical effect of such interchange will be, and the nature of that effect depends fundamentally upon political and social factors, not upon the nature of the scientific information that is exchanged.

What I have said thus far about the unknowability of goal applies to science. What of technology, which by definition has a definable goal? Should an effort be made to guide technology toward peaceful ends? Professor Wiener thinks that it should. While objecting to the military interference with scientific publication that took place during the war and is still going on, he himself feels competent to perform intelligent censorship. He proposes to perform this censorship on the basis of the practical use that is contemplated for his own ideas. He states flatly, for example, that the only possible use of guided missiles is to murder foreign civilians indiscriminately.

Overlooking the astonishing lack of logic that is involved in imposing one's own censorship while simultaneously rejecting that of others, I feel that Wiener is wrong in this attitude. In a peaceful world, work even on guided missiles would proceed, though not on the same scale or with such desperate intensity as now. Guided missiles would be developed for a wholly peaceful and scientific purpose, not a military one. Given peace, they will carry man's instruments, and finally man himself, through outer space to the planets and the stars.

Here, as before—here even in the branch of engineering that Wiener regards as the farthest-north of militarism—here still the principle holds. If the world is "postured for peace," as the Senators say (some of them say it in a way which implies that the posture involves a barrel), science, technology, and the useful arts contribute to the enrichment and the improvement of peaceful life. If the world is racked with suspicion, preparing for war, or in the throes of combat, the identical arts, techniques, skills, and individuals will contribute to the frightfulness and the horror of war. The decision rests on the contemporary character of world thought and world organization.

This is the basis for my assertion that the "social responsibility of the scientist" is identical with the social responsibility of every thinking man. Each must do his best to make sure that science, the canning industry, young men, the railroads—in short, the entire rubric of our society—are used for harmless and laudable purposes, and not for war. This desirable end can be attained only in a world where measures short of war are applied to solve international frictions. The scientist can no more choose whether he works for war or for peace than the Western Electric Company can choose whether the telephone instruments it manufactures are used on domestic circuits or as Army phones on a field of battle. The scientist does science, and Western Electric makes telephones. The use of either product is determined by society as a whole.

Anyone who feels a *special* sense of guilt because he helped create an atomic bomb, or anyone who believes that the creators of the atomic bomb should feel so, is confusing two quite different things. He is identifying the profound immorality of murder with the relatively insignificant matter of improving the means of murder. God told Moses, "Thou shalt not kill"—not "Thou shalt not kill with atomic energy, for that is so effective as to be sinful." The immorality of war is shared by all. Technical improvements in weapons can influence only the logistics and the strategy of any war that may occur; whether a war occurs or not is the crucial matter, and this is determined by the current "posture" of the world.

Among the social and political factors that influence the posture of the world at any given time, the state of armament of the nations is of great importance. So is the rate at which this state of armament is increasing or decreasing. There is some evidence to suggest that arms beget war, and presumably this is what causes Wiener and others of similar views to do personally whatever they can to retard the arming of our nation. Wiener's refusal to supply the report for which he was asked, though a purely formal matter, can only be regarded as an action taken in the belief that arms are bad in themselves, and that the more feebly this nation is armed, the less likely is war. Such a belief may be partly or entirely correct. I simply do not know whether, in a feral world, it is wiser for a nation to be strong or to be weak. And since I do not know, I do not feel it my privilege, much less my duty, to challenge by individual action the clear decision in favor of armaments that has been made by our government.

By coincidence, Wiener's position in this particular matter bears a very close relationship to an important misconception widely held among those having no knowledge of science. The latter view can be called, for short, the small-war philosophy. The small-war men desire to restrain technology (which they often miscall "science") with a view to making the next war as much like the last as possible. The bombs that dropped on North America in World War II were few and small, the reasoning runs. If we can only stop weapon development at its present level, the coming war will leave our children the chance to live it through.

There are two important defects in this reasoning. First, it cannot work. Under present political arrangements, the only weapon development it lies in our power to stop is that of our own country, and stopping this could in no way guarantee that World War III would resemble World War II. Second, the small-war philosophy entirely misses the moral point; one war differs from another by not one whit of principle. The effectiveness of the weapons used in a war in no way increases or diminishes the moral guilt of murder.

I am dubious of proposals for instant unilateral disarmament and uncompromising individual pacifism. It seems to me that this country offers the best current approximation to freedom of the individual, under law, that can be found anywhere in our admittedly imperfect world. The status of the individual in our society contrasts markedly with the freedom that the individual is said to enjoy in Russia. I recognize fully that most of the desirable freedoms of the individual would be submerged, even in this country, if we had another war; but I feel that the tradition of their former existence would bring them back, if we had a succeeding peace. Given lasting peace, I am sure that the freedom of the individual would emerge everywhere in the world, under any form of government whatever; because the craving for this freedom is one of the basic human hungers, and our present peaceful technology is so abundant that we can fill even this expensive appetite, if war can be avoided. Even though I am thus convinced that freedom of the individual will appear eventually under any form of government, I am interested in preserving the form that has so far afforded the greatest freedom: our own.

Thus it seems to me deplorable but understandable that this country, while desiring and working toward peace, feels it necessary to be strong in a military sense. I shall be seriously worried about our arms only if we commence to put reliance in them as our guarantee of peace. Armaments are neither designed for this role nor useful in it. So long as we continue in a sincere effort to create a successful world organization by participation in and modification of the United Nations, it is idle to object to our possession of arms in a world of the present sort. Worse, it may be dangerous as well. I am sure that we should be regarded as a nation of lunatics if we engaged today in any thorough unilateral disarmament.

The scientist, on whom so much attention has focused for the past year and a half, is in a difficult position at the present time. Because he wishes to re-establish the traditional internationalism of his profession, he is a Communist. Because he served his country well in the war just past, he is an irresponsible armsmonger, with a childish delight in frightful new technical weapons. Because he is concerned over the damage that an uncritical policy of continued secrecy can do to our scientific and technological progress as a nation—whether for peace or war—he is an idealist who wants to give the bomb to Russia, and he "nauseates" Mr. Baruch. Because some scientists, such as Wiener, are devout pacifists, the scientist is an un-American fellow who cannot be trusted. Because certain other scientists are still working for the Army and Navy, helping to arm our nation in accordance with the overwhelmingly expressed desire of the people of the country, science is the whore of the military. Because, among the perhaps ten thousand scientists and engineers who had contact with the atomic energy project, one has been convicted of a breach of secrecy, scientists are Red spies.

What I am claiming here is that scientists are people like everybody else. In common with all other citizens of the world, they have a heavy responsibility to work toward a world-wide political organization, social philosophy, and public morality that can be adequate to prevent wars between nations. To suggest that the scientist has an outstanding responsibility in terms of this entirely unscientific problem is misleading and harmful, for it encourages the lazy to fob their own responsibility off onto someone else. Wiener, in the name of science, is cheerfully accepting a unique social responsibility, while lasting peace demands that the responsibility be shared by all.

Finally, I reject the defeatist withdrawal from the world as it is, that is implicit in Wiener's letter. The only hope for man today is to work for a better world within the framework of what we have, imperfect as this is. It *can* be improved, and such improvement must arise not from withdrawal, but from intelligent and vigorous participation in existing affairs. Most scientists stand ready to do their part.

J. BRONOWSKI

Dr. Jacob Bronowski was born in 1908 in Poland, but has spent most of his career in England. Trained as a mathematician, he received the Ph.D. from Cambridge in 1933 and was for some years a senior lecturer at Hull. In 1945 he was scientific deputy to the British Chiefs of Staff Mission to Japan. He has been head of the Projects Division of UNESCO and held a variety of posts conducting and directing research into industrial development for British government agencies. One of his main interests has been the relation between science and the arts, and he is well known in England for broadcasts on atomic energy and other science subjects and for his radio dramas. Among his writings are The Poet's Defense *(1939),* William Blake: a Man without a Mask *(1944),* The Common Sense of Science *(1951),* Science and Human Values *(1959),* The Western Intellectual Tradition from Leonardo to Hegel *(1960), and* Insight *(1964). The present essay, originally written as an address to the International Liaison Committee of the Organizations for Peace, was published in the January, 1956,* Bulletin of the Atomic Scientists.

THE REAL RESPONSIBILITIES
OF THE SCIENTIST

We live in times of very difficult decisions for scientists, for statesmen, and for the lay public. Many of these decisions are forced on us by new scientific discoveries, and the difficulties in making them are created by the distance between the scientist and the public. (Indeed, there is a frightening distance even between scientists in one field and those in another.) This sense of distance is, I think, a grave threat to the survival of the kind of society in which science can flourish at all.

People hate scientists. There is no use in beating about the bush here. The scientist is in danger of becoming the scapegoat for the helplessness which the public feels. And if an immense revulsion of public feeling does lead to the destruction of the scientific tradition, then the world may again enter a dark age as it did after the Goths destroyed Rome. It is not impossible that the whole mechanical and intellectual society which we know could be abolished by a great wave of fanaticism.

That is the danger which faces us, because people hate scientists. But even if this danger does not materialize, something as terrible can happen —and is happening. This is that the scientist is forced, by the hatred of public opinion, to side with established authority and government. He becomes a prisoner of the hatred of the lay public, and by that becomes the tool of authority.

My purpose is not to underline these obvious dangers, which we may hide from ourselves but which in our hearts we all know to exist. My purpose is to try to give a picture, as I see it, of the real responsibilities of scientists, government, and public, in order that, beginning from this diagnosis, we may begin to cure the great and threatening division between them.

What the lay public does when it hates the scientist is what it does also when it hates policemen and ministers of state and all symbols of authority. It tries to shift the responsibility for decisions from its own shoulders to the shoulders of other people. "They have done this," it says. And "They" is always the law, the government—or in this case, the scientist.

You must allow me here to make a digression which is not strictly part of my theme, but which I think needs saying. It is this: that we must not forget that scientists do bear a heavy responsibility. I am of course about to explain that really the public and governments bear the main responsibility. But this does not shift from us, the scientists, the grave onus of having acquiesced in the abuse of science. We have contrived weapons and policies with our public conscience, which each of us individually would never have undertaken with his private conscience. Men are only murderers in large groups. They do not individually go out and strangle their neighbor. And scientists are only murderers in large groups— collectively. For scientists are very ordinary human beings. Any collection of people in any laboratory contains good and bad, people with consciences and without, and what we have allowed to happen is the conquest of science by the minority without conscience which exists in every group.

It is sad that scientists have been exceptionally corruptible. Look into your own experience. Most of us have come from poor parents. We have worked our own way up. The practice of science has enabled us to earn salaries which would be unthinkable to us if we had stayed peddling whatever our fathers peddled. Quite suddenly, the possession of a special skill has opened to us a blue door in the antechambers of prime ministers. We sit at conference tables, we have become important people, because we happen to be able to be murderers. And therefore scientists have been bought with large salaries and fellowships and rewards quite inappropriate to their merits, because a policy was furthered by their techniques. The scientist has proved to be the easiest of all men to blind with the attractions of public life.

Having said this I now propose to stop abusing the scientist. I think it is right that we should all make this confession of guilt—I have been as guilty as anyone else—but this is all spilt milk, this is all water over the dam. We must now look toward what we can do to remedy what has happened. And it cannot be remedied by a gigantic strike of scientists, who will suddenly refuse to have anything to do with commercial or war research, because the society of scientists contains too many fallible human beings to make this practicable.

When the public dreams of such a strike, when it says: "scientists ought not to have invented this or disclosed that secret," it is already demanding something of the individual scientist which lies beyond his personal responsibility.

The voters of Great Britain elect for the purpose of making their policy six hundred and thirty members of Parliament. They do not elect the people who go to Harwell or the people who go to my own research laboratory. That is: we have already deputed to those whom we elect the responsibility for framing policy in peace and war, and it is quite wrong to ask a body of professional experts like the scientists to take this responsibility from the men whom our society has named.

The individual scientist is not the keeper of the public conscience, because that is not what he was chosen for. The population at large, through its deputed ministers, has chosen scientists to execute certain public orders which are thought to represent the public will. And you cannot ask the scientist to be executioner of this will, and judge as well. If you have given a body of scientists this particular hangman's task, you cannot ask them also to form a collective opposition to it. The collective responsibility belongs to the lay public and through that, to those who were elected by that public to carry it out.

Thus when Einstein on August 2, 1939, wrote a letter to President Roosevelt in order to draw his attention to the possibility of an atomic bomb, he was acting with exemplary correctness. He was disclosing to the elected head of government a matter of public importance on which the decision was not his, the writer's, but was the President's to make.

We must explain to people that they are asking of scientists quite the wrong collective decision when they say, "you should not have invented this" or "you should not have disclosed that." This is asking us all to betray the public in the same way as Dr. Klaus Fuchs did, by asking scientists to make decisions which are for the nation to make. The only man who ever, on his own responsibility, was willing to shoulder public responsibility in this way, was Dr. Fuchs. But so far from being hailed as the only sane scientist, he was treated as quite the opposite—as of course he was, since scientists have no right to betray the will of the nation. Yet Fuchs did just what the public asks of every scientist—he decided what to do with a scientific invention.

Very well. We will agree that the scientist is not the keeper of the nation's policy. Then what is he the keeper of? He is the keeper of his own private conscience. His responsibility is not to be seduced as a person. He has the right to act individually as a conscientious objector. Indeed, I believe he has the duty to act as a conscientious objector. I would like to repeat this point. It is in this country an offense to betray the armed forces or to seduce their members from their allegiance. It is not an offense to refuse to be a soldier. And I believe that this is exactly like the position of the scientist. He has no business to act as if he commands the army, but he has a business to settle with his own conscience: the serious business whether he personally will engage in forms of research of which he does not morally approve.

My claim then is that the individual scientist should exercise his own personal conscience. This is his duty. What is the duty of governments in this respect? It is to make it possible for him to exercise his conscience. The responsibility of governments in this is to create the conditions in which a scientist can say: No! to projects in which he does not want to take part. He must even be able to give advice which is distasteful to those in authority, and still must not be hounded out of public life or prevented from making a living.

In all countries the serious threat to scientists who have once touched the fringes of secret subjects is that they are then caught in something from which they can never escape again. They do not get a passport, in case somebody captures them. They cannot get a job because, if they do not want to do this, then they are too dangerous or awkward to be trusted with anything else. This is what we must prevent governments from doing, and this can only be prevented by the opinion of quite ordinary citizens. This is the duty which citizens owe to scientists, to insist that governments shall make it possible for scientists to be conscientious objectors if they wish.

I have explored this subject in general terms, and I would now like to be specific. I would like to tell you precisely what I think is the responsibility of the public, of the scientists, and of governments.

The responsibility of the public is to make the decisions of policy on which their future depends, and to make them themselves. And in a democracy the apparatus for this is to elect those people in whose judgment you have confidence—and to elect them on the issues which in fact face the world. Now you can only elect such people, you can only put pressure on them about public issues, if you are well informed. The greatest lack in public opinion today is lack of information about what is possible and not possible in science. This sets my teeth on edge every time I read a scientific newsflash. I will quote one of many instances which I find distasteful: the use of the phrase "cobalt bomb." This is a technical term for a piece of medical equipment, but has suddenly become transformed into something to describe how a hydrogen bomb might be clothed. As a result, of the fifty million people in this country, forty-nine million nine hundred odd thousand have heard the words "cobalt bomb," but are helplessly confused between radioactive treatment and something that you blow people up with. The public must be well informed; and the public gets not only the government it deserves, but the newspapers it deserves.

If this is once granted, the next step I think is simple. If it is once granted that we believe in democratic election, and that in our generation this can only be carried out by a public informed on the scientific issues on which the fate of nations hangs, then the duty of the scientist is clear. The duty of the scientist is to inform the public. The duty of the scientist is to create the public opinion for right policies, and this he can only create if the public shares his knowledge.

My generation has a heavy task here, because it ought to spend the bulk of its time—alas—not in laboratories at all, but in explaining to the voting public what is going on in the laboratories. What are the choices which face us? What could be done with antibiotics, with new materials, with coal (if you like), and with alternative forms of energy? These are urgent questions and yet, however many times we raise them, the layman still does not understand the scale of the changes which our work is making, and on which the answers must hang.

There is a slightly irreverent story about this. At the time the Smyth Report was published in America there was published in this country a White Paper on the British contribution to atomic energy. One of the documents in it is the directive which Mr. Winston Churchill, as he then was, gave about the setting up of an atomic energy project. This directive begins with the words, "Though personally satisfied with the power of existing explosives. . . ." This bland phrase is a monument to a nonscientific education. For it could only have been written by a man, an intelligent man, who simply does not understand how big a million is. The difference between atomic explosives and ordinary explosives is the difference between the length of a nuclear bond and a molecular bond; and this is a factor of more than a million. To suppose somehow that in multiplying the energy of an explosive by a million, you are doing nothing very different from multiplying it by two, or five, or ten—this is simply not to grasp the scale of the world.

And the public does not grasp it. To say "ten to the sixth" to anybody, however educated, is still to invite the reproof today that one is stressing mere numerical details. One of our tasks, as scientists, must be to educate people in the scale of things.

While I am telling improper stories—improper only in the amusing sense—I will tell you that everybody who works in industrial research has this trouble all the time, when he discusses the economics of new processes. We put forward the result of research, or we simply estimate what would happen if a piece of research proved successful. And at once we get back a balance sheet from the finance department which says: The current process makes a profit of 2/2d a ton, and what you have in mind might make a loss of 8d a ton; it is therefore not worth pursuing. This, if you please, is the comment on a piece of research which, if it works on the full scale, might cut costs by a factor of five. But no accountant understands a factor of five; he budgets in shillings and pence, and what is liable to loss is to him as good as lost. One cannot explain a factor of five, or a factor of a million, to people who have not been brought up in a scientific tradition. This is what I mean when I say that the scientist has a duty to become a teacher to the public in understanding the pace, the nature, the scale of the changes which are possible in our lifetime.

I have detailed the duties of the public and of the scientist. What are the duties of government? The duties of government are to give its public the opportunity to learn, and therefore to give scientists the opportunity to teach. And I have already suggested that these duties are twofold. One is to give scientists freedom to live their own lives if they do not want to go on with research projects which seem to them without conscience. The other is the duty to allow scientists to speak freely on subjects of world importance.

As for the second, everyone who has ever been connected with the atomic energy projects knows how it is met today. We spend our time waiting for some American journalist to publish some piece of information which we know to be accurate, so that we may then quote it as being the opinion of the *New York Times*. I am being frank about this: I do it all the time. I read what the greatest indiscreet senator said to the small indiscreet reporters, and I know that nine statements are nonsense and one statement is accurate. Then I quote the one that is accurate—but not as my opinion.

Of course it is natural that governments resist the explosive opinions of scientists. All governments, all societies are resistant to change. Rather over two thousand years ago, Plato was anxious to exile poets from his society; and in our lifetime, for the same reason, governments are in effect anxious to exile or at least silence scientists. They are anxious to exile all dissidents, because dissidents are the people who will change society.

There is a simple difference between governments and scientists. Governments believe that society ought to stay the way it is for good—and particularly, that there ought to be no more elections. Scientists believe that society ought to be stable, but this does not mean the same thing to them as being static. We scientists want to see an *evolving* society, because when the physical world is evolving (and we are helping to evolve it) the forms of society and government cannot be kept the same.

Having described the duties of the public, of scientists, and of governments, let me now underline what I have said by describing what happens in all three cases if these duties are not kept. If governments do not allow scientists freedom of conscience, to work at what they like and to refuse to work at what they do not like, and to speak freely about why they do so, then you get the gravest of all disasters—the disaster of state intolerance. This is a disaster because it saps both sides of the moral contract. For there is a moral contract between society and its individuals which allows the individual to be a dissident; and if the state breaks this moral contract, then it leaves the individual no alternative but to become a terrorist. I do not know whether the great state trials in Russia were just or were false. But I know that if they were just, if men like Radek and Trotsky and Zinoviev really committed those enormities, then this in itself condemns the system of government which does not allow any other form of protest than such a form. The grave danger to our society too is that this becomes the only choice which is left open to scientists, if state intolerance imprisons them and tries to turn them into a secret Egyptian priest-craft.

The great sin of the public is acquiescence in this secrecy. I am horrified by the feeling that I get, from such trifling things as American advertisements, that people really enjoy the sense that they are not to be trusted. There is an advertisement running in the *New Yorker* at the moment (I think for a clothing firm) which shows a man who has just got out of an airplane. He has a face like a prizefighter, he is well-dressed and wears what in New York is called a sharp hat, and he carries a bag in one hand which is chained to his wrist. He is carrying secret documents. This is the holy of holies. This is what we are to admire—the man with his mouth shut tight who is not trusting you and me, because of course you and I are not to be trusted. When people come to believe this, when they themselves believe that it is better for them not to know, then totalitarianism is on the doorstep. Then you are ready for Hitler to get up and say: "I am the man who will take your communal responsibilities. I will make your decisions for you."

And the third in our scheme, the scientist, must preserve the tradition of quarrelling, of questioning, and of dissent on which science (and I believe all post-Renaissance civilization) has been built. He must do this for two reasons. First, there is the mundane reason which is obvious in the failure of German research after Hitler took power. It is this: that you do not get good science as soon as you have reduced the scientists to yes-men. It is the nature of scientists to be thoroughly contrary people— let us own up to that. It is the nature of science as an activity to doubt your word and mine. As soon as you get a science, such as atomic energy research in totalitarian Germany, in which the young men are no longer allowed to question what the great men have said, then that science is dead. You can find in the files of the German Atomic Energy Commission that several young men made what I suppose must be called very good suggestions, but they were not followed because (such is the influence of totalitarianism) Heisenberg always knew the answers already.

This does not happen in English laboratories yet. Mr. Churchill begins by saying that he is satisfied with existing explosives, but after the comma he does give scientists the opportunity to be dissatisfied. This tradition, this independence and tolerance, is I believe the base of all our values; and this is what we as scientists must preserve.

I have given you the simple practical grounds for allowing scientists to be awkward, but I believe also that imaginatively and intellectually this is equally important. The sense of intellectual heresy is the lifeblood of our civilization. And the heresy of scientists cannot be confined to their science. Newton was thoroughly and rightly contrary in science, and he was also a thorough heretic in religious matters. For the same reason, people like Oppenheimer and Einstein are found to associate with such unreliable characters. You cannot say to scientists: "When you get into the laboratory at nine in the morning you are going to become a dissenter; and when you go out at five-thirty you are going to become a citizen who touches his cap and who is politically sound." The intellect is not divided into these simple categories.

I have said that the duty of the scientist is today publicly to become a teacher. Let me end by saying something of what he is to teach. There is, of course, the scientific method. There are things about the scale and order of size, of which I have spoken. There are the possibilities which are open to us in controlling nature and ourselves. Above all, he can teach men to ask whether the distance between promise and achievement in our age need be quite so large; whether there must be such a gap between what society is capable of doing and what it does. All this, every scientist can teach.

But every scientist can also teach something deeper. He can teach men to resist all forms of acquiescence, of indifference, and all imposition of secrecy and denial. We must resist the attitude of officials, that there ought to be a good reason why something should be published before you allow it. We must teach even officials that there will have to be a very good reason indeed before anyone is silenced by secrecy.

Mr. Gordon Dean, former chairman of the American Atomic Energy Commission, has just been complaining against secrecy on practical grounds. He says that the commercial reactors which are being built in America are still on the secret list and that this is handicapping American business in its competition with English business for world reactor markets. God works in a mysterious way and it may be that by this anxiety to sell atomic power, science will be liberated. At any rate, let us not look askance at any ally in the drive against silence. My message, in this and in all else, has been the scientist's duty to speak. There is one thing above all others that the scientist has a duty to teach to the public and to governments: it is the duty of heresy.

JOHN HAYBITTLE

John Leslie Haybittle is principal physicist at Addenbrookes Hospital, Cambridge, England. He received his M.A. from Cambridge University in 1946 and has contributed articles on physics to technical journals. The present more philosophical article appeared in the May, 1964, Bulletin of the Atomic Scientists.

ETHICS FOR THE SCIENTIST

In discussing the ethical responsibilities of scientists, I am concerned only with the responsibilities of the individual scientist for the consequences that result from his own scientific work. I am not concerned with the responsibilities of science as a branch of human activity, or with the collective responsibilities of its practitioners as a social group. Ethics cannot be attributed to an abstraction such as science, and the ethics of scientists cannot be separated from the ethics of each individual scientist. When an attempt is made to distinguish between collective and individual responsibility, confusion always results. Dr. J. Bronowski, in "The Real Responsibilities of the Scientist" (January 1956 *Bulletin*), made just such an attempt, and some quotations from his article should clarify the point I am trying to make.

"In assessing collective responsibility," he writes, "we must explain to people that they are asking of scientists quite the wrong collective decision when they say 'you should not have invented this' or 'you should not have disclosed that.' This is asking us all to betray the public in the same way as Dr. Klaus Fuchs did, by asking scientists to make decisions which are for the nation to make. . . . Scientists have no right to betray the will of the nation."

He then goes on to discuss the responsibility of the individual scientist: "He is the keeper of his private conscience. He has the right to act individually as a conscientious objector. . . . He has a business to settle with his own conscience, the serious business whether he personally will engage in forms of research of which he does not morally approve."

These two statements seem to be irreconcilable when translated into the concrete terms of any particular situation. I would agree that the public is asking the wrong questions of scientists as a body, but the questions are valid ones when put to an individual scientist and require an answer. If he gives the answer "I acted so because I have no right to betray the will of the nation," then he must also admit that he has no right to act individually as a conscientious objector. Refusal to do scientific work on, for example, the development of atomic weapons is obviously frustrating the will of the nation if its democratically elected government has decided it needs atomic weapons for its defense.

The problem of ethical responsibility for actions that may affect the whole community is not, of course, confined to scientists, and in making provision for conscientious objectors, most Western democracies have accepted the principle that the individual can frustrate the will of the nation. (It is debatable whether the principle would still be accepted if a greater proportion of the population decided to be conscientious objectors.) However, insofar as conscientious objection is allowed in any sphere of action, the responsibility of the individual for the consequences of his actions is greatly increased. And this applies to the scientist in any country where, in spite of economic and other pressures, he still has some measure of freedom to choose the type of work he will do, the results he will publish, and even, if he thinks fit, to decide not to practice science at all.

Ethical problems do not only arise in connection with war, but this is nevertheless the area in which scientists today are likely to find their consciences most troubled. To practice science for the specific purpose of developing weapons involves an ethical judgment that cannot be avoided by trying to cast all responsibility onto those who have to make decisions as to when and where these weapons are used.

Once again I find myself disagreeing with Dr. Bronowski who, in his book *Science and Human Values* (London: Hutchinson, 1961) writes, "Science has nothing to be ashamed of even in the ruins of Nagasaki. The shame is theirs who appeal to other values than the human imaginative values that science has evolved." By "science" he presumably means scientists, since feelings of shame cannot be attributed to an abstraction, but his choice of words, although perhaps unintentional, illustrates a weakness to which we, as scientists, are peculiarly prone. We too easily tend to reject our individual share of responsibility for any consequences of our work about which we may feel uneasy, and pass the responsibility on to "them," by implication usually the politicians, the decisionmakers. This is in contrast to the attitude adopted when the results of scientific work are generally accepted as good and where nonscientific administrators and politicians have played their part by making decisions that we happen to believe were right. If there is shame in the ruins of Nagasaki, then it must be borne in part by those who provided the means, even though they may not have decided the ends.

The ethical responsibility of a scientist may be stated plainly as follows. Where the possible uses of the end-product of any scientific work are known, then those scientists doing the work share a part of the responsibility for those uses whether they be good or bad. The scientist, therefore, cannot with an easy conscience escape from the burden of making what may be essentially moral and political decisions about the work he will do and the results he will publish.

Can the scientific discipline guide the individual in making these decisions? How much help can he obtain from the moral component that is "right in the grain of science itself"?

To answer these questions we must distinguish between the two processes that occur in making an ethical decision. First, in deciding upon a course of action, an individual must consider the end which he hopes to achieve. Such ends may range from making himself happy to furthering the greatest happiness of the greatest number, from keeping himself and his family alive to preserving the nation or the human race, from pleasing himself to pleasing God; and the ends he really aims at may often be very different from those he openly proclaims. The practice of science can, in my opinion, give no guidance in this choice of ends. Science has its own ends which are strictly limited. They are the furtherance of man's understanding of himself and his environment and the increase of his power to control and alter that environment. The purposes for which he shall use this understanding and power cannot be decided without some basic hypothesis or faith which is not deducible by the scientific process.

The second aspect of decisionmaking is the choice of means, and here it would at first sight appear that the scientific method can make a contribution. Scientists are trained to attack the problem "How may such-and-such a result be obtained?" and have achieved undreamt of success in solving such problems in the material world. Nevertheless, the application of scientific techniques to the problems of society and human relationships does not always meet with similar success. The reason for this is that, although we can still observe, collect data, and build hypotheses, we are severely limited in our capacity to experiment under conditions where all the possible variables are strictly controlled. This is not to say that results obtained by the social scientist and psychologist, in conjunction with the anthropologist and the human biologist, may not have great relevance to ethics. But in so many of the major ethical problems facing mankind today, significant scientific results are scanty, experiments cannot be made, and vital decisions cannot be deferred. At the national level we must now act either on the assumption that nuclear weapons will deter aggression, preserve peace, and insure the continued existence of the values we uphold, or we must act on the contrary assumption. If we choose the wrong assumption, then we shall not be in the position of the scientist who may, when his experiment fails to produce the expected results, devise a new experiment to test an alternative hypothesis. The same considerations apply in many of the problems that face us at the personal level. Bringing up our children is an experiment which we have to carry out, but which we can seldom repeat if we judge our first attempt to be a failure.

We have therefore to be guided in our actions and our associated ethical judgments, not by a scientific theory resting on unimpeachable experimentally determined facts, but by a combination of our reason and our beliefs concerning human values and the real source of power in the universe. Dr. Bronowski has argued, and here I agree, that certain values are directly cultivated by the practice of science, namely, truth to fact, freedom of thought and speech, tolerance, dissent, justice, honor, human dignity, and self-respect; and that "if these values did not exist, then the society of scientists would have to invent them to make the practice of science possible." But these values, impressive as they may sound, are, in my view, secondary to those "of tenderness, of kindliness, of human intimacy and love" which, as Dr. Bronowski says, "are not generated by the practice of science." If the latter values are accepted, then the scientific values will automatically follow, and in certain circumstances, the demands of truth, justice, and honor must in fact give way to the greater demand of love. Without love, even freedom of thought and speech, tolerance, and dissent lose their ethical imperative. Here I am no longer attempting an impartial discussion, but, as is inevitable when one talks of values, I am revealing my own particular bias, a belief in the supreme power of love at all levels of human relationships.

The solution of most ethical problems depends finally upon a valuation of individual man in relationships to other men and the community, and upon an estimate of the real sources of power that determine the outcome of these relationships. This is the province of religion, using that term in its widest sense, and it is, I believe, within the context of a religious outlook that the scientist must form his ethical judgments. Science alone is not enough. It is wisdom without compassion. If we, as scientists, fail to recognize this fact, then science itself may fall into disrepute through its lack of success in fields where the power of its method is limited.

PAUL WEISS

Paul Alfred Weiss was born in Vienna in 1898. He took his Ph.D. at the University there in 1922, came to the United States in 1931, and became an American citizen in 1939. Recipient of numerous fellowships and honors for his work in physiology, he was Professor of Zoology at Chicago from 1933 to 1954. Since then he has been a member of the Rockefeller Institute for Medical Research in New York, which he now heads. A veritable statesman of science, Dr. Weiss has served on the National Research Council and on other governmental and international boards. In addition, he edits several journals in the field of biology. "The Message of Science," first published in 1959, is here reprinted from the collection The Atomic Age, *ed. M. Grodzins and E. Rabinowitch (New York, 1963).*

THE MESSAGE OF SCIENCE

To testify as a scientist on the new vistas of man's future is a great privilege, indeed. However, though speaking as a scientist, I cannot speak for Science—that abstract allegory lodged in so many people's minds, half glorified, half damned, but without real body. Real science is earthy; just one of many branches of the human enterprise; one to be cultivated, but not a cult. Science must make more men its devotees, but none its priests. I therefore speak for no one but myself.

Man's hope lies in the advance of civilization. Science is part of it. To understand its role requires insight into science's nature, power, and limitations. I thus shall dwell on these three points:

First, that man will continue to reap rich fruit from scientific progress.

Second, that understanding the process of science—not just its products —understanding science as a way of thinking, gives man a firmer grounding in reality against his floundering and fumbling in abstractions.

And, third, that science's task is to serve man by mastering nature, and not to become man's master. In serving man, science must close ranks with other servants of humanity—the creative arts, philosophy, religion—all striving for a new integrated humanism. Science, which has helped dethrone man from his self-appropriated station at the center of the universe, can help him now to grow into his rightful stature.

Man, whatever else he be, is in and of nature. Nature is orderly. To cope with nature, man wants to understand this order; to understand it by discovering the underlying rules. Once he has found a rule, he has gained control over that phase of nature—intellectual control in comprehension, and veritable physical control, which culminates in the practical accomplishments of technology, medicine, and agriculture. Science is man's rational tool to find those rules. And by finding them, it replaces notion by reason; magic by method; contention by evidence; and wishful thinking by sober appraisal. The book of rules is what we know as knowledge.

Scientific knowledge grows like an organic tree, not as a compilation of collector's items. Facts, observations, and discoveries as items are but the nutrients on which the tree of knowledge feeds, and not until they have been thoroughly absorbed and assimilated have they truly enlarged the body of knowledge. Nurtured in the fertile soil of healthy economics and in a beneficent climate of public understanding and intellectual freedom, the tree grows and bears fruit—that rich fruit of tangible scientific deliveries that for too many is all they know of science: cheap power, better communications, less disease, fewer disasters, more efficient agriculture, enhanced production, and reduced waste—gains in man's striving for material betterment.

That this utility will mount immensely in the new age that lies ahead goes without saying. Ever new fruit-bearing branches keep sprouting from the tree in luxuriant proliferation. To predict just which of them are destined to yield bumper crops would be gratuitous; for science has a way of making the greatest spurts of growth in the most unexpected—and therefore unpredictable—directions. Let me then simply say in general that mankind can rely on reaping ever greater material benefits from science.

But is that all that science has to offer? To be sure, we must not sneer at gains in hardware and in pills. If through the works of science more men will attain a higher than marginal standard of living—with starvation, pestilence, and pain ever more narrowly retrenched—this will be quite a feat. But there is something more science can offer. Enchanted by the fruits shown on the market, we let ourselves too glibly be distracted from looking at the process by which the tree that bore those fruits has grown. This growth process itself conveys a message—my second point—and it is this: If science has been so patently successful, could man not emulate that success formula in some of his other, thus far less successful, undertakings?

The formula is no secret. It is called "scientific spirit." Its power stems from the strict mental discipline and critical detachment that it imparts to those who live and practice by its code. And if living by this code can help men lead more satisfying lives so as more fully to enjoy and share promised release from want and drudgery; if, just as an example, scientific advances will not only bring man more leisure time, but scientific spirit will spark him to enjoy it in creative self-improvement instead of as a passive on-looker at prefabricated mass performances; if science will not just extend man's life span but render the content of that life span more purposeful; if science can convince man that many of the evils and errors and convulsions of the present age stem from his ignorance and neglect of the very code of science; then science will truly have given him another noble gift: a basis for responsible and judicious self-direction as a design for living.

For we take it to be axiomatic that within the frame set him by God or nature, or under whatever symbol you wish to refer to that principle which sets his limits, man is free to choose his course for better or for worse. And in this choice, a dose of scientific spirit can help him to avoid predictably disastrous turns and missteps. Man may make foolish uses of scientific *products*, but the scientific *spirit* can teach him reason. At any rate, science is not to blame for man's misdirecting scientific knowledge to evil ends.

Now, just what is it that marks this spirit as superior to the mere application of logic, the golden rule, or just plain common sense? The answer is: the categorical demand for validation and verification of each premise, each contention, and each conclusion by the most rigorous and critical tests of evidence. Every rule and law has to be tested and enforced, and nowhere else is the penalty for error or infringement so prompt and telling. Misjudging public pressures may do no more than sweep a politician out of office, but miscalculating wind or water pressures in the design of towers or dams will surely doom those structures to collapse. Thus, by reward and punishment, the scientific method teaches man to discipline his thinking and his actions based on thought.

This discipline of the scientific method, broadly applied, can go far toward clearing the underbrush of superstition and prejudice that hamper civilization in its march. By its incisiveness, the scientific spirit will leave its mark wherever men strive to overcome obscurity and obscurantism.

But it has limitations. According to the code of science, no positive assertions are final. All propositions are approximations, and indeed are provisional pending conclusive proof that all alternative propositions are untenable. Viewed in this light, science is seen to advance more by denying what is wrong than by asserting what is right—by reducing and eventually eradicating errors, rather than by heading straight toward some preconceived final truth.

Mankind is facing the vast realm of the unknown, which must be conquered. From any point along that frontier of knowledge, the imagination and curiosity of individual men start treks that radiate in all directions into this virgin jungle. Through trial and error, one gradually comes to single out the right path, as the successful survivor from the multitude of tested and discarded blind alleys. Now, what endows a trek into the wilderness with such survival value? What makes it right? Simply the fact that it has not remained a blind and isolated venture, but has met other new or familiar lines that had struck out from other points, merging with them in mutual reinforcement. Success lies in the confluence of thoughts from many diverse directions.

This is of first importance. A blind path driven into the unknown stays blind, its fate unknown, until it meets with other paths, the intersection giving both a valid check of their respective bearings. The unknown is not conquered until it has become so thoroughly pervaded by this network of trails that trains of thought can travel from any place or subject without encountering stops or gaps or frontiers with a "do not trespass" sign. This is what gives to science its coherence and consistency, with a stable interconvertible intellectual currency of terms and units, modes of operation, and standards of proof or disproof. But remember that the way in which science gains this structural unity and strength is by gradually removing the inconsistencies and incongruities within the system; by the systematic reduction of margins for error.

In taking this course, science has adopted the time-tested method of organic evolution, but on an infinitely faster scale. According to current concepts, organic forms evolve as follows: With each species a major stock of heritable characteristics is passed down conservatively from generation to generation. Every so often, changes—so-called mutations— spring up in the basic repertory, which when recombined in the offspring from slightly divergent parents, may lead to novel characters. These emergent properties, never before subject to the test of survival value, more often than not turn out to be failures, blind alleys. The few new products which are improvements assert themselves by their competitive success and mark an enduring forward step in the advancement of the species, provided they benefit the total interbreeding population.

Mutations, thus, are like the blind probings of advancing knowledge; in both, success comes not from designing the fit but from routing out the unfit. Yet, thought processes—the probings of the mind—while following the model of genetics, are infinitely faster in going through their tests. The unit of genetic probing is the time it takes for a generation to test its endowment and either win or lose the test; for man this unit is about a quarter century—one generation. Knowledge's mutations—the novel ideas emerging from spontaneous inspirations or from hybrid crossing in a single mind of two unrelated parent lines of thought—take much less time to prove their soundness; so little time in fact, that in a single generation we have witnessed the most startling advances of modern physics, chemistry, medicine, and agriculture.

This then gives man his unprecedented chance for rapid progress; but progress, let me repeat, arises, as in evolution, from the incessant weeding out of error. Thus truth in scientific terms is not approached as one would seek a goal: by heading straight toward a distant beacon, visible or visualized. The individual scientist may proceed that way, but as for science as a whole, what it regards as truth is but that strip of possibilities left over after all demonstrable untruths have been trimmed away. And this will remain a fairly broad band of uncertainty, including the indeterminate, the unknown, the indeterminable, and the unknowable.

It is a sobering experience for the scientist thus to acknowledge the finite boundaries of his reach. It takes humility and courage to live with partial answers, and it disturbs complacency. Yet, if this critical scientific spirit can cure more men of their cocksureness that they already know the answers to questions yet unsolved, then science will have given man a new resolve to search and strive again, not just conform; to face his problems, not accept pat solutions; to exercise his ingenuity, instead of dully abdicating to authority. The scientific spirit will thus rekindle flames which one of science's products—mechanization—threatens to smother.

But then again, by the same token, science must judge its own scope with no less critical detachment. This precept is not popular. With the exuberance of youth, science has often maintained not only that it is a cure-all for mankind's ills, but that it can prescribe ultimate goals to guide man's conduct. A mature science cannot condone such juvenile extremism. It must take into account the other claimants to a share in human destiny. And if it is to thrive and serve humanity, it must range itself among them as a partner, and not set itself on top as a ruler.

The creative arts, philosophy, the kernel of religions (not of creeds), the lessons of the course of history, all of these are companions of science in shaping mankind's fate. Never mind that they at times have also shown monopolistic arrogance; this does not exculpate the scientist from blame if he does likewise. His own code holds him to curtailing error, and positive conclusions must remain confined to what is testable and can either be verified or negated. True, this code entitles science to pry into those other areas as auditor of their accounts, and sure enough, it finds a host of errors in their books. But the accounting done, there still remains wide open that broad band of beliefs in which the scientist can have no say, being beyond his testing range; there rest the mysteries of the basic order and direction of the universe and of the ethical, aesthetic, and moral principles by which men live.

Of course, there have been scientific (and also pseudo-scientific) doctrines purporting to explain such things as beauty, decency, or sympathy. They may be right, but by science's own dictum they cannot prove it, because they cannot prove that those of opposite doctrine are wrong. So science would do well to concede and retreat to its proper province. Where science tries to be objective, barring the arbitrariness of the observing subject, the arts in contrast express man's urge to break out from the strait jacket of reality and find an outlet for his subjectivity. While science preferably deals with classes of phenomena that are predictable, all history in contrast relates the singular, unique, and unpredictable. Science may be able to tell us what probably will not happen, but it cannot tell us precisely what will happen next. Religions in their plurality reflect ethnic, social, and psychologic differentiations among men that history and science might treat rationally. But by science's own verdict, religion—as man's awareness of the limits of his rational cognition—retains its unassailable position alongside science, because it cannot be invalidated.

Science to be consistent must take this position of critical and modest self-appraisal and sober recognition of its own limits. No sophistry or verbal trickery, or wishful thinking or political design, can hide this need for those who see the broad perspective of our times. If science claims no greater share of man's allegiance than it can ask for on scientific grounds; if it will behave as educator rather than as conqueror; then the resentments, the suspicions, and the injunctions of those who have feared the aggressive expansionism of a youthful science will subside, and the barriers of prejudice can be let down on all sides. Civilization needs us all. Let us be friends. That is what I call "closing ranks."

What we must look and work for is a broad humanism where science is accepted not grudgingly, but understandingly by all men in all walks of life, not for its fruits alone, but for the ideal of rational thought which it can carry to its highest culmination. Yet at the same time, the men of science must ever be on guard against the danger of specialist isolation in tunnels of mechanical robotism and rote performance to the neglect of other human values. Science must neither let itself become dehumanized nor power-drunk. It has a mighty, not almighty, mission—and this concludes my message as a scientist.

I have spoken of science, but not for science. Some men of science share my views, others do not. Which have the greater number on their side, I do not know; nor does it matter, for the soundness of such arguments is not decided, like elections, by majority vote. New mutations or new ideas, when they arise, are always at first in the minority; but fitness makes such budding germs of progress spread.

I have spoken as an individual, and so should those speak who would controvert me. Science legitimizes such diversity. The averages, groups, and classes with which it deals embrace, but cannot define, the unique character of individual events or persons. As such an individual, and from my station of independent judgment and free thought expression I take courage to make a final plea: alarmed by signs that an abuse of science may lead to humans being treated as merely "cases" for a gigantic statistical processing mill in which they are to be leveled to standards of the average, the common, and the mediocre, I make a plea to science to reacclaim diversity as source of progress (for uniformity means death), including the diversity of human minds in their responsible expressions. And then I make another plea to the nonscientific humanists not to regard themselves as prime custodians of civilization, shunning science as if it were inhuman. Let none of us lodge in the master's mansion, but let us all move down into the servants' quarters, so that we all may work together united for human progress in harmonious cooperation. The tasks are large, our forces limited. No group can do the job alone. So, let us all close ranks, the men of science with those in other walks of life, for humanism and against the dehumanization of our culture.

Technology and
Human Values

None of the essays gathered below deals solely or even mainly with the benefits we have derived from technology. In the first place, the matter is too plain, too axiomatic, to require elaborate treatment. The reader does not have to be reminded of the achievements of American industry, of the rise in our standard of living, of the medical alleviation of our pain and the lengthening of our lives. The successful application of science to our practical problems has been truly described as "one of the miracles of mankind." But unless it be in the course of passionate partisan defense of free enterprise or of the democratic way of life, almost no responsible writer today can discuss technological progress without considerable misgivings and without considerable acknowledgment of the losses that seem often to accompany the gains. These misgivings were already felt by Jonathan Swift when applied science was still in its infancy. Lerner and Ellul write with the experience of two hundred years of the industrial age behind them, and Mowrer, focussing on the single problem, population, wryly speculates on our "progress" in the future. Rachel Carson similarly deals with a concrete problem: the losses incurred by our use of chemical pesticides. The satirical story of E. B. White invites, among other things, some speculation on its relation to Swift's. In one form or another, all of these writers ask the same question: In the pursuit of material progress, in the pride of technical know-how, what human values have we lost? The question is taken up again in several other sections of this book, particularly in the following one on work and leisure.

JONATHAN SWIFT

Swift (1667–1745), born of an English family in Dublin, became an Anglican clergyman during a period of disappointment over his hopes for a political career in England. He nevertheless pursued politics and by 1710 had achieved a powerful position in the Tory party. In 1713 he was rewarded for his service to the Tory government—in the manner of those times—with the Deanship of St. Patrick's, Dublin. However, he spent little time in Ireland until the fall of the Tory party forced his return the following year; for the rest of his life he became a champion of the Irish people against English oppression. Meanwhile, he had become an intimate of the best English writers of his time, a leading political pamphleteer, and had begun the series of writings that make him the greatest of English satirists. Especially notable are A Tale of a Tub *and* The Battle of the Books, *published in 1704,* A Modest Proposal *(1720), and the incomparable* Gulliver's Travels *(1726). It is from the third part of this work, "A Voyage to Laputa, Balnibarbi, Luggnagg, Glubbdubdrib, and Japan," that the present account (Chapter 5) is taken. Some of the specific details in the description would have been recognized by Swift's contemporaries as comic versions of actual experiments reported in the* Transactions of the Royal Society, *the leading scientific group in England. The suggestion for the abolition of words probably refers to Thomas Sprat's ideal of an economical scientific prose that would express "so many 'Things,' almost in an equal number of 'Words.'" Critics have sometimes been inclined to apologize for the attitude towards scientific experiment here expressed by Swift. They point out that no one at the time (Sir Isaac Newton was still alive) could have predicted the enormous achievements of science and technology, and Swift does seem to have attacked "projectors" in part because of the impracticality of their schemes. But*

in the context of the other readings in this section, the reader may find that Swift's satire still contains some prophecy in it.

THE GRAND ACADEMY
OF LAGADO

This Academy is not an entire single Building, but a Continuation of several Houses on both Sides of a Street; which growing waste, was purchased and applyed to that Use.

I was received very kindly by the Warden, and went for many Days to the Academy. Every Room hath in it one or more Projectors; and I believe I could not be in fewer than five Hundred Rooms.

The first Man I saw was of a meagre Aspect, with sooty Hands and Face, his Hair and Beard long, ragged and singed in several Places. His Clothes, Shirt, and Skin were all of the same Colour. He had been Eight Years upon a Project for extracting Sun-Beams out of Cucumbers, which were to be put into Vials hermetically sealed, and let out to warm the Air in raw inclement Summers. He told me, he did not doubt in Eight Years more, that he should be able to supply the Governors Gardens with Sun-shine at a reasonable Rate; but he complained that his Stock was low, and intreated me to give him something as an Encouragement to Ingenuity, especially since this had been a very dear Season for Cucumbers. I made him a small Present, for my Lord had furnished me with Money on purpose, because he knew their Practice of begging from all who go to see them.

I went into another Chamber, but was ready to hasten back, being almost overcome with a horrible Stink. My Conductor pressed me forward, conjuring me in a Whisper to give no Offence, which would be highly resented; and therefore I durst not so much as stop my Nose. The Projector of this Cell was the most ancient Student of the Academy. His Face and Beard were of a pale Yellow; his Hands and Clothes dawbed over with Filth. When I was presented to him, he gave me a very close Embrace, (a Compliment I could well have excused.) His Employment from his first coming into the Academy, was an Operation to reduce human Excrement to its original Food, by separating the several Parts, removing the Tincture which it receives from the Gall, making the Odour exhale, and scumming off the Saliva. He had a weekly Allowance from the Society, of a Vessel filled with human Ordure, about the Bigness of a *Bristol* Barrel.

I saw another at work to calcine Ice into Gunpowder; who likewise shewed me a Treatise he had written concerning the Malleability of Fire, which he intended to publish.

There was a most ingenious Architect who had contrived a new Method for building Houses, by beginning at the Roof, and working downwards to the Foundation; which he justified to me by the like Practice of those two prudent Insects the Bee and the Spider.

There was a Man born blind, who had several Apprentices in his own Condition: Their Employment was to mix Colours for Painters, which their Master taught them to distinguish by feeling and smelling. It was indeed my Misfortune to find them at that Time not very perfect in their Lessons; and the Professor himself happened to be generally mistaken: This Artist is much encouraged and esteemed by the whole Fraternity.

In another Apartment I was highly pleased with a Projector, who had found a Device of plowing the Ground with Hogs, to save the Charges of Plows, Cattle, and Labour. The Method is this: In an Acre of Ground you bury at six Inches Distance, and eight deep, a Quantity of Acorns, Dates, Chesnuts, and other Maste or Vegetables whereof these Animals are fondest; then you drive six Hundred or more of them into the Field, where in a few Days they will root up the whole Ground in search of their Food, and make it fit for sowing, at the same time manuring it with their Dung. It is true, upon Experiment they found the Charge and Trouble very great, and they had little or no Crop. However, it is not doubted that this Invention may be capable of great Improvement.

I went into another Room, where the Walls and Ceiling were all hung round with Cobwebs, except a narrow Passage for the Artist to go in and out. At my Entrance he called aloud to me not to disturb his Webs. He lamented the fatal Mistake the World had been so long in of using Silk-Worms, while we had such plenty of domestick Insects, who infinitely excelled the former, because they understood how to weave as well as spin. And he proposed farther, that by employing Spiders, the Charge of dying Silks would be wholly saved; whereof I was fully convinced when he shewed me a vast Number of Flies most beautifully coloured, wherewith he fed his Spiders; assuring us, that the Webs would take a Tincture from them; and as he had them of all Hues, he hoped to fit every Body's Fancy, as soon as he could find proper Food for the Flies, of certain Gums, Oyls, and other glutinous Matter, to give a Strength and Consistence to the Threads.

There was an Astronomer who had undertaken to place a Sun-Dial upon the great Weather-Cock on the Town-House, by adjusting the annual and diurnal Motions of the Earth and Sun, so as to answer and coincide with all accidental Turnings of the Wind.

I was complaining of a small Fit of the Cholick; upon which my Conductor led me into a Room, where a great Physician resided, who was famous for curing that Disease by contrary Operations from the same Instrument. He had a large Pair of Bellows, with a long slender Muzzle of Ivory. This he conveyed eight Inches up the Anus, and drawing in the Wind, he affirmed he could make the Guts as lank as a dried Bladder. But when the Disease was more stubborn and violent, he let in the Muzzle while the Bellows was full of Wind, which he discharged into the Body of the Patient; then withdrew the Instrument to replenish it, clapping his Thumb strongly against the Orifice of the Fundament; and this being repeated three or four Times, the adventitious Wind would rush out, bringing the noxious along with it (like Water put into a Pump) and the Patient recovers. I saw him try both Experiments upon a Dog, but could not discern any Effect from the former. After the latter, the Animal was ready to burst, and made so violent a Discharge, as was very offensive to me and my Companions. The Dog died on the Spot, and we left the Doctor endeavouring to recover him by the same Operation.

I visited many other Apartments, but shall not trouble my Reader with all the Curiosities I observed, being studious of Brevity.

I had hitherto seen only one Side of the Academy, the other being appropriated to the Advancers of speculative Learning; of whom I shall say something when I have mentioned one illustrious Person more, who is called among them *the universal Artist*. He told us, he had been Thirty Years employing his Thoughts for the Improvement of human Life. He had two large Rooms full of wonderful Curiosities, and Fifty Men at work. Some were condensing Air into a dry tangible Substance, by extracting the Nitre, and letting the aqueous or fluid Particles percolate: Others softening Marble for Pillows and Pin-cushions; others petrifying the Hoofs of a living Horse to preserve them from foundring. The Artist himself was at that Time busy upon two great Designs: The first, to sow Land with Chaff, wherein he affirmed the true seminal Virtue to be contained, as he demonstrated by several Experiments which I was not skilful enough to comprehend. The other was, by a certain Composition of Gums, Minerals, and Vegetables outwardly applied, to prevent the Growth of Wool upon two young Lambs; and he hoped in a reasonable Time to propagate the Breed of naked Sheep all over the Kingdom.

We crossed a Walk to the other Part of the Academy, where, as I have already said, the Projectors in speculative Learning resided.

The first Professor I saw was in a very large Room, with Forty Pupils about him. After Salutation, observing me to look earnestly upon a Frame, which took up the greatest Part of both the Length and Breadth of the Room; he said, perhaps I might wonder to see him employed in a Project for improving speculative Knowledge by practical and mechanical Operations. But the World would soon be sensible of its Usefulness; and he flattered himself, that a more noble exalted Thought never sprang in any other Man's Head. Every one knew how laborious the usual Method is of attaining to Arts and Sciences; whereas by his Contrivance, the most ignorant Person at a reasonable Charge, and with a little bodily Labour, may write Books in Philosophy, Poetry, Politicks, Law, Mathematicks and Theology, without the least Assistance from Genius or Study. He then led me to the Frame, about the Sides whereof all his Pupils stood in Ranks. It was Twenty Foot square, placed in the Middle of the

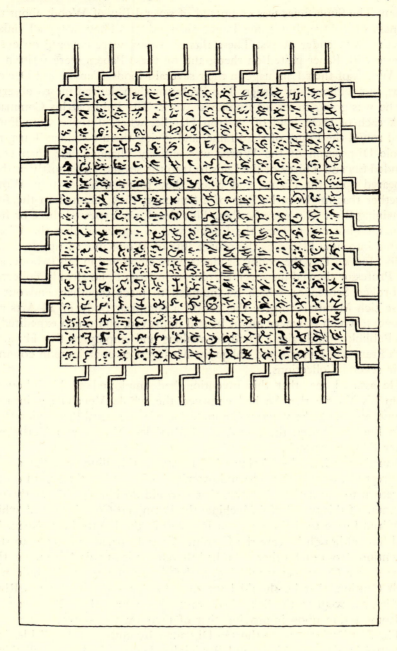

Room. The Superficies was composed of several Bits of Wood, about the Bigness of a Dye, but some larger than others. They were all linked together by slender Wires. These Bits of Wood were covered on every Square with Paper pasted on them; and on these Papers were written all the Words of their Language in their several Moods, Tenses, and Declensions, but without any Order. The Professor then desired me to observe, for he was going to set his Engine at work. The Pupils at his Command took each of them hold of an Iron Handle, whereof there were Forty fixed round the Edges of the Frame; and giving them a sudden Turn, the whole Disposition of the Words was entirely changed. He then commanded Six and Thirty of the Lads to read the several Lines softly as they appeared upon the Frame; and where they found three or four Words together that might make Part of a Sentence, they dictated to the four remaining Boys who were Scribes. This Work was repeated three or four Times, and at every Turn the Engine was so contrived that the Words shifted into new Places, as the square Bits of Wood moved upside down.

Six Hours a-Day the young Students were employed in this Labour; and the Professor shewed me several Volumes in large Folio already collected, of broken Sentences, which he intended to piece together; and out of those rich Materials to give the World a compleat Body of all Arts and Sciences; which however might be still improved, and much expedited, if the Publick would raise a Fund for making and employing five Hundred such Frames in *Lagado*, and oblige the Managers to contribute in common their several Collections.

He assured me, that this Invention had employed all his Thoughts from his Youth; that he had emptyed the whole Vocabulary into his Frame, and made the strictest Computation of the general Proportion there is in Books between the Numbers of Particles, Nouns, and Verbs, and other Parts of Speech.

I made my humblest Acknowledgments to this illustrious Person for his great Communicativeness; and promised if ever I had the good Fortune to return to my native Country, that I would do him Justice, as the sole Inventer of this wonderful Machine; the Form and Contrivance of which I desired Leave to delineate upon Paper as in the Figure here annexed. I told him, although it were the Custom of our Learned in *Europe* to steal Inventions from each other, who had thereby at least this Advantage, that it became a Controversy which was the right Owner; yet I would take such Caution, that he should have the Honour entire without a Rival.

We next went to the School of Languages, where three Professors sat in Consultation upon improving that of their own Country.

The first Project was to shorten Discourse by cutting Polysyllables into one, and leaving out Verbs and Participles; because in Reality all things imaginable are but Nouns.

The other, was a Scheme for entirely abolishing all Words whatsoever: And this was urged as a great Advantage in Point of Health as well as

Brevity. For, it is plain, that every Word we speak is in some Degree a Diminution of our Lungs by Corrosion; and consequently contributes to the shortning of our Lives. An Expedient was therefore offered, that since Words are only Names for *Things*, it would be more convenient for all Men to carry about them, such *Things* as were necessary to express the particular Business they are to discourse on. And this Invention would certainly have taken Place, to the great Ease as well as Health of the Subject, if the Women in Conjunction with the Vulgar and Illiterate had not threatned to raise a Rebellion, unless they might be allowed the Liberty to speak with their Tongues, after the Manner of their Forefathers: Such constant irreconcileable Enemies to Science are the common People. However, many of the most Learned and Wise adhere to the new Scheme of expressing themselves by *Things*; which hath only this Inconvenience attending it; that if a Man's Business be very great, and of various Kinds, he must be obliged in Proportion to carry a greater Bundle of *Things* upon his Back, unless he can afford one or two strong Servants to attend him. I have often beheld two of those Sages almost sinking under the Weight of their Packs, like Pedlars among us; who when they met in the Streets would lay down their Loads, open their Sacks, and hold Conversation for an Hour together; then put up their Implements, help each other to resume their Burthens, and take their Leave.

But, for short Conversations a Man may carry Implements in his Pockets and under his Arms, enough to supply him, and in his House he cannot be at a Loss; therefore the Room where Company meet who practice this Art, is full of all *Things* ready at Hand, requisite to furnish Matter for this Kind of artificial Converse.

Another great Advantage proposed by this Invention, was, that it would serve as an universal Language to be understood in all civilized Nations, whose Goods and Utensils are generally of the same Kind, or nearly resembling, so that their Uses might easily be comprehended. And thus, Embassadors would be qualified to treat with foreign Princes or Ministers of State, to whose Tongues they were utter Strangers.

I was at the Mathematical School, where the Master taught his Pupils after a Method scarce imaginable to us in *Europe*. The Proposition and Demonstration were fairly written on a thin Wafer, with Ink composed of a Cephalick Tincture. This the Student was to swallow upon a fasting Stomach, and for three Days following eat nothing but Bread and Water. As the Wafer digested, the Tincture mounted to his Brain, bearing the Proposition along with it. But the Success hath not hitherto been answerable, partly by some Error in the *Quantum* or Composition, and partly by the Perverseness of Lads; to whom this Bolus is so nauseous, that they generally steal aside, and discharge it upwards before it can operate; neither have they been yet persuaded to use so long an Abstinence as the Prescription requires.

MAX LERNER

THE CULTURE
OF MACHINE LIVING

This is Chapter 6 of the fourth part of America as a Civilization. *For information on the author and his works, see page 164 above.*

•

Any principle that comes to dominate a culture can do so only by making itself part of the life processes of the people. This has happened in the case of America, and it is one of the reasons we can speak seriously, and not as a literary flourish, of the culture of machine living. Siegfried Giedion points out that the machine has mechanized such fundamentals as the soil (mechanized agriculture), bread (mechanized milling), death (assembly-line slaughtering pens and the use of by-products by the big meat packers), and the household (the kitchen revolution, the household-appliance revolution, mechanized laundering, and the mechanized bathroom). The analysis can be carried further. Mechanization has extended to transport (boats, trains, autos, busses, trucks, subways, planes), to living outside the home (hotels, motels, sleeping cars, "automats"), and to the basic phases of the communications revolution (newsprint, book publishing, magazines, telephone, telegraph, movies, radio, TV).

Aside from these arterial forms of American living there is also the interminable gadgetry. From the automatic vending machines to the automatic gas stations, from the gadgeted car to the gadgeted bed, America has taken on the aspect of a civilization cluttered with artifacts and filled with the mechanized bric-a-brac of machine living. The Big Technology of the mass-production industries is supplemented by the Little Technology of everyday living.

One could draw a gloomy picture of machine living in America and depict it as the Moloch swallowing the youth and resilience of American manhood. From Butler's *Erewhon* to Capek's *R.U.R.*, European thinkers have seized on the machine as the cancer of modern living. Some have even suggested that there is a daimon in Western man, and especially in the American, that is driving him to the monstrous destruction of his instinctual life and indeed of his whole civilization.

Part of the confusion flows from the failure to distinguish at least three phases of the machine culture. One is what I have just described: *machine living* as such, the use of machinery in work and in leisure and in the constant accompaniments of the day. The second is cultural *standardization*, aside from the machine, but a standardization that flows from machine production. The third is *conformism* in thought, attitude, and action. All three are parts of the empire of the machine but at varying removes and with different degrees of danger for the human spirit.

The danger in machine living itself is chiefly the danger of man's arrogance in exulting over the seemingly easy triumphs over Nature which he calls "progress," so that he cuts himself off increasingly from the organic processes of life itself. Thus with the soil: the erosion of the American earth is not, as some seem to believe, the result of the mechanization of agriculture; a farmer can use science and farm technology to the full, and he need not exhaust or destroy his soil but can replenish it, as has been shown in the TVA, which is itself a triumph of technology. But the machines have been accompanied by a greed for quick results and an irreverence for the soil which are responsible for destroying the balance between man and the environment. What is true of the soil is true of the household: the mechanized household appliances have not destroyed the home or undermined family life; rural electrification has made the farmer's wife less a drudge, and the mass production of suburban houses has given the white-collar family a better chance than it had for sun and living space. What threatens family life is not the "kitchen revolution" or the "housing revolution" but the restless malaise of the spirit, of which the machine is more product than creator.

Even in a society remarkable for its self-criticism the major American writers have not succumbed to the temptation of making the machine into a Devil. Most of the novelists have amply expressed the frustrations of American life, and some (Dreiser, Dos Passos, Farrell and Algren come to mind) have mirrored in their style the pulse beats of an urban mechanized civilization. But except for a few isolated works, like Elmer Rice's *Adding Machine* and Eugene O'Neill's *Dynamo*, the writers have refrained from the pathetic fallacy of ascribing the ills of the spirit to the diabolism of the machine. The greatest American work on technology and its consequences—Lewis Mumford's massive four-volume work starting with *Man and Technics* and ending with *The Conduct of Life* —makes the crucial distinction between what is due to the machine itself and what is due to the human institutions that guide it and determine its uses.

It is here, moving from machine living to cultural standardization, that the picture becomes bleaker. Henry Miller's phrase for its American form is "the air-conditioned nightmare." Someone with a satiric intent could do a withering take-off on the rituals of American standardization.

Most American babies (he might say) are born in standardized hospitals, with a standardized tag put around them to keep them from getting confused with other standardized products of the hospital. Many of them grow up either in uniform rows of tenements or of small-town or suburban houses. They are wheeled about in standard perambulators, shiny or shabby as may be, fed from standardized bottles with standardized nipples according to standardized formulas, and tied up with standardized diapers. In childhood they are fed standardized breakfast foods out of standardized boxes with pictures of standardized heroes on them. They are sent to monotonously similar schoolhouses, where almost uniformly standardized teachers ladle out to them standardized information out of standardized textbooks. They pick up the routine wisdom of the streets in standard slang and learn the routine terms which constrict the range of their language within dishearteningly narrow limits. They wear out standardized shoes playing standardized games, or as passive observers they follow through standardized newspaper accounts or standardized radio and TV programs the highly ritualized antics of grown-up professionals playing the same games. They devour in millions of uniform pulp comic books the prowess of standardized supermen.

As they grow older they dance to canned music from canned juke boxes, millions of them putting standard coins into standard slots to get standardized tunes sung by voices with standardized inflections of emotion. They date with standardized girls in standardized cars. They see automatons thrown on millions of the same movie and TV screens, watching stereotyped love scenes adapted from made-to-order stories in standardized magazines.

They spend the days of their years with monotonous regularity in factory, office, and shop, performing routinized operations at regular intervals. They take time out for standardized "coffee breaks" and later a quick standardized lunch, come home at night to eat processed or canned food, and read syndicated columns and comic strips. Dressed in standardized clothes they attend standardized club meetings, church services, and socials. They have standardized fun at standardized big-city conventions. They are drafted into standardized armies, and if they escape the death of mechanized warfare they die of highly uniform diseases, and to the accompaniment of routine platitudes they are buried in standardized graves and celebrated by standardized obituary notices.

Caricature? Yes, perhaps a crude one, but with a core of frightening validity in it. Every society has its routines and rituals, the primitive groups being sometimes more tyrannously restricted by convention than the industrial societies. The difference is that where the primitive is bound by the rituals of tradition and group life, the American is bound by the rituals of the machine, its products, and their distribution and consumption.

The role of the machine in this standardized living must be made clear. The machine mechanizes life, and since mass production is part of Big Technology, the machine also makes uniformity of life possible. But it does not compel such uniformity. The American who shaves with an electric razor and his wife who buys a standardized "home permanent" for her hair do not thereby have to wear a uniformly vacuous expression through the day. A newspaper that uses the press association wire stories and prints from a highly mechanized set of presses does not thereby have to take the same view of the world that every other paper takes. A novelist who uses a typewriter instead of a quill pen does not have to turn out machine-made historical romances.

The answer is that some do and some don't. What the machine and the mass-produced commodities have done has been to make conformism easier. To buy and use what everyone else does, and live and think as everyone else does, becomes a short cut involving no need for one's own thinking. Those Americans have been captured by conformist living who have been capturable by it.

Cultural stereotypes are an inherent part of all group living, and they become sharper with mass living. There have always been unthinking people leading formless, atomized lives. What has happened in America is that the economics of mass production has put a premium on uniformity, so that America produces more units of more commodities (although sometimes of fewer models) than other cultures. American salesmanship has sought out every potential buyer of a product, so that standardization makes its way by the force of the distributive mechanism into every life. Yet for the person who has a personality pattern and style of his own, standardization need not mean anything more than a set of conveniences which leave a larger margin of leisure and greater scope for creative living. "That we may be enamored by the negation brought by the machine," as Frank Lloyd Wright has put it, "may be inevitable for a time. But I like to imagine this novel negation to be only a platform underfoot to enable a greater splendor of life to be ours than any known to Greek or Roman, Goth or Moor. We should know a life beside which the life they knew would seem not only limited in scale and narrow in range but pale in richness of the color of imagination and integrity of spirit."

Which is to say that technology is the shell of American life, but a shell that need not hamper or stultify the modes of living and thinking. The real dangers of the American mode of life are not in the machine or even in standardization as much as they are in conformism. The dangers do not flow from the contrivances that men have fashioned to lighten their burdens, or from the material abundance which, if anything, should make a richer cultural life possible. They flow rather from the mimesis of the dominant and successful by the weak and mediocre, from the intolerance of diversity, and from the fear of being thought different from one's fellows. This is the essence of conformism.

It would be hard to make the connection between technology and conformism, unless one argues that men fashion their minds in the image of their surroundings, and that in a society of automatism, human beings themselves will become automatons. But this is simply not so. What relation there is between technology and conformism is far more subtle and less mystical. It is a double relation. On the one hand, as Jefferson foresaw, the simpler society of small-scale manufacture did not involve concentration of power in a small group, was not vulnerable to breakdown, and did not need drastic governmental controls; a society of big-scale industry has shown that it does. In that sense the big machines carry with them an imperative toward the directed society, which in turn—whether in war or peace—encourages conformism. On the second score, as De Tocqueville saw, a society in which there is no recognized elite group to serve as the arbiter of morals, thought, and style is bound to be a formless one in which the ordinary person seeks to heal his insecurity by attuning himself to the "tyranny of opinion"—to what others do and say and what they think of him. He is ruled by imitation and prestige rather than a sense of his own worth.

These are dangerous trends, but all of social living is dangerous. The notable fact is that in spite of its machines and standardization America has proved on balance less conformist than some other civilizations where the new technology has played less of a role. One thinks of the totalitarian experience of Italy, of Spain and Portugal, of Germany, of Russia and the East European countries, of Japan, of China. Some, like the Germans, the Japanese, and the Russian and Chinese Communists have been seized with an admiration for the machine; the others have had clerical and feudal traditions, and have lagged in industrial development. The totalitarian spirit can come to reside in a culture no matter what the shell of its technology is. There is no unvarying relation between machines and rigidity of living and thinking.

Americans have, it is true, an idolatry of production and consumption as they have an idolatry of success. But they have not idolized authority or submitted unquestioningly to human or supernatural oracles. They have had their cranks, eccentrics, and anarchists, and they still cling to individualism, even when it is being battered hard. It will take them some time before they can become "man in equipoise," balancing what science and the machine can do as against the demands of the life processes. But where they have failed, the failure has been less that of the machines they have wrought than of the very human fears, greeds, and competitive drives that have accompanied the building of a powerful culture.

It has been suggested that the American, like the Faustian, made a bargain with the Big Technology: a bargain to transform his ways of life and thought in the image of the machine, in return for the range of power and riches the machine would bring within his reach. It is a fine allegory. But truer than the Faustian bargain, with its connotations of the sale of one's soul to the Devil, is the image of Prometheus stealing fire from the gods in order to light a path of progress for men. The path is not yet clear, nor the meaning of progress, nor where it is leading: but the bold intent, the irreverence, and the secular daring have all become part of the American experience.

JACQUES ELLUL

Jacques Ellul, born in Bordeaux in 1912, has studied at the Universities of Bordeaux and Paris. He holds a doctorate in law and is now Professor of Law at Bordeaux. Among his various writings, those on technology have attracted the greatest attention in the United States. His book La Technique *(1954) appeared in English as* The Technological Society *(1964). He is also the author of* Le fondement théologique du droit *(1946), translated in 1960* (The Theological Foundation of Law); Présence au monde moderne *(1948);* Histoire des institutions, *two vols. (1955–56); and* Propagandes *(1962). The present essay, translated by John Wilkinson, appeared in* The Technological Order, *ed. Carl F. Stover (Detroit, 1963). Wilkinson remarks that "'Technique' as it is used by Ellul is most nearly equivalent to what we commonly think of as 'the technological order' or 'the technological society.'"*

TECHNICAL PROGRESS
IS ALWAYS AMBIGUOUS

It cannot be maintained that technical progress is in itself either good or bad. In the evolution of Technique, contradictory elements are always indissolubly connected. Let us consider these elements under the following four rubrics:

1. All technical progress exacts a price;
2. Technique raises more problems than it solves;
3. Pernicious effects are inseparable from favorable effects; and
4. Every technique implies unforeseeable effects.

1. ALL TECHNICAL PROGRESS EXACTS A PRICE

What is meant here is not that technical progress exacts a price in money or in intellectual effort, but that, when technical progress adds something on the one hand, it inevitably subtracts something on the other. It is always difficult to interpret satisfactorily the bald statement that "technical progress is an established fact," because some people cling to traditional social forms, tending to deny any value at all to such progress, and deeming that nothing can be called progress if it casts doubt on established social values. Other persons, on the contrary, hold that Technique produces extraordinary things of a prodigious novelty, bringing about the consequent disappearance of all sorts of valueless junk.

The fact is that, viewed objectively, technological progress produces values of unimpeachable merit, while simultaneously destroying values no less important. As a consequence, it cannot be maintained that there is absolute progress or absolute regress.

Let me give a few simple examples of this reciprocal action. In the first place, let us consider the fact that modern man, thanks to hygiene in particular and to technical progress in general, enjoys a greater life span than ever before. Life expectancy in France today is approximately 60 years, compared, say, to 35 years in 1890 and 30 years about 1800.[1] But, even with this indubitable extension of the average life span, all physicians are in agreement that, proportionately to this extension, life has become very much more precarious, i.e., our general state of health has become very much more fragile. Human beings of the present have neither the same resistance as their ancestors to disease or to natural conditions, nor the same endurance; they suffer from a certain nervous "fragility" and a loss of general vitality, sensitiveness of their senses, and so on. In the 60 years during which such studies have been carried out, regression in all these respects has been marked. Thus, though we live longer, we live a reduced life with nothing resembling the vital energy of our ancestors. It is clear that diminution on the one hand has been accompanied by augmentation on the other.

In the sphere of labor, the technical progress of the present has effected

---

[1] I must remark that I am very sceptical of the way in which mean life spans are calculated for periods antedating 1800. When the historian says that life expectancy was 20 years in the thirteenth century, his statement can hardly be looked upon as more than a mere joke. There are no means *in principle* of establishing life expectancies for the past.

a considerable economy of muscular effort; but, at the same time this progress has come to demand a greater and greater nervous effort so that tension and wear and tear on our nerves have inversely increased. Here again, a kind of equilibrium has asserted itself between savings and expense.

To take an instance from the sphere of economics, technical progress allows the creation of new industries. But a just view of the matter would compel us to take into consideration the accompanying destruction of resources. To take a French example, the so-called Lacq case is beginning to be well known. An industrial complex for the exploitation of sulphur and natural gas has been established at Lacq, a simple technical fact. But, from the economic point of view, this is far from being the case, since a serious agricultural problem has arisen because of the excessive destruction of farm products in the region. Up to now, the government has not seen fit to take the matter seriously, although it has been officially estimated in reports to the Chamber that, for 1960, agricultural losses have aggregated two billion francs. Now, the vineyards of Jurançon are being attacked by the sulfurous gases and are disappearing, a not inconsiderable economic loss.

To calculate from the economist's point of view the profits of an industry of this kind, it would at the minimum be necessary to deduct the value of what has been destroyed, in this case two billion francs. It would likewise be necessary to deduct the very considerable expenses of all the necessary protective devices, hospitals (which, incidentally, have not yet been constructed), schools,—in short, of the whole urban complex which has not yet been brought into being but which is nevertheless indispensable. We must have knowledge of how to calculate the *whole*. The Lacq enterprise, counting all the expenses of which we have been speaking, must be reckoned a "deficit" enterprise.

Our last example has to do with the problem of the intellectual culture of the masses. True, today's technical means permit a mass culture to exist. Television allows people who never visited a theatre in their lives to see performances of the great classics. *Paris-Match*, through its articles, allows masses of people who would be in total ignorance without such articles to attain to a certain literary (and even to a certain aesthetic) culture. But, on the other side of the ledger, it must be recorded that this same technical progress leads to an ever increasing cultural superficiality. Technical progress absolutely forbids certain indispensable conditions of a genuine culture, viz., reflection and opportunity for assimilation. We are indeed witnessing the creation of knowledge, since we are in possession of the means of knowing what we could never have known before; but it is nevertheless a superficial development because it is one which is purely *quantitative*.

The intellectual no longer has any time to meditate on a book and must choose between two alternatives: *Either* he reads through a whole collection of books rapidly, of which a little later but a few fragments survive—

scattered bits of vague knowledge; *or*, he takes a year to peruse a few books thoroughly. I should like to know who today has the time to take Pascal or Montaigne seriously. To do them justice would require months and months; but today's Technique forbids any such thing. Exactly the same holds for the problem of the "Musée Imaginaire," which Malraux has put so well. We can be in contact with the whole painting and sculpture of humanity; but this availability has no cultural value comparable to that enjoyed by Poussin, who, in his voyage to Rome, passed several years in studying, statue by statue, the ensemble of artistic works at his disposal. He clearly knew nothing of Polynesian or Chinese art, but what he did know had infinitely more educational value for him because it penetrated his personality slowly.

So, once again, we see that Technique allows us to progress quantitatively to the level of culture spoken of, but at the same time interdicts us from making any progress in depth. In the circumstances, is it really possible to speak of "culture" at all? All technical progress exacts a price. We cannot believe that Technique brings us nothing; but we must not think that what it brings it brings free of charge.

2. THE PROBLEMS POSED BY TECHNICAL PROGRESS

The second aspect of the ambiguity of technical progress concerns the following point: When Technique evolves, it does so by solving a certain number of problems, and by raising others.

The further we advance into the technological society, the more convinced we become that, in any sphere whatever, there are nothing but technical problems. We conceive all problems in their technical aspect, and think that solutions to them can only appear by means of further perfecting techniques. In a certain sense, we are right; it is true that Technique permits us to solve the majority of the problems we encounter. But we are compelled to note (perhaps not often enough) that each technical evolution raises new problems, and that, as a consequence, there is never *one* technique which solves *one* problem. The technological movement is more complicated; one technique solves one problem, but at the same time creates others.

Let us take some simple examples of this fact. We are well acquainted with the details of the gravest sociological problem faced by the nineteenth century, i.e., that of the proletariat, a problem which we are only now in process of solving (with difficulty). The phenomenon of the proletariat is not to be considered a simple one, and Marx himself did not describe it as "merely" the exploitation of the workers by certain wicked capitalists. His explanation of the "proletarian condition" was very much more profound; he demonstrated that the proletariat was a result of the division and the mechanization of labor. He expressly states that "it is necessary to pass through the stage represented by the proletariat." For Marx, therefore, the problem is not, say, a moral one, with "bad guys exploiting good guys." Marx never puts the problem in this way; he always poses it as lying outside good or bad moral qualities, external to value judgments, and on the level of fact. And the fact is the fact of the division of labor, and of the machine, giving rise to a society in which exploitation is inevitable, i.e., drawing off surplus values. The phenomenon of the proletariat is therefore, even in the Marxian analysis, the result of technical progress. The machine and the division of labor allowed, from the economic point of view, an extraordinary expansion, but, at the same time, and as a result of the same movement, posed the social problem which it has taken a whole century to resolve.

Let us consider in the same way the extension of the above problem as it appears in the questions which will eventually but certainly be posed by the so-called "automation." Again, automation is not just another simple economic fact; indeed, we are gradually coming to realize that it will entail difficulties which, from our present point of view, can only be characterized as insurmountable. *First* of all, automation implies a production of goods in a relatively constant series of types. This means that when production has been automated, it is no longer possible to vary types, so that an unavoidable condition of immobilism with regard to production must ensue. An automated production line, considered in its full context of operation, is so expensive that amortization must occur over terms so long that the exclusive production of certain types of goods without any possibility of modification must be a consequence. *But,* up to the present, no commercial market of the capitalist world is suited to the absorption of the production of an unchanging line of goods. No presently existing Western economic organization, *on the commercial plane,* is prepared to find an answer to automated production.

Another difficulty of automation is the fact that it will result in a massive diminution of the necessary labor force. The simplistic reaction to this problem will clearly be to hold that the solution is easy. It is not necessary to cut down on the number of the workers but only to diminish the number of daily working hours of each. This solution is quite clearly impossible for a very simple reason. Automation cannot be applied to any arbitrarily selected industry or production, and this for reasons which are basic and not due to the temporary exigencies of, say, the money market. Certain kinds of production can and will be automated; certain others cannot and will never be automated. Consequently, it is not possible to cut down working hours over the working class as a whole. There are industrial sectors in which the workers would conceivably work one hour per day, whereas in others the workers would have to continue working a normal day of eight hours. Hence, as a result of automation, there will be extended sectors of the economy emptied of manpower, while other sectors will continue on the normal standard.

Diebold estimates that in the single year 1955–1956, in the United States, automation reduced the total number of working hours by seven per cent. In the automated plants of the Ford Motor Company there was a reduction of personnel by 25 per cent; and in 1957, in industrial branches in which automation gained most (in particular in the manufacture of electric bulbs and in the very highly automated chemical industry), it was possible to dispense with the services of 800,000 workers. In other words, automation does not result in labor saving favorable to the workers, but is expressed through unemployment and employment disequilibration.

It might be alleged that the situation described is true of capitalist countries but cannot be identical in socialist. This statement is not exact; in socialist countries the problem likewise is posed, primarily because of socialist egalitarianism. The problem is the same for the Soviet Union, for example, where automation is commencing, as for the United States. There will be specialized workers in some industries who will be freed from the necessity to work in one way or another, while in other branches of industry the eight-hour day will have to remain in force, a situation clearly unacceptable to the egalitarian theories of socialism.

A *second* problem is bound to arise in connection with the *retraining* of the "liberated" workers for jobs in new industrial sectors in which there is a shortage of manpower. But, such retraining more often than not presents enormous difficulties, since the disemployed worker is generally semi-skilled (or unskilled) and a completely new apprenticeship is implied of such a nature as to steer him toward other branches of industry.

A *third* difficulty occasioned by automation is the problem of *wages*. The wage problem produced by automation has, up till now, not been solved. How is it possible to fix a wage scale for automated industrial plants? It cannot be done on the piecework plan—machines do all the work. It cannot be done on the basis of time put in on the job. If it is desired to reduce unemployment by reducing the work day to, say, two or three hours, a given worker would only be employed for a very short period each day. Should such a worker, then, be paid according to a wage schedule which pays him for two hours of work at the equivalent of a worker who must work eight? The injustice of such a procedure is clear. How, then, should wages be calculated in an automated industry? One is forced to the admission that the relation between wages and productivity, on the one hand, and between wages and job time, on the other, *must* disappear. Wages will be calculated only as a function of the purchasing power given to the worker (with a view to maximum consumption) by dividing the total production value by the total number of workers. Such a method is really the only one feasible. Since 1950, in Russia, it has actually been tried twice. But the results were unsatisfactory, and it very soon became necessary to return to the system of hourly wages, since, in the present state of affairs, the necessary calculations prove unfeasible. But then the difficulties mentioned above (inherent in calculating either according to job-time or according to production) return, and, at the moment, wage calculation in automated industries is completely shrouded in uncertainties.

Still another problem is presented by the fact that modern economic crises most often result from a "distortion" between the different economic sectors, more exactly, from unequal growth of the different sectors. Here, automation must prove to be an economic factor much to be feared: There will not only be disparity of economic growth between the automated and the non-automated industrial sectors, but still more between industry and agriculture. *Either* capitalist countries must look forward to an increase of crises due to automation, *or* they must adopt planning aimed at rectifying the distortions (and planning by authoritarian measures, as in the Soviet Union). At the present time, even the Soviet planners find that their planning is insufficient to meet the problems of automation, since it is not "flexible" enough, on the one hand, and not "extensive" enough to re-equilibrate the out-of-phase sectors, on the other.

Here, then, are a number of problems (and there are a great many others) with which we must expect to be confronted by the fact of automation, all of which furnish us with examples of our thesis that Technique raises, in proportion to its progress, problems of greater and greater difficulty.

Let me indicate one final example of this, i.e., the problem of overpopulation, resulting from the application of medical and prophylactic health techniques, the final result of which is the suppression of infant mortality and the prolongation of human life. The phenomenon of overpopulation, in its turn, produces the tragic phenomenon of underconsumption. A century hence, all of us *without exception* will be menaced by a general underconsumption which will afflict the whole human race, *if* the expansion of the world's population increases. Here we are confronted by a problem clearly provoked by certain techniques, certain *positive techniques*.

The common factor of all these examples is that technical progress raises whole complexes of problems which we are in no position to solve. Examples of such problems are literally innumerable.

3. THE EVIL EFFECTS OF TECHNIQUE ARE INSEPARABLE FROM THE GOOD

An idea frequently to be encountered in superficial inquiries concerning Technique is the following: "At bottom, everything depends on the way Technique is employed; mankind has only to use Technique for the good and avoid using it for the bad." A common example of this notion is the usual recommendation to employ techniques for the beneficent purposes of peace and eschew them for the maleficent purposes of war. All then will go well.

Our thesis is that technical progress contains simultaneously the good *and* the bad. Consider automation, the problem which we have just been discussing. It is indisputable that technological unemployment is the result of mechanical progress. It cannot be otherwise. All mechanical progress necessarily entails a saving of labor and, consequently, a necessary technological unemployment. Here we have an ill-omened effect indissolubly connected with one which is in itself beneficial. The progress of mechanization necessarily entails unemployment. The technological unemployment so produced can be resolved by either of two means, which are the only two means economically or politically possible, viz., spreading it out either in *space* or in *time*.

A capitalist economist holds that the solution to unemployment is "that technological unemployment ultimately dies out of itself." This means that the workers who have been "freed" (the optimistic formula for unemployment) because of technical advances, will ultimately find jobs, either by directing themselves toward industries with manpower shortages or through the fact that new inventions will produce new opportunities of employment and new vocations. The standard example cited in defense of this thesis is that of the vocational opportunities connected with the invention of the automobile. Admittedly, this technological device did suppress a certain number of vocations, but it brought innumerable others into being with the final result that a vast number of persons are now employed by the servicing required by this industry. Hence, the machine in question has actually created employment.

All of this is indeed true. It is nevertheless a terribly heartless view of the situation, because it neglects to mention the *interim* period. It is all very well to say that the worker rendered jobless will, *with the lapse of a certain time*, again find employment . . . and that, after he has been reclassified, unemployment will die out. But, humanly speaking, what is the situation of the unemployed worker in the interim? Here the problem of spreading out unemployment in time is posed.

In the Soviet Union, unemployment of a technological nature (which not only exists but springs from the same sources) is spread out in space. By this I mean that when, in one place new machines are applied and workers "liberated" the affected workers will, without having to wait very long, receive a work-card which tells them in effect: "Two thousand kilometers from here a job has been assigned to you; you are hereby directed to remove yourself to such and such a factory." In one way, such a procedure seems a little less inhuman; but, in another way, it seems just as inhuman as the time procedure of the capitalists, since no account is taken of one's attachments to family, friends, locality, and so on. The human being is only a pawn to be moved about. It is hard to tell, between the capitalist and the socialist ways of handling the problem, which solution presents the worse indecencies.

A further example of the inseparable mingling of good and bad effects is furnished by the noteworthy study of the American sociological historian, J. U. Nef, concerning "industry and war." Nef shows how industrialism, i.e., the development of industry taken as a whole, necessarily prods industrialized societies in the direction of war. His analysis has nothing to do with the inner essence of industrialism; the phenomena described by him lie purely at the level of the human being.

First, industrialism gives an increasing population the means to live. It is a law sociologically irrefutable that, the denser the population, the greater the number of wars. This phenomenon is, of course, well known as a *practical* matter to all sociologists, but only Nef has studied it carefully.

Second, industrialism creates the media of the press, transmission of information, and transport, and finally the means of making war, all of which make it more and more difficult and even almost impossible to distinguish between the aggressor and the aggressed. At the present, no one knows (and perhaps no one can know) which side has commenced hostilities, a fact not solely due to armaments, but also to facility of transport. The extraordinary rapidity of transport allows an aggression to be launched within 24 hours, or even less, without anyone being able to foresee it. Here, the influence of the press is extremely important, since the press function is to confuse and addle the facts so that no one is able to gain any correct intelligence of them.

Finally, Nef indicates that the new means of destruction created by industrialism have greatly reduced the trouble, the difficulties, and the anguish implied in the act of killing people. A bombardier or artillerist has no feeling at all of killing anyone; he is in fact able to reach the conclusion that he has killed someone only with the aid of a syllogism. In hand-to-hand combat all the tiresome difficulties of conscience about the evil of murder keep obtruding themselves. In such ways, then, positive elements of industry result essentially (by very complex expedients) in favoring war and even in provoking it, even if no one has the *intention* of using Technique "badly."

Let us consider, as a final example of the relation between good effects and bad effects, the press and information.

It seems to be a simple matter, for example, to distinguish between information and propaganda. But, closer study of the problem reveals that it is practically impossible to make such a distinction. Considering but a few elements of the situation, the problem of information is today no longer that of the necessity of transmitting *honest* information—everybody agrees on this point. On the moral level it is a commonplace that we ought to transmit true information. I merely inquire, "How do we get it?" To remain on the *moral* level is simply not to understand the situation. The *concrete* situation, to take but a single example, is something like the following: Over the wires and into the offices of the Associated Press pass daily up to 300,000 words of world news, approximately equal to an enormous volume of 1000 pages. From this mass of words, it is necessary for the Associated Press, in competition with all the other world agencies, to choose, cut, and re-expedite as quickly as possible, perhaps a twentieth part of the whole to its subscribers. How is it possible to select from such a flood just what should be retained, what is true, what is possibly false, etc.? The editors have no criteria, they are at the mercy of whatever comes in, and (even when they judge in good faith and knowledge) they must essentially judge subjectively. Then again, even if the editor had only true news, how should he assign it a coefficient of importance? To do so is his business, and here the stereotypes of the editor are true enough: The Catholic editor will deem the news of the latest Vatican Council of great significance, information which has not the slightest importance to the Communist editor. What we have to do with here is not a question of bad faith, but of a difference of perspective on the world. The result is that we never know, even under the most favorable circumstances, if a given piece of information is subjective. And we must always bear in mind that this information, whatever it is, has been worked over by at least four or five different pairs of hands.

My reasons for maintaining that good effects are inseparable from bad are now, I trust, clear. And, as communications improve, the freer will be the flow of the news and the more available to all agencies concerned. These factors will play an ever greater role, making the difficulties of editing proportionately more difficult, and the chance of selecting absurd rather than sound news ever greater.

4. ALL TECHNICAL PROGRESS CONTAINS UNFORESEEABLE EFFECTS

The final aspect of the ambiguity of technical progress resides in the following state of affairs: When scientists carry out their researches in one or another discipline and hit upon new technical means, they generally see clearly in what sphere the new technique will be applicable. Certain results are expected and gotten. *But*, there are always secondary effects which had not been anticipated, which in the primary stage of the technical progress in question could not *in principle* have been anticipated. This unpredictability arises from the fact that predictability implies complete possibility of experimenting in *every* sphere, an inconceivable state of affairs.

The most elementary example is furnished by drugs. You have a cold in the head; you take an aspirin. The headache disappears, but aspirin has other actions besides doing away with headaches. In the beginning we were totally oblivious of these side effects; but, I should imagine, by now everyone has read articles warning against the use of aspirin because of its possible dangerous effects, say, on the blood picture. Grave hemorrhages have appeared in people who habitually took two or three aspirins daily. Yet aspirin was thought the perfect remedy a scant ten years ago— on the ground that no side effects were to be feared. Now, such effects begin to appear even in what was, and is, probably the most harmless of all drugs.

Another spectacular example is that of DDT, a chemical which in 1945 was thought to be a prodigiously successful means for the destruction of all kinds of vermin and insects. One of the most admirable things about DDT was that it was said to be completely innocuous toward human beings. DDT was sprinkled over the whole surface of the globe. Then, by accident, it was discovered that in certain areas veal cattle were wasting away and dying. Research revealed that DDT in oily solution causes anemia. Cattle had been dusted with DDT in order to get rid of insects; they had subsequently licked themselves clean and ingested the DDT. The chemical in question passed into their milk and by this route found its way into oily solution, i.e., in the milk fat. Calves suckled by such cows died of anemia, and it is needless to add that the same milk was ingested by human infants. Identical problems are potentially raised by *all* chemicals consumed by animals or men. Recall the recent example of thalidomide.

This is an example of the so-called secondary effects, effects which are essentially unpredictable and only revealed after the technique in question has been applied on a grand scale, i.e., when it is no longer possible to retrace one's steps.

Another interesting example is furnished by the psycho-sociological studies of the particular psychology of big city dwellers, where, once more, we are confronted with the effect of the technical environment on the human being. One of the principal elements of big city life is the feeling of isolation, loneliness, absence of human contacts, etc. One of the leading ideas of Le Corbusier in his *Maison des Hommes* was the admission that "big city dwellers do not know one another." "Let us create," said Le Corbusier, "great blocks of dwellings where people will meet one another as they did in the village, with everything (grocer, baker, butcher) included in the block so that people will get to know one another and a community will come into being. . . ." The result of Le Corbusier's creation was exactly the opposite of what had been planned; problems of loneliness and isolation in such blocks of dwellings proved to be much more tragic than in the normal and traditional city.

Then, it was held (and this is the penultimate word in city planning) that it was necessary to rediscover human groupings *on a human scale*, not on the scale of a block with, say, 5000 separate dwelling units. In the works and writings of sociologists and of city planners of perhaps seven or eight years ago we read: "At bottom, the only ones who understood what a city was were the people of the Middle Ages, who knew how to create a true city corresponding to the demands of a genuine city-planning technique, i.e., a human community centered about a small square surrounded by small houses, toward which converged the (straight) city streets, etc. . . ." The new city planners in keeping with these theories, applied them to the suburbs of Chicago, and in particular, to the well known "village" of Park Forest. There, it was thought, was to be found the distinctively human formula, one which really allows the human being his full scope. But, the most recent sociological and psychological analyses show this model community to represent nothing less than a new and unexpected difficulty. This time, people are traumatized because they are perpetually under the eyes and under the surveillance of their neighbors. The affected group is indeed much reduced in size; but no one dares to budge, because everybody knows just what everybody else is up to, a frightfully constricting situation, to say the least. It is clear that, even with the best intentions and with the application of hypermodern and profound research in psychology and sociology, we only succeed in coming to results in every case which could not possibly have been anticipated.

I shall give one last example of these unforeseeable effects, this time from agriculture, viz., the massive cultivation of certain plants like corn and cotton. The cultivation of these plants in the "new countries" seems to represent undeniable progress. The deforestation of land too heavily forested is a felicitous operation, profitable from every point of view, and consequently, represents technical progress. But, it could not have been anticipated that corn and cotton are plants which not only impoverish the soil, but even annihilate it by the twofold action of removing certain natural elements and destroying the relation between the humus and the soil particles. Both these last are destroyed by the roots of cotton and corn to the degree that, after 30 or 40 years of cultivation of these agricultural products, the soil is transformed into a veritable dust bowl. A strong wind need only to pass over it to reduce it to bare rock.

The phenomenon is world wide, and is to be encountered in the United States, Brazil, and Russia, among others. It is a bone of contention between Khrushchev and certain Soviet agricultural specialists. Khrushchev essentially emphasizes the cultivation of corn, as is well known; but many Soviet specialists insist that this emphasis is a very dangerous one. It allows a very rapid economic progress for, say, 20 years, only to be followed by a destruction of hitherto fertile lands which may last for centuries.

The inquiries of Castro and Vogt have shown that, at the present, in certain regions 20 per cent of cultivated land is threatened with destruction in this way. If this factor is considered in connection with that of population growth, a very considerable difficulty seems to lurk in the offing. If arable land continues to diminish in extent beyond possibility of recovery, our chances of survival diminish correspondingly. Here we have an example of typical and unpredictable secondary effects, effects which in corn and cotton agriculture do not reveal themselves except after 30 years of experience. It is again impossible, therefore, to say whether technical progress is in essence good or bad.

We are launched into a world of an astonishing degree of complexity; at every step we let loose new problems and raise new difficulties. We succeed progressively in solving these difficulties, but only in such a way that when one has been resolved we are confronted by another. Such is the progress of technology in our society. All I have been able to do is to give a few fragmentary examples. What would be necessary in order to comprehend the problem in its entirety is a systematic and detailed study of all these points.

EDGAR ANSEL MOWRER

E. A. Mowrer, a prominent foreign correspondent and political analyst, was born in 1913 and attended the Universities of Michigan and Chicago and the Sorbonne. He covered World War I in France for the Chicago Daily News, *and remained in Europe as head of the* News *bureau in Berlin. His uncompromising stories of the rise of the Nazi regime forced his departure from Germany and won him the 1932 Pulitzer Prize for Journalism. After stints in China, Japan, France, and England, he became during World War II Deputy Director of the U. S. Office of Facts and Figures (later the Office of War Information) and traveled widely in Asia and Europe. Among his books are* Immortal Italy *(1922),* Germany Puts Back the Clock *(1932),* The Dragon Awakes: A Report from China *(1938),* Challenge and Decision *(1950), and* An End to Make-Believe *(1961). The present essay first appeared in the* Saturday Review, *December 8, 1956.*

SAWDUST, SEAWEED, AND SYNTHETICS

A great-grandfather of mine left Central Illinois as "too darned civilized" when he failed to sight a deer on his own birthday. Another close relative finds my house in the New Hampshire woods "too lonely," although the nearest neighbor is less than a quarter of a mile away! Even under ideal conditions there are always some people who will think the world is too crowded. In a scientific sense, however, it is important to ask: How many people are too many?

To begin with, any humane or logical blueprint of an optimum earth must allow for varying degrees of human density, from the 137 people per acre in Manhattan (87,680 per square mile) to the utter emptiness of Antarctica.

The earth's present density (forty-two per square mile of land) still permits almost everybody able to travel to find somewhat the sort of environment that means the most. But not for long—not at the present rate of human increase. Java suffers from no less than 1,000 souls per square mile. There a drive through the so-called countryside resembles, for the number of people encountered, the U.S. seacoast between Miami Beach and Fort Lauderdale, Florida—an unending suburb! And the eastern seaboard of the United States, taken as a single area, already counts 180 to the square mile, over three times the national average.

Thanks to her readiness to accept the Lord's living bounty our country is confounding the population "experts" of the Twenties and Thirties who dolefully predicted a stationary or diminishing American population. In fact, a great change has come over American society. The average young American woman, according to Betsy Talbot Blackwell, editor of *Mademoiselle,* "follows the current trend of marrying in her late teens or early twenties, and raising as many children as the good Lord gives her." The American people have increased no less than 31 million in the past twenty years. Two and eight-tenths millions joined the throng in 1955, and each successive sunrise (as of October 1956) sees 7,200 more citizens than the previous dawn.

Certainly these child-eager American young women, taken together, seem to have reversed what demographers thought was a one-way street, namely, the so-called Demographic Transition. This was the breakthrough from an original situation as a high birth-rate, high death-rate country to a low birth-rate, low death-rate country. It was thought to occur whenever a population reached a certain standard of living. Instead, an American birth-rate that from 1935 to 1945 was about 20 per 1,000 has since the end of World War II stayed around 25 per 1,000. The United States is setting a new pattern: middle birth-rate with low death-rate. As a result future estimates have been drastically revised upward. One demographer predicts a U.S. population of 193,400,000 for 1975 and no less than 320 million for the year 2000! Although population forecasting is obviously more of an art than a science present calculations might well turn out to be correct. For the American reversal of the prewar trend, if it continues, is something new—a rising living standard provoking more rather than less conception.

Anyhow, for two-thirds of the world's population births are still running close to the physiological maximum. Costa Rica (1952) chalked up no less a birth-rate than 54.6 per 1,000 inhabitants. India is another example. India's population, thanks to a high death-rate, remained virtually stable for two or three thousand years prior to 1850—and the country was well fed and prosperous. Since the British cut the death-rate the number of Indians has zoomed skyward with no promise of relief. Ceylon's population is growing by 3 per cent a year! Before Perry Japan had a stable population. Since that gentleman "opened" it the Japanese have multiplied like weeds. Under American occupation after World War II they grew almost visibly—and still do. Some have calculated that the world's people will by the year 2106 have reached 20 billion.

Nature's explosive fecundity is as awesome as the power of the atom. A well-fed amoeba will double in an hour. Given adequate food and favorable circumstances it could by the sixth day have produced enough amoebas to exceed the weight of the entire earth! One type of plant louse breeds so quickly that if all its progeny survived the lice would in ten generations weigh as much as 500 million stout men (Huxley). If every codfish egg became adult and reproduced, within six years the Atlantic Ocean would be a solid mass of cod. Certain protozoa might, theoretically, fill *all known space* in a few years.

Human beings cannot quite keep up but some try hard. The Hutterites of the USA and Canada have increased by some nineteen times in the last seventy years. At the present rate they would in 250 years more equal the present population of the United States. The original 6,000 French settlers of Canada have multiplied no less than 700 times in a little over 300 years. Let present death rates sink further—as seems likely if mankind avoids a major atomic war—and there seem no *a priori* limits on the number of people except those of available food and other primary resources.

Already the vehemence of our growth threatens with extinction many other forms of organic life. A contemporary zoologist, N. J. Berrill, believes that the earth produces roughly the same amount of life at all times. It follows that when one organic element, in this case the human race, starts roaring its expansive way across the earth's surface other elements fade and die out. Hence, the present growing "prevalence of people" must—Berrill holds—seem to all other life *"like a cancer whose strange cells multiply without restraint, ruthlessly demanding the nourishment that all the body has need of."* And he concludes that sooner or later the body (or the community) is starved of support and perishes.

As a whole Americans are still barely aware of any problem. Our tradition is one of limitless spaces to be filled, limitless resources to be developed. Businessmen are purring over the flood of new customers. Even trained economists look upon the torrent of new babies primarily in terms of the ever-expanding market. The spectacle of suburbs mushrooming out over once pastoral landscapes around our cities may at some point cause a reconsideration. But in proportion to other countries ours is still only moderately populated. As against less than one acre of cultivated land per person in most parts of the earth, our own ratio, though down to just over two acres per head, is still sufficient to flood the country with unconsumed food which the Government lets rot rather than sell, give, or throw away. Botanist Karl Sax states that even "with present agricultural techniques, the United States and Canada could provide ample food for a population of 200 million and a subsistence diet for nearly 1 billion." So Americans need not yet fear hunger. Not so a country like India. There—according to chemist Harrison Brown—nine-tenths of the *total labor* is already devoted to obtaining food. Unless the birth rate falls sharply no improvement seems conceivable.

Such rapid human increase has started a first-class controversy among experts, both recognized and self-proclaimed. Obviously, unlimited reproduction must *at some point*—unless offset by a growing death rate— lead to starvation. The dispute is about the location of that point.

Viewers-with-alarm (who go back to the Church father Tertullian) see the limit as fairly close at hand. And anyhow, even if we do not soon run out of food we are—they believe—rapidly using up many other essential resources (including cheap water) whose exhaustion or decline would shortly force us back into a purely agricultural condition. On the other hand, specialists of equal prestige regard natural growth as a sign of laudable virility which will correct itself before it becomes dangerous.

The argument—with the specialists so divided—is as confusing as all-important. Nonetheless, if a layman may presume, it seems largely irrelevant to the real question. The demographers are mostly overlooking the essential point. This is not what is the earth's *maximum*, but what is its *optimum* population? *At what density are human beings most able to live the Good Life?* If by stepping up the fertility of our women we can provide more favorable surroundings for their children, well and good. If, on the other hand, further urbanization and suburbanization will prevent the fullest individual development of which people are capable then it is time to slow down.

It is surprising how few population students seem to have centered their investigation upon this point. Even the promising title "Ideal Size for Our Population" (*New York Times* Magazine, May 1, 1955), by the sociologist Kingsley Davis, is deceptive. Mr. Davis at one point writes bravely: "Some (person) will, as I do, see certain disadvantages in an ever larger number of people—disadvantages which do not concern tangibles such as food and housing but rather the intangible but nonetheless treasured aspects of life." But then he spoils the effect: "These may seem *trivial* considerations and *in a way they are.*" (My italics.)

Personal freedom, nature, beauty, privacy, solitude, variety, savor— trivial? Surely Mr. Davis would admit that all are essential components of valid human living even at the present dubious level.

It is, or should be, perfectly obvious that the greater the crowding, the larger the number of people in proportion to diminishing natural resources, the more the authorities will be obliged to curtail their liberties, not because they are necessarily opposed to freedom but because they must do so if living is to be made endurable for any of them. The result could well be the hive, or world-wide welfare state, which looks after the material needs of all its citizens while strictly controlling their actions; in short, a kind of benevolent "Nineteen Eighty-four" where Big Brother is looking at each person just about every minute.

Now the drive for freedom, we know, is not only anchored in the freeman's soul, it is a part of his biological nature. The reaction against constraint is one of the earliest and deepest to appear in higher animals. It will hardly disappear in man, or if it does seems bound to reappear later. Constraint and an overdense population are inseparable.

What of that close relationship between man and the rest of nature which crowding is already tending to distort? How far can mankind lose contact with both the organic substratum and the macrocosmic framework of his life and prosper spiritually?

Many individuals have little or no desire for natural surroundings. Nature—except human nature—leaves them unmoved. Some have nonetheless been greatly creative.

Yet how many more human creators have felt just the other way! Poets of all times and places, most painters and sculptors, the majority of great writers, many abstract thinkers, the greatest scientists have avowed an intimate need of nature. In some of them the thirst for natural things, for the full sky, landscapes, trees, flowers, wild animals, the tang of the autumn wind, the tumbling seas and tranquil lakes, has been an obsession. They have truly fed upon nature in all its aspects. The implication is clear that severed from nature man's imagination and inquiring mind would diminish, perhaps wither utterly.

How long could a rashly multiplying mankind continue to find enough beauty? So far in history people seem to have derived beauty chiefly from two things—nature, primitive or cultivated, and the nature-inspired products of man's own mind and hands. Where would they seek it if a growing population should cover most of the earth with utilitarian devices —and desecrate the remainder in the process?

To be sure, modern expressionistic, abstract, and functional art claims to supply the thirsting soul with all that previous generations got from *natural* content, *natural* expression, and *natural* ornament. Architects not only justify their banal (not to say primitive) designs but glorify them on the theory that "function determines form" and that a successfully embodied "function" has a beauty of its own superior to the "illustrative" or "ornamental" designs of the past.

To what extent are these claims fulfilled? Opinions differ widely. Where the evidence is still inconclusive one can but express a personal conviction. I literally grew up in a generation of writers and artists frantically striving to free themselves from naturalistic form and conscious meaning. And I conclude that wherever and whenever man no longer has a full natural environment on which to feed his sense of beauty he will succumb to dreariness. Think of today's slums and slagheaps, garbage dumps, and polluted rivers. Consider our ruined landscapes, commercially exploited U.S. highways, all the monotonous Levittowns. How avoid the conclusion that too many people and sufficient beauty—natural or man-made—seem incompatible?

What of the diminishing privacy that accompanies crowding? Privacy is freedom from observation, disturbance, and interference, whether with thoughts, emotions, or acts. It is privately that people receive their most powerful and original impulses. But who—today—wants privacy? Certainly not the "integration-minded" American teachers who rate pupil conformity and popularity above ability to learn or express. Not those millions who instinctively flock together like sparrows when there is plenty of room elsewhere.

Perhaps the need for privacy begins only with individuals of a certain kind. And perhaps even among them only those understand its value who have seen what life without it can become—the awful promiscuity of the boat-dwellers on the Pearl River at Canton, China; or crowded Calcutta on a summer night during the monsoon; or Russian workers packed four families in a room and unable to open the window lest they freeze! Even without these sights many Americans who passed some time in crowded military camps in wartime learned how essential some privacy can become to happiness. Certainly without it the creative portion of mankind would find it more difficult to achieve that concentration essential to maximum mental creativity.

Solitude is something else. One can—with sufficient will power—find solitude in a crowd, in a suburban rose garden, or indoors in a great city, windows closed and doors barred. Some great minds have done so. But surely that solitude is best where the possibility of being alone is coupled with privacy, silence, and the exciting quality of remoteness which only untouched nature seems to possess. Certain supreme beauties move one more the further away from cities they lie—the empty starlit sky, the glint of moonlight on a lake, towering mountains. Clearly for the few drawn to contemplation and the search for truth, who are the teachers of the race, a world with no remaining wilderness would be poor indeed.

Needs differ, even among animals—as any dog-lover can testify. Any good society must provide for varying preferences—for crowd-warmth as well as for freedom, nature, natural beauty, privacy, and solitude. So, if we say that an optimum population for this planet is one that can most fully enjoy the *savor* of life we have to admit that savor is hard to define. It includes all sorts of things—freedom, nature, beauty, spaciousness, the sense of adventure—and a certain smacking of the lips. It can even (at least for me) be *symbolized* by the type of available food.

It is here that the demographers reveal their appalling inhumanity. Solemnly they calculate the amount of nourishment necessary to fill ever more billions of bellies. Looking for the maximum nourishment obtainable, some are already counting on wood pulp and algae. Through tens of millions of acres of forests or algae "farms" in the sea and floating islands whose inhabitants would cut down their physical activities so as to need a minimum of calories, the earth—they reason—might conceivably nourish no less than 200 billion creatures—though whether they could any longer at that point be called human I cannot say. Some masterminds go further. A British physicist, J. D. Bernal, has suggested solving the food problem by synthesizing an edible something from coal, limestone, and air. (This has, I believe, been done and I would wish Communists like Bernal no worse than having to live on it.) On such a basis, zoologist Berrill acidly comments, there might develop "a population so universally dense that there would be sitting room only." Yet if maximum multiplication is a man's aim (or fate) here is a promising approach.

It inspires a less promising conclusion: Raising as many children as the good Lord sends may—short of catastrophe—at some point require everyone to live upon *sawdust, seaweed,* and/or *synthetics.* Provided one cared to live at all. Personally I should not. Suffering we can stand if we must. But not the tedium of a savorless existence.

Sir Charles Darwin insists that man, like any other organism, will regularly reproduce right up to the starvation limit. Some people have always been hungry. Some are hungry today. Some always will be hungry. Nothing that man does can change it. Perhaps not. But if man's will cannot limit the size of his family how can Sir Charles know that his statement is anything but a conditioned reflex, empty of either truth or falsehood? Determinism anywhere makes argument useless. Besides, other distinguished specialists believe that mankind can control its numbers if it puts its mind to it.

One other objection to limiting population deserves more consideration. It runs that by limiting the number of human beings we would actually worsen the race by limiting the occurrence of superior men and women. If—one may reason—"teachers of the human race" occur in anything like a regular proportion, then the more people, the more outstanding individuals on earth at any time and the faster civilization will grow.

What little we know about the frequency of greatness does not sustain this view. Observed evidence is all the other way. Athens, Alexandria, Florence, Cordova, medieval Paris—these seem to have brought forth genius in all fields far more thickly than modern New York or London, not to speak of Canton or Calcutta. Renaissance Italy, Germany, France, Britain, and the Low Countries, Persia at one period—with relatively few inhabitants—appear to have been proportionately richer in high-quality individuals than today's teeming supernations. A serious investigation of population density and human quality might well indicate an optimum size to cities as well as an optimum human density. Such an investigation would be difficult. And maintaining the optimum, once it was found, even harder. After all, in our own times two countries, Ireland and Sweden, have kept their numbers under control with admirable results.

One ingenious way to control population has been stated by an inhabitant of Lin Yutang's imaginary island of Thainos: "Very simple. We have a system of proportionate taxation. The larger the family the higher the tax. That stops it, all right."

Difficult to enact and enforce? Perhaps. But compare it with an alternative remedy currently proposed. Dr. Fritz Zwicky suggests that those who find the earth too crowded simply bomb large pieces out of frigid planets like Jupiter, Saturn, and Neptune, create out of the material salvaged a hundred new planets with climates and motions like the earth's, and go live on them. He even offers, given ten years and enough money, to build an interplanetary ship. Which is more utopian: to call upon people to limit the number of their offspring or to rearrange the Solar System?

Until the advent of nuclear weapons it could be argued that no Great Power, however desirous of promoting the quality rather than the quantity of its citizens, dare do so lest it be militarily overwhelmed by a conceivably inferior but more numerous enemy. But the H-bombs seem to have become the "equalizers" of nations much as the six-shooter was that of individuals. Certainly they have made it unlikely that man can surmount the next half-century without a holocaust that would solve the population problem for some time unless he establishes some sort of supernational authority. On this account the threat of multiplication to where "the earth is covered with a writhing mass of human beings much as a dead cow is covered with a writhing mass of maggots" is presumably just a poetic nightmare. Yet the dilemma of some not-too-distant future is real enough—an increasingly dreary, shrinking life for ever more people, or an ever nobler, broader life for a limited number. There is no escape. So maybe the average American young woman had better start helping God to keep human quality up by some limitation on human numbers.

RACHEL CARSON

Rachel Carson (1907–1964), biologist and writer, was educated at Pennsylvania College for Women and Johns Hopkins. She taught zoology at the University of Maryland, worked sixteen years for the U. S. Fish and

Wildlife Service, and contributed many articles to both popular and scientific periodicals. Her remarkable combination of scientific knowledge, love of nature, and superbly expressive literary style accounted for the universal admiration of The Sea Around Us *(1951). Her other books are* Under the Sea Wind *(1941),* The Edge of the Sea *(1955), and* Silent Spring *(1962). The last, written in a more polemical vein, touched off an international controversy over the effect of pesticides. We here include Chapter 15, followed by the references given by the author for this chapter.*

NATURE FIGHTS BACK

To have risked so much in our efforts to mold nature to our satisfaction and yet to have failed in achieving our goal would indeed be the final irony. Yet this, it seems, is our situation. The truth, seldom mentioned but there for anyone to see, is that nature is not so easily molded and that the insects are finding ways to circumvent our chemical attacks on them.

"The insect world is nature's most astonishing phenomenon," said the Dutch biologist C. J. Briejèr. "Nothing is impossible to it; the most improbable things commonly occur there. One who penetrates deeply into its mysteries is continually breathless with wonder. He knows that anything can happen, and that the completely impossible often does."

The "impossible" is now happening on two broad fronts. By a process of genetic selection, the insects are developing strains resistant to chemicals. This will be discussed in the following chapter. But the broader problem, which we shall look at now, is the fact that our chemical attack is weakening the defenses inherent in the environment itself, defenses designed to keep the various species in check. Each time we breach these defenses a horde of insects pours through.

From all over the world come reports that make it clear we are in a serious predicament. At the end of a decade or more of intensive chemical control, entomologists were finding that problems they had considered solved a few years earlier had returned to plague them. And new problems had arisen as insects once present only in insignificant numbers had increased to the status of serious pests. By their very nature chemical controls are self-defeating, for they have been devised and applied without taking into account the complex biological systems against which they have been blindly hurled. The chemicals may have been pretested against a few individual species, but not against living communities.

In some quarters nowadays it is fashionable to dismiss the balance of nature as a state of affairs that prevailed in an earlier, simpler world— a state that has now been so thoroughly upset that we might as well forget it. Some find this a convenient assumption, but as a chart for a course of action it is highly dangerous. The balance of nature is not the same today as in Pleistocene times, but it is still there: a complex, precise, and highly integrated system of relationships between living things which cannot safely be ignored any more than the law of gravity can be defied with impunity by a man perched on the edge of a cliff. The balance of nature is not a *status quo;* it is fluid, ever shifting, in a constant state of adjustment. Man, too, is part of this balance. Sometimes the balance is in his favor; sometimes—and all too often through his own activities—it is shifted to his disadvantage.

Two critically important facts have been overlooked in designing the modern insect control programs. The first is that the really effective control of insects is that applied by nature, not by man. Populations are kept in check by something the ecologists call the resistance of the environment, and this has been so since the first life was created. The amount of food available, conditions of weather and climate, the presence of competing or predatory species, all are critically important. "The greatest single factor in preventing insects from overwhelming the rest of the world is the internecine warfare which they carry out among themselves," said the entomologist Robert Metcalf. Yet most of the chemicals now used kill all insects, our friends and enemies alike.

The second neglected fact is the truly explosive power of a species to reproduce once the resistance of the environment has been weakened. The fecundity of many forms of life is almost beyond our power to imagine, though now and then we have suggestive glimpses. I remember from student days the miracle that could be wrought in a jar containing a simple mixture of hay and water merely by adding to it a few drops of material from a mature culture of protozoa. Within a few days the jar would contain a whole galaxy of whirling, darting life—uncountable trillions of the slipper animalcule, *Paramecium,* each small as a dust grain, all multiplying without restraint in their temporary Eden of favorable temperatures, abundant food, absence of enemies. Or I think of shore rocks white with barnacles as far as the eye can see, or of the spectacle of passing through an immense school of jellyfish, mile after mile, with seemingly no end to the pulsing, ghostly forms scarcely more substantial than the water itself.

We see the miracle of nature's control at work when the cod move through winter seas to their spawning grounds, where each female deposits several millions of eggs. The sea does not become a solid mass of cod as it would surely do if all the progeny of all the cod were to survive. The checks that exist in nature are such that out of the millions of young produced by each pair only enough, on the average, survive to adulthood to replace the parent fish.

Biologists used to entertain themselves by speculating as to what would happen if, through some unthinkable catastrophe, the natural restraints were thrown off and all the progeny of a single individual survived. Thus

Thomas Huxley a century ago calculated that a single female aphis (which has the curious power of reproducing without mating) could produce progeny in a single year's time whose total weight would equal that of the inhabitants of the Chinese empire of his day.

Fortunately for us such an extreme situation is only theoretical, but the dire results of upsetting nature's own arrangements are well known to students of animal populations. The stockman's zeal for eliminating the coyote has resulted in plagues of field mice, which the coyote formerly controlled. The oft repeated story of the Kaibab deer in Arizona is another case in point. At one time the deer population was in equilibrium with its environment. A number of predators—wolves, pumas, and coyotes—prevented the deer from outrunning their food supply. Then a campaign was begun to "conserve" the deer by killing off their enemies. Once the predators were gone, the deer increased prodigiously and soon there was not enough food for them. The browse line on the trees went higher and higher as they sought food, and in time many more deer were dying of starvation than had formerly been killed by predators. The whole environment, moreover, was damaged by their desperate efforts to find food.

The predatory insects of field and forests play the same role as the wolves and coyotes of the Kaibab. Kill them off and the population of the prey insect surges upward.

No one knows how many species of insects inhabit the earth because so many are yet to be identified. But more than 700,000 have already been described. This means that in terms of the number of species, 70 to 80 per cent of the earth's creatures are insects. The vast majority of these insects are held in check by natural forces, without any intervention by man. If this were not so, it is doubtful that any conceivable volume of chemicals—or any other methods—could possibly keep down their populations.

The trouble is that we are seldom aware of the protection afforded by natural enemies until it fails. Most of us walk unseeing through the world, unaware alike of its beauties, its wonders, and the strange and sometimes terrible intensity of the lives that are being lived about us. So it is that the activities of the insect predators and parasites are known to few. Perhaps we may have noticed an oddly shaped insect of ferocious mien on a bush in the garden and been dimly aware that the praying mantis lives at the expense of other insects. But we see with understanding eye only if we have walked in the garden at night and here and there with a flashlight have glimpsed the mantis stealthily creeping upon her prey. Then we sense something of the drama of the hunter and the hunted. Then we begin to feel something of that relentlessly pressing force by which nature controls her own.

The predators—insects that kill and consume other insects—are of many kinds. Some are quick and with the speed of swallows snatch their prey from the air. Others plod methodically along a stem, plucking off and devouring sedentary insects like the aphids. The yellowjackets capture soft-bodied insects and feed the juices to their young. Muddauber wasps build columned nests of mud under the eaves of houses and stock them with insects on which their young will feed. The horseguard wasp hovers above herds of grazing cattle, destroying the blood-sucking flies that torment them. The loudly buzzing syrphid fly, often mistaken for a bee, lays its eggs on leaves of aphis-infested plants; the hatching larvae then consume immense numbers of aphids. Ladybugs or lady beetles are among the most effective destroyers of aphids, scale insects, and other plant-eating insects. Literally hundreds of aphids are consumed by a single ladybug to stoke the little fires of energy which she requires to produce even a single batch of eggs.

Even more extraordinary in their habits are the parasitic insects. These do not kill their hosts outright. Instead, by a variety of adaptations they utilize their victims for the nurture of their own young. They may deposit their eggs within the larvae or eggs of their prey, so that their own developing young may find food by consuming the host. Some attach their eggs to a caterpillar by means of a sticky solution; on hatching, the larval parasite bores through the skin of the host. Others, led by an instinct that simulates foresight, merely lay their eggs on a leaf so that a browsing caterpillar will eat them inadvertently.

Everywhere, in field and hedgerow and garden and forest, the insect predators and parasites are at work. Here, above a pond, the dragonflies dart and the sun strikes fire from their wings. So their ancestors sped through swamps where huge reptiles lived. Now, as in those ancient times, the sharp-eyed dragonflies capture mosquitoes in the air, scooping them in with basket-shaped legs. In the waters below, their young, the dragonfly nymphs, or naiads, prey on the aquatic stages of mosquitoes and other insects.

Or there, almost invisible against a leaf, is the lacewing, with green gauze wings and golden eyes, shy and secretive, descendant of an ancient race that lived in Permian times. The adult lacewing feeds mostly on plant nectars and the honeydew of aphids, and in time she lays her eggs, each on the end of a long stalk which she fastens to a leaf. From these emerge her children—strange, bristled larvae called aphis lions, which live by preying on aphids, scales, or mites, which they capture and suck dry of fluid. Each may consume several hundred aphids before the ceaseless turning of the cycle of its life brings the time when it will spin a white silken cocoon in which to pass the pupal stage.

And there are many wasps, and flies as well, whose very existence depends on the destruction of the eggs or larvae of other insects through parasitism. Some of the egg parasites are exceedingly minute wasps, yet by their numbers and their great activity they hold down the abundance of many crop-destroying species.

All these small creatures are working—working in sun and rain, during the hours of darkness, even when winter's grip has damped down the fires of life to mere embers. Then this vital force is merely smoldering, awaiting the time to flare again into activity when spring awakens the insect world. Meanwhile, under the white blanket of snow, below the frost-hardened soil, in crevices in the bark of trees, and in sheltered caves, the parasites and the predators have found ways to tide themselves over the season of cold.

The eggs of the mantis are secure in little cases of thin parchment attached to the branch of a shrub by the mother who lived her life span with the summer that is gone.

The female *Polistes* wasp, taking shelter in a forgotten corner of some attic, carries in her body the fertilized eggs, the heritage on which the whole future of her colony depends. She, the lone survivor, will start a small paper nest in the spring, lay a few eggs in its cells, and carefully rear a small force of workers. With their help she will then enlarge the nest and develop the colony. Then the workers, foraging ceaselessly through the hot days of summer, will destroy countless caterpillars.

Thus, through the circumstances of their lives, and the nature of our own wants, all these have been our allies in keeping the balance of nature tilted in our favor. Yet we have turned our artillery against our friends. The terrible danger is that we have grossly underestimated their value in keeping at bay a dark tide of enemies that, without their help, can overrun us.

The prospect of a general and permanent lowering of environmental resistance becomes grimly and increasingly real with each passing year as the number, variety, and destructiveness of insecticides grows. With the passage of time we may expect progressively more serious outbreaks of insects, both disease-carrying and crop-destroying species, in excess of anything we have ever known.

"Yes, but isn't this all theoretical?" you may ask. "Surely it won't really happen—not in my lifetime, anyway."

But it is happening, here and now. Scientific journals had already recorded some 50 species involved in violent dislocations of nature's balance by 1958. More examples are being found every year. A recent review of the subject contained references to 215 papers reporting or discussing unfavorable upsets in the balance of insect populations caused by pesticides.

Sometimes the result of chemical spraying has been a tremendous upsurge of the very insect the spraying was intended to control, as when blackflies in Ontario became 17 times more abundant after spraying than they had been before. Or when in England an enormous outbreak of the cabbage aphid—an outbreak that had no parallel on record—followed spraying with one of the organic phosphorus chemicals.

At other times spraying, while reasonably effective against the target insect, has let loose a whole Pandora's box of destructive pests that had never previously been abundant enough to cause trouble. The spider mite, for example, has become practically a worldwide pest as DDT and other insecticides have killed off its enemies. The spider mite is not an insect. It is a barely visible eight-legged creature belonging to the group that includes spiders, scorpions, and ticks. It has mouth parts adapted for piercing and sucking, and a prodigious appetite for the chlorophyll that makes the world green. It inserts these minute and stiletto-sharp mouth parts into the outer cells of leaves and evergreen needles and extracts the chlorophyll. A mild infestation gives trees and shrubbery a mottled or salt-and-pepper appearance; with a heavy mite population, foliage turns yellow and falls.

This is what happened in some of the western national forests a few years ago, when in 1956 the United States Forest Service sprayed some 885,000 acres of forested lands with DDT. The intention was to control the spruce budworm, but the following summer it was discovered that a problem worse than the budworm damage had been created. In surveying the forests from the air, vast blighted areas could be seen where the magnificent Douglas firs were turning brown and dropping their needles. In the Helena National Forest and on the western slopes of the Big Belt Mountains, then in other areas of Montana and down into Idaho the forests looked as though they had been scorched. It was evident that this summer of 1957 had brought the most extensive and spectacular infestation of spider mites in history. Almost all of the sprayed area was affected. Nowhere else was the damage evident. Searching for precedents, the foresters could remember other scourges of spider mites, though less dramatic than this one. There had been similar trouble along the Madison River in Yellowstone Park in 1929, in Colorado 20 years later, and then in New Mexico in 1956. *Each of these outbreaks had followed forest spraying with insecticides.* (The 1929 spraying, occurring before the DDT era, employed lead arsenate.)

Why does the spider mite appear to thrive on insecticides? Besides the obvious fact that it is relatively insensitive to them, there seem to be two other reasons. In nature it is kept in check by various predators such as ladybugs, a gall midge, predaceous mites and several pirate bugs, all of them extremely sensitive to insecticides. The third reason has to do with population pressure within the spider mite colonies. An undisturbed colony of mites is a densely settled community, huddled under a protective webbing for concealment from its enemies. When sprayed, the colonies disperse as the mites, irritated though not killed by the chemicals, scatter out in search of places where they will not be disturbed. In so doing they find a far greater abundance of space and food than was available in the former colonies. Their enemies are now dead so there is no need for the mites to spend their energy in secreting protective webbing. Instead, they pour all their energies into producing more mites. It is not uncommon for their egg production to be increased threefold—all through the beneficent effect of insecticides.

In the Shenandoah Valley of Virginia, a famous apple-growing region, hordes of a small insect called the red-banded leaf roller arose to plague the growers as soon as DDT began to replace arsenate of lead. Its depredations had never before been important; soon its toll rose to 50 per cent of the crop and it achieved the status of the most destructive pest of apples, not only in this region but throughout much of the East and Midwest, as the use of DDT increased.

The situation abounds in ironies. In the apple orchards of Nova Scotia in the late 1940's the worst infestations of the codling moth (cause of "wormy apples") were in the orchards regularly sprayed. In unsprayed orchards the moths were not abundant enough to cause real trouble.

Diligence in spraying had a similarly unsatisfactory reward in the eastern Sudan, where cotton growers had a bitter experience with DDT. Some 60,000 acres of cotton were being grown under irrigation in the Gash Delta. Early trials of DDT having given apparently good results, spraying was intensified. It was then that trouble began. One of the most destructive enemies of cotton is the bollworm. But the more cotton was sprayed, the more bollworms appeared. The unsprayed cotton suffered less damage to fruits and later to mature bolls than the sprayed, and in twice-sprayed fields the yield of seed cotton dropped significantly. Although some of the leaf-feeding insects were eliminated, any benefit that might thus have been gained was more than offset by bollworm damage. In the end the growers were faced with the unpleasant truth that their cotton yield would have been greater had they saved themselves the trouble and expense of spraying.

In the Belgian Congo and Uganda the results of heavy applications of DDT against an insect pest of the coffee bush were almost "catastrophic." The pest itself was found to be almost completely unaffected by the DDT, while its predator was extremely sensitive.

In America, farmers have repeatedly traded one insect enemy for a worse one as spraying upsets the population dynamics of the insect world. Two of the mass-spraying programs recently carried out have had precisely this effect. One was the fire ant eradication program in the South; the other was the spraying for the Japanese beetle in the Midwest.

When a wholesale application of heptachlor was made to the farmlands in Louisiana in 1957, the result was the unleashing of one of the worst enemies of the sugarcane crop—the sugarcane borer. Soon after the heptachlor treatment, damage by borers increased sharply. The chemical aimed at the fire ant had killed off the enemies of the borer. The crop was so severely damaged that farmers sought to bring suit against the state for negligence in not warning them that this might happen.

The same bitter lesson was learned by Illinois farmers. After the devastating bath of dieldrin recently administered to the farmlands in eastern Illinois for the control of the Japanese beetle, farmers discovered that corn borers had increased enormously in the treated area. In fact, corn grown in fields within this area contained almost twice as many of the destructive larvae of this insect as did the corn grown outside. The farmers may not yet be aware of the biological basis of what has happened, but they need no scientists to tell them they have made a poor bargain. In trying to get rid of one insect, they have brought on a scourge of a much more destructive one. According to Department of Agriculture estimates, total damage by the Japanese beetle in the United States adds up to about 10 million dollars a year, while damage by the corn borer runs to about 85 million.

It is worth noting that natural forces had been heavily relied on for control of the corn borer. Within two years after this insect was accidentally introduced from Europe in 1917, the United States Government had mounted one of its most intensive programs for locating and importing parasites of an insect pest. Since that time 24 species of parasites of the corn borer have been brought in from Europe and the Orient at considerable expense. Of these, 5 are recognized as being of distinct value in control. Needless to say, the results of all this work are now jeopardized as the enemies of the corn borer are killed off by the sprays.

If this seems absurd, consider the situation in the citrus groves of California, where the world's most famous and successful experiment in biological control was carried out in the 1880's. In 1872 a scale insect that feeds on the sap of citrus trees appeared in California and within the next 15 years developed into a pest so destructive that the fruit crop in many orchards was a complete loss. The young citrus industry was threatened with destruction. Many farmers gave up and pulled out their trees. Then a parasite of the scale insect was imported from Australia, a small lady beetle called the vedalia. Within only two years after the first shipment of the beetles, the scale was under complete control throughout the citrus-growing sections of California. From that time on one could search for days among the orange groves without finding a single scale insect.

Then in the 1940's the citrus growers began to experiment with glamorous new chemicals against other insects. With the advent of DDT and the even more toxic chemicals to follow, the populations of the vedalia in many sections of California were wiped out. Its importation had cost the government a mere $5000. Its activities had saved the fruit growers several millions of dollars a year, but in a moment of heedlessness the benefit was canceled out. Infestations of the scale insect quickly reappeared and damage exceeded anything that had been seen for fifty years.

"This possibly marked the end of an era," said Dr. Paul DeBach of the Citrus Experiment Station in Riverside. Now control of the scale has become enormously complicated. The vedalia can be maintained only by repeated releases and by the most careful attention to spray schedules, to minimize their contact with insecticides. And regardless of what the citrus growers do, they are more or less at the mercy of the owners of adjacent acreages, for severe damage has been done by insecticidal drift.

All these examples concern insects that attack agricultural crops. What of those that carry disease? There have already been warnings. On Nissan Island in the South Pacific, for example, spraying had been carried on intensively during the Second World War, but was stopped when hostilities came to an end. Soon swarms of a malaria-carrying mosquito reinvaded the island. All of its predators had been killed off and there had not been time for new populations to become established. The way was therefore clear for a tremendous population explosion. Marshall Laird, who has described this incident, compares chemical control to a treadmill; once we have set foot on it we are unable to stop for fear of the consequences.

In some parts of the world disease can be linked with spraying in quite a different way. For some reason, snail-like mollusks seem to be almost immune to the effects of insecticides. This has been observed many times. In the general holocaust that followed the spraying of salt marshes in eastern Florida, aquatic snails alone survived. The scene as described was a macabre picture—something that might have been created by a surrealist brush. The snails moved among the bodies of the dead fishes and the moribund crabs, devouring the victims of the death rain of poison.

But why is this important? It is important because many aquatic snails serve as hosts of dangerous parasitic worms that spend part of their life cycle in a mollusk, part in a human being. Examples are the blood flukes, or schistosoma, that cause serious disease in man when they enter the body by way of drinking water or through the skin when people are bathing in infested waters. The flukes are released into the water by the host snails. Such diseases are especially prevalent in parts of Asia and Africa. Where they occur, insect control measures that favor a vast increase of snails are likely to be followed by grave consequences.

And of course man is not alone in being subject to snail-borne disease. Liver disease in cattle, sheep, goats, deer, elk, rabbits, and various other warm-blooded animals may be caused by liver flukes that spend part of their life cycles in fresh-water snails. Livers infested with these worms are unfit for use as human food and are routinely condemned. Such rejections cost American cattlemen about 3½ million dollars annually. Anything that acts to increase the number of snails can obviously make this problem an even more serious one.

Over the past decade these problems have cast long shadows, but we have been slow to recognize them. Most of those best fitted to develop natural controls and assist in putting them into effect have been too busy laboring in the more exciting vineyards of chemical control. It was reported in 1960 that only 2 per cent of all the economic entomologists in the country were then working in the field of biological controls. A substantial number of the remaining 98 per cent were engaged in research on chemical insecticides.

Why should this be? The major chemical companies are pouring money into the universities to support research on insecticides. This creates attractive fellowships for graduate students and attractive staff positions. Biological-control studies, on the other hand, are never so endowed—for the simple reason that they do not promise anyone the fortunes that are to be made in the chemical industry. These are left to state and federal agencies, where the salaries paid are far less.

This situation also explains the otherwise mystifying fact that certain outstanding entomologists are among the leading advocates of chemical control. Inquiry into the background of some of these men reveals that their entire research program is supported by the chemical industry. Their professional prestige, sometimes their very jobs depend on the perpetuation of chemical methods. Can we then expect them to bite the hand that literally feeds them? But knowing their bias, how much credence can we give to their protests that insecticides are harmless?

Amid the general acclaim for chemicals as the principal method of insect control, minority reports have occasionally been filed by those few entomologists who have not lost sight of the fact that they are neither chemists nor engineers, but biologists.

F. H. Jacob in England has declared that "the activities of many so-called economic entomologists would make it appear that they operate in the belief that salvation lies at the end of a spray nozzle . . . that when they have created problems of resurgence or resistance or mammalian toxicity, the chemist will be ready with another pill. That view is not held here . . . Ultimately only the biologist will provide the answers to the basic problems of pest control."

"Economic entomologists must realize," wrote A. D. Pickett of Nova Scotia, "that they are dealing with living things . . . their work must be more than simply insecticide testing or a quest for highly destructive chemicals." Dr. Pickett himself was a pioneer in the field of working out sane methods of insect control that take full advantage of the predatory and parasitic species. The method which he and his associates evolved is today a shining model but one too little emulated. Only in the integrated control programs developed by some California entomologists do we find anything comparable in this country.

Dr. Pickett began his work some thirty-five years ago in the apple orchards of the Annapolis Valley in Nova Scotia, once one of the most concentrated fruit-growing areas in Canada. At that time it was believed that insecticides—then inorganic chemicals—would solve the problems of insect control, that the only task was to induce fruit growers to follow the recommended methods. But the rosy picture failed to materialize. Somehow the insects persisted. New chemicals were added, better spraying equipment was devised, and the zeal for spraying increased, but the insect problem did not get any better. Then DDT promised to "obliterate the nightmare" of codling moth outbreaks. What actually resulted from its use was an unprecedented scourge of mites. "We move from crisis to crisis, merely trading one problem for another," said Dr. Pickett.

At this point, however, Dr. Pickett and his associates struck out on a new road instead of going along with other entomologists who continued to pursue the will-o'-the-wisp of the ever more toxic chemical. Recognizing that they had a strong ally in nature, they devised a program that makes maximum use of natural controls and minimum use of insecticides. Whenever insecticides are applied only minimum dosages are used— barely enough to control the pest without avoidable harm to beneficial species. Proper timing also enters in. Thus, if nicotine sulphate is applied before rather than after the apple blossoms turn pink one of the important predators is spared, probably because it is still in the egg stage.

Dr. Pickett uses special care to select chemicals that will do as little harm as possible to insect parasites and predators. "When we reach the point of using DDT, parathion, chlordane, and other new insecticides as routine control measures in the same way we have used the inorganic chemicals in the past, entomologists interested in biological control may as well throw in the sponge," he says. Instead of these highly toxic, broad-spectrum insecticides, he places chief reliance on ryania (derived from ground stems of a tropical plant), nicotine sulphate, and lead arsenate. In certain situations very weak concentrations of DDT or malathion are used (1 or 2 ounces per 100 gallons—in contrast to the usual 1 or 2 pounds per 100 gallons). Although these two are the least toxic of the modern insecticides, Dr. Pickett hopes by further research to replace them with safer and more selective materials.

How well has this program worked? Nova Scotia orchardists who are following Dr. Pickett's modified spray program are producing as high a proportion of first-grade fruit as are those who are using intensive chemical applications. They are also getting as good production. They are getting these results, moreover, at a substantially lower cost. The outlay for insecticides in Nova Scotia apple orchards is only from 10 to 20 per cent of the amount spent in most other apple-growing areas.

More important than even these excellent results is the fact that the modified program worked out by these Nova Scotian entomologists is not doing violence to nature's balance. It is well on the way to realizing the philosophy stated by the Canadian entomologist G. C. Ullyett a decade ago: "We must change our philosophy, abandon our attitude of human superiority and admit that in many cases in natural environments we find ways and means of limiting populations of organisms in a more economical way than we can do it ourselves."

PRINCIPAL SOURCES OF INFORMATION

Page 635
Briejèr, C. J., "The Growing Resistance of Insects to Insecticides," *Atlantic Naturalist*, Vol. 13 (1958), No. 3, pp. 149–55.

Page 636
Metcalf, Robert L., "The Impact of the Development of Organo-phosphorus Insecticides upon Basic and Applied Science," *Bull. Entomol. Soc. Am.*, Vol. 5 (March 1959), pp. 3–15.

Page 637
Ripper, W. E., "Effect of Pesticides on Balance of Arthropod Popula-tions," *Annual Rev. Entomol.*, Vol. 1 (1956), pp. 403–38.

Page 637
Allen, Durward L., *Our Wildlife Legacy*. New York: Funk & Wag-nalls, 1954. Pp. 234–36.

Page 637
Sabrosky, Curtis W., "How Many Insects Are There?" *Yearbook of Agric.*, U.S. Dept. of Agric., 1952, pp. 1–7.

Page 638
Bishopp, F. C., "Insect Friends of Man," *Yearbook of Agric.*, U.S. Dept. of Agric., 1952, pp. 79–87.

Page 638
Klots, Alexander B., and Elsie B. Klots, "Beneficial Bees, Wasps, and Ants," *Handbook on Biological Control of Plant Pests*, pp. 44–46. Brooklyn Botanic Garden. Reprinted from *Plants and Gardens*, Vol. 16 (1960), No. 3.

Page 638
Hagen, Kenneth S., "Biological Control with Lady Beetles," *Hand-book on Biological Control of Plant Pests*, pp. 28–35.

Page 638
Schlinger, Evert I., "Natural Enemies of Aphids," *Handbook on Bio-logical Control of Plant Pests*, pp. 36–42.

Page 639
Bishopp, "Insect Friends of Man."

Page 639
Ripper, "Effect of Pesticides on Arthropod Populations."

Page 639
Davies, D. M., "A Study of the Black-fly Population of a Stream in Algonquin Park, Ontario," *Transactions*, Royal Canadian Inst., Vol. 59 (1950), pp. 121–59.

Page 639
Ripper, "Effect of Pesticides on Arthropod Populations."

Page 640
Johnson, Philip C., *Spruce Spider Mite Infestations in Northern Rocky*

Mountain Douglas-Fir Forests. Research Paper 55, Intermountain Forest and Range Exper. Station, U.S. Forest Service, Ogden, Utah, 1958.

Pages 640–41

Davis, Donald W., "Some Effects of DDT on Spider Mites," *Jour. Econ. Entomol.*, Vol. 45 (1952), No. 6, pp. 1011–19.

Page 641

Gould, E., and E. O. Hamstead, "Control of the Red-banded Leaf Roller," *Jour. Econ. Entomol.*, Vol. 41 (1948), pp. 887–90.

Page 641

Pickett, A. D., "A Critique on Insect Chemical Control Methods," *Canadian Entomologist*, Vol. 81 (1949), No. 3, pp. 1–10.

Page 641

Joyce, R. J. V., "Large-Scale Spraying of Cotton in the Gash Delta in Eastern Sudan," *Bull. Entomol. Research*, Vol. 47 (1956), pp. 390–413.

Page 641

Long, W. H., et al., "Fire Ant Eradication Program Increases Damage by the Sugarcane Borer," *Sugar Bull.*, Vol. 37 (1958), No. 5, pp. 62–63.

Pages 641–42

Luckmann, William H., "Increase of European Corn Borers Following Soil Application of Large Amounts of Dieldrin," *Jour. Econ. Entomol.*, Vol. 53 (1960), No. 4, pp. 582–84.

Page 642

Haeussler, G. J., "Losses Caused by Insects," *Yearbook of Agric.*, U.S. Dept. of Agric., 1952, pp. 141–46.

Page 642

Clausen, C. P., "Parasites and Predators," *Yearbook of Agric.*, U.S. Dept. of Agric., 1952, pp. 380–88.

Page 642

———, *Biological Control of Insect Pests in the Continental United States.* U.S. Dept. of Agric. Technical Bulletin No. 1139 (June 1956), pp. 1–151.

Page 642

DeBach, Paul, "Application of Ecological Information to Control of Citrus Pests in California," *Proc.*, 10th Internatl. Congress of Entomologists (1956), Vol. 3 (1958), pp. 187–94.

Page 643

Laird, Marshall, "Biological Solutions to Problems Arising from the Use of Modern Insecticides in the Field of Public Health," *Acta Tropica*, Vol. 16 (1959), No. 4, pp. 331–55.

Page 643

Harrington, R. W., and W. L. Bidlingmayer, "Effects of Dieldrin on Fishes and Invertebrates of a Salt Marsh," *Jour. Wildlife Management*, Vol. 22 (1958), No. 1, pp. 76–82.

Page 643
Liver Flukes in Cattle. U.S. Dept. of Agric. Leaflet No. 493 (1961).
Page 644
Fisher, Theodore W., "What Is Biological Control?" *Handbook on
Biological Control of Plant Pests,* pp. 6–18. Brooklyn Botanic Garden.
Reprinted from *Plants and Gardens,* Vol. 16 (1960), No. 3.
Page 644
Jacob, F. H., "Some Modern Problems in Pest Control," *Science
Progress,* No. 181 (1958), pp. 30–45.
Page 644
Pickett, A. D., and N. A. Patterson, "The Influence of Spray Programs
on the Fauna of Apple Orchards in Nova Scotia. IV. A Review,"
Canadian Entomologist, Vol. 85 (1953), No. 12, pp. 472–78.
Pages 644–45
Pickett, A. D., "Controlling Orchard Insects," *Agric. Inst. Rev.,* March–
April 1953.
Page 645
——, "The Philosophy of Orchard Insect Control," 79th *Annual Re-
port,* Entomol. Soc. of Ontario (1948), pp. 1–5.
Page 645
——, "The Control of Apple Insects in Nova Scotia." Mimeo.
Page 645
Ullyett, G. C., "Insects, Man and the Environment," *Jour. Econ.
Entomol.,* Vol. 44 (1951), No. 4, pp. 459–64.

E. B. WHITE

*Elwyn Brooks White, born in 1899, was graduated from Cornell in 1921
and joined the staff of* The New Yorker *in 1926. He regularly wrote its
"Notes and Comment" section until 1938. His sensitive, humorous character and his witty yet natural and exact literary style, along with the
congenial talents of James Thurber and a few others, were largely responsible for the extraordinary reputation of* New Yorker *writing at that time.
He contributed a monthly column, entitled "One Man's Meat," to*

Harper's *from 1938 to 1943 and resumed writing for* The New Yorker *on a free-lance basis in 1945. Since 1937 he has taken periodic refuge in a Maine farm, which he manages and writes about with enthusiasm. He has been awarded honorary degrees from Dartmouth, Maine, Bowdoin, Hamilton, and Harvard, and received a National Institute of Arts and Letters gold medal in 1960 for his contribution to literature. White has published two excellent children's books,* Stuart Little *(1945) and* Charlotte's Web *(1952), two volumes of poetry, collections of his magazine pieces, and other books. Among the best known are* Is Sex Necessary?, *written with James Thurber (1929);* Every Day Is Saturday *(1934);* One Man's Meat *(1942);* The Wild Flag *(1946); and* The Elements of Style *(1959), a reverent re-editing of the textbook of his former teacher William Strunk, Jr. The story we present below, taken from* The Second Tree From the Corner *(1954), was first published in* The New Yorker *in February, 1950.*

THE MORNING OF THE DAY
THEY DID IT

My purpose is to tell how it happened and to set down a few impressions of that morning while it is fresh in memory. I was in a plane that was in radio communication with the men on the platform. To put the matter briefly, what was intended as a military expedient turned suddenly into a holocaust. The explanation was plain enough to me, for, like millions of others, I was listening to the conversation between the two men and was instantly aware of the quick shift it took. That part is clear. What is not so clear is how I myself survived, but I am beginning to understand that, too. I shall not burden the reader with an explanation, however, as the facts are tedious and implausible. I am now in good health and fair spirits, among friendly people on an inferior planet, at a very great distance from the sun. Even the move from one planet to another has not relieved me of the nagging curse that besets writing men—the feeling that they must produce some sort of record of their times.

The thing happened shortly before twelve noon. I came out of my house on East Harding Boulevard at quarter of eight that morning, swinging my newspaper and feeling pretty good. The March day was mild and springlike, the warmth and the smells doubly welcome after the rotten weather we'd been having. A gentle wind met me on the Boulevard, frisked me, and went on. A man in a leather cap was loading bedsprings into a van in front of No. 220. I remember that as I walked along I worked my tongue around the roof of my mouth, trying to dislodge a prune skin. (These details have no significance; why write them down?)

A few blocks from home there was a Contakt plane station and I hurried in, caught the 8:10 plane, and was soon aloft. I always hated a jet-assist takeoff right after breakfast, but it was one of the discomforts that went with my job. At ten thousand feet our small plane made contact with the big one, we passengers were transferred, and the big ship went on up to fifty thousand, which was the height television planes flew at. I was a script writer for one of the programs. My tour of duty was supposed to be eight hours.

I should probably explain here that at the period of which I am writing, the last days of the planet earth, telecasting was done from planes circling the stratosphere. This eliminated the coaxial cable, a form of relay that had given endless trouble. Coaxials worked well enough for a while, but eventually they were abandoned, largely because of the extraordinary depredations of earwigs. These insects had developed an alarming resistance to bugspray and were out of control most of the time. Earwigs increased in size and in numbers, and the forceps at the end of their abdomen developed so that they could cut through a steel shell. They seemed to go unerringly for coaxials. Whether the signals carried by the cables had anything to do with it I don't know, but the bugs fed on these things and were enormously stimulated. Not only did they feast on the cables, causing the cables to disintegrate, but they laid eggs in them in unimaginable quantities, and as the eggs hatched the television images suffered greatly, there was more and more flickering on the screen, more and more eyestrain and nervous tension among audiences, and of course a further debasement of taste and intellectual life in general. Finally the coaxials were given up, and after much experimenting by Westinghouse and the Glenn Martin people a satisfactory substitute was found in the high-flying planes. A few of these planes, spotted around the country, handled the whole television load nicely. Known as Stratovideo planes, they were equipped with studios; many programs originated in the air and were transmitted directly, others were beamed to the aircraft from ground stations and then relayed. The planes flew continuously, twenty-four hours a day, were refuelled in air, and dropped down to ten thousand feet every eight hours to meet the Contakt planes and take on new shifts of workers.

I remember that as I walked to my desk in the Stratoship that morning, the nine-o'clock news had just ended and a program called "Author, Please!" was going on, featuring Melonie Babson, a woman who had written a best-seller on the theme of euthanasia, called "Peace of Body." The program was sponsored by a dress-shield company.

I remember, too, that a young doctor had come aboard the plane with the rest of us. He was a newcomer, a fellow named Cathcart, slated to be the physician attached to the ship. He had introduced himself to me in the Contakt plane, had asked the date of my Tri-D shot, and had noted it down in his book. (I shall explain about these shots presently.) This doctor certainly had a brief life in our midst. He had hardly been introduced around and shown his office when our control room got a radio call asking if there was a doctor in the stratosphere above Earth-point F-plus-6, and requesting medical assistance at the scene of an accident.

F-plus-6 was almost directly below us, so Dr. Cathcart felt he ought to respond, and our control man gave the word and asked for particulars and instructions. It seems there had been a low-altitude collision above F-plus-6 involving two small planes and killing three people. One plane was a Diaheliper, belonging to an aerial diaper service that flew diapers to rural homes by helicopter. The other was one of the familiar government-owned sprayplanes that worked at low altitudes over croplands, truck gardens, and commercial orchards, delivering a heavy mist of the deadly Tri-D solution, the pesticide that had revolutionized agriculture, eliminated the bee from nature, and given us fruits and vegetables of undreamed-of perfection but very high toxicity.

The two planes had tangled and fallen onto the observation tower of a whooping-crane sanctuary, scattering diapers over an area of half a mile and releasing a stream of Tri-D. Cathcart got his medical kit, put on his parachute, and paused a moment to adjust his pressurizer, preparatory to bailing out. Knowing that he wouldn't be back for a while, he asked if anybody around the shop was due for a Tri-D shot that morning, and it turned out that Bill Foley was. So the Doctor told Foley to come along, and explained that he would give him his injection on the way down. Bill threw me a quick look of mock anguish, and started climbing into his gear. This must have been six or seven minutes past nine.

It seems strange that I should feel obliged to explain Tri-D shots. They were a commonplace at this time—as much a part of a person's life as his toothbrush. The correct name for them was Anti-Tri-D, but people soon shortened the name. They were simply injections that everyone had to receive at regular twenty-one-day intervals, to counteract the lethal effect of food, and the notable thing about them was the great importance of the twenty-one-day period. To miss one's Tri-D shot by as much as a couple of hours might mean serious consequences, even death. Almost every day there were deaths reported in the papers from failure to get the injection at the proper time. The whole business was something like insulin control in diabetes. You can easily imagine the work it entailed for doctors in the United States, keeping the entire population protected against death by poisoning.

As Dr. Cathcart and Bill eased themselves out of the plane through the chute exit, I paused briefly and listened to Miss Babson, our author of the day.

"It is a grand privilege," she was saying, "to appear before the television audience this morning and face this distinguished battery of critics, including my old sparring partner, Ralph Armstrong, of the *Herald Tribune*. I suppose after Mr. Armstrong finishes with me I will be a pretty good candidate for euthanasia myself. Ha. But seriously, ladies and gentlemen, I feel that a good book is its own defense."

The authoress had achieved a state of exaltation already. I knew that her book, which she truly believed to be great, had been suggested to her by an agent over a luncheon table and had been written largely by somebody else, whom the publisher had had to bring in to salvage the thing. The final result was a run-of-the-can piece of rubbish easily outselling its nearest competitor.

Miss Babson continued, her exaltation stained with cuteness:

"I have heard my novel criticized on the ground that the theme of euthanasia is too daring, and even that it is anti-Catholic. Well, I can remember, way back in the dark ages, when a lot of things that are accepted as commonplace today were considered daring or absurd. My own father can recall the days when dairy cows were actually bred by natural methods. The farmers of those times felt that the artificial-breeding program developed by our marvellous experiment stations was highfalutin nonsense. Well, we all know what has happened to the dairy industry, with many of our best milch cows giving milk continuously right around the clock, in a steady stream. True, the cows do have to be propped up and held in position in special stanchions and fed intravenously, but I always say it isn't the hubbub that counts, it's the butterfat. And I doubt if even Mr. Armstrong here would want to return to the days when a cow just gave a bucket of milk and then stopped to rest."

Tiring of the literary life, I walked away and looked out a window. Below, near the layer of cumulus, the two chutes were visible. With the help of binoculars I could see Bill manfully trying to slip his chute over next to the Doc, and could see Cathcart fumbling for his needle. Our telecandid man was at another window, filming the thing for the next newscast, as it was a new wrinkle in the Tri-D world to have somebody getting his shot while parachuting.

I had a few chores to do before our program came on, at eleven-five. "Town Meeting of the Upper Air" was the name of it. "Town Meeting" was an unrehearsed show, but I was supposed to brief the guests, distribute copies of whatever prepared scripts there were, explain the cuing, and make everybody happy generally. The program we were readying that morning had had heavy advance billing, and there was tremendous interest in it everywhere, not so much because of the topic ("Will the fear of retaliation stop aggression?") or even the cast of characters, which included Major General Artemus T. Recoil, but because of an incidental stunt we were planning to pull off. We had arranged a radio hookup with the space platform, a gadget the Army had succeeded in establishing six hundred miles up, in the regions of the sky beyond the pull of gravity. The Army, after many years of experimenting with rockets, had not only got the platform established but had sent two fellows there in a Spaceship, and also a liberal supply of the New Weapon.

The whole civilized world had read about this achievement, which swung the balance of power so heavily in our favor, and everyone was aware that the damned platform was wandering around in its own orbit at a dizzy distance from the earth and not subject to gravitational pull. Every kid in America had become an astrophysicist overnight and talked knowingly of exhaust velocities, synergy curves, and Keplerian ellipses. Every subway rider knew that the two men on the platform were breathing oxygen thrown off from big squash vines that they had taken along. The *Reader's Digest* had added to the fun by translating and condensing several German treatises on rockets and space travel, including the great *Wege zur Raumschiffahrt*. But to date, because of security regulations and technical difficulties, there had been no radio-television hookup. Finally we got clearance from Washington, and General Recoil agreed to interview the officers on the platform as part of the "Town Meeting" program. This was big stuff—to hear directly from the Space Platform for Checking Aggression, known pretty generally as the SPCA.

I was keyed up about it myself, but I remember that all that morning in the plane I felt disaffected, and wished I were not a stratovideo man. There were often days like that in the air. The plane, with its queer cargo and its cheap goings on, would suddenly seem unaccountably remote from the world of things I admired. In a physical sense we were never very remote: the plane circled steadily in a fixed circle of about ten miles diameter, and I was never far from my own home on East Harding Boulevard. I could talk to Ann and the children, if I wished, by radiophone.

In many respects mine was a good job. It paid two hundred and twenty-five dollars a week, of which two hundred and ten was withheld. I should have felt well satisfied. Almost everything in the way of social benefits was provided by the government—medical care, hospitalization, education for the children, accident insurance, fire and theft, old-age retirement, Tri-D shots, vacation expense, amusement and recreation, welfare and well-being, Christmas and good will, rainy-day resource, staples and supplies, beverages and special occasions, babysitzfund—it had all been worked out. Any man who kept careful account of his pin money could get along all right, and I guess I should have been happy. Ann never complained much, except about one thing. She found that no matter how we saved and planned, we never could afford to buy flowers. One day, when she was a bit lathered up over household problems, she screamed, "God damn it, I'd rather live dangerously and have one dozen yellow freesias!" It seemed to prey on her mind.

Anyway, this was one of those oppressive days in the air for me.

Something about the plane's undeviating course irritated me; the circle we flew seemed a monstrous excursion to nowhere. The engine noise (we flew at subsonic speed) was an unrelieved whine. Usually I didn't notice the engines, but today the ship sounded in my ears every minute, reminding me of a radiotherapy chamber, and there was always the palpable impact of vulgar miracles—the very nature of television—that made me itchy and fretful.

Appearing with General Recoil on "Town Meeting of the Upper Air" were to be Mrs. Florence Gill, president of the Women's Auxiliary of the Sons of Original Matrons; Amory Buxton, head of the Economics and Withholding Council of the United Nations; and a young man named Tollip, representing one of the small, ineffectual groups that advocated world federation. I rounded up this stable of intellects in the reception room, went over the procedure with them, gave the General a drink (which seemed to be what was on his mind), and then ducked out to catch the ten-o'clock news and to have a smoke.

I found Pete Everhardt in the control room. He looked bushed. "Quite a morning, Nuncle," he said. Pete not only had to keep his signal clean on the nine-o'clock show (Melonie Babson was a speaker who liked to range all over the place when she talked) but he had to keep kicking the ball around with the two Army officers on the space platform, for fear he would lose them just as they were due to go on. And on top of that he felt obliged to stay in touch with Dr. Cathcart down below, as a matter of courtesy, and also to pick up incidental stuff for subsequent newscasts.

I sat down and lit a cigarette. In a few moments the day's authoress wound up her remarks and the news started, with the big, tense face of Ed Peterson on the screen dishing it out. Ed was well equipped by nature for newscasting; he had the accents of destiny. When he spread the news, it penetrated in depth. Each event not only seemed fraught with meaning, it seemed fraught with Ed. When he said "I predict . . ." you felt the full flow of his pipeline to God.

To the best of my recollection the ten-o'clock newscast on this awful morning went as follows:

(Announcer) "Good morning. Tepky's Hormone-Enriched Dental Floss brings you Ed Peterson and the news."

(Ed) "Flash! Three persons were killed and two others seriously injured a few minutes ago at Earthpoint F-plus-6 when a government sprayplane collided with a helicopter of the Diaheliper Company. Both pilots were thrown clear. They are at this moment being treated by a doctor released by parachute from Stratovideo Ship 3, from which I am now speaking. The sprayplane crashed into the observation tower of a whooping-crane sanctuary, releasing a deadly mist of Tri-D and instantly killing three wardens who were lounging there watching the love dance of the cranes. Diapers were scattered widely over the area, and these sterile garments proved invaluable to Dr. Herbert L. Cathcart in bandaging the wounds of the injured pilots, Roy T. Bliss and Homer Schenck. [Here followed a newsreel shot showing Cathcart winding a diaper around the head of one of the victims.] You are now at the scene of the disaster," droned Ed. "This is the first time in the history of television that an infant's napkin has appeared in the role of emergency bandage. Another first for American Tel. & Vid.!

"Washington! A Senate committee, with new facts at its disposal, will reopen the investigation to establish the blame for Pearl Harbor.

"Chicago! Two members of the Department of Sanitation were removed from the payroll today for refusal to take the loyalty oath. Both are members of New Brooms, one of the four hundred thousand organizations on the Attorney General's subversive list.

"Hollywood! It's a boy at the Roscoe Pews. Stay tuned to this channel for a closeup of the Caesarean section during the eleven-o'clock roundup!

"New York! Flash! The Pulitzer Prize in editorial writing has been awarded to Frederick A. Mildly, of the New York *Times,* for his nostalgic editorial 'The Old Pumphandle.'

"Flash! Donations to the Atlantic Community Chest now stand at a little over seven hundred billion dollars. Thanks for a wonderful job of giving—I mean that from my heart.

"New York! The vexing question of whether Greek athletes will be allowed to take part in next year's Olympic Games still deadlocks the Security Council. In a stormy session yesterday the Russian delegate argued that the presence of Greek athletes at the games would be a threat to world peace. Most of the session was devoted to a discussion of whether the question was a procedural matter or a matter of substance.

"Flash! Radio contact with the two United States Army officers on the Space Platform for Checking Aggression, known to millions of listeners as the SPCA, has definitely been established, despite rumors to the contrary. The television audience will hear their voices in a little more than one hour from this very moment. You will *not* see their faces. Stay tuned! This is history, ladies and gentlemen—the first time a human voice freed from the pull of gravity has been heard on earth. The spacemen will be interviewed by Major General Artemus T. Recoil on the well-loved program 'Town Meeting of the Upper Air.'

"I predict: that because of SPCA and the Army's Operation Space, the whole course of human destiny will be abruptly changed, and that the age-old vision of peace is now on the way to becoming a reality."

Ed finished and went into his commercial, which consisted of digging a piece of beef gristle out of his teeth with dental floss.

I rubbed out my cigarette and walked back toward my cell. In the studio next ours, "The Bee" was on the air, and I paused for a while to watch. "The Bee" was a program sponsored by the Larry Cross

Pollination Company, aimed principally at big orchardists and growers
—or rather at their wives. It was an interminable mystery-thriller sort
of thing, with a character called the Bee, who always wore a green hood
with two long black feelers. Standing there in the aisle of the plane,
looking into the glass-enclosed studio, I could see the Bee about to
strangle a red-haired girl in slinky pajamas. This was America's pollination hour, an old standby, answer to the housewife's dream. The Larry
Cross outfit was immensely rich. I think they probably handled better
than eighty per cent of all fertilization in the country. Bees, as I have
said, had become extinct, thanks to the massive doses of chemicals, and
of course this had at first posed a serious agricultural problem, as vast
areas were without natural pollination. The answer came when the Larry
Cross firm was organized, with the slogan "We Carry the Torch for
Nature." The business mushroomed, and branch offices sprang up all
over the nation. During blossom time, field crews of highly trained men
fanned out and pollinized everything by hand—a huge job and an arduous
one. The only honey in the United States was synthetic—a blend of
mineral oil and papaya juice. Ann hated it with a morbid passion.

When I reached my studio I found everybody getting ready for the
warmup. The Town Crier, in his fusty costume, stood holding his bell
by the clapper, while the makeup man touched up his face for him.
Mrs. Gill, the S.O.M. representative, sat gazing contemptuously at young
Tollip. I had riffled through her script earlier, curious to find out what
kind of punch she was going to throw. It was about what I expected.
Her last paragraph contained the suggestion that all persons who advocated a revision of the Charter of the United Nations be automatically
deprived of their citizenship. "If these well-meaning but misguided
persons," ran the script, "with their utopian plans for selling this nation
down the river are so anxious to acquire world citizenship, I say let's
make it easy for them—let's take away the citizenship they've already
got and see how they like it. As a lineal descendant of one of the Sons
of Original Matrons, I am sick and tired of these cuckoo notions of one
world, which come dangerously close to simple treachery. We've enough
to do right here at home without . . ."

And so on. In my mind's ear I could already hear the moderator's
salutary and impartial voice saying, "Thank you, Mrs. Florence Gill."

At five past eleven, the Crier rang his bell. "Hear ye! See ye! Town
Meetin' today! Listen to both sides and make up your own minds!"
Then George Cahill, the moderator, started the ball rolling.

I glanced at Tollip. He looked as though his stomach were filling
up with gas. As the program got under way, my own stomach began
to inflate, too, the way it often did a few hours after breakfast. I remember very little of the early minutes of that morning's Town Meeting.
I recall that the U.N. man spoke first, then Mrs. Gill, then Tollip (who
looked perfectly awful). Finally the moderator introduced General Re-

coil, whose stomach enjoyed the steadying effects of whiskey and who spoke in a loud, slow, confident voice, turning frequently to smile down on the three other guests.

"We in the Army," began the General, "don't pretend that we know all the answers to these brave and wonderful questions. It is not the Army's business to know whether aggression is going to occur or not. Our business is to put on a good show if it *does* occur. The Army is content to leave to the United Nations and to idealists like Mr. Tollip the troublesome details of political progress. I certainly don't know, ladies and gentlemen, whether the fear of retaliation is going to prevent aggression, but I *do* know that there is no moss growing on we of Operation Space. As for myself, I guess I am what you might call a retaliatin' fool. [Laughter in the upper air.] Our enemy is well aware that we are now in a most unusual position to retaliate. That knowledge on the part of our enemy is, in my humble opinion, a deterrent to aggression. If I didn't believe that, I'd shed this uniform and get into a really well-paid line of work, like professional baseball."

Will this plane never quit circling? (I thought). Will the words never quit going round and round? Is there no end to this noisy carrousel of indigestible ideas? Will no one ever catch the brass ring?

"But essentially," continued the General, "our job is not to deal with the theoretical world of Mr. Tollip, who suggests that we merge in some vast superstate with every Tom, Dick, and Harry, no matter what their color or race or how underprivileged they are, thus pulling down our standard of living to the level of the lowest common denominator. Our job is not to deal with the diplomatic world of Mr. Buxton, who hopes to find a peaceful solution around a conference table. No, the Army must face the world as it is. We know the enemy is strong. In our dumb way, we think it is just horse sense for us to be stronger. And I'm proud, believe me, ladies and gentlemen, proud to be at one end of the interplanetary conversation that is about to take place on this very, *very* historic morning. The achievement of the United States Army in establishing the space platform—which is literally a man-made planet—is unparalleled in military history. We have led the way into space. We have given Old Lady Gravity the slip. We have got there, and we have got there fustest with the mostest. [Applause.]

"I can state without qualification that the New Weapon, in the capable hands of the men stationed on our platform, brings the *entire* globe under our dominion. We can pinpoint any spot, anywhere, and sprinkle it with our particular brand of thunder. Mr. Moderator, I'm ready for this interview if the boys out there in space are ready."

Everyone suspected that there might be a slipup in the proceedings at this point, that the mechanical difficulties might prove insuperable. I glanced at the studio clock. The red sweep hand was within a few jumps of eleven-thirty—the General had managed his timing all right.

Cahill's face was tenser than I had ever seen it before. Because of the advance buildup, a collapse at this moment would put him in a nasty hole, even for an old experienced m.c. But at exactly eleven-thirty the interview started, smooth as silk. Cahill picked it up from the General.

"And now, watchers of television everywhere, you will hear a conversation between Major General Artemus T. Recoil, who pioneered Operation Space, and two United States Army officers on the platform —Major James Obblington, formerly of Brooklyn, New York, now of Space, and Lieutenant Noble Trett, formerly of Sioux City, Iowa, now of Space. Go ahead, General Recoil!"

"Come in, Space!" said the General, his tonsils struggling in whiskey's undertow, his eyes bearing down hard on the script. "Can you hear me, Major Obblington and Lieutenant Trett?"

"I hear you," said a voice. "This is Trett." The voice, as I remember it, astonished me because of a certain laconic quality that I had not expected. I believe it astonished everyone. Trett's voice was cool, and he sounded as though he were right in the studio.

"Lieutenant Trett," continued the General, "tell the listeners here on earth, tell us, in your position far out there in free space, do you feel the pull of gravity?"

"No, sir, I don't," answered Trett. In spite of the "sir," Trett sounded curiously listless, almost insubordinate.

"Yet you are perfectly comfortable, sitting there on the platform, with the whole of earth spread out before you like a vast target?"

"Sure I'm comfortable."

The General waited a second, as though expecting amplification, but it failed to come. "Well, ah, how's the weather up there?" he asked heartily.

"There isn't any," said Trett.

"No weather? No weather in space? That's very interesting."

"The hell it is," said Trett. "It's God-damn dull. This place is a dump. Worse than some of the islands in the Pacific."

"Well, I suppose it must get on your nerves a bit. That's all part of the game. Tell us, Lieutenant, what's it like to be actually a part of the solar system, with your own private orbit?"

"It's all right, except I'd a damn sight rather get drunk," said Trett.

I looked at Cahill. He was swallowing his spit. General Recoil took a new hold on his script.

"And you say you don't feel the pull of gravity, not even a little?"

"I just told you I didn't feel any pull," said Trett. His voice now had a surly quality.

"Well, ah," continued the General, who was beginning to tremble, "can you describe, briefly, for the television audience—" But it was at this point that Trett, on the platform, seemed to lose interest in talking with General Recoil and started chinning with Major Obblington, his sidekick in space. At first the three voices clashed and blurred, but the General, on a signal from the moderator, quit talking, and the conversation that ensued between Trett and Obblington was audible and clear. Millions of listeners must have heard the dialogue.

"Hey, Obie," said Trett, "you want to know something else I don't feel the pull of, besides gravity?"

"What?" asked his companion.

"Conscience," said Trett cheerfully. "I don't feel my conscience pulling me around."

"Neither do I," said Obblington. "I ought to feel some pulls but I don't."

"I also don't feel the pull of duty."

"Check," said Obblington.

"And what is even more fantastic, I don't feel the pull of dames."

Cahill made a sign to the General. Stunned and confused by the turn things had taken, Recoil tried to pick up the interview and get it back on the track. "Lieutenant Trett," he commanded, "you will limit your remarks to the—"

Cahill waved him quiet. The next voice was the Major's.

"Jesus, now that you mention it, I don't feel the pull of dames, either! Hey, Lieutenant—you suppose gravity has anything to do with sex?"

"God damn if *I* know," replied Trett. "I know I don't *weigh* anything, and when you don't weigh anything, you don't seem to *want* anything."

The studio by this time was paralyzed with attention. The General's face was swollen, his mouth was half open, and he struggled for speech that wouldn't come.

Then Trett's cool, even voice again: "See that continent down there, Obie? That's where old Fatso Recoil lives. You feel drawn toward that continent in any special way?"

"Naa," said Obblington.

"You feel like doing a little shooting, Obie?"

"You're rootin' tootin' I feel like shootin'."

"Then what are we waiting for?"

I am, of course, reconstructing this conversation from memory. I am trying to report it faithfully. When Trett said the words "Then what are we waiting for?" I quit listening and dashed for the phones in the corridor. As I was leaving the studio, I turned for a split second and looked back. The General had partially recovered his power of speech. He was mumbling something to Cahill. I caught the words "phone" and "Defense Department."

The corridor was already jammed. I had only one idea in my head— to speak to Ann. Pete Everhardt pushed past me. He said crisply, "This is it." I nodded. Then I glanced out of a window. High in the east a crazy ribbon of light was spreading upward. Lower down, in a terrible parabola, another streak began burning through. The first blast was felt only slightly in the plane. It must have been at a great distance. It was followed immediately by two more. I saw a piece of wing break up, saw one of the

starboard engines shake itself loose from its fastenings and fall. Near the
phone booths, the Bee, still in costume, fumbled awkwardly for a parachute. In the crush one of his feelers brushed my face. I never managed
to reach a phone. All sorts of things flashed through my mind. I saw Ann
and the children, their heads in diapers. I saw again the man in the leather
cap, loading bedsprings. I heard again Pete's words, "This is it," only I
seemed to hear them in translation: "Until the whole wide world to
nothingness do sink." (How durable the poets are!) As I say, I never
managed the phone call. My last memory of the morning is of myriads
of bright points of destruction where the Weapon was arriving, each pyre
in the characteristic shape of an artichoke. Then a great gash, and the
plane tumbling. Then I lost consciousness.

I cannot say how many minutes or hours after that the earth finally
broke up. I do not know. There is, of course, a mild irony in the fact that
it was the United States that was responsible. Insofar as it can be said of
any country that it had human attributes, the United States was well-
meaning. Of that I am convinced. Even I, at this date and at this distance,
cannot forget my country's great heart and matchless ingenuity. I can't in
honesty say that I believe we were wrong to send the men to the platform
—it's just that in any matter involving love, or high explosives, one can
never foresee all the factors. Certainly I can't say with any assurance that
Tollip's theory was right; it seems hardly likely that anyone who suffered
so from stomach gas could have been on the right track. I did feel sympathetic toward some of his ideas, perhaps because I suffered from flatulence
myself. Anyway, it was inevitable that it should have been the United
States that developed the space platform and the new weapon that made
the H-bomb obsolete. It was inevitable that what happened, at last, was
conceived in good will.

Those times—those last days of earth! I think about them a lot. A sort
of creeping ineptitude had set in. Almost everything in life seemed wrong
to me, somehow, as though we were all hustling down a blind alley. Many
of my friends seemed mentally confused, emotionally unstable, and I have
an idea I seemed the same to them. In the big cities, horns blew before the
light changed, and it was clear that motorists no longer had the capacity to
endure the restrictions they had placed on their own behavior. When the
birds became extinct (all but the whooping crane), I was reasonably sure
that human beings were on the way out, too. The cranes survived only
because of their dance—which showmen were quick to exploit. (Every
sanctuary had its television transmitter, and the love dance became a more
popular spectacle than heavyweight prizefighting.) Birds had always been
the symbol of freedom. As soon as I realized that they were gone, I felt
that the significance had gone from my own affairs. (I was a cranky man,
though—I must remember that, too—and am not trying here to suggest
anything beyond a rather strong personal sadness at all this.)

Those last days! There were so many religions in conflict, each ready to save the world with its own dogma, each perfectly intolerant of the other. Every day seemed a mere skirmish in the long holy war. It was a time of debauch and conversion. Every week the national picture magazines, as though atoning for past excesses, hid their cheesecake carefully away among four-color reproductions of the saints. Television was the universal peepshow—in homes, schools, churches, bars, stores, everywhere. Children early formed the habit of gaining all their images at second hand, by looking at a screen; they grew up believing that anything perceived directly was vaguely fraudulent. Only what had been touched with electronics was valid and real. I think the decline in the importance of direct images dated from the year television managed to catch an eclipse of the moon. After that, nobody ever looked at the sky, and it was as though the moon had joined the shabby company of buskers. There was really never a moment when a child, or even a man, felt free to look away from the television screen—for fear he might miss the one clue that would explain everything.

In many respects I like the planet I'm on. The people here have no urgencies, no capacity for sustained endeavor, but merely tackle things by fits and starts, leaving undone whatever fails to hold their interest, and so, by witlessness and improvidence, escape many of the errors of accomplishment. I like the apples here better than those on earth. They are often wormy, but with a most wonderful flavor. There is a saying here: "Even a very lazy man can eat around a worm."

But I would be lying if I said I didn't miss that other life, I loved it so.

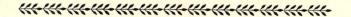

Work and Leisure

We have long been aware that man's use of power machinery makes possible a great deal of productivity and leisure and that these in turn create some psychological and social problems. But as Miss Hilton points out in the first essay in this section, technology is now taking a new turn. Whereas in the past we had been living in an age of "mechanization," the use of machines controlled by men, we are now rapidly moving into an age of "cybernation," machines controlled by themselves. Soon enough, Miss Hilton and her colleagues suggest, the machines won't need us any more. No longer faced with either the necessity or the opportunity for work, what will we do with ourselves?

Thus, the essays in this section take up in a new mood the age-old question of work and leisure and their relation to human happiness. They provide, too, some interesting comparisons of approach and tone. Russell Lynes is perhaps the most conventional and optimistic, viewing the problem principally as one of boredom and consumption and suggesting a happy solution. Fromm, a psychoanalyst, darkly analyzes the effect of industrialism on the attitude toward work, and Swados, a novelist with much experience of factory life, vigorously describes the complex behavior of workers in a modern industrial town.

ALICE MARY HILTON

Miss Hilton (born in 1924) has had a remarkably varied education. She holds a B.A. with honors in comparative literature from Oxford, has studied at the Sorbonne, at Heidelberg, and at the Claremont Graduate School, and has a degree in electrical engineering from U.C.L.A., where she also did graduate work in mathematics. Since the early 1950's, when the first computers impressed her of the vast social changes to come, she has worked for public understanding of cybernation. In 1964 she joined a group of publishers, scholars, and labor leaders in presenting to President Johnson a memorandum on the "Triple Revolution"—in weaponry, cybernation, and civil rights—which advocated, among other things, a guaranteed income as a right of all Americans. At present the head of the Institute for Cybercultural Research in New York, she is a prolific lecturer and writer of articles and has authored two books, Logic, Computing Machines, and Automation *(1963) and* The Cybercultural Revolution *(1965). The present essay—here reprinted in shortened form—first appeared in the* Michigan Quarterly Review, *October, 1964. An earlier version served as a resource paper for the June, 1964, Seminar on Work, Leisure, and Education in a Changing Industrialized Democracy, sponsored by the Center for Continuing Liberal Education at the Pennsylvania State University, under the direction of Professor Maxwell H. Goldberg, CCLE Associate Director for the Humanities.*

CYBERCULTURE—THE AGE OF ABUNDANCE AND LEISURE

In a Chicago suburb, in a bakery as large as a football field, bread and rolls and cakes and cookies are produced for millions of households throughout the country by a team of machines, called a system.

Factories have been growing larger, production has increased, and machines have become complex for more than a century, and size, increase in productivity, or the complexity of machine systems have long ago ceased to be newsworthy. In this bakery the revolutionary change, unknown before this decade, is not its size, productivity, or complexity—impressive though they are—but its cybernation (or true automation) which means that the entire huge operation is run by a completely self-sufficient and self-contained machine system. The enormously complex business is guided, directed, controlled, and monitored by an electronic computing machine, the central and integral part of the machine system that serves as nerve and message center.

The mixing and blending of flour, sugar, milk, butter, and all the other solid and liquid ingredients is directed and constantly supervised by the computing machine whose electronic pulses busily carry instructions to the other machines and bring information from sensory devices about conditions, performance, and progress back to the central computing machine. The mixing and blending is done according to recipes, or "programs," stored on magnetic tape, punch cards, tiny doughnut-shaped "cores," magnetic drums, or similar devices.

Apart from the mixing, blending, and baking, the computing machine controls supplies so that raw materials are ordered and thriftily kept at the proper level—not so much as to waste storage space or risk spoiling, and not so little as to keep any of the mixing and baking centers idle. Baking time and oven temperatures are computed and continually adjusted to the slightest change in outside conditions. The baking process is constantly monitored and controlled. Conveyor belts, for the transport of raw materials to mixing centers, dough to baking containers, containers to ovens, cooling racks, freezing plants, dispatch centers, and trucks, are directed.

And the entire production process—from ordering of raw materials to shipping of finished goods—is only *one* of the functions of the cybernated system. The computing machine also performs management functions for the business end of the bakery operation by controlling and monitoring the component machines to calculate, for example, the optimum number of rolls to be delivered on any day to each customer—not fewer than he might sell, but not so many that he will return them—always considering weather conditions, the day of the week, impending holidays, and many other variables that might influence consumption. This calculation is transmitted to raw-material dispatch centers, mixing centers, and so forth, right to the shipping department and the delivery trucks. And everywhere adjustments are made, orders corrected, space re-allocated, all in order to assure the optimum efficiency and economy of operations.

The computing machine is programmed to process the payroll for the company's diminishing number of employees and the invoices for its increasing number of customers; to compute the market prognosis, adjusted in accordance with trends in taste, seasons, advertising, and any other influences the programmers have thought of; to provide information about past experience to modify advertising; to calculate any changes thereby required in the production, purchasing, and distribution patterns; and to monitor all phases of operation to assure that instructions (with all modifications) are carried out. In other words, the system is capable of an interchange of information that permits the most complex relationships in continuous cycles of adjustments, feedback, modifications, and learning, at speeds expressed in as unfathomable a unit as a "micro-second" or a "nano-second." Still the potential applications of the system are not exhausted; and, like every other cybernated machine system in use now, it is underused. The real potentials of cybernated machine systems are barely imagined yet; they are limited only by the system's storage capacity—the feasible number of magnetic tapes, cores, drums, and other devices that contain instructions and data.

. . .

Only a few years ago, a bakery with equal output would have employed an army of bakers and sweepers, clerks and dispatchers, their attendant foremen and supervisors, engineers, and junior and intermediate level executives and managers. All the blue-collar and white-collar workers—of all levels—have been replaced by a silent machine system that labors twenty-four hours every day, never taking off a weekend or a holiday, never succumbing to illness, never demanding retirement benefits. And millions of dollars that used to be distributed as wages and salaries have shrunk to an annual rental fee of a few hundred-thousand dollars for the machine system.

. . .

A cybernated bakery can produce hundreds of thousands of loaves of bread—and a vast array of cakes and cookies and rolls—while the modern housewife bakes her single loaf. And contrary to popular opinion and nostalgic reminiscences, the machine bakes delicious bread if the recipe calls for the right proportions of excellent raw materials, and home-made bread can be dull. Whenever the reverse is true, it is not so because of the inherent qualities of machine- versus home-baking, but because of the economics of marketing and mechanized mass production. Re-tooling mechanized equipment was expensive; therefore, products were standardized, bland, non-objectionable, so that they could be sold to the largest possible number of consumers.

Happily, with cybernation adjustments for almost infinite variety are very cheap and easily provided for in the program. But, though it is possible to cater to individual taste and encourage diversity, in a cybercultural society, individualism and excellence are achieved by human decisions. Although excellent results are possible with cybernation, it is not necessarily inherent in the process. Inherent in cybernation is the fact that machines do not forget ingredients, and that they never let the bread burn because the telephone has to be answered, or the baby's tears dried. A machine does not have headaches or rush off to a PTA meeting. Neither does it suddenly feel adventurous enough to add a little sesame seed or a dash of sherry. And it never adds an extra pat of butter just because it is an extra lovely day. The machine does follow the recipe competently, reliably, and consistently; and every hour it supplies bread and cakes and rolls and cookies for hundreds of thousands of families without any need for one drop of sweat to form on the face of a single human being.

. . .

In Washington, *Pravda* is translated daily from Russian into understandable, if not always the most elegant or poetic, English. The "translator" is a computing machine.

In Los Angeles, the *Times* is printed from a tape—all columns are automatically justified, and words are correctly divided and hyphenated, according to programmed instructions.

In Seattle, airplane wings, automatic pilots, and fuel lines are designed by the computing machine that also controls the machine tools, the transfer machines, the circuit printers. Squadrons of engineers, regiments of draftsmen, platoons of production managers, divisions of metal workers are no longer needed.

In Texas and New Jersey, in the oil refineries—the silent, lifeless ghost towns of this century—crude oil is processed into different grades of gasoline and various by-products—the proportions determined automatically and flexibly as consumers' demands vary. Crude oil is piped in—gasoline and by-products emerge, hour after hour, day after day, without pause for sleep or rest or play, without coffee breaks or vacations, sick leaves or strikes. There are no workers, no supervisors, no executives; just a few highly trained engineers standing by in the central control room, watching their brainchild fend for itself.

Thus, a new era, the age of abundance and leisure, is being born. It started quietly, a little more than a decade ago, with seemingly unrelated installations of new equipment. Nobody blamed it on (or called it) automation, or cybernation, in the beginning, when a new transfer machine in a Cleveland metal-working plant was self-adjusted to keep parts moving from machine-tool to machine-tool so that no bottlenecks or pauses interrupted the smooth flow of production. "It will never pay," most competitors said, but they kept their skeptical eyes on the new method. The few workers replaced by one simple machine found other jobs, or they were so close to retirement that nobody made much of a fuss. Most of them had some savings, and there would be Social Security soon, and loans were easy to get, if you wanted to move to Florida to grow oranges or run a gas station.

The few union leaders alert enough to realize that there was something different about these new machines—the fore-runners of cybernated systems—started to think about the guaranteed annual wage and a shorter work week. But a few years were to pass before anyone talked about spreading the work left by the machines. After a year or two, when more manufacturers ordered new "numerically controlled" machine tools, it was emphatically asserted that the unions had nothing to worry about, because it would take months—even years—before the new machines could be delivered, tested, and operating. And, they claimed, even years later nobody would have to worry about losing his job. No, workers would not have to be fired—not too many, anyway—because new workers weren't being hired and that way everything would balance by a process that later was to become commonly known as the "attrition" of human beings by retirement, illness, and death. "Optimism" prevailed. American ingenuity was duly admired, and anyone who wondered about those who were (not yet) being fired and those who were (no longer) being hired was suspected of subversion, or at least of political unorthodoxy. In general, Americans have always had—at least until quite recently —implicit faith that every advance in technology must, without fail, lead us upwards and onwards.

. . .

Walter Reuther's demands for a guaranteed annual wage were considered impractical, Norbert Wiener's tales of chess-playing machines were discussed as science fiction, and soon the reports about "automation" were shrugged off as conflicting and confusing. A Ford spokesman said that automation reduces labor tremendously; but at a roundtable discussion sponsored by *Fortune*, a management official said: "I don't think we are consciously trying to ease the burden of our workers, nor consciously trying to improve their standard of living. *These things take care of themselves*" (italics added). And another expert said that automation ". . . will produce an unemployment situation, in comparison with which . . . the depression of the thirties will seem a pleasant joke." But, said the Ford spokesman, there wasn't a thing to worry about, because "the hand trucker of today, replaced by a conveyor belt, might become tomorrow's electronics engineer . . ."

Nobody really explained just how the hand trucker would achieve this metamorphosis, and nobody mentioned publicly that, before a hand trucker can learn to be an electronics engineer, a machine will have been developed to beat him at the game. It became so confusing for the public and so awkward for the "experts" that the talk about automation subsided. In the late fifties one took the risk of being called a "nag" and a "bore," or (more politely, though less accurately) a pessimist and (simultaneously) a dreamer who did not understand the "laws of economics" that "inevitably assured" that an increase in the Gross National Product "naturally" brought about a rise in employment. In the late 1950's the laws of economics were . . . well Laws! And it could always be proved that, if a man didn't like to sit around waiting for "attrition" or occupy himself with busy-work, he could quit and move on to another job or fight in Korea.

That was the beginning of the cybercultural revolution that is freeing *all* men from drudgery through "cybernation,"—the computing-machine production process—as, centuries ago, slavery freed *some* men from the need to labor in order to sustain life. The cybernated slaves of the twentieth century labor under the efficient direction of computing machines.

. . .

The persistent and emphatic assertion that "in the long run" full employment will be possible in the future as it has been in the past (at least occasionally), if only the Gross National Product is helped (or permitted) to grow, is due to the vast ignorance and the common confusion of mechanization with cybernation. The conclusions are fairly logical, but they are based upon completely false premises. It might be possible to assume that *full* employment can be restored when *more* machines turn out *more* goods, although each machine requires *fewer* people to direct it. But with the least amount of common sense one must surely recognize the fact that *no* employment at all can result when machines require *no* human direction, or intervention, no matter how much is produced and consumed.

Man no longer figures in the economic equation as a producer. There is no method of re-arranging the need for manpower and labor statistics that can alter the fact that, no matter what the Gross National Product, zero requirement for human labor spells unemployment. That is the fact—that is the irreversible trend towards which humanity has been headed for centuries. And when the first cybernated machine system was installed, the trend was accelerated into a cosmic gallop. Even if we wanted to, we could not erase centuries of human development nor could we unmake the computing machine.

Instead of asking where science and technology should stop, we must ask ourselves—and give much careful thought to our answer—where science and technology, and every other creation of the human mind, *should lead!* This generation has reached (or been led to) a cultural revolution.

Revolution means a turning, a complete change that may be for the better, or for worse, depending upon the point of view. The cybercultural revolution could proceed in an orderly and intelligent way, without grievous hardship to individuals; we could assure that it is beneficent for humanity and conserve the basic values of our society. But the danger of drifting amidst human misery towards chaos, violence, bloodshed, and finally total destruction of all we hold dear into a society so inhuman and horrible as to make Huxley's or Orwell's imagined horrors seem happy lands is at least as real as the promise of achieving a humane society—a great civilization.

It is not the *fact of change* that we must fear, but our failure to choose our destiny, and thereby to make the worst possible choice. Cybernation, *per se*, is neither good nor evil. It exists. Emancipating human beings from heavy toil, from the danger of precarious mine shafts, the poison fumes of chemical plants, the mind-destroying drudgery of attending machines, the stultifying boredom of bookkeeping is surely not deplorable. The history of civilization consists of the desire of human beings to live human lives, and their efforts to free themselves from necessary drudgery. For the first time in human history, this struggle *can* be brought to a successful conclusion.

. . .

It is not cybernation we need fear, but our social infantilism that—so far —has prevented us from creating a society in which human beings can acquire the means to live in reasonable comfort, and without fear, and find a sense of worth and human dignity in leisure. This is a period of transition of undetermined length that must be coped with. The very fact that it *is* a period of transition causes many problems that must be solved —at the very time when our long-range goals must be determined. So many terribly difficult social and political decisions of such frightening importance and such lasting impact have to be made that we are almost paralysed with fear.

What happens to the bakers in Chicago, the translators in Washington, the printers in Los Angeles, the draftsmen in Seattle, the engineers in Texas and New Jersey, the men from the assembly lines in Ohio, the clerks in Connecticut, the cotton-pickers in Louisiana?

Should they find jobs, when there are no jobs that machines can't do more efficiently and more economically than human beings? What should they do during this period of transition? And what must society do about them? And what should happen to their children, and their children's children?

. . .

No amount of misguided "optimism" can obscure the fact that every human production worker produces sixty per cent more than he produced in the 1930's—and even so staggering a fact is a gross understatement. For during two-thirds of this period, cybernation did not exist. Although considerable effort was made during the war to make every worker as productive as possible, the curve of productivity increased only slightly during the longest part (including war) of this period; and it took a sharp rise only recently. The workweek has been reduced by one-sixth since 1945, but—nevertheless—in nineteen years we have acquired ten-and-one-half million unemployed workers.

. . .

Official unemployment statistics never count the unknown number who are not eligible for registration with unemployment offices: those who no longer hope; those who are employed but unoccupied, doing busy-labor or feather-bedding; the women who have retired to their kitchens and to their neuroses. And unemployment rises, although we consume more than we ever did—which, according to pre-cybercultural economic pundits, *should* assure full employment and prosperity for all.

Busy-labor is by no means restricted to union members. Nobody knows how many engineers are perfecting their doodling while the front-office bids for a new contract; nobody has ever compiled statistics of the assistant-managers who are tacitly permitted to fill their desks with the tenth carbon copies of memoranda sent out by tenth vice-presidents, in order to contribute (with their very presence) to the prestige of the person on the next rung of the executive ladder, and because a line of succession must be maintained.

Unemployment is swelled less by those who have been fired than by those who are no longer hired. They leave school, are discharged from the army, become a problem. They may not be eligible for unemployment insurance, but they want to eat. The process of "attrition" would work (perhaps) if in every seven seconds a new baby were not born in the United States, if nobody ever left school, and if our accelerating cybernation could be balanced with a decreasing population. But death in the United States occurs once in twenty seconds, or once while three babies are born. And every day there are more with a claim to the abundance that pours forth, but without a permit to share its use; and every week 50,000 more dreary jobs are done by the machines.

. . .

Our problems, far from being technological or economic, result directly from persistently clinging to obsolete ethical concepts which few really believe although they diligently give lip service. Our problems remain insoluble as long as we ignore moral values that always have been true and must remain true, if we are to remain human beings. To prevent the all-destroying thermonuclear war that endangers us, to survive the less dramatic but more persistent dangers inherent in our failure to reconcile scientific-technological sophistication with social-political infantilism, we must carefully distinguish between permanent values and transient concepts. Then only can we create a new ethos suitable for the age of leisure and abundance; and then only can we re-affirm and conserve what is true at all times and for all human beings. Respect for human life and for the inviolable importance of the individual—his rights, his dignity, his worth—are permanent values. But the ethos that exalts thrift and diligence, that decrees that man shall eat his bread in the sweat of his face, is of transient worth. This ethos was indeed fine and decent—and imperative for the survival of human life and the beginning of civilization—during the millennia of scarcity and necessary drudgery, when only human beings could guide the plow along the furrows and control the anvil in the forge.

The ethos of scarcity has lost all meaning. It is not decent—but clearly unethical and immoral—for human beings to starve while grain rots in the granaries; and it is not decent—but clearly unethical and immoral—if a human being must envy a mule who, no longer needed to pull a wagon, may graze in peace; and it is not decent—but clearly unethical and immoral—for a human being to hope for permission to continue the mind-destroying labor which can be done by a machine. Such a human being is mistreated—his worth and dignity as an individual are not respected, his human rights are violated; he is murdered more brutally than if he were hanged, when his humanity is killed and he is driven to exist in the condition worse than that of a mule and of a thing.

It takes much time, or a great disaster, to change the prejudices of a society. And we do not have time, and must avoid the great and final disaster. Faced with an ever-increasing number of the unemployed, we must neither permit hopelessness and despair to overtake us, nor persist in panic and terror in unworkable methods. To review our ideals, discard our prejudices, and define our goals, is difficult, but surely not impossible. We cannot afford to ignore the present and immediate problems and we must improvise and do what we can now to the best of our ability to alleviate every instance of suffering.

No solution is sound if it merely deals with the problems of today, if it merely feeds the hungry today in the hope that tomorrow they will not be so tactless as to starve in our sight. Unless we take care of tomorrow's problems today, the poor will be here tomorrow—more of them, hungrier than ever, more discouraged than ever, and angrier than ever.

As we improvise and patch up the worst holes, we must take a good look at the whole fabric of society and invent new patterns for a world of leisure and abundance, and of the good life. Although we want to get through this period of transition with as little pain as possible, it is dangerous to mistake an analgesic for a cure, and to use palliatives that are injurious to the vision of the end—of a society of human beings living human lives and achieving human tasks.

ERICH FROMM

Dr. Fromm, born in Germany in 1900, studied sociology and psychology at Heidelberg, Frankfurt, and Munich, and received the Ph.D. from Heidelberg in 1922. He then trained in psychoanalysis at Munich and at the Psychoanalytic Institute in Berlin. In 1934 he settled in the United States and eventually became an American citizen. He has lectured at Columbia, was for a long time on the faculty of Bennington College, and in 1951 began teaching psychoanalysis at the National Autonomous University of Mexico. His particular interest is the application of psychoanalytic theory to the problems of culture and society, and he has published a number of widely read books in this area. Among them are Escape from Freedom *(1941),* Man for Himself *(1947),* The Sane Society *(1955),* The Art of Loving *(1956),* May Man Prevail *(1961), and* The Heart of Man *(1964). The present selection is a self-contained part of Chapter 5 of* The Sane Society. *Earlier in his book (p. 120), Fromm defines "alienation" as follows: "By alienation is meant a mode of experience in which the person experiences himself as an alien. He has become, one might say, estranged from himself. He does not experience himself as the center of his world, as the creator of his own acts—but his acts and their consequences have become his masters, whom he obeys, or whom he may even worship. The alienated person is out of touch with himself as he is out of touch with any other person."*

WORK IN AN ALIENATED SOCIETY

What becomes the meaning of *work* in an alienated society?

We have already made some brief comments about this question in the general discussion of alienation. But since this problem is of utmost importance, not only for the understanding of present-day society, but also for any attempt to create a saner society, I want to deal with the nature of work separately and more extensively in the following pages.

Unless man exploits others, he has to work in order to live. However primitive and simple his method of work may be, by the very fact of production, he has risen above the animal kingdom; rightly has he been defined as "the animal that produces." But work is not only an inescapable necessity for man. Work is also his liberator from nature, his creator as a social and independent being. *In the process of work, that is, the molding and changing of nature outside of himself, man molds and changes himself.* He emerges from nature by mastering her; he develops his powers of co-operation, of reason, his sense of beauty. He separates himself from nature, from the original unity with her, but at the same time unites himself with her again as her master and builder. The more his work develops, the more his individuality develops. In molding nature and re-creating her, he learns to make use of his powers, increasing his skill and creativeness. Whether we think of the beautiful paintings in the caves of Southern France, the ornaments on weapons among primitive people, the statues and temples of Greece, the cathedrals of the Middle Ages, the chairs and tables made by skilled craftsmen, or the cultivation of flowers, trees or corn by peasants—all are expressions of the creative transformation of nature by man's reason and skill.

In Western history, craftsmanship, especially as it developed in the thirteenth and fourteenth centuries, constitutes one of the peaks in the evolution of creative work. Work was not only a useful activity, but one which carried with it a profound satisfaction. The main features of craftsmanship have been very lucidly expressed by C. W. Mills. "There is no ulterior motive in work other than the product being made and the processes of its creation. The details of daily work are meaningful because they are not detached in the worker's mind from the product of the work. The worker is free to control his own working action. The craftsman is thus able to learn from his work; and to use and develop his capacities and skills in its prosecution. There is no split of work and play, or work and culture. The craftsman's way of livelihood determines and infuses his entire mode of living."[1]

With the collapse of the medieval structure, and the beginning of the modern mode of production, the meaning and function of work changed fundamentally, especially in the Protestant countries. Man, being afraid of his newly won freedom, was obsessed by the need to subdue his doubts and fears by developing a feverish activity. The outcome of this activity, success or failure, decided his salvation, indicating whether he was among the saved or the lost souls. *Work, instead of being an activity satisfying in itself and pleasureable, became a duty and an obsession.* The more it was possible to gain riches by work, the more it became a pure

[1] C. W. Mills, *White Collar*, Oxford University Press, New York, 1951, p. 220.

means to the aim of wealth and success. Work became, in Max Weber's terms, the chief factor in a system of "inner-worldly asceticism," an answer to man's sense of aloneness and isolation.

However, work in this sense existed only for the upper and middle classes, those who could amass some capital and employ the work of others. For the vast majority of those who had only their physical energy to sell, work became nothing but forced labor. The worker in the eighteenth or nineteenth century who had to work sixteen hours if he did not want to starve was not doing it because he served the Lord in this way, nor because his success would show that he was among the "chosen" ones, but because he was forced to sell his energy to those who had the means of exploiting it. The first centuries of the modern era find the meaning of work divided into that of *duty* among the middle class, and that of *forced labor* among those without property.

The religious attitude toward work as a duty, which was still so prevalent in the nineteenth century, has been changing considerably in the last decades. Modern man does not know what to do with himself, how to spend his lifetime meaningfully, and he is driven to work in order to avoid an unbearable boredom. But work has ceased to be a moral and religious obligation in the sense of the middle-class attitude of the eighteenth and nineteenth centuries. Something new has emerged. Ever-increasing production, the drive to make bigger and better things, have become aims in themselves, new ideals. Work has become alienated from the working person.

What happens to the industrial worker? He spends his best energy for seven or eight hours a day in producing "something." He needs his work in order to make a living, but his role is essentially a passive one. He fulfills a small isolated function in a complicated and highly organized process of production, and is never confronted with "his" product as a whole, at least not as a producer, but only as a consumer, provided he has the money to buy "his" product in a store. He is concerned neither with the whole product in its physical aspects nor with its wider economic and social aspects. He is put in a certain place, has to carry out a certain task, but does not participate in the organization or management of the work. He is not interested, nor does he know why one produces this, instead of another commodity—what relation it has to the needs of society as a whole. The shoes, the cars, the electric bulbs, are produced by "the enterprise," using the machines. He is a part of the machine, rather than its master as an active agent. The machine, instead of being in his service to do work for him which once had to be performed by sheer physical energy, has become his master. Instead of the machine being the substitute for human energy, man has become a substitute for the machine. *His work can be defined as the performance of acts which cannot yet be performed by machines.*

Work is a means of getting money, not in itself a meaningful human activity. P. Drucker, observing workers in the automobile industry, expresses this idea very succinctly: "For the great majority of automobile workers, the only meaning of the job is in the pay check, not in anything connected with the work or the product. Work appears as something unnatural, a disagreeable, meaningless and stultifying condition of getting the pay check, devoid of dignity as well as of importance. No wonder that this puts a premium on slovenly work, on slow-downs, and on other tricks to get the same pay check with less work. No wonder that this results in an unhappy and discontented worker—because a pay check is not enough to base one's self-respect on."[2]

This relationship of the worker to his work is an outcome of the whole social organization of which he is a part. Being "employed,"[3] he is not an active agent, has no responsibility except the proper performance of the isolated piece of work he is doing, and has little interest except the one of bringing home enough money to support himself and his family. Nothing more is expected of him, or wanted from him. He is part of the equipment hired by capital, and his role and function are determined by this quality of being a piece of equipment. In recent decades, increasing attention has been paid to the psychology of the worker, and to his attitude toward his work, to the "human problem of industry"; but this very formulation is indicative of the underlying attitude; there is a human being spending most of his lifetime at work, and what should be discussed is the *"industrial problem of human beings,"* rather than *"the human problem of industry."*

Most investigations in the field of industrial psychology are concerned with the question of how the productivity of the individual worker can be increased, and how he can be made to work with less friction; psychology has lent its services to "human engineering," an attempt to treat the worker and employee like a machine which runs better when it is well oiled. While Taylor was primarily concerned with a better organization of the technical use of the worker's physical powers, most industrial psychologists are mainly concerned with the manipulation of the worker's psyche. The underlying idea can be formulated like this: if he works better when he is happy, then let us make him happy, secure, satisfied, or anything else, provided it raises his output and diminishes friction. In the name of "human relations," the worker is treated with all devices which suit a completely alienated person; even happiness and human values are recommended in the interest of better relations with the public. Thus, for instance, according to *Time* magazine, one of the best-known American psychiatrists said to a group of fifteen hundred Supermarket executives: "It's going to be an increased satisfaction to our customers if we

---

[2] Cf. Peter F. Drucker, *Concept of the Corporation*, The John Day Company, New York, 1946, p. 179.

[3] The English "employed" like the German *angestellt* are terms which refer to things rather than to human beings.

are happy. . . . It is going to pay off in cold dollars and cents to management, if we could put some of these general principles of values, human relationships, really into practice." One speaks of "human relations" and one means the most in-human relations, those between alienated automatons; one speaks of happiness and means the perfect routinization which has driven out the last doubt and all spontaneity.

The alienated and profoundly unsatisfactory character of work results in two reactions: one, the ideal of complete *laziness;* the other a deep-seated, though often unconscious *hostility* toward work and everything and everybody connected with it.

It is not difficult to recognize the widespread longing for the state of complete laziness and passivity. Our advertising appeals to it even more than to sex. There are, of course, many useful and labor saving gadgets. But this usefulness often serves only as a rationalization for the appeal to complete passivity and receptivity. A package of breakfast cereal is being advertised as *"new—easier to eat."* An electric toaster is advertised with these words: ". . . the most distinctly different toaster in the world! Everything is done *for* you with this new toaster. You need not even bother to lower the bread. Power-action, through a unique electric motor, *gently takes the bread right out of your fingers!"* How many courses in languages, or other subjects are announced with the slogan "effortless learning, no more of the old drudgery." Everybody knows the picture of the elderly couple in the advertisement of a life-insurance company, who have retired at the age of sixty, and spend their life in the complete bliss of having nothing to do except just travel.

Radio and television exhibit another element of this yearning for laziness: the idea of "push-button power"; by pushing a button, or turning a knob on my machine, I have the power to produce music, speeches, ball games, and on the television set, to command events of the world to appear before my eyes. The pleasure of driving cars certainly rests partly upon this same satisfaction of the wish for push-button power. By the effortless pushing of a button, a powerful machine is set in motion; little skill and effort is needed to make the driver feel that he is the ruler of space.

But there is far more serious and deep-seated reaction to the meaninglessness and boredom of work. It is a hostility toward work which is much less conscious than our craving for laziness and inactivity. Many a businessman feels himself the prisoner of his business and the commodities he sells; he has a feeling of fraudulency about his product and a secret contempt for it. He hates his customers, who force him to put up a show in order to sell. He hates his competitors because they are a threat; his employees as well as his superiors, because he is in a constant competitive fight with them. Most important of all, he hates himself, because he sees his life passing by, without making any sense beyond the momentary intoxication of success. Of course, this hate and contempt for others and for oneself, and for the very things one produces, is mainly unconscious, and only occasionally comes up to awareness in a fleeting thought, which is sufficiently disturbing to be set aside as quickly as possible.

HARVEY SWADOS

Harvey Swados was born in 1920, attended the University of Michigan, served in the Merchant Marine in World War II, and has divided his life since between writing and teaching. He has been visiting professor at San Francisco State College and at Iowa State University and is a regular member of the literature faculty at Sarah Lawrence. He is a novelist, short-story writer, and an outspoken critic of American culture; many of his articles have been published in such magazines as The Nation, Saturday Review, Esquire, *and* The Saturday Evening Post. *His published fiction includes the novels* Out Went the Candle *(1955),* False Coin *(1960), and* The Will *(1963); and two collections of stories:* On the Line *(1957) and* Nights in the Gardens of Brooklyn *(1961). In 1962 he published* A Radical's America, *essays on labor and the laboring classes, and* Years of Conscience: The Muckrakers, *an anthology. The present essay is from* The Nation, *February, 1958.*

LESS WORK—LESS LEISURE

AKRON, OHIO

I regard the five-day week as an unworthy ideal . . . More work and better work is a more inspiring and worthier motto than less work and more pay . . . It is better not to trifle or tamper with God's laws.
—JOHN E. EDGERTON, *President of the National Association of Manufacturers (1926).*

Times have changed since the gentleman quoted above invoked the
Deity in opposition to Henry Ford's revolutionary five-day week. Not
that hard-pressed executives ceased thereafter to cite divine guidance
as the source of their labor relations. A decade after Mr. Edgerton pointed
to the Lord, sit-down strikers at the largest rubber plant in the world,
Akron's Goodyear plant, provided one of the first tests of the new C.I.O.,
and in a nineteen-below-zero St. Valentine's Day blizzard, the scraggly
crowd of determined workers marched up Market Street into the teeth of
the gale. Little more than a year later, in March, 1937, the 10,000 workers
of the Akron Firestone plant struck after four years of futile effort to
get the company to recognize their union. Harvey Firestone was at his
estate in Miami Beach. The teletype from Akron to Harbel Villa kept
Mr. Firestone informed, but, we are assured by the authorized Firestone
biographer, it "did not alleviate his feeling of distress at this cleavage.
'When the strike broke out in Akron it jarred me for a day or two.
Then I concluded there must be some reason for it and that we could not
help it, but the thing we should do was not to fight it but to stand on
what we thought was right and then let matters stand, as it was God's will
we were to have a strike and there was a good reason for it, and it would
be righted in the right time. . . .'"

In the Akron of today, it is hard indeed to realize that it was only twenty
years ago that Harvey Firestone sent that philosophical message to his
son, that it was only twenty years ago that the Firestone strikers threw
up shacks of canvas, wood and tin as picket shelters at the freezing
factory gates. Now this industrial city is clean, prosperous and not
slum-ridden, and to the casual visitor the workers themselves are transformed, too; they are no longer the grimly huddled proletarians of those
terrible and dramatic days. At a glance, they seem to epitomize the publicity ideal of the smiling middle-class American. And the union that
helped to lead them out of the pit of the depression, the United Rubber
Workers, is today not merely a well-housed and comfortably situated
fraternal organization; it is a democratically-operated, decently-adminis-
tered labor union, properly and profoundly concerned with the naggingly
complex problems of its membership, and still so proud of its militant
origins that it disputes with its big brother union, the Auto Workers,
the claim to originating the weapon of the sit-down strike.

Just as it is hard to realize that the affable, self-assured workers cruising
Akron's streets in late-model cars are often the same men who pounded
up those streets as defiant strikers two decades ago, so it is hard to believe
that much of the present leadership of their union, from President L. H.
Buckmaster on down, consists of the very same men who founded the
union and endured beatings and imprisonment in the course of their early
struggles. Yet you will bump into them as you travel around town—
George Bass in the International Office, Joe Childs at a restaurant, Jack
Little at a meeting of his local; men whose names are already legendary,

but who give the impression—along with the union's rank-and-file activists and "politicians"—of being more worried about the immediate future than proud of their accomplishments in what is already the remote past. Indeed, one might almost be tempted to characterize this mood, particularly among the rank and file, as one of uncertainty, of tentativeness of direction, of lack of confidence in whatever the ultimate goals may be. It is a mood strikingly different from the explosive élan of those who went out and built the C.I.O. because they were convinced beyond question that they were going to convert the rotten life of the American worker into the good life.

Ever since those dismal depression days, a portion of Akron's rubber workers have worked a six-hour day and a six-day week. The six-hour day was first instituted by the companies as a work-sharing (or poverty-sharing) device, but soon became so popular with the workers that they wrote it into their union constitution (one of their constitutionally-enshrined objectives is "To establish the six-hour day and the thirty-hour work-week with wage increases to compensate for the shorter time so that there will be no reduction in weekly earnings from such action"), and into their contracts with the Big Four of the rubber industry. Today it is an emotionally-charged article of belief, and even the most cursory inquirer in Akron soon becomes convinced that the delegate from Local 101 to the union's 1956 Los Angeles convention was hardly exaggerating when he cried from the floor: "We in the six-hour plant regard it as almost a religion."

It is this unique long-time experience with the shorter work-day that has lately made Akron a focus of interest as a possible forecast of what all America will be like in the era of the less-than-forty-hour week, an era that presently seems inevitable even if the Deity should once again be invoked by those who oppose its arrival. Already the town has been researched and written-up by *Fortune* and the *Wall Street Journal*, and it is increasingly referred to by those who write about and ponder the problems that will attend the shorter work-week: will people use the increased leisure wisely? will workers tend to hunt up second jobs? what will the social effects eventually be?

Unquestionably, the outlines of the social pattern of the future are here to be seen. But the first thing the visitor learns is the complexity of that pattern, and certainly before we are so brash as to generalize from this unique industrial instance we should at least note some of the special factors that must be taken into consideration in any speculation about the uses of leisure.

First, although about 30,000 rubber workers do work a six-hour day, six days a week, with the plants operating four shifts a day, they represent only about 15 per cent of the employees of the rubber industry. Most rubber workers, by special contractual agreements, are now on a straight eight-hour day with premium pay if they work the sixth day.

Second, even in some of the six-hour shops there are departments or divisions (mostly the crafts) which work eight-hour shifts.

Third, in only two cities outside Akron do Rubber Workers' locals have six-hour contracts.

(These first three points acquire a special significance when you realize that the hourly rate for the eight-hour man is contractually lower, even for the same work, than that of the man in the six-hour plant—but that he may take home somewhat more money if his plant regularly works a sixth or overtime day. To put it mildly, the union membership is not united on the question of which working day is better.)

Fourth, Akron cannot be regarded as a typical American industrial city, if only because its population is virtually homogeneous with a relatively small percentage of immigrants. They call Akron "the capital of West Virginia." It would seem obvious that people who have come up by the thousands out of the hill country to make steady money building tires are going to use their leisure somewhat differently from those who came over from Europe to make ladies' garments or pig iron, but also to escape oppression and to build a future for their children.

Fifth, the city is relatively characterless—partly because the Southerners are still so deeply rooted in their home country that they return at every opportunity, and partly because the rubber barons have not seen fit to dispense largesse in any considerable amount in the community which produces their wealth or to indulge locally in those leisure-class hobbies which have given other cities their symphonies and art galleries.

Sixth, it seems most unlikely that any general shortening of working hours across the country will follow the unique Akron pattern. More probably we are going to see unions pressing for work-weeks like the Garment Workers' seven-hour, five-day week, or the Auto Workers' momentarily-abandoned, but very much alive proposed eight-hour, four-day week. The difference in effect of each system is almost incalculable. For example, who is going to be more willing and able to work at a second job: the man who works a six-hour, six-day week, or the one who will work an eight-hour, four-day week?

Seventh, there has been no large-scale, careful study of the uses of leisure by Akron rubber workers. With the exception of a cursory union survey, there has not been an attempt to find out exactly how many of them hold down a second job. Therefore, given the complexity of the six-hour-eight-hour pattern, no one can say with confidence that the man who works shorter hours does in fact lead a measurably different life—in terms of what he does with his off-hours—than his fellow on the more traditional eight-hour day. In all honesty we must be limited at this point to impressionistic hunches and conjectures, which in the present instance are based on observation and on conversation with workers.

What can we learn from the experience of these Americans who have been living with the short workday for a generation? Quite a lot. First of all, the research director of the Akron Chamber of Commerce estimates that there are about 52,000 women workers in an Akron labor force of 195,000 persons. Now it is true that one out of three in the national labor force of some 65,000,000 is a woman, and that the Akron ratio is apparently somewhat smaller. But when you remember that Akron is primarily a city of heavy industry, the figure is staggering—particularly when you learn that some 60 per cent of the Akron working women are married. In short, 30,000 housewives in this area are not only housewives but wage-earners too, and not on an emergency war-time basis but as steady workers, accumulating seniority, looking for paid vacations and working toward retirement pensions alongside their men.

Not exactly alongside, however. The wife in Chicago or New York who works will probably leave home with her husband in the morning and meet him at home for supper. Not so in Akron, where the four six-hour rubber-plant shifts make it easier for the wife to work a shift which will still enable her to keep house, and for the husband to work one which will enable him to baby-sit while his wife works. If, in addition, he has a *second* job, which as we will see is often the case, he is going to be able to spend only a few hours a week alone with his wife. Their children, often looked after by grandma or by baby-sitters, are causing heads to shake anxiously over increasing juvenile delinquency. Togetherness is never going to penetrate very far into the household where the adults are holding down multiple jobs; for every three marriage licenses issued here last year, there was one suit filed for divorce. And we have to bear in mind that this looks more and more like a permanent phenomenon, as working wives strive not just for that extra paycheck (the federal government takes a healthy bite out of it every year), but for security, for hospitalization, medical care, vacations, pensions.

We might note parenthetically at this point that a Gallup poll taken last year indicated that, on a national basis, women were opposed to the idea of a four-day week by a three-to-one margin. No reasons were given, but it seems only logical that a housewife who normally puts in a twelve-hour day and must continue to do so (like the farmers, who were predictably opposed to the four-day week by a four-to-one margin) would resent such a lightening of the burden of others. Besides, there is the fear that the husband who is off for three days may become less responsible, drink more, run around more. Nevertheless, I should be very much surprised if a poll were to show anything like this feeling among the women of Akron, who have learned from experience that the shorter day gives them more of what they want—even if it is only the opportunity to go out and become wage-earners themselves.

What else have the Akron rubber workers been doing with those extra hours? The stroller down South Main Street on a Monday evening, when the stores are open late, will get one or two ideas, provided he isn't run over (per capita auto registration here last year was second only to Los Angeles). Husbands and wives are clustered in the brilliantly-lit do-it-yourself supermarkets, picking over wall-coverings for the bathroom and floor-coverings for the rumpus room. Home ownership is high—seven out of ten Akron families live in their own homes—and men who work only six hours a day can put in a good deal of time fixing and repairing, building a garage, paving a driveway, adding an extra room.

The bowling alleys are jammed, the poolrooms do well, the neighboring waters are stocked with power boats, and last year Summit County sold the fantastic number of 67,400 hunting and fishing licenses to local residents (there are a little over 300,000 people in Akron).

The churches can't complain, either. The people up from West Virginia, Kentucky and Tennessee take their religion seriously, many of them tithe as a matter of course and of conscience, and they go in heavily for revivalism and fundamentalism. The Temple of Healing Stripes has free bus service to its Divine Healing Services; evangelists hold Old Fashioned Brush-Arbor Revivals and show Signs! Wonders! Miracles! every night in the summertime; and Rex Humbard is supervising construction of the Cathedral of Tomorrow, Calvary Temple, The Largest Church Auditorium Built In This Generation.

Other cultural manifestations are somewhat more muted. Living theatre is practically non-existent, there is no professional symphony, and although the Public Library is good, one can search the city in vain for a bookshop devoted to selling new books. (There are, to be sure, several which specialize in ecclesiastical tracts of various denominations, and a shop in the very shadow of a rubber plant which, despite the protestations of its owner that he caters to a steady clientele of "bookworms," seems to attract primarily young workers looking for what the proprietor calls "strictly legal" sex and girlie books.)

At this level, then, Akron rubber workers do not seem to spend their extra off-hours very differently from their brothers across America. What the others are doing, *they* are doing—and then some. We can even say this of the one big question not touched on thus far, the second job. A Federal Census Bureau survey published in the summer of 1957 found some 3,700,000 persons to be multiple job-holders. This figure is about double what it had been six years before, and it works out to about 5.5 per cent of the country's total employed.

Now there cannot be a single person in Akron who would claim—although everyone is guessing—that the percentage of rubber workers holding down two jobs is that low. Best guesses seem to agree that anywhere from one in seven down to one in five rubber workers holds a second full-time job, with a small fraction even managing two jobs on different shifts at different rubber plants. In addition, something like 40 per cent engage in some sort of part-time outside work. With such a discrepancy between the Akron picture and the national picture, the inference would seem obvious, although there are many rubber workers who heatedly deny it: the shorter day, even with a higher pay scale, increases the number of men who obtain second jobs as garage attendants, taxi drivers, bellhops, grocers, butchers, clerks, insurance salesmen, realtors, brokers, barbers, repairmen, bakers—yes, and engineers too.

I am afraid that what I have said thus far has a cold and clammy ring to it but the general picture must be clear before we can attempt to understand its meaning in the lives of the individual actors—the workers themselves. It is to be expected that *Time*, surveying the "moonlighting" (two-job) situation, should point out that there are those who "hail moonlighters as heirs to the spirit of the nation's founders and insist that hard work never hurt anybody." But when Arthur Schlesinger, Jr., asserted last fall that "The most dangerous threat hanging over American society is the threat of leisure . . . and those who have the least preparation for leisure will have the most of it," one wonders whether he realized that it was the *enforced* leisure of the layoff that was soon to threaten American workers, and that all too often it was the memory of previous enforced leisure that was driving them into moonlighting, into destroying their leisure by racing from one job to the other while the jobs were still there to be had?

It is unlikely that Mr. Schlesinger was thinking in these terms. One can agree with his warning only if one takes a long-term view; it can hardly be immediately comforting to those workers who have not accumulated sufficient seniority to avoid being laid off in the current slump, like the two ladies with fourteen years' seniority who sat biting their lips, jobless, in an Akron coffee shop. Or (to cite a perhaps less suspect source), like Kenneth Marxmiller of the Caterpillar plant in Peoria. "It affects my wife more than me," said Mr. Marxmiller to a *Life* reporter (January 27, 1958). "She just sits and cries. . . ."

Nor is it likely that Mr. Schlesinger could foresee how rapidly his analysis would be vulgarized into the grossest sort of caricature. The *Saturday Evening Post* of January 11, 1958, has a short story entitled Holiday for Howie and subtitled: *At first glance it seemed terrific, a four-day work week! But then he found there was a catch in it.* . . . The catch, it turns out, is that Howie rapidly gets bored with all that leisure. He takes to sleeping late on those long weekends, and when his wife declines to go gallivanting around the country with him (her responsibility to house and children continues on his days off), he looks up an old school friend, now a rich bachelor leading an idle, dissolute life. They drink together, which is what Howie had been looking forward to, but the friend reveals that he is not really happy or free; he is drinking himself to death from boredom and loneliness. Shocked, Howie goes to the beach to Think Things Out:

He hadn't learned to handle time. All he could do was try to kill it. . . . And all the while, crazily, more time being made. Household gadgets to save time for the housewife, for what? So that she can spend the afternoon playing cards? And all the freeways built to save time, for what? So that people traveling at breakneck speed can get home ten minutes earlier to have an extra cocktail before dinner? And science adding years to a man's life, for what? So that at eighty he can learn to dance? . . . Speed, and time to be filled, is that all our civilization has contributed? He felt like crying and he didn't know why.

Lying there, Howie discovers the secret—Time opens out for him into Eternity. He hurries home to explain this to his wife—a large order—and to tell her that he has decided to take a second job, one which will fill two of his three free days, because:

". . . Time is not for me. Some people can handle it. I can't. . . ."

"Oh, Howie." There was love and admiration in her muffled voice. And vague regret.

"Cheer up, Doll. Think what we can do with the extra money— lots of things. Think what we can get—a new car, with all the gadgets! Color TV! Air conditioning! We'll really be living! Smile, Doll!"

THE END

It is characteristic of the corrupt sub-literature of the mass media, as it used to be of Fascist propaganda; that it is thoroughly capable of seizing on some of the most agonizing and centrally important human problems and distorting them into grotesque and semi-comic horror stories, which relate only weirdly to the way people really think and feel.

Then what do the workers believe? Every Akron worker with any consciousness of his position in society starts with one unalterable and clearly-understood premise: he is a member of a declining labor force. On November 1, 1951, the Goodrich plant in Akron had 11,475 employees on its rolls; on May 4, 1956, it had 8,500 employees. It is true that the company moved some of its operations to more modern and hence more competitive plants elsewhere, as well as to plants working eight-hour shifts (with lower hourly rates); but this only serves to sharpen the worker's realization that automation, rationalization and continually developing industrial technology are, before his very eyes, cutting down on the number of human beings needed to manufacture goods.

He sees himself in a situation not unlike that of the farmer. With productivity steadily increasing at the rate of about 3 per cent a year, he will be able to protect himself and his family only by moving from the manufacture of goods to the delivery of services, as the farmers have gradually moved to the cities (the two-job situation can be partially interpreted as the beginning of such a shift—very often the second job is a service job, whether it be cutting hair or selling real estate), or by spending less hours per week producing goods. I was not too surprised to hear several workers say that they believed eventually the government would have to subsidize labor as it has subsidized the farmer. "You can call this socialism if you want," one added aggressively. "The point is the problem is bigger than we are and it has to be solved in a big way."

Here again is something the Akron worker has come to see: the problem of the shorter work-week, of increased leisure versus a second job, is bigger than he is, it is bigger even than his 220,000-member union, and it has implications that may make it too big even for his senior partner, the million-membered Auto Workers Union, whose lead he has traditionally followed (although the development of the plastic industry and of such products as foam rubber and pliofilm are making Akron somewhat less directly dependent on Detroit's prosperity). And he is badly split.

He is split not only when an eight-hour local opposes a six-hour local (the international union, which has been seriously trying to achieve work-week uniformity so that it can bargain across the country for pay-rate uniformity, presented its program clumsily to the last convention and was voted down by the six-hour men and the abstainers). He is split in discussions within his own local. And most serious and pregnant of all, he is sorely split in his own mind.

Every rubber worker with whom I spoke was agreed that the rising unemployment in Akron would vanish at once if all men working second jobs were to leave them. Were they therefore agreed that all two-jobbers should be compelled to give up the second job? No.

Again, no one knows for sure, but there seems to be a consensus that the men who are out moonlighting are mostly in the thirty-five to fifty age bracket. Men older than that often have their homes paid off; their wants are more modest; they are looking forward to retirement and pension. They are over the hump. The youngsters in the six-hour shops have never worked any longer hours; this seems plenty long enough to spend in a filthy, noisy place where the acrid stench of hot rubber is never absent. And some of them can and do go to Akron University while they are working. It is the men who remember the depression who apparently comprise the bulk of the two-jobbers—they and the young men with wives and children who have concurrent payments to meet (sometimes of staggering amounts) on house, car, TV, furniture and appliances. And, as the very men who oppose the two-job frenzy demand: "Can you blame them?"

What is wrong, then, with a man going out and getting a second job? In reply the workers themselves will tell you horror stories far more shocking than any dreamed up by a slick fictioneer. They will tell you of a Negro worker found to have twelve years of seniority at one rubber plant and thirteen at another, and finally forced to choose between them, when the fact that he had been working seventy-two hours a week not for a few months, but for a dozen years, was brought to light. They will tell you of workers taking second jobs at small independent eight-hour rubber shops and being told frankly by their new boss that he had secured contracts on the basis of their working for him for less than the union scale in the Big Four. They will tell you of two men splitting an eight-hour shift at a gas station in their "leisure" time, and thus depriving one job-hunter of full-time work. They will tell you of their brother union members driving cabs for scab wages, cutting hair for scab wages, painting houses for scab wages. They will tell you of their terrible shame when a member of their union's policy committee was found working a second job as a salesman in a department store even while the store was being picketed by the Retail Clerks' union for not paying a decent minimum wage. They will insist that the rubber companies themselves look the other way when a worker takes a second job (unless his efficiency is drastically lowered), because they know that the man with two jobs will be less likely to attend union meetings, that he will more easily accede to downgrading, that in general he will be far less militant than the man who relies solely on the income from his job in the rubber plant.

And then, almost in the same breath, they will say that this is a free country; that you can't stop a man from trying to get ahead; that if a man wants to drive himself to death for the privilege of sleeping in a $30,000 house it is his privilege; and that it is only reasonable for a man still as basically insecure as an industrial worker to make it while he can, to catch up while times are still good, to acquire some of the luxuries while they are still within his grasp.

Is this a preview of America's (and indeed the industrialized world's) future? As the work-week shrinks, will we be treated to the spectacle not of thousands, but of millions of workers scrambling to undercut one another, protected in the primary job by their union and bidding their labor for secondary employment at ruinously low rates? Will leisure become a term of mockery covering *longer* hours spent in working to obtain, and then to replace, household objects carefully engineered for rapid obsolescence? On this point, at any rate, some of the workers mix faith and optimism. They tend to agree, although they put it differently, with the magazine *Factory Management and Maintenance* (November, 1956), that the "Crux of the matter, on either a four- or five-day week, is whether general economic conditions and the worker's pay scale would put pressure on him to carry a second job for the added income, or allow him to enjoy the added leisure of a four-day week with a single job."

But the road toward that happy day is going to be, and is now, hard, rocky and painful. "Certainly it should not be expected that there should be eight hours of pay for six hours of work," Goodyear's Board Chairman P. W. Litchfield and President E. J. Thomas told their employees in 1953. Despite the fact that they did not invoke the Deity, they were not fooling. Employers generally are going to resist the better pay-less hours onslaught with everything they've got; unions will be forced by the logic of the situation to carry that onslaught forward with everything they've got.

When the dust has settled—and a good many human beings have suffered in the struggle to achieve it—we will probably find ourselves in the era of the shorter work-week. *Then* Mr. Schlesinger's warning of a populace trained to work but not to live will be seen in all its force—and in all likelihood it may be too late to do anything about it in a missile-maddened, consumption-crazy society premised on lunacy and buttressed by hypocrisy. It is not to be expected that the unions, deeply absorbed as they are in daily grievance wrangles and protracted contractual fights, are going to devote themselves to thoroughgoing studies and forecasts of the leisure hours of their membership. Besides, as one tough but weary old militant put it to me ruefully: "We've been so worried these past years about subversives that we haven't hired or inspired any of the young hotheads. The banks and the law firms aren't afraid of the independent-minded kids—they snap them up—but we've been scared of radicals here in the union and as a result we're not attracting the kind of minds who could help us plan for a different future, the way we used to attract them when we were first organizing."

The problem of what two hundred million of us will do with our increasing leisure time—and just as we have been watching Akron, so two billion will be watching the two hundred million—is so awesome in its magnitude as to be terrifying. Isn't that all the more reason for it to capture the imagination of our younger generation of social scientists, as the conquest of other worlds is supposed to be capturing the imagination of the physical scientists?

We must persist in the confidence that the best of the new intellectuals will break free of the internal isolationism, the exclusive concern with career and family, which has preoccupied them in common with most Americans for the past decade and more, and will undertake audaciously the task of outlining a social order in which both work and leisure will be rationally based. What is needed is a social order in which, most important of all, the masses of man will be protected against the swelling flood of "entertainment" opiates in order that they may be energized to search freely for new patterns of spontaneous living for themselves and their children.

RUSSELL LYNES

Mr. Lynes (born 1910) graduated from Yale in 1932 and began a mixed career in publishing and education while working for Harper and Brothers. He then became, successively, director of publications for Vassar College, principal of Shipley School in Bryn Mawr, Pennsylvania, and assistant editor and then in 1949 managing editor of Harper's Magazine. A sprightly student of art as well as of letters, he has lectured widely in colleges and museums and is a director of the Municipal Art Society, New York, and the Archives of American Art. His main publications, on American taste and mores, are Highbrow, Lowbrow, Middlebrow (1949), The Taste-makers (1954), and Domesticated Americans (1963). The following selection first appeared in the July, 1958, Harper's.

TIME ON OUR HANDS

Recently I discovered among some papers that my mother had stowed away in a deserted file a clipping from a magazine of the 1920s. It was headed "Schedule for a One-Maid House." The house, it said, "has seven rooms: a living-room, dining-room, porch, kitchen, maid's room and bath, three bedrooms, and two baths." The schedule starts with:

6:45 A.M. *Wash and Dress*

and ends with:

8:00 P.M. *Plans for the evening will be adapted to the household convenience.*

Bridget, if that was her name, was busy in the intervening hours with cleaning, cooking, bed-making, baking, and polishing silver and brass. Her respite came sometime between 1:30 and 3:00 P.M. when, according to the schedule, she was to "clear table, wash dishes, go to own room to rest, bathe, and change dress." At 3:00 she was back in the kitchen, "ready to answer door, etc."

Leisure was not much of a problem for Bridget at work in a one-maid house. Her schedule covers six days (on Saturday it says: "Bake cake for Sunday") and like everyone else she had Sunday as her only day off. (She doesn't seem to have had "maid's night out" on the customary Thursday.)

The familiar picture of the maid on her day off was of a girl dressed "fit to kill" on her way to meet her friends at church. The equally familiar picture of the man of the house was father asleep in a hammock buried under the Sunday paper. Leisure in those days was merely a restorative for work. Now leisure has become work in its own right . . . and a worry to lots of earnest Americans.

Last year at the commencement exercises at New York University a clergyman said to the graduating class: "America can be undone by her misuse of leisure. Life is getting easier physically, and this makes life harder morally."

There are, of course, a great many professional and business men who wonder what all this talk about leisure is; somehow it is no problem to them—or so they think. There are also a good many women, especially young married women, who would give their heirlooms for a few minutes to themselves. They have only to wait.

But leisure is making some thoughtful people uneasy. In January the American Council of Churches met in Columbus to discuss the spare time of our increasingly urbanized populace. The Twentieth Century Fund is deep in an investigation of leisure and the University of Chicago is (with the help of Ford Foundation funds) making a study of the nature of leisure and how people use it. Corporations not only worry about the leisure of their employees; they do something about it. Schoolteachers and social workers and local politicians worry about it, about footloose youngsters, about long summer vacations for teen-agers, and about juvenile delinquency. City planners, safety experts, highway engineers watch the growing number of hours when families are not at work and feel they have to go somewhere. Where? To what extent is the boredom of leisure responsible for young drug addicts, for the common cold, for muggings on city streets?

Every new scientific development, whether it is aimed at saving our skins or washing our dishes, leads in one way or another to reducing still further the sweat of the public brow. The four-day week which looms on the immediate horizon (and which causes such consternation in the corporate breast) is, of course, less the product of labor's demands than of manufacturing genius. Machines not men have created the three-day weekend, and men are worried about what to do with it. Not long ago the Oil, Chemical, and Atomic Workers Union made a survey of its membership. It asked them: ". . . if and when the Union enters a bargaining program for shorter hours" how would they like this additional leisure to be distributed? Would a housewife, for example, "want her husband at home three consecutive days?" Good question.

The attitude of many large corporations has been somewhat different. They have attacked the problem of employee leisure head on. They have provided all sorts of sports facilities, music clubs, theater groups, and bowling leagues. IBM has its own golf courses for its employees. Bell and Howell has baseball fields lighted for night games. Ford's River Rouge plant has an indoor shooting range, tennis courts, baseball diamonds (nine of them), and horseshoe pits. Corning Glass has its own museum, visiting repertory theater, and changing exhibitions, in addition to automatic bowling alleys, basketball courts, and dancing classes.

Business is not sentimental about the new leisure. "Many of these off-the-job or after-hours activities," the head of employee relations for General Motors has said, "have not only a therapeutic value, but can actually sharpen or increase employees' skills." And the President of Bell and Howell has said, "Everyone in the organization gains from a well-planned recreational program."

But these efforts to sponge up the ocean of the so-called leisure time which has engulfed us can only put a few drops in the bucket. The truth is that while the new leisure has come on us fairly gradually, it has found us not at all prepared. If we are to cope agreeably with it, we are going to have to change our minds about some shibboleths and even some rather basic beliefs. To do this, we need to understand what has happened to the pattern of our leisure and where it is likely to lead.

Leisure is not a new problem born of automation, but it is a new problem for a great many kinds of people who were never much concerned with it when Bridget was working her seventy- or eighty-hour week in the one-maid house. America has had a leisure class since the industrialization of our country began, and in the 1850s the art critic James Jackson Jarves complained in shocked tones of the number of scions of wealthy families who threw themselves into rivers because they were so bored that life seemed not worth living. (Mr. Jarves wanted to interest such young men in the arts as a suitable outlet for their energies and money.) These young men, whom we would call the idle rich, had on a large scale the same problem that nearly everybody in America has today on a small scale. In its simplest terms, the primary problem of leisure is how to avoid boredom.

We used to be more accomplished at being bored than we are today, or at least we seem to have taken boredom with better grace in the days of party calls and decorous parlor games. We assumed a high moral tone toward leisure, and in some respects this tone persists. "The devil finds work for idle hands," our parents said and shook their heads; and when they said, "All work and no play makes Jack a dull boy," they meant, of course, that Jack should work most of the time but not quite all of it. Primarily leisure was thought of as a way to get a man back on his feet so that after Sunday he could put in sixty or so productive hours from Monday through Saturday. Leisure for women (few women in those days had jobs) was something quite else—it was the custody of culture and good works. Women in their spare time were expected to cultivate the arts, foster the education of their children, and play the role of Lady Bountiful in the community.

It was a neat division of family functions and a tidy way of life. Father's leisure was restorative; mother's was extremely productive. But more has changed than just the roles of men and women; the whole complex machinery of leisure has changed.

Briefly the changes are these:

In the last few decades what had started about a century ago as a trickle of people from the country and small towns to the cities became a torrent. Cities filled like cisterns and overflowed into suburbs, and as we shifted from a predominantly agricultural economy to a predominantly industrial one, we changed the nature of much of our leisure from what might be called a natural one to an artificial one, from pleasures provided by nature to pleasures concocted by man. Ways of using leisure began to come in packages—in cars, in movies, in radios, and most recently in television sets, and what was once the sauce only for the city goose became the sauce for the country gander as well. City culture is now within easy reach of everyone everywhere and everyone has the same access to talent that only a few decades ago used to be reserved for the rich and the urbane.

During the time when we were changing from a rural to an urban culture, the length of the work-week fell from sixty hours or more to forty or thirty-five. Gradually the five-day week became an almost universal reality, and the four-day week is on the immediate horizon. With more leisure time, men have, quite naturally, taken on some of the household chores that only a short while ago they wouldn't have been caught dead at, and have assumed some of the cultural responsibilities which were once the domain of their wives. They have also, with time on their hands and cars at their disposal, turned again to many kinds of rural recreation . . . to fishing and hunting, especially, but also to sailing and skiing. The most solitary of all sports, fishing, is also the most popular of all sports with American men.

But the greatest assault on old patterns of leisure and on the shibboleths about devil's work for idle hands, has been industry's discovery that it needs the consuming time of workers as much as it needs their producing time. In an economy, geared as ours is to making life comfortable for everyone, it is essential to business that people have time to enjoy their comfort and to use up the things that make life comfortable.

A tremendous part of our production plant is committed to promoting leisure—to automobiles, to television sets, to time-saving gadgets, to sports equipment, and to hundreds of services which are unnecessary to life but which contribute to relaxed living. Our economy, in other words, is more and more involved with Time Off. Think of the industries, the purveyors of pleasure, that would collapse if we were to go back to the sixty-hour week. It looks as though we were far more likely (and not because of pressures from labor but the demands of technology and automation) to go to a twenty-eight hour week.

Urbanization, the shorter working day and week, and the changing roles of the sexes have, heaven knows, produced tremendous changes in the ways Americans live. But the premium put on the consuming time of the worker by our economic system presents us with a tidily packaged moral dilemma. When idleness is a public virtue, what becomes of the moral value of work? What are we going to substitute for the old adages on which we were brought up? What are we going to tell our children? What will happen to the economy if we go on saying that virtue is its own reward, that work is good for the soul, and that leisure is only a reward for toil? What happens to the Calvinist ethic?

This is a problem I would rather refer to a dilettante than to an economist or a clergyman or certainly to an engineer. The economist would consider it from the point of view of wealth, the clergyman of the after life, and the engineer of production. The dilettante can be counted on to look at it from the point of view of life, liberty, and especially the pursuit of happiness.

I would like to contend in all seriousness, at this moment when there is such a cry for engineers and when our theological seminaries are bursting at the doors, that what we need is more dilettantes. Compared with good dilettantes, good engineers and good clergymen are a dime a dozen. Every newspaper account of the engineering shortage is contradicted by another story of how big corporations are hoarding engineers the way people hoarded butter during the war. Recently, Dr. Robert J. Havighurst of the University of Chicago made it quite clear that the number of engineers and technologists being trained in our technical schools is more than adequate to our needs; the shortage, he said, is in good teachers. In the long run our civilization will be measured more accurately by our know-why than by our know-how.

It is probably because in the triumvirate of our ideals—life, liberty, and the pursuit of happiness—the last of these has always seemed to our Calvinist society rather naughty, that we have come to look down our noses at the dilettante. We have dismissed him as a trifler; we have despised him as a parasite on other people's work, the fritterer, the gadfly. But there was a time when the word dilettante was by no means the term of opprobrium it has become.

Originally *dilettante* meant a lover of the fine arts (it comes from the Latin word for delight) and it was used to distinguish the consumer from the producer. Its application spread beyond the arts in England,

and in the eighteenth century the Society of the Dilettanti was a club of influential men interested not only in the arts but in the sciences and in archaeology. It meant the man of intellectual curiosity who devoted part of his time to the intelligent cultivation of the arts and sciences, to the resources of leisure and the satisfactions of the mind.

If you transplant the idea of the eighteenth-century dilettante from England to America, you discover that he was Thomas Jefferson and Benjamin Franklin—one a farmer who dabbled in architecture and introduced a new style to America, the other a printer who dabbled in natural science and flew a kite into a thunderstorm. You discover several others who got together and started a talkfest that became the Philosophical Society of Philadelphia, and others who, dabbling in the arts, somehow founded a string of distinguished museums across the nation and filled them with masterpieces, and, of course, a good many bad guesses. These men were dilettantes. There is no other word that fits them.

In the nineteenth century the word came on hard times. "The connoisseur is 'one who knows,' as opposed to the dilettante who 'only thinks he knows'," said F. W. Fairholt in the 1850s. Fairholt, an antiquary who wrote among other things *A Dictionary of Terms in Art*, was, there is no question, a connoisseur, and like all experts he was impatient of non-scholars who pretended to the delights he reserved for himself and his kind. A connoisseur, he said, "is cognisant of the true principles of Art, and can fully appreciate them. He is of a higher grade than the amateur, and more nearly approaches the artists." In his definition of an amateur he puts the emphasis on his "skill" as a performer and his non-professionalism, just as we do today, and in his definition of the dilettante, while he acknowledges the seriousness of the original meaning of the word, he bemoans the dilettante's pretentiousness and his use of the arts for purposes of social climbing. He admits (as people who consider themselves connoisseurs today rarely admit, however far they may go in buttering up the dilettante for their own purposes) that the arts need the enthusiasm that the dilettante's support brings to them.

The trouble (and it is a trouble) is that, with the decline of the word *dilettante*, there is no word left to describe the enthusiast who is more serious than the fan, less knowledgeable than the connoisseur, and hasn't the skill that makes an amateur. (The amateur is, after all, basically a performer.) What we need in our society, I contend again, is more real dilettantes, and we need to extend the meaning of the word to many delights besides the arts and sciences.

The dilettante is just a consumer. He is a man who takes the pursuit of happiness seriously, not frivolously, and he works at it. He is part sensualist, part intellectual, and part enthusiast. He is also likely to be a proselytizer for those causes in which his interests are involved, and to be rather scornful of those people who do not take their pleasures seriously and who are passive instead of active in the cultivation of them. But whatever else he may be he is not lazy. He may or may not have a job that he finds interesting, but he does not use his leisure in a miscellaneous and undirected fashion. He knows what he wants out of life and will go to a lot of trouble to get it. Primarily, in Voltaire's sense, he wants to cultivate his own garden.

You will find dilettantes everywhere and in every aspect of our culture. I found one a few weeks ago driving a taxi in New York. He was a man in his early sixties.

"I only drive this hack three days a week," he said. "The other four days I go fishing. I like to fish and I'm pretty good at it."

By the time he had delivered me home I knew what he fished for at what times of the year, what bait he used and where and in what weather, and which were the best fishing boats and captains going out of New York harbor. I asked him what he did with all the fish he caught.

"I got a son-in-law runs a saloon," he said. "I give them to his customers."

Probably the most common and in some ways the most accomplished of American dilettantes is the baseball fan, though the national pastime is being crowded out of its position as top banana of entertainment these days by serious music. The baseball fan knows his subject with something very close to genuine scholarship. He is an expert in the minutiae of its history and understands the nuances and subtleties of its performance. He takes as much pleasure from the refinements of its details as from the outcome of any single game, and he enjoys the company of others with whom he can argue the relative virtues of performance and make comparisons with other similar situations. He demands skill on the field of a truly professional caliber, and he lets his displeasure with anything less be known in the most direct and uncompromising manner. He is, by and large, a less tolerant dilettante than the one whose interest is devoted to art, for his expert eye is less subject to changes in fashion. Unquestionably without him the standards of baseball would long since have gone to pot.

The simple fact is that the dilettante is the ideal consumer, not ideal, perhaps, from the point of view of those producers who would like their customers to accept their products with blind confidence, but ideal from the point of view of maintaining standards of quality . . . whether material or cultural. He takes his functions as a consumer seriously. He takes the trouble to know what he likes and to sort out the shoddy and the meretricious from the sound and reasonable. If he is a dilettante of music, for example, he demands the best performance from his record-player. He is unimpressed by an imitation mahogany cabinet in the Chippendale manner, but he knows that the components of his hi-fi equipment are the very best that he can afford. (He can, in fact, be credited with the very great improvement in mass-produced sound equipment; it was his interest in high-fidelity that spread the word to the general public and raised the level of public acceptance.)

We are likely to associate the dilettante only with the arts, which is one reason why he has such a bad name in America. In the rambunctious and expansive days of the nineteenth century when America was growing and fighting its way across the continent, toil was man's business; culture was left to women. So were most other refinements of life, and the arts were thought of as sissy and men who showed any interest in them as something less than virile. A man who didn't sleep through a concert or an opera was regarded with suspicion. It was only when a man retired from business that it was considered suitable for him to spend his money on art—not necessarily because he liked it or knew anything about it but because it gave him social prestige. Except in a few Eastern Seaboard cities, the arts were women's work, and there was no time and place for the dilettante.

The nature of our new-found leisure is rapidly changing the old stereotypes. The businessman who doesn't make some pretense at an interest in culture, who doesn't support the local symphony and museum, who isn't on the library board or out raising money for his college is looked upon as not doing his duty, much less serving his own interests. Babbitt isn't Babbitt any more. Babbitt is by way of becoming a dilettante. A lot worse things could happen to him. In no time at all being a dilettante will not be considered un-American.

The point at which the dilettante becomes an "expert" but not a "professional" is an indistinct one. Two successful businessmen who have, in their leisure time, become naturalists of considerable reputation are an officer of J. P. Morgan & Co., R. Gordon Wasson, who has recently produced an important book of original research on mushrooms, and Boughton Cobb, a textile manufacturer who is one of the world's leading authorities on ferns. A few years ago an ancient language known to scholars as "Minoan Linear B" that had had scholars completely at sea for years was "broken" by an English architect, Michael Ventris, for whom cryptanalysis was a leisure activity. These three men became experts, not professionals, dilettantes in the best sense, not amateurs.

Obviously not many men in any generation are going to be able to extend their leisure activities to such levels of distinction. But leisure without direction, without the satisfaction of accomplishment of some sort is debilitating to anyone brought up in an atmosphere, like ours, in which the virtues of work have been so long extolled and are so deeply imbedded in our mythology. The greatest satisfaction of the dilettante is not in doing but in discovering, in discriminating, and in enjoying the fruits of his knowledge and his taste.

There will, of course, always be those who can only find satisfaction in making something, the eternal do-it-yourselfers, the cabinetmakers, and needlepointers, and gardeners, and model builders, and rug hookers.

These are the amateur craftsmen who often achieve professional competence. There are also those who will find their only satisfactions apart from work in sensuous pleasures, in sports, and food and drink, and love. The dilettante finds his satisfactions primarily in the mind. He is the ideal traveler, the perfect audience, the coveted reader, and the perceptive collector.

But he is not by any means necessarily a highbrow. Indeed the ideal dilettante is not. He may be a professional intellectual or he may not, but he does not pose as what he isn't. His tastes and his knowledge may well run to abstruse and esoteric things, to the dances of Tibet or the jewelry of pre-Columbian Mexico, but they may just as well run to the square dance and baseball cards. The dilettante of jazz, the man who knows the names of the instrumentalists in all of the great bands of the last thirty years, is as important a dilettante as the man who knows his Mozart by Koechel numbers. It is genuine, not simulated, enthusiasm that counts. The function of the dilettante is to encourage a high degree of performance in whatever field of interest happens to be his, to be an informed, but by no means conventional, critic, and to be a watchdog. He must be both an enthusiast and an irritant who will praise what measures up to his standards and needle producers into doing as well as they know how, and better. He is an incorrigible asker of hard questions. He keeps controversy in our culture alive, and if he is sometimes proved to be dead wrong, he is at least never dead on his feet. He is the want-to-know-why man and the traditional anathema of the know-how man.

Several months ago I found myself in an argument, or the beginnings of one, in a radio interview with a well-known broadcaster. "Our colleges need to produce more and better trained men," he said, and I countered with the suggestion that they needed to produce better educated men. "We need experts," he said.

"We need dilettantes," I replied, and the word so surprised him that he gingerly changed the subject to safer ground.

I would like to change my position, but only slightly. What we need are trained men with the capacity for being dilettantes. There can be no argument with the fact that an industrialized society must have a great many highly trained men and women with specialized knowledge and skills. But in this country the consumers and the producers are the same people; all of us work both sides of the economic street. We are, the great majority of us, the part-time idle rich, and no nation, so far as I know, has ever found itself in such a position before. Ours is a society in which no man's nose need be permanently to the grindstone, and where every man is a potential dilettante.

We have thought of our know-how as our most exportable commodity, and when somebody else demonstrated, moon-fashion, a superior know-how, we took it as a blow to our "national prestige." In fact our most exportable commodity has been a cultural one, a way of life that balances work and leisure for almost everyone and distributes the fruits of labor with astonishing, if not complete, evenness. Our most effective know-how has been the production of leisure, a commodity filled with promise and booby traps. It is the engineer with his slide rule who knows how to produce leisure, but it is the dilettante who knows how to use it and make it productive.

It will be as dilettantes and consumers that we will, in the long run, determine the quality of our culture. We will determine not only the gadgets of our civilization but the fate of its arts as well. We will determine whether the pursuit of happiness has, after all, been worth it.

The Fate of the City

The thoughtful reader who lives in a large city or one of its suburbs will not need an introduction to this problem. Technology, the growth of populations, and the flight from the farm are radically changing the boundaries and complexions of cities everywhere. The tendency of large urban centers to grow out and coalesce suggests that some day, for instance, our east and west coasts will have become urban sprawls extending for hundreds of miles from Boston to Washington and from San Francisco to the Mexican border. What kind of life will there be in these "cities" of the future?

There has already been a great deal of strenuous and expensive coping with the successive problems of crowding, traffic, ugliness, noise, decay, and pollution as they have arisen in city after city, and there has been some "city planning" and some "urban renewal." The prospect, however, is profoundly unsatisfactory to some thinkers, chief among them Lewis Mumford, whose essay begins this section and whose views are specifically challenged by Robert Moses in the essay following. We next print a foreign poet and novelist's shocked description of the territory between San Francisco and Palo Alto, California. It is followed by John Burchard's sensitive analysis, based on worldwide study, of the complex elements in the beauty of cities. Jane Jacobs in two essays presents an approach to city planning which Mumford calls sentimental but which merits the wide attention it has nevertheless received.

LEWIS MUMFORD

Lewis Mumford (born in 1895) has been called a "man of the renaissance" for the breadth of his knowledge and influence in the areas of literature, history, art, architecture, and city planning. Although he holds no academic degrees and is neither a professional architect nor city planner, he has held many professorships, lectureships, and awards in these fields. In 1961 he was the first American to receive the Royal Gold Medal for architecture from Queen Elizabeth II, and he received the Award of Merit of the American Institute of Architects in 1962. He was brought up an Episcopalian, but he considers himself a "religious humanist" in the tradition of Emerson and Whitman. A strong influence on his intellectual development was Sir Patrick Geddes, a Scottish biologist and sociologist who was a pioneer in civic and regional studies. One of the major themes in Mumford's writings is that man's only hope lies in a rediscovery of human feelings and values. "In a mature society," he has said, "man himself, not his machines or his organizations, is the chief work of art." In the 1920's and 1930's he wrote a number of books important to students of American art and literature and more recently a more general series, including Technics and Civilization *(1934),* The Culture of Cities *(1938),* The Condition of Man *(1944),* The Conduct of Life *(1951), and* The City in History *(1961), which won the National Book Award in 1962. "The Disappearing City" (October, 1962) was the first in a series of five articles entitled "The Future of the City" written for* The Architectural Record.

THE DISAPPEARING CITY

Nobody can be satisfied with the form of the city today. Neither as a working mechanism, as a social medium, nor as a work of art does the city fulfill the high hopes that modern civilization has called forth—or even meet our reasonable demands. Yet the mechanical processes of fabricating urban structures have never before been carried to a higher point: the energies even a small city now commands would have roused the envy of an Egyptian Pharaoh in the Pyramid Age. And there are moments in approaching New York, Philadelphia or San Francisco by car when, if the light is right and the distant masses of the buildings are sufficiently far away, a new form of urban splendor, more dazzling than that of Venice or Florence, seems to have been achieved.

Too soon one realizes that the city as a whole, when one approaches it closer, does not have more than a residue of this promised form in an occasional patch of good building. For the rest, the play of light and shade, of haze and color, has provided for the mobile eye a pleasure that will not bear closer architectural investigation. The illusion fades in the presence of the car-choked street, the blank glassy buildings, the glare of competitive architectural advertisements, the studied monotony of high-rise slabs in urban renewal projects: in short, new buildings and new quarters that lack any esthetic identity and any human appeal except that of superficial sanitary decency and bare mechanical order.

In all the big cities of America, the process of urban rebuilding is now proceeding at a rapid rate, as a result of putting both the financial and legal powers of the state at the service of the private investor and builder. But both architecturally and socially the resulting forms have been so devoid of character and individuality that the most sordid quarters, if they have been enriched over the years by human intercourse and human choice, suddenly seem precious even in their ugliness, even in their disorder.

Whatever people made of their cities in the past, they expressed a visible unity that bound together, in ever more complex form, the cumulative life of the community; the face and form of the city still recorded that which was desirable, memorable, admirable. Today a rigid mechanical order takes the place of social diversity, and endless assembly-line urban units automatically expand the physical structure of the city while destroying the contents and meaning of city life. The paradox of this period of rapid "urbanization" is that the city itself is being effaced. Minds still operating under an obsolete 19th century ideology of unremitting physical expansion oddly hail this outcome as "progress."

The time has come to reconsider the whole process of urban design. We must ask ourselves what changes are necessary if the city is again to become architecturally expressive, and economically workable, without our having to sacrifice its proper life to the mechanical means for keeping that life going. The architect's problem is again to make the city visually "imageable"—to use Kevin Lynch's term. Admittedly neither the architect nor the planner can produce, solely out of his professional skill, the conditions necessary for building and rebuilding adequate urban communities; but their own conscious reorientation on these matters is a necessary part of a wider transformation in which many other groups, professions and institutions must in the end participate.

The multiplication and expansion of cities which took place in the 19th century in all industrial countries occurred at a moment when the great city builders of the past—the kings and princes, the bishops and the guilds—were all stepping out of the picture; and the traditions that had guided them, instead of being modified and improved, were recklessly discarded by both municipal authorities and business enterprisers.

Genuine improvements took place indeed in the internal organization of cities during the 19th century: the first substantial improvements since the introduction of drains, piped drinking water, and water closets into the cities and palaces of Sumer, Crete and Rome. But the new organs of sanitation, hygiene and communication had little effect on the visible city, while the improvements of transportation by railroad, elevated railroad and trolley car brought in visual disorder and noise and, in the case of railroad cuts and marshalling yards, disrupted urban space as recklessly as expressways and parking lots do today. In both the underground and the above-ground city, these new gains in mechanical efficiency were mainly formless, apart from occasional by-products like a handsome railroad station or a bridge.

In consequence, the great mass of metropolitan buildings since the 19th century has been disorganized and formless, even when it has professed to be mechanically efficient. Almost until today, dreams of improvement were either cast into archaic, medieval, classic or renascence molds, unchanged except in scale, or into purely industrial terms of mechanical innovations, collective "Crystal Palaces," such as H. G. Wells pictured in his scientific romances, and even Ebenezer Howard first proposed for a garden city shopping mall. In America, despite the City Beautiful movement of the Nineties, urban progress is still identified with high buildings, wide avenues, long vistas: the higher, the wider, the longer, the better.

Current suggestions for further urban improvement still tend to fall automatically into a purely mechanical mold: gouging new expressways into the city, multiplying skyscrapers, providing moving sidewalks, building garages and underground shelters, projecting linear Roadtowns, or covering the entire area with a metal and plastic dome to make possible total control of urban weather—on the glib theory that uniform conditions are "ideal" ones. So long as the main human functions and purposes of the city are ignored, these subsidiary processes tend to dominate the architect's imagination. All the more because the resulting fragments of urbanoid tissue can be produced anywhere, at a profit, in limitless quantities. We are now witnessing the climax of this process.

The great exception to the routine processes of 19th century urban expansion was the replanning of the center of Paris. Paris became in fact *the* model 19th century city. Here, in a consistent organic development that began under Colbert and was carried to a temporary climax under Baron Haussmann during the Second Empire, a new central structure was created—first in the handsome monumental masonry of the Seine embankment, and then in the great boulevards and new parks. By creating a new outlet for sociability and conversation in the tree-lined promenade and the sidewalk café, accessible even to older quarters that were still dismally congested and hygienically deplorable, the planners of Paris democratized and humanized the otherwise sterile Baroque plan. The beauty and order of this new frame, which at once preserved the complexities of the older neighborhoods and opened up new quarters threaded with broad public greens, attracted millions of visitors to Paris and—what was more important—helped increase the daily satisfaction of its inhabitants.

But while Paris improved its rich historic core, it lost out in form, as badly as London or Berlin, Philadelphia or Chicago, on its spreading periphery. The vitality and individuality that had been heightened by the boulevards, parks and parkways of Paris were dependent upon historic institutions and many-sided activities that the new quarters lacked. Left to themselves, these residential quarters were deserts of pretentious monotony. Today central Paris, too, is being annihilated by the same forces that produce the vast areas of urban nonentity that surround the living core of our own big cities. These forces are choking Paris today as they have choked cities in the United States, as new as Fort Worth and as old as Boston.

Not the weakest of these destructive forces are those that operate under the guise of "up-to-date planning," in extravagant engineering projects, like the new motorway along the Left Bank of the Seine—a self-negating improvement just as futile as the motorways that have deprived Boston and Cambridge of access to their most convenient and potentially most delightful recreation area along the Charles. This new order of planning makes the city more attractive temporarily to motor cars, and infinitely less attractive permanently to human beings. On the suburban outskirts of our cities everywhere in both Europe and America, high-rise apartments impudently counterfeit the urbanity they have actually left behind. Present-day building replaces the complex structure of the city with loose masses of "urbanoid" tissue.

This formless urbanization, which is both dynamic and destructive, has become almost universal. Though it utilizes one kind of structure in metropolitan renewal projects and a slightly different kind in suburbia, the two types have basically the same defect. They have been built by people who lack historical or sociological insight into the nature of the city, considered as anything but the largest number of consumers that can be brought together in the most accessible manufacturing and marketing area.

If this theory were an adequate one, it would be hard to account for the general exodus that has been taking place from the center of big cities for the last generation or more; and even harder to account for the fact that suburbs continue to spread relentlessly around every big metropolis, forming ever-widening belts of population at low residential density per acre, ever further removed from the jobs and cultural opportunities that big cities are by their bigness supposed to make more accessible. In both cases, cities, villages and countryside, once distinct entities with individuality and identity, have become homogenized masses. Therewith one of the main functions of architecture, to symbolize and express the social idea, has disappeared.

During the last generation an immense amount of literature on cities has belatedly appeared, mostly economic and social analysis of a limited kind, dealing with the subsidiary and peripheral aspects of urban life. Most of these studies have been entirely lacking in concrete architectural understanding and historical perspective. Though they emphasize dynamic processes and technological change, they quaintly assume that the very processes of change now under observation are themselves unchanging; that is, that they may be neither retarded, halted nor redirected nor brought within a more complex pattern that would reflect more central human needs and would alter their seeming importance.

For the exponents of aimless dynamism, the only method of controlling the urban processes now visible is to hasten them and widen their province. Those who favor this automatic dynamism treat the resultant confusions and frustrations as the very essence of city life, and cheerfully write off the accompanying increase in nervous tensions, violence, crime and health-depleting sedatives, tranquillizers and atmospheric poisons.

The effect of this literature has been, no doubt, to clarify the economic and technical processes that are actually at work in Western urban society. But that clarification, though it may help the municipal administrator in performing his daily routines and making such plans as can be derived from five-year projections, has so far only served to reinforce and speed up the disruptive processes that are now in operation. From the standpoint of the architect and the city planning, such analysis would be useful only if it were attached to a formative idea of the city; and such an idea of the city is precisely what is lacking.

"Idea" comes from the original Greek term for "image." Current proposals for city improvement are so imageless that city planning schools in America, for the last half-generation, have been turning out mainly administrators, statisticians, economists, traffic experts. For lack of an image of the modern city, contemporary "experts" covertly fall back on already obsolete clichés, such as Le Corbusier's Voisin plan for Paris. Following the humanly functionless plans and the purposeless processes that are now producing total urban disintegration, they emerge, like the sociologist Jean Gottmann, with the abstract concept of "Megalopolis" —the last word in imageless urban amorphousness. And unfortunately, people who have no insight into the purposes of urban life have already begun to talk of this abstraction as the new "form" of the city.

The emptiness and sterility of so much that now goes under the rubric of modern city design is now being widely felt. Hence the interest that has been awakened by books like Jane Jacobs' *The Death and Life of Great American Cities,* with its keen appreciation of some of the more intimate aspects of urban life, and with its contrasting criticism, largely deserved, of radical human deficiencies in the standardized, high-rise, "urban renewal" projects.

But unfortunately Mrs. Jacobs, despite her healthy reaction against bad design, has, to match her phobia about open spaces, an almost pathological aversion to good urban design. In order to avoid officious municipal demolition and regulation, she would return to Victorian *laissez faire;* in order to overcome regimentation, she would invite chaos. Mrs. Jacobs has made a sentimental private utopia out of a very special case—a few streets in a little urban backwater—a special neighborhood of New York that happily retained its historical identity longer than any other area except Brooklyn Heights. In any large sense, she lacks an image of the modern city. Her new model is only the old muddle from which less whimsical planners are belatedly trying to escape.

The fact is that 20th century planning still lacks a fresh multi-dimensional image of the city, partly because we have not discussed and sorted out the true values, functions and purposes of modern culture from many pseudo-values and apparently automatic processes that promise power or profit to those who promote them.

What has passed for a fresh image of the city turns out to be two forms of anti-city. One of these is a multiplication of standard, de-individualized high-rise structures, almost identical in form, whether they enclose offices, factories, administrative headquarters or family apartments, set in the midst of a spaghetti tangle of traffic arteries, expressways, parking lots and garages. The other is the complementary but opposite image of urban scatter and romantic seclusion often called suburban, though it has in fact broken away from such order as the 19th century suburb had actually achieved, and even lacks such formal coherence as Frank Lloyd Wright proposed to give it in his plans for Broadacre City. As an agent of human interaction and cooperation, as a stage for the social drama, the city is rapidly sinking out of sight.

If either the architect or the planner is to do better in the future, he must understand the historical forces that produced the original miscarriage of the city, and the contemporary pressures that have brought about this retreat and revolt.

ROBERT MOSES

Robert Moses, although he has impeccable academic credentials, is a thoroughly unacademic man and has had more to do with actually chang- ing the face of New York City than any other person. Born in 1888, Mr. Moses graduated from Yale, was a Rhodes Scholar, holds a doctorate in political science from Columbia, twenty-four honorary degrees, and fifty- two awards for public service. He became head of both the New York State and Long Island park commissions in 1924, and since then has built innumerable parks, playgrounds, beaches, dams, bridges, tunnels, public buildings, housing projects, and two world's fairs. His programs have frequently involved fierce controversy—one of his severest critics is Lewis Mumford. Mr. Moses defends his methods by commenting that this is the way to get things done. "Are Cities Dead?" from the January, 1962, Atlantic Monthly, is a fair sample of his vigorous style.

ARE CITIES DEAD?

I picked up a New York City paper one morning recently and was ap- palled by the space and emphasis given to an obscure assistant professor with no record of administration, who, enjoying a foundation grant and speaking for a regional civic organization, prophesied imminent chaos and the early disintegration of our metropolis. He maintained that there are 1467 municipal agencies, fiercely independent, viciously uncoordi- nated, and shamelessly spending taxpayers' money in frantic insanity.

These counsels of despair come just as the Congress plans a Depart- ment of Urban Affairs of Cabinet rank. If the new Secretary begins by believing that American cities are doomed in spite of the increasingly rapid shift from rural to urban centers, he will accomplish little. If emphasis is on anything but local initiative, the effect will be zero, and we shall have merely elevated a bureau to an expensive department and put another bureaucrat in orbit. Anyway, if we are to have a new Secretary, let us see that he believes in cities.

There are plenty of things that are wrong with our cities. These things should not be slurred over or forgotten. There are many failures which should be appraised. But why exaggerate? Why imply that the faults are beyond redemption? Why minimize notable evidence of progress? Why ignore the remarkable people and achievements which make our big cities the powerful magnets they are?

One of the most-quoted Jeremiahs who inveigh against the condition of our cities is Lewis Mumford, author of *The City in History*. He is widely acclaimed in the academic world. I object to these Jeremiahs primarily because they attempt to poison a rising generation of ordinarily optimistic young Americans. There is another good reason for deprecating this school of thought: those who undermine the very foundations and *raison d'être* of cities, and not merely the incidental mistakes of individuals, make municipal administration increasingly unattractive and relegate it finally to the lowest politics and the poorest talent.

Suppose we were to ask some of our best and most ambitious mayors, battling valiantly for limited, immediate objectives, whether concentrations of population are beyond improvement, whether the *raison d'être* of the metropolis is gone, and whether their plans for redevelopment are essentially futile. I mean men like Lee of New Haven, Dilworth of Philadelphia, Miriani of Detroit, and former Mayor Morrison of New Orleans. Are the citizens who believe in such men now to be told that their trust has been betrayed?

There is, indeed, much wrong with cities—big and little—but the answer is not to abandon or completely to rebuild them on abstract principles. Only on paper can you disperse concentrations of population and create small urban stars with planned satellites around them. In the course of many years devoted to reclamation of water front, manufacturing of topsoil to cover thousands of acres of new parks, buying and preserving large areas of natural woodlands and shores in advance of the realtor and subdivider, planting thousands of trees along parkways and expressways, building hundreds of playgrounds, planning cultural centers in place of decaying tenements, tightening zoning and building laws, restricting billboards, opposing entrenched power companies and other utility corporations to keep the basic natural public resources inalienable, and stopping water pollution, I never caught a glimpse of the breast beaters who are now touted as pundits in this field. I saw none of them in our long battle to establish eleven thousand acres of Jamaica Bay within New York City as a permanent, protected, unspoiled natural game refuge. Is Jamaica Bay a symbol of urban rot, or is it just too small and obscure to attract the attention of the critics?

Recently, a number of planners and civic leaders in New York wrote a letter to the press advocating the conversion to a park of the whole of

Welfare Island, a wedge in the East River presently occupied by hospitals. I tried this twenty-five years ago, before new hospitals and a bridge on the wrong side of the river were built, but the hospital commissioner poured abuse on me and was supported by the then mayor. It is too late now, because of the huge investment in modern institutions and vehicular access. Meanwhile, we have built adequate parks on Randall's and Ward's islands a little way up the East River and a pedestrian bridge to Ward's, which the paper planners never mention.

In his Baccalaureate Address for 1961, President A. Whitney Griswold of Yale said, among other things:

"I shall not attempt to recite here all the worst things that are said about us or to refute them by pointing out that just as bad (or worse) things go on in the countries which say them. Neither shall I attempt to itemize the shortcomings which we ourselves acknowledge. It is enough to remind ourselves of the nature of the great, national, hundred per cent American jeremiad. It goes like this. We are soft. We are spoiled. We are lazy, flabby, undisciplined, in poor physical condition, poorly educated, beguiled with gadgets, bedazzled by sex, uninterested in anything but our own comfort, unprepared for the responsibilities fate has placed upon us, unready for our destiny. In a word, we are decadent. Do I exaggerate the case? Listen to an American voice in the chorus of American self-criticism. I quote.

The arena, the tall tenement, the mass contests and exhibitions, the football matches, the international beauty contests, the strip tease made ubiquitous by advertisement, the constant titillation of the senses by sex, liquor and violence—all in true Roman style. . . . These are symptoms of the end: Magnifications of demoralized power, minifications of life. When these signs multiply, Necropolis is near, though not a stone has yet crumbled. For the barbarian has already captured the city from within. Come, hangman! Come, vulture!

"This is not an editorial from *Pravda* or one of the lighter touches from a tirade by Castro," President Griswold continued. "It is a view of present-day American life by Lewis Mumford in his most recent book, *The City in History*. It is a view that is shared, or at any rate expressed, by many Americans from pulpits, classrooms, editorial offices, and high places in the government.

"Are things really that bad? If they are, heaven help us—and heaven will not help us until we help ourselves. If things are not that bad, why do Mr. Mumford and so many of his fellow citizens say they are? Perhaps they haven't got the facts straight. . . . May be the whole of Western civilization is decadent and, since we are the leaders of it, we are the most decadent of all."

The physical beauties of a city can, no doubt, be exaggerated, but **no** balanced observer will ignore them. Europeans coming to New York City for the first time are ecstatic about the view of lower Manhattan in the early morning from a great liner as it passes through upper New York Bay; mid-Manhattan seen from the Triborough Bridge at sundown; the jeweled diadem spread before the jet flyer at night; the clean gossamer cobwebs of its suspension bridges; the successive bustle and tomblike silences of its streets; the fantastic daring, imagination, and aspiration of its builders. Visitors are, of course, aware of New York's congested traffic, but is the slowdown any worse than that in London or Paris?

Admittedly, the gasoline motor has provided us with problems which did not exist in ancient Rome. But the jaundiced eye of the city historian sees no signs of achievement and progress. He is obsessed with the harlotry and the decline and fall of Rome and Babylon, and the beams and motes blot out Jones Beach.

Here is one example of this counsel of despair:

"Such form as the metropolis achieves is crowd-form: the swarming bathing beach by the sea or the body of spectators in the boxing arena or the football stadium. With the increase of private motor cars, the streets and avenues become parking lots, and to move traffic at all, vast expressways gouge through the city and increase the demand for further parking lots and garages. In the act of making the core of the metropolis accessible, the planners of congestion have already almost made it uninhabitable. . . .

"We must restore to the city the maternal, life-nurturing functions, the autonomous activities, the symbiotic associations that have long been neglected or suppressed. For the city should be an organ of love; and the best economy of cities is the care and culture of men."

Nowhere does the author even remotely tell us how these "symbiotic associations" can be revived and encouraged or where he would start with this renaissance.

As to housing, we read many similar grotesque misstatements. For example, Mumford says: "Stuyvesant Town was built by a private insurance company with generous aid by the State: but its residential density of 393 per acre remains that of a slum. Despite its inner open spaces, this housing would require eighty additional acres to provide the park and playground space now regarded as desirable, nineteen more than the entire project without buildings."

Here are the facts. The state had nothing to do with this project. It is not a slum in any sense. It is not overpopulated. New York City and the Metropolitan Life Insurance Company substituted for filthy tenements excellent, modern, low-rental housing with plenty of light and air and views all around on less than 20 per cent land coverage. Everyone familiar with housing and recreation knows that no such huge additional space as eighty acres is needed for parks and playgrounds in a project totaling seventy-two acres.

Similar distortions appear in dicta regarding traffic.

"In the interest of an unimpeded traffic flow highway engineers produce vast clover leaves even in low density areas with limited cross traffic, where there is no reason whatever why the arterial flow should not be occasionally halted as in a city street."

Every competent engineer knows that halting through traffic at a clover leaf would produce strangulation and is the negation of all accepted standards for limited-access highways.

The prosperous suburbanite is as proud of his ranch home as the owner of the most gracious villa of Tuscany. In the suburbs the hiker finds the long brown path leading wherever he chooses, by day, in filtered sunlight, or by evening, in the midst of the rhythmic orchestration of tree frogs. The little identical suburban boxes of average people, which differ only in color and planting, represent a measure of success unheard of by hundreds of millions on other continents. Small plots reflect not merely the rapacity of realtors but the caution of owners who do not want too much grass to cut and snow to shovel—details too intimate for the historians.

The real-estate subdivisions east of the city are not all there is to Long Island. The South Shore is my home. It is still mostly unspoiled, well protected, and largely in public ownership. Those of us who work at the problems that critics chatter about go down to the sea in cars and ships for respite, to fish, swim, soak up sun, and refresh our spirits, and in off seasons to wander in the anonymous enveloping ocean mist. Our fog appears, not stealing in on cat feet, but as a ghostly emanation of the sea, in silence punctuated only by the muffled bell and intermittent warning of the buoys along the hidden channels. Here we knit up the ravell'd sleave of care. Who are these pundits to say we have neglected our problems or that others might solve them better?

The cultures, amenities, and attractions of cities, suburbs, exurbs, and open country are manifestly different but complement each other. The sanest, best-balanced people are those who spend part of the year in each area and do not stay continuously under urban pressure. In that way they get the best of the city and of the more or less open spaces. A shack nearby or shelter in some vast wilderness will shortly be within the reach of most families.

In Mr. Mumford's recent gloom book, Baron Haussmann, a giant among planners, who saved Paris and turned it into a modern city, is contemptuously dismissed as a bulldozer and sadistic wrecker of fine old neighborhoods.

Here is some further pontification:

"To keep the advantages first discovered in the closed city, we must create a more porous pattern, richer in both social and esthetic variety. Residential densities of about one hundred people per net acre, exclusive of streets and sidewalks, will provide usable private gardens and encourage small public inner parks for meeting and relaxing. This can be achieved without erecting the sterile, space-mangling high-rise slabs that now grimly parade, in both Europe and America, as the ultimate contribution of 'modern' architecture."

Can anyone possibly believe that garden apartments housing over one hundred persons an acre are uncivilized and that small public inner parks have not been repeatedly considered and found wholly unworkable?

To sum up, let me ask the Gamaliels of the city a few pointed questions.

By what practical and acceptable means would they limit the growth of population?

How would they reduce the output of cars, and if they could, what would take the place of the car as an employer of workers or as a means of transport in a motorized civilization?

If more cars are inevitable, must there not be roads for them to run on? If so, they must be built somewhere, and built in accordance with modern design. Where? This is a motor age, and the motorcar spells mobility.

Is the present distinction between parkways, landscaped limited-access expressways, boulevards, ordinary highways, and city streets unscientific? If so, what do the critics propose as a substitute?

Is mass commuter railroad transportation the sole and entire answer to urban street congestion? Is conflict between rubber and rails in fact irrepressible? Are there not practical combinations of public, quasi-public, and private financing which can solve the riddle? And what of the people who prefer cars and car pools and find them more comfortable, faster, and even cheaper than rails?

If a family likes present city life, should it be forced to live according to avant-garde architectural formulas? Do most professional planners in fact know what people think and want? The incredible affection of slum dwellers for the old neighborhood and their stubborn unwillingness to move are the despair of experts. The forensic medicine men who perform the autopsies on cities condemn these uncooperative families to hell and imply that they could be transplanted painlessly to New Delhi, Canberra, Brasilia, and Utopia. We do not smoke such opium. We have to live with our problems.

Is it a mark of genius to exhibit lofty indifference to population growth, contempt for invested capital, budgets, and taxes; to be oblivious to the need of the average citizen to make a living and to his preferences, immediate concerns, and troubles?

What do the critics of cities offer as a substitute for the highly taxed central city core which supports the surrounding, quieter, less densely settled, and less exploited segments of the municipal pie? Have they an alternative to real-estate taxes?

Pending responsible answers to these questions, those of us who have work to do and obstacles to overcome, who cannot hide in ivory towers writing encyclopedic theses, whose usefulness is measured by results, must carry on.

DAN JACOBSON

Dan Jacobson is a poet, story-writer, and essayist who was born (1929) and educated in South Africa and now lives in London. His first jobs were in teaching, journalism, and business. In 1956–1957 he held a Fellowship in Creative Writing at Stanford University, and No Further West *(1957) is a record of the impression California made on him. We reprint below its second chapter. Mr. Jacobson has written many stories and reviews for magazines in both England and the United States. He reviews books for the* New Statesman *and the* Guardian. *Some of his other writings are* A Dance in the Sun *(1956),* A Long Way from London *(1958),* Evidence of Love *(1960), and* Time of Arrival and Other Essays *(1962).*

THE SEVERED TENDON

Why hadn't anyone *told* me? That was the question I asked of myself in awe, in fear, in anger, in despair. What I saw was all new, brand-new, and of a size and a populousness and a busyness that I couldn't begin to comprehend. Why hadn't anyone told me about it? Why hadn't I been warned?

And I asked this question though what we saw of Palo Alto by daylight on our first morning there confirmed my first impression that the town was very similar to the small towns I had known in South Africa. There was the same sense of space, newness, and sandiness; there were the same wide tarred streets, empty in the sun; there were the same lawns of grass shrivelling at the edges; the leaves of familiar trees hung down spiritlessly in front of houses that were often of a style I had known in South Africa; there was a main street, with its shop windows and department stores stretching away from the pavements, and few people about.

But the difficulty was that this main street wasn't main at all, and the town wasn't a small one, if it existed at all; and of that I wasn't sure. What I saw in the days following our arrival seemed to be a single sprawl that stretched all the thirty miles between San Francisco and Palo Alto and for another thirty miles beyond; and what it was anywhere along the length was precisely what it was anywhere else along its length. And what *that* was—I had no word for it. It was a sprawl, a mess, a nightmare of repetition and disjunction and incoherence, all grown permanent and powerful.

There were shops, identical houses in tracts, drive-ins, motels, factories, shopping centres, supermarkets, giant billboards, filling-stations, used-car lots all along El Camino Real. There were identical houses in tracts, drive-ins, motels, shopping-centres, supermarkets, giant billboards all along the Bayshore Highway; there were whole towns of identical houses in tracts between the Bayshore Highway and El Camino Real; and further again, and further yet, there were used-car lots and giant billboards and shopping centres and supermarkets . . .

And all the buildings sprawled wide, drunkenly, sharing no style, no size, having no relation to one another but that imposed on them by the single thing they did share: a frontage of the road, a view of the traffic, a gaze across to the other side of the road where there were other motels, drive-ins, gas-stations and other names—The Crown, Crazy Jack's, Ole Olsen's, Top-T Service, and a supermarket spaciously spelling out its name with a single letter in each of its stucco arches. They were all spread away from one another, pushed apart physically. Every car of the thousands that rushed at all times and along all the length of the roads had to have a place for it when it swung off the road and stopped. So, sprawling enough in themselves, the places spread their grounds wider still, in hope that one car or a hundred would stop in this drive-in rather than the fifty others over the last few miles, this supermarket rather than the last. Perhaps the car would stop because in front of this supermarket someone had taken the trouble to advertise—in black letters six inches high against a white illuminated background—*Celery: 10 Cents a Stick.* How could anyone go to so much trouble to sell sticks of celery, one wondered; but one wondered about nothing very long on that road, because next there was a car mounted on a platform twenty feet high, and slowly the whole platform turned round, bearing the car on its palm. Below it, and stretching away from it was a used-car lot, and another, all decorated with streamers and bunting and strings of plastic whirligigs, as if royalty were soon to pass by, to inspect the acres upon acres of used cars, glittering in their lots on the sand. Then a service-station, or two, or three, a motel with all its Swiss-style gabled little chalets in a row along the road, a second-hand furniture mart, a liquor store, more used-car lots. It was impossible to tell which of all the cars in rows belonged to one lot and which to another, for there were no fences between them;

but there were names on poles, names on billboards, names as high as the little wooden offices that bore them, and each name was different from the last—unless it was a name that had been seen before, fifty times before, in front of other lots, on other hoardings, further back along the road.

The used-car lots covered their spaces, they stretched down the road, and then beyond them there rose the grandeur of a new shopping centre. This one looked something like the Palais de Chaillot in Paris. It was white, it gleamed, it flung its arms open as if to embrace not a terraced garden but a plain of parked cars as wide as that first one we saw in front of the airport. These shopping centres were things that we had never seen before—places that under a single sprawling roof housed enough shops to supply the wants of a town. That one was like the Palais de Chaillot; the next was quaint, rural, timbered, with flagged walks, low buildings with overhanging eaves, at every corner a loudspeaker playing soft music. In this shopping centre there was a shop that sold only electronically-operated garage doors; but otherwise there was nothing in it that was not repeated shabbily or elegantly by some single shop belonging to the sprawl directly and not through the *imperium in imperio* of the shopping centre. They both contributed to the sprawl, and who could say which contribution was the greater—that of the shopping centre, with all its elegant arcades and galleries, or of this shabby drive-in shaped like a Mexican hat, with its brim over the place where cars were parked?

But what did shabby mean here, and what did elegant mean? Here was a shack of shingles and nails all smeared and disfigured with the great letters that give it its name—but within there was wall-to-wall carpeting, marble-topped desks, mobiles hanging from the ceilings, and sheer glass partitions; there was a neon sign blazing away so fiercely that it almost hid the little barn behind it where food was served. And the cars in the used-car lots, were they shabby or are they elegant? And that hospital for dogs, where on the roof a neon dog wagged its long neon tail?

But it was gone too, behind us, in a moment, for one always travelled by car down the roads, one never walked.

Those highways were able along their length to provide you with any material thing you might ever need. There were all the shops of various kinds; there were banks, travel-agencies, money-lenders, real-estate agents who would sell you a house, and furniture stores that would sell you the furniture to fill it with. There were bookstores and shops selling the latest selection of records, and little establishments that offered tropical fish in bowls, and imported Danish cutlery. There were the shops and the facilities for whole cities of prosperous people; but the curious, the frightening thing was that all the shops and facilities belonged only to the highways and to no city.

Nowhere along their length did the highways seem to contract, confine themselves, centre themselves for a community around them. There were no parks along the highways, no statues, no plaques commemorating notable events; there were no vistas, no views, no streets that radiated from this point or that; there was nowhere that one could turn and look back the way one had come. The highways ran with all their businesses and townships from San Francisco to Palo Alto and beyond, simply ploughing across the country; and it was as if some kind of vital tendon had been severed, so that they could grasp nothing to themselves, could enclose nothing in themselves, could make no order of themselves, but could only lie sprawling, incoherent, centreless, viewless, shapeless, faceless—offering all the products a community might need and yet making the establishment of a community impossible.

For it was by the roads and from the roads that the towns like ours seemed to live. Every morning half of the male inhabitants of the towns seemed to get into their cars and go thundering along the highways to San Francisco or elsewhere, and every evening they thundered back again. The women drove along the highways to do their shopping; the very air of the towns was filled night and day with the whisper of the traffic on the highways. As our town seemed to be, so seemed all the others —flat, indistinguishable appendages to the highways, equal parts of a brand-new nameless sprawl across a country.

JOHN ELY BURCHARD

Dean Burchard was born in 1898, and graduated from Massachusetts Institute of Technology with a B.S. in architectural engineering in 1923 and an M.S. degree two years later. A specialist in housing, in library construction, and in structural defense, he spent many years in industry, worked five years for the government (receiving a Presidential Medal of Merit for war services), and in 1944 joined the administration of M.I.T. He became Dean of the School of Humanities and Social Studies and is at present Dean Emeritus. He was president of the American Academy of Arts and Sciences from 1954 to 1956. Among his writings are The Evolving House, with *A. F. Bemis, three volumes (1933–1936);* A Method for Analyzing Economic Distribution of Shelter *(1940); and* The Architecture of America, *with Albert Bush-Brown (1960). He has edited* Mid-Century, The Social Implications of Scientific Progress *(1950), and* The Historian and the City, *with Oscar Handlin (1963). "The Urban Aesthetic" is taken from* Metropolis in Ferment, *ed. Martin Meyerson, volume 314 of the* Annals of the American Academy of Political and Social Science *(November, 1957).*

THE URBAN AESTHETIC

The works of J. K. Huysmans are no longer fashionable, but makers of cities would do well to recall the experiences of his hero, des Esseintes. This man understood that the true aesthetic experience exacts the use of all of the senses, not the optical alone; and that this experience is more sensuous than intellectual.

So it is for the city of today, even though architects and planners seem often to ignore it. The character of a fine or a mean city is composed of its smells, its noises, even its taste as well as its sights. Its sights include people, their clothing, their conveyances, their flowers, trees, fountains. A city has an unseen history which also forms its aesthetic. A city is not architecture alone, perhaps not even principally.

Cities have noises. There are the shrill engine whistles at the Gare St. Lazare, the chants of the street peddlers of Naples, the bells of the betjaks in Jakarta, the horns in the fogs of San Francisco Bay, the subterranean rumble of the subways of Manhattan, the unmuffled motorcycle engines on the Corso.

Cities have people and people have tongues. Street voices do not sound the same even in a single country. The sharpness of Albany is countered by the softness of New Orleans, the flatness of Omaha by the twang of Portsmouth, New Hampshire. None is like the diapasons of Hamburg, the falsetto upturnings of London, the liquids of Rome or Helsinki, the wails or bleats of Bombay or Cairo. When they stop talking some people in some cities sing, some listen to sidewalk orchestras, some are silent. Thus cities do not sound alike.

Cities have smells. Wood smoke and manure provide the warm fall atmosphere of Bourges; coal gas cares for Lille, or Birmingham, or Washington, Pennsylvania; oil for Galveston; fish drying in the sun for Ålesund; coffee roasting for Boston; while, when the wind is in the southwest, Chicago knows the sick sweet odor of drying blood and recently ardent flesh. Mainz is redolent with honeysuckle. Thus cities do not smell alike.

Nor are all the visual motifs of a city architectural. People wear clothes: The bizarre open shirt of Hollywood and Vine is not the careful gray flannel of Grand Central, or the big hat of Fort Worth, or the bowler of the City of London. The summer skirts of Stockholm do not resemble the kimonos of Kobe, or the saris of Madras, or the serapes of Bogotá.

People are carried about. Some cities have elephants, or camels or goats, many have mules and horses, some have rickshaws, some have sleds, and a few have sedan chairs even now. More have bicycles, and when you see many you can be sure you are in flat Amsterdam and not flat Chicago. Most common today, of course, are motorcars but even these do not look alike in every city; even the automobile scenery changes. You will not, praise be, see many swept wings east of Suez. Not yet.

Cities have history, at least great cities do, and historical spots have their own aesthetic. Some cities like Helsinki bear the formidable memories of many different occupations in architectural forms which have not been destroyed; some like Athens and Rome wear their proudest jewels in their magnificent ruins; some like Paris or London offer a wide canvas of undisturbed historical development. For many the historical aesthetic may be mainly an aesthetic of the memory: The door through which assassins sought to reach a Henry of Navarre; the ancient site of a wilderness fort such as Duquesne, or Dearborn; the pavement, long since replaced, on which a Crispus Attucks fell. Often the memory is served only by a plaque. But even such tremulous whispers from the past will cause the sensitive to prickle.

Some cities have sidewalk cafés and some do not; some have awnings, or umbrellas, or arcades and some do not; some are adorned with mosaic pavements and the result is different from that of cobble stones or asphalt. Some have pleasant street signs or street lamps. Some support flowers everywhere; some have rejected plants. Some are best known for their chimney pots. Some have amusement gardens, but a Tivoli, a Skansen, or a Liseberg is quite a different thing from a Sutro's Baths or a Coney Island, to say nothing of a Revere Beach. Some have rivers, or canals, or lakes; some are moist with fountains; some are dry and hard.

All these things add to the aesthetic of a city, but most of them are the result of time and tradition. Few have been consciously created in the way a hotel manager might sprinkle an elevator in the Ritz-Carlton with perfume. Yet the city of the future will be incomplete if all these aspects of personality, while possible in an old economics of scarcity and overwork, are discarded as obsolete or impossible in the new economics of plenty and leisure. It would be ironic if the brave new city could sport no flowers because there is now no one left with time or inclination to tend to them.

The city that we love or detest is the summation of all such things: Of its smells, its noises, its people, its voices, its clothes, its vehicles, its animals; it is the sum too of its markets and its sidewalks, of its trees, flowers, water, and sculpture, of its clean or grimy air, of its abundant or covered sun, of the color of its sky, of its terrain, of a way of life, and a history. When the city is lucky, and this does not always happen, it possesses an architecture which has understood and loved all these nonarchitectural considerations. When we synthesize all these, the image of a given city springs quickly to mind as any exercise in calling names will prove. Most of us will have immediate and moderately reliable responses to names such as Bangkok, Benares, Hong Kong, Kyoto, Katmandu, Nuremberg, Florence, Venice, Athens, Cairo, Caracas, or Honolulu as well as to the great world capitals like Rome, Berlin, Paris, London, Stockholm, Tokyo. In America a few cities evoke such images, but these are more likely to be New York, Philadelphia, Washington, Boston, San Francisco, or New Orleans than Houston, Kansas City, or Buffalo. We can even conjecture reasonable images of cities we have not seen, cities like Samarkand, Isfahan, or Leopoldville. Happy the city that proffers such a positive image. Unhappy the city that does not.

There has been a decline in the number of positive images. Newly created cities like New Delhi or Canberra need at least time. But the lesser cities of the world look more and more alike every day, and at a slower pace as we know more about each other, as we adopt each other's conveniences and merge them with our own, the same thing is happening to the greater cities. Whether or not it is better for French health that Coca Cola replace Pernod, it is probably not better for the French aesthetic. A slow leveling process is going on all over the world. Of course, it is theoretically possible to level up as well as down, but an improvement in standards of sanitation is not necessarily synonymous with an improvement in aesthetic standards. On the aesthetic side it may be that Gresham's Law is at work in the world. The symbols of Western "progress," coveted in too many places, are not always pretty symbols. The symbols of the Soviet Union are, if anything, less pretty. Thus sanitation will remove the indigenous smells, mass production the indigenous costumes, mass communication the indigenous tastes, education the indigenous tongues. Mass transport will diminish the importance of indigenous materials. History cannot be expunged quite so easily, but many people would like now to forget much of their history, and not all peoples recall the past with pride. The camel will not survive forever on the streets of Tashkent, or the llama in Lima, or the water buffalo in Rangoon. Skylines will change, not always for the better; architectural deviations will become less conspicuous. To the designer of American embassies, Copenhagen and Stockholm were unfortunately not different cities. But even where the city centers that provided the character have been well protected, they become engulfed by the anonymous and expanding peripheral suburb.

The life of man in the large modern city has so changed that the visual aspects of the old city he may once have known and cherished can have only a tangential effect upon his life. Thus in his own impression, they are not at all as his memory might recall them even when they have not been physically changed. Nor do they look to him quite as they may to a stranger. Once this was not important, but in the modern world nearly every one in a large city is, in a curious way, something of a stranger.

This is not to say that the city dweller thinks of himself as exotic. The exotic city so many of us want to visit is always over the range in Erewhon. We want to visit Erewhon and return to praise it, but the more important word is not "praise" but rather "return." In an increasingly nomadic world there can be fewer homes to return to, more determination to make every place like home, fewer exotic experiences. For the exotic and the indigenous are, naturally, the same thing only seen through different eyes. If the final world is to be one great Conrad Hilton chain, this will have some effect upon the aesthetics of the cities. The quaint Alice Foote MacDougall repetition of the pretty picturesque will not do for modern men. We need not expect to hear muezzins calling from the minarets of Hilton-Mecca. As an incorrigible and sentimental romantic I may regret this, but I cannot ignore it.

Yet this leveling raises hard questions for the designer of new, as yet unbuilt, cities, perhaps even harder ones for those who will rebuild the old cities. The questions are even humiliating if he is sensitive enough to understand them.

The largest humiliation is that so little of the urban aesthetic is his to control. He cannot write the whole symphony. He will not, perhaps fortunately, be able to design the noises, the smells, the costumes, the vehicles, even the major elements of the terrain. He can neither select them nor expunge them, but he will be a bad designer if he ignores them.

Nor can he remake or relive history. Yet he must be careful not to destroy it for there can be no great urban aesthetic which forgets history or tries to pretend that people have not trod the streets before. History offers particular pitfalls. It will not do, on the one hand, to wax sentimental about it and to create more Williamsburgs or Santa Barbaras. But it will not do to extirpate it either, and it will be wrong to destroy fine things for new projects. Boston without the old churches, the Bulfinch State House, Richardson's Trinity Church, McKim's Public Library, the Boston Common, and the Charles River Basin would not be much of a city. Solicitude for what has gone before cannot be limited to refraining from tearing them down. The designers of the two insurance buildings which destroyed the urban sky line of Boston were as much vandals as though they had torn down Trinity Church for a shopping center.

In America the willingness to refrain from encroachment is almost nonexistent for we have not even learned not to tear down. The bulldozer is in some ways more glamorous for us than the bricks it pushes into the earth. Yet we must somehow learn the truth. There may be a greater architect in America today than Henry Hobson Richardson ever was, there may be even two or three. But nothing that such a contemporary can design for Pittsburgh on the particular site of the Allegheny Court House and Jail will ever contribute as much to the aesthetics of Pittsburgh as this great stone monument from an earlier day and by another great artist. The Jail and Court House may become obsolete for their original purposes. They cannot become obsolete as part of the meaning of Pittsburgh. Cities are like human beings, and they cannot void their past experience. They should not even try. This is a lesson better understood in Europe than in America. A primary and inexorable problem for the modern urban aesthetic is to respect and understand history without being servile to her. For us of today there is less risk of servility than there is of disrespect. We must never forget that there were brave men before Agamemnon—or Le Corbusier.

Many otherwise great designers have not possessed this sensitive understanding of history. They have been willing either to tear down fine old buildings, to restore them arrogantly, or to enter into an unfortunate and juxtaposed competition with them. But even if history is understood and appropriately revered, there remain other humiliating limitations.

The designer will scarcely be permitted, for example, to design whole cities except in books. Frank Lloyd Wright must share Bagdad with Aalto and others, however much he may protest; this is probably just as well, no matter how towering the genius. Cities take a long time to make, and order or consistency are not the only ways to a fine urban aesthetic; they may indeed offer the most limited way.

I have heard revealing debates about Broadway at night which will illustrate this point. Broadway is vulgar, strident, brassy, confused, and wonderful. Orderly minds perceiving the fundamental beauty wish that it might all be taken in hand by a single brain or at least by a group of sympathetic brains and brought into order, its colors subdued, its competitive excesses suppressed. But this would, of course, be exactly wrong. The greatness of this magnificent nocturnal honky-tonk is precisely that it is unbridled. There are other ways of using neon as the basin of the Charles River at Boston, also unplanned, will attest. But more liveliness on the Charles and more order on Broadway would simply downgrade both.

This produces the rather negative conclusion that, though there are some fine examples of beautiful cities with master plans that have been observed, there are more examples of beautiful cities in which no such order can be found. The problem is then how to achieve the fine effects of laissez-faire without the disadvantages, disorder, and excessive competition; or how to achieve the fine effects of master planning without the disadvantage of stodginess or pedantry. This is an impossible question, but to me it seems that a city is too big a piece of sculpture for any one man to carve, and I am still more apprehensive about sculpture by a committee,

The architect-designer must face one further humiliation. Some cities are most famous, not as cities but because they possess individual buildings of the greatest consequence. But there are also cities of great beauty which own no buildings of the absolutely highest quality or in which the few such buildings as do exist have no dominant influence on the whole aesthetic. Two examples will suffice.

Old San Francisco from the Presidio to the Oakland Bridge offers one of the finest visual impressions furnished by any city in the world, an impression which cannot be diminished by the less elegant ensembles of the surrounding East Bay, Peninsula, or Marin County. The streets are badly planned and march their gridiron in defiance of the contours. The buildings lack individual distinction with hardly an exception. Here there is no Louvre, no St. Peter's, no Forum Romanum, no Parthenon, no Hagia Sofia, no Taj Mahal. Not even the Coit tower or the belfry of the Ferry offers much punctuation. Anonymous and individually undistinguished buildings push their white walls up the hills to make one of the most beautiful cityscapes in the world.

The Götaplatsen of Göteborg, a handsome square, centers around one of Milles' finest fountains. As the Kungsportsavenyn slopes gently away from it towards the harbor, it leaves a square of excellent consequence, nearer to the Piazza San Marco than anything to be found in Stockholm, the so-called "Venice of the North." Yet not one of the three buildings which frame the square, neither the City Theatre, nor the Art Museum and gallery nor the Concert Hall adorns the square with a really fine façade. The façades, indeed, embrace great absurdities; but the relation of their walls, the rise of their steps, the quality of the pavements, and perhaps above all the tubs of flowers rising bank on bank combine to support the play of water on the colossal and archaic Poseidon and his humorous entourage to produce a remarkable over-all effect. Would the effect be greater or less had the enveloping buildings been made by greater geniuses, had they more brilliance in their own individual rights? One should not be too quick to say. What can be said with confidence and with no denial of the great quality of 860 Lake Shore Drive in Chicago is that such a Miesian building would be utterly out of place on the Götaplatsen.

A great urban aesthetic arises not from a cluster of architectural chefs-d'oeuvre but from a sensitivity on the part of each successive builder to the amenities that are already there. No good architect would dream of destroying the beautiful natural terrain of an isolated site but would, instead, try to marry his building to the land and the vegetation, and the water, and the sky. It is easier to forget and it is common to forget that there is also an urban terrain and that this, too, is entitled to respect, even to love. Urban aesthetics are not to be made over as lightly as ladies' clothes.

The qualification must naturally be remembered that when we speak of the beauty of a city we speak usually of only a small part. Beautiful

San Francisco does not include what is happening on the eastern and southern ridges of the Bay or down in the erstwhile walnut groves and artichoke farms. When we speak of the charms of Göteborg we are not talking about the brutal array of multistoried tenements that accumulate on its periphery, tenements with perhaps less to recommend them than the Dudok-influenced apartments nearer town and of an earlier day which it is now the fashion to repudiate. Beautiful Philadelphia is not Levittown, and beautiful Sydney is not the string of abominable villas which line the coast for twenty-five miles toward the Pittwater.

A troublesome question arises here. As believers in the possibility of better things we have to admire the occasional efforts to do something fine on the periphery whether it be at Baldwin Hills Village or at Vällingby outside of Stockholm. But when we are content not to be doctrinaire we must also concede that even the best of these, as of now, have failed to achieve something that was implicit in the old city and that is too fine to give up without a struggle. In terms of superior safety, health, convenience, democratic standards, indeed in terms of most social standards which are currently accepted, they represent a considerable step forward and not only in comparison to the slum. But something is still missing from this new suburban aesthetic: Something of beauty, something of humor, something of informality, something of surprise, something in short of nature.

No city is really beautiful, nor can any peripheral development achieve beauty, if nature is too much ignored. The hills, the rivers, the lakes, the sea, cannot be installed by man. But trees, flowers, fountains, pleasant pavements can. So can wide avenues, pedestrian walks, vistas, stopping points, other punctuation marks. New projects like Vällingby or even shopping centers like Northlands in Detroit have done fairly well with those things that can be made of brick, or stone, or glass. They seem to have tried but in pallid way to introduce sculpture and painting; but either they have not spent enough for their art or not enough contemporary artists are ready for the challenge as for example the fountain makers of Rome, Nuremberg, Stockholm, and Göteborg were, each in his different day. Probably it is a little of each. The flower beds are not abundant enough and luxuriant enough, and they do not receive enough care; the trees are too few and too small; the water runs through spouts that are ungenerous. Meanwhile the parks of the old center where the grass is deep and green, the trees opulent—these are now too far away from too many people. Of course new projects may mature with age, and of course it does take a longer time to make a tree than it does to make a flat; but when trees are destroyed in the making of flats, the pressures of obsolescence may see to it that a Vällingby never does mature. The suspicion remains that the tree, the moss, the fern, the flower, the water, and the sculpture are not greatly admired or coveted by the artists of the new complexes as they have ceased to be admired by most contemporary sculptors who may not be really competent now to produce a fine fountain if given the chance, and perhaps not very interested in the chance either.

In more concrete terms let me suggest five specific problems of the visual aesthetic of the modern city, the problem of preserving or producing the gateway, the problem of preserving or creating magnets, the problem of accommodating to new time scales, the problem of aesthetics around the clock, and the problem of developing individuality and character in the periphery.

As we think of old—or even new—fine cities we will often think of them in terms of a major approach or gateway: The spire of Chartres across the wheat fields of La Beauce, the towers of lower Manhattan as one steams up toward the Battery, the air approach to Chicago across the false front of the skyscrapers of Michigan Avenue. There are cities of hills and sea: San Francisco, Rio de Janeiro, Lisbon, Sydney, Wellington, Oslo. There are cities that rise from the ocean: Boston, New York, Copenhagen. There are cities of the big rivers or estuaries: London, St. Louis, Rome, Paris, St. Paul, Melbourne, Vienna. There are cities of the plains: Moscow, Salisbury, Lincoln in England or Nebraska. All of these, except perhaps the cities of the plains, have a particular appearance that must be seen from a particular direction, and historically there has been one dominating approach which has established the image of such a city. This overriding and individual image is not unimportant for the aesthetics of a city. The ancient approaches to such an image were leisurely and from the level of the street or the surface of the sea or river. One had time to see the image grow and change, to watch its details emerge from the mass. One looked up at the spires, not down. Each skyline had a regional and an identifiable characteristic. Thus the gateway to the city was visually as well as strategically important. As cities grew they developed other approaches: Those of the railroads were somber, dingy, and desolate; those of the automobile roads strips of chaotic vulgarity; those of the aeroplane utterly unpredictable and dependent upon the wind direction at the time of arrival. Yet through all this, great cities possessed and still possess a dominant visual approach whether it is that of the Battery, the Great North Road, the Bois de Boulogne, or the Golden Gate.

Very often the most glamorous approach became the way of the visitor, not that of the native. But for a long time the native had his own, if more bucolic, way. We can see vestiges of these still in Philadelphia, Boston, New York, London, or Paris. Here there was a continuous change of scale and pace and texture from countryside through village, to park-like suburb, here reaching some main theme of the city such as a great river or lake, then parks, boulevards, and thus to the heart of town which truly was a heart, not a series of disconnected and independent blood vessels. To be sure this experience with its morning crescendo and its evening diminuendo might soon come to be reserved for the few who lived in the park-like suburb or even in the country. To be sure the experience was quite different for the many who might have to approach Paris via the Porte St. Denis, or London via the Isle of Dogs, or New York across the petroleum-perfume of Bayonne and the piggeries of Secaucus. But this did not alter the fact that other approaches had been possible and might have been available to all. It did not alter the even more relentless fact that urban "progress" instead of making the best available to all tended rather to take it away even from the few. There is hardly a city left in the world to reach which is not only a frustration to all of its citizens, but a visual abomination as well for all those who have not forgotten how to see. The doughnut stand, the drive-in movie, and the used-car lot have outmoded the tree—hardly a tribute to the aesthetic contributions of "small business." At a higher level Le Corbusier's written sketches for the boscage of Chandrigarh seem more literary than arboreal.

The question of the approach ought to be a dominant one today, complicated though it is by the fact that the approach must now be made from so many directions and at so many different speeds. A cityscape can no longer be a bas relief; it must be a sculpture in the round, elegant from all points of view, from above as well as from below. It must be compatible with many speeds of approach and viewing, say from three miles an hour to more than three hundred. This means that scales and details have to agree on two quite different sets of coordinates. If the experience of the gateway is to be satisfactory the problem of reconciliation is gigantic and it may be a small wonder that the failures have been herculean.

Once one had reached the older city he found internal and localized satisfactions, usually, though not always, on a more intimate, more human and personal scale. These were the parts of the city I call magnets. Some of them might be for purely utilitarian purposes: Markets, exchanges, public buildings, even the rostrums of Hyde Park. Others served specific pleasures: Concert-hall or opera-house squares, circuses, or specific spiritual needs such as the parvis of the cathedral. Some were for general recreation: A zoo, a botanical garden, a pond in the Tuileries for the sailing of toy boats, the lakes of Stockholm for grown-up boats, the promenades for strollers. We all know how fortunate is the city which has many such magnets, how dismal the city with none. They may be monumental like the Place de la Concorde, or of normal scale like the Place Vendôme, or intimate like Gramercy Park, open like the Presidio, closed like Grosvenor Square before the Americans came. Best of all the city could provide a range of scales. Not all these magnets needed to be important.

At the corner of Fifty-Ninth Street and Fifth Avenue in New York is a tiny such square, hard by the Plaza Hotel, a kind of pendant period to Central Park. Surrounded by undistinguished buildings, adorned with small trees and benches, this square, principally this cube of open air, enriches a region of several blocks. Had such spaces been multiplied every five or six blocks throughout Manhattan Island how immeasurably finer the city would have been! How different and more gracious would have been the life of Philadelphia had the original scheme been followed and had it been studded with many Rittenhouse Squares!

Our cities have many such magnets to be sure. Rockefeller Center is one, and Grand Central Terminal has been one, and Place de l'Opéra used to be. But there are not enough magnets at the center and almost none on the periphery. As the periphery swells, the central magnets become more remote and less adequate; the peripheral shopping center and local movie theater are hardly an adequate replacement. The problem here is whether magnets can successfully be invented or must rise naturally. What activates a magnet? Why are some parks visited and loved and others left empty? Such questions cannot be answered simply by reference to the transportation network. We need to find out how much and how effectively such magnets can be decentralized before we can tell how successful it will be to restore the central city as one great magnet, even if this is but a collection of lesser magnets in a central place.

But whatever screen may represent the whole city and however the screen may be divided into neighborhoods, the problem of the two-time scales will again arise, the scale of the vehicular which is large, remote, and fast and the scale of the pedestrian which is small, intimate, and slow.

It must be suggested that, whatever their purposes, both the big and little magnets need much development. We need to be cautious lest certain simple amenities such as those of variety and surprise are not wiped out in the city as the store chain wipes out the boutique. This problem is particularly pressing in America where we so sharply separate our places of abode from our places of work, an Americanism which is violated only by the Chinese, some Italians, and a few artists.

The problem of the changing time scale has perhaps been emphasized enough in the foregoing. There needs only to be this warning for those who identify technological change with progress. The new never quite expunges the old. The Olympian view from the airplane will not supersede all other views. Nor will the restricted and truncated urban panorama permitted by the onrushing automobile window. But there will still be those who must walk in the street or even want to. All the new urban design must not be for those who no longer walk, who prefer motion to repose. The city will still need places for people to sit out of doors and near to the ground. All the new beauties should not be out of their ken.

It is unnecessary to say much either about the 24-hour city. Urban aesthetics cannot, as in the Middle Ages, content itself with a dayscape that vanishes at dusk. Indeed the most beautiful cityscapes of today may be those from airplanes at night. Then the defects of form and substance are mercifully obscured and only the lights remain. The individual excesses of the neon tubes are also concealed by distance and rapid changes of position.

But this is not the only night view of cities which are used more and more at night. For the man in the street the potentials for beauty in the electric light rest almost unexploited. We have our brilliant accidents like the accident of Broadway. We have our stereotyped flood lighting which simply pretends that a building designed for the day is actually being seen by day at 1:00 A.M., but which does not manage the deception very well. We have a few hints of how buildings might be designed in conjunction with streets so that their day aspect when lighted from without gives way to a quite different but equally charming night aspect when lighted from within. Such night lightings might produce design subtleties quite beyond those possible by day. The potentials exist even in old buildings as the illuminations at the Château de Chambord would suggest, but much wider possibilities for enchantment are contained in the modern modes. Combinations of lights—colored as well as white—of moving waters, of plants, not building by building but in urban groupings, could make the city of night even more alluring than the city of day. These things can come to pass, though, only if designers permit themselves more fantasy than their sobrieties now permit or than the Museum of Modern Art might approve from anyone subsequent to Klee, Léger, or Miró.

These considerations of day and night, of the new time scales, of the preservation and the extension of magnets and gateways are all important, but are overshadowed by the formidable battle against the plasmodial and anonymously ugly growth of the urban periphery the world over. A Vällingby is not a great solution but simply much better than the things around it. How far it falls short of what is possible becomes clear when we compare it with the refinement and repose of some of the best parts of any of the good old cities, American or European. The modern world has much to recommend it, and anyway it is the only world we have, but it need not pay the price of abandoning refinement and repose.

There are two main theories as to how one might do better by those who live in the periphery, which means most of us. One might make the old center such a marvelous magnet and the approaches so handsome and convenient that we would always flock there for our leisure and be content with dormitories for the rest of the time. That is the implication of the projects of a Robert Moses although they are not so expressly stated. This somehow seems inadequate, perhaps even too impersonal.

The other and probably better way, which might have been the way of Los Angeles and which could still be the way of Dallas, was the way of Venice if we are to believe Sansovino,

There are also, praise the Lord, on the island of the Giudecca several buildings of importance of which two, at the moment, seem more important than the others. The one at the near point of the island is the palace of Andrea Dandolo . . . the other almost at the other end of the island, of the Vendramin family. These and many other buildings nearby of more or less importance form a vast and great city which will appear to the subtle not as one but as many separate cities all joined together. If her situation is considered without the bridges, one will see that she is divided into many large towns and cities surrounded by their canals, over which one passes from one to the other by way of bridges, which are generally built of stone but sometimes of wood, and which join her various parts together. The shops which are spread all over the city also make her appear many cities joined into one because every quarter has not only one but many churches, its own public square and wells, its bakeries, wineshops, its guild of tailors, greengrocers, pharmacists, school teachers, carpenters, shoemakers and finally in great abundance all else required for human needs, to the extent that leaving one quarter and entering another one would say without doubt one was leaving one city and entering another—to the great convenience and satisfaction of the inhabitants and to the great surprise of strangers.[1]

This is the way sanity lies. The greatest lesson some European cities today could teach American city planners and architects—and traveling citizens—is that every pleasure does not lie at the other end of a ride in an automobile. The misfortune is that the lesson seems to be going the other way.

That the metropolis is necessary if only to support the great magnets like the symphony orchestra, the topflight opera, the diversity of tastes is evident. But that the periphery must supply the other magnets seems equally evident. It will not do to say that a varied personality on the periphery is impossible because the general taste craves uniformity. History does not suggest that it was ever very different, and it is the task of the planner and the city designer not so much to dictate public taste as to seek incessantly to find the best of this taste and to encourage it to thrive. The public taste is not as bad as hucksters make it appear to be.

I must leave it to others to decide whether this will come about and how it is to be brought about. I can only suggest that it will not appear, I fear, through the actions of a few dictatorial master planners, however talented they may be. I doubt that there is any human genius which is individually able to comprehend or provide the whole urban aesthetic. The results can be expected only at the hands of many men in many places, individual men and not men of committees, but architects, and

---

[1] Extract from "Venice, a Very Noble City" described by Mr. Francesco Sansovino, 1581. Translated by Giovanna Lawford and cited in Francis Henry Taylor, *The Taste of Angels* (Boston: Little, Brown and Company, 1948), Appendix C, p. 617.

sculptors, and painters, and planners working in consort and even sometimes in opposition. Their common qualities should be those of a respect
and even an affection for the past, a solicitude for the future, and an
understanding of the present. These qualities should transcend their
desires to be known as dominant and famous individual personalities or
their hope to create *the* architecture of the present against which the
work of all other men will be measured and found wanting. The wise
young men of our time will not be those who slavishly follow one great
master whether Miës, or Wright, or Le Corbusier, or even Aalto—
who in these matters might be the best to follow—but rather young
men who can see that these great men have in no case found a classic
answer to our problems but have made enough suggestions upon which
to build a great future, and that their ideas, moreover, are not altogether
mutually exclusive. But equally essential will be a sensitive concern not
only about one's own buildings but also about the buildings of the past,
and so far as possible the buildings of the future, buildings of others.
We shall need a new band of sculptors more interested in delight than in
their own despairs, more interested in materials other than metal, more
interested in life processes as well as intellectual ones. We shall need
designers who are not pessimists, who respect curves as well as straight
lines, who can still see and admire and partly understand a sunset, the
waving of a reed in a lake, the budding of a flower, the music of falling
water, the sawing of the cicadas in the hot dusk at the close of a sultry
day.

JANE JACOBS

*Jane Jacobs was born in 1916 in Scranton, Pennsylvania, and came to New
York at the age of 18. She worked at a variety of jobs, sold some magazine
articles, and explored the city. In 1947, three years after her marriage to
an architect, she moved into a three-story slum building on Hudson Street
in the western part of Greenwich Village and immediately began to rehabilitate it. She became chairman of the Committee to Save the West
Village, and led a battle which prevented New York City from redevelop-*

*ing a fourteen-block portion of her neighborhood. From 1952 to 1962
she was an editor of* Architectural Forum *and in 1961 published her very
controversial book,* The Death and Life of Great American Cities. *We
reprint two parts of the book which were adapted for magazine publication. The first essay, "Violence in the City Streets," is from the September,
1961,* Harper's. *The second essay, "How City Planners Hurt Cities," is
from* The Saturday Evening Post, *October 14, 1961. "To approach a
city," Mrs. Jacobs has written, "as if it were a larger architectural problem, capable of being given order by converting it into a disciplined
work of art, is to make the mistake of substituting art for life."*

VIOLENCE IN THE CITY STREETS

To build city districts that are custom-made for easy crime is idiotic.
Yet that is what we do. Today barbarism has taken over many city
streets—or people fear it has, which comes to much the same thing
in the end.

"I live in a lovely quiet residential area," says a friend of mine who is
hunting for another place to live. "The only disturbing sound at night
is the occasional scream of someone being mugged."

It does not take many incidents of violence to make people fear the
streets. And as they fear them, they use them less, which makes the
streets still more unsafe.

This problem is not limited to the older parts of cities. Sidewalk and
doorstep insecurity are as serious in cities that have made conscientious
efforts to rebuild as they are in those cities that have lagged. Nor is it
illuminating to tag minority groups, or the poor, or the outcasts, with
responsibility for city danger. Some of the safest—as well as some
of the most dangerous—sidewalks in New York, for example, are those
along which poor people or minority groups live. And this is true elsewhere.

Deep and complicated social ills underlie delinquency and crime—in
suburbs and towns as well as great cities. But if we are to maintain a
city society that can diagnose and keep abreast of these profoundly
difficult problems, the starting point must be to strengthen the workable
forces that now exist for maintaining urban safety and civilization. In
fact we do precisely the opposite.

First, we must understand that the public peace—the sidewalk and
street peace—of cities is not kept primarily by the police, necessary
though they are. It is kept primarily by an intricate, almost unconscious,
network of voluntary controls and standards among the people themselves. In some city areas—notably older public-housing projects and

streets with very high population turnover—the keeping of public side-walk law and order is left almost entirely to the police and special guards. Such places are jungles.

Nor can the problem be solved by spreading people out more thinly, trading the characteristics of cities for the characteristics of suburbs. If this were possible, then Los Angeles should be in good shape because superficially it is almost all suburban. It has virtually no districts compact enough to qualify as dense city. Yet Los Angeles' crime figures are flabbergasting. Among the seventeen standard metropolitan areas with populations over a million, Los Angeles stands pre-eminent in crime, especially the crimes associated with personal attack, which make people fear the streets. (Los Angeles, for example, has a forcible rape rate more than twice as high as either of the next two cities, which happen to be St. Louis and Philadelphia, three times as high as the rate for Chicago, and more than four times the rate for New York.)

The reasons for Los Angeles' high crime rates are complex, and at least in part obscure. But of this we can be sure: thinning out a city does not insure safety from crime and fear of crime. This is demonstrable too in cities where pseudosuburbs or superannuated suburbs are ideally suited to rape, muggings, beatings, holdups, and the like. The all-important question is: How much easy opportunity does any city street offer to crime? It may be that there is some absolute amount of crime in a given city, which will find an outlet somehow (I do not believe this). In any case, different kinds of city streets garner radically different shares of barbarism.

Some city streets afford no such opportunity. The streets of the North End of Boston are outstanding examples. City planners officially consider this area a "slum" but the streets are probably as safe as any place on earth. Although most of the North End's residents are Italian or of Italian descent, the district's streets are heavily and constantly used also by people of every race and background. Some of the strangers from outside work in or close to the district; some come to shop and stroll; many make a point of cashing their paychecks in North End stores and immediately making their big weekly purchases in streets where they know they will not be parted from their money between the getting and the spending.

Frank Havey, director of the North End Union, the local settlement house, says, "In twenty-eight years I have never heard of a single case of rape, mugging, molestation of a child, or other street crime of that sort in the district. And if there had been any, I would have heard of it even if it did not reach the papers." Half-a-dozen times or so in the past three decades, says Havey, would-be molesters have made a try toward luring a child or, late at night, attacking a woman. In every such case the try was thwarted by passers-by, by kibitzers from windows, or shopkeepers.

Meantime, in the Elm Hill Avenue section of Roxbury, a part of inner Boston that is suburban in superficial character, prudent people stay off the streets at night because of the ever-present possibility of street assaults with no kibitzers to protect the victims. For this and other related reasons—dispiritedness and dullness—most of Roxbury has run down. It has become a place to leave.

Roxbury's disabilities, and especially its Great Blight of Dullness, are all too common in other cities too. But differences like these in public safety within the same city are worth noting. The once fine Elm Hill Avenue section's basic troubles are not due to a criminal or a discriminated-against or a poverty-stricken population. Its troubles are due to the fundamental fact that it is physically unsuited to function with vitality as a city district, and so cannot function safely.

Even within supposedly similar parts of supposedly similar places, drastic differences in public safety exist. For example, at Washington Houses, a public-housing project in New York, a tenants' group put up three Christmas trees in mid-December 1958. The biggest tree—a huge one—went into the project's inner "street," a landscaped central mall. Two smaller trees were placed at the outer corners of the project where it abuts a busy avenue and lively cross streets. The first night, the large tree and all its trimmings were stolen. The two smaller ones remained intact, lights, ornaments, and all, until they were taken down at New Year's. The inner mall is *theoretically* the most safe and sheltered place in the project. But, says a social worker who has been helping the tenants' group, "People are no safer in that mall than the Christmas tree. On the other hand, the place where the other trees were safe, where the project is just one corner out of four, happens to be safe for people."

Everyone knows that a well-used city street is apt to be safe. A deserted one is apt to be unsafe. But how does this work, really? And what makes a city street well used or shunned? Why is the inner side-walk mall in Washington Houses—which is supposed to be an attraction—shunned when the sidewalks of the old city just to its west are not? What about streets that are busy part of the time and then empty abruptly? A city street equipped to make a safety asset out of the presence of strangers, as successful city neighborhoods always do, must have three main qualities:

First, there must be a clear demarcation between public and private spaces. They cannot ooze into each other as they do typically in housing projects where streets, walks, and play areas may seem at first glance to be open to the public but in effect are special preserves. (The fate of Washington Houses' large Christmas tree is a classic example of what happens when the distinction between public and private space is blurred, and the area which should be under public surveillance has no clear practicable limits.)

Second, there must be *eyes* upon the street, eyes belonging to what we might call its natural proprietors. To insure the safety of both residents and strangers, the buildings on a street must be oriented to it. They cannot turn their backs or blank sides on it and leave it blind.

And third, the sidewalk must have users on it fairly continuously, both to add more effective eyes and to induce plenty of people in buildings along the street to watch the sidewalks. Nobody enjoys sitting on a stoop or looking out a window at an empty street. But large numbers of people entertain themselves, off and on, by watching street activity.

In settlements smaller than cities, public behavior (if not crime) is controlled to some extent by a web of reputation, gossip, approval, disapproval, and sanctions. All of these are powerful if people know each other and word travels. But a city's streets must control not only the behavior of city people but also of visitors who want to have a big time away from the gossip and sanctions at home. It is a wonder cities have solved such a difficult problem at all. And yet in many streets they do it magnificently.

The issue of unsafe streets cannot be evaded by trying to make some other features of a locality safe instead—for example, interior courtyards, or sheltered play spaces. The streets of a city are where strangers come and go. The streets must not only defend the city against predatory strangers. They must also insure the safety of the many peaceable strangers who pass through. Moreover no normal person can spend his life in some artificial haven, and this includes children. Everyone must use the streets.

On the surface, we seem to have here some simple aims: To try for streets where the public space is unequivocally public and to see that these public street spaces have eyes on them as continually as possible.

But it is far from simple to accomplish these things. You can't make people use streets without reason. You can't make people watch streets if they do not want to. The safety of the street works best—and with least taint of hostility or suspicion—where people are using and enjoying the city streets voluntarily.

The basic requisite for such surveillance is a substantial quantity of stores and other public places sprinkled along the sidewalks; it is especially important that places frequented during the evening and night be among them. Stores, bars, and restaurants—the chief examples—abet sidewalk safety in different and complex ways.

First, they give people concrete reasons for using the sidewalks.

Second, they draw people along the sidewalks past places which have few attractions in themselves; this influence does not carry very far geographically, so there must be many—and different—enterprises in a city district if they are to give walkers reason for criss-crossing paths and populating barren stretches on the street.

Third, small businessmen and their employees are typically strong proponents of peace and order themselves; they hate broken windows, holdups, and nervous customers. If present in sufficient abundance, they are great street watchers and sidewalk guardians.

Fourth, the activity generated by people on errands, or people aiming for food or drink, in itself attracts more people to the street.

This last point seems incomprehensible to city planners and architectural designers. They operate on the premise that city people seek emptiness, obvious order, and quiet. Nothing could be less true. The love of people for watching activity and other people is evident in cities everywhere. This trait reaches an almost ludicrous extreme on upper Broadway in New York, where the street is divided by a narrow, central mall, right in the middle of traffic. Benches have been placed at the cross-street intersections of this long mall, and on any day when the weather is even barely tolerable they are filled with people watching the pedestrians, the traffic, and each other.

Eventually Broadway reaches Columbia University and Barnard College, one to the right, the other to the left. Here all is obvious order and quiet. No more stores and the activity they generate, almost no more pedestrians—and no more watchers on the benches. I have tried them and can see why. No place could be more boring. Even the students shun it. They do their outdoor loitering, homework, and street watching on the steps overlooking the busiest campus crossing.

It is just so elsewhere. A lively street always has both its users and watchers. Last year I was in the Lower East Side of Manhattan, waiting for a bus on a street full of errand-goers, children playing, and loiterers on the stoops. In a minute or so a woman opened a third floor tenement window, vigorously yoo-hooed at me, and shouted down that "The bus doesn't run here on Saturdays!" Then she directed me around the corner. This woman was one of thousands of New Yorkers who casually take care of the streets. They notice strangers. They observe everything going on. If they need to take action, whether to direct a stranger or to call the police, they do so. Such action usually requires, to be sure, a certain self-assurance about the actor's proprietorship of the street and the support he will get if necessary, and this raises special problems I will not deal with here. But the fundamental thing is the watching itself.

Not everyone in cities helps to take care of the streets, and many a resident or worker is unaware of why his neighborhood is safe. Consider, for example, a recent incident which occurred on the street where I live.

My block is a small one, but it contains a remarkable range of buildings, varying from several vintages of tenements to three- or four-story houses. Some of these have been converted into low-rent flats with stores on the ground floor; some, like ours, have been returned to single-family use. Across the street are some four-story brick tenements with stores below. Half of them were converted twelve years ago into small high-rent elevator apartments.

From my second-story window I happened to see a suppressed struggle going on between a man and a little girl. He seemed to be trying to get her to go with him, by turns cajoling her, and then acting nonchalant. The child was making herself rigid against the wall.

I wondered whether I should intervene, but then it became unnecessary. The wife of the butcher emerged from their shop with a determined look on her face. Joe Cornacchia came out of his delicatessen and stood solidly to the other side. Several heads poked out of the tenement windows above; one was withdrawn quickly, and its owner reappeared a moment later in the doorway behind the man. Two men from the bar next to the butcher shop came to the doorway and waited. On my side of the street, the locksmith, the fruit man, and the laundry proprietor came out of their shops, and other eyes peered from windows. That man did not know it, but he was surrounded. Nobody was going to allow a little girl to be dragged off, even if nobody knew who she was. I am sorry—for dramatic reasons—to have to report that the little girl turned out to be the man's daughter.

Throughout this little drama, perhaps five minutes in all, *no eyes appeared in the windows of the high-rent apartments*. It was the only building of which this was true. When we first moved to our block, I used to hope that soon all the old tenements would be rehabilitated in the same way. I know better now, and am filled with gloom by the recent news that such a transformation is scheduled for the rest of the block. The high-rent tenants, most of whom are so transient[1] we cannot even keep track of their faces, have not the remotest idea of who takes care of their street, or how. A city neighborhood can absorb and protect a substantial number of these birds of passage. But if and when they *become* the neighborhood, the streets will gradually grow less secure, and if things get bad enough they will drift away to another neighborhood which is mysteriously safer.

In some rich neighborhoods, where there is little do-it-yourself surveillance, street watchers are hired. The monotonous sidewalks of residential Park Avenue in New York, for example, are surprisingly little used; their logical users are populating instead the interesting sidewalks of Lexington and Madison Avenues to the east and west, filled with bars, stores, and restaurants. A network of doormen and superintendents, of delivery boys and nursemaids—a form of *hired* neighborhood—keeps residential Park Avenue supplied with eyes. At night, dog walkers safely venture forth and supplement the doormen. But this street is blank of built-in eyes, and devoid of concrete reasons for using or watching it. If its rents were to slip below the point where they could support a plentiful hired neighborhood of doormen and elevator men, it would become a woefully dangerous street.

---

[1] Some, according to the storekeepers, live on beans and bread and spend their sojourn looking for a place to live where all their money will not go for rent.

Once a street has effective demarcation between private and public spaces and has a basic supply of activity and eyes, it is equipped to handle strangers, in fact the more the merrier.

Strangers can be a safety asset, particularly at night. The street on which I live is fortunate in having a locally supported bar, another around the corner, and a famous one—the White Horse—that draws continuous troops of strangers. (Dylan Thomas used to go there, and mentioned it in his writing.) This bar, indeed, works two distinct shifts. In the morning and early afternoon it is a social gathering place for Irish longshoremen and other craftsmen in the area, as it always was. But beginning in midafternoon it changes to kind of a college bull session combined with a literary cocktail party, and this continues until the early hours of the morning. On a cold winter's night, when the doors of the White Horse open, a solid wave of conversation surges out—very warming. The comings and goings from this bar do much to keep our street reasonably populated until three in the morning, make it safe to come home to. The only instance I know of a beating in our street occurred in the dead hours between the closing of the bar and dawn. (The beating was halted by one of our neighbors who saw it from his window.)

I know a street uptown where a church youth and community center, with many night dances and other activities, performs about the same service as the White Horse bar. Orthodox planning is much imbued with puritanical conceptions of how people should spend their free time. But there is room in cities for many differences in people's tastes, proclivities, and occupations. And these differences are in fact *needed*. Utopians and other compulsive managers of other people's leisure openly prefer one kind of legal enterprise over others—youth centers and restaurants are "better" than bars and poolrooms. This kind of thinking is worse than irrelevant for cities. It is harmful. The greater and more plentiful the range of all legitimate interests—in the strictly legal sense—that city streets and their enterprises can satisfy, the better for the streets and for the safety of the city.

Bars, and indeed all commerce, have a bad name in many city districts precisely because they do draw strangers and the strangers do not work out as an asset.

This is especially true in the dispirited gray belts of great cities and in once-fashionable (or at least once-solid) inner residential areas gone into decline. Because these neighborhoods are so dangerous, and the streets typically so dark, it is commonly believed that their troubles with strangers may result from insufficient street lighting. Good lighting is important, but darkness alone does not account for the gray areas' deep, functional sickness, the Great Blight of Dullness.

Bright lights do give some reassurance to people who need or want to go out. Thus lights induce these people to contribute their own eyes to the upkeep of the street. Moreover, as is obvious, good lighting makes the eyes count for more because their range is greater. Each additional pair of eyes, and every increase in their range, is that much to the good. But unless eyes are there, and unless in the brains behind those eyes is the almost unconscious reassurance of general street support in upholding civilization, lights can do no good. Horrifying public crimes can, and do, occur in well-lighted subway stations when no effective eyes are present (although a few people may be). They virtually never occur in darkened theatres where many people and eyes are present.

To explain the troubling effect of strangers on the streets of gray city areas, it is useful to examine the peculiarities of another and figurative kind of street—the corridors of high-rising, public-housing projects which have become standard all over America. The elevators and corridors of these projects are, in a sense, streets piled up in the sky to permit the ground to become deserted parks like the mall at Washington Houses where the tree was stolen.

These interior parts of the building are not only streets in the sense that they serve the comings and goings of residents—few of whom may know each other or recognize, necessarily, who is a resident and who is not. They are streets also in the sense of being accessible to the public. They have been designed in an imitation of upper-class standards for apartment living without upper-class cash for doormen and elevator men. Anyone can go into these buildings, unquestioned, and use the elevator and corridors. These blind-eyed streets, although completely accessible to public use, are closed to public view and thus lack the checks and inhibitions exerted by eye-policed city streets.

The New York Housing Authority some years back experimented with corridors open to public view in a Brooklyn project which I shall call Blenheim Houses although that is not its name. (I do not wish to add to its troubles by advertising it.)

Because the buildings of Blenheim Houses are sixteen stories high, the open corridors cannot really be watched from the ground or from other buildings. But their psychological openness has had some effect. More importantly, the corridors were well designed to induce surveillance from within the buildings themselves. They were equipped to serve as play space, and as narrow porches, as well as passageways. This all turned out to be so lively and interesting that the tenants added still another use: picnic grounds—this in spite of continual pleas and threats from the management which did not *plan* that the balcony corridors should serve as picnic grounds. (One of the main tenets of planners is that the Plan should anticipate everything and then permit no changes.) The tenants are devoted to the balcony-corridors which are, as a result, under intense surveillance. There has been no problem of crime in these corridors nor of vandalism either. Not even light bulbs are stolen or broken.

Nonetheless, Blenheim Houses has a fearsome problem of vandalism and scandalous behavior. The lighted balconies which are, as the manager puts it, "the brightest and most attractive scene in sight," draw strangers, especially teen-agers, from all over Brooklyn. But these strangers do not halt at the visible corridors. They go into other "streets" of the buildings, streets that lack surveillance—the elevators and, more important in this case, the fire stairs and their landings. The housing police run up and down after the malefactors—who behave barbarously and viciously in the blind-eyed, sixteen-story stairways—and the malefactors elude them. It is easy to run the elevators up to a high floor, jam the doors so the elevators cannot be brought down, and then play hell with a building and anyone you can catch. So serious is the problem and apparently so uncontrollable, that the advantage of the safe corridors is all but canceled out—at least in the harried manager's eyes.

What happens at Blenheim Houses is somewhat the same as in dull gray areas of cities. Their pitifully few and thinly spaced patches of life are like the visible corridors at Blenheim Houses. They do attract strangers. But the relatively deserted, blind streets leading from these places are like the fire stairs at Blenheim Houses. They lack the kind of street life which could equip them to handle strangers safely, and the presence of strangers in them is thus an automatic menace.

The temptation in such cases is to blame the balconies—or the commerce or bars that serve as a magnet. A typical train of thought is exemplified in the Hyde Park–Kenwood renewal project now under way in Chicago. This piece of gray area adjoining the University of Chicago contains many splendid houses and grounds, but for thirty years it has been plagued with a frightening street-crime problem, accompanied in recent years by considerable physical decay. The "cause" of Hyde Park–Kenwood's decline has been brilliantly identified, by the city planners, as the presence of "blight." By this they mean that too many of the college professors and other middle-class families steadily deserted this dull and dangerous area and their places were often, quite naturally, taken by those with little economic or social choice among living places.

What does the Hyde Park–Kenwood plan do? It designates and removes these chunks of blight and replaces them with housing projects designed, as usual, to minimize use of the streets. The plan also adds still more empty spaces here and there, blurs even further the district's already poor distinctions between private and public space, and amputates the existing commerce, which is no great shakes.

The early plans for this renewal included, for example, a relatively large imitation-suburban shopping center. But further thought gave the planners a faint glimmer of the realities. A large center—larger than that required for the standard shopping needs of the renewal district's residents—"might draw into the area extraneous people," as one of the architectural planners put it. A small shopping center was thereupon settled on. Large or small matters little.

It matters little because Hyde Park–Kenwood, like all city districts, is, in real life, surrounded by "extraneous" people—hundreds of thousands of them. The area is an embedded part of Chicago. It cannot wish away its location. It cannot bring back its one-time condition, long gone, of semi-suburbia. To plan as if it could, and to evade its deep, functional inadequacies, can have only one of two possible results so far as safety is concerned:

(1) Extraneous people will continue to come into the area as they please, including some who are not at all nice, and the opportunity for street crime will be a little easier, if anything, because of the added emptiness. (2) Or a determined effort can be made to keep extraneous people out of the area. Indeed, according to the *New York Times*, the adjoining University of Chicago—the institution that was the moving spirit in getting the plan under way—took the extraordinary measure of loosing police dogs every night to patrol its campus. The dogs are trained to hold at bay any human in this dangerous unurban inner keep. The barriers formed by new projects at the edges of Hyde Park–Kenwood, plus extraordinary policing, may be able to keep out strangers. If so, the price will be hostility from the surrounding city and an ever more beleaguered feeling within the fort. And who can be sure, either, that all those thousands rightfully within the fort are trustworthy in the dark?

I do not wish to single out one area, or in this case one plan, as uniquely opprobrious. Hyde Park–Kenwood is significant mainly because the diagnosis and the corrective measures of its plan typify in slightly more ambitious form plans conceived for cities all over the country. And in city after city, we are seeing the results of orthodox city planning of this kind: great cyclone fences are erected to "protect" sequestered projects and developments from their surroundings and special police are hired to chase intruding boys—while the crime rates rise, and people cling to their cars at night. Hyde Park–Kenwood, in short, is not a local aberration but an example of how we are deliberately building unsafe cities.

In this article I have pointed to some lively and well-used city streets and neighborhoods where lives are secure and civilized and public violence and barbarism are rare. I am not suggesting, however, that we should therefore try to imitate routinely and mechanically the districts that do display strength and success as fragments of city life. That would be impossible, and, moreover, even the best city streets and districts can stand improvement, especially in their amenity. But if life in our cities is to be safe and satisfying, we must first be aware of where it now succeeds and fails, and why. Then we shall at least have some idea both of the kind of city we want and the failure of most urban planning today to achieve anything resembling it. And this first step we have not yet begun to take.

HOW CITY PLANNERS
HURT CITIES

City planners and rebuilders are killing our cities, not on purpose, but because they do not understand how cities work. Their well-meant but ignorant actions, supported by public money and political power, can be fearsomely destructive.

We are continually assured that planners are producing healthful city environments for us. But most planners and rebuilders do not recognize a healthful city environment when they see one, much less know how to create one. Consider, for example, a district called the North End, in Boston.

Twenty years ago, when I first saw the North End, its buildings were badly overcrowded. Rundown brick houses had been converted into flats. Four- or five-story walk-ups had been built to house immigrants first from Ireland, then Eastern Europe and finally from Sicily. You did not have to look far to see that the district was taking a severe physical beating and was desperately poor.

When I saw the North End again in 1959, I was amazed. Scores of buildings had been rehabilitated. Instead of mattresses against the windows, there were Venetian blinds and glimpses of fresh paint. Many of the small, converted houses were now occupied by one or two families instead of three or four. Some of the families in the tenements had uncrowded themselves by throwing two flats together, equipping them with new bathrooms and kitchens. Mingled among the buildings were splendid food stores. Small industries—upholstery making, metalworking, food processing, and the like—rimmed the neighborhood. The streets were alive with children playing, people shopping, strolling and talking.

I had seen a lot of Boston in the past few days, most of it dull, gloomy and decaying. This place struck me as the healthiest district in the city. To find out more about it, I went into a bar and phoned a Boston planner I know.

"Why in the world are you down in the North End?" he said. "Nothing's going on there. Eventually, yes, but not yet. That's a slum!"

"It doesn't seem like a slum to me," I said.

"Why that's the worst slum in the city. It has 275 dwelling units to the net acre! [Excluding streets, nonresidential land, etc.] I hate to admit we have anything like that in Boston, but it's a fact."

"Do you have any other figures on it?" I asked.

He did. Statistics showed that the neighborhood's delinquency, disease and infant-mortality rates are among the lowest in the city. The child population is just about average. The death rate is low, 8.8 per 1000, against the average city rate of 11.2.

"You should have more slums like this," I said. "Don't tell me there are plans to wipe this out. You ought to be down here learning as much as you can from it."

"I know how you feel," he said. "I often go down there myself just to walk around the streets and feel that wonderful, cheerful street life. You'd be crazy about it in summer. But we have to rebuild it eventually. We've got to get those people off the street."

My planner friend's instincts told him the North End was a healthful place. Statistics confirmed it. But his training as a city planner told him the North End *had* to be a "bad" place. It has little park land. Children play on the sidewalks. It has small blocks. In city-planning parlance, the district is "badly cut up by wasteful streets." It also has "mixed uses" —another sin. It is made up of the plans of hundreds of people—not planners. Such freedom represents, as one of the wise men of city planning put it, "a chaotic accident . . . the summation of the haphazard, antagonistic whims of many self-centered, ill-advised individuals."

Under the seeming chaos of a lively place like the North End is a marvelous and intricate order—a complicated array of urban activities. These activities support and supplement each other, keeping the neighborhood interesting and vital. The planners would kill it.

The North End is not unique. In city after city, there are districts that refuse to decay, districts that hold people even when their incomes rise and their "status" improves, districts that spontaneously repair and renovate in spite of discouragement by government officials and mortgage lenders. These interesting and vital areas are the ones that have everything possible wrong with them—according to city-planning theory. Equally significant, in city after city the districts in decline and decay are frequently the ones that ought to be successful—according to planning theory.

The Morningside Heights area in New York City is such an example. According to theory, it should not be in trouble. It has a great abundance of park land, campus areas, playgrounds and other open spaces. It has plenty of grass. It occupies high and pleasant ground with magnificent river views. It is a famous educational center. It has good hospitals and fine churches. It has no industries. Its residential streets are zoned against "incompatible uses."

Yet by the early 1950's Morningside Heights was becoming the kind of slum in which people fear to walk the streets. Columbia University, other institutions and the planners from the city government got together. At great cost the most blighted part of the area was wiped out. In the torn-down area a middle-income project complete with shopping center was built. Nearby a fenced-off low-income project was erected. The projects were hailed as a great demonstration in city saving.

After that Morningside Heights went downhill even faster. It continues to pile up new mountains of crime and troubles to this day. The "remedy" didn't work. Dull, sorted-out "quiet residential areas" in cities fail because they are inconvenient, uninteresting and dangerous. The dark, empty grounds of housing projects breed crime. And it is much the same with dark, empty streets of "quiet residential areas" in big cities.

Our cities need help desperately. If places like Morningside Heights are to be helped, the help must be based not on imitations of genteel, "good" addresses, but on understanding the real needs of those who live in big cities. A little involvement with the life of city streets, a little recognition that empty grass festooned with used tissue paper is no treat for anyone, a little common sense—these are the first requirements.

The New York City neighborhood where I live is considered a mess by planners. They have plans to sort out its differing land uses from one another and isolate residences from working places with a buffer strip. Such a strip would be useful primarily to muggers. For months residents and businessmen of the neighborhood have been combating the scheme to simplify and regiment the area with Federal funds. Simplification would be the avenue to its ruin.

One need only watch the sidewalks to see how the neighborhood is built upon a complicated set of activities. Each day Hudson Street, my street, is the scene of an endlessly varied parade of persons, some of them neighbors, many of them strangers. This scene is all composed of interesting movement and change.

I make my first entrance a little after eight A.M. when I put out the garbage can. Around me, droves of junior-high-school students and people coming to work in the district walk by the center of the stage. While I sweep the sidewalk, I watch the signs and rituals of morning. Mr. Halpert unlocking his laundry hand-cart from its mooring to a cellar door. Joe Cornacchia's son-in-law stacking out empty crates from the delicatessen. The barber bringing out his sidewalk folding chair. Mr. Goldstein arranging coils of wire that proclaim the hardware store is open. The primary children, heading for St. Luke's to the south. The children for St. Veronica's heading west. The children for P.S. 41 heading east. Well-dressed and even elegant women, and men with briefcases, emerge now from doorways and side streets. Simultaneously numbers of women in house dresses emerge and pause for quick conversations. Longshoremen who are not working gather at the White Horse Tavern or the International Bar for beer and conversation.

As noontime arrives, the executives and business lunchers from the industries in the neighborhood throng the Dorgene Restaurant and the Lion's Head coffee house down the street. If there were no workers to support these places at noon, we residents would not have them to use at night. Character dancers come onstage: a strange old man with strings of old shoes over his shoulders; motor-scooter riders with big black beards and girl friends who bounce on the back of their scooters. Mr. Koochagian, the tailor, waters the plants in his window, gives them a look from the outside and accepts a compliment on them from two passers-by. The baby carriages come out.

As the residents return home from work in other places, the ballet reaches its crescendo. This is the time of roller skates and stilts and tricycles and games with bottle tops and plastic cowboys. This is the time of bundles and packages and zigzagging from the drugstore to the fruit stand. This is the time when teenagers, all dressed up, are pausing to ask if their slips show or their collars look right. This is the time when anybody you know in the neighborhood will go by.

As darkness thickens and Mr. Halpert moors the laundry cart to the cellar door again, the ballet goes on under lights. It eddies back and forth, intensifying at the bright spotlight pools of Joe's sidewalk pizzeria, the bars and the drugstore. On Hudson Street we do not barricade ourselves indoors when darkness falls.

I know the deep night ballet from waking long after midnight to tend a baby. Sitting in the dark I have seen the shadows and heard the sounds of the sidewalk. Mostly it is snatches of party conversation. When the bars have closed, it is the sound of singing. Sometimes there is anger or sad weeping; sometimes a flurry of searching for a string of broken beads. One night a young man came along bellowing invectives at two girls who apparently were disappointing him. Doors opened, a wary semicircle of men and women formed around him; the police came. Out came the heads, too, along Hudson Street, offering opinion, "Drunk. . . . Crazy. . . . A wild kid from the suburbs." (It turned out he *was* a wild kid from the suburbs.)

I have not begun to describe the many differences that keep our sidewalks bustling. Among businesses and industries alone there are more than fifty different kinds within a few blocks. On Hudson Street, just as in the North End of Boston, we are the lucky possessors of a complex city order that is anything but the chaos that city planners proclaim it to be. Such neighborhoods as ours engender intense affection among those who live or work in them. As a result, they are stable places where people of many different incomes and tastes remain permanently—by choice.

The true problem of city planning and rebuilding in a free society is how to cultivate more city districts that are free; lively and fertile places for the differing plans of thousands of individuals—not planners. Nothing could be farther from the aims of planners today. They have been trained to think of people as interchangeable statistics to be pushed around, to think of city vitality and mixture as a mess. Planners are the enemies of cities because they offer us only the poisonous promise of making every place in a city more like dull and standardized Morningside Heights. They have failed to pursue the main point: to study the success and failure of the real life of the cities. With their eyes on simple-minded panaceas, they destroy success and health. Planners will become helpful only when they abandon what they have learned about what "ought" to be good for cities.

When they learn how fulfilling life in a city really can be, then they will finally stop working against the very goals they set out to achieve.

The Function of Art

Citizens have been telling artists what to do at least since Plato's day (see above, p. 363), and artists have responded variously, sometimes with a sublime incoherence but occasionally with that resonant authority that is theirs alone. The fact that more than half of the essays in this section are by artists—one painter and four writers—gives the artists more than their usual share of representation in the debate on the function of art. The rest is given over to the philosopher, the social theorist, the editor, and the professor, each of whom perpetuates Plato's function in his own way. What all have in common, however, is the conviction that art is important. Mrs. Langer's magisterial essay stresses the role of art in the rendering of imagination and feeling, of subjective reality. Matisse, the painter, with deceptively artless simplicity, writes "notes" on painting that imply an aesthetic related to Mrs. Langer's. The Marxist critic Ernst Fischer finds in art the link between the limited life of the individual and a richer, more communal existence, and he attempts to define the special "function of art in a class society at war within itself." The Editors of *Life* take a position in part surprisingly close to Fischer's, issuing a call for art—in this case the novel—as an expression of the central character of our culture and our aspirations. Camus and Orwell justify the art that has political purpose. De Quincey distinguishes didactic purpose from emotive; Pater, likewise an English essayist of the nineteenth century, gives what is widely taken to be the classical expression of "the love of art for art's sake." We conclude the section with a small anthology of poems, in which the reader may test Matisse's remark, "that the best explanation an artist can give of his aims and ability is afforded by his work." Before the poems we have printed Highet's essay "What Use Is Poetry?," particularly for those readers to whom the invitation to read poetry will be a new experience.

SUSANNE K. LANGER

THE CULTURAL IMPORTANCE
OF ART

Originally a lecture delivered at Syracuse University, this essay was first published in Aesthetic Form and Education, *ed. M. F. Andrews (1958). It later appeared as Chapter 5 in Mrs. Langer's* Philosophical Sketches *(1962), and it is this text which we reprint below. For information about the author and her writings, see page 59.*

•

Every culture develops some kind of art as surely as it develops language. Some primitive cultures have no real mythology or religion, but all have some art—dance, song, design (sometimes only on tools or on the human body). Dance, above all, seems to be the oldest elaborated art.

The ancient ubiquitous character of art contrasts sharply with the prevalent idea that art is a luxury product of civilization, a cultural frill, a piece of social veneer.

It fits better with the conviction held by most artists, that art is the epitome of human life, the truest record of insight and feeling, and that the strongest military or economic society without art is poor in comparison with the most primitive tribe of savage painters, dancers, or idol carvers. Wherever a society has really achieved culture (in the ethnological sense, not the popular sense of "social form") it has begotten art, not late in its career, but at the very inception of it.

Art is, indeed, the spearhead of human development, social and individual. The vulgarization of art is the surest symptom of ethnic decline. The growth of a new art or even a great and radically new style always bespeaks a young and vigorous mind, whether collective or single.

What sort of thing is art, that it should play such a leading role in human development? It is not an intellectual pursuit, but is necessary to intellectual life; it is not religion, but grows up with religion, serves it, and in large measure determines it.

We cannot enter here on a long discussion of what has been claimed as the essence of art, the true nature of art, or its defining function; in a single lecture dealing with one aspect of art, namely its cultural influence, I can only give you by way of preamble my own definition of art, with categorical brevity. This does not mean that I set up this definition in a categorical spirit, but only that we have no time to debate it; so you are asked to accept it as an assumption underlying these reflections.

Art, in the sense here intended—that is, the generic term subsuming painting, sculpture, architecture, music, dance, literature, drama, and film—may be defined as the practice of creating perceptible forms expressive of human feeling. I say "perceptible" rather than "sensuous" forms because some works of art are given to imagination rather than to the outward senses. A novel, for instance, usually is read silently with the eye, but is not made for vision, as a painting is; and though sound plays a vital part in poetry, words even in poetry are not essentially sonorous structures like music. Dance requires to be seen, but its appeal is to deeper centers of sensation. The difference between dance and mobile sculpture makes this immediately apparent. But all works of art are purely perceptible forms that seem to embody some sort of feeling.

"Feeling" as I am using it here covers much more than it does in the technical vocabulary of psychology, where it denotes only pleasure and displeasure, or even in the shifting limits of ordinary discourse, where it sometimes means sensation (as when one says a paralyzed limb has no feeling in it), sometimes sensibility (as we speak of hurting someone's feelings), sometimes emotion (e.g., as a situation is said to harrow your feelings, or to evoke tender feeling), or a directed emotional attitude (we say we feel strongly *about* something), or even our general mental or physical condition, feeling well or ill, blue, or a bit above ourselves. As I use the word, in defining art as the creation of perceptible forms expressive of human feeling, it takes in all those meanings; it applies to everything that may be felt.

Another word in the definition that might be questioned is "creation." I think it is justified, not pretentious, as perhaps it sounds, but that issue is slightly beside the point here; so let us shelve it. If anyone prefers to speak of the "making" or "construction" of expressive forms, that will do here just as well.

What does have to be understood is the meaning of "form," and more particularly "expressive form"; for that involves the very nature of art and therefore the question of its cultural importance.

The word "form" has several current uses; most of them have some relation to the sense in which I am using it here, though a few, such as "a form to be filled in for tax purposes" or "a mere matter of form," are fairly remote, being quite specialized. Since we are speaking of art, it might be good to point out that the meaning of stylistic pattern—"the sonata form," "the sonnet form"—is not the one I am assuming here.

I am using the word in a simpler sense, which it has when you say, on a foggy night, that you see dimly moving forms in the mist; one of them emerges clearly, and is the form of a man. The trees are gigantic forms; the rills of rain trace sinuous forms on the windowpane. The rills are not fixed things; they are forms of motion. When you watch gnats weaving in the air, or flocks of birds wheeling overhead, you see dynamic forms —forms made by motion.

It is in this sense of an apparition given to our perception that a work of art is a form. It may be a permanent form like a building or a vase or a picture, or a transient, dynamic form like a melody or a dance, or even a form given to imagination, like the passage of purely imaginary, apparent events that constitutes a literary work. But it is always a perceptible, self-identical whole; like a natural being, it has a character of organic unity, self-sufficiency, individual reality. And it is thus, as an appearance, that a work of art is good or bad or perhaps only rather poor—as an appearance, not as a comment on things beyond it in the world, or as a reminder of them.

This, then, is what I mean by "form"; but what is meant by calling such forms "expressive of human feeling"? How do apparitions "express" anything—feeling or anything else? First of all, let us ask just what is meant here by "express," what sort of "expression" we are talking about.

The word "expression" has two principal meanings. In one sense it means self-expression—giving vent to our feelings. In this sense it refers to a symptom of what we feel. Self-expression is a spontaneous reaction to an actual, present situation, an event, the company we are in, things people say, or what the weather does to us; it bespeaks the physical and mental state we are in and the emotions that stir us.

In another sense, however, "expression" means the presentation of an idea, usually by the proper and apt use of words. But a device for presenting an idea is what we call a symbol, not a symptom. Thus a word is a symbol, and so is a meaningful combination of words.

A sentence, which is a special combination of words, expresses the idea of some state of affairs, real or imagined. Sentences are complicated symbols. Language will formulate new ideas as well as communicate old ones, so that all people know a lot of things that they have merely heard or read about. Symbolic expression, therefore, extends our knowledge beyond the scope of our actual experience.

If an idea is clearly conveyed by means of symbols we say it is well expressed. A person may work for a long time to give his statement the best possible form, to find the exact words for what he means to say, and to carry his account or his argument most directly from one point to another. But a discourse so worked out is certainly not a spontaneous reaction. Giving expression to an idea is obviously a different thing from giving expression to feelings. You do not say of a man in a rage that his anger is well expressed. The symptoms just are what they are; there is no critical standard for symptoms. If, on the other hand, the angry man tries to tell you what he is fuming about, he will have to collect himself, curtail his emotional expression, and find words to express his ideas. For to tell a story coherently involves "expression" in quite a different sense: this sort of expression is not "self-expression," but may be called "conceptual expression."

Language, of course, is our prime instrument of conceptual expression. The things we can say are in effect the things we can think. Words are the terms of our thinking as well as the terms in which we present our thoughts, because they present the objects of thought to the thinker himself. Before language communicates ideas, it gives them form, makes them clear, and in fact makes them what they are. Whatever has a name is an object for thought. Without words, sense experience is only a flow of impressions, as subjective as our feelings; words make it objective, and carve it up into *things* and *facts* that we can note, remember, and think about. Language gives outward experience its form, and makes it definite and clear.

There is, however, an important part of reality that is quite inaccessible to the formative influence of language: that is the realm of so-called "inner experience," the life of feeling and emotion. The reason why language is so powerless here is not, as many people suppose, that feeling and emotion are irrational; on the contrary, they seem irrational because language does not help to make them conceivable, and most people cannot conceive anything without the logical scaffolding of words. The unfitness of language to convey subjective experience is a somewhat technical subject, easier for logicians to understand than for artists; but the gist of it is that the form of language does not reflect the natural form of feeling, so that we cannot shape any extensive concepts of feeling with the help of ordinary, discursive language. Therefore the words whereby we refer to feeling only name very general kinds of inner experience—excitement, calm, joy, sorrow, love, hate, and so on. But there is no language to describe just how one joy differs, sometimes radically, from another. The real nature of feeling is something language as such—as discursive symbolism —cannot render.

For this reason, the phenomena of feeling and emotion are usually treated by philosophers as irrational. The only pattern discursive thought can find in them is the pattern of outward events that occasion them. There are different degrees of fear, but they are thought of as so many degrees of the same simple feeling.

But human feeling is a fabric, not a vague mass. It has an intricate dynamic pattern, possible combinations and new emergent phenomena. It is a pattern of organically interdependent and interdetermined tensions and resolutions, a pattern of almost infinitely complex activation and cadence. To it belongs the whole gamut of our sensibility—the sense of straining thought, all mental attitude and motor set. Those are the deeper reaches that underlie the surface waves of our emotion, and make human life a life of feeling instead of an unconscious metabolic existence interrupted by feelings.

It is, I think, this dynamic pattern that finds its formal expression in the arts. The expressiveness of art is like that of a symbol, not that of an emotional symptom; it is as a formulation of feeling for our conception that a work of art is properly said to be expressive. It may serve somebody's need of self-expression besides, but that is not what makes it good or bad art. In a special sense one may call a work of art a symbol of feeling, for, like a symbol, it formulates our ideas of inward experience, as discourse formulates our ideas of things and facts in the outside world. A work of art differs from a genuine symbol—that is, a symbol in the full and usual sense—in that it does not point beyond itself to something else. Its relation to feeling is a rather special one that we cannot undertake to analyze here; in effect, the feeling it expresses appears to be directly given with it —as the sense of a true metaphor, or the value of a religious myth—and is not separable from its expression. We speak of the feeling *of*, or the feeling *in*, a work of art, not the feeling it means. And we speak truly; a work of art presents something like a direct vision of vitality, emotion, subjective reality.

The primary function of art is to objectify feeling so that we can contemplate and understand it. It is the formulation of so-called "inward experience," the "inner life," that is impossible to achieve by discursive thought, because its forms are incommensurable with the forms of language and all its derivatives (e.g., mathematics, symbolic logic). Art objectifies the sentience and desire, self-consciousness and world-consciousness, emotions and moods, that are generally regarded as irrational because words cannot give us clear ideas of them. But the premise tacitly assumed in such a judgment—namely, that anything language cannot express is formless and irrational—seems to me to be an error. I believe the life of feeling is not irrational; its logical forms are merely very different from the structures of discourse. But they are so much like the dynamic forms of art that art is their natural symbol. Through plastic works, music, fiction, dance, or dramatic forms we can conceive what vitality and emotion feel like.

This brings us, at last, to the question of the cultural importance of the arts. Why is art so apt to be the vanguard of cultural advance, as it was in Egypt, in Greece, in Christian Europe (think of Gregorian music and Gothic architecture), in Renaissance Italy—not to speculate about ancient cavemen, whose art is all that we know of them? One thinks of culture as economic increase, social organization, the gradual ascendancy of rational thinking and scientific control of nature over superstitious imagination and magical practices. But art is not practical; it is neither philosophy nor science; it is not religion, morality, or even social comment (as many drama critics take comedy to be). What does it contribute to culture that could be of major importance?

It merely presents forms—sometimes intangible forms—to imagination. Its direct appeal is to that faculty, or function, that Lord Bacon considered the chief stumbling block in the way of reason, and that enlightened writers like Stuart Chase never tire of condemning as the source of all nonsense and bizarre erroneous beliefs. And so it is; but it is also the source of all insight and true beliefs. Imagination is probably the oldest mental trait that is typically human—older than discursive reason; it is probably the common source of dream, reason, religion, and all true general observation. It is this primitive human power—imagination—that engenders the arts and is in turn directly affected by their products.

Somewhere at the animalian starting line of human evolution lie the beginnings of that supreme instrument of the mind—language. We think of it as a device for communication among the members of a society. But communication is only one, and perhaps not even the first, of its functions. The first thing it does is to break up what William James called the "blooming, buzzing confusion" of sense perception into units and groups, events and chains of events—things and relations, causes and effects. All these patterns are imposed on our experience by language. We think, as we speak, in terms of objects and their relations.

But the process of breaking up our sense experience in this way, making reality conceivable, memorable, sometimes even predictable, is a process of imagination. Primitive conception is imagination. Language and imagination grow up together in a reciprocal tutelage.

What discursive symbolism—language in its literal use—does for our awareness of things about us and our own relation to them, the arts do for our awareness of subjective reality, feeling and emotion; they give form to inward experiences and thus make them conceivable. The only way we can really envisage vital movement, the stirring and growth and passage of emotion, and ultimately the whole direct sense of human life, is in artistic terms. A musical person thinks of emotions musically. They cannot be discursively talked about above a very general level. But they may nonetheless be known—objectively set forth, publicly known—and there is nothing necessarily confused or formless about emotions.

As soon as the natural forms of subjective experience are abstracted to the point of symbolic presentation, we can use those forms to imagine feeling and understand its nature. Self-knowledge, insight into all phases of life and mind, springs from artistic imagination. That is the cognitive value of the arts.

But their influence on human life goes deeper than the intellectual level. As language actually gives form to our sense experience, grouping our impressions around those things which have names, and fitting sensations to the qualities that have adjectival names, and so on, the arts we live with

—our picture books and stories and the music we hear—actually form our emotive experience. Every generation has its styles of feeling. One age shudders and blushes and faints, another swaggers, still another is godlike in a universal indifference. These styles in actual emotion are not insincere. They are largely unconscious—determined by many social causes, but *shaped* by artists, usually popular artists of the screen, the jukebox, the shop window, and the picture magazine. (That, rather than incitement to crime, is my objection to the comics.) Irwin Edman remarks in one of his books that our emotions are largely Shakespeare's poetry.

This influence of art on life gives us an indication of why a period of efflorescence in the arts is apt to lead a cultural advance: it formulates a new way of feeling, and that is the beginning of a cultural age. It suggests another matter for reflection, too—that a wide neglect of artistic education is a neglect in the education of feeling. Most people are so imbued with the idea that feeling is a formless, total organic excitement in men as in animals that the idea of educating feeling, developing its scope and quality, seems odd to them, if not absurd. It is really, I think, at the very heart of personal education.

There is one other function of the arts that benefits not so much the advance of culture as its stabilization—an influence on individual lives. This function is the converse and complement of the objectification of feeling, the driving force of creation in art: it is the education of vision that we receive in seeing, hearing, reading works of art—the development of the artist's eye, that assimilates ordinary sights (or sounds, motions, or events) to inward vision, and lends expressiveness and emotional import to the world. Wherever art takes a motif from actuality—a flowering branch, a bit of landscape, a historic event, or a personal memory, any model or theme from life—it transforms it into a piece of imagination, and imbues its image with artistic vitality. The result is an impregnation of ordinary reality with the significance of created form. This is the subjectification of nature that makes reality itself a symbol of life and feeling.

The arts objectify subjective reality, and subjectify outward experience of nature. Art education is the education of feeling, and a society that neglects it gives itself up to formless emotion. Bad art is corruption of feeling. This is a large factor in the irrationalism which dictators and demagogues exploit.

HENRI MATISSE

One of the most notable twentieth-century painters, Matisse was born in France in 1869. He first studied under Adolphe Bougereau, whom he found too academic; he then studied under Gustave Moreau, spending a great deal of time copying paintings of old masters at the Louvre. When he discovered the impressionists, he changed radically, joined the new school, and became one of its most memorable representatives. His first successful original painting, "Dinner Table," was exhibited in 1897, and in the next years Matisse painted a whole series of what have since been called masterpieces. He has also done some sculpting, worked with lithographs and etchings, illustrated many books, and designed two ballet sets—one for Diaghilev. In 1943 he left Paris for Vence, a small village in the hills behind Nice; he continued to paint and also designed the chapel of the Rosary for the Dominican nuns there. Matisse died in Nice in 1954 at the age of 85. "Notes of a Painter" was originally published in La Grande Revue, *Paris, on December 25, 1908. We have taken our text from the English translation, by Margaret Scolari Barr, which was published first in* Henri-Matisse (The Museum of Modern Art, 1931) *and later in* Matisse: His Art and His Public, *by Alfred H. Barr, Jr. (1951). We have omitted the paragraph headings added by the editor.*

NOTES OF A PAINTER

A painter who addresses the public not in order to present his works but to reveal some of his ideas on the art of painting exposes himself to several dangers. In the first place, I know that some people like to think of painting as dependent upon literature and therefore like to see in it not general ideas suited to pictorial art, but rather specifically literary ideas. I fear, therefore, that the painter who risks himself in the field of the literary man may be regarded with disapproval; in any case, I myself am fully convinced that the best explanation an artist can give of his aims and ability is afforded by his work.

However, such painters as Signac, Desvallières, Denis, Blanche, Guérin, Bernard etc. have written on such matters in various periodicals. In my turn I shall endeavor to make clear my pictorial intentions and aspirations without worrying about the writing.

One of the dangers which appears to me immediately is that of contradicting myself. I feel very strongly the bond between my old works and my recent ones. But I do not think the way I thought yesterday. My fundamental thoughts have not changed but have evolved and my modes of expression have followed my thoughts. I do not repudiate any of my paintings but I would not paint one of them in the same way had I to do it again. My destination is always the same but I work out a different route to get there.

If I mention the name of this or that artist it will be to point out how our manners differ so that it may seem that I do not appreciate his work. Thus I may be accused of injustice towards painters whose efforts and aims I best understand, or whose accomplishments I most appreciate. I shall use them as examples not to establish my superiority over them but to show clearly through what they have done, what I am attempting to do.

What I am after, above all, is expression. Sometimes it has been conceded that I have a certain technical ability but that, my ambition being limited, I am unable to proceed beyond a purely visual satisfaction such as can be procured from the mere sight of a picture. But the purpose of a painter must not be conceived as separate from his pictorial means, and these pictorial means must be the more complete (I do not mean complicated) the deeper is his thought. I am unable to distinguish between the feeling I have for life and my way of expressing it.

Expression to my way of thinking does not consist of the passion mirrored upon a human face or betrayed by a violent gesture. The whole arrangement of my picture is expressive. The place occupied by figures or objects, the empty spaces around them, the proportions, everything plays a part. Composition is the art of arranging in a decorative manner the various elements at the painter's disposal for the expression of his feelings. In a picture every part will be visible and will play the rôle conferred upon it, be it principal or secondary. All that is not useful in the picture is detrimental. A work of art must be harmonious in its entirety; for superfluous details would, in the mind of the beholder, encroach upon the essential elements.

Composition, the aim of which is expression, alters itself according to the surface to be covered. If I take a sheet of paper of given dimensions I will jot down a drawing which will have a necessary relation to its format—I would not repeat this drawing on another sheet of different dimensions, for instance on a rectangular sheet if the first one happened to be square. And if I had to repeat it on a sheet of the same shape but

ten times larger I would not limit myself to enlarging it: a drawing must
have a power of expansion which can bring to life the space which surrounds it. An artist who wants to transpose a composition onto a larger
canvas must conceive it over again in order to preserve its expression; he
must alter its character and not just fill in the squares into which he has
divided his canvas.

Both harmonies and dissonances of color can produce very pleasurable
effects. Often when I settle down to work I begin by noting my immediate and superficial color sensations. Some years ago this first result
was often enough for me—but today if I were satisfied with this my picture would remain incomplete. I would have put down the passing sensations of a moment; they would not completely define my feelings and
the next day I might not recognize what they meant. I want to reach
that state of condensation of sensations which constitutes a picture. Perhaps I might be satisfied momentarily with a work finished at one sitting
but I would soon get bored looking at it; therefore, I prefer to continue
working on it so that later I may recognize it as a work of my mind.
There was a time when I never left my paintings hanging on the wall because they reminded me of moments of nervous excitement and I did not
like to see them again when I was quiet. Nowadays I try to put serenity
into my pictures and work at them until I feel that I have succeeded.

Supposing I want to paint the body of a woman: first of all I endow it
with grace and charm but I know that something more than that is
necessary. I try to condense the meaning of this body by drawing its
essential lines. The charm will then become less apparent at first glance
but in the long run it will begin to emanate from the new image. This
image at the same time will be enriched by a wider meaning, a more
comprehensively human one, while the charm, being less apparent, will
not be its only characteristic. It will be merely one element in the general
conception of the figure.

Charm, lightness, crispness—all these are passing sensations. I have a
canvas on which the colors are still fresh and I begin work on it again. The
colors will probably grow heavier—the freshness of the original tones will
give way to greater solidity, an improvement to my mind, but less seduc-
tive to the eye.

The impressionist painters, Monet, Sisley especially, had delicate, vibrat-
ing sensations; as a result their canvases are all alike. The word "impres-
sionism" perfectly characterizes their intentions for they register fleeting
impressions. This term, however, cannot be used with reference to more
recent painters who avoid the first impression and consider it deceptive.
A rapid rendering of a landscape represents only one moment of its
appearance. I prefer, by insisting upon its essentials, to discover its more
enduring character and content, even at the risk of sacrificing some of its
pleasing qualities.

Underneath this succession of moments which constitutes the superficial existence of things animate and inanimate and which is continually obscuring and transforming them, it is yet possible to search for a truer, more essential character which the artist will seize so that he may give to reality a more lasting interpretation. When we go into the XVII and XVIII century sculpture rooms in the Louvre and look for instance at a Puget, we realize that the expression is forced and exaggerated in a very disquieting way. Then, again, if we go to the Luxembourg the attitude in which the painters seize their models is always the one in which the muscular development will be shown to greatest advantage. But movement thus interpreted corresponds to nothing in nature and if we catch a motion of this kind by a snapshot the image thus captured will remind us of nothing that we have seen. Indication of motion has meaning for us only if we do not isolate any one sensation of movement from the preceding and from the following one.

There are two ways of expressing things; one is to show them crudely, the other is to evoke them artistically. In abandoning the literal representation of movement it is possible to reach towards a higher ideal of beauty. Look at an Egyptian statue: it looks rigid to us; however, we feel in it the image of a body capable of movement and which despite its stiffness is animated. The Greeks too are calm; a man hurling a discus will be shown in the moment in which he gathers his strength before the effort or else, if he is shown in the most violent and precarious position implied by his action, the sculptor will have abridged and condensed it so that balance is re-established, thereby suggesting a feeling of duration. Movement in itself is unstable and is not suited to something durable like a statue unless the artist has consciously realized the entire action of which he represents only a moment.

It is necessary for me to define the character of the object or of the body that I wish to paint. In order to do this I study certain salient points very carefully: if I put a black dot on a sheet of white paper the dot will be visible no matter how far I stand away from it—it is a clear notation; but beside this dot I place another one, and then a third. Already there is confusion. In order that the first dot may maintain its value I must enlarge it as I proceed putting other marks on the paper.

If upon a white canvas I jot down some sensations of blue, of green, of red—every new brushstroke diminishes the importance of the preceding ones. Suppose I set out to paint an interior: I have before me a cupboard; it gives me a sensation of bright red—and I put down a red which satisfies me; immediately a relation is established between this red and the white of the canvas. If I put a green near the red, if I paint in a yellow floor, there must still be between this green, this yellow and the white of the canvas a relation that will be satisfactory to me. But these several tones mutually weaken one another. It is necessary, therefore, that the various elements that I use be so balanced that they do not destroy one another. To do this I must organize my ideas; the relation between tones must be so established that they will sustain one another. A new combination of colors will succeed the first one and will give more completely my interpretation. I am forced to transpose until finally my picture may seem completely changed when, after successive modifications, the red has succeeded the green as the dominant color. I cannot copy nature in a servile way, I must interpret nature and submit it to the spirit of the picture—when I have found the relationship of all the tones the result must be a living harmony of tones, a harmony not unlike that of a musical composition.

For me all is in the conception—I must have a clear vision of the whole composition from the very beginning. I could mention the name of a great sculptor who produces some admirable pieces but for him a composition is nothing but the grouping of fragments and the result is a confusion of expression. Look instead at one of Cézanne's pictures: all is so well arranged in them that no matter how many figures are represented and no matter at what distance you stand, you will be able always to distinguish each figure clearly and you will always know which limb belongs to which body. If in the picture there is order and clarity it means that this same order and clarity existed in the mind of the painter and that the painter was conscious of their necessity. Limbs may cross, may mingle, but still in the eyes of the beholder they will remain attached to the right body. All confusion will have disappeared.

The chief aim of color should be to serve expression as well as possible. I put down my colors without a preconceived plan. If at the first step and perhaps without my being conscious of it one tone has particularly pleased me, more often than not when the picture is finished I will notice that I have respected this tone while I have progressively altered and transformed the others. I discover the quality of colors in a purely instinctive way. To paint an autumn landscape I will not try to remember what colors suit this season, I will only be inspired by the sensation that the season gives me; the icy clearness of the sour blue sky will express the season just as well as the tonalities of the leaves. My sensation itself may vary, the autumn may be soft and warm like a protracted summer or quite cool with a cold sky and lemon yellow trees that give a chilly impression and announce winter.

My choice of colors does not rest on any scientific theory; it is based on observation, on feeling, on the very nature of each experience. Inspired by certain pages of Delacroix, Signac is preoccupied by complementary colors and the theoretical knowledge of them will lead him to use a certain tone in a certain place. I, on the other hand, merely try to find a color that will fit my sensation. There is an impelling proportion of tones that can induce me to change the shape of a figure or to transform my composition. Until I have achieved this proportion in all the parts of the composition I strive towards it and keep on working. Then a moment comes when every part has found its definite relationship and from then on it would be impossible for me to add a stroke to my picture without having to paint it all over again. As a matter of fact, I think that the theory of complementary colors is not absolute. In studying the paintings of artists whose knowledge of colors depends only upon instinct and sensibility and on a consistency of their sensations, it would be possible to define certain laws of color and so repudiate the limitations of the accepted color theory.

What interests me most is neither still life nor landscape but the human figure. It is through it that I best succeed in expressing the nearly religious feeling that I have towards life. I do not insist upon the details of the face. I do not care to repeat them with anatomical exactness. Though I happen to have an Italian model whose appearance at first suggests nothing but a purely animal existence yet I succeed in picking out among the lines of his face those which suggest that deep gravity which persists in every human being. A work of art must carry in itself its complete significance and impose it upon the beholder even before he can identify the subject matter. When I see the Giotto frescoes at Padua I do not trouble to recognize which scene of the life of Christ I have before me but I perceive instantly the sentiment which radiates from it and which is instinct in the composition in every line and color. The title will only serve to confirm my impression.

What I dream of is an art of balance, of purity and serenity devoid of troubling or depressing subject matter, an art which might be for every mental worker, be he business man or writer, like an appeasing influence, like a mental soother, something like a good armchair in which to rest from physical fatigue.

Often a discussion arises upon the value of different processes, and their relation to different temperaments. A distinction is made between artists who work directly from nature and those who work purely from their imagination. I think neither of these methods should be preferred to the exclusion of the other. Often both are used in turn by the same man; sometimes he needs tangible objects to provide him with sensations and thus excite his creative power; at other times when his pictorial sensations are already present in his mind he needs contact with reality before he can organize them into a picture. However, I think that one can judge of the vitality and power of an artist when after having received impressions from nature he is able to organize his sensations to return in the same mood on different days, voluntarily to continue receiving these impressions (whether nature appears the same or not); this power proves he is sufficiently master of himself to subject himself to discipline.

The simplest means are those which enable an artist to express himself best. If he fears the obvious he cannot avoid it by strange representations, bizarre drawing, eccentric color. His expression must derive inevitably from his temperament. He must sincerely believe that he has only painted what he has seen. I like Chardin's way of expressing it: "I put on color until it resembles (is a good likeness)," or Cézanne: "I want to secure a likeness," or Rodin: "Copy nature!" or Leonardo: "He who can copy can do (create)." Those who work in an affected style, deliberately turning their backs on nature, are in error—an artist must recognize that when he uses his reason his picture is an artifice and that when he paints he must feel that he is copying nature—and even when he consciously departs from nature he must do it with the conviction that it is only the better to interpret her.

Some will object perhaps that a painter should have some other outlook upon painting and that I have only uttered platitudes. To this I shall answer that there are no new truths. The rôle of the artist, like that of the scholar, consists in penetrating truths as well known to him as to others but which will take on for him a new aspect and so enable him to master them in their deepest significance. Thus if the aviators were to explain to us the researches which led to their leaving earth and rising in the air they would be merely confirming very elementary principles of physics neglected by less successful inventors.

An artist has always something to learn when he is given information about himself—and I am glad now to have learned which is my weak point. M. Peladan in the "Revue Hébdomadaire" reproaches a certain number of painters, amongst whom I think I should place myself, for calling themselves *"Fauves"* (wild beasts) and yet dressing like everyone else so that they are no more noticeable than the floor walkers in a department store. Does genius count for so little? In the same article this excellent writer pretends that I do not paint honestly and I feel that I should perhaps be annoyed though I admit that he restricts his statement by adding, "I mean honestly with respect to the Ideal and the Rules." The trouble is that he does not mention where these rules are—I am willing to admit that they exist but were it possible to learn them what sublime artists we would have!

Rules have no existence outside of individuals: otherwise Racine would be no greater genius than a good professor. Any of us can repeat a fine sentence but few can also penetrate the meaning. I have no doubt that from a study of the works of Raphael or Titian a more complete set of rules can be drawn than from the works of Manet or Renoir but the rules followed by Manet and Renoir were suited to their artistic temperaments and I happen to prefer the smallest of their paintings to all the work of those who have merely imitated the "Venus of Urbino" or the "Madonna of the Goldfinch." Such painters are of no value to anyone because, whether we want to or not, we belong to our time and we share in its opinions, preferences and delusions. All artists bear the imprint of their time but the great artists are those in which this stamp is most deeply impressed. Our epoch for instance is better represented by Courbet than by Flandrin, by Rodin better than by Fremiet. Whether we want to or not between our period and ourselves an indissoluble bond is established and M. Peladan himself cannot escape it. The aestheticians of the future may perhaps use his books as evidence if they get it in their heads to prove that no one of our time understood a thing about the art of Leonardo da Vinci.

ERNST FISCHER

Ernst Fischer was born in Austria in 1899. A member of the Social Democratic Party, he edited the Vienna Arbeiter Zeitung (Workers' Newspaper) *from 1927 to 1934. That year he emigrated to Prague and became a member of the Communist party. He spent a number of years in Moscow where he was active in literary circles, and during World War II became a radio commentator. In 1945 he returned to Austria, became active in politics, and served from 1945 to 1959 as a member of Parliament in the National Assembly. He is the author of many political and literary works. The selection we print below is the opening chapter of his* The Necessity of Art: A Marxist Approach, *trans. Anna Bostock (1963), originally published as* Von der Notwendigkeit der Kunst *in 1959.*

THE FUNCTION OF ART

'Poetry is indispensable—if I only knew what for.' With this charmingly paradoxical epigram Jean Cocteau has summed up the necessity of art—as well as its questionable role in the late bourgeois world.

The painter Mondrian spoke of the possible 'disappearance' of art. Reality would, he believed, increasingly displace the work of art, which was essentially a substitute for an equilibrium that reality lacked at present. 'Art will disappear as life gains more equilibrium.'

Art as a 'life substitute', art as a means of putting man in a state of equilibrium with the surrounding world—the idea contains a partial recognition of the nature of art and its necessity. And since a perpetual equilibrium between man and the surrounding world cannot be expected to exist even in the most highly developed society, the idea suggests, too, that art was not merely necessary in the past but will always remain so.

Yet is art really no more than a substitute? Does it not also express a deeper relationship between man and the world? Indeed, can the function of art be summed up at all in a single formula? Does it not have to satisfy many and various needs? And if, as we reflect upon the origins of art, we become aware of its initial function, has not that function also changed with the changing of society, and have not new functions come into being?

This book is an attempt to answer questions such as these, founded on the conviction that art has been, still is, and always will be necessary.

As a first step we must realize that we are inclined to take an astonishing phenomenon too much for granted. And it is certainly astonishing: countless millions read books, listen to music, watch the theatre, go to the cinema. Why? To say that they seek distraction, relaxation, entertainment, is to beg the question. Why is it distracting, relaxing, entertaining to sink oneself in someone else's life and problems, to identify oneself with a painting or a piece of music or with the characters in a novel, play, or film? Why do we respond to such 'unreality' as though it were reality intensified? What strange, mysterious entertainment is this? And if one answers that we want to escape from an unsatisfactory existence into a richer one, into experience without risk, then the next question arises: why is our own existence not enough? Why this desire to fulfil our unfulfilled lives through other figures, other forms, to gaze from the darkness of an auditorium at a lighted stage where something that is only play can so utterly absorb us?

Evidently man wants to be more than just himself. He wants to be a *whole* man. He is not satisfied with being a separate individual; out of the partiality of his individual life he strives towards a 'fulness' that he senses and demands, towards a fulness of life of which individuality with all its limitations cheats him, towards a more comprehensible, a more just world, a world that *makes sense*. He rebels against having to consume himself within the confines of his own life, within the transient, chance limits of his own personality. He wants to refer to something that is more than 'I', something outside himself and yet essential to himself. He longs to absorb the surrounding world and make it his own; to extend his inquisitive, world-hungry 'I' in science and technology as far as the remotest constellations and as deep as the innermost secrets of the atom; to unite his limited 'I' in art with a communal existence; to make his individuality *social*.

If it were man's nature to be no more than an individual, this desire would be incomprehensible and senseless, for as an individual he would then *be* a whole: he would be all that he was capable of being. Man's desire to be increased and supplemented indicates that he is more than an individual. He feels that he can attain wholeness only if he takes possession of the experiences of others that might potentially be his own. Yet what a man apprehends as his potential includes everything that humanity as a whole is capable of. Art is the indispensable means for this merging of the individual with the whole. It reflects his infinite capacity for association, for sharing experiences and ideas.

And yet: is this definition of art as the means of becoming one with the whole of reality, as the individual's way to the world at large, as the expression of his desire to identify himself with what he is not, perhaps too romantic? Is it not rash to conclude, on the basis of our own near-hysterical sense of identification with the hero of a film or a novel, that this is the universal and original function of art? Does art not also contain the opposite of this 'Dionysian' losing of oneself? Does it not also contain the 'Apollonian' element of entertainment and satisfaction which consists precisely in the fact that the onlooker does *not* identify himself with what is represented but *gains distance* from it, overcomes the direct power of reality through its deliberate representation, and finds, in art, that happy freedom of which the burdens of everyday life deprive him? And is not the same duality—on the one hand the absorption in reality, on the other the excitement of controlling it—also evident in the way the artist himself works? For make no mistake about it, work for an artist is a highly conscious, rational process at the end of which the work of art emerges as mastered reality—not at all a state of intoxicated inspiration.

In order to be an artist it is necessary to seize, hold, and transform experience into memory, memory into expression, material into form. Emotion for an artist is not everything; he must also know his trade and enjoy it, understand all the rules, skills, forms, and conventions whereby nature —the shrew—can be tamed and subjected to the contract of art. The passion that consumes the dilettante *serves* the true artist: the artist is not mauled by the beast, he tames it.

Tension and dialectical contradiction are inherent in art; not only must art derive from an intense experience of reality, it must also be *constructed*, it must gain form through objectivity. The free play of art is the result of mastery. Aristotle, so often misunderstood, held that the function of drama was to purify the emotions, to overcome terror and pity, so that the spectator identifying himself with Orestes or Oedipus was liberated from that identification and lifted above the blind workings of fate. The ties of life are temporarily cast off, for art 'captivates' in a different way from reality, and this pleasant temporary captivity is precisely the nature of the 'entertainment', of that pleasure which is derived even from tragic works.

Bertolt Brecht said of this pleasure, this liberating quality of art:

> Our theatre must encourage the thrill of comprehension and train people in the pleasure of changing reality. Our audiences must not

only hear how Prometheus was set free, but also train themselves in the pleasure of freeing him. They must be taught to feel, in our theatre, all the satisfaction and enjoyment felt by the inventor and the discoverer, all the triumph felt by the liberator.

Brecht points out that in a society of class struggle, the 'immediate' effect of a work of art demanded by the ruling aesthetic is to suppress the social distinctions within the audience and thus, while the work is being enjoyed, create a collective not divided into classes but 'universally human'. On the other hand, the function of 'non-Aristotelian drama' which Brecht advocated was precisely to divide the audience by removing the conflict between feeling and reason which has come about in the capitalist world.

> Both feeling and reason degenerated in the age of capitalism when that age was drawing towards its end, and entered into a bad, unproductive conflict with each other. But the rising new class and those who fight on its side are concerned with feeling and reason engaged in *productive* conflict. Our feelings impel us towards the maximum effort of reasoning, and our reason purifies our feelings.

In the alienated world in which we live, social reality must be presented in an arresting way, in a new light, through the 'alienation' of the subject and the characters. The work of art must grip the audience not through passive identification but through an appeal to reason which demands action and decision. The rules according to which human beings live together must be treated in the drama as 'temporary and imperfect' so as to make the spectator do something more productive than merely watch, stimulating him to think along with the play and finally to pass judgment: 'That's not the way to do it. This is very strange, almost unbelievable. This must stop.' And so the spectator, who is a working man or woman, will come to the theatre to

> . . . enjoy, as entertainment, his own terrible and never-ending labours by which he is meant to support himself, and suffer the shock of his own incessant change. Here he may *produce himself* in the easiest fashion: for the easiest fashion of existence is in art.

Without claiming that Brecht's 'epic theatre' is the only possible kind of militant working-class drama, I quote Brecht's important theory as an illustration of the dialectic of art and of the way that the function of art changes in a changing world.

The *raison d'être* of art never stays entirely the same. The function of art in a class society at war within itself differs in many respects from its original function. But nevertheless, despite different social situations, there is something in art that expresses an unchanging truth. It is this that enables us, who live in the twentieth century, to be moved by prehistoric cave paintings or very ancient songs. Karl Marx described the epic as the art form of an undeveloped society,[1] and then added:

> But the difficulty is not in grasping the idea that Greek art and epos are bound up with certain forms of social development. It rather lies in understanding why they still constitute with us a source of aesthetic enjoyment and in certain respects prevail as the standard and model beyond attainment.

He then offered the following answer:

> Why should the social childhood of mankind, where it had obtained its most beautiful development, not exert an eternal charm as an age that will never return? There are ill-bred children and precocious children. Many of the ancient nations belong to the latter class. The Greeks were normal children. The charm their art has for us does not conflict with the primitive character of the social order from which it had sprung. It is rather the product of the latter, and is rather due to the fact that the unripe social conditions under which the art arose and under which alone it could appear can never return.

Today we may doubt whether, compared with other nations, the ancient Greeks were 'normal children'. Indeed, in another connexion Marx and Engels themselves drew attention to the problematic aspects of the Greek world with its contempt for work, its degradation of women, its eroticism reserved solely for courtesans and boys. And since then we have discovered a great deal more about the seamy side of Greek beauty, serenity, and harmony. Today our ideas of the ancient world coincide only in part with those of Winckelmann, Goethe, and Hegel. Archaeological, ethnological, and cultural discoveries no longer allow us to accept classical Greek art as belonging to our 'childhood'. On the contrary, we see in it something relatively late and mature, and in its perfection in the age of Pericles we detect hints of decadence and decline. Many works, once praised as 'classical', by the sculptors who followed the great Phidias, a large number of those heroes, athletes, discus throwers, and charioteers, strike us today as empty and meaningless compared with Egyptian or Mycenean works. But to go deeper into these matters would take us too far from the question Marx raised and the answer he supplied.

What matters is that Marx saw the time-conditioned art of an undeveloped social stage as a *moment of humanity*, and recognized that in this lay its power to act beyond the historical moment, to exercise an eternal fascination.

We may put it like this: all art is conditioned by time, and represents

---

[1] *A Contribution to the Critique of Political Economy*, Kegan Paul, Trench Trübner, 1904.

humanity in so far as it corresponds to the ideas and aspirations, the needs and hopes of a particular historical situation. But, at the same time, art goes beyond this limitation and, within the historical moment, also creates a moment of humanity, promising constant development. We should never underestimate the degree of continuity throughout the class struggle, despite periods of violent change and social upheaval. Like the world itself, the history of mankind is not only a contradictory discontinuum but also a continuum. Ancient, apparently long-forgotten things are preserved within us, continue to work upon us—often without our realizing it—and then, suddenly, they come to the surface and speak to us like the shadows in Hades whom Odysseus fed with his blood. In different periods, depending on the social situation and the needs of rising or declining classes, different things which have been latent or lost are brought again into the light of day, awakened to new life. And just as it was no coincidence that Lessing and Herder, in their revolt against the feudal and the courtly and all the contemporary false posturings with wig and alexandrine, discovered Shakespeare for the Germans, so it is no coincidence that, today, Western Europe in its denial of humanism and in the fetish-like character of its institutions reaches back to the fetishes of pre-history and constructs false myths to hide its real problems.

Different classes and social systems, while developing their own ethos, have contributed to the forming of a universal human ethos. The concept of freedom, though it always corresponds to the conditions and aims of a class or a social system, nevertheless tends to grow into an all-embracing idea. In the same way, constant features of mankind are captured even in time-conditioned art. In so far as Homer, Aeschylus, and Sophocles mirrored the simple conditions of a society based on slavery, they are time-bound and out of date. But in so far as, in that society, they discovered the greatness of man, gave artistic form to his conflicts and passions, and hinted at his infinite potentiality, they remain as modern as ever. Prometheus bringing fire to earth, Odysseus in his wanderings and his return, the fate of Tantalus and his children, all this has preserved its original power for us. Though we may regard the subject-matter of *Antigone*—a struggle for the right to give honourable burial to a blood relative—as archaic, though we may need historical commentaries in order to understand it, the figure of Antigone is as moving today as it ever was, and so long as there are human beings in the world they will be moved by her words: 'My nature is to join in love, not hate.' The more we come to know of long-forgotten works of art, the clearer become their common and continuous elements, despite their variety. Fragment joins fragment to make humanity.

We may conclude from a constantly growing wealth of evidence that art in its origins was *magic*, a magic aid towards mastering a real but unexplored world. Religion, science, and art were combined in a latent form—germinally as it were—in magic. This magic role of art has progressively given way to the role of illuminating social relationships, of enlightening men in societies becoming opaque, of helping men to recognize and change social reality. A highly complex society with its multiple relationships and social contradictions can no longer be represented in the manner of a myth. In such a society, which demands literal recognition and all-embracing consciousness, there is bound to be an overwhelming need to break through the rigid forms of earlier ages where the magic element still operated, and to arrive at more open forms—at the freedom, say, of the novel. Either of the two elements of art may predominate at a particular time, depending on the stage of society reached —sometimes the magically suggestive, at other times the rational and enlightening; sometimes dreamlike intuition, at other times the desire to sharpen perception. But whether art soothes or awakens, casts shadows or brings light, it is never merely a clinical description of reality. Its function is always to move the *whole* man, to enable the 'I' to identify itself with another's life, to make its own what it is not and yet is capable of being. Even a great didactic artist like Brecht does not act purely through reason and argument, but also through feeling and suggestion. He not only confronts the audience with a work of art, he also lets them 'get inside' it. He himself was aware of this, and pointed out that it was not a problem of absolute contrasts but of shifting stresses. 'In this way the emotionally suggestive or the purely rationally persuasive may predominate as a means of communication.'

True as it is that the essential function of art for a class destined to change the world is not that of *making magic* but of *enlightening* and *stimulating action*, it is equally true that a magical residue in art cannot be entirely eliminated, for without that minute residue of its original nature, art ceases to be art.

In all the forms of its development, in dignity and fun, persuasion and exaggeration, sense and nonsense, fantasy and reality, art always has a little to do with magic.

Art is necessary in order that man should be able to recognize and change the world. But art is also necessary by virtue of the magic inherent in it.

THE EDITORS OF *LIFE*

WANTED: AN AMERICAN NOVEL

The following editorial appeared in the September 12, 1955, issue of Life.

•

Sloan Wilson, a young writer whose first novel (*The Man in the Gray Flannel Suit*) is moving up best-seller lists, recently made a statement in defense of his book's happy ending which is worth repeating: "The world's treated me awfully well," he said, "and I guess it's crept into my work. . . . These are, we forget, pretty good times. Yet too many novelists are still writing as if we were back in the Depression years."

Wilson put his finger on a strange contradiction. Ours is the most powerful nation in the world. It has had a decade of unparalleled prosperity. It has gone further than any other society in the history of man toward creating a truly classless society. Yet it is still producing a literature which sounds sometimes as if it were written by an unemployed homosexual living in a packing-box shanty on the city dump while awaiting admission to the county poorhouse.

This is doubly strange because past American eras have produced art which faithfully mirrored their times; *The Great Gatsby* still speaks eloquently of Prohibition's frauds and deceits, *Main Street* of the high tide of provincial self-satisfaction, *The Grapes of Wrath* with a just anger for the unnecessary humiliations of Depression, while *Look Homeward, Angel* may well speak for a timeless America. But who speaks for America today? One might argue, with some plausibility, that the fearful indecisions of an atomic age keep a representative literature from being born, but when has life ever been secure? Atomic fear or not, the incredible accomplishments of our day are surely the raw stuff of saga.

Wilson's uneven book may be flimsy art but it is at least affirmative. Happily there are a few other signs of a trend away from degeneracy and negation. For example, Lionel Shapiro's *Sixth of June*, though it revolves about a triangle, is not resolved by adultery. Herman Wouk's *Marjorie Morningstar* is a mutiny, says *Time*, against "three decades of

U.S. fiction dominated by skeptical criticism, sexual emancipation, social protest and psychoanalytical sermonizing." Wouk's book even endorses premarital chastity. And there is visible in other work what Critic Maxwell Geismar calls "a return to the security of a religious universe."

A change is needed. Nobody wants Pollyanna literature. Poets have always had what Robert Frost admits is "a vested interest in human misery"; agony begets art. Maybe art mistrusts prosperity. But at least the breeches-busting Paul Bunyan of the U.S. today seems to deserve better literature than the papaya-smelly, overripe school of the Truman Capotes, or the obscenity-obsessed school of "new realism" exemplified by a parade of war novels which mostly read like the diary of a professional grievance collector with a dirty mind and total recall. James Gould Cozzens' *Guard of Honor* was one of the few military novels that rang true with dignity. In most of the others the enemy is not the one shooting at us but our own officers and Army.

Europeans are already prejudiced against America by savage animadversions in their own classics against our "vulgar" democracy ("If I had remained another day in that horrible . . . United States, where there is neither hope nor faith, nor charity," wrote Balzac, "I should have died without being sick"). Small wonder that our own self-depreciation helps them enlarge the evil image to that which France's Michel Mohrt describes in his new study of American novels: "a hypocritical society based on the power of money, racial prejudice, sexual taboos. Exile, alcohol, suicide seem the only escape." Such a onetime exile, Henry (*Tropic of Cancer*) Miller, puts it more savagely in the current *Chicago Review*. The American seen through the eyes of our leading writers, he asserts, is "a digit in machine-made formulas . . . he has neither face nor name but is shuffled about like the victim of a soulless society on an electronic chessboard operated by a dummy hidden in the cells of a publisher's diseased brain. . . ." The writing, he adds, "reeks of embalming fluid."

It is understandable that American groups which feel the most isolated should produce the most anguished writing, and that so much of it should come from the South. Its ante bellum slave society was in some ways similar to the feudal Russian system whose injustices and tensions produced a Dostoevski and a Tolstoi. William Faulkner has a patent kinship with Dostoevski and his preoccupation with guilt. But Faulkner, for all his enormous gifts, can be searched in vain for that quality of redemption, through love and brotherhood, which always shines amid Dostoevski's horrors. It shines also amid the worst havoc of Tolstoi's overturned world (Moscow, too, was burned, even if not by Sherman).

To find this redeeming quality of spiritual purpose today's reader must turn not to novels but to nonfiction like Russell Davenport's *The Dignity of Man* or to the British book, *The Conquest of Everest*. That conquest

held a deeper meaning than the achievement. The European Hillary and
the Asian Tenzing are a hopeful symbol for a wider brotherhood yet
to be achieved. Their final triumph expresses the unquenchable reaching
of man's soul for a truth higher than reality, for a good better than himself, the qualities which modern literature so often deny. In every healthy
man there is a wisdom deeper than his conscious mind, reaching beyond
memory to the primeval rivers, a yea-saying to the goodness and joy of
life. This is what is most missing from our hothouse literature—the joy
of life itself.

ALBERT CAMUS

WHAT CAN THE ARTIST DO IN THE WORLD OF TODAY?

*At least two interviews with Camus have been translated into English
under the title* The Artist and His Time. *We present below a section of
the 1953 interview printed in* The Myth of Sisyphus and Other Essays,
*translated by Justin O'Brien (1955). For information about the author and
his writings, see page 261.*

•

He is not asked either to write about co-operatives or, conversely, to lull
to sleep in himself the sufferings endured by others throughout history.
And since you have asked me to speak personally, I am going to do so
as simply as I can. Considered as artists, we perhaps have no need to
interfere in the affairs of the world. But considered as men, yes. The
miner who is exploited or shot down, the slaves in the camps, those in
the colonies, the legions of persecuted throughout the world—they need
all those who can speak to communicate their silence and to keep in
touch with them. I have not written, day after day, fighting articles and
texts, I have not taken part in the common struggles because I desire the
world to be covered with Greek statues and masterpieces. The man who

has such a desire does exist in me. Except that he has something better to do in trying to instill life into the creatures of his imagination. But from my first articles to my latest book I have written so much, and perhaps too much, only because I cannot keep from being drawn toward every-day life, toward those, whoever they may be, who are humiliated and debased. They need to hope, and if all keep silent or if they are given a choice between two kinds of humiliation, they will be forever deprived of hope and we with them. It seems to me impossible to endure that idea, nor can he who cannot endure it lie down to sleep in his tower. Not through virtue, as you see, but through a sort of almost organic intoler-ance, which you feel or do not feel. Indeed, I see many who fail to feel it, but I cannot envy their sleep.

This does not mean, however, that we must sacrifice our artist's nature to some social preaching or other. I have said elsewhere why the artist was more than ever necessary. But if we intervene as men, that experience will have an effect upon our language. And if we are not artists in our language first of all, what sort of artists are we? Even if, militants in our lives, we speak in our works of deserts and of selfish love, the mere fact that our lives are militant causes a special tone of voice to people with men that desert and that love. I shall certainly not choose the moment when we are beginning to leave nihilism behind to stupidly deny the values of creation in favor of the values of humanity, or vice versa. In my mind neither one is ever separated from the other and I measure the greatness of an artist (Molière, Tolstoy, Melville) by the balance he managed to maintain between the two. Today, under the pressure of events, we are obliged to transport that tension into our lives likewise. This is why so many artists, bending under the burden, take refuge in the ivory tower or, conversely, in the social church. But as for me, I see in both choices a like act of resignation. We must simultaneously serve suffering and beauty. The long patience, the strength, the secret cunning such service calls for are the virtues that establish the very renascence we need.

One word more. This undertaking, I know, cannot be accomplished without dangers and bitterness. We must accept the dangers: the era of chairbound artists is over. But we must reject the bitterness. One of the temptations of the artist is to believe himself solitary, and in truth he hears this shouted at him with a certain base delight. But this is not true. He stands in the midst of all, in the same rank, neither higher nor lower, with all those who are working and struggling. His very vocation, in the face of oppression, is to open the prisons and to give a voice to the sorrows and joys of all. This is where art, against its enemies, justifies itself by proving precisely that it is no one's enemy. By itself art could probably not produce the renascence which implies justice and liberty. But without it, that renascence would be without forms and, consequently, would be nothing. Without culture, and the relative freedom it implies, society, even when perfect, is but a jungle. This is why any authentic creation is a gift to the future.   (1953)

GEORGE ORWELL

WHY I WRITE

This essay is taken from Orwell's collection, Such, Such Were the Joys *(1953). For further information about the author and his writings, see page 74.*

•

From a very early age, perhaps the age of five or six, I knew that when I grew up I should be a writer. Between the ages of about seventeen and twenty-four I tried to abandon this idea, but I did so with the consciousness that I was outraging my true nature and that sooner or later I should have to settle down and write books.

I was the middle child of three, but there was a gap of five years on either side, and I barely saw my father before I was eight. For this and other reasons I was somewhat lonely, and I soon developed disagreeable mannerisms which made me unpopular throughout my schooldays. I had the lonely child's habit of making up stories and holding conversations with imaginary persons, and I think from the very start my literary ambitions were mixed up with the feeling of being isolated and under-valued. I knew that I had a facility with words and a power of facing unpleasant facts, and I felt that this created a sort of private world in which I could get my own back for my failure in everyday life. Nevertheless the volume of serious—*i.e.* seriously intended—writing which I produced all through my childhood and boyhood would not amount to half a dozen pages. I wrote my first poem at the age of four or five, my mother taking it down to dictation. I cannot remember anything about it except that it was about a tiger and the tiger had "chair-like teeth"— a good enough phrase, but I fancy the poem was a plagiarism of Blake's "Tiger, Tiger." At eleven, when the war of 1914–18 broke out, I wrote a patriotic poem which was printed in the local newspaper, as was another, two years later, on the death of Kitchener. From time to time, when I was a bit older, I wrote bad and usually unfinished "nature poems" in the Georgian style. I also, about twice, attempted a short story which was a ghastly failure. That was the total of the would-be serious work that I actually set down on paper during all those years.

However, throughout this time I did in a sense engage in literary activities. To begin with there was the made-to-order stuff which I produced quickly, easily and without much pleasure to myself. Apart from school work, I wrote *vers d'occasion*, semi-comic poems which I could turn out at what now seems to me astonishing speed—at fourteen I wrote a whole rhyming play, in imitation of Aristophanes, in about a week—and helped to edit school magazines, both printed and in manuscript. These magazines were the most pitiful burlesque stuff that you could imagine, and I took far less trouble with them than I now would with the cheapest journalism. But side by side with all this, for fifteen years or more, I was carrying out a literary exercise of a quite different kind: this was the making up of a continuous "story" about myself, a sort of diary existing only in the mind. I believe this is a common habit of children and adolescents. As a very small child I used to imagine that I was, say, Robin Hood, and picture myself as the hero of thrilling adventures, but quite soon my "story" ceased to be narcissistic in a crude way and became more and more a mere description of what I was doing and the things I saw. For minutes at a time this kind of thing would be running through my head: "He pushed the door open and entered the room. A yellow beam of sunlight, filtering through the muslin curtains, slanted on to the table, where a matchbox, half open, lay beside the inkpot. With his right hand in his pocket he moved across to the window. Down in the street a tortoiseshell cat was chasing a dead leaf," etc., etc. This habit continued till I was about twenty-five, right through my non-literary years. Although I had to search, and did search, for the right words, I seemed to be making this descriptive effort almost against my will, under a kind of compulsion from outside. The "story" must, I suppose, have reflected the styles of the various writers I admired at different ages, but so far as I remember it always had the same meticulous descriptive quality.

When I was about sixteen I suddenly discovered the joy of mere words, *i.e.* the sounds and associations of words. The lines from *Paradise Lost*—

> So hee with difficulty and labour hard
> Moved on: with difficulty and labour hee,

which do not now seem to me so very wonderful, sent shivers down my backbone; and the spelling "hee" for "he" was an added pleasure. As for the need to describe things, I knew all about it already. So it is clear what kind of books I wanted to write, in so far as I could be said to want to write books at that time. I wanted to write enormous naturalistic novels with unhappy endings, full of detailed descriptions and arresting similes, and also full of purple passages in which words were used partly for the sake of their sound. And in fact my first completed novel, *Burmese Days*, which I wrote when I was thirty but projected much earlier, is rather that kind of book.

I give all this background information because I do not think one can assess a writer's motives without knowing something of his early development. His subject matter will be determined by the age he lives in—at least this is true in tumultuous, revolutionary ages like our own—but before he ever begins to write he will have acquired an emotional attitude from which he will never completely escape. It is his job, no doubt, to discipline his temperament and avoid getting stuck at some immature stage, or in some perverse mood: but if he escapes from his early influences altogether, he will have killed his impulse to write. Putting aside the need to earn a living, I think there are four great motives for writing, at any rate for writing prose. They exist in different degrees in every writer, and in any one writer the proportions will vary from time to time, according to the atmosphere in which he is living. They are:

(1) Sheer egoism. Desire to seem clever, to be talked about, to be remembered after death, to get your own back on grownups who snubbed you in childhood, etc., etc. It is humbug to pretend that this is not a motive, and a strong one. Writers share this characteristic with scientists, artists, politicians, lawyers, soldiers, successful businessmen—in short, with the whole top crust of humanity. The great mass of human beings are not acutely selfish. After the age of about thirty they abandon individual ambition—in many cases, indeed, they almost abandon the sense of being individuals at all—and live chiefly for others, or are simply smothered under drudgery. But there is also the minority of gifted, wilful people who are determined to live their own lives to the end, and writers belong in this class. Serious writers, I should say, are on the whole more vain and self-centred than journalists, though less interested in money.

(2) Esthetic enthusiasm. Perception of beauty in the external world, or, on the other hand, in words and their right arrangement. Pleasure in the impact of one sound on another, in the firmness of good prose or the rhythm of a good story. Desire to share an experience which one feels is valuable and ought not to be missed. The esthetic motive is very feeble in a lot of writers, but even a pamphleteer or a writer of textbooks will have pet words and phrases which appeal to him for non-utilitarian reasons; or he may feel strongly about typography, width of margins, etc. Above the level of a railway guide, no book is quite free from esthetic considerations.

(3) Historical impulse. Desire to see things as they are, to find out true facts and store them up for the use of posterity.

(4) Political purpose—using the word "political" in the widest possible

sense. Desire to push the world in a certain direction, to alter other people's idea of the kind of society that they should strive after. Once again, no book is genuinely free from political bias. The opinion that art should have nothing to do with politics is itself a political attitude.

It can be seen how these various impulses must war against one another, and how they must fluctuate from person to person and from time to time. By nature—taking your "nature" to be the state you have attained when you are first adult—I am a person in whom the first three motives would outweigh the fourth. In a peaceful age I might have written ornate or merely descriptive books, and might have remained almost unaware of my political loyalties. As it is I have been forced into becoming a sort of pamphleteer. First I spent five years in an unsuitable profession (the Indian Imperial Police, in Burma), and then I underwent poverty and the sense of failure. This increased my natural hatred of authority and made me for the first time fully aware of the existence of the working classes, and the job in Burma had given me some understanding of the nature of imperialism: but these experiences were not enough to give me an accurate political orientation. Then came Hitler, the Spanish civil war, etc. By the end of 1935 I had still failed to reach a firm decision. I remember a little poem that I wrote at that date, expressing my dilemma:

> A happy vicar I might have been
> Two hundred years ago,
> To preach upon eternal doom
> And watch my walnuts grow;
>
> But born, alas, in an evil time,
> I missed that pleasant haven,
> For the hair has grown on my upper lip
> And the clergy are all clean-shaven.
>
> And later still the times were good,
> We were so easy to please,
> We rocked our troubled thoughts to sleep
> On the bosoms of the trees.
>
> All ignorant we dared to own
> The joys we now dissemble;
> The greenfinch on the apple bough
> Could make my enemies tremble.
>
> But girls' bellies and apricots,
> Roach in a shaded stream,
> Horses, ducks in flight at dawn,
> All these are a dream.
>
> It is forbidden to dream again;
> We maim our joys or hide them;

Horses are made of chromium steel
And little fat men shall ride them.

I am the worm who never turned,
The eunuch without a harem;
Between the priest and the commissar
I walk like Eugene Aram;

And the commissar is telling my fortune
While the radio plays,
But the priest has promised an Austin Seven,
For Duggie always pays.

I dreamed I dwelt in marble halls,
And woke to find it true;
I wasn't born for an age like this;
Was Smith? Was Jones? Were you?

The Spanish war and other events in 1936–7 turned the scale and thereafter I knew where I stood. Every line of serious work that I have written since 1936 has been written, directly or indirectly, *against* totalitarianism and *for* democratic socialism, as I understand it. It seems to me nonsense, in a period like our own, to think that one can avoid writing of such subjects. Everyone writes of them in one guise or another. It is simply a question of which side one takes and what approach one follows. And the more one is conscious of one's political bias, the more chance one has of acting politically without sacrificing one's esthetic and intellectual integrity.

What I have most wanted to do throughout the past ten years is to make political writing into an art. My starting point is always a feeling of partisanship, a sense of injustice. When I sit down to write a book, I do not say to myself, "I am going to produce a work of art." I write it because there is some lie that I want to expose, some fact to which I want to draw attention, and my initial concern is to get a hearing. But I could not do the work of writing a book, or even a long magazine article, if it were not also an esthetic experience. Anyone who cares to examine my work will see that even when it is downright propaganda it contains much that a full-time politician would consider irrelevant. I am not able, and I do not want, completely to abandon the world-view that I acquired in childhood. So long as I remain alive and well I shall continue to feel strongly about prose style, to love the surface of the earth, and to take a pleasure in solid objects and scraps of useless information. It is no use trying to suppress that side of myself. The job is to reconcile my ingrained likes and dislikes with the essentially public, non-individual activities that this age forces on all of us.

It is not easy. It raises problems of construction and of language, and it raises in a new way the problem of truthfulness. Let me give just one example of the cruder kind of difficulty that arises. My book about the Spanish civil war, *Homage to Catalonia*, is, of course, a frankly political book, but in the main it is written with a certain detachment and regard for form. I did try very hard in it to tell the whole truth without violating my literary instincts. But among other things it contains a long chapter, full of newspaper quotations and the like, defending the Trotskyists who were accused of plotting with Franco. Clearly such a chapter, which after a year or two would lose its interest for any ordinary reader, must ruin the book. A critic whom I respect read me a lecture about it. "Why did you put in all that stuff?" he said. "You've turned what might have been a good book into journalism." What he said was true, but I could not have done otherwise. I happened to know, what very few people in England had been allowed to know, that innocent men were being falsely accused. If I had not been angry about that I should never have written the book.

In one form or another this problem comes up again. The problem of language is subtler and would take too long to discuss. I will only say that of late years I have tried to write less picturesquely and more exactly. In any case I find that by the time you have perfected any style of writing, you have always outgrown it. *Animal Farm* was the first book in which I tried, with full consciousness of what I was doing, to fuse political purpose and artistic purpose into one whole. I have not written a novel for seven years, but I hope to write another fairly soon. It is bound to be a failure, every book is a failure, but I do know with some clarity what kind of book I want to write.

Looking back through the last page or two, I see that I have made it appear as though my motives in writing were wholly public-spirited. I don't want to leave that as the final impression. All writers are vain, selfish and lazy, and at the very bottom of their motives there lies a mystery. Writing a book is a horrible, exhausting struggle, like a long bout of some painful illness. One would never undertake such a thing if one were not driven on by some demon whom one can neither resist nor understand. For all one knows that demon is simply the same instinct that makes a baby squall for attention. And yet it is also true that one can write nothing readable unless one constantly struggles to efface one's own personality. Good prose is like a window pane. I cannot say with certainty which of my motives are the strongest, but I know which of them deserve to be followed. And looking back through my work, I see that it is invariably where I lacked a *political* purpose that I wrote lifeless books and was betrayed into purple passages, sentences without meaning, decorative adjectives and humbug generally.

[1947]

THOMAS DE QUINCEY

De Quincey (1785–1859) is most popularly known for his Confessions of an English Opium-Eater *(1822), based on an addiction that had begun with his taking opium for pain. He was, however, a very wide-ranging writer on other subjects, and a good literary critic. He attended Oxford University, became for a time closely associated with the poets Wordsworth and Coleridge, was a friend of the essayist Charles Lamb, and was an important contributor to the leading literary periodicals of his time. It is from a long review of "The Works of Alexander Pope, Esquire. By W. Roscoe, Esq." in the August, 1848,* North British Review *that we take the following passage, almost an essay in itself and traditionally given the present title.*

THE LITERATURE OF KNOWLEDGE AND THE LITERATURE OF POWER

What is it that we mean by *literature?* Popularly, and amongst the thoughtless, it is held to include everything that is printed in a book. Little logic is required to disturb *that* definition; the most thoughtless person is easily made aware that in the idea of *literature* one essential element is—some relation to a general and common interest of man, so that what applies only to a local—or professional—or merely personal interest, even though presenting itself in the shape of a book, will not belong to literature. So far the definition is easily narrowed; and it is as easily expanded. For not only is much that takes a station in books not literature; but inversely, much that really *is* literature never reaches a station in books. The weekly sermons of Christendom, that vast pulpit literature which acts so extensively upon the popular mind—to warn, to uphold, to renew, to comfort, to alarm, does not attain the sanctuary of libraries in the ten thousandth part of its extent. The drama again, as, for instance, the finest of Shakspere's plays in England, and all leading Athenian plays in the noontide of the Attic stage, operated as a literature on the public mind, and were (according to the strictest letter of that term) *published* through the audiences that witnessed[1] their representation some time before they were published as things to be read; and they were published in this scenical mode of publication with much more effect than they could have had as books, during ages of costly copying or of costly printing.

Books, therefore, do not suggest an idea co-extensive and interchangeable with the idea of literature; since much literature, scenic, forensic, or didactic, (as from lecturers and public orators,) may never come into books; and much that *does* come into books, may connect itself with no literary interest. But a far more important correction, applicable to the common vague idea of literature, is to be sought—not so much in a better definition of literature, as in a sharper distinction of the two functions which it fulfils. In that great social organ, which collectively we call literature, there may be distinguished two separate offices that may blend and often *do* so, but capable severally of a severe insulation, and naturally fitted for reciprocal repulsion. There is first the literature of *knowledge,* and secondly, the literature of *power.* The function of the first is—to *teach;* the function of the second is—to *move:* the first is a rudder, the second an oar or a sail. The first speaks to the *mere* discursive understanding; the second speaks ultimately it may happen to the higher understanding or reason, but always *through* affections of pleasure and sympathy. Remotely, it may travel towards an object seated in what Lord Bacon calls *dry* light; but proximately it does and must operate, else it ceases to be a literature of *power,* on and through that *humid* light which clothes itself in the mists and glittering *iris* of human passions, desires, and genial emotions. Men have so little reflected on the higher functions of literature, as to find it a paradox if one should describe it as a mean or subordinate purpose of books to give information. But this is a paradox only in the sense which makes it honourable to be paradoxical. Whenever we talk in ordinary language of seeking information or gaining knowledge, we understand the words as connected with something of absolute novelty. But it is the grandeur of all truth which *can* occupy a very high place in human interests, that it is never absolutely novel to the meanest of minds: it exists eternally by way of germ or latent principle in the lowest as in the highest, needing to be developed but never to be planted. To be capable of transplantation is the immediate criterion of a truth that ranges on a lower scale. Besides which, there is a rarer thing than truth, namely, *power* or deep sympathy

---

[1] Charles I., for example, when Prince of Wales, and many others in his father's court, gained their known familiarity with Shakspere—not through the original quartos, so slenderly diffused, nor through the first folio of 1623, but through the court representations of his chief dramas at Whitehall.

with truth. What is the effect, for instance, upon society—of children? By the pity, by the tenderness, and by the peculiar modes of admiration, which connect themselves with the helplessness, with the innocence, and with the simplicity of children, not only are the primal affections strengthened and continually renewed, but the qualities which are dearest in the sight of heaven—the frailty for instance, which appeals to forbearance, the innocence which symbolizes the heavenly, and the simplicity which is most alien from the worldly, are kept up in perpetual remembrance, and their ideals are continually refreshed. A purpose of the same nature is answered by the higher literature, viz. the literature of power. What do you learn from Paradise Lost? Nothing at all. What do you learn from a cookery-book? Something new, something that you did not know before, in every paragraph. But would you therefore put the wretched cookery-book on a higher level of estimation than the divine poem? What you owe to Milton is not any knowledge, of which a million separate items are still but a million of advancing steps on the same earthly level; what you owe—is *power*, that is, exercise and expansion to your own latent capacity of sympathy with the infinite, where every pulse and each separate influx is a step upwards—a step ascending as upon a Jacob's ladder from earth to mysterious altitudes above the earth. *All* the steps of knowledge, from first to last, carry you farther on the same plane, but could never raise you one foot above your ancient level of earth: whereas, the very *first* step in power is a flight —is an ascending into another element where earth is forgotten.

Were it not that human sensibilities are ventilated and continually called out into exercise by the great phenomena of infancy, or of real life as it moves through chance and change, or of literature as it recombines these elements in the mimicries of poetry, romance, &c., it is certain that, like any animal power or muscular energy falling into disuse, all such sensibilities would gradually droop and dwindle. It is in relation to these great *moral* capacities of man that the literature of power, as contra-distinguished from that of knowledge, lives and has its field of action. It is concerned with what is highest in man: for the Scriptures themselves never condescend to deal by suggestion or co-operation, with the mere discursive understanding: when speaking of man in his intellectual capacity, the Scriptures speak not of the understanding, but of *"the understanding heart,"*—making the heart, i. e., the great *intuitive* (or non-discursive) organ, to be the interchangeable formula for man in his highest state of capacity for the infinite. Tragedy, romance, fairy-tale, or epopee, all alike restore to man's mind the ideals of justice, of hope, of truth, of mercy, of retribution, which else, (left to the support of daily life in its realities,) would languish for want of sufficient illustration. What is meant for instance by *poetic justice?*—It does not mean a justice that differs by its object from the ordinary justice of human jurisprudence; for then it must be confessedly a very bad kind of justice; but it means a justice that differs from common forensic justice by the degree in which it *attains* its object, a justice that is more omnipotent over its own ends, as dealing—not with the refractory elements of earthly life—but with elements of its own creation, and with materials flexible to its own purest preconceptions. It is certain that, were it not for the literature of power, these ideals would often remain amongst us as mere arid notional forms; whereas, by the creative forces of man put forth in literature, they gain a vernal life of restoration, and germinate into vital activities. The commonest novel, by moving in alliance with human fears and hopes, with human instincts of wrong and right, sustains and quickens those affections. Calling them into action, it rescues them from torpor. And hence the pre-eminency over all authors that merely *teach*, of the meanest that *moves;* or that teaches, if at all, indirectly *by* moving. The very highest work that has ever existed in the literature of knowledge, is but a *provisional* work: a book upon trial and sufferance, and *quamdiu bene se gesserit*. Let its teaching be even partially revised, let it be but expanded, nay, even let its teaching be but placed in a better order, and instantly it is superseded. Whereas the feeblest works in the literature of power, surviving at all, survive as finished and unalterable amongst men. For instance, the *Principia* of Sir Isaac Newton was a book *militant* on earth from the first. In all stages of its progress it would have to fight for its existence: 1*st*, as regards absolute truth; 2*dly*, when that combat is over, as regards its form or mode of presenting the truth. And as soon as a La Place, or anybody else, builds higher upon the foundations laid by this book, effectually he throws it out of the sunshine into decay and darkness; by weapons won from this book he superannuates and destroys this book, so that soon the name of Newton remains, as a mere *nominis umbra*, but his book, as a living power, has transmigrated into other forms. Now, on the contrary, the Iliad, the Prometheus of Æschylus,—the Othello or King Lear,—the Hamlet or Macbeth,—and the Paradise Lost, are not militant but triumphant for ever as long as the languages exist in which they speak or can be taught to speak. They never *can* transmigrate into new incarnations. To reproduce *these* in new forms, or variations, even if in some things they should be improved, would be to plagiarize. A good steam-engine is properly superseded by a better. But one lovely pastoral valley is not superseded by another, nor a statue of Praxiteles by a statue of Michael Angelo. These things are not separated by imparity, but by disparity. They are not thought of as unequal under the same standard, but as differing in *kind*, and as equal under a different standard. Human works of immortal beauty and works of nature in one respect stand on the same footing: they never absolutely repeat each other: never approach so near as not to differ; and they differ not as better and worse, or simply by more and less: they differ by undecipherable and incommunicable differences, that cannot be caught by mimicries, nor be reflected in the mirror of copies, nor become ponderable in the scales of vulgar comparison.

Applying these principles to Pope, as a representative of fine literature in general, we would wish to remark the claim which he has, or which any equal writer has, to the attention and jealous winnowing of those critics in particular who watch over public morals. Clergymen, and all the organs of public criticism put in motion by clergymen, are more especially concerned in the just appreciation of such writers, if the two canons are remembered, which we have endeavoured to illustrate, viz., that all works in this class, as opposed to those in the literature of knowledge, 1st, work by far deeper agencies; and, 2dly, are more permanent; in the strictest sense they are κτήματα ἐς ἀεί [possessions forever]: and what evil they do, or what good they do, is commensurate with the national language, sometimes long after the nation has departed. At this hour, 500 years since their creation, the tales of Chaucer,[2] never equalled on this earth for tenderness, and for life of picturesqueness, are read familiarly by many in the charming language of their natal day, and by others in the modernizations of Dryden, of Pope, and Wordsworth. At this hour, 1800 years since their creation, the Pagan tales of Ovid, never equalled on this earth for the gaiety of their movement and the capricious graces of their narrative, are read by all Christendom. This man's people and their monuments are dust: but *he* is alive: he has survived them, as he told us that he had it in his commission to do, by a thousand years; "and *shall* a thousand more."

All the literature of knowledge builds only ground-nests, that are swept away by floods, or confounded by the plough; but the literature of power builds nests in aerial altitudes of temples sacred from violation, or of forests inaccessible to fraud. *This* is a great prerogative of the *power* literature: and it is a greater which lies in the mode of its influence. The *knowledge* literature, like the fashion of this world, passeth away. An Encyclopædia is its abstract; and, in this respect, it may be taken for its speaking symbol—that, before one generation has passed, an Encyclopædia is superannuated; for it speaks through the dead memory and unimpassioned understanding, which have not the *rest* of higher faculties, but are continually enlarging and varying their phylacteries. But all literature, properly so called—literature κατ᾽ ἐξοχην [i.e., great literature], for the very same reason that it is so much more durable than the literature of knowledge, is (and by the very same proportion it is) more intense and electrically searching in its impressions. The directions in which the tragedy of this planet has trained our human feelings to play, and the combinations into which the poetry of this planet has thrown our human passions of love and hatred, of admiration and contempt, exercises

---

[2] The Canterbury Tales were not made public until 1380 or thereabouts: but the composition must have cost 30 or more years; not to mention that the work had probably been finished for some years before it was divulged.

a power bad or good over human life, that cannot be contemplated when seen stretching through many generations, without a sentiment allied to awe.[3] And of this let every one be assured—that he owes to the impassioned books which he has read, many a thousand more of emotions than he can consciously trace back to them. Dim by their origination, these emotions yet arise in him, and mould him through life like the forgotten incidents of childhood.

---

[3] The reason why the broad distinctions between the two literatures of power and knowledge so little fix the attention, lies in the fact, that a vast proportion of books—history, biography, travels, miscellaneous essays, &c., lying in a middle zone, confound these distinctions by interblending them. All that we call "amusement" or "entertainment," is a diluted form of the power belonging to passion, and also a mixed form; and where threads of direct *instruction* intermingle in the texture with these threads of *power*, this absorption of the duality into one representative *nuance* neutralises the separate perception of either. Fused into a *tertium quid*, or neutral state, they disappear to the popular eye as the repelling forces, which in fact they are.

WALTER PATER

Pater (1839–1894) spent most of his life as a student and Fellow at Oxford. His great reputation as an essayist and critic is partly based on the many articles on literature and art he published in the serious reviews of his time. A trip to Italy in 1865 sharpened his already great interest in the visual arts, and his resulting essays on renaissance subjects were collected and published in 1873 as Studies in the History of the Renaissance. *The present essay is the book's "Conclusion," as it appeared in the third edition of this work (1888). It was printed with the following note: "This brief 'Conclusion' was omitted in the second edition of this book, as I conceived it might possibly mislead some of those young men into whose hands it might fall. On the whole, I have thought it best to reprint it here, with some slight changes which bring it closer to my original meaning. I have dealt more fully in* Marius the Epicurean *with the thoughts suggested by it."* Marius the Epicurean *is Pater's most famous longer work, a "philosophical romance" about the intellectual and spiritual life of a young Roman of the time of Marcus Aurelius. It is written in the rich, polished*

style for which Pater is noted, and expounds in great detail the author's own philosophy of beauty.

CONCLUSION FROM
THE RENAISSANCE

Λέγει που Ἡράκλειτος ὅτι πάντα χωρεῖ καὶ οὐδὲν μένει

[Heraclitus says somewhere that all things move and nothing stays]

To regard all things and principles of things as inconstant modes or fashions has more and more become the tendency of modern thought. Let us begin with that which is without—our physical life. Fix upon it in one of its more exquisite intervals, the moment, for instance, of delicious recoil from the flood of water in summer heat. What is the whole physical life in that moment but a combination of natural elements to which science gives their names? But these elements, phosphorus and lime and delicate fibres, are present not in the human body alone: we detect them in places most remote from it. Our physical life is a perpetual motion of them— the passage of the blood, the wasting and repairing of the lenses of the eye, the modification of the tissues of the brain by every ray of light and sound—processes which science reduces to simpler and more elementary forces. Like the elements of which we are composed, the action of these forces extends beyond us; it rusts iron and ripens corn. Far out on every side of us those elements are broadcast, driven by many forces; and birth and gesture and death and the springing of violets from the grave are but a few out of ten thousand resultant combinations. That clear, perpetual outline of face and limb is but an image of ours, under which we group them—a design in a web, the actual threads of which pass out beyond it. This at least of flamelike our life has, that it is but the concurrence, renewed from moment to moment, of forces parting sooner or later on their ways.

Or if we begin with the inward world of thought and feeling, the whirlpool is still more rapid, the flame more eager and devouring. There it is no longer the gradual darkening of the eye and fading of colour from the wall,—the movement of the shore-side, where the water flows down indeed, though in apparent rest,—but the race of the midstream, a drift of momentary acts of sight and passion and thought. At first sight experience seems to bury us under a flood of external objects, pressing upon us with a sharp and importunate reality, calling us out of ourselves in a thousand forms of action. But when reflexion begins to act upon those objects they are dissipated under its influence; the cohesive force seems suspended like a trick of magic; each object is loosed into a group of impressions—colour, odour, texture—in the mind of the observer. And if we continue to dwell in thought on this world, not of objects in the solidity with which language invests them, but of impressions unstable, flickering, inconsistent, which burn and are extinguished with our consciousness of them, it contracts still further; the whole scope of observation is dwarfed to the narrow chamber of the individual mind. Experience, already reduced to a swarm of impressions, is ringed round for each one of us by that thick wall of personality through which no real voice has ever pierced on its way to us, or from us to that which we can only conjecture to be without. Every one of those impressions is the impression of the individual in his isolation, each mind keeping as a solitary prisoner its own dream of a world. Analysis goes a step farther still, and assures us that those impressions of the individual mind to which, for each one of us, experience dwindles down, are in perpetual flight; that each of them is limited by time, and that as time is infinitely divisible, each of them is infinitely divisible also; all that is actual in it being a single moment, gone while we try to apprehend it, of which it may ever be more truly said that it has ceased to be than that it is. To such a tremulous wisp constantly reforming itself on the stream, to a single sharp impression, with a sense in it, a relic more or less fleeting, of such moments gone by, what is real in our life fines itself down. It is with this movement, with the passage and dissolution of impressions, images, sensations, that analysis leaves off—that continual vanishing away, that strange, perpetual weaving and unweaving of ourselves.

Philosophiren, says Novalis, *ist dephlegmatisiren vivificiren*. The service of philosophy, of speculative culture, towards the human spirit is to rouse, to startle it into sharp and eager observation. Every moment some form grows perfect in hand or face; some tone on the hills or the sea is choicer than the rest; some mood of passion or insight or intellectual excitement is irresistibly real and attractive for us,—for that moment only. Not the fruit of experience, but experience itself, is the end. A counted number of pulses only is given to us of a variegated, dramatic life. How may we see in them all that is to be seen in them by the finest senses? How shall we pass most swiftly from point to point, and be present always at the focus where the greatest number of vital forces unite in their purest energy?

To burn always with this hard, gemlike flame, to maintain this ecstasy, is success in life. In a sense it might even be said that our failure is to form habits: for, after all, habit is relative to a stereotyped world, and meantime it is only the roughness of the eye that makes any two persons, things, situations, seem alike. While all melts under our feet, we may well catch at any exquisite passion, or any contribution to knowledge that seems by a lifted horizon to set the spirit free for a moment, or any stirring of the senses, strange dyes, strange colours, and curious odours, or work of the artist's hands, or the face of one's friend. Not to discriminate every

moment some passionate attitude in those about us, and in the brilliancy
of their gifts some tragic dividing of forces on their ways, is, on this short
day of frost and sun, to sleep before evening. With this sense of the
splendour of our experience and of its awful brevity, gathering all we
are into one desperate effort to see and touch, we shall hardly have time
to make theories about the things we see and touch. What we have to do
is to be for ever curiously testing new opinions and courting new impressions, never acquiescing in a facile orthodoxy of Comte, or of Hegel,
or of our own. Philosophical theories or ideas, as points of view, instruments of criticism, may help us to gather up what might otherwise pass
unregarded by us. "Philosophy is the microscope of thought." The theory
or idea or system which requires of us the sacrifice of any part of this
experience, in consideration of some interest into which we cannot enter,
or some abstract theory we have not identified with ourselves, or what
is only conventional, has no real claim upon us.

One of the most beautiful passages in the writings of Rousseau is that
in the sixth book of the *Confessions*, where he describes the awakening
in him of the literary sense. An undefinable taint of death had always
clung about him, and now in early manhood he believed himself smitten
by mortal disease. He asked himself how he might make as much as
possible of the interval that remained; and he was not biassed by anything
in his previous life when he decided that it must be by intellectual excitement, which he found just then in the clear, fresh writings of Voltaire.
Well! we are all *condamnés*, as Victor Hugo says: we are all under sentence of death but with a sort of indefinite reprieve—*les hommes sont
tous condamnés à mort avec des sursis indéfinis:* we have an interval, and
then our place knows us no more. Some spend this interval in listlessness,
some in high passions, the wisest, at least among "the children of this
world," in art and song. For our one chance lies in expanding that interval,
in getting as many pulsations as possible into the given time. Great passions may give us this quickened sense of life, ecstasy and sorrow of love,
the various forms of enthusiastic activity, disinterested or otherwise,
which come naturally to many of us. Only be sure it is passion—that it
does yield you this fruit of a quickened, multiplied consciousness. Of
this wisdom, the poetic passion, the desire of beauty, the love of art for
art's sake, has most; for art comes to you professing frankly to give
nothing but the highest quality to your moments as they pass, and simply
for those moments' sake.

GILBERT HIGHET

Gilbert Highet, classical scholar, teacher, and writer, was born in Scotland in 1906. Educated at the University of Glasgow and Oxford University, he was appointed Fellow and Lecturer in Classics at St. John's College, Oxford, where he taught for five years and edited a literary and political review, New Oxford Outlook. *In 1937 he came to the United States to join the faculty of Columbia University where he now holds a professorship in Latin. Mr. Highet was chief book reviewer for* Harper's, *a post he left in 1954 to become an editor of the Book-of-the-Month Club. His own writings include* The Classical Tradition *(1949),* The Art of Teaching *(1950),* People, Places, and Books *(1953),* A Clerk of Oxenford *(1954), from which we reprint the essay below,* The Powers of Poetry *(1960), and* The Anatomy of Satire *(1962).*

WHAT USE IS POETRY?

Children ask lots and lots of questions, about religion, about sex, about the stars. But there are some questions which they never ask: they leave grown-ups to ask them and to answer them. Often this means that the questions are silly: that they are questions about nonexistent problems, or questions to which the answer is obvious. Sometimes it means that the questions *should* be asked, but that the answer is difficult or multiplex.

So, children never ask what is the good of music. They just like singing and dancing, and even drumming on a low note of the piano. In the same way, they never ask what is the use of poetry. They all enjoy poems and songs, and very often come to like them before they can even talk properly; but it never occurs to them that they ought to find reasons for their enjoyment. But grown-ups do inquire about the justification of poetry: they ask what is the point of putting words in a special order and extracting special sound effects from them, instead of speaking plainly and directly. And often—because they get no adequate answer, either from the poets or from the professors—they conclude that poetry is only a set of tricks like conjuring, or a complicated game like chess; and they turn away from it in discouragement . . . until, perhaps, a poetic film like *Henry V* shocks them into realizing something of its power; or, as they grow older, they find that a poem learned in childhood sticks in their mind and becomes clearer and more beautiful with age.

What is the use of poetry?

There must be a number of different answers to the question. Just as a picture can be meant to give pleasure, or to carry a puzzle, or to convey information, so poems are meant for many different things. We can begin to get some of the answers if we look at the poetry that children them-selves naturally enjoy, and then see how it is connected with the most famous grown-up poems.

The first pleasure of poetry is the simplest. It is the same pleasure that we have in music—the pleasure of following a pattern of sound. Everyone loves talking, and most people like what might be called doodling in sound. So, if you look through the *Oxford Dictionary of Nursery Rhymes*, you will find several tongue-twisters, like this:

> Peter Piper picked a peck of pickled pepper;
> A peck of pickled pepper Peter Piper picked;
> If Peter Piper picked a peck of pickled pepper,
> Where's the peck of pickled pepper Peter Piper picked?

On a grown-up level, many a famous poem is little more than a pattern of sound: for instance, Shakespeare's love song:

> It was a lover and his lass,
>   With a hey and a ho and a hey nonino,
> That o'er the green cornfield did pass,
>   In the spring time, the only pretty ring time,
>   When birds do sing, hey ding a ding ding;
>   Sweet lovers love the spring.

Much of the best poetry of Swinburne is pattern-making in sound, with a very light core of meaning. Here are four exquisite lines which really mean very little more than the sound of spring showers:

> When the hounds of spring are on winter's traces,
>   The mother of months in meadow or plain
> Fills the shadows and windy places
>   With lisp of leaves and ripple of rain.

Small meaning, but lovely rhythm and melody.

Now, there is a second pleasure in poetry. This is that it is sometimes better than prose for telling a story. It even gives authority to a story which is illogical or incredible, or even gruesome. That is one reason children love the poem that tells of the tragic fate of Jack and Jill. There is an interesting variant of it: the cumulative story, in which one detail is piled up on another until the whole story has been set forth with the simple exactitude of a primitive painting: for instance, 'The House That Jack Built,' and the funeral elegy, 'Who Killed Cock Robin?' and the famous old Jewish rhyme, 'Had Gadyo,' about the kid bought for two pieces of money—which is said to symbolize a vast stretch of the history of the Jewish people. Another variant is the limerick, which is simply a funny story in verse. Many a man who would protest that he knew no poetry, and cared nothing for it, could still recite eight or ten limericks in the right company.

In serious adult poetry there are many superb stories, including the two oldest books in Western literature, the *Iliad* and the *Odyssey*. Every good collection of poems will include some of the most dramatic tales ever told, the English and Scottish ballads, which are still occasionally sung in our own southern states. One of the strangest things about the stories told as ballads is their terrible abruptness and directness. They leave out a great deal. They give only a few details, a name or two; they draw the outlines, harsh and black or blood-red, and they concentrate on the actions and the passions. Such is the ballad about an ambush in which a knight was killed by his own wife's brother. It is called 'The Dowie Houms of Yarrow' (that means the sad fields beside the river Yarrow, in the Scottish borders), and it opens immediately with the quarrel, almost with the clash of swords:

> Late at een, drinkin' the wine,
>   And ere they paid the lawin',
> They set a combat them between,
>   To fight it in the dawin'.

Within only a few verses, the knight has been surrounded, and treacherously murdered, fighting against heavy odds; and when his widow goes out to find his body, her anguish is described in one of the most terrible stanzas in all poetry:

> She kissed his cheek, she kamed his hair,
>   As oft she did before, O;
> She drank the red blood frae him ran,
>   On the dowie houms o' Yarrow.

That story in poetry and a few others like 'Edward, Edward'—in which a mother persuades her son to kill his own father, and drives him mad—are absolutely unforgettable.

But besides storytelling, poetry has another use, known all over the world. This is mnemonic. Put words into a pattern, and they are easier to remember. I should never have known the lengths of the months if I had not learned:

> Thirty days hath September,
> April, June, and November;
> All the rest have thirty-one,
> Excepting February alone,
> And that has twenty-eight days clear
> And twenty-nine in each leap year.

This is certainly four hundred years old, for it occurs in an English manuscript dated about 1555, and there is a French poem, with the same rhyme scheme, written three hundred years earlier. (It might be easier to change the calendar, but mankind is by nature conservative.) On a simpler level there are many nursery rhymes in every language which are designed to teach children the very simplest things; for instance, counting and performing easy actions:

> One, two,
> Buckle my shoe,
> Three, four,
> Shut the door.

And even earlier, before the child can speak, he is lucky if his mother can recite the poem that goes over his five toes or fingers, one after another:

> This little pig went to market,
> This little pig stayed at home,

up to the comical climax when the child is meant to squeak too, and to enjoy staying at home.

Adults also remember facts better if they are put into verse. Nearly every morning I repeat to myself:

> Early to bed and early to rise
> Makes a man healthy and wealthy and wise.

And nearly every evening I change it to Thurber's parody:

> Early to rise and early to bed
> Makes a male healthy and wealthy and dead;

or occasionally to George Ade's variant:

> Early to bed and early to rise
> Will make you miss all the regular guys.

This is the source of what they call didactic poetry, poetry meant to teach. The best-known example of it is the Book of Proverbs in the Bible, which ought to be translated into rhythmical prose, or even verse. The third oldest book in Greek literature, not much younger than Homer, is a farmer's handbook all set out in poetry, so that it could be learned off by heart and remembered: it is the *Works and Days* by Hesiod. To teach has long been one of the highest functions of the poet: great poetry can be written in order to carry a message of philosophical or practical truth—or sometimes an ironical counsel, as in this strange poem by Sir Walter Scott:

> Look not thou on beauty's charming;
> Sit thou still when kings are arming;
> Taste not when the winecup glistens;
> Speak not when the people listens;
> Stop thine ear against the singer;
> From the red gold keep thy finger;
> Vacant heart and hand and eye,
> Easy live and quiet die.

There is one peculiar variation on the poem that conveys information. This is the riddle poem, which tells you something—but only if you are smart enough to see through its disguise. There are some such riddles in the Bible: Samson created a good one, about the dead lion with a hive of wild bees inside it. Legend has it that Homer died of chagrin because he could not solve a rather sordid poetic puzzle. The nursery rhyme 'Humpty Dumpty' was really a riddle to begin with (before Lewis Carroll and his illustrator gave it away). We are supposed to guess what was the mysterious person or thing which fell down, and then could not possibly be put together again, not even by all the king's horses and all the king's men, and nowadays by all the republic's scientific experts: the answer is an egg. There is a beautiful folk song made up of three such riddles: the cherry without a stone, the chicken without a bone, and the baby that does not cry. It is at least five hundred years old, and yet for four hundred years it was passed on from one singer to another, without ever being printed.

Again, there are some famous and splendid poems that deal with mystical experience in riddling terms, phrases which have two meanings, or three, or one concealed: these are also didactic, informative, and yet riddles. One such poem, by an American poet, deals with the paradox of God—the complete God, who includes all the appearances of the universe, both the appearance of good and the appearance of evil. This is Emerson's 'Brahma.'

> If the red slayer think he slays,
> Or if the slain think he is slain,

They know not well the subtle ways
    I keep, and pass, and turn again.

Far or forgot to me is near;
    Shadow and sunlight are the same;
The vanished gods to me appear;
    And one to me are shame and fame.

They reckon ill who leave me out;
    When me they fly, I am the wings;
I am the doubter and the doubt,
    And I the hymn the Brahmin sings.

The strong gods pine for my abode,
    And pine in vain the sacred Seven;
But thou, meek lover of the good!
    Find me, and turn thy back on heaven.

This is a riddle which is meant not for children but for adults. There are similar riddles in the Bible, sometimes equally beautiful. Such is the meditation on old age at the end of that mysterious and rather unorthodox book called *Koheleth,* or *Ecclesiastes:*

Remember now thy Creator in the days of thy youth,
    while the evil days come not,
     nor the years draw nigh, when thou shalt say, I have
                            no pleasure in them;

while the sun or the light or the moon or the stars be
    not darkened, nor the clouds return after the rain;

in the day when the keepers of the house shall tremble,
    and the strong men shall bow themselves,
    and the grinders cease because they are few,
    and those that look out of the windows be darkened,
and the doors shall be shut in the streets,
    when the sound of the grinding is low,
    and he shall rise up at the voice of the bird,
    and all the daughters of music shall be brought low,
also when they shall be afraid of that which is high,
    and fears shall be in the way,
    and the almond tree shall flourish,
    and the grasshopper shall be a burden,
    and desire shall fail:
      because man goeth to his long home
      and the mourners go about the streets;

or ever the silver cord be loosed,
    or the golden bowl be broken,

> or the pitcher be broken at the fountain
> or the wheel broken at the cistern.

> Then shall the dust return to the earth as it was;
> and the spirit shall return unto God who gave it.

All these enigmatic and memorable phrases are descriptions of the symptoms of the last and almost the bitterest fact in life, old age. They show that it is pathetic, and yet they make it beautiful.

Such poetry is unusual. Or rather, its manner is unusual and its subject is a fact of common experience. It is possible for poets to speak plainly and frankly about everyday life; and that is one more of the uses of poetry—one of the best known. Poetry can express general experience: can say what many men and women have thought and felt. The benefit of this is that it actually helps ordinary people, by giving them words. Most of us are not eloquent. Most of us—especially in times of intense emotion—cannot say what we feel; often we hardly know what we feel. There, in our heart, there is the turmoil, be it love or protest or exultation or despair: it stirs us, but all our gestures and words are inadequate. As the emotion departs, we know that an opportunity was somehow missed, an opportunity of realizing a great moment to the full. It is in this field that poetry comes close to religion. Religion is one of the experiences which the ordinary man finds most difficult to compass in words. Therefore he nearly always falls back on phrases which have been composed for him by someone more gifted. Many, many thousands of times, in battles and concentration camps and hospitals, beside death beds, and even on death beds, men and women have repeated a very ancient poem only six verses long, and have found comfort in it, such as no words of their own would have brought them. It begins, 'The Lord is my shepherd; I shall not want.'

If we look at poetry or any of the arts from this point of view, we shall gain a much greater respect for them. They are not amusements or decorations; they are aids to life. Ordinary men and women find living rather difficult. One of their chief difficulties is to apprehend their own thoughts and feelings, and to respond to them by doing the right things and saying the right sentences. It is the poets who supply the words and sentences. They too have felt as we do, but they have been able to speak, while we are dumb.

Not only that. By expressing common emotions clearly and eloquently, the poets help us to understand them in other people. It is difficult to understand—for any grown-up it is difficult to understand—what goes on in the mind of a boy or girl. Parents are often so anxious and serious that they have forgotten what it was like to be young, and vague, and romantic. It is a huge effort, rather an unpleasantly arduous effort, to think oneself back into boyhood. Yet there are several poems which will allow us to understand it, and even to enjoy the experience. One of them is a fine lyric by Longfellow, called 'My Lost Youth':

> I remember the gleams and glooms that dart
>   Across the schoolboy's brain;
> The song and the silence in the heart,
> That in part are prophecies, and in part
>   Are longings wild and vain.
>   And the voice of that fitful song
>   Sings on, and is never still:
>   'A boy's will is the wind's will,
> And the thoughts of youth are long, long thoughts.'
>
> There are things of which I may not speak;
>   There are dreams that cannot die;
> There are thoughts that make the strong heart weak,
> And bring a pallor into the cheek,
>   And a mist before the eye.
>   And the words of that fatal song
>   Come over me like a chill:
>   'A boy's will is the wind's will,
> And the thoughts of youth are long, long thoughts.'

If you have a young son who seems to be woolgathering half the time, and who sometimes does not even answer when he is spoken to, you should read and reflect on that poem of Longfellow.

This function of poetry is not the only one, but it is one of the most vital: to give adequate expression to important general experiences. In 1897, when Queen Victoria celebrated her Diamond Jubilee, the Poet Laureate was that completely inadequate little fellow, Alfred Austin; but the man who wrote the poem summing up the emotions most deeply felt during the Jubilee was Rudyard Kipling. It is called 'Recessional.' It is a splendid poem, almost a hymn—Biblical in its phrasing and deeply prophetic in its thought:

> The tumult and the shouting dies—
>   The captains and the kings depart—
> Still stands Thine ancient sacrifice,
>   An humble and a contrite heart.
> Lord God of Hosts, be with us yet,
> Lest we forget, lest we forget!

However, as you think over the poems you know, you will realize that many of them seem to be quite different from this. They are not even trying to do the same thing. They do not express important general experiences in universally acceptable words. On the contrary, they express strange and individual experiences in abstruse and sometimes unintelligible words. We enjoy them not because they say what we have often thought but because they say what we should never have dreamed of thinking. If a poem like Kipling's 'Recessional' or Longfellow's 'Lost Youth' is close to religion, then this other kind of poetry is close to magic: its words sound like spells; its subjects are often dreams, visions, and myths.

Such are the two most famous poems by Coleridge: 'The Ancient Mariner' and 'Kubla Khan.' They are scarcely understandable. They are unbelievable. Beautiful, yes, and haunting, yes, but utterly illogical; crazy. Coleridge himself scarcely knew their sources, deep in his memory and his subconscious—sources on which a modern scholar has written a superb book. Both of them end with a mystical experience that none of us has ever had: 'The Ancient Mariner' telling how, like the Wandering Jew, he must travel forever from country to country, telling his story with 'strange power of speech'; and 'Kubla Khan' with the poet himself creating a magical palace:

> I would build that dome in air,
> That sunny dome! those caves of ice!
> And all who heard should see them there,
> And all should cry, Beware! Beware!
> His flashing eyes, his floating hair!
> Weave a circle round him thrice,
> > And close your eyes with holy dread,
> > For he on honey-dew hath fed,
> And drunk the milk of Paradise.

Not long after those fantastic verses were written, young Keats was composing a lyric, almost equally weird, which is now considered one of the finest odes in the English language. It ends with the famous words which we all know, and which few of us believe:

> Beauty is truth, truth beauty,—that is all
> Ye know on earth, and all ye need to know.

It is the 'Ode on a Grecian Urn'; but how many of us have ever stood, like Keats, meditating on the paintings that surround a Greek vase? and, even if we have, how many of us have thought that

> Heard melodies are sweet, but those unheard
> Are sweeter?

It is a paradox. The entire ode is a paradox: not an expression of ordinary life, but an extreme extension of it, almost a direct contradiction of usual experience.

Most modern poetry is like this. It tells of things almost unknown to ordinary men and women, even to children. If it has power over them at all, it is because it enchants them by its strangeness. Such is the poetry of Verlaine, and Mallarmé, and Rimbaud; of the difficult and sensitive Austrian poet Rilke; in our own language, such is most of Auden's poetry, and Ezra Pound's; and what could be more unusual than most of T. S. Eliot—although he is the most famous poet writing today? Suppose we test this. Let us take something simple. Spring. What have the poets said about the first month of spring, about April? Most of them say it is charming and frail:

> April, April,
> Laugh thy girlish laughter;
> Then, the moment after,
> Weep thy girlish tears!

That is Sir William Watson: turn back, and see Shakespeare talking of

> The uncertain glory of an April day;

turn forward, and hear Browning cry

> O to be in England
> Now that April's there!

and then hundreds of years earlier, see Chaucer beginning his *Canterbury Tales* with a handshake of welcome to 'Aprille, with his shoures soote.' Indeed, that is what most of us feel about April: it is sweet and delicate and youthful and hopeful. But T. S. Eliot begins *The Waste Land* with a grim statement which is far outside ordinary feelings:

> April is the cruellest month, breeding
> Lilacs out of the dead land, mixing
> Memory and desire, stirring
> Dull roots with spring rain.

And the entire poem, the best known of our generation, is a description of several agonizing experiences which most of us not only have never had but have not even conceived as possible. Yet there is no doubt that it is good poetry, and that it has taken a permanent place in our literature, together with other eccentric and individual visions.

But some of us do not admit it to be poetry—or rather claim that, if it is so extreme and unusual, poetry is useless. This is a mistake. The universe is so vast, the universe is so various, that we owe it to ourselves to try to understand every kind of experience—both the usual and the remote, both the intelligible and the mystical. Logic is not enough. Not all the truth about the world, or about our own lives, can be set down in straightforward prose, or even in straightforward poetry. Some important truths are too subtle even to be uttered in words. A Japanese, by arranging a few flowers in a vase, or Rembrandt, by drawing a dark room with an old man sitting in it, can convey meanings which no one could ever utter in speech. So also, however extravagant a romantic poem may seem, it can tell us something about our world which we ought to know.

It is easier for us to appreciate this nowadays than it would have been for our grandfathers in the nineteenth century, or for their great-grandfathers in the eighteenth century. Our lives are far less predictable; and it is far less possible to use logic alone in organizing and understanding them. Therefore there are justifications, and good ones, for reading and memorizing not only what we might call universal poetry but also strange and visionary poetry. We ourselves, at some time within the mysterious future, may well have to endure and to try to understand some experience absolutely outside our present scope: suffering of some unforeseen kind, a magnificent and somber duty, a splendid triumph, the development of some new power within us. We shall be better able to do so if we know what the poets (yes, and the musicians) have said about such enhancements and extensions of life. Many a man has lived happily until something came upon him which made him, for the first time, think of committing suicide. Such a man will be better able to understand himself and to rise above the thought if he knows the music that Rachmaninoff wrote when he, too, had such thoughts and conquered them, or if he reads the play of *Hamlet,* or if he travels through Dante's *Comedy*, which begins in utter despair and ends in the vision of

> love, that moves the sun and the other stars.

And even if we ourselves are not called upon to endure such extremes, there may be those around us, perhaps very close to us, who are faced with situations the ordinary mind cannot assimilate: sudden wealth, the temptations of great beauty, the gift of creation, profound sorrow, unmerited guilt. The knowledge of what the poets have said about experiences beyond the frontiers of logic will help us at least to sympathize with them in these experiences. Such understanding is one of the most difficult and necessary efforts of the soul. Shelley compared the skylark, lost in the radiance of the sun, to

> a Poet hidden
> In the light of thought
> Singing hymns unbidden,
> Till the world is wrought
> To sympathy with hopes and fears it heeded not.

To create such sympathy is one of the deepest functions of poetry, and one of the most bitterly needed.

SIX POEMS ON ART

JOHN KEATS

1795-1821

ODE ON A GRECIAN URN

I

Thou still unravish'd bride of quietness,
   Thou foster-child of silence and slow time,
Sylvan historian, who canst thus express
   A flowery tale more sweetly than our rhyme:
What leaf-fring'd legend haunts about thy shape
   Of deities or mortals, or of both,
      In Tempe or the dales of Arcady?
What men or gods are these? What maidens loth?
   What mad pursuit? What struggle to escape?
      What pipes and timbrels? What wild ecstasy?

II

Heard melodies are sweet, but those unheard
   Are sweeter; therefore, ye soft pipes, play on;
Not to the sensual ear, but, more endear'd,
   Pipe to the spirit ditties of no tone:
Fair youth, beneath the trees, thou canst not leave
   Thy song, nor ever can those trees be bare;
      Bold Lover, never, never canst thou kiss
Though winning near the goal—yet, do not grieve;
   She cannot fade, though thou hast not thy bliss,
      For ever wilt thou love, and she be fair!

III

Ah, happy, happy boughs! that cannot shed
   Your leaves, nor ever bid the Spring adieu;
And, happy melodist, unwearied,
   For ever piping songs for ever new;
More happy love! more happy, happy love!
   For ever warm and still to be enjoy'd,
     For ever panting, and for ever young;
All breathing human passion far above,
   That leaves a heart high-sorrowful and cloy'd,
     A burning forehead, and a parching tongue.

IV

Who are these coming to the sacrifice?
   To what green altar, O mysterious priest,
Lead'st thou that heifer lowing at the skies,
   And all her silken flanks with garlands dressed?
What little town by river or sea shore,
   Or mountain-built with peaceful citadel,
     Is emptied of this folk, this pious morn?
And, little town, thy streets for evermore
   Will silent be; and not a soul to tell
     Why thou art desolate, can e'er return.

V

O Attic shape! Fair attitude! with brede
   Of marble men and maidens overwrought
With forest branches and the trodden weed;
   Thou, silent form, dost tease us out of thought
As doth eternity: Cold Pastoral!
   When old age shall this generation waste,
     Thou shalt remain, in midst of other woe
Than ours, a friend to man, to whom thou say'st,
   'Beauty is truth, truth beauty,'—that is all
     Ye know on earth, and all ye need to know.

(1819)

WILLIAM BUTLER YEATS
1865–1939

SAILING TO BYZANTIUM

I

That is no country for old men. The young
In one another's arms, birds in the trees
—Those dying generations—at their song,
The salmon-falls, the mackerel-crowded seas,
Fish, flesh, or fowl, commend all summer long
Whatever is begotten, born, and dies.
Caught in that sensual music all neglect
Monuments of unaging intellect.

II

An aged man is but a paltry thing,
A tattered coat upon a stick, unless
Soul clap its hands and sing, and louder sing
For every tatter in its mortal dress,
Nor is there singing school but studying
Monuments of its own magnificence;
And therefore I have sailed the seas and come
To the holy city of Byzantium.

III

O sages standing in God's holy fire
As in the gold mosaic of a wall,
Come from the holy fire, perne in a gyre,
And be the singing-masters of my soul.
Consume my heart away; sick with desire
And fastened to a dying animal
It knows not what it is; and gather me
Into the artifice of eternity.

IV

Once out of nature I shall never take
My bodily form from any natural thing,
But such a form as Grecian goldsmiths make
Of hammered gold and gold enamelling

To keep a drowsy Emperor awake;
Or set upon a golden bough to sing
To lords and ladies of Byzantium
Of what is past, or passing, or to come.

(1928)

ROBERT FROST

1874–1963

FOR ONCE, THEN, SOMETHING

Others taunt me with having knelt at well-curbs
Always wrong to the light, so never seeing
Deeper down in the well than where the water
Gives me back in a shining surface picture
Me myself in the summer heaven godlike
Looking out of a wreath of fern and cloud puffs.
Once, when trying with chin against a well-curb,
I discerned, as I thought, beyond the picture,
Through the picture, a something white, uncertain,
Something more of the depths—and then I lost it.
Water came to rebuke the too clear water.
One drop fell from a fern, and lo, a ripple
Shook whatever it was lay there at bottom,
Blurred it, blotted it out. What was that whiteness?
Truth? A pebble of quartz? For once, then, something.

(1923)

MARIANNE MOORE

1887–

POETRY

I, too, dislike it: there are things that are important beyond
        all this fiddle.
    Reading it, however, with a perfect contempt for it, one
        discovers in

it after all, a place for the genuine.
    Hands that can grasp, eyes
    that can dilate, hair that can rise
       if it must, these things are important not because a

high-sounding interpretation can be put upon them but be-
       cause they are
   useful. When they become so derivative as to become
       unintelligible,
   the same thing may be said for all of us, that we
    do not admire what
    we cannot understand: the bat
      holding on upside down or in quest of something to

eat, elephants pushing, a wild horse taking a roll, a tireless
      wolf under
   a tree, the immovable critic twitching his skin like a horse
      that feels a flea, the base-
   ball fan, the statistician—
    nor is it valid
      to discriminate against 'business documents and

school-books'; all these phenomena are important. One
      must make a distinction
   however: when dragged into prominence by half poets,
      the result is not poetry,
   nor till the poets among us can be
    'literalists of
    the imagination'—above
      insolence and triviality and can present

for inspection, 'imaginary gardens with real toads in them',
      shall we have
   it. In the meantime, if you demand on the one hand,
   the raw material of poetry in
    all its rawness and
    that which is on the other hand
      genuine, you are interested in poetry.

                                    (1921)

W. H. AUDEN

1907–

SEPTEMBER 1, 1939

I sit in one of the dives
On Fifty-Second Street
Uncertain and afraid
As the clever hopes expire
Of a low dishonest decade:
Waves of anger and fear
Circulate over the bright
And darkened lands of the earth,
Obsessing our private lives;
The unmentionable odour of death
Offends the September night.

Accurate scholarship can
Unearth the whole offence
From Luther until now
That has driven a culture mad,
Find what occurred at Linz,
What huge imago made
A psychopathic god:
I and the public know
What all schoolchildren learn,
Those to whom evil is done
Do evil in return.

Exiled Thucydides knew
All that a speech can say
About Democracy,
And what dictators do,
The elderly rubbish they talk
To an apathetic grave;
Analysed all in his book,
The enlightenment driven away,
The habit-forming pain,
Mismanagement and grief:
We must suffer them all again.

Into this neutral air
Where blind skyscrapers use

Their full height to proclaim
The strength of Collective Man,
Each language pours its vain
Competitive excuse:
But who can live for long
In an euphoric dream;
Out of the mirror they stare,
Imperialism's face
And the international wrong.

Faces along the bar
Cling to their average day:
The lights must never go out,
The music must always play,
All the conventions conspire
To make this fort assume
The furniture of home;
Lest we should see where we are,
Lost in a haunted wood,
Children afraid of the night
Who have never been happy or good.

The windiest militant trash
Important Persons shout
It is not so crude as our wish:
What mad Nijinsky wrote
About Diaghilev
Is true of the normal heart;
For the error bred in the bone
Of each woman and each man
Craves what it cannot have,
Not universal love
But to be loved alone.

From the conservative dark
Into the ethical life
The dense commuters come,
Repeating their morning vow;
"I *will* be true to the wife,
I'll concentrate more on my work,"
And helpless governors wake
To resume their compulsory game:
Who can release them now,
Who can reach the deaf,
Who can speak for the dumb?

All I have is a voice
To undo the folded lie,
The romantic lie in the brain
Of the sensual man-in-the-street
And the lie of Authority
Whose buildings grope the sky:
There is no such thing as the State
And no one exists alone;
Hunger allows no choice
To the citizen or the police;
We must love one another or die.

Defenceless under the night
Our world in stupor lies;
Yet dotted everywhere,
Ironic points of light
Flash out wherever the Just
Exchange their messages:
May I, composed like them
Of Eros and of dust,
Beleaguered by the same
Negation and despair,
Show an affirming flame.

(1940)

DYLAN THOMAS

1914–1953

IN MY CRAFT OR SULLEN ART

In my craft or sullen art
Exercised in the still night
When only the moon rages
And the lovers lie abed
With all their griefs in their arms,
I labour by singing light
Not for ambition or bread
Or the strut and trade of charms
On the ivory stages
But for the common wages
Of their most secret heart.
Not for the proud man apart
From the raging moon I write
On these spindrift pages
Nor for the towering dead
With their nightingales and psalms
But for the lovers, their arms
Round the griefs of the ages,
Who pay no praise or wages
Nor heed my craft or art.

(1945)

On the Standards of Taste

"De gustibus non disputandum est" goes the venerable saying, "There's no disputing about tastes"; and in a society devoted like ours to equality and to individualism, the idea has many adherents. To many people, indeed, there seems to be something offensive and snobbish—positively undemocratic—in the idea of a hierarchy of tastes: that one person's taste can be bad and another one's good. Can tastes be anything more than merely different? "I like what I like," is the popular answer, "and furthermore, nobody is going to tell me what to like." But on the other side there stands a group of critics and philosophers—and even teachers—whose very presence suggests that there are useful standards of taste, and that "good" taste can be cultivated and improved. The following essays take up this question; in presenting them we frankly exhibit our own bias on the side of those who believe in standards.

Russell Lynes's well-known essay proves in generous and amusing detail that our tastes differ socially in predictable ways, that whole groups of us have consciously or unconsciously accepted rigid standards of taste. But Lynes does not indicate as strongly as does Kronenberger that there may be a defensible hierarchy of tastes. "Every catalogue of bad taste is a comedy of over-assurance," Kronenberger wisely says. But this does not prevent his comparing the old vulgarity with the new. E. M. Forster and Virginia Woolf focus our attention on taste in books. Both of them are talented writers who address the reader sympathetically. Each in his own way teaches both discrimination and independence in taste. Marya Mannes comes out boldly and directly for standards, for educated appreciation of purpose and craftsmanship, and it is on this note—and with her last sentence—that we are pleased to end this collection.

RUSSELL LYNES

HIGHBROW, LOWBROW,
MIDDLEBROW

This essay first appeared in the February, 1949, Harper's. For information on the author and his writings, see page 690.

•

I

My wife's grandmother, the wife of a distinguished lawyer, once declined to dine with the Cartiers of jewelry fame because they were, as she put it, "in trade." Life for grandmother was relatively simple where social distinctions were concerned, but while there are still a few people who think and act much as she did, the passage of time has eliminated a great deal of that particular kind of snobbishness from American society. We are replacing it with another kind. The old structure of the upper class, the middle class, and the lower class is on the wane. It isn't wealth or family that makes prestige these days. It's high thinking.

Our heroes now are not the Carnegies or the Morgans but the intellectuals—the atomic scientists, the cultural historians, the writers, the commentators, the thinkers of global thoughts who, we assume for lack of another faith, know better than anyone else how we should cope with what we call with new resonance our national destiny. What we want are oracles, and the best substitutes we can find are the intellectuals. Einstein makes headlines as Milliken never did. Toynbee's popularity is to be reckoned with as Spengler's never was. Even Calvert whiskey has selected as Men of Distinction more artists, architects, writers, and commentators than it has industrialists or financiers. What we are headed for is a sort of social structure in which the highbrows are the elite, the middlebrows are the bourgeoisie, and the lowbrows are *hoi polloi*.

For the time being this is perhaps largely an urban phenomenon, and the true middlebrow may readily be mistaken in the small community for a genuine highbrow, but the pattern is emerging with increasing clarity, and the new distinctions do not seem to be based either on money or on breeding. Some lowbrows are as rich as Billy Rose, and as flamboyant, some as poor as Rosie O'Grady and as modest. Some middlebrows run industries; some run the women's auxiliary of the Second Baptist Church. Some highbrows eat caviar with their Proust; some eat hamburger when they can afford it. It is true that most highbrows are in the ill-paid professions, notably the academic, and that most middlebrows are at least reasonably well off. Only the lowbrows can be found in about equal percentages at all financial levels. There may be a time, of course, when the highbrows will be paid in accordance with their own estimate of their worth, but that is not likely to happen in any form of society in which creature comforts are in greater demand than intellectual uplift. Like poets they will have to be content mostly with prestige. The middlebrows are influential today, but neither the highbrows nor the lowbrows like them; and if we ever have intellectual totalitarianism, it may well be the lowbrows and the highbrows who will run things, and the middlebrows who will be exiled in boxcars to a collecting point probably in the vicinity of Independence, Missouri.

While this social shift is still in its early stages, and the dividing lines are still indistinct and the species not yet frozen, let us assume a rather lofty position, examine the principal categories, with their subdivisions and splinter groups, and see where we ourselves are likely to fetch up in the new order.

II

The highbrows come first. Edgar Wallace, who was certainly not a highbrow himself, was asked by a newspaper reporter in Hollywood some years ago to define one. "What is a highbrow?" he said. "A highbrow is a man who has found something more interesting than women."

Presumably at some time in every man's life there are things he finds more interesting than women; alcohol, for example, or the World Series. Mr. Wallace has only partially defined the highbrow. Brander Matthews came closer when he said that "a highbrow is a person educated beyond his intelligence," and A. P. Herbert came closest of all when he wrote that "a highbrow is the kind of person who looks at a sausage and thinks of Picasso."

It is this association of culture with every aspect of daily life, from the design of his razor to the shape of the bottle that holds his sleeping pills, that distinguishes the highbrow from the middlebrow or the lowbrow. Spiritually and intellectually the highbrow inhabits a precinct well up the slopes of Parnassus, and his view of the cultural scene is from above. His vision pinpoints certain lakes and quarries upon which his special affections are concentrated—a perturbed lake called Rilke or a deserted quarry called Kierkegaard—but he believes that he sees them, as he sees the functional design of his razor, always in relation to the broader cultural scene. There is a certain air of omniscience about the highbrow, though that air is in many cases the thin variety encountered on the tops of high mountains from which the view is extensive but the details are lost.

You cannot tell a man that he is a lowbrow any more than you can tell a woman that her clothes are in bad taste, but a highbrow does not mind being called a highbrow. He has worked hard, read widely, traveled far, and listened attentively in order to satisfy his curiosity and establish his squatters' rights in this little corner of intellectualism, and he does not care who knows it. And this is true of both kinds of highbrow—the militant, or crusader, type and the passive, or dilettante, type. These types in general live happily together; the militant highbrow carries the torch of culture, the passive highbrow reads by its light.

The carrier of the torch makes a profession of being a highbrow and lives by his calling. He is most frequently found in university and college towns, a member of the liberal-arts faculty, teaching languages (ancient or modern), the fine arts, or literature. His spare time is often devoted to editing a magazine which is read mainly by other highbrows, ambitious undergraduates, and the editors of middlebrow publications in search of talent. When he writes for the magazine himself (or for another "little" magazine) it is usually criticism or criticism *of* criticism. He leaves the writing of fiction and poetry to others more bent on creation than on what has been created, for the highbrow is primarily a critic and not an artist— a taster, not a cook. He is often more interested in where the arts have been, and where they are going, than in the objects themselves. He is devoted to the proposition that the arts must be pigeon-holed, and that their trends should be plotted, or as W. H. Auden puts it—

> Our intellectual marines,
> Landing in Little Magazines,
> Capture a trend.

This gravitation of the highbrows to the universities is fairly recent. In the twenties, when the little magazines were devoted to publishing experimental writing rather than criticism of exhumed experimental writing, the highbrows flocked to Paris, New York, and Chicago. The *transatlantic review, transition,* and the *Little Review,* of the lower-case era of literature, were all published in Paris; BROOM was published in New York; *Poetry* was (and still is) published in Chicago. The principal little magazines now, with the exception of *Partisan Review,* a New York product but written mostly by academics, are published in the colleges —the *Kenyon Review,* the *Sewanee Review,* the *Virginia Quarterly,* and so on—and their flavor reflects this. But this does not mean that highbrows do not prefer the centers in which cultural activities are the most varied and active, and these are still London, Paris, New York, and more recently Rome. Especially in the fine arts, the highbrow has a chance to make a living in the metropolis where museums are centered and where art is bought and sold as well as created. This is also true of commercial publishing, in which many highbrows find suitable, if not congenial, refuge.

But no matter where they may make their homes, all highbrows live in a world which they believe is inhabited almost entirely by Philistines —those who through viciousness or smugness or the worship of materialism gnaw away at the foundations of culture. And the highbrow sees as his real enemy the middlebrow, whom he regards as a pretentious and frivolous man or woman who uses culture to satisfy social or business ambitions; who, to quote Clement Greenberg in *Partisan Review*, is busy "devaluating the precious, infecting the healthy, corrupting the honest, and stultifying the wise."

It takes a man who feels strongly to use such harsh words, but the militant highbrow has no patience with his enemies. He is a serious man who will not tolerate frivolity where the arts are concerned. It is part of his function as a highbrow to protect the arts from the culture-mongers, and he spits venom at those he suspects of selling the Muses short.

The fact that nowadays everyone has access to culture through schools and colleges, through the press, radio, and museums, disturbs him deeply; for it tends to blur the distinctions between those who are serious and those who are frivolous. "Culturally what we have," writes William Phillips in *Horizon*, "is a democratic free-for-all in which every individual, being as good as every other one, has the right to question any form of intellectual authority." To this Mr. Greenberg adds, "It becomes increasingly difficult to tell who is serious and who not."

The highbrow does not like to be confused, nor does he like to have his authority questioned, except by other highbrows of whose seriousness he is certain. The result is precisely what you would expect: the highbrows believe in, and would establish, an intellectual elite, "a fluid body of intellectuals . . . whose accepted role in society is to perpetuate traditional ideas and values and to create new ones." Such an elite would like to see the middlebrow eliminated, for it regards him as the undesirable element in our, and anybody else's, culture.

"It must be obvious to anyone that the volume and social weight of middlebrow culture," Mr. Greenberg writes, "borne along as it has been by the great recent increase in the American middle class, have multiplied at least tenfold in the past three decades. This culture presents a more serious threat to the genuine article than the old-time pulp dime novel, Tin Pan Alley, *Schund* variety ever has or will. Unlike the latter, which has its social limits clearly marked out for it, middlebrow culture attacks distinctions as such and insinuates itself everywhere. . . . Insidiousness is of its essence, and in recent years its avenues of penetration have become infinitely more difficult to detect and block."

By no means all highbrows are so intolerant or so desperate as this, or so ambitious for authority. Many of them, the passive ones, are merely consumers totally indifferent to the middlebrows or supercilious about them. Others without a great deal of hope but in ardent good faith expend themselves in endeavor to widen the circle of those who can enjoy the arts in their purest forms. Many museums, colleges, and publishing houses are at least partly staffed by highbrows who exert a more than half-hearted effort to make the arts exciting and important to the public. But they are aware that most of their labors are wasted. In his heart of hearts nearly every highbrow believes with Ortega y Gasset that "the average citizen [is] a creature incapable of receiving the sacrament of art, blind and deaf to pure beauty." When, for example, the Metropolitan Museum planned to expand its facilities a few years ago, an art dealer who can clearly be classified as a highbrow remarked: "All this means is less art for more people."

There are also many highbrows who are not concerned in the least with the arts or with literature, and who do not fret themselves about the upstart state of middlebrow culture. These are the specialized high-brows who toil in the remote corners of science and history, of philology and mathematics. They are concerned with their investigations of fruit-flies or Elizabethan taxation or whatever it may be, and they do not talk about them, as the dilettante always talks of the arts, to the first person they can latch onto at a cocktail party. When not in their laboratories or the library, they are often as not thoroughly middlebrow in their attitudes and tastes.

The real highbrow's way of life is as intellectualized as his way of thinking, and as carefully plotted. He is likely to be either extremely self-conscious about his physical surroundings and creature comforts or else sublimely, and rather ostentatiously, indifferent to them. If he affects the former attitude, he will within the limits of his income surround himself with works of art. If he cannot afford paintings he buys draw-ings. Color reproductions, except as casual reminders tucked in the frame of a mirror or thrown down on a table, are beneath him. The facsimile is no substitute in his mind for the genuine, and he would rather have a slight sketch by a master, Braque or Picasso or even Jackson Pollock, than a fully-realized canvas by an artist he considers not quite first-rate. Drawings by his friends he hangs in the bathroom. His furniture, if it is modern, consists of identifiable pieces by Aalto, or Breuer, or Mies van der Rohe, or Eames; it does not come from department stores. If he finds modern unsympathetic, he will tend to use Biedermaier or the more "entertaining" varieties of Victorian, which he collects piece by piece with an eye to the slightly eccentric. If he has antiques, you may be sure they are not maple; the cult of "early American" is offensive to him.

The food that he serves will be planned with the greatest care, either very simple (a perfect French omelette made with sweet butter) or elaborate recipes from *Wine and Food* magazine published in London and edited by André Simon. If he cannot afford a pound of butter with every guinea fowl, he will in all probability resort to the casserole, and peasant cookery with the sparer parts of animals and birds seasoned meticulously with herbs that he gets from a little importer in the wholesale district. His wine is more likely to be a "perfectly adequate little red wine" for eighty-nine cents a half-gallon than an imported French vintage. (Anybody with good advice can buy French wines, but the discovery of a good domestic bottle shows perception and educated taste.) He wouldn't dream of washing his salad bowl. His collection of phonograph records is likely to bulk large at the ends and sag in the middle—a predominance of Bach-and-before at one end and Stravinsky, Schönberg, Bartok, and New Orleans jazz at the other. The nineteenth century is represented, perhaps, by Beethoven quartets and late sonatas, and some French "art songs" recorded by Maggie Teyte. His radio, if he has one, is turned on rarely; he wouldn't have a television set in the house.

The highbrow who disregards his creature comforts does it with a will. He lives with whatever furniture happens to come his way in a disorganized conglomeration of Victorian, department store, and Mexican bits and pieces. He takes care of his books in that he knows where each one is no matter in what disorder they may appear. Every other detail of domestic life he leaves to his wife, of whose taste he is largely unaware, and he eats what she gives him without comment. If he is a bachelor, he eats in a cafeteria or drugstore or diner and sometimes spills soup on the open pages of his book. He is oblivious to the man who sits down opposite him, and if Edgar Wallace is right, to the woman who shares his table. He is not a man without passions, but they have their place. Dress is a matter of indifference to him.

The highbrows about whom I have been writing are mainly consumers and not creators—editors, critics, and dilettantes. The creative artists who are generally considered highbrows—such men as T. S. Eliot, E. M. Forster, Picasso, and Stravinsky—seem to me to fall in another category, that of the professional man who, while he may be concerned with communicating with a limited (and perhaps largely highbrow) audience, is primarily a doer and not a done-by. When Eliot or Forster or Picasso or Stravinsky sits down at his work-table, I do not know whether he says to himself, "I am going to create Art," but I very much doubt if that is what is in his mind. He is concerned rather with the communication of ideas within the frame of a poem, a novel, a painting, or a ballet suite, and if it turns out to be art (which many think it frequently does) that is to him a by-product of creation, an extra dividend of craftsmanship, intelligence, and sensibility. But when this happens he is taken up by the highbrow consumer and made much of. In fact he may become, whether he likes it or not, a vested interest, and his reputation will be every bit as carefully guarded by the highbrows as a hundred shares of Standard Oil of New Jersey by the middlebrows. He will be sold—at a par decided upon by the highbrows—to the middlebrows, who are natural gamblers in the commodities of culture.

In a sense it is this determination of par that is the particular contribution of the highbrow. Others may quarrel with his evaluations but the fact remains that unless there were a relatively small group of self-appointed intellectuals who took it upon themselves to ransack the studios of artists, devour the manuscripts of promising writers, and listen at the keyholes of young composers, many talented men and women might pass unnoticed and our culture be the poorer. Their noncommercial attitude toward discovery of talent is useful, though they have an obsession with the evils of the monetary temptations with which America strews the artist's path. They stand as a wavering bulwark against the enticements of Hollywood and the advertising agencies, and they are saddened by the writers and painters who have set out to be serious men, as Hemingway did, and then become popular by being taken up by the middlebrows. They even go so far as to say that a story published in *Partisan Review* is a better story than if it were published in the *New Yorker* or *Harper's Bazaar*, for the reason that "what we have is at once a general raising and lowering of the level, for with the blurring of distinctions new writing tends to become more and more serious and intellectual and less and less bold and extreme. . . ."

This attitude, which is the attitude of the purist, is valuable. The ground in which the arts grow stays fertile only when it is fought over by both artists and consumers, and the phalanx of highbrows in the field, a somewhat impenetrable square of warriors, can be counted on to keep the fray alive.

III

The highbrow's friend is the lowbrow. The highbrow enjoys and respects the lowbrow's art—jazz for instance—which he is likely to call a spontaneous expression of folk culture. The lowbrow is not interested, as the middlebrow is, in pre-empting any of the highbrow's function or in any way threatening to blur the lines between the serious and the frivolous. In fact he is almost completely oblivious of the highbrow unless he happens to be taken up by him—as many jazz musicians, primitive painters, and ballad writers have been—and then he is likely to be flattered, a little suspicious, and somewhat amused. A creative lowbrow like the jazz musician is a prominent citizen in his own world, and the fact that he is taken up by the highbrows has very little effect on his social standing therein. He is tolerant of the highbrow, whom he regards as somewhat odd and out-of-place in a world in which people do things and enjoy them without analyzing why or worrying about their cultural implications.

The lowbrow doesn't give a hang about art *qua* art. He knows what he likes, and he doesn't care why he likes it—which implies that all children are lowbrows. The word "beautiful," which has long since ceased to mean anything to the highbrow, is a perfectly good word to the lowbrow. Beautiful blues, beautiful sunsets, beautiful women, all things that do something to a man inside without passing through the mind, associations without allusions, illusions without implications. The arts created by the lowbrow are made in the expression of immediate pleasure or grief, like most forms of jazz; or of usefulness, like the manufacturing of a tool or a piece of machinery or even a bridge across the Hudson. The form, to use a highbrow phrase, follows the function. When the lowbrow arts follow this formula (which they don't always do), then the highbrow finds much in them to admire, and he calls it the vernacular. When, however, the lowbrow arts get mixed up with middlebrow ideas of culture, then the highbrow turns away in disgust. Look, for example, at what happened to the circus, a traditional form of lowbrow art. They got in Norman Bel Geddes to fancy it up, and now its special flavor of authenticity is gone—all wrapped up in pink middlebrow sequins. This is not to say that the lowbrow doesn't like it just as much as he ever did. It is the highbrow who is pained.

Part of the highbrow's admiration for the lowbrow stems from the lowbrow's indifference to art. This makes it possible for the highbrow to blame whatever he doesn't like about lowbrow taste on the middlebrow. If the lowbrow reads the comics, the highbrow understands; he is frequently a connoisseur of the comics himself. But if he likes grade-B double features, the highbrow blames that on the corrupting influence of the middlebrow moneybags of Hollywood. If he participates in give-away quiz programs, it is because the radio pollsters have decided that the average mental age of the listening audience is thirteen, and that radio is venal for taking advantage of the adolescent.

The lowbrow consumer, whether he is an engineer of bridges or a bus driver, wants to be comfortable and to enjoy himself without having to worry about whether he has good taste or not. It doesn't make any difference to him that a chair is a bad Grand Rapids copy of an eighteenth-century *fauteuil* as long as he's happy when he sits down in it. He doesn't care whether the movies are art, or the radio improving, so long as he has fun while he is giving them his attention and getting a fair return of pleasure from his investment. It wouldn't occur to him to tell a novelist what kind of book he should write, or a movie director what kind of movie to make. If he doesn't like a book he ignores it; if he doesn't like a movie he says so, whether it is a "Blondie" show or "Henry V." If he likes jive or square-dancing, he doesn't worry about whether they are fashionable or not. If other people like the ballet, that's all right with him, so long as he doesn't have to go himself. In general the lowbrow attitude toward the arts is live and let live. Lowbrows are not Philistines. One has to know enough about the arts to argue about them with highbrows to be a Philistine.

IV

The popular press, and also much of the unpopular press, is run by the middlebrows, and it is against them that the highbrow inveighs.

"The true battle," Virginia Woolf wrote in an unmailed letter to the *New Statesman*, ". . . lies not between highbrow and lowbrow, but between highbrows and lowbrows joined together in blood brotherhood against the bloodless and pernicious pest who comes between."

The pests divide themselves into two groups: the Upper Middlebrows and the Lower Middlebrows. It is the upper middlebrows who are the principal purveyors of highbrow ideas and the lower middlebrows who are the principal consumers of what the upper middlebrows pass along to them.

Many publishers, for example, are upper middlebrows—as are most educators, museum directors, movie producers, art dealers, lecturers, and the editors of most magazines which combine national circulation with an adult vocabulary. These are the men and women who devote themselves professionally to the dissemination of ideas and cultural artifacts and, not in the least incidentally, make a living along the way. They are the cultural do-gooders, and they see their mission clearly and pursue it with determination. Some of them are disappointed highbrows; some of them try to work both sides of the street; nearly all of them straddle the fence between highbrow and middlebrow and enjoy their equivocal position.

The conscientious publisher, for instance, believes in the importance of literature and the dignity of publishing as a profession. He spends a large part of his time on books that will not yield him a decent return on his investment. He searches out writers of promise; he pores over the "little" magazines (or pays other people to); he leafs through hundreds and hundreds of pages of manuscript. He advises writers, encourages them, coaxes them to do their best work; he even advances them money. But he is not able to be a publisher at all (unless he is willing to put his personal fortune at the disposal of financially naïve muses) if he does not publish to make money. In order to publish slender volumes of poetry he must also publish fat volumes of historical romance, and in order to encourage the first novel of a promising young writer he must sell tens of thousands of copies of a book by an old hand who grinds out one best seller a year. He must take the measure of popular taste and cater to it at the same time that he tries to create a taste for new talent. If he is a successful publisher he makes money, lives comfortably, patronizes the other arts, serves on museum boards and committees for the Prevention of This and the Preservation of That, contributes to the symphony, and occasionally buys pictures by contemporary painters.

The highbrow suspects that the publisher does not pace his book-lined office contriving ways to serve the muses and that these same muses have to wait their turn in line until the balance sheet has been served. He believes that the publisher is really happy only when he can sell a couple of hundred thousand copies of a novel about a hussy with a horsewhip or a book on how to look forty when forty-five. To the highbrow he is a tool to be cultivated and used, but not to be trusted.

The museum director is in much the same position, caught between the muses and the masses. If he doesn't make a constant effort to swell the door-count, his middlebrow trustees want to know why he isn't serving the community; if he does, the highbrows want to know why he is pandering to popular taste and not minding his main business—the service of scholarship and the support of artists currently certified to be "serious." Educators are in the same position, bound to be concerned with mass education often at the expense of the potential scholar, and editors of all magazines except those supported by private angels or cultural institutions know that they must not only enlighten but entertain if they are to have enough readers to pay the bills. To the highbrow this can lead to nothing but compromise and mediocrity.

The upper-middlebrow consumer takes his culture seriously, as seriously as his job allows, for he is gainfully employed. In his leisure hours he reads Toynbee or Sartre or Osbert Sitwell's serialized memoirs. He goes to museum openings and to the theater and he keeps up on the foreign films. He buys pictures, sometimes old masters if he can afford them, sometimes contemporary works. He has a few etchings and lithographs, and he is not above an occasional color reproduction of a Van Gogh or a Cézanne. Writers and painters are his friends and dine at his house; if, however, his own son were to express an interest in being an artist, he would be dismayed ("so few artists ever really pull it off")—though he would keep a stiff upper lip and hope the boy would learn better before it was too late. His house is tastefully decorated, sometimes in the very latest mode, a model of the modern architect's dream of functionalism, in which case he can discourse on the theory of the open plan and the derivations of the international style with the zest and uncertain vocabulary of a convert. If his house is "traditional" in character, he will not put up with Grand Rapids copies of old pieces; he will have authentic ones, and will settle for Victorian if he cannot afford Empire. He, or his wife, will ransack second-hand shops for entertaining bibelots and lamps or a piece of Brussels carpet for the bedroom. He never refers to curtains as "drapes." He talks about television as potentially a new art form, and he listens to the Saturday afternoon opera broadcasts. His library contains a few of the more respectable current best sellers which he reads out of "curiosity" rather than interest. (Membership in any sort of book club he considers beneath him.) There are a few shelves of first editions, some of them autographed by friends who have dined at his house, some of them things (like a presentation copy of *Jurgen*) that he "just happened to pick up" and a sampling of American and British poets. There is also a shelf of paper-bound French novels—most of them by nineteenth-century writers. The magazines on his table span the areas from *Time* and the *New Yorker* to *Harper's* and the *Atlantic*, with an occasional copy of the *Yale* and *Partisan Reviews*, and the *Art News*.

From this it can be seen that he supports the highbrows—buys some of the books they recommend and an occasional picture they have looked upon with favor—and contributes to organized efforts to promote the arts both by serving on boards and shelling out money. In general he is modest about expressing his opinion on cultural matters in the presence of highbrows but takes a slightly lordly tone when he is talking to other middlebrows. If he discovers a "little" painter or poet the chances are excellent that the man has already been discovered and promoted by a highbrow or by an upper-middlebrow entrepreneur (art dealer or publisher). Once in a while he will take a flyer on an unknown artist, and hang his picture inconspicuously in the bedroom. He takes his function as a patron of the arts seriously, but he does it for the pleasure it gives him to be part of the cultural scene. If he does it for "money, fame, power, or prestige," as Virginia Woolf says he does, these motives are so obscured by a general sense of well-being and well-meaning that he would be shocked and surprised to be accused of venality.

v

If the upper middlebrow is unsure of his own tastes, but firm in his belief that taste is extremely important, the lower middlebrow is his counterpart. The lower middlebrow ardently believes that he knows what he likes, and yet his taste is constantly susceptible to the pressures that put him in knickerbockers one year and rust-colored slacks the next. Actually he is unsure about almost everything, especially about what he likes. This may explain his pronouncements on taste, which he considers an effete and questionable virtue, and his resentment of the arts; but it may also explain his strength.

When America and Americans are characterized by foreigners and highbrows, the middlebrows are likely to emerge as the dominant group in our society—a dreadful mass of insensible back-slappers, given to sentimentality as a prime virtue, the willing victims of slogans and the whims of the bosses, both political and economic. The picture painted by middlebrow exploiters of the middlebrow, such as the advertisers of nationally advertised brands, is strikingly similar to that painted by the highbrow; their attitudes and motives are quite different (the highbrow paints with a snarl, the advertiser with a gleam), but they both make the middlebrow out to be much the same kind of creature. The villain of the highbrow and the hero of the advertisers is envisaged as "the typical American family"—happy little women, happy little children, all spotless or sticky in the jam pot, framed against dimity curtains in the windows or decalcomania flowers on the cupboard doors. Lower-middlebrowism is a world pictured without tragedy, a world of new two-door sedans, and Bendix washers, and reproductions of hunting prints over the living-room mantel. It is a world in which the ingenuity and patience of the housewife are equaled only by the fidelity of her husband and his love of home, pipe, and radio. It is a world that smells of soap. But it is a world of ambition as well, the constant striving for a better way of life—better furniture, bigger refrigerators, more books in the bookcase, more evenings at the movies. To the advertisers this is Americanism; to the highbrows this is the dead weight around the neck of progress, the gag in the mouth of art.

The lower middlebrows are not like this, of course, and unlike the highbrows and the upper middlebrows, whose numbers are tiny by comparison, they are hard to pin down. They live everywhere, rubbing elbows with lowbrows in apartment houses like vast beehives, in row houses all alike from the outside except for the planting, in large houses at the ends of gravel driveways, in big cities, in medium cities and suburbs, and in small towns, from Boston to San Francisco, from Seattle to Jacksonville. They are the members of the book clubs who read difficult books along with racy and innocuous ones that are sent along by Messrs. Fadiman, Canby, Beecroft *et al.* They are the course-takers who swell the enrollments of adult education classes in everything from "The Technique of the Short Story" to "Child Care." They are the people who go to hear the lecturers that swarm out from New York lecture bureaus with tales of travel on the Dark Continent and panaceas for saving the world from a fate worse than capitalism. They eat in tea shoppes and hold barbecues in their backyards. They are hell-bent on improving their minds as well as their fortunes. They decorate their homes under the careful guidance of *Good Housekeeping* and the *Ladies' Home Journal,* or, if they are well off, of *House and Garden,* and are subject to fads in furniture so long as these don't depart too radically from the traditional and the safe, from the copy of Colonial and the reproduction of Sheraton. In matters of taste, the lower-middlebrow world is largely dominated by women. They select the furniture, buy the fabrics, pick out the wallpapers, the pictures, the books, the china. Except in the selection of his personal apparel and the car, it is almost *infra dig* for a man to have taste; it is not considered quite manly for the male to express opinions about things which come under the category of "artistic."

Nonetheless, as a member of the school board or the hospital board he decides which design shall be accepted when a new building goes up. The lower middlebrows are the organizers of the community fund, the members of the legislature, the park commissioners. They pay their taxes and they demand services in return. There are millions of them, conscientious stabilizers of society, slow to change, slow to panic. But they are not as predictable as either the highbrows or the bosses, political or economic, think they are. They can be led, they can be seduced, but they cannot be pushed around.

VI

Highbrow, lowbrow, upper middlebrow, and lower middlebrow—the lines between them are sometimes indistinct, as the lines between upper class, lower class, and middle class have always been in our traditionally fluid society. But gradually they are finding their own levels and confining themselves more and more to the company of their own kind. You will not find a highbrow willingly attending a Simon & Schuster cocktail party any more than you will find an upper middlebrow at a Rotary Club luncheon or an Elks' picnic.

The highbrows would like, of course, to eliminate the middlebrows and devise a society that would approximate an intellectual feudal system in which the lowbrows do the work and create folk arts, and the highbrows do the thinking and create fine arts. All middlebrows, presumably, would have their radios taken away, be suspended from society until they had agreed to give up their subscriptions to the Book-of-the-Month, turned their color reproductions over to a Commission for the Dissolution of Middlebrow Taste, and renounced their affiliation with all educational and other cultural institutions whatsoever. They would be taxed for the support of all writers, artists, musicians, critics, and critics-of-criticism whose production could be certified "serious"—said writers, artists, musicians, and critics to be selected by representatives of qualified magazines with circulations of not more than five thousand copies. Middlebrows, both upper and lower, who persisted in "devaluating the precious, infecting the healthy, corrupting the honest, and stultifying the wise" would be disposed of forthwith.

But the highbrows haven't a chance; things have gone too far. Everybody but the genuine lowbrow (who is more wooed than wedded by the highbrow) is jockeying for position in the new cultural class order. *Life* magazine, sensing the trend, has been catching us up on the past of Western Civilization in sixteen-page, four-color capsules. *Mademoiselle* walks off with the first prizes in the annual short-story contests. The Pepsi-Cola Company stages the most elaborate and highest-paying art competition in the country. Even *Partisan Review,* backed by a new angel, runs full-page ads in the *New York Times* Book Review. The Book-of-the-Month Club ships out a couple of hundred thousand copies of Toynbee's *A Study of History* as "dividends."

If life for grandmother, who wouldn't dine with the Cartiers, was simple in its social distinctions, life is becoming equally simple for us. The rungs of the ladder may be different, it may even be a different ladder, but it's onward and upward just the same. You may not be known by which fork you use for the fish these days, but you will be known by which key you use for your *Finnegans Wake*.

LOUIS KRONENBERGER

Louis Kronenberger, editor, drama critic, and teacher, was born in Cincinnati in 1904 and educated at the University there. From 1926 to 1935 he did editorial work for two New York publishing houses. Then he joined the staff of Fortune *and two years later moved to* Time *and became its drama critic until 1961. After a two-year lectureship at Columbia he became, in 1952, Professor of Theatre Arts at Brandeis University. At the same time he began an eight-year editorship of the annual volume of* The Best Plays. *He has also edited several anthologies. In addition to some novels, he has written a great deal of non-fiction, including* Kings and Desperate Men: Life in Eighteenth Century England *(1942),* The Thread of Laughter *(1952),* Company Manners: A Cultural Inquiry into American Life *(1954),* The Republic of Letters *(1955),* Marlborough's Duchess *(1958), and* The Cart and the Horse *(1964), from which we take the present essay.*

FASHIONS IN VULGARITY

I

Nothing, in a sense, would be easier to chronicle than a history of bad taste. The past is strewn with horrible examples; we need only look at the drearier or declining sections of cities, or in junk or antique shops, or—since on occasion vulgarity begins at home—in our own family attics. There are McKinley-period trophies in architecture, German-beermug-era trophies in décor. Everywhere there are reminders of a false refinement; or novels that ladies quite as much as ladies' maids once wept over. Every age yields fictional accounts of moneyed upstarts—Trimalchio in ancient Rome, M. Jourdain in seventeenth-century France, the Veneerings in nineteenth-century England. Was "bad taste" ever more rife than among Victorian England's indigestible wedding-cakes in stone? Yet, was "vulgarity" ever so ridiculous as with the great Lord Chesterfield, who deemed it vulgar to laugh aloud; or with the French classical drama, that forbade mention of the handkerchief, since on its exalted stage not noses were blown, but trumpets.

Yet, though nothing were more easily compiled than a chronicle of bad taste, nothing, after a time, calls out more for revision. Let fifty years go by, and it is not the items in the catalogue that shriek bad taste; it is the cataloguer. Not what he excoriated will seem vulgar, but what he extolled. In the early 1920's a critic of décor, championing the most functional furniture, might have whacked away at the curlycued accessories of the Victorians. Today all too many people wish their keepsakes had been kept, sigh in vain for their grandparents' square pianos and rosewood sofas; and shudder at the metal frames and tubular stems that passed for furniture. Clearly, since taste began, one generation's fashion has become the next generation's fright.

In the degree, then, that it posits touchstones and untouchables, proclaims What's Done and proscribes What Will Never Do, every catalogue of bad taste is a comedy of over-assurance. Virtually the same era that banished the handkerchief from the drama, and laughter from the drawing-room, cheerfully made butts of cuckolds and sport of madmen. The Augustans, while thinking it effeminate for men to carry umbrellas, deemed it manly for them to carry muffs. The Victorians, while forbidding mention of most illnesses and all sex, doted on rancid practical jokes. Yet, for all such warnings of booby traps, there is perhaps some point in our trying to discover vulgarity's more permanent traits. From the past, we get at least a clue in its verbal alliances, in the company it kept. There was once constant reference to "vulgar display," to "vulgar curiosity," to "vulgar presumption." Vulgar display, probably the arch offender, calls up visions of too much finery and jewelry, of bric-a-brac and be-silvered-and-china'd dining-room tables—or simply of too much dinner. All this particularly brings the last century to mind, for with it emerged large, prosperous middle-class families that, by requiring large houses, encouraged lavish living. Moreover, an age that admired plump, high-busted women put no tax on heavy meals. Then, too, so prudish an age banned so many other forms of indulgence as perhaps to make lavishness less an initial desire than a kind of last resort. A respectable matron dared not smoke a cigarette; on the other hand she could virtuously eat three slices of cake.

Actually, even the more tasteful Victorians never stigmatized display in itself; they merely stigmatized this thing or that on display. Passing up, for the moment, any distinction between vulgarity and bad taste, we still might note that vulgarity isn't avoided merely through good taste in individual selection; there must also be a sense of proportion about the whole. Nor need we confine ourselves to the marble and plush atrocities of upstarts: the desire to exhibit on a vast scale has much ancient and aristocratic warrant. Most lordly establishments impart a too strutting sense of ownership, of greedy heaping-up and senseless size. Measured against a perfect taste, the patrician's giving material form to his pride of rank can be just as vulgar as the parvenu's proclaiming his lack of any.

There was that other once-common phrase, "vulgar presumption." It has largely fallen into disuse, not because people have stopped being presumptuous but because the phrase became a caste reproof—something applied to whomever one deemed one's social inferior. The culprit might often be vulgar enough, whether from a bumptious attempt to get on or a blatant attempt to dazzle; but he was hardly presumptuous: it was rather his detractors who presumed. But of course the class bias that stamps so many things vulgar goes very deep—indeed to the roots of the word itself, to *vulgus* or the common people. Something, in other words, was vulgar that had a lower-class stamp—or at least the stamp of a lower class than one's own.

This class bias is not uninstructive; but though we have still to define vulgarity, plainly in its subtler connotations today it has not just over-flowed "lower class" banks; it has been rechanneled in a different direction. We might even contend that it is only the common people—along with some decidedly uncommon ones—who are not vulgar. What were once designated the lower orders may be coarse or crude, may indeed be common or cheap or disgusting. But the things they do that are most beyond the pale—belch or spit, eat with their knives or sleep in their underwear—do not quite fit our current sense of "vulgar." It is crude to eat with your knife; what is vulgar is to drink tea with your little finger extended. It is disgusting to pick your teeth; what is vulgar is to use a gold toothpick. It is illiterate to say "aint I"; what is vulgar is to say "aren't I." The common people, as a group, are not vulgar if only because they don't know enough or care enough to be.

It is among those who would once have been termed their betters that we encounter vulgarity full blast. We encounter it, that is, when signs of education have entered in; when there is a certain awareness of social or cultural or esthetic right and wrong; when there is a craving to attract notice or seem to belong. We are never, said La Rochefoucauld, so ridiculous through the qualities we have as through those we pretend to; and we are never, he might have added, so cheap. For, together with such pretensions, there almost always goes the attempt to mask them—the coy tactic, the devious maneuvre. Vulgarity, I would think, involves motivation. People are vulgar when, for self-interested reasons, they resort to unworthy methods—whenever they do something to falsify or floodlight their prestige or importance, their claims to position or talent or knowledge. They are equally vulgar when, from the same kind of motives, they fail to do something. One of the columnists told of a Broadway figure who displayed a new gold cigarette case. "I'm sick of gold," he remarked —"what I'd have really liked was a platinum cigarette case: but my friends would have thought it was silver."

At an innocuous level, vulgarity is mere vanity—people's wanting to look their best, or better than their best. Oliver Cromwell might exhort the portraitist to paint him warts and all; most of us desire to have the warts removed, and dimples added. Few of us speak as readily of the ancestor who was hanged as of the ancestor who was knighted. But if we weren't a little vulgar in matters of this sort we might be something much worse, we might be unbearably priggish. It is not till people, in manifesting superiority, begin to seem sniffy and cheap—or no better than what they disparage—that vulgarity turns offensive. The well-placed have for generations made a vulgar ploy of vulgarity: Jones, they will remark, had "the bad taste" to refer to something they didn't want mentioned; or Smith had "the insolence" to remind them of something they preferred to forget. This sort of high-handedness always has vulgar blood; high-handedness, indeed, must pass an esthetic test of being more stylish or witty than it is arrogant and rude. Equally, there are right and wrong snubs. The wrong ones can be as illbred as anything they wish to pulverize. For a nice snub, consider the very nobly born Frenchman to whom some one not half so wellborn was bragging of his vast family mansion with its great high-domed dining-room. "With us," the Frenchman finally murmured, "it's just the other way. Our dining-room is so low that all we can eat is fried sole."

Obviously, there are ways in which human and artistic vulgarity differ. Vulgarity in life is not just an esthetic offense; it has a falseness or impurity about it, an *inner* cheapness. Vulgar people often display perfect form; can talk well, live smartly, even get discreetly ahead in the world. But as they grow superficially more presentable, they grow, if anything, inwardly more insensitive. There is even a kind of vulgarity so self-assured as to take pride in flaunting itself: a very famous theater personage sent out, as a Christmas card, a picture of himself posing for a beer ad. Vulgarity in art, on the other hand, usually involves form as well as substance, and questions of esthetic effect. But it, too, largely derives from a false or flashy motive, from a greater wish to be impressive than sound. Often in men of much talent we find a streak of it—of excess or exhibitionism, specious beauty or spurious virtue. Swinburne can be too lilting or lush; Wilde and Disraeli use too much pomade; Tennessee Williams can be lavishly sensational, William Saroyan ostentatiously humane.

On the other hand, we must distinguish between styles in art and the vulgarization of a style. Thus, gingerbread architecture with its childlike Hansel-and-Gretel playfulness may be far less vulgar than "classical" mansions that look like U.S. subtreasuries. One may not respond to the baroque of Tiepolo's frescoes or Prandtauer's architecture; but except where misapplied, baroque is not vulgar in the least. Indeed, the real test of taste perhaps only arises at the level of the ornamented or theatrical. Any one, by playing safe, by wearing only grey and navy blue, by sticking to the best Georgian spoons, by reading Virgil or Racine, can be unassailably tasteful. The test of taste comes in one's particular use of bright paint and loud colors, or harps and trumpets, or marble and jewels. Almost any one can grasp the vulgarity in Liszt and the lack of it in Mozart; it is more difficult to grasp the vulgar lapses in Wagner and the lack of them in Berlioz. And certainly one great form of vulgarity is the fear of vulgarity; it flaws the work of even a Henry James.

II

Vulgarity does not stand still: there are fashions in it, it shows progress, it gains on one front and loses on another. The world of today differs strikingly from that of two centuries ago—machinery and mass production, literacy and mass communication, democracy and relatively classless living have proved banes and blessings alike. Material display—the overmuch, the over-large, the over-stuffed, the over-shiny—has in great part been streamlined into submission. Our material tastes have not only learned from the excesses of the past, they are shaped by the exigencies of the present. What with a general lack of space today, and lack of servants; with doctors and diets, with the rise of sport and decline of prudery, most people eat, dress, live, travel, entertain more simply. To gorge or splurge is curiously unchic. Most people indeed live like most other people, in a world of deep-freezes, dishwashers, station wagons, casseroles and baby-sitters. A pantry maid is almost as remote as a coach-and-four; and a man may see the same dress on his secretary as on his wife. And with so much social and cultural leveling off, vulgar display has steeply declined.

The new vulgarity is different. The old vulgarity followed that classic rule for the playwright—always show rather than tell. The vulgar used to show how grand they were by the size of their houses, the massiness of their plate, the snootiness of their butlers; by how they over-dressed, over-tipped, overrode those about them. They never said they were rich; they never had to.

Today the old stage formula has been discarded for the blunter vulgarity of *announcing* one's importance. Self-display has passed over into self-advertisement; and it is not so much the business world that conducts itself so as the world of journalism, of Hollywood and Broadway, of TV and "the communication arts." In that world people, beyond frequently engaging paid publicists, distribute their own testimonials, write their own plugs, sing their own praises, stress their own good deeds. And when not patting their own backs, they are slapping—or stabbing—other people's. When they cannot command the limelight, they invade it. This is an age of name-dropping—and of last-name-dropping even more—when on meeting a famous man of sixty, a man of twenty-four straightway calls him Bill. And as the first name flourishes in speech, so does the first person in writing. Serious writers turn out waggish pieces as a way of plugging their books. Columnists brag, when the most piffling news story breaks, how they had predicted it months before. Into the body of their newspaper stints people inject commercials about their TV appearances. Even all sense of occasion has vanished. At a small private New Year's Eve party, while the guests were watching, on TV, the crowds gathered in Times Square, one television man sang out loudly to another: "They wanted *me* to handle this—but we couldn't get together on the dough." The remark, to be sure, isn't much more vulgar than the sort of gathering that makes it possible. In the professional world today, entertainment tends to be the merest form of self-advancement, of blandly feeding the mouth that bites you, of managing to be seen, of striking up useful connections on sofas, of cooking up deals over drinks. Even those hostesses who are above the battle and imagine they are exhibiting lions are actually racing rats.

All this, however appalling, is today perhaps inevitable. What with ratings and samplings, press-agentry and polls, people who are supposed to mold and influence others must more and more promote themselves, make shop-windows of their offices, show windows of their homes. Truman Capote, in his book about the visit of the *Porgy and Bess* troupe to the Soviet Union, told how, while most of those on board the train going into Russia relaxed and joked, a columnist was kidded for sitting in a compartment alone, pounding relentlessly away at his typewriter. "People don't get into my income-tax bracket," he explained, "by looking at scenery."

Furthermore, the whole fashion in entertaining, or interviewing, or "educating" mass audiences today tends to throw privacy to the winds, to make publicity not just an unreprehensible, but a greatly respected, side of modern life. To use zoological terms once more—it keeps getting harder to use strictly human ones—there now goes on a kind of human horse show, in which blue-ribboned personalities are trotted up and down, are photographed, queried, televised; or are just put on view as distinguished hosts or pedigreed hostesses endorsing Scotch or bed-sheets or soap. For the amateurs in all this, the appeal to vanity may be enough: for the professionals, it is part of a fierce struggle to survive. Big-name feuding is no longer mere internecine strife; it is a spectator sport. Which of two feuders will come out ahead is on a par with which of two football teams.

The worst part of all this is that it has *become* such a spectator sport. It was said, long ago, that evil communications corrupt good manners: it might be said more pertinently today that mass communication corrupts good manners, that we are all being gradually worn down, that without even being aware of it, we are acquiescing in what would have appalled us twenty-five years ago. And how not, with the very air we breathe commercialized, with the very lives we live treated as so much copy? Quite literally, it is the gossip columnist's business to write about what is none of his business. The quiz programs with their venal lure and test-of-virtue stakes have vanished; but another kind of quiz program survives, where interviewers ask people—before millions of listeners—questions that their closest friends might hesitate to ask them when alone.

It is perfectly true that it takes two to make up such interviews—and millions, listening in, to make a go of them. Clearly, were there no people willing to be questioned, and no large audiences intent upon the answers, such programs could not exist. But, psychologically and sociologically, the thing is not so simple. With the person interviewed, vanity; love of the limelight; the fear that it will go elsewhere, are strong inducements; and in an age when publicity has become respectable and when psychiatry has licensed people to Tell All, fewer and fewer are those who when invited will say No. But what has happened to the performer is really less important than what has happened to the public. Of course, the average person is full of curiosity and enjoys gossip. But to argue that—because he's something of a peeping tom—it's his inquisitiveness that produces such interviews, is pure peeping-tommyrot. We bring up our children, we order our lives, we regulate our society on the contrary principle that our shoddier instincts should not be deliberately pandered to. Those most genuinely concerned for freedom of speech are no less concerned for the right of privacy; nor are they misled when sensationalism appears purporting to be the servant of truth, or when psychiatry is commercially invoked to chaperone smut. The motive of the scandal magazines is all too clear. It is where the motive is masked, when privacy is invaded on the pretext of a sociological search warrant, that a more menacing vulgarization appears; and as the product of such corrupting alliances, what sort of children will inhabit the world of tomorrow? For in time values not only get tarnished: they even get turned around. A few years ago George S. Kaufman, by complaining that *Stille Nacht* was being turned into a kind of cheap Christmas commercial, roused a storm of furious protest against himself: in the face of such things, who shall dare to argue that people can distinguish God from Mammon?

We live in a world where TV is now sovereign, is so enthroned that 50,000,000 Americans sit bareheaded before it for hours on end, enduring blare for the sake of glare, and forever plagued by those powers behind the throne—the sponsors with their intrusions. *Of course* there are good television programs; but that is sociologically beyond the point. The point is that for tens of millions of people TV has become habit-forming, brain-softening, taste-degrading; has altered for the worse the whole cultural climate of American life. Privacy was in sufficient danger before TV appeared; and TV has given it its death blow. And as all liking for privacy vanishes, all dislike for publicity must vanish too. Men that one would have supposed had distinction are nowadays Men of Distinction by way

of the ads. Indeed, the better known a man is for his taste or good character, the more he is sought out, the more he is importuned, to sully or
betray them. When those who shape our manners shout at parties about
not getting together over the dough, or send out their beer blurbs as
Christmas cards, who shall maintain that the vulgarity that once featured
a clock planted in a Venus de Milo's belly has disappeared? Some of us
might even put back the clock if we could.

E. M. FORSTER

*Edward Morgan Forster, British novelist and critic, was born in 1879
and educated at King's College, Cambridge. Shortly after his graduation,
in a period of five years, he published four of his five novels:* Where
Angels Fear to Tread *(1905),* The Longest Journey *(1907),* A Room
With a View *(1908), and* Howard's End *(1910), which many regard as
his masterpiece. In 1911, the year after* Howard's End *was published,
Forster went to India for the first time. He spent the World War I years
in Alexandria, doing civilian war work, but returned to London after the
war, became a reviewer for the* New Statesman, Spectator, *and other
papers, and served for a brief period as literary editor of the* Labor Daily
Herald. *He again traveled to India in 1921, and thereafter completed his
fifth, last, and best-known novel,* A Passage to India *(1924). He has also
published two collections of short stories,* Celestial Omnibus *(1912) and*
The Eternal Moment *(1928), but since the late twenties his writing has
been mainly non-fiction. In 1927 he delivered the Clark lectures at King's
College, Cambridge, which he published the same year as* Aspects of the
Novel. *Two collections of reviews and articles followed:* Abinger Harvest
(1936) and Two Cheers for Democracy *(1951), from which we take the
essay below. In 1953 Forster was awarded membership in the Order of
Companions of Honour by Queen Elizabeth.*

A BOOK THAT INFLUENCED ME

It was rather a little book, and that introduces my first point. One's impulse, on tackling the question of influence, is to search for a great book, and to assume that here is the force which has moulded one's outlook and character. Looking back upon my own half-century of reading, I have no doubt which my three great books have been: Dante's *Divine Comedy*, Gibbon's *Decline and Fall*, and Tolstoy's *War and Peace*. All three are great both in quality and in bulk. Bulk is not to be despised. Combined with quality, it gives a long book a pull over a short one, and permits us to call it monumental. Here are three monuments. But they have not influenced me in the least, though I came across them all at an impressionable age. They impressed me by their massiveness and design, and made me feel small in the right way, and to make us feel small in the right way is a function of art; men can only make us feel small in the wrong way. But to realise the vastness of the universe, the limits of human knowledge, the even narrower limits of human power, to catch a passing glimpse of the mediaeval universe, or of the Roman Empire on its millennial way, or of Napoleon collapsing against the panorama of Russian daily life—that is not to be influenced. It is to be extended. Perhaps those three books were too monumental, and human beings are not much influenced by monuments. They gaze, say "Oh!" and pass on unchanged. They are more likely to be influenced by objects nearer their own size. Anyhow, that has been my own case.

The book in question is Samuel Butler's *Erewhon*, a work of genius, but with Dante, Gibbon and Tolstoy setting our standards not to be called great. It has been better described as "a serious book not written too seriously."

Published as far back as 1872, it is difficult to classify—partly a yarn, partly an account of Utopia, partly a satire on Victorian civilisation. It opens with some superb descriptions of mountain scenery: this part is taken from Butler's New Zealand experiences. The hero is a bit of a scamp, and not so much a living character as a vehicle for the author's likes and dislikes, and for his mischievousness. He has left England under a cloud for a distant colony, with the intention of converting some lost tribe to Christianity at a handsome profit. He hears that beyond the mountain range there are terrible figures, and still more terrible sounds. He sets out, and presently discovers enormous and frightful statues, through whose hollow heads the wind moans. They are the guardians of Erewhon. Struggling past them, he enters the unknown country, and the fantasy proper begins. The descent on the further side beyond the statues is exquisitely related, and the scenery now suggests the Italian slopes of the Alps. He is politely imprisoned by the mountaineers until instructions as to his disposal can come up from the capital. But there are two hitches. One of them occurs when his watch is discovered on him. The other is with his jailer's daughter, Yram (Erewhonian for Mary). He and she get on well, and when he catches a cold he makes the most of it, in the hope of being cosseted by her. She flies into a fury.

By now he has learnt the language, and is summoned to the capital. He is to be the guest of a Mr. Nosnibor and the account of Mr. Nosnibor puzzles him. "He is," says his informant, "a most delightful man, who has but lately recovered from embezzling a large sum of money under singularly distressing circumstances; you are sure to like him." What can this all mean? It's wrong to have a watch, wrong to catch a cold, but embezzlement is only a subject for sympathy. The reader is equally puzzled, and skilfully does Butler lead us into the heart of this topsy-turvy country, without explaining its fantasies too soon. Take the Musical Banks. Erewhon, it seems, has two banking systems, one of them like ours, the other is Musical Banking. Mr. Nosnibor, as befits a dubious financier, goes constantly to the first sort of bank, but never attends the offices of the second, though he is ostensibly its ardent supporter. Mrs. Nosnibor and her daughters go once a week. Each bank has its own coinage, the coins of the musical banks being highly esteemed, but of no commercial value, as the hero soon discovers when he tries to tip one of its officials with them. Just as in Swift we read for a bit about the Yahoos without realising that he intends them for ourselves, so we read about the Musical Banks, and only gradually realise that they caricature the Church of England and its connections with Capitalism. There was a great row over this chapter as soon as it was understood; the "enfant terrible," as he called himself, had indeed heaved a brick. He also shocked people by reversing the positions of crime and illness. In Erewhon it is wicked to be ill—that is why Yram was angry when the hero had a cold. Embezzlement, on the other hand, is a disease. Mr. Nosnibor is treated for it professionally and very severely. "Poor papa," says his charming daughter, "I really do not think he will steal any more." And as for possessing a watch—all machinery invented after a certain date has been destroyed by the Erewhonians, lest it breed new machines, who may enslave men. And there are further brilliant inventions —for instance, the College of Unreason, who teach a Hypothetical Language, never used outside their walls, and in whom we must reluctantly recognize the ancient universities of Oxford and Cambridge, and their schools of Latin and Greek. And there is the worship of the Goddess Ydgrun (Mrs. Grundy); for worship is mostly bad, yet it produces a few fine people, the High Ydgrunites. These people were conventional in the right way: they hadn't too many ideals, and they were always willing to drop a couple to oblige a friend. In the High Ydgrunites we come to what Butler thought desirable. Although a rebel, he was not a reformer. He believed in the conventions, provided they are observed humanely. Grace and graciousness, good temper, good looks, good health and good sense; tolerance, intelligence, and willingness to abandon any moral standard at a pinch. That is what he admired.

The book ends, as it began, in the atmosphere of adventure. The hero elopes with Miss Nosnibor in a balloon. The splendid descriptions of natural scenery are resumed, they fall into the sea and are rescued, and we leave him as secretary of the Erewhon Evangelisation Company in London, asking for subscriptions for the purpose of converting the country to Christianity with the aid of a small expeditionary force. "An uncalled-for joke?" If you think so, you have fallen into one of Butler's little traps. He wanted to make uncalled-for jokes. He wanted to write a serious book not too seriously.

Why did this book influence me? For one thing, I have the sort of mind which likes to be taken unawares. The frontal full-dress presentation of an opinion often repels me, but if it be insidiously slipped in sidewise I may receive it, and Butler is a master of the oblique. Then, what he had to say was congenial, and I lapped it up. It was the food for which I was waiting. And this brings me to my next point. I suggest that the only books that influence us are those for which we are ready, and which have gone a little farther down our particular path than we have yet got ourselves. I suggest, furthermore, that when you feel that you could almost have written the book yourself—that's the moment when it's influencing you. You are not influenced when you say, "How marvellous! What a revelation! How monumental. Oh!" You are being extended. You are being influenced when you say "I might have written that myself if I hadn't been so busy." I don't suppose that I could have written the *Divine Comedy* or the *Decline and Fall*. I don't even think I could have written the *Antigone* of Sophocles, though of all the great tragic utterances that comes closest to my heart, that is my central faith. But I do think (quite erroneously) that I could have turned out this little skit of Erewhon if the idea of it had occurred to me. Which is strong evidence that it has influenced me.

Erewhon also influenced me in its technique. I like that idea of fantasy, of muddling up the actual and the impossible until the reader isn't sure which is which, and I have sometimes tried to do it when writing myself. However, I mustn't start on technique. Let me rather get in an observation which was put to me the other day by a friend. What about the books which influence us negatively, which give us the food we don't want, or, maybe, are unfit for, and so help us to realize what we do want? I have amused myself by putting down four books which have influenced me negatively. They are books by great writers, and I have appreciated them. But they are not my sort of book. They are: *The Confessions* of St. Augustine, Macchiavelli's *Prince*, Swift's *Gulliver*, and Carlyle on *Heroes and Hero Worship*. All these books have influenced me negatively, and impelled me away from them towards my natural food. I know that St. Augustine's *Confessions* is a "good" book, and I want to be good. But not in St. Augustine's way. I don't want the goodness which entails an asceticism close to cruelty. I prefer the goodness of William Blake. And Macchiavelli—he is clever—and unlike some of my compatriots I want to be clever. But not with Macchiavelli's cold, inhuman cleverness. I prefer the cleverness of Voltaire. And indignation—Swift's indignation in *Gulliver* is too savage for me; I prefer Butler's in *Erewhon*. And strength—yes, I want to be strong, but not with the strength of Carlyle's dictator heroes, who foreshadow Hitler. I prefer the strength of Antigone.

VIRGINIA WOOLF

Virginia Woolf (1882–1941) was the daughter of a prominent English scholar and critic, Sir Leslie Stephen, and was educated mainly in her father's library and in extensive travels. In 1917, she and her husband, Leonard Woolf, began printing on a hand press their own writings and those of other (then obscure) authors like Katherine Mansfield, T. S. Eliot, and E. M. Forster. This was the beginning of the celebrated Hogarth Press and center of the so-called "Bloomsbury Group" of intellectuals and writers. Mrs. Woolf is particularly noted for her novels, among which we mention Mrs. Dalloway *(1925),* To the Lighthouse *(1927),* Orlando *(1928), and* The Waves *(1931) as a few of the best. They are considered important experiments in novelistic form: she disregards ordinary factual description of characters and action, concentrating instead on psychological penetration and on variations in temporal perspective and rhythm. Mrs. Woolf also wrote many reviews and essays, on art and literature, and on the problems of social and economic reform. Her literary essays were collected in* The Common Reader *(1925; second series, 1932),* The Death of the Moth *(1942), and* The Moment and Other Essays *(1947). Her social writings may be found in* A Room of One's Own *(1929) and* Three Guineas *(1938). The present essay is from* The Common Reader, *second series, where it is described as "a paper read at a School."*

HOW SHOULD ONE READ A BOOK?

In the first place, I want to emphasize the note of interrogation at the end of my title. Even if I could answer the question for myself, the answer would apply only to me and not to you. The only advice, indeed, that one person can give another about reading is to take no advice, to follow your own instincts, to use your own reason, to come to your own conclusions. If this is agreed between us, then I feel at liberty to put forward a few ideas and suggestions because you will not allow them to fetter that independence which is the most important quality that a reader can possess. After all, what laws can be laid down about books? The battle of Waterloo was certainly fought on a certain day; but is *Hamlet* a better play than *Lear?* Nobody can say. Each must decide that question for himself. To admit authorities, however heavily furred and gowned, into our libraries and let them tell us how to read, what to read, what value to place upon what we read, is to destroy the spirit of freedom which is the breath of those sanctuaries. Everywhere else we may be bound by laws and conventions—there we have none.

But to enjoy freedom, if the platitude is pardonable, we have of course to control ourselves. We must not squander our powers, helplessly and ignorantly, squirting half the house in order to water a single rose-bush; we must train them, exactly and powerfully, here on the very spot. This, it may be, is one of the first difficulties that faces us in a library. What is "the very spot"? There may well seem to be nothing but a conglomeration and huddle of confusion. Poems and novels, histories and memoirs, dictionaries and blue-books; books written in all languages by men and women of all tempers, races, and ages jostle each other on the shelf. And outside the donkey brays, the women gossip at the pump, the colts gallop across the fields. Where are we to begin? How are we to bring order into this multitudinous chaos and so get the deepest and widest pleasure from what we read?

It is simple enough to say that since books have classes—fiction, biography, poetry—we should separate them and take from each what it is right that each should give us. Yet few people ask from books what books can give us. Most commonly we come to books with blurred and divided minds, asking of fiction that it shall be true, of poetry that it shall be false, of biography that it shall be flattering, of history that it shall enforce our own prejudices. If we could banish all such preconceptions when we read, that would be an admirable beginning. Do not dictate to your author; try to become him. Be his fellow-worker and accomplice. If you hang back, and reserve and criticize at first, you are preventing yourself from getting the fullest possible value from what you read. But if you open your mind as widely as possible, then signs and hints of almost imperceptible fineness, from the twist and turn of the first sentences, will bring you into the presence of a human being unlike any other. Steep yourself in this, acquaint yourself with this, and soon you will find that your author is giving you, or attempting to give you, something far more definite. The thirty-two chapters of a novel— if we consider how to read a novel first—are an attempt to make something as formed and controlled as a building: but words are more impalpable than bricks; reading is a longer and more complicated process than seeing. Perhaps the quickest way to understand the elements of what a novelist is doing is not to read, but to write; to make your own experiment with the dangers and difficulties of words. Recall, then, some event that has left a distinct impression on you—how at the corner of the street, perhaps, you passed two people talking. A tree shook; an electric light danced; the tone of the talk was comic, but also tragic; a whole vision, an entire conception, seemed contained in that moment.

But when you attempt to reconstruct it in words, you will find that it breaks into a thousand conflicting impressions. Some must be subdued; others emphasized; in the process you will lose, probably, all grasp upon the emotion itself. Then turn from your blurred and littered pages to the opening pages of some great novelist—Defoe, Jane Austen, Hardy. Now you will be better able to appreciate their mastery. It is not merely that we are in the presence of a different person—Defoe, Jane Austen, or Thomas Hardy—but that we are living in a different world. Here, in *Robinson Crusoe*, we are trudging a plain high road; one thing happens after another; the fact and the order of the fact is enough. But if the open air and adventure mean everything to Defoe they mean nothing to Jane Austen. Hers is the drawing-room, and people talking, and by the many mirrors of their talk revealing their characters. And if, when we have accustomed ourselves to the drawing-room and its reflections, we turn to Hardy, we are once more spun round. The moors are round us and the stars are above our heads. The other side of the mind is now exposed—the dark side that comes uppermost in solitude, not the light side that shows in company. Our relations are not towards people, but towards Nature and destiny. Yet different as these worlds are, each is consistent with itself. The maker of each is careful to observe the laws of his own perspective, and however great a strain they may put upon us they will never confuse us, as lesser writers so frequently do, by introducing two different kinds of reality into the same book. Thus to go from one great novelist to another—from Jane Austen to Hardy, from Peacock to Trollope, from Scott to Meredith—is to be wrenched and uprooted; to be thrown this way and then that. To read a novel is a difficult and complex art. You must be capable not only of great fineness of perception, but of great boldness of imagination if you are going to make use of all that the novelist—the great artist—gives you.

But a glance at the heterogeneous company on the shelf will show you that writers are very seldom "great artists"; far more often a book makes no claim to be a work of art at all. These biographies and autobiographies, for example, lives of great men, of men long dead and forgotten, that stand cheek by jowl with the novels and poems, are we to refuse to read them because they are not "art"? Or shall we read them, but read them in a different way, with a different aim? Shall we read them in the first place to satisfy that curiosity which possesses us sometimes when in the evening we linger in front of a house where the lights are lit and the blinds not yet drawn, and each floor of the house shows us a different section of human life in being? Then we are consumed with curiosity about the lives of these people—the servants gossiping, the gentlemen dining, the girl dressing for a party, the old woman at the window with her knitting. Who are they, what are they, what are their names, their occupations, their thoughts, and adventures?

Biographies and memoirs answer such questions, light up innumerable such houses; they show us people going about their daily affairs, toiling, failing, succeeding, eating, hating, loving, until they die. And sometimes as we watch, the house fades and the iron railings vanish and we are out at sea; we are hunting, sailing, fighting; we are among savages and soldiers; we are taking part in great campaigns. Or if we like to stay here in England, in London, still the scene changes; the street narrows; the house becomes small, cramped, diamond-paned, and malodorous. We see a poet, Donne, driven from such a house because the walls were so thin that when the children cried their voices cut through them. We can follow him, through the paths that lie in the pages of books, to Twickenham; to Lady Bedford's Park, a famous meeting-ground for nobles and poets; and then turn our steps to Wilton, the great house under the downs, and hear Sidney read the *Arcadia* to his sister; and ramble among the very marshes and see the very herons that figure in that famous romance; and then again travel north with that other Lady Pembroke, Anne Clifford, to her wild moors, or plunge into the city and control our merriment at the sight of Gabriel Harvey in his black velvet suit arguing about poetry with Spenser. Nothing is more fascinating than to grope and stumble in the alternate darkness and splendour of Elizabethan London. But there is no staying there. The Temples and the Swifts, the Harleys and the St. Johns beckon us on; hour upon hour can be spent disentangling their quarrels and deciphering their characters; and when we tire of them we can stroll on, past a lady in black wearing diamonds, to Samuel Johnson and Goldsmith and Garrick; or cross the channel, if we like, and meet Voltaire and Diderot, Madame du Deffand; and so back to England and Twickenham—how certain places repeat themselves and certain names!—where Lady Bedford had her Park once and Pope lived later, to Walpole's home at Strawberry Hill. But Walpole introduces us to such a swarm of new acquaintances, there are so many houses to visit and bells to ring that we may well hesitate for a moment, on the

Miss Berrys' doorstep, for example, when behold, up comes Thackeray; he is the friend of the woman whom Walpole loved; so that merely by going from friend to friend, from garden to garden, from house to house, we have passed from one end of English literature to another and wake to find ourselves here again in the present, if we can so differentiate this moment from all that have gone before. This, then, is one of the ways in which we can read these lives and letters; we can make them light up the many windows of the past; we can watch the famous dead in their familiar habits and fancy sometimes that we are very close and can surprise their secrets, and sometimes we may pull out a play or a poem that they have written and see whether it reads differently in the presence of the author. But this again rouses other questions. How far, we must ask ourselves, is a book influenced by its writer's life—how far is it safe to let the man interpret the writer? How far shall we resist or give way to the sympathies and antipathies that the man himself rouses in us—so sensitive are words, so receptive of the character of the author? These are questions that press upon us when we read lives and letters, and we must answer them for ourselves, for nothing can be more fatal than to be guided by the preferences of others in a matter so personal.

But also we can read such books with another aim, not to throw light on literature, not to become familiar with famous people, but to refresh and exercise our own creative powers. Is there not an open window on the right hand of the bookcase? How delightful to stop reading and look out! How stimulating the scene is, in its unconsciousness, its irrelevance, its perpetual movement—the colts galloping round the field, the woman filling her pail at the well, the donkey throwing back his head and emitting his long, acrid moan. The greater part of any library is nothing but the record of such fleeting moments in the lives of men, women, and donkeys. Every literature, as it grows old, has its rubbish-heap, its record of vanished moments and forgotten lives told in faltering and feeble accents that have perished. But if you give yourself up to the delight of rubbish-reading you will be surprised, indeed you will be overcome, by the relics of human life that have been cast out to moulder. It may be one letter—but what a vision it gives! It may be a few sentences—but what vistas they suggest! Sometimes a whole story will come together with such beautiful humour and pathos and completeness that it seems as if a great novelist had been at work, yet it is only an old actor, Tate Wilkinson, remembering the strange story of Captain Jones; it is only a young subaltern serving under Arthur Wellesley and falling in love with a pretty girl at Lisbon; it is only Maria Allen letting fall her sewing in the empty drawing-room and sighing how she wishes she had taken Dr. Burney's good advice and had never eloped with her Rishy. None of this has any value; it is negligible in the extreme; yet how absorbing it is now and again to go through the rubbish-heaps and find rings and scissors and broken noses buried in the huge past and try to piece them together while the colt gallops round the field, the woman fills her pail at the well, and the donkey brays.

But we tire of rubbish-reading in the long run. We tire of searching for what is needed to complete the half-truth which is all that the Wilkinsons, the Bunburys, and the Maria Allens are able to offer us. They had not the artist's power of mastering and eliminating; they could not tell the whole truth even about their own lives; they have disfigured the story that might have been so shapely. Facts are all that they can offer us, and facts are a very inferior form of fiction. Thus the desire grows upon us to have done with half-statements and approximations; to cease from searching out the minute shades of human character, to enjoy the greater abstractness, the purer truth of fiction. Thus we create the mood, intense and generalised, unaware of detail, but stressed by some regular, recurrent beat, whose natural expression is poetry; and that is the time to read poetry when we are almost able to write it.

> Western wind, when wilt thou blow?
> The small rain down can rain.
> Christ, if my love were in my arms,
> And I in my bed again!

The impact of poetry is so hard and direct that for the moment there is no other sensation except that of the poem itself. What profound depths we visit then—how sudden and complete is our immersion! There is nothing here to catch hold of; nothing to stay us in our flight. The illusion of fiction is gradual; its effects are prepared; but who when they read these four lines stops to ask who wrote them, or conjures up the thought of Donne's house or Sidney's secretary; or enmeshes them in the intricacy of the past and the succession of generations? The poet is always our contemporary. Our being for the moment is centred and constricted, as in any violent shock of personal emotion. Afterwards, it is true, the sensation begins to spread in wider rings through our minds; remoter senses are reached; these begin to sound and to comment and we are aware of echoes and reflections. The intensity of poetry covers an immense range of emotion. We have only to compare the force and directness of

> I shall fall like a tree, and find my grave,
>   Only remembering that I grieve,

with the wavering modulation of

> Minutes are numbered by the fall of sands,
> As by an hour glass; the span of time
> Doth waste us to our graves, and we look on it;
> An age of pleasure, revelled out, comes home
> At last, and ends in sorrow; but the life,

> Weary of riot, numbers every sand,
> Wailing in sighs, until the last drop down,
> So to conclude calamity in rest,

or place the meditative calm of

> whether we be young or old,
> Our destiny, our being's heart and home,
> Is with infinitude, and only there;
> With hope it is, hope that can never die,
> Effort, and expectation, and desire,
> And something evermore about to be,

beside the complete and inexhaustible loveliness of

> The moving Moon went up the sky,
> And no where did abide:
> Softly she was going up,
> And a star or two beside—

or the splendid fantasy of

> And the woodland haunter
> Shall not cease to saunter
>   When, far down some glade,
> Of the great world's burning,
> One soft flame upturning
> Seems, to his discerning,
>   Crocus in the shade.

to bethink us of the varied art of the poet; his power to make us at once actors and spectators; his power to run his hand into character as if it were a glove, and be Falstaff or Lear; his power to condense, to widen, to state, once and for ever.

"We have only to compare"—with those words the cat is out of the bag, and the true complexity of reading is admitted. The first process, to receive impressions with the utmost understanding, is only half the process of reading; it must be completed, if we are to get the whole pleasure from a book, by another. We must pass judgment upon these multitudinous impressions; we must make of these fleeting shapes one that is hard and lasting. But not directly. Wait for the dust of reading to settle; for the conflict and the questioning to die down; walk, talk, pull the dead petals from a rose, or fall asleep. Then suddenly without our willing it, for it is thus that Nature undertakes these transitions, the book will return, but differently. It will float to the top of the mind as a whole. And the book as a whole is different from the book received currently in separate phrases. Details now fit themselves into their places. We see the shape from start to finish; it is a barn, a pig-sty, or a cathedral.

Now then we can compare book with book as we compare building with building. But this act of comparison means that our attitude has changed; we are no longer the friends of the writer, but his judges; and just as we cannot be too sympathetic as friends, so as judges we cannot be too severe. Are they not criminals, books that have wasted our time and sympathy; are they not the most insidious enemies of society, corrupters, defilers, the writers of false books, faked books, books that fill the air with decay and disease? Let us then be severe in our judgments; let us compare each book with the greatest of its kind. There they hang in the mind the shapes of the books we have read solidified by the judgments we have passed on them—*Robinson Crusoe, Emma, The Return of the Native*. Compare the novels with these—even the latest and least of novels has a right to be judged with the best. And so with poetry—when the intoxication of rhythm has died down and the splendour of words has faded a visionary shape will return to us and this must be compared with *Lear*, with *Phèdre*, with *The Prelude;* or if not with these, with whatever is the best or seems to us to be the best in its own kind. And we may be sure that the newness of new poetry and fiction is its most superficial quality and that we have only to alter slightly, not to recast, the standards by which we have judged the old.

It would be foolish, then, to pretend that the second part of reading, to judge, to compare, is as simple as the first—to open the mind wide to the fast flocking of innumerable impressions. To continue reading without the book before you, to hold one shadow-shape against another, to have read widely enough and with enough understanding to make such comparisons alive and illuminating—that is difficult; it is still more difficult to press further and to say, "Not only is the book of this sort, but it is of this value; here it fails; here it succeeds; this is bad; that is good". To carry out this part of a reader's duty needs such imagination, insight, and learning that it is hard to conceive any one mind sufficiently endowed; impossible for the most self-confident to find more than the seeds of such powers in himself. Would it not be wiser, then, to remit this part of reading and to allow the critics, the gowned and furred authorities of the library, to decide the question of the book's absolute value for us? Yet how impossible! We may stress the value of sympathy; we may try to sink our own identity as we read. But we know that we cannot sympathise wholly or immerse ourselves wholly; there is always a demon in us who whispers, "I hate, I love", and we cannot silence him. Indeed, it is precisely because we hate and we love that our relation with the poets and novelists is so intimate that we find the presence of another person intolerable. And even if the results are abhorrent and our judgments are wrong, still our taste, the nerve of sensation that sends shocks through us, is our chief illuminant; we learn through feeling; we cannot suppress our own idiosyncrasy without impoverishing it. But as time goes on perhaps we can train our taste; perhaps we can make it submit to some control. When it has fed greedily and lavishly upon books of all sorts—poetry, fiction, history, biography—and has stopped reading and looked for long spaces upon the variety, the incongruity of the living world, we shall find that it is changing a little; it is not so greedy, it is more reflective. It will begin to bring us not merely judgments on particular books, but it will tell us that there is a quality common to certain books. Listen, it will say, what shall we call *this?* And it will read us perhaps *Lear* and then perhaps the *Agamemnon* in order to bring out that common quality. Thus, with our taste to guide us, we shall venture beyond the particular book in search of qualities that group books together; we shall give them names and thus frame a rule that brings order into our perceptions. We shall gain a further and a rarer pleasure from that discrimination. But as a rule only lives when it is perpetually broken by contact with the books themselves—nothing is easier and more stultifying than to make rules which exist out of touch with facts, in a vacuum— now at last, in order to steady ourselves in this difficult attempt, it may be well to turn to the very rare writers who are able to enlighten us upon literature as an art. Coleridge and Dryden and Johnson, in their considered criticism, the poets and novelists themselves in their unconsidered sayings, are often surprisingly relevant; they light up and solidify the vague ideas that have been tumbling in the misty depths of our minds. But they are only able to help us if we come to them laden with questions and suggestions won honestly in the course of our own reading. They can do nothing for us if we herd ourselves under their authority and lie down like sheep in the shade of a hedge. We can only understand their ruling when it comes in conflict with our own and vanquishes it.

If this is so, if to read a book as it should be read calls for the rarest qualities of imagination, insight, and judgment, you may perhaps conclude that literature is a very complex art and that it is unlikely that we shall be able, even after a lifetime of reading, to make any valuable contribution to its criticism. We must remain readers; we shall not put on the further glory that belongs to those rare beings who are also critics. But still we have our responsibilities as readers and even our importance. The standards we raise and the judgments we pass steal into the air and become part of the atmosphere which writers breathe as they work. An influence is created which tells upon them even if it never finds its way into print. And that influence, if it were well instructed, vigorous and individual and sincere, might be of great value now when criticism is necessarily in abeyance; when books pass in review like the procession of animals in a shooting gallery, and the critic has only one second in which to load and aim and shoot and may well be pardoned if he mistakes rabbits for tigers, eagles for barndoor fowls, or misses altogether and wastes his shot upon some peaceful cow grazing in a further field. If behind the erratic gunfire of the press the author felt that there was another kind of criticism, the opinion of people reading for the love of reading, slowly and unprofessionally, and judging with great sympathy and yet with great severity, might this not improve the quality of his work? And if by our means books were to become stronger, richer, and more varied, that would be an end worth reaching.

Yet who reads to bring about an end however desirable? Are there not some pursuits that we practise because they are good in themselves, and some pleasures that are final? And is not this among them? I have sometimes dreamt, at least, that when the Day of Judgment dawns and the great conquerors and lawyers and statesmen come to receive their rewards—their crowns, their laurels, their names carved indelibly upon imperishable marble—the Almighty will turn to Peter and will say, not without a certain envy when He sees us coming with our books under our arms, "Look, these need no reward. We have nothing to give them here. They have loved reading".

MARYA MANNES

Marya Mannes is the daughter of two musicians and the niece of Walter Damrosch, the famous symphony conductor. She was born in 1904 in New York and educated privately there. She worked as feature editor of Vogue *until World War II, then served three years in the Office of War Information. After a brief resumption of feature editing for* Glamour *(1946), she published a novel (1948) and in 1952 began her present association with* The Reporter: *she is a staff writer and the author of the satiric verses signed SEC. Mrs. Mannes has also lectured frequently, written plays, appeared on radio, and had her own television program. She has received many honors and awards, especially for her pungent and critical magazine essays on American art, morals, and culture. Some of these have been published in the collections* More in Anger *(1958),* The New York I Know *(1961), and* But Will It Sell? *(1955), from which we take the present essay.*

HOW DO YOU KNOW IT'S GOOD?

Suppose there were no critics to tell us how to react to a picture, a play, or a new composition of music. Suppose we wandered innocent as the dawn into an art exhibition of unsigned paintings. By what standards, by what values would we decide whether they were good or bad, talented or untalented, successes or failures? How can we ever know that what we think is right?

For the last fifteen or twenty years the fashion in criticism or appreciation of the arts has been to deny the existence of any valid criteria and to make the words "good" or "bad" irrelevant, immaterial, and inapplicable. There is no such thing, we are told, as a set of standards, first acquired through experience and knowledge and later imposed on the subject under discussion. This has been a popular approach, for it relieves the critic of the responsibility of judgment and the public of the necessity of knowledge. It pleases those resentful of disciplines, it flatters the empty-minded by calling them open-minded, it comforts the confused. Under the banner of democracy and the kind of equality which our forefathers did *not* mean, it says, in effect, "Who are you to tell us what is good or bad?" This is the same cry used so long and so effectively by the producers of mass media who insist that it is the public, not they, who decides what it wants to hear and see, and that for a critic to say that *this* program is bad and *this* program is good is purely a reflection of personal taste. Nobody recently has expressed this philosophy more succinctly than Dr. Frank Stanton, the highly intelligent president of CBS television. At a hearing before the Federal Communications Commission, this phrase escaped him under questioning: "One man's mediocrity is another man's good program."

There is no better way of saying "No values are absolute." There is another important aspect to this philosophy of *laissez faire:* It is the fear, in all observers of all forms of art, of guessing wrong. This fear is well come by, for who has not heard of the contemporary outcries against artists who later were called great? Every age has its arbiters who do not grow with their times, who cannot tell evolution from revolution or the difference between frivolous faddism, amateurish experimentation, and profound and necessary change. Who wants to be caught *flagrante delicto* with an error of judgment as serious as this? It is far safer, and certainly easier, to look at a picture or a play or a poem and to say "This is hard to understand, but it may be good," or simply to welcome it as a new form. The word "new"—in our country especially—has magical connotations. What is new must be good; what is old is probably bad. And if a critic can describe the new in language that nobody can understand, he's safer still. If he has mastered the art of saying nothing with exquisite complexity, nobody can quote him later as saying anything.

But all these, I maintain, are forms of abdication from the responsibility of judgment. In creating, the artist commits himself; in appreciating, you have a commitment of your own. For after all, it is the audience which makes the arts. A climate of appreciation is essential to its flowering, and the higher the expectations of the public, the better the performance of the artist. Conversely, only a public ill-served by its critics could have accepted as art and as literature so much in these last years that has been neither. If anything goes, everything goes; and at the bottom of the junkpile lie the discarded standards too.

But what are these standards? How do you get them? How do you know they're the right ones? How can you make a clear pattern out of so many intangibles, including that greatest one, the very private I?

Well for one thing, it's fairly obvious that the more you read and see and hear, the more equipped you'll be to practice that art of association which is at the basis of all understanding and judgment. The more you live and the more you look, the more aware you are of a consistent pattern—as universal as the stars, as the tides, as breathing, as night and day—underlying everything. I would call this pattern and this rhythm an order. Not order—*an* order. Within it exists an incredible diversity of forms. Without it lies chaos. I would further call this order—this incredible diversity held within one pattern—health. And I would call chaos—the wild cells of destruction—sickness. It is in the end up to you to distinguish between the diversity that is health and the chaos that is sickness, and you can't do this without a process of association that can link a bar of Mozart with the corner of a Vermeer painting, or a Stravinsky score with a Picasso abstraction; or that can relate an aggressive act with a Franz Kline painting and a fit of coughing with a John Cage composition.

There is no accident in the fact that certain expressions of art live for all time and that others die with the moment, and although you may not always define the reasons, you can ask the questions. What does an artist say that is timeless; how does he say it? How much is fashion, how much is merely reflection? Why is Sir Walter Scott so hard to read now, and Jane Austen not? Why is baroque right for one age and too effulgent for another?

Can a standard of craftsmanship apply to art of all ages, or does each have its own, and different, definitions? You may have been aware, inadvertently, that craftsmanship has become a dirty word these years because, again, it implies standards—something done well or done badly. The result of this convenient avoidance is a plentitude of actors who can't project their voices, singers who can't phrase their songs, poets who can't communicate emotion, and writers who have no vocabulary—not to speak of painters who can't draw. The dogma now is that craftsmanship gets in the way of expression. You can do better if you don't know *how* you do it, let alone *what* you're doing.

I think it is time you helped reverse this trend by trying to rediscover craft: the command of the chosen instrument, whether it is a brush, a word, or a voice. When you begin to detect the difference between freedom and sloppiness, between serious experimentation and egotherapy, between skill and slickness, between strength and violence, you are on your way to separating the sheep from the goats, a form of segregation denied us for quite a while. All you need to restore it is a small bundle of standards and a Geiger counter that detects fraud, and we might begin our tour of the arts in an area where both are urgently needed: contemporary painting.

I don't know what's worse: to have to look at acres of bad art to find the little good, or to read what the critics say about it all. In no other field of expression has so much double-talk flourished, so much confusion prevailed, and so much nonsense been circulated: further evidence of the close interdependence between the arts and the critical climate they inhabit. It will be my pleasure to share with you some of this double-talk so typical of our times.

Item one: preface for a catalogue of an abstract painter:

"Time-bound meditation experiencing a life; sincere with plastic piety at the threshold of hallowed arcana; a striving for pure ideation giving shape to inner drive; formalized patterns where neural balances reach a fiction." End of quote. Know what this artist paints like now?

Item two: a review in the *Art News*:

". . . a weird and disparate assortment of material, but the monstrosity which bloomed into his most recent cancer of aggregations is present in some form everywhere. . . ." Then, later, "A gluttony of things and processes terminated by a glorious constipation."

Item three, same magazine, review of an artist who welds automobile fragments into abstract shapes:

"Each fragment . . . is made an extreme of human exasperation, torn at and fought all the way, and has its rightness of form as if by accident. *Any technique that requires order or discipline would just be the human ego.* No, these must be egoless, uncontrolled, undesigned and different enough to give you a bang—fifty miles an hour around a telephone pole. . . ."

"Any technique that requires order or discipline would just be the human ego." What does he mean—"just be"? What are they really talking about? Is this journalism? Is it criticism? Or is it that other convenient abdication from standards of performance and judgment practiced by so many artists and critics that they, like certain writers who deal only in sickness and depravity, "reflect the chaos about them"? Again, whose chaos? Whose depravity?

I had always thought that the prime function of art was to create order *out* of chaos—again, not the order of neatness or rigidity or convention or artifice, but the order of clarity by which one will and one vision could draw the essential truth out of apparent confusion. I still do. It is not enough to use parts of a car to convey the brutality of the machine. This is as slavishly representative, and just as easy, as arranging dried flowers under glass to convey nature.

Speaking of which, i.e., the use of real materials (burlap, old gloves, bottletops) in lieu of pigment, this is what one critic had to say about an exhibition of Assemblage at the Museum of Modern Art last year:

"Spotted throughout the show are indisputable works of art, accounting for a quarter or even a half of the total display. But the remainder are works of non-art, anti-art, and art substitutes that are the aesthetic counterparts of the social deficiencies that land people in the clink on charges of vagrancy. These aesthetic bankrupts . . . have no legitimate ideological roof over their heads and not the price of a square intellectual meal, much less a spiritual sandwich, in their pockets."

I quote these words of John Canaday of *The New York Times* as an example of the kind of criticism which puts responsibility to an intelligent public above popularity with an intellectual coterie. Canaday has the courage to say what he thinks and the capacity to say it clearly: two qualities notably absent from his profession.

Next to art, I would say that appreciation and evaluation in the field of music is the most difficult. For it is rarely possible to judge a new composition at one hearing only. What seems confusing or fragmented at first might well become clear and organic a third time. Or it might not. The only salvation here for the listener is, again, an instinct born of experience and association which allows him to separate intent from accident, design from experimentation, and pretense from conviction. Much of contemporary music is, like its sister art, merely a reflection of the composer's own fragmentation: an absorption in self and symbols at the expense of communication with others. The artist, in short, says to the public: If you don't understand this, it's because you're dumb. I maintain that you are not. You may have to go part way or even halfway to meet the artist, but if you must go the whole way, it's his fault, not yours. Hold fast to that. And remember it too when you read new poetry, that estranged sister of music.

"A multitude of causes, unknown to former times, are now acting with a combined force to blunt the discriminating powers of the mind, and, unfitting it for all voluntary exertion, to reduce it to a state of almost savage torpor. The most effective of these causes are the great national events which are daily taking place and the increasing accumulation of men in cities, where the uniformity of their occupations produces a craving for extraordinary incident, which the rapid communication of intelligence hourly gratifies. To this tendency of life and manners, the literature and theatrical exhibitions of the country have conformed themselves."

This startlingly applicable comment was written in the year 1800 by William Wordsworth in the preface to his "Lyrical Ballads"; and it has been cited by Edwin Muir in his recently published book "The Estate of Poetry." Muir states that poetry's effective range and influence have diminished alarmingly in the modern world. He believes in the inherent and indestructible qualities of the human mind and the great and permanent objects that act upon it, and suggests that the audience will increase when "poetry loses what obscurity is left in it by attempting greater themes, for great themes have to be stated clearly." If you keep that firmly in mind and resist, in Muir's words, "the vast dissemination of secondary objects that isolate us from the natural world," you have gone a long way toward equipping yourself for the examination of any work of art.

When you come to theatre, in this extremely hasty tour of the arts, you can approach it on two different levels. You can bring to it anticipation and innocence, giving yourself up, as it were, to the life on the stage and reacting to it emotionally, if the play is good, or listlessly, if the play is boring; a part of the audience organism that expresses its favor by silence or laughter and its disfavor by coughing and rustling. Or you can bring to it certain critical faculties that may heighten, rather than diminish, your enjoyment.

You can ask yourselves whether the actors are truly in their parts or merely projecting themselves; whether the scenery helps or hurts the mood; whether the playwright is honest with himself, his characters, and you. Somewhere along the line you can learn to distinguish between the true creative act and the false arbitrary gesture; between fresh observation and stale cliché; between the avant-garde play that is pretentious drivel and the avant-garde play that finds new ways to say old truths.

Purpose and craftsmanship—end and means—these are the keys to your judgment in all the arts. What is this painter trying to say when he slashes a broad band of black across a white canvas and lets the edges dribble down? Is it a statement of violence? Is it a self-portrait? If it is *one* of these, has he made you believe it? Or is this a gesture of the ego or a form of therapy? If it shocks you, what does it shock you into?

And what of this tight little painting of bright flowers in a vase? Is the painter saying anything new about flowers? Is it different from a million other canvases of flowers? Has it any life, any meaning, beyond its statement? Is there any pleasure in its forms or texture? The question is not whether a thing is abstract or representational, whether it is "modern" or conventional. The question, inexorably, is whether it is good. And this is a decision which only you, on the basis of instinct, experience, and association, can make for yourself. It takes independence and courage. It involves, moreover, the risk of wrong decision and the humility, after the passage of time, of recognizing it as such. As we grow and change and learn, our attitudes can change too, and what we once thought obscure or "difficult" can later emerge as coherent and illuminating. Entrenched prejudices, obdurate opinions are as sterile as no opinions at all.

Yet standards there are, timeless as the universe itself. And when you have committed yourself to them, you have acquired a passport to that elusive but immutable realm of truth. Keep it with you in the forests of bewilderment. And never be afraid to speak up.

INDEX

A   NOTE   ON   THE   TYPE

The text of this book was set on the Linotype in Janson, a recutting made direct from type cast from matrices long thought to have been made by the Dutchman Anton Janson, who was a practicing type founder in Leipzig during the years 1668–87. However, it has been conclusively demonstrated that these types are actually the work of Nicholas Kis (1650–1702), a Hungarian, who most probably learned his trade from the master Dutch type founder Dirk Voskens. The type is an excellent example of the influential and sturdy Dutch types that prevailed in England up to the time William Caslon developed his own incomparable designs from these Dutch faces.

This book was composed, printed and bound by The Haddon Craftsmen, Inc., Scranton, Pa. Binding design by GUY FLEMING.